SportingNews
BOOKS

PRO FOOTBALL GUIDE

2005 EDITION

CONTENTS

Sporting News Contributors:
Editors: Corrie Anderson, Dave Sloan
Cover Design by: Chad Painter; **Page layout by:** Chad Painter, Kristin Bressert

ON THE COVER: Tom Brady and Champ Bailey by Albert Dickson / TSN, Donovan McNabb by Jay Drowns / TSN. BACK COVER: Tony Gonzalez by Albert Dickson / TSN.

NFL statistics compiled by STATS, Inc., a News Corporation company; 8130 Lehigh Avenue, Morton Grove, IL 60053. STATS is a trademark of Sports Team Analysis and Tracking Systems, Inc.

10 9 8 7 6 5 4 3 2 1

2005 SEASON

NFL directory

Team information

Schedule

College draft

Playoff plan

NFL DIRECTORY

COMMISSIONER'S OFFICE

Address
280 Park Avenue
New York, NY 10017
Phone
212-450-2000
212-681-7573 (FAX)
Commissioner
Paul Tagliabue
Exec. vp and COO of league and football development
Roger Goodell
Exec. vp of comm. & public affairs
Joe Browne

Exec. vp of media, president and COO of NFL Network
Steve Bornstein
Exec. vice president for labor relations
Harold Henderson
Executive vice president
Jeff Pash

COMMUNICATIONS
Vice president of public relations
Greg Aiello

Sr. dir. of international public affairs
Pete Abitante
Director of community affairs
Beth Colleton
Director of media services
Leslie Hammond
Director of corporate communications
Brian McCarthy
AFC Info Manager
Steve Alic
NFC Info Manager
Michael Signora

OTHER ORGANIZATIONS

NFL FILMS, INC.

Address
1 NFL Plaza
Mt. Laurel, NJ 08054
Phone
856-222-3500
President
Steve Sabol

PRO FOOTBALL HALL OF FAME

Address
2121 George Halas Drive, N.W.
Canton, OH 44708
Phone
330-456-8207
330-456-8175 (FAX)
Executive director
John W. Bankert
Vp/communications & exhibits
Joe Horrigan
Vp/operations and marketing
Dave Motts
Vp/merchandising & licensing
Judy Kuntz

NFL PLAYERS ASSOCIATION

Address
2021 L Street, N.W.
Washington, DC 20036
Phone
202-463-2200
202-835-9775 (FAX)
Executive director
Gene Upshaw
Assistant executive director
Doug Allen
Assistant director of retired players
Dee Becker
General counsel
Richard Berthelsen
Director of communications
Carl Francis
Director of player development
Stacey Robinson
Director of research department
Michael Duberstein
Dir. of agent admin. & salary cap
Joe Nahra

NFL ALUMNI ASSOCIATION

Address
3696 N. Federal Highway
Suite 202
Ft. Lauderdale, FL 33308-6263
Phone
954-630-2100
954-630-2535 (FAX)
Executive director/CEO
Frank Krauser
Chairman of the board
Randy Minniear
Vice president/alumni relations
Martin Lerch
Vp/director of communications
Remy Mackowski
Manager of player appearances
Amy Glanzman

DIVISIONAL ALIGNMENT

AMERICAN FOOTBALL CONFERENCE

AFC EAST	AFC NORTH	AFC SOUTH	AFC WEST
Buffalo Bills	Baltimore Ravens	Houston Texans	Denver Broncos
Miami Dolphins	Cincinnati Bengals	Indianapolis Colts	Kansas City Chiefs
New England Patriots	Cleveland Browns	Jacksonville Jaguars	Oakland Raiders
New York Jets	Pittsburgh Steelers	Tennessee Titans	San Diego Chargers

NATIONAL FOOTBALL CONFERENCE

NFC EAST	NFC NORTH	NFC SOUTH	NFC WEST
Dallas Cowboys	Chicago Bears	Atlanta Falcons	Arizona Cardinals
New York Giants	Detroit Lions	Carolina Panthers	St. Louis Rams
Philadelphia Eagles	Green Bay Packers	New Orleans Saints	San Francisco 49ers
Washington Redskins	Minnesota Vikings	Tampa Bay Buccaneers	Seattle Seahawks

ARIZONA CARDINALS
NFC WEST DIVISION

2005 SEASON

CLUB DIRECTORY

President
William V. Bidwill
Vice president
William V. Bidwill Jr.
Vice president and general counsel
Michael J. Bidwill
Vice president-football operations
Rod Graves
Senior director of football operations
John Idzik
Pro personnel assistant
Rodd Newhouse
National scouting coordinator
Jerry Hardaway
Director of media relations
Mark Dalton
Media relations manager
Chris Melvin
Director of community relations
Luis Zendejas

Head coach
Dennis Green

Assistant coaches
Frank Bush (linebackers)
Ryan Capretta (asst. strength & conditioning)
Rick Courtright (defensive quality control)
Carl Hargrave (tight ends)
Bill Khayat (off. quality control)
Mike Kruczek (quarterbacks)
Daryl Lawrence (asst. strength & conditioning)
Everett Lindsay (offensive line)
Kevin O'Dea (special teams)
Clancy Pendergast (defensive coordinator)
Deek Pollard (defensive line)
Keith Rowen (offensive coordinator)
Richard Solomon (def. backs)
Steve Wetzel (strength & conditioning)
Kirby Wilson (running backs)
Mike Wilson (wide receivers)

OFFSEASON MOVES

Key additions
S Robert Griffith	Rel./Browns
LB Orlando Huff	FA/Seahawks
CB Rhett Nelson	Rel./Vikings
DE Chike Okeafor	FA/Seahawks
OT Oliver Ross	FA/Steelers
QB Kurt Warner	FA/Giants

Key losses
OT Anthony Clement	Rel./Broncos
LB Levar Fisher	FA/Saints
CB Renaldo Hill	FA/Raiders
TE Freddie Jones	FA/Panthers
QB Shaun King	Free agent
LB Ronald McKinnon	Free agent
WR Nate Poole	Free agent
RB Emmitt Smith	Retired
G Cameron Spikes	Free agent
CB Duane Starks	Trade/Patriots
DB Michael Stone	FA/Rams
LB Raynoch Thompson	Rel./Packers
DE Kyle Vanden Bosch	FA/Titans
WR Karl Williams	Free agent
LB LeVar Woods	Rel./Bears

SCHEDULE

Sept.	11—at N.Y. Giants	4:15
Sept.	18—ST. LOUIS	4:05
Sept.	25—at Seattle	4:05
Oct.	2—SAN FRANCISCO	8:30
Oct.	9—CAROLINA	4:15
Oct.	16—Open date	
Oct.	23—TENNESSEE	4:15
Oct.	30—at Dallas	2:00
Nov.	6—SEATTLE	5:05
Nov.	13—at Detroit	2:00
Nov.	20—at St. Louis	2:00
Nov.	27—JACKSONVILLE	5:05
Dec.	4—at San Francisco	5:05
Dec.	11—WASHINGTON	5:05
Dec.	18—at Houston	2:00
Dec.	24—PHILADELPHIA (Sat.)	5:05
Jan.	1—at Indianapolis	2:00

All times are Eastern.
All games Sunday unless noted.

DRAFT CHOICES

Antrel Rolle, CB, Miami (first round/eighth pick overall).
J.J. Arrington, RB, California (2/44).
Eric Green, CB, Virginia Tech (3/75).
Darryl Blackstock, OLB, Virginia (3/95).
Elton Brown, G, Virginia (4/111).
Lance Mitchell, ILB, Oklahoma (5/168).
LeRon McCoy, Indiana (Pa.) (7/226).

MISCELLANEOUS TEAM DATA

Stadium (capacity, surface):
Sun Devil Stadium (73,243, grass)
Business address:
P.O. Box 888
Phoenix, AZ 85001-0888
Business phone:
602-379-0101
Ticket information:
602-379-0102
Team colors:
Cardinal red, black and white
Flagship radio station:
KTAR, 620 AM/KMVP 860 AM

Website:
www.azcardinals.com
Training site:
Northern Arizona University
Flagstaff, Ariz.
520-523-1818

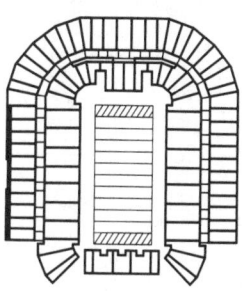

ARIZONA CARDINALS

No.	QUARTERBACKS	Ht./Wt.	Born	NFL Exp.	College	How acq.	'04 Games GP/GS
12	McCown, Josh	6-4/212	7-4-79	4	Sam Houston State	D3a/02	14/13
16	Navarre, John	6-6/250	9-9-80	1	Michigan	D7/04	1/1
13	Warner, Kurt	6-2/200	6-22-71	8	Northern Iowa	FA/05	10/9
	RUNNING BACKS						
20	Anderson, Damien	5-11/212	7-17-79	4	Northwestern	FA/02	4/0
28	Arrington, J.J.	5-9/214	1-23-83	R	California	D2/05	—
30	Ayanbadejo, Obafemi (FB)	6-2/231	3-5-75	7	San Diego State	FA/04	16/5
32	Croom, Larry	5-10/205	10-29-81	2	UNLV	FA/04	6/1
22	Hambrick, Troy	6-1/233	11-6-76	6	Savannah State	FA/04	10/0
42	Hodgins, James (FB)	6-1/274	4-30-77	7	San Jose State	FA/03	0/0
33	Scobey, Josh	6-0/216	12-11-79	3	Kansas State	D6/02	12/0
31	Shipp, Marcel	5-11/230	8-8-78	5	Massachusetts	FA/01	0/0
	RECEIVERS						
49	Blizzard, Bobby (TE)	6-4/272	3-22-80	1	North Carolina	FA/05	0/0
81	Boldin, Anquan	6-1/218	10-3-80	3	Florida State	D2/03	10/9
83	Edwards, Eric (TE)	6-5/256	8-4-80	2	LSU	FA/04	16/1
11	Fitzgerald, Larry	6-3/223	8-31-83	2	Pittsburgh	D1/04	16/16
84	Hamilton, Lawrence	6-3/204	8-31-80	3	Stephen F. Austin	FA/04	1/0
80	Johnson, Bryant	6-2/214	3-7-81	3	Penn State	D1a/03	16/11
19	McCoy, LeRon	6-1/211	1-24-82	R	Indiana (Pa.)	D7/05	—
87	Newhouse, Reggie	6-1/191	2-16-81	1	Baylor	FA/04	3/0
	OFFENSIVE LINEMEN						
73	Bridges, Jeremy (G)	6-4/301	4-19-80	2	Southern Mississippi	FA/04	14/8
61	Brown, Elton (G)	6-5/329	5-22-82	R	Virginia	D4/05	—
75	Davis, Leonard (T)	6-6/381	9-5-78	5	Texas	D1/01	15/15
60	Leckey, Nick (C)	6-3/286	3-12-82	2	Kansas State	D6/04	16/0
62	Newton, Jim (T)	6-9/297	10-13-78	1	Utah State	FA/05	0/0
66	Reuber, Alan (T)	6-6/323	1-26-81	1	Texas A&M	W-Min./04	3/0
78	Ross, Oliver (T)	6-5/322	9-27-74	7	Iowa State	FA/05	16/16
71	Stepanovich, Alex (C)	6-4/301	9-25-81	2	Ohio State	D4/04	16/16
74	Wells, Reggie (G)	6-4/323	11-3-80	3	Clarion	D6a/03	16/16
	DEFENSIVE LINEMEN						
92	Berry, Bertrand (E)	6-3/275	8-15-75	8	Notre Dame	FA/04	16/16
91	Bryant, Wendell (T)	6-5/303	9-12-80	4	Wisconsin	D1/02	3/0
98	Davis, Russell (T)	6-4/310	3-28-75	7	North Carolina	W-Chi./00	16/16
90	Dockett, Darnell (T)	6-4/301	5-27-81	2	Florida State	D3/04	16/15
95	King, Kenny (T)	6-3/285	4-23-81	3	Alabama	D5/03	0/0
72	Kolodziej, Ross (T)	6-3/295	5-11-78	4	Wisconsin	FA/04	13/4
56	Okeafor, Chike (E)	6-4/265	3-27-76	7	Purdue	FA/05	16/16
97	Pace, Calvin (E)	6-4/262	10-28-80	3	Wake Forest	D1b/03	14/0
67	Smith, Antonio (E)	6-3/274	10-21-81	1	Oklahoma State	D5/04	2/0
94	Zellner, Peppi (E)	6-5/262	3-14-75	7	Fort Valley State	T-Oak./04	16/14
	LINEBACKERS						
55	Blackstock, Darryl	6-4/241	5-30-83	R	Virginia	D3b/05	—
58	Dansby, Karlos	6-4/243	11-3-81	2	Auburn	D2/04	15/11
51	Darling, James	6-1/247	12-29-74	9	Washington State	FA/01	15/15
54	Hayes, Gerald	6-1/242	10-10-80	3	Pittsburgh	D3/03	16/1
57	Huff, Orlando	6-2/250	8-14-78	5	Fresno State	FA/05	16/14
59	Joe, Leon	6-1/235	10-26-81	2	Maryland	W-Chi./04	5/0
53	Keys, Isaac	6-3/245	6-6-78	2	Morehouse	FA/04	3/0
52	Mitchell, Lance	6-2/247	10-9-81	R	Oklahoma	D5/05	—
	DEFENSIVE BACKS						
43	Green, Eric (CB)	5-11/197	3-16-82	R	Virginia Tech	D3a/05	—
34	Griffith, Robert (S)	5-11/200	11-30-70	12	San Diego State	FA/05	16/16
29	Harris, Quentin (S)	6-1/214	1-26-77	4	Syracuse	FA/02	16/4
27	Macklin, David (CB)	5-10/200	7-14-78	6	Penn State	FA/04	16/16
37	Mayes, Adrian (S)	6-1/211	11-17-80	2	LSU	FA/04	4/0
38	Nelson, Rhett (CB)	6-0/201	2-16-80	2	Colorado State	FA/05	4/0
25	Ohalete, Ifeanyi (S)	6-2/222	5-22-79	5	USC	FA/04	16/13
21	Rolle, Antrel (CB)	6-0/202	12-16-82	R	Miami	D1/05	—
35	Shazor, Ernest (S)	6-3/226	7-4-83	1	Michigan	FA/05	—
26	Tate, Robert (CB)	5-11/193	10-19-73	8	Cincinnati	FA/02	14/0
24	Wilson, Adrian (S)	6-3/222	10-12-79	5	North Carolina State	D3/01	16/16
	SPECIALISTS						
10	Player, Scott (P)	6-1/213	12-17-69	8	Florida State	FA/98	16/0
1	Rackers, Neil (K)	6-0/206	8-16-76	6	Illinois	FA/03	16/0

Abbreviations: D1—draft pick, first round; W—claimed on waivers; T—obtained in trade; FA—free-agent acquisition.

2004 regular-season record: 6-10
Position: 3rd in NFC West

Sept.12—at St. Louis	L	10-17
Sept.19—NEW ENGLAND	L	12-23
Sept.26—at Atlanta	L	3-6
Oct. 3—NEW ORLEANS	W	34-10
Oct. 10—at San Francisco (OT)	L	28-31
Oct. 17—Open date		
Oct. 24—SEATTLE	W	25-17
Oct. 31—at Buffalo	L	14-38
Nov. 7—at Miami	W	24-23
Nov.14—N.Y. GIANTS	W	17-14
Nov.21—at Carolina	L	10-35
Nov.28—N.Y. JETS	L	3-13
Dec. 5—at Detroit	L	12-26
Dec.12—SAN FRANCISCO (OT)	L	28-31
Dec.19—ST. LOUIS	W	31-7
Dec.26—at Seattle	L	21-24
Jan. 2—TAMPA BAY	W	12-7

SCORING BY PERIODS

	Q1	Q2	Q3	Q4	OT	Pts.
Cardinals	40	78	57	109	0	284
Opponents	64	100	63	89	6	322

TEAM STATISTICS

	Ariz.	Opp.
TOTAL FIRST DOWNS	280	282
Rushing	86	101
Passing	152	153
Penalty	42	28
3rd Down: Made/Att.	84/241	66/209
3rd Down Pct.	34.9	31.6
4th Down: Made/Att.	5/12	8/14
4th Down Pct.	41.7	57.1
POSSESSION AVG.	30:53	29:07
TOTAL NET YARDS	4550	5141
Avg. per Game	284.4	321.3
Total Plays	1047	993
Avg. per Play	4.3	5.2
NET YARDS RUSHING	1668	2105
Avg. per Game	104.3	131.6
Total Rushes	475	450
NET YARDS PASSING	2882	3036
Avg. per Game	180.1	189.8
Sacked/Yards Lost	39/320	38/229
Gross Yards	3202	3265
Att./Completions	533/299	505/271
Completion Pct.	56.1	53.7
Had Intercepted	18	15
PUNTS/AVERAGE	99/42.7	97/41.9
NET PUNTING AVG.	99/36.4	97/35.8
PENALTIES/YARDS	124/948	139/1121
FUMBLES/LOST	34/11	32/15
TOUCHDOWNS	31	35
Rushing	15	12
Passing	14	18
Returns	2	5

SCORING (NON-KICKERS)

	Tot. TD	RTD	PTD	MTD	2Pt.	Tot. Pts.
E. Smith	9	9	0	0	0	54
Fitzgerald	8	0	8	0	0	48

	Tot. TD	RTD	PTD	MTD	2Pt.	Tot. Pts.
Ayanbadejo	4	3	1	0	0	24
McCown	2	2	0	0	1	14
Hambrick	2	1	1	0	0	12
F. Jones	2	0	2	0	0	12
Boldin	1	0	1	0	0	6
B. Johnson	1	0	1	0	0	6
Starks	1	0	0	1	0	6
Wilson	1	0	0	1	0	6
Cardinals	31	15	14	2	1	190
Opponents	35	12	18	5	4	218

2-Pt. conversions: Cardinals 1-3; Opponents 4-5.

(KICKERS)

	XPM/XPA	FGM/FGA	Pts.
Rackers	28/28	22/29	94
Cardinals	28/28	22/29	94
Opponents	29/30	25/26	104

RUSHING

	Att.	Yds.	Avg.	Lg.	TD
E. Smith	267	937	3.5	t29	9
Hambrick	63	283	4.5	62	1
Ayanbadejo	30	122	4.1	23	3
McCown	36	112	3.1	12	2
Scobey	27	89	3.3	10	0
Croom	29	76	2.6	20	0
King	9	30	3.3	16	0
Fitzgerald	8	14	1.8	10	0
Williams	2	6	3.0	3	0
Boldin	1	3	3.0	3	0
Anderson	1	2	2.0	2	0
B. Johnson	2	-6	-3.0	1	0
Cardinals	475	1668	3.5	62	15
Opponents	450	2105	4.7	74	12

RECEIVING

	No.	Yds.	Avg.	Lg.	TD
Fitzgerald	58	780	13.4	48	8
Boldin	56	623	11.1	t31	1
B. Johnson	49	537	11.0	40	1
F. Jones	45	426	9.5	40	2
Ayanbadejo	19	171	9.0	t21	1
Scobey	18	191	10.6	42	0
Williams	18	197	10.9	33	0
E. Smith	15	105	7.0	18	0
Edwards	5	51	10.2	19	0
Poole	5	70	14.0	24	0
Hambrick	4	16	4.0	9	1
Diamond	3	19	6.3	8	0
Croom	2	16	8.0	8	0
McCown	1	-5	-5.0	-5	0
Newhouse	1	5	5.0	5	0
Cardinals	299	3202	10.7	48	14
Opponents	271	3265	12.0	t75	18

INTERCEPTIONS

	No.	Yds.	Avg.	Lg.	TD
Macklin	4	18	4.5	16	0
Wilson	3	62	20.7	27	0
Starks	3	46	15.3	t41	1

	No.	Yds.	Avg.	Lg.	TD
Darling	1	65	65.0	65	0
Dockett	1	20	20.0	20	0
Dansby	1	2	2.0	2	0
Hill	1	2	2.0	2	0
Harris	1	-1	-1.0	-1	0
Cardinals	15	214	14.3	65	1
Opponents	18	263	14.6	76	1

SACKS: Berry 14.5, Dansby 5.0, Pace 4.5, Dockett 3.5, Zellner 2.0, Darling 1.0, R. Davis 1.0, Harris 1.0, Hill 1.0, Kolodziej 1.0, Starks 1.0, Thompson 1.0, Wilson 1.0, Macklin 0.5. Cardinals 38.0; Opponents 39.0.

PUNTING

	No.	Yds.	Avg.	In. 20	Lg.
Player	98	4230	43.2	32	57
Cardinals	99	4230	42.7	32	57
Opponents	97	4064	41.9	25	68

PUNT RETURNS

	No.	FC	Yds.	Avg.	Lg.	TD
Williams	42	12	286	6.8	38	0
Starks	7	1	43	6.1	15	0
Cardinals	49	14	329	6.7	38	0
Opponents	56	16	486	8.7	t71	1

KICK RETURNS

	No.	Yds.	Avg.	Lg.	TD
Scobey	32	723	22.6	71	0
Croom	16	314	19.6	35	0
B. Johnson	6	135	22.5	47	0
Ayanbadejo	3	50	16.7	21	0
Edwards	3	40	13.3	14	0
Hayes	3	6	2.0	6	0
Vanden Bosch	1	7	7.0	7	0
Williams	1	18	18.0	18	0
Cardinals	65	1293	19.9	71	0
Opponents	46	1017	22.1	t87	1

FIELD GOALS

	1-19	20-29	30-39	40-49	50+
Rackers	0/0	6/6	5/7	6/7	5/9
Cardinals	0/0	6/6	5/7	6/7	5/9
Opponents	0/0	13/13	7/7	3/4	2/2

Rackers: (22G) (51G, 52G, 58N) (30G) (26G, 33G) () (55G, 55G, 50G) (64N) (29G) (41G) (50N) (28G) (20G) (42G, 33G) (34N, 44G, 22G) (48G) (52N) (40G, 45G, 35N, 39G, 31G, 47N) Opponents: (50G, 28G, 22G) (29G, 28G, 24G) (25G, 23G) (20G) (37G, 42G, 32G) (54G) (25G) (30G, 29G, 28G) (44B) () (28G, 46G) (45G, 22G, 31G, 36G) (31G) () (34G)

PASSING

	Att.	Cmp.	Yds.	Pct.	Avg. Gain	TD	Pct. TD	Int.	Pct. Int.	Long	Sack/Lost	Rating
McCown	408	233	2511	57.1	6.15	11	2.7	10	2.5	48	31/263	74.1
King	84	47	502	56.0	5.98	1	1.2	4	4.8	40	6/42	57.7
Navarre	40	18	168	45.0	4.20	1	2.5	4	10.0	t33	1/8	25.8
E. Smith	1	1	21	100.0	21.00	1	100.0	0	0.0	t21	0/0	158.3
Cardinals	533	299	3202	56.1	6.01	14	2.6	18	3.4	48	39/320	68.5
Opponents	505	271	3265	53.7	6.47	18	3.6	15	3.0	t75	38/229	73.2

ATLANTA FALCONS
NFC SOUTH DIVISION

2005 SEASON

CLUB DIRECTORY

Owner and CEO
Arthur Blank
President/general manager
Rich McKay
Vice president of player personnel
Ron Hill
Vice president of communications and community affairs
Susan Bass
Vp of football communications
Reggie Roberts
Senior Director of media relations
Frank Kleha
Director of college scouting
Phil Emery
Director of pro personnel
Les Snead
Director of football administration
Brian Xanders

Head coach
Jim Mora

Assistant coaches
Dennis Allen (defensive asst.)
Clancy Barone (tight ends)
Chris Beake (linebackers)
Rocky Colburn (asst.strength & conditioning)
Chris Dalman (offensive asst.)
Joe DeCamillis (special teams coordinator)
Ed Donatell (def. coordinator)
Alex Gibbs (consultant/offensive line)
Jeff Jagodzinski (offensive line)
Bill Johnson (defensive line)
Mike Johnson (quarterbacks)
Greg Knapp (off. coordinator)
Brett Maxie (defensive backs)
Al Miller (strength & conditioning)
Robert Prince (offensive asst.)
George Stewart (wide receivers)
Emmitt Thomas (secondary/senior defensive asst.)
Ollie Wilson (running backs)

SCHEDULE

Sept.	12—PHILADELPHIA (Mon.)	9:00
Sept.	18—at Seattle	4:05
Sept.	25—at Buffalo	1:00
Oct.	2—MINNESOTA	4:15
Oct.	9—NEW ENGLAND	1:00
Oct.	16—at New Orleans	1:00
Oct.	24—N.Y. JETS (Mon.)	9:00
Oct.	30—Open date	
Nov.	6—at Miami	2:00
Nov.	13—GREEN BAY	5:15
Nov.	20—TAMPA BAY	2:00
Nov.	24—at Detroit (Thurs.)	1:30
Dec.	4—at Carolina	2:00
Dec.	12—NEW ORLEANS (Mon.)	10:00
Dec.	18—at Chicago	9:30
Dec.	24—at Tampa Bay (Sat.)	2:00
Jan.	1—CAROLINA	2:00

All times are Eastern.
All games Sunday unless noted.

OFFSEASON MOVES

Key additions
S Rich Coady	FA/Rams
P Toby Gowin	FA/Jets
LB Ed Hartwell	FA/Ravens
S Ronnie Heard	FA/49ers
G Matt Lehr	FA/Rams
DE Brandon Mitchell	FA/Seahawks
K Todd Peterson	FA/49ers
LB Ike Reese	FA/Eagles
OT Barry Stokes	FA/Giants

Key losses
CB Aaron Beasley	Free agent
LB Chris Draft	Rel./Panthers
K Jay Feely	FA/Giants
G Roberto Garza	FA/Bears
S Cory Hall	Released
DE Travis Hall	Released
DT Ed Jasper	Released
P Chris Mohr	Released
LB Matt Stewart	FA/Browns
DE Joe Tafoya	Waiv./Seahawks
LB Artie Ulmer	Free agent

DRAFT CHOICES

Sharod "Roddy" White, WR, UAB (first round/27th pick overall).
Jonathan Babineaux, DT, Iowa (2/59).
Jordan Beck, ILB, Cal State Polytechnic (3/90).
Chauncey Davis, DE, Florida State (4/128).
Michael Boley, OLB, Southern Miss (5/160).
Frank Omiyale, OT, Tennessee Tech (5/163).
Deandra Cobb, RB, Michigan State (6/201).
Darrell Shropshire, DT, South Carolina (7/241).

MISCELLANEOUS TEAM DATA

Stadium (capacity, surface):
Georgia Dome
(71,228, artificial)
Business address:
4400 Falcon Parkway
Flowery Branch, GA 30542
Business phone:
770-965-3115
Ticket information:
404-223-8444
Team colors:
Black, red, silver and white
Flagship radio station:
Z-93 (92.9 FM)
Website:
www.atlantafalcons.com

Training site:
Furman University
Greenville, S.C.
864-294-2600

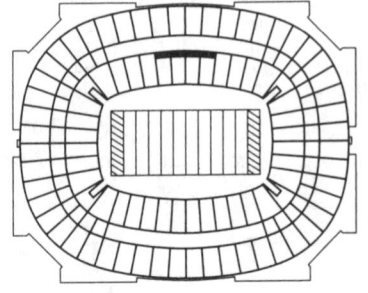

2005 TRAINING CAMP ROSTER

No.	QUARTERBACKS	Ht./Wt.	Born	NFL Exp.	College	How acq.	'04 Games GP/GS
14	Detmer, Ty	6-0/189	10-30-67	14	BYU	FA/04	0/0
8	Schaub, Matt	6-5/237	6-25-81	2	Virginia	D3/04	6/1
7	Vick, Michael	6-0/215	6-26-80	5	Virginia Tech	D1/01	15/15
	RUNNING BACKS						
34	Cobb, DeAndra	5-10/196	5-18-81	R	Michigan State	D6/05	—
45	Duckett, T.J.	6-0/254	2-17-81	4	Michigan State	D1/02	13/0
41	Dudley, Kevin (FB)	6-0/238	1-2-82	R	Michigan	FA/05	—
28	Dunn, Warrick	5-9/180	1-5-75	9	Florida State	FA/02	16/16
33	Griffith, Justin (FB)	5-11/232	4-13-81	3	Mississippi State	D4/03	12/11
44	McCrary, Fred (FB)	6-0/247	9-19-72	9	Mississippi State	FA/04	3/2
32	McLendon, T.A.	5-10/235	2-21-83	R	N.C. State	FA/05	—
35	Wright, Jason	5-10/210	7-12-82	2	Northwestern	FA/04	2/0
	RECEIVERS						
80	Beverly, Eric (TE)	6-3/300	3-28-74	8	Miami (Ohio)	FA/04	13/3
85	Blakley, Dwayne (TE)	6-4/257	8-10-79	2	Missouri	FA/04	15/1
83	Crumpler, Alge (TE)	6-2/262	12-23-77	5	North Carolina	D2/01	14/14
86	Finneran, Brian	6-5/210	1-31-76	7	Villanova	FA/00	12/1
12	Jenkins, Michael	6-4/217	6-18-82	2	Ohio State	D1b/04	16/0
81	Price, Peerless	5-11/190	10-27-76	7	Tennessee	T-Buf./03	16/15
48	Rackley, Derek (TE)	6-4/250	7-18-77	6	Minnesota	FA/00	16/0
89	White, Dez	6-1/215	8-23-79	6	Georgia Tech	FA/04	16/15
84	White, Roddy	6-1/201	11-2-81	R	UAB	D1/05	—
	OFFENSIVE LINEMEN						
64	Bibla, Martin (G)	6-3/306	10-4-79	4	Miami	D4/02	11/0
65	Forney, Kynan (G)	6-3/307	9-8-78	5	Hawaii	D7b/01	16/16
73	Herndon, Steve (G)	6-4/292	5-25-77	5	Georgia	FA/04	15/1
66	King, Austin (C)	6-5/303	4-11-81	3	Northwestern	FA/04	4/0
61	Lehr, Matt (G)	6-2/293	4-25-79	5	Virginia Tech	FA/05	7/2
69	Mabry, Mike (C)	6-1/295	4-26-80	1	Central Florida	FA/04	0/0
62	McClure, Todd (C)	6-1/286	2-16-77	7	LSU	D7a/99	16/16
67	Moore, Michael (G)	6-2/318	11-1-76	5	Troy	FA/03	1/1
70	Omiyale, Frank (T)	6-4/310	11-23-82	R	Tennessee Tech	D5b/05	—
71	Peck, Jared (T)	6-5/290	5-6-79	2	North Dakota State	FA/04	1/0
76	Shaffer, Kevin (T)	6-5/290	3-2-80	4	Tulsa	D7b/02	15/15
79	Stokes, Barry (T)	6-4/310	12-20-73	8	Eastern Michigan	FA/05	0/0
74	Weiner, Todd (T)	6-4/297	9-16-75	8	Kansas State	FA/02	16/16
	DEFENSIVE LINEMEN						
95	Babineaux, Jonathan (T)	6-2/281	10-12-81	R	Iowa	D2/05	—
75	Coleman, Rod (T)	6-2/285	8-16-76	7	East Carolina	FA/04	13/13
77	Davis, Chauncey (E)	6-1/258	1-27-83	R	Florida State	D4/05	—
93	Glymph, Junior (E)	6-5/270	9-2-80	2	Carson-Newman	FA/04	3/0
97	Kerney, Patrick (E)	6-5/273	12-30-76	7	Virginia	D1/99	16/15
96	Lake, Antwan (E)	6-4/308	7-10-79	3	West Virginia	FA/04	16/2
94	Lavalais, Chad (T)	6-1/293	4-15-79	2	LSU	D5/04	16/6
92	Mitchell, Brandon (T)	6-3/290	6-19-75	9	Texas A&M	FA/05	15/0
71	Shropshire, Darrell (T)	6-2/301	3-18-83	R	South Carolina	D7/05	—
91	Smith, Brady (E)	6-5/274	6-5-73	10	Colorado State	FA/00	16/16
99	Vaughn, Khaleed (E)	6-4/276	5-20-81	2	Clemson	FA/04	3/0
	LINEBACKERS						
52	Beck, Jordan	6-2/231	4-18-83	R	Cal Poly	D3/05	—
59	Boley, Michael	6-2/228	8-24-82	R	Southern Mississippi	D5a/05	—
56	Brooking, Keith	6-2/245	10-30-75	8	Georgia Tech	D1/98	16/16
50	Hartwell, Ed	6-1/250	5-27-78	5	Western Illinois	FA/05	16/15
53	Kramer, Jordan	6-1/230	12-7-79	3	Idaho	FA/05	4/0
98	Reese, Ike	6-2/222	10-16-73	8	Michigan State	FA/05	16/1
51	Williams, Demorrio	6-0/232	7-6-80	2	Nebraska	D4/04	16/1
	DEFENSIVE BACKS						
29	Carpenter, Keion (S)	5-11/205	10-31-77	7	Virginia Tech	FA/02	0/0
27	Coady, Rich (S)	6-1/210	1-26-76	7	Texas A&M	FA/05	16/5
21	Hall, DeAngelo (CB)	5-10/197	11-19-83	2	Virginia Tech	D1a/04	10/9
38	Heard, Ronnie (S)	6-3/215	10-5-76	6	Mississippi	FA/05	16/14
47	Joyce, Eric (CB)	5-10/200	1-21-78	4	Tennessee State	FA/05	0/0
23	Mathis, Kevin (CB)	5-9/185	4-29-74	9	Texas A&M-Comm.	FA/02	15/12
25	McCadam, Kevin (S)	6-1/219	3-6-79	4	Virginia Tech	D5a/02	16/2
30	Morton, Christian (CB)	6-0/180	4-28-81	2	Illinois	FA/04	2/0
42	Pruitt, Etric (S)	6-0/196	8-16-81	2	Southern Mississippi	D6/04	3/0
20	Rossum, Allen (CB)	5-8/178	10-22-75	8	Notre Dame	FA/02	16/1
24	Scott, Bryan (S)	6-1/219	4-13-81	3	Penn State	D2/03	16/16
36	Webster, Jason (CB)	5-9/187	9-8-77	6	Texas A&M	FA/04	10/9
	SPECIALISTS						
4	Gowin, Toby (P)	5-10/167	3-30-75	9	North Texas	FA/05	16/0
2	Peterson, Todd (K)	5-11/180	2-4-70	12	Georgia	FA/05	16/0

Abbreviations: D1—draft pick, first round; T—obtained in trade; FA—free-agent acquisition.

ATLANTA FALCONS

ATLANTA FALCONS

2004 regular-season record: 11-5
Position: 1st in NFC South

Sept.12—at San Francisco	W	21-19
Sept.19—ST. LOUIS	W	34-17
Sept.26—ARIZONA	W	6-3
Oct. 3—at Carolina	W	27-10
Oct. 10—DETROIT	L	10-17
Oct. 17—SAN DIEGO	W	21-20
Oct. 24—at Kansas City	L	10-56
Oct. 31—at Denver	W	41-28
Nov. 7—Open date		
Nov.14—TAMPA BAY	W	24-14
Nov. 21—at N.Y. Giants	W	14-10
Nov.28—NEW ORLEANS	W	24-21
Dec. 5—at Tampa Bay	L	0-27
Dec.12—OAKLAND	W	35-10
Dec.18—CAROLINA (OT)	W	34-31
Dec.26—at New Orleans	L	13-26
Jan. 2—at Seattle	L	26-28

2004 postseason record: 1-1

Jan. 15—ST. LOUIS*	W	47-17
Jan. 23—at Philadelphia†	L	10-27

*NFC divisional playoff game. †NFC championship game.

SCORING BY PERIODS

	Q1	Q2	Q3	Q4	OT	Pts.
Falcons	71	118	42	106	3	340
Opponents	57	105	76	99	0	337

TEAM STATISTICS

	Atl.	Opp.
TOTAL FIRST DOWNS ..	284	310
Rushing	133	107
Passing	120	183
Penalty	31	20
3rd Down: Made/Att. ..	73/201	72/200
3rd Down Pct.	36.3	36.0
4th Down: Made/Att.	10/18	10/16
4th Down Pct.	55.6	62.5
POSSESSION AVG.	29:10	30:50
TOTAL NET YARDS	5084	5207
Avg. per Game	317.8	325.4
Total Plays	969	999
Avg. per Play	5.2	5.2
NET YARDS RUSHING ..	2672	1681
Avg. per Game	167.0	105.1
Total Rushes	524	434
NET YARDS PASSING....	2412	3526
Avg. per Game	150.8	220.4
Sacked/Yards Lost	50/280	48/312
Gross Yards	2692	3838
Att./Completions	395/217	517/328
Completion Pct.	54.9	63.4
Had Intercepted	16	19
PUNTS/AVERAGE	76/40.6	80/43.3
NET PUNTING AVG.	76/36.9	80/36.4
PENALTIES/YARDS	109/905	129/930
FUMBLES/LOST	26/14	24/13
TOUCHDOWNS	41	41
Rushing	20	20

	Atl.	Opp.
Passing	15	19
Returns	6	2

SCORING (NON-KICKERS)

	Tot. TD	RTD	PTD	MTD	2Pt.	Tot. Pts.
Dunn	9	9	0	0	0	54
Duckett	8	8	0	0	0	48
Crumpler	6	0	6	0	0	36
Price	3	0	3	0	0	18
Vick	3	3	0	0	0	18
Finneran	2	0	2	0	0	12
Mathis	2	0	0	2	0	12
White	2	0	2	0	0	12
Coleman	1	0	0	1	0	6
Griffith	1	0	1	0	0	6
D. Hall	1	0	0	1	0	6
Pritchett	1	0	1	0	0	6
Rossum	1	0	0	1	0	6
B. Smith	1	0	0	1	0	6
Falcons	41	20	15	6	0	246
Opponents	41	20	19	2	1	250

2-Pt. conversions: Falcons 0-1; Opponents 1-2.

(KICKERS)

	XPM/XPA	FGM/FGA	Pts.
Feely	40/40	18/23	94
Falcons	40/40	18/23	94
Opponents	39/39	16/18	87

RUSHING

	Att.	Yds.	Avg.	Lg.	TD
Dunn	265	1106	4.2	60	9
Vick	120	902	7.5	58	3
Duckett	104	509	4.9	35	8
Griffith	9	39	4.3	10	0
Price	3	34	11.3	16	0
Schaub	8	26	3.3	11	0
Pritchett	6	18	3.0	8	0
White	3	14	4.7	26	0
Layne	1	12	12.0	12	0
Wright	3	10	3.3	8	0
Jenkins	1	2	2.0	2	0
Rossum	1	0	0.0	0	0
Falcons	524	2672	5.1	60	20
Opponents	434	1681	3.9	29	20

RECEIVING

	Att.	Yds.	Avg.	Lg.	TD
Crumpler	48	774	16.1	t49	6
Price	45	575	12.8	50	3
White	30	370	12.3	54	2
Dunn	29	294	10.1	59	0
Finneran	23	258	11.2	26	2
Griffith	22	220	10.0	62	1
Jenkins	7	119	17.0	46	0
Blakley	4	35	8.8	13	0
Duckett	3	15	5.0	11	0
McCrary	2	23	11.5	14	0

	Att.	Yds.	Avg.	Lg.	TD
Pritchett	2	5	2.5	4	1
Feely	1	-2	-2.0	-2	0
Layne	1	6	6.0	6	0
Falcons	217	2692	12.4	62	15
Opponents	328	3838	11.7	t80	19

INTERCEPTIONS

	No.	Yds.	Avg.	Lg.	TD
Beasley	4	115	28.8	85	0
Brooking	3	41	13.7	27	0
Mathis	2	101	50.5	t66	2
D. Hall	2	50	25.0	t48	1
Rossum	2	22	11.0	14	0
Coleman	1	39	39.0	t39	1
Draft	1	33	33.0	33	0
Scott	1	22	22.0	22	0
Webster	1	18	18.0	18	0
B. Smith	1	1	1.0	1	0
Kerney	1	0	0.0	0	0
Falcons	19	442	23.3	85	4
Opponents	16	201	12.6	75	0

SACKS: Kerney 13.0, Coleman 11.5, B. Smith 6.0, T. Hall 3.0, Brooking 2.5, Scott 2.5, Williams 2.5, Jasper 2.0, Stewart 1.5, Beasley 1.0, Glymph 1.0, Rossum 1.0, D. Hall 0.5. Falcons 48.0; Opponents 50.0.

PUNTING

	No.	Yds.	Avg.	In. 20	Lg.
Mohr	76	3082	40.6	19	56
Falcons	76	3082	40.6	19	56
Opponents	80	3466	43.3	20	67

PUNT RETURNS

	No.	FC	Yds.	Avg.	Lg.	TD
Rossum	37	14	457	12.4	t75	1
Falcons	37	17	457	12.4	t75	1
Opponents	33	21	134	4.1	25	0

KICK RETURNS

	No.	Yds.	Avg.	Lg.	TD
Rossum	58	1250	21.6	49	0
Griffith	1	31	31.0	31	0
D. Hall	1	48	48.0	48	0
Pritchett	1	2	2.0	2	0
Falcons	61	1331	21.8	49	0
Opponents	56	1117	19.9	t96	1

FIELD GOALS

	1-19	20-29	30-39	40-49	50+
Feely	1/1	7/7	7/9	3/6	0/0
Falcons	1/1	7/7	7/9	3/6	0/0
Opponents	0/0	7/7	4/5	2/3	3/3

Feely: () (35G, 25G) (25G, 23G) (47G, 30G) (27G) () (19G) (24G, 43G, 49N) (33G) (46N) (37N, 31G) () () (37G, 45N, 38G) (25G, 20G) (33G, 39N, 40G) Opponents: (23G, 32G) (46G) (30G) (26G) (48N, 23G) (53G, 28G) () () () (24G) (48G, 38G, 37B) (50G, 30G) (52G) (21G) (22G)

PASSING

	Att.	Cmp.	Yds.	Pct.	Avg. Gain	TD	Pct. TD	Int.	Pct. Int.	Long	Sack/Lost	Rating
Vick	321	181	2313	56.4	7.21	14	4.4	12	3.7	62	46/266	78.1
Schaub	70	33	330	47.1	4.71	1	1.4	4	5.7	59	4/14	42.0
Price	1	1	25	100.0	25.00	0	0.0	0	0.0	25	0/0	118.8
Mohr	3	2	24	66.7	8.00	0	0.0	0	0.0	26	0/0	91.0
Falcons	395	217	2692	54.9	6.82	15	3.8	16	4.1	62	50/280	72.0
Opponents	517	328	3838	63.4	7.42	19	3.7	19	3.7	t80	48/312	82.8

BALTIMORE RAVENS
AFC NORTH DIVISION

2005 SEASON

CLUB DIRECTORY

Owner
Steve Bisciotti
President
Dick Cass
General manager
Ozzie Newsome
Vice president of football administration
Pat Moriarty
Director of player development
O.J. Brigance
Director of college scouting
Eric DeCosta
Director of pro personnel
George Kokinis
Senior vice president/public & community relations
Kevin Byrne
Dir. of publications/asst. dir. of P.R.
Francine Lubera
Senior director of operations
Bob Eller

Head coach
Brian Billick

Assistant coaches
Clarence Brooks (defensive line)
Jim Fassel (offensive coordinator)
John Fassel (coaching assistant)
Chris Foerster (offensive line/assistant head coach)
Jedd Fisch (offensive asst.)
Jeff FitzGerald (linebackers)
Jeff Friday (strength & conditioning)
Wade Harman (tight ends/asst. offensive line)
Johnnie Lynn (secondary)
Rick Neuheisel (quarterbacks)
Mike Pettine (outside linebackers)
Paul Ricci (asst. strength & conditioning)
Rex Ryan (defensive coordinator)
David Shaw (wide receivers)
Matt Simon (running backs)
Bennie Thompson (special teams asst.)
Dennis Thurman (secondary)
Gary Zauner (special teams coordinator)

OFFSEASON MOVES

Key additions
WR Derrick Mason	Rel./Titans
LB Jim Nelson	FA/Colts
LB Tommy Polley	FA/Rams
CB Samari Rolle	Rel./Titans
G Keydrick Vincent	FA/Steelers

Key losses
OL Bennie Anderson	FA/Bills
CB Gary Baxter	FA/Browns
LB Peter Boulware	Released
DE Marques Douglas	FA/49ers
LB Ed Hartwell	FA/Falcons
WR Kevin Johnson	Rel./Lions
C Casey Rabach	FA/Redskins
WR Travis Taylor	FA/Vikings
RB Jamel White	FA/Lions

SCHEDULE

Sept.	11—INDIANAPOLIS	8:30
Sept.	18—at Tennessee	1:00
Sept.	25—Open date	
Oct.	2—N.Y. JETS	4:05
Oct.	9—at Detroit	1:00
Oct.	16—CLEVELAND	1:00
Oct.	23—at Chicago	4:15
Oct.	31—at Pittsburgh (Mon.)	10:00
Nov.	6—CINCINNATI	2:00
Nov.	13—at Jacksonville	2:00
Nov.	20—PITTSBURGH	5:15
Nov.	27—at Cincinnati	2:00
Dec.	4—HOUSTON	2:00
Dec.	11—at Denver	5:15
Dec.	19—GREEN BAY (Mon.)	10:00
Dec.	25—MINNESOTA	9:30
Jan.	1—at Cleveland	2:00

All times are Eastern.
All games Sunday unless noted.

DRAFT CHOICES

Mark Clayton, WR, Oklahoma (first round/22nd pick overall).
Dan Cody, DE, Oklahoma (2/53).
Adam Terry, OT, Syracuse (2/64).
Jason Brown, C, North Carolina (4/124).
Justin Green, FB, Montana (5/158).
Derek Anderson, QB, Oregon State (6/213).
Mike Smith, ILB, Texas Tech (7/234).

MISCELLANEOUS TEAM DATA

Stadium (capacity, surface):
M&T Bank Stadium (69,084, Sportexe Momentum Turf)
Business address:
1 Winning Drive
Owings Mills, MD 21117
Business phone:
410-701-4000
Ticket information:
410-261-RAVE (7283)
Team colors:
Purple, black and metallic gold
Flagship radio stations:
WJFK, 1300 AM & WQSR, 102.7 FM
Website:
www.baltimoreravens.com
Training site:
McDaniel College
Westminster, Md.
410-701-4000

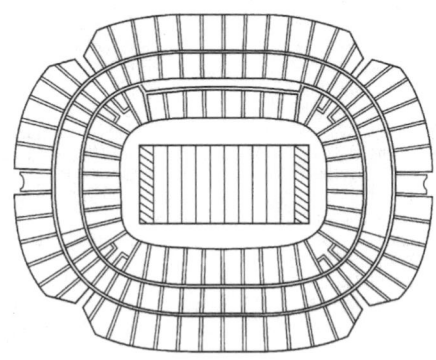

BALTIMORE RAVENS

No.	QUARTERBACKS	Ht./Wt.	Born	NFL Exp.	College	How acq.	'04 Games GP/GS
14	Anderson, Derek	6-6/239	6-15-83	R	Oregon State	D6/05	—
7	Boller, Kyle	6-3/220	6-17-81	3	California	D1b/03	16/16
2	Wright, Anthony	6-1/215	2-14-76	7	South Carolina	FA/02	0/0
	RUNNING BACKS						
33	Green, Justin (FB)	5-11/250	4-30-82	R	Montana	D5/05	—
31	Lewis, Jamal	5-11/245	8-29-79	6	Tennessee	D1a/00	12/12
34	Mughelli, Ovie (FB)	6-1/255	6-10-80	3	Wake Forest	D4b/03	3/0
39	Ricard, Alan (FB)	5-11/237	1-17-77	5	Louisiana-Monroe	FA/00	16/9
36	Sams, B.J. (KR)	5-10/185	10-29-80	2	McNeese State	FA/04	16/1
32	Smith, Musa	6-0/232	5-31-82	3	Georgia	D3/03	9/0
29	Taylor, Chester	5-11/213	9-22-79	4	Toledo	D6c/02	16/4
	RECEIVERS						
12	Abney, Derek	5-9/180	12-19-80	1	Kentucky	D7a/04	0/0
89	Clayton, Mark	5-10/193	7-2-82	R	Oklahoma	D1/05	—
81	Darling, Devard	6-1/215	4-16-82	1	Washington State	D3/04	3/0
87	Dinkins, Darnell (TE)	6-3/255	1-20-77	3	Pittsburgh	FA/02	10/4
86	Heap, Todd (TE)	6-5/252	3-16-80	5	Arizona State	D1/01	6/6
80	Hymes, Randy	6-3/211	8-7-79	3	Grambling State	FA/02	14/7
11	Johnson, Patrick	5-10/196	8-10-76	7	Oregon	FA/05	0/0
82	Jones, Terry (TE)	6-3/260	12-3-79	4	Alabama	D5/02	15/10
85	Mason, Derrick	5-10/190	1-17-74	9	Michigan State	FA/05	16/16
84	Moore, Clarence	6-6/211	9-24-82	2	Northern Arizona	D6b/04	15/6
88	Smith, Trent (TE)	6-5/245	9-15-79	2	Oklahoma	D7/03	0/0
83	Wilcox, Daniel (TE)	6-1/245	3-23-77	2	Appalachian State	FA/04	16/5
	OFFENSIVE LINEMEN						
60	Brown, Jason (C)	6-3/313	5-5-83	R	North Carolina	D4/05	—
77	Brown, Orlando (T)	6-7/360	12-12-70	10	South Carolina State	FA/03	14/13
65	Caylor, Drew (C)	6-5/291	1-27-81	R	Stanford	D6c/04	0/0
62	Flynn, Mike (C)	6-3/305	6-15-74	8	Maine	FA/97	9/5
59	Maese, Joe (LS)	6-0/245	12-2-78	5	New Mexico	D6/01	15/0
64	Mulitalo, Edwin (G)	6-3/345	9-1-74	7	Arizona	D4b/99	15/15
75	Ogden, Jonathan (T)	6-9/345	7-31-74	10	UCLA	D1a/96	12/12
79	Pashos, Tony (T)	6-6/337	8-3-80	2	Illinois	D5b/03	6/0
69	Rimpf, Brian (G)	6-5/319	2-11-81	1	East Carolina	D7/04	1/0
78	Terry, Adam (T)	6-8/330	9-1-82	R	Syracuse	D2b/05	—
68	Vincent, Keydrick (G)	6-5/325	4-13-78	5	Mississippi	FA/05	16/16
	DEFENSIVE LINEMEN						
93	Edwards, Dwan (T)	6-3/315	5-16-81	2	Oregon State	D2/04	4/0
91	Franklin, Aubrayo (T)	6-1/320	8-27-80	3	Tennessee	D5a/03	6/0
97	Gregg, Kelly (T)	6-0/310	11-1-76	6	Oklahoma	FA/00	14/14
95	Johnson, Jarret (E)	6-3/285	8-14-81	3	Alabama	D4a/03	16/0
92	Kemoeatu, Maake (T)	6-5/340	1-10-79	4	Utah	FA/02	14/3
55	Suggs, Terrell (E)	6-3/260	10-11-82	3	Arizona State	D1a/03	16/16
98	Weaver, Anthony (E)	6-3/290	7-28-80	4	Notre Dame	D2/02	16/15
	LINEBACKERS						
94	Cody, Dan	6-3/270	12-1-81	R	Oklahoma	D2a/05	—
54	Green, Roderick	6-2/250	4-26-82	2	Central Missouri St.	D5/04	9/0
52	Lewis, Ray	6-1/245	5-15-75	10	Miami	D1b/96	15/15
56	Nelson, Jim	6-1/234	4-16-75	7	Penn State	FA/05	15/1
50	Polley, Tommy	6-3/240	1-18-78	5	Florida State	FA/05	15/13
57	Scott, Bart	6-2/235	8-18-80	4	Southern Illinois	FA/02	13/0
51	Smith, Mike	6-2/238	9-2-81	R	Texas Tech	D7/05	—
96	Thomas, Adalius	6-2/270	8-18-77	6	Southern Mississippi	D6a/00	16/16
	DEFENSIVE BACKS						
24	Carter, Dale (CB)	6-1/194	11-28-69	13	Tennessee	FA/04	0/0
47	Demps, Will (S)	6-0/205	11-7-79	4	San Diego State	FA/02	16/16
28	Johnson, Jarvis (S)	5-10/195	11-22-82	R	Rutgers	FA/05	—
21	McAlister, Chris (CB)	6-1/206	6-14-77	7	Arizona	D1/99	15/14
20	Reed, Ed (S)	5-11/200	9-11-78	4	Miami	D1/02	16/16
22	Rolle, Samari (CB)	6-0/175	8-10-76	8	Florida State	FA/05	12/11
37	Sanders, Deion (CB)	6-1/198	8-9-67	14	Florida State	FA/04	9/2
49	Williams, Chad (S)	5-9/207	1-22-79	4	Southern Mississippi	D6d/02	16/1
	SPECIALISTS						
3	Stover, Matt (K)	5-11/178	1-27-68	16	Louisiana Tech	FA/91	16/0
15	Zastudil, Dave (P)	6-3/215	10-26-78	4	Ohio	D4a/02	13/0

Abbreviations: D1—draft pick, first round; FA—free-agent acquisition.

2004 regular-season record: 9-7
Position: 2nd in AFC North

Sept.12—at Cleveland	L	3-20
Sept.19—PITTSBURGH	W	30-13
Sept.26—at Cincinnati	W	23-9
Oct. 4—KANSAS CITY	L	24-27
Oct. 10—at Washington	W	17-10
Oct. 17—Open date		
Oct. 24—BUFFALO	W	20-6
Oct. 31—at Philadelphia	L	10-15
Nov. 7—CLEVELAND	W	27-13
Nov.14—at N.Y. Jets (OT)	W	20-17
Nov.21—DALLAS	W	30-10
Nov.28—at New England	L	3-24
Dec. 5—CINCINNATI	L	26-27
Dec.12—N.Y. GIANTS	W	37-14
Dec.19—at Indianapolis	L	10-20
Dec.26—at Pittsburgh	L	7-20
Jan. 2—MIAMI	W	30-23

SCORING BY PERIODS

	Q1	Q2	Q3	Q4	OT	Pts.
Ravens	63	89	75	87	3	317
Opponents	46	59	57	106	0	268

TEAM STATISTICS

	Bal.	Opp.
TOTAL FIRST DOWNS	260	273
Rushing	103	88
Passing	135	158
Penalty	22	27
3rd Down: Made/Att.	81/231	75/218
3rd Down Pct.	35.1	34.4
4th Down: Made/Att.	4/15	2/8
4th Down Pct.	26.7	25.0
POSSESSION AVG.	29:36	30:24
TOTAL NET YARDS	4375	4803
Avg. per Game	273.4	300.2
Total Plays	991	1009
Avg. per Play	4.4	4.8
NET YARDS RUSHING	2063	1681
Avg. per Game	128.9	105.1
Total Rushes	491	469
NET YARDS PASSING	2312	3122
Avg. per Game	144.5	195.1
Sacked/Yards Lost	35/247	39/264
Gross Yards	2559	3386
Att./Completions	465/258	501/276
Completion Pct.	55.5	55.1
Had Intercepted	11	21
PUNTS/AVERAGE	97/40.6	94/40.1
NET PUNTING AVG.	97/34.6	94/33.1
PENALTIES/YARDS	94/894	101/798
FUMBLES/LOST	26/12	23/13
TOUCHDOWNS	33	27
Rushing	11	9
Passing	13	14
Returns	9	4

SCORING (NON-KICKERS)

				Tot.			Tot.
	TD	RTD	PTD	MTD	2Pt.	Pts.	
J. Lewis	7	7	0	0	0	42	
Moore	4	0	4	0	1	26	
Heap	3	0	3	0	0	18	
Sams	3	1	0	2	0	18	
Hymes	2	0	2	0	0	12	
McAlister	2	0	0	2	0	12	
Reed	2	0	0	2	0	12	
C. Taylor	2	2	0	0	0	12	
Boller	1	1	0	0	0	6	
Dinkins	1	0	1	0	0	6	
J. Johnson	1	0	0	1	0	6	
K. Johnson	1	0	1	0	0	6	
T. Jones	1	0	1	0	0	6	
Sanders	1	0	0	1	0	6	
Wilcox	1	0	1	0	0	6	
Williams	1	0	0	1	0	6	
Ravens	33	11	13	9	1	200	
Opponents	27	9	14	4	1	166	

2-Pt. conversions: Ravens 1-3; Opponents 1-3.

(KICKERS)

	XPM/XPA	FGM/FGA	Pts.
Stover	30/30	29/32	117
Ravens	30/30	29/32	117
Opponents	24/24	26/31	102

RUSHING

	Att.	Yds.	Avg.	Lg.	TD
J. Lewis	235	1006	4.3	t75	7
C. Taylor	160	714	4.5	47	2
Boller	53	189	3.6	19	1
White	14	62	4.4	16	0
Smith	12	48	4.0	13	0
Ricard	10	36	3.6	14	0
Sams	4	19	4.8	8	1
K. Johnson	1	0	0.0	0	0
Stewart	1	-1	-1.0	-1	0
Sanders	1	-10	-10.0	-10	0
Ravens	491	2063	4.2	t75	11
Opponents	469	1681	3.6	t35	9

RECEIVING

	No.	Yds.	Avg.	Lg.	TD
K. Johnson	35	373	10.7	35	1
T. Taylor	34	421	12.4	47	0
C. Taylor	30	184	6.1	23	0
Heap	27	303	11.2	37	3
Hymes	26	323	12.4	t57	2
Wilcox	25	219	8.8	20	1
Moore	24	293	12.2	52	4
T. Jones	20	152	7.6	19	1
Ricard	11	39	3.5	8	0
J. Lewis	10	116	11.6	46	0
Dinkins	9	94	10.4	18	1
Darling	2	5	2.5	4	0
Smith	2	31	15.5	25	0

	No.	Yds.	Avg.	Lg.	TD
White	2	4	2.0	6	0
Sams	1	2	2.0	2	0
Ravens	258	2559	9.9	t57	13
Opponents	276	3386	12.3	t76	14

INTERCEPTIONS

	No.	Yds.	Avg.	Lg.	TD
Reed	9	358	39.8	t106	1
Williams	3	156	52.0	94	1
Sanders	3	87	29.0	t48	1
McAlister	1	51	51.0	t51	1
Baxter	1	33	33.0	33	0
A. Thomas	1	8	8.0	8	0
J. Johnson	1	6	6.0	t6	1
Weaver	1	1	1.0	1	0
Demps	1	0	0.0	0	0
Ravens	21	700	33.3	t106	5
Opponents	11	172	15.6	71	0

SACKS: Suggs 10.5, A. Thomas 8.0, Douglas 5.5, Weaver 4.0, Demps 2.5, Baxter 2.0, Reed 2.0, Williams 2.0, Gregg 1.5, R. Lewis 1.0. Ravens 39.0; Opponents 35.0.

PUNTING

	No.	Yds.	Avg.	In. 20	Lg.
Murphy	18	777	43.2	6	54
Stewart	5	177	35.4	2	42
Stover	1	33	33.0	0	33
Zastudil	73	2948	40.4	26	61
Ravens	97	3935	40.6	34	61
Opponents	94	3767	40.1	24	59

PUNT RETURNS

	No.	FC	Yds.	Avg.	Lg.	TD
Sams	55	12	575	10.5	t78	2
Sanders	5	0	41	8.2	23	0
Ravens	60	12	616	10.3	t78	2
Opponents	36	21	281	7.8	18	0

KICK RETURNS

	No.	Yds.	Avg.	Lg.	TD
Sams	59	1251	21.2	64	0
Dinkins	1	7	7.0	7	0
J. Johnson	1	6	6.0	6	0
Ravens	61	1264	20.7	64	0
Opponents	65	1509	23.2	t95	2

FIELD GOALS

	1-19	20-29	30-39	40-49	50+
Stover	2/2	9/9	7/8	9/10	2/3
Ravens	2/2	9/9	7/8	9/10	2/3
Opponents	1/1	13/13	3/4	8/10	1/3

Stover: (42G) (35G, 27G, 34G) (21G) (50G) (33G) (24G, 50N, 19G) (44G) (44G, 39G, 43G, 36G) (24G, 42G) (50G) (22G) (20G, 22G, 38G, 45G) (46G, 44G, 27G) (42G, 31B) (44N) (25G, 19G, 33G) **Opponents:** (37G, 25G) (48N) (29G, 47G, 26G) (42G, 38G) (26G) (24G, 21G) (20G, 41G, 43G) (50G, 29G) (20G) (19G, 41N) (28G, 40G, 48G) (53N, 41G, 24G) () (24G, 33G, 33N) (23G, 40G) (53N)

PASSING

	Att.	Cmp.	Yds.	Pct.	Avg. Gain	TD	Pct. TD	Int.	Pct. Int.	Long	Sack/Lost	Rating
Boller	464	258	2559	55.6	5.52	13	2.8	11	2.4	t57	35/247	70.9
Hymes	1	0	0	0.0	0.00	0	0.0	0	0.0	...	0/0	39.6
Ravens	465	258	2559	55.5	5.50	13	2.8	11	2.4	t57	35/247	70.7
Opponents	501	276	3386	55.1	6.76	14	2.8	21	4.2	t76	39/264	68.0

BUFFALO BILLS
AFC EAST DIVISION

2005 SEASON

CLUB DIRECTORY

Owner
Ralph C. Wilson Jr.
President/general manager
Tom Donahoe
Assistant general manager
Tom Modrak
Vice president/communications
Scott Berchtold
Director of pro personnel
John Guy
Coordinator of college scouting
Doug Majeski
Director of community affairs
Gretchen Geitter
Media relations manager
Bill Hudock

Head coach
Mike Mularkey

Assistant coaches
Bobby April (special teams coordinator)
Don Blackmon (linebackers)
Tom Clements (off. coordinator)
Jerry Gray (def. coordinator)
Tim Krumrie (defensive line)
Chuck Lester (defensive asst.)
Jim McNally (offensive line)
Mike Miller (tight ends)
Brad Roll (strength & conditioning)
Eric Studesville (running backs)
Steve Szabo (defensive backs)
Tyke Tolbert (wide receivers)
Frank Verducci (offensive line)
Sam Wyche (quarterbacks)

OFFSEASON MOVES

Key additions
OL Bennie Anderson	FA/Ravens
OL Mike Gandy	FA/Bears
QB Kelly Holcomb	FA/Browns
RB ReShard Lee	FA/Cowboys

Key losses
QB Drew Bledsoe	Rel./Cowboys
OT Jonas Jennings	FA/49ers
OT Marcus Price	FA
S Pierson Prioleau	FA/Redskins
G Mike Pucillo	FA
S Izell Reese	FA
DT Pat Williams	FA/Vikings

SCHEDULE

Sept.	11—HOUSTON	1:00
Sept.	18—at Tampa Bay	1:00
Sept.	25—ATLANTA	1:00
Oct.	2—at New Orleans	1:00
Oct.	9—MIAMI	1:00
Oct.	16—N.Y. JETS	4:15
Oct.	23—at Oakland	4:15
Oct.	30—at New England	9:30
Nov.	6—Open date	
Nov.	13—KANSAS CITY	2:00
Nov.	20—at San Diego	5:15
Nov.	27—CAROLINA	2:00
Dec.	4—at Miami	2:00
Dec.	11—NEW ENGLAND	2:00
Dec.	17—DENVER (Sat.)	9:30
Dec.	24—at Cincinnati (Sat.)	2:00
Jan.	1—at N.Y. Jets	2:00

All times are Eastern.
All games Sunday unless noted.

DRAFT CHOICES

Roscoe Parrish, WR, Miami (second round/55th pick overall).
Kevin Everett, TE, Miami (3/86).
Raymond "Duke" Preston, C, Illinois (4/122).
Eric King, CB, Wake Forest (5/156).
Justin Geisinger, G, Vanderbilt (6/197).
Lionel Gates, RB, Louisville (7/236).

MISCELLANEOUS TEAM DATA

Stadium (capacity, surface):
Ralph Wilson Stadium (73,967, AstroPlay)
Business address:
One Bills Drive
Orchard Park, N.Y. 14127
Business phone:
716-648-1800
Ticket information:
877-BB-TICKS
Team colors:
Dark navy, red, royal and nickel gray
Flagship radio station:
WGRF, 96.9 FM (97 ROCK)
Website:
www.buffalobills.com
Training site:
St. John Fisher College
Rochester, N.Y.
716-648-1800

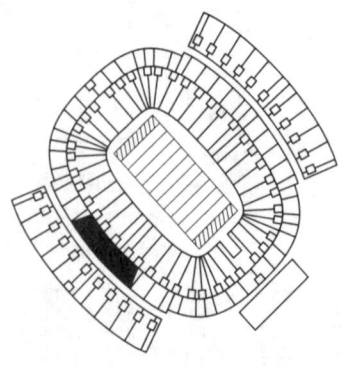

BUFFALO BILLS

No.	QUARTERBACKS	Ht./Wt.	Born	NFL Exp.	College	How acq.	'04 Games GP/GS
10	Holcomb, Kelly	6-2/212	7-9-73	9	Middle Tenn. State	FA/05	4/2
7	Losman, J.P.	6-2/217	3-12-81	2	Tulane	D1b/04	4/0
6	Matthews, Shane	6-3/199	6-1-70	12	Florida	FA/04	3/0
	RUNNING BACKS						
30	Brown, Dante	6-1/215	7-28-80	3	Memphis	FA/04	1/0
35	Burns, Joe	5-9/215	9-15-79	4	Georgia Tech	FA/02	16/0
25	Gates, Lionel (FB)	6-0/223	3-13-82	R	Louisville	D7/05	—
20	Henry, Travis	5-9/215	10-29-78	5	Tennessee	D2b/01	10/5
	Lee, ReShard	5-10/220	10-12-80	2	Middle Tennessee St.	FA/05	14/0
21	McGahee, Willis	6-0/228	10-20-81	3	Miami	D1/03	16/11
31	Shelton, Daimon (FB)	6-0/262	9-15-72	8	Sacramento State	FA/04	16/12
40	Williams, Shaud	5-7/193	10-2-80	2	Alabama	FA/04	4/0
	RECEIVERS						
89	Aiken, Sam	6-2/204	12-14-80	3	North Carolina	D4b/03	16/0
84	Campbell, Mark (TE)	6-6/255	12-6-75	6	Michigan	T-Cle./03	12/12
87	Euhus, Tim (TE)	6-5/249	10-2-80	2	Oregon State	D4/04	12/5
83	Evans, Lee	5-10/197	3-11-81	2	Wisconsin	D1a/04	16/11
85	Everett, Kevin (TE)	6-4/241	2-5-82	R	Miami	D3/05	—
86	Haddad, Drew	5-11/187	8-15-78	3	Buffalo	FA/04	1/0
80	Moulds, Eric	6-2/210	7-17-73	10	Mississippi State	D1/96	16/16
88	Neufeld, Ryan (TE)	6-4/250	11-22-75	5	UCLA	FA/03	16/5
11	Parrish, Roscoe	5-10/168	7-16-82	R	Miami	D2/05	—
82	Reed, Josh	5-10/208	5-1-80	4	Louisiana State	D2a/02	12/1
19	Smith, Jonathan	5-10/194	11-28-81	2	Georgia Tech	D7b/04	9/0
81	Trafford, Rod (TE)	6-3/250	11-28-78	2	South Carolina	FA/04	4/0
	OFFENSIVE LINEMEN						
66	Anderson, Bennie (G)	6-5/345	2-17-77	5	Tennessee State	FA/05	16/12
50	Bannan, Justin (G)	6-3/305	4-18-79	4	Colorado	D5/02	10/0
47	Dorenbos, Jon (LS)	6-0/250	7-21-80	3	UTEP	FA/03	13/0
69	Gandy, Mike (T)	6-4/310	1-3-79	5	Notre Dame	FA/05	5/5
73	Geisinger, Justin (G)	6-3/322	5-24-82	R	Vanderbilt	D6/05	—
79	McFarland, Dylan (T)	6-5/290	7-11-80	1	Montana	D7a/04	2/0
71	Peters, Jason (T)	6-4/328	1-22-82	2	Arkansas		5/1
75	Preston, Duke (C)	6-5/311	6-12-82	R	Illinois	D4/05	—
72	Smith, Lawrence (T)	6-3/295	8-16-79	2	Tennessee State	FA/04	16/8
64	Sobieski, Ben (T)	6-5/315	5-3-79	3	Iowa	D5/03	0/0
70	Teague, Trey (C/T)	6-5/300	12-27-74	8	Tennessee	FA/02	12/12
65	Tucker, Ross (G/C)	6-4/316	3-2-79	5	Princeton	W-Dal./03	16/12
58	Villarrial, Chris (G)	6-3/318	6-9-73	10	Indiana (Pa.)	FA/04	16/16
68	Williams, Mike (T)	6-6/360	1-11-80	4	Texas	D1/02	15/15
	DEFENSIVE LINEMEN						
95	Adams, Sam (T)	6-4/335	6-13-73	12	Texas A&M	FA/03	16/16
97	Anderson, Tim (T)	6-3/304	11-22-80	2	Ohio State	D3/04	3/0
67	Brown, LaWaylon (T)	6-4/315	6-12-80	1	Oklahoma State	FA/05	0/0
92	Denney, Ryan (E)	6-7/275	6-15-77	4	BYU	D2b/02	16/5
98	Edwards, Ron (T)	6-3/320	7-12-79	5	Texas A&M	D3a/01	16/2
63	Gause, George (E)	6-4/275	6-20-82	R	South Carolina	FA/05	0/0
90	Kelsay, Chris (E)	6-4/275	10-31-79	3	Nebraska	D2/03	16/10
99	Osunde, Uyi (E)	6-3/255	2-28-82	1	Connecticut	FA/04	0/0
77	Sape, Lauvale (T)	6-1/296	8-29-80	3	Utah	D6/03	0/0
94	Schobel, Aaron (E)	6-4/262	9-1-77	5	TCU	D2a/01	16/16
	LINEBACKERS						
55	Crowell, Angelo	6-1/235	8-16-81	3	Virginia	D3/03	16/0
59	Fletcher, London	5-10/245	5-19-75	8	John Carroll	FA/02	16/16
53	Haggan, Mario	6-3/248	3-3-80	3	Mississippi State	D7/03	16/0
96	Posey, Jeff	6-4/241	8-14-75	8	Southern Mississippi	FA/03	16/15
51	Spikes, Takeo	6-2/242	12-17-76	8	Auburn	FA/03	16/16
57	Stamer, Josh	6-2/238	10-11-77	3	South Dakota	FA/03	16/0
	DEFENSIVE BACKS						
26	Baker, Rashad (S)	5-10/198	2-22-82	2	Tennessee	FA/04	14/3
22	Clements, Nate (CB)	6-0/209	12-12-79	5	Ohio State	D1/01	16/16
33	Greer, Jabari (CB)	5-11/169	2-2-82	2	Tennessee	FA/04	12/1
29	King, Eric (CB)	5-8/189	5-10-82	R	Wake Forest	D5/05	—
24	McGee, Terrence (CB)	5-9/195	10-14-80	3	Northwestern State	D4a/03	16/13
36	Milloy, Lawyer (S)	6-0/190	11-14-73	10	Washington	FA/03	11/11
28	Thomas, Kevin (CB)	6-0/182	7-28-78	4	UNLV	D6/02	16/1
23	Vincent, Troy (S)	6-1/200	6-8-71	14	Wisconsin	FA/04	7/7
27	Wire, Coy (S)	6-0/205	11-7-78	4	Stanford	D3/02	12/3
	SPECIALISTS						
9	Lindell, Rian (K)	6-3/235	1-20-77	6	Washington State	FA/03	16/0
8	Moorman, Brian (P)	6-0/175	2-5-76	5	Pittsburg State	FA/01	16/0

Abbreviations: D1—draft pick, first round; W—claimed on waivers; T—obtained in trade; FA—free-agent acquisition.

BUFFALO BILLS

2004 regular-season record: 9-7
Position: 3rd in AFC East

Sept.12—JACKSONVILLE	L	10-13
Sept.19—at Oakland	L	10-13
Sept.26—Open date		
Oct. 3—NEW ENGLAND	L	17-31
Oct. 10—at N.Y. Jets	L	14-16
Oct. 17—MIAMI	W	20-13
Oct. 24—at Baltimore	L	6-20
Oct. 31—ARIZONA	W	38-14
Nov. 7—N.Y. JETS	W	22-17
Nov. 14—at New England	L	6-29
Nov. 21—ST. LOUIS	W	37-17
Nov. 28—at Seattle	W	38-9
Dec. 5—at Miami	W	42-32
Dec. 12—CLEVELAND	W	37-7
Dec. 19—at Cincinnati	W	33-17
Dec. 26—at San Francisco	W	41-7
Jan. 2—PITTSBURGH	L	24-29

	Tot. TD	RTD	PTD	MTD	2Pt.	Tot. Pts.
McGee	3	0	0	3	0	18
Clements	2	0	0	2	0	12
Euhus	2	0	2	0	0	12
Spikes	2	0	0	2	0	12
S. Williams	2	2	0	0	0	12
Peters	1	0	0	1	0	6
J. Smith	1	0	0	1	0	6
P. Williams	1	0	0	1	0	8
Bills	46	15	21	10	0	278
Opponents	29	6	20	3	1	176

2-Pt. conversions: Bills 0-1; Opponents 1-2.

(KICKERS)

	XPM/XPA	FGM/FGA	Pts.
Lindell	45/45	24/28	117
Bills	45/45	24/28	117
Opponents	27/27	27/32	108

SCORING BY PERIODS

	Q1	Q2	Q3	Q4	OT	Pts.
Bills	89	101	80	125	0	395
Opponents	78	100	12	94	0	284

TEAM STATISTICS

	Buf.	Opp.
TOTAL FIRST DOWNS	271	258
Rushing	102	79
Passing	149	150
Penalty	20	29
3rd Down: Made/Att.	77/215	77/214
3rd Down Pct.	35.8	36.0
4th Down: Made/Att.	10/21	11/15
4th Down Pct.	47.6	73.3
POSSESSION AVG.	30:21	29:39
TOTAL NET YARDS	4691	4228
Avg. per Game	293.2	264.3
Total Plays	982	978
Avg. per Play	4.8	4.3
NET YARDS RUSHING	1874	1604
Avg. per Game	117.1	100.3
Total Rushes	483	447
NET YARDS PASSING	2817	2624
Avg. per Game	176.1	164.0
Sacked/Yards Lost	38/215	45/319
Gross Yards	3032	2943
Att./Completions	461/262	486/261
Completion Pct.	56.8	53.7
Had Intercepted	17	24
PUNTS/AVERAGE	78/43.1	79/40.7
NET PUNTING AVG.	78/36.5	79/33.0
PENALTIES/YARDS	121/1047	120/865
FUMBLES/LOST	26/12	31/15
TOUCHDOWNS	46	29
Rushing	15	6
Passing	21	20
Returns	10	3

SCORING (NON-KICKERS)

	Tot. TD	RTD	PTD	MTD	2Pt.	Tot. Pts.
McGahee	13	13	0	0	0	78
Evans	9	0	9	0	0	54
Campbell	5	0	5	0	0	30
Moulds	5	0	5	0	0	30

RUSHING

	Att.	Yds.	Avg.	Lg.	TD
McGahee	284	1128	4.0	41	13
Henry	94	326	3.5	19	0
S. Williams	42	167	4.0	t27	2
Evans	5	85	17.0	48	0
Burns	20	73	3.7	21	0
Bledsoe	22	37	1.7	17	0
Moorman	2	23	11.5	34	0
Moulds	5	19	3.8	12	0
Losman	2	15	7.5	10	0
J. Smith	2	11	5.5	8	0
Reed	2	-1	-0.5	6	0
Matthews	2	-3	-1.5	-1	0
Greer	1	-6	-6.0	-6	0
Bills	483	1874	3.9	48	15
Opponents	447	1604	3.6	58	6

RECEIVING

	No.	Yds.	Avg.	Lg.	TD
Moulds	88	1043	11.9	49	5
Evans	48	843	17.6	t69	9
McGahee	22	169	7.7	16	0
Campbell	17	203	11.9	27	5
Shelton	17	114	6.7	24	0
Reed	16	153	9.6	20	0
Aiken	11	148	13.5	54	0
Euhus	11	98	8.9	17	2
Henry	10	45	4.5	10	0
Neufeld	6	61	10.2	29	0
Shaw	5	59	11.8	20	0
J. Smith	3	21	7.0	11	0
Trafford	3	25	8.3	10	0
S. Williams	3	19	6.3	10	0
Burns	1	7	7.0	7	0
Thomas	1	24	24.0	24	0
Bills	262	3032	11.6	t69	21
Opponents	261	2943	11.3	t51	20

INTERCEPTIONS

	No.	Yds.	Avg.	Lg.	TD
Clements	6	77	12.8	35	1
Spikes	5	122	24.4	t62	2
McGee	3	21	7.0	21	0
Milloy	2	20	10.0	11	0

	No.	Yds.	Avg.	Lg.	TD
Reese	1	33	33.0	33	0
Baker	1	26	26.0	26	0
P. Williams	1	20	20.0	t20	1
Vincent	1	8	8.0	8	0
Kelsay	1	3	3.0	3	0
Posey	1	3	3.0	3	0
Adams	1	0	0.0	0	0
Stamer	1	0	0.0	0	0
Bills	24	333	13.9	t62	4
Opponents	17	357	21.0	94	1

SACKS: Schobel 8.0, Adams 5.0, Kelsay 4.5, Edwards 4.0, Milloy 4.0, Fletcher 3.5, Denney 3.0, Spikes 3.0, P. Williams 2.5, McGee 2.0, Greer 1.0, Posey 1.0, Thomas 1.0, Vincent 1.0, Wire 1.0, Clements 0.5. Bills 45.0; Opponents 38.0.

PUNTING

	No.	Yds.	Avg.	In. 20	Lg.
Lindell	1	37	37.0	0	37
Moorman	77	3325	43.2	17	80
Bills	78	3362	43.1	17	80
Opponents	79	3218	40.7	18	69

PUNT RETURNS

	No.	FC	Yds.	Avg.	Lg.	TD
Clements	35	10	327	9.3	t86	1
J. Smith	9	0	157	17.4	t70	1
Reed	1	0	7	7.0	7	0
S. Williams	1	0	0	0.0	0	0
Bills	46	10	491	10.7	t86	2
Opponents	37	6	315	8.5	34	0

KICK RETURNS

	No.	Yds.	Avg.	Lg.	TD
McGee	52	1370	26.3	t104	3
Fletcher	4	86	21.5	23	0
Shelton	2	25	12.5	15	0
Clements	1	14	14.0	14	0
Kelsay	1	14	14.0	14	0
Moulds	1	2	2.0	2	0
Neufeld	1	3	3.0	3	0
J. Smith	1	28	28.0	28	0
Bills	63	1542	24.5	t104	3
Opponents	77	1406	18.3	65	0

FIELD GOALS

	1-19	20-29	30-39	40-49	50+
Lindell	0/0	13/14	10/11	1/3	0/0
Bills	0/0	13/14	10/11	1/3	0/0
Opponents	2/2	11/12	8/9	6/7	0/2

Lindell: (42N, 25G) (32G) (33G) () (43N, 43G, 20G) (24G, 21G) (25G) (20G, 30G) () (21G, 35G, 33G) (25G) (38N) (23G, 21G, 37G) (23G, 39G, 21G, 33G) (23G, 31G) (37G, 28N) Opponents: (25G, 27G) (21G, 33G) (42G) (29N, 37G, 36G, 38G) (47G, 28G) (24G, 50N, 19G) (64N) (36N, 41G) (27G, 24G, 20G, 45G, 37G) (41G) (19G) (47G) (45N) (24G) () (22G, 21G, 31G, 37G, 33G)

PASSING

	Att.	Cmp.	Yds.	Pct.	Avg. Gain	TD	Pct. TD	Int.	Pct. Int.	Long	Sack/Lost	Rating
Bledsoe	450	256	2932	56.9	6.52	20	4.4	16	3.6	t69	37/215	76.6
Matthews	3	2	44	66.7	14.67	1	33.3	0	0.0	t33	0/0	149.3
Losman	5	3	32	60.0	6.40	0	0.0	1	20.0	17	1/0	39.2
Moorman	3	1	24	33.3	8.00	0	0.0	0	0.0	24	0/0	63.2
Bills	461	262	3032	56.8	6.58	21	4.6	17	3.7	t69	38/215	76.7
Opponents	486	261	2943	53.7	6.06	20	4.1	24	4.9	t51	45/319	65.2

CAROLINA PANTHERS
NFC SOUTH DIVISION

2005 SEASON

CLUB DIRECTORY

Owner & founder
Jerry Richardson
President of Carolina Panthers
Mark Richardson
President of Carolinas Stadium Corp.
Jon Richardson
General manager
Marty Hurney
Director of player development
Donnie Shell
Director of communications
Charlie Dayton
Director of pro scouting
Mark Koncz
Director of college scouting
Tony Softli
Director of community relations
Riley Fields

Head coach
John Fox

Assistant coaches
Danny Crossman (special teams)
Paul Ferraro (special teams asst.)
Ken Flajole (linebackers)
Mike Gillhamer (defensive asst./secondary)
Dan Henning (offensive coordinator)
David Magazu (tight ends)
Mike Maser (offensive line)
Mike McCoy (quarterbacks/offensive asst.)
Rod Perry (secondary)
Jerry Simmons (strength & conditioning)
Jim Skipper (running backs)
Sal Sunseri (defensive line)
Mike Trgovac (def. coordinator)
Richard Williamson (wide receivers)

OFFSEASON MOVES

Key additions
S Idrees Bashir	FA/Colts
LB Chris Draft	Rel./Falcons
TE Freddie Jones	FA/Cardinals
CB Ken Lucas	FA/Seahawks
S Marlon McCree	FA/Texans
P Tom Rouen	FA/Seahawks
G Mike Wahle	Rel./Packers

Key losses
LB Brian Allen	FA/Redskins
G Doug Brzezinski	Released
CB Artrell Hawkins	Released
WR Muhsin Muhammad	Released/Bears
QB Rodney Peete	Released
S Travares Tillman	FA/Dolphins

SCHEDULE

Sept.	11—NEW ORLEANS	1:00
Sept.	18—NEW ENGLAND	1:00
Sept.	25—at Miami	1:00
Oct.	3—GREEN BAY (Mon.)	9:00
Oct.	9—at Arizona	4:15
Oct.	16—at Detroit	1:00
Oct.	23—Open week	
Oct.	30—MINNESOTA	2:00
Nov.	6—at Tampa Bay	2:00
Nov.	13—N.Y. JETS	5:05
Nov.	20—at Chicago	2:00
Nov.	27—at Buffalo	2:00
Dec.	4—ATLANTA	2:00
Dec.	11—TAMPA BAY	2:00
Dec.	18—at New Orleans	2:00
Dec.	24—DALLAS (Sat.)	2:00
Jan.	1—at Atlanta	2:00

All times are Eastern.
All games Sunday unless noted.

DRAFT CHOICES

Thomas Davis, FS, Georgia (first round/14th pick overall).
Eric Shelton, RB, Louisville (2/54).
Evan Mathis, G, Alabama (3/79).
Atiyyah Ellison, DT, Missouri (3/89).
Stefan Lefors, QB, Louisville (4/121).
Adam Seward, ILB, UNLV (5/149).
Geoff Hangartner, C, Texas A&M (5/169).
Ben Emanuel, FS, UCLA (5/171).
Jovan Haye, DE, Vanderbilt (6/189).
Joe Berger, OT, Michigan Tech (6/207).

MISCELLANEOUS TEAM DATA

Stadium (capacity, surface):
Bank of America Stadium
(73,298, grass)
Business address:
800 S. Mint St.
Charlotte, NC 28202-1502
Business phone:
704-358-7000
Ticket information:
704-358-7800
Team colors:
Blue, black and silver
Flagship radio station:
WRFX-99.7 FM
Website:
www.panthers.com
Training site:
Wofford College
Spartanburg, S.C.
704-358-7000

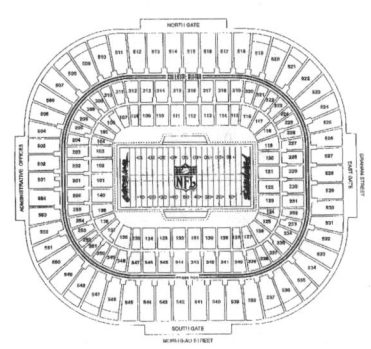

CAROLINA PANTHERS

No.	QUARTERBACKS	Ht./Wt.	Born	NFL Exp.	College	How acq.	'04 Games GP/GS
17	Delhomme, Jake	6-2/215	1-10-75	7	Louisiana-Lafayette	FA/03	16/16
15	LeFors, Stefan	5-11/201	6-7-81	R	Louisville	D4/05	—
12	Rutherford, Rod	6-2/223	12-12-80	1	Pittsburgh	FA/04	0/0
16	Weinke, Chris	6-4/232	7-31-72	5	Florida State	D4/01	1/0
	RUNNING BACKS						
49	Cramer, Casey	6-2/235	1-5-82	2	Dartmouth	FA/04	6/1
48	Davis, Stephen	6-0/230	3-1-74	10	Auburn	FA/03	2/2
26	Foster, DeShaun	6-0/222	1-10-80	4	UCLA	D2/02	4/3
37	Goings, Nick (FB)	6-0/225	1-26-78	5	Pittsburgh	FA/01	16/8
45	Hoover, Brad (FB)	6-0/245	11-11-76	6	Western Carolina	FA/00	14/9
35	Shelton, Eric	6-1/246	6-23-83	R	Louisville	D2/05	—
32	Smart, Rod	5-11/201	1-9-77	5	Western Kentucky	W-Phi./02	3/0
	RECEIVERS						
18	Carter, Drew	6-3/200	9-5-81	1	Ohio State	D5/04	0/0
83	Colbert, Keary	5-10/193	5-21-82	2	USC	D2/04	15/15
84	Gaines, Michael (TE)	6-3/280	3-30-80	2	Central Florida	D7/04	15/6
88	Hankton, Karl	6-2/202	7-24-70	7	Trinity	FA/00	15/0
85	Jones, Freddie (TE)	6-4/265	9-16-74	9	North Carolina	FA/05	16/15
86	Mangum, Kris (TE)	6-4/252	8-15-73	8	Mississippi	D7/97	15/10
81	Proehl, Ricky	6-0/190	3-7-68	16	Wake Forest	FA/03	16/3
82	Seidman, Mike (TE)	6-4/261	2-11-81	3	UCLA	D3a/03	16/6
89	Smith, Steve	5-9/185	5-12-79	5	Utah	D3/01	1/1
	OFFENSIVE LINEMEN						
74	Berger, Joe (T)	6-5/290	5-25-82	R	Michigan Tech	D6b/05	—
64	Ferrario, Bill (G)	6-2/315	9-22-78	4	Wisconsin	FA/04	0/0
78	Fordham, Todd (T)	6-5/319	10-9-73	9	Florida State	T-Pit./04	15/7
69	Gross, Jordan (T)	6-4/300	7-20-80	3	Utah	D1/03	16/16
63	Hangartner, Geoff (C)	6-5/301	4-22-82	R	Texas A&M	D5b/05	—
61	Kadela, Dave (T)	6-6/304	5-6-78	3	Virginia Tech	FA/03	1/0
73	Mathis, Evan (G/C)	6-5/304	11-1-81	R	Alabama	D3a/05	—
60	Mitchell, Jeff (C)	6-4/300	1-29-74	10	Florida	FA/01	16/16
76	Reyes, Tutan (G)	6-3/305	10-28-77	6	Mississippi	W-TB/02	14/12
68	Wahle, Mike (G)	6-6/304	3-29-77	8	Navy	FA/05	16/16
70	Wharton, Travelle (T)	6-4/312	5-19-81	2	South Carolina	D3/04	11/11
	DEFENSIVE LINEMEN						
99	Buckner, Brentson (T)	6-2/310	9-30-71	12	Clemson	FA/01	15/15
67	Carstens, Jordan (T)	6-5/300	1-22-81	2	Iowa State	FA/04	12/1
98	Ellison, Atiyyah (T)	6-3/303	9-29-81	R	Missouri	D3b/05	—
92	Haye, Jovan (E)	6-2/284	6-21-82	R	Vanderbilt	D6a/05	—
77	Jenkins, Kris (T)	6-4/335	8-3-79	5	Maryland	D2/01	4/4
91	Jordan, Omari (T)	6-4/315	4-15-78	2	Buffalo	FA/04	4/0
94	Moorehead, Kindal (T)	6-2/285	10-14-78	3	Alabama	D5/03	14/12
90	Peppers, Julius (E)	6-6/283	1-18-80	4	North Carolina	D1/02	16/16
62	Pinkney, Cleveland (T)	6-1/300	9-14-77	3	South Carolina	FA/03	5/0
97	Rasmussen, Kemp (E)	6-3/265	5-25-79	4	Indiana	FA/02	12/0
93	Rucker, Mike (E)	6-5/275	2-28-75	7	Nebraska	D2b/99	16/16
96	Wallace, Al (E)	6-5/275	3-25-74	6	Maryland	T-Mia./02	16/0
	LINEBACKERS						
50	Ciurciu, Vinny	6-0/235	5-2-80	3	Boston College	FA/03	16/4
52	Draft, Chris	5-11/232	2-26-76	8	Stanford	FA/05	14/13
56	Kyle, Jason	6-3/242	5-12-72	11	Arizona State	FA/01	16/0
55	Morgan, Dan	6-2/245	12-19-78	5	Miami	D1/01	12/12
46	Seward, Adam	6-3/253	6-15-82	R	UNLV	D5a/05	—
53	Short, Brandon	6-3/253	7-11-77	6	Penn State	FA/04	16/2
57	Tufts, Sean	6-3/236	3-26-82	2	Colorado	D6/04	3/0
54	Witherspoon, Will	6-1/231	8-19-80	3	Georgia	D3/02	16/16
	DEFENSIVE BACKS						
33	Bashir, Idrees (S)	6-2/198	12-7-78	5	Memphis	FA/05	13/13
28	Branch, Colin (S)	5-11/205	3-2-80	3	Stanford	D4/03	16/15
47	Davis, Thomas (S)	6-1/231	3-22-83	R	Georgia	D1/05	—
36	Emanuel, Ben (S)	6-3/213	6-18-82	R	UCLA	D5c/05	—
20	Gamble, Chris (CB)	6-1/181	3-11-83	2	Ohio State	D1/04	16/16
23	Lucas, Ken (CB)	6-0/205	1-23-79	5	Mississippi	FA/05	16/16
24	Manning, Ricky (CB)	5-8/185	11-18-80	3	UCLA	D3b/03	16/16
27	McCree, Marlon (S)	5-11/202	3-17-77	5	Kentucky	FA/05	16/1
30	Minter, Mike (S)	5-10/195	1-15-74	9	Nebraska	D2/97	16/16
21	Wesley, Dante (CB)	6-0/211	4-5-79	4	Arkansas-Pine Bluff	D4/02	13/0
	SPECIALISTS						
6	Cheek, Steve (P)	6-4/205	4-18-77	2	Humboldt State	FA/05	12/0
4	Kasay, John (K)	5-10/198	10-27-69	15	Georgia	FA/95	14/0
8	Rouen, Tom (P)	6-3/225	6-9-68	13	Colorado	FA/05	4/0

Abbreviations: D1—draft pick, first round; W—claimed on waivers; T—obtained in trade; FA—free-agent acquisition.

2004 regular-season record: 7-9
Position: 3rd in NFC South

Date		Result	Score
Sept.13	GREEN BAY	L	14-24
Sept.19	at Kansas City	W	28-17
Sept.26	Open date		
Oct. 3	ATLANTA	L	10-27
Oct. 10	at Denver	L	17-20
Oct. 17	at Philadelphia	L	8-30
Oct. 24	SAN DIEGO	L	6-17
Oct. 31	at Seattle	L	17-23
Nov. 7	OAKLAND	L	24-27
Nov. 14	at San Francisco	W	37-27
Nov. 21	ARIZONA	W	35-10
Nov. 28	TAMPA BAY	W	21-14
Dec. 5	at New Orleans	W	32-21
Dec. 12	ST. LOUIS	W	20-7
Dec. 18	at Atlanta (OT)	L	31-34
Dec. 26	at Tampa Bay	W	37-20
Jan. 2	NEW ORLEANS	L	18-21

SCORING BY PERIODS

	Q1	Q2	Q3	Q4	OT	Pts.
Panthers	78	90	62	125	0	355
Opponents	80	79	92	85	3	339

TEAM STATISTICS

	Car.	Opp.
TOTAL FIRST DOWNS	308	307
Rushing	85	98
Passing	192	177
Penalty	31	32
3rd Down: Made/Att.	83/206	99/215
3rd Down Pct.	40.3	46.0
4th Down: Made/Att.	3/8	6/12
4th Down Pct.	37.5	50.0
POSSESSION AVG.	29:56	30:04
TOTAL NET YARDS	5225	5382
Avg. per Game	326.6	336.4
Total Plays	991	1021
Avg. per Play	5.3	5.3
NET YARDS RUSHING	1582	1904
Avg. per Game	98.9	119.0
Total Rushes	422	474
NET YARDS PASSING	3643	3478
Avg. per Game	227.7	217.4
Sacked/Yards Lost	33/246	34/225
Gross Yards	3889	3703
Att./Completions	536/311	513/303
Completion Pct.	58.0	59.1
Had Intercepted	15	26
PUNTS/AVERAGE	79/43.1	64/41.1
NET PUNTING AVG.	79/36.9	64/37.9
PENALTIES/YARDS	123/1020	117/1078
FUMBLES/LOST	23/11	29/12
TOUCHDOWNS	42	40
Rushing	10	19
Passing	29	18
Returns	3	3

SCORING (NON-KICKERS)

	Tot. TD	RTD	PTD	MTD	2Pt.	Tot. Pts.
Muhammad	16	0	16	0	0	96
Goings	7	6	1	0	0	42
Colbert	5	0	5	0	1	32
Mangum	3	0	3	0	0	18
Seidman	2	0	2	0	1	14
Foster	2	2	0	0	0	12
Hoover	2	0	2	0	0	12
Peppers	2	0	0	2	0	12
Bennett	1	1	0	0	0	6
Delhomme	1	1	0	0	0	6
Moorehead	1	0	0	1	0	6
Panthers	42	10	29	3	2	256
Opponents	40	19	18	3	0	240

2-Pt. conversions: Panthers 2-2; Opponents 0-1.

(KICKERS)

	XPM/XPA	FGM/FGA	Pts.
Kasay	27/28	19/22	84
Chandler	8/8	0/2	8
Sauerbrun	4/4	1/1	7
Panthers	39/40	20/25	99
Opponents	39/39	20/28	99

RUSHING

	Att.	Yds.	Avg.	Lg.	TD
Goings	217	821	3.8	t57	6
Foster	59	255	4.3	74	2
Hoover	68	246	3.6	16	0
Davis	24	92	3.8	12	0
Delhomme	25	71	2.8	13	1
Harris	15	53	3.5	19	0
Bennett	6	17	2.8	11	1
Muhammad	3	15	5.0	13	0
Proehl	1	9	9.0	9	0
Smart	3	4	1.3	3	0
Peete	1	-1	-1.0	-1	0
Panthers	422	1582	3.7	71	10
Opponents	474	1904	4.0	71	19

RECEIVING

	No.	Yds.	Avg.	Lg.	TD
Muhammad	93	1405	15.1	51	16
Colbert	47	754	16.0	63	5
Goings	45	394	8.8	37	1
Mangum	34	323	9.5	26	3
Proehl	34	497	14.6	34	0
Hoover	21	161	7.7	34	2
Seidman	13	123	9.5	27	2
Foster	9	76	8.4	42	0
S. Smith	6	60	10.0	15	0
Gaines	4	34	8.5	14	0
Davis	2	32	16.0	22	0
Hankton	2	25	12.5	20	0
Smart	1	5	5.0	5	0
Panthers	311	3889	12.5	63	29
Opponents	303	3703	12.2	t75	18

INTERCEPTIONS

	No.	Yds.	Avg.	Lg.	TD
Gamble	6	15	2.5	13	0
Witherspoon	4	48	12.0	25	0
Manning Jr.	4	46	11.5	30	0
Branch	3	79	26.3	76	0
Peppers	2	143	71.5	97	1
Morgan	2	20	10.0	11	0

	No.	Yds.	Avg.	Lg.	TD
Allen	1	21	21.0	21	0
Moorehead	1	17	17.0	t17	1
Fields	1	14	14.0	14	0
Hawkins	1	9	9.0	9	0
Buckner	1	8	8.0	8	0
Panthers	26	420	16.2	97	2
Opponents	15	321	21.4	t64	3

SACKS: Peppers 11.0, Fields 4.0, Buckner 3.5, Rucker 3.5, Witherspoon 3.0, Minter 2.0, Moorehead 2.0, Morgan 2.0, Jenkins 1.0, Jordan 1.0, Wallace 1.0. Panthers 34.0; Opponents 33.0.

PUNTING

	No.	Yds.	Avg.	In. 20	Lg.
Kasay	2	51	25.5	0	34
Sauerbrun	76	3351	44.1	25	65
Panthers	79	3402	43.1	25	65
Opponents	64	2630	41.1	21	67

PUNT RETURNS

	No.	FC	Yds.	Avg.	Lg.	TD
Broussard	10	8	43	4.3	13	0
Gamble	9	2	69	7.7	16	0
Baker	8	3	49	6.1	18	0
Hawkins	1	0	4	4.0	4	0
Panthers	28	14	165	5.9	18	0
Opponents	38	12	303	8.0	34	0

KICK RETURNS

	No.	Yds.	Avg.	Lg.	TD
Broussard	24	555	23.1	49	0
Bennett	8	177	22.1	43	0
Smart	8	169	21.1	33	0
Robertson	6	180	30.0	49	0
Proehl	3	64	21.3	27	0
Baker	2	39	19.5	23	0
Colbert	2	30	15.0	19	0
Foster	2	16	8.0	14	0
Hoover	2	30	15.0	16	0
Seidman	2	20	10.0	12	0
Rasmussen	1	12	12.0	12	0
Wesley	1	15	15.0	15	0
Panthers	61	1307	21.4	49	0
Opponents	69	1477	21.4	66	0

FIELD GOALS

	1-19	20-29	30-39	40-49	50+
Kasay	0/0	11/11	4/4	1/2	3/5
Chandler	0/0	0/0	0/2	0/0	0/0
Sauerbrun	0/0	0/0	1/1	0/0	0/0
Panthers	0/0	11/11	5/7	1/2	3/5
Opponents	1/1	5/7	7/10	7/9	0/1

Kasay: () () (26G) (53G, 52N) () (28G, 21G, 46N) (30G) (38G) (37G, 25G) () () (30G, 50G, 46G, 25G, 21G, 21G) (27G, 20G) (21G) (26G) (54G, 60B); Chandler: () () () () () () () () (38N, 38B) () () () () (); Sauerbrun: () () () () () () () () () (34G) () () () () () () (). Opponents: (41G) (33G, 47N) (47G, 30G) (32G, 33G) (48G, 34G, 43G) (29N, 44G) (27G, 45G, 22G) (26G, 19G) (28G, 46G) (50N, 28G) (39N, 26B, 37N) () () (37G, 45N, 38G) () (38N)

PASSING

	Att.	Cmp.	Yds.	Pct.	Avg. Gain	TD	Pct. TD	Int.	Pct. Int.	Long	Sack/Lost	Rating
Delhomme	533	310	3886	58.2	7.29	29	5.4	15	2.8	63	33/246	87.3
Peete	1	1	3	100.0	3.00	0	0.0	0	0.0	3	0/0	79.2
Proehl	1	0	0	0.0	0.00	0	0.0	0	0.0	...	0/0	39.6
S. Smith	1	0	0	0.0	0.00	0	0.0	0	0.0	...	0/0	39.6
Panthers	536	311	3889	58.0	7.26	29	5.4	15	2.8	63	33/246	87.0
Opponents	513	303	3703	59.1	7.22	18	3.5	26	5.1	t75	34/225	72.0

CAROLINA PANTHERS

CHICAGO BEARS
NFC NORTH DIVISION

2005 SEASON

CLUB DIRECTORY

Chairman of the board
Michael B. McCaskey
President/CEO
Ted Phillips
General manager
Jerry Angelo
Vice president
Timothy E. McCaskey
Senior director of administration
John Bostrom
Senior director of corporate communications
Scott Hagel
Senior director of corporate sales & marketing
Dave Greeley
Senior director of business development & alumni relations
Brian McCaskey
Senior director of ticket operations
George McCaskey
Senior director of finance & treasurer
Karen Murphy
Director of pro personnel
Bobby DePaul
Director of college scouting
Greg Gabriel

Head coach
Lovie Smith

Assistant coaches
Bob Babich (linebackers)
Mike Bajakian (off. quality control)
Rob Boras (tight ends)
Charlie Coiner (asst. special teams)
Darryl Drake (wide receivers)
Perry Fewell (defensive backs)
Harold Goodwin (asst. off. line)
Torrian Gray (asst. def. backs)
Harry Heistand (offensive line)
Don Johnson (defensive line)
Lloyd Lee (def. quality control)
Ron Rivera (def. coordinator)
Tim Spencer (running backs)
Dave Toub (special teams coordinator)
Ron Turner (off. coordinator)
Wade Wilson (quarterbacks)

OFFSEASON MOVES

Key additions
WR Eddie Berlin	FA/Titans
K Doug Brien	Released/Jets
G Roberto Garza	FA/Falcons
OT Fred Miller	Released/Titans
WR Muhsin Muhammad	Rel./Panthers
LB LeVar Woods	Rel./Cardinals

Key losses
OL Mike Gandy	FA/Bills
OT Aaron Gibson	FA
QB Jonathan Quinn	Released
WR David Terrell	Rel./Patriots
RB Anthony Thomas	FA/Cowboys
G Rex Tucker	Released/Rams

SCHEDULE

Sept.	11—at Washington	1:00
Sept.	18—DETROIT	1:00
Sept.	25—CINCINNATI	1:00
Oct.	2—Open date	
Oct.	9—at Cleveland	1:00
Oct.	16—MINNESOTA	1:00
Oct.	23—BALTIMORE	4:15
Oct.	30—at Detroit	2:00
Nov.	6—at New Orleans	2:00
Nov.	13—SAN FRANCISCO	2:00
Nov.	20—CAROLINA	2:00
Nov.	27—at Tampa Bay	2:00
Dec.	4—GREEN BAY	2:00
Dec.	11—at Pittsburgh	2:00
Dec.	18—ATLANTA	9:30
Dec.	25—at Green Bay	6:00
Jan.	1—at Minnesota	2:00

All times are Eastern.
All games Sunday unless noted.

DRAFT CHOICES

Cedric Benson, RB, Texas (first round/fourth pick overall).
Mark Bradley, WR, Oklahoma (2/39).
Kyle Orton, QB, Purdue (4/106).
Airese Currie, WR, Clemson (5/140).
Chris Harris, S, Louisiana-Monroe (6/181).
Rodriques Wilson, SS, South Carolina (7/220).

MISCELLANEOUS TEAM DATA

Stadium (capacity, surface):
Soldier Field (61,500, grass)
Business address:
Halas Hall at Conway Park
1000 Football Drive
Lake Forest, IL 60045
Business phone:
847-295-6600
Ticket information:
847-295-6600
Team colors:
Navy blue, orange and white
Flagship radio station:
WBBM, 780 AM
Website:
www.chicagobears.com
Training site:
Olivet Nazarene University
Bourbonnais, Ill.
847-295-6600

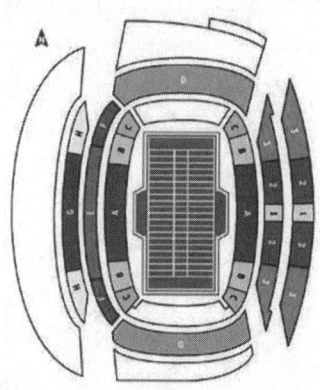

2005 TRAINING CAMP ROSTER

CHICAGO BEARS

No.	QUARTERBACKS	Ht./Wt.	Born	NFL Exp.	College	How acq.	'04 Games GP/GS
8	Grossman, Rex	6-1/218	8-23-80	3	Florida	D1b/03	3/3
9	Hutchinson, Chad	6-5/237	2-21-77	4	Stanford	FA/04	5/5
16	Krenzel, Craig	6-4/228	7-1-81	2	Ohio State	D5b/04	6/5
18	Orton, Kyle	6-3/226	11-14-82	R	Purdue	D4/05	—
	RUNNING BACKS						
32	Benson, Cedric	5-10/222	12-28-82	R	Texas	D1/05	—
47	Johnson, Bryan (FB)	6-1/242	1-18-78	5	Boise State	T-Was./04	12/6
20	Jones, Thomas	5-10/220	8-19-78	6	Virginia	FA/04	14/14
37	McKie, Jason (FB)	5-11/240	5-22-80	3	Temple	FA/02	15/2
29	Peterson, Adrian	5-10/210	7-1-79	4	Georgia Southern	D6a/02	14/0
	RECEIVERS						
82	Berlin, Eddie	5-11/195	1-14-78	5	Northern Iowa	FA/05	16/1
80	Berrian, Bernard	6-1/185	12-27-80	2	Fresno State	D3/04	16/1
14	Bradley, Mark	6-2/198	1-29-82	R	Oklahoma	D2/05	—
88	Clark, Desmond (TE)	6-3/255	4-20-77	7	Wake Forest	FA/03	15/13
17	Currie, Airese	5-10/186	11-16-82	R	Clemson	D5/05	—
12	Gage, Justin	6-4/210	1-25-81	3	Missouri	D5b/03	16/2
18	Johnson, Ron	6-2/218	5-23-80	3	Minnesota	FA/05	0/0
89	Lyman, Dustin (TE)	6-5/254	8-5-76	6	Wake Forest	D3b/00	16/10
87	Muhammad, Muhsin	6-2/217	5-5-73	10	Michigan State	FA/05	16/16
84	Wade, Bobby	5-10/192	2-25-81	3	Arizona	D5a/03	16/14
	OFFENSIVE LINEMEN						
68	Anderson, Bryan (G)	6-4/325	3-30-80	2	Pittsburgh	D7/03	4/0
74	Brown, Ruben (G)	6-3/300	2-13-72	11	Pittsburgh	FA/04	9/9
75	Colombo, Marc (T)	6-8/325	10-8-78	3	Boston College	D1/02	8/2
79	Edwards, Steve (G)	6-5/330	2-20-79	3	Central Florida	FA/02	15/8
63	Garza, Roberto (C/G)	6-2/296	3-26-79	5	Texas A&M-Kingsville	FA/05	16/15
57	Kreutz, Olin (C)	6-2/292	6-9-77	8	Washington	D3/98	16/16
65	Mannelly, Patrick (LS)	6-5/265	4-18-75	8	Duke	D6b/98	16/0
60	Metcalf, Terrence (G)	6-3/318	1-28-78	4	Mississippi	D3b/02	13/5
69	Miller, Fred (T)	6-7/320	2-6-73	10	Baylor	FA/05	16/16
72	Mitchell, Qasim (T)	6-6/355	12-3-79	3	North Carolina A&T	FA/03	16/14
76	Tait, John (T)	6-6/315	1-26-75	7	BYU	FA/04	13/13
	DEFENSIVE LINEMEN						
70	Boone, Alfonso (T)	6-4/318	1-11-76	5	Mt. San Antonio JC	FA/00	12/2
96	Brown, Alex (E)	6-3/262	6-4-79	4	Florida	D4/02	16/16
67	Campbell, Darrell (T)	6-4/290	7-6-81	1	Notre Dame	FA/05	0/0
91	Harris, Tommie (T)	6-3/300	4-29-83	2	Oklahoma	D1/04	16/16
97	Haynes, Michael (E)	6-3/274	9-13-80	3	Penn State	D1a/03	16/4
71	Idonije, Israel (T)	6-7/290	11-17-80	2	Manitoba (Canada)	FA/03	15/0
73	Jackson, Jonathan (E)	6-3/250	10-17-82	R	Oklahoma	FA/05	—
99	Johnson, Tank (T)	6-3/300	12-7-81	2	Washington	D2/04	16/1
93	Ogunleye, Adewale (E)	6-4/260	8-9-77	5	Indiana	T-Mia./04	12/12
98	Pierson, Shurron (E)	6-2/250	5-31-82	3	South Florida	T-Oak./04	2/0
95	Scott, Ian (T)	6-2/305	11-8-81	3	Florida	D4b/03	14/13
	LINEBACKERS						
55	Briggs, Lance	6-1/238	11-12-80	3	Arizona	D3/03	16/16
58	Cain, Jeremy	6-1/235	12-8-81	2	Massachusetts	FA/04	5/0
92	Hillenmeyer, Hunter	6-4/238	10-28-80	3	Vanderbilt	FA/03	16/11
59	Odom, Joe	6-1/235	12-14-79	3	Purdue	D6a/03	16/5
52	Reese, Marcus	6-1/233	6-15-81	2	UCLA	FA/03	11/2
54	Urlacher, Brian	6-4/258	5-25-78	6	New Mexico	D1/00	9/9
53	Woods, LeVar	6-3/244	3-15-78	5	Iowa	FA/05	14/3
	DEFENSIVE BACKS						
23	Azumah, Jerry (CB)	5-10/192	9-1-77	7	New Hampshire	D5c/99	12/8
30	Brown, Mike (S)	5-10/212	2-13-78	5	Nebraska	D2/00	2/2
25	Gray, Bobby (S)	6-0/210	4-30-78	4	Louisiana Tech	D5a/02	10/4
43	Green, Mike (S)	6-0/195	12-6-76	6	Northwestern State	D7b/00	16/16
46	Harris, Chris (S)	6-1/206	8-6-82	R	Louisiana-Monroe	D6/05	—
32	Johnson, Todd (S)	6-1/200	12-18-78	2	Florida	D4a/03	16/10
22	Marshall, Alfonso (CB)	6-1/183	1-17-81	2	Miami	D7/04	7/0
26	McMillon, Todd (CB)	5-11/188	9-26-74	6	Northern Arizona	FA/00	14/1
21	McQuarters, R.W. (CB)	5-10/195	12-21-76	8	Oklahoma State	T-SF/00	16/14
33	Tillman, Charles (CB)	6-1/196	2-23-81	3	Louisiana-Lafayette	D2/03	8/7
31	Vasher, Nathan (CB)	5-10/180	11-17-81	2	Texas	D4a/04	16/7
60	Wilson, Rodriques (S)	6-2/217	11-12-81	R	South Carolina	D7/05	—
24	Worrell, Cameron (S)	5-11/199	12-14-79	3	Fresno State	FA/03	13/0
	SPECIALISTS						
10	Brien, Doug (K)	6-0/185	11-24-70	12	California	FA/05	16/0
2	Edinger, Paul (K)	5-8/175	1-17-78	6	Michigan State	D6b/00	16/0
4	Maynard, Brad (P)	6-1/186	2-9-74	9	Ball State	FA/01	16/0

Abbreviations: D1—draft pick, first round; T—obtained in trade; FA—free-agent acquisition.

CHICAGO BEARS

2004 regular-season record: 5-11
Position: 4th in NFC North

Sept.12—DETROIT	L	16-20
Sept.19—at Green Bay	W	21-10
Sept.26—at Minnesota	L	22-27
Oct. 3—PHILADELPHIA	L	9-19
Oct. 10—Open date		
Oct. 17—WASHINGTON	L	10-13
Oct. 24—at Tampa Bay	L	7-19
Oct. 31—SAN FRANCISCO	W	23-13
Nov. 7—at N.Y. Giants	W	28-21
Nov.14—at Tennessee (OT)	W	19-17
Nov.21—INDIANAPOLIS	L	10-41
Nov.25—at Dallas	L	7-21
Dec. 5—MINNESOTA	W	24-14
Dec.12—at Jacksonville	L	3-22
Dec.19—at HOUSTON	L	5-24
Dec.26—at Detroit	L	13-19
Jan. 2—GREEN BAY	L	14-31

SCORING BY PERIODS

	Q1	Q2	Q3	Q4	OT	Pts.
Bears	34	80	36	79	2	231
Opponents	78	117	50	86	0	331

TEAM STATISTICS

	Chi.	Opp.
TOTAL FIRST DOWNS ..	230	302
Rushing	84	109
Passing	121	165
Penalty	25	28
3rd Down: Made/Att. ..	56/223	67/220
3rd Down Pct.	25.1	30.5
4th Down: Made/Att.	6/19	4/15
4th Down Pct.	31.6	26.7
POSSESSION AVG.	28:20	31:40
TOTAL NET YARDS	3816	5390
Avg. per Game	238.5	336.9
Total Plays	967	1046
Avg. per Play	3.9	5.2
NET YARDS RUSHING ..	1624	2050
Avg. per Game	101.5	128.1
Total Rushes	430	496
NET YARDS PASSING....	2192	3340
Avg. per Game	137.0	208.8
Sacked/Yards Lost	66/449	35/173
Gross Yards	2641	3513
Att./Completions	471/249	515/287
Completion Pct.	52.9	55.7
Had Intercepted	16	17
PUNTS/AVERAGE	110/42.6	92/40.4
NET PUNTING AVG.	110/38.3	92/32.0
PENALTIES/YARDS	124/956	120/914
FUMBLES/LOST	35/21	21/12
TOUCHDOWNS	26	36
Rushing	10	9
Passing	9	23
Returns	7	4

SCORING (NON-KICKERS)

	Tot. TD	RTD	PTD	MTD	2Pt.	Tot. Pts.
Jones	7	7	0	0	0	42
Berrian	2	0	2	0	0	12
Johnson	2	0	2	0	0	12
McKie	2	0	2	0	0	12
McQuarters	2	0	0	2	0	12
Thomas	2	2	0	0	0	12
Azumah	1	0	0	1	0	6
Briggs	1	0	0	1	0	6
M. Brown	1	0	0	1	0	6
Clark	1	0	1	0	0	6
Grossman	1	1	0	0	0	6
Haynes	1	0	0	1	0	6
Lyman	1	0	1	0	0	6
Terrell	1	0	1	0	0	6
Vasher	1	0	0	1	0	6
Krenzel	0	0	0	0	1	2
Bears	26	10	9	7	1	164
Opponents	36	9	23	4	0	218

2-Pt. conversions: Bears 1-4; Opponents 0-1.

(KICKERS)

	XPM/XPA	FGM/FGA	Pts.
Edinger	22/22	15/24	67
Bears	22/22	15/24	67
Opponents	35/35	26/36	113

RUSHING

	Att.	Yds.	Avg.	Lg.	TD
Jones	240	948	4.0	54	7
Thomas	122	404	3.3	t41	2
Wade	12	76	6.3	14	0
Grossman	11	48	4.4	8	1
Krenzel	18	41	2.3	12	0
Quinn	3	35	11.7	23	0
Berrian	8	28	3.5	25	0
Peterson	6	19	3.2	13	0
Hutchinson	6	14	2.3	11	0
Terrell	3	10	3.3	20	0
McKie	1	1	1.0	1	0
Bears	430	1624	3.8	54	10
Opponents	496	2050	4.1	40	9

RECEIVING

	No.	Yds.	Avg.	Lg.	TD
Jones	56	427	7.6	45	0
Terrell	42	699	16.6	63	1
Wade	42	481	11.5	40	0
Clark	24	282	11.8	31	1
Thomas	17	132	7.8	30	0
Berrian	15	225	15.0	t49	2
Johnson	14	55	3.9	14	2
McKie	13	70	5.4	t15	2
Gage	12	156	13.0	32	0
Lyman	11	73	6.6	13	1
Peterson	2	30	15.0	30	0
Gilmore	1	11	11.0	11	0
Bears	249	2641	10.6	63	9
Opponents	287	3513	12.2	69	23

INTERCEPTIONS

	No.	Yds.	Avg.	Lg.	TD
Vasher	5	177	35.4	t71	1
Azumah	4	128	32.0	t70	1
McQuarters	2	85	42.5	t45	1
Green	2	0	0.0	0	0
Haynes	1	45	45.0	t45	1
Urlacher	1	42	42.0	42	0
Briggs	1	38	38.0	t38	1
Gray	1	31	31.0	31	0
Bears	17	546	32.1	t71	5
Opponents	16	222	13.9	45	1

SACKS: A. Brown 6.0, Urlacher 5.5, Ogunleye 5.0, Harris 3.5, Boone 2.5, Hillenmeyer 2.5, Haynes 2.0, Scott 2.0, Azumah 1.5, Green 1.5, Idonije 1.0, Worrell 1.0, Briggs 0.5, T. Johnson 0.5. Bears 35.0; Opponents 66.0.

PUNTING

	No.	Yds.	Avg.	In. 20	Lg.
Edinger	2	53	26.5	1	30
Maynard	108	4638	42.9	34	58
Bears	110	4691	42.6	35	58
Opponents	92	3713	40.4	18	57

PUNT RETURNS

	No.	FC	Yds.	Avg.	Lg.	TD
McQuarters ..	44	13	435	9.9	t75	1
Berrian	2	2	10	5.0	12	0
Gage	0	0	56	-	56	0
Gray	0	0	9	-	9	0
Bears	46	15	510	11.1	t75	1
Opponents	57	21	380	6.7	29	0

KICK RETURNS

	No.	Yds.	Avg.	Lg.	TD
Azumah	42	924	22.0	73	0
Berrian	17	385	22.6	41	0
Jones	6	112	18.7	23	0
McKie	3	65	21.7	25	0
Peterson	3	57	19.0	22	0
McQuarters	2	46	23.0	37	0
Johnson	1	18	18.0	18	0
Bears	74	1607	21.7	73	0
Opponents	54	1160	21.5	43	0

FIELD GOALS

	1-19	20-29	30-39	40-49	50+
Edinger	0/0	6/7	2/5	4/7	3/5
Bears	0/0	6/7	2/5	4/7	3/5
Opponents	0/0	11/11	6/8	7/11	2/6

Edinger: (27B) (45N) (34G, 23G, 39N, 32G) (25G) (46G) () (52G, 45G, 53N, 27G) (22G, 21G) (39N, 29G) (51G) (48N) (53G, 52N) (47N, 42G) (39N, 43G) () () Opponents: (27G, 21G) (25G, 45N) (46N, 42G, 24G) (51G, 42G, 42G, 40G, 39N, 45N) (41G, 26G) (22G, 22G) (48G, 51G, 50N) () (58N, 33G, 52B) (34G, 20G) (52N) (38N) (30G, 25G) (42N, 20G) (31G, 39G, 34G, 40G) (20G)

PASSING

	Att.	Cmp.	Yds.	Pct.	Avg. Gain	TD	Pct. TD	Int.	Pct. Int.	Long	Sack/Lost	Rating
Hutchinson	161	92	903	57.1	5.61	4	2.5	3	1.9	63	23/160	73.6
Krenzel	127	59	718	46.5	5.65	3	2.4	6	4.7	t49	23/158	52.5
Grossman	84	47	607	56.0	7.23	1	1.2	3	3.6	40	5/22	67.9
Quinn	98	51	413	52.0	4.21	1	1.0	3	3.1	32	15/109	53.7
Edinger	1	0	0	0.0	0.00	0	0.0	1	100.0	...	0/0	0.0
Bears	471	249	2641	52.9	5.61	9	1.9	16	3.4	63	66/449	61.7
Opponents	515	287	3513	55.7	6.82	23	4.5	17	3.3	69	35/173	78.1

CINCINNATI BENGALS
AFC NORTH DIVISION

2005 SEASON

CLUB DIRECTORY

President
Mike Brown
Sr. vice president—player personnel
Pete Brown
Executive vice president
Katie Blackburn
Vice president—player personnel
Paul Brown
Director of business development
Troy Blackburn
Director of football operations
Jim Lippincott
Director of player personnel
Duke Tobin
Public relations director
Jack Brennan
Director of player relations
Eric Ball

Head coach
Marvin Lewis

Assistant coaches
Paul Alexander (asst. head
    coach/offensive line)
Jim Anderson (running backs)
Bob Bratkowski (off. coordinator)
Chuck Bresnahan (def. coordinator)
Louie Cioffi (asst. defensive backs)
Kevin Coyle (defensive backs)
Paul Guenther (staff asst.)
Jay Hayes (defensive line)
Jonathan Hayes (tight ends)
Ricky Hunley (linebackers)
Chip Morton (strength & condi-
    tioning)
Ray Oliver (asst. strength & con-
    ditioning)
Darrin Simmons (special teams)
Bob Surace (asst. offensive line)
Hue Jackson (wide receivers)
Ken Zampese (quarterbacks)

OFFSEASON MOVES

Key additions
DE Elton Patterson	FA/Jaguars
DT Bryan Robinson	FA/Dolphins

Key losses
S Rogers Beckett	Released
LB Frank Chamberlin	FA/Texans
C Jerry Fontenot	Free agent
LB Kevin Hardy	Released
LB LaDairis Jackson	Released
S Ricot Joseph	Released
P Kyle Richardson	FA/Browns
CB Dennis Weathersby	Released
DT Tony Williams	FA/Jaguars

SCHEDULE

Sept.	11—at Cleveland	1:00
Sept.	18—MINNESOTA	1:00
Sept.	25—at Chicago	1:00
Oct.	2—HOUSTON	1:00
Oct.	9—at Jacksonville	8:30
Oct.	16—at Tennessee	1:00
Oct.	23—PITTSBURGH	1:00
Oct.	30—GREEN BAY	2:00
Nov.	6—at Baltimore	2:00
Nov.	13—Open date	
Nov.	20—INDIANAPOLIS	2:00
Nov.	27—BALTIMORE	2:00
Dec.	4—at Pittsburgh	2:00
Dec.	11—CLEVELAND	2:00
Dec.	18—at Detroit	5:05
Dec.	24—BUFFALO (Sat.)	2:00
Jan.	1—at Kansas City	2:00

All times are Eastern.
All games Sunday unless noted.

DRAFT CHOICES

David Pollack, DE, Georgia (first
round/17th pick overall).
Odell Thurman, ILB, Georgia (2/48).
Chris Henry, WR, West Virginia (3/83).
Eric Ghiaciuc, C, Central Michigan
(4/119).
Adam Kieft, OT, Central Michigan (5/153).
Tab Perry, WR, UCLA (6/190).
Jonathan Fanene, DE, Utah (7/233).

MISCELLANEOUS TEAM DATA

Stadium (capacity, surface):
Paul Brown Stadium
(65,326, synthetic)
Business address:
One Paul Brown Stadium
Cincinnati, OH 45202-3492
Business phone:
513-621-3550
Ticket information:
513-621-TDTD (8383)
Team colors:
Black, orange and white
Flagship radio stations:
WCKY-AM (1360 Homer); WOFX-FM (92.5
The Fox); WLW-AM (700 The Big One)
Website:
www.bengals.com
Training site:
Georgetown College
Georgetown, Ky.
502-868-6300

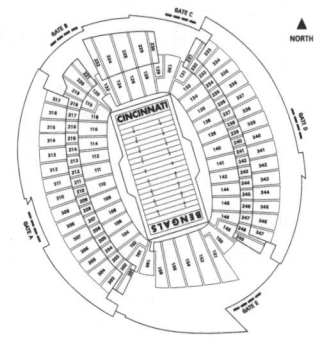

CINCINNATI BENGALS

No.	QUARTERBACKS	Ht./Wt.	Born	NFL Exp.	College	How acq.	'04 Games GP/GS
4	Bramlet, Casey	6-4/225	4-2-81	2	Wyoming	D7/04	0/0
3	Kitna, Jon	6-2/220	9-21-72	9	Central Washington	FA/01	4/3
9	Palmer, Carson	6-5/230	12-27-79	3	USC	D1/03	13/13
	RUNNING BACKS						
31	Johnson, Jeremi (FB)	5-11/265	9-4-80	3	Western Kentucky	D4b/03	16/6
32	Johnson, Rudi	5-10/220	10-1-79	4	Auburn	D4/01	16/16
23	Perry, Chris	6-0/224	12-27-81	2	Michigan	D1/04	2/0
33	Watson, Kenny	5-11/218	3-13-78	4	Penn State	FA/03	16/0
35	Wilson, Quincy	5-9/225	4-26-81	1	West Virginia	FA/04	0/0
	RECEIVERS						
47	Dickerson, Kori (TE)	6-4/240	12-6-78	1	USC	W-Was./05	—
15	Henry, Chris	6-4/197	5-17-83	R	West Virginia	D3/05	—
84	Houshmandzadeh, T.J.	6-1/197	9-26-77	5	Oregon State	D7/01	16/13
85	Johnson, Chad	6-1/192	1-9-78	5	Oregon State	D2/01	16/16
82	Kelly, Reggie (TE)	6-4/255	2-22-77	7	Mississippi State	FA/03	16/15
12	Perry, Tab	6-3/229	1-20-82	R	UCLA	D6/05	—
88	Russell, Cliff	5-11/193	2-8-79	3	Utah	FA/04	13/1
89	Schobel, Matt (TE)	6-5/257	11-4-78	4	TCU	D3/02	16/1
48	St. Louis, Brad (TE/LS)	6-3/247	8-19-76	6	SW Missouri State	D7/00	16/0
86	Stewart, Tony (TE)	6-5/260	8-9-79	5	Penn State	FA/02	16/9
80	Warrick, Peter	5-11/192	6-19-77	6	Florida State	D1/00	4/1
87	Washington, Kelley	6-3/218	8-21-79	3	Tennessee	D3/03	16/2
	OFFENSIVE LINEMEN						
71	Anderson, Willie (T)	6-5/340	7-11-75	10	Auburn	D1/96	16/16
79	Andrews, Stacy (T)	6-5/346	6-2-81	1	Mississippi	D4/04	1/0
74	Braham, Rich (C)	6-4/305	11-6-70	11	West Virginia	FA/00	10/10
69	Ghiaciuc, Eric (C)	6-4/302	5-28-81	R	Central Michigan	D4/05	—
76	Jones, Levi (T)	6-5/310	8-24-79	4	Arizona State	D1/02	16/16
70	Kieft, Adam (T)	6-7/337	8-21-82	R	Central Michigan	D5/05	—
75	Kooistra, Scott (G)	6-6/320	10-14-80	3	North Carolina State	D7/03	16/0
50	Moore, Larry (G)	6-3/300	6-1-75	8	BYU	FA/02	13/1
65	Steinbach, Eric (G)	6-6/297	4-4-80	3	Iowa	D2/03	16/15
62	Sulfsted, Alex (G)	6-3/320	12-21-77	3	Miami (Ohio)	FA/01	3/0
63	Williams, Bobbie (G)	6-4/330	9-25-76	4	Arkansas	FA/04	16/16
	DEFENSIVE LINEMEN						
96	Askew, Matthias (T)	6-5/308	7-1-82	2	Michigan State	D4a/04	5/0
92	Clemons, Duane (E)	6-5/275	5-23-74	10	California	FA/03	14/14
68	Fanene, Jonathan (E)	6-3/290	3-19-82	R	Utah	D7/05	—
91	Geathers, Robert (E)	6-2/271	8-11-83	2	Georgia	D4b/04	14/1
98	Martin, Terrance (E)	6-2/290	7-6-79	3	North Carolina State	FA/03	2/0
60	Moore, Langston (T)	6-1/303	7-17-81	2	South Carolina	D6/03	15/8
78	Patterson, Elton (E)	6-2/271	6-13-81	2	Central Florida	FA/05	8/0
72	Powell, Carl (E)	6-2/285	1-4-74	6	Louisville	FA/03	10/2
98	Robinson, Bryan (T)	6-4/296	6-22-74	9	Fresno State	FA/05	16/13
93	Scott, Greg (E)	6-4/258	10-2-79	2	Hampton	W-Was./03	1/0
90	Smith, Justin (E)	6-4/270	9-30-79	5	Missouri	D1/01	16/16
97	Thornton, John (T)	6-3/297	10-2-76	7	West Virginia	FA/03	16/16
	LINEBACKERS						
53	Abdullah, Khalid	6-2/227	3-6-79	2	Mars Hill	D5/03	0/0
59	Johnson, Landon	6-1/227	3-13-81	2	Purdue	D3/04	16/11
58	Miller, Caleb	6-3/225	9-3-80	2	Arkansas	D3/04	13/3
99	Pollack, David	6-2/261	6-19-82	R	Georgia	D1/05	—
56	Simmons, Brian	6-3/244	6-21-75	7	North Carolina	D1b/98	15/15
45	Thurman, Odell	6-1/237	7-9-83	R	Georgia	D2/05	—
52	Webster, Nate	6-0/235	11-29-77	6	Miami	FA/04	3/3
55	Wilkins, Marcus	6-2/235	1-2-80	4	Texas	FA/02	16/0
	DEFENSIVE BACKS						
21	Bauman, Rashad (CB)	5-8/184	5-7-79	4	Oregon	D3a/02	4/0
27	Brooks, Greg (CB)	5-11/177	12-16-80	1	Southern Mississippi	D6/04	0/0
22	Herring, Kim (S)	6-0/212	9-10-75	8	Penn State	FA/01	12/10
20	James, Tory (CB)	6-2/186	5-18-73	9	LSU	FA/03	16/16
34	Kaesviharn, Kevin (S)	6-1/194	8-29-76	5	Augustana (S.D.)	FA/01	15/6
42	Mitchell, Anthony (S)	6-1/198	12-13-74	6	Tuskegee	FA/99	12/0
24	O'Neal, Deltha (CB)	5-11/191	1-30-77	6	California	T-Den./04	12/10
25	Ratliff, Keiwan (CB)	5-11/190	4-19-81	2	Florida	D2/04	16/5
30	Roberts, Terrell (CB)	5-10/197	4-7-81	3	Oregon State	FA/03	11/1
26	Shabazz, Siddeeq (S)	5-11/200	2-5-81	3	New Mexico State	FA/05	15/0
40	Williams, Madieu (S)	6-1/193	10-18-81	2	Maryland	D2/04	16/13
	SPECIALISTS						
17	Graham, Shayne (K)	6-0/197	12-9-77	5	Virginia Tech	W-Car./03	16/0
19	Larson, Kyle (P)	6-1/204	9-2-80	2	Nebraska	FA/04	16/0

Abbreviations: D1—draft pick, first round; W—claimed on waivers; T—obtained in trade; FA—free-agent acquisition.

2004 regular-season record: 8-8
Position: 3rd in AFC North

Sept.12—at N.Y. Jets	L	24-31
Sept.19—MIAMI	W	16-13
Sept.26—BALTIMORE	L	9-23
Oct. 3—at Pittsburgh	L	17-28
Oct. 10—Open date		
Oct. 17—at Cleveland	L	17-34
Oct. 25—DENVER	W	23-10
Oct. 31—at Tennessee	L	20-27
Nov. 7—DALLAS	W	26-3
Nov. 14—at Washington	W	17-10
Nov. 21—PITTSBURGH	L	14-19
Nov. 28—CLEVELAND	W	58-48
Dec. 5—at Baltimore	W	27-26
Dec. 12—at New England	L	28-35
Dec. 19—BUFFALO	L	17-33
Dec. 26—N.Y. GIANTS	W	23-22
Jan. 2—at Philadelphia	W	38-10

SCORING BY PERIODS

	Q1	Q2	Q3	Q4	OT	Pts.
Bengals	69	108	96	101	0	374
Opponents	75	117	82	98	0	372

TEAM STATISTICS

	Cin.	Opp.
TOTAL FIRST DOWNS ..	286	303
Rushing	93	123
Passing	172	158
Penalty	21	22
3rd Down: Made/Att. ..	88/219	80/218
3rd Down Pct.	40.2	36.7
4th Down: Made/Att.	6/12	5/15
4th Down Pct.	50.0	33.3
POSSESSION AVG.	29:20	30:40
TOTAL NET YARDS	5140	5365
Avg. per Game	321.3	335.3
Total Plays	1004	1031
Avg. per Play	5.1	5.2
NET YARDS RUSHING ..	1839	2062
Avg. per Game	114.9	128.9
Total Rushes	437	474
NET YARDS PASSING....	3301	3303
Avg. per Game	206.3	206.4
Sacked/Yards Lost	31/219	37/257
Gross Yards	3520	3560
Att./Completions	536/324	520/313
Completion Pct.	60.4	60.2
Had Intercepted	22	20
PUNTS/AVERAGE	84/41.7	79/41.9
NET PUNTING AVG.	84/35.5	79/35.7
PENALTIES/YARDS	103/810	106/887
FUMBLES/LOST	17/10	40/16
TOUCHDOWNS	42	41
Rushing	14	11
Passing	23	23
Returns	5	7

SCORING (NON-KICKERS)

		Tot.					Tot.
	TD	RTD	PTD	MTD	2Pt.		Pts.
Ru. Johnson ..	12	12	0	0	0		72
C. Johnson	9	0	9	0	0		54
Houshmandzadeh	4	0	4	0	0		24
Schobel	4	0	4	0	0		24
Washington	3	0	3	0	0		18
Geathers	1	0	0	1	0		6
J. Johnson	1	0	1	0	0		6
Kaesviharn...	1	0	1	0	0		6
Larson	1	1	0	0	0		6
O'Neal	1	0	0	1	0		6
Palmer	1	1	0	0	0		6
Simmons	1	0	0	1	0		6
Stewart	1	0	1	0	0		6
Watson	1	0	1	0	0		6
M. Williams ...	1	0	0	1	0		6
Bengals	42	14	23	5	0		252
Opponents...	41	11	23	7	0		248

2-Pt. conversions: Bengals 0-1; Opponents 0-1.

(KICKERS)

	XPM/XPA	FGM/FGA	Pts.
Graham	41/41	27/31	122
Bengals	41/41	27/31	122
Opponents	40/40	28/31	124

RUSHING

	Att.	Yds.	Avg.	Lg.	TD
Ru. Johnson ..	361	1454	4.0	52	12
Watson	26	161	6.2	25	0
Houshmandzadeh	6	51	8.5	16	0
Palmer	18	47	2.6	14	1
Kitna	10	42	4.2	15	0C.
Johnson	4	39	9.8	18	0
Russell	3	15	5.0	13	0
Warrick	2	14	7.0	8	0
Larson	1	11	11.0	t11	1
J. Johnson	3	5	1.7	4	0
Perry	2	1	0.5	1	0
Washington ..	1	-1	-1.0	-1	0
Bengals	437	1839	4.2	52	14
Opponents	474	2062	4.4	t75	11

RECEIVING

	No.	Yds.	Avg.	Lg.	TD
C. Johnson	95	1274	13.4	t53	9
Houshmandzadeh	73	978	13.4	62	4
Washington ..	31	378	12.2	28	3
Watson	25	171	6.8	21	1
Schobel	21	201	9.6	t76	4
J. Johnson	16	53	3.3	9	1
Ru. Johnson ...	15	84	5.6	30	0
Kelly	15	85	5.7	14	0
Warrick	11	127	11.5	30	0
Stewart	10	48	4.8	9	1
Walter	8	67	8.4	18	0
Perry	3	33	11.0	13	0
Russell	1	21	21.0	21	0
Bengals	324	3520	10.9	t76	23
Opponents	313	3560	11.4	t99	23

INTERCEPTIONS

	No.	Yds.	Avg.	Lg.	TD
James	8	66	8.3	23	0
O'Neal	4	60	15.0	t31	1
M. Williams ..	3	51	17.0	t51	1
Simmons	2	61	30.5	t50	1
Geathers	1	36	36.0	t36	1
Herring	1	0	0.0	0	0
Powell	1	-2	-2.0	-2	0
Bengals	20	272	13.6	t51	4
Opponents	22	446	20.3	t62	4

SACKS: J. Smith 8.0, Clemons 6.5, Hardy 4.0, Geathers 3.5, Thornton 3.0, L. Johnson 2.0, Powell 2.0, M. Williams 2.0, Lan. Moore 1.0, O'Neal 1.0, Simmons 1.0, Webster 1.0. Bengals 37.0; Opponents 31.0.

PUNTING

	No.	Yds.	Avg.	In. 20	Lg.
Larson	83	3499	42.2	21	66
Bengals	84	3499	41.7	21	66
Opponents	79	3309	41.9	23	69

PUNT RETURNS

	No.	FC	Yds.	Avg.	Lg.	TD
Ratliff	17	5	207	12.2	49	0
Houshmandzadeh	11	7	88	8.0	28	0
O'Neal	7	6	33	4.7	17	0
Bengals	35	18	328	9.4	49	0
Opponents....	51	10	378	7.4	63	0

KICK RETURNS

	No.	Yds.	Avg.	Lg.	TD
Russell	39	872	22.4	40	0
Watson	13	240	18.5	32	0
Houshmandzadeh	10	227	22.7	32	0
Stewart	3	20	6.7	10	0
Kelly	1	14	14.0	14	0
Lan. Moore ..	1	15	15.0	15	0
O'Neal	1	15	15.0	15	0
Bengals	68	1403	20.6	40	0
Opponents	80	1573	19.7	41	0

FIELD GOALS

	1-19	20-29	30-39	40-49	50+
Graham	0/0	7/7	10/12	7/8	3/4
Bengals	0/0	7/7	10/12	7/8	3/4
Opponents	0/0	13/13	8/8	7/10	0/0

Graham: (22G) (38N, 48G, 36G, 39G) (29G, 47G, 26G) (34G) (32G, 44N) (53G, 34G, 35G) (28G, 50G) (35G, 47G, 45G, 30G) (41G) () (21G, 32G, 36G) (53N, 41G, 24G) () (24G) (42G) (37N, 50G) **Opponents:** (21G) (43G, 47G) (21G) () (23G, 33G) (49N, 29G) (23G, 45G) (24G) (47N, 33G) (32G) (23G, 29G) (20G, 22G, 38G, 45G) () (23G, 39G, 21G, 33G) (31G, 36G, 44G, 41G, 28G) (45N, 46G)

PASSING

	Att.	Cmp.	Yds.	Pct.	Avg. Gain	TD	Pct. TD	Int.	Pct. Int.	Long	Sack/Lost	Rating
Palmer	432	263	2897	60.9	6.71	18	4.2	18	4.2	t76	25/178	77.3
Kitna	104	61	623	58.7	5.99	5	4.8	4	3.8	30	6/41	75.9
Bengals	536	324	3520	60.4	6.57	23	4.3	22	4.1	t76	31/219	77.0
Opponents	520	313	3560	60.2	6.85	23	4.4	20	3.8	t99	37/257	79.5

CINCINNATI BENGALS

CLEVELAND BROWNS
AFC NORTH DIVISION

2005 SEASON

CLUB DIRECTORY

Owner
Randy Lerner
President and chief executive officer
John Collins
Senior vice president and general manager
Phil Savage
Executive vice president and chief financial officer
Doug Jacobs
Executive vice president and chief operating officer
Lew Merletti
Vice president of communications
Bill Bonsiewicz
Vice president of new media and publishing
Vic Carucci
Vice president of event and stadium operations
Don Renzulli
Vice president of broadcasting and production
George Veras

Head coach
Romeo Crennel

Assistant coaches
Dave Atkins (running backs)
Maurice Carthon (off. coordinator)
Ben Coates (tight ends)
Carl Crennel II (offensive quality control)
Jeff Davidson (offensive line)
Todd Grantham (def. coordinator)
Mike Haluchak (linebackers)
John Lott (head strength and conditioning)
Randy Melvin (defensive line)
Terry Robiskie (wide receivers)
Jerry Rosburg (special teams coordinator)
Rip Scherer (quarterbacks)
Bob Trott (defensive asst.)
Mel Tucker (defensive backs)
Jeff Uhlenhake (offensive line asst.)
Cory Undlin (defensive quality control)

SCHEDULE

Sept.	11—CINCINNATI	1:00
Sept.	18—at Green Bay	4:15
Sept.	25—at Indianapolis	1:00
Oct.	2—Open date	
Oct.	9—CHICAGO	1:00
Oct.	16—at Baltimore	1:00
Oct.	23—DETROIT	1:00
Oct.	30—at Houston	2:00
Nov.	6—TENNESSEE	2:00
Nov.	13—at Pittsburgh	9:30
Nov.	20—MIAMI	2:00
Nov.	27—at Minnesota	2:00
Dec.	4—JACKSONVILLE	2:00
Dec.	11—at Cincinnati	2:00
Dec.	18—at Oakland	5:05
Dec.	24—PITTSBURGH (Sat.)	2:00
Jan.	1—BALTIMORE	2:00

All times are Eastern.
All games Sunday unless noted.

DRAFT CHOICES

Braylon Edwards, WR, Michigan (first round/third pick overall).
Brodney Pool, FS, Oklahoma (2/34).
Charlie Frye, QB, Akron (3/67).
Antonio Perkins, CB, Oklahoma (4/103).
David McMillan, DE, Kansas (5/139).
Nick Speegle, OLB, New Mexico (6/176).
Andrew Hoffman, DT, Virginia (6/203).
Jon Dunn, OT, Virginia Tech (7/217).

OFFSEASON MOVES

Key additions

G Joe Andruzzi	FA/Patriots
CB Gary Baxter	FA/Ravens
G Cosey Coleman	FA/Buccaneers
QB Trent Dilfer	Trade/Seahawks
RB Reuben Droughns	Trade/Broncos
DT Jason Fisk	Rel./Chargers
P Kyle Richardson	FA/Bengals
S Brian Russell	FA/Vikings
LB Matt Stewart	FA/Falcons

Key losses

LB Kevin Bentley	FA/Seahawks
DE Courtney Brown	Rel./Broncos
OL Damion Cook	FA/Dolphins
DE Ebenezer Ekuban	Trade/Broncos
QB Jeff Garcia	Rel./Lions
LB Barry Gardner	FA/Jets
G Kelvin Garmon	Released
OT Joaquin Gonzalez	FA/Colts
S Robert Griffith	Rel./Cardinals
CB Anthony Henry	FA/Cowboys
QB Kelly Holcomb	FA/Bills
LB Warrick Holdman	FA/Redskins
S Earl Little	Rel./Packers
QB Luke McCown	Trade/Bucs
DT Michael Myers	Trade/Broncos
S Lewis Sanders	FA/Texans
DT Gerard Warren	Trade/Broncos

MISCELLANEOUS TEAM DATA

Stadium (capacity, surface):
Cleveland Browns Stadium (73,200, grass)
Business address:
76 Lou Groza Boulevard
Berea, Ohio 44017
Business phone:
440-891-5000
Ticket information:
440-891-5050
Team colors:
Brown, orange and white
Flagship radio station:
WMMS, 100.7 FM
Website:
www.clevelandbrowns.com
Training site:
76 Lou Groza Boulevard
Berea, Ohio
440-891-5000

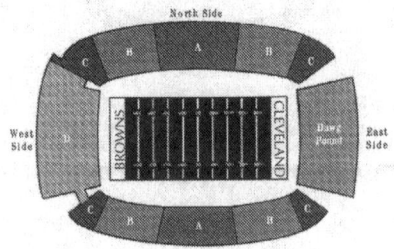

CLEVELAND BROWNS

No.	QUARTERBACKS	Ht./Wt.	Born	NFL Exp.	College	How acq.	'04 Games GP/GS
8	Dilfer, Trent	6-4/225	3-13-72	12	Fresno State	T-Sea./05	5/2
9	Frye, Charlie	6-4/217	8-28-81	R	Akron	D3/05	—
5	Harris, Josh	6-1/238	9-9-82	1	Bowling Green	FA/04	0/0
	RUNNING BACKS						
34	Droughns, Reuben	5-11/207	8-21-78	6	Oregon	T-Den./05	16/15
23	Echemandu, Adimchinobe	5-10/226	11-21-80	2	California	D7/04	4/0
31	Green, William	6-0/215	12-17-79	4	Boston College	D1/02	15/12
40	Miller, Ben (FB)	6-3/250	8-18-79	1	Air Force	FA/02	0/0
42	Smith, Terrelle (FB)	6-0/255	3-12-78	6	Arizona State	FA/04	16/9
44	Suggs, Lee	6-0/210	8-11-80	3	Virginia Tech	D4/03	10/4
	RECEIVERS						
89	Alston, Richard	6-0/213	11-20-80	2	East Carolina	FA/04	9/0
81	Bryant, Antonio	6-1/196	3-9-81	4	Pittsburgh	T-Dal./04	15/8
87	Davis, Andre'	6-1/195	6-12-79	4	Virginia Tech	D2/02	7/7
17	Edwards, Braylon	6-3/211	2-21-83	R	Michigan	D1/05	—
82	Heiden, Steve (TE)	6-5/265	9-21-76	7	South Dakota State	T-SD/02	13/13
49	Heinrich, Keith (TE)	6-5/255	3-19-79	4	Sam Houston State	FA/03	7/0
19	Jackson, Frisman	6-3/220	6-12-79	4	Western Illinois	FA/02	10/0
86	Northcutt, Dennis	5-11/175	12-22-77	6	Arizona	D2/00	16/11
83	Shea, Aaron (TE)	6-3/255	12-5-76	6	Michigan	D4b/00	15/8
80	Winslow, Kellen (TE)	6-4/250	7-21-83	2	Miami	D1/04	2/2
	OFFENSIVE LINEMEN						
63	Andruzzi, Joe (G)	6-3/312	8-23-75	9	Southern Connecticut	FA/05	16/16
78	Bogle, Phil (T/G)	6-3/332	9-27-79	2	New Haven	FA/05	0/0
65	Chambers, Kirk (T)	6-7/313	3-19-79	2	Stanford	D6/04	6/0
60	Coleman, Cosey (G)	6-4/322	10-27-78	6	Tennessee	FA/05	16/16
75	Collins, Javiar (T/G)	6-6/322	4-13-78	5	Northwestern	FA/04	0/0
70	DeMar, Enoch (G)	6-4/320	9-7-80	3	Indiana	FA/03	15/11
71	Dunn, Jon (T)	6-7/328	12-12-81	R	Virginia Tech	D7/05	—
50	Faine, Jeff (C)	6-3/300	4-6-81	3	Notre Dame	D1/03	13/13
67	Fowler, Melvin (G/C)	6-3/305	3-31-79	4	Maryland	D3/02	15/3
64	Pontbriand, Ryan (C/LS)	6-2/255	10-1-79	3	Rice	D5a/03	16/0
73	Randall, Greg (T/G)	6-5/322	6-23-78	5	Michigan State	FA/05	0/0
72	Tucker, Ryan (T)	6-6/320	6-12-75	9	TCU	FA/02	7/7
77	Verba, Ross (T)	6-4/305	10-31-73	9	Iowa	FA/01	16/16
	DEFENSIVE LINEMEN						
98	Eason, Nick (E)	6-3/301	5-29-80	3	Clemson	FA/04	1/0
95	Fisk, Jason (T)	6-3/295	9-4-72	11	Stanford	FA/05	15/1
94	Gordon, Amon (E)	6-2/305	10-13-81	2	Stanford	D5/04	6/0
91	Hoffman, Andrew (T)	6-4/296	2-15-82	R	Virginia	D6b/05	—
90	Jackson, Corey (E)	6-6/255	11-6-78	2	Nevada	FA/03	1/0
97	McKinley, Alvin (E/T)	6-3/310	6-9-78	6	Mississippi State	W-Car./01	16/2
92	McMillan, David (E)	6-3/246	9-20-81	R	Kansas	D5/05	—
99	Roye, Orpheus (E)	6-4/320	1-21-73	10	Florida State	FA/00	15/14
	LINEBACKERS						
52	Boyer, Brant	6-1/240	6-27-71	12	Arizona	FA/01	0/0
57	Coates, Sherrod	6-2/242	12-22-78	3	Western Kentucky	FA/03	5/0
54	Davis, Andra	6-1/255	12-23-78	4	Florida	D5/02	11/11
56	Kurpeikis, Justin	6-3/254	7-17-77	3	Penn State	FA/05	5/0
59	Speegle, Nick	6-6/250	11-29-81	R	New Mexico	D6a/05	—
55	Stewart, Matt	6-3/232	8-31-79	5	Vanderbilt	FA/05	16/15
58	Taylor, Ben	6-2/245	8-31-78	4	Virginia Tech	D4b/02	3/2
51	Thompson, Chaun	6-2/250	5-22-80	3	West Texas A&M	D2/03	16/13
53	Unck, Mason	6-3/235	3-30-80	2	Arizona State	FA/03	11/0
	DEFENSIVE BACKS						
24	Baxter, Gary (CB)	6-2/215	11-24-78	5	Baylor	FA/05	16/16
28	Bodden, Leigh (CB)	6-1/200	9-24-81	3	Duquesne	FA/03	8/1
35	Carter, Dyshod	5-10/195	6-18-78	3	Kansas State	FA/04	6/0
25	Crocker, Chris (S)	5-11/194	3-9-80	3	Marshall	D3/03	12/5
22	Jameson, Michael (CB)	5-11/205	7-14-79	5	Texas A&M	D6/01	16/0
26	Jones, Sean (S)	6-1/212	3-2-82	2	Georgia	D2/04	0/0
39	Lehan, Michael (CB)	6-0/190	11-25-79	3	Minnesota	D5b/03	10/2
33	McCutcheon, Daylon (CB)	5-10/190	12-9-76	7	USC	D3a/99	12/10
30	Perkins, Antonio (CB)	6-0/190	1-9-82	R	Oklahoma	D4/05	—
21	Pool, Brodney (S)	6-2/208	5-24-84	R	Oklahoma	D2/05	—
27	Russell, Brian (S)	6-2/204	2-5-78	4	San Diego State	FA/05	16/16
	SPECIALISTS						
4	Dawson, Phil (K)	5-11/200	1-23-75	7	Texas	FA/99	16/0
3	Frost, Derrick (P)	6-4/200	11-25-80	2	Northern Iowa	FA/03	16/0
10	Richardson, Kyle (P)	6-2/210	3-2-73	8	Arkansas State	FA/05	0/0

Abbreviations: D1—draft pick, first round; W—claimed on waivers; T—obtained in trade; FA—free-agent acquisition.

CLEVELAND BROWNS

2004 regular-season record: 4-12
Position: 4th in AFC North

Date		Result	Score
Sept.12	BALTIMORE	W	20-3
Sept.19	at Dallas	L	12-19
Sept.26	at N.Y. Giants	L	10-27
Oct. 3	WASHINGTON	W	17-13
Oct. 10	at Pittsburgh	L	23-34
Oct. 17	CINCINNATI	W	34-17
Oct. 24	PHILADELPHIA (OT)	L	31-34
Oct. 31	Open date		
Nov. 7	at Baltimore	L	13-27
Nov.14	PITTSBURGH	L	10-24
Nov.21	N.Y. JETS	L	7-10
Nov.28	at Cincinnati	L	48-58
Dec. 5	NEW ENGLAND	L	15-42
Dec.12	at Buffalo	L	7-37
Dec.19	SAN DIEGO	L	0-21
Dec.26	at Miami	L	7-10
Jan. 2	at Houston	W	22-14

SCORING BY PERIODS

	Q1	Q2	Q3	Q4	OT	Pts.
Browns	67	62	55	92	0	276
Opponents	107	107	72	101	3	390

TEAM STATISTICS

	Cle.	Opp.
TOTAL FIRST DOWNS	245	307
Rushing	94	141
Passing	125	144
Penalty	26	22
3rd Down: Made/Att.	59/203	78/216
3rd Down Pct.	29.1	36.1
4th Down: Made/Att.	7/16	7/16
4th Down Pct.	43.8	43.8
POSSESSION AVG.	28:03	31:57
TOTAL NET YARDS	4481	5215
Avg. per Game	280.1	325.9
Total Plays	921	1024
Avg. per Play	4.9	5.1
NET YARDS RUSHING	1657	2314
Avg. per Game	103.6	144.6
Total Rushes	441	532
NET YARDS PASSING	2824	2901
Avg. per Game	176.5	181.3
Sacked/Yards Lost	41/252	32/190
Gross Yards	3076	3091
Att./Completions	439/251	460/277
Completion Pct.	57.2	60.2
Had Intercepted	21	15
PUNTS/AVERAGE	85/40.0	85/41.6
NET PUNTING AVG.	85/35.4	85/33.9
PENALTIES/YARDS	115/854	109/890
FUMBLES/LOST	32/19	20/13
TOUCHDOWNS	29	45
Rushing	6	22
Passing	21	17
Returns	2	6

SCORING (NON-KICKERS)

	Tot. TD	RTD	PTD	MTD	2Pt.	Tot. Pts.
Heiden	5	0	5	0	1	32
Bryant	4	0	4	0	0	24
Shea	4	0	4	0	0	24
Morgan	3	0	3	0	0	18
Suggs	3	2	1	0	0	18
Andre Davis	2	0	2	0	0	12
Garcia	2	2	0	0	0	12
Green	2	2	0	0	0	12
Northcutt	2	0	2	0	0	12
Alston	1	0	0	1	0	6
Crocker	1	0	0	1	0	6
Browns	29	6	21	2	1	176
Opponents	45	22	17	6	1	274

2-Pt. conversions: Browns 1-1; Opponents 1-1.

(KICKERS)

	XPM/XPA	FGM/FGA	Pts.
Dawson	28/28	24/29	100
Browns	28/28	24/29	100
Opponents	44/44	24/28	116

RUSHING

	Att.	Yds.	Avg.	Lg.	TD
Suggs	199	744	3.7	39	2
Green	163	585	3.6	46	2
Garcia	35	169	4.8	21	2
J. Jackson	12	81	6.8	38	0
Echemandu	8	25	3.1	6	0
McCown	6	25	4.2	11	0
Northcutt	8	19	2.4	8	0
Smith	4	9	2.3	4	0
F. Jackson	1	4	4.0	4	0
Frost	1	1	1.0	1	0
Holcomb	3	-2	-0.7	0	0
Andre Davis	1	-3	-3.0	-3	0
Browns	441	1657	3.8	46	6
Opponents	532	2314	4.3	52	22

RECEIVING

	No.	Yds.	Avg.	Lg.	TD
Northcutt	55	806	14.7	t58	2
Bryant	42	546	13.0	t55	4
Heiden	28	287	10.3	30	5
Shea	26	252	9.7	35	4
Suggs	20	178	8.9	t59	1
Andre Davis	16	416	26.0	t99	2
Green	14	84	6.0	17	0
F. Jackson	13	168	12.9	24	0
Morgan	9	144	16.0	t46	3
Smith	7	39	5.6	16	0
J. Jackson	6	22	3.7	13	0
King	5	49	9.8	16	0
Winslow	5	50	10.0	21	0
Echemandu	3	25	8.3	19	0
Heinrich	1	1	1.0	1	0

	No.	Yds.	Avg.	Lg.	TD
Mustard	1	9	9.0	9	0
Browns	251	3076	12.3	t99	21
Opponents	277	3091	11.2	t72	17

INTERCEPTIONS

	No.	Yds.	Avg.	Lg.	TD
Henry	4	83	20.8	51	0
Andra Davis	3	35	11.7	30	0
L. Sanders	2	36	18.0	24	0
McCutcheon	2	0	0.0	2	0
Gardner	1	30	30.0	30	0
Little	1	28	28.0	28	0
Crocker	1	20	20.0	t20	1
Griffith	1	18	18.0	18	0
Browns	15	250	16.7	51	1
Opponents	21	232	11.0	t106	2

SACKS: Ekuban 8.0, Lang 7.0, Warren 4.0, McKinley 3.0, Thompson 2.5, Crocker 2.0, Rogers 1.5, Griffith 1.0, Myers 1.0, Roye 1.0, Andra Davis 0.5, Holdman 0.5. Browns 32.0; Opponents 41.0.

PUNTING

	No.	Yds.	Avg.	In. 20	Lg.
Frost	85	3404	40.0	24	54
Browns	85	3404	40.0	24	54
Opponents	85	3537	41.6	21	62

PUNT RETURNS

	No.	FC	Yds.	Avg.	Lg.	TD
Northcutt	36	12	432	12.0	44	0
Browns	36	12	432	12.0	44	0
Opponents	48	10	313	6.5	49	0

KICK RETURNS

	No.	Yds.	Avg.	Lg.	TD
Alston	46	1016	22.1	t93	1
Brown	13	243	18.7	30	0
King	5	95	19.0	24	0
F. Jackson	4	70	17.5	22	0
J. Jackson	2	39	19.5	23	0
Mustard	2	13	6.5	9	0
Shea	2	19	9.5	13	0
L. Sanders	1	9	9.0	10	0
Browns	75	1504	20.1	t93	1
Opponents	59	1336	22.6	t93	1

FIELD GOALS

	1-19	20-29	30-39	40-49	50+
Dawson	0/0	11/11	6/8	6/9	1/1
Browns	0/0	11/11	6/8	6/9	1/1
Opponents	0/0	7/8	9/9	6/9	2/2

Dawson: (37G, 25G) (45G, 23G, 49G, 22G) (49G) (30G) (24G, 34G, 46G) (23G, 33G) (38G) (50G, 29G) (31G) (42N, 34N) (23G, 29G) () (45N) (39N) (43N) (45G, 22G, 29G, 45G, 22G) Opponents: (42G) (30G, 49N) (43G, 25G) (31G, 26G) (47G, 26G) (32G, 44N) (38G, 50G) (44G, 39G, 43G, 36G) (20G, 24N) (43B, 41G) (21G, 32G, 36G) () (23G, 21G, 37G) () (51G) ()

PASSING

	Att.	Cmp.	Yds.	Pct.	Avg. Gain	TD	Pct. TD	Int.	Pct. Int.	Long	Sack/Lost	Rating
Garcia	252	144	1731	57.1	6.87	10	4.0	9	3.6	t99	24/99	76.7
Holcomb	87	59	737	67.8	8.47	7	8.0	5	5.7	t55	5/31	96.8
McCown	98	48	608	49.0	6.20	4	4.1	7	7.1	t58	12/122	52.6
Echemandu	1	0	0	0.0	0.00	0	0.0	0	0.0	...	0/0	39.6
F. Jackson	1	0	0	0.0	0.00	0	0.0	0	0.0	...	0/0	39.6
Browns	439	251	3076	57.2	7.01	21	4.8	21	4.8	t99	41/252	74.9
Opponents	460	277	3091	60.2	6.72	17	3.7	15	3.3	t72	32/190	79.0

DALLAS COWBOYS
NFC EAST DIVISION

2005 SEASON

CLUB DIRECTORY

Owner/president/general manager
Jerry Jones
COO/executive vice president/director of player personnel
Stephen Jones
Chief sales & marketing officer/vice president/general counsel
Jerry Jones Jr.
Director, college and pro scouting
Jeff Ireland
Director, football operations
Bruce Mays
Director of community relations
Emily Robbins
Director of public relations
Rich Dalrymple

Head coach
Bill Parcells

Assistant coaches
Ted Bowles (secondary)
Bruce DeHaven (special teams)
Gary Gibbs (linebackers)
Todd Haley (wide receivers)
Joe Juraszek (strength & conditioning)
David Lee (quarterbacks/offensive quality control)
Anthony Lynn (running backs)
Mike MacIntyre (asst. secondary/defensive quality control)
Paul Pasqualoni (tight ends)
Sean Payton (asst. head coach/passing game coordinator)
Kacy Rodgers (defensive line)
Tony Sparano (running game coordinator/offensive line)
Mike Zimmer (def. coordinator)

OFFSEASON MOVES

Key additions
QB Drew Bledsoe	Released/Bills
DT Jason Ferguson	FA/Jets
CB Aaron Glenn	Rel./Texans
CB Anthony Henry	FA/Browns
G Marco Rivera	FA/Packers
RB Anthony Thomas	FA/Bears

Key losses
FB Richie Anderson	Released
LB Dexter Coakley	FA/Rams
C Gennaro DiNapoli	Released
QB Vinny Testaverde	Free agent
DE Marcellus Wiley	Rel./Jaguars
WR Randal Williams	Released

SCHEDULE

Sept.	11—at San Diego	4:15
Sept.	19—WASHINGTON (Mon.)	9:00
Sept.	25—at San Francisco	4:05
Oct.	2—at Oakland	4:15
Oct.	9—PHILADELPHIA	4:15
Oct.	16—N.Y. GIANTS	1:00
Oct.	23—at Seattle	4:05
Oct.	30—ARIZONA	2:00
Nov.	6—Open date	
Nov.	14—at Philadelphia (Mon.)	10:00
Nov.	20—DETROIT	2:00
Nov.	24—DENVER (Thurs.)	5:15
Dec.	4—at N.Y. Giants	2:00
Dec.	11—KANSAS CITY	5:15
Dec.	18—at Washington	2:00
Dec.	24—at Carolina (Sat.)	2:00
Jan.	1—ST. LOUIS	9:30

All times are Eastern.
All games Sunday unless noted.

DRAFT CHOICES

Demarcus Ware, DE, Troy State (first round/11th pick overall).
Marcus Spears, DE, LSU (1/20).
Kevin Burnett, OLB, Tennessee (2/42).
Marion Barber, RB, Minnesota (4/109).
Chris Canty, DE, Virginia (4/132).
Justin Beriault, FS, Ball State (6/208).
Rob Petitti, OT, Pittsburgh (6/209).
Jeremiah "Jay" Ratliff, DE, Auburn (7/224).

MISCELLANEOUS TEAM DATA

Stadium (capacity, surface):
Texas Stadium
(65,675, artificial)
Business address:
One Cowboys Parkway
Irving, TX 75063
Business phone:
972-556-9900
Ticket information:
972-785-5000
Team colors:
Blue, metallic silver blue and white
Flagship radio station:
KLUV, 98.7 FM
Website:
www.dallascowboys.com
Training site:
Residence Inn
Oxnard, CA.

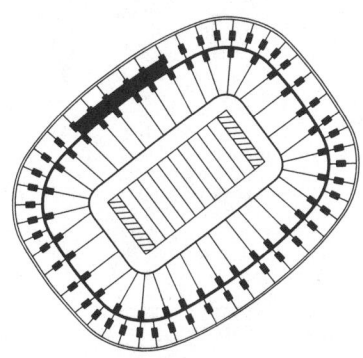

DALLAS COWBOYS

No.	QUARTERBACKS	Ht./Wt.	Born	NFL Exp.	College	How acq.	'04 Games GP/GS
11	Bledsoe, Drew	6-5/238	2-14-72	13	Washington State	FA/05	16/16
7	Henson, Drew	6-4/233	2-13-80	2	Michigan	T-Hou./04	7/1
9	Romo, Tony	6-2/219	4-21-80	2	Eastern Illinois	FA/03	6/0
	RUNNING BACKS						
24	Barber, Marion	5-11/221	6-10-83	R	Minnesota	D4a/05	—
36	Barnes, Darian (FB)	6-2/241	2-28-80	4	Hampton	T-TB/04	16/10
34	Bickerstaff, Erik	6-0/230	7-26-80	2	Wisconsin	FA/03	0/0
21	Jones, Julius	5-10/205	8-14-81	2	Notre Dame	D2/04	8/7
39	Polite, Lousaka (FB)	6-0/246	9-14-81	1	Pittsburgh	FA/04	1/0
32	Thomas, Anthony	6-2/225	11-7-77	5	Michigan	FA/05	12/2
	RECEIVERS						
86	Campbell, Dan (TE)	6-5/262	4-13-76	7	Texas A&M	FA/03	3/2
18	Copper, Terrance	6-0/201	3-12-82	2	East Carolina	FA/04	10/0
84	Crayton, Patrick	6-0/200	4-7-79	2	NW Oklahoma State	D7b/04	8/0
83	Glenn, Terry	5-11/193	7-23-74	10	Ohio State	T-GB/03	6/6
19	Johnson, Keyshawn	6-4/214	7-22-72	10	USC	T-TB/04	16/16
10	Merritt, Ahmad	5-10/195	2-5-77	3	Wisconsin	FA/05	0/0
81	Morgan, Quincy	6-1/215	9-23-77	5	Kansas State	T-Cle./04	15/12
88	Pierce, Brett (TE)	6-5/250	1-7-81	2	Stanford	FA/04	8/1
85	Robinson, Jeff (LS)	6-4/250	2-20-70	12	Idaho	FA/02	16/0
80	Ryan, Sean (TE)	6-5/257	3-27-80	2	Boston College	D5/04	6/1
82	Witten, Jason (TE)	6-5/261	5-6-82	3	Tennessee	D3/03	16/15
	OFFENSIVE LINEMEN						
76	Adams, Flozell (T)	6-7/343	5-18-75	8	Michigan State	D2/98	16/16
73	Allen, Larry (G)	6-3/325	11-27-71	12	Sonoma State	D2/94	16/16
65	Gurode, Andre (G)	6-4/314	3-6-78	4	Colorado	D2a/02	14/13
52	Johnson, Al (C)	6-5/296	1-27-79	2	Wisconsin	D2/03	16/15
60	Noll, Ben (G)	6-4/300	11-14-81	2	Pennsylvania	FA/04	1/1
72	Peterman, Stephen (G)	6-4/318	1-11-82	1	LSU	D3/04	0/0
79	Petitti, Rob (T)	6-6/347	5-21-82	R	Pittsburgh	D6b/05	—
62	Rivera, Marco (G)	6-4/307	4-26-72	9	Penn State	FA/05	16/16
75	Rogers, Jacob (T)	6-6/305	8-17-81	2	USC	D2/04	2/0
77	Tucker, Torrin (T)	6-6/315	12-25-79	3	Southern Mississippi	FA/03	13/13
78	Vollers, Kurt (T)	6-7/300	4-4-79	4	Notre Dame	W-Ind./02	13/3
71	Walter, Tyson (C)	6-4/303	3-17-78	4	Ohio State	D6a/02	13/1
	DEFENSIVE LINEMEN						
92	Brooks, Jermaine (T)	6-3/290	4-11-79	1	Arkansas	FA/04	0/0
99	Canty, Chris (E)	6-7/286	11-10-82	R	Virginia	D4b/05	—
91	Carson, Leonardo (T)	6-2/292	2-11-77	6	Auburn	FA/03	15/15
93	Coleman, Kenyon (E)	6-5/284	4-10-79	3	UCLA	T-Oak./03	12/0
98	Ellis, Greg (E)	6-6/271	8-14-75	8	North Carolina	D1/98	16/16
95	Ferguson, Jason (T)	6-3/305	11-28-74	8	Georgia	FA/05	16/14
97	Glover, La'Roi (T)	6-2/282	7-4-74	10	San Diego State	FA/02	16/16
90	Ogbogu, Eric (E)	6-4/269	7-18-75	7	Maryland	FA/03	15/1
66	Ratliff, Jay (T)	6-3/293	8-29-81	R	Auburn	D7/05	—
96	Spears, Marcus (E)	6-4/298	3-8-83	R	LSU	D1b/05	—
94	Ware, Demarcus (E)	6-3/247	7-31-82	R	Troy	D1a/05	—
	LINEBACKERS						
57	Burnett, Kevin	6-3/237	12-24-82	R	Tennessee	D2/05	—
56	James, Bradie	6-2/245	1-17-81	3	LSU	D4/03	16/2
59	Nguyen, Dat	5-11/238	9-25-75	7	Texas A&M	D3/99	16/16
54	O'Neil, Keith	6-0/235	8-26-80	3	Northern Arizona	FA/03	16/0
58	Shanle, Scott	6-2/237	11-23-79	3	Nebraska	W-St.L./03	16/3
51	Singleton, Al	6-2/236	8-7-75	9	Temple	FA/03	13/12
53	Thornton, Kalen	6-3/240	5-12-82	2	Texas	FA/04	16/0
	DEFENSIVE BACKS						
40	Beriault, Justin (S)	6-2/199	8-23-81	R	Ball State	D6a/05	—
29	Davis, Keith (S)	5-10/193	12-30-78	3	Sam Houston State	FA/02	15/0
30	Frazier, Lance (CB)	5-10/183	5-23-81	2	West Virginia	FA/04	12/8
20	Glenn, Aaron (CB)	5-9/185	7-16-72	12	Texas A&M	FA/05	16/16
42	Henry, Anthony (CB)	6-1/205	11-3-76	5	South Florida	FA/05	14/14
47	Hunter, Pete (CB)	6-2/208	5-25-80	4	Virginia Union	D5/02	3/3
33	Jones, Nathan (CB)	5-10/184	6-13-82	2	Rutgers	D7a/04	16/1
41	Newman, Terence (CB)	5-11/190	9-4-78	3	Kansas State	D1/03	16/16
35	Reeves, Jacques (CB)	5-11/190	10-8-82	2	Purdue	D7b/04	15/1
38	Scott, Lynn (S)	6-0/211	6-23-77	5	NW Oklahoma State	FA/01	16/9
25	Thornton, Bruce (CB)	5-10/198	1-31-80	1	Georgia	D4/04	1/0
31	Williams, Roy (S)	6-0/226	8-14-80	4	Oklahoma	D1/02	16/16
	SPECIALISTS						
3	Cundiff, Billy (K)	6-1/201	3-30-80	4	Drake	FA/02	16/0
1	McBriar, Mat (P)	6-1/210	7-8-79	2	Hawaii	FA/04	16/0

Abbreviations: D1—draft pick, first round; W—claimed on waivers; T—obtained in trade; FA—free-agent acquisition.

2004 regular-season record: 6-10
Position: 3rd in NFC East

Sept.12—at Minnesota	L	17-35
Sept.19—CLEVELAND	W	19-12
Sept.27—at Washington	W	21-18
Oct. 3—Open date		
Oct. 10—N.Y. GIANTS	L	10-26
Oct. 17—PITTSBURGH	L	20-24
Oct. 24—at Green Bay	L	20-41
Oct. 31—DETROIT	W	31-21
Nov. 7—at Cincinnati	L	3-26
Nov.15—PHILADELPHIA	L	21-49
Nov.21—at Baltimore	L	10-30
Nov.25—CHICAGO	W	21-7
Dec. 6—at Seattle	W	43-39
Dec.12—NEW ORLEANS	L	13-27
Dec.19—at Philadelphia	L	7-12
Dec.26—WASHINGTON	W	13-10
Jan. 2—at N.Y. Giants	L	24-28

SCORING BY PERIODS

	Q1	Q2	Q3	Q4	OT	Pts.
Cowboys	63	82	72	76	0	293
Opponents	47	120	83	155	0	405

TEAM STATISTICS

	Dal.	Opp.
TOTAL FIRST DOWNS	296	297
Rushing	101	88
Passing	171	180
Penalty	24	29
3rd Down: Made/Att.	78/214	75/192
3rd Down Pct.	36.4	39.1
4th Down: Made/Att.	9/17	2/7
4th Down Pct.	52.9	28.6
POSSESSION AVG.	30:37	29:23
TOTAL NET YARDS	5197	5285
Avg. per Game	324.8	330.3
Total Plays	1004	960
Avg. per Play	5.2	5.5
NET YARDS RUSHING	1769	1764
Avg. per Game	110.6	110.3
Total Rushes	449	425
NET YARDS PASSING	3428	3521
Avg. per Game	214.3	220.1
Sacked/Yards Lost	36/208	33/197
Gross Yards	3636	3718
Att./Completions	519/308	502/310
Completion Pct.	59.3	61.8
Had Intercepted	23	13
PUNTS/AVERAGE	76/42.3	78/41.8
NET PUNTING AVG.	76/35.1	78/35.8
PENALTIES/YARDS	105/867	104/879
FUMBLES/LOST	26/14	20/9
TOUCHDOWNS	33	49
Rushing	14	14
Passing	19	31
Returns	0	4

SCORING (NON-KICKERS)

	Tot. TD	RTD	PTD	MTD	2Pt.	Tot. Pts.
J. Jones	7	7	0	0	0	42
Witten	6	0	6	0	0	38
Johnson	6	0	6	0	0	36
George	4	4	0	0	0	24
Glenn	2	0	2	0	0	12
Robinson	2	0	2	0	0	12
Anderson	1	1	0	0	0	6
Barnes	1	0	1	0	0	6
Copper	1	0	1	0	0	6
Crayton	1	0	1	0	0	6
Lee	1	1	0	0	0	6
Testaverde	1	1	0	0	0	6
Cowboys	33	14	19	0	1	202
Opponents	49	14	31	4	2	298

2-Pt. conversions: Cowboys 1-2; Opponents 2-4.

(KICKERS)

	XPM/XPA	FGM/FGA	Pts.
Cundiff	31/31	20/26	91
Cowboys	31/31	20/26	91
Opponents	44/45	21/23	107

RUSHING

	Att.	Yds.	Avg.	Lg.	TD
J. Jones	197	819	4.2	53	7
George	132	432	3.3	24	4
Anderson	57	246	4.3	27	1
Lee	27	128	4.7	14	1
Testaverde	21	38	1.8	10	1
Coakley	1	33	33.0	33	0
Morgan	2	23	11.5	24	0
Johnson	2	13	6.5	13	0
Ra. Williams	1	13	13.0	13	0
Ward	1	11	11.0	11	0
Barnes	5	10	2.0	8	0
Henson	1	7	7.0	7	0
Copper	1	-1	-1.0	-1	0
Glenn	1	-3	-3.0	-3	0
Cowboys	449	1769	3.9	53	14
Opponents	425	1764	4.2	t90	14

RECEIVING

	No.	Yds.	Avg.	Lg.	TD
Witten	87	980	11.3	t42	6
Johnson	70	981	14.0	39	6
Anderson	26	207	8.0	28	0
Glenn	24	400	16.7	48	2
Morgan	22	260	11.8	53	0
J. Jones	17	109	6.4	37	0
Bryant	16	266	16.6	48	0
Crayton	12	162	13.5	t39	1
Barnes	10	59	5.9	14	1
George	9	83	9.2	28	0
Copper	7	84	12.0	22	1
Campbell	2	16	8.0	9	0
Robinson	2	2	1.0	t1	2
Lee	1	4	4.0	4	0
Polite	1	4	4.0	4	0
Ward	1	5	5.0	5	0
Ra. Williams	1	14	14.0	14	0
Cowboys	308	3636	11.8	53	19
Opponents	310	3718	12.0	t76	31

INTERCEPTIONS

	No.	Yds.	Avg.	Lg.	TD
Newman	4	31	7.8	21	0
Nguyen	3	19	6.3	19	0
Ro. Williams	2	53	26.5	33	0
Frazier	2	2	1.0	2	0
Hunter	1	2	2.0	2	0
L. Scott	1	2	2.0	2	0
Cowboys	13	109	8.4	33	0
Opponents	23	526	22.9	t101	4

SACKS: Ellis 9.0, Glover 7.0, Ogbogu 4.5, Dixon 3.0, Wiley 3.0, Coleman 1.0, Hunter 1.0, N. Jones 1.0, Nguyen 1.0, L. Scott 1.0, Williams 1.0, Carson 0.5. Cowboys 33.0; Opponents 36.0.

PUNTING

	No.	Yds.	Avg.	In. 20	Lg.
Cundiff	1	34	34.0	1	34
McBriar	75	3182	42.4	22	68
Cowboys	76	3216	42.3	23	68
Opponents	78	3260	41.8	22	58

PUNT RETURNS

	No.	FC	Yds.	Avg.	Lg.	TD
Frazier	24	9	229	9.5	55	0
Ward	14	6	114	8.1	13	0
Crayton	4	1	34	8.5	17	0
Newman	2	0	13	6.5	7	0
Cowboys	44	16	390	8.9	55	0
Opponents	39	16	410	10.5	43	0

KICK RETURNS

	No.	Yds.	Avg.	Lg.	TD
Lee	41	964	23.5	62	0
Copper	16	307	19.2	39	0
Reeves	13	199	15.3	27	0
N. Jones	2	43	21.5	25	0
Morgan	2	25	12.5	19	0
B. Thornton	2	43	21.5	24	0
Lehr	1	9	9.0	9	0
Pierce	1	13	13.0	13	0
Cowboys	78	1603	20.6	62	0
Opponents	62	1083	17.5	34	0

FIELD GOALS

	1-19	20-29	30-39	40-49	50+
Cundiff	1/1	6/6	4/4	9/13	0/2
Cowboys	1/1	6/6	4/4	9/13	0/2
Opponents	1/1	6/6	4/4	7/8	3/4

Cundiff: (27G) (30G, 49N) () (41G, 52N) (47G, 39G) (46G, 24G) (40G) (24G) () (19G, 41N) (52N) (39G, 49G, 47G) (42N, 34G, 41G) (46N) (26G, 23G) (40G, 24G, 45G)
Opponents: () (45G, 23G, 49G, 22G) (19G) (31G, 51G, 47G, 26G) (51G) (26G, 40G) () (35G, 47G, 45G, 30G) () (50G) (48N) (21G) (39G, 44G) () (25G, 57N) ()

PASSING

	Att.	Cmp.	Yds.	Pct.	Avg. Gain	TD	Pct. TD	Int.	Pct. Int.	Long	Sack/Lost	Rating
Testaverde	495	297	3532	60.0	7.14	17	3.4	20	4.0	53	34/182	76.4
Henson	18	10	78	55.6	4.33	1	5.6	1	5.6	16	2/26	61.8
Anderson	1	1	26	100.0	26.00	0	0.0	0	0.0	t26	0/0	158.3
Crayton	1	0	0	0.0	0.00	0	0.0	0	0.0	...	0/0	39.6
Glenn	1	0	0	0.0	0.00	0	0.0	0	0.0	...	0/0	39.6
Johnson	2	0	0	0.0	0.00	0	0.0	1	50.0	...	0/0	0.0
McBriar	1	0	0	0.0	0.00	0	0.0	0	100.0	...	0/0	39.6
Cowboys	519	308	3636	59.3	7.01	19	3.7	23	4.4	53	36/208	74.5
Opponents	502	310	3718	61.8	7.41	31	6.2	13	2.6	t76	33/197	94.2

DENVER BRONCOS
AFC WEST DIVISION

2005 SEASON

CLUB DIRECTORY

President/chief executive officer
Pat Bowlen
Executive vp of business operations
Joe Ellis
General manager
Ted Sundquist
Vice president of public relations
Jim Saccomano
Director of operations
Chip Conway
Director of pro personnel
Rick Smith
Director of college scouting
Jim Goodman
Vice president of community development
Cindy Galloway-Kellogg
Director of media relations
Paul Kirk

Head coach/executive vp of football operations
Mike Shanahan

Assistant coaches
Ronnie Bradford (special teams coach)
Tim Brewster (tight ends)
Jacob Burney (defensive line)
Frank Bush (special teams)
Troy Calhoun (asst. to the head coach)
Larry Coyer (def. coordinator)
Rick Dennison (offensive line)
Kirk Doll (linebackers)
Gary Kubiak (offensive coordinator)
Pat McPherson (quarterbacks)
Andre Patterson (defensive front)
Jim Ryan (defensive asst.)
Greg Saporta (asst. strength & conditioning)
Bob Slowik (defensive backs)
Cedric Smith (asst. strength & conditioning)
Jimmy Spencer (asst. defensive backs)
Bobby Turner (running backs)
Rich Tuten (strength & conditioning)
Steve Watson (wide receivers)

OFFSEASON MOVES

Key additions
TE Stephen Alexander	FA/Lions
DE Courtney Brown	Rel./Browns
LB Keith Burns	FA/Buccaneers
OT Anthony Clement	Rel./Cardinals
RB Ron Dayne	FA/Giants
DE Ebenezer Ekuban	Trade/Browns
LB Ian Gold	Rel./Bucs
DT Michael Myers	Trade/Browns
DT Gerard Warren	Trade/Browns

Key losses
RB Reuben Droughns	Trade/Browns
DE Reggie Hayward	FA/Jaguars
CB Kelly Herndon	FA/Seahawks
DE Ellis Johnson	Free agent
S Kenoy Kennedy	FA/Lions
G Dan Neil	Released
LB Donnie Spragan	FA/Dolphins

SCHEDULE

Sept. 11—at Miami	1:00
Sept. 18—SAN DIEGO	4:15
Sept. 26—KANSAS CITY (Mon.)	9:00
Oct. 2—at Jacksonville	1:00
Oct. 9—WASHINGTON	4:15
Oct. 16—NEW ENGLAND	4:15
Oct. 23—at N.Y. Giants	4:15
Oct. 30—PHILADELPHIA	5:15
Nov. 6—Open Week	
Nov. 13—at Oakland	5:05
Nov. 20—N.Y. JETS	5:15
Nov. 24—at Dallas (Thurs.)	5:15
Dec. 4—at Kansas City	5:15
Dec. 11—BALTIMORE	5:15
Dec. 17—at Buffalo (Sat.)	9:30
Dec. 24—OAKLAND (Sat.)	5:15
Dec. 31—at San Diego (Sat.)	5:30

All times are Eastern.
All games Sunday unless noted.

DRAFT CHOICES

Darrent Williams, CB, Oklahoma State (second round/56th pick overall).
Karl Paymah, CB, Washington State (3/76).
Domonique Foxworth, CB, Maryland (3/97).
Maurice Clarett, RB, Ohio State (3/101).
Chris Myers, G, Miami (6/200).
Paul Ernster, K, Northern Arizona (7/239).

MISCELLANEOUS TEAM DATA

Stadium (capacity, surface):
Invesco Field at Mile High
(76,125, grass)
Business address:
13655 Broncos Parkway
Englewood, CO 80112
Business phone:
303-649-9000
Ticket information:
720-258-3333
Team colors:
Orange, navy blue and white
Flagship radio station:
KOA, 850 AM
Website:
www.denverbroncos.com
Training site:
Dove Valley Headquarters
Englewood, CO
303-649-9000

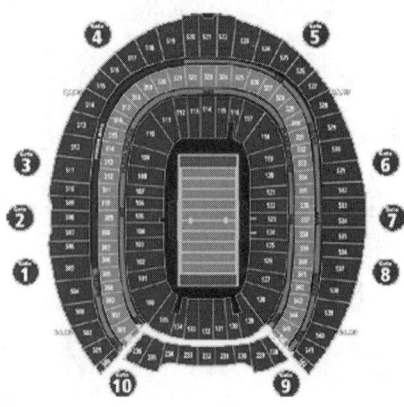

No.	QUARTERBACKS	Ht./Wt.	Born	NFL Exp.	College	How acq.	'04 Games GP/GS
13	Kanell, Danny	6-3/218	11-21-73	8	Florida State	FA/03	1/0
8	Mauck, Matt	6-1/213	12-12-79	1	LSU	D7a/04	0/0
16	Plummer, Jake	6-2/212	12-19-74	9	Arizona State	FA/03	16/16
	RUNNING BACKS						
38	Anderson, Mike	6-0/230	9-21-73	6	Utah	D6/00	0/0
26	Bell, Tatum	5-11/213	3-2-81	2	Oklahoma State	D2a/04	14/0
20	Clarett, Maurice	6-0/234	10-29-83	R	Ohio State	D3c/05	—
33	Dayne, Ron	5-10/245	3-14-78	6	Wisconsin	FA/05	14/2
21	Griffin, Quentin	5-7/195	1-12-81	3	Oklahoma	D4a/03	6/4
39	Johnson, Kyle (FB)	6-0/242	12-15-78	2	Syracuse	FA/03	14/3
37	Sapp, Cecil (FB)	5-11/229	12-12-78	2	Colorado State	FA/03	5/0
	RECEIVERS						
81	Adams, Charlie	6-2/190	10-23-79	3	Hofstra	FA/04	4/0
82	Alexander, Stephen (TE)	6-4/250	11-7-75	8	Oklahoma	FA/05	16/15
86	Hape, Patrick (TE)	6-4/262	6-6-74	9	Alabama	FA/01	16/5
14	Jackson, Nate	6-3/223	6-4-79	3	Menlo	T-S.F./03	12/0
83	Leach, Mike (TE)	6-2/245	10-18-76	6	William & Mary	FA/02	16/0
85	Lelie, Ashley	6-3/200	2-16-80	4	Hawaii	D1/02	16/16
87	Luke, Triandos	5-10/189	12-24-81	2	Alabama	D6a/04	10/0
88	Putzier, Jeb (TE)	6-4/256	1-20-79	4	Boise State	D6/02	16/5
80	Smith, Rod	6-0/200	5-15-70	11	Missouri Southern	FA/94	16/16
17	Watts, Darius	6-2/188	12-19-81	2	Marshall	D2b/04	16/2
	OFFENSIVE LINEMEN						
69	Alexander, P.J. (G)	6-4/297	12-23-78	3	Syracuse	FA/03	5/0
65	Carlisle, Cooper (G)	6-5/295	8-11-77	6	Florida	D4b/00	16/4
67	Clement, Anthony (T)	6-8/337	4-10-76	8	Louisiana-Lafayette	FA/05	16/7
72	Foster, George (T)	6-5/338	6-9-80	3	Georgia	D1/03	16/16
74	Green, Cornell (T)	6-6/315	8-25-76	6	Central Florida	FA/04	0/0
50	Hamilton, Ben (C/G)	6-4/283	8-18-77	5	Minnesota	D4a/01	16/16
78	Lepsis, Matt (T)	6-4/290	1-13-74	9	Colorado	FA/97	16/16
62	Myers, Chris (G)	6-5/300	9-15-81	R	Miami	D6/05	—
66	Nalen, Tom (C)	6-3/286	5-13-71	12	Boston College	D7c/94	16/16
	DEFENSIVE LINEMEN						
98	Brown, Courtney (E)	6-4/290	2-14-78	6	Penn State	FA/05	2/2
92	Coleman, Marco (E)	6-3/270	12-18-69	14	Georgia Tech	FA/04	16/16
96	Davis, Dorsett (E)	6-5/305	1-24-79	4	Mississippi State	D3/02	0/0
91	Ekuban, Ebenezer (E)	6-3/275	5-29-76	7	North Carolina	T-Cle./05	16/11
94	Elliss, Luther (T)	6-5/318	3-22-73	11	Utah	FA/04	8/0
68	Fatafehi, Mario (T)	6-2/300	1-27-79	5	Kansas State	FA/03	16/16
99	Johnson, Raylee (E)	6-3/272	6-1-70	13	Arkansas	FA/04	14/1
76	Myers, Michael (T)	6-2/300	1-20-76	8	Alabama	T-Cle./05	16/7
95	Palepoi, Anton (E)	6-3/283	1-19-78	4	UNLV	FA/04	12/0
75	Pope, Monsanto (T)	6-3/300	1-27-78	4	Virginia	D7b/02	16/15
93	Pryce, Trevor (E)	6-5/295	8-3-75	9	Clemson	D1/97	2/1
61	Warren, Gerard (T)	6-4/325	7-25-78	5	Florida	T-Cle./05	13/13
	LINEBACKERS						
51	Burns, Keith	6-2/235	5-16-72	12	Oklahoma State	FA/05	16/0
55	Chukwurah, Patrick	6-1/250	3-1-79	5	Wyoming	FA/04	14/0
52	Gold, Ian	6-0/223	8-23-78	6	Michigan	FA/05	16/13
53	Green, Louis	6-3/228	9-23-79	2	Alcorn State	FA/03	6/0
58	Pierce, Terry	6-1/251	6-21-81	3	Kansas State	D2/03	15/0
57	Sykes, Jashon	6-2/236	9-25-79	3	Colorado	FA/02	3/0
55	Williams, D.J.	6-1/242	7-20-82	2	Miami	D1/04	16/14
56	Wilson, Al	6-0/240	6-21-77	7	Tennessee	D1/99	16/16
	DEFENSIVE BACKS						
45	Alexander, Roc (CB)	5-10/186	9-23-81	2	Washington	FA/04	16/1
24	Bailey, Champ (CB)	6-0/192	6-22-78	6	Georgia	T-Was./04	16/16
42	Brandon, Sam (S)	6-2/200	7-5-79	4	UNLV	D4/02	9/0
25	Ferguson, Nick (S)	5-11/201	11-27-74	6	Georgia Tech	FA/03	16/1
22	Foxworth, Domonique (CB)	5-11/178	3-27-83	R	Maryland	D3b/05	—
47	Lynch, John (S)	6-2/220	9-25-71	13	Stanford	FA/04	15/15
23	Middlebrooks, Willie (CB)	6-1/200	2-12-79	5	Minnesota	D1/01	12/2
41	Paymah, Karl (CB)	6-0/198	11-29-82	R	Washington State	D3a/05	—
28	Shoate, Jeff (CB)	5-10/189	3-23-81	2	San Diego State	D5/04	7/0
35	Walls, Lenny (CB)	6-4/192	9-26-79	4	Boston College	FA/02	7/1
27	Williams, Darrent (CB)	5-8/188	9-27-82	R	Oklahoma State	D2/05	—
32	Young, Chris (S)	6-0/210	1-23-80	3	Georgia Tech	D7a/02	10/0
	SPECIALISTS						
6	Baker, Jason (P)	6-1/201	5-17-78	5	Iowa	W-Ind./04	10/0
1	Elam, Jason (K)	5-11/200	3-8-70	13	Hawaii	D3b/93	16/0
3	Ernster, Paul (K)	6-0/217	1-26-82	R	Northern Arizona	D7/05	—

Abbreviations: D1—draft pick, first round; W—claimed on waivers; T—obtained in trade; FA—free-agent acquisition.

DENVER BRONCOS

DENVER BRONCOS

2004 regular-season record: 10-6
Position: 2nd in AFC West

Sept.12—KANSAS CITY	W	34-24
Sept.19—at Jacksonville	L	6-7
Sept.26—SAN DIEGO	W	23-13
Oct. 3—at Tampa Bay	W	16-13
Oct. 10—CAROLINA	W	20-17
Oct. 17—at Oakland	W	31-3
Oct. 25—at Cincinnati	L	10-23
Oct. 31—ATLANTA	L	28-41
Nov. 7—HOUSTON	W	31-13
Nov.14—Open date		
Nov.21—at New Orleans	W	34-13
Nov.28—OAKLAND	L	24-25
Dec. 5—at San Diego	L	17-20
Dec.12—MIAMI	W	20-17
Dec.19—at Kansas City	L	17-45
Dec.25—at Tennessee	W	37-16
Jan. 2—INDIANAPOLIS	W	33-14

2004 postseason record: 0-1

Jan. 9—at Indianapolis#	L	24-49

#AFC wild-card game.

SCORING BY PERIODS

	Q1	Q2	Q3	Q4	OT	Pts.
Broncos	102	138	50	91	0	381
Opponents	68	121	67	48	0	304

TEAM STATISTICS

	Den.	Opp.
TOTAL FIRST DOWNS ..	351	235
Rushing	127	83
Passing	184	130
Penalty	40	22
3rd Down: Made/Att. ..	78/206	65/209
3rd Down Pct.	37.9	31.1
4th Down: Made/Att.	7/14	5/14
4th Down Pct.	50.0	35.7
POSSESSION AVG.	32:37	27:23
TOTAL NET YARDS	6332	4459
Avg. per Game	395.8	278.7
Total Plays	1070	918
Avg. per Play	5.9	4.9
NET YARDS RUSHING ..	2333	1512
Avg. per Game	145.8	94.5
Total Rushes	534	396
NET YARDS PASSING....	3999	2947
Avg. per Game	249.9	184.2
Sacked/Yards Lost	15/90	38/266
Gross Yards	4089	3213
Att./Completions	521/303	484/272
Completion Pct.	58.2	56.2
Had Intercepted	20	12
PUNTS/AVERAGE	70/40.5	95/44.7
NET PUNTING AVG.	70/34.3	95/38.2
PENALTIES/YARDS	93/880	120/1062
FUMBLES/LOST	23/9	24/8
TOUCHDOWNS	42	35
Rushing	13	16
Passing	27	17
Returns	2	2

SCORING (NON-KICKERS)

	Tot. TD	RTD	PTD	MTD	2Pt.	Tot. Pts.
Droughns	8	6	2	0	0	48
Lelie	7	0	7	0	0	42
Smith	7	0	7	0	0	42
Hape	4	0	4	0	0	24
Bell	3	3	0	0	0	18
Griffin	3	2	1	0	0	18
K. Johnson	2	0	2	0	0	12
Putzier	2	0	2	0	0	12
Carswell	1	0	1	0	0	6
Hearst	1	1	0	0	0	6
Johnson	1	0	0	1	0	6
Plummer	1	1	0	0	0	6
Watts	1	0	1	0	0	6
Wilson	1	0	0	1	0	6
Broncos	42	13	27	2	0	252
Opponents	35	16	17	2	0	210

2-Pt. conversions: Broncos 0-0; Opponents 0-3.

(KICKERS)

	XPM/XPA	FGM/FGA	Pts.
Elam	42/42	29/34	129
Broncos	42/42	29/34	129
Opponents	31/32	21/26	94

RUSHING

	Att.	Yds.	Avg.	Lg.	TD
Droughns	275	1240	4.5	t51	6
Bell	75	396	5.3	29	3
Griffin	85	311	3.7	t47	2
Plummer	62	202	3.3	22	1
Hearst	20	81	4.1	11	1
Smith	5	33	6.6	14	0
Watts	5	33	6.6	10	0
Sapp	4	32	8.0	18	0
Lelie	3	5	1.7	8	0
Broncos	534	2333	4.4	t51	13
Opponents	396	1512	3.8	44	16

RECEIVING

	No.	Yds.	Avg.	Lg.	TD
Smith	79	1144	14.5	t85	7
Lelie	54	1084	20.1	58	7
Putzier	36	572	15.9	39	2
Droughns	32	241	7.5	t23	2
Watts	31	385	12.4	28	1
Carswell	22	198	9.0	20	1
Griffin	10	68	6.8	22	1
K. Johnson	9	126	14.0	31	2
Hape	8	35	4.4	11	4
N. Jackson	8	73	9.1	20	0
Luke	6	52	8.7	12	0
Bell	5	80	16.0	58	0
Hearst	2	20	10.0	15	0
Bailey	1	11	11.0	11	0
Broncos	303	4089	13.5	t85	27
Opponents	272	3213	11.8	t71	17

INTERCEPTIONS

	No.	Yds.	Avg.	Lg.	TD
Bailey	3	0	0.0	0	0
K. Herndon	2	17	8.5	15	0
Wilson	2	17	8.5	10	1
Hayward	1	76	76.0	76	0
Johnson	1	32	32.0	t32	1
Kennedy	1	21	21.0	21	0
Williams	1	10	10.0	10	0
Lynch	1	2	2.0	2	0
Broncos	12	175	14.6	76	2
Opponents	20	344	17.2	97	1

SACKS: Hayward 10.5, Johnson 3.0, Palepoi 3.0, Coleman 2.5, Fatafehi 2.5, Wilson 2.5, Elliss 2.0, Kennedy 2.0, Lynch 2.0, Williams 2.0, Chukwurah 1.0, K. Herndon 1.0, Johnson 1.0, Middlebrooks 1.0, Pope 1.0, Spragan 1.0. Broncos 38.0; Opponents 15.0.

PUNTING

	No.	Yds.	Avg.	In. 20	Lg.
Baker	15	591	39.4	7	48
Knorr	54	2243	41.5	12	66
Broncos	70	2834	40.5	19	66
Opponents	95	4250	44.7	36	65

PUNT RETURNS

	No.	FC	Yds.	Avg.	Lg.	TD
Smith	22	8	223	10.1	30	0
Luke	19	8	135	7.1	21	0
Adams	2	1	42	21.0	39	0
Broncos	43	17	400	9.3	39	0
Opponents	32	11	295	9.2	50	0

KICK RETURNS

	No.	Yds.	Avg.	Lg.	TD
Alexander	19	386	20.3	32	0
Luke	15	306	20.4	32	0
Droughns	14	344	24.6	48	0
Griffin	4	52	13.0	21	0
Sapp	1	34	34.0	34	0
Broncos	53	1122	21.2	48	0
Opponents	68	1635	24.0	t97	1

FIELD GOALS

	1-19	20-29	30-39	40-49	50+
Elam	0/0	10/10	7/8	9/12	3/4
Broncos	0/0	10/10	7/8	9/12	3/4
Opponents	0/0	6/6	7/8	3/5	5/7

Elam: (43G, 45G) (44G, 22G, 51N) (22G, 23G, 43G) (49G, 50G, 23G) (32G, 33G) (33G) (49N, 29G) () (52G) (48G, 34G) (32G, 43B) (43N, 31G) (20G, 50G) (27G) (22G, 34N, 22G, 30G) (45G, 23G, 40G, 40G)

Opponents: (58N, 50G) () (23G, 51G) (28G, 30G) (53G, 52N) (35G) (53G, 34G, 35G) (24G, 43G, 49N) (37N) (24G, 36G) (48N) (23G, 23G) (32G) (39G) (44G, 43G, 50G) ()

PASSING

	Att.	Cmp.	Yds.	Pct.	Avg. Gain	TD	Pct. TD	Int.	Pct. Int.	Long	Sack/Lost	Rating
Plummer	521	303	4089	58.2	7.85	27	5.2	20	3.8	t85	15/90	84.5
Broncos	521	303	4089	58.2	7.85	27	5.2	20	3.8	t85	15/90	84.5
Opponents	484	272	3213	56.2	6.64	17	3.5	12	2.5	t71	38/266	78.0

DETROIT LIONS
NFC NORTH DIVISION

2005 SEASON

CLUB DIRECTORY

Chairman and owner
William Clay Ford
Vice chairman
William Clay Ford Jr.
President and CEO
Matt Millen
Executive vice president and COO
Tom Lewand
Sr. vp of finance and CFO
Tom Lesnan
Sr. vp of communications & marketing
Bill Keenist
Asst. G.M. & sr. vp of legal affairs
Martin Mayhew
Director of pro personnel
Sheldon White
Director of college scouting
Scott McEwen
Director of media relations
Matt Barnhart
Manager of football operations
Craig Vandermause

Head coach
Steve
Mariucci

Assistant coaches
Jason Arapoff (strength & conditioning)
Malcom Blacken (asst. strength & conditioning)
Larry Brooks (defensive line)
Don Clemons (defensive asst.)
George Catavolos (defensive backs)
Fred Graves (wide receivers)
Johnny Holland (linebackers)
Dick Jauron (defensive coordinator)
Sean Kugler (asst. offensive line/tight ends)
Stan Kwan (asst. special teams/offensive asst.)
Kevin Lartigue (asst. to the head coach)
Pat Morris (offensive line)
Greg Olson (quarterbacks)
Chuck Priefer (special teams)
Tom Rathman (running backs)
Phil Snow (defensive asst.)
Andy Sugarman (tight ends)
Ted Tollner (off. coordinator)

OFFSEASON MOVES

Key additions

G Rick DeMulling	FA/Colts
QB Jeff Garcia	Rel./Browns
WR Kevin Johnson	Rel./Ravens
S Kenoy Kennedy	FA/Broncos
G Kyle Kosier	FA/49ers
TE Marcus Pollard	Rel./Colts
RB Jamel White	FA/Ravens

Key losses

TE Stephen Alexander	FA/Broncos
CB Rod Babers	Free agent
WR Az Hakim	Released
G Matt Joyce	Released
S Brock Marion	Released
OT Stockar McDougle	FA/Dolphins
QB Mike McMahon	FA/Eagles
DT Kelvin Pritchett	Free agent
WR Tai Streets	Free agent
WR Reggie Swinton	FA/Texans
S Brian Walker	Released

SCHEDULE

Sept.	11—GREEN BAY	4:15
Sept.	18—at Chicago	1:00
Sept.	25—Open date	
Oct.	2—at Tampa Bay	1:00
Oct.	9—BALTIMORE	1:00
Oct.	16—CAROLINA	1:00
Oct.	23—at Cleveland	1:00
Oct.	30—CHICAGO	2:00
Nov.	6—at Minnesota	2:00
Nov.	13—ARIZONA	2:00
Nov.	20—at Dallas	2:00
Nov.	24—ATLANTA (Thurs.)	1:30
Dec.	4—MINNESOTA	2:00
Dec.	11—at Green Bay	9:30
Dec.	18—CINCINNATI	5:05
Dec.	24—at New Orleans (Sat.)	2:00
Jan.	1—at Pittsburgh	2:00

All times are Eastern.
All games Sunday unless noted.

DRAFT CHOICES

Mike Williams, WR, Southern California (first round/10th pick overall).
Shaun Cody, DT, Southern California (2/37).
Stanley Wilson, CB, Stanford (3/72).
Dan Orlovsky, QB, Connecticut (5/145).
Bill Swancutt, DE, Oregon State (6/184).
Jonathan Goddard, DE, Marshall (6/206).

MISCELLANEOUS TEAM DATA

Stadium (capacity, surface):
Ford Field
(65,000, FieldTurf)
Business address:
222 Republic Drive
Allen Park, MI 48101
Business phone:
313-216-4000
Ticket information:
313-262-2000
Team colors:
Honolulu blue and silver
Flagship radio station:
WKRK, 97.1 FM
Website:
www.detroitlions.com

Training site:
222 Republic Drive
Allen Park, MI 48101
313-216-4000

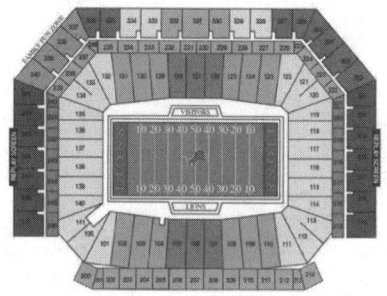

DETROIT LIONS

No.	QUARTERBACKS	Ht./Wt.	Born	NFL Exp.	College	How acq.	'04 Games GP/GS
5	Garcia, Jeff	6-1/200	2-24-70	7	San Jose State	FA/05	11/10
3	Harrington, Joey	6-4/220	10-21-78	4	Oregon	D1/02	16/16
9	Orlovsky, Dan	6-4/238	8-18-83	R	Connecticut	D5/05	—
	RUNNING BACKS						
24	Bryson, Shawn	6-1/230	11-20-76	7	Tennessee	FA/03	16/1
34	Jones, Kevin	5-11/221	8-21-82	2	Virginia Tech	D1b/04	15/14
43	Matthews, Will (FB)	6-3/250	4-30-81	R	Texas	FA/05	—
21	Pinner, Artose	5-10/235	1-5-78	3	Kentucky	D4/03	9/2
30	Schlesinger, Cory (FB)	6-0/247	6-23-72	11	Nebraska	D6b/95	13/11
27	Smith, Paul (FB)	5-11/234	1-31-78	5	UTEP	FA/03	0/0
23	White, Jamel	5-9/222	2-11-78	6	South Dakota	FA/05	13/0
	RECEIVERS						
18	Drummond, Eddie	5-9/190	4-12-80	4	Penn State	FA/02	11/1
82	FitzSimmons, Casey (TE)	6-4/258	10-10-80	3	Carroll	FA/03	16/2
86	Hamilton, Paris	6-1/195	7-26-81	R	Minnesota	FA/05	—
85	Johnson, Kevin	5-11/195	7-15-76	7	Syracuse	FA/05	16/5
87	Kircus, David	6-1/185	2-19-80	3	Grand Valley State	D6/03	7/0
81	Pollard, Marcus (TE)	6-3/247	2-8-72	11	Bradley	FA/05	13/13
80	Rogers, Charles	6-3/202	5-23-81	3	Michigan State	D1/03	1/1
84	Savoy, Steve	5-11/191	2-27-82	R	Utah	FA/05	—
10	Vines, Scottie	6-2/220	4-17-79	2	Wyoming	FA/04	6/1
88	Williams, Mike	6-5/229	1-4-84	R	USC	D1/05	—
11	Williams, Roy	6-2/212	12-20-81	2	Texas	D1/04	14/12
	OFFENSIVE LINEMEN						
76	Backus, Jeff (T)	6-5/305	9-21-77	5	Michigan	D1/01	16/16
70	Bubin, Sean (T)	6-7/307	1-26-81	1	Illinois	FA/04	0/0
79	Butler, Kelly (T)	6-7/334	7-24-82	1	Purdue	D6/04	0/0
64	DeMulling, Rick (G)	6-4/304	7-21-77	5	Idaho	FA/05	11/11
68	Hopson, Tyrone (C)	6-2/294	5-28-76	4	Eastern Kentucky	FA/04	11/0
69	Kosier, Kyle (T)	6-5/309	11-27-78	4	Arizona State	FA/05	16/16
62	Loverne, David (G)	6-3/299	5-22-76	7	San Jose State	FA/04	15/13
67	Muhlbach, Don (LS)	6-5/262	8-17-81	2	Texas A&M	FA/04	8/0
51	Raiola, Dominic (C)	6-1/295	12-30-78	5	Nebraska	D2a/01	16/16
71	Rogers, Victor (T)	6-6/331	11-10-78	4	Colorado	D7c/02	1/0
65	Woody, Damien (G)	6-3/325	11-3-77	7	Boston College	FA/04	16/16
	DEFENSIVE LINEMEN						
94	Bell, Marcus	6-2/339	6-1-79	5	Memphis	D4b/01	16/0
75	Cody, Shaun (T)	6-4/292	1-22-83	R	USC	D2/05	—
95	DeVries, Jared (E)	6-4/275	6-11-76	7	Iowa	D3/99	15/0
98	Edwards, Kalimba (E)	6-6/265	12-26-79	4	South Carolina	D2/02	16/0
96	Hall, James (E)	6-2/280	2-4-77	6	Michigan	FA/00	16/16
78	Redding, Cory (E)	6-4/290	11-15-80	3	Texas	D3/03	16/16
92	Rogers, Shaun (T)	6-4/345	3-12-79	5	Texas	D2b/01	16/16
61	Shull, Andrew (E)	6-5/260	4-2-81	1	Kansas State	FA/05	0/0
90	Swancutt, Bill (E)	6-4/264	9-4-82	R	Oregon State	D6a/05	—
72	Wilkinson, Dan (T)	6-4/335	3-13-73	12	Ohio State	FA/04	16/16
	LINEBACKERS						
97	Bailey, Boss	6-3/235	10-14-79	3	Georgia	D2/03	0/0
55	Curry, Donte'	6-1/233	7-22-78	5	Morris Brown	W-Was./02	12/0
52	Davis, James	6-2/240	4-26-79	3	West Virginia	D5b/03	16/15
99	Goddard, Jonathan	6-0/242	5-11-81	R	Marshall	D6b/05	—
50	Holmes, Earl	6-2/242	4-28-73	10	Florida A&M	FA/03	16/14
54	Lehman, Teddy	6-2/238	11-18-81	2	Oklahoma	D2/04	16/16
59	Lewis, Alex	6-0/227	6-11-81	2	Wisconsin	D5/04	15/1
57	Littleton, Jody (LS)	6-1/235	10-23-74	4	Baylor	FA/03	8/0
58	Rainer, Wali	6-2/240	4-19-77	7	Virginia	FA/03	16/0
	DEFENSIVE BACKS						
32	Bly, Dre' (CB)	5-9/185	5-22-77	7	North Carolina	FA/03	13/13
25	Bryant, Fernando (CB)	5-10/175	3-26-77	7	Alabama	FA/04	10/10
29	Cash, Chris (CB)	5-10/185	7-13-80	4	USC	D6/02	11/5
39	Echols, Mike (CB)	5-9/190	10-13-78	3	Wisconsin	FA/04	0/0
36	Fox, Vernon (S)	5-9/200	10-9-79	4	Fresno State	FA/04	14/0
35	Goodman, Andre' (CB)	5-10/185	8-11-78	4	South Carolina	D3/02	11/4
42	Holt, Terrence (S)	6-2/208	3-5-80	3	North Carolina State	D5a/03	16/0
26	Kennedy, Kenoy (S)	6-1/215	11-15-77	6	Arkansas	FA/05	16/16
38	Smith, Keith (CB)	5-11/192	3-20-80	2	McNeese State	D3/04	15/2
28	Walker, Bracy (S)	6-0/202	10-28-70	12	North Carolina	FA/02	16/16
33	Wilson, Stanley (CB)	5-11/189	11-5-82	R	Stanford	D3/05	—
	SPECIALISTS						
4	Hanson, Jason (K)	5-11/182	6-17-70	14	Washington State	D2b/92	16/0
2	Harris, Nick (P)	6-2/218	7-23-78	5	California	FA/03	16/0

Abbreviations: D1—draft pick, first round; W—claimed on waivers; FA—free-agent acquisition.

2004 regular-season record: 6-10
Position: 3rd in NFC North

Sept.12—at Chicago	W	20-16
Sept.19—HOUSTON	W	28-16
Sept.26—PHILADELPHIA	L	13-30
Oct. 3—Open date		
Oct. 10—at Atlanta	W	17-10
Oct. 17—GREEN BAY	L	10-38
Oct. 24—at N.Y. Giants	W	28-13
Oct. 31—at Dallas	L	21-31
Nov. 7—WASHINGTON	L	10-17
Nov. 14—at Jacksonville (OT)	L	17-23
Nov. 21—at Minnesota	L	19-22
Nov. 25—INDIANAPOLIS	L	9-41
Dec. 5—ARIZONA	W	26-12
Dec. 12—at Green Bay	L	13-16
Dec. 19—MINNESOTA	L	27-28
Dec. 26—CHICAGO	W	19-13
Jan. 2—at Tennessee	L	19-24

SCORING BY PERIODS

	Q1	Q2	Q3	Q4	OT	Pts.
Lions	60	97	45	94	0	296
Opponents	86	80	92	86	6	350

TEAM STATISTICS

	Det.	Opp.
TOTAL FIRST DOWNS	263	320
Rushing	92	118
Passing	142	167
Penalty	29	35
3rd Down: Made/Att.	66/210	98/231
3rd Down Pct.	31.4	42.4
4th Down: Made/Att.	6/16	7/19
4th Down Pct.	37.5	36.8
POSSESSION AVG.	28:03	31:57
TOTAL NET YARDS	4693	5401
Avg. per Game	293.3	337.6
Total Plays	949	1071
Avg. per Play	4.9	5.0
NET YARDS RUSHING	1777	1887
Avg. per Game	111.1	117.9
Total Rushes	407	498
NET YARDS PASSING	2916	3514
Avg. per Game	182.3	219.6
Sacked/Yards Lost	37/208	38/222
Gross Yards	3124	3736
Att./Completions	505/285	535/328
Completion Pct.	56.4	61.3
Had Intercepted	13	14
PUNTS/AVERAGE	93/40.5	84/43.5
NET PUNTING AVG.	93/34.2	84/36.9
PENALTIES/YARDS	121/1000	114/976
FUMBLES/LOST	12/7	20/10
TOUCHDOWNS	32	43
Rushing	7	10
Passing	19	29
Returns	6	4

SCORING (NON-KICKERS)

	Tot. TD	RTD	PTD	MTD	2Pt.	Tot. Pts.
Williams	8	0	8	0	0	48
Jones	6	5	1	0	0	36
Drummond	4	0	0	4	0	24
Hakim	3	0	3	0	0	18
Schlesinger	3	0	3	0	0	18
Pinner	2	2	0	0	0	12
Streets	1	0	1	0	1	8
Alexander	1	0	1	0	0	6
Bly	1	0	0	1	0	6
Kircus	1	0	1	0	0	6
Swinton	1	0	1	0	0	6
Bra. Walker	1	0	0	1	0	6
Lions	32	7	19	6	1	196
Opponents	43	10	29	4	1	262

2-Pt. conversions: Lions 1-4; Opponents 1-4.

(KICKERS)

	XPM/XPA	FGM/FGA	Pts.
Hanson	28/28	24/28	100
Lions	28/28	24/28	100
Opponents	37/38	17/20	88

RUSHING

	Att.	Yds.	Avg.	Lg.	TD
Jones	241	1133	4.7	74	5
Bryson	50	264	5.3	28	0
Harrington	48	175	3.6	17	0
Pinner	57	174	3.1	14	2
McMahon	2	18	9.0	14	0
Drummond	1	9	9.0	9	0
Schlesinger	4	7	1.8	2	0
Swinton	1	3	3.0	3	0
Williams	1	1	1.0	1	0
Hakim	1	0	0.0	0	0
N. Harris	1	-7	-7.0	-7	0
Lions	407	1777	4.4	74	7
Opponents	498	1887	3.8	43	10

RECEIVING

	No.	Yds.	Avg.	Lg.	TD
Williams	54	817	15.1	46	8
Bryson	44	322	7.3	30	0
Alexander	41	377	9.2	30	1
Hakim	31	533	17.2	t39	3
Jones	28	180	6.4	34	1
Streets	28	260	9.3	22	1
Swinton	18	213	11.8	28	1
Pinner	11	72	6.5	26	0
FitzSimmons	10	103	10.3	27	0
Schlesinger	10	91	9.1	30	3
Trejo	4	37	9.3	18	0
Kircus	3	68	22.7	t50	1
Vines	3	51	17.0	26	0
Lions	285	3124	11.0	62	19
Opponents	328	3736	11.4	t82	29

INTERCEPTIONS

	No.	Yds.	Avg.	Lg.	TD
Bly	4	107	26.8	t55	1
Marion	3	43	14.3	24	0
Lewis	1	33	33.0	33	0
Hall	1	30	30.0	30	0
K. Smith	1	2	2.0	2	0
Lehman	1	1	1.0	1	0
Cash	1	0	0.0	0	0
Goodman	1	0	0.0	-	0
Bra. Walker	1	0	0.0	0	0
Lions	14	216	15.4	t55	1
Opponents	13	194	14.9	43	2

SACKS: Hall 11.5, Edwards 4.5, S. Rogers 4.0, Davis 3.5, DeVries 3.0, Redding 3.0, Bell 2.0, Lewis 2.0, Wilkinson 1.5, Lehman 1.0, Pritchett 1.0, Bra. Walker 1.0. Lions 38.0; Opponents 37.0.

PUNTING

	No.	Yds.	Avg.	In. 20	Lg.
N. Harris	92	3765	40.9	32	60
Lions	93	3765	40.5	32	60
Opponents	84	3658	43.5	25	64

PUNT RETURNS

	No.	FC	Yds.	Avg.	Lg.	TD
Drummond	24	8	316	13.2	t83	2
Swinton	16	9	104	6.5	18	0
Lions	40	17	420	10.5	t83	2
Opponents	46	24	441	9.6	56	0

KICK RETURNS

	No.	Yds.	Avg.	Lg.	TD
Drummond	41	1092	26.6	t99	2
Swinton	18	410	22.8	43	0
Bryson	2	27	13.5	14	0
Trejo	2	12	6.0	10	0
D. Curry	1	-1	-1.0	-1	0
DeVries	1	5	5.0	5	0
Schlesinger	1	23	23.0	23	0
Lions	66	1568	23.8	t99	2
Opponents	54	1058	19.6	52	0

FIELD GOALS

	1-19	20-29	30-39	40-49	50+
Hanson	0/0	9/9	10/11	5/8	0/0
Lions	0/0	9/9	10/11	5/8	0/0
Opponents	1/1	6/8	5/5	4/4	1/2

Hanson: (27G, 21G) (47N) () (48N, 23G) (48G) () () (40G) (32N, 21G) (48G) (20G, 34G, 48N, 32G) (45G, 22G, 31G, 36G) (31G, 36G) (32G, 23G) (31G, 39G, 34G, 40G) (26G, 26G) Opponents: (27B) (34G) (26G, 47G, 39G) (27G) (50G) (19G, 25G) (40G) (24G, 51N) (31G) () () (42G, 33G) (36G, 28G, 23G) () () (40G, 27B)

PASSING

	Att.	Cmp.	Yds.	Pct.	Avg. Gain	TD	Pct. TD	Int.	Pct. Int.	Long	Sack/Lost	Rating
Harrington	489	274	3047	56.0	6.23	19	3.9	12	2.5	62	36/196	77.5
McMahon	15	11	77	73.3	5.13	0	0.0	1	6.7	19	1/12	56.8
Williams	1	0	0	0.0	0.00	0	0.0	0	0.0	...	0/0	39.6
Lions	505	285	3124	56.4	6.19	19	3.8	13	2.6	62	37/208	76.7
Opponents	535	328	3736	61.3	6.98	29	5.4	14	2.6	t82	38/222	89.4

DETROIT LIONS

GREEN BAY PACKERS
NFC NORTH DIVISION

2005 SEASON

CLUB DIRECTORY

President/chief executive officer
Robert E. Harlan
Executive vp & chief operating officer
John Jones
Executive vp, general manager and
director of football operations
Ted Thompson
Vp of player finance/general counsel
Andrew Brandt
Director of pro personnel
Reggie McKenzie
Director of college scouting
John Dorsey
Director of public relations
Jeff Blumb
Manager of community relations
Cathy Dworak

Executive
vp/head coach
Mike Sherman

Assistant coaches
Joe Baker (secondary/safeties)
Jim Bates (defensive coordinator)
Larry Beightol (offensive line)
Edgar Bennett (running backs)
Darrell Bevell (quarterbacks)
John Bonamego (special teams
coordinator)
James Campen (asst. offensive
line/quality control)
Mark Duffner (linebackers)
James Franklin (wide receivers)
Charlie Jackson (defensive quality
control)
Mark Lovat (strength & condition-
ing asst.)
Brad Miller (asst. special teams)
Robert Nunn (defensive tackles)
Joe Philbin (tight ends/asst. offen-
sive line)
Tom Rossley (off. coordinator)
Barry Rubin (strength & condition-
ing)
Bob Sanders (defensive line/defen-
sive ends)
Vince Tobin (special asst.)
Lionel Washington (defensive
nickel package/cornerbacks)
Vince Workman (weight room asst.)

OFFSEASON MOVES

Key additions
S Todd Franz	FA/Redskins
S Arturo Freeman	Rel./Dolphins
OT Adrian Klemm	FA/Patriots
S Earl Little	Rel./Browns
G Matt O'Dwyer	FA/Buccaneers
LB Raynoch Thompson	Rel./Cardinals

Key losses
P Bryan Barker	Free agent
CB Michael Hawthorne	Rel./Rams
CB Bhawoh Jue	FA/Chargers
LB Torrance Marshall	Free agent
G Marco Rivera	FA/Cowboys
S Darren Sharper	Rel./Vikings
G Mike Wahle	Rel./Panthers

SCHEDULE

Sept.	11—at Detroit	4:15
Sept.	18—CLEVELAND	4:15
Sept.	25—TAMPA BAY	1:00
Oct.	3—at Carolina (Mon.)	9:00
Oct.	9—NEW ORLEANS	1:00
Oct.	16—Open week	
Oct.	23—at Minnesota	1:00
Oct.	30—at Cincinnati	2:00
Nov.	6—PITTSBURGH	5:15
Nov.	13—at Atlanta	5:15
Nov.	21—MINNESOTA (Mon.)	10:00
Nov.	27—at Philadelphia	5:15
Dec.	4—at Chicago	2:00
Dec.	11—DETROIT	9:30
Dec.	19—at Baltimore (Mon.)	10:00
Dec.	25—CHICAGO	6:00
Jan.	1—SEATTLE	5:15

All times are Eastern.
All games Sunday unless noted.

DRAFT CHOICES

Aaron Rodgers, QB, California (first round/24th pick overall).
Nick Collins, FS, Bethune-Cookman (2/51).
Terrence Murphy, WR, Texas A&M (2/58).
Marviel Underwood, FS, San Diego State (4/115).
Brady Poppinga, OLB, BYU (4/125).
Junius Coston, C, N. Carolina A&T (5/143).
Michael Hawkins, CB, Oklahoma (5/167).
Mike Montgomery, DT, Texas A&M (6/180).
Craig Bragg, WR, UCLA (6/195).
Kurt Campbell, CB, Albany (7/245).
William Whitticker, G, Michigan State (7/246).

MISCELLANEOUS TEAM DATA

Stadium (capacity, surface):
Lambeau Field
(72,601, grass)
Business address:
P.O. Box 10628
Green Bay, WI 54307-0628
Business phone:
920-569-7500
Ticket information:
920-569-7100
Team colors:
Dark green, gold and white
Flagship radio station:
WTMJ, 620 AM
Website:
www.packers.com
Training site:
Clarke Hinkle Field
Green Bay, Wis.
920-569-7500

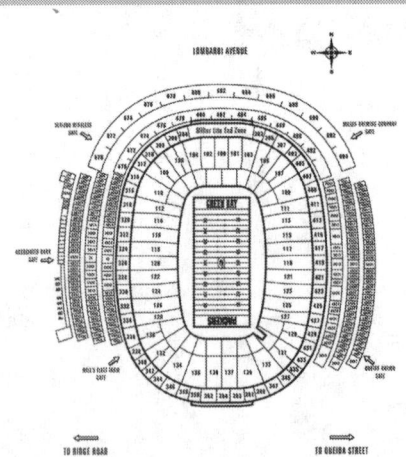

No.	QUARTERBACKS	Ht./Wt.	Born	NFL Exp.	College	How acq.	'04 Games GP/GS
4	Favre, Brett	6-2/224	10-10-69	15	Southern Mississippi	T-Atl./92	16/16
16	Nall, Craig	6-3/228	4-21-79	2	Northwestern State	D5b/02	5/0
7	O'Sullivan, J.T.	6-2/220	8-25-79	1	California-Davis	T-NO/04	2/0
12	Rodgers, Aaron	6-1/223	12-2-83	R	California	D1/05	—
	RUNNING BACKS						
44	Davenport, Najeh	6-1/250	2-8-79	4	Miami	D4/02	11/1
40	Fisher, Tony	6-1/222	10-12-79	4	Notre Dame	FA/02	16/0
30	Green, Ahman	6-0/218	2-16-77	8	Nebraska	T-Sea./00	15/15
33	Henderson, William (FB)	6-1/251	2-19-71	11	North Carolina	D3b/95	16/8
22	Luchey, Nick (FB)	6-2/273	3-30-77	7	Miami	FA/03	16/6
	RECEIVERS						
17	Bragg, Craig	6-1/196	3-15-82	R	UCLA	D6b/05	—
83	Chatman, Antonio	5-9/184	2-12-79	3	Cincinnati	FA/03	16/2
80	Driver, Donald	6-0/192	2-2-75	7	Alcorn State	D7b/99	16/11
89	Ferguson, Robert	6-1/210	12-17-79	4	Texas A&M	D2/01	13/5
88	Franks, Bubba (TE)	6-6/265	1-6-78	6	Miami	D1/00	16/14
87	Martin, David (TE)	6-4/262	3-13-79	5	Tennessee	D6/01	9/3
86	Murphy, Terrence	6-0/202	12-15-82	R	Texas A&M	D2b/05	—
82	Steele, Ben (TE)	6-5/250	5-27-78	2	Mesa State	FA/04	15/0
84	Walker, Javon	6-3/215	10-14-78	4	Florida State	D1/02	16/12
	OFFENSIVE LINEMEN						
71	Barry, Kevin (G/T)	6-4/335	7-20-79	4	Arizona	FA/02	13/3
72	Bedell, Brad (T)	6-4/306	2-12-77	4	Colorado	T-Mia./04	4/0
76	Clifton, Chad (T)	6-5/330	6-26-76	6	Tennessee	D2/00	16/16
62	Coston, Junius (C)	6-3/310	11-5-83	R	North Carolina A&T	D5a/05	—
69	Curtin, Brennan (T)	6-9/334	6-30-80	1	Notre Dame	D6/03	0/0
60	Davis, Rob (LS)	6-3/283	12-10-68	10	Shippensburg	FA/97	16/0
58	Flanagan, Mike (C)	6-5/297	11-10-73	8	UCLA	D3a/96	3/3
70	Klemm, Adrian (G)	6-3/312	5-21-77	4	Hawaii	FA/05	2/0
78	Morley, Steve (G)	6-7/332	8-18-81	1	St. Mary's (Can.)	FA/04	0/0
73	O'Dwyer, Matt (G)	6-5/305	9-1-72	11	Northwestern	FA/05	4/0
67	Ruegamer, Grey (C)	6-4/305	6-11-76	6	Arizona State	FA/03	15/11
65	Tauscher, Mark (T)	6-4/320	6-17-77	5	Wisconsin	D7a/00	16/16
63	Wells, Scott (C)	6-2/300	1-7-81	2	Tennessee	D7/04	5/2
79	Whitticker, William (G)	6-5/329	8-2-82	R	Michigan State	D7b/05	—
	DEFENSIVE LINEMEN						
90	Cole, Colin (T)	6-2/299	6-24-80	2	Iowa	FA/04	3/1
94	Gbaja-Biamila, Kabeer (E)	6-4/252	9-24-77	6	San Diego State	D5a/00	16/15
97	Hunt, Cletidus (T)	6-4/310	1-2-76	7	Kentucky State	D3b/99	16/14
75	Jackson, Grady (T)	6-2/340	1-21-73	9	Knoxville	W-NO/03	10/10
77	Jenkins, Cullen (E/T)	6-3/292	1-20-81	2	Central Michigan	FA/04	16/6
74	Kampman, Aaron (E)	6-4/284	11-30-79	4	Iowa	D5a/02	16/16
64	Lee, James (T)	6-5/325	3-12-80	2	Oregon State	D5a/03	9/1
96	Montgomery, Mike (T)	6-5/276	8-18-83	R	Texas A&M	D6a/05	—
98	Peterson, Kenny (E)	6-3/295	11-21-78	3	Ohio State	D3/03	9/0
91	Truluck, R-Kal (E)	6-4/260	9-30-74	4	Cortland State	T-KC/04	14/1
95	Washington, Donnell (T)	6-6/323	2-6-81	1	Clemson	D3/04	0/0
99	Williams, Corey (E)	6-4/310	8-17-80	2	Arkansas State	D6/04	12/0
	LINEBACKERS						
56	Barnett, Nick	6-2/233	5-27-81	3	Oregon State	D1/03	16/16
52	Campbell, Kurt	6-1/225	7-30-82	R	Albany (N.Y.)	D7a/05	—
59	Diggs, Na'il	6-4/237	7-8-78	6	Ohio State	D4a/00	14/14
53	Lenon, Paris	6-2/245	11-26-77	4	Richmond	FA/01	16/4
50	Navies, Hannibal	6-3/249	7-19-77	7	Colorado	FA/03	15/14
51	Poppinga, Brady	6-3/259	9-21-79	R	BYU	D4b/05	—
55	Thompson, Ray	6-3/224	11-21-77	6	Tennessee	FA/05	11/3
	DEFENSIVE BACKS						
28	Carroll, Ahmad (CB)	5-10/185	8-4-83	2	Arkansas	D1/04	14/11
36	Collins, Nick (S)	5-11/206	8-16-83	R	Bethune-Cookman	D2a/05	—
29	Franz, Todd (S)	6-0/202	4-12-76	4	Tulsa	FA/05	16/0
35	Freeman, Arturo (S)	6-1/210	10-27-76	6	South Carolina	FA/05	16/9
31	Harris, Al (CB)	6-1/185	12-7-74	8	Texas A&M-Kingsville	T-Phi./03	16/16
27	Hawkins, Michael (CB)	6-1/175	7-15-83	R	Oklahoma	D5b/05	—
26	Horton, Jason (CB)	6-0/193	2-16-80	2	North Carolina A&T	FA/04	14/0
21	Little, Earl (S)	6-1/205	3-10-73	8	Miami	FA/05	16/11
23	Roman, Mark (S)	5-11/200	3-26-77	6	LSU	FA/04	16/15
24	Thomas, Joey (CB)	6-1/195	8-29-80	2	Montana State	D3a/04	14/0
25	Underwood, Marviel (S)	5-10/205	2-17-82	R	San Diego State	D4a/05	—
	SPECIALISTS						
8	Longwell, Ryan (K)	6-0/202	8-16-74	9	California	W-SF/97	16/0
11	Sander, B.J. (P)	6-4/217	1-5-80	1	Ohio State	D3/04	0/0

Abbreviations: D1—draft pick, first round; W—claimed on waivers; T—obtained in trade; FA—free-agent acquisition.

GREEN BAY PACKERS

2004 regular-season record: 10-6
Position: 1st in NFC North

Sept.13—at Carolina	W	24-14
Sept.19—CHICAGO	L	10-21
Sept.26—at Indianapolis	L	31-45
Oct. 3—N.Y. GIANTS	L	7-14
Oct. 11—TENNESSEE	L	27-48
Oct. 17—at Detroit	W	38-10
Oct. 24—DALLAS	W	41-20
Oct. 31—at Washington	W	28-14
Nov. 7—Open date		
Nov.14—MINNESOTA	W	34-31
Nov.21—at Houston	W	16-13
Nov.29—ST. LOUIS	W	45-17
Dec. 5—at Philadelphia	L	17-47
Dec.12—DETROIT	W	16-13
Dec.19—JACKSONVILLE	L	25-28
Dec.24—at Minnesota	W	34-31
Jan. 2—at Chicago	W	31-14

2004 postseason record: 0-1
Jan. 9—MINNESOTA#   L   17-31
#NFC wild-card game.

SCORING BY PERIODS

	Q1	Q2	Q3	Q4	OT	Pts.
Packers	57	146	107	114	0	424
Opponents	82	147	58	93	0	380

TEAM STATISTICS

	G.B.	Opp.
TOTAL FIRST DOWNS	354	307
Rushing	98	92
Passing	228	181
Penalty	28	34
3rd Down: Made/Att.	98/207	69/197
3rd Down Pct.	47.3	35.0
4th Down: Made/Att.	8/14	5/9
4th Down Pct.	57.1	55.6
POSSESSION AVG.	30:28	29:32
TOTAL NET YARDS	6357	5541
Avg. per Game	397.3	346.3
Total Plays	1053	967
Avg. per Play	6.0	5.7
NET YARDS RUSHING	1908	1878
Avg. per Game	119.3	117.4
Total Rushes	441	409
NET YARDS PASSING	4449	3663
Avg. per Game	278.1	228.9
Sacked/Yards Lost	14/101	40/280
Gross Yards	4550	3943
Att./Completions	598/382	518/314
Completion Pct.	63.9	60.6
Had Intercepted	19	8
PUNTS/AVERAGE	66/40.1	81/39.2
NET PUNTING AVG.	66/33.4	81/34.6
PENALTIES/YARDS	116/950	112/942
FUMBLES/LOST	22/10	17/7
TOUCHDOWNS	50	47

	G.B.	Opp.
Rushing	9	12
Passing	36	33
Returns	5	2

SCORING (NON-KICKERS)

	Tot. TD	RTD	PTD	MTD	2Pt.	Tot. Pts.
Walker	12	0	12	0	0	72
Driver	9	0	9	0	1	56
Green	8	7	1	0	0	48
Franks	7	0	7	0	0	42
Henderson	3	0	3	0	0	18
Sharper	3	0	0	3	0	18
Davenport	2	2	0	0	0	12
Fisher	2	0	2	0	0	12
Ferguson	1	0	1	0	1	8
Carroll	1	0	0	1	0	6
Chatman	1	0	1	0	0	6
Hawthorne	1	0	0	1	0	6
Packers	50	9	36	5	2	304
Opponents	47	12	33	2	0	282

2-Pt. conversions: Packers 2-2; Opponents 0-0.

(KICKERS)

	XPM/XPA	FGM/FGA	Pts.
Longwell	48/48	24/28	120
Packers	48/48	24/28	120
Opponents	47/47	17/25	98

RUSHING

	Att.	Yds.	Avg.	Lg.	TD
Green	259	1163	4.5	t90	7
Davenport	71	359	5.1	t40	2
Fisher	65	224	3.4	24	0
W. Williams	6	42	7.0	28	0
Chatman	4	36	9.0	18	0
Favre	16	36	2.3	17	0
Luchey	10	24	2.4	4	0
Pederson	2	15	7.5	9	0
Nall	3	7	2.3	9	0
Driver	3	4	1.3	14	0
O'Sullivan	2	-2	-1.0	-1	0
Packers	441	1908	4.3	t90	9
Opponents	409	1878	4.6	54	12

RECEIVING

	No.	Yds.	Avg.	Lg.	TD
Walker	89	1382	15.5	t79	12
Driver	84	1208	14.4	50	9
Green	40	275	6.9	48	1
Fisher	38	277	7.3	25	2
Franks	34	361	10.6	29	7
Henderson	34	239	7.0	t38	3
Ferguson	24	367	15.3	48	1
Chatman	22	246	11.2	21	1
Martin	5	88	17.6	35	0
Davenport	4	33	8.3	12	0
Steele	4	42	10.5	27	0

PASSING

	Att.	Cmp.	Yds.	Pct.	Avg. Gain	TD	Pct. TD	Int.	Pct. Int.	Long	Sack/Lost	Rating
Favre	540	346	4088	64.1	7.57	30	5.6	17	3.1	t79	12/93	92.4
Nall	33	23	314	69.7	9.52	4	12.1	0	0.0	43	2/8	139.4
Pederson	23	11	120	47.8	5.22	0	0.0	2	8.7	24	0/0	27.4
Green	1	1	20	100.0	20.00	1	100.0	0	0.0	t20	0/0	158.3
Fisher	1	1	8	100.0	8.00	1	100.0	0	0.0	t8	0/0	139.6
Packers	598	382	4550	63.9	7.61	36	6.0	19	3.2	t79	14/101	93.8
Opponents	518	314	3943	60.6	7.61	33	6.4	8	1.5	t68	40/280	99.1

	No.	Yds.	Avg.	Lg.	TD
Luchey	2	20	10.0	11	0
Thurman	2	12	6.0	9	0
Packers	382	4550	11.9	t79	36
Opponents	314	3943	12.6	t68	33

INTERCEPTIONS

	No.	Yds.	Avg.	Lg.	TD
Sharper	4	97	24.3	t43	2
Harris	1	29	29.0	29	0
Jue	1	23	23.0	23	0
Barnett	1	16	16.0	16	0
Carroll	1	0	0.0	0	0
Packers	8	165	20.6	t43	2
Opponents	19	166	8.7	31	1

SACKS: Gbaja-Biamila 13.5, Jenkins 4.5, Kampman 4.5, Roman 3.5, Barnett 3.0, Truluck 2.5, Carroll 2.0, Hunt 2.0, Diggs 1.0, G. Jackson 1.0, Lee 1.0, C. Williams 1.0, Navies 0.5. Packers 40.0; Opponents 14.0.

PUNTING

	No.	Yds.	Avg.	In. 20	Lg.
Barker	66	2644	40.1	16	64
Packers	66	2644	40.1	16	64
Opponents	81	3176	39.2	31	58

PUNT RETURNS

	No.	FC	Yds.	Avg.	Lg.	TD
Chatman	32	27	245	7.7	28	0
Sharper	1	0	9	9.0	9	0
Packers	33	27	254	7.7	28	0
Opponents	34	10	301	8.9	40	0

KICK RETURNS

	No.	Yds.	Avg.	Lg.	TD
Chatman	25	565	22.6	59	0
Ferguson	21	526	25.0	71	0
Davenport	14	286	20.4	27	0
Thurman	3	59	19.7	28	0
Carroll	2	31	15.5	16	0
Henderson	2	16	8.0	10	0
Whitley	2	33	16.5	20	0
Peterson	1	6	6.0	6	0
Packers	70	1522	21.7	71	0
Opponents	79	1594	20.2	58	0

FIELD GOALS

	1-19	20-29	30-39	40-49	50+
Longwell	0/0	8/8	8/9	6/8	2/3
Packers	0/0	8/8	8/9	6/8	2/3
Opponents	0/0	5/5	5/8	7/12	0/0

Longwell: (41G) (25G, 45N) (38G, 52N) () (39G, 53G) (50G) (26G, 40G) (37G, 39G) (43G, 33G) (49N, 23G, 39G, 46G) (27G) (40G) (36G, 28G, 23G) (35G, 31N) (42G, 29G) (20G) Opponents: () (45N) (45G) (49N, 30N, 33N) (36G, 38G, 42B) (48G) (46G, 24G) (35N) (21G) (40N, 46G, 40G) (42N, 34G) (22G, 45G, 47G, 22G) (31G, 36G) () (29G) ()

HOUSTON TEXANS
AFC SOUTH DIVISION

2005 SEASON

CLUB DIRECTORY

Chairman and chief executive officer
Robert C. McNair
Vice chairman
Philip Burguieres
Sr. vp and general manager, football
Charley Casserly
Vice president/communications
Tony Wyllie
Director of pro scouting
Chuck Banker
Coordinator of college scouting
Mike Maccagnan
Director of operations
Barry Asimos
Media relations manager
Rocky Harris
Director of community relations
Regina Woolfolk

Head coach
Dom Capers

Assistant coaches
Kippy Brown (wide receivers)
Vic Fangio (def. coordinator)
Chick Harris (running backs)
Jon Hoke (defensive backs)
Mike London (defensive line)
Joe Marciano (special teams coord.)
Tony Marciano (tight ends)
Steve Marshall (offensive line/tackles)
Tony Oden (defensive asst./asst. defensive backs)
Tom Olivadotti (linebackers)
Chris Palmer (off. coordinator)
Joe Pendry (offensive line/centers & guards)
Dan Riley (strength & conditioning)
Greg Roman (quarterbacks)
Eric Sutulovich (asst. special teams)
Ray Wright (asst. strength & conditioning)

OFFSEASON MOVES

Key additions
CB Phillip Buchanon	Trade/Raiders
LB Frank Chamberlin	FA/Bengals
LB Morlon Greenwood	FA/Dolphins
LB Zeke Moreno	FA/Chargers
OT Victor Riley	FA/Saints
S Lewis Sanders	FA/Browns
DL Daleroy Stewart	FA/49ers
WR Reggie Swinton	FA/Lions

Key losses
S Eric Brown	Released
LB Jay Foreman	Rel./Raiders
CB Aaron Glenn	Rel./Cowboys
S Marlon McCree	FA/Panthers
LB Jamie Sharper	Rel./Seahawks
CB Kenny Wright	FA/Jaguars

SCHEDULE

Sept.	11—at Buffalo	1:00
Sept.	18—PITTSBURGH	1:00
Sept.	25—Open week	
Oct.	2—at Cincinnati	1:00
Oct.	9—TENNESSEE	1:00
Oct.	16—at Seattle	8:30
Oct.	23—INDIANAPOLIS	1:00
Oct.	30—CLEVELAND	2:00
Nov.	6—at Jacksonville	2:00
Nov.	13—at Indianapolis	2:00
Nov.	20—KANSAS CITY	9:30
Nov.	27—ST. LOUIS	2:00
Dec.	4—at Baltimore	2:00
Dec.	11—at Tennessee	2:00
Dec.	18—ARIZONA	2:00
Dec.	24—JACKSONVILLE (Sat.)	2:00
Jan.	1—at San Francisco	5:05

All times are Eastern.
All games Sunday unless noted.

DRAFT CHOICES

Travis Johnson, DT, Florida State (first round/16th pick overall).
Vernand Morency, RB, Oklahoma State (3/73).
Jerome Mathis, WR, Hampton (4/114).
Drew Hodgdon, C, Arizona State (5/151).
Ceandris Brown, SS, Louisiana-Lafayette (6/188).
Kenneth Pettway, OLB, Grambling State (7/227).

MISCELLANEOUS TEAM DATA

Stadium (capacity, surface):
Reliant Stadium (71,054, grass)
Business address:
Two Reliant Park
Houston, TX 77054
Business phone:
832-667-2000
Ticket information:
832-667-2002
Team colors:
Deep steel blue, battle red, liberty white
Flagship radio station:
KILT, 610 AM
Website:
www.houstontexans.com
Training site:
Reliant Park practice facility
Houston, TX
832-667-2000

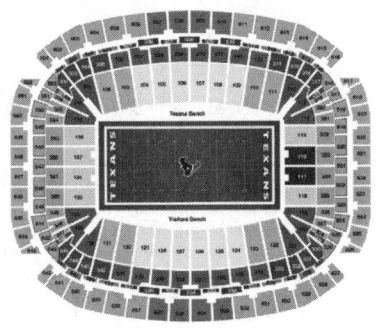

HOUSTON TEXANS

No.	QUARTERBACKS	Ht./Wt.	Born	NFL Exp.	College	How acq.	'04 Games GP/GS
12	Banks, Tony	6-4/229	4-5-73	10	Michigan State	FA/02	5/0
8	Carr, David	6-3/220	7-21-79	4	Fresno State	D1/02	16/16
4	Ragone, Dave	6-3/225	10-3-79	3	Louisville	D3c/03	0/0
2	Symons, B.J.	6-0/210	11-19-80	1	Texas Tech	D7/04	—
	RUNNING BACKS						
47	Baxter, Jarrod (FB)	6-1/243	3-9-79	4	New Mexico	D5a/02	8/1
37	Davis, Domanick	5-9/221	10-1-80	3	LSU	D4/03	15/15
25	Hollings, Tony	5-10/218	12-1-81	3	Georgia Tech	SD/03	7/0
34	Morency, Vernand	5-9/212	2-4-80	R	Oklahoma State	D3/05	—
44	Norris, Moran (FB)	6-1/254	6-16-78	5	Kansas	W-NO/02	12/4
32	Wells, Jonathan	6-1/252	7-21-79	4	Ohio State	D4/02	16/1
	RECEIVERS						
88	Armstrong, Derick	6-2/206	4-2-79	3	Arkansas-Monticello	FA/03	14/1
85	Bradford, Corey	6-1/201	12-8-75	8	Jackson State	FA/02	15/10
87	Bruener, Mark (TE)	6-4/258	9-16-72	11	Washington	FA/04	16/11
86	Gaffney, Jabar	6-1/205	12-1-80	4	Florida	D2a/02	16/12
80	Johnson, Andre	6-3/219	7-11-81	3	Miami	D1/03	16/16
13	Mathis, Jerome	5-11/181	7-26-83	R	Hampton	D4/05	—
82	Miller, Billy (TE)	6-3/245	4-24-77	7	USC	FA/02	16/8
45	Rivers, Marcellus (TE)	6-4/250	10-26-78	5	Oklahoma State	FA/05	16/3
17	Starling, Kendrick	6-0/193	12-27-79	2	San Jose State	FA/04	8/0
	OFFENSIVE LINEMEN						
67	Brown, Milford (G)	6-4/331	8-15-80	4	Florida State	SD6/02	2/2
63	Hodgdon, Drew (G)	6-3/309	11-15-81	R	Arizona State	D5/05	—
73	Jones, Garrick (T)	6-5/323	12-2-78	3	Arkansas State	W-KC/03	0/0
76	McKinney, Steve (C)	6-4/302	10-15-75	8	Texas A&M	FA/02	16/16
48	Pittman, Bryan (LS)	6-3/275	1-20-77	3	Washington	FA/03	16/0
69	Pitts, Chester (G)	6-4/329	6-26-79	4	San Diego State	D2b/02	16/16
68	Riley, Victor (T)	6-5/340	11-4-74	8	Auburn	FA/05	16/15
78	Wand, Seth (T)	6-7/330	8-6-79	3	NW Missouri State	D3b/03	16/16
77	Washington, Todd (C)	6-3/317	9-19-76	8	Virginia Tech	FA/03	15/0
70	Weary, Fred (G)	6-4/308	9-30-77	4	Tennessee	D3a/02	2/1
72	Wiegert, Zach (G)	6-5/305	8-16-72	11	Nebraska	FA/03	13/13
	DEFENSIVE LINEMEN						
97	Davis, Jason (E)	6-3/290	5-12-80	1	West Virginia	FA/03	0/0
95	Deloach, Jerry (T)	6-2/335	7-17-77	5	California	T-Was./02	15/3
94	Ioane, Junior (T)	6-4/332	7-21-77	6	Arizona State	W-Oak./03	3/0
75	Johnson, Travis (E)	6-4/290	4-26-82	R	Florida State	D1/05	—
91	Payne, Seth (T)	6-4/315	2-12-75	9	Cornell	ED/02	16/12
92	Sears, Corey (E)	6-3/314	4-15-73	7	Mississippi State	FA/02	15/0
99	Smith, Robaire (E)	6-4/328	11-15-77	6	Michigan State	FA/04	16/16
64	Stewart, Daleroy (E)	6-4/298	11-2-78	4	Southern Mississippi	FA/05	11/0
96	Walker, Gary (E)	6-2/324	2-28-73	11	Auburn	ED/02	15/15
	LINEBACKERS						
50	Anderson, Charlie	6-4/243	12-8-81	2	Mississippi	D6/04	15/0
59	Chamberlin, Frank	6-1/235	1-2-78	5	Boston College	FA/05	0/0
54	Evans, Troy	6-1/237	12-3-77	4	Cincinnati	FA/02	13/0
56	Greenwood, Morlon	6-0/238	7-17-78	5	Syracuse	FA/05	16/15
58	Moreno, Zeke	6-2/235	10-10-78	5	USC	FA/05	9/0
53	Orr, Shantee	6-0/250	5-28-81	3	Michigan	FA/05	4/0
98	Peek, Antwan	6-3/238	10-29-79	3	Cincinnati	D3a/03	14/1
55	Pettway, Kenneth	6-4/255	11-13-82	R	Grambling State	D7/05	—
51	Polk, DaShon	6-2/240	3-13-77	6	Arizona	FA/04	16/4
52	Wong, Kailee	6-2/246	5-23-76	7	Stanford	FA/02	16/16
	DEFENSIVE BACKS						
33	Bell, Jason (CB)	6-0/186	4-1-78	5	UCLA	W-Dal./02	9/0
24	Brown, Ceandris (S)	6-2/210	1-27-83	R	Louisiana-Lafayette	D6/05	—
31	Buchanon, Phillip (CB)	5-10/185	9-19-80	4	Miami	T-Oak./05	14/14
42	Coleman, Marcus (S)	6-2/206	5-24-74	10	Texas Tech	ED/02	12/12
26	Earl, Glenn (S)	6-1/215	6-10-81	2	Notre Dame	D4/04	12/9
38	Faggins, Demarcus (CB)	5-10/180	6-13-79	4	Kansas State	D6a/02	16/2
20	Lord, Jammal (S)	6-2/220	1-10-81	1	Nebraska	D6b/04	1/0
23	Robinson, Dunta (CB)	5-10/174	4-11-82	2	South Carolina	D1/04	16/16
21	Sanders, Lewis (CB)	6-1/210	6-22-78	6	Maryland	FA/05	16/5
30	Simmons, Jason (S)	5-9/199	3-30-76	8	Arizona State	FA/02	10/6
	SPECIALISTS						
3	Brown, Kris (K)	5-11/205	12-23-76	7	Nebraska	FA/02	16/0
7	Stanley, Chad (P)	6-3/216	1-29-76	6	Stephen F. Austin	FA/02	16/0

Abbreviations: D1—draft pick, first round; W—claimed on waivers; T—obtained in trade; FA—free-agent acquisition; SD—Supplemental draft; ED—expansion draft.

2004 regular-season record: 7-9
Position: 3rd in AFC South

Sept.12—SAN DIEGO	L	20-27
Sept.19—at Detroit	L	16-28
Sept.26—at Kansas City	W	24-21
Oct. 3—OAKLAND	W	30-17
Oct. 10—MINNESOTA (OT)	L	28-34
Oct. 17—at Tennessee	W	20-10
Oct. 24—Open date		
Oct. 31—JACKSONVILLE	W	20-6
Nov. 7—at Denver	L	13-31
Nov.14—at Indianapolis	L	14-49
Nov.21—GREEN BAY	L	13-16
Nov.28—TENNESSEE	W	31-21
Dec. 5—at N.Y. Jets	L	7-29
Dec.12—INDIANAPOLIS	L	14-23
Dec.19—at Chicago	W	24-5
Dec.26—at Jacksonville	W	21-0
Jan. 2—CLEVELAND	L	14-22

SCORING BY PERIODS

	Q1	Q2	Q3	Q4	OT	Pts.
Texans	33	101	60	115	0	309
Opponents	61	105	85	82	6	339

TEAM STATISTICS

	Hou.	Opp.
TOTAL FIRST DOWNS	300	304
Rushing	103	89
Passing	174	194
Penalty	23	21
3rd Down: Made/Att.	81/211	89/205
3rd Down Pct.	38.4	43.4
4th Down: Made/Att.	13/21	1/6
4th Down Pct.	61.9	16.7
POSSESSION AVG.	29:59	30:01
TOTAL NET YARDS	5128	5458
Avg. per Game	320.5	341.1
Total Plays	1001	971
Avg. per Play	5.1	5.6
NET YARDS RUSHING	1882	1843
Avg. per Game	117.6	115.2
Total Rushes	481	417
NET YARDS PASSING	3246	3615
Avg. per Game	202.9	225.9
Sacked/Yards Lost	49/301	24/161
Gross Yards	3547	3776
Att./Completions	471/286	530/344
Completion Pct.	60.7	64.9
Had Intercepted	14	22
PUNTS/AVERAGE	73/41.2	69/41.7
NET PUNTING AVG.	73/35.7	69/36.4
PENALTIES/YARDS	106/928	123/979
FUMBLES/LOST	22/11	22/8
TOUCHDOWNS	37	39
Rushing	16	4
Passing	16	32
Returns	5	3

SCORING (NON-KICKERS)

	Tot. TD	RTD	PTD	MTD	2Pt.	Tot. Pts.
D. Davis	14	13	1	0	0	84
An. Johnson	6	0	6	0	0	36
Wells	5	3	2	0	1	32
Bradford	3	0	3	0	0	18
Gaffney	2	0	2	0	0	12
Anderson	1	0	0	1	0	6
Armstrong	1	0	1	0	0	6
Coleman	1	0	0	1	0	6
Faggins	1	0	0	1	0	6
Miller	1	0	1	0	0	6
Peek	1	0	0	1	0	6
Sharper	1	0	0	1	0	6
Texans	37	16	16	5	1	224
Opponents	39	4	32	3	0	236

2-Pt. conversions: Texans 1-3; Opponents 0-1.

(KICKERS)

	XPM/XPA	FGM/FGA	Pts.
K. Brown	34/34	17/24	85
Texans	34/34	17/24	85
Opponents	37/37	22/29	103

RUSHING

	Att.	Yds.	Avg.	Lg.	TD
D. Davis	302	1188	3.9	44	13
Carr	73	299	4.1	24	0
Wells	82	299	3.6	14	3
Hollings	11	47	4.3	13	0
Gaffney	4	30	7.5	10	0
An. Johnson	4	12	3.0	14	0
Stanley	1	5	5.0	5	0
Baxter	2	1	0.5	1	0
Simmons	1	1	1.0	1	0
Norris	1	0	0.0	0	0
Texans	481	1882	3.9	44	16
Opponents	417	1843	4.4	t55	4

RECEIVING

	No.	Yds.	Avg.	Lg.	TD
An. Johnson	79	1142	14.5	t54	6
D. Davis	68	588	8.6	38	1
Gaffney	41	632	15.4	69	2
Armstrong	29	415	14.3	44	1
Bradford	27	399	14.8	47	3
Miller	17	178	10.5	27	1
Wells	11	79	7.2	28	2
Hollings	5	46	9.2	27	0
Bruener	4	52	13.0	27	0
Norris	4	13	3.3	7	0
Baxter	1	3	3.0	3	0
Texans	286	3547	12.4	69	16
Opponents	344	3776	11.0	t80	32

INTERCEPTIONS

	No.	Yds.	Avg.	Lg.	TD
Robinson	6	146	24.3	61	0
Glenn	5	40	8.0	23	0
Faggins	3	47	15.7	t43	1
Wong	3	0	0.0	0	0
Coleman	2	116	58.0	t102	1
McCree	1	24	24.0	24	0
Peek	1	20	20.0	20	0
Simmons	1	0	0.0	0	0
Texans	22	393	17.9	t102	2
Opponents	14	157	11.2	t77	1

SACKS: Wong 5.5, Babin 4.0, Robinson 3.0, Payne 2.0, Peek 2.0, Sharper 2.0, Smith 2.0, Polk 1.0, Wright 1.0, G. Walker 0.5. Texans 24.0; Opponents 49.0.

PUNTING

	No.	Yds.	Avg.	In. 20	Lg.
Stanley	73	3009	41.2	19	57
Texans	73	3009	41.2	19	57
Opponents	69	2880	41.7	24	64

PUNT RETURNS

	No.	FC	Yds.	Avg.	Lg.	TD
Moses	36	13	309	8.6	27	0
Glenn	4	0	22	5.5	18	0
Robinson	0	0	-2	-	-2	0
Texans	40	13	329	8.2	27	0
Opponents	30	24	265	8.8	46	0

KICK RETURNS

	No.	Yds.	Avg.	Lg.	TD
Moses	59	1303	22.1	49	0
Gaffney	2	31	15.5	27	0
Norris	2	25	12.5	15	0
Washington	2	27	13.5	16	0
Wells	2	27	13.5	18	0
Hollings	1	23	23.0	23	0
Starling	1	14	14.0	14	0
Texans	69	1450	21.0	49	0
Opponents	60	1386	23.1	t99	1

FIELD GOALS

	1-19	20-29	30-39	40-49	50+
K. Brown	0/0	7/7	3/5	6/9	1/3
Texans	0/0	7/7	3/5	6/9	1/3
Opponents	0/0	7/7	3/7	10/13	2/2

K. Brown: (37G, 20G) (34G) (28G, 49G, 49G) (46G, 57N, 21G, 44G) () (21G, 50G) (38G, 21G) (37N) (55N) (40N, 46G, 40G) (29G, 41B) () () (42N, 20G) (34B) ()
Opponents: (48G, 29G) (47N) () (35N, 50G) () (40G) (44G, 49N, 36G) (52G) (39N) (49N, 23G, 39G, 46G) () (41G, 26G, 25G) (30G, 43G, 44G) (39N, 43G) (31N) (45G, 22G, 29G, 45G, 22G)

PASSING

	Att.	Cmp.	Yds.	Pct.	Avg. Gain	TD	Pct. TD	Int.	Pct. Int.	Long	Sack/Lost	Rating
Carr	466	285	3531	61.2	7.58	16	3.4	14	3.0	69	49/301	83.5
Banks	2	1	16	50.0	8.00	0	0.0	0	0.0	16	0/0	77.1
Gaffney	3	0	0	0.0	0.00	0	0.0	0	0.0	...	0/0	39.6
Texans	471	286	3547	60.7	7.53	16	3.4	14	3.0	69	49/301	83.0
Opponents	530	344	3776	64.9	7.12	32	6.0	22	4.2	t80	24/161	88.7

HOUSTON TEXANS

INDIANAPOLIS COLTS
AFC SOUTH DIVISION

INDIANAPOLIS COLTS

2005 SEASON

CLUB DIRECTORY

Owner and CEO
James Irsay
President
Bill Polian
Senior executive vice president
Pete Ward
Vice president of player personnel
Chris Polian
Assistant general manager/scouting
Dom Anile
Executive vice president
Bob Terpening
Executive director of administration
Bill Brooks
Vice president of public relations
Craig Kelley
Director of pro personnel
Clyde Powers
Director of college scouting
Mike Butler
Director of player development
Steve Champlin
**Director of community relations/
marketing communications**
Nicole Duncan

Head coach
Tony Dungy

Assistant coaches
Jim Caldwell (asst. coach/ quarterbacks)
Clyde Christensen (wide receivers)
Richard Howell (asst. strength & conditioning)
Gene Huey (running backs)
Ron Meeks (def. coordinator)
Pete Metzelaars (offensive quality control)
Tom Moore (off. coordinator)
Howard Mudd (offensive line)
Mike Murphy (linebackers)
Russ Purnell (special teams)
Diron Reynolds (defensive quality control)
John Teerlinck (defensive line)
Ricky Thomas (tight ends)
Jon Torine (strength & conditioning)
Alan Williams (defensive backs)

OFFSEASON MOVES

Key additions
OT Joaquin Gonzalez — FA/Browns
Key losses
S Idrees Bashir — FA/Panthers
S Cory Bird — Free agent
G Rick DeMulling — FA/Lions
K Martin Gramatica — Free agent
LB Rob Morris — Free agent
LB Jim Nelson — FA/Ravens
TE Marcus Pollard — Rel./Lions
DE Brad Scioli — Released

SCHEDULE

Sept.	11—at Baltimore	8:30
Sept.	18—JACKSONVILLE	1:00
Sept.	25—CLEVELAND	1:00
Oct.	2—at Tennessee	1:00
Oct.	9—at San Francisco	4:05
Oct.	17—ST. LOUIS (Mon.)	9:00
Oct.	23—at Houston	1:00
Oct.	30—Open week	
Nov.	7—at New England (Mon.)	10:00
Nov.	13—HOUSTON	2:00
Nov.	20—at Cincinnati	2:00
Nov.	28—PITTSBURGH (Mon.)	10:00
Dec.	4—TENNESSEE	2:00
Dec.	11—at Jacksonville	2:00
Dec.	18—SAN DIEGO	2:00
Dec.	24—at Seattle (Sat.)	5:15
Jan.	1—ARIZONA	2:00

All times are Eastern.
All games Sunday unless noted.

DRAFT CHOICES

Marlin Jackson, CB, Michigan (first round/29th pick overall).
Kelvin Hayden, CB, Illinois (2/60).
Vicent Burns, DE, Kentucky (3/92).
Dylan Gandy, G, Texas Tech (4/129).
Matt Giordano, FS, California (4/135).
Jonathan Welsh, DE, Wisconsin (5/148).
Robert Hunt, C, North Dakota State (5/165).
Tyjaun Hagler, OLB, Cincinnati (5/173).
Dave Rayner, K, Michigan State (6/202).
Anthony Davis, RB, Wisconsin (7/243).

MISCELLANEOUS TEAM DATA

Stadium (capacity, surface):
RCA Dome (55,506, artificial)
Business address:
P.O. Box 535000
Indianapolis, IN 46253
Business phone:
317-297-2658
Ticket information:
317-297-7000
Team colors:
Royal blue and white
Flagship radio stations:
WNDE, 1260 AM
WFBQ, 94.7 FM
Website:
www.colts.com
Training site:
Rose Hulman Technical Institute
Terre Haute, Ind.
317-297-2658

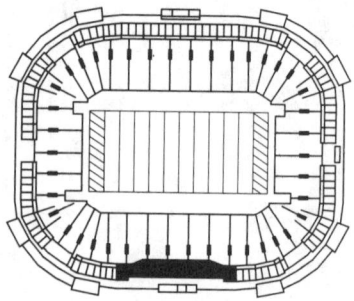

2005 TRAINING CAMP ROSTER

INDIANAPOLIS COLTS

No.	QUARTERBACKS	Ht./Wt.	Born	NFL Exp.	College	How acq.	'04 Games GP/GS
5	Brown, Travis	6-3/215	7-17-77	3	Northern Arizona	FA/04	0/0
18	Manning, Peyton	6-5/230	3-24-76	8	Tennessee	D1/98	16/16
12	Sorgi, Jim	6-5/196	12-3-80	2	Wisconsin	D6b/04	4/0
	RUNNING BACKS						
35	Carthon, Ran	6-0/218	2-10-81	1	Florida	FA/05	0/0
41	Davis, Anthony	5-7/200	5-21-82	R	Wisconsin	D7/05	—
32	James, Edgerrin	6-0/214	8-1-78	7	Miami	D1/99	16/16
23	Mungro, James	5-9/214	2-13-78	4	Syracuse	W-Det./02	15/0
33	Rhodes, Dominic	5-9/203	1-17-79	4	Midwestern State	FA/01	16/0
34	Wall, J.T. (FB)	6-0/250	9-12-79	1	Georgia	FA/05	0/0
	RECEIVERS						
44	Clark, Dallas (TE)	6-3/252	6-12-79	3	Iowa	D1/03	15/13
81	Fletcher, Bryan (TE)	6-5/235	3-23-79	1	UCLA	FA/04	0/0
88	Harrison, Marvin	6-0/175	8-25-72	10	Syracuse	D1/96	16/16
80	Hartsock, Ben (TE)	6-4/262	7-5-80	2	Ohio State	D3/04	16/3
85	Moorehead, Aaron	6-3/200	11-5-80	3	Illinois	FA/03	7/0
84	Pyatt, Brad	5-11/195	4-16-80	3	Northern Colorado	FA/03	8/0
48	Snow, Justin (TE/LS)	6-3/240	12-21-76	6	Baylor	FA/00	16/0
83	Stokley, Brandon	5-11/197	6-23-76	7	Louisiana-Lafayette	FA/03	16/3
47	Utecht, Ben (TE)	6-6/249	6-30-81	1	Minnesota	FA/04	0/0
86	Walters, Troy	5-7/172	12-15-76	6	Stanford	W-Min./02	5/0
87	Wayne, Reggie	6-0/198	11-17-78	5	Miami	D1/01	16/16
	OFFENSIVE LINEMEN						
71	Diem, Ryan (T)	6-6/331	7-1-79	5	Northern Illinois	D4/01	16/16
76	Freitas, Makoa (T)	6-4/307	11-23-79	3	Arizona	D6b/03	16/0
57	Gandy, Dylan (G)	6-3/300	3-8-82	R	Texas Tech	D4a/05	—
78	Glenn, Tarik (T)	6-5/332	5-25-76	9	California	D1/97	16/16
74	Gonzalez, Joaquin (T)	6-5/315	9-7-79	4	Miami	FA/05	16/11
72	Hunt, Rob (G)	6-4/301	3-3-81	R	North Dakota State	D5b/05	—
61	Hutton, Trevor (G)	6-5/305	2-28-80	2	Utah State	FA/04	4/0
65	Lilja, Ryan (G)	6-2/285	10-15-81	2	Kansas State	FA/04	7/6
64	Portis, Marico (G)	6-3/313	11-29-79	1	Alabama	FA/05	0/0
63	Saturday, Jeff (C)	6-2/295	6-8-75	7	North Carolina	FA/99	14/14
73	Scott, Jake (G)	6-5/280	4-16-81	2	Idaho	D5/04	12/9
	DEFENSIVE LINEMEN						
92	Adibi, Nathaniel (E)	6-3/249	1-25-81	1	Virginia Tech	FA/05	0/0
79	Brock, Raheem (E)	6-4/274	6-10-78	4	Temple	D7/02	16/16
94	Burns, Vincent (T)	6-2/268	6-21-81	R	Kentucky	D3/05	—
93	Freeney, Dwight (E)	6-1/268	2-19-80	4	Syracuse	D1/02	16/16
98	Mathis, Robert (E)	6-2/235	2-26-81	3	Alabama A&M	D5a/03	16/1
90	Reagor, Montae (T)	6-2/285	6-29-77	7	Texas Tech	FA/03	16/16
68	Stewart, Jason (DT)	6-1/285	11-14-80	1	Fresno State	FA/04	0/0
91	Thomas, Josh (E)	6-5/271	6-26-81	2	Syracuse	FA/04	11/0
75	Tripplett, Larry (T)	6-2/295	1-18-79	4	Washington	D2/02	16/0
99	Welsh, Jonathan (DE)	6-3/233	6-9-82	R	Wisconsin	D5a/05	—
96	Williams, Josh (T)	6-3/285	8-9-76	6	Michigan	D4/00	16/15
	LINEBACKERS						
58	Brackett, Gary	5-11/235	5-23-80	3	Rutgers	FA/03	15/1
51	Gardner, Gilbert	6-1/228	5-9-82	2	Purdue	D3/04	11/0
95	Hagler, Tyjuan	6-0/236	12-3-81	R	Cincinnati	D5c/05	—
59	June, Cato	6-0/227	11-18-79	3	Michigan	D6a/03	16/16
55	Pope, Kendyll	6-1/220	3-9-81	1	Florida State	D4/04	2/0
97	Rogers, Nick	6-2/251	5-31-79	4	Georgia Tech	D6/02	11/0
50	Thornton, David	6-2/230	11-1-78	4	North Carolina	D4/02	16/15
52	Whiteside, Keyon	6-0/229	1-31-80	3	Tennessee	D5b/03	7/0
	DEFENSIVE BACKS						
26	Bacon, Waine (S)	5-10/191	4-11-79	2	Alabama	D6b/03	11/0
42	David, Jason (CB)	5-8/172	6-12-82	2	Washington State	D4b/04	16/11
20	Doss, Mike (S)	5-10/207	3-24-81	3	Ohio State	D2/03	10/9
43	Giordano, Matt (S)	5-10/194	10-16-82	R	California	D4b/05	—
25	Harper, Nick (CB)	5-10/182	9-10-74	5	Fort Valley State	FA/01	14/14
40	Hayden, Kelvin (CB)	5-10/198	7-23-83	R	Illinois	D2/05	—
27	Hutchins, Von (CB)	5-9/181	2-14-81	2	Mississippi	D6/04	16/1
28	Jackson, Marlin (CB)	6-0/196	6-30-83	R	Michigan	D1/05	—
29	Jefferson, Joseph (CB)	6-1/202	2-15-80	3	Western Kentucky	D3/02	9/3
21	Sanders, Bob (S)	5-8/206	2-24-81	2	Iowa	D2/04	6/4
38	Sapp, Gerome (S)	6-1/216	2-8-81	3	Notre Dame	FA/04	13/0
30	Strickland, Donald (CB)	5-10/187	11-24-80	3	Colorado	D3/03	4/4
	SPECIALISTS						
15	Rayner, Dave (K)	6-2/209	10-26-82	R	Michigan State	D6/05	—
17	Smith, Hunter (P)	6-2/209	8-9-77	7	Notre Dame	D7a/99	16/0
13	Vanderjagt, Mike (K)	6-5/211	3-24-70	8	West Virginia	FA/98	15/0

Abbreviations: D1—draft pick, first round; W—claimed on waivers; FA—free-agent acquisition.

INDIANAPOLIS COLTS

2004 regular-season record: 12-4
Position: 1st in AFC South

Sept. 9—at New England	L	24-27	
Sept.19—at Tennessee	W	31-17	
Sept.26—GREEN BAY	W	45-31	
Oct. 3—at Jacksonville	W	24-17	
Oct. 10—OAKLAND	W	35-14	
Oct. 17—Open date			
Oct. 24—JACKSONVILLE	L	24-27	
Oct. 31—at Kansas City	L	35-45	
Nov. 8—MINNESOTA	W	31-28	
Nov.14—HOUSTON	W	49-14	
Nov.21—at Chicago	W	41-10	
Nov.25—at Detroit	W	41-9	
Dec. 5—TENNESSEE	W	51-24	
Dec.12—at Houston	W	23-14	
Dec.19—BALTIMORE	W	20-10	
Dec.26—SAN DIEGO (OT)	W	34-31	
Jan. 2—at Denver	L	14-33	

2004 postseason record: 1-1

Jan. 9—DENVER#	W	49-24	
Jan. 16—at New England*	L	3-20	

#AFC wild-card game. *AFC divisional play-off game.

SCORING BY PERIODS

	Q1	Q2	Q3	Q4	OT	Pts.
Colts	120	157	118	124	3	522
Opponents	78	102	73	98	0	351

TEAM STATISTICS

	Ind.	Opp.
TOTAL FIRST DOWNS ..	379	331
Rushing	94	103
Passing	238	209
Penalty	47	19
3rd Down: Made/Att. ..	70/164	91/217
3rd Down Pct.	42.7	41.9
4th Down: Made/Att.	4/7	9/28
4th Down Pct.	57.1	32.1
POSSESSION AVG.	28:40	31:20
TOTAL NET YARDS	6475	5929
Avg. per Game	404.7	370.6
Total Plays	968	1042
Avg. per Play	6.7	5.7
NET YARDS RUSHING ..	1852	2037
Avg. per Game	115.8	127.3
Total Rushes	427	440
NET YARDS PASSING....	4623	3892
Avg. per Game	288.9	243.3
Sacked/Yards Lost	14/109	45/340
Gross Yards	4732	4232
Att./Completions	527/353	557/364
Completion Pct.	67.0	65.4
Had Intercepted	10	19
PUNTS/AVERAGE	54/45.2	52/42.7
NET PUNTING AVG.	54/36.8	52/37.9
PENALTIES/YARDS	106/801	116/877
FUMBLES/LOST	19/7	36/17
TOUCHDOWNS	66	39

	Ind.	Opp.
Rushing	10	12
Passing	51	26
Returns	5	1

SCORING (NON-KICKERS)

	Tot. TD	RTD	PTD	MTD	2Pt.	Tot. Pts.
Harrison	15	0	15	0	0	90
Wayne	12	0	12	0	0	72
Stokley	10	0	10	0	0	60
James	9	9	0	0	1	56
Pollard..........	6	0	6	0	0	36
Clark	5	0	5	0	0	30
Mungro	3	0	3	0	0	18
Rhodes	2	1	0	1	0	12
David	1	0	0	1	0	6
Hutchins	1	0	0	1	0	6
Morris	1	0	0	1	0	6
Sanders	1	0	0	1	0	6
Colts	66	10	51	5	1	398
Opponents......	39	12	26	1	3	240

2-Pt. conversions: Colts 1-1; Opponents 3-3.

(KICKERS)

	XPM/XPA	FGM/FGA	Pts.
Vanderjagt	59/60	20/25	119
Bryant	5/5	0/1	5
Colts	64/65	20/26	124
Opponents	36/36	25/31	111

RUSHING

	Att.	Yds.	Avg.	Lg.	TD
James	334	1548	4.6	40	9
Rhodes	53	254	4.8	55	1
Manning	25	38	1.5	19	0
Mungro	5	19	3.8	8	0
H. Smith	1	2	2.0	2	0
Wayne...........	1	-4	-4.0	-4	0
Sorgi.............	8	-5	-0.6	2	0
Colts	427	1852	4.3	55	10
Opponents	440	2037	4.6	47	12

RECEIVING

	No.	Yds.	Avg.	Lg.	TD
Harrison	86	1113	12.9	59	15
Wayne	77	1210	15.7	t71	12
Stokley	68	1077	15.8	t69	10
James	51	483	9.5	56	0
Pollard..........	29	309	10.7	31	6
Clark	25	423	16.9	t80	5
Mungro	7	36	5.1	16	3
Hartsock	4	33	8.3	17	0
Pyatt	2	12	6.0	7	0
Rhodes	2	24	12.0	20	0
Moorehead	1	7	7.0	7	0
Walters	1	5	5.0	5	0
Colts	353	4732	13.4	t80	51
Opponents	364	4232	11.6	t79	26

INTERCEPTIONS

	No.	Yds.	Avg.	Lg.	TD
David	4	36	9.0	t34	1
Harper...........	3	12	4.0	12	0
June	2	71	35.5	71	0
Doss	2	32	16.0	32	0
Brackett	2	2	1.0	2	0
Hutchins	1	77	77.0	t77	1
Morris	1	17	17.0	17	0
Thornton........	1	5	5.0	5	0
Bacon	1	0	0.0	0	0
Jefferson........	1	0	0.0	0	0
Nelson	1	0	0.0	0	0
Colts	19	252	13.3	t77	2
Opponents	10	191	19.1	65	0

SACKS: Freeney 16.0, Mathis 10.5, Brock 6.5, Reagor 5.0, Morris 3.0, Scioli 2.0, Doss 1.0, Thomas 1.0. Colts 45.0; Opponents 14.0.

PUNTING

	No.	Yds.	Avg.	In. 20	Lg.
H. Smith	54	2443	45.2	21	62
Colts	54	2443	45.2	21	62
Opponents	52	2220	42.7	16	64

PUNT RETURNS

	No.	FC	Yds.	Avg.	Lg.	TD
David...........	8	4	50	6.3	13	0
Pyatt	8	5	47	5.9	13	0
Walters	7	6	40	5.7	14	0
Moorehead ..	1	0	34	34.0	34	0
Colts	24	15	171	7.1	34	0
Opponents....	29	13	395	13.6	t91	1

KICK RETURNS

	No.	Yds.	Avg.	Lg.	TD
Rhodes	48	1188	24.8	t88	1
Pyatt	10	230	23.0	32	0
Mungro	7	111	15.9	24	0
Walters	1	16	16.0	16	0
Colts	66	1545	23.4	t88	1
Opponents	92	1960	21.3	71	0

FIELD GOALS

	1-19	20-29	30-39	40-49	50+
Vanderjagt	0/0	6/6	9/11	5/7	0/1
Bryant...........	0/0	0/0	0/0	0/1	0/0
Colts	0/0	6/6	9/11	5/8	0/1
Opponents	0/0	6/6	7/9	9/11	3/5

Vanderjagt: (32G, 48N) (28G) (45G) (46G) () (34G) (54N) (35G) (39N) (34G, 20G) () (47G, 20G, 37G) (30G, 43G, 44G) (24G, 33G, 33N) (36G, 26G, 23G, 47N, 30G) () Bryant: () () () () (44N) () () () () () () () () () () () Opponents: (32G, 43G) (39G) (38G, 52N) (35N, 48G, 42G, 22G) () (26G, 32G, 26G, 53G) (32G) (42G, 23G) (55N) (51G) (20G, 34G, 48N, 32G) (45G, 43B) () (42G, 31B) (50G) (45G, 23G, 40G, 40G)

PASSING

	Att.	Cmp.	Yds.	Pct.	Avg. Gain	TD	Pct. TD	Int.	Pct. Int.	Long	Sack/Lost	Rating
Manning	497	336	4557	67.6	9.17	49	9.9	10	2.0	t80	13/101	121.1
Sorgi......................	29	17	175	58.6	6.03	2	6.9	0	0.0	t71	1/8	99.1
Saturday	1	0	0	0.00	0.00	0	0.0	0	0.0	...	0/0	39.6
Colts	527	353	4732	67.0	8.98	51	9.7	10	1.9	t80	14/109	119.7
Opponents	557	364	4232	65.4	7.60	26	4.7	19	3.4	t79	45/340	89.5

JACKSONVILLE JAGUARS
AFC SOUTH DIVISION

2005 SEASON

CLUB DIRECTORY

Chairman & CEO
Wayne Weaver
Senior vice president/football operations
Paul Vance
Vice president of communications & media
Dan Edwards
Vice president of player personnel
James Harris
Director of pro personnel
Charles Bailey
Director of college scouting
Gene Smith
Director of football operations
Skip Richardson

Head coach
Jack Del Rio

Assistant coaches
Ken Anderson (quarterbacks)
Mark Asanovich (strength & conditioning)
Paul Boudreau (offensive line)
Dave Campo (asst. head coach/secondary)
Les Ebert (asst. strength & conditioning)
Ray Hamilton (defensive line)
Andy Heck (asst. offensive line)
Todd Howard (asst. defensive line)
Mark Michaels (asst. special teams)
Kennedy Pola (running backs)
Alvin Reynolds (defensive backs)
Alfredo Roberts (tight ends)
Pete Rodriguez (special teams coordinator)
Carl Smith (off. coordinator)
Mike Smith (def. coordinator)
Brian VanGorder (linebackers)
Steve Walters (wide receivers)

OFFSEASON MOVES

Key additions
DT Martin Chase — Rel./Giants
CB Terry Cousin — Rel./Giants
DE Reggie Hayward — FA/Broncos
OL Brent Smith — Rel./Jets
DE Marcellus Wiley — Rel./Cowboys
DT Tony Williams — FA/Bengals
CB Kenny Wright — FA/Texans
LB Nate Wayne — Rel./Eagles
Key losses
CB Juran Bolden — Rel./Bucs
FB Marc Edwards — Released
DE Jason Gildon — Free agent
LB Tommy Hendricks — Released
DE Elton Patterson — FA/Bengals
CB Dewayne Washington — Released
OT Bob Whitfield — FA/Giants
OT Sammy Williams — Released

SCHEDULE

Sept.	11—SEATTLE	1:00
Sept.	18—at Indianapolis	1:00
Sept.	25—at N.Y. Jets	1:00
Oct.	2—DENVER	1:00
Oct.	9—CINCINNATI	8:30
Oct.	16—at Pittsburgh	1:00
Oct.	23—Open week	
Oct.	30—at St. Louis	2:00
Nov.	6—HOUSTON	2:00
Nov.	13—BALTIMORE	2:00
Nov.	20—at Tennessee	2:00
Nov.	27—at Arizona	5:05
Dec.	4—at Cleveland	2:00
Dec.	11—INDIANAPOLIS	2:00
Dec.	18—SAN FRANCISCO	2:00
Dec.	24—at Houston (Sat.)	2:00
Jan.	1—TENNESSEE	5:05

All times are Eastern.
All games Sunday unless noted.

DRAFT CHOICES

Matt Jones, WR, Arkansas (first round/21st pick overall).
Khalif Barnes, OT, Washington (2/52).
Scott Starks, CB, Wisconsin (3/87).
Alvin Pearman, RB, Virginia (4/127).
Gerald Sensabaugh, SS, North Carolina (5/157).
Chad Owens, WR, Hawaii (6/185).
Pat Thomas, OLB, North Carolina State (6/194).
Chris Roberson, CB, Eastern Michigan (7/237).

MISCELLANEOUS TEAM DATA

Stadium (capacity, surface):
ALLTEL Stadium (67,164, grass)
Business address:
One ALLTEL Stadium Place
Jacksonville, FL 32202
Business phone:
904-633-6000
Ticket information:
904-633-2000
Team colors:
Teal, black and gold
Flagship radio station:
WOKV, 690 AM
Website:
www.jaguars.com
Training site:
ALLTEL Stadium
Jacksonville, Fla.
904-633-6000

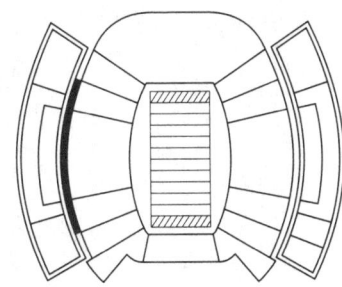

JACKSONVILLE JAGUARS

No.	QUARTERBACKS	Ht./Wt.	Born	NFL Exp.	College	How acq.	'04 Games GP/GS
9	Garrard, David	6-2/244	2-14-78	4	East Carolina	D4a/02	4/2
5	Gray, Quinn	6-3/246	5-21-79	1	Florida A&M	FA/03	0/0
7	Leftwich, Byron	6-5/245	1-14-80	3	Marshall	D1/03	14/14
	RUNNING BACKS						
32	Allen, David	5-9/195	2-5-78	3	Kansas State	FA/02	5/0
45	Fuamatu-Ma'afala, C. (FB)	6-0/252	3-4-77	8	Utah	FA/03	7/1
33	Jones, Greg (FB)	6-1/250	4-4-81	2	Florida State	D2/04	16/3
34	Pearman, Alvin	5-9/208	8-10-82	R	Virginia	D4/05	—
28	Taylor, Fred	6-1/234	1-27-76	7	Florida	D1a/98	14/14
22	Toefield, LaBrandon	5-11/232	9-24-80	3	LSU	D4b/03	14/0
	RECEIVERS						
80	Brady, Kyle (TE)	6-6/278	1-14-72	11	Penn State	FA/99	11/8
16	Edwards, Troy	5-10/195	4-7-77	7	Louisiana Tech	FA/03	16/4
85	Hankton, Cortez	6-0/200	1-20-81	3	Texas Southern	FA/03	12/0
18	Jones, Matt	6-6/242	4-22-83	R	Arkansas	D1/05	—
84	Owens, Chad	5-7/183	4-3-82	R	Hawaii	D6a/05	—
82	Smith, Jimmy	6-1/208	2-9-69	12	Jackson State	FA/95	16/16
19	Wilford, Ernest	6-4/223	1-14-79	2	Virginia Tech	D4/04	15/3
11	Williams, Reggie	6-4/223	5-17-83	2	Washington	D1/04	16/15
87	Wrighster, George (TE)	6-2/260	4-1-81	3	Oregon	D4a/03	4/3
83	Yoder, Todd (TE)	6-4/250	3-18-78	6	Vanderbilt	FA/04	16/8
88	Zelenka, Joe (TE)	6-3/270	3-9-76	7	Wake Forest	FA/01	16/0
	OFFENSIVE LINEMEN						
69	Barnes, Khalif (T)	6-6/305	4-21-82	R	Washington	D2/05	—
77	Compton, Mike (G/T)	6-6/310	9-18-70	12	West Virginia	FA/04	13/0
67	Manuwai, Vince (G)	6-2/312	7-12-80	3	Hawaii	D3/03	16/16
63	Meester, Brad (C)	6-3/300	3-23-77	6	Northern Iowa	D2/00	16/16
65	Naeole, Chris (G)	6-3/320	12-25-74	9	Colorado	FA/02	16/16
72	Pearson, Mike (T)	6-7/297	8-22-80	4	Florida	D2/02	4/4
66	Romberg, Brett (C)	6-3/293	10-10-79	2	Miami	FA/03	0/0
76	Salaam, Ephraim (T)	6-7/295	6-19-76	8	San Diego State	FA/04	15/12
73	Smith, Brent (G)	6-5/305	11-21-73	6	Mississippi State	FA/05	4/1
74	Williams, Maurice (T)	6-5/310	1-26-79	5	Michigan	D2/01	16/16
	DEFENSIVE LINEMEN						
58	Cordova, Jorge (E)	6-1/241	9-25-81	R	Nevada	D3/04	0/0
96	Hayward, Reggie (E)	6-5/270	3-14-79	5	Iowa State	FA/05	16/15
98	Henderson, John (T)	6-7/328	1-9-79	4	Tennessee	D1/02	16/16
91	Maddox, Anthony (T)	6-1/295	11-22-78	R	Delta State	D4a/04	2/0
93	McCray, Bobby (E)	6-5/251	11-1-81	R	Florida	D7/04	16/7
92	Meier, Rob (E/T)	6-5/293	8-29-77	6	Washington State	D7b/00	11/8
95	Spicer, Paul (E)	6-4/287	8-18-75	5	Saginaw Valley	FA/00	2/2
99	Stroud, Marcus (T)	6-6/312	6-25-78	5	Georgia	D1/01	16/16
75	Wiley, Marcellus (E)	6-4/278	11-30-74	9	Columbia	FA/05	16/15
94	Williams, Tony (T)	6-2/296	7-9-75	9	Memphis	FA/05	6/6
	LINEBACKERS						
51	Ayodele, Akin	6-2/251	9-17-79	4	Purdue	D3/02	16/16
55	Favors, Greg	6-1/244	9-30-74	8	Mississippi State	FA/04	15/11
50	Gilbert, Tony	6-1/244	10-16-79	3	Georgia	FA/03	16/0
54	Peterson, Mike	6-1/230	6-17-76	7	Florida	FA/03	16/16
52	Smith, Daryl	6-2/234	4-14-82	2	Georgia Tech	D2/04	15/13
53	Thomas, Pat	6-2/230	1-26-83	R	North Carolina State	D6b/05	—
	Wayne, Nate	6-0/237	1-12-75	7	Mississippi	FA/05	9/7
	DEFENSIVE BACKS						
35	Cooper, Deke (S)	6-2/210	10-18-77	4	Notre Dame	FA/03	16/0
21	Cousin, Terry (CB)	5-9/185	4-11-75	9	South Carolina	FA/05	16/5
20	Darius, Donovin (S)	6-1/225	8-12-75	8	Syracuse	D1b/98	16/16
37	Grant, Deon (S)	6-2/210	3-14-79	5	Tennessee	FA/04	16/16
27	Mathis, Rashean (CB)	6-1/200	8-27-80	3	Bethune-Cookman	D2/03	16/16
26	Richardson, David (CB)	6-0/202	9-9-81	2	Cal Poly	FA/04	2/0
38	Roberson, Chris (CB)	5-11/185	6-3-83	R	Eastern Michigan	D7/05	—
43	Sensabaugh, Gerald (S)	6-0/210	6-13-83	R	North Carolina	D5/05	—
41	Sorensen, Nick (S)	6-3/210	7-31-78	5	Virginia Tech	FA/03	16/0
31	Starks, Scott (CB)	5-8/172	6-27-83	R	Wisconsin	D3/05	—
24	Thomas, Kiwaukee (CB)	5-11/192	6-19-77	6	Georgia Southern	D5/00	16/2
29	Thompson, Chris (CB)	6-0/187	5-19-82	R	Nicholls State	D5b/04	0/0
25	Wright, Kenny (CB)	6-1/207	9-14-77	7	Northwestern State	FA/05	16/0
	SPECIALISTS						
2	Hanson, Chris (P)	6-1/223	10-25-76	5	Marshall	FA/01	16/0
6	Marler, Seth (K)	6-1/200	3-27-81	2	Tulane	FA/03	0/0
10	Scobee, Josh (K)	6-1/190	6-23-82	R	Louisiana Tech	D5a/04	16/0

Abbreviations: D1—draft pick, first round; FA—free-agent acquisition.

2004 regular-season record: 9-7
Position: 2nd in AFC South

Sept.12—at Buffalo	W	13-10
Sept.19—DENVER	W	7-6
Sept.26—at Tennessee	W	15-12
Oct. 3—INDIANAPOLIS	L	17-24
Oct. 10—at San Diego	L	21-34
Oct. 17—KANSAS CITY	W	22-16
Oct. 24—at Indianapolis	W	27-24
Oct. 31—at Houston	L	6-20
Nov. 7—Open date		
Nov.14—DETROIT (OT)	W	23-17
Nov.21—TENNESSEE	L	15-18
Nov. 28—at Minnesota	L	16-27
Dec. 5—PITTSBURGH	L	16-17
Dec.12—CHICAGO	W	22-3
Dec.19—at Green Bay	W	28-25
Dec.26—HOUSTON	L	0-21
Jan. 2—at Oakland	W	13-6

SCORING BY PERIODS

	Q1	Q2	Q3	Q4	OT	Pts.
Jaguars	35	75	56	89	6	261
Opponents	61	86	34	99	0	280

TEAM STATISTICS

	Jac.	Opp.
TOTAL FIRST DOWNS ..	279	290
Rushing	88	83
Passing	161	181
Penalty	30	26
3rd Down: Made/Att. ..	80/217	84/205
3rd Down Pct.	36.9	41.0
4th Down: Made/Att.	10/18	5/10
4th Down Pct.	55.6	50.0
POSSESSION AVG.	30:28	29:32
TOTAL NET YARDS	5009	5134
Avg. per Game	313.1	320.9
Total Plays	991	972
Avg. per Play	5.1	5.3
NET YARDS RUSHING ..	1850	1777
Avg. per Game	115.6	111.1
Total Rushes	446	438
NET YARDS PASSING....	3159	3357
Avg. per Game	197.4	209.8
Sacked/Yards Lost	32/156	37/217
Gross Yards	3315	3574
Att./Completions	513/305	497/306
Completion Pct.	59.5	61.6
Had Intercepted	11	16
PUNTS/AVERAGE	84/42.8	74/44.1
NET PUNTING AVG.	84/35.5	74/35.1
PENALTIES/YARDS	109/940	118/966
FUMBLES/LOST	23/11	30/12
TOUCHDOWNS	26	31
Rushing	9	7
Passing	17	18
Returns	0	6

SCORING (NON-KICKERS)

	Tot.					Tot.
	TD	RTD	PTD	MTD	2Pt.	Pts.
J. Smith	6	0	6	0	0	36
G. Jones	3	3	0	0	0	18
F. Taylor	3	2	1	0	0	18
Wilford	2	0	2	0	1	14
Hankton	2	0	2	0	0	12
Leftwich	2	2	0	0	0	12
R. Williams	1	0	1	0	2	10
B. Jones	1	0	1	0	1	8
Brady	1	0	1	0	0	6
T. Edwards	1	0	1	0	0	6
Fuamatu-Ma'afala	1	1	0	0	0	6
Garrard	1	1	0	0	0	6
Toefield	1	0	1	0	0	6
Wrighster	1	0	1	0	0	6
Jaguars	26	9	17	0	4	168
Opponents	31	7	18	6	2	190

2-Pt. conversions: Jaguars 4-4; Opponents 2-3.

(KICKERS)

	XPM/XPA	FGM/FGA	Pts.
Scobee	21/21	24/31	93
Jaguars	21/21	24/31	93
Opponents	27/28	21/28	90

RUSHING

	Att.	Yds.	Avg.	Lg.	TD
F. Taylor	260	1224	4.7	46	2
Toefield	51	169	3.3	16	0
G. Jones	62	162	2.6	12	3
Leftwich	39	148	3.8	17	2
Garrard	12	76	6.3	12	1
Fuamatu-Ma'afala	20	69	3.5	10	1
T. Edwards	2	2	1.0	2	0
Jaguars	446	1850	4.1	46	9
Opponents	438	1777	4.1	47	7

RECEIVING

	No.	Yds.	Avg.	Lg.	TD
J. Smith	74	1172	15.8	65	6
T. Edwards	50	533	10.7	36	1
F. Taylor	36	345	9.6	t64	1
Toefield	28	151	5.4	16	1
R. Williams	27	268	9.9	26	1
Wilford	19	271	14.3	46	2
Brady	14	103	7.4	21	1
Yoder	14	157	11.2	56	0
Wrighster	10	69	6.9	12	1
Hankton	9	81	9.0	t14	2
M. Edwards	7	41	5.9	15	0
B. Jones	6	87	14.5	t26	1
Fuamatu-Ma'afala	4	19	4.8	8	0
G. Jones	3	13	4.3	9	0
Allen	2	8	4.0	5	0
Leftwich	1	-7	-7.0	-7	0
Lewis	1	4	4.0	4	0

	No.	Yds.	Avg.	Lg.	TD
Jaguars	305	3315	10.9	65	17
Opponents	306	3574	11.7	54	18

INTERCEPTIONS

	No.	Yds.	Avg.	Lg.	TD
Darius	5	80	16.0	37	0
Mathis	5	42	8.4	21	0
Grant	2	4	2.0	4	0
Washington ..	2	0	0.0	0	0
Cooper	1	0	0.0	0	0
D. Smith	1	0	0.0	0	0
Jaguars	16	126	7.9	37	0
Opponents	11	163	14.8	t43	1

SACKS: Favors 5.5, Henderson 5.5, Peterson 5.0, Stroud 4.5, McCray 3.5, Gildon 3.0, Ayodele 2.0, D. Smith 2.0, Barnes 1.0, Cooper 1.0, Grant 1.0, Patterson 1.0, Meier 0.5, Ransom 0.5. Jaguars 37.0; Opponents 32.0.

PUNTING

	No.	Yds.	Avg.	In. 20	Lg.
Hanson	84	3592	42.8	28	69
Jaguars	84	3592	42.8	28	69
Opponents	74	3265	44.1	19	80

PUNT RETURNS

	No.	FC	Yds.	Avg.	Lg.	TD
Lewis	23	7	227	9.9	50	0
Allen	15	2	144	9.6	32	0
T. Edwards	3	1	26	8.7	14	0
Mathis	1	0	8	8.0	8	0
Jaguars	42	10	405	9.6	50	0
Opponents	38	13	429	11.3	t83	2

KICK RETURNS

	No.	Yds.	Avg.	Lg.	TD
Lewis	21	386	18.4	26	0
T. Edwards	15	335	22.3	45	0
Allen	11	210	19.1	25	0
G. Jones	5	90	18.0	23	0
Toefield	3	43	14.3	19	0
Brady	1	15	15.0	15	0
M. Edwards ..	1	8	8.0	8	0
Jaguars	57	1087	19.1	45	0
Opponents	50	995	19.9	52	0

FIELD GOALS

	1-19	20-29	30-39	40-49	50+
Scobee	0/0	10/10	8/11	5/7	1/3
Jaguars	0/0	10/10	8/11	5/7	1/3
Opponents	0/0	9/9	7/10	5/8	0/1

Scobee: (25G, 27G) () () (35N, 48G, 42G, 22G) () (51N) (26G, 32G, 26G, 53G) (44G, 49N, 36G) (31G) (35G, 48G, 44N) (33G, 32G, 42G) (32N, 20G, 29G, 36G, 60N) (30G, 25G) () (31N) (26G, 22G) Opponents: (42N, 25G) (44G, 22G, 51N) (26G, 40G) (46G) (21G, 28G) (31G, 42N) (34G) (38G, 21G) (32N, 21G) (41G) (25G, 33G) (37G) (47N, 42G) (35G, 31N) (34B) (35G, 27G)

PASSING

	Att.	Cmp.	Yds.	Pct.	Avg. Gain	TD	Pct. TD	Int.	Pct. Int.	Long	Sack/Lost	Rating
Leftwich	441	267	2941	60.5	6.67	15	3.4	10	2.3	65	25/114	82.2
Garrard	72	38	374	52.8	5.19	2	2.8	1	1.4	t36	6/35	71.2
Jaguars	513	305	3315	59.5	6.46	17	3.3	11	2.1	65	32/156	80.7
Opponents	497	306	3574	61.6	7.19	18	3.6	16	3.2	54	37/217	82.0

JACKSONVILLE JAGUARS

KANSAS CITY CHIEFS
AFC WEST DIVISION

2005 SEASON

CLUB DIRECTORY

Founder
Lamar Hunt
Chairman of the board
Clark Hunt
Vice chairman of the board
Jack Steadman
President/g.m./chief executive officer
Carl Peterson
Executive vice president/assistant g.m.
Dennis Thum
Senior vice president
Bill Newman
Vp of football operations and player personnel
Lynn Stiles
Vp of pro personnel
Bill Kuharich
Director of college scouting
Chuck Cook
Director of public relations
Bob Moore
Director of community relations
Brenda Sniezek

Head coach
Dick Vermeil

Assistant coaches
Gunther Cunningham (def. coordinator)
Vernon Dean (asst. defensive backs)
Irv Eatman (offensive line)
Frank Gansz Jr. (special teams)
Peter Giunta (defensive backs)
Carl Hairston (defensive line)
Jeff Hurd (strength & conditioning)
Charlie Joiner (wide receivers)
Bob Karmelowicz (defensive line)
Billy Long (asst. strength & conditioning)
Chad O'Shea (asst. special teams)
Fred Pagac (linebackers)
Al Saunders (asst. head coach/ offensive coordinator)
Bob Saunders (offensive asst.)
James Saxon (running backs)
Terry Shea (quarterbacks)
Mike Solari (offensive line)
Jason Verduzco (tight ends)
Darvin Wallis (defensive asst./ quality control)
Mike White (director of football administration)

OFFSEASON MOVES

Key additions
LB Kendrell Bell	FA/Steelers
DE Carlos Hall	Trade/Titans
FB Robert Holcombe	Rel./Titans
S Sammy Knight	FA/Dolphins
CB Patrick Surtain	Trade/Dolphins

Key losses
LB Monty Beisel	FA/Patriots
RB Derrick Blaylock	FA/Jets
DE Vonnie Holliday	Rel./Dolphins

SCHEDULE

Sept.	11—N.Y. JETS	1:00
Sept.	18—at Oakland	8:30
Sept.	26—at Denver (Mon.)	9:00
Oct.	2—PHILADELPHIA	1:00
Oct.	9—Open week	
Oct.	16—WASHINGTON	1:00
Oct.	23—at Miami	1:00
Oct.	30—at San Diego	5:05
Nov.	6—OAKLAND	2:00
Nov.	13—at Buffalo	2:00
Nov.	20—at Houston	9:30
Nov.	27—NEW ENGLAND	2:00
Dec.	4—DENVER	5:15
Dec.	11—at Dallas	5:15
Dec.	17—at N.Y. Giants (Sat.)	6:00
Dec.	24—SAN DIEGO (Sat.)	2:00
Jan.	1—CINCINNATI	2:00

All times are Eastern.
All games Sunday unless noted.

DRAFT CHOICES

Derrick Johnson, OLB, Texas (first round/15th pick overall).
Dustin Colquitt, P, Tennessee (3/99).
Craphonso Thorpe, WR, Florida State (4/116).
Boomer Grigsby, ILB, Illinois State (5/138).
Alphonso Hodge, CB, Miami (Ohio) (5/147).
Will Svitek, OT, Stanford (6/187).
Khari Long, DE, Baylor (6/199).
James Kilian, QB, Tulsa (7/229).
Jeremy Parquet, OT, Southern Mississippi (7/238).

MISCELLANEOUS TEAM DATA

Stadium (capacity, surface):
Arrowhead Stadium
(79,451, grass)
Business address:
One Arrowhead Drive
Kansas City, MO 64129
Business phone:
816-920-9300
Ticket information:
816-920-9400
Team colors:
Red, gold and white
Flagship radio station:
KCFX, 101 FM
Website:
www.kcchiefs.com
Training site:
U. of Wisconsin-River Falls
River Falls, Wis.
715-425-4580

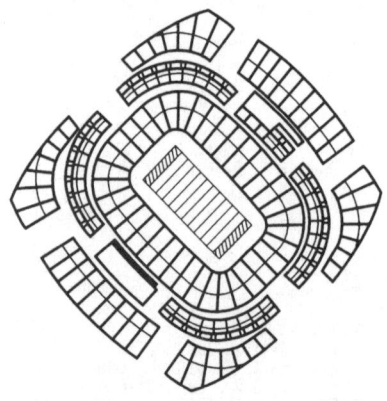

No.	QUARTERBACKS	Ht./Wt.	Born	NFL Exp.	College	How acq.	'04 Games GP/GS
15	Collins, Todd	6-4/228	11-5-71	11	Michigan	W-Buf./98	2/0
10	Green, Trent	6-3/217	7-9-70	12	Indiana	T-St.L./01	16/16
11	Huard, Damon	6-3/212	7-9-73	9	Washington	FA/04	0/0
5	Kilian, James	6-4/215	10-24-80	R	Tulsa	D7a/05	—
	RUNNING BACKS						
39	Holcombe, Robert (FB)	5-11/220	12-11-75	8	Illinois	FA/05	16/8
31	Holmes, Priest	5-9/213	10-7-73	9	Texas	FA/01	8/8
27	Johnson, Larry	6-1/230	11-19-79	3	Penn State	D1/03	10/3
49	Richardson, Tony (FB)	6-1/238	12-17-71	11	Auburn	FA/95	16/16
	RECEIVERS						
85	Boerigter, Marc	6-3/220	5-4-78	4	Hastings	FA/02	0/0
89	Dunn, Jason (TE)	6-6/276	11-15-73	9	Eastern Kentucky	FA/00	16/0
83	Gammon, Kendall (LS)	6-4/255	10-23-68	14	Pittsburg State	FA/00	16/0
88	Gonzalez, Tony (TE)	6-5/251	2-27-76	9	California	D1/97	16/16
82	Hall, Dante	5-8/187	9-20-78	6	Texas A&M	D5a/00	16/6
9	Hill, Darrell	6-3/200	6-19-79	4	Northern Illinois	FA/05	14/0
87	Kennison, Eddie	6-1/201	1-20-73	10	LSU	FA/01	14/14
14	McIntyre, Jeris	6-0/203	7-4-81	1	Auburn	D6/04	0/0
80	Morton, Johnnie	6-0/185	10-7-71	12	USC	FA/02	13/12
18	Parker, Samie	5-11/190	3-25-81	2	Oregon	D4a/04	4/0
12	Thorpe, Craphonso	6-1/188	6-27-83	R	Florida State	D4/05	—
84	Wilson, Kris	6-2/251	8-22-81	1	Pittsburgh	D2b/04	3/0
	OFFENSIVE LINEMEN						
65	Black, Jordan (T)	6-5/304	1-28-80	3	Notre Dame	D5/03	16/4
67	Bober, Chris (C)	6-5/310	12-24-76	6	Nebraska-Omaha	FA/04	12/2
72	Parquet, Jeremy (T)	6-7/323	4-11-82	R	Southern Mississippi	D7b/05	—
77	Roaf, Willie (T)	6-5/320	4-18-70	13	Louisiana Tech	T-N.O./02	16/16
79	Sampson, Kevin (T)	6-4/312	6-19-81	2	Syracuse	D7/04	6/0
68	Shields, Will (G)	6-3/320	9-15-71	13	Nebraska	D3/93	16/16
71	Svitek, Will (T)	6-7/300	1-8-82	R	Stanford	D6a/05	—
54	Waters, Brian (G)	6-3/318	2-18-77	6	North Texas	FA/00	16/16
76	Welbourn, John (G)	6-5/310	3-30-76	7	California	T-Phi./04	10/10
62	Wiegmann, Casey (C)	6-2/285	7-20-73	10	Iowa	FA/01	16/16
74	Williams, Brett (T)	6-5/321	5-2-80	3	Florida State	D4/03	5/0
	DEFENSIVE LINEMEN						
69	Allen, Jared (E)	6-6/265	4-3-82	2	Idaho State	D4b/04	15/10
93	Browning, John (T)	6-5/297	9-30-73	10	West Virginia	D3/96	16/7
75	Dalton, Lional (T)	6-1/315	2-21-75	8	Eastern Michigan	FA/04	16/13
92	Hall, Carlos (E)	6-4/261	1-16-79	4	Arkansas	T-Ten./05	14/14
98	Hicks, Eric (E)	6-6/280	6-17-76	8	Maryland	FA/98	16/16
73	Long, Khari (E)	6-4/257	5-23-82	R	Baylor	D6b/05	—
61	Sharpe, Montique (T)	6-2/296	3-10-80	2	Wake Forest	D7a/03	0/0
94	Siavii, Junior (T)	6-5/336	11-14-78	2	Oregon	D2a/04	12/0
90	Sims, Ryan (T)	6-4/315	5-4-80	4	North Carolina	D1/02	15/13
55	Stills, Gary (E)	6-2/250	7-11-74	7	West Virginia	D3a/99	16/0
96	Wilkerson, Jimmy (E)	6-2/280	1-4-81	3	Oklahoma	D6/03	15/0
	LINEBACKERS						
59	Barber, Shawn	6-2/240	1-14-75	8	Richmond	FA/03	8/8
99	Bell, Kendrell	6-1/257	7-2-78	5	Georgia	FA/05	3/0
52	Caver, Quinton	6-4/241	8-22-78	5	Arkansas	FA/03	16/4
97	Fox, Keyaron	6-3/235	1-24-82	2	Georgia Tech	D3/04	12/0
51	Fujita, Scott	6-5/250	4-28-79	4	California	D5/02	16/16
95	Grigsby, James	6-0/242	11-15-81	R	Illinois State	D5a/05	—
56	Johnson, Derrick	6-2/234	11-22-82	R	Texas	D1/05	—
57	Maslowski, Mike	6-1/243	7-11-74	7	Wisconsin-La Crosse	FA/99	0/0
50	Mitchell, Kawika	6-1/253	10-10-79	3	South Florida	D2/03	15/12
	DEFENSIVE BACKS						
24	Bartee, William (CB)	6-1/200	6-25-77	6	Oklahoma	D2/00	14/9
26	Battle, Julian (CB)	6-2/205	7-11-81	3	Tennessee	D3/03	12/1
42	Harts, Shaunard (S)	6-0/210	8-4-78	4	Boise State	D7a/01	16/6
47	Hodge, Alphonso (CB)	5-11/203	5-30-82	R	Miami (Ohio)	D5b/05	—
29	Knight, Sammy (S)	6-0/215	9-10-75	9	USC	FA/05	16/16
22	McCleon, Dexter (CB)	5-10/195	10-9-73	9	Clemson	FA/03	13/6
23	Surtain, Patrick (CB)	5-11/192	6-19-76	8	Southern Mississippi	T-Mia./05	15/15
44	Warfield, Eric (CB)	6-0/200	3-3-76	8	Nebraska	D7a/98	16/16
25	Wesley, Greg (S)	6-2/206	3-19-78	6	Arkansas-Pine Bluff	D3/00	12/11
21	Woods, Jerome (S)	6-3/205	3-17-73	10	Memphis	D1/96	10/10
	SPECIALISTS						
2	Colquitt, Dustin (P)	6-2/211	5-6-82	R	Tennessee	D3/05	—
1	Tynes, Lawrence (K)	6-1/202	5-3-78	2	Troy	FA/04	16/0

Abbreviations: D1—draft pick, first round; W—claimed on waivers; T—obtained in trade; FA—free-agent acquisition.

KANSAS CITY CHIEFS

KANSAS CITY CHIEFS

2004 regular-season record: 7-9
Position: 3rd in AFC West

Sept.12—at Denver	L	24-34	
Sept.19—CAROLINA	L	17-28	
Sept.26—HOUSTON	L	21-24	
Oct. 4—at Baltimore	W	27-24	
Oct. 10—Open date			
Oct. 17—at Jacksonville	L	16-22	
Oct. 24—ATLANTA	W	56-10	
Oct. 31—INDIANAPOLIS	W	45-35	
Nov. 7—at Tampa Bay	L	31-34	
Nov. 14—at New Orleans	L	20-27	
Nov. 22—NEW ENGLAND	L	19-27	
Nov. 28—SAN DIEGO	L	31-34	
Dec. 5—at Oakland	W	34-27	
Dec. 13—at Tennessee	W	49-38	
Dec. 19—DENVER	W	45-17	
Dec. 25—OAKLAND	W	31-30	
Jan. 2—at San Diego	L	17-24	

SCORING BY PERIODS

	Q1	Q2	Q3	Q4	OT	Pts.
Chiefs	113	137	93	140	0	483
Opponents	81	152	73	129	0	435

TEAM STATISTICS

	K.C.	Opp.
TOTAL FIRST DOWNS ..	398	327
Rushing	138	97
Passing	228	190
Penalty	32	40
3rd Down: Made/Att. ..	91/193	71/185
3rd Down Pct.	47.2	38.4
4th Down: Made/Att.	4/14	5/16
4th Down Pct.	28.6	31.3
POSSESSION AVG.	32:14	27:46
TOTAL NET YARDS	6695	6037
Avg. per Game	418.4	377.3
Total Plays	1089	960
Avg. per Play	6.1	6.3
NET YARDS RUSHING ..	2289	1834
Avg. per Game	143.1	114.6
Total Rushes	496	397
NET YARDS PASSING....	4406	4203
Avg. per Game	275.4	262.7
Sacked/Yards Lost	32/227	41/250
Gross Yards	4633	4453
Att./Completions	561/370	522/312
Completion Pct.	66.0	59.8
Had Intercepted	17	13
PUNTS/AVERAGE	55/39.5	64/42.2
NET PUNTING AVG.	55/31.5	64/35.8
PENALTIES/YARDS	117/963	117/957
FUMBLES/LOST	20/10	23/8
TOUCHDOWNS	62	53
Rushing	31	18
Passing	27	32
Returns	4	3

SCORING (NON-KICKERS)

	Tot. TD	RTD	PTD	MTD	2Pt.	Tot. Pts.
Holmes	15	14	1	0	0	90
L. Johnson	11	9	2	0	0	66
Blaylock	9	8	1	0	0	54
Kennison	8	0	8	0	1	50
Gonzalez	7	0	7	0	0	42
Dunn	3	0	3	0	0	18
Morton	3	0	3	0	0	18
Hall	2	0	0	2	0	12
Horn	1	0	1	0	0	6
Mitchell	1	0	0	1	0	6
Parker	1	0	1	0	0	6
Warfield	1	0	0	1	0	6
Chiefs	62	31	27	4	1	374
Opponents	53	18	32	3	2	322

2-Pt. conversions: Chiefs 1-2; Opponents 2-2.

(KICKERS)

	XPM/XPA	FGM/FGA	Pts.
Tynes	58/60	17/23	109
Chiefs	58/60	17/23	109
Opponents	50/51	21/27	113

RUSHING

	Att.	Yds.	Avg.	Lg.	TD
Holmes	196	892	4.6	t33	14
L. Johnson	120	581	4.8	t46	9
Blaylock	118	539	4.6	24	8
Green	25	85	3.4	13	0
Hall	8	56	7.0	17	0
Richardson	12	56	4.7	13	0
Morton	7	43	6.1	14	0
Kennison	2	15	7.5	15	0
Horn	1	12	12.0	12	0
Gonzalez	1	5	5.0	5	0
Collins	1	4	4.0	4	0
Easy	4	1	0.3	4	0
Cheek	1	0	0.0	0	0
Chiefs	496	2289	4.6	t46	31
Opponents	397	1834	4.6	t78	18

RECEIVING

	No.	Yds.	Avg.	Lg.	TD
Gonzalez	102	1258	12.3	32	7
Kennison	62	1086	17.5	t70	8
Morton	55	795	14.5	52	3
Blaylock	25	246	9.8	30	1
Hall	25	230	9.2	22	0
L. Johnson	22	278	12.6	40	2
Holmes	19	187	9.8	52	1
Richardson	19	118	6.2	22	0
Dunn	17	120	7.1	17	3
Horn	15	178	11.9	30	1
Parker	9	137	15.2	t48	1
Chiefs	370	4633	12.5	t70	27
Opponents	312	4453	14.3	65	32

INTERCEPTIONS

	No.	Yds.	Avg.	Lg.	TD
Wesley	4	92	23.0	65	0
Warfield	4	49	12.3	t43	1
McCleon	2	23	11.5	23	0
Barber	1	10	10.0	10	0
Sapp	1	0	0.0	0	0
Beisel	1	-1	-1.0	-1	0
Chiefs	13	173	13.3	65	1
Opponents	17	244	14.4	t102	1

SACKS: Allen 9.0, Hicks 5.0, Browning 4.5, Fujita 4.5, Dalton 4.0, Beisel 2.5, Stills 2.5, Sims 2.0, Bartee 1.5, Barber 1.0, Mitchell 1.0, Siavii 1.0, Woods 1.0, Wilkerson 0.5. Chiefs 41.0; Opponents 32.0.

PUNTING

	No.	Yds.	Avg.	In. 20	Lg.
Baker	9	340	37.8	3	52
Cheek	42	1643	39.1	8	55
Murphy	4	189	47.3	1	58
Chiefs	55	2172	39.5	12	58
Opponents	64	2703	42.2	23	66

PUNT RETURNS

	No.	FC	Yds.	Avg.	Lg.	TD
Hall	23	17	232	10.1	46	0
Harts	1	0	0	0.0	0	0
Chiefs	24	17	232	9.7	46	0
Opponents	24	13	301	12.5	t75	2

KICK RETURNS

	No.	Yds.	Avg.	Lg.	TD
Hall	68	1718	25.3	t97	2
Horn	4	44	11.0	17	0
Blaylock	1	22	22.0	22	0
Kennison	1	36	36.0	36	0
Stills	1	0	0.0	0	0
Chiefs	75	1820	24.3	t97	2
Opponents	85	1908	22.4	44	0

FIELD GOALS

	1-19	20-29	30-39	40-49	50+
Tynes	0/0	5/5	7/8	3/6	2/4
Chiefs	0/0	5/5	7/8	3/6	2/4
Opponents	1/1	6/7	5/5	8/9	1/5

Tynes: (58N, 50G) (33G, 47N) () (42G, 38G) (31G, 42N) () (32G) (31G) (24G, 44G) (44G, 24G) (28G) (28G, 22G) () (39G) (43B, 50N, 38G) (50G, 33N) Opponents: (43G, 45G) () (28G, 49G, 49G) (50G) (51N) (19G) (54N) (46N) (39G, 38G) (37G, 28G) (29N, 52N, 25G, 43G) (27G, 36G) (50N, 27G) (27G) (40G, 45G, 46G) (34G)

PASSING

	Att.	Cmp.	Yds.	Pct.	Avg. Gain	TD	Pct. TD	Int.	Pct. Int.	Long	Sack/Lost	Rating
Green	556	369	4591	66.4	8.26	27	4.9	17	3.1	t70	32/227	95.2
Collins	5	1	42	20.0	8.40	0	0.0	0	0.0	42	0/0	62.1
Chiefs	561	370	4633	66.0	8.26	27	4.8	17	3.0	t70	32/227	94.9
Opponents	522	312	4453	59.8	8.53	32	6.1	13	2.5	65	41/250	97.5

MIAMI DOLPHINS
AFC EAST DIVISION

2005 SEASON

CLUB DIRECTORY

Owner/chairman of the board
H. Wayne Huizenga
CEO, Dolphin Enterprises
Joe Bailey
General manager
Rick Spielman
Exec. vp & chief operating officer
Bryan Wiedmeier
Sr. vice president/operations
Bill Galante
Director of pro personnel
George Paton
Director of college scouting
Ron Labadie
Sr. vice president/media relations
Harvey Greene
Director of media relations
Neal Gulkis
Director of operations
Rhett Ticconi

Head coach
Nick Saban

Assistant coaches
Keith Armstrong (special teams)
Charlie Baggett (asst. head coach/wide receivers)
Tim Davis (asst. offensive line)
Derek Dooley (tight ends)
George Edwards (linebackers)
Eric Fears (asst. strength & conditioning)
John Gamble (strength & conditioning)
Jason Garrett (quarterbacks)
Judd Garrett (offensive quality control)
Bert Hill (associate strength & conditioning)
Hudson Houck (offensive line)
Travis Jones (asst. defensive line)
Scott Linehan (off. coordinator)
Will Muschamp (asst. head coach/defense)
Mel Phillips (secondary)
Glenn Pires (defensive quality control)
Dan Quinn (defensive line)
Richard Smith (def. coordinator)
Bobby Williams (running backs)

OFFSEASON MOVES

Key additions
DE Kevin Carter	Rel./Titans
OL Damion Cook	FA/Browns
CB Mario Edwards	Rel./Bucs
FB Heath Evans	FA/Seahawks
QB Gus Frerotte	FA/Vikings
DE Vonnie Holliday	Rel./Chiefs
S Tebucky Jones	FA/Saints
OT Stockar McDougle	FA/Lions
LB Donnie Spragan	FA/Broncos
S Travares Tillman	FA/Panthers

Key losses
WR David Boston	Released
QB Jay Fiedler	Rel./Jets
S Arturo Freeman	Rel./Packers
LB Morlon Greenwood	FA/Texans
S Sammy Knight	FA/Chiefs
FB Rob Konrad	Retired
DT Bryan Robinson	FA/Bengals
CB Patrick Surtain	Trade/Chiefs
DE Jay Williams	Rel./Rams
S Shawn Wooden	Released

SCHEDULE

Sept.	11—DENVER	1:00
Sept.	18—at N.Y. Jets	4:15
Sept.	25—CAROLINA	1:00
Oct.	2—Open week	
Oct.	9—at Buffalo	1:00
Oct.	16—at Tampa Bay	1:00
Oct.	23—KANSAS CITY	1:00
Oct.	30—at New Orleans	2:00
Nov.	6—ATLANTA	2:00
Nov.	13—NEW ENGLAND	2:00
Nov.	20—at Cleveland	2:00
Nov.	27—at Oakland	5:05
Dec.	4—BUFFALO	2:00
Dec.	11—at San Diego	5:15
Dec.	18—N.Y. JETS	2:00
Dec.	24—TENNESSEE (Sat.)	2:00
Jan.	1—at New England	2:00

All times are Eastern.
All games Sunday unless noted.

DRAFT CHOICES

Ronnie Brown, RB, Auburn (first round, second pick overall).
Matt Roth, DE, Iowa (2/46).
Channing Crowder, ILB, Florida (3/70).
Travis Daniels, CB, Louisiana State (4/104).
Anthony Alabi, OT, Texas Christian (5/162).
Kevin Vickerson, DT, Michigan State (7/216).

MISCELLANEOUS TEAM DATA

Stadium (capacity, surface):
Dolphins Stadium
(75,540, grass)
Business address:
7500 S.W. 30th St.
Davie, FL 33314
Business phone:
954-452-7000
Ticket information:
888-346-7849
Team colors:
Aqua, coral, blue and white
Flagship radio station:
790 AM The Ticket
Website:
www.miamidolphins.com

Training site:
Nova Southeastern University
Davie, Fla.
954-452-7000

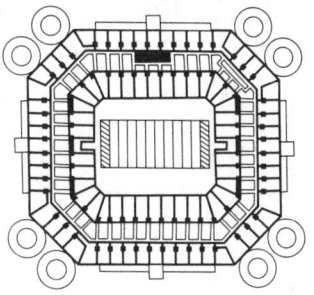

MIAMI DOLPHINS

No.	QUARTERBACKS	Ht./Wt.	Born	NFL Exp.	College	How acq.	'04 Games GP/GS
8	Berlin, Brock	6-0/213	7-4-81	R	Miami	FA/05	—
7	Feeley, A.J.	6-3/225	5-16-77	5	Oregon	T-Phi/04	11/8
11	Frerotte, Gus	6-3/237	7-31-71	12	Tulsa	FA/05	16/0
18	Rosenfels, Sage	6-4/222	3-6-78	5	Iowa State	T-Was/02	3/1
	RUNNING BACKS						
23	Brown, Ronnie	6-0/233	12-12-81	R	Auburn	D1/05	—
44	Evans, Heath (FB)	6-0/245	12-30-78	5	Auburn	D3/01	15/0
30	Gordon, Lamar	6-1/228	1-7-80	4	North Dakota State	D3a/02	3/2
43	Harris, Kay-Jay	6-0/229	3-27-79	R	West Virginia	FA/05	—
32	Martin, Jamar (FB)	5-11/244	4-12-80	3	Ohio State	W-Dal/04	9/1
28	Minor, Travis	5-10/205	6-30-79	5	Florida State	D3a/01	11/4
31	Morris, Sammy (FB)	6-0/220	3-23-77	6	Texas Tech	D5/00	13/8
	RECEIVERS						
86	Booker, Marty	6-0/212	7-31-76	7	Louisiana-Monroe	T-Chi/04	15/15
80	Boston, David	6-2/240	8-19-78	7	Ohio State	T-SD/04	0/0
84	Chambers, Chris	5-11/210	8-12-78	5	Wisconsin	D2/01	15/15
82	Gilmore, Bryan	6-0/195	1-21-78	5	Midwestern State	FA/00	16/2
85	Lee, Donald (TE)	6-3/255	8-31-80	3	Mississippi State	D5a/03	16/10
81	McMichael, Randy (TE)	6-3/250	6-28-79	4	Georgia	D4/02	16/16
89	Perry, Ed (TE)	6-4/265	9-1-74	9	James Madison	D6d/97	16/0
88	Thompson, Derrius	6-2/220	7-5-77	7	Baylor	FA/03	16/3
83	Welker, Wes	5-9/190	5-1-81	2	Texas Tech	FA/04	15/0
	OFFENSIVE LINEMEN						
67	Alabi, Anthony (T)	6-5/310	2-16-81	R	TCU	D5/05	—
72	Carey, Vernon (T)	6-5/325	7-31-81	2	Miami	D1/04	14/2
76	Cook, Damion (T)	6-5/330	4-16-79	5	Bethune-Cookman	FA/05	15/6
66	Hadnot, Rex (G)	6-2/323	1-28-82	2	Houston	D6/04	14/7
78	James, Jeno (G)	6-3/315	1-12-77	6	Auburn	FA/04	14/14
60	Jerman, Greg (G)	6-5/310	1-24-79	4	Baylor	FA/02	1/0
73	McDougle, Stockar (T)	6-6/335	1-11-77	6	Oklahoma	FA/05	16/16
77	McIntosh, Damion (T)	6-4/325	3-25-77	6	Kansas State	FA/04	14/14
68	McKinney, Seth (C)	6-3/305	6-12-79	4	Texas A&M	D3/02	16/16
71	Pape, Tony (T)	6-6/315	9-29-81	1	Michigan	D7a/04	0/0
74	Smith, Wade (E)	6-4/315	4-26-81	3	Memphis	D3a/04	6/2
70	St. Clair, John (T)	6-4/320	7-31-77	6	Virginia	FA/04	14/14
61	Thomas, Jason (G)	6-3/310	7-10-77	3	Hampton	FA/05	0/0
69	Whitley, Taylor (G)	6-4/315	2-21-80	3	Texas A&M	D3b/03	16/11
	DEFENSIVE LINEMEN						
96	Bowens, David (E)	6-3/260	7-3-77	6	Western Illinois	FA/01	16/15
95	Bowens, Tim (T)	6-4/325	2-7-73	12	Mississippi	D1/94	2/2
93	Carter, Kevin (E)	6-5/290	9-21-73	11	Florida	FA/05	16/16
64	Chester, Larry (T)	6-2/325	10-17-75	8	Temple	FA/02	2/2
91	Holliday, Vonnie (E/T)	6-5/290	12-11-75	8	North Carolina	FA/05	9/3
94	Romero, Dario (T)	6-3/305	4-13-78	4	Eastern Washington	FA/02	14/1
98	Roth, Matt (E)	6-3/272	10-14-82	R	Iowa	D2/05	—
75	Shaw, Josh (T)	6-2/290	9-7-79	2	Michigan State	FA/04	5/0
99	Taylor, Jason (E)	6-6/245	9-1-74	9	Akron	D3a/97	16/16
92	Vickerson, Kevin (T)	6-4/295	1-8-83	R	Michigan State	D7/05	—
90	Zgonina, Jeff (T)	6-2/285	5-24-70	13	Purdue	FA/03	16/14
	LINEBACKERS						
50	Ayanbadejo, Brendon	6-1/230	9-6-76	3	UCLA	FA/03	16/2
22	Bua, Tony	5-11/212	2-11-80	2	Arkansas	D5/04	7/0
52	Crowder, Channing	6-2/247	12-2-83	R	Florida	D3/05	—
57	Jenkins, Corey	6-0/222	8-25-76	3	South Carolina	D6a/03	7/0
58	Moore, Eddie	6-0/230	7-5-80	3	Tennessee	D2/03	13/3
56	Pope, Derrick	5-11/233	5-4-82	2	Alabama	D7/04	16/3
55	Seau, Junior	6-3/250	1-19-69	16	USC	T-SD/03	8/8
59	Spragan, Donnie	6-3/239	7-12-76	5	Stanford	FA/05	16/14
54	Thomas, Zach	5-11/230	9-1-73	10	Texas Tech	D5c/96	13/13
	DEFENSIVE BACKS						
36	Akins, Chris (S)	5-11/195	11-29-76	6	Arkansas-Pine Bluff	FA/04	0/0
37	Bell, Yeremiah (S)	6-1/200	3-3-78	2	Eastern Kentucky	D6c/03	13/0
21	Daniels, Travis (CB)	6-2/194	9-8-82	R	LSU	D4/05	—
20	Edwards, Mario (CB)	6-0/199	12-1-75	7	Florida State	FA/05	15/3
45	Eiland, Deandre' (S)	5-11/202	6-4-82	1	South Carolina	FA/04	0/0
25	Howard, Reggie (CB)	6-0/190	5-17-77	6	Memphis	FA/04	15/3
24	Jones, Tebucky (S)	6-2/220	10-6-74	8	Syracuse	FA/05	16/16
29	Madison, Sam (CB)	5-11/185	4-23-74	9	Louisville	D2/97	16/16
26	Tillman, Travares (S)	6-1/190	10-8-77	5	Georgia Tech	FA/05	6/1
38	Williams, Quintin (S)	5-11/204	9-24-82	2	Wake Forest	FA/04	6/0
	SPECIALISTS						
10	Mare, Olindo (K)	5-10/195	6-6-73	9	Syracuse	FA/97	11/0
1	Turk, Matt (P)	6-5/235	6-16-68	11	Wis.-Whitewater	FA/04	16/0

Abbreviations: D1—draft pick, first round; W—claimed on waivers; T—obtained in trade; FA—free-agent acquisition.

MIAMI DOLPHINS

2004 regular-season record: 4-12
Position: 4th in AFC East

Sept.11—TENNESSEE	L	7-17
Sept.19—at Cincinnati	L	13-16
Sept.26—PITTSBURGH	L	3-13
Oct. 3—N.Y. JETS	L	9-17
Oct. 10—at New England	L	10-24
Oct. 17—at Buffalo	L	13-20
Oct. 24—ST. LOUIS	W	31-14
Nov. 1—at N.Y. Jets	L	14-41
Nov. 7—ARIZONA	L	23-24
Nov. 14—Open date		
Nov. 21—at Seattle	L	17-24
Nov. 28—at San Francisco	W	24-17
Dec. 5—BUFFALO	L	32-42
Dec. 12—at Denver	L	17-20
Dec. 20—NEW ENGLAND	W	29-28
Dec. 26—CLEVELAND	W	10-7
Jan. 2—at Baltimore	L	23-30

SCORING BY PERIODS

	Q1	Q2	Q3	Q4	OT	Pts.
Dolphins	79	59	34	103	0	275
Opponents	79	88	95	92	0	354

TEAM STATISTICS

	Mia.	Opp.
TOTAL FIRST DOWNS	267	281
Rushing	71	107
Passing	165	139
Penalty	31	35
3rd Down: Made/Att.	80/232	72/223
3rd Down Pct.	34.5	32.3
4th Down: Made/Att.	8/16	8/11
4th Down Pct.	50.0	72.7
POSSESSION AVG.	28:20	31:40
TOTAL NET YARDS	4404	4894
Avg. per Game	275.3	305.9
Total Plays	1022	1009
Avg. per Play	4.3	4.9
NET YARDS RUSHING	1339	2302
Avg. per Game	83.7	143.9
Total Rushes	384	539
NET YARDS PASSING	3065	2592
Avg. per Game	191.6	162.0
Sacked/Yards Lost	52/326	36/223
Gross Yards	3391	2815
Att./Completions	586/309	434/244
Completion Pct.	52.7	56.2
Had Intercepted	26	15
PUNTS/AVERAGE	99/41.5	102/41.0
NET PUNTING AVG.	99/36.9	102/33.3
PENALTIES/YARDS	112/852	107/852
FUMBLES/LOST	42/16	22/10
TOUCHDOWNS	31	42
Rushing	10	12
Passing	19	20
Returns	2	10

SCORING (NON-KICKERS)

	Tot. TD	RTD	PTD	MTD	2Pt.	Tot. Pts.
Chambers	7	0	7	0	1	44
Morris	6	6	0	0	0	36
McMichael	4	0	4	0	1	26
Thompson	4	0	4	0	0	24
Minor	3	3	0	0	0	18
Booker	1	0	1	0	0	6
Feeley	1	1	0	0	0	6
Gilmore	1	0	1	0	0	6
Konrad	1	0	1	0	0	6
Lee	1	0	1	0	0	6
Pope	1	0	0	1	0	6
Welker	1	0	0	1	0	6
Dolphins	31	10	19	2	2	192
Opponents	42	12	20	10	0	252

2-Pt. conversions: Dolphins 2-4; Opponents 0-0.

(KICKERS)

	XPM/XPA	FGM/FGA	Pts.
Mare	18/18	12/16	54
Bryant	7/7	3/3	16
Gramatica	0/1	3/3	9
Welker	1/1	1/1	4
Dolphins	26/27	19/23	83
Opponents	42/42	20/28	102

RUSHING

	Att.	Yds.	Avg.	Lg.	TD
Morris	132	523	4.0	t35	6
Minor	109	388	3.6	34	3
Henry	46	141	3.1	53	0
Chambers	9	76	8.4	24	0
Gordon	35	64	1.8	11	0
Fiedler	12	59	4.9	26	0
Forsey	19	53	2.8	15	0
Konrad	2	18	9.0	15	0
Feeley	14	13	0.9	t7	1
King	4	9	2.3	3	0
Turk	1	3	3.0	3	0
Booker	1	-8	-8.0	-8	0
Dolphins	384	1339	3.5	53	10
Opponents	539	2302	4.3	62	12

RECEIVING

	No.	Yds.	Avg.	Lg.	TD
McMichael	73	791	10.8	t42	4
Chambers	69	898	13.0	t76	7
Booker	50	638	12.8	45	1
Thompson	23	359	15.6	36	4
Morris	22	124	5.6	24	0
Gilmore	15	206	13.7	37	1
Gordon	13	74	5.7	20	0
Lee	13	110	8.5	t15	1
Minor	13	75	5.8	20	0
Konrad	8	69	8.6	t20	1
Martin	4	15	3.8	7	0
Henry	3	12	4.0	7	0
Bellamy	1	8	8.0	8	0
Easlick	1	4	4.0	4	0
King	1	8	8.0	8	0
Dolphins	309	3391	11.0	t76	19
Opponents	244	2815	11.5	t69	20

INTERCEPTIONS

	No.	Yds.	Avg.	Lg.	TD
Freeman	4	59	14.8	47	0
Knight	4	32	8.0	32	0
Surtain	4	2	0.5	2	0
B. Ayanbadejo	1	2	2.0	2	0
J. Williams	1	0	0.0	0	0
Taylor	1	-3	-3.0	-3	0
Dolphins	15	92	6.1	47	0
Opponents	26	464	17.8	t66	8

SACKS: Taylor 9.5, D. Bowens 7.0, Zgonina 5.0, Romero 3.5, Pope 2.0, Thomas 2.0, J. Williams 2.0, Ahanotu 1.0, Edwards 1.0, Poole 1.0, Seau 1.0, Surtain 1.0. Dolphins 36.0; Opponents 52.0.

PUNTING

	No.	Yds.	Avg.	In. 20	Lg.
Mare	1	19	19.0	0	19
Turk	98	4088	41.7	29	67
Dolphins	99	4107	41.5	29	67
Opponents	102	4177	41.0	30	63

PUNT RETURNS

	No.	FC	Yds.	Avg.	Lg.	TD
Welker	43	12	464	10.8	71	0
Brightful	9	2	89	9.9	36	0
Gilmore	0	0	11	-	11	0
Dolphins	52	14	564	10.8	71	0
Opponents	45	19	258	5.7	24	0

KICK RETURNS

	No.	Yds.	Avg.	Lg.	TD
Welker	57	1313	23.0	t95	1
Brightful	5	126	25.2	32	0
Gilmore	5	114	22.8	53	0
Morris	1	27	27.0	27	0
Poole	1	22	22.0	22	0
Wyrick	1	58	58.0	58	0
Dolphins	70	1660	23.7	t95	1
Opponents	51	1114	21.8	t104	1

FIELD GOALS

	1-19	20-29	30-39	40-49	50+
Mare	0/0	1/2	6/7	3/4	2/3
Bryant	0/0	1/1	0/0	2/2	0/0
Gramatica	0/0	2/2	1/1	0/0	0/0
Welker	0/0	1/1	0/0	0/0	0/0
Dolphins	0/0	5/6	7/8	5/6	2/3
Opponents	2/2	5/5	4/7	6/11	3/3

Mare: (46N) (43G, 47G) (34G) (36G, 37G, 23G) () () () () (34N, 39G) (22N, 50G) (47G) (32G) (30G) (51G) (53N); Bryant: () () () (47G, 28G) (43G) () () () () () () ; Gramatica: () () () () () () () (30G, 29G, 28G) () () () () (); Welker: () () () () (29G) () () () () () () () () () Opponents: (33N, 22G) (38N, 48G, 36G, 39G) (40G, 44N, 45N, 51G) (53G) (40G, 47N) (43N, 43G, 20G) () (49G, 43G) (29G) (33G) (19G) (38N) (20G, 50G) () (43N) (25G, 19G, 33G)

PASSING

	Att.	Cmp.	Yds.	Pct.	Avg. Gain	TD	Pct. TD	Int.	Pct. Int.	Long	Sack/Lost	Rating
Feeley	356	191	1893	53.7	5.32	11	3.1	15	4.2	38	23/136	61.7
Fiedler	190	101	1186	53.2	6.24	7	3.7	8	4.2	t71	25/165	67.1
Rosenfels	39	16	264	41.0	6.77	1	2.6	3	7.7	t76	3/16	41.0
Booker	1	1	48	100.0	48.00	0	0.0	0	0.0	48	0/0	118.8
Dolphins	586	309	3391	52.7	5.79	19	3.2	26	4.4	t76	52/326	62.5
Opponents	434	244	2815	56.2	6.49	20	4.6	15	3.5	t69	36/223	76.9

MINNESOTA VIKINGS
NFC NORTH DIVISION

2005 SEASON

CLUB DIRECTORY

Owners
Red & Charline McCombs
President
Gary Woods
Vp of football operations
Rob Brzezinski
Director of college scouting
Scott Studwell
Director of pro scouting
Paul Wiggin
Director of football administration
Dave Blando
Senior consultant/player personnel
Frank Gilliam
Coordinator of pro personnel
Jeff Robinson
Director of public relations
Bob Hagan
Director of community relations
Brad Madson

Head coach
Mike Tice

Assistant coaches
Brian Baker (defensive line)
Pete Bercich (linebackers)
Wes Chandler (wide receivers)
Ted Cottrell (asst. head coach/defensive coordinator)
Dean Dalton (running backs)
Todd Downing (offensive quality control)
Mark Ellis (asst. strength & conditioning)
Randy Hanson (offensive asst./asst. quarterbacks)
Chuck Knox Jr. (coverage coordinator/defensive backs)
Steve Loney (offensive coordinator/offensive line)
Rich Olson (quarterbacks)
Jim Panagos (asst. defensive line/asst. special teams)
Sid Pillai (coaches' support administrator)
Kevin Ross (asst. defensive backs)
Kurtis Schultz (strength & conditioning)
John Tice (tight ends/asst. offensive line)
Rusty Tillman (special teams)

OFFSEASON MOVES

Key additions
LB Sam Cowart	Trade/Jets
LB Napoleon Harris	Trade/Raiders
QB Brad Johnson	Rel./Bucs
S Darren Sharper	Rel./Packers
CB Fred Smoot	FA/Redskins
WR Travis Taylor	FA/Ravens
DT Pat Williams	FA/Bills

Key losses
LB Chris Claiborne	FA/Rams
WR Kenny Clark	Released
QB Gus Frerotte	FA/Dolphins
DT Chris Hovan	FA/Buccaneers
DE Kenny Mixon	Released
WR Randy Moss	Trade/Raiders
LB Mike Nattiel	Released
RB Larry Ned	Released
CB Rhett Nelson	Rel./Cardinals
S Brian Russell	FA/Browns
CB Terrance Shaw	Released

SCHEDULE

Sept.	11—TAMPA BAY	1:00
Sept.	18—at Cincinnati	1:00
Sept.	25—NEW ORLEANS	1:00
Oct.	2—at Atlanta	4:15
Oct.	9—Open week	
Oct.	16—at Chicago	1:00
Oct.	23—GREEN BAY	1:00
Oct.	30—at Carolina	2:00
Nov.	6—DETROIT	2:00
Nov.	13—at N.Y. Giants	2:00
Nov.	21—at Green Bay (Mon.)	10:00
Nov.	27—CLEVELAND	2:00
Dec.	4—at Detroit	2:00
Dec.	11—ST. LOUIS	2:00
Dec.	18—PITTSBURGH	2:00
Dec.	25—at Baltimore	9:30
Jan.	1—CHICAGO	2:00

All times are Eastern.
All games Sunday unless noted.

DRAFT CHOICES

Troy Williamson, WR, South Carolina (first round/seventh pick overall)
Erasmus James, DE, Wisconsin (1/18).
Marcus Johnson, OT, Mississippi (2/49).
Dustin Fox, CB, Ohio State (3/80).
Ciatrick Fason, RB, Florida (4/112).
C.J. Mosley, DT, Missouri (6/191).
Adrian Ward, CB, Texas-El Paso (7/219).

MISCELLANEOUS TEAM DATA

Stadium (capacity, surface):
Metrodome (64,121, FieldTurf)
Business address:
9520 Viking Drive
Eden Prairie, MN 55344
Business phone:
952-828-6500
Ticket information:
612-338-4537
Team colors:
Purple, gold and white
Flagship radio station:
KFAN, 1130 AM
Website:
www.vikings.com

Training site:
Minnesota State University-
Mankato
Mankato, Minn.
952-828-6500

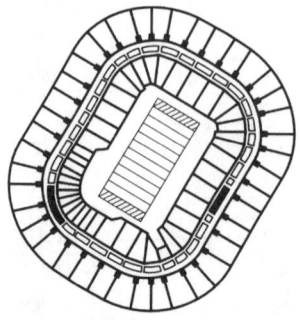

MINNESOTA VIKINGS

No.	QUARTERBACKS	Ht./Wt.	Born	NFL Exp.	College	How acq.	'04 Games GP/GS
11	Culpepper, Daunte	6-4/264	1-28-77	6	Central Florida	D1a/99	16/16
13	Hill, Shaun	6-3/226	1-9-80	1	Maryland	FA/02	1/0
14	Johnson, Brad	6-5/226	9-13-68	12	Florida State	FA/05	4/4
	RUNNING BACKS						
23	Bennett, Michael	5-9/209	8-13-78	5	Wisconsin	D1/01	11/7
35	Fason, Ciatrick	6-1/207	12-29-82	R	Florida	D4/05	—
30	Moore, Mewelde	5-11/209	7-24-82	2	Tulane	D4/04	10/3
32	Smith, Onterrio	5-10/214	12-8-80	3	Oregon	D4/03	11/6
20	Williams, Moe	6-1/205	7-26-74	10	Kentucky	FA/02	14/1
	RECEIVERS						
86	Angulo, Richard (TE)	6-7/260	8-13-80	2	Western New Mexico	W-St.L./03	0/0
44	Berton, Sean (TE)	6-4/272	10-31-79	3	North Carolina State	FA/03	14/7
81	Burleson, Nate	6-0/192	8-19-81	3	Nevada	D3/03	16/15
16	Campbell, Kelly	5-10/173	7-23-80	4	Georgia Tech	FA/02	16/3
83	Dugan, Jeff (TE)	6-4/258	4-8-81	2	Maryland	D7/04	14/2
82	Howry, Keenan	5-10/172	6-17-81	3	Oregon	D7/03	3/0
40	Kleinsasser, Jim (TE)	6-3/272	1-31-77	6	North Dakota	D2/99	1/1
17	Nelson, Ben	6-2/185	8-21-79	2	St. Cloud State	FA/03	3/0
89	Owens, Richard (TE)	6-4/273	11-4-80	2	Louisville	FA/04	7/2
87	Robinson, Marcus	6-3/215	2-27-75	8	South Carolina	FA/04	16/7
89	Taylor, Travis	6-1/210	3-30-78	6	Florida	FA/05	10/9
85	Wiggins, Jermaine (TE)	6-2/260	1-18-75	6	Georgia	FA/04	14/13
19	Williamson, Troy	6-1/201	4-30-83	R	South Carolina	D1a/05	—
	OFFENSIVE LINEMEN						
78	Birk, Matt (C)	6-4/309	7-23-76	8	Harvard	D6/98	12/11
65	Dorsey, Nat (T)	6-7/322	9-9-83	2	Georgia Tech	D4/04	13/7
73	Goldberg, Adam (G)	6-7/310	8-12-80	2	Wyoming	FA/04	13/6
67	Herrera, Anthony (G)	6-2/315	6-14-80	1	Tennessee	FA/04	0/0
72	Johnson, Marcus (G)	6-6/321	12-1-81	R	Mississippi	D2/05	—
76	Liwienski, Chris (G)	6-5/325	8-2-75	6	Indiana	FA/99	16/16
46	Loeffler, Cullen (C)	6-5/241	1-27-81	2	Texas	FA/03	16/0
74	McKinnie, Bryant (T)	6-8/335	9-23-79	4	Miami	D1/02	16/16
75	Rosenthal, Mike (T)	6-7/318	6-10-77	6	Notre Dame	FA/03	2/2
71	Snell, Shannon (G)	5-10/320	4-27-82	1	Florida	FA/05	0/0
60	Withrow, Cory (C)	6-2/287	4-5-75	6	Washington State	FA/99	12/5
	DEFENSIVE LINEMEN						
99	James, Erasmus (E)	6-4/263	11-4-82	R	Wisconsin	D1b/05	—
97	Johnson, Spencer (T)	6-3/286	12-12-81	2	Auburn	FA/04	9/7
51	Johnstone, Lance (E)	6-4/250	6-11-73	10	Temple	FA/01	16/1
90	Martin, Steve (T)	6-4/320	5-31-74	10	Missouri	FA/04	12/0
96	Mosley, C.J. (T)	6-3/305	8-6-83	R	Missouri	D6/05	—
98	Scott, Darrion (E)	6-3/289	10-25-81	2	Ohio State	D3/04	12/0
95	Udeze, Kenechi (E)	6-3/281	3-5-83	2	USC	D1/04	16/15
93	Williams, Kevin (T)	6-5/311	8-16-80	3	Oklahoma State	D1/03	16/16
94	Williams, Pat (T)	6-3/317	10-24-72	8	Texas A&M	FA/05	16/15
	LINEBACKERS						
55	Cowart, Sam	6-2/245	2-26-75	7	Florida State	T-NYJ/05	9/2
50	Davis, Rod	6-2/239	4-2-81	2	Southern Mississippi	D5/04	14/0
58	Harris, Napoleon	6-2/255	2-25-79	4	Northwestern	T-Oak./05	14/9
56	Henderson, E.J.	6-1/245	8-3-80	3	Maryland	D2/03	14/14
52	Newman, Keith	6-2/248	1-19-77	7	North Carolina	FA/03	15/14
57	Smith, Raonall	6-2/241	10-22-78	3	Washington State	D2/02	7/3
53	Stewart, Quincy	6-1/220	3-27-78	4	Louisiana Tech	FA/05	1/0
54	Thomas, Dontarrious	6-2/241	9-2-80	2	Auburn	D2/04	16/5
66	Wiley, Grant	6-0/235	3-11-81	1	West Virginia	FA/04	0/0
	DEFENSIVE BACKS						
33	Brown, Ralph (CB)	5-10/185	9-16-78	5	Nebraska	FA/04	12/0
21	Chavous, Corey (S)	6-1/205	1-15-76	8	Vanderbilt	FA/02	16/16
37	Fox, Dustin (S)	5-11/190	10-8-82	R	Ohio State	D3/05	—
22	Irvin, Ken (CB)	5-11/182	7-11-72	10	Memphis	FA/03	0/0
31	Jones, Rushen (CB)	5-10/201	4-4-80	3	Vanderbilt	FA/03	2/0
24	Offord, Willie (S)	6-1/216	12-22-78	4	South Carolina	D3/02	16/0
42	Sharper, Darren (S)	6-2/210	11-3-75	9	William & Mary	FA/05	15/13
21	Smoot, Fred (CB)	5-11/174	4-17-79	5	Mississippi State	FA/05	15/15
47	Ward, Adrian (CB)	5-10/170	7-1-82	R	UTEP	D7/05	—
29	Williams, Brian (CB)	5-11/198	7-2-79	4	North Carolina State	D4a/02	16/16
26	Winfield, Antoine (CB)	5-9/180	6-24-77	7	Ohio State	FA/04	14/12
	SPECIALISTS						
2	Bennett, Darren (P)	6-5/235	1-9-65	11	None	FA/04	15/0
5	Dorsch, Travis (K)	6-6/227	9-4-79	1	Purdue	FA/04	0/0
8	Elling, Aaron (K)	6-2/201	5-31-78	3	Wyoming	FA/03	8/0

Abbreviations: D1—draft pick, first round; W—claimed on waivers; T—obtained in trade; FA—free-agent acquisition.

MINNESOTA VIKINGS

2004 regular-season record: 8-8
Position: 2nd in NFC North

Sept.12—DALLAS	W	35-17
Sept.20—at Philadelphia	L	16-27
Sept.26—CHICAGO	W	27-22
Oct. 3—Open date		
Oct. 10—at Houston (OT)	W	34-28
Oct. 17—at New Orleans	W	38-31
Oct. 24—TENNESSEE	W	20-3
Oct. 31—N.Y. GIANTS	L	13-34
Nov. 8—at Indianapolis	L	28-31
Nov. 14—at Green Bay	L	31-34
Nov. 21—DETROIT	W	22-19
Nov. 28—JACKSONVILLE	W	27-16
Dec. 5—at Chicago	L	14-24
Dec. 12—SEATTLE	L	23-27
Dec. 19—at Detroit	W	28-27
Dec. 24—GREEN BAY	L	31-34
Jan. 2—at Washington	L	18-21

2004 postseason record: 1-1

Jan. 9—at Green Bay#	W	31-17
Jan. 16—at Philadelphia*	L	14-27

#NFC wild-card game. *NFC divisional play-off game.

SCORING BY PERIODS

	Q1	Q2	Q3	Q4	OT	Pts.
Vikings	54	136	73	136	6	405
Opponents	78	135	54	128	0	395

TEAM STATISTICS

	Min.	Opp.
TOTAL FIRST DOWNS ..	351	350
Rushing	98	110
Passing	225	220
Penalty	28	20
3rd Down: Made/Att. ..	102/195	90/196
3rd Down Pct.	52.3	45.9
4th Down: Made/Att.	6/10	10/16
4th Down Pct.	60.0	62.5
POSSESSION AVG.	30:02	29:58
TOTAL NET YARDS	6339	5902
Avg. per Game	396.2	368.9
Total Plays	985	1018
Avg. per Play	6.4	5.8
NET YARDS RUSHING ..	1823	2006
Avg. per Game	113.9	125.4
Total Rushes	387	435
NET YARDS PASSING....	4516	3896
Avg. per Game	282.3	243.5
Sacked/Yards Lost	46/238	39/234
Gross Yards	4754	4130
Att./Completions	552/380	544/338
Completion Pct.	68.8	62.1
Had Intercepted	12	11
PUNTS/AVERAGE	57/39.3	59/42.2
NET PUNTING AVG.	57/35.3	59/36.2
PENALTIES/YARDS	117/884	110/974
FUMBLES/LOST	20/9	25/11
TOUCHDOWNS	50	46

	Min.	Opp.
Rushing	8	15
Passing	39	30
Returns	3	1

SCORING (NON-KICKERS)

	TD	RTD	PTD	MTD	2Pt.	Tot. Pts.
Moss	13	0	13	0	0	78
Burleson	10	0	9	1	1	62
Robinson	8	0	8	0	0	48
O. Smith	4	2	0	2	1	26
Wiggins	4	0	4	0	0	24
M. Williams	4	3	1	0	0	24
Culpepper	2	2	0	0	1	14
M. Bennett	2	1	1	0	0	12
Campbell	1	0	1	0	0	6
Claiborne	1	0	0	1	0	6
K. Williams	1	0	0	1	0	6
Vikings	50	8	39	3	3	306
Opponents	46	15	30	1	1	280

2-Pt. conversions: Vikings 3-4; Opponents 1-3.

(KICKERS)

	XPM/XPA	FGM/FGA	Pts.
Andersen	45/45	18/22	99
Vikings	45/45	18/22	99
Opponents	43/43	24/27	115

RUSHING

	Att.	Yds.	Avg.	Lg.	TD
O. Smith	124	544	4.4	38	2
Culpepper	88	406	4.6	16	2
Moore	65	379	5.8	33	0
M. Bennett	70	276	3.9	25	1
M. Williams	30	161	5.4	49	3
Burleson	6	49	8.2	11	0
Campbell	3	4	1.3	16	0
Russell	1	4	4.0	4	0
Vikings	387	1823	4.7	49	8
Opponents	435	2006	4.6	53	15

RECEIVING

	No.	Yds.	Avg.	Lg.	TD
Wiggins	71	705	9.9	39	4
Burleson	68	1006	14.8	t68	9
Moss	49	767	15.7	t82	13
Robinson	47	657	14.0	t50	8
O. Smith	36	394	10.9	t63	2
Moore	27	238	8.8	26	0
M. Bennett	21	207	9.9	t38	1
M. Williams	21	233	11.1	28	1
Campbell	19	364	19.2	61	1
Berton	9	78	8.7	14	0
Owens	8	69	8.6	18	0
Kleinsasser	2	24	12.0	18	0
Howry	1	3	3.0	3	0
Ned	1	9	9.0	9	0
Vikings	380	4754	12.5	t82	39
Opponents	338	4130	12.2	62	30

INTERCEPTIONS

	No.	Yds.	Avg.	Lg.	TD
Winfield	3	89	29.7	56	0
B. Williams	2	14	7.0	14	0
Russell	1	41	41.0	41	0
Shaw	1	22	22.0	22	0
R. Smith	1	19	19.0	19	0
Claiborne	1	15	15.0	t15	1
K. Williams	1	7	7.0	7	0
Chavous	1	0	0.0	0	0
Vikings	11	207	18.8	56	1
Opponents	12	207	17.3	52	0

SACKS: K. Williams 11.5, Johnstone 11.5, Udeze 5.0, Newman 3.5, Mixon 2.5, Hovan 1.5, Claiborne 1.0, Henderson 1.0, Johnson 1.0, Martin 0.5, Thomas 0.5. Vikings 39.0; Opponents 46.0.

PUNTING

	No.	Yds.	Avg.	In. 20	Lg.
D. Bennett	57	2240	39.3	18	61
Vikings	57	2240	39.3	18	61
Opponents	59	2488	42.2	24	55

PUNT RETURNS

	No.	FC	Yds.	Avg.	Lg.	TD
Burleson	25	9	214	8.6	t91	1
Moore	4	1	28	7.0	17	0
Howry	2	3	33	16.5	21	0
Vikings	31	14	275	8.9	t91	1
Opponents	26	15	169	6.5	15	0

KICK RETURNS

	No.	Yds.	Avg.	Lg.	TD
Campbell	35	760	21.7	55	0
Moore	20	386	19.3	33	0
O. Smith	9	155	17.2	24	0
Burleson	2	51	25.5	29	0
Howry	2	45	22.5	24	0
Ross	2	33	16.5	19	0
Berton	1	3	3.0	3	0
Davis	1	15	15.0	15	0
Johnson	1	0	0.0	0	0
Vikings	73	1448	19.8	55	0
Opponents	75	1869	24.9	t92	1

FIELD GOALS

	1-19	20-29	30-39	40-49	50+
Andersen	1/1	8/8	5/7	4/6	0/0
Vikings	1/1	8/8	5/7	4/6	0/0
Opponents	0/0	5/10	12	7/7	2/3

Andersen: () (42G, 19G, 39G, 44N) (46N, 42G, 24G) () (39G) (29G, 29G) (38N) (42G, 23G) (21G) () (25G, 33G) (38N) (48G, 32G, 31G) () (29G) (23G) Opponents: (27G) (37G, 47G) (34G, 23G, 39N, 32G) () (45G) (40G) (50G, 30G) (35G) (43G, 33G) (48G) (33G, 32G, 42G) (53G, 52N) (38N, 33G, 28G) (32G, 23G) (42G, 29G) ()

PASSING

	Att.	Cmp.	Yds.	Pct.	Avg. Gain	TD	Pct. TD	Int.	Pct. Int.	Long	Sack/Lost	Rating
Culpepper	548	379	4717	69.2	8.61	39	7.1	11	2.0	t82	46/238	110.9
Moss	2	1	37	50.0	18.50	0	0.0	1	50.0	37	0/0	56.3
Frerotte	1	0	0	0.0	0.00	0	0.0	0	0.0	...	0/0	39.6
Moore	1	0	0	0.0	0.00	0	0.0	0	0.0	...	0/0	39.6
Vikings	552	380	4754	68.8	8.61	39	7.1	12	2.2	t82	46/238	109.8
Opponents	544	338	4130	62.1	7.59	30	5.5	11	2.0	62	39/234	95.5

NEW ENGLAND PATRIOTS
AFC EAST DIVISION

2005 SEASON

CLUB DIRECTORY

Chairman and owner
Robert K. Kraft
Vice chairman
Jonathan A. Kraft
Vp and chief marketing officer
Lou Imbriano
Vp of community affairs & corporate philanthropy
Rena Clark
Vice president of player personnel
Scott Pioli
Director of college scouting
Thomas Dimitroff
Director of pro personnel
Nick Caserio
Director of operations
Brian Smith
Executive director of media relations
Stacey James

Head coach
Bill Belichick

Assistant coaches
Joel Collier (asst. secondary)
Brian Daboll (wide receivers)
Ivan Fears (running backs)
Pepper Johnson (defensive line)
Eric Mangini (defensive coordinator)
Pete Mangurian (tight ends)
Josh McDaniels (quarterbacks)
Harold Nash (asst. strength and conditioning)
Matt Patricia (asst. offensive line)
Dean Pees (linebackers)
Dante Scarnecchia (asst. head coach/offensive line)
Brad Seely (special teams)
Mike Woicik (strength and conditioning)

SCHEDULE

Sept.	8—OAKLAND (Thurs.)	9:00
Sept.	18—at Carolina	1:00
Sept.	25—at Pittsburgh	4:15
Oct.	2—SAN DIEGO	1:00
Oct.	9—at Atlanta	1:00
Oct.	16—at Denver	4:15
Oct.	23—Open week	
Oct.	30—BUFFALO	9:30
Nov.	7—INDIANAPOLIS (Mon.)	10:00
Nov.	13—at Miami	2:00
Nov.	20—NEW ORLEANS	2:00
Nov.	27—at Kansas City	2:00
Dec.	4—N.Y. JETS	5:15
Dec.	11—at Buffalo	2:00
Dec.	17—TAMPA BAY (Sat.)	2:30
Dec.	26—at N.Y. Jets (Mon.)	10:00
Jan.	1—MIAMI	2:00

All times are Eastern.
All games Sunday unless noted.

OFFSEASON MOVES

Key additions
LB Monty Beisel	FA/Chiefs
LB Chad Brown	Rel./Seahawks
CB Ike Charlton	FA/Giants '03
WR Tim Dwight	Rel./Chargers
QB Doug Flutie	Rel./Chargers
LB Wesly Mallard	FA/Giants
QB Chris Redman	FA/Ravens '03
CB Chad Scott	Rel./Steelers
CB Duane Starks	Trade/Cardinals
WR David Terrell	Rel./Bears

Key losses
G Joe Andruzzi	FA/Browns
WR Troy Brown	Free agent
OT Adrian Klemm	FA/Packers
CB Ty Law	Released
CB Omare Lowe	FA/Seahawks
QB Jim Miller	FA/Giants
WR David Patten	FA/Redskins
LB Roman Phifer	Released
NT Keith Traylor	Released

DRAFT CHOICES

Logan Mankins, G, Fresno State (first round, 32nd pick overall).
Ellis Hobbs, CB, Iowa State (3/84).
Nick Kaczur, G, Toledo (3/100).
James Sanders, SS, Fresno State (4/133).
Ryan Claridge, OLB, Nevada-Las Vegas (5/170).
Matt Cassel, QB, Southern California (7/230).
Andy Stokes, TE, William Penn (7/255).

MISCELLANEOUS TEAM DATA

Stadium (capacity, surface):
Gillette Stadium
(68,756, grass)
Business address:
One Patriot Place
Foxborough, MA 02035
Business phone:
508-543-8200
Ticket information:
508-543-1776
Team colors:
Red, white, blue and silver
Flagship radio station:
WBCN, 104.1 FM
Website:
www.patriots.com

Training site:
Gillette Stadium
Foxborough, MA
508-543-8200

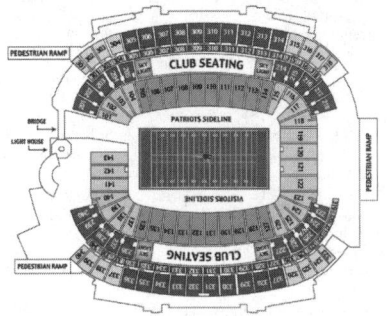

NEW ENGLAND PATRIOTS

No.	QUARTERBACKS	Ht./Wt.	Born	NFL Exp.	College	How acq.	'04 Games GP/GS
12	Brady, Tom	6-4/225	8-3-77	6	Michigan	D6b/00	16/16
16	Cassel, Matt	6-5/230	5-17-82	R	USC	D7a/05	—
6	Davey, Rohan	6-2/245	4-14-78	4	LSU	D4a/02	4/0
2	Flutie, Doug	5-10/180	10-23-62	12	Boston College	FA/05	2/1
7	Redman, Chris	6-3/223	7-7-77	3	Louisville	FA/05	0/0
	RUNNING BACKS						
34	Cobbs, Cedric	6-0/225	1-9-81	2	Arkansas	D4b/04	3/0
28	Dillon, Corey	6-1/225	10-24-74	9	Washington	T-Cin./04	15/14
33	Faulk, Kevin	5-8/202	6-5-76	7	LSU	D2/99	11/1
35	Pass, Patrick (FB)	5-10/217	12-31-77	6	Georgia	D7b/00	14/4
	RECEIVERS						
83	Branch, Deion	5-9/193	7-18-79	4	Louisville	D2/02	9/9
86	Dwight, Tim	5-8/180	7-13-75	8	Iowa	FA/05	12/0
88	Fauria, Christian (TE)	6-4/250	9-22-71	11	Colorado	FA/02	16/10
87	Givens, David	6-0/215	8-16-80	4	Notre Dame	D7b/02	15/12
82	Graham, Daniel (TE)	6-3/257	11-16-78	4	Colorado	D1/02	14/14
81	Johnson, Bethel	5-11/200	2-11-79	3	Texas A&M	D2b/03	13/1
14	Sam, P.K.	6-3/210	2-26-83	1	Florida State	D5/04	2/0
46	Stokes, Andy (TE)	6-5/245	6/2/81	R	William Penn	D7b/05	—
10	Terrell, David	6-3/212	3-13-79	5	Michigan	FA/05	16/15
84	Watson, Ben (TE)	6-3/253	12-18-80	1	Georgia	D1b/04	1/1
	OFFENSIVE LINEMEN						
68	Ashworth, Tom (T)	6-6/305	10-10-77	4	Colorado	FA/01	6/6
76	Gorin, Brandon (T)	6-6/308	7-17-78	4	Purdue	FA/03	14/10
71	Hochstein, Russ (G)	6-4/305	10-7-77	5	Nebraska	FA/03	16/2
77	Kaczur, Nick (T)	6-4/319	7-28-79	R	Toledo	D3b/05	—
67	Koppen, Dan (C)	6-2/296	9-12-79	3	Boston College	D5/03	16/16
72	Light, Matt (T)	6-4/305	6-23-78	5	Purdue	D2/01	16/16
70	Mankins, Logan (G/T)	6-4/307	12-18-77	R	Fresno State	D1/05	—
64	Mruczkowski, Gene (G/C)	6-2/305	6-6-80	3	Purdue	FA/03	10/0
61	Neal, Stephen (G)	6-4/305	10-9-76	4	Cal State Bakersfield	FA/01	16/14
66	Paxton, Lonie (C)	6-2/260	3-13-78	6	Sacramento State	FA/00	16/0
	DEFENSIVE LINEMEN						
96	Bailey, Rodney (E)	6-3/306	10-7-79	5	Ohio State	FA/04	0/0
97	Green, Jarvis (E)	6-3/290	1-12-79	4	LSU	D4b/02	16/1
91	Hill, Marquise (E)	6-6/300	8-7-82	2	LSU	D2/04	1/0
99	Kelley, Ethan (T)	6-2/310	2-12-80	2	Baylor	D7/03	1/0
93	Seymour, Richard (E)	6-6/310	10-6-79	5	Georgia	D1/01	15/15
92	Thomas, Santonio (T)	6-4/308	7/2/81	R	Miami	FA/05	—
94	Warren, Ty (E)	6-5/300	2-6-81	3	Texas A&M	D1/03	16/16
75	Wilfork, Vince (T)	6-2/325	11-4-81	2	Miami	D1a/04	16/6
	LINEBACKERS						
48	Banta-Cain, Tully	6-2/250	8-28-80	3	California	D7b/03	16/0
56	Beisel, Monty	6-3/238	8-20-78	5	Kansas State	FA/05	11/9
94	Brown, Chad	6-2/245	7-12-70	13	Colorado	FA/05	7/7
54	Bruschi, Tedy	6-1/247	6-9-73	10	Arizona	D3/96	16/16
58	Chatham, Matt	6-4/250	6-28-77	6	South Dakota	W-St.L./00	5/0
47	Claridge, Ryan	6-2/254	4/12/81	R	UNLV	D5/05	—
59	Colvin, Rosevelt	6-3/250	9-5-77	7	Purdue	FA/03	16/1
51	Davis, Don	6-1/235	12-17-72	10	Kansas	FA/03	16/2
53	Izzo, Larry	5-10/228	9-26-74	10	Rice	FA/01	16/0
52	Johnson, Ted	6-4/253	12-4-72	11	Colorado	D2/95	16/15
90	Klecko, Dan	5-11/275	1-12-81	3	Temple	D4a/03	6/2
53	Mallard, Wesly	6-1/230	11-21-78	4	Oregon	FA/05	4/0
55	McGinest, Willie	6-5/270	12-11-71	12	USC	D1/94	16/16
50	Vrabel, Mike	6-4/261	8-14-75	9	Ohio State	FA/01	16/15
	DEFENSIVE BACKS						
41	Charlton, Ike (CB)	5-11/199	10-6-77	5	Virginia Tech	FA/05	0/0
21	Gay, Randall (CB)	5-11/186	5-5-82	2	LSU	FA/04	15/9
37	Harrison, Rodney (S)	6-1/220	12-15-72	12	Western Illinois	FA/03	16/16
25	Hobbs, Ellis (CB)	5-9/188	5-16-83	R	Iowa State	D3a/05	—
38	Poole, Tyrone (CB)	5-8/188	2-3-72	10	Fort Valley State	FA/01	5/4
42	Reid, Dexter (S)	5-11/203	3-18-81	2	North Carolina	D4a/04	13/2
22	Samuel, Asante (CB)	5-10/185	1-6-81	3	Central Florida	D4b/03	13/8
36	Sanders, James (S)	5-10/207	11-11-83	R	Fresno State	D4/05	—
30	Scott, Chad (CB)	6-1/202	9-6-74	9	Maryland	FA/05	7/7
39	Scott, Guss (S)	5-10/205	5-21-82	1	Florida	D3/04	0/0
23	Starks, Duane (CB)	5-10/174	5-23-74	8	Miami	T-Ari./05	15/8
26	Wilson, Eugene (S)	5-10/195	8-17-80	3	Illinois	D2a/03	15/14
	SPECIALISTS						
8	Miller, Josh (P)	6-4/225	7-14-70	10	Arizona	FA/04	16/0
4	Vinatieri, Adam (K)	6-0/202	12-28-72	10	South Dakota State	FA/96	16/0

Abbreviations: D1—draft pick, first round; W—claimed on waivers; T—obtained in trade; FA—free-agent acquisition.

2004 regular-season record: 14-2
Position: 1st in AFC East

Sept. 9—INDIANAPOLIS	W	27-24
Sept.19—at Arizona	W	23-12
Sept.26—Open date		
Oct. 3—at Buffalo	W	31-17
Oct. 10—MIAMI	W	24-10
Oct. 17—SEATTLE	W	30-20
Oct. 24—N.Y. JETS	W	13-7
Oct. 31—at Pittsburgh	L	20-34
Nov. 7—at St. Louis	W	40-22
Nov.14—BUFFALO	W	29-6
Nov.22—at Kansas City	W	27-19
Nov.28—BALTIMORE	W	24-3
Dec. 5—at Cleveland	W	42-15
Dec.12—CINCINNATI	W	35-28
Dec.20—at Miami	L	28-29
Dec.26—at N.Y. Jets	W	23-7
Jan. 2—SAN FRANCISCO	W	21-7

2004 postseason record: 3-0

Jan. 16—INDIANAPOLIS*	W	20-3
Jan. 23—at Pittsburgh†	W	41-27
Feb. 6—at Philadelphia‡	W	24-21

*AFC divisional playoff game. †AFC championship game. ‡Super Bowl 39.

SCORING BY PERIODS

	Q1	Q2	Q3	Q4	OT	Pts.
Patriots	87	159	102	89	0	437
Opponents	55	94	45	66	0	260

TEAM STATISTICS

	N.E.	Opp.
TOTAL FIRST DOWNS	344	290
Rushing	120	83
Passing	193	177
Penalty	31	30
3rd Down: Made/Att.	93/206	81/209
3rd Down Pct.	45.1	38.8
4th Down: Made/Att.	4/10	13/30
4th Down Pct.	40.0	43.3
POSSESSION AVG.	31:22	28:38
TOTAL NET YARDS	5722	4972
Avg. per Game	357.6	310.8
Total Plays	1035	988
Avg. per Play	5.5	5.0
NET YARDS RUSHING	2134	1572
Avg. per Game	133.4	98.3
Total Rushes	524	405
NET YARDS PASSING	3588	3400
Avg. per Game	224.3	212.5
Sacked/Yards Lost	26/162	45/311
Gross Yards	3750	3711
Att./Completions	485/293	538/315
Completion Pct.	60.4	58.6
Had Intercepted	14	20
PUNTS/AVERAGE	56/42.0	69/41.5
NET PUNTING AVG.	56/33.7	69/36.8
PENALTIES/YARDS	101/822	118/1014
FUMBLES/LOST	24/13	31/16
TOUCHDOWNS	49	31
Rushing	15	9
Passing	29	18
Returns	5	4

SCORING (NON-KICKERS)

	Tot. TD	RTD	PTD	MTD	2Pt.	Tot. Pts.
Dillon	13	12	1	0	1	80
Graham	7	0	7	0	0	42
Patten	7	0	7	0	0	42
Branch	4	0	4	0	0	24
Faulk	3	2	1	0	0	18
Givens	3	0	3	0	0	18
Fauria	2	0	2	0	0	12
B. Johnson	2	0	1	1	0	12
Vrabel	2	0	2	0	0	12
Abdullah	1	1	0	0	0	6
T. Brown	1	0	1	0	0	6
Gay	1	0	1	0	0	6
J. Green	1	0	0	1	0	6
Samuel	1	0	0	1	0	6
Seymour	1	0	0	1	0	6
Patriots	49	15	29	5	1	296
Opponents	31	9	18	4	3	192

2-Pt. conversions: Patriots 1-1; Opponents 3-8.

(KICKERS)

	XPM/XPA	FGM/FGA	Pts.
Vinatieri	48/48	31/33	141
Patriots	48/48	31/33	141
Opponents	23/23	15/18	68

RUSHING

	Att.	Yds.	Avg.	Lg.	TD
Dillon	345	1635	4.7	44	12
Faulk	54	255	4.7	20	2
Pass	39	141	3.6	19	0
Cobbs	22	50	2.3	13	0
Brady	43	28	0.7	10	0
Abdullah	13	13	1.0	5	1
B. Johnson	2	8	4.0	11	0
Patten	1	5	5.0	5	0
Izzo	1	0	0.0	0	0
Davey	4	-1	-0.3	3	0
Patriots	524	2134	4.1	44	15
Opponents	405	1572	3.9	34	9

RECEIVING

	No.	Yds.	Avg.	Lg.	TD
Givens	56	874	15.6	50	3
Patten	44	800	18.2	t48	7
Branch	35	454	13.0	t26	4
Graham	30	364	12.1	48	7
Pass	28	215	7.7	22	0
Faulk	26	248	9.5	t31	1
T. Brown	17	184	10.8	22	1
Fauria	16	195	12.2	25	2
Dillon	15	103	6.9	20	1
B. Johnson	10	174	17.4	48	1
Weaver	8	93	11.6	25	0
Klecko	3	18	6.0	11	0
Vrabel	2	3	1.5	t2	2
Watson	2	16	8.0	14	0
Abdullah	1	9	9.0	9	0
Patriots	293	3750	12.8	50	29
Opponents	315	3711	11.8	t65	18

INTERCEPTIONS

	No.	Yds.	Avg.	Lg.	TD
Wilson	4	51	12.8	24	0
Bruschi	3	70	23.3	36	0
T. Brown	3	22	7.3	17	0
Gay	2	23	11.5	13	0
Harrison	2	12	6.0	12	0
Samuel	1	34	34.0	t34	1
McGinest	1	27	27.0	27	0
Phifer	1	26	26.0	26	0
Poole	1	21	21.0	21	0
Banta-Cain	1	4	4.0	4	0
Law	1	0	0.0	0	0
Patriots	20	290	14.5	36	1
Opponents	14	242	17.3	65	1

SACKS: McGinest 9.5, Vrabel 5.5, Colvin 5.0, Seymour 5.0, J. Green 4.0, Bruschi 3.5, Warren 3.5, Harrison 3.0, Wilfork 2.0, Banta-Cain 1.5, Phifer 1.5, T. Johnson 1.0. Patriots 45.0; Opponents 26.0.

PUNTING

	No.	Yds.	Avg.	In. 20	Lg.
Jo. Miller	56	2350	42.0	19	69
Patriots	56	2350	42.0	19	69
Opponents	69	2866	41.5	21	63

PUNT RETURNS

	No.	FC	Yds.	Avg.	Lg.	TD
Faulk	20	11	133	6.7	16	0
T. Brown	12	3	83	6.9	23	0
B. Johnson	4	1	8	2.0	6	0
Poole	2	0	6	3.0	6	0
Branch	1	0	0	0.0	0	0
Gay	1	0	0	0.0	0	0
Patriots	40	15	230	5.8	23	0
Opponents	31	7	365	11.8	71	1

KICK RETURNS

	No.	Yds.	Avg.	Lg.	TD
B. Johnson	41	1016	24.8	t93	1
Pass	6	115	19.2	24	0
Faulk	4	73	18.3	24	0
Kasper	3	61	20.3	21	0
Banta-Cain	1	21	21.0	21	0
Patten	1	16	16.0	16	0
Patriots	56	1302	23.3	t93	1
Opponents	86	2003	23.3	t98	1

FIELD GOALS

	1-19	20-29	30-39	40-49	50+
Vinatieri	0/0	13/13	7/7	11/12	0/1
Patriots	0/0	13/13	7/7	11/12	0/1
Opponents	1/1	5/5	5/6	2/3	2/3

Vinatieri: (32G, 43G) (29G, 28G, 24G) (42G) (40G, 47N) (40G, 39G, 30G) (41G, 27G) (43G, 25G) (43G, 31G, 45G, 36G) (27G, 24G, 20G, 45G, 37G) (37G, 28G) (28G, 40G, 48G) () () () (28G, 29G, 50N, 26G) ()
Opponents: (32G, 48N) (51G, 52G, 58N) (33G) (29G) (33G, 40G, 28G, 31G) () (19G, 29G) () () (44G, 24G) (22G) () (30G) () (39N)

PASSING

	Att.	Cmp.	Yds.	Pct.	Avg. Gain	TD	Pct. TD	Int.	Pct. Int.	Long	Sack/Lost	Rating
Brady	474	288	3692	60.8	7.79	28	5.9	14	3.0	50	26/162	92.6
Davey	10	4	54	40.0	5.40	0	0.0	0	0.0	20	0/0	57.9
Vinatieri	1	1	4	100.0	4.00	1	100.0	0	0.0	t4	0/0	122.9
Patriots	485	293	3750	60.4	7.73	29	6.0	14	2.9	50	26/162	92.5
Opponents	538	315	3711	58.6	6.90	18	3.3	20	3.7	t65	45/311	75.3

NEW ENGLAND PATRIOTS

NEW ORLEANS SAINTS
NFC SOUTH DIVISION

2005 SEASON

CLUB DIRECTORY

Owner
Tom Benson
Owner/executive
Rita LeBlanc
Executive vice president/general manager of football operations
Mickey Loomis
Director of player personnel
Rick Mueller
Senior football administrator
Russ Ball
Director of College Scouting
Rick Reiprish
College scouting coordinator
Rick Thompson
Director of media & public relations
Greg Bensel

Head coach
Jim Haslett

Assistant coaches
Joe Alley (coaching assistant)
Adam Bailey (asst. strength & conditioning)
Chip Beake (offensive asst.)
Greg Brown (defensive asst. /cornerbacks)
Al Everest (special teams coordinator)
Rock Gullickson (strength & conditioning)
Jack Henry (associate head coach/running game coordinator)
Ty Knott (defensive asst./quality control)
Winston Moss (linebackers)
Bob Palcic (tight ends)
John Pease (defensive line)
Jim Pyne (asst. offensive line)
Jimmy Robinson (wide receivers)
Willy Robinson (senior defensive asst./secondary)
Johnny Roland (running backs)
Turk Schonert (quarterbacks)
Mike Sheppard (off. coordinator)
Rick Venturi (def. coordinator)

SCHEDULE

Sept. 11—at Carolina		1:00
Sept. 18—N.Y. GIANTS		1:00
Sept. 25—at Minnesota		1:00
Oct. 2—BUFFALO		1:00
Oct. 9—at Green Bay		1:00
Oct. 16—ATLANTA		1:00
Oct. 23—at St. Louis		1:00
Oct. 30—MIAMI		2:00
Nov. 6—CHICAGO		2:00
Nov. 13—Open date		
Nov. 20—at New England		2:00
Nov. 27—at N.Y. Jets		9:30
Dec. 4—TAMPA BAY		2:00
Dec. 12—at Atlanta (Mon.)		10:00
Dec. 18—CAROLINA		2:00
Dec. 24—DETROIT (Sat.)		2:00
Jan. 1—at Tampa Bay		2:00

All times are Eastern.
All games Sunday unless noted.

OFFSEASON MOVES

Key additions
LB Levar Fisher	FA/Cardinals
OT Jermane Mayberry	FA/Eagles
TE Shad Meier	FA/Titans
RB Antowain Smith	FA/Titans
DB Dwight Smith	FA/Buccaneers
CB Jimmy Williams	FA/49ers

Key losses
CB Ashley Ambrose	Released
S Tebucky Jones	FA/Dolphins
WR Jerome Pathon	FA/Seahawks
OT Victor Riley	FA/Texans
DE Kenny Smith	FA/Raiders

DRAFT CHOICES

Jammal Brown, OT, Oklahoma (first round/13th pick overall).
Josh Bullocks, FS, Nebraska (2/40).
Alfred Fincher, ILB, Connecticut (3/82).
Chase Lyman, WR, California (4/118).
Adrian McPherson, QB, Florida State (5/152).
Jason Jefferson, DT, Wisconsin (6/193).
Jimmy Verdon, DT, Arizona State (7/232).

MISCELLANEOUS TEAM DATA

Stadium (capacity, surface):
Louisiana Superdome
(64,900, Sportexe Momentum)
Business address:
5800 Airline Drive
Metairie, LA 70003
Business phone:
504-733-0255
Ticket information:
504-731-1700
Team colors:
Old gold, black and white
Flagship radio station:
WWL-870 AM
Website:
www.neworleanssaints.com
Training site:
5800 Airline Drive
Metairie, LA 70003
504-733-0255

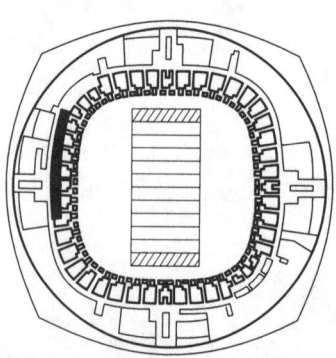

NEW ORLEANS SAINTS

No.	QUARTERBACKS	Ht./Wt.	Born	NFL Exp.	College	How acq.	'04 Games GP/GS
4	Bouman, Todd	6-2/226	8-1-72	8	St. Cloud State	T-Min./03	16/0
2	Brooks, Aaron	6-4/220	3-24-76	7	Virginia	T-GB/00	16/16
12	Kingsbury, Kliff	6-4/231	8-9-79	2	Texas Tech	FA/05	0/0
5	McPherson, Adrian	6-3/218	5-8-83	R	Florida State	D5/05	—
	RUNNING BACKS						
44	Karney, Mike (FB)	5-11/258	7-6-81	2	Arizona State	D5/04	16/8
25	McAfee, Fred	5-10/193	6-20-68	14	Mississippi College	FA/00	11/0
26	McAllister, Deuce	6-1/232	12-27-78	5	Mississippi	D1/01	14/14
32	Smith, Antowain	6-2/232	3-14-72	9	Houston	FA/05	13/4
27	Stecker, Aaron	5-10/213	11-13-75	6	Western Illinois	FA/04	16/3
	RECEIVERS						
85	Conwell, Ernie (TE)	6-2/255	8-17-72	10	Washington	FA/03	16/10
88	Gardner, Talman	6-1/210	3-10-80	3	Florida State	D7/03	11/1
89	Hall, Lamont (TE)	6-4/260	11-16-74	6	Clemson	FA/04	16/2
19	Henderson, Devery	5-11/200	3-26-82	2	LSU	D2/04	1/0
87	Horn, Joe	6-1/213	1-16-72	10	Itawamba JC	FA/00	16/16
84	Lewis, Michael	5-8/173	11-14-71	5	None	FA/01	14/1
80	Meier, Shad (TE)	6-4/255	6-7-78	5	Kansas State	FA/05	14/7
83	Stallworth, Donte'	6-0/196	11-10-80	4	Tennessee	D1a/02	16/10
82	Williams, Boo (TE)	6-4/265	6-22-79	5	Arkansas	FA/00	16/8
	OFFENSIVE LINEMEN						
65	Bentley, LeCharles (C)	6-2/313	11-7-79	4	Ohio State	D2/02	16/16
70	Brown, Jammal (T)	6-6/313	3-30-81	R	Oklahoma	D1/05	—
71	Folau, Spencer (T)	6-5/310	4-5-73	9	Idaho	FA/02	16/3
72	Gandy, Wayne (T)	6-4/315	2-10-71	12	Auburn	FA/03	16/16
61	Holland, Montrae (G)	6-2/322	5-21-80	3	Florida State	D4/03	13/13
47	Houser, Kevin (C)	6-2/252	8-23-77	6	Ohio State	FA/02	16/0
64	Jacox, Kendyl (G)	6-2/325	6-10-75	8	Kansas State	FA/02	13/13
75	Mayberry, Jermane (G)	6-4/325	8-29-73	10	Texas A&M-Kingsville	FA/04	12/12
67	Nesbit, Jamar (G/C)	6-4/328	12-17-76	7	South Carolina	FA/04	16/4
78	Stinchcomb, Jon (T)	6-5/315	8-27-79	3	Georgia	D2/03	4/0
	DEFENSIVE LINEMEN						
92	Bryant, Tony (E)	6-6/282	9-3-76	6	Florida State	FA/04	16/0
94	Grant, Charles (E)	6-3/290	9-3-78	4	Georgia	D1b/02	16/16
95	Green, Howard (T)	6-2/320	1-12-79	3	LSU	FA/03	14/12
93	Howard, Darren (E)	6-3/275	11-19-76	6	Kansas State	D2/00	13/12
99	Jefferson, Jason (T)	6-1/306	12-20-81	R	Wisconsin	D6/05	—
77	Leisle, Rodney (T)	6-3/315	2-5-81	1	UCLA	D5/04	2/0
91	Smith, Will (E)	6-3/282	8-4-81	2	Ohio State	D1/04	16/4
97	Sullivan, Johnathan (T)	6-3/315	1-21-81	3	Georgia	D1/03	7/4
79	Verdon, Jimmy (T)	6-3/280	11-4-81	R	Arizona State	D7/05	—
98	Whitehead, Willie (T)	6-3/300	1-26-73	7	Auburn	FA/99	8/0
66	Young, Brian (T)	6-2/298	7-8-77	6	UTEP	FA/04	15/15
	LINEBACKERS						
50	Allen, James	6-2/245	11-11-79	4	Oregon State	D3/02	16/10
57	Bockwoldt, Colby	6-1/237	4-14-81	2	BYU	D7/04	16/7
90	Fincher, Alfred	6-1/241	8-15-83	R	Connecticut	D3/05	—
54	Fisher, Levar	6-2/239	7-2-79	3	North Carolina State	FA/05	0/0
58	Grant, Cie	6-0/235	11-27-79	3	Ohio State	D3/03	0/0
52	Hodge, Sedrick	6-4/246	9-13-78	5	North Carolina	D3a/01	9/6
53	Knight, Roger	6-0/245	10-11-78	4	Wisconsin	FA/01	15/0
59	Rodgers, Derrick	6-0/230	10-14-71	9	Arizona State	T-Mia./03	8/8
56	Ruff, Orlando	6-3/253	9-28-76	7	Furman	FA/03	14/8
55	Watson, Courtney	6-1/246	9-18-80	2	Notre Dame	D2/04	12/8
	DEFENSIVE BACKS						
20	Bellamy, Jay (S)	5-11/200	7-8-72	12	Rutgers	FA/01	16/16
35	Brown, Fakhir (CB)	5-11/192	9-21-77	6	Grambling	FA/02	16/10
29	Bullocks, Josh (S)	6-0/207	2-28-83	R	Nebraska	D2/05	—
21	Craft, Jason (CB)	5-10/187	2-13-76	7	Colorado State	T-Jac./04	14/0
37	Gleason, Steve (S)	5-11/212	3-19-77	5	Washington State	FA/00	15/0
34	McKenzie, Mike (CB)	6-0/194	4-26-76	7	Memphis	T-GB/04	11/10
40	Mitchell, Mel (S)	6-1/222	2-10-79	4	Western Kentucky	D5/02	15/0
24	Smith, Dwight (S)	5-10/201	8-13-78	5	Akron	FA/05	16/16
22	Thomas, Fred (CB)	5-9/185	9-11-73	10	Tennessee-Martin	FA/00	15/7
28	Williams, Jimmy (CB)	5-11/190	3-10-79	5	Vanderbilt	FA/05	12/6
	SPECIALISTS						
17	Berger, Mitch (P)	6-4/228	6-24-72	11	Colorado	FA/03	16/0
3	Carney, John (K)	5-11/185	4-20-64	16	Notre Dame	FA/01	16/0

Abbreviations: D1—draft pick, first round; T—obtained in trade; FA—free-agent acquisition.

NEW ORLEANS SAINTS

2004 regular-season record: 8-8
Position: 2nd in NFC South

Sept.12—SEATTLE	L	7-21
Sept.19—SAN FRANCISCO	W	30-27
Sept.26—at St. Louis (OT)	W	28-25
Oct. 3—at Arizona	L	10-34
Oct. 10—TAMPA BAY	L	17-20
Oct. 17—MINNESOTA	L	31-38
Oct. 24—at Oakland	W	31-26
Oct. 31—Open date		
Nov. 7—at San Diego	L	17-43
Nov. 14—KANSAS CITY	W	27-20
Nov. 21—DENVER	L	13-34
Nov. 28—at Atlanta	L	21-24
Dec. 5—CAROLINA	L	21-32
Dec. 12—at Dallas	W	27-13
Dec. 19—at Tampa Bay	W	21-17
Dec. 26—ATLANTA	W	26-13
Jan. 2—at Carolina	W	21-18

SCORING BY PERIODS

	Q1	Q2	Q3	Q4	OT	Pts.
Saints	29	132	83	101	3	348
Opponents	117	110	70	108	0	405

TEAM STATISTICS

	N.O.	Opp.
TOTAL FIRST DOWNS	291	343
Rushing	82	118
Passing	177	193
Penalty	32	32
3rd Down: Made/Att.	70/210	80/210
3rd Down Pct.	33.3	38.1
4th Down: Made/Att.	9/18	6/7
4th Down Pct.	50.0	85.7
POSSESSION AVG.	28:18	31:42
TOTAL NET YARDS	5193	6141
Avg. per Game	324.6	383.8
Total Plays	989	1067
Avg. per Play	5.3	5.8
NET YARDS RUSHING	1606	2253
Avg. per Game	100.4	140.8
Total Rushes	406	485
NET YARDS PASSING	3587	3888
Avg. per Game	224.2	243.0
Sacked/Yards Lost	41/223	37/207
Gross Yards	3810	4095
Att./Completions	542/309	545/324
Completion Pct.	57.0	59.4
Had Intercepted	16	13
PUNTS/AVERAGE	85/43.6	71/40.8
NET PUNTING AVG.	85/39.0	71/34.5
PENALTIES/YARDS	129/1141	119/965
FUMBLES/LOST	23/10	31/20
TOUCHDOWNS	40	44
Rushing	15	16
Passing	21	24
Returns	4	4

SCORING (NON-KICKERS)

	Tot. TD	RTD	PTD	MTD	2Pt.	Tot. Pts.
Horn	11	0	11	0	1	68
McAllister	9	9	0	0	0	54
Stallworth	5	0	5	0	0	30
Brooks	4	4	0	0	0	24
Stecker	3	2	0	1	0	18
B. Williams	2	0	2	0	0	12
Bockwoldt	1	0	0	1	0	6
Conwell	1	0	1	0	0	6
L. Hall	1	0	1	0	0	6
M. Lewis	1	0	0	1	0	6
Mitchell	1	0	0	1	0	6
Pathon	1	0	1	0	0	6
Saints	40	15	21	4	1	244
Opponents	44	16	24	4	2	270

2-Pt. conversions: Saints 1-2; Opponents 2-2.

(KICKERS)

	XPM/XPA	FGM/FGA	Pts.
Carney	38/38	22/27	104
Saints	38/38	22/27	104
Opponents	42/42	31/35	135

RUSHING

	Att.	Yds.	Avg.	Lg.	TD
McAllister	269	1074	4.0	71	9
Stecker	58	244	4.2	t42	2
Brooks	58	173	3.0	15	4
McAfee	2	54	27.0	53	0
Stallworth	6	37	6.2	26	0
K. Carter	10	17	1.7	8	0
Karney	3	7	2.3	4	0
Saints	406	1606	4.0	71	15
Opponents	485	2253	4.6	60	16

RECEIVING

	No.	Yds.	Avg.	Lg.	TD
Horn	94	1399	14.9	57	11
Stallworth	58	767	13.2	45	5
McAllister	34	228	6.7	20	0
Pathon	34	581	17.1	38	1
B. Williams	33	362	11.0	22	2
Stecker	29	174	6.0	26	0
Conwell	10	102	10.2	28	1
M. Lewis	8	127	15.9	30	0
Karney	6	42	7.0	17	0
Brooks	1	1	1.0	1	0
Gardner	1	23	23.0	23	0
L. Hall	1	4	4.0	t4	1
Saints	309	3810	12.3	57	21
Opponents	324	4095	12.6	59	24

INTERCEPTIONS

	No.	Yds.	Avg.	Lg.	TD
McKenzie	5	19	3.8	14	0
Ambrose	3	19	6.3	19	0
Brown	2	0	0.0	0	0
Jones	1	55	55.0	55	0
Ch. Grant	1	8	8.0	8	0
Ruff	1	0	0.0	0	0
Saints	13	101	7.8	55	0
Opponents	16	260	16.3	76	1

SACKS: Howard 11.0, Ch. Grant 10.5, W. Smith 7.5, Young 2.5, Bryant 2.0, Watson 2.0, Bockwoldt 1.0, Sullivan 0.5. Saints 37.0; Opponents 41.0.

PUNTING

	No.	Yds.	Avg.	Lg.	TD
Berger	85	3704	43.6	28	63
Saints	85	3704	43.6	28	63
Opponents	71	2896	40.8	17	60

PUNT RETURNS

	No.	FC	Yds.	Avg.	Lg.	TD
M. Lewis	34	11	382	11.2	53	0
Stallworth	6	1	6	1.0	4	0
Saints	40	12	388	9.7	53	0
Opponents	43	25	310	7.2	t59	1

KICK RETURNS

	No.	Yds.	Avg.	Lg.	TD
M. Lewis	51	1215	23.8	t96	1
Stecker	18	469	26.1	t98	1
McAfee	8	137	17.1	26	0
L. Hall	3	20	6.7	8	0
Ruff	1	9	9.0	9	0
W. Smith	1	17	17.0	17	0
Whitehead	1	12	12.0	12	0
Saints	83	1879	22.6	t98	2
Opponents	74	1710	23.1	63	0

FIELD GOALS

	No.	Yds.	Avg.	Lg.	TD
Carney	0/0	3/3	12/15	5/6	2/3
Saints	0/0	3/3	12/15	5/6	2/3
Opponents	0/0	10/10	9/10	8/10	4/5

Carney: () (32G, 36G, 37G) (52G, 53G, 39G, 51N, 38G, 31G) (20G) (47G) (45G) (41G) (46N, 37G) (39G, 38G) (24G, 36G) (48G, 38G, 37B) () (39G, 44G) (38N) (22G) (38N)
Opponents: () (30G, 33G) (53G) (26G, 33G) (23G, 53G, 41N) (39G) (28G, 42G, 44G, 40G) (40G, 27G) (24G, 44G) (48G, 34G) (37N, 31G) (30G, 50G, 46G, 25G, 21G, 21G) (42N, 34G, 41G) (37G) (25G, 20G) (54G, 60B)

PASSING

	Att.	Cmp.	Yds.	Pct.	Avg. Gain	TD	Pct. TD	Int.	Pct. Int.	Long	Sack/Lost	Rating
Brooks	542	309	3810	57.0	7.03	21	3.9	16	3.0	57	41/223	79.5
Saints	542	309	3810	57.0	7.03	21	3.9	16	3.0	57	41/223	79.5
Opponents	545	324	4095	59.4	7.51	24	4.4	13	2.4	59	37/207	87.7

NEW YORK GIANTS
NFC EAST DIVISION

2005 SEASON

CLUB DIRECTORY

President/co-CEO
Wellington T. Mara
Chairman/co-CEO
Preston Robert Tisch
COO/general counsel
John K. Mara
Vice president/general manager
Ernie Accorsi
Assistant general manager
Kevin Abrams
Director/player personnel
Jerry Reese
Director/pro personnel
Dave Gettleman
Director/research and development
Raymond J. Walsh Jr.
Vice president for player evaluation
Chris Mara
Director/college scouting
Jerry Shay
Vice president of communications
Pat Hanlon
Director of community relations
Allison Stangeby

OFFSEASON MOVES

Key additions
WR Plaxico Burress	FA/Steelers
DT Kendrick Clancy	FA/Steelers
K Jay Feely	FA/Falcons
QB Tim Hasselbeck	FA/Redskins
OT Kareem McKenzie	FA/Jets
LB Antonio Pierce	FA/Redskins
OT Bob Whitfield	FA/Jaguars

Key losses
DE Lorenzo Bromell	Released
DT Martin Chase	Rel./Jaguars
CB Terry Cousin	Rel./Jaguars
RB Ron Dayne	FA/Broncos
DT Norman Hand	Released
WR Ike Hilliard	FA/Buccaneers
DL Lance Legree	FA/Jets
LB Wesly Mallard	FA/Patriots
TE Marcellus Rivers	Free agent
OL Barry Stokes	Released
S Omar Stoutmire	Released
QB Kurt Warner	FA/Cardinals
DL Keith Washington	Released

Head coach
Tom Coughlin

Assistant coaches
Andy Barnett (asst. strength & conditioning)
John DeFilippo (offensive quality control)
Dave DeGuglielmo (asst. offensive line)
Pat Flaherty (offensive line)
Kevin Gilbride (quarterbacks)
John Hufnagel (off. coordinator)
Jerald Ingram (running backs)
Tim Lewis (def. coordinator)
Dave Merritt (defensive asst.)
Ron Milus (defensive secondary)
Jerry Palmieri (strength & conditioning)
Michael Pope (tight ends)
Mike Priefer (asst. special teams)
Bill Sheridan (linebackers)
Mike Sullivan (wide receivers)
Mike Sweatman (special teams coordinator)
Mike Waufle (defensive line)

SCHEDULE

Sept. 11—ARIZONA	4:15
Sept. 18—at New Orleans	1:00
Sept. 25—at San Diego	8:30
Oct. 2—ST. LOUIS	1:00
Oct. 9—Open date	
Oct. 16—at Dallas	1:00
Oct. 23—DENVER	4:15
Oct. 30—WASHINGTON	2:00
Nov. 6—at San Francisco	5:05
Nov. 13—MINNESOTA	2:00
Nov. 20—PHILADELPHIA	2:00
Nov. 27—at Seattle	5:15
Dec. 4—DALLAS	2:00
Dec. 11—at Philadelphia	5:05
Dec. 17—KANSAS CITY (Sat.)	6:00
Dec. 24—at Washington (Sat.)	2:00
Dec. 31—at Oakland (Sat.)	9:00

All times are Eastern.
All games Sunday unless noted.

DRAFT CHOICES

Corey Webster, CB, LSU (second round/43rd pick overall).
Justin Tuck, DE, Notre Dame (3/74).
Brandon Jacobs, RB, Southern Illinois (4/110).
Eric Moore, DE, Florida State (6/186).

MISCELLANEOUS TEAM DATA

Stadium (capacity, surface):
Giants Stadium
(80,242, artificial)
Business address:
East Rutherford, N.J. 07073
Business phone:
201-935-8111
Ticket information:
201-935-8222
Team colors:
Blue, white and red
Flagship radio station:
WFAN, 660 AM
Website:
www.giants.com
Training site:
University at Albany
Albany, N.Y.
201-935-8111

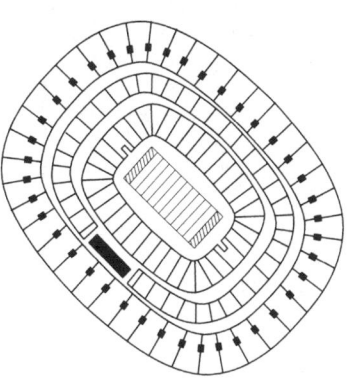

NEW YORK GIANTS

No.	QUARTERBACKS	Ht./Wt.	Born	NFL Exp.	College	How acq.	'04 Games GP/GS
8	Hasselbeck, Tim	6-1/211	4-6-78	3	Boston College	W-Was./05	0/0
	Lorenzen, Jared	6-4/275	2-14-81	1	Kentucky	FA/04	0/0
10	Manning, Eli	6-4/218	1-3-81	2	Mississippi	T-SD/04	9/7
3	Palmer, Jesse	6-2/225	10-5-78	3	Florida	D4b/01	0/0
	RUNNING BACKS						
21	Barber, Tiki	5-10/200	4-7-75	9	Virginia	D2/97	16/14
30	Cloud, Mike	5-10/205	7-1-75	7	Boston College	FA/03	10/0
20	Finn, Jim (FB)	6-0/245	12-2-76	6	Pennsylvania	FA/03	16/9
47	Grant, Ryan	6-1/218	12-9-82	R	Notre Dame	FA/05	—
27	Jacobs, Brandon	6-4/256	7-6-82	R	Southern Illinois	D4/05	—
44	Lawton, Luke (FB)	5-11/237	8-26-80	1	McNeese State	FA/04	0/0
34	Ward, Derrick	5-11/233	8-30-80	2	Ottawa (Kan.)	D7c/04	5/0
	RECEIVERS						
17	Burress, Plaxico	6-5/226	8-12-77	6	Michigan State	FA/05	11/11
84	Carter, Tim	6-0/200	9-21-79	4	Auburn	D2/02	5/0
89	Jones, Mark	5-9/185	11-3-80	2	Tennessee	W-TB/04	14/0
88	Luzar, Chris (TE)	6-7/265	2-12-79	3	Virginia	D4b/02	0/0
87	Ponder, Willie	6-0/205	2-14-80	3	Southeast Missouri	D6a/03	11/0
82	Shiancoe, Visanthe (TE)	6-4/250	6-18-80	3	Morgan State	D3/03	16/7
80	Shockey, Jeremy (TE)	6-5/253	8-18-80	4	Miami	D1/02	15/15
86	Taylor, Jamaar	6-0/197	2-25-81	2	Texas A&M	D6/04	8/0
81	Toomer, Amani	6-3/208	9-8-74	10	Michigan	D2/96	15/14
85	Tyree, David	6-0/205	1-3-80	3	Syracuse	D6c/03	16/1
	OFFENSIVE LINEMEN						
66	Diehl, David (G)	6-5/315	9-15-80	3	Illinois	D5/03	16/16
78	Hilliard, Jason (T)	6-6/328	6-29-81	1	Louisville	FA/04	2/0
62	Lucier, Wayne (C)	6-3/300	12-5-79	3	Colorado	D7/03	15/9
67	McKenzie, Kareem (T)	6-6/327	5-24-79	5	Penn State	FA/05	16/16
60	O'Hara, Shaun (C)	6-3/306	6-23-77	6	Rutgers	FA/00	12/12
77	Petitgout, Luke (T)	6-6/310	6-16-76	7	Notre Dame	D1/99	16/16
69	Seubert, Rich (G)	6-5/305	3-30-79	4	Western Illinois	FA/01	0/0
76	Snee, Chris (G)	6-2/314	1-8-82	2	Boston College	D2/04	11/11
71	Whitfield, Bob (T)	6-5/310	10-18-71	14	Stanford	FA/05	10/0
65	Whittle, Jason (G)	6-4/305	3-7-75	7	Southwest Missouri	T-TB/04	16/16
68	Winey, Brandon (T)	6-6/311	1-27-78	3	LSU	FA/03	13/0
	DEFENSIVE LINEMEN						
97	Allen, Kenderick (T)	6-6/315	9-14-78	3	LSU	FA/03	5/2
70	Clancy, Kendrick (T)	6-1/292	9-17-78	6	Mississippi	FA/05	8/0
99	Duckett, Damane (T)	6-6/300	1-21-81	2	East Carolina	FA/04	6/1
94	Joseph, William (T)	6-5/315	9-3-79	3	Miami	D1/03	15/4
90	Kuehl, Ryan (T)	6-5/280	1-18-72	8	Virginia	FA/03	16/0
93	Moore, Eric (E)	6-4/255	2-28-81	R	Florida State	D6/05	—
64	Orr, Raheem (E)	6-3/258	11-8-80	1	Rutgers	FA/04	2/0
98	Robbins, Fred (T)	6-4/325	3-25-77	6	Wake Forest	FA/04	15/15
92	Strahan, Michael (E)	6-5/275	11-21-71	13	Texas Southern	D2/93	8/8
91	Tuck, Justin (E)	6-4/256	3-29-83	R	Notre Dame	D3/05	—
72	Umenyiora, Osi (E)	6-3/280	11-16-80	3	Troy	D2/03	16/7
96	Williams, Davern (T)	6-3/305	2-13-80	2	Troy	FA/04	2/1
	LINEBACKERS						
51	Emmons, Carlos	6-5/250	9-3-73	10	Arkansas State	FA/04	15/15
52	Green, Barrett	6-0/225	10-29-77	6	West Virginia	FA/04	10/9
54	Greisen, Nick	6-1/245	8-10-79	4	Wisconsin	D5/02	15/7
55	Hollowell, T.J.	6-0/235	4-8-81	2	Nebraska	FA/04	4/0
59	Lewis, Kevin	6-1/235	10-6-78	6	Duke	FA/00	16/16
57	Maxwell, James	6-4/242	8-8-81	2	Gardner-Webb	FA/04	14/0
53	Pierce, Antonio	6-1/240	10-26-78	5	Arizona	FA/05	16/16
58	Torbor, Reggie	6-2/254	1-25-81	2	Auburn	D4/04	16/1
	DEFENSIVE BACKS						
26	Alexander, Brent (S)	5-11/200	7-10-71	12	Tennessee State	FA/00	16/16
25	Allen, Will (CB)	5-10/196	8-5-78	5	Syracuse	D1/01	16/16
22	Brewer, Jack (S)	6-0/194	1-8-79	4	Minnesota	W-Min./04	13/0
29	Burns, Curry (S)	6-0/216	2-12-81	2	Louisville	D7/03	8/2
39	Deloatch, Curtis (CB)	6-2/217	10-4-81	2	North Carolina A&T	FA/04	16/0
24	Peterson, Will (CB)	6-0/200	6-15-79	5	Western Illinois	D3/01	16/15
41	Walker, Frank (CB)	5-10/198	8-6-80	3	Tuskegee	D6b/03	13/1
23	Webster, Corey (CB)	6-0/204	3-2-82	R	LSU	D2/05	—
36	Williams, Shaun (S)	6-2/218	10-10-76	7	UCLA	D1/98	2/2
28	Wilson, Gibril (S)	6-0/197	11-12-81	2	Tennessee	D5/04	8/7
	SPECIALISTS						
18	Feagles, Jeff (P)	6-1/215	3-7-66	18	Miami	FA/03	16/0
2	Feely, Jay (K)	5-10/206	5-23-76	5	Michigan	FA/05	16/0

Abbreviations: D1—draft pick, first round; W—claimed on waivers; T—obtained in trade; FA—free-agent acquisition.

2004 regular-season record: 6-10
Position: 2nd in NFC East

Sept.12—at Philadelphia	L	17-31
Sept.19—WASHINGTON	W	20-14
Sept.26—CLEVELAND	W	27-10
Oct. 3—at Green Bay	W	14-7
Oct. 10—at Dallas	W	26-10
Oct. 17—Open date		
Oct. 24—DETROIT	L	13-28
Oct. 31—at Minnesota	W	34-13
Nov. 7—CHICAGO	L	21-28
Nov.14—at Arizona	L	14-17
Nov.21—ATLANTA	L	10-14
Nov.28—PHILADELPHIA	L	6-27
Dec. 5—at Washington	L	7-31
Dec.12—at Baltimore	L	14-37
Dec.18—PITTSBURGH	L	30-33
Dec.26—at Cincinnati	L	22-23
Jan. 2—DALLAS	W	28-24

SCORING BY PERIODS

	Q1	Q2	Q3	Q4	OT	Pts.
Giants	72	79	55	97	0	303
Opponents	72	114	71	90	0	347

TEAM STATISTICS

	NYG	Opp.
TOTAL FIRST DOWNS	281	310
Rushing	105	112
Passing	143	170
Penalty	33	28
3rd Down: Made/Att.	56/190	87/208
3rd Down Pct.	29.5	41.8
4th Down: Made/Att.	4/19	6/14
4th Down Pct.	21.1	42.9
POSSESSION AVG.	28:52	31:08
TOTAL NET YARDS	4722	5187
Avg. per Game	295.1	324.2
Total Plays	951	1005
Avg. per Play	5.0	5.2
NET YARDS RUSHING	1904	2157
Avg. per Game	119.0	134.8
Total Rushes	424	498
NET YARDS PASSING	2818	3030
Avg. per Game	176.1	189.4
Sacked/Yards Lost	52/279	40/250
Gross Yards	3097	3280
Att./Completions	475/269	467/292
Completion Pct.	56.6	62.5
Had Intercepted	13	14
PUNTS/AVERAGE	77/40.1	77/38.9
NET PUNTING AVG.	77/34.4	77/33.8
PENALTIES/YARDS	118/977	120/1007
FUMBLES/LOST	29/11	27/14
TOUCHDOWNS	34	41
Rushing	18	13
Passing	12	28
Returns	4	0

SCORING (NON-KICKERS)

	Tot. TD	RTD	PTD	MTD	2Pt.	Tot. Pts.
Barber	15	13	2	0	0	90
Shockey	6	0	6	0	0	36
Cloud	3	3	0	0	0	18
T. Carter	1	0	1	0	0	6
Dayne	1	1	0	0	0	6
Green	1	0	0	1	0	6
Ponder	1	0	1	0	0	6
Rivers	1	0	1	0	0	6
Shiancoe	1	0	1	0	0	6
Tyree	1	0	1	0	0	6
Umenyiora	1	0	0	1	0	6
Ward	1	0	0	1	0	6
Warner	1	1	0	0	0	6
Giants	34	18	12	4	0	204
Opponents	41	13	28	0	2	250

2-Pt. conversions: Giants 0-1; Opponents 2-4.

(KICKERS)

	XPM/XPA	FGM/FGA	Pts.
Christie	33/33	22/28	99
Giants	33/33	22/28	99
Opponents	37/37	20/25	97

RUSHING

	Att.	Yds.	Avg.	Lg.	TD
Barber	322	1518	4.7	t72	13
Dayne	52	179	3.4	15	1
Cloud	21	90	4.3	26	3
Manning	6	35	5.8	15	0
I. Hilliard	3	34	11.3	17	0
Warner	13	30	2.3	13	1
T. Carter	2	23	11.5	15	0
Finn	3	7	2.3	5	0
Ponder	1	-4	-4.0	-4	0
Taylor	1	-8	-8.0	-8	0
Giants	424	1904	4.5	t72	18
Opponents	498	2157	4.3	50	13

RECEIVING

	No.	Yds.	Avg.	Lg.	TD
Shockey	61	666	10.9	38	6
Barber	52	578	11.1	t62	2
Toomer	51	747	14.6	48	0
I. Hilliard	49	437	8.9	43	0
Finn	15	112	7.5	15	0
T. Carter	12	182	15.2	t38	1
Tyree	10	155	15.5	49	1
Taylor	6	146	24.3	52	0
Rivers	5	36	7.2	13	1
Shiancoe	5	25	5.0	9	1
Cloud	1	3	3.0	3	0
Dayne	1	7	7.0	7	0
Ponder	1	3	3.0	3	0
Giants	269	3097	11.5	t62	12
Opponents	292	3280	11.2	53	28

INTERCEPTIONS

	No.	Yds.	Avg.	Lg.	TD
Wilson	3	39	13.0	39	0
Alexander	3	3	1.0	2	0
F. Walker	2	20	10.0	10	0
Peterson	2	9	4.5	9	0
Robbins	1	13	13.0	13	0
Burns	1	12	12.0	12	0
W. Allen	1	11	11.0	11	0
Cousin	1	6	6.0	6	0
Giants	14	113	8.1	39	0
Opponents	13	134	10.3	41	0

SACKS: Umenyiora 7.0, Robbins 5.0, Strahan 4.0, Torbor 3.0, Wilson 3.0, Alexander 2.0, Greisen 2.0, Joseph 2.0, Legree 2.0, Allen 1.0, W. Allen 1.0, Duckett 1.0, Emmons 1.0, Hand 1.0, Lewis 1.0, Maxwell 1.0, Washington 1.0, Wiley 0.5, Williams 0.5. Giants 40.0; Opponents 52.0.

PUNTING

	No.	Yds.	Avg.	In. 20	Lg
Christie	1	19	19.0	1	19
Feagles	74	3069	41.5	23	55
Giants	77	3088	40.1	24	55
Opponents	77	2997	38.9	19	58

PUNT RETURNS

	No.	FC	Yds.	Avg.	Lg.	TD
Jones	34	11	227	6.7	29	0
I. Hilliard	4	0	26	6.5	15	0
Giants	38	11	253	6.7	29	0
Opponents	38	15	356	9.4	42	0

KICK RETURNS

	No.	Yds.	Avg.	Lg.	TD
Ponder	36	967	26.9	t91	1
Ward	16	436	27.3	t92	1
Cloud	8	175	21.9	38	0
Jones	2	37	18.5	20	0
Dayne	1	11	11.0	11	0
Finn	1	16	16.0	16	0
Rivers	1	8	8.0	8	0
Shiancoe	1	8	8.0	8	0
Giants	66	1658	25.1	t92	2
Opponents	66	1278	19.4	49	0

FIELD GOALS

	1-19	20-29	30-39	40-49	50+
Christie	1/1	8/8	6/8	4/7	3/4
Giants	1/1	8/8	6/8	4/7	3/4
Opponents	0/0	6/6	2/3	12/14	0/2

Christie: (53G) (47N, 38G, 22G, 51B) (43G, 25G) (49N, 30N, 33N) (31G, 51G, 47G, 26G) (19G, 25G) (50G, 30G) () (44B) (24G) (22G, 31G) () () (22G) (31G, 36G, 44G, 41G, 28G) () Opponents: (45G, 53N) (41N) (49G) () (41G, 52N) () (38N) (22G, 21G) (41G) (46N) (47G, 42G) (46G) (46G, 44G, 27G) (33G, 21G, 36G, 28G) (42G) (40G, 24G, 45G)

PASSING

	Att.	Cmp.	Yds.	Pct.	Avg. Gain	TD	Pct. TD	Int.	Pct. Int.	Long	Sack/Lost	Rating
Warner	277	174	2054	62.8	7.42	6	2.2	4	1.4	t62	39/196	86.5
Manning	197	95	1043	48.2	5.29	6	3.0	9	4.6	52	13/83	55.4
Feagles	1	0	0.0	0.0	0.00	0	0.0	0	0.0	...	0/0	39.6
Giants	475	269	3097	56.6	6.52	12	2.5	13	2.7	t62	52/279	73.5
Opponents	467	292	3280	62.5	7.02	28	6.0	14	3.0	53	40/250	90.9

NEW YORK GIANTS

NEW YORK JETS
AFC EAST DIVISION

2005 SEASON

CLUB DIRECTORY

Chairman and CEO
Robert Wood Johnson IV
President
Jay Cross
Exec. vice president/general manager
Terry Bradway
Senior vp football operations/asst. G.M.
Mike Tannenbaum
Vp, player development
Kevin Winston
Director, pro personnel
JoJo Wooden
Assistant director, pro personnel
Brian Gaine
Director, football administration
Dawn Aponte
Senior director, college scouting
Jesse Kaye
National scout
Joey Clinkscales
Vp, public relations
Ron Colangelo

Head coach
Herman
Edwards

Assistant coaches
Sal Alosi (asst. director of physical development)
Jeremy Bates (quarterbacks)
Tim Berbenich (offensive asst.)
Corwin Brown (defensive backs)
Bob Casullo (tight ends)
Dick Curl (asst. to the head coach/running backs)
Pep Hamilton (wide receivers)
Mike Heimerdinger (offensive coordinator)
Donnie Henderson (defensive coordinator)
Denny Marcin (defensive line)
Doug Marrone (offensive line)
Chris Mattura (defensive asst.)
Markus Paul (director of physical development)
Bob Sutton (linebackers)
Nate Wainwright (asst. coach)
Mike Westhoff (asst. head coach /special teams coordinator)
John Zernhelt (tight ends)

OFFSEASON MOVES

Key additions
RB Derrick Blaylock	FA/Chiefs
WR Laveranues Coles	Trade/Redskins
QB Jay Fiedler	Rel./Dolphins
LB Barry Gardner	FA/Browns
TE Doug Jolley	Trade/Raiders
DL Lance Legree	FA/Giants

Key losses
TE Anthony Becht	FA/Buccaneers
K Doug Brien	Rel./Bears
LB Sam Cowart	Trade/Vikings
DT Josh Evans	Retired
DT Jason Ferguson	FA/Cowboys
P Toby Gowin	FA/Falcons
RB LaMont Jordan	FA/Raiders
OT Kareem McKenzie	FA/Giants
WR Santana Moss	Trade/Jets
QB Ricky Ray	Released
OL Brent Smith	Rel./Jaguars

SCHEDULE

Sept.	11—at Kansas City	1:00
Sept.	18—MIAMI	4:15
Sept.	25—JACKSONVILLE	1:00
Oct.	2—at Baltimore	4:05
Oct.	9—TAMPA BAY	1:00
Oct.	16—at Buffalo	4:15
Oct.	24—at Atlanta (Mon.)	9:00
Oct.	30—Open date	
Nov.	6—SAN DIEGO	2:00
Nov.	13—at Carolina	5:05
Nov.	20—at Denver	5:15
Nov.	27—NEW ORLEANS	9:30
Dec.	4—at New England	5:15
Dec.	11—OAKLAND	2:00
Dec.	18—at Miami	2:00
Dec.	26—NEW ENGLAND (Mon.)	10:00
Jan.	1—BUFFALO	2:00

All times are Eastern.
All games Sunday unless noted.

DRAFT CHOICES

Mike Nugent, K, Ohio State (second round/47th pick overall).
Justin Miller, CB, Clemson (2/57).
Sione Pouha, DT, Utah (3/88).
Kerry Rhodes, FS, Louisville (4/123).
Andre Maddox, SS, North Carolina State (5/161).
Cedric Houston, RB, Tennessee (6/182).
Joel Dreessen, TE, Colorado State (6/198).
Harry Williams, WR, Tuskegee (7/240).

MISCELLANEOUS TEAM DATA

Stadium (capacity, surface):
The Meadowlands
(80,062, artificial)
Business address:
1000 Fulton Avenue
Hempstead, NY 11550
50 W. 57th,
New York, NY 10019
Business phone:
516-560-8100, 212-969-1800
Ticket information:
516-560-8200
Team colors:
Green and white
Flagship radio station:
ESPN Radio

Website:
www.newyorkjets.com
Training site:
Hofstra University
Hempstead, N.Y.
516-560-8288

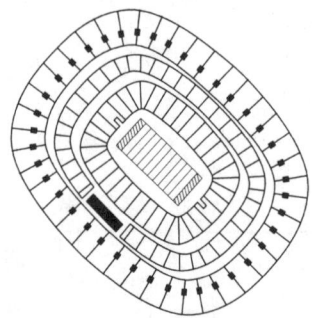

NEW YORK JETS

No.	QUARTERBACKS	Ht./Wt.	Born	NFL Exp.	College	How acq.	'04 Games GP/GS
5	Bollinger, Brooks	6-1/205	11-15-79	3	Wisconsin	D6/03	1/0
9	Fiedler, Jay	6-2/225	12-29-71	10	Dartmouth	FA/05	8/7
10	Pennington, Chad	6-3/225	6-26-76	6	Marshall	D1c/00	13/13
	RUNNING BACKS						
35	Askew, B.J. (FB)	6-3/233	8-19-80	3	Michigan	D3/03	16/0
23	Blaylock, Derrick	5-9/210	8-23-79	5	Stephen F. Austin	FA/05	12/5
39	Houston, Cedric	5-11/225	6-28-82	R	Tennessee	D6a/05	—
30	Joyce, Delvin	5-7/195	9-21-78	3	James Madison	FA/05	0/0
28	Martin, Curtis	5-11/210	5-1-73	11	Pittsburgh	FA/98	16/16
33	Sowell, Jerald (FB)	6-0/237	1-21-74	9	Tulane	W-GB/97	16/16
	RECEIVERS						
86	Baker, Chris (TE)	6-3/258	11-18-79	4	Michigan State	D3/02	16/0
84	Carter, Jonathan	6-0/180	3-20-79	4	Troy	W-NYG/02	13/1
80	Chrebet, Wayne	5-10/188	8-14-73	11	Hofstra	FA/95	16/1
87	Coles, Laveranues	5-11/193	12-29-77	6	Florida State	T-Was./05	16/16
89	Cotchery, Jerricho	6-0/207	6-16-82	2	North Carolina State	D4a/04	12/0
85	Dearth, James (TE)	6-4/270	1-22-76	5	Tarleton State	FA/00	16/0
49	Dreessen, Joel (TE)	6-4/260	7-26-82	R	Colorado State	D6b/05	—
88	Jolley, Doug (TE)	6-4/250	1-2-79	4	Brigham Young	T-Oak./05	16/13
81	McCareins, Justin	6-2/215	12-11-78	5	Northern Illinois	T-Ten./04	16/16
18	Williams, Harry	6-3/180	8-10-82	R	Tuskegee	D7/05	—
	OFFENSIVE LINEMEN						
77	Cavka, Marko (T)	6-7/294	4-4-81	1	Sacramento State	D6/04	0/0
69	Fabini, Jason (T)	6-7/304	8-25-74	8	Cincinnati	D4/98	16/16
78	Goodwin, Jonathan (C/G)	6-3/318	12-2-78	4	Michigan	D5/02	15/3
79	Jones, Adrian (T)	6-4/296	6-10-81	2	Kansas	D4b/04	12/0
66	Kendall, Pete (G)	6-5/280	7-9-73	10	Boston College	FA/04	15/15
68	Mawae, Kevin (C)	6-4/289	1-23-71	12	LSU	FA/98	16/16
65	Moore, Brandon (G)	6-3/295	6-3-80	3	Illinois	FA/02	13/13
64	Yovanovits, Dave (G)	6-3/294	3-6-81	3	Temple	D7/03	4/0
	DEFENSIVE LINEMEN						
94	Abraham, John (E)	6-4/256	5-6-78	6	South Carolina	D1b/00	12/12
92	Ellis, Shaun (E)	6-5/285	6-24-77	6	Tennessee	D1a/00	15/15
98	Harper, Alan (T)	6-1/285	9-6-79	4	Fresno State	D4/02	11/0
97	Johnson, Trevor (E)	6-4/260	2-26-81	2	Nebraska	D7b/04	16/0
70	Legree, Lance (T)	6-1/300	12-22-77	5	Notre Dame	FA/05	15/7
91	Pouha, Sione (T)	6-3/330	2-3-79	R	Utah	D3/05	—
93	Reed, James (T)	6-0/286	2-3-77	5	Iowa State	D7a/01	16/0
63	Robertson, Dewayne (T)	6-1/317	10-16-81	3	Kentucky	D1/03	16/16
99	Thomas, Bryan (E)	6-4/266	6-7-79	4	UAB	D1/02	14/6
	LINEBACKERS						
50	Barton, Eric	6-2/245	9-29-77	7	Maryland	FA/04	16/15
55	Brown, Mark	6-0/238	5-19-80	2	Auburn	FA/03	12/6
53	Gardner, Barry	6-1/245	12-13-76	7	Northwestern	FA/05	14/5
54	Hobson, Victor	6-0/252	2-3-80	3	Michigan	D2/03	12/0
57	McClover, Darrell	6-2/226	8-25-81	2	Miami	D7a/04	16/0
51	Vilma, Jonathan	6-1/230	4-16-82	2	Miami	D1/04	16/14
52	Wright, Kenyatta	6-0/240	2-19-78	5	Oklahoma State	FA/03	16/0
	DEFENSIVE BACKS						
29	Abraham, Donnie (CB)	5-10/192	10-8-73	10	East Tennessee St.	FA/02	16/16
36	Barrett, David (CB)	5-10/195	12-22-77	6	Arkansas	FA/04	16/16
45	Celestin, Oliver (S)	6-0/207	2-25-81	2	Texas Southern	FA/04	8/0
26	Coleman, Erik (S)	5-10/200	5-6-82	2	Washington State	D5/04	16/16
41	Maddox, Andre (S)	6-1/205	10-8-82	R	North Carolina State	D5/05	—
38	McGraw, Jon (S)	6-3/206	4-2-79	4	Kansas State	D2/02	12/1
24	Mickens, Ray (CB)	5-8/180	1-4-73	9	Texas A&M	D3/96	0/0
34	Miller, Justin (CB)	5-10/202	2-14-84	R	Clemson	D2b/05	—
20	Pagel, Derek (S)	6-1/208	10-24-79	3	Iowa	D5a/03	5/0
37	Rhodes, Kerry (S)	6-2/209	8-2-82	R	Louisville	D4/05	—
21	Strait, Derrick (CB)	5-11/189	8-27-80	2	Oklahoma	D3/04	5/1
25	Tongue, Reggie (S)	6-0/204	4-11-73	10	Oregon State	FA/04	16/16
42	Washington, Rashad (S)	6-1/217	3-15-80	2	Kansas State	D7d/04	6/0
	SPECIALISTS						
4	Knorr, Micah (P)	6-2/199	1-9-75	6	Utah State	FA/05	12/0
1	Nugent, Mike (K)	5-10/182	3-2-82	R	Ohio State	D2a/05	—

Abbreviations: D1—draft pick, first round; W—claimed on waivers; T—obtained in trade; FA—free-agent acquisition.

NEW YORK JETS

2004 regular-season record: 10-6
Position: 2nd in AFC East

Sept.12—CINCINNATI	W	31-24
Sept.19—at San Diego	W	34-28
Sept.26—Open date		
Oct. 3—at Miami	W	17-9
Oct. 10—BUFFALO	W	16-14
Oct. 17—SAN FRANCISCO	W	22-14
Oct. 24—at New England	L	7-13
Nov. 1—MIAMI	W	41-14
Nov. 7—at Buffalo	L	17-22
Nov. 14—BALTIMORE (OT)	L	17-20
Nov. 21—at Cleveland	W	10-7
Nov. 28—at Arizona	W	13-3
Dec. 5—HOUSTON	W	29-7
Dec. 12—at Pittsburgh	L	6-17
Dec. 19—SEATTLE	W	37-14
Dec. 26—NEW ENGLAND	L	7-23
Jan. 2—at St. Louis (OT)	L	29-32

2004 postseason record: 1-1

Jan. 8—at San Diego (OT)#	W	20-17
Jan. 15—at Pittsburgh (OT)*	L	17-20

#AFC wild-card game. *AFC divisional play-off game.

SCORING BY PERIODS

	Q1	Q2	Q3	Q4	OT	Pts.
Jets	51	94	95	93	0	333
Opponents	34	104	34	83	6	261

TEAM STATISTICS

	NYJ	Opp.
TOTAL FIRST DOWNS ..	313	282
Rushing	135	87
Passing	163	169
Penalty	15	26
3rd Down: Made/Att. ..	91/214	79/208
3rd Down Pct.	42.5	38.0
4th Down: Made/Att.	4/8	5/13
4th Down Pct.	50.0	38.5
POSSESSION AVG.	31:51	28:09
TOTAL NET YARDS	5438	4878
Avg. per Game	339.9	304.9
Total Plays	996	966
Avg. per Play	5.5	5.0
NET YARDS RUSHING ..	2388	1566
Avg. per Game	149.3	97.9
Total Rushes	527	432
NET YARDS PASSING....	3050	3312
Avg. per Game	190.6	207.0
Sacked/Yards Lost	31/181	37/220
Gross Yards	3231	3532
Att./Completions	438/282	497/289
Completion Pct.	64.4	58.1
Had Intercepted	11	19
PUNTS/AVERAGE	80/38.2	89/40.1
NET PUNTING AVG.	80/33.5	89/34.8
PENALTIES/YARDS	91/693	86/720

	NYJ	Opp.
FUMBLES/LOST	19/5	29/14
TOUCHDOWNS	38	30
Rushing	15	8
Passing	19	21
Returns	4	1

SCORING (NON-KICKERS)

	Tot. TD	RTD	PTD	MTD	2Pt.	Tot. Pts.
C. Martin	14	12	2	0	0	84
Moss	5	0	5	0	0	30
Baker	4	0	4	0	0	24
McCareins	4	0	4	0	0	24
D. Abraham	2	0	0	2	0	12
Jordan	2	2	0	0	0	12
Becht	1	0	1	0	0	6
Carter	1	0	1	0	0	6
Chrebet	1	0	1	0	0	6
Cotchery	1	0	0	1	0	6
Pennington	1	1	0	0	0	6
Sowell	1	0	1	0	0	6
Vilma	1	0	0	1	0	6
Jets	38	15	19	4	0	228
Opponents	30	8	21	1	1	184

2-Pt. conversions: Jets 0-4; Opponents 1-1.

(KICKERS)

	XPM/XPA	FGM/FGA	Pts.
Brien	33/34	24/29	105
Jets	33/34	24/29	105
Opponents	29/29	16/19	77

RUSHING

	Att.	Yds.	Avg.	Lg.	TD
C. Martin	371	1697	4.6	t25	12
Jordan	93	479	5.2	33	2
Pennington	34	126	3.7	16	1
Sowell	2	28	14.0	19	0
Askew	6	23	3.8	14	0
Q. Carter	12	20	1.7	9	0
Moss	6	18	3.0	12	0
Bollinger	1	2	2.0	2	0
McCareins	2	-5	-2.5	-2	0
Jets	527	2388	4.5	33	15
Opponents	432	1566	3.6	53	8

RECEIVING

	No.	Yds.	Avg.	Lg.	TD
McCareins	56	770	13.8	43	4
Moss	45	838	18.6	t69	5
Sowell	45	342	7.6	34	0
C. Martin	41	245	6.0	22	2
Chrebet	31	397	12.8	t35	1
Baker	18	182	10.1	23	4
Jordan	15	112	7.5	25	0
Becht	13	100	7.7	19	1
Carter	10	173	17.3	t46	1
Cotchery	6	60	10.0	18	0

	No.	Yds.	Avg.	Lg.	TD
Askew	2	12	6.0	11	0
Jets	282	3231	11.5	t69	19
Opponents	289	3532	12.2	65	21

INTERCEPTIONS

	No.	Yds.	Avg.	Lg.	TD
Coleman	4	43	10.8	37	0
Vilma	3	58	19.3	t38	1
Buckley	3	30	10.0	18	0
D. Abraham ..	2	66	33.0	t66	1
Barrett	2	14	7.0	14	0
McGraw	2	0	0.0	0	0
Tongue	1	23	23.0	23	0
Barton	1	7	7.0	7	0
Hobson	1	2	2.0	2	0
Jets	19	243	12.8	t66	2
Opponents	11	332	30.2	78	0

SACKS: Ellis 11.0, J. Abraham 9.5, J. Ferguson 3.5, Robertson 3.0, Barton 2.5, Coleman 2.0, Reed 2.0, Vilma 2.0, B. Thomas 1.5. Jets 37.0; Opponents 31.0.

PUNTING

	No.	Yds.	Avg.	In. 20	Lg.
Gowin	80	3057	38.2	22	58
Jets	80	3057	38.2	22	58
Opponents	89	3571	40.1	26	64

PUNT RETURNS

	No.	FC	Yds.	Avg.	Lg.	TD
Moss	27	7	225	8.3	46	0
McCareins	14	6	88	6.3	26	0
Jets	41	13	313	7.6	46	0
Opponents	34	14	221	6.5	25	0

KICK RETURNS

	No.	Yds.	Avg.	Lg.	TD
Carter	17	374	22.0	40	0
Jordan	14	284	20.3	40	0
Cotchery	13	362	27.8	t94	1
Askew	2	18	9.0	13	0
Jets	46	1038	22.6	t94	1
Opponents	72	1557	21.6	t87	1

FIELD GOALS

	1-19	20-29	30-39	40-49	50+
Brien	0/0	9/10	4/6	10/11	1/2
Jets	0/0	9/10	4/6	10/11	1/2
Opponents	0/0	9/9	5/6	2/3	0/1

Brien: (21G) (28G, 23G) (53G) (29N, 37G, 36G, 38G) (43G) () (49G, 43G) (36N, 41G) (20G) (43B, 41G) (28G, 46G) (41G, 26G, 25G) (43G, 41G) (21G, 30N) () (47G, 33G, 27G, 53N) **Opponents:** (22G) () (36G, 37G, 23G) () () (41G, 27G) () (20G, 30G) (24G, 42G) (42N, 34N) (20G) () (34G) () (28G, 29G, 50N, 26G) (31G)

PASSING

	Att.	Cmp.	Yds.	Pct.	Avg. Gain	TD	Pct. TD	Int.	Pct. Int.	Long	Sack/Lost	Rating
Pennington	370	242	2673	65.4	7.22	16	4.3	9	2.4	48	18/103	91.0
Q. Carter	58	35	498	60.3	8.59	3	5.2	1	1.7	t69	12/70	98.2
Bollinger	9	5	60	55.6	6.67	0	0.0	0	0.0	26	1/8	76.2
Jordan	1	0	0	0.0	0.00	0	0.0	1	100.0	...	0/0	0.0
Jets	438	282	3231	64.4	7.38	19	4.3	11	2.5	t69	31/181	90.5
Opponents	497	289	3532	58.1	7.11	21	4.2	19	3.8	65	37/220	78.3

OAKLAND RAIDERS
AFC WEST DIVISION

2005 SEASON

CLUB DIRECTORY

Owner
Al Davis
Chief executive
Amy Trask
Personnel executive
Mike Lombardi
Senior administrator
Morris Bradshaw
Finance
Marc Badain, Tom Blanda
Public relations director
Mike Taylor

Head coach
Norv Turner

Assistant coaches
Joe Avezzano (special teams)
Martin Bayless (special teams asst.)
Fred Biletnikoff (wide receivers)
Willie Brown (squad development)
Sam Clancy (defensive line)
Jim Colletto (offensive line)
Jeff Fish (strength & conditioning)
Chris Griswold (defensive asst.)
Pat Jones (outside linebackers)
Clayton Lopez (defensive backs)
Don Martindale (inside linebackers)
Keith Millard (asst. defensive line)
Skip Peete (running backs)
Jimmy Raye (asst. head coach/offensive coordinator)
Rob Ryan (defensive coordinator)
John Shoop (quarterbacks)
Chris Turner (offensive asst.)

OFFSEASON MOVES

Key additions
DE Derrick Burgess	FA/Eagles
LB Jay Foreman	Rel./Texans
CB Renaldo Hill	FA/Cardinals
RB LaMont Jordan	FA/Jets
WR Randy Moss	Trade/Vikings
DE Kenny Smith	FA/Saints

Key losses
S Ray Buchanan	Released
CB Phillip Buchanon	Trade/Texans
LB Napoleon Harris	Trade/Vikings
TE Doug Jolley	Trade/Jets
OL Frank Middleton	Released
DT John Parrella	Released
RB Tyrone Wheatley	Released
TE Roland Williams	Rel./Rams
RB Amos Zereoue	Free agent

SCHEDULE

Sept.	8—at New England (Thurs.)	9:00
Sept.	18—KANSAS CITY	8:30
Sept.	25—at Philadelphia	1:00
Oct.	2—DALLAS	4:15
Oct.	9—Open week	
Oct.	16—SAN DIEGO	4:15
Oct.	23—BUFFALO	4:15
Oct.	30—at Tennessee	2:00
Nov.	6—at Kansas City	2:00
Nov.	13—DENVER	5:05
Nov.	20—at Washington	2:00
Nov.	27—MIAMI	5:05
Dec.	4—at San Diego	9:30
Dec.	11—at N.Y. Jets	2:00
Dec.	18—CLEVELAND	5:05
Dec.	24—at Denver (Sat.)	5:15
Dec.	31—N.Y. GIANTS	9:00

All times are Eastern.
All games Sunday unless noted.

DRAFT CHOICES

Fabian Washington, CB, Nebraska (first round/23rd pick overall).
Stanford Routt, CB, Houston (3/38).
Andrew Walter, QB, Arizona State (3/69).
Kirk Morrison, ILB, San Diego State (3/78).
Anttaj Hawthorne, DT, Wisconsin (6/175).
Ryan Riddle, DE, California (6/212).
Pete McMahon, OT, Iowa (6/214).

MISCELLANEOUS TEAM DATA

Stadium (capacity, surface):
Network Associates Coliseum
(63,142, grass)
Business address:
1220 Harbor Bay Parkway
Alameda, CA 94502
Business phone:
510-864-5000
Ticket information:
800-949-2626
Team colors:
Silver and black
Flagship radio station:
KSFO, 560 AM
Website:
www.raiders.com
Training site:
Napa, Calif.
707-256-1000

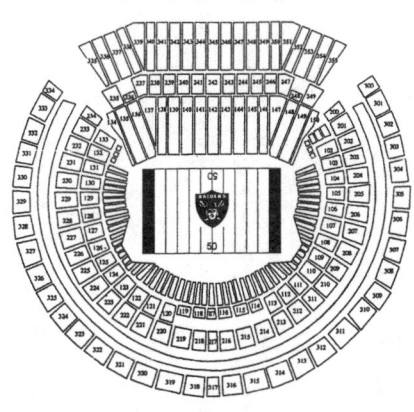

OAKLAND RAIDERS

No.	QUARTERBACKS	Ht./Wt.	Born	NFL Exp.	College	How acq.	'04 Games GP/GS
5	Collins, Kerry	6-5/245	12-30-72	11	Penn State	FA/04	14/13
8	Tuiasosopo, Marques	6-1/220	3-22-79	5	Washington	D2/01	0/0
16	Walter, Andrew	6-5/234	5-11-82	R	Arizona State	D3a/05	—
	RUNNING BACKS						
32	Crockett, Zack (FB)	6-2/240	12-2-72	11	Florida State	FA/99	16/9
20	Fargas, Justin	6-1/220	1-25-80	3	USC	D3b/03	12/0
44	Hetherington, Chris (FB)	6-3/245	11-27-72	9	Yale	FA/03	5/2
34	Jordan, LaMont	5-10/230	11-11-78	5	Maryland	FA/05	16/0
27	Redmond, J.R.	5-11/215	9-28-77	6	Arizona State	FA/03	16/1
	RECEIVERS						
83	Anderson, Courtney (TE)	6-7/270	11-19-80	2	San Jose State	D7a/04	9/4
89	Curry, Ronald	6-2/220	5-28-79	3	North Carolina	D7/02	12/3
10	Francis, Carlos	5-9/190	1-3-81	2	Texas Tech	D4/04	5/0
85	Gabriel, Doug	6-2/215	8-27-80	3	Central Florida	D5/03	16/5
82	Johnson, Teyo (TE)	6-6/260	11-29-81	3	Stanford	D2/03	8/1
19	Morant, Johnnie	6-4/220	12-7-81	2	Syracuse	D5/04	4/0
18	Moss, Randy	6-4/210	2-13-77	8	Marshall	T-Min./05	13/13
84	Porter, Jerry	6-2/220	7-14-78	6	West Virginia	D2/00	16/16
15	Stone, John	5-11/180	7-7-79	2	Wake Forest	FA/03	4/0
87	Whitted, Alvis	6-0/185	9-4-74	8	North Carolina State	FA/02	11/5
	OFFENSIVE LINEMEN						
70	Badger, Brad (G)	6-4/320	1-11-75	9	Stanford	FA/02	16/12
76	Gallery, Robert (T)	6-7/325	7-26-80	2	Iowa	D1/04	16/15
64	Grove, Jake (G/C)	6-4/300	1-22-80	2	Virginia Tech	D2/04	9/8
71	Hulsey, Corey (G)	6-4/325	7-26-77	4	Clemson	FA/03	3/0
69	McMahon, Pete (T)	6-8/329	10-15-81	R	Iowa	D6c/05	—
65	Sims, Barry (T)	6-5/300	12-1-74	7	Utah	FA/99	16/16
78	Slaughter, Chad (G)	6-8/340	6-4-78	5	Alcorn State	FA/03	10/0
67	Stone, Ron (G)	6-5/325	7-20-71	13	Boston College	FA/04	5/5
62	Treu, Adam (C/LS)	6-5/300	6-24-74	9	Nebraska	D3/97	16/16
66	Walker, Langston (G/T)	6-8/345	9-3-79	4	California	D2a/02	16/1
	DEFENSIVE LINEMEN						
91	Brayton, Tyler (E)	6-6/280	11-20-79	3	Colorado	D1b/03	15/15
58	Burgess, Derrick (E)	6-2/266	8-12-78	4	Mississippi	FA/05	12/11
98	Hamilton, Bobby (E)	6-5/285	7-1-71	11	Southern Mississippi	FA/04	16/15
77	Hawthorne, Anttaj (T)	6-2/310	11-15-81	R	Wisconsin	D6a/05	—
96	Irons, Grant (E)	6-6/285	7-7-79	4	Notre Dame	FA/02	8/2
93	Kelly, Tommy (T)	6-6/300	12-27-80	2	Mississippi State	FA/04	10/3
57	Riddle, Ryan (E)	6-1/251	7-5-81	R	California	D6b/05	—
90	Sands, Terdell (T)	6-7/335	10-31-79	3	Chattanooga	FA/03	15/0
99	Sapp, Warren (T)	6-2/300	12-19-72	11	Miami	FA/04	16/16
97	Smith, Kenny (T)	6-4/303	9-8-77	5	Alabama	FA/05	0/0
92	Washington, Ted (T)	6-5/365	4-13-68	15	Louisville	FA/04	16/16
	LINEBACKERS						
55	Clark, Danny	6-2/245	5-9-77	6	Illinois	FA/04	16/16
56	Foreman, Jay	6-1/240	2-18-76	7	Nebraska	FA/05	11/11
94	Gbaja-Biamila, Akbar	6-5/270	5-6-79	3	San Diego State	FA/03	14/0
59	Grant, DeLawrence	6-3/280	11-18-79	5	Oregon State	D3/01	9/9
51	Johnson, Tim	6-0/245	2-7-78	4	Youngstown State	FA/02	16/0
52	Morrison, Kirk	6-1/238	2-19-82	R	San Diego State	D3b/05	—
56	Smith, Travian	6-4/240	8-26-75	8	Oklahoma	D5b/98	8/4
50	Tuitele, Maugaula	6-1/250	5-26-78	4	Colorado State	FA/02	1/0
54	Williams, Sam	6-5/265	7-28-80	3	Fresno State	D3a/03	9/4
	DEFENSIVE BACKS						
23	Anderson, Marques (S)	5-11/210	5-26-79	4	UCLA	T-GB/04	14/10
21	Asomugha, Nnamdi (CB)	6-2/210	7-6-81	3	California	D1a/03	16/7
40	Cooper, Jarrod (S)	6-0/215	3-31-78	5	Kansas State	W-Car./04	15/0
36	Gibson, Derrick (S)	6-2/215	3-22-79	5	Florida State	D1/01	0/0
22	Hill, Renaldo (CB/S)	5-11/189	11-12-78	5	Michigan State	FA/05	13/10
26	Routt, Stanford (CB)	6-1/190	7-23-83	R	Houston	D2/05	—
30	Schweigert, Stuart (S)	6-1/210	6-21-81	2	Purdue	D3/04	16/3
25	Walker, Denard (CB)	6-1/190	8-9-73	9	LSU	FA/04	16/5
27	Washington, Fabian (CB)	5-10/183	6-9-83	R	Nebraska	D1/05	—
29	Williams, Brock (CB)	5-10/195	8-11-79	3	Notre Dame	W-Chi./04	2/0
24	Woodson, Charles (CB)	6-1/200	10-7-76	8	Michigan	D1a/98	13/12
	SPECIALISTS						
11	Janikowski, Sebastian (K)	6-2/250	3-2-78	6	Florida State	D1/00	16/0
9	Lechler, Shane (P)	6-2/225	8-7-76	6	Texas A&M	D5/00	16/0

Abbreviations: D1—draft pick, first round; W—claimed on waivers; T—obtained in trade; FA—free-agent acquisition.

2004 regular-season record: 5-11
Position: 4th in AFC West

Sept.12—at Pittsburgh	L	21-24
Sept.19—BUFFALO	W	13-10
Sept.26—TAMPA BAY	W	30-20
Oct. 3—at Houston	L	17-30
Oct. 10—at Indianapolis	L	14-35
Oct. 17—DENVER	L	3-31
Oct. 24—NEW ORLEANS	L	26-31
Oct. 31—at San Diego	L	14-42
Nov. 7—at Carolina	W	27-24
Nov. 14—Open date		
Nov. 21—SAN DIEGO	L	17-23
Nov. 28—at Denver	W	25-24
Dec. 5—KANSAS CITY	L	27-34
Dec. 12—at Atlanta	L	10-35
Dec. 19—TENNESSEE	W	40-35
Dec. 25—at Kansas City	L	30-31
Jan. 2—JACKSONVILLE	L	6-13

SCORING BY PERIODS

	Q1	Q2	Q3	Q4	OT	Pts.
Raiders	51	121	60	88	0	320
Opponents	68	155	89	130	0	442

TEAM STATISTICS

	Oak.	Opp.
TOTAL FIRST DOWNS	275	367
Rushing	75	115
Passing	176	210
Penalty	24	42
3rd Down: Made/Att.	71/200	101/213
3rd Down Pct.	35.5	47.4
4th Down: Made/Att.	7/14	7/15
4th Down Pct.	50.0	46.7
POSSESSION AVG.	26:47	33:13
TOTAL NET YARDS	5153	5936
Avg. per Game	322.1	371.0
Total Plays	939	1072
Avg. per Play	5.5	5.5
NET YARDS RUSHING	1295	2012
Avg. per Game	80.9	125.8
Total Rushes	327	537
NET YARDS PASSING	3858	3924
Avg. per Game	241.1	245.3
Sacked/Yards Lost	30/161	25/182
Gross Yards	4019	4106
Att./Completions	582/330	510/315
Completion Pct.	56.7	61.8
Had Intercepted	22	9
PUNTS/AVERAGE	73/46.7	68/41.3
NET PUNTING AVG.	73/37.2	68/37.3
PENALTIES/YARDS	134/1013	102/837
FUMBLES/LOST	23/13	14/9
TOUCHDOWNS	35	56
Rushing	10	21
Passing	24	30
Returns	1	5

SCORING (NON-KICKERS)

	Tot. TD	RTD	PTD	MTD	2Pt.	Tot. Pts.
Porter	9	0	9	0	0	54
Curry	6	0	6	0	0	36
Wheatley	4	4	0	0	0	24
Zereoue	3	3	0	0	0	18
Whitted	2	0	2	0	1	14
Crockett	2	2	0	0	0	12
Gabriel	2	0	2	0	0	12
T. Johnson	2	2	0	0	0	12
Jolley	2	0	2	0	0	12
C. Anderson	1	0	1	0	0	6
Buchanon	1	0	0	1	0	6
Fargas	1	1	0	0	0	6
Raiders	35	10	24	1	1	214
Opponents	56	21	30	5	1	338

2-Pt. conversions: Raiders 1-3; Opponents 1-2.

(KICKERS)

	XPM/XPA	FGM/FGA	Pts.
Janikowski	31/32	25/28	106
Raiders	31/32	25/28	106
Opponents	53/54	17/25	104

RUSHING

	Att.	Yds.	Avg.	Lg.	TD
Zereoue	112	425	3.8	t55	3
Wheatley	85	327	3.8	60	4
Crockett	48	232	4.8	47	2
Fargas	35	126	3.6	15	1
Redmond	21	119	5.7	18	0
Collins	16	36	2.3	8	0
Gannon	5	26	5.2	20	0
Gabriel	2	7	3.5	4	0
Hetherington	1	4	4.0	4	0
Curry	1	-3	-3.0	-3	0
Porter	1	-4	-4.0	-4	0
Raiders	327	1295	4.0	60	10
Opponents	537	2012	3.7	34	21

RECEIVING

	No.	Yds.	Avg.	Lg.	TD
Porter	64	998	15.6	52	9
Curry	50	679	13.6	63	6
Zereoue	39	284	7.3	13	0
Gabriel	33	551	16.7	t58	2
Redmond	32	233	7.3	22	0
Jolley	27	313	11.6	t34	2
Crockett	16	87	5.4	11	0
Wheatley	15	78	5.2	20	0
C. Anderson	13	175	13.5	28	1
Fargas	11	68	6.2	21	0
T. Johnson	9	131	14.6	25	2
Whitted	9	227	25.2	57	2
Rice	5	67	13.4	18	0
Hetherington	3	28	9.3	14	0
J. Stone	3	80	26.7	55	0
Morant	1	20	20.0	20	0
Raiders	330	4019	12.2	63	24
Opponents	315	4106	13.0	t85	30

INTERCEPTIONS

	No.	Yds.	Avg.	Lg.	TD
Buchanon	3	69	23.0	37	1
D. Walker	1	45	45.0	45	0
Buchanan	1	27	27.0	27	0
C. Woodson	1	25	25.0	25	0
Brayton	1	24	24.0	24	0
M. Anderson	1	23	23.0	23	0
T. Johnson	1	8	8.0	8	0
Raiders	9	221	24.6	45	1
Opponents	22	356	16.2	61	3

SACKS: Kelly 4.0, Washington 3.0, Brayton 2.5, Sapp 2.5, C. Woodson 2.5, Clark 2.0, Grant 2.0, Asomugha 1.0, Cooper 1.0, Gbaja-Biamila 1.0, Hamilton 1.0, Irons 1.0, T. Johnson 0.5. Raiders 25.0; Opponents 30.0.

PUNTING

	No.	Yds.	Avg.	In. 20	Lg.
Lechler	73	3409	46.7	22	67
Raiders	73	3409	46.7	22	67
Opponents	68	2808	41.3	21	63

PUNT RETURNS

	No.	FC	Yds.	Avg.	Lg.	TD
Buchanon	21	1	121	5.8	18	0
Gabriel	2	2	7	3.5	7	0
C. Woodson	1	0	4	4.0	4	0
Raiders	24	9	132	5.5	18	0
Opponents	35	10	413	11.8	50	0

KICK RETURNS

	No.	Yds.	Avg.	Lg.	TD
Gabriel	53	1140	21.5	64	0
Francis	14	259	18.5	33	0
Redmond	8	153	19.1	31	0
Curry	4	63	15.8	25	0
Hetherington	1	23	23.0	23	0
Porter	1	6	6.0	6	0
J. Stone	1	20	20.0	20	0
Whitted	1	36	36.0	36	0
Raiders	83	1700	20.5	64	0
Opponents	62	1458	23.5	50	0

FIELD GOALS

	1-19	20-29	30-39	40-49	50+
Janikowski	1/1	7/7	7/8	8/10	2/2
Raiders	1/1	7/7	7/8	8/10	2/2
Opponents	1/1	5/5	7/7	4/10	0/2

Janikowski: (28G, 38G) (21G, 33G) (23G, 40G, 46N, 39G) (35N, 50G) () (35G) (28G, 42G, 44G, 40G) () (26G, 19G) (31G) (48N) (27G, 36G) (52G) (42G) (40G, 45G, 46G) (35G, 27G) Opponents: (42G) (32G) (36G, 30G, 44N) (46G, 57N, 21G, 44G) (44N) (33G) (41G) () (38G) (42N, 19G) (32G, 43B) (28G, 22G) () (41N) (43B, 50N, 38G) (26G, 22G)

PASSING

	Att.	Cmp.	Yds.	Pct.	Avg. Gain	TD	Pct. TD	Int.	Pct. Int.	Long	Sack/Lost	Rating
Collins	513	289	3495	56.3	6.81	21	4.1	20	3.9	63	25/144	74.8
Gannon	68	41	524	60.3	7.71	3	4.4	2	2.9	t58	5/17	86.9
Curry	1	0	0	0.0	0.00	0	0.0	0	0.0	...	0/0	39.6
Raiders	582	330	4019	56.7	6.91	24	4.1	22	3.8	63	30/161	76.1
Opponents	510	315	4106	61.8	8.05	30	5.9	9	1.8	t85	25/182	99.4

OAKLAND RAIDERS

PHILADELPHIA EAGLES
NFC EAST DIVISION

2005 SEASON

CLUB DIRECTORY

Chairman/chief executive officer
Jeffrey Lurie
President
Joe Banner
Sr. vp/business operations
Mark Donovan
Vice president of player personnel
Tom Heckert
Director of pro personnel
Scott Cohen
Assistant director of player personnel
Jason Licht
Director of football media relations
Derek Boyko
Manager of community relations
Julie Dubin

Head coach & exec. vp for football operations
Andy Reid

Assistant coaches
Tommy Brasher (defensive line)
Juan Castillo (offensive line)
Brad Childress (off. coordinator)
Dave Culley (wide receivers)
Ted Daisher (special teams quality control)
John Harbaugh (special teams coordinator)
Jim Johnson (def. coordinator)
Tom Kanavy (strength & conditioning asst.)
Sean McDermott (secondary/safeties)
Tom Melvin (tight ends)
Marty Mornhinweg (asst. head coach)
Mike Reed (defensive asst./quality control)
Bill Shuey (offensive asst./quality control)
Pat Shurmur (quarterbacks)
Steve Spagnuolo (linebackers)
Trent Walters (secondary)
Ted Williams (running backs)
Mike Wolf (strength & conditioning)

OFFSEASON MOVES

Key additions
QB Mike McMahon — FA/Lions
Key losses
QB Jeff Blake — Free agent
DE Derrick Burgess — FA/Raiders
RB Dorsey Levens — Free agent
OT Jermane Mayberry — FA/Saints
WR Freddie Mitchell — Released
LB Ike Reese — FA/Falcons
LB Nate Wayne — Rel./Jaguars

SCHEDULE

Sept.	12—at Atlanta (Mon.)	9:00
Sept.	18—SAN FRANCISCO	1:00
Sept.	25—OAKLAND	1:00
Oct.	2—at Kansas City	1:00
Oct.	9—at Dallas	4:15
Oct.	16—Open date	
Oct.	23—SAN DIEGO	1:00
Oct.	30—at Denver	5:15
Nov.	6—at Washington	9:30
Nov.	14—DALLAS (Mon.)	10:00
Nov.	20—at N.Y. Giants	2:00
Nov.	27—GREEN BAY	5:15
Dec.	5—SEATTLE (Mon.)	10:00
Dec.	11—N.Y. GIANTS	5:05
Dec.	18—at St. Louis	5:15
Dec.	24—at Arizona (Sat.)	5:05
Jan.	1—WASHINGTON	4:15

All times are Eastern.
All games Sunday unless noted.

DRAFT CHOICES

Mike Patterson, DT, Southern California (first round/31st pick overall).
Reggie Brown, WR, Georgia (2/35).
Matt McCoy, OLB, San Diego State (2/63).
Ryan Moats, RB, Louisiana Tech (3/77).
Sean Considine, FS, Iowa (4/102).
Todd Herremans, OT, Saginaw Valley State (4/126).
Trent Cole, OLB, Cincinnati (5/146).
Scott Young, G, Brigham Young (5/172).
Calvin Armstrong, OT, Washington State (6/211).
Keyonta Marshall, DT, Grand Valley State (7/247).
David Bergeron, ILB, Stanford (7/252).

MISCELLANEOUS TEAM DATA

Stadium (capacity, surface):
Lincoln Financial Field
(68,400, grass)
Business address:
NovaCare Complex
One NovaCare Way
Philadelphia, PA 19145
Business phone:
215-463-2500
Ticket information:
215-463-5500
Team colors:
Midnight green, silver and white
Flagship radio station:
WYSP, 94.1 FM
Website:
www.philadelphiaeagles.com
Training site:
Lehigh University
Bethlehem, Pa.
215-463-2500

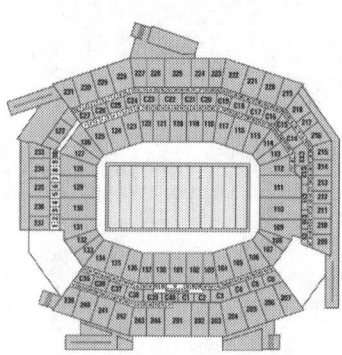

PHILADELPHIA EAGLES

No.	QUARTERBACKS	Ht./Wt.	Born	NFL Exp.	College	How acq.	'04 Games GP/GS
10	Detmer, Koy	6-1/195	7-5-73	7	Colorado	D7a/97	16/1
4	McMahon, Mike	6-2/215	2-8-79	5	Rutgers	FA/05	1/0
5	McNabb, Donovan	6-2/240	11-25-76	7	Syracuse	D1/99	15/15
	RUNNING BACKS						
28	Buckhalter, Correll	6-0/222	10-6-78	3	Nebraska	D4/01	0/0
34	Mahe, Reno	5-10/212	6-3-80	3	BYU	FA/03	11/0
23	Moats, Ryan	5-8/210	12-17-82	R	Louisiana Tech	D3/05	—
49	Parry, Josh	6-2/250	4-5-78	2	San Jose State	FA/04	13/4
48	Ritchie, Jon (FB)	6-2/250	9-4-74	8	Stanford	FA/03	3/0
41	Tapeh, Thomas (FB)	6-1/243	3-28-80	2	Minnesota	D5/04	7/0
36	Westbrook, Brian	5-10/205	9-2-79	4	Villanova	D3/02	13/12
	RECEIVERS						
88	Bartrum, Mike (TE)	6-4/245	6-23-70	12	Marshall	FA/00	16/0
86	Brown, Reggie	6-1/197	1-13-81	R	Georgia	D2a/05	—
16	Jenkins, Justin	6-0/207	12-10-80	1	Mississippi State	FA/04	0/0
83	Lewis, Greg	6-0/180	2-12-80	3	Illinois	FA/03	16/3
80	McMullen, Billy	6-4/210	3-8-80	3	Virginia	D3/03	8/0
81	Owens, Terrell	6-3/226	12-7-73	10	Chattanooga	T-SF/04	14/14
87	Pinkston, Todd	6-3/180	4-23-77	6	Southern Mississippi	D2a/00	16/16
82	Smith, L.J. (TE)	6-3/258	5-13-80	3	Rutgers	D2/03	16/8
	OFFENSIVE LINEMEN						
73	Andrews, Shawn (G)	6-4/340	12-25-82	1	Arkansas	D1/04	1/1
76	Armstrong, Calvin (T)	6-7/325	3-31-82	R	Washington State	D6/05	—
61	Clarke, Adrien (G)	6-5/330	3-26-81	1	Ohio State	D7/04	0/0
66	Darilek, Trey (G)	6-5/310	4-23-81	2	UTEP	D4/04	3/0
63	Fraley, Hank (C)	6-2/300	9-21-77	5	Robert Morris	W-Pit./00	16/16
79	Herremans, Todd (T)	6-6/321	10-13-82	R	Saginaw Valley	D4b/05	—
77	Hicks, Artis (T/G)	6-4/320	11-28-78	3	Memphis	FA/02	14/13
67	Jackson, Jamaal (C)	6-4/330	5-8-80	1	Delaware State	FA/03	0/0
69	Runyan, Jon (T)	6-7/330	11-27-73	10	Michigan	FA/00	16/16
68	Sciullo, Steve (G)	6-5/325	8-27-80	3	Marshall	D4/03	15/5
72	Thomas, Tra (T)	6-7/349	11-20-74	8	Florida State	D1/98	15/15
71	Young, Scott (G)	6-4/312	7-15-81	R	BYU	D5b/05	—
	DEFENSIVE LINEMEN						
53	Douglas, Hugh (E)	6-2/281	8-23-71	11	Central State	FA/03	16/3
65	Green, Jamaal (E)	6-2/272	6-5-80	2	Miami	D4/03	8/0
94	Kalu, N.D. (E)	6-3/265	8-3-75	8	Rice	FA/01	0/0
93	Kearse, Jevon (E)	6-4/265	9-3-76	7	Florida	FA/04	14/14
79	Marshall, Keyonta (T)	6-1/290	8-13-81	R	Grand Valley State	D7a/05	—
95	McDougle, Jerome (E)	6-2/264	12-15-78	3	Miami	D1/03	11/0
98	Patterson, Mike (T)	5-11/292	9-1-83	R	USC	D1/05	—
91	Rayburn, Sam (T)	6-3/303	10-20-80	3	Tulsa	FA/03	16/2
90	Simon, Corey (T)	6-2/293	3-2-77	6	Florida State	D1/00	16/16
78	Thomas, Hollis (T)	6-0/306	1-10-74	9	Northern Illinois	FA/96	13/2
97	Walker, Darwin (T)	6-3/294	6-15-77	5	Tennessee	W-Ari./00	16/16
	LINEBACKERS						
57	Adams, Keith	5-11/223	11-22-79	5	Clemson	W-Dal./02	16/2
58	Bergeron, David	6-4/245	12-4-81	R	Stanford	D7b/05	—
58	Cole, Trent	6-2/257	10-5-82	R	Cincinnati	D5a/05	—
55	Jones, Dhani	6-1/240	2-22-78	5	Michigan	FA/04	16/15
59	Labinjo, Mike	6-0/241	7-8-80	2	Michigan State	FA/04	3/0
51	McCoy, Matt	6-0/234	10-14-82	R	San Diego State	D2b/05	—
56	Richmond, Greg	6-1/235	7-15-81	1	Oklahoma State	FA/04	0/0
52	Short, Jason	6-4/254	7-15-78	2	Eastern Michigan	FA/03	11/0
50	Simoneau, Mark	6-0/245	1-16-77	6	Kansas State	FA/04	14/13
54	Trotter, Jeremiah	6-1/262	1-20-77	8	Stephen F. Austin	FA/02	16/9
	DEFENSIVE BACKS						
24	Brown, Sheldon (CB)	5-10/200	3-19-79	4	South Carolina	D2b/02	16/16
37	Considine, Sean (S)	6-0/206	10-28-81	R	Iowa	D4a/05	—
20	Dawkins, Brian (S)	6-0/210	10-13-73	10	Clemson	D2b/96	15/15
29	Hood, Roderick (CB)	5-11/196	10-3-81	3	Auburn	FA/03	16/2
32	Lewis, Michael (S)	6-1/211	4-29-80	4	Colorado	D2a/02	16/16
27	Mikell, Quintin (S)	5-10/206	9-16-80	3	Boise State	FA/03	14/0
30	Reed, J.R. (S)	5-11/202	2-11-82	2	South Florida	D4a/04	14/1
26	Sheppard, Lito (CB)	5-10/194	4-8-81	4	Florida	D1/02	15/15
21	Ware, Matt (CB)	6-2/210	12-2-82	2	UCLA	D3/04	12/0
31	Wynn, Dexter (CB)	5-9/177	2-25-81	2	Colorado State	D6/04	12/0
	SPECIALISTS						
2	Akers, David (K)	5-10/200	12-9-74	7	Louisville	FA/99	16/0
8	Johnson, Dirk (P)	6-0/205	6-1-75	3	Northern Colorado	FA/03	16/0

Abbreviations: D1—draft pick, first round; W—claimed on waivers; T—obtained in trade; FA—free-agent acquisition.

PHILADELPHIA EAGLES

2004 regular-season record: 13-3
Position: 1st in NFC East

Sept.12—N.Y. GIANTS	W	31-17	
Sept.20—MINNESOTA	W	27-16	
Sept.26—at Detroit	W	30-13	
Oct. 3—at Chicago	W	19-9	
Oct. 10—Open date			
Oct. 17—CAROLINA	W	30-8	
Oct. 24—at Cleveland (OT)	W	34-31	
Oct. 31—BALTIMORE	W	15-10	
Nov. 7—at Pittsburgh	L	3-27	
Nov. 14—at Dallas	W	49-21	
Nov. 21—WASHINGTON	W	28-6	
Nov. 28—at N.Y. Giants	W	27-6	
Dec. 5—GREEN BAY	W	47-17	
Dec. 12—at Washington	W	17-14	
Dec. 19—DALLAS	W	12-7	
Dec. 27—at St. Louis	L	7-20	
Jan. 2—CINCINNATI	L	10-38	

2004 postseason record: 2-1

Jan. 16—MINNESOTA*	W	27-14
Jan. 23—ATLANTA†	W	27-10
Feb. 6—NEW ENGLAND‡	L	21-24

*NFC divisional playoff game. †NFC championship game. ‡Super Bowl 39.

SCORING BY PERIODS

	Q1	Q2	Q3	Q4	OT	Pts.
Eagles	100	121	79	83	3	386
Opponents	54	83	41	82	0	260

TEAM STATISTICS

	Phi.	Opp.
TOTAL FIRST DOWNS	301	299
Rushing	87	101
Passing	188	165
Penalty	26	33
3rd Down: Made/Att.	72/195	82/229
3rd Down Pct.	36.9	35.8
4th Down: Made/Att.	0/4	9/19
4th Down Pct.	0.0	47.4
POSSESSION AVG.	28:26	31:34
TOTAL NET YARDS	5618	5115
Avg. per Game	351.1	319.7
Total Plays	960	1039
Avg. per Play	5.9	4.9
NET YARDS RUSHING	1639	1903
Avg. per Game	102.4	118.9
Total Rushes	376	442
NET YARDS PASSING	3979	3212
Avg. per Game	248.7	200.8
Sacked/Yards Lost	37/229	47/263
Gross Yards	4208	3475
Att./Completions	547/336	550/334
Completion Pct.	61.4	60.7
Had Intercepted	11	17
PUNTS/AVERAGE	73/42.0	89/42.5
NET PUNTING AVG.	73/37.1	89/35.4
PENALTIES/YARDS	124/952	119/1001
FUMBLES/LOST	17/11	29/11
TOUCHDOWNS	44	30

	Att.	Cmp.	Yds.	Pct.
McNabb	469	300	3875	64.0
Detmer	40	18	207	45.0
Blake	37	18	126	48.6
Bartrum	1	0	0	0.0
Eagles	547	336	4208	61.4
Opponents	550	334	3475	60.7

	Phi.	Opp.
Rushing	10	13
Passing	32	16
Returns	2	1

SCORING (NON-KICKERS)

	Tot. TD	RTD	PTD	MTD	2Pt.	Tot. Pts.
Owens	14	0	14	0	0	84
Westbrook	9	3	6	0	0	54
Smith	5	0	5	0	0	30
Levens	4	4	0	0	0	24
C. Lewis	3	0	3	0	0	18
McNabb	3	3	0	0	0	18
F. Mitchell	2	0	2	0	0	12
Sheppard	2	0	0	2	0	12
Bartrum	1	0	1	0	0	6
Pinkston	1	0	1	0	0	6
Eagles	44	10	32	2	0	264
Opponents	30	13	16	1	1	182

2-Pt. conversions: Eagles 0-2; Opponents 1-3.

(KICKERS)

	XPM/XPA	FGM/FGA	Pts.
Akers	41/42	27/32	122
Eagles	41/42	27/32	122
Opponents	27/27	17/24	78

RUSHING

	Att.	Yds.	Avg.	Lg.	TD
Westbrook	177	812	4.6	50	3
Levens	94	410	4.4	45	4
McNabb	41	220	5.4	28	3
Mahe	23	91	4.0	22	0
McCoo	9	54	6.0	12	0
Tapeh	12	42	3.5	10	0
G. Lewis	4	16	4.0	11	0
Blake	3	6	2.0	8	0
Owens	3	-5	-1.7	6	0
Detmer	10	-7	-0.7	2	0
Eagles	376	1639	4.4	50	10
Opponents	442	1903	4.3	t72	13

RECEIVING

	No.	Yds.	Avg.	Lg.	TD
Owens	77	1200	15.6	t59	14
Westbrook	73	703	9.6	50	6
Pinkston	36	676	18.8	80	1
Smith	34	377	11.1	31	5
C. Lewis	29	267	9.2	21	3
F. Mitchell	22	377	17.1	60	2
G. Lewis	17	183	10.8	25	0
Mahe	14	123	8.8	30	0
Levens	9	92	10.2	23	0
Parry	9	75	8.3	22	0
Bartrum	5	45	9.0	17	1
Ritchie	4	36	9.0	11	0
McMullen	3	24	8.0	15	0
McCoo	2	15	7.5	8	0
Tapeh	2	15	7.5	13	0
Eagles	336	4208	12.5	80	32
Opponents	334	3475	10.4	52	16

INTERCEPTIONS

	No.	Yds.	Avg.	Lg.	TD
Sheppard	5	172	34.4	t101	2
Dawkins	4	40	10.0	32	0
Brown	2	33	16.5	33	0
Reese	2	22	11.0	15	0
Hood	1	20	20.0	20	0
Jones	1	0	0.0	0	0
M. Lewis	1	0	0.0	0	0
Mikell	1	0	0.0	0	0
Eagles	17	287	16.9	t101	2
Opponents	11	140	12.7	41	1

SACKS: Kearse 7.5, Rayburn 6.0, Simon 5.5, Walker 4.5, Brown 3.0, Dawkins 3.0, H. Douglas 3.0, Burgess 2.5, McDougle 2.0, Simoneau 1.5, Green 1.0, Reese 1.0, Sheppard 1.0, Trotter 1.0, Wayne 1.0, Wynn 1.0, Jones 0.5. Eagles 47.0; Opponents 37.0.

PUNTING

	No.	Yds.	Avg.	In. 20	Lg.
Akers	1	36	36.0	0	36
D. Johnson	72	3032	42.1	20	62
Eagles	73	3068	42.0	20	62
Opponents	89	3785	42.5	29	68

PUNT RETURNS

	No.	FC	Yds.	Avg.	Lg.	TD
Mahe	19	8	109	5.7	25	0
Wynn	18	7	194	10.8	40	0
Sheppard	2	5	42	21.0	39	0
Westbrook	2	0	14	7.0	14	0
Reed	0	0	18	-	18	0
Eagles	41	20	377	9.2	40	0
Opponents	34	13	221	6.5	25	0

KICK RETURNS

	No.	Yds.	Avg.	Lg.	TD
Reed	33	761	23.1	66	0
Hood	15	336	22.4	45	0
Mahe	3	44	14.7	22	0
G. Lewis	2	28	14.0	15	0
Parry	2	24	12.0	14	0
Wynn	1	21	21.0	21	0
Eagles	56	1214	21.7	66	0
Opponents	73	1693	23.2	73	0

FIELD GOALS

	1-19	20-29	30-39	40-49	50+
Akers	0/0	4/4	6/7	15/18	2/3
Eagles	0/0	4/4	6/7	15/18	2/3
Opponents	1/1	5/5	5/7	4/9	2/2

Akers: (45G, 53N) (37G, 47G) (26G, 47G, 39G) (51G, 42G, 42G, 40G, 39N, 45N) (48G, 34G, 43G) (38G, 50G) (20G, 41G, 43G) (33G) () () (47G, 42G) (22G, 45G, 47G, 22G) (48N, 38G) () () (45N, 46G)

Opponents: (53G) (42G, 19G, 39G, 44N) () (25G) () (38G) (44G) (33N, 42G, 31G) () (35G, 24G, 48N) (22G, 31G) (40G) (43N) (46N) (44N, 28G, 29G) (37N, 50G)

PASSING

	Att.	Cmp.	Yds.	Pct.	Avg. Gain	TD	Pct. TD	Int.	Pct. Int.	Long	Sack/Lost	Rating
McNabb	469	300	3875	64.0	8.26	31	6.6	8	1.7	80	32/192	104.7
Detmer	40	18	207	45.0	5.18	0	0.0	2	5.0	31	2/16	40.3
Blake	37	18	126	48.6	3.41	1	2.7	1	2.7	21	2/17	54.6
Bartrum	1	0	0	0.0	0.00	0	0.0	0	0.0	...	0/0	39.6
Eagles	547	336	4208	61.4	7.69	32	5.9	11	2.0	80	37/229	96.4
Opponents	550	334	3475	60.7	6.32	16	2.9	17	3.1	52	47/263	75.8

PITTSBURGH STEELERS
AFC NORTH DIVISION

2005 SEASON

CLUB DIRECTORY

Chairman
Daniel M. Rooney
President
Arthur J. Rooney II
Vice president
John R. McGinley
Vice president
Arthur J. Rooney Jr.
Administration advisor
Charles H. Noll
Director of football operations
Kevin Colbert
Communications coordinator
TBA
Public relations/media manager
David Lockett
Pro personnel coordinator
Doug Whaley
College scouting coordinator
Ron Hughes

Head coach
Bill Cowher

Assistant coaches
Bruce Arians (wide receivers)
Keith Butler (linebackers)
James Daniel (tight ends)
Chet Fuhrman (conditioning)
Russ Grimm (asst. head
    coach/offensive line)
Dick Hoak (running backs)
Ray Horton (asst. defensive
    backs)
Dick LeBeau (def. coordinator)
John Mitchell (defensive line)
Darren Perry (defensive backs)
Matt Raich (offensive quality
    control)
Lou Spanos (defensive quality
    control)
Kevin Spencer (special teams)
Mark Whipple (quarterbacks)
Ken Whisenhunt (offensive coor-
    dinator)

OFFSEASON MOVES

Key additions
WR Cedrick Wilson   FA/49ers
Key losses
LB Kendrell Bell   FA/Chiefs
WR Plaxico Burress   FA/Giants
DT Kendrick Clancy   FA/Giants
TE Jay Riemersma   Released
OT Oliver Ross   FA/Cardinals
CB Chad Scott   Rel./Patriots
G Keydrick Vincent   FA/Ravens

SCHEDULE

Sept.	11—TENNESSEE	1:00
Sept.	18—at Houston	1:00
Sept.	25—NEW ENGLAND	4:15
Oct.	2—Open week	
Oct.	10—at San Diego	9:00
Oct.	16—JACKSONVILLE	1:00
Oct.	23—at Cincinnati	1:00
Oct.	31—BALTIMORE	10:00
Nov.	6—at Green Bay	5:15
Nov.	13—CLEVELAND	9:30
Nov.	20—at Baltimore	5:15
Nov.	28—at Indianapolis	10:00
Dec.	4—CINCINNATI	2:00
Dec.	11—CHICAGO	2:00
Dec.	18—at Minnesota	2:00
Dec.	24—at Cleveland	2:00
Jan.	1—DETROIT	2:00

All times are Eastern.
All games Sunday unless noted.

DRAFT CHOICES

Heath Miller, TE, Virginia (first
round/30th pick overall).
Bryant McFadden, CB, Florida State
(2/62).
Trai Essex, OT, Northwestern (3/93).
Fred Gibson, WR, Georgia (4/131).
Rian Wallace, ILB, Temple (5/166).
Chris Kemoeatu, G, Utah (6/204).
Shaun Nua, DE, Brigham Young (7/228).
Noah Herron, RB, Northwestern (7/244).

MISCELLANEOUS TEAM DATA

Stadium (capacity, surface):
Heinz Field
(64,350, grass)
Business address:
3400 South Water St.
Pittsburgh, PA 15203-2349
Business phone:
412-432-7800
Ticket information:
412-323-1200
Team colors:
Black and gold
Flagship radio station:
WDVE, 102.5 FM
Website:
www.steelers.com
Training site:
St. Vincent College
Latrobe, Pa.
412-539-8515

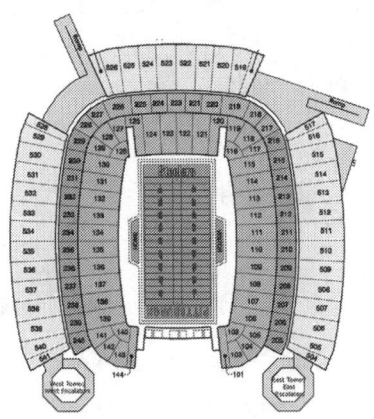

PITTSBURGH STEELERS

No.	QUARTERBACKS	Ht./Wt.	Born	NFL Exp.	College	How acq.	'04 Games GP/GS
16	Batch, Charlie	6-2/216	12-5-74	8	Eastern Michigan	FA/02	0/0
8	Maddox, Tommy	6-4/219	9-2-71	9	UCLA	FA/01	4/3
7	Roethlisberger, Ben	6-5/241	3-2-81	2	Miami (Ohio)	D1/04	14/13
2	St. Pierre, Brian	6-2/230	11-28-79	3	Boston College	D5/03	1/0
	RUNNING BACKS						
36	Bettis, Jerome	5-11/255	2-16-72	13	Notre Dame	T-St.L./96	15/6
34	Haynes, Verron (FB)	5-9/222	2-17-79	4	Georgia	D5/02	13/0
38	Herron, Noah	5-11/224	4-3-82	R	Northwestern	D7b/05	—
35	Kreider, Dan (FB)	5-11/255	3-11-77	6	New Hampshire	FA/00	16/9
39	Parker, Willie	5-10/209	11-11-80	2	North Carolina	FA/04	8/0
22	Staley, Duce	5-11/242	2-27-75	9	South Carolina	FA/04	10/10
	RECEIVERS						
49	Battaglia, Marco (TE)	6-3/250	1-25-73	9	Rutgers	FA/05	0/0
48	Cushing, Matt (TE)	6-4/251	7-2-75	7	Illinois	FA/03	16/0
11	Gibson, Fred	6-4/202	10-26-81	R	Georgia	D4/05	—
88	Kranchick, Matt (TE)	6-7/260	12-13-79	1	Penn State	D6b/04	2/0
89	Mays, Lee	6-2/193	9-18-78	4	UTEP	D6/02	16/1
83	Miller, Heath (TE)	6-5/256	12-22-82	R	Virginia	D1/05	—
81	Morey, Sean	5-11/200	2-26-76	4	Brown	FA/04	16/0
82	Randle El, Antwaan	5-10/192	8-17-79	4	Indiana	D2/02	16/7
87	Rasby, Walter (TE)	6-3/252	9-7-72	11	Wake Forest	FA/04	10/8
84	Tuman, Jerame (TE)	6-4/253	3-24-76	7	Michigan	FA/03	16/16
86	Ward, Hines	6-0/215	3-8-76	8	Georgia	D3b/98	16/16
80	Wilson, Cedrick	5-10/183	12-17-78	5	Tennessee	FA/05	15/15
	OFFENSIVE LINEMEN						
72	Brooks, Barrett (T)	6-4/325	5-5-72	10	Kansas State	FA/03	5/0
	Claxton, Ben (C)	6-2/288	7-30-80	1	Mississippi	FA/05	0/0
79	Essex, Trai (T)	6-4/324	12-5-82	R	Northwestern	D3/05	—
66	Faneca, Alan (G)	6-5/307	12-7-76	8	LSU	D1/98	16/16
64	Hartings, Jeff (C)	6-3/299	9-7-72	10	Penn State	FA/01	16/16
74	Jones, Jim (G)	6-3/319	1-27-78	2	Notre Dame	FA/04	0/0
68	Kemoeatu, Chris (G)	6-3/344	1-4-83	R	Utah	D6/05	—
56	Okobi, Chukky (C)	6-1/318	10-18-78	5	Purdue	D5/01	16/0
54	Schneck, Mike (LS)	6-0/237	8-4-77	7	Wisconsin	FA/99	16/0
73	Simmons, Kendall (G)	6-3/313	3-11-79	4	Auburn	D1/02	0/0
77	Smith, Marvel (T)	6-5/321	8-6-78	6	Arizona State	D2/00	16/16
78	Starks, Max (T)	6-7/337	1-10-82	2	Florida	D3/04	10/0
	DEFENSIVE LINEMEN						
98	Hampton, Casey (NT)	6-1/325	9-3-77	5	Texas	D1/01	6/6
76	Hoke, Chris (NT)	6-3/296	4-6-76	5	BYU	FA/02	14/10
99	Keisel, Brett (E)	6-5/285	9-19-78	4	BYU	D7b/02	13/0
90	Kirschke, Travis (E)	6-3/298	9-6-74	9	UCLA	FA/04	16/1
96	Nua, Shaun (DE)	6-5/270	5-22-81	R	BYU	D7a/05	—
91	Smith, Aaron (E)	6-5/298	4-9-76	7	Northern Colorado	D4/99	16/15
69	Taylor, Eric (DE)	6-2/305	12-14-81	1	Memphis	FA/04	0/0
67	von Oelhoffen, Kimo (E)	6-4/299	1-30-71	12	Boise State	FA/00	16/16
	LINEBACKERS						
51	Farrior, James	6-2/243	1-6-75	9	Virginia	FA/02	16/16
50	Foote, Larry	6-0/239	6-12-80	4	Michigan	D4/02	16/16
53	Haggans, Clark	6-4/243	1-10-77	6	Colorado State	D5a/00	13/13
92	Harrison, James	6-0/242	5-4-78	2	Kent State	FA/04	16/4
95	Jackson, Alonzo	6-4/268	9-15-80	3	Florida State	D2/03	7/0
57	Kriewaldt, Clint	6-1/248	3-16-76	7	Wis.-Stevens Point	FA/03	15/0
55	Porter, Joey	6-3/250	3-22-77	7	Colorado State	D3a/99	15/15
94	Wallace, Rian	6-3/243	5-24-82	R	Temple	D5/05	—
	DEFENSIVE BACKS						
23	Carter, Tyrone (S)	5-8/190	3-31-76	6	Minnesota	FA/04	9/0
21	Colclough, Ricardo (CB)	5-11/186	4-18-82	2	Tusculum	D2/04	16/0
25	Duff, Vontez (CB)	5-11/204	3-8-82	1	Notre Dame	FA/04	0/0
28	Hope, Chris (S)	5-11/206	9-29-80	4	Florida State	D3/02	16/16
29	Iwuoma, Chidi (CB)	5-8/184	2-19-78	5	California	FA/02	14/0
31	Logan, Mike (S)	6-1/211	9-15-74	9	West Virginia	FA/01	3/0
20	McFadden, Bryant (CB)	6-0/190	11-21-81	R	Florida State	D2/05	—
43	Polamalu, Troy (S)	5-10/212	4-19-81	3	USC	D1/03	16/16
33	Stuvaints, Russell (S)	6-0/202	8-28-80	3	Youngstown State	FA/04	15/0
24	Taylor, Ike (CB)	6-1/191	5-5-80	3	Louisiana-Lafayette	D4/03	13/1
26	Townsend, Deshea (CB)	5-10/190	9-8-75	8	Alabama	D4a/98	15/15
27	Williams, Willie (CB)	5-9/194	12-26-70	13	Western Carolina	FA/98	16/10
	SPECIALISTS						
17	Gardocki, Chris (P)	6-1/192	2-7-70	14	Clemson	FA/04	16/0
3	Reed, Jeff (K)	5-11/232	4-9-79	4	North Carolina	FA/02	16/0

Abbreviations: D1—draft pick, first round; T—obtained in trade; FA—free-agent acquisition.

2004 regular-season record: 15-1
Position: 1st in AFC North

Sept.12—OAKLAND	W	24-21
Sept.19—at Baltimore	L	13-30
Sept.26—at Miami	W	13-3
Oct. 3—CINCINNATI	W	28-17
Oct. 10—CLEVELAND	W	34-23
Oct. 17—at Dallas	W	24-20
Oct. 24—Open date		
Oct. 31—NEW ENGLAND	W	34-20
Nov. 7—PHILADELPHIA	W	27-3
Nov.14—at Cleveland	W	24-10
Nov.21—at Cincinnati	W	19-14
Nov.28—WASHINGTON	W	16-7
Dec. 5—at Jacksonville	W	17-16
Dec.12—N.Y. JETS	W	17-6
Dec.18—at N.Y. Giants	W	33-30
Dec.26—BALTIMORE	W	20-7
Jan. 2—at Buffalo	W	29-24

2004 postseason record: 1-1

Jan. 15—N.Y. JETS (OT)*	W	20-17
Jan. 23—NEW ENGLANDÜ	L	27-41

*AFC divisional playoff game. ÜAFC championship game.

SCORING BY PERIODS

	Q1	Q2	Q3	Q4	OT	Pts.
Steelers	123	90	47	112	0	372
Opponents	79	42	66	64	0	251

TEAM STATISTICS

	Pit.	Opp.
TOTAL FIRST DOWNS	310	248
Rushing	134	79
Passing	147	146
Penalty	29	23
3rd Down: Made/Att.	94/219	63/193
3rd Down Pct.	42.9	32.6
4th Down: Made/Att.	7/12	7/13
4th Down Pct.	58.3	53.8
POSSESSION AVG.	34:00	26:00
TOTAL NET YARDS	5184	4134
Avg. per Game	324.0	258.4
Total Plays	1012	882
Avg. per Play	5.1	4.7
NET YARDS RUSHING	2464	1299
Avg. per Game	154.0	81.2
Total Rushes	618	357
NET YARDS PASSING	2720	2835
Avg. per Game	170.0	177.2
Sacked/Yards Lost	36/250	41/225
Gross Yards	2970	3060
Att./Completions	358/228	484/269
Completion Pct.	63.7	55.6
Had Intercepted	13	19
PUNTS/AVERAGE	67/43.0	79/42.7
NET PUNTING AVG.	67/37.4	79/36.3
PENALTIES/YARDS	99/837	104/875
FUMBLES/LOST	20/8	28/13
TOUCHDOWNS	41	26
Rushing	16	8
Passing	20	14
Returns	5	4

SCORING (NON-KICKERS)

	Tot. TD	RTD	PTD	MTD	2Pt.	Tot. Pts.
Bettis	13	13	0	0	0	78
Burress	5	0	5	0	0	30
Ward	5	1	4	0	0	30
Randle El	3	0	3	0	0	18
Tuman	3	0	3	0	0	18
Haynes	2	0	2	0	0	12
Riemersma	2	0	2	0	0	12
Farrior	1	0	0	1	0	6
Harrison	1	0	0	1	0	6
Kreider	1	0	1	0	0	6
Polamalu	1	0	0	1	0	6
Roethlisberger	1	1	0	0	0	6
Staley	1	1	0	0	0	6
Stuvaints	1	0	0	1	0	6
Townsend	1	0	0	1	0	6
Steelers	41	16	20	5	0	248
Opponents	26	8	14	4	1	158

2-Pt. conversions: Steelers 0-1; Opponents 1-2.

(KICKERS)

	XPM/XPA	FGM/FGA	Pts.
Reed	40/40	28/33	124
Steelers	40/40	28/33	124
Opponents	24/24	23/27	93

RUSHING

	Att.	Yds.	Avg.	Lg.	TD
Bettis	250	941	3.8	29	13
Staley	192	830	4.3	38	1
Haynes	55	272	4.9	18	0
Parker	32	186	5.8	58	0
Roethlisberger	56	144	2.6	20	1
Randle El	8	34	4.3	12	0
Ward	7	25	3.6	t16	1
Kreider	4	18	4.5	6	0
Maddox	9	15	1.7	10	0
Da. Brown	1	2	2.0	2	0
St. Pierre	4	-3	-0.8	2	0
Steelers	618	2464	4.0	58	16
Opponents	357	1299	3.6	35	8

RECEIVING

	No.	Yds.	Avg.	Lg.	TD
Ward	80	1004	12.6	58	4
Randle El	43	601	14.0	39	3
Burress	35	698	19.9	48	5
Haynes	18	142	7.9	26	2
Kreider	10	75	7.5	13	1
Mays	9	137	15.2	46	0
Tuman	9	89	9.9	26	3
Riemersma	7	82	11.7	t26	2
Bettis	6	46	7.7	20	0
Staley	6	55	9.2	21	0
Parker	3	16	5.3	12	0
Cushing	1	17	17.0	17	0
Morey	1	8	8.0	8	0
Steelers	228	2970	13.0	58	20
Opponents	269	3060	11.4	t58	14

INTERCEPTIONS

	No.	Yds.	Avg.	Lg.	TD
Polamalu	5	58	11.6	t26	1
Farrior	4	113	28.3	41	1
Townsend	4	54	13.5	t39	1
Hope	1	41	41.0	41	0
Scott	1	23	23.0	23	0
Porter	1	3	3.0	3	0
Foote	1	1	1.0	1	0
I. Taylor	1	0	0.0	0	0
Williams	1	0	0.0	0	0
Steelers	19	293	15.4	41	3
Opponents	13	190	14.6	t51	3

SACKS: A. Smith 8.0, Porter 7.0, Haggans 6.0, Townsend 4.0, Farrior 3.0, Foote 3.0, Colclough 1.5, Harrison 1.0, Hoke 1.0, Kirschke 1.0, Polamalu 1.0, von Oelhoffen 1.0, Williams 1.0, Kriewaldt 0.5. Steelers 41.0; Opponents 36.0.

PUNTING

	No.	Yds.	Avg.	In. 20	Lg.
Gardocki	67	2879	43.0	24	61
Steelers	67	2879	43.0	24	61
Opponents	79	3375	42.7	26	63

PUNT RETURNS

	No.	FC	Yds.	Avg.	Lg.	TD
Randle El	42	13	347	8.3	60	0
Colclough	1	0	13	13.0	13	0
Haynes	1	0	5	5.0	5	0
Steelers	44	13	365	8.3	60	0
Opponents	34	8	252	7.4	33	0

KICK RETURNS

	No.	Yds.	Avg.	Lg.	TD
Colclough	26	566	21.8	48	0
Randle El	21	527	25.1	41	0
I. Taylor	11	184	16.7	22	0
Cushing	3	45	15.0	20	0
Kirschke	1	13	13.0	13	0
Steelers	62	1335	21.5	48	0
Opponents	74	1595	21.6	t91	1

FIELD GOALS

	1-19	20-29	30-39	40-49	50+
Reed	1/1	8/9	12/13	5/8	2/2
Steelers	1/1	8/9	12/13	5/8	2/2
Opponents	0/0	7/8	11/12	5/6	0/1

Reed: (42G) (48N) (40G, 44N, 45N, 51G) () (47G, 26G) (51G) (19G, 29G) (33N, 42G, 31G) (20G, 24N) (32G) (33G, 36G, 32G) (37G) (34G) (33G, 21G, 36G, 28G) (23G, 40G) (22G, 21G, 31G, 37G, 33G)

Opponents: (28G, 38G) (35G, 27G, 34G) (34G) (34G) (24G, 34G, 46G) (47G, 39G) (43G, 25G) (33G) (31G) () () (32N, 20G, 29G, 36G, 60N) (43G, 41G) (22G) (44N) (37G, 28N)

PASSING

	Att.	Cmp.	Yds.	Pct.	Avg. Gain	TD	Pct. TD	Int.	Pct. Int.	Long	Sack/Lost	Rating
Roethlisberger	295	196	2621	66.4	8.88	17	5.8	11	3.7	58	30/213	98.1
Maddox	60	30	329	50.0	5.48	1	1.7	2	3.3	39	6/37	58.3
Bettis	1	1	10	100.0	10.00	1	100.0	0	0.0	t10	0/0	147.9
Randle El	1	1	10	100.0	10.00	1	100.0	0	0.0	t10	0/0	147.9
St. Pierre	1	0	0	0.0	0.00	0	0.0	0	0.0	...	0/0	39.6
Steelers	358	228	2970	63.7	8.30	20	5.6	13	3.6	58	36/250	93.2
Opponents	484	269	3060	55.6	6.32	14	2.9	19	3.9	t58	41/225	68.0

ST. LOUIS RAMS
NFC WEST DIVISION

2005 SEASON

CLUB DIRECTORY

Chairman/owner
Georgia Frontiere
Vice chairman/owner
Stan Kroenke
President
John Shaw
President/football operations
Jay Zygmunt
General manager
Charley Armey
Executive vice president
Bob Wallace
Director of player personnel
Lawrence McCutcheon
Vice president/operations
John Oswald
Director of football media
Duane Lewis

Head coach
Mike Martz

Assistant coaches
Charles Bankins (asst. special teams)
John Benton (offensive line)
Gill Byrd (secondary asst.)
Pat Carter (offensive asst.)
Chris Clausen (strength & conditioning)
Henry Ellard (wide receivers)
Steve Fairchild (off. coordinator)
Frank Falks (tight ends)
Bill Kollar (defensive line)
Dana LeDuc (strength & conditioning)
Bob Ligashesky (special teams)
Larry Marmie (def. coordinator)
John Matsko (offensive line)
Wilbert Montgomery (running backs)
John Ramsdell (quarterbacks)
Kurt Schottenheimer (secondary coach)
Matt Sheldon (special asst.)
Joe Vitt (asst. head coach/linebackers)

OFFSEASON MOVES

Key additions
LB Chris Claiborne	FA/Vikings
LB Dexter Coakley	FA/Cowboys
CB Michael Hawthorne	Rel./Packers
DB Michael Stone	FA/Cardinals
G Rex Tucker	Rel./Bears
DE Jay Williams	Rel./Dolphins
TE Roland Williams	Rel./Raiders

Key losses
QB Chris Chandler	Released
TE Cam Cleeland	Free agent
S Rich Coady	FA/Falcons
S Antuan Edwards	Free agent
DT Bryce Fisher	FA/Seahawks
G Matt Lehr	FA/Falcons
LB Tommy Polley	FA/Ravens

SCHEDULE

Sept.	11—at San Francisco	4:15
Sept.	18—at Arizona	4:05
Sept.	25—TENNESSEE	1:00
Oct.	2—at N.Y. Giants	1:00
Oct.	9—SEATTLE	1:00
Oct.	17—at Indianapolis (Mon.)	9:00
Oct.	23—NEW ORLEANS	1:00
Oct.	30—JACKSONVILLE	2:00
Nov.	6—Open week	
Nov.	13—at Seattle	5:15
Nov.	20—ARIZONA	2:00
Nov.	27—at Houston	2:00
Dec.	4—WASHINGTON	5:05
Dec.	11—at Minnesota	2:00
Dec.	18—PHILADELPHIA	5:15
Dec.	24—SAN FRANCISCO (Sat.)	2:00
Jan.	1—at Dallas	9:30

All times are Eastern.
All games Sunday unless noted.

DRAFT CHOICES

Alex Barron, OT, Florida State (first round/19th pick overall).
Ronald Bartell, CB, Howard (2/50).
Oshiomogho Atogwe, FS, Stanford (3/66).
Richie Incognito, C, Nebraska (3/81).
Jerome Carter, SS, Florida State (4/117).
Claude Terrell, G, New Mexico (4/134).
Jerome Collins, TE, Notre Dame (5/144).
Dante Ridgeway, WR, Ball State (6/192).
Reggie Hodges, P, Ball State (6/210).
Ryan Fitzpatrick, QB, Harvard (7/250).
Madison Hedgecock, FB, North Carolina (7/251).

MISCELLANEOUS TEAM DATA

Stadium (capacity, surface):
Edward Jones Dome (66,000, artificial)
Business address:
1 Rams Way
St. Louis, MO 63045
Business phone:
314-982-7267
Ticket information:
314-425-8830
Team colors:
Rams millennium blue, Rams century gold
Flagship radio station:
KLOU, 103.3 FM; KATZ, 1600 AM; KTRS, 550 AM
Training site:
Rams Park
St. Louis, MO 63045

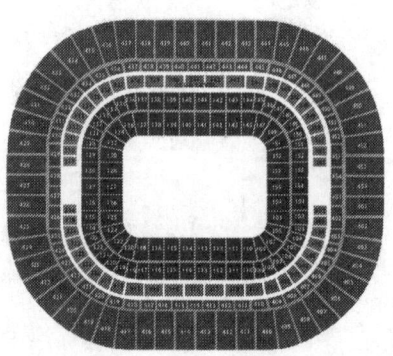

ST. LOUIS RAMS

No.	QUARTERBACKS	Ht./Wt.	Born	NFL Exp.	College	How acq.	'04 Games GP/GS
10	Bulger, Marc	6-3/215	4-5-77	5	West Virginia	FA/01	14/14
12	Fitzpatrick, Ryan	6-2/221	11-24-82	R	Harvard	D7a/05	—
11	Martin, Jamie	6-2/205	2-8-70	11	Weber State	FA/04	1/0
9	Smoker, Jeff	6-3/223	6-13-81	1	Michigan State	D6/04	0/0
	RUNNING BACKS						
27	Cason, Aveion	5-10/204	7-12-79	5	Illinois State	W-Ari./04	3/0
28	Faulk, Marshall	5-10/211	2-26-73	12	San Diego State	T-Ind./99	14/14
44	Goodspeed, Joey (FB)	6-1/247	2-22-78	4	Notre Dame	FA/02	16/5
33	Harris, Arlen	5-10/212	4-22-80	3	Virginia	FA/03	14/1
38	Hedgecock, Madison (FB)	6-3/266	8-27-81	R	North Carolina	D7b/05	—
39	Jackson, Steven	6-2/233	7-22-83	2	Oregon State	D1/04	14/3
45	Massey, Chris (LS)	6-0/245	8-21-79	4	Marshall	D7/02	16/0
	RECEIVERS						
80	Bruce, Isaac	6-0/188	11-10-72	12	Memphis	D2/94	16/16
48	Collins, Jerome (TE)	6-4/258	8-18-82	R	Notre Dame	D5/05	—
83	Curtis, Kevin	5-11/186	7-17-78	3	Utah State	D3/03	15/0
82	Furrey, Mike	6-0/185	5-12-77	3	Northern Iowa	FA/03	8/0
81	Holt, Torry	6-0/190	6-5-76	7	North Carolina State	D1/99	16/16
49	Jensen, Erik (TE)	6-2/253	10-11-80	1	Iowa	D7a/04	0/0
89	Looker, Dane	6-0/194	4-5-76	4	Washington	FA/02	14/0
86	Manumaleuna, B. (TE)	6-2/288	1-4-80	5	Arizona	D4b/01	16/16
84	McDonald, Shaun	5-10/183	6-13-81	3	Arizona State	D4a/03	16/0
87	Ridgeway, Dante	5-11/212	4-18-84	R	Ball State	D6a/05	—
88	Williams, Roland (TE)	6-5/265	4-27-75	8	Syracuse	W-Oak/05	12/3
	OFFENSIVE LINEMEN						
70	Barron, Alex (T)	6-7/320	9-28-82	R	Florida State	D1/05	—
61	Incognito, Richie (C)	6-3/305	7-5-83	R	Nebraska	D3b/05	—
67	McCollum, Andy (C)	6-4/300	6-2-70	12	Toledo	FA/99	16/16
76	Pace, Orlando (T)	6-7/325	11-4-75	9	Ohio State	D1/97	16/16
60	Saipaia, Blaine (G)	6-3/310	8-25-78	2	Colorado State	FA/04	8/5
63	Tercero, Scott (T)	6-4/303	10-28-81	2	California	D6/03	8/4
75	Terrell, Claude (G)	6-2/343	4-20-82	R	New Mexico	D4b/05	—
62	Timmerman, Adam (G)	6-4/310	8-14-71	11	South Dakota State	FA/99	16/16
66	Tucker, Rex (G)	6-5/315	12-20-76	5	Texas A&M	W-Chi./05	6/5
64	Turner, Larry (C)	6-2/290	3-8-82	2	Eastern Kentucky	D7b/04	14/1
77	Williams, Grant (T)	6-7/320	5-10-74	10	Louisiana Tech	T-NE/02	16/11
	DEFENSIVE LINEMEN						
97	Green, Brandon (E)	6-3/270	9-5-80	2	Rice	FA/05	3/0
95	Hargrove, Anthony (E)	6-3/269	7-20-83	2	Georgia Tech	D3/04	15/2
98	Howard, Brian (T)	6-4/278	9-9-81	2	Idaho	FA/04	15/1
97	Jackson, Tyoka (E)	6-2/280	11-22-71	11	Penn State	FA/01	14/0
73	Kennedy, Jimmy (T)	6-4/320	11-15-79	3	Penn State	D1/03	9/5
92	Lewis, Damione (T)	6-2/301	3-1-78	5	Miami	D1a/01	16/10
91	Little, Leonard (E)	6-3/261	10-19-74	8	Tennessee	D3/98	16/16
79	Pickett, Ryan (T)	6-2/310	10-8-79	5	Ohio State	D1c/01	16/16
96	Williams, Jay (E)	6-3/270	10-13-71	11	Wake Forest	W-Mia./05	16/1
	LINEBACKERS						
54	Chillar, Brandon	6-2/253	10-21-82	2	UCLA	D4/04	16/5
59	Claiborne, Chris	6-3/259	7-26-78	7	USC	FA/05	12/12
52	Coakley, Dexter	5-10/231	10-20-72	9	Appalachian State	FA/05	16/16
57	Faulk, Trev	6-3/254	8-6-81	2	LSU	FA/03	13/2
55	Thomas, Robert	6-1/237	7-17-80	4	UCLA	D1/02	14/11
50	Tinoisamoa, Pisa	6-1/235	7-15-81	3	Hawaii	D2/03	16/16
58	Wahlroos, Drew	6-3/235	6-7-80	2	Colorado	FA/04	6/0
	DEFENSIVE BACKS						
20	Anderson, Dwight (CB)	5-10/172	7-5-81	2	South Dakota	FA/04	12/0
31	Archuleta, Adam (S)	6-0/223	11-27-77	5	Arizona State	D1b/01	16/14
41	Atogwe, Oshiomogho (S)	5-11/203	6-28-81	R	Stanford	D3a/05	—
32	Bartell, Ronald (CB)	6-1/208	2-22-82	R	Howard	D2/05	—
23	Butler, Jerametrius (CB)	5-10/181	11-28-78	5	Kansas State	D5/01	16/16
42	Carter, Jerome (S)	5-11/219	10-25-82	R	Florida State	D4a/05	—
23	Fair, Terry (CB)	5-9/184	7-20-76	6	Tennessee	W-Pit./05	0/0
22	Fisher, Travis (CB)	5-10/189	9-12-79	4	Central Florida	D2/02	10/10
21	Garrett, Kevin (CB)	5-10/194	7-29-80	3	Southern Methodist	D5c/03	14/1
24	Groce, DeJuan (CB)	5-10/192	2-17-80	3	Nebraska	D4b/03	11/4
26	Hawthorne, Michael (CB)	6-3/204	1-26-77	6	Purdue	FA/05	16/5
34	Stone, Michael (S)	6-0/201	2-13-78	4	Memphis	FA/05	14/0
	SPECIALISTS						
4	Hodges, Reggie (P)	6-0/226	1-26-87	R	Ball State	D6b/05	—
14	Wilkins, Jeff (K)	6-2/205	4-19-72	12	Youngstown State	FA/97	16/0

Abbreviations: D1—draft pick, first round; W—claimed on waivers; T—obtained in trade; FA—free-agent acquisition.

ST. LOUIS RAMS

2004 REVIEW

2004 regular-season record: 8-8
Position: 2nd in NFC West

Sept.12—ARIZONA	W	17-10
Sept.19—at Atlanta	L	17-34
Sept.26—NEW ORLEANS (OT)	L	25-28
Oct. 3—at San Francisco	W	24-14
Oct.10—at Seattle (OT)	W	33-27
Oct.18—TAMPA BAY	W	28-21
Oct.24—at Miami	L	14-31
Oct.31—Open date		
Nov. 7—NEW ENGLAND	L	22-40
Nov.14—SEATTLE	W	23-12
Nov.21—at Buffalo	L	17-37
Nov.29—at Green Bay	L	17-45
Dec. 5—SAN FRANCISCO	W	16-6
Dec.12—at Carolina	L	7-20
Dec.19—at Arizona	L	7-31
Dec.27—PHILADELPHIA	W	20-7
Jan. 2—N.Y. JETS (OT)	W	32-29

2004 postseason record: 1-1

Jan. 8—at Seattle#	W	27-20
Jan.15—at Atlanta*	L	17-47

#NFC wild-card game. *NFC divisional play-off game.

SCORING BY PERIODS

	Q1	Q2	Q3	Q4	OT	Pts.
Rams	69	115	40	86	9	319
Opponents	78	127	90	94	3	392

TEAM STATISTICS

	St.L.	Opp.
TOTAL FIRST DOWNS	321	311
Rushing	96	118
Passing	203	172
Penalty	22	21
3rd Down: Made/Att.	89/211	76/209
3rd Down Pct.	42.2	36.4
4th Down: Made/Att.	13/19	12/17
4th Down Pct.	68.4	70.6
POSSESSION AVG.	31:05	28:55
TOTAL NET YARDS	5877	5353
Avg. per Game	367.3	334.6
Total Plays	1011	1006
Avg. per Play	5.8	5.3
NET YARDS RUSHING	1624	2179
Avg. per Game	101.5	136.2
Total Rushes	381	480
NET YARDS PASSING	4253	3174
Avg. per Game	265.8	198.4
Sacked/Yards Lost	50/362	34/241
Gross Yards	4615	3415
Att./Completions	580/372	492/292
Completion Pct.	64.1	59.3
Had Intercepted	22	6
PUNTS/AVERAGE	68/41.9	71/42.5
NET PUNTING AVG.	68/34.0	71/37.6
PENALTIES/YARDS	127/993	109/827
FUMBLES/LOST	27/17	18/9

	St.L.	Opp.
TOUCHDOWNS	37	43
Rushing	11	13
Passing	23	24
Returns	3	6

SCORING (NON-KICKERS)

	Tot. TD	RTD	PTD	MTD	2Pt.	Tot. Pts.
Holt	10	0	10	0	0	60
Bruce	6	0	6	0	0	36
M. Faulk	4	3	1	0	2	28
S. Jackson	4	4	0	0	1	26
Bulger	3	3	0	0	0	18
McDonald	3	0	3	0	0	18
Curtis	2	0	2	0	1	14
Little	2	0	0	2	0	12
Archuleta	1	0	0	1	0	6
Goodspeed	1	1	0	0	0	6
Manumaleuna	1	0	1	0	0	6
Rams	37	11	23	3	4	230
Opponents	43	13	24	6	1	260

2-Pt. conversions: Rams 4-4; Opponents 1-4.

(KICKERS)

	XPM/XPA	FGM/FGA	Pts.
J. Wilkins	32/32	19/24	89
Rams	32/32	19/24	89
Opponents	39/39	31/36	132

RUSHING

	Att.	Yds.	Avg.	Lg.	TD
M. Faulk	195	774	4.0	40	3
S. Jackson	134	673	5.0	48	4
Bulger	19	89	4.7	t19	3
Harris	20	63	3.2	14	0
Curtis	3	24	8.0	15	0
Goodspeed	3	6	2.0	t2	1
C. Chandler	1	2	2.0	2	0
McDonald	4	0	0.0	7	0
Cleeland	1	-2	-2.0	-2	0
J. Wilkins	1	-5	-5.0	-5	0
Rams	381	1624	4.3	48	11
Opponents	480	2179	4.5	t42	13

RECEIVING

	No.	Yds.	Avg.	Lg.	TD
Holt	94	1372	14.6	t75	10
Bruce	89	1292	14.5	56	6
M. Faulk	50	310	6.2	25	1
McDonald	37	494	13.4	t52	3
Curtis	32	421	13.2	t41	2
S. Jackson	19	189	9.9	28	0
Manumaleuna	15	174	11.6	48	1
Looker	13	183	14.1	29	0
Goodspeed	11	71	6.5	13	0
Cleeland	7	57	8.1	15	0
Harris	4	44	11.0	21	0
Furrey	1	8	8.0	8	0

	No.	Yds.	Avg.	Lg.	TD
Rams	372	4615	12.4	t75	23
Opponents	292	3415	11.7	t71	24

INTERCEPTIONS

	No.	Yds.	Avg.	Lg.	TD
Butler	5	15	3.0	10	0
T. Fisher	1	30	30.0	30	0
Rams	6	45	7.5	30	0
Opponents	22	191	8.7	t38	1

SACKS: B. Fisher 8.5, Little 7.0, Lewis 5.0, T. Jackson 4.0, Archuleta 2.0, Pickett 2.0, Polley 2.0, Tinoisamoa 1.5, Flowers 1.0, Hargrove 1.0. Rams 34.0; Opponents 50.0.

PUNTING

	No.	Yds.	Avg.	In.20	Lg.
Landeta	40	1733	43.3	9	63
Stemke	28	1115	39.8	12	56
Rams	68	2848	41.9	21	63
Opponents	71	3014	42.5	17	65

PUNT RETURNS

	No.	FC	Yds.	Avg.	Lg.	TD
McDonald	30	18	143	4.8	39	0
Rams	30	18	143	4.8	39	0
Opponents	35	17	416	11.9	t86	1

KICK RETURNS

	No.	Yds.	Avg.	Lg.	TD
Harris	47	951	20.2	29	0
Cason	14	310	22.1	31	0
Furrey	8	157	19.6	23	0
Anderson	4	71	17.8	25	0
S. Jackson	4	79	19.8	23	0
Manumaleuna	2	13	6.5	13	0
Coady	1	-1	-1.0	-1	0
M. Faulk	1	0	0.0	0	0
Flowers	1	0	0.0	0	0
Goodspeed	1	9	9.0	9	0
Groce	1	15	15.0	15	0
Rams	84	1604	19.1	31	0
Opponents	66	1680	25.5	t94	1

FIELD GOALS

	1-19	20-29	30-39	40-49	50+
J. Wilkins	0/0	7/7	5/6	3/6	4/5
Rams	0/0	7/7	5/6	3/6	4/5
Opponents	0/0	8/8	11/12	9/11	3/5

J. Wilkins: (50G, 28G, 22G) (46G) (53G) (20G, 33N) (39G, 36G) (56N, 44N) () () (36G, 47G, 23G) (41G) (42N, 34G) (29G, 52G, 52G) () () (44N, 28G, 29G) (31G)
Opponents: (22G) (35G, 25G) (52G, 53G, 39G, 51N, 38G, 31G) () (48G, 43N, 34G) (35N, 48N) (43G) (43G, 31G, 45G, 36G) (28G, 30G, 45G, 41G) (21G, 35G, 33G) (27G) (51G, 40G) (27G, 20G) (48G) () (47G, 33G, 27G, 53N)

PASSING

	Att.	Cmp.	Yds.	Pct.	Avg. Gain	TD	Pct. TD	Int.	Pct. Int.	Long	Sack/Lost	Rating
Bulger	485	321	3964	66.2	8.17	21	4.3	14	2.9	56	41/302	93.7
C. Chandler	62	35	463	56.5	7.47	2	3.2	8	12.9	t75	7/54	51.4
Martin	30	16	188	53.3	6.27	0	0.0	0	0.0	26	2/6	72.6
Bruce	2	0	0	0.0	0.00	0	0.0	0	0.0	...	0/0	39.6
J. Wilkins	1	0	0	0.0	0.00	0	0.0	0	0.0	...	0/0	39.6
Rams	580	372	4615	64.1	7.96	23	4.0	22	3.8	t75	50/362	86.1
Opponents	492	292	3415	59.3	6.94	24	4.9	6	1.2	t71	34/241	91.6

SAN DIEGO CHARGERS
AFC WEST DIVISION

2005 SEASON

CLUB DIRECTORY

Owner
Alex G. Spanos
President/CEO
Dean A. Spanos
Executive vice president
Michael A. Spanos
Executive vice president/general manager
A.J. Smith
Executive vp & chief operating officer
Jim Steeg
Assistant general manager/director of player personnel
Buddy Nix
Vice president of football operations
Ed McGuire
Vice president/chief financial & administrative officer
Jeanne Bonk
Vice president/chief marketing officer
Ken Derrett
Director of college scouting
Jimmy Raye
Director of pro scouting
Fran Foley
Director of public relations
Bill Johnston
Director of public affairs & corporate community relations
Kimberley Layton

OFFSEASON MOVES

Key additions
CB Bhawoh Jue — FA/Packers
Key losses
WR Tim Dwight — Rel./Patriots
DT Jason Fisk — Rel./Browns
QB Doug Flutie — Rel./Patriots
LB Zeke Moreno — FA/Texans

Head coach
Marty Schottenheimer

Assistant coaches
Cam Cameron (off. coordinator)
Pete Carmichael Jr. (asst. wide receivers/quality control)
Rob Chudzinski (tight ends)
Steve Crosby (special teams)
Albert Lewis (asst. secondary)
James Lofton (wide receivers)
Greg Manusky (linebackers)
Carl Mauck (offensive line)
Wayne Nunnely (defensive line)
John Pagano (asst. linebackers/quality control)
Wade Phillips (def. coordinator)
Dave Redding (strength & conditioning)
Matt Schiotz (asst. strength & conditioning)
Brian Schottenheimer (quarterbacks)
Clarence Shelmon (running backs)
Brian Stewart (secondary)
John Wuehrmann (coaching administrator)

SCHEDULE

Sept.	11—DALLAS	4:15
Sept.	18—at Denver	4:15
Sept.	25—N.Y. GIANTS	8:30
Oct.	2—at New England	1:00
Oct.	10—PITTSBURGH (Mon.)	9:00
Oct.	16—at Oakland	4:15
Oct.	23—at Philadelphia	1:00
Oct.	30—KANSAS CITY	5:05
Nov.	6—at N.Y. Jets	2:00
Nov.	13—Open week	
Nov.	20—BUFFALO	5:15
Nov.	27—at Washington	2:00
Dec.	4—OAKLAND	9:30
Dec.	11—MIAMI	5:15
Dec.	18—at Indianapolis	2:00
Dec.	24—at Kansas City (Sat.)	2:00
Dec.	31—DENVER (Sat.)	5:30

All times are Eastern.
All games Sunday unless noted.

DRAFT CHOICES

Shawne Merriman, OLB, Maryland (first round/12th pick overall).
Luis Castillo, DT, Northwestern (1/28).
Vincent Jackson, WR, Northern Colorado (2/61).
Darren Sproles, RB, Kansas State (4/130).
Wesley Britt, OT, Alabama (5/164).
Wes Sims, G, Oklahoma (6/177).
Scott Mruczkowski, C, Bowling Green (7/242).

MISCELLANEOUS TEAM DATA

Stadium (capacity, surface):
Qualcomm Stadium
(70,000, grass)
Business address:
P.O. Box 609609
San Diego, CA 92160-9609
Business phone:
858-874-4500
Ticket information:
877-CHARGERS
Team colors:
Navy blue, white and gold
Flagship radio station:
KIOZ, Rock 105.3 FM
Website:
www.chargers.com
Training site:
Chargers Park
San Diego, CA
858-874-4500

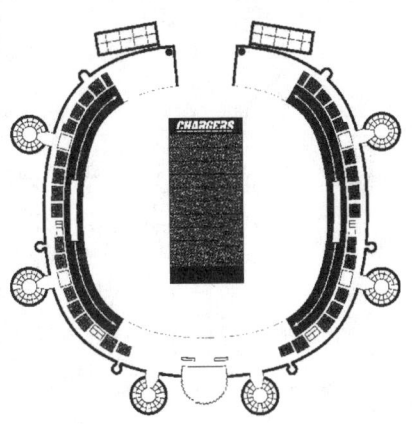

SAN DIEGO CHARGERS

No.	QUARTERBACKS	Ht./Wt.	Born	NFL Exp.	College	How acq.	'04 Games GP/GS
9	Brees, Drew	6-0/209	1-15-79	5	Purdue	D2/01	15/15
12	Lemon, Cleo	6-2/215	8-16-79	2	Arkansas State	FA/03	0/0
17	Rivers, Philip	6-5/228	12-8-81	2	North Carolina State	T-NYG/04	2/0
	RUNNING BACKS						
24	Chatman, Jesse	5-8/247	9-22-79	4	Eastern Washington	FA/02	15/0
41	Neal, Lorenzo (FB)	5-11/255	12-27-70	13	Fresno State	FA/03	16/10
34	Pinnock, Andrew (FB)	5-10/260	3-12-80	3	South Carolina	D7/03	1/0
43	Sproles, Darren	5-6/181	6-20-83	R	Kansas State	D4/05	—
21	Tomlinson, LaDainian	5-10/221	6-23-79	5	TCU	D1/01	15/15
33	Turner, Michael	5-10/237	2-13-82	2	Northern Illinois	D5b/04	14/1
	RECEIVERS						
82	Caldwell, Reche	6-0/215	3-28-79	4	Florida	D2b/02	6/6
13	Floyd, Malcom	6-5/201	9-8-81	2	Wyoming	FA/04	4/2
85	Gates, Antonio (TE)	6-4/260	6-18-80	3	Kent State	FA/03	15/15
83	Jackson, Vincent	6-5/241	1-14-83	R	Northern Colorado	D2/05	—
89	Krause, Ryan (TE)	6-3/256	6-16-81	1	Nebraska-Omaha	D6/04	1/1
87	McCardell, Keenan	6-1/191	1-6-70	14	UNLV	T-TB/04	7/6
81	Osgood, Kassim	6-5/209	5-20-80	3	San Diego State	FA/03	16/7
88	Parker, Eric	6-0/180	4-14-79	4	Tennessee	FA/02	15/13
84	Peelle, Justin (TE)	6-4/255	3-15-79	4	Oregon	D4/02	16/4
	OFFENSIVE LINEMEN						
50	Binn, David (LS)	6-3/223	2-6-72	12	California	FA/94	16/0
65	Brandt, David (G)	6-4/311	9-25-77	4	Michigan	T-Was./03	3/0
67	Britt, Wesley (T)	6-8/314	11-21-81	R	Alabama	D5/05	—
68	Dielman, Kris (G)	6-4/310	2-3-81	3	Indiana	FA/03	15/0
77	Fonoti, Toniu (G)	6-4/350	11-26-81	3	Nebraska	D2a/02	16/16
79	Goff, Mike (G)	6-5/311	1-6-76	8	Iowa	FA/04	16/16
62	Hallen, Bob (C)	6-3/305	3-9-75	8	Kent State	FA/04	2/0
61	Hardwick, Nick (C)	6-4/295	9-12-81	2	Purdue	D3/04	14/14
75	Jordan, Leander (T)	6-4/316	9-15-77	6	Indiana (Pa.)	FA/04	5/0
66	Joseph, Carlos (T)	6-6/342	7-14-80	1	Miami	D7c/04	0/0
63	Mruczkowski, Scott (C)	6-4/321	4-5-82	R	Bowling Green	D7/05	—
72	Oben, Roman (T)	6-4/305	10-9-72	10	Louisville	T-TB/04	16/16
70	Olivea, Shane (T)	6-3/312	10-7-81	2	Ohio State	D7b/04	16/16
60	Sims, Wes (T)	6-4/317	4-8-81	R	Oklahoma	D6/05	—
71	Van Buren, Courtney (T)	6-6/350	2-22-80	3	Arkansas-Pine Bluff	D3/03	1/0
	DEFENSIVE LINEMEN						
96	Ball, Dave (E)	6-5/277	1-4-81	2	UCLA	D5a/04	6/0
97	Bingham, Ryon (T)	6-3/303	6-6-81	1	Nebraska	D7a/04	0/0
93	Castillo, Luis (NT)	6-3/306	8-4-83	R	Northwestern	D1b/05	—
74	Cesaire, Jacques (E)	6-2/295	8-30-80	3	S. Connecticut State	FA/03	16/12
90	Dingle, Adrian (E)	6-3/296	6-25-77	7	Clemson	D5a/99	10/2
99	Olshansky, Igor (E)	6-6/309	5-3-82	2	Oregon	D2/04	16/16
94	Pollard, Robert (E)	6-2/278	6-28-81	1	TCU	FA/04	1/0
78	Scott, DeQuincy (E)	6-1/260	3-5-78	4	Southern Mississippi	FA/01	14/2
76	Williams, Jamal (NG)	6-3/348	4-28-76	8	Oklahoma State	SD2/98	15/15
	LINEBACKERS						
54	Cooper, Stephen	6-1/235	6-19-79	3	Maine	FA/03	16/2
59	Edwards, Donnie	6-2/227	4-6-73	10	UCLA	FA/02	16/16
53	Foley, Steve	6-4/265	9-11-75	7	Louisiana-Monroe	FA/04	16/16
58	Godfrey, Randall	6-2/245	4-6-73	10	Georgia	FA/04	15/15
51	Leber, Ben	6-3/244	12-7-78	4	Kansas State	D3/02	16/16
91	Merriman, Shawne	6-4/253	5-25-84	R	Maryland	D1a/05	—
95	Phillips, Shaun	6-3/262	5-13-81	2	Purdue	D4/04	16/0
52	Polk, Carlos	6-2/250	2-22-77	5	Nebraska	D4/01	1/0
56	Wilhelm, Matt	6-2/254	2-2-81	3	Ohio State	D4/03	7/0
	DEFENSIVE BACKS						
45	Butler, Robb (S)	6-0/217	9-14-81	2	Robert Morris	FA/04	5/0
36	Curry, Markus (CB)	5-11/181	4-7-81	1	Michigan	FA/05	—
22	Davis, Sammy (CB)	6-0/195	4-8-80	3	Texas A&M	D1/03	12/10
25	Fletcher, Jamar (CB)	5-10/186	8-28-79	5	Wisconsin	T-Mia./04	16/0
29	Florence, Drayton (CB)	6-0/195	12-19-80	3	Tuskegee	D2a/03	13/5
42	Hart, Clinton (S)	6-0/205	7-20-77	3	Central Florida CC	W-Phi./04	14/0
23	Jammer, Quentin (CB)	6-0/204	6-19-79	4	Texas	D1/02	16/16
27	Jue, Bhawoh (S)	6-0/199	5-24-79	5	Penn State	FA/05	16/4
48	Kiel, Terrence (S)	5-11/207	11-24-80	3	Texas A&M	D2b/03	16/16
31	Milligan, Hanik (S)	6-3/200	11-3-79	3	Houston	D6/03	14/0
20	Wilson, Jerry (S)	5-11/190	7-17-73	10	Southern (La.)	FA/02	16/16
	SPECIALISTS						
10	Kaeding, Nate (K)	6-0/187	3-26-82	2	Iowa	D3a/04	16/0
5	Scifres, Mike (P)	6-2/236	10-8-80	3	Western Illinois	D5/03	16/0

Abbreviations: D1—draft pick, first round; W—claimed on waivers; T—obtained in trade; FA—free-agent acquisition; SD2—supplemental draft, second round.

2004 regular-season record: 12-4
Position: 1st in AFC West

Sept.12—at Houston	W	27-20
Sept.19—N.Y. JETS	L	28-34
Sept.26—at Denver	L	13-23
Oct. 3—TENNESSEE	W	38-17
Oct. 10—JACKSONVILLE	W	34-21
Oct. 17—at Atlanta	L	20-21
Oct. 24—at Carolina	W	17-6
Oct. 31—OAKLAND	W	42-14
Nov. 7—NEW ORLEANS	W	43-17
Nov. 14—Open date		
Nov. 21—at Oakland	W	23-17
Nov. 28—at Kansas City	W	34-31
Dec. 5—DENVER	W	20-17
Dec. 12—TAMPA BAY	W	31-24
Dec. 19—at Cleveland	W	21-0
Dec. 26—at Indianapolis (OT)	L	31-34
Jan. 2—KANSAS CITY	W	24-17

2004 postseason record: 0-1
Jan. 8—N.Y. JETS (OT)#   L   17-20
#AFC wild-card game.

SCORING BY PERIODS

	Q1	Q2	Q3	Q4	OT	Pts.
Chargers	92	138	106	110	0	446
Opponents	37	97	52	124	3	313

TEAM STATISTICS

	S.D.	Opp.
TOTAL FIRST DOWNS	328	320
Rushing	131	79
Passing	160	200
Penalty	37	41
3rd Down: Made/Att.	97/208	69/196
3rd Down Pct.	46.6	35.2
4th Down: Made/Att.	5/8	13/24
4th Down Pct.	62.5	54.2
POSSESSION AVG.	31:30	28:30
TOTAL NET YARDS	5542	5360
Avg. per Game	346.4	335.0
Total Plays	996	991
Avg. per Play	5.6	5.4
NET YARDS RUSHING	2185	1307
Avg. per Game	136.6	81.7
Total Rushes	525	355
NET YARDS PASSING	3357	4053
Avg. per Game	209.8	253.3
Sacked/Yards Lost	21/149	29/142
Gross Yards	3506	4195
Att./Completions	450/288	607/372
Completion Pct.	64.0	61.3
Had Intercepted	8	23
PUNTS/AVERAGE	69/43.1	64/42.4
NET PUNTING AVG.	69/38.4	64/37.0
PENALTIES/YARDS	108/875	109/940
FUMBLES/LOST	27/10	19/10
TOUCHDOWNS	55	36
Rushing	24	15
Passing	29	19
Returns	2	2

SCORING (NON-KICKERS)

	Tot. TD	RTD	PTD	MTD	2Pt.	Tot. Pts.
Tomlinson	18	17	1	0	0	108
Gates	13	0	13	0	0	78
E. Parker	4	0	4	0	0	24
Caldwell	3	0	3	0	0	18
Chatman	3	3	0	0	0	18
Brees	2	2	0	0	0	12
Dwight	2	0	1	1	0	12
Flutie	2	2	0	0	0	12
Osgood	2	0	2	0	0	12
Peelle	2	0	2	0	0	12
Edwards	1	0	0	1	0	6
Floyd	1	0	1	0	0	6
Krause	1	0	1	0	0	6
McCardell	1	0	1	0	0	6
Chargers	55	24	29	2	0	332
Opponents	36	15	19	2	2	220

2-Pt. conversions: Chargers 0-0; Opponents 2-2.

(KICKERS)

	XPM/XPA	FGM/FGA	Pts.
Kaeding	54/55	20/25	114
Chargers	54/55	20/25	114
Opponents	33/34	20/27	93

RUSHING

	Att.	Yds.	Avg.	Lg.	TD
Tomlinson	339	1335	3.9	42	17
Chatman	65	392	6.0	52	3
Turner	20	104	5.2	30	0
Brees	53	85	1.6	22	2
Dwight	4	54	13.5	48	0
Neal	16	53	3.3	8	0
E. Parker	4	53	13.3	38	0
Caldwell	4	45	11.3	20	0
Flutie	5	39	7.8	20	2
Pinnock	9	26	2.9	11	0
McCardell	1	3	3.0	3	0
Shaw	1	1	1.0	1	0
Rivers	4	-5	-1.3	-1	0
Chargers	525	2185	4.2	52	24
Opponents	355	1307	3.7	26	15

RECEIVING

	No.	Yds.	Avg.	Lg.	TD
Gates	81	964	11.9	t72	13
Tomlinson	53	441	8.3	t74	1
E. Parker	47	690	14.7	t79	4
McCardell	31	393	12.7	31	1
Caldwell	18	310	17.2	t58	3
Osgood	15	308	20.5	65	2
Neal	13	66	5.1	12	0
Peelle	10	84	8.4	t17	2
Krause	5	81	16.2	29	1
Turner	4	8	2.0	7	0
Floyd	3	49	16.3	27	1
Pinnock	3	26	8.7	14	0
Chatman	2	17	8.5	17	0
Dwight	2	31	15.5	t23	1
Brees	1	38	38.0	38	0
Chargers	288	3506	12.2	t79	29
Opponents	372	4195	11.3	50	19

INTERCEPTIONS

	No.	Yds.	Avg.	Lg.	TD
Edwards	5	49	9.8	t30	1
Florence	4	54	13.5	40	0
Wilson	3	12	4.0	12	0
Kiel	2	31	15.5	31	0
Foley	2	4	2.0	4	0
Hart	1	13	13.0	13	0
Jammer	1	12	12.0	12	0
Davis	1	4	4.0	4	0
Dingle	1	1	1.0	1	0
Fletcher	1	0	0.0	0	0
Phillips	1	0	0.0	0	0
Wilhelm	1	0	0.0	0	0
Chargers	23	180	7.8	40	1
Opponents	8	66	8.3	25	0

SACKS: Foley 10.0, Phillips 4.0, J. Williams 4.0, Godfrey 2.0, Leber 2.0, Scott 1.5, Dingle 1.0, Edwards 1.0, Fisk 1.0, Kiel 1.0, Olshansky 1.0, Cesaire 0.5. Chargers 29.0; Opponents 21.0.

PUNTING

	No.	Yds.	Avg.	In. 20	Lg.
Scifres	69	2974	43.1	29	60
Chargers	69	2974	43.1	29	60
Opponents	64	2713	42.4	13	59

PUNT RETURNS

	No.	FC	Yds.	Avg.	Lg.	TD
E. Parker	27	10	237	8.8	32	0
Dwight	1	5	6	6.0	6	0
Florence	1	0	0	0.0	0	0
Chargers	29	15	243	8.4	32	0
Opponents	23	23	164	7.1	38	0

KICK RETURNS

	No.	Yds.	Avg.	Lg.	TD
Dwight	50	1222	24.4	t87	1
Chatman	4	89	22.3	35	0
Welker	4	102	25.5	33	0
Butler	2	35	17.5	24	0
Neal	1	12	12.0	12	0
Turner	1	18	18.0	18	0
Chargers	62	1478	23.8	t87	1
Opponents	83	1846	22.2	t96	2

FIELD GOALS

	1-19	20-29	30-39	40-49	50+
Kaeding	1/1	9/11	2/2	5/6	3/5
Chargers	1/1	9/11	2/2	5/6	3/5
Opponents	0/0	11/11	6/9	2/6	1/1

Kaeding: (48G, 29G) () (23G, 51G) (31G) (21G, 28G) (53G, 28G) (29N, 44G) () (40G, 27G) (42N, 19G) (29N, 52N, 25G, 43G) (23G, 23G) (51N, 40G) () (50G) (34G)
Opponents: (37G, 20G) (28G, 23G) (22G, 23G, 43G) (24G) () () (28G, 21G, 46N) () (46N, 37G) (31G) (28G) (43N, 31G) (30N, 41G) (39N) (36G, 26G, 23G, 47N, 30G) (50G, 33N)

PASSING

	Att.	Cmp.	Yds.	Pct.	Avg. Gain	TD	Pct. TD	Int.	Pct. Int.	Long	Sack/Lost	Rating
Brees	400	262	3159	65.5	7.90	27	6.8	7	1.8	t79	18/131	104.8
Flutie	38	20	276	52.6	7.26	1	2.6	0	0.0	29	1/7	85.0
Tomlinson	2	1	38	50.0	19.00	0	0.0	0	0.0	38	1/1	95.8
Rivers	8	5	33	62.5	4.13	1	12.5	0	0.0	t13	1/10	110.9
McCardell	1	0	0	0.0	0.00	0	0.0	0	0.0	...	0/0	39.6
Scifres	1	0	0	0.0	0.00	0	0.0	1	100.0	...	0/0	0.0
Chargers	450	288	3506	64.0	7.79	29	6.4	8	1.8	t79	21/149	102.0
Opponents	607	372	4195	61.3	6.91	19	3.1	23	3.8	50	29/142	76.6

SAN DIEGO CHARGERS

SAN FRANCISCO 49ERS
NFC WEST DIVISION

2005 SEASON

CLUB DIRECTORY

Owner
Denise DeBartolo-York
Owner
John York
Owner
The DeBartolo Corporation
CFO
Larry MacNeil
Vice president/operations
Murlan Fowell
Vice president business affairs/general counsel
Ed Goines
Vice president player personnel
Scot McCloughan
Director of football operations
Paraag Marathe
Director of football administration
Terry Tumey
Ticket manager
Lynn Carrozzi
Director of security
Fred Formosa
Director of public relations
Kirk Reynolds
Equipment manager
Steve Urbianak
Head athletic trainer
Todd Lazenby
Video operations director
Robert Yanagi

Head coach
Mike Nolan

Assistant coaches
Duane Carlisle (asst. strength & conditioning)
A.J. Christoff (secondary)
Billy Davis (defensive coordinator)
Bishop Harris (running backs)
Pete Hoener (tight ends)
Jim Hostler (quarterbacks)
Vance Joseph (secondary asst.)
Larry Mac Duff (special teams coordinator)
Ben McAdoo (asst. offensive line/quality control)
Mike McCarthy (offensive coordinator)
Johnny Parker (strength and conditioning)
Jeff Rodgers (special teams quality control)
Mike Singletary (asst. head coach/linebackers)
Jerry Sullivan (wide receivers)
Jason Tarver (defensive asst./defensive quality control)
George Warhop (offensive line)

OFFSEASON MOVES

Key additions
OT Jonas Jennings	FA/Bills
K Joe Nedney	Rel./Titans
DE Marques Douglas	FA/Ravens

Key losses
K Todd Peterson	FA/Falcons
WR Cedrick Wilson	FA/Steelers
S Ronnie Heard	FA/Falcons
CB Jimmy Williams	FA/Saints
DL Daleroy Stewart	FA/Texans
G Kyle Kosier	FA/Lions
DE Brandon Whiting	Free agent

SCHEDULE

Sept. 11—ST. LOUIS	4:15
Sept. 18—at Philadelphia	1:00
Sept. 25—DALLAS	4:05
Oct. 2—at Arizona	8:30
Oct. 9—INDIANAPOLIS	4:05
Oct. 16—Open week	
Oct. 23—at Washington	1:00
Oct. 30—TAMPA BAY	5:15
Nov. 6—N.Y. GIANTS	5:05
Nov. 13—at Chicago	2:00
Nov. 20—SEATTLE	5:05
Nov. 27—at Tennessee	2:00
Dec. 4—ARIZONA	5:05
Dec. 11—at Seattle	5:05
Dec. 18—at Jacksonville	2:00
Dec. 24—at St. Louis (Sat.)	2:00
Jan. 1—HOUSTON	5:05

All times are Eastern.
All games Sunday unless noted.

DRAFT CHOICES

Alex Smith, QB, Utah (first round/first pick overall).
David Baas, C, Michigan (2/33).
Frank Gore, RB, Miami (3/65).
Adam Snyder, G, Oregon (3/94).
Ronald Fields, DT, Mississippi State (5/137).
Rasheed Marshall, WR, West Virginia (5/174).
Derrick Johnson, CB, Washington (6/205).
Daven Holly, CB, Cincinnati (7/215).
Marcus Maxwell, WR, Oregon (7/223).
Patrick Estes, TE, Virginia (7/248).
Billy Bajema, TE, Oklahoma State (7/249).

MISCELLANEOUS TEAM DATA

Stadium (capacity, surface):
Monster Park at Candlestick Point (69,734, grass)
Business address:
4949 Centennial Blvd.
Santa Clara, CA 95054-1229
Business phone:
408-562-4949
Ticket information:
415-656-4900
Team colors:
Forty Niners gold and cardinal
Flagship radio station:
KNBR 680 AM
Website:
www.sf49ers.com
Training site:
4949 Centennial Blvd.
Santa Clara, CA 95054-1229
408-562-4949

SAN FRANCISCO 49ERS

No.	QUARTERBACKS	Ht./Wt.	Born	NFL Exp.	College	How acq.	'04 Games GP/GS
7	Dorsey, Ken	6-4/218	4-22-81	3	Miami	D7/03	9/7
3	Pickett, Cody	6-3/227	6-30-80	1	Washington	D7a/04	2/0
13	Rattay, Tim	6-0/200	3-15-77	6	Louisiana Tech	D7a/00	9/9
11	Smith, Alex	6-4/212	5-7-84	R	Utah	D1/05	—
	RUNNING BACKS						
32	Barlow, Kevan	6-1/238	1-7-79	5	Pittsburgh	D3/01	15/14
40	Beasley, Fred (FB)	6-0/246	9-18-74	8	Auburn	D6/98	14/10
21	Gore, Frank	5-9/217	5-14-83	R	Miami	D3a/05	—
43	Hicks, Maurice	5-11/200	7-22-78	2	North Carolina A&T	FA/04	9/2
22	Jackson, Terry (FB)	6-0/232	1-10-76	7	Florida	D5/99	16/0
	RECEIVERS						
47	Bajema, Billy (TE)	6-5/261	10-31-82	R	Oklahoma State	D7d/05	—
83	Battle, Arnaz	6-1/217	2-22-80	3	Notre Dame	D6/03	14/0
48	Estes, Patrick (TE)	6-6/268	2-4-83	R	Virginia	D7c/05	—
10	Fleck, P.J.	5-10/191	11-29-80	1	Northern Illinois	FA/04	1/0
88	Hamilton, Derrick	6-4/203	11-30-81	1	Clemson	D3/04	2/0
86	Jennings, Brian (TE)	6-5/245	10-14-76	6	Arizona State	D7b/00	16/0
82	Johnson, Eric (TE)	6-3/256	9-15-79	5	Yale	D7b/01	16/14
85	Lloyd, Brandon	6-0/192	7-5-81	3	Illinois	D4/03	13/13
84	Marshall, Rasheed	6-0/190	7-11-81	R	West Virginia	D5b/05	—
19	Maxwell, Marcus	6-4/205	7-8-83	R	Oregon	D7b/05	—
49	Walker, Aaron (TE)	6-6/252	3-14-80	3	Florida	D5/03	16/4
81	Woods, Rashaun	6-2/202	10-17-80	2	Oklahoma State	D1/04	14/0
	OFFENSIVE LINEMEN						
64	Baas, David (G/C)	6-4/319	9-28-81	R	Michigan	D2/05	—
61	Downey, Khiawatha (T)	6-4/333	9-20-79	1	Indiana (Pa.)	FA/04	0/0
78	Gragg, Scott (T)	6-8/315	2-28-72	11	Montana	FA/00	16/16
77	Harris, Kwame (T)	6-7/310	3-15-82	3	Stanford	D1/03	14/7
66	Heitmann, Eric (G)	6-3/305	2-24-80	4	Stanford	D7a/02	16/16
75	Jennings, Jonas (T)	6-3/325	11-21-77	5	Georgia	FA/05	14/14
68	Murphy, Rob (G)	6-5/310	1-18-77	4	Ohio State	FA/03	15/0
62	Newberry, Jeremy (C)	6-5/310	3-23-76	8	California	D2/98	2/1
65	Smiley, Justin (G)	6-3/301	11-11-81	2	Alabama	D2a/04	16/9
	Snyder, Adam (T)	6-5/316	1-30-82	R	Oregon	D3b/05	—
	DEFENSIVE LINEMEN						
91	Adams, Anthony (NT)	6-0/300	6-18-80	3	Penn State	D2/03	14/12
92	Brown, Tony (E)	6-1/280	9-29-80	2	Memphis	FA/04	16/4
93	Cooper, Chris (E)	6-5/285	12-27-77	5	Nebraska-Omaha	FA/04	10/2
94	Douglas, Marques (E)	6-2/290	3-5-77	6	Howard	FA/05	16/15
95	Engelberger, John (E)	6-4/268	10-18-76	6	Virginia Tech	D2a/00	16/15
	Fields, Ronald (T)	6-1/322	9-13-81	R	Mississippi State	D5a/05	—
71	Smith, Corey (E)	6-2/250	11-2-79	3	North Carolina State	FA/04	5/0
90	Sopoaga, Isaac (NT)	6-2/321	9-4-81	1	Hawaii	D4a/04	0/0
99	Williams, Andrew (E)	6-2/263	4-18-79	3	Miami	D3/03	7/3
97	Young, Bryant (E)	6-3/291	1-27-72	12	Notre Dame	D1/94	16/16
	LINEBACKERS						
96	Carter, Andre	6-4/265	5-12-79	5	California	D1/01	7/6
56	Moore, Brandon	6-1/242	1-16-79	4	Oklahoma	FA/02	12/1
98	Peterson, Julian	6-3/235	7-28-78	6	Michigan State	D1a/00	5/5
51	Rasheed, Saleem	6-2/229	6-15-81	4	Alabama	D3/02	14/2
54	Seigler, Richard	6-2/238	10-19-80	2	Oregon State	D4b/04	7/0
50	Smith, Derek	6-2/245	1-18-75	9	Arizona State	FA/01	14/14
53	Ulbrich, Jeff	6-0/249	2-17-77	6	Hawaii	D3b/00	16/14
55	Winborn, Jamie	5-11/242	5-14-79	5	Vanderbilt	D2/01	14/10
	DEFENSIVE BACKS						
20	Adams, Mike (S)	5-11/193	3-24-81	2	Delaware	FA/04	8/0
35	Carpenter, Dwaine (S)	6-1/203	11-4-76	3	North Carolina A&T	FA/03	15/6
27	Hanson, Joselio (CB)	5-9/175	8-13-81	2	Texas Tech	FA/03	13/3
26	Holly, Daven (CB)	5-10/186	8-8-82	R	Cincinnati	D7a/05	—
23	Johnson, Derrick (CB)	5-11/188	2-9-82	R	Washington	D6/05	—
28	Lewis, Keith (S)	6-0/202	10-20-81	2	Oregon	D6b/04	16/0
38	Parker, Arnold (S)	6-2/215	7-1-81	1	Utah	FA/05	0/0
33	Parrish, Tony (S)	6-0/210	11-23-75	8	Washington	FA/02	16/16
29	Plummer, Ahmed (CB)	6-0/191	3-26-76	6	Ohio State	D1b/00	6/6
31	Reed, Rayshun (CB)	5-10/185	4-10-81	2	Troy	FA/04	7/1
24	Rumph, Mike (CB)	6-2/205	11-8-79	4	Miami	D1/02	2/2
36	Spencer, Shawntae (CB)	6-1/181	2-22-82	2	Pittsburgh	D2b/04	16/12
	SPECIALISTS						
4	Lee, Andy (P)	6-0/206	8-11-82	2	Pittsburgh	D6/04	16/0
6	Nedney, Joe (K)	6-5/225	3-22-73	9	San Jose State	FA/05	0/0

Abbreviations: D1—draft pick, first round; FA—free-agent acquisition.

SAN FRANCISCO 49ERS

2004 regular-season record: 2-14
Position: 4th in NFC West

Sept.12—ATLANTA	L	19-21
Sept.19—at New Orleans	L	27-30
Sept.26—at Seattle	L	0-34
Oct. 3—ST. LOUIS	L	14-24
Oct. 10—ARIZONA (OT)	W	31-28
Oct. 17—at N.Y. Jets	L	14-22
Oct. 24—Open date		
Oct. 31—at Chicago	L	13-23
Nov. 7—SEATTLE	L	27-42
Nov.14—CAROLINA	L	27-37
Nov.21—at Tampa Bay	L	3-35
Nov.28—MIAMI	L	17-24
Dec. 5—at St. Louis	L	6-16
Dec.12—at Arizona (OT)	W	31-28
Dec.18—WASHINGTON	L	16-26
Dec.26—BUFFALO	L	7-41
Jan. 2—at New England	L	7-21

SCORING BY PERIODS

	Q1	Q2	Q3	Q4	OT	Pts.
49ers	68	62	35	88	6	259
Opponents	86	141	84	141	0	452

TEAM STATISTICS

	S.F.	Opp.
TOTAL FIRST DOWNS	280	322
Rushing	83	121
Passing	172	179
Penalty	25	22
3rd Down: Made/Att.	72/222	83/206
3rd Down Pct.	32.4	40.3
4th Down: Made/Att.	14/19	6/9
4th Down Pct.	73.7	66.7
POSSESSION AVG.	29:00	31:00
TOTAL NET YARDS	4585	5481
Avg. per Game	286.6	342.6
Total Plays	1026	1014
Avg. per Play	4.5	5.4
NET YARDS RUSHING	1449	1995
Avg. per Game	90.6	124.7
Total Rushes	413	495
NET YARDS PASSING	3136	3486
Avg. per Game	196.0	217.9
Sacked/Yards Lost	52/319	29/194
Gross Yards	3455	3680
Att./Completions	561/325	490/308
Completion Pct.	57.9	62.9
Had Intercepted	21	9
PUNTS/AVERAGE	96/41.6	80/40.9
NET PUNTING AVG.	96/35.3	80/35.8
PENALTIES/YARDS	103/859	107/867
FUMBLES/LOST	33/19	24/12
TOUCHDOWNS	29	54
Rushing	10	22
Passing	16	27
Returns	3	5

SCORING (NON-KICKERS)

	Tot. TD	RTD	PTD	MTD	2Pt.	Tot. Pts.
Barlow	7	7	0	0	0	42
Lloyd	6	0	6	0	1	38
Conway	3	0	3	0	1	20
Wilson	3	0	3	0	0	18
Hicks	2	2	0	0	0	12
E. Johnson	2	0	2	0	0	12
Battle	1	0	0	1	0	6
Bush	1	0	1	0	0	6
Carpenter	1	0	0	1	0	6
Robertson	1	1	0	0	0	6
D. Smith	1	0	0	1	0	6
Woods	1	0	1	0	0	6
Rattay	0	0	0	0	1	2
49ers	29	10	16	3	3	182
Opponents	54	22	27	5	1	326

2-Pt. conversions: 49ers 3-6; Opponents 1-3.

(KICKERS)

	XPM/XPA	FGM/FGA	Pts.
T. Peterson	23/23	18/22	77
49ers	23/23	18/22	77
Opponents	51/51	25/29	126

RUSHING

	Att.	Yds.	Avg.	Lg.	TD
Barlow	244	822	3.4	60	7
Hicks	96	362	3.8	35	2
Jackson	26	101	3.9	13	0
Robertson	16	71	4.4	16	1
Rattay	12	55	4.6	15	0
Beasley	9	15	1.7	4	0
Dorsey	5	7	1.4	3	0
Wilson	1	6	6.0	6	0
Battle	2	5	2.5	7	0
Pickett	1	5	5.0	5	0
Isom	1	0	0.0	0	0
49ers	413	1449	3.5	60	10
Opponents	495	1995	4.0	29	22

RECEIVING

	No.	Yds.	Avg.	Lg.	TD
E. Johnson	82	825	10.1	25	2
Wilson	47	641	13.6	39	3
Lloyd	43	565	13.1	52	6
Conway	38	403	10.6	37	3
Barlow	35	212	6.1	15	0
Jackson	21	139	6.6	22	0
Hicks	16	154	9.6	19	0
Beasley	10	44	4.4	9	0
Walker	10	115	11.5	30	0
Battle	8	143	17.9	65	0
Woods	7	160	22.9	59	1
Robertson	4	34	8.5	14	0
Bush	2	10	5.0	6	1
Isom	1	1	1.0	1	0
Ware	1	9	9.0	9	0

	No.	Yds.	Avg.	Lg.	TD
49ers	325	3455	10.6	65	16
Opponents	308	3680	11.9	60	27

INTERCEPTIONS

	No.	Yds.	Avg.	Lg.	TD
Parrish	4	64	16.0	26	0
Carpenter	1	31	31.0	31	0
Ulbrich	1	19	19.0	19	0
Heard	1	14	14.0	14	0
Winborn	1	1	1.0	1	0
M. Adams	1	0	0.0	0	0
49ers	9	129	14.3	31	0
Opponents	21	479	22.8	85	4

SACKS: Engelberger 6.0, Winborn 4.5, Young 3.0, J. Peterson 2.5, Carpenter 2.0, Carter 2.0, D. Smith 1.5, Brown 1.0, C. Cooper 1.0, Hanson 1.0, Leverette 1.0, B. Moore 1.0, Ulbrich 1.0, J. Williams 1.0, Parrish 0.5. 49ers 29.0; Opponents 52.0

PUNTING

	No.	Yds.	Avg.	In. 20	Lg.
Lee	96	3990	41.6	25	81
49ers	96	3990	41.6	25	81
Opponents	80	3268	40.9	28	61

PUNT RETURNS

	No.	FC	Yds.	Avg.	Lg.	TD
Battle	31	20	266	8.6	t71	1
Wilson	2	1	21	10.5	13	0
Fleck	1	0	10	10.0	10	0
J. Peterson	1	0	6	6.0	6	0
49ers	35	21	303	8.7	t71	1
Opponents	51	17	445	8.7	35	0

KICK RETURNS

	No.	Yds.	Avg.	Lg.	TD
Hicks	31	623	20.1	35	0
Robertson	25	560	22.4	37	0
Battle	13	257	19.8	40	0
Wilson	10	196	19.6	36	0
J. Williams	3	58	19.3	23	0
Jackson	2	22	11.0	14	0
49ers	84	1716	20.4	40	0
Opponents	56	1119	20.0	73	0

FIELD GOALS

	1-19	20-29	30-39	40-49	50+
T. Peterson	1/1	3/3	7/8	5/6	2/4
49ers	1/1	3/3	7/8	5/6	2/4
Opponents	0/0	10/11	7/9	4/4	4/5

T. Peterson: (23G, 32G) (30G, 33G) (46N) () (37G, 42G, 32G) () (48G, 51G, 50N) (27G, 30G) (28G, 46G) (50N, 47G) (19G) (51G, 40G) (31G) () () (39N) Opponents: () (32G, 36G, 37G) (35G, 28G) (20G, 33N) () (43G) (52G, 45G, 53N, 27G) () (37G, 25G, 34G) () (50N, 50G) (29G, 52G, 52G) (34N, 44G, 22G) (49G, 25G, 20G, 26G) (23G, 31G) ()

PASSING

	Att.	Cmp.	Yds.	Pct.	Avg. Gain	TD	Pct. TD	Int.	Pct. Int.	Long	Sack/Lost	Rating
Rattay	325	198	2169	60.9	6.67	10	3.1	10	3.1	65	37/211	78.1
Dorsey	226	123	1231	54.4	5.45	6	2.7	9	4.0	59	13/94	62.4
Pickett	10	4	55	40.0	5.50	0	0.0	2	20.0	18	2/14	18.8
49ers	561	325	3455	57.9	6.16	16	2.9	21	3.7	65	52/319	69.9
Opponents	490	308	3680	62.9	7.51	27	5.5	9	1.8	60	29/194	96.5

SEATTLE SEAHAWKS
NFC WEST DIVISION

2005 SEASON

CLUB DIRECTORY

Owner
Paul Allen
President of football operations
Bob Whitsitt
CEO
Tod Leineke
General manager
Bob Ferguson
Vice president of football administration
Mike Reinfeldt
Vice president/administration
Gary Wright
Director of communication & broadcasting
Dave Pearson
Community outreach director
Sandy Gregory
Director of pro personnel
Will Lewis

Executive vp of football operations/ head coach
Mike Holmgren

Assistant coaches
Teryl Austin (defensive backs)
Dwaine Board (defensive line)
Bob Casullo (asst. special teams)
Mike Clark (strength & conditioning)
Nolan Cromwell (wide receivers)
Gil Haskell (off. coordinator)
Darren Krein (asst. strength & conditioning)
Bill Laveroni (offensive line)
Jim Lind (tight ends)
John Marshall (linebackers)
Stump Mitchell (running backs)
Gary Reynolds (quality control/offense)
Ray Rhodes (def. coordinator)
Zerick Rollins (defensive line/quality control)
Jim Zorn (quarterbacks)

OFFSEASON MOVES

Key additions
LB Kevin Bentley	FA/Browns
DT Chartric Darby	FA/Buccaneers
CB Andre Dyson	FA/Titans
DT Bryce Fisher	FA/Rams
CB Kelly Herndon	FA/Broncos
WR Joe Jurevicius	Rel./Bucs
CB Omare Lowe	FA/Patriots
WR Jerome Pathon	FA/Saints
LB Jamie Sharper	Rel./Texans
DE Joe Tafoya	Waiv./Falcons

Key losses
LB Chad Brown	Rel./Patriots
QB Trent Dilfer	Trade/Browns
FB Heath Evans	FA/Dolphins
LB Orlando Huff	FA/Cardinals
CB Ken Lucas	FA/Panthers
DE Brandon Mitchell	FA/Falcons
DE Chike Okeafor	FA/Cardinals
WR Jerry Rice	Released
S Damien Robinson	Released
P Tom Rouen	FA/Panthers
LB Anthony Simmons	Released
OT Chris Terry	Released

SCHEDULE

Sept.	11—at Jacksonville	1:00
Sept.	18—ATLANTA	4:05
Sept.	25—ARIZONA	4:05
Oct.	2—at Washington	1:00
Oct.	9—at St. Louis	1:00
Oct.	16—HOUSTON	8:30
Oct.	23—DALLAS	4:05
Oct.	30—Open week	
Nov.	6—at Arizona	5:05
Nov.	13—ST. LOUIS	5:15
Nov.	20—at San Francisco	5:05
Nov.	27—N.Y. GIANTS	5:15
Dec.	5—at Philadelphia (Mon.)	10:00
Dec.	11—SAN FRANCISCO	5:05
Dec.	18—at Tennessee	2:00
Dec.	24—Indianapolis (Sat.)	5:15
Jan.	1—at Green Bay	5:15

All times are Eastern.
All games Sunday unless noted.

DRAFT CHOICES

Chris Spencer, C, Mississippi (first round, 26th pick overall).
Lofa Tatupu, ILB, Southern California (2/45).
David Greene, QB, Georgia (3/85).
Leroy Hill, OLB, Clemson (3/98).
Ray Willis, OT, Florida State (4/105).
Jeb Huckeba, OLB, Arkansas (5/159).
Tony Jackson, TE, Iowa (6/196).
Cornelius Wortham, OLB, Alabama (7/235).
Doug Nienhuis, OT, Oregon State (7/254).

MISCELLANEOUS TEAM DATA

Stadium (capacity, surface):
Quest Field (67,000, artificial)
Business address:
11220 N.E. 53rd Street
Kirkland, WA 98033
Business phone:
425-827-9777
Ticket information:
800-635-4295
Team colors:
Seahawks blue, Seahawks navy and Seahawks bright green
Flagship radio station:
KIRO, 710 AM
Website:
www.seahawks.com
Training site:
Eastern Washington University
Cheney, Wash.
425-827-9777

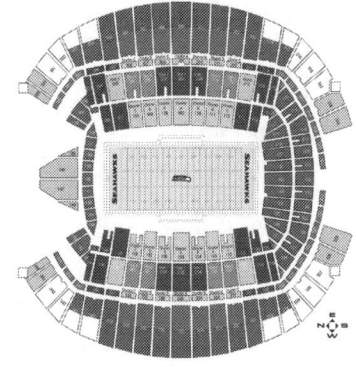

SEATTLE SEAHAWKS

No.	QUARTERBACKS	Ht./Wt.	Born	NFL Exp.	College	How acq.	'04 Games GP/GS
11	Greene, David	6-3/231	6-22-82	R	Georgia	D3a/05	—
8	Hasselbeck, Matt	6-4/223	9-25-75	7	Boston College	T-GB/01	14/14
15	Wallace, Seneca	5-11/196	8-6-80	3	Iowa State	D4a/03	0/0
	RUNNING BACKS						
37	Alexander, Shaun	5-11/225	8-30-77	6	Alabama	D1a/00	16/16
32	Carter, Kerry	6-1/238	12-19-80	3	Stanford	FA/03	16/0
44	Jackson, Tony (FB)	6-2/264	7-5-82	R	Iowa	D6/05	—
20	Morris, Maurice	5-11/202	12-1-79	4	Oregon	D2a/02	15/0
38	Strong, Mack (FB)	6-0/245	9-11-71	13	Georgia	FA/93	16/13
	RECEIVERS						
85	Bannister, Alex	6-5/207	4-23-79	5	Eastern Kentucky	D5/01	7/1
84	Engram, Bobby	5-10/188	1-7-73	10	Penn State	FA/01	13/7
18	Hackett, D.J.	6-2/199	7-31-81	1	Colorado	D5/04	0/0
83	Hannam, Ryan (TE)	6-2/248	2-24-80	4	Northern Iowa	D5b/02	16/0
82	Jackson, Darrell	6-0/201	12-6-78	6	Florida	D3/00	16/16
19	Jurevicius, Joe	6-5/230	12-23-74	8	Penn State	FA/05	10/3
88	Mili, Itula (TE)	6-4/260	4-20-73	9	BYU	D6/97	15/4
16	Pathon, Jerome	6-0/195	12-16-75	8	Washington	FA/05	15/7
81	Robinson, Koren	6-1/205	3-19-80	5	North Carolina State	D1a/01	10/8
86	Stevens, Jerramy (TE)	6-7/260	11-13-79	4	Washington	D1/02	16/5
87	Wallace, Taco	6-1/190	4-14-81	2	Kansas State	D7/03	2/0
	OFFENSIVE LINEMEN						
52	Darche, Jean-Philippe (C)	6-0/246	2-28-75	6	McGill	FA/00	16/0
62	Gray, Chris (G)	6-4/308	6-19-70	13	Auburn	FA/98	16/16
73	Hunter, Wayne (T)	6-5/303	7-2-81	3	Hawaii	D3/03	1/0
76	Hutchinson, Steve (G)	6-5/313	11-1-77	5	Michigan	D1b/01	16/16
71	Jones, Walter (T)	6-5/315	1-19-74	9	Florida State	D1b/97	16/16
75	Locklear, Sean (G)	6-4/301	5-29-81	2	North Carolina State	D3/04	16/0
72	Nienhuis, Doug (T)	6-6/307	2-16-82	R	Oregon State	D7b/05	—
65	Spencer, Chris (C)	6-3/309	3-28-82	R	Mississippi	D1/05	—
61	Tobeck, Robbie (C)	6-4/297	3-6-70	12	Washington State	FA/00	16/16
74	Willis, Ray (T)	6-6/327	8-13-82	R	Florida State	D4/05	—
77	Womack, Floyd (T)	6-4/333	11-15-78	5	Mississippi State	D4c/01	15/8
70	Wunsch, Jerry (G)	6-6/339	1-21-74	9	Wisconsin	FA/02	5/0
	DEFENSIVE LINEMEN						
99	Bernard, Rocky (T)	6-3/293	4-19-79	4	Texas A&M	D5a/02	14/1
78	Cochran, Antonio (E)	6-4/299	6-21-76	7	Georgia	D4/99	16/7
92	Darby, Chartric (T)	6-0/298	10-22-75	5	South Carolina State	FA/05	16/16
91	Fisher, Bryce (E)	6-3/272	5-12-77	5	Air Force	FA/05	16/14
97	Huckeba, Jeb (E)	6-4/252	5-20-82	R	Arkansas	D5/05	—
95	Moore, Rashad (T)	6-3/324	3-16-79	3	Tennessee	D6/03	16/12
93	Terrill, Craig (T)	6-2/290	6-27-80	2	Purdue	D6/04	4/0
90	Tubbs, Marcus (T)	6-4/320	5-16-81	2	Texas	D1/04	11/3
96	Wistrom, Grant (E)	6-4/272	7-3-76	8	Nebraska	FA/04	9/9
98	Woodard, Cedric (T)	6-2/310	9-5-77	6	Texas	W-Bal./00	16/16
	LINEBACKERS						
50	Bates, Solomon	6-1/243	4-18-82	3	Arizona State	D4b/03	10/3
57	Bentley, Kevin	6-1/240	12-29-79	4	Northwestern	FA/05	16/3
56	Hill, Leroy	6-1/224	9-14-82	R	Clemson	D3b/05	—
58	Kacyvenski, Isaiah	6-1/252	10-3-77	6	Harvard	D4b/00	16/13
53	Koutouvides, Niko	6-2/238	3-25-81	2	Purdue	D4/04	16/2
54	Lewis, D.D.	6-1/241	1-8-79	4	Texas	FA/02	0/0
55	Sharper, Jamie	6-3/239	11-23-74	9	Virginia	FA/05	16/16
51	Tatupu, Lofa	5-11/226	11-15-82	R	USC	D2/05	—
59	White, Tracy	6-0/230	4-14-81	3	Howard	FA/05	10/2
46	Wortham, Cornelius	6-1/234	1-25-82	R	Alabama	D7a/05	—
	DEFENSIVE BACKS						
27	Babineaux, Jordan (S)	6-0/200	8-31-82	2	Southern Arkansas	FA/04	6/0
34	Bierria, Terreal (S)	6-3/211	10-10-80	3	Georgia	D4/02	15/12
28	Boulware, Michael (S)	6-3/223	9-17-81	2	Florida State	D2/04	16/4
22	Dyson, Andre (CB)	5-10/183	5-25-79	5	Utah	FA/05	16/16
26	Hamlin, Ken (S)	6-2/209	1-20-81	3	Arkansas	D2/03	16/16
31	Herndon, Kelly (CB)	5-10/180	11-3-76	4	Toledo	FA/05	16/16
41	Lowe, Omare (CB)	6-1/196	4-20-78	3	Washington	W-NE/05	3/0
33	Manuel, Marquand (S)	6-0/209	7-11-79	4	Florida	W-Cin./04	15/0
42	Richard, Kris (CB)	5-11/190	10-28-78	4	USC	D3/02	16/0
24	Taylor, Bobby (CB)	6-3/216	12-28-73	11	Notre Dame	FA/04	10/0
23	Trufant, Marcus (CB)	5-11/199	12-25-80	3	Washington State	D1/03	16/16
	SPECIALISTS						
3	Brown, Josh (K)	6-0/202	4-29-79	3	Nebraska	D7/03	16/0
9	Jones, Donnie (P)	6-2/222	7-5-80	2	LSU	D7/04	7/0

Abbreviations: D1—draft pick, first round; W—claimed on waivers; T—obtained in trade; FA—free-agent acquisition.

2004 REVIEW

2004 regular-season record: 9-7
Position: 1st in NFC West

Sept.12—at New Orleans	W	21-7
Sept.19—at Tampa Bay	W	10-6
Sept.26—SAN FRANCISCO	W	34-0
Oct. 3—Open date		
Oct. 10—ST. LOUIS (OT)	L	27-33
Oct. 17—at New England	L	20-30
Oct. 24—at Arizona	L	17-25
Oct. 31—CAROLINA	W	23-17
Nov. 7—at San Francisco	W	42-27
Nov.14—at St. Louis	L	12-23
Nov.21—MIAMI	W	24-17
Nov.28—BUFFALO	L	9-38
Dec. 6—DALLAS	L	39-43
Dec.12—at Minnesota	W	27-23
Dec.19—at N.Y. Jets	L	14-37
Dec.26—ARIZONA	W	24-21
Jan. 2—ATLANTA	W	28-26

2004 postseason record: 0-1

Jan. 8—ST. LOUIS#	L	20-27

#NFC wild-card game.

SCORING BY PERIODS

	Q1	Q2	Q3	Q4	OT	Pts.
Seahawks	86	129	70	86	0	371
Opponents	89	113	52	113	6	373

TEAM STATISTICS

	Sea.	Opp.
TOTAL FIRST DOWNS ..	320	311
Rushing	110	102
Passing	189	191
Penalty	21	18
3rd Down: Made/Att. ..	76/210	97/229
3rd Down Pct.	36.2	42.4
4th Down: Made/Att.	6/11	6/9
4th Down Pct.	54.5	66.7
POSSESSION AVG.	29:00	31:00
TOTAL NET YARDS	5634	5621
Avg. per Game	352.1	351.3
Total Plays	1034	1047
Avg. per Play	5.4	5.4
NET YARDS RUSHING ..	2095	2031
Avg. per Game	130.9	126.9
Total Rushes	468	452
NET YARDS PASSING....	3539	3590
Avg. per Game	221.2	224.4
Sacked/Yards Lost	34/176	36/218
Gross Yards	3715	3808
Att./Completions	532/304	559/340
Completion Pct.	57.1	60.8
Had Intercepted	18	23
PUNTS/AVERAGE	79/38.4	74/41.8
NET PUNTING AVG.	79/34.3	74/37.3
PENALTIES/YARDS	79/669	91/748
FUMBLES/LOST	19/9	25/12
TOUCHDOWNS	43	42
Rushing	17	17
Passing	23	24
Returns	3	1

SCORING (NON-KICKERS)

	Tot. TD	RTD	PTD	MTD	2Pt.	Tot. Pts.
Alexander	20	16	4	0	0	120
Jackson	7	0	7	0	1	44
Stevens	3	0	3	0	1	20
Rice	3	0	3	0	0	18
Engram	2	0	2	0	0	12
K. Robinson ..	2	0	2	0	0	12
Boulware	1	0	0	0	0	6
Hasselbeck	1	1	0	0	0	6
Lucas	1	0	0	1	0	6
Mili	1	0	1	0	0	6
Simmons	1	0	1	0	0	6
Urban	1	0	1	0	0	6
Seahawks	43	17	23	3	2	262
Opponents	42	17	24	1	0	254

2-Pt. conversions: Seahawks 2-3; Opponents 0-2.

(KICKERS)

	XPM/XPA	FGM/FGA	Pts.
J. Brown	40/40	23/25	109
Seahawks	40/40	23/25	109
Opponents	38/39	27/32	119

RUSHING

	Att.	Yds.	Avg.	Lg.	TD
Alexander	353	1696	4.8	44	16
Strong	36	131	3.6	11	0
Morris	30	126	4.2	12	0
Hasselbeck	27	90	3.3	19	1
H. Evans	7	20	2.9	7	0
Carter	4	15	3.8	6	0
Dilfer	10	14	1.4	11	0
K. Robinson ..	1	3	3.0	3	0
Seahawks	468	2095	4.5	44	17
Opponents	452	2031	4.5	53	17

RECEIVING

	No.	Yds.	Avg.	Lg.	TD
Jackson	87	1199	13.8	t56	7
Engram	36	499	13.9	60	2
K. Robinson ..	31	495	16.0	33	2
Stevens	31	349	11.3	32	3
Rice	25	362	14.5	56	3
Alexander	23	170	7.4	24	4
Mili	23	240	10.4	20	1
Strong	21	99	4.7	13	0
Morris	9	53	5.9	12	0
Hannam	8	110	13.8	36	0
Urban	6	117	19.5	33	1
Bannister	2	10	5.0	8	0
H. Evans	2	12	6.0	9	0
Seahawks	304	3715	12.2	60	23
Opponents	340	3808	11.2	63	24

INTERCEPTIONS

	No.	Yds.	Avg.	Lg.	TD
Lucas	6	46	7.7	25	1
Trufant	5	141	28.2	58	0
Boulware	5	69	13.8	t63	1
Hamlin	4	48	12.0	24	0
Simmons	1	23	23.0	t23	1
Bierria	1	10	10.0	10	0
Cochran	1	0	0.0	0	0
Seahawks	23	337	14.7	t63	3
Opponents	18	158	8.8	t48	1

SACKS: Okeafor 8.5, Cochran 6.5, R. Bernard 3.5, Wistrom 3.5, Hamlin 2.0, Moore 2.0, Boulware 1.0, C. Brown 1.0, Huff 1.0, Kacyvenski 1.0, Koutouvides 1.0, Mitchell 1.0, Trufant 1.0, Tubbs 1.0, White 1.0, Woodard 1.0. Seahawks 36.0; Opponents 34.0.

PUNTING

	No.	Yds.	Avg.	In. 20	Lg.
J. Brown	1	35	35.0	0	35
D. Jones	26	988	38.0	6	51
Rouen	26	1093	42.0	10	60
Walter	24	920	38.3	4	50
Seahawks	79	3036	38.4	20	60
Opponents	74	3091	41.8	31	60

PUNT RETURNS

	No.	FC	Yds.	Avg.	Lg.	TD
Morris	15	4	75	5.0	22	0
Engram	10	19	118	11.8	48	0
Richard	4	3	31	7.8	14	0
Hannam	1	0	6	6.0	6	0
Seahawks	30	26	230	7.7	48	0
Opponents	33	21	244	7.4	39	0

KICK RETURNS

	No.	Yds.	Avg.	Lg.	TD
Morris	47	994	21.1	34	0
Carter	21	448	21.3	36	0
H. Evans	3	51	17.0	21	0
Locklear	1	12	12.0	12	0
Mili	1	12	12.0	12	0
Stevens	1	12	12.0	12	0
Seahawks	74	1529	20.7	36	0
Opponents	77	1677	21.8	51	0

FIELD GOALS

	1-19	20-29	30-39	40-49	50+
J. Brown	1/1	7/7	8/9	6/7	1/1
Seahawks	1/1	7/7	8/9	6/7	1/1
Opponents	0/0	6/6	12/15	6/7	3/4

J. Brown: () (44G) (35G, 28G) (48G, 43N, 34G) (33G, 40G, 28G, 31G) (54G) (27G, 45G, 22G) () (28G, 30G, 45G, 41G) (33G) (19G) (21G) (38N, 33G, 28G) () (34G) ()
Opponents: () (24G, 27G) (46N) (39G, 36G) (40G, 39G, 30G) (55G, 55G, 50G) (30G) (27G, 30G) (36G, 47G, 23G) (34N, 39G) (25G) (39G, 49G, 47G) (48G, 32G, 31G) (21G, 30N) (52N) (33G, 39N, 40G)

PASSING

	Att.	Cmp.	Yds.	Pct.	Avg. Gain	TD	Pct. TD	Int.	Pct. Int.	Long	Sack/Lost	Rating
Hasselbeck	474	279	3382	58.9	7.14	22	4.6	15	3.2	60	30/155	83.1
Dilfer	58	25	333	43.1	5.74	1	1.7	3	5.2	56	4/21	46.1
Seahawks	532	304	3715	57.1	6.98	23	4.3	18	3.4	60	34/176	79.1
Opponents	559	340	3808	60.8	6.81	24	4.3	23	4.1	63	36/218	78.3

SEATTLE SEAHAWKS

TAMPA BAY BUCCANEERS
NFC SOUTH DIVISION

2005 SEASON

CLUB DIRECTORY

Owner
Malcolm Glazer
Executive vice president
Bryan Glazer
Executive vice president
Joel Glazer
Executive vice president
Edward Glazer
General manager
Bruce Allen
Director of football operations
Mark Arteaga
Senior director/business administration
Mike Newquist
Director of college scouting
Ruston Webster
Director of public relations
Jeff Kamis
Director of player development
Cedric Saunders
Director of pro personnel
Mark Dominik
Personnel executive
Doug Williams

OFFSEASON MOVES

Key additions
TE Anthony Becht	FA/Jets
CB Juran Bolden	Rel./Jaguars
K Matt Bryant	FA/Dolphins
WR Ike Hilliard	FA/Giants
DT Chris Hovan	FA/Vikings
QB Luke McCown	Trade/Browns

Key losses
LB Keith Burns	FA/Broncos
G Cosey Coleman	FA/Browns
DT Chartric Darby	FA/Seahawks
CB Mario Edwards	Rel./Dolphins
LB Ian Gold	Rel./Broncos
QB Brad Johnson	Rel./Vikings
WR Joe Jurevicius	Rel./Seahawks
G Matt O'Dwyer	FA/Packers
DB Dwight Smith	FA/Saints

Head coach
Jon Gruden

Assistant coaches
Joe Barry (linebackers)
Richard Bisaccia (special teams)
Garrett Giemont (strength & conditioning coordinator)
Jay Gruden (offensive asst.)
Paul Hackett (quarterbacks)
Monte Kiffin (def. coordinator)
Aaron Kromer (senior asst.)
Richard Mann (wide receivers)
Rod Marinelli (asst. head coach/defensive line)
Ron Middleton (tight ends/asst. special teams)
Mike Morris (asst. strength & conditioning)
Raheem Morris (asst. defensive backs coach)
Bill Muir (offensive coordinator/offensive line)
Kyle Shanahan (offensive quality control)
Mike Tomlin (defensive backs)
Art Valero (running backs)
Joe Woods (defensive quality control)

SCHEDULE

Sept.	11—at Minnesota	1:00
Sept.	18—BUFFALO	1:00
Sept.	25—at Green Bay	1:00
Oct.	2—DETROIT	1:00
Oct.	9—at N.Y. Jets	1:00
Oct.	16—MIAMI	1:00
Oct.	23—Open week	
Oct.	30—at San Francisco	5:15
Nov.	6—CAROLINA	2:00
Nov.	13—WASHINGTON	2:00
Nov.	20—at Atlanta	2:00
Nov.	27—CHICAGO	2:00
Dec.	4—at New Orleans	2:00
Dec.	11—at Carolina	2:00
Dec.	17—at New England (Sat.)	2:30
Dec.	24—ATLANTA	2:00
Jan.	1—NEW ORLEANS	2:00

All times are Eastern.
All games Sunday unless noted.

DRAFT CHOICES

Carnell Williams, RB, Auburn (first round/fifth pick overall).
Barrett Ruud, ILB, Nebraska (2/36).
Alex Smith, TE, Stanford (3/71).
Chris Colmer, OT, North Carolina State (3/91).
Dan Buenning, G, Wisconsin (4/107).
Donte Nicholson, SS, Oklahoma (5/141).
Larry Brackins, WR, Pearl River CC (5/155).
Anthony Bryant, DT, Alabama (6/178).
Rick Razzano, FB, Mississippi (7/221).
Paris Warren, WR, Utah (7/225).
Hamza Abdullah, SS, Washington State (7/231).
J.R. Russell, WR, Louisville (7/253).

MISCELLANEOUS TEAM DATA

Stadium (capacity, surface):
Raymond James Stadium
(65,699, grass)
Business address:
One Buccaneer Place
Tampa, FL 33607
Business phone:
813-870-2700
Ticket information:
813-879-2827
Team colors:
Buccaneer red, pewter, black and orange
Flagship radio station:
Thunder 103.5 FM
Website:
www.buccaneers.com
Training site:
Disney Wide World of Sports
Orlando, Fla.
407-939-2827

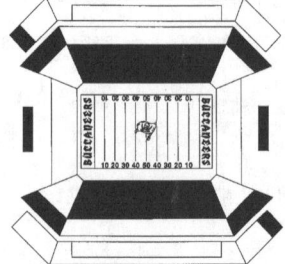

No.	QUARTERBACKS	Ht./Wt.	Born	NFL Exp.	College	How acq.	'04 Games GP/GS
8	Griese, Brian	6-3/214	3-18-75	8	Michigan	FA/04	11/10
12	McCown, Luke	6-3/212	7-12-81	R	Louisiana Tech	T-Cle./05	0/0
2	Simms, Chris	6-4/220	8-29-80	3	Texas	D3/03	5/2
	RUNNING BACKS						
40	Alstott, Mike (FB)	6-1/248	12-21-73	10	Purdue	D2/96	14/11
43	Cook, Jameel (FB)	5-10/237	2-8-79	5	Illinois	D6a/01	12/5
30	Garner, Charlie	5-10/190	2-13-72	12	Tennessee	FA/04	3/3
33	Graham, Earnest	5-9/215	1-15-80	2	Florida	FA/04	9/0
32	Pittman, Michael	6-0/218	8-14-75	8	Fresno State	FA/02	13/13
44	Razzano, Rick	5-11/240	1-28-81	R	Mississippi	D7a/05	—
36	Smart, Ian	5-8/192	10-28-80	2	C.W. Post	FA/04	4/0
24	Williams, Carnell	5-11/217	4-21-82	R	Auburn	D1/05	—
	RECEIVERS						
88	Becht, Anthony (TE)	6-5/272	8-8-77	6	West Virginia	FA/05	16/16
16	Brackins, Larry	6-4/205	11-5-82	R	Pearl River CC	D5b/05	—
80	Clayton, Michael	6-4/197	10-13-82	2	LSU	D1/04	16/13
84	Galloway, Joey	5-11/197	11-20-71	11	Ohio State	T-Dal./04	10/7
89	Heller, Will (TE)	6-6/250	2-28-81	3	Georgia Tech	FA/03	10/2
19	Hilliard, Ike	5-11/210	4-5-76	9	Florida	FA/05	16/15
46	Lawrie, Nate (TE)	6-5/262	10-17-81	1	Yale	D6/04	2/0
83	Moore, Dave (TE)	6-2/250	11-11-69	14	Pittsburgh	FA/04	15/0
14	Russell, J.R.	6-3/206	12-5-81	R	Louisville	D7d/05	—
86	Shepherd, Edell	6-1/175	5-18-80	3	San Jose State	FA/03	0/0
81	Smith, Alex (TE)	6-4/258	5-22-82	R	Stanford	D3a/05	—
15	Warren, Paris	6-0/213	9-6-82	R	Utah	D7b/05	—
	OFFENSIVE LINEMEN						
60	Buckles, Doug (G)	6-5/311	6-18-82	R	Mississippi	FA/05	—
72	Buenning, Dan (G)	6-4/320	10-26-81	R	Wisconsin	D4/05	—
61	Colmer, Chris (T)	6-5/310	11-21-80	R	North Carolina State	D3b/05	—
69	Davis, Anthony (T/G)	6-4/322	3-27-80	2	Virginia Tech	FA/04	2/0
70	Deese, Derrick (T)	6-3/289	5-17-70	14	USC	FA/04	16/16
79	Mahan, Sean (C)	6-3/301	5-28-80	3	Notre Dame	D5/03	16/8
71	Martin, Matt (T)	6-6/300	10-12-79	3	Kansas State	FA/04	0/0
75	Steussie, Todd (T)	6-6/320	12-1-70	12	California	FA/04	16/5
78	Stinchcomb, Matt (G)	6-6/310	6-3-77	7	Georgia	FA/04	16/16
77	Terry, Jeb (G)	6-5/311	4-10-81	1	North Carolina	D5/04	4/0
76	Wade, John (C)	6-5/299	1-25-75	8	Marshall	FA/03	8/8
67	Walker, Kenyatta (T)	6-5/302	2-1-79	5	Florida	D1/01	13/11
	DEFENSIVE LINEMEN						
64	Bryant, Anthony (T)	6-3/336	11-6-81	R	Alabama	D6/05	—
99	Cowsette, Del (T)	6-1/296	9-3-77	3	Maryland	FA/05	0/0
66	Gregory, Damian (T)	6-2/305	1-21-77	4	Illinois State	W-Mia./02	6/0
95	Hovan, Chris (T)	6-2/296	5-12-78	6	Boston College	FA/05	13/9
92	McFarland, Anthony (T)	6-0/300	12-18-77	7	LSU	D1/99	8/8
97	Rice, Simeon (E)	6-5/268	2-24-74	10	Illinois	FA/01	16/16
93	Savage, Josh (E)	6-4/276	9-28-80	2	Utah	FA/04	6/0
94	Spires, Greg (E)	6-1/265	8-12-74	8	Florida State	FA/02	16/16
90	White, Dewayne (E)	6-2/273	10-19-79	3	Louisville	D2/03	16/3
96	Wyms, Ellis (T)	6-3/279	4-12-79	5	Mississippi State	D6b/01	6/0
	LINEBACKERS						
55	Brooks, Derrick	6-0/235	4-18-73	11	Florida State	D1b/95	16/16
54	Buhl, Josh	6-0/210	5-4-81	1	Kansas State	FA/05	—
58	Cooper, Marquis	6-3/213	3-11-82	2	Washington	D3/04	14/0
50	Gooch, Jeff	5-11/226	10-31-74	10	Austin Peay	FA/04	16/1
45	Grootegoed, Matt	5-11/218	5-6-82	R	USC	FA/05	—
56	Nece, Ryan	6-3/224	2-24-79	4	UCLA	FA/02	16/0
53	Quarles, Shelton	6-1/225	9-11-71	9	Vanderbilt	FA/97	15/15
51	Ruud, Barrett	6-1/242	5-20-83	R	Nebraska	D2/05	—
	DEFENSIVE BACKS						
35	Abdullah, Hamza (S)	6-2/213	8-20-83	R	Washington State	D7c/05	—
26	Allen, Will (S)	6-1/193	6-17-82	2	Ohio State	D4/04	16/0
20	Barber, Ronde (CB)	5-10/184	4-7-75	9	Virginia	D3b/97	16/16
21	Bolden, Juran (CB)	6-2/207	6-27-74	8	Mississippi Delta JC	FA/05	13/0
27	Cox, Torrie (CB)	5-10/181	10-29-80	3	Pittsburgh	D6/03	10/0
34	Jackson, Dexter (S)	6-0/205	7-28-77	7	Florida State	FA/03	6/1
25	Kelly, Brian (CB)	5-11/193	1-14-76	8	USC	D2b/98	16/16
28	Nicholson, Donte (S)	6-1/216	12-18-81	R	Oklahoma	D5a/05	—
23	Phillips, Jermaine (S)	6-1/214	3-27-79	4	Georgia	D5/02	9/9
29	Whitaker, Ronyell (CB)	5-9/196	3-19-79	1	Virginia Tech	FA/03	0/0
	SPECIALISTS						
9	Bidwell, Josh (P)	6-3/220	3-13-76	6	Oregon	FA/04	16/0
3	Bryant, Matt (K)	5-9/200	5-29-75	3	Baylor	FA/05	4/0
4	France, Todd (K)	6-3/185	2-13-80	1	Toledo	FA/05	0/0

Abbreviations: D1—draft pick, first round; W—claimed on waivers; T—obtained in trade; FA—free-agent acquisition.

TAMPA BAY BUCCANEERS

TAMPA BAY BUCCANEERS

2004 regular-season record: 5-11
Position: 4th in NFC South

Sept. 12—at Washington	L	10-16
Sept. 19—SEATTLE	L	6-10
Sept. 26—at Oakland	L	20-30
Oct. 3—DENVER	L	13-16
Oct. 10—at New Orleans	W	20-17
Oct. 18—at St. Louis	L	21-28
Oct. 24—CHICAGO	W	19-7
Oct. 31—Open date		
Nov. 7—KANSAS CITY	W	34-31
Nov. 14—at Atlanta	L	14-24
Nov. 21—SAN FRANCISCO	W	35-3
Nov. 28—at Carolina	L	14-21
Dec. 5—ATLANTA	W	27-0
Dec. 12—at San Diego	L	24-31
Dec. 19—NEW ORLEANS	L	17-21
Dec. 26—CAROLINA	L	20-37
Jan. 2—at Arizona	L	7-12

SCORING BY PERIODS

	Q1	Q2	Q3	Q4	OT	Pts.
Buccaneers	48	101	83	69	0	301
Opponents	68	91	69	76	0	304

TEAM STATISTICS

	T.B.	Opp.
TOTAL FIRST DOWNS	271	258
Rushing	74	101
Passing	175	131
Penalty	22	26
3rd Down: Made/Att.	75/199	77/218
3rd Down Pct.	37.7	35.3
4th Down: Made/Att.	4/6	3/8
4th Down Pct.	66.7	37.5
POSSESSION AVG.	29:43	30:17
TOTAL NET YARDS	4963	4552
Avg. per Game	310.2	284.5
Total Plays	949	961
Avg. per Play	5.2	4.7
NET YARDS RUSHING	1489	1973
Avg. per Game	93.1	123.3
Total Rushes	393	480
NET YARDS PASSING	3474	2579
Avg. per Game	217.1	161.2
Sacked/Yards Lost	44/299	45/264
Gross Yards	3773	2843
Att./Completions	512/340	436/247
Completion Pct.	66.4	56.7
Had Intercepted	18	16
PUNTS/AVERAGE	83/41.8	87/44.4
NET PUNTING AVG.	83/36.8	87/40.2
PENALTIES/YARDS	117/916	112/897
FUMBLES/LOST	32/18	21/11
TOUCHDOWNS	37	35
Rushing	9	8
Passing	24	21
Returns	4	6

SCORING (NON-KICKERS)

	TD	RTD	PTD	MTD	2Pt.	Tot. Pts.
Pittman	10	7	3	0	0	60
Clayton	7	0	7	0	0	42
Galloway	6	0	5	1	0	36
Dilger	3	0	3	0	1	20
Alstott	2	2	0	0	0	12
Barber	2	0	0	2	0	12
Jurevicius	2	0	2	0	0	12
Brown	1	0	1	0	0	6
Cook	1	0	1	0	0	6
Cox	1	0	0	1	0	6
Heller	1	0	1	0	0	6
Schroeder	1	0	1	0	0	6
Buccaneers	37	9	24	4	1	224
Opponents	35	8	21	6	0	210

2-Pt. conversions: Buccaneers 1-4;
Opponents 0-0.

(KICKERS)

	XPM/XPA	FGM/FGA	Pts.
Gramatica	21/22	11/19	54
Taylor	11/11	4/5	23
Buccaneers	32/33	15/24	77
Opponents	34/35	20/31	94

RUSHING

	Att.	Yds.	Avg.	Lg.	TD
Pittman	219	926	4.2	t78	7
Alstott	67	230	3.4	32	2
Garner	30	111	3.7	25	0
Graham	13	73	5.6	13	0
Clayton	5	30	6.0	15	0
Smart	2	26	13.0	25	0
B. Johnson	5	23	4.6	7	0
J. White	13	20	1.5	10	0
Galloway	2	19	9.5	14	0
Griese	30	17	0.6	7	0
Simms	7	14	2.0	12	0
Buccaneers	393	1489	3.8	t78	9
Opponents	480	1973	4.1	t64	8

RECEIVING

	No.	Yds.	Avg.	Lg.	TD
Clayton	80	1193	14.9	t75	7
Pittman	41	391	9.5	68	3
Dilger	39	345	8.8	t45	3
Galloway	33	416	12.6	t36	5
Alstott	29	202	7.0	20	0
Jurevicius	27	333	12.3	t42	2
Brown	24	200	8.3	21	1
Lee	15	207	13.8	35	0
Heller	12	98	8.2	22	1
Garner	9	62	6.9	31	0
Cook	7	44	6.3	9	1
Schroeder	7	156	22.3	54	1
J. White	4	17	4.3	12	0
Dudley	3	48	16.0	24	0
Moore	3	17	5.7	10	0
Smart	2	10	5.0	5	0
Baber	1	7	7.0	7	0
Coleman	1	4	4.0	4	0
Comella	1	12	12.0	12	0
Griese	1	-4	-4.0	-4	0
Lawrie	1	15	15.0	15	0
Buccaneers	340	3773	11.1	t75	24
Opponents	247	2843	11.5	t79	21

INTERCEPTIONS

	No.	Yds.	Avg.	Lg.	TD
Kelly	4	101	25.3	75	0
Barber	3	23	7.7	23	0
D. Smith	3	13	4.3	13	0
Cox	1	55	55.0	t55	1
Gold	1	31	31.0	31	0
Brooks	1	3	3.0	3	0
Nece	1	2	2.0	2	0
Allen	1	0	0.0	0	0
Phillips	1	0	0.0	0	0
Ivy	0	11	...	11	0
Buccaneers	16	239	14.9	75	1
Opponents	18	328	18.2	t46	4

SACKS: Rice 12.0, Spires 8.0, D. White 6.0,
Ahanotu 3.5, Quarles 3.5, Barber 3.0,
Brooks 3.0, McFarland 3.0, Bradley 1.0,
Phillips 1.0, Gold 0.5, Gooch 0.5.
Buccaneers 45.0; Opponents 44.0.

PUNTING

	No.	Yds.	Avg.	In. 20	Lg.
Bidwell	82	3472	42.3	23	60
Buccaneers	82	3472	41.8	23	60
Opponents	87	3867	44.4	34	81

PUNT RETURNS

	No.	FC	Yds.	Avg.	Lg.	TD
Galloway	20	8	142	7.1	t59	1
Brown	6	12	48	8.0	14	0
Schroeder	6	1	21	3.5	12	0
Clayton	1	1	2	2.0	2	0
Buccaneers	33	22	213	6.5	t59	1
Opponents	31	24	279	9.0	53	0

KICK RETURNS

	No.	Yds.	Avg.	Lg.	TD
Cox	33	866	26.2	59	0
Murphy	8	208	26.0	54	0
Smart	8	167	20.9	27	0
J. White	4	99	24.8	44	0
Graham	3	52	17.3	18	0
Schroeder	2	29	14.5	16	0
Comella	1	20	20.0	20	0
D. White	1	9	9.0	9	0
Buccaneers	60	1450	24.2	59	0
Opponents	58	1315	22.7	t98	1

FIELD GOALS

	1-19	20-29	30-39	40-49	50+
Gramatica	0/0	6/7	3/6	1/5	1/1
Taylor	0/0	2/3	1/1	1/1	0/0
Buccaneers	0/0	6/7	5/9	2/6	2/2
Opponents	0/0	4/4	7/11	8/11	1/5

Gramatica: (47G) (24G, 27G) (36G, 30G,
44N) (28G, 30G) (23G, 53G, 41N) (35N,
48N) (22G, 22G) (46N) () () (39N, 26B,
37N) () () () (); Taylor: () () () () () () ()
() () () (50G, 30G) (30N, 41G) (37G) ()
Opponents: (50N, 20G, 30G, 34G) (44G)
(23G, 40G, 46N, 39G) (49G, 50G, 23G)
(47G) (56N, 44N) () (31G) (33G) (50N, 47G)
(38N, 38B) () (51N, 40G) (38N) (26G) (40G,
45G, 35N, 39G, 31G, 47N)

PASSING

	Att.	Cmp.	Yds.	Pct.	Avg. Gain	TD	Pct. TD	Int.	Pct. Int.	Long	Sack/Lost	Rating
Griese	336	233	2632	69.3	7.83	20	6.0	12	3.6	68	26/169	97.5
B. Johnson	103	65	674	63.1	6.54	3	2.9	3	2.9	54	8/55	79.5
Simms	73	42	467	57.5	6.40	1	1.4	3	4.1	t75	10/75	64.1
Buccaneers	512	340	3773	66.4	7.37	24	4.7	18	3.5	t75	44/299	89.1
Opponents	436	247	2843	56.7	6.52	21	4.8	16	3.7	t79	45/264	77.2

TENNESSEE TITANS
AFC SOUTH DIVISION

2005 SEASON

CLUB DIRECTORY

Owner
K.S. "Bud" Adams Jr.
Executive vice president/general manager
Floyd Reese
Vice president of administration
Don MacLachlan
Director of player personnel
Rich Snead
Director of media relations and services
Robbie Bohren
Vice president for community affairs
Bob Hyde

**Head coach/
executive
vice
president**
Jeff Fisher

Assistant coaches
Chuck Cecil (defensive asst./
quality control)
Norm Chow (offensive coordinator)
Dave McGinnis (linebackers)
George Henshaw (asst. head
coach/offense)
Ned James (offensive asst./quality control)
Craig Johnson (quarterbacks)
Alan Lowry (special teams)
Mike Munchak (offensive line)
Jim Schwartz (def. coordinator)
Ray Sherman (wide receivers)
Sherman Smith (running backs)
Jim Washburn (defensive line)
Steve Watterson (strength &
conditioning)
Everett Withers (defensive backs)

OFFSEASON MOVES

Key additions
DE Kyle Vanden Bosch   FA/Cardinals
Key losses
WR Eddie Berlin   FA/Bears
DE Kevin Carter   Rel./Dolphins
CB Andre Dyson   FA/Seahawks
DE Carlos Hall   Trade/Chiefs
FB Robert Holcombe   Rel./Chiefs
WR Derrick Mason   Rel./Ravens
TE Shad Meier   FA/Saints
OT Fred Miller   Rel./Bears
K Joe Nedney   Rel./49ers
CB Samari Rolle   Rel./Ravens
RB Antowain Smith   FA/Saints

SCHEDULE

Sept. 11—at Pittsburgh	1:00
Sept. 18—BALTIMORE	1:00
Sept. 25—at St. Louis	1:00
Oct. 2—INDIANAPOLIS	1:00
Oct. 9—at Houston	1:00
Oct. 16—CINCINNATI	1:00
Oct. 23—at Arizona	4:15
Oct. 30—OAKLAND	2:00
Nov. 6—at Cleveland	2:00
Nov. 13—Open week	
Nov. 20—JACKSONVILLE	2:00
Nov. 27—SAN FRANCISCO	2:00
Dec. 4—at Indianapolis	2:00
Dec. 11—HOUSTON	2:00
Dec. 18—SEATTLE	2:00
Dec. 24—at Miami	2:00
Jan. 1—at Jacksonville	5:05

All times are Eastern.
All games Sunday unless noted.

DRAFT CHOICES

Adam "Pacman" Jones, CB, West
Virginia (first round/sixth pick overall).
Michael Roos, OT, Eastern Washington
(2/41).
Courtney Roby, WR, Indiana (3/68).
Brandon Jones, WR, Oklahoma (3/96).
Vincent Fuller, FS, Virginia Tech (4/108).
David Stewart, OT, Mississippi State
(4/113).
Roydell Williams, WR, Tulane (4/136).
Damien Nash, RB, Missouri (5/142).
Daniel Loper, OT, Texas Tech (5/150).
Bo Scaife, TE, Texas (6/179).
Reynaldo Hill, CB, Florida (7/218).

MISCELLANEOUS TEAM DATA

Stadium (capacity, surface):
Coliseum
(68,804, grass)
Business address:
460 Great Circle Road
Nashville, TN 37228
Business phone:
615-565-4000
Ticket information:
615-565-4200
Team colors:
Navy, red, Titan blue and white
Flagship radio station:
WKDF, 103.3 FM
Website:
www.titansonline.com
Training site:
460 Great Circle Road
Nashville, TN 37228
615-565-4000

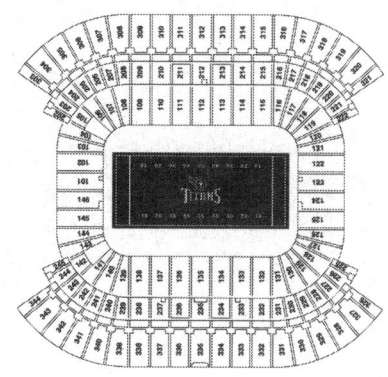

TENNESSEE TITANS

No.	QUARTERBACKS	Ht./Wt.	Born	NFL Exp.	College	How acq.	'04 Games GP/GS
8	Guidugli, Gino	6-4/230	3-13-83	1	Cincinnati	FA/05	—
9	McNair, Steve	6-2/235	2-14-73	11	Alcorn State	D1/95	8/8
7	Volek, Billy	6-2/214	4-28-76	6	Fresno State	FA/00	10/8
19	White, Jason	6-2/226	6-19-80	1	Oklahoma	FA/05	—
	RUNNING BACKS						
29	Brown, Chris	6-3/219	4-17-81	3	Colorado	D3/03	11/11
44	Fleming, Troy (FB)	6-0/230	10-1-80	2	Tennessee	D6/04	16/0
5	Larkins, Corey	5-7/200	10-23-81	1	Tennessee	FA/05	—
20	Nash, Damien	5-11/215	4-14-82	R	Missouri	D5a/05	—
39	Reyes, Walter	5-10/210	5-22-81	1	Syracuse	FA/05	—
	RECEIVERS						
10	Anderson, Jason	6-3/195	6-25-82	1	Wake Forest	FA/05	—
83	Bennett, Drew	6-5/206	8-26-78	5	UCLA	FA/01	16/16
11	Bush, Chris	6-1/193	7-22-81	1	Tulane	FA/05	—
87	Calico, Tyrone	6-4/222	11-9-80	3	Middle Tenn. State	D2/03	1/0
81	Jones, Brandon	6-1/208	10-6-82	R	Oklahoma	D3b/05	—
88	Kinney, Erron (TE)	6-5/275	7-28-77	6	Florida	D3a/00	9/9
82	Roby, Courtney	6-0/189	1-10-83	R	Indiana	D3a/05	—
80	Scaife, Bo (TE)	6-2/249	1-6-81	R	Texas	D6/05	—
84	Troupe, Ben (TE)	6-4/262	9-1-82	2	Florida	D2a/04	14/6
86	Williams, Roydell	6-0/192	3-14-81	R	Tulane	D4c/05	—
	OFFENSIVE LINEMEN						
64	Amano, Eugene (G/C)	6-3/295	8-1-82	2	Southeast Missouri	D7b/04	15/2
60	Bell, Jacob (T)	6-4/306	3-2-81	2	Miami (Ohio)	D5a/04	15/14
77	Hartwig, Justin (C)	6-4/305	11-21-78	4	Kansas	D6/02	15/15
72	Hopkins, Brad (T)	6-3/305	9-5-70	13	Illinois	D1/93	11/11
70	Loper, Daniel (T)	6-6/306	1-15-82	R	Texas Tech	D5b/05	—
75	Olson, Benji (G)	6-4/320	6-5-75	8	Washington	D5/98	15/15
69	Piller, Zach (G)	6-5/321	5-2-76	7	Florida	D3/99	1/1
71	Roos, Michael (T)	6-5/320	10-5-82	R	Eastern Washington	D2/05	—
76	Stewart, David (T)	6-7/323	8-28-82	R	Mississippi State	D4b/05	—
78	Williams, Todd (T)	6-5/330	9-4-78	3	Florida State	D7/03	6/0
	DEFENSIVE LINEMEN						
78	Clauss, Jared (T)	6-4/294	4-7-81	2	Iowa	D7/04	14/1
92	Haynesworth, Albert (T)	6-6/320	6-17-81	4	Tennessee	D1/02	10/10
73	Johnson, Shawn (E)	6-5/275	3-21-80	1	Delaware	FA/05	—
91	LaBoy, Travis (E)	6-3/253	8-10-81	2	Hawaii	D2b/04	13/2
99	Long, Rien (T)	6-6/300	8-7-81	3	Washington State	D4/03	15/3
98	Odom, Antwan (E)	6-4/277	9-24-81	2	Alabama	D2c/04	16/8
95	Schobel, Bo (E)	6-5/264	3-24-81	2	TCU	D4a/04	5/2
90	Starks, Randy (T)	6-3/307	12-14-83	2	Maryland	D3a/04	14/8
93	Vanden Bosch, Kyle (E)	6-4/278	11-17-78	4	Nebraska	FA/05	16/1
	LINEBACKERS						
58	Amato, Ken	6-2/245	5-18-77	3	Montana State	FA/03	16/0
50	Boiman, Rocky	6-4/236	1-24-80	4	Notre Dame	D4c/02	7/6
53	Bulluck, Keith	6-3/235	4-4-77	6	Syracuse	D1/00	16/16
54	Calmus, Rocky	6-3/238	8-1-79	4	Oklahoma	D3/02	4/3
55	Kassell, Brad	6-3/242	1-7-80	4	North Texas	FA/02	15/14
51	Reynolds, Robert	6-3/242	5-20-81	2	Ohio State	D5b/04	14/1
59	Sirmon, Peter	6-2/237	2-18-77	5	Oregon	D4b/00	0/0
56	Spencer, Cody	6-2/242	6-1-81	2	North Texas	W-Oak./04	7/0
	DEFENSIVE BACKS						
24	Beckham, Tony (CB)	6-1/187	10-1-78	4	Wisconsin-Stout	D4b/02	5/1
22	Fuller, Vincent (S)	6-1/189	8-3-82	R	Virginia Tech	D4a/05	—
30	Gardner, Rich (CB)	5-10/199	2-1-81	2	Penn State	D3b/04	15/1
21	Hill, Reynaldo (CB)	5-11/187	8-28-82	R	Florida	D7/05	—
32	Jones, Adam (CB)	5-10/187	9-30-83	R	West Virginia	D1/05	—
23	Nickey, Donnie (S)	6-3/215	4-25-80	3	Ohio State	D5/03	15/6
40	Sandy, Justin (S)	6-0/214	2-22-82	1	Northern Iowa	FA/04	1/0
31	Schulters, Lance (S)	6-2/202	5-27-75	8	Hofstra	FA/02	3/3
28	Thompson, Lamont (S)	6-1/220	7-30-78	4	Washington State	FA/03	16/13
36	Waddell, Michael (CB)	5-10/187	1-9-81	2	North Carolina	D4/04	16/4
25	Williams, Tank (S)	6-3/223	6-30-80	4	Stanford	D2/02	9/9
26	Woolfolk, Andre (CB)	6-2/197	1-26-80	3	Oklahoma	D1/03	10/2
	SPECIALISTS						
15	Hentrich, Craig (P)	6-3/213	5-18-71	12	Notre Dame	FA/98	16/0
3	Kimrin, Ola (K)	6-3/230	2-29-72	2	UTEP	W-Was./05	5/0

Abbreviations: D1—draft pick, first round; W—claimed on waivers; T—obtained in trade; FA—free-agent acquisition.

2004 regular-season record: 5-11
Position: 4th in AFC South

Sept.11—at Miami	W	17-7
Sept.19—INDIANAPOLIS	L	17-31
Sept.26—JACKSONVILLE	L	12-15
Oct. 3—at San Diego	L	17-38
Oct. 11—at Green Bay	W	48-27
Oct. 17—HOUSTON	L	10-20
Oct. 24—at Minnesota	L	3-20
Oct. 31—CINCINNATI	W	27-20
Nov. 7—Open date		
Nov.14—CHICAGO (OT)	L	17-19
Nov.21—at Jacksonville	W	18-15
Nov.28—at Houston	L	21-31
Dec. 5—at Indianapolis	L	24-51
Dec.13—KANSAS CITY	L	38-49
Dec.19—at Oakland	L	35-40
Dec.25—DENVER	L	16-37
Jan. 2—DETROIT	W	24-19

SCORING BY PERIODS

	Q1	Q2	Q3	Q4	OT	Pts.
Titans	106	111	49	78	0	344
Opponents	76	117	99	145	2	439

TEAM STATISTICS

	Ten.	Opp.
TOTAL FIRST DOWNS	308	318
Rushing	85	99
Passing	200	189
Penalty	23	30
3rd Down: Made/Att.	74/217	62/186
3rd Down Pct.	34.1	33.3
4th Down: Made/Att.	12/27	9/12
4th Down Pct.	44.4	75.0
POSSESSION AVG.	31:40	28:20
TOTAL NET YARDS	5487	5724
Avg. per Game	342.9	357.8
Total Plays	1053	977
Avg. per Play	5.2	5.9
NET YARDS RUSHING	1871	1917
Avg. per Game	116.9	119.8
Total Rushes	420	421
NET YARDS PASSING	3616	3807
Avg. per Game	226.0	237.9
Sacked/Yards Lost	44/317	32/220
Gross Yards	3933	4027
Att./Completions	589/356	524/333
Completion Pct.	60.4	63.5
Had Intercepted	19	18
PUNTS/AVERAGE	79/42.9	74/43.6
NET PUNTING AVG.	79/38.2	74/38.8
PENALTIES/YARDS	110/923	95/774
FUMBLES/LOST	33/12	22/12
TOUCHDOWNS	41	52
Rushing	12	18
Passing	27	29
Returns	2	5

SCORING (NON-KICKERS)

	Tot. TD	RTD	PTD	MTD	2Pt.	Tot. Pts.
Bennett	11	0	11	0	0	66
Mason	7	0	7	0	0	42
Brown	6	6	0	0	0	36
Smith	4	4	0	0	0	24
Kinney	3	0	3	0	0	18
Fleming	2	0	2	0	0	12
Meier	2	0	2	0	0	12
McNair	1	1	0	0	1	8
Berlin	1	0	1	0	0	6
Bulluck	1	0	0	1	0	6
Thompson	1	0	0	1	0	6
Troupe	1	0	1	0	0	6
Volek	1	1	0	0	0	6
Titans	41	12	27	2	1	248
Opponents	52	18	29	5	1	320

2-Pt. conversions: Titans 1-2; Opponents 1-2.

(KICKERS)

	XPM/XPA	FGM/FGA	Pts.
Anderson	37/37	17/22	88
Elling	2/2	1/2	5
Hentrich	0/0	1/3	3
Titans	39/39	19/27	96
Opponents	50/50	23/28	119

RUSHING

	Att.	Yds.	Avg.	Lg.	TD
Brown	220	1067	4.9	52	6
Smith	137	509	3.7	43	4
McNair	23	128	5.6	23	1
Holcombe	17	62	3.6	20	0
Volek	11	50	4.5	14	1
Fleming	7	40	5.7	13	0
Bennett	1	12	12.0	12	0
Hentrich	1	8	8.0	8	0
Johnson	2	-2	-1.0	-1	0
Mason	1	-3	-3.0	-3	0
Titans	420	1871	4.5	52	12
Opponents	421	1917	4.6	55	18

RECEIVING

	No.	Yds.	Avg.	Lg.	TD
Mason	96	1168	12.2	t37	7
Bennett	80	1247	15.6	t48	11
Troupe	33	329	10.0	33	1
Kinney	25	193	7.7	21	3
Meier	25	127	5.1	29	2
Smith	22	169	7.7	31	0
Berlin	20	278	13.9	31	1
Brown	20	147	7.4	21	0
Fleming	19	164	8.6	37	2
Holcombe	11	60	5.5	9	0
Calico	2	13	6.5	9	0
McAddley	2	38	19.0	36	0
Volek	1	0	0.0	0	0
Titans	356	3933	11.0	t48	27
Opponents	333	4027	12.1	62	29

INTERCEPTIONS

	No.	Yds.	Avg.	Lg.	TD
Dyson	6	135	22.5	44	0
Thompson	4	77	19.3	t37	1
Bulluck	2	25	12.5	25	0
Woolfolk	1	25	25.0	25	0
Ta. Williams	1	13	13.0	13	0
McGarrahan	1	11	11.0	11	0
Rolle	1	0	0.0	0	0
Waddell	1	0	0.0	0	0
Gardner	1	-1	-1.0	-1	0
Titans	18	285	15.8	44	1
Opponents	19	306	16.1	t51	2

SACKS: Carter 6.0, Bulluck 5.0, Long 5.0, Starks 4.5, LaBoy 3.5, Hall 2.5, Odom 2.0, Haynesworth 1.0, Schulters 1.0, Ta. Williams 1.0, McGarrahan 0.5. Titans 32.0; Opponents 44.0.

PUNTING

	No.	Yds.	Avg.	In. 20	Lg.
Elling	6	272	45.3	1	58
Hentrich	73	3117	42.7	20	64
Titans	79	3389	42.9	21	64
Opponents	74	3223	43.6	24	66

PUNT RETURNS

	No.	FC	Yds.	Avg.	Lg.	TD
Mason	24	12	93	3.9	13	0
Waddell	9	3	54	6.0	18	0
Berlin	7	1	26	3.7	13	0
Titans	40	16	173	4.3	20	0
Opponents	31	26	195	6.3	t75	1

KICK RETURNS

	No.	Yds.	Avg.	Lg.	TD
McAddley	38	849	22.3	45	0
Fleming	18	316	17.6	30	0
Waddell	17	342	20.1	33	0
Holcombe	3	26	8.7	14	0
Bennett	1	-8	-8.0	-8	0
Kinney	1	21	21.0	21	0
Schobel	1	12	12.0	12	0
Titans	79	1558	19.7	45	0
Opponents	69	1389	20.1	35	0

FIELD GOALS

	1-19	20-29	30-39	40-49	50+
Anderson	0/0	4/5	4/4	9/12	0/1
Hentrich	0/0	0/0	0/0	0/0	1/3
Elling	0/0	1/1	0/1	0/0	0/0
Titans	0/0	5/6	4/5	9/12	1/4
Opponents	0/0	12/12	5/7	3/6	3/3

Anderson: () (39G) (26G, 40G) (24G) (36G, 38G, 42B) (40G) (40G) (23G, 45G) (33G) (41G) () (45G, 43B) (50N, 27G) (41N) (44G, 43G) (40G, 27B); Hentrich: () () () () () () () () (58N, 52B) () () () () (50G) (); Elling: (33N, 32G) () () () () () () () () () () () () () () () Opponents: (46N) (28G) () (31G) (39G, 53G) (21G, 50G) (29G, 29G) (28G, 50G) (39N, 29G) (35G, 48G, 44N) (29G, 41B) (47G, 20G, 37G) () (42G) (22G, 34N, 22G, 30G) (26G, 26G)

PASSING

	Att.	Cmp.	Yds.	Pct.	Avg. Gain	TD	Pct. TD	Int.	Pct. Int.	Long	Sack/Lost	Rating
Volek	357	218	2486	61.1	6.96	18	5.0	10	2.8	t48	30/216	87.1
McNair	215	129	1343	60.0	6.25	8	3.7	9	4.2	t37	13/95	73.1
Johnson	12	6	68	50.0	5.67	0	0.0	0	0.0	33	1/6	67.4
Bennett	1	1	26	100.0	26.00	1	100.0	0	0.0	t26	0/0	158.3
Hentrich	4	2	10	50.0	2.50	0	0.0	0	0.0	6	0/0	56.3
Titans	589	356	3933	60.4	6.68	27	4.6	19	3.2	t48	44/317	82.1
Opponents	524	333	4027	63.5	7.69	29	5.5	18	3.4	62	32/220	91.2

WASHINGTON REDSKINS
NFC EAST DIVISION

2005 SEASON

CLUB DIRECTORY

Owner, chairman and CEO
Daniel M. Snyder
Chief operating officer
Dave Pauken
Senior vice president of stadium operations
Michael Dillow
Vice president of football operations
Vinny Cerrato
Director of pro personnel
Scott Campbell
Director of public relations
Patrick Wixted

Head coach
Joe Gibbs

Assistant coaches
Greg Blache (def. coord./def. line)
Don Breaux (off. coordinator)
Joe Bugel (asst. head coach/offense)
Jack Burns (offensive asst.)
Earnest Byner (running backs)
Bobby Crumpler (strength & conditioning)
John Dunn (head strength & conditioning)
Coy Gibbs (quality control/offense)
John Hastings (strength & conditioning)
Stan Hixon (wide receivers)
Steve Jackson (third down/safeties)
Bill Lazor (offensive asst.)
Dale Lindsey (linebackers)
Bill Musgrave (quarterbacks)
Kirk Olivadotti (defensive asst./special teams)
Rennie Simmons (tight ends)
Danny Smith (special teams)
DeWayne Walker (secondary/cornerbacks)
Gregg Williams (asst. head coach/defense)

OFFSEASON MOVES

Key additions
LB Brian Allen	FA/Panthers
LB Warrick Holdman	FA/Browns
WR Santana Moss	Trade/Jets
WR David Patten	FA/Patriots
S Pierson Prioleau	FA/Bills
C Casey Rabach	FA/Ravens

Key losses
WR Lavernues Coles	Trade/Jets
S Todd Franz	FA/Packers
DT Jermaine Haley	Released
QB Tim Hasselbeck	Rel./Giants
OT Vaughn Parker	Released
LB Antonio Pierce	FA/Giants
CB Fred Smoot	FA/Vikings

SCHEDULE

Sept.	11—CHICAGO	1:00
Sept.	19—at Dallas (Mon.)	9:00
Sept.	25—Open week	
Oct.	2—SEATTLE	1:00
Oct.	9—at Denver	4:15
Oct.	16—at Kansas City	1:00
Oct.	23—SAN FRANCISCO	1:00
Oct.	30—at N.Y. Giants	2:00
Nov.	6—PHILADELPHIA	9:30
Nov.	13—at Tampa Bay	2:00
Nov.	20—OAKLAND	2:00
Nov.	27—SAN DIEGO	2:00
Dec.	4—at St. Louis	5:05
Dec.	11—at Arizona	5:05
Dec.	18—DALLAS	2:00
Dec.	24—N.Y. GIANTS (Sat.)	2:00
Jan.	1—at Philadelphia	5:15

All times are Eastern.
All games Sunday unless noted.

DRAFT CHOICES

Carlos Rogers, CB, Auburn (first round/ninth pick overall).
Jason Campbell, QB, Auburn (1/25).
Manuel White, FB, UCLA (4/120).
Robert McCune, ILB, Louisville (5/154).
Jared Newberry, OLB, Stanford (6/183).
Nehemiah Broughton, FB, The Citadel (7/222).

MISCELLANEOUS TEAM DATA

Stadium (capacity, surface):
FedEx Field (91,665, grass)
Business address:
21300 Redskin Park Drive
Ashburn, VA 20147
Business phone:
703-726-7000
Ticket information:
301-276-6050
Team colors:
Burgundy and gold
Flagship radio station:
WJFK, 106.7 FM
Website:
www.redskins.com
Training site:
Redskins Park
Ashburn, VA
703-726-7000

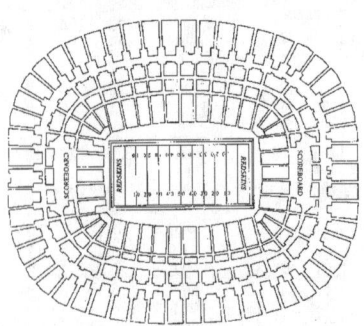

WASHINGTON REDSKINS

No.	QUARTERBACKS	Ht./Wt.	Born	NFL Exp.	College	How acq.	'04 Games GP/GS
8	Brunell, Mark	6-1/217	9-17-70	12	Washington	T-Jac./04	9/9
17	Campbell, Jason	6-4/223	12-31-81	R	Auburn	D1b/05	—
11	Ramsey, Patrick	6-2/223	2-14-79	4	Tulane	D1/02	9/7
	RUNNING BACKS						
46	Betts, Ladell	5-10/222	8-27-79	4	Iowa	D2/02	16/1
36	Broughton, Nehemiah	5-11/250	11-4-82	R	The Citadel	D7/05	—
40	Cartwright, Rock	5-7/223	12-3-79	4	Kansas State	D7c/02	13/0
47	Cooley, Chris (FB)	6-3/265	7-11-82	2	Utah State	D3/04	16/9
20	Morton, Chad	5-8/203	4-4-77	6	USC	FA/03	6/0
26	Portis, Clinton	5-11/205	9-1-81	4	Miami	T-Den./04	15/15
45	Sellers, Mike (FB)	6-3/260	7-21-75	6	Walla Walla CC	FA/01	16/1
48	White, Manuel	6-2/239	7-2-82	R	UCLA	D4/05	—
	RECEIVERS						
43	Baber, Billy (TE)	6-3/255	1-17-79	3	Virginia	FA/05	1/0
86	Brown, Antonio	5-10/175	3-3-78	3	West Virginia	FA/03	3/0
84	Jacobs, Taylor	6-0/198	5-30-81	3	Florida	D2/03	15/4
85	McCants, Darnerien	6-3/214	8-1-77	4	Delaware State	D5/01	5/1
89	Moss, Santana	5-10/185	6-1-79	5	Miami	T-NYJ/05	15/14
80	Patten, David	5-10/190	8-19-74	9	Western Carolina	FA/05	16/11
88	Royal, Robert (TE)	6-4/257	5-15-79	3	LSU	D5b/02	14/9
83	Thrash, James	6-0/200	4-28-75	9	Missouri Southern	T-Phi./04	16/3
	OFFENSIVE LINEMEN						
71	Albright, Ethan (C)	6-5/265	5-1-71	11	North Carolina	FA/01	16/0
67	Brown, Ray (G)	6-5/318	12-12-62	18	Arkansas State	FA/04	16/14
66	Dockery, Derrick (G)	6-6/345	9-7-80	3	Texas	D3/03	16/16
64	Friedman, Lennie (G)	6-3/283	10-13-76	6	Duke	FA/03	5/2
76	Jansen, Jon (T)	6-6/305	1-28-76	6	Michigan	D2/99	0/0
69	Molinaro, Jim (T)	6-6/309	4-27-81	2	Notre Dame	D6/04	11/0
61	Rabach, Casey (C)	6-4/301	9-24-77	4	Wisconsin	FA/05	16/16
52	Raymer, Cory (C)	6-3/300	3-3-73	10	Wisconsin	FA/04	15/14
60	Samuels, Chris (T)	6-5/310	7-28-77	6	Alabama	D1b/00	16/16
77	Thomas, Randy (G)	6-5/306	1-19-76	7	Mississippi State	FA/03	15/15
63	Wilson, Mark (T)	6-6/295	11-11-80	2	California	D5/04	2/1
	DEFENSIVE LINEMEN						
73	Boschetti, Ryan (T)	6-4/300	10-7-81	2	UCLA	FA/04	3/1
93	Daniels, Phillip (E)	6-3/288	3-4-73	10	Georgia	FA/04	5/5
92	Evans, Demetric (E)	6-3/300	9-3-79	4	Georgia	FA/01	12/8
96	Griffin, Cornelius (T)	6-3/300	12-3-76	6	Alabama	FA/04	15/15
75	Noble, Brandon (T)	6-2/304	4-10-74	6	Penn State	FA/03	16/7
95	Salave'a, Joe (T)	6-3/295	3-23-75	7	Arizona	FA/04	15/9
94	Warner, Ron (E)	6-3/270	9-26-75	4	Kansas	FA/01	14/2
72	Williams, Melvin (E)	6-2/278	2-2-79	3	Kansas State	FA/04	3/0
97	Wynn, Renaldo (E)	6-3/292	9-3-74	9	Notre Dame	FA/02	16/16
	LINEBACKERS						
55	Allen, Brian	6-0/232	4-1-78	5	Florida State	FA/05	14/0
56	Arrington, LaVar	6-3/253	6-20-78	6	Penn State	D1a/00	4/2
51	Barnes, Brandon	6-2/247	6-12-81	2	Missouri	FA/04	12/0
58	Barrow, Mike	6-2/245	4-19-70	12	Miami	FA/04	0/0
50	Campbell, Khary	6-3/250	4-4-79	4	Bowling Green	FA/02	9/0
57	Clemons, Chris	6-3/234	10-30-81	2	Georgia	FA/04	6/0
48	Holdman, Warrick	6-1/234	11-22-75	7	Texas A&M	FA/05	16/14
98	Marshall, Lemar	6-2/227	12-17-76	4	Michigan State	FA/01	16/14
59	McCune, Robert	5-11/243	3-9-79	R	Louisville	D5/05	—
99	Newberry, Jared	6-1/234	11-11-81	R	Stanford	D6/05	—
53	Washington, Marcus	6-3/247	10-17-77	6	Auburn	FA/04	16/16
	DEFENSIVE BACKS						
41	Bowen, Matt (S)	6-1/207	11-12-76	6	Iowa	FA/03	5/5
25	Clark, Ryan (S)	5-11/200	10-12-79	4	LSU	FA/02	15/11
27	Harris, Walt (CB)	5-11/192	8-10-74	10	Mississippi State	FA/04	16/2
34	Lott, Andre (S)	5-10/196	5-31-79	4	Tennessee	D5a/02	4/3
29	Prioleau, Pierson (S)	5-11/188	8-6-77	7	Virginia Tech	FA/05	16/2
32	Rogers, Carlos (CB)	6-0/199	7-2-81	R	Auburn	D1a/05	—
24	Springs, Shawn (CB)	6-0/204	3-11-75	9	Ohio State	FA/04	15/15
21	Taylor, Sean (S)	6-2/231	4-1-83	2	Miami	D1/04	15/13
38	Wilds, Garnell (CB)	5-11/196	6-8-81	1	Virginia Tech	FA/04	2/0
	SPECIALISTS						
5	Chandler, Jeff (K)	6-2/218	6-18-79	3	Florida	FA/04	5/0
10	Hall, John (K)	6-3/240	3-17-74	9	Wisconsin	FA/03	8/0
19	Tupa, Tom (P)	6-4/225	2-6-66	17	Ohio State	FA/04	16/0

Abbreviations: D1—draft pick, first round; T—obtained in trade; FA—free-agent acquisition.

WASHINGTON REDSKINS

2004 regular-season record: 6-10
Position: 4th in NFC East

Sept.12—TAMPA BAY	W	16-10
Sept.19—at N.Y. Giants	L	14-20
Sept.27—DALLAS	L	18-21
Oct. 3—at Cleveland	L	13-17
Oct. 10—BALTIMORE	L	10-17
Oct. 17—at Chicago	W	13-10
Oct. 24—Open date		
Oct. 31—GREEN BAY	L	14-28
Nov. 7—at Detroit	W	17-10
Nov.14—CINCINNATI	L	10-17
Nov.21—at Philadelphia	L	6-28
Nov.28—at Pittsburgh	L	7-16
Dec. 5—N.Y. GIANTS	W	31-7
Dec.12—PHILADELPHIA	L	14-17
Dec.18—at San Francisco	W	26-16
Dec.26—at Dallas	L	10-13
Jan. 2—MINNESOTA	W	21-18

SCORING BY PERIODS

	Q1	Q2	Q3	Q4	OT	Pts.
Redskins	54	80	34	72	0	240
Opponents	44	78	69	74	0	265

TEAM STATISTICS

	Was.	Opp.
TOTAL FIRST DOWNS ..	269	251
Rushing	91	67
Passing	156	153
Penalty	22	31
3rd Down: Made/Att. ..	70/221	70/226
3rd Down Pct.	31.7	31.0
4th Down: Made/Att.	4/11	7/17
4th Down Pct.	36.4	41.2
POSSESSION AVG.	31:19	28:41
TOTAL NET YARDS	4397	4281
Avg. per Game	274.8	267.6
Total Plays	1023	974
Avg. per Play	4.3	4.4
NET YARDS RUSHING ..	1765	1304
Avg. per Game	110.3	81.5
Total Rushes	471	419
NET YARDS PASSING....	2632	2977
Avg. per Game	164.5	186.1
Sacked/Yards Lost	38/242	40/245
Gross Yards	2874	3222
Att./Completions	514/288	515/294
Completion Pct.	56.0	57.1
Had Intercepted	17	18
PUNTS/AVERAGE	104/43.7	104/40.2
NET PUNTING AVG.	104/35.2	104/35.9
PENALTIES/YARDS	115/1047	97/797
FUMBLES/LOST	20/10	17/8
TOUCHDOWNS	26	30
Rushing	6	7
Passing	18	17
Returns	2	6

SCORING (NON-KICKERS)

	Tot.TD	RTD	PTD	MTD	2Pt.	Tot.Pts.
Portis	7	5	2	0	0	42
Cooley	6	0	6	0	0	36
Gardner	5	0	5	0	0	30
Royal	4	0	4	0	0	24
Betts	1	1	0	0	0	6
Coles	1	0	1	0	0	6
Harris	1	0	0	1	0	6
Pierce	1	0	0	1	0	6
Jacobs	0	0	0	0	1	2
Redskins	26	6	18	2	1	158
Opponents	30	7	17	6	2	186

2-Pt. conversions: Redskins 1-1; Opponents 2-2.

(KICKERS)

	XPM/XPA	FGM/FGA	Pts.
Hall	13/13	8/11	37
Kimrin	6/6	6/10	24
Chandler	6/6	5/6	21
Redskins	25/25	19/27	82
Opponents	28/28	17/20	79

RUSHING

	Att.	Yds.	Avg.	Lg.	TD
Portis	343	1315	3.8	t64	5
Betts	90	371	4.1	27	1
Brunell	19	62	3.3	21	0
Ramsey	10	19	1.9	17	0
Gardner	3	7	2.3	11	0
Cartwright	2	0	0.0	2	0
Coles	3	-3	-1.0	7	0
Jacobs	1	-6	-6.0	-6	0
Redskins	471	1765	3.7	t64	6
Opponents	419	1304	3.1	26	7

RECEIVING

	No.	Yds.	Avg.	Lg.	TD
Coles	90	950	10.6	45	1
Gardner	51	650	12.7	51	5
Portis	40	235	5.9	18	2
Cooley	37	314	8.5	31	6
Thrash	17	203	11.9	31	0
Jacobs	16	178	11.1	45	0
Betts	15	108	7.2	20	0
Royal	8	70	8.8	23	4
McCants	5	71	14.2	27	0
Rasby	5	52	10.4	13	0
Kozlowski	3	29	9.7	13	0
Sellers	1	14	14.0	14	0
Redskins	288	2874	10.0	51	18
Opponents	294	3222	11.0	80	17

INTERCEPTIONS

	No.	Yds.	Avg.	Lg.	TD
Springs	5	117	23.4	38	0
Taylor	4	85	21.3	45	0
Smoot	3	17	5.7	17	0
Pierce	2	94	47.0	t78	1
Harris	2	31	15.5	31	0
R. Warner	1	39	39.0	39	0
Franz	1	22	22.0	22	0
Redskins	18	405	22.5	t78	1
Opponents	17	201	11.8	t70	1

SACKS: Griffin 6.0, Springs 6.0, Washington 4.5, R. Warner 3.5, Clemons 3.0, Wynn 3.0, Evans 2.5, Bowen 2.0, Salave'a 2.0, Marshall 1.5, Arrington 1.0, Daniels 1.0, Haley 1.0, Noble 1.0, Pierce 1.0, Taylor 1.0. Redskins 40.0; Opponents 38.0.

PUNTING

	No.	Yds.	Avg.	In.20	Lg.
Tupa	103	4544	44.1	30	61
Redskins	104	4544	43.7	30	61
Opponents	104	4180	40.2	26	58

PUNT RETURNS

	No.	FC	Yds.	Avg.	Lg.	TD
Thrash	19	8	162	8.5	43	0
Morton	13	12	80	6.2	14	0
Brown	10	2	89	8.9	39	0
Redskins	42	23	331	7.9	43	0
Opponents	65	11	727	11.2	t78	1

KICK RETURNS

	No.	Yds.	Avg.	Lg.	TD
Betts	23	528	23.0	70	0
Morton	16	358	22.4	49	0
Thrash	9	186	20.7	36	0
Sellers	4	56	14.0	17	0
Brown	1	66	66.0	66	0
Kozlowski	1	4	4.0	4	0
Molinaro	1	5	5.0	5	0
Redskins	55	1203	21.9	70	0
Opponents	57	1223	21.5	t92	1

FIELD GOALS

	1-19	20-29	30-39	40-49	50+
Hall	1/1	3/3	3/3	1/3	0/1
Kimrin	0/0	3/3	2/3	1/3	0/1
Chandler	0/0	4/4	0/0	1/1	0/1
Redskins	1/1	10/10	5/6	3/7	0/3
Opponents	0/0	4/4	9/9	4/6	0/1

Hall: (50N, 20G, 30G, 34G) (41N) (19G) (31G, 26G) (26G) () () () () (46G) (43N) () () (); Kimrin: () () () () () (41G, 26G) (35N) (24G, 51N) (47N, 33G) (35G, 24G, 48N) () () () () () (); Chandler: () () () () () () () () (49G, 25G, 20G, 26G) (25G, 57N) () Opponents: (47G) (47N, 38G, 22G, 51B) () (30G) (33G) (46G) (37G, 39G) (40G) (41G) () (33G, 36G, 32G) () (48N, 38G) () (26G, 23G) (23G)

PASSING

	Att.	Cmp.	Yds.	Pct.	Avg.Gain	TD	Pct.TD	Int.	Pct.Int.	Long	Sack/Lost	Rating
Ramsey	272	169	1665	62.1	6.12	10	3.7	11	4.0	51	23/137	74.8
Brunell	237	118	1194	49.8	5.04	7	3.0	6	2.5	49	15/105	63.9
Portis	2	1	15	50.0	7.50	1	50.0	0	0.0	t15	0/0	114.6
Gardner	3	0	0	0.0	0.00	0	0.0	0	0.0	...	0/0	39.6
Redskins	514	288	2874	56.0	5.59	18	3.5	17	3.3	51	38/242	70.0
Opponents	515	294	3222	57.1	6.26	17	3.3	18	3.5	80	40/245	72.2

SCHEDULE

PRESEASON

(All times Eastern)

HALL OF FAME WEEKEND

SATURDAY, AUGUST 6

Atlanta vs. Indianapolis at Tokyo, Japan........................ 5:00

MONDAY, AUGUST 8

Chicago vs. Miami at Canton, Ohio 8:00

WEEK 1

THURSDAY, AUGUST 11

San Diego at Green Bay.. 8:00

FRIDAY, AUGUST 12

Detroit at N.Y. Jets.. 7:00
New England at Cincinnati 7:30
Chicago at St. Louis 8:00
Kansas City at Minnesota 8:00
Seattle at New Orleans... 8:00
Tampa Bay at Tennessee.. 8:00

SATURDAY, AUGUST 13

Baltimore at Atlanta 7:30
Miami at Jacksonville 7:30
Buffalo at Indianapolis 8:00
Denver at Houston.. 8:00
N.Y. Giants at Cleveland.. 8:00
Washington at Carolina.. 8:00
Dallas at Arizona.. 10:00
Oakland at San Francisco 10:00

MONDAY, AUGUST 15

Philadelphia at Pittsburgh...................................... 8:00

WEEK 2

THURSDAY, AUGUST 18

New Orleans at New England.................................. 8:00

FRIDAY, AUGUST 19

Tennessee at Atlanta... 7:30
Minnesota at N.Y. Jets... 8:00
Cincinnati at Washington.. 8:00

SATURDAY, AUGUST 20

Cleveland at Detroit 1:00
Green Bay at Buffalo... 6:00
Jacksonville at Tampa Bay...................................... 7:30
Miami at Pittsburgh... 7:30
Carolina at N.Y. Giants.. 8:00
Chicago at Indianapolis 8:00
Oakland at Houston... 8:00
Philadelphia at Baltimore....................................... 8:00
Arizona at Kansas City... 8:30
San Francisco at Denver 9:00

SUNDAY, AUGUST 21

St. Louis at San Diego... 4:00

MONDAY, AUG. 22

Dallas at Seattle 8:00

WEEK 3

THURSDAY, AUGUST 25

Atlanta at Jacksonville 8:00

FRIDAY, AUGUST 26

Cincinnati at Philadelphia....................................... 7:30
Pittsburgh at Washington.. 8:00
Baltimore at New Orleans....................................... 8:00
Buffalo at Chicago 8:00
Carolina at Cleveland 8:00
New England at Green Bay 8:00
N.Y. Jets at N.Y. Giants.. 8:00
San Diego at Minnesota... 8:00
Arizona at Oakland.. 9:30
Tennessee at San Francisco.................................... 10:00

SATURDAY, AUGUST 27

Tampa Bay at Miami.. 7:30
Indianapolis at Denver 8:00
Houston at Dallas.. 8:00
Seattle at Kansas City 8:30

MONDAY, AUGUST 29

St. Louis at Detroit 8:00

WEEK 4

THURSDAY, SEPTEMBER 1

Atlanta at Miami... 7:30
Houston at Tampa Bay... 7:30
N.Y. Jets at Philadelphia 7:30
Cleveland at Chicago 8:00
Green Bay at Tennessee... 8:00
Jacksonville at Dallas.. 8:00
N.Y. Giants at New England 8:00
Pittsburgh at Carolina.. 8:00
Washington at Baltimore... 8:00
New Orleans at Oakland... 9:00
San Francisco at San Diego.................................... 10:00

FRIDAY, SEPTEMBER 2

Detroit at Buffalo 7:00
Indianapolis at Cincinnati....................................... 7:30
Kansas City at St. Louis... 8:00
Minnesota at Seattle.. 9:00
Denver at Arizona... 10:00

REGULAR SEASON

(All times Eastern)

WEEK 1

THURSDAY, SEPTEMBER 8

Oakland at New England... 9:00

SUNDAY, SEPTEMBER 11

Chicago at Washington... 1:00
Cincinnati at Cleveland... 1:00
Denver at Miami... 1:00
Houston at Buffalo... 1:00
New Orleans at Carolina 1:00
N.Y. Jets at Kansas City... 1:00
Seattle at Jacksonville 1:00
Tampa Bay at Minnesota... 1:00
Tennessee at Pittsburgh 1:00
Arizona at N.Y. Giants.. 4:15
Dallas at San Diego 4:15
Green Bay at Detroit 4:15
St. Louis at San Francisco...................................... 4:15
Indianapolis at Baltimore.. 8:30

MONDAY, SEPTEMBER 12

Philadelphia at Atlanta 9:00

WEEK 2

SUNDAY, SEPTEMBER 18

Baltimore at Tennessee	1:00
Buffalo at Tampa Bay	1:00
Detroit at Chicago	1:00
Jacksonville at Indianapolis	1:00
Minnesota at Cincinnati	1:00
New England at Carolina	1:00
N.Y. Giants at New Orleans	1:00
Pittsburgh at Houston	1:00
San Francisco at Philadelphia	1:00
Atlanta at Seattle	4:05
St. Louis at Arizona	4:05
Cleveland at Green Bay	4:15
Miami at N.Y. Jets	4:15
San Diego at Denver	4:15
Kansas City at Oakland	8:30

MONDAY, SEPTEMBER 19

Washington at Dallas	9:00

WEEK 3

SUNDAY, SEPTEMBER 25

Atlanta at Buffalo	1:00
Carolina at Miami	1:00
Cincinnati at Chicago	1:00
Cleveland at Indianapolis	1:00
Jacksonville at N.Y. Jets	1:00
New Orleans at Minnesota	1:00
Oakland at Philadelphia	1:00
Tampa Bay at Green Bay	1:00
Tennessee at St. Louis	1:00
Arizona at Seattle	4:05
Dallas at San Francisco	4:05
New England at Pittsburgh	4:15
N.Y. Giants at San Diego	8:30

MONDAY, SEPTEMBER 26

Kansas City at Denver	9:00

Open date: Baltimore, Detroit, Houston, Washington

WEEK 4

SUNDAY, OCTOBER 2

Buffalo at New Orleans	1:00
Denver at Jacksonville	1:00
Detroit at Tampa Bay	1:00
Houston at Cincinnati	1:00
Indianapolis at Tennessee	1:00
Philadelphia at Kansas City	1:00
San Diego at New England	1:00
Seattle at Washington	1:00
St. Louis at N.Y. Giants	1:00
N.Y. Jets at Baltimore	4:05
Dallas at Oakland	4:15
Minnesota at Atlanta	4:15
San Francisco at Arizona	8:30

MONDAY, OCTOBER 3

Green Bay at Carolina	9:00

Open date: Chicago, Cleveland, Miami, Pittsburgh

WEEK 5

SUNDAY, OCTOBER 9

Baltimore at Detroit	1:00
Chicago at Cleveland	1:00
Miami at Buffalo	1:00
New England at Atlanta	1:00
New Orleans at Green Bay	1:00
Seattle at St. Louis	1:00
Tampa Bay at N.Y. Jets	1:00
Tennessee at Houston	1:00
Indianapolis at San Francisco	4:05
Carolina at Arizona	4:15
Philadelphia at Dallas	4:15
Washington at Denver	4:15
Cincinnati at Jacksonville	8:30

MONDAY, OCTOBER 10

Pittsburgh at San Diego	9:00

Open date: Kansas City, Minnesota, N.Y. Giants, Oakland

WEEK 6

SUNDAY, OCTOBER 16

Atlanta at New Orleans	1:00
Carolina at Detroit	1:00
Cincinnati at Tennessee	1:00
Cleveland at Baltimore	1:00
Jacksonville at Pittsburgh	1:00
Miami at Tampa Bay	1:00
Minnesota at Chicago	1:00
N.Y. Giants at Dallas	1:00
Washington at Kansas City	1:00
New England at Denver	4:15
N.Y. Jets at Buffalo	4:15
San Diego at Oakland	4:15
Houston at Seattle	8:30

MONDAY, OCTOBER 17

St. Louis at Indianapolis	9:00

Open date: Arizona, Green Bay, Philadelphia, San Francisco

WEEK 7

SUNDAY, OCTOBER 23

Detroit at Cleveland	1:00
Green Bay at Minnesota	1:00
Indianapolis at Houston	1:00
Kansas City at Miami	1:00
New Orleans at St. Louis	1:00
Pittsburgh at Cincinnati	1:00
San Diego at Philadelphia	1:00
San Francisco at Washington	1:00
Dallas at Seattle	4:05
Baltimore at Chicago	4:15
Buffalo at Oakland	4:15
Denver at N.Y. Giants	4:15
Tennessee at Arizona	4:15

MONDAY, OCTOBER 24

N.Y. Jets at Atlanta	9:00

Open date: Carolina, Jacksonville, New England, Tampa Bay

WEEK 8

SUNDAY, OCTOBER 30

Arizona at Dallas	1:00
Chicago at Detroit	1:00
Cleveland at Houston	1:00
Green Bay at Cincinnati	1:00
Jacksonville at St. Louis	1:00
Miami at New Orleans	1:00
Minnesota at Carolina	1:00
Oakland at Tennessee	1:00
Washington at N.Y. Giants	1:00
Kansas City at San Diego	4:05
Philadelphia at Denver	4:15
Tampa Bay at San Francisco	4:15
Buffalo at New England	8:30

MONDAY, OCTOBER 31

Baltimore at Pittsburgh	9:00

Open date: Atlanta, Indianapolis, N.Y. Jets, Seattle

WEEK 9

SUNDAY, NOVEMBER 6

Atlanta at Miami	1:00
Carolina at Tampa Bay	1:00
Chicago at New Orleans	1:00
Cincinnati at Baltimore	1:00
Detroit at Minnesota	1:00
Houston at Jacksonville	1:00
Oakland at Kansas City	1:00
San Diego at N.Y. Jets	1:00
Tennessee at Cleveland	1:00
N.Y. Giants at San Francisco	4:05
Seattle at Arizona	4:05
Pittsburgh at Green Bay	4:15
Philadelphia at Washington	8:30

MONDAY, NOVEMBER 7

Indianapolis at New England	9:00

Open date: Buffalo, Dallas, Denver, St. Louis

WEEK 10

SUNDAY, NOVEMBER 13

Arizona at Detroit	1:00
Baltimore at Jacksonville	1:00
Houston at Indianapolis	1:00
Kansas City at Buffalo	1:00
Minnesota at N.Y. Giants	1:00
New England at Miami	1:00
San Francisco at Chicago	1:00
Washington at Tampa Bay	1:00
Denver at Oakland	4:05
N.Y. Jets at Carolina	4:05
Green Bay at Atlanta	4:15
St. Louis at Seattle	4:15
Cleveland at Pittsburgh	8:30

MONDAY, NOVEMBER 14

Dallas at Philadelphia	9:00

Open date: Cincinnati, New Orleans, San Diego, Tennessee

WEEK 11

SUNDAY, NOVEMBER 20

Arizona at St. Louis	1:00
Carolina at Chicago	1:00
Detroit at Dallas	1:00
Indianapolis at Cincinnati	1:00
Jacksonville at Tennessee	1:00
Miami at Cleveland	1:00
New Orleans at New England	1:00
Oakland at Washington	1:00
Philadelphia at N.Y. Giants	1:00
Tampa Bay at Atlanta	1:00
Seattle at San Francisco	4:05
Buffalo at San Diego	4:15
N.Y. Jets at Denver	4:15
Pittsburgh at Baltimore	4:15
Kansas City at Houston	8:30

MONDAY, NOVEMBER 21

Minnesota at Green Bay	9:00

WEEK 12

THURSDAY, NOVEMBER 24

Atlanta at Detroit	12:30
Denver at Dallas	4:15

SUNDAY, NOVEMBER 27

Baltimore at Cincinnati	1:00
Carolina at Buffalo	1:00
Chicago at Tampa Bay	1:00
Cleveland at Minnesota	1:00
New England at Kansas City	1:00
San Diego at Washington	1:00
San Francisco at Tennessee	1:00
St. Louis at Houston	1:00
Jacksonville at Arizona	4:05
Miami at Oakland	4:05
Green Bay at Philadelphia	4:15
N.Y. Giants at Seattle	4:15
New Orleans at N.Y. Jets	8:30

MONDAY, NOVEMBER 28

Pittsburgh at Indianapolis	9:00

WEEK 13

SUNDAY, DECEMBER 4

Atlanta at Carolina	1:00
Buffalo at Miami	1:00
Cincinnati at Pittsburgh	1:00
Dallas at N.Y. Giants	1:00
Green Bay at Chicago	1:00
Houston at Baltimore	1:00
Jacksonville at Cleveland	1:00
Minnesota at Detroit	1:00
Tampa Bay at New Orleans	1:00
Tennessee at Indianapolis	1:00
Arizona at San Francisco	4:05
Washington at St. Louis	4:05
Denver at Kansas City	4:15
N.Y. Jets at New England	4:15
Oakland at San Diego	8:30

MONDAY, DECEMBER 5

Seattle at Philadelphia	9:00

WEEK 14

SUNDAY, DECEMBER 11

Chicago at Pittsburgh	1:00
Cleveland at Cincinnati	1:00
Houston at Tennessee	1:00
Indianapolis at Jacksonville	1:00
New England at Buffalo	1:00
Oakland at N.Y. Jets	1:00
St. Louis at Minnesota	1:00
Tampa Bay at Carolina	1:00
N.Y. Giants at Philadelphia	4:05
San Francisco at Seattle	4:05
Washington at Arizona	4:05
Baltimore at Denver	4:15
Kansas City at Dallas	4:15
Miami at San Diego	4:15
Detroit at Green Bay	8:30

MONDAY, DECEMBER 12

New Orleans at Atlanta	9:00

WEEK 15

SATURDAY, DECEMBER 17

Tampa Bay at New England	1:30
Kansas City at N.Y. Giants	5:00
Denver at Buffalo	8:30

SUNDAY, DECEMBER 18

Arizona at Houston	1:00
Carolina at New Orleans	1:00
Dallas at Washington	1:00
N.Y. Jets at Miami	1:00
Pittsburgh at Minnesota	1:00

San Diego at Indianapolis	1:00
Seattle at Tennessee	1:00
San Francisco at Jacksonville	1:00
Cincinnati at Detroit	4:05
Cleveland at Oakland	4:05
Philadelphia at St. Louis	4:15
Atlanta at Chicago	8:30

MONDAY, DECEMBER 19

Green Bay at Baltimore	9:00

WEEK 16

SATURDAY, DECEMBER 24

Atlanta at Tampa Bay	1:00
Buffalo at Cincinnati	1:00
Dallas at Carolina	1:00
Detroit at New Orleans	1:00
Jacksonville at Houston	1:00
N.Y. Giants at Washington	1:00
Pittsburgh at Cleveland	1:00
San Diego at Kansas City	1:00
San Francisco at St. Louis	1:00
Tennessee at Miami	1:00
Philadelphia at Arizona	4:05
Indianapolis at Seattle	4:15
Oakland at Denver	4:15

SUNDAY, DECEMBER 25

Chicago at Green Bay	5:00
Minnesota at Baltimore	8:30

MONDAY, DECEMBER 26

New England at N.Y. Jets	9:00

WEEK 17

SATURDAY, DECEMBER 31

Denver at San Diego	4:30
N.Y. Giants at Oakland	8:00

SUNDAY, JANUARY 1

Arizona at Indianapolis	1:00
Baltimore at Cleveland	1:00
Buffalo at N.Y. Jets	1:00
Carolina at Atlanta	1:00
Chicago at Minnesota	1:00
Cincinnati at Kansas City	1:00
Detroit at Pittsburgh	1:00
Miami at New England	1:00
New Orleans at Tampa Bay	1:00
Houston at San Francisco	4:05
Tennessee at Jacksonville	4:05
Seattle at Green Bay	4:15
Washington at Philadelphia	4:15
St. Louis at Dallas	8:30

NATIONALLY TELEVISED GAMES

(All times Eastern)

PRESEASON

Sat.	Aug.	6—	Atlanta vs. Indianapolis (5 a.m., ESPN2) (Replay: 6:00, ESPN)
Mon.	Aug.	8—	Chicago vs. Miami (8:00, ABC)
Thurs.	Aug.	11—	San Diego at Green Bay (8:00, ESPN)
Mon.	Aug.	15—	Philadelphia at Pittsburgh (8:00, ESPN)
Thurs.	Aug.	18—	New Orleans at New England (8:00, FOX)
Fri.	Aug.	19—	Minnesota at N.Y. Jets (8:00, CBS)
Mon.	Aug.	22—	Dallas at Seattle (8:00, ABC)
Thurs.	Aug.	25—	Atlanta at Jacksonville (8:00, ESPN)
Fri.	Aug.	26—	Pittsburgh at Washington (8:00, FOX)
Sat.	Aug.	27—	Indianapolis at Denver (8:00, CBS)
Mon.	Aug.	29—	St. Louis at Detroit (8:00, ABC)

REGULAR SEASON

Thurs.	Sept.	8—	Oakland at New England (9:00, ABC)
Sun.	Sept.	11—	Dallas at San Diego (4:15, FOX) Indianapolis at Baltimore (8:30, ESPN)
Mon.	Sept.	12—	Philadelphia at Atlanta (9:00, ABC)
Sun.	Sept.	18—	Cleveland at Green Bay (4:15, CBS) Kansas City at Oakland (8:30, ESPN)
Mon.	Sept.	19—	Washington at Dallas (9:00, ABC)
Sun.	Sept.	25—	New England at Pittsburgh (4:15, CBS) New York Giants at San Diego (8:30, ESPN)
Mon.	Sept.	26—	Kansas City at Denver (9:00, ABC)
Sun.	Oct.	2—	Dallas at Oakland (4:15, FOX) San Francisco at Arizona (Mexico) (8:30, ESPN)
Mon.	Oct.	3—	Green Bay at Carolina (9:00, ABC)
Sun.	Oct.	9—	Philadelphia at Dallas (4:15, FOX) Cincinnati at Jacksonville (8:30, ESPN)
Mon.	Oct.	10—	Pittsburgh at San Diego (9:00, ABC)
Sun.	Oct.	16—	New England at Denver (4:15, CBS) Houston at Seattle (8:30, ESPN)
Mon.	Oct.	17—	St. Louis at Indianapolis (9:00, ABC)
Sun.	Oct.	23—	Denver at New York Giants (4:15, CBS)
Mon.	Oct.	24—	New York Jets at Atlanta (9:00, ABC)
Sun.	Oct.	30—	Philadelphia at Denver (4:15, FOX) Buffalo at New England (8:30, ESPN)
Mon.	Oct.	31—	Baltimore at Pittsburgh (9:00, ABC)
Sun.	Nov.	6—	Pittsburgh at Green Bay (4:15, CBS) Philadelphia at Washington (8:30, ESPN)
Mon.	Nov.	7—	Indianapolis at New England (9:00, ABC)
Sun.	Nov.	13—	Green Bay at Atlanta (4:15, FOX) Cleveland at Pittsburgh (8:30, ESPN)
Mon.	Nov.	14—	Dallas at Philadelphia (9:00, ABC)
Sun.	Nov.	20—	New York Jets at Denver (4:15, CBS) Kansas City at Houston (8:30, ESPN)
Mon.	Nov.	21—	Minnesota at Green Bay (9:00, ABC)
Thurs.	Nov.	24—	Atlanta at Detroit (2:30, FOX) Denver at Dallas (4:00, CBS)
Sun.	Nov.	27—	Green Bay at Philadelphia (4:15, FOX) New Orleans at New York Jets (8:30, ESPN)
Mon.	Nov.	28—	Pittsburgh at Indianapolis (9:00, ABC)
Sun.	Dec.	4—	New York Jets at New England (4:15, CBS) Oakland at San Diego (8:30, ESPN)
Mon.	Dec.	5—	Seattle at Philadelphia (9:00, ABC)
Sun.	Dec.	11—	Kansas City at Dallas (4:15, CBS) Detroit at Green Bay (8:30, ESPN)
Mon.	Dec.	12—	New Orleans at Atlanta (9:00, ABC)
Sat.	Dec.	17—	Tampa Bay at New England (1:30, FOX) Kansas City at New York Giants (5:00, CBS) Denver at Buffalo (8:30, ESPN)
Sun.	Dec.	18—	Philadelphia at St. Louis (4:15, FOX) Atlanta at Chicago (8:30, ESPN)
Mon.	Dec.	19—	Green Bay at Baltimore (9:00, ABC)
Sat.	Dec.	24—	Oakland at Denver (4:15, CBS)
Sun.	Dec.	25—	Chicago at Green Bay (5:00, FOX) Minnesota at Baltimore (8:30, ESPN)
Mon.	Dec.	26—	New England at New York Jets (9:00, ABC)
Sat.	Dec.	31—	Denver at San Diego (4:30, CBS) New York Giants at Oakland (8:00, ESPN)
Sun.	Jan.	1—	Seattle at Green Bay (4:15, FOX) St. Louis at Dallas (8:30, ESPN)

POSTSEASON

Sat.	Jan.	7—	AFC, NFC wild-card playoffs (ABC)
Sun.	Jan.	8—	AFC, NFC wild-card playoffs (CBS, FOX)
Sat.	Jan.	14—	AFC, NFC divisional playoffs (CBS, FOX)
Sun.	Jan.	15—	AFC, NFC divisional playoffs (CBS, FOX)
Sun.	Jan.	22—	AFC, NFC championship games (CBS, FOX)
Sun.	Feb.	5—	Super Bowl XL, Ford Field, Detroit (ABC)
Sun.	Feb.	13—	Pro Bowl, Aloha Stadium, Honolulu (ESPN)

(All times Eastern)

Sun.	Sept. 11—	Seattle at Jacksonville	1:00
		Dallas at San Diego	4:15
Sun.	Sept. 18—	Buffalo at Tampa Bay	1:00
		Minnesota at Cincinnati	1:00
		New England at Carolina	1:00
		Cleveland at Green Bay	4:15
Sun.	Sept. 25—	Atlanta at Buffalo	1:00
		Carolina at Miami	1:00
		Cincinnati at Chicago	1:00
		Oakland at Philadelphia	1:00
		Tennessee at St. Louis	1:00
		N.Y. Giants at San Diego	8:30
Sun.	Oct. 2—	Buffalo at New Orleans	1:00
		Philadelphia at Kansas City	1:00
		Dallas at Oakland	4:15
Sun.	Oct. 9—	Baltimore at Detroit	1:00
		Chicago at Cleveland	1:00
		New England at Atlanta	1:00
		Tampa Bay at N.Y. Jets	1:00
		Indianapolis at San Francisco	4:05
		Washington at Denver	4:15
Sun.	Oct. 16—	Miami at Tampa Bay	1:00
		Washington at Kansas City	1:00
		Houston at Seattle	8:30
Mon.	Oct. 17—	St. Louis at Indianapolis	9:00
Sun.	Oct. 23—	Detroit at Cleveland	1:00
		San Diego at Philadelphia	1:00
		Baltimore at Chicago	4:15
		Tennessee at Arizona	4:15
		Denver at N.Y. Giants	4:15
Mon.	Oct. 24—	N.Y. Jets at Atlanta	9:00
Sun.	Oct. 30—	Green Bay at Cincinnati	1:00
		Jacksonville at St. Louis	1:00
		Miami at New Orleans	1:00
		Philadelphia at Denver	4:15
Sun.	Nov. 6—	Atlanta at Miami	1:00
		Pittsburgh at Green Bay	4:15
Sun.	Nov. 13—	N.Y. Jets at Carolina	4:05
Sun.	Nov. 20—	New Orleans at New England	1:00
		Oakland at Washington	1:00
Thurs.	Nov. 24—	Denver at Dallas	4:15
Sun.	Nov. 27—	Carolina at Buffalo	1:00
		Cleveland at Minnesota	1:00
		San Diego at Washington	1:00
		San Francisco at Tennessee	1:00
		St. Louis at Houston	1:00
		Jacksonville at Atlanta	4:05
		New Orleans at N.Y. Jets	8:30
Sun.	Dec. 11—	Chicago at Pittsburgh	1:00
		Kansas City at Dallas	4:15
Sat.	Dec. 17—	Tampa Bay at New England	1:30
		Kansas City at N.Y. Giants	5:00
Sun.	Dec. 18—	Arizona at Houston	1:00
		Pittsburgh at Minnesota	1:00
		Seattle at Tennessee	1:00
		San Francisco at Jacksonville	1:00
		Cincinnati at Detroit	4:05
Mon.	Dec. 19—	Green Bay at Baltimore	9:00
Sat.	Dec. 24—	Indianapolis at Seattle	4:15
Sun.	Dec. 25—	Minnesota at Baltimore	8:30
Sat.	Dec. 31—	N.Y. Giants at Oakland	8:00
Sun.	Jan. 1—	Arizona at Indianaplis	1:00
		Detroit at Pittsburgh	1:00
		Houston at San Francisco	4:05

2005 STRENGTH OF SCHEDULE

(Teams are ranked from most difficult to easiest schedules, based on 2005 opponents' combined 2004 records. Ties based on percentage were broken using number of opponents who made the playoffs.)

	Team	Opp. Wins	Opp. Losses	Opp. Ties	Opp. Pct.						
1.	Miami (1)	140	116	0	.547	17.	Green Bay (T13)	127	129	0	.496
2.	San Diego (T13)	139	117	0	.543	18.	New Orleans (17)	126	130	0	.492
3.	New England (T5)	138	118	0	.539	19.	Carolina (T20)	126	130	0	.492
4.	Kansas City (T23)	137	119	0	.535	20.	Tampa Bay (T26)	126	130	0	.492
5.	N.Y. Jets (T5)	137	119	0	.535		Tennessee (T26)	126	130	0	.492
6.	Baltimore (T13)	136	120	0	.531	22.	N.Y. Giants (29)	125	131	0	.488
	Buffalo (T5)	136	120	0	.531	23.	Detroit (T20)	125	131	0	.488
8.	Oakland (T5)	135	121	0	.527	24.	Chicago (T18)	123	133	0	.480
9.	Cleveland (T26)	135	121	0	.527	25.	Minnesota (T18)	123	133	0	.480
10.	Cincinnati (T5)	134	122	0	.523	26.	Dallas (32)	122	134	0	.477
	Denver (T23)	134	122	0	.523	27.	San Francisco (T5)	113	127	0	.471
12.	Pittsburgh (30)	130	126	0	.508	28.	Washington (T20)	119	137	0	.465
13.	Jacksonville (T3)	129	127	0	.504	29.	Seattle (T3)	117	139	0	.457
14.	Houston (T5)	129	127	0	.504	30.	Philadelphia (T31)	116	140	0	.453
	Indianapolis (T13)	129	127	0	.504	31.	Arizona (2)	115	141	0	.449
16.	Atlanta (T23)	128	128	0	.500	32.	St. Louis (T5)	114	142	0	.445

NOTE: Number in parentheses is 2004 preseason rank.

COLLEGE DRAFT

ROUND-BY-ROUND SELECTIONS, APRIL 23-24, 2005

FIRST ROUND

Team	Player selected	Pos.	College	Draft pick origination
1. San Francisco	Alex Smith	QB	Utah	
2. Miami	Ronnie Brown	RB	Auburn	
3. Cleveland	Braylon Edwards	WR	Michigan	
4. Chicago	Cedric Benson	RB	Texas	
5. Tampa Bay	Carnell Williams	RB	Auburn	
6. Tennessee	Adam "Pacman" Jones	CB	West Virginia	
7. Minnesota	Troy Williamson	WR	South Carolina	From Oakland
8. Arizona	Antrel Rolle	CB	Miami	From Miami
9. Washington	Carlos Rogers	CB	Auburn	
10. Detroit	Mike Williams	WR	Southern California	
11. Dallas	Demarcus Ware	DE	Troy State	
12. San Diego	Shawne Merriman	OLB	Maryland	From N.Y. Giants
13. New Orleans	Jammal Brown	OT	Oklahoma	From Houston
14. Carolina	Thomas Davis	FS	Georgia	
15. Kansas City	Derrick Johnson	OLB	Texas	
16. Houston	Travis Johnson	DT	Florida State	From New Orleans
17. Cincinnati	David Pollack	DE	Georgia	
18. Minnesota	Erasmus James	DE	Wisconsin	
19. St. Louis	Alex Barron	OT	Florida State	
20. Dallas	Marcus Spears	DE	Louisiana State	From Buffalo
21. Jacksonville	Matt Jones	WR	Arkansas	
22. Baltimore	Mark Clayton	WR	Oklahoma	
23. Oakland	Fabian Washington	CB	Nebraska	From Seattle
24. Green Bay	Aaron Rodgers	QB	California	
25. Washington	Jason Campbell	QB	Auburn	From Denver
26. Seattle	Chris Spencer	C	Mississippi	From N.Y. Jets through Oakland
27. Atlanta	Sharod "Roddy" White	WR	Alabama-Birmingham	
28. San Diego	Luis Castillo	DT	Northwestern	
29. Indianapolis	Marlin Jackson	CB	Michigan	
30. Pittsburgh	Heath Miller	TE	Virginia	
31. Philadelphia	Mike Patterson	DT	Southern California	
32. New England	Logan Mankins	G	Fresno State	

SECOND ROUND

Team	Player selected	Pos.	College	Draft pick origination
33. San Francisco	David Baas	C	Michigan	
34. Cleveland	Brodney Pool	FS	Oklahoma	
35. Philadelphia	Reggie Brown	WR	Georgia	From Miami
36. Tampa Bay	Barrett Ruud	ILB	Nebraska	
37. Detroit	Shaun Cody	DT	Southern California	From Tennessee
38. Oakland	Stanford Routt	CB	Houston	
39. Chicago	Mark Bradley	WR	Oklahoma	
40. New Orleans	Josh Bullocks	FS	Nebraska	From Washington
41. Tennessee	Michael Roos	OT	Eastern Washington	From Detroit
42. Dallas	Kevin Burnett	OLB	Tennessee	
43. N.Y. Giants	Corey Webster	CB	Louisiana State	
44. Arizona	J.J. Arrington	RB	California	
45. Seattle	Lofa Tatupu	ILB	Southern California	From Carolina
46. Miami	Matt Roth	DE	Iowa	From Kansas City
47. N.Y. Jets	Mike Nugent	K	Ohio State	From Houston through Oakland
48. Cincinnati	Odell Thurman	ILB	Georgia	
49. Minnesota	Marcus Johnson	OT	Mississippi	
50. St. Louis	Ronald Bartell	CB	Howard	
51. Green Bay	Nick Collins	FS	Bethune-Coookman	From New Orleans
52. Jacksonville	Khalif Barnes	OT	Washington	
53. Baltimore	Dan Cody	DE	Oklahoma	
54. Carolina	Eric Shelton	RB	Louisville	From Seattle
55. Buffalo	Roscoe Parrish	WR	Miami	
56. Denver	Darrent Williams	CB	Oklahoma State	
57. N.Y. Jets	Justin Miller	CB	Clemson	
58. Green Bay	Terrence Murphy	WR	Texas A&M	
59. Atlanta	Jonathan Babineaux	DT	Iowa	
60. Indianapolis	Kelvin Hayden	CB	Illinois	
61. San Diego	Vincent Jackson	WR	Northern Colorado	
62. Pittsburgh	Bryant McFadden	CB	Florida State	
63. Philadelphia	Matt McCoy	OLB	San Diego State	
64. Baltimore	Adam Terry	OT	Syracuse	From New England

THIRD ROUND

Team	Player selected	Pos.	College	Draft pick origination
65. San Francisco	Frank Gore	RB	Miami	
66. St. Louis	Oshiomogho Atogwe	FS	Stanford	From Miami
67. Cleveland	Charlie Frye	QB	Akron	
68. Tennessee	Courtney Roby	WR	Indiana	
69. Oakland	Andrew Walter	QB	Arizona State	
70. Miami	Channing Crowder	ILB	Florida	From Chicago
71. Tampa Bay	Alex Smith	TE	Stanford	
72. Detroit	Stanley Wilson	CB	Stanford	
73. Houston	Vernand Morency	RB	Oklahoma State	From Dallas
74. N.Y. Giants	Justin Tuck	DE	Notre Dame	
75. Arizona	Eric Green	CB	Virginia Tech	
76. Denver	Karl Paymah	CB	Washington State	From Washington
77. Philadelphia	Ryan Moats	RB	Louisiana Tech	From Kansas City
78. Oakland	Kirk Morrison	ILB	San Diego State	From Houston
79. Carolina	Evan Mathis	G	Alabama	
80. Minnesota	Dustin Fox	CB	Ohio State	
81. St. Louis	Richie Incognito	C	Nebraska	
82. New Orleans	Alfred Fincher	ILB	Connecticut	
83. Cincinnati	Chris Henry	WR	West Virginia	
84. New England	Ellis Hobbs	CB	Iowa State	From Baltimore
85. Seattle	David Greene	QB	Georgia	
86. Buffalo	Kevin Everett	TE	Miami	
87. Jacksonville	Scott Starks	CB	Wisconsin	
88. N.Y. Jets	Sione Pouha	DT	Utah	
89. Carolina	Atiyyah Ellison	DT	Missouri	From Green Bay
Denver (Forfeited)				
90. Atlanta	Jordan Beck	ILB	Cal State Polytechnic	
91. Tampa Bay	Chris Colmer	OT	North Carolina State	From San Diego
92. Indianapolis	Vincent Burns	DE	Kentucky	
93. Pittsburgh	Trai Essex	OT	Northwestern	
94. San Francisco	Adam Snyder	G	Oregon	From Philadelphia
95. Arizona	Darryl Blackstock	OLB	Virginia	From New England
96. Tennessee*	Brandon Jones	WR	Oklahoma	
97. Denver*	Domonique Foxworth	CB	Maryland	
98. Seattle*	Leroy Hill	OLB	Clemson	
99. Kansas City*	Dustin Colquitt	P	Tennessee	
100. New England*	Nick Kaczur	G	Toledo	
101. Denver*	Maurice Clarett	RB	Ohio State	

FOURTH ROUND

Team	Player selected	Pos.	College	Draft pick origination
102. Philadelphia	Sean Considine	FS	Iowa	From San Francisco
103. Cleveland	Antonio Perkins	CB	Oklahoma	
104. Miami	Travis Daniels	CB	Louisiana State	
105. Seattle	Ray Willis	OT	Florida State	From Oakland
106. Chicago	Kyle Orton	QB	Purdue	
107. Tampa Bay	Dan Buenning	G	Wisconsin	
108. Tennessee	Vincent Fuller	FS	Virginia Tech	
109. Dallas	Marion Barber	RB	Minnesota	
110. N.Y. Giants	Brandon Jacobs	RB	Southern Illinois	
111. Arizona	Elton Brown	G	Virginia	
112. Minnesota	Ciatrick Fason	RB	Florida	From Washington
113. Tennessee	David Stewart	OT	Mississippi State	From Detroit
114. Houston	Jerome Mathis	WR	Hampton	
115. Green Bay	Marviel Underwood	FS	San Diego State	From Carolina
116. Kansas City	Craphonso Thorpe	WR	Florida State	
117. St. Louis	Jerome Carter	SS	Florida State	
118. New Orleans	Chase Lyman	WR	California	
119. Cincinnati	Eric Ghiaciuc	C	Central Michigan	
120. Washington	Manuel White	FB	UCLA	From Minnesota
121. Carolina	Stefan Lefors	QB	Louisville	From Seattle
122. Buffalo	Raymond "Duke" Preston	C	Illinois	
123. N.Y. Jets	Kerry Rhodes	FS	Louisville	From Jacksonville
124. Baltimore	Jason Brown	C	North Carolina	
125. Green Bay	Brady Poppinga	OLB	Brigham Young	
126. Philadelphia	Todd Herremans	OT	Saginaw Valley State	From Den. through Cle., Sea., Car. and G.B.
127. Jacksonville	Alvin Pearman	RB	Virginia	From N.Y. Jets
128. Atlanta	Chauncey Davis	DE	Florida State	
129. Indianapolis	Dylan Gandy	G	Texas Tech	

Team	Player selected	Pos.	College	Draft pick origination
130. San Diego	Darren Sproles	RB	Kansas State	
131. Pittsburgh	Fred Gibson	WR	Georgia	
132. Dallas	Chris Cant	DE	Virginia	From Philadelphia
133. New England	James Sanders	SS	Fresno State	
134. St. Louis*	Claude Terrell	G	New Mexico	
135. Indianapolis*	Matt Giordano	FS	California	
136. Tennessee*	Williams, Roydell	WR	Tulane	

FIFTH ROUND

Team	Player selected	Pos.	College	Draft pick origination
137. San Francisco	Ronald Fields	DT	Mississippi State	
138. Kansas City	Boomer Grigsby	ILB	Illinois State	From Miami
139. Cleveland	David McMillan	DE	Kansas	
140. Chicago	Airese Currie	WR	Clemson	
141. Tampa Bay	Donte Nicholson	SS	Oklahoma	
142. Tennessee	Damien Nash	RB	Missouri	
143. Green Bay	Junius Coston	C	North Carolina A&T	From Oakland
144. St. Louis	Jerome Collins	TE	Notre Dame	From N.Y. Giants through S.D. and T.B.
145. Detroit	Dan Orlovsky	QB	Connecticut	From Arizona through New England
146. Philadelphia	Trent Cole	OLB	Cincinnati	From Washington
147. Kansas City	Alphonso Hodge	CB	Miami (Ohio)	From Detroit
148. Indianapolis	Jonathan Welsh	DE	Wisconsin	From Dallas through Philadelphia
149. Carolina	Adam Seward	ILB	UNLV	
150. Tennessee	Daniel Loper	OT	Texas Tech	From Kansas City
151. Houston	Drew Hodgdon	C	Arizona State	
152. New Orleans	Adrian McPherson	QB	Florida State	
153. Cincinnati	Adam Kieft	OT	Central Michigan	
154. Washington	Robert McCune	ILB	Louisville	From Minnesota
155. Tampa Bay	Larry Brackins	WR	Pearl River CC	From St. Louis
156. Buffalo	Eric King	CB	Wake Forest	
157. Jacksonville	Gerald Sensabaugh	SS	North Carolina	
158. Baltimore	Justin Green	FB	Montana	
159. Seattle	Jub Huckeba	OLB	Arkansas	
160. Atlanta	Michael Boley	OLB	Southern Mississippi	From Denver
161. N.Y. Jets	Andre Maddox	SS	North Carolina State	
162. Miami	Anthony Alabi	OT	Texas Christian	From Green Bay through Kansas City
163. Atlanta	Frank Omiyale	OT	Tennessee Tech	
164. San Diego	Wesley Britt	OT	Alabama	
165. Indianapolis	Robert Hunt	C	North Dakota State	
166. Pittsburgh	Rian Wallace	ILB	Temple	
167. Green Bay	Michael Hawkins	FS	Oklahoma	From Philadelphia
168. Arizona	Lance Mitchell	ILB	Oklahoma	From New England
169. Carolina*	Geoff Hangartner	C	Texas A&M	
170. New England*	Ryan Claridge	OLB	Nevada-Las Vegas	
171. Carolina*	Ben Emanuel	FS	UCLA	
172. Philadelphia*	Scott Young	G	Brigham Young	
173. Indianapolis*	Tyjaun Hagler	OLB	Cincinnati	
174. San Francisco*	Rasheed Marshall	WR	West Virginia	

SIXTH ROUND

Team	Player selected	Pos.	College	Draft pick origination
175. Oakland	Anttaj Hawthorne	DT	Wisconsin	From Phil. through G.B. and N.E.
176. Cleveland	Nick Speegle	OLB	New Mexico	
177. San Diego	Wes Sims	G	Oklahoma	From Miami
178. Tampa Bay	Anthony Bryant	DT	Alabama	
179. Tennessee	Bo Scaife	TE	Texas	
180. Green Bay	Mike Montgomery	DT	Texas A&M	From Oakland
181. Chicago	Chris Harris	SS	Louisiana-Monroe	
182. N.Y. Jets	Cedric Houston	RB	Tennessee	From Arizona through Oakland
183. Washington	Jared Newberry	OLB	Stanford	
184. Detroit	Bill Swancutt	DE	Oregon State	
185. Jacksonville	Chad Owens	WR	Hawaii	From Dallas through Oakland and N.Y. Jets
186. N.Y. Giants	Eric Moore	DE	Florida State	
187. Kansas City	Will Svitek	OT	Stanford	
188. Houston	Ceandris Brown	SS	Louisiana-Lafayette	
189. Carolina	Jovan Haye	DE	Vanderbilt	
190. Cincinnati	Tab Perry	WR	UCLA	
191. Minnesota	C.J. Mosley	DT	Missouri	
192. St. Louis	Dante Ridgeway	WR	Ball State	
193. New Orleans	Jason Jefferson	DT	Wisconsin	
194. Jacksonville	Pat Thomas	OLB	North Carolina State	

Team	Player selected	Pos.	College	Draft pick origination
195. Green Bay	Craig Bragg	WR	UCLA	From Baltimore through New England
196. Seattle	Tony Jackson	TE	Iowa	
197. Buffalo	Justin Geisinger	G	Vanderbilt	
198. N.Y. Jets	Joel Dreessen	TE	Colorado State	
199. Kansas City	Khari Long	DE	Baylor	From Green Bay
200. Denver	Chris Myers	G	Miami	
201. Atlanta	Deandra Cobb	RB	Michigan State	
202. Indianapolis	Dave Rayner	K	Michigan State	
203. Cleveland	Andrew Hoffman	DT	Virginia	From Tampa Bay
204. Pittsburgh	Chris Kemoeatu	G	Utah	
205. San Francisco	Derrick Johnson	CB	Washington	From Philadelphia
206. Detroit	Jonathan Goddard	DE	Marshall	From New England
207. Carolina*	Joe Berger	OT	Michigan Tech	
208. Dallas*	Justin Beriault	FS	Ball State	
209. Dallas*	Rob Petitti	OT	Pittsburgh	
210. St. Louis*	Reggie Hodges	P	Ball State	
211. Philadelphia*	Calvin Armstrong	OT	Washington State	
212. Oakland*	Ryan Riddle	DE	California	
213. Baltimore*	Derek Anderson	QB	Oregon State	
214. Oakland*	Pete McMahon	OT	Iowa	

SEVENTH ROUND

Team	Player selected	Pos.	College	Draft pick origination
215. San Francisco	Daven Holly	CB	Cincinnati	
216. Miami	Kevin Vickerson	DT	Michigan State	
217. Cleveland	Jon Dunn	OT	Virginia Tech	
218. Tennessee	Reynaldo Hill	CB	Florida	
219. Minnesota	Adrian Ward	CB	Texas-El Paso	From Oakland
220. Chicago	Rodriques Wilson	SS	South Carolina	
221. Tampa Bay	Rick Razzano	FB	Mississippi	
222. Washington	Nehemiah Broughton	FB	The Citadel	
223. San Francisco	Marcus Maxwell	WR	Oregon	From Detroit
224. Dallas	Jeremiah "Jay" Ratliff	DE	Auburn	
225. Tampa Bay	Paris Warren	WR	Utah	From N.Y. Giants
226. Arizona	LeRon McCoy	WR	Indiana (Pa.)	
227. Houston	Kenneth Pettway	OLB	Grambling State	
228. Pittsburgh	Shaun Nua	DE	Brigham Young	From Carolina
229. Kansas City	James Kilian	QB	Tulsa	
230. New England	Matt Cassel	QB	Southern California	From Min. through N.Y. Jets and Oak.
231. Tampa Bay	Hamza Abdullah	SS	Washington State	From St. Louis
232. New Orleans	Jimmy Verdon	DT	Arizona State	
233. Cincinnati	Jonathan Fanene	DE	Utah	
234. Baltimore	Mike Smith	ILB	Texas Tech	
235. Seattle	Cornelius Wortham	OLB	Alabama	
236. Buffalo	Lionel Gates	RB	Louisville	
237. Jacksonville	Chris Roberson	CB	Eastern Michigan	
238. Kansas City	Jeremy Parquet	OT	Southern Mississippi	From Green Bay
239. Denver	Paul Ernster	P	Northern Arizona	
240. N.Y. Jets	Harry Williams	WR	Tuskegee	
241. Atlanta	Darrell Shropshire	DT	South Carolina	
242. San Diego	Scott Mruczkowski	C	Bowling Green	
243. Indianapolis	Anthony Davis	RB	Wisconsin	
244. Pittsburgh	Noah Herron	RB	Northwestern	
245. Green Bay	Kurt Campbell	SS	Albany (N.Y.)	From Philadelphia
246. Green Bay	William Whitticker	G	Michigan State	From New England
247. Philadelphia*	Keyonta Marshall	DT	Grand Valley State	
248. San Francisco*	Patrick Estes	TE	Virginia	
249. San Francisco*	Billy Bajema	TE	Oklahoma State	
250. St. Louis*	Ryan Fitzpatrick	QB	Harvard	
251. St. Louis*	Madison Hedgecock	FB	North Carolina	
252. Philadelphia*	David Bergeron	ILB	Stanford	
253. Tampa Bay*	J.R. Russell	WR	Louisville	
254. Seattle*	Doug Nienhuis	OT	Oregon State	
255. New England*	Andy Stokes	TE	William Penn	

*Compensatory selection

2005 DRAFT DISTRIBUTIONS
SELECTIONS PER ROUND BY TEAM

Club	1	2	3	4	5	6	7	Total Picks
Tampa Bay	1	1	2	1	2	1	4	12
Green Bay	1	2	0	2	2	2	2	11
Philadelphia	1	2	1	2	2	1	2	11
San Francisco	1	1	2	0	2	1	4	11
St. Louis	1	1	2	2	1	2	2	11
Tennessee	1	1	2	3	2	1	1	11
Carolina	1	1	2	1	3	2	0	10
Indianapolis	1	1	1	2	3	1	1	10
Kansas City	1	0	1	1	2	2	2	9
Seattle	1	1	2	1	1	1	2	9
Atlanta	1	1	1	1	2	1	1	8
Cleveland	1	1	1	1	1	2	1	8
Dallas	2	1	0	2	0	2	1	8
Jacksonville	1	1	1	1	1	2	1	8
N.Y. Jets	0	2	1	1	1	2	1	8
Pittsburgh	1	1	1	1	1	1	2	8
Arizona	1	1	2	1	1	0	1	7
Baltimore	1	2	0	1	1	1	1	7
Cincinnati	1	1	1	1	1	1	1	7
Minnesota	2	1	1	1	0	1	1	7
New England	1	0	2	1	1	0	2	7
New Orleans	1	1	1	1	1	1	1	7
Oakland	1	1	2	0	0	3	0	7
San Diego	2	1	0	1	1	1	1	7
Buffalo	0	1	1	1	1	1	1	6
Chicago	1	1	0	1	1	1	1	6
Denver	0	1	3	0	0	1	1	6
Detroit	1	1	1	0	1	2	0	6
Houston	1	0	1	1	1	1	1	6
Miami	1	1	1	1	1	0	1	6
Washington	2	0	0	1	1	1	1	6
N.Y. Giants	0	1	1	1	0	1	0	4
Total Picks	32	32	38	35	38	40	41	255

SELECTIONS BY COLLEGE

College		College		College		College	
Oklahoma	11	N.C. State	3	Alabama-Birmingham	1	Michigan Tech	1
Florida State	9	Northwestern	3	Albany (N.Y.)	1	Minnesota	1
Virginia	7	Ohio State	3	Baylor	1	Montana	1
Wisconsin	7	Oregon State	3	Bethune-Cookman	1	North Carolina A&T	1
Georgia	6	San Diego State	3	Bowling Green	1	North Dakota State	1
Louisville	6	South Carolina	3	Cal State Polytecnic	1	Northern Arizona	1
Stanford	6	Tennessee	3	Colorado State	1	Northern Colorado	1
Auburn	5	Texas	3	Eastern Michigan	1	Pearl River CC	1
California	5	Texas A&M	3	Eastern Washington	1	Pittsburgh	1
Iowa	5	Texas Tech	3	Grambling State	1	Purdue	1
Miami	5	Virginia Tech	3	Grand Valley State	1	Saginaw Valley State	1
Southern California	5	Washington State	3	Hampton	1	Southern Illinois	1
Utah	5	West Virginia	3	Harvard	1	Syracuse	1
Alabama	4	Arkansas	2	Hawaii	1	Temple	1
Michigan State	4	Central Michigan	2	Houston	1	Tennessee Tech	1
Nebraska	4	Connecticut	2	Howard	1	Texas Christian	1
UCLA	4	Fresno State	2	Illinois State	1	Texas-El Paso	1
Arizona State	3	Illinois	2	Indiana	1	The Citadel	1
Ball State	3	Maryland	2	Indiana (Pa.)	1	Toledo	1
Brigham Young	3	Mississippi State	2	Iowa State	1	Troy State	1
Cincinnati	3	New Mexico	2	Kansas	1	Tulane	1
Clemson	3	Notre Dame	2	Kansas State	1	Tulsa	1
Florida	3	Oregon	2	Kentucky	1	Tuskegee	1
LSU	3	Southern Mississippi	2	Louisiana Tech	1	Wake Forest	1
Michigan	3	UNLV	2	Louisiana-Lafayette	1	William Penn	1
Mississippi	3	Vanderbilt	2	Louisiana-Monroe	1		
Missouri	3	Washington	2	Marshall	1		
North Carolina	3	Akron	1	Miami (Ohio)	1		

SELECTIONS BY POSITION

Wide receivers	31	Quarterbacks	14
Cornerbacks	28	Free safeties	13
Offensive tackles	24	Centers	11
Defensive ends	21	Strong safeties	10
Running backs	20	Tight ends	10
Defensive tackles	18	Fullbacks	5
Outside linebackers	17	Punters	3
Guards	14	Kickers	2
Inside linebackers	14		

PLAYOFF PLAN

TIEBREAKING PROCEDURES

(Note: Tie games count as one-half win and one-half loss for both clubs.)

DIVISION TIES

TWO CLUBS

1. Head-to-head (best won-lost-tied percentage in games between the clubs).
2. Best won-lost-tied percentage in games played within the division.
3. Best won-lost-tied percentage in common games.
4. Best won-lost-tied percentage in games played within the conference.
5. Strength of victory.
6. Strength of schedule.
7. Best combined ranking among conference teams in points scored and points allowed.
8. Best combined ranking among all teams in points scored and points allowed.
9. Best net points in common games.
10. Best net points in all games.
11. Best net touchdowns in all games.
12. Coin toss.

THREE OR MORE CLUBS

(Note: If two clubs remain tied after other clubs are eliminated during any step, tiebreaker reverts to Step 1 of two-club format.)

1. Head-to-head (best won-lost-tied percentage in games between the clubs).
2. Best won-lost-tied percentage in games played within the division.
3. Best won-lost-tied percentage in common games.
4. Best won-lost-tied percentage in games played within the conference.
5. Strength of victory.
6. Strength of schedule.
7. Best combined ranking among conference teams in points scored and points allowed.
8. Best combined ranking among all teams in points scored and points allowed.
9. Best net points in common games.
10. Best net points in all games.
11. Best net touchdowns in all games.
12. Coin toss.

WILD-CARD TIES

If necessary to break ties to determine the three wild-card clubs from each conference, the following steps will be taken:

1. If all the tied clubs are from the same division, apply division tiebreaker.
2. If the tied clubs are from different divisions, apply the steps listed in the right-hand column.
3. When the first wild-card team has been identified, the procedure is repeated to name the second wild-card club (i.e. eliminate all but the highest-ranked club in each division prior to proceeding to Step 2), and repeated a third time, if necessary, to identify the third wild-card team. In situations where three teams from the same division are involved in the procedure, the original seeding of the teams remains the same for subsequent applications of the tiebreaker if the top-ranked team in that division qualifies for a wild-card berth.

TWO CLUBS

1. Head-to-head, if applicable.
2. Best won-lost-tied percentage in the games played within the conference.
3. Best won-lost-tied percentage in common games, minimum of four.
4. Strength of victory.
5. Strength of schedule.
6. Best combined ranking among conference teams in points scored and points allowed.
7. Best combined ranking among all teams in points scored and points allowed.
8. Best net points in conference games.
9. Best net points in all games.
10. Best net touchdowns in all games.
11. Coin toss.

THREE OR MORE CLUBS

(Note: If two clubs remain tied after other clubs are eliminated, tiebreaker reverts to Step 1 of two-club format.)

1. Apply division tiebreaker to eliminate all but highest-ranked club in each division prior to proceeding to Step 2. The original seeding within a division upon application of the division tiebreaker remains the same for all subsequent applications of the procedure that are necessary to identify the wild-card participants.
2. Head-to-head sweep (apply only if one club has defeated each of the others or one club has lost to each of the others).
3. Best won-lost-tied percentage in the games played within the conference.
4. Best won-lost-tied percentage in common games, minimum of four.
5. Strength of victory.
6. Strength of schedule.
7. Best combined ranking among conference teams in points scored and points allowed.
8. Best combined ranking among all teams in points scored and points allowed.
9. Best net points in conference games.
10. Best net points in all games.
11. Best net touchdowns in all games.
12. Coin toss.

OTHER TIEBREAKING PROCEDURES

1. In comparing records against common opponents among tied teams, the best won-lost-tied percentage is the deciding factor since teams may have played an unequal number of games.
2. To determine home-field priority among division winners, apply wild-card tiebreakers.
3. To determine home-field priority for wild-card qualifiers, apply division tiebreakers (if teams are from the same division) or wild-card tiebreakers (if teams are from different divisions).

2004 REVIEW

Final Standings

Weeks 1 through 17

Wild-card games

Divisional playoffs

Conference championships

Super Bowl 39

Pro Bowl

Player participation

Attendance

Trades

FINAL STANDINGS

AMERICAN FOOTBALL CONFERENCE

EAST DIVISION

	W	L	T	Pct.	Pts.	Opp.	Home	Away	Vs. AFC	Vs. NFC	Vs. AFC East
New England*	14	2	0	.875	437	260	8-0	6-2	10-2	4-0	5-1
N.Y. Jets†	10	6	0	.625	333	261	6-2	4-4	7-5	3-1	3-3
Buffalo	9	7	0	.563	395	284	5-3	4-4	5-7	4-0	3-3
Miami	4	12	0	.250	275	354	3-5	1-7	2-10	2-2	1-5

NORTH DIVISION

	W	L	T	Pct.	Pts.	Opp.	Home	Away	Vs. AFC	Vs. NFC	Vs. AFC North
Pittsburgh*	15	1	0	.938	372	251	8-0	7-1	11-1	4-0	5-1
Baltimore	9	7	0	.563	317	268	6-2	3-5	6-6	3-1	3-3
Cincinnati	8	8	0	.500	374	372	5-3	3-5	4-8	4-0	2-4
Cleveland	4	12	0	.250	276	390	3-5	1-7	3-9	1-3	2-4

SOUTH DIVISION

	W	L	T	Pct.	Pts.	Opp.	Home	Away	Vs. AFC	Vs. NFC	Vs. AFC South
Indianapolis*	12	4	0	.750	522	351	7-1	5-3	8-4	4-0	5-1
Jacksonville	9	7	0	.563	261	280	4-4	5-3	6-6	3-1	2-4
Houston	7	9	0	.438	309	339	3-5	4-4	6-6	1-3	4-2
Tennessee	5	11	0	.313	344	439	2-6	3-5	3-9	2-2	1-5

WEST DIVISION

	W	L	T	Pct.	Pts.	Opp.	Home	Away	Vs. AFC	Vs. NFC	Vs. AFC West
San Diego*	12	4	0	.750	446	313	7-1	5-3	9-3	3-1	5-1
Denver†	10	6	0	.625	381	304	6-2	4-4	7-5	3-1	3-3
Kansas City	7	9	0	.438	483	435	4-4	3-5	6-6	1-3	3-3
Oakland	5	11	0	.313	320	442	3-5	2-6	3-9	2-2	1-5

*Division champion. †Wild-card team.

NATIONAL FOOTBALL CONFERENCE

EAST DIVISION

	W	L	T	Pct.	Pts.	Opp.	Home	Away	Vs. AFC	Vs. NFC	Vs. NFC East
Philadelphia*	13	3	0	.813	386	260	7-1	6-2	2-2	11-1	6-0
N.Y. Giants	6	10	0	.375	303	347	3-5	3-5	1-3	5-7	3-3
Dallas	6	10	0	.375	293	405	4-4	2-6	1-3	5-7	2-4
Washington	6	10	0	.375	240	265	3-5	3-5	0-4	6-6	1-5

NORTH DIVISION

	W	L	T	Pct.	Pts.	Opp.	Home	Away	Vs. AFC	Vs. NFC	Vs. NFC North
Green Bay*	10	6	0	.625	424	380	4-4	6-2	1-3	9-3	5-1
Minnesota†	8	8	0	.500	405	395	5-3	3-5	3-1	5-7	3-3
Detroit	6	10	0	.375	296	350	3-5	3-5	1-3	5-7	2-4
Chicago	5	11	0	.313	231	331	2-6	3-5	1-3	4-8	2-4

SOUTH DIVISION

	W	L	T	Pct.	Pts.	Opp.	Home	Away	Vs. AFC	Vs. NFC	Vs. NFC South
Atlanta*	11	5	0	.688	340	337	7-1	4-4	3-1	8-4	4-2
New Orleans	8	8	0	.500	348	405	3-5	5-3	2-2	6-6	3-3
Carolina	7	9	0	.438	355	339	3-5	4-4	1-3	6-6	3-3
Tampa Bay	5	11	0	.313	301	304	4-4	1-7	1-3	4-8	2-4

WEST DIVISION

	W	L	T	Pct.	Pts.	Opp.	Home	Away	Vs. AFC	Vs. NFC	Vs. NFC West
Seattle*	9	7	0	.563	371	373	5-3	4-4	1-3	8-4	3-3
St. Louis†	8	8	0	.500	319	392	6-2	2-6	1-3	7-5	5-1
Arizona	6	10	0	.375	284	322	5-3	1-7	1-3	5-7	2-4
San Francisco	2	14	0	.125	259	452	1-7	1-7	0-4	2-10	2-4

*Division champion. †Wild-card team.

AFC PLAYOFFS

AFC wild-card: N.Y. Jets 20, SAN DIEGO 17 (OT)
INDIANAPOLIS 49, Denver 24
AFC semifinals: PITTSBURGH 20, N.Y. Jets 17 (OT)
NEW ENGLAND 20, Indianapolis 3
AFC championship: New England 41, PITTSBURGH 27

NFC PLAYOFFS

NFC wild-card: St. Louis 27, SEATTLE 20
Minnesota 31, GREEN BAY 17
NFC semifinals: ATLANTA 47, St. Louis 17
PHILADELPHIA 27, Minnesota 14
NFC championship: PHILADELPHIA 27, Atlanta 10

SUPER BOWL XXXIX

New England 24, PHILADELPHIA 21

2004 REVIEW *Final standings*

WEEK 1

STANDINGS

AMERICAN FOOTBALL CONFERENCE

EAST DIVISION
	W	L	T	Pct.	PF	PA
New England	1	0	0	1.000	27	24
N.Y. Jets	1	0	0	1.000	31	24
Buffalo	0	1	0	.000	10	13
Miami	0	1	0	.000	7	17

NORTH DIVISION
	W	L	T	Pct.	PF	PA
Cleveland	1	0	0	1.000	20	3
Pittsburgh	1	0	0	1.000	24	21
Baltimore	0	1	0	.000	3	20
Cincinnati	0	1	0	.000	24	31

SOUTH DIVISION
	W	L	T	Pct.	PF	PA
Jacksonville	1	0	0	1.000	13	10
Tennessee	1	0	0	1.000	17	7
Houston	0	1	0	.000	20	27
Indianapolis	0	1	0	.000	24	27

WEST DIVISION
	W	L	T	Pct.	PF	PA
Denver	1	0	0	1.000	34	24
San Diego	1	0	0	1.000	27	20
Kansas City	0	1	0	.000	24	34
Oakland	0	1	0	.000	21	24

NATIONAL FOOTBALL CONFERENCE

EAST DIVISION
	W	L	T	Pct.	PF	PA
Philadelphia	1	0	0	1.000	31	17
Washington	1	0	0	1.000	16	10
Dallas	0	1	0	.000	17	35
N.Y. Giants	0	1	0	.000	17	31

NORTH DIVISION
	W	L	T	Pct.	PF	PA
Detroit	1	0	0	1.000	20	16
Green Bay	1	0	0	1.000	24	14
Minnesota	1	0	0	1.000	35	17
Chicago	0	1	0	.000	16	20

SOUTH DIVISION
	W	L	T	Pct.	PF	PA
Atlanta	1	0	0	1.000	21	19
Carolina	0	1	0	.000	14	24
New Orleans	0	1	0	.000	7	21
Tampa Bay	0	1	0	.000	10	16

WEST DIVISION
	W	L	T	Pct.	PF	PA
Seattle	1	0	0	1.000	21	7
St. Louis	1	0	0	1.000	17	10
Arizona	0	1	0	.000	10	17
San Francisco	0	1	0	.000	19	21

TOP PERFORMANCES

100-YARD RUSHING GAMES
Player, Team & Opponent	Att.	Yds.	TD
Curtis Martin, NYJ vs. Cin.	29	96	1
Quentin Griffin, Den. vs. K.C.	23	156	2
Priest Holmes, K.C. at Den.	26	151	3
Clinton Portis, Was. vs. T.B.	29	148	1
Edgerrin James, Ind. at N.E.	30	142	0
Shaun Alexander, Sea. at N.O.	28	135	2
Marshall Faulk, St.L. vs. Ariz.	22	128	0
Tiki Barber, NYG at Phi.	9	125	1
LaDainian Tomlinson, S.D. at Hou.	26	121	1
Ahman Green, G.B. at Car.	33	119	2
Brian Westbrook, Phi. vs. NYG	17	119	0
Chris Brown, Ten. at Mia.	16	100	0

300-YARD PASSING GAMES
Player, Team & Opponent	Att.	Cmp.	Yds.	TD	Int.
Vinny Testaverde, Dal. at Min.	50	29	355	1	0
Tom Brady, N.E. vs. Ind.	38	26	335	3	1
Donovan McNabb, Phi. vs. NYG	36	26	330	4	0
Rich Gannon, Oak. at Pit.	37	20	305	2	2

100-YARD RECEIVING GAMES
Player, Team & Opponent	Rec.	Yds.	TD
David Terrell, Chi. vs. Det.	5	126	0
Antonio Gates, S.D. at Hou.	8	123	0
Isaac Bruce, St.L. vs. Ariz.	9	112	1
Antonio Bryant, Dal. at Min.	8	112	0
Keyshawn Johnson, Dal. at Min.	9	111	0
Joe Horn, N.O. vs. Sea.	6	110	0
Eddie Kennison, K.C. at Den.	6	101	0

RESULTS

THURSDAY, SEPTEMBER 9
NEW ENGLAND 27, Indianapolis 24
SATURDAY, SEPTEMBER 11
Tennessee 17, MIAMI 7
SUNDAY, SEPTEMBER 12
San Diego 27, HOUSTON 20
ST. LOUIS 17, Arizona 10
Jacksonville 13, BUFFALO 10
WASHINGTON 16, Tampa Bay 10
N.Y. JETS 31, Cincinnati 24
CLEVELAND 20, Baltimore 3
PITTSBURGH 24, Oakland 21
Detroit 20, CHICAGO 16
Seattle 21, NEW ORLEANS 7
PHILADELPHIA 31, N.Y. Giants 17
MINNESOTA 35, Dallas 17
Atlanta 21, SAN FRANCISCO 19
DENVER 34, Kansas City 24
MONDAY, SEPTEMBER 13
Green Bay 24, CAROLINA 14

2004 REVIEW Week 1

PATRIOTS 27, COLTS 24
Thursday, September 9

Indianapolis	0	17	0	7—24
New England	3	10	14	0—27

First Quarter
N.E.—FG, Vinatieri 32, 4:51.

Second Quarter
Ind.—FG, Vanderjagt 32, 1:20.
Ind.—Rhodes 3 run (Vanderjagt kick), 6:58.
N.E.—Branch 16 pass from Brady (Vinatieri kick), 11:56.
Ind.—Harrison 3 pass from Manning (Vanderjagt kick), 14:18.
N.E.—FG, Vinatieri 43, 15:00.

Third Quarter
N.E.—Patten 25 pass from Brady (Vinatieri kick), 4:12.
N.E.—Graham 8 pass from Brady (Vinatieri kick), 13:37.

Fourth Quarter
Ind.—Stokley 7 pass from Manning (Vanderjagt kick), 3:55.
Attendance—68,756.

	Indianapolis	New England
First downs	28	22
Rushes-yards	42-202	17-82
Passing	244	320
Punt returns	2-20	2-6
Kickoff returns	4-89	5-107
Interception returns	1-12	1-5
Comp.-att.-int.	16-29-1	26-38-1
Sacked-yards lost	1-12	2-15
Punts	2-41	3-47
Fumbles-lost	2-2	2-1
Penalties-yards	3-20	8-55
Time of possession	31:41	28:19

INDIVIDUAL STATISTICS

RUSHING—Indianapolis, James 30-142, Rhodes 10-42, Manning 2-18. New England, Dillon 15-86, Brady 1-(minus 1), B. Johnson 1-(minus 3).

PASSING—Indianapolis, Manning 16-29-1-256. New England, Brady 26-38-1-335.

RECEIVING—Indianapolis, Harrison 7-44, Stokley 4-77, James 3-29, Clark 1-64, Wayne 1-42. New England, Branch 7-86, Graham 7-57, Patten 4-86, Givens 4-80, Watson 2-16, B. Johnson 1-5, Fauria 1-5.

MISSED FIELD GOAL ATTEMPTS—Indianapolis, Vanderjagt 48.

INTERCEPTIONS—Indianapolis, Harper 1-12. New England, Bruschi 1-5.

KICKOFF RETURNS—Indianapolis, Rhodes 4-89. New England, B. Johnson 5-107.

PUNT RETURNS—Indianapolis, Pyatt 2-20. New England, Poole 1-6, Branch 1-0.

SACKS—Indianapolis, Brock 1, Freeney 1. New England, McGinest 1.

TITANS 17, DOLPHINS 7
Saturday, September 11

Tennessee	0	7	7	3—17
Miami	0	0	0	7— 7

Second Quarter
Ten.—Kinney 1 pass from McNair (Elling kick), 13:11.

Third Quarter
Ten.—Thompson 37 interception return (Elling kick), 12:34.

Fourth Quarter
Ten.—FG, Elling 22, 8:12.
Mia.—McMichael 15 pass from Feeley (Mare kick), 11:38.
Attendance—69,987.

	Tennessee	Miami
First downs	15	14
Rushes-yards	36-182	20-65
Passing	61	198
Punt returns	2-9	2-11
Kickoff returns	0-0	4-99
Interception returns	3-48	0-0
Comp.-att.-int.	9-14-0	26-44-3
Sacked-yards lost	2-12	3-12
Punts	6-45	5-43
Fumbles-lost	4-1	2-0
Penalties-yards	7-55	13-71
Time of possession	30:29	29:31

INDIVIDUAL STATISTICS

RUSHING—Tennessee, Brown 16-100, A. Smith 11-40, Holcombe 7-31, McNair 2-11. Miami, Gordon 12-32, Minor 5-25, Chambers 1-6, Morris 1-2, Fiedler 1-0.

PASSING—Tennessee, McNair 9-14-0-73. Miami, Feeley 21-31-1-168, Fiedler 5-13-2-42.

RECEIVING—Tennessee, Mason 3-51, Bennett 3-15, Brown 1-5, A. Smith 1-1, Kinney 1-1. Miami, McMichael 8-79, Chambers 6-35, Gordon 5-30, Booker 4-36, Minor 1-20, Morris 1-6, Easlick 1-4.

MISSED FIELD GOAL ATTEMPTS—Tennessee, Elling 33. Miami, Mare 46.

INTERCEPTIONS—Tennessee, Thompson 1-37, A. Dyson 1-11, Rolle 1-0.

KICKOFF RETURNS—Miami, Brightful 3-77, Poole 1-22.

PUNT RETURNS—Tennessee, Mason 2-9. Miami, Brightful 2-11.

SACKS—Tennessee, Long 1, Odom 1, Starks 1. Miami, Seau 1, J. Williams 1.

CHARGERS 27, TEXANS 20
Sunday, September 12

San Diego	3	7	10	7—27
Houston	3	10	7	0—20

First Quarter
Hou.—FG, K. Brown 37, 3:11.
S.D.—FG, Kaeding 48, 8:25.

Second Quarter
Hou.—FG, K. Brown 20, :53.
S.D.—Tomlinson 1 run (Kaeding kick), 5:09.
Hou.—D. Davis 2 run (K. Brown kick), 10:17.

Third Quarter
S.D.—Caldwell 36 pass from Brees (Kaeding kick), 5:48.
Hou.—D. Davis 1 run (K. Brown kick), 10:24.
S.D.—FG, Kaeding 29, 15:00.

Fourth Quarter
S.D.—E. Parker 19 pass from Brees (Kaeding kick), 6:26.
Attendance—70,255.

	San Diego	Houston
First downs	17	20
Rushes-yards	32-122	29-110
Passing	202	226
Punt returns	1-13	2-25
Kickoff returns	4-102	6-154
Interception returns	2-0	0-0
Comp.-att.-int.	17-24-0	19-25-2
Sacked-yards lost	1-7	2-3
Punts	4-39	2-46
Fumbles-lost	2-0	2-2
Penalties-yards	8-60	6-83
Time of possession	31:10	28:50

INDIVIDUAL STATISTICS

RUSHING—San Diego, Tomlinson 26-121, Brees 5-(minus 2), Neal 1-3. Houston, D. Davis 21-87, Carr 3-12, Hollings 3-10, Baxter 2-1.

PASSING—San Diego, Brees 17-24-0-209. Houston, Carr 19-25-2-229.

RECEIVING—San Diego, Gates 8-123, Caldwell 4-65, Tomlinson 3-(minus 4), E. Parker 2-25. Houston, D. Davis 5-70, An. Johnson 4-58, Gaffney 4-40, Bradford 3-24, Hollings 1-27, Bruener 1-7, Baxter 1-3.

MISSED FIELD GOAL ATTEMPTS—None.

INTERCEPTIONS—San Diego, Wilson 1-0, Foley 1-0.

KICKOFF RETURNS—San Diego, Welker 4-102. Houston, Moses 6-154.

PUNT RETURNS—San Diego, E. Parker 1-13. Houston, Moses 2-25.

SACKS—San Diego, Kiel 1, Phillips 1. Houston, Wong 1.

RAMS 17, CARDINALS 10
Sunday, September 12

Arizona	0	3	7	0—10
St. Louis	0	6	3	8—17

Second Quarter
St.L.—FG, J. Wilkins 50, 3:39.
Ariz.—FG, Rackers 22, 6:50.
St.L.—FG, J. Wilkins 28, 12:21.

Third Quarter
St.L.—FG, J. Wilkins 22, 9:10.
Ariz.—E. Smith 11 run (Rackers kick), 14:03.

Fourth Quarter
St.L.—Bruce 8 pass from Bulger (M. Faulk run), :33.
Attendance—65,538.

	Arizona	St. Louis
First downs	14	27
Rushes-yards	23-103	30-176

	Arizona	St. Louis
Passing	157	272
Punt returns	1-7	2-13
Kickoff returns	5-138	2-34
Interception returns	1-(-1)	0-0
Comp.-att.-int.	18-29-0	23-34-1
Sacked-yards lost	2-24	0-0
Punts	8-43	3-40
Fumbles-lost	0-0	2-2
Penalties-yards	8-59	7-55
Time of possession	26:10	33:50

INDIVIDUAL STATISTICS

RUSHING—Arizona, E. Smith 16-87, Scobey 2-9, Hambrick 2-2, McCown 1-5, B. Johnson 1-1, Fitzgerald 1-(minus 1). St. Louis, M. Faulk 22-128, S. Jackson 7-50, Cleeland 1-(minus 2).

PASSING—Arizona, McCown 18-29-0-181. St. Louis, Bulger 23-34-1-272.

RECEIVING—Arizona, F. Jones 6-39, Fitzgerald 4-70, Scobey 3-23, B. Johnson 3-19, Poole 1-24, K. Williams 1-6. St. Louis, Bruce 9-112, Holt 7-96, Looker 1-34, M. Faulk 2-17, McDonald 2-13.

MISSED FIELD GOAL ATTEMPTS—None.

INTERCEPTIONS—Arizona, Harris 1-(minus 1).

KICKOFF RETURNS—Arizona, Scobey 5-138. St. Louis, S. Jackson 1-20, Harris 1-14.

PUNT RETURNS—Arizona, K. Williams 1-7. St. Louis, McDonald 2-13.

SACKS—St. Louis, B. Fisher 1, Lewis 1.

JAGUARS 13, BILLS 10
Sunday, September 12

Jacksonville	0	3	3	7—13
Buffalo	7	0	0	3—10

First Quarter
Buf.—Moulds 17 pass from Bledsoe (Lindell kick), 12:12.

Second Quarter
Jac.—FG, Scobee 25, 14:43.

Third Quarter
Jac.—FG, Scobee 27, 10:28.

Fourth Quarter
Buf.—FG, Lindell 25, 4:45.
Jac.—Wilford 7 pass from Leftwich (Scobee kick), 15:00.
Attendance—72,389.

	Jacksonville	Buffalo
First downs	14	16
Rushes-yards	23-83	36-95
Passing	142	147
Punt returns	4-34	1-5
Kickoff returns	3-59	2-43
Interception returns	0-0	2-35
Comp.-att.-int.	18-36-2	17-26-0
Sacked-yards lost	2-5	1-6
Punts	6-47	5-45
Fumbles-lost	0-0	3-2
Penalties-yards	9-50	7-78
Time of possession	26:07	33:53

INDIVIDUAL STATISTICS

RUSHING—Jacksonville, F. Taylor 17-61, Toefield 3-8, Leftwich 2-11, G. Jones 1-3. Buffalo, Henry 23-75, McGahee 9-31, Bledsoe 3-(minus 4), Reed 1-(minus 7).

PASSING—Jacksonville, Leftwich 18-36-2-147. Buffalo, Bledsoe 17-26-0-153.

RECEIVING—Jacksonville, T. Edwards 5-37, J. Smith 4-83, Wrighster 2-12, R. Williams 2-9, M. Edwards 2-6, Toefield 2-(minus 7), Wilford 1-7. Buffalo, Moulds 8-75, Henry 3-9, Reed 2-18, Evans 2-12, Campbell 1-27, McGahee 1-12.

MISSED FIELD GOAL ATTEMPTS—Buffalo, Lindell 42.

INTERCEPTIONS—Buffalo, Reese 1-33, Clements 1-2.

KICKOFF RETURNS—Jacksonville, Lewis 3-59. Buffalo, McGee 2-43.

PUNT RETURNS—Jacksonville, Lewis 4-34. Buffalo, Clements 1-5.

SACKS—Jacksonville, Barnes 1. Buffalo, Fletcher 1, Edwards 1.

REDSKINS 16, BUCCANEERS 10
Sunday, September 12

Tampa Bay	0	3	7	0—10
Washington	7	3	0	6—16

First Quarter
Was.—Portis 64 run (Hall kick), 3:31.

Second Quarter
Was.—FG, Hall 20, :28.
T.B.—FG, Gramatica 47, 2:03.

Third Quarter
T.B.—Barber 9 fumble return (Gramatica kick), 10:16.

Fourth Quarter
Was.—FG, Hall 30, 6:05.
Was.—FG, Hall 34, 14:44.
Attendance—90,098.

	Tampa Bay	Washington
First downs	10	13
Rushes-yards	15-30	39-166
Passing	139	125
Punt returns	5-21	3-18
Kickoff returns	5-138	3-63
Interception returns	0-0	1-16
Comp.-att.-int.	24-37-1	13-24-0
Sacked-yards lost	4-30	0-0
Punts	9-40	7-50
Fumbles-lost	3-1	3-1
Penalties-yards	6-44	3-23
Time of possession	27:13	32:47

INDIVIDUAL STATISTICS

RUSHING—Tampa Bay, Garner 11-25, Alstott 4-5. Washington, Portis 29-148, Betts 5-17, Brunell 5-1.

PASSING—Tampa Bay, B. Johnson 24-37-1-169. Washington, Brunell 13-24-0-125.

RECEIVING—Tampa Bay, Clayton 7-53, Brown 4-23, Alstott 3-17, Dilger 3-12, Dudley 2-31, Schroeder 2-26, Garner 1-4, J. White 1-3, Galloway 1-0. Washington, Gardner 4-61, Portis 4-15, Coles 3-27, Cooley 1-16, Betts 1-6.

MISSED FIELD GOAL ATTEMPTS—Washington, Hall 50.

INTERCEPTIONS—Washington, Pierce 1-16.

KICKOFF RETURNS—Tampa Bay, Murphy 4-125, Schroeder 1-13. Washington, Morton 2-48, Sellers 1-15.

PUNT RETURNS—Tampa Bay, Schroeder 5-21. Washington, Morton 3-18.

SACKS—Washington, Bowen 2, Arrington 1, Wynn 0.5, R. Warner 0.5.

JETS 31, BENGALS 24
Sunday, September 12

Cincinnati	7	3	7	7—24
N.Y. Jets	14	0	10	7—31

First Quarter
Cin.—Ru. Johnson 9 run (Graham kick), 2:24.
NYJ—C. Martin 3 pass from Pennington (Brien kick), 6:12.
NYJ—J. Carter 46 pass from Pennington (Brien kick), 11:51.

Second Quarter
Cin.—FG, Graham 22, 11:43.

Third Quarter
NYJ—D. Abraham 41 fumble return (Brien kick), 3:04.
Cin.—Watson 6 pass from Palmer (Graham kick), 8:40.
NYJ—FG, Brien 21, 14:34.

Fourth Quarter
NYJ—C. Martin 24 run (Brien kick), 5:25.
Cin.—C. Johnson 53 pass from Palmer (Graham kick), 8:32.
Attendance—77,230.

	Cincinnati	N.Y. Jets
First downs	19	24
Rushes-yards	28-113	34-219
Passing	238	219
Punt returns	0-0	2-13
Kickoff returns	5-127	5-100
Interception returns	0-0	1-4
Comp.-att.-int.	18-27-1	20-27-0
Sacked-yards lost	1-10	1-5
Punts	3-50	2-39
Fumbles-lost	1-1	3-1
Penalties-yards	6-49	1-7
Time of possession	29:13	30:47

INDIVIDUAL STATISTICS

RUSHING—Cincinnati, Ru. Johnson 23-67, Watson 2-28, Palmer 2-10, Warrick 1-8. New York, C. Martin 29-196, Pennington 2-(minus 2), Sowell 1-19, Moss 1-8, Q. Carter 1-(minus 2).

PASSING—Cincinnati, Palmer 18-27-1-248. New York, Pennington 20-27-0-224.

RECEIVING—Cincinnati, C. Johnson 5-99, Warrick 5-76, Houshmandzadeh 3-38, Watson 2-15, Washington 1-9, J. Johnson 1-8, R. Kelly 1-3. New York, McCareins 5-66, Moss 4-55, Sowell 3-20, C. Martin 3-7, Chrebet 2-21, J. Carter 1-46, Jordan 1-5, Baker 1-4.

MISSED FIELD GOAL ATTEMPTS—None.
INTERCEPTIONS—New York, Coleman 1-4.
KICKOFF RETURNS—Cincinnati, Houshmandzadeh 5-127. New York, J. Carter 5-100.
PUNT RETURNS—New York, Moss 2-13.
SACKS—Cincinnati. New York, J. Abraham 1.

BROWNS 20, RAVENS 3
Sunday, September 12

Baltimore	0	0	3	0—	3
Cleveland	0	3	7	10—	20

Second Quarter
Cle.—FG, Dawson 37, 7:18.

Third Quarter
Bal.—FG, Stover 42, 9:03.
Cle.—Morgan 46 pass from Garcia (Dawson kick), 14:36.

Fourth Quarter
Cle.—FG, Dawson 25, 7:42.
Cle.—Garcia 3 run (Dawson kick), 10:40.
Attendance—73,068.

	Baltimore	Cleveland
First downs	16	10
Rushes-yards	26-88	29-85
Passing	166	165
Punt returns	6-5	2-19
Kickoff returns	4-78	1-30
Interception returns	0-0	2-2
Comp.-att.-int.	22-38-2	15-24-0
Sacked-yards lost	3-25	2-15
Punts	7-39	7-45
Fumbles-lost	2-1	0-0
Penalties-yards	6-46	6-50
Time of possession	30:59	29:01

INDIVIDUAL STATISTICS
RUSHING—Baltimore, J. Lewis 20-57, C. Taylor 3-14, Boller 2-16, Ricard 1-1. Cleveland, Green 22-65, J. Jackson 4-7, Garcia 3-13.
PASSING—Baltimore, Boller 22-38-2-191. Cleveland, Garcia 15-24-0-180.
RECEIVING—Baltimore, Heap 9-86, K. Johnson 5-43, Hymes 5-39, Wilcox 2-18, T. Taylor 1-5. Cleveland, Winslow 4-39, Green 4-27, Northcutt 3-12, J. Jackson 2-5, Andre. Davis 1-51, Morgan 1-46.
MISSED FIELD GOAL ATTEMPTS—None.
INTERCEPTIONS—Cleveland, Andra. Davis 1-2, Henry 1-0.
KICKOFF RETURNS—Baltimore, Sams 4-78. Cleveland, De. Brown 1-30.
PUNT RETURNS—Baltimore, Sams 5-0, Sanders 1-5. Cleveland, Northcutt 2-19.
SACKS—Baltimore, R. Lewis 1, Baxter 1. Cleveland, Lang 3.

STEELERS 24, RAIDERS 21
Sunday, September 12

Oakland	0	7	3	11—	21
Pittsburgh	7	7	7	3—	24

First Quarter
Pit.—Bettis 1 run (Reed kick), 8:31.

Second Quarter
Pit.—Bettis 1 run (Reed kick), 3:52.
Oak.—Gabriel 58 pass from Gannon (Janikowski kick), 13:23.

Third Quarter
Oak.—FG, Janikowski 28, 6:43.
Pit.—Bettis 1 run (Reed kick), 11:48.

Fourth Quarter
Oak.—FG, Janikowski 38, 4:28.
Oak.—Whitted 38 pass from Gannon (Whitted pass from Gannon), 10:09.
Pit.—FG, Reed 24, 14:53.
Attendance—60,147.

	Oakland	Pittsburgh
First downs	18	17
Rushes-yards	22-61	33-107
Passing	297	130
Punt returns	1-13	2-22
Kickoff returns	5-96	5-111
Interception returns	0-0	2-36
Comp.-att.-int.	20-37-2	13-22-0
Sacked-yards lost	3-8	2-12
Punts	3-44	6-44
Fumbles-lost	5-2	2-1
Penalties-yards	5-31	3-20
Time of possession	30:43	29:17

INDIVIDUAL STATISTICS
RUSHING—Oakland, Wheatley 11-24, Fargas 7-17, Crockett 2-10, Redmond 1-7, Gabriel 1-3. Pittsburgh, Staley 24-91, Bettis 5-1, Maddox 3-13, Haynes 1-2.
PASSING—Oakland, Gannon 20-37-2-305. Pittsburgh, Maddox 13-22-0-142.
RECEIVING—Oakland, Porter 4-44, Gabriel 3-81, Redmond 3-29, Rice 2-22, Fargas 2-19, Whitted 1-38, Wheatley 1-20, Jolley 1-19, C. Anderson 1-13, Curry 1-12, Crockett 1-8. Pittsburgh, Ward 7-99, Burress 1-13, Riemersma 1-12, Randle 1-11, Tuman 1-6, Staley 1-3, Haynes 1-(minus 2).
MISSED FIELD GOAL ATTEMPTS—None.
INTERCEPTIONS—Pittsburgh, Farrior 1-36, Townsend 1-0.
KICKOFF RETURNS—Oakland, Francis 4-94, Gabriel 1-2. Pittsburgh, Randle El 3-76, Colclough 1-23, Cushing 1-12.
PUNT RETURNS—Oakland, Buchanon 1-13. Pittsburgh, Randle El 2-22.
SACKS—Oakland, Brayton 1, Team 1. Pittsburgh, Haggans 2, A. Smith 1.

LIONS 20, BEARS 16
Sunday, September 12

Detroit	0	3	10	7—	20
Chicago	7	0	0	9—	16

First Quarter
Chi.—T. Jones 2 run (Edinger kick), 7:22.

Second Quarter
Det.—FG, Hanson 27, 14:44.

Third Quarter
Det.—Bra. Walker 92 blocked FG return (Hanson kick), 2:43.
Det.—FG, Hanson 21, 7:23.

Fourth Quarter
Chi.—T. Jones 2 run (Edinger kick), 2:20.
Det.—Hakim 4 pass from Harrington (Hanson kick), 5:06.
Chi.—Safety, 13:07.
Attendance—61,535.

	Detroit	Chicago
First downs	13	18
Rushes-yards	29-77	32-128
Passing	185	214
Punt returns	1-2	4-80
Kickoff returns	3-74	6-132
Interception returns	2-0	1-0
Comp.-att.-int.	14-26-1	16-35-2
Sacked-yards lost	2-2	3-13
Punts	8-38	7-46
Fumbles-lost	0-0	3-2
Penalties-yards	9-80	9-95
Time of possession	29:42	30:18

INDIVIDUAL STATISTICS
RUSHING—Detroit, Jones 15-36, Pinner 5-21, Bryson 3-18, Harrington 3-6, Schlesinger 1-2, Williams 1-1, N. Harris 1-(minus 1). Chicago, T. Jones 21-67, Grossman 4-21, Thomas 3-13, Terrell 1-20, Wade 1-5, McKie 1-1, Berrian 1-1.
PASSING—Detroit, Harrington 14-26-1-187. Chicago, Grossman 16-35-2-227.
RECEIVING—Detroit, Williams 4-69, Hakim 3-29, Alexander 2-15, Jones 1-34, Schlesinger 1-30, Pinner 1-5, FitzSimmons 1-4, Streets 1-1. Chicago, T. Jones 6-38, Terrell 5-126, Clark 1-28, Wade 1-12, McKie 1-10, Gage 1-9, B. Johnson 1-4.
MISSED FIELD GOAL ATTEMPTS—Chicago, Edinger 27.
INTERCEPTIONS—Detroit, Goodman 1-0, Bra. Walker 1-0. Chicago, Green 1-0.
KICKOFF RETURNS—Detroit, Drummond 3-74. Chicago, Da. Jones 4-70, McQuarters 1-37, McKie 1-25.
PUNT RETURNS—Detroit, Drummond 1-2. Chicago, McQuarters 3-12, Berrian 1-12.
SACKS—Detroit, Hall 1, Pritchett 1, S. Rogers 0.5, Edwards 0.5. Chicago, Urlacher 1, Haynes 1.

SEAHAWKS 21, SAINTS 7
Sunday, September 12

Seattle	0	14	7	0—	21
New Orleans	0	7	0	0—	7

Second Quarter
Sea.—Alexander 14 pass from Hasselbeck (J. Brown kick), :08.
Sea.—Alexander 6 run (J. Brown kick), 8:22.
N.O.—Conwell 6 pass from Brooks (Carney kick), 12:06.

Third Quarter
Sea.—Alexander 9 run (J. Brown kick), 11:54.
Attendance—64,900.

	Seattle	New Orleans
First downs	21	12
Rushes-yards	43-169	19-74

– 118 –

	Seattle	New Orleans
Passing	246	207
Punt returns	3-26	4-24
Kickoff returns	2-46	4-129
Interception returns	1-0	1-0
Comp.-att.-int.	19-29-1	18-37-1
Sacked-yards lost	0-0	2-16
Punts	7-39	7-42
Fumbles-lost	1-1	2-2
Penalties-yards	5-45	8-68
Time of possession	33:37	26:23

INDIVIDUAL STATISTICS

RUSHING—Seattle, Alexander 28-135, Strong 7-25, Morris 4-10, Hasselbeck 4-(minus 1). New Orleans, McAllister 16-57, Brooks 2-16, Stallworth 1-1.

PASSING—Seattle, Hasselbeck 19-29-1-246. New Orleans, Brooks 18-37-1-223.

RECEIVING—Seattle, Jackson 7-98, Engram 3-55, K. Robinson 3-35, Alexander 2-31, Strong 2-9, Mili 1-15, H. Evans 1-3. New Orleans, Horn 6-110, Stallworth 3-36, Conwell 3-32, B. Williams 3-13, McAllister 2-20, Karney 1-12.

MISSED FIELD GOAL ATTEMPTS—None.

INTERCEPTIONS—Seattle, Boulware 1-0. New Orleans, Ambrose 1-0.

KICKOFF RETURNS—Seattle, Morris 2-46. New Orleans, M. Lewis 4-129.

PUNT RETURNS—Seattle, Engram 3-26. New Orleans, M. Lewis 4-24.

SACKS—Seattle, R. Bernard 1, Okeafor 0.5, Wistrom 0.5.

EAGLES 31, GIANTS 17
Sunday, September 12

N.Y. Giants	7	3	0	7—17
Philadelphia	14	10	7	0—31

First Quarter
NYG—Dayne 3 run (Christie kick), 6:43.
Phi.—Owens 20 pass from McNabb (Akers kick), 8:42.
Phi.—Owens 3 pass from McNabb (Akers kick), 12:43.

Second Quarter
Phi.—Smith 14 pass from McNabb (Akers kick), 8:45.
Phi.—FG, Akers 45, 12:46.
NYG—FG, Christie 53, 13:46.

Third Quarter
Phi.—Owens 12 pass from McNabb (Akers kick), 9:38.

Fourth Quarter
NYG—Barber 72 run (Christie kick), 12:35.
Attendance—67,532.

	N.Y. Giants	Philadelphia
First downs	19	21
Rushes-yards	23-170	27-141
Passing	243	313
Punt returns	1-8	3-50
Kickoff returns	5-119	3-67
Interception returns	0-0	0-0
Comp.-att.-int.	19-37-0	26-36-0
Sacked-yards lost	5-26	2-17
Punts	5-43	4-34
Fumbles-lost	3-1	0-0
Penalties-yards	5-30	8-50
Time of possession	27:50	32:10

INDIVIDUAL STATISTICS

RUSHING—New York, Dayne 13-45, Barber 9-125, Warner 1-0. Philadelphia, Westbrook 17-119, McNabb 4-12, Mahe 3-7, Tapeh 3-3.

PASSING—New York, Warner 16-28-0-203, Manning 3-9-0-66. Philadelphia, McNabb 26-36-0-330.

RECEIVING—New York, Barber 5-75, T. Carter 4-51, Toomer 4-41, I. Hilliard 3-59, Shockey 1-4. Philadelphia, Owens 8-68, C. Lewis 6-58, Pinkston 3-76, Smith 3-50, Westbrook 3-42, Ritchie 2-14, F. Mitchell 1-22.

MISSED FIELD GOAL ATTEMPTS—Philadelphia, Akers 53.

INTERCEPTIONS—None.

KICKOFF RETURNS—New York, Ponder 5-119. Philadelphia, Reed 3-67.

PUNT RETURNS—New York, Jones 1-8. Philadelphia, Mahe 3-50.

SACKS—New York, Lewis 1, Strahan 1. Philadelphia, Brown 1, H. Douglas 1, McDougle 1, Simoneau 0.5, Dh. Jones 0.5, Simon 0.5, Burgess 0.5.

VIKINGS 35, COWBOYS 17
Sunday, September 12

Dallas	3	7	7	0—17
Minnesota	0	14	14	7—35

First Quarter
Dal.—FG, Cundiff 27, 3:58.

Second Quarter
Min.—O. Smith 63 pass from Culpepper (M. Andersen kick), 3:34.
Min.—M. Robinson 3 pass from Culpepper (M. Andersen kick), 14:30.
Dal.—Glenn 32 pass from Testaverde (Cundiff kick), 14:55.

Third Quarter
Min.—Moss 3 pass from Culpepper (M. Andersen kick), 2:35.
Dal.—Lee 7 run (Cundiff kick), 4:24.
Min.—Moss 1 pass from Culpepper (M. Andersen kick), 8:59.

Fourth Quarter
Min.—Campbell 43 pass from Culpepper (M. Andersen kick), 8:04.
Attendance—64,105.

	Dallas	Minnesota
First downs	27	23
Rushes-yards	21-71	28-136
Passing	352	279
Punt returns	1-12	1-1
Kickoff returns	6-152	4-71
Interception returns	0-0	0-0
Comp.-att.-int.	29-51-0	18-24-0
Sacked-yards lost	1-3	2-0
Punts	3-33	3-34
Fumbles-lost	4-2	1-0
Penalties-yards	9-119	5-40
Time of possession	29:44	30:16

INDIVIDUAL STATISTICS

RUSHING—Dallas, George 8-25, Anderson 6-10, Lee 5-35, Barnes 1-1, Testaverde 1-0. Minnesota, O. Smith 15-76, M. Williams 6-27, Culpepper 6-25, Moore 1-8.

PASSING—Dallas, Testaverde 29-50-0-355, McBriar 0-1-0-0. Minnesota, Culpepper 17-23-0-242, Moss 1-1-0-37.

RECEIVING—Dallas, K. Johnson 9-111, Bryant 8-112, Glenn 5-84, Anderson 4-31, Witten 3-17. Minnesota, Moss 4-27, M. Robinson 3-54, Burleson 3-34, Kleinsasser 2-24, Wiggins 2-18, O. Smith 1-63, Campbell 1-43, M. Williams 1-8, Moore 1-8.

MISSED FIELD GOAL ATTEMPTS—None.

INTERCEPTIONS—None.

KICKOFF RETURNS—Dallas, Lee 3-97, Reeves 2-46, Lehr 1-9. Minnesota, O. Smith 3-54, Moore 1-17.

PUNT RETURNS—Dallas, Ward 1-12. Minnesota, Moore 1-1.

SACKS—Dallas, Dixon 1, Hunter 1. Minnesota, K. Williams 1.

FALCONS 21, 49ERS 19
Sunday, September 12

Atlanta	7	7	0	7—21
San Francisco	0	3	3	13—19

First Quarter
Atl.—Crumpler 15 pass from Vick (Feely kick), 10:48.

Second Quarter
Atl.—Dunn 2 run (Feely kick), 8:43.
S.F.—FG, T. Peterson 23, 13:46.

Third Quarter
S.F.—FG, T. Peterson 32, 7:49.

Fourth Quarter
Atl.—Dunn 9 run (Feely kick), 6:03.
S.F.—Wilson 8 pass from Rattay (T. Peterson kick), 8:46.
S.F.—E. Johnson 16 pass from Rattay (pass failed), 14:20.
Attendance—65,584.

	Atlanta	San Francisco
First downs	14	21
Rushes-yards	28-95	23-93
Passing	132	266
Punt returns	3-19	3-4
Kickoff returns	4-49	3-57
Interception returns	1-85	1-19
Comp.-att.-int.	13-22-1	27-46-1
Sacked-yards lost	4-31	3-20
Punts	8-40	6-41
Fumbles-lost	2-0	1-1
Penalties-yards	7-72	10-57
Time of possession	26:33	33:27

INDIVIDUAL STATISTICS

RUSHING—Atlanta, Dunn 19-63, Vick 6-10, Duckett 2-6, P. Price 1-16. San Francisco, Barlow 19-76, Jackson 3-19, Battle 1-(minus 2).

PASSING—Atlanta, Vick 13-22-1-163. San Francisco, Rattay 18-31-1-175, Dorsey 9-15-0-111.

RECEIVING—Atlanta, Crumpler 6-82, P. Price 4-62, Finneran 1-16, Griffith 1-2, Duckett 1-1. San Francisco, E. Johnson 8-86, Wilson 7-94, Lloyd 4-29, Jackson 3-31, Conway 2-24, Barlow 1-15, Battle 1-6, Isom 1-1.

MISSED FIELD GOAL ATTEMPTS—None.

INTERCEPTIONS—Atlanta, Beasley 1-85. San Francisco, Ulbrich 1-19.

KICKOFF RETURNS—Atlanta, Rossum 4-49. San Francisco, Battle 3-57.

PUNT RETURNS—Atlanta, Rossum 3-19. San Francisco, Battle 3-4.

SACKS—Atlanta, Scott 1, R. Coleman 1, B. Smith 1. San Francisco, Winborn 2, J. Peterson 1, J. Williams 1.

BRONCOS 34, CHIEFS 24
Sunday, September 12

Kansas City	7	0	17	0—24
Denver	3	14	7	10—34

First Quarter
K.C.—Holmes 2 run (Tynes kick), 4:14.
Den.—FG, Elam 43, 9:41.

Second Quarter
Den.—Griffin 1 pass from Plummer (Elam kick), 1:53.
Den.—Griffin 25 run (Elam kick), 6:16.

Third Quarter
K.C.—FG, Tynes 50, 2:07.
K.C.—Holmes 4 run (Tynes kick), 3:37.
Den.—Griffin 47 run (Elam kick), 5:06.
K.C.—Holmes 33 run (Tynes kick), 9:10.

Fourth Quarter
Den.—FG, Elam 45, 1:39.
Den.—Hape 2 pass from Plummer (Elam kick), 12:48.
   Attendance—75,939.

	Kansas City	Denver
First downs	15	24
Rushes-yards	28-167	36-192
Passing	151	221
Punt returns	1-26	4-55
Kickoff returns	1-17	4-113
Interception returns	2-9	1-0
Comp.-att.-int.	16-32-1	18-29-2
Sacked-yards lost	1-23	1-9
Punts	5-45	2-57
Fumbles-lost	0-0	3-1
Penalties-yards	9-70	4-35
Time of possession	28:24	31:36

INDIVIDUAL STATISTICS

RUSHING—Kansas City, Holmes 26-151, Richardson 1-13, Green 1-3. Denver, Griffin 23-156, Plummer 8-23, Bell 2-11, Hearst 2-5, Smith 1-(minus 3).

PASSING—Kansas City, Green 16-32-1-174. Denver, Plummer 18-29-2-230.

RECEIVING—Kansas City, Kennison 6-101, Morton 3-30, Gonzalez 2-17, Hall 2-17, Holmes 2-(minus 2), Blaylock 1-11. Denver, Smith 7-76, Lelie 4-88, Putzier 2-25, Watts 1-22, Bailey 1-11, Hearst 1-5, Hape 1-2, Griffin 1-1.

MISSED FIELD GOAL ATTEMPTS—Kansas City, Tynes 58.

INTERCEPTIONS—Kansas City, Barber 1-10, Beisel 1-(minus 1). Denver, Bailey 1-0.

KICKOFF RETURNS—Kansas City, Hall 1-17. Denver, Droughns 2-58, R. Alexander 2-55.

PUNT RETURNS—Kansas City, Hall 1-26. Denver, Smith 4-55.

SACKS—Kansas City, Siavii 1. Denver, Hayward 0.5, Fatafehi 0.5.

PACKERS 24, PANTHERS 14
Monday, September 13

Green Bay	3	7	14	0—24
Carolina	0	7	0	7—14

First Quarter
G.B.—FG, Longwell 41, 11:32.

Second Quarter
Car.—Hoover 1 pass from Delhomme (Kasay kick), 7:17.
G.B.—Green 6 run (Longwell kick), 11:35.

Third Quarter
G.B.—Green 3 run (Longwell kick), 4:01.
G.B.—Green 3 pass from Favre (Longwell kick), 12:59.

Fourth Quarter
Car.—Muhammad 30 pass from Delhomme (Kasay kick), 10:14.
   Attendance—73,656.

	Green Bay	Carolina
First downs	22	17
Rushes-yards	47-152	13-38
Passing	127	262
Punt returns	3-26	0-0
Kickoff returns	2-43	5-90
Interception returns	1-16	0-0
Comp.-att.-int.	15-22-0	23-40-1
Sacked-yards lost	2-16	2-22
Punts	5-31	5-43
Fumbles-lost	1-0	2-1
Penalties-yards	8-77	9-59
Time of possession	38:04	21:56

INDIVIDUAL STATISTICS

RUSHING—Green Bay, Green 33-119, Fisher 9-32, Davenport 4-2, Favre 1-(minus 1). Carolina, Davis 9-26, Foster 3-12, Delhomme 1-0.

PASSING—Green Bay, Favre 15-22-0-143. Carolina, Delhomme 23-39-1-284, S. Smith 0-1-0-0.

RECEIVING—Green Bay, Driver 3-39, J. Walker 2-37, Franks 2-27, Fisher 2-18, Henderson 2-7, Green 2-(minus 3), Martin 1-13, Ferguson 1-5. Carolina, S. Smith 6-60, Muhammad 4-65, Foster 4-22, Proehl 2-56, Hankton 2-25, Davis 1-22, Mangum 1-15, Goings 1-13, Smart 1-5, Hoover 1-1.

MISSED FIELD GOAL ATTEMPTS—None.

INTERCEPTIONS—Green Bay, Barnett 1-16.

KICKOFF RETURNS—Green Bay, Davenport 2-43. Carolina, Smart 3-74, Foster 2-16.

PUNT RETURNS—Green Bay, Chatman 3-26.

SACKS—Green Bay, Barnett 1, Roman 0.5, Navies 0.5. Carolina, Jenkins 1, Buckner 1.

WEEK 2

STANDINGS

AMERICAN FOOTBALL CONFERENCE

EAST DIVISION

	W	L	T	Pct.	PF	PA
New England	2	0	0	1.000	50	36
N.Y. Jets	2	0	0	1.000	65	52
Buffalo	0	2	0	.000	20	26
Miami	0	2	0	.000	20	33

NORTH DIVISION

	W	L	T	Pct.	PF	PA
Baltimore	1	1	0	.500	33	33
Cincinnati	1	1	0	.500	40	44
Cleveland	1	1	0	.500	32	22
Pittsburgh	1	1	0	.500	37	51

SOUTH DIVISION

	W	L	T	Pct.	PF	PA
Jacksonville	2	0	0	1.000	20	16
Indianapolis	1	1	0	.500	55	44
Tennessee	1	1	0	.500	34	38
Houston	0	2	0	.000	36	55

WEST DIVISION

	W	L	T	Pct.	PF	PA
Denver	1	1	0	.500	40	31
Oakland	1	1	0	.500	34	34
San Diego	1	1	0	.500	55	54
Kansas City	0	2	0	.000	41	62

NATIONAL FOOTBALL CONFERENCE

EAST DIVISION

	W	L	T	Pct.	PF	PA
Philadelphia	2	0	0	1.000	58	33
Dallas	1	1	0	.500	36	47
N.Y. Giants	1	1	0	.500	37	45
Washington	1	1	0	.500	30	30

NORTH DIVISION

	W	L	T	Pct.	PF	PA
Detroit	2	0	0	1.000	48	32
Chicago	1	1	0	.500	37	30
Green Bay	1	1	0	.500	34	35
Minnesota	1	1	0	.500	51	44

SOUTH DIVISION

	W	L	T	Pct.	PF	PA
Atlanta	2	0	0	1.000	55	36
Carolina	1	1	0	.500	42	41
New Orleans	1	1	0	.500	37	48
Tampa Bay	0	2	0	.000	16	26

WEST DIVISION

	W	L	T	Pct.	PF	PA
Seattle	2	0	0	1.000	31	13
St. Louis	1	1	0	.500	34	44
Arizona	0	2	0	.000	22	40
San Francisco	0	2	0	.000	46	51

TOP PERFORMANCES

100-YARD RUSHING GAMES

Player, Team & Opponent	Att.	Yds.	TD
DeShaun Foster, Car. at K.C.	32	174	1
Corey Dillon, N.E. at Ariz.	32	158	0
Chris Brown, Ten. vs. Ind.	26	152	1
Thomas Jones, Chi. at G.B.	23	152	1
Ahman Green, G.B. vs. Chi.	24	128	0
Edgerrin James, Ind. at Ten.	21	124	2
Curtis Martin, NYJ at S.D.	32	119	2
Kevan Barlow, S.F. at N.O.	20	114	2
Michael Vick, Atl. vs. St.L.	12	109	0

300-YARD PASSING GAMES

Player, Team & Opponent	Att.	Cmp.	Yds.	TD	Int.
Daunte Culpepper, Min. at Phi.	47	37	343	1	1
Vinny Testaverde, Dal. vs. Cle.	35	23	322	1	3
David Carr, Hou. at Det.	34	23	313	2	1

100-YARD RECEIVING GAMES

Player, Team & Opponent	Rec.	Yds.	TD
Hines Ward, Pit. at Bal.	6	151	1
Torry Holt, St.L. at Atl.	9	121	1
David Givens, N.E. at Ariz.	6	120	0
Reggie Wayne, Ind. at Ten.	7	119	1
Donte' Stallworth, N.O. vs. S.F.	9	113	1
Curtis Conway, S.F. at N.O.	8	112	0
Derrick Mason, Ten. vs. Ind.	8	104	0
Isaac Bruce, St.L. at Atl.	8	102	0
Javon Walker, G.B. vs. Chi.	7	102	0
Laveranues Coles, Was. at NYG	9	100	0

RESULTS

SUNDAY, SEPTEMBER 19

JACKSONVILLE 7, Denver 6
Carolina 28, KANSAS CITY 17
BALTIMORE 30, Pittsburgh 13
DETROIT 28, Houston 16
ATLANTA 34, St. Louis 17
Indianapolis 31, TENNESSEE 17
Chicago 21, GREEN BAY 10
N.Y. GIANTS 20, Washington 14
NEW ORLEANS 30, San Francisco 27
Seattle 10, TAMPA BAY 6
N.Y. Jets 34, SAN DIEGO 28
OAKLAND 13, Buffalo 10
DALLAS 19, Cleveland 12
New England 23, ARIZONA 12
CINCINNATI 16, Miami 13

MONDAY, SEPTEMBER 20

PHILADELPHIA 27, Minnesota 16

JAGUARS 7, BRONCOS 6
Sunday, September 19

Denver	0	6	0	0—6
Jacksonville	0	7	0	0—7

Second Quarter
Jac.—Wilford 12 pass from Leftwich (Scobee kick), 2:21.
Den.—FG, Elam 44, 5:23.
Den.—FG, Elam 22, 15:00.
Attendance—69,127.

	Denver	Jacksonville
First downs	20	8
Rushes-yards	35-106	22-67
Passing	250	109
Punt returns	3-32	5-78
Kickoff returns	2-49	1-24
Interception returns	0-0	0-0
Comp.-att.-int.	23-39-0	8-16-0
Sacked-yards lost	0-0	2-11
Punts	7-41	9-44
Fumbles-lost	3-1	1-0
Penalties-yards	7-57	10-85
Time of possession	37:08	22:52

INDIVIDUAL STATISTICS
RUSHING—Denver, Griffin 25-66, Plummer 6-24, Bell 4-16. Jacksonville, F. Taylor 16-54, G. Jones 2-9, Leftwich 2-8, Toefield 2-(minus 4).

PASSING—Denver, Plummer 23-39-0-250. Jacksonville, Leftwich 8-16-0-120.

RECEIVING—Denver, Smith 6-83, Griffin 5-29, Lelie 3-53, Carswell 3-35, N. Jackson 2-25, Putzier 2-12, Watts 1-11, Droughns 1-2. Jacksonville, J. Smith 3-69, T. Edwards 2-15, R. Williams 1-19, Wilford 1-12, Toefield 1-5.

MISSED FIELD GOAL ATTEMPTS—Denver, Elam 51.

INTERCEPTIONS—None.

KICKOFF RETURNS—Denver, Droughns 2-49. Jacksonville, Lewis 1-24.

PUNT RETURNS—Denver, Smith 3-32. Jacksonville, Lewis 5-78.

SACKS—Denver, Hayward 1, Williams 1.

PANTHERS 28, CHIEFS 17
Sunday, September 19

Carolina	7	0	7	14—28
Kansas City	3	7	7	0—17

First Quarter
K.C.—FG, Tynes 33, 4:51.
Car.—Mangum 3 pass from Delhomme (Kasay kick), 13:50.
Second Quarter
K.C.—Holmes 1 run (Tynes kick), 2:26.
Third Quarter
Car.—Colbert 9 pass from Delhomme (Kasay kick), 8:13.
K.C.—Warfield 43 interception return (Tynes kick), 11:26.
Fourth Quarter
Car.—Seidman 1 pass from Delhomme (Kasay kick), :05.
Car.—Foster 3 run (Kasay kick), 4:25.
Attendance—78,136.

	Carolina	Kansas City
First downs	23	17
Rushes-yards	39-183	23-109
Passing	175	172
Punt returns	3-18	2-19
Kickoff returns	2-61	4-59
Interception returns	1-13	2-43
Comp.-att.-int.	16-29-2	17-34-1
Sacked-yards lost	1-5	3-15
Punts	6-40	5-44
Fumbles-lost	1-0	1-1
Penalties-yards	6-51	8-88
Time of possession	35:15	24:45

INDIVIDUAL STATISTICS
RUSHING—Carolina, Foster 32-174, Smart 3-4, Goings 2-6, Delhomme 1-0, Hoover 1-(minus 1). Kansas City, Holmes 16-66, Blaylock 3-13, Hall 2-15, Green 2-15.

PASSING—Carolina, Delhomme 16-29-2-180. Kansas City, Green 17-34-1-187.

RECEIVING—Carolina, Proehl 4-48, Hoover 4-37, Colbert 3-46, Muhammad 2-26, Goings 1-19, Mangum 1-3, Seidman 1-1. Kansas City, Morton 5-76, Gonzalez 4-63, Holmes 3-16, Richardson 3-7, Kennison 1-20, Blaylock 1-5.

MISSED FIELD GOAL ATTEMPTS—Kansas City, Tynes 47.

INTERCEPTIONS—Carolina, Gamble 1-13. Kansas City, Warfield 2-43.
KICKOFF RETURNS—Carolina, Smart 2-61. Kansas City, Hall 4-59.
PUNT RETURNS—Carolina, Baker 3-18. Kansas City, Hall 2-19.
SACKS—Carolina, Peppers 2, Morgan 1. Kansas City, Browning 1.

RAVENS 30, STEELERS 13
Sunday, September 19

Pittsburgh	0	0	0	13—13
Baltimore	7	6	7	10—30

First Quarter
Bal.—J. Lewis 3 run (Stover kick), 6:02.
Second Quarter
Bal.—FG, Stover 35, 3:25.Bal.—FG, Stover 27, 14:42.
Third Quarter
Bal.—J. Lewis 1 run (Stover kick), 3:01.
Fourth Quarter
Pit.—Randle El 3 pass from Roethlisberger (Reed kick), 1:56.
Bal.—FG, Stover 34, 6:31.
Pit.—Ward 12 pass from Roethlisberger (pass failed), 8:50.
Bal.—McAlister 51 interception return (Stover kick), 12:04.
Attendance—69,859.

	Pittsburgh	Baltimore
First downs	17	15
Rushes-yards	25-93	41-172
Passing	217	87
Punt returns	3-11	6-82
Kickoff returns	7-139	3-46
Interception returns	0-0	2-59
Comp.-att.-int.	16-33-2	10-18-0
Sacked-yards lost	4-26	2-11
Punts	7-41	7-42
Fumbles-lost	1-1	0-0
Penalties-yards	9-77	10-123
Time of possession	26:52	33:08

INDIVIDUAL STATISTICS
RUSHING—Pittsburgh, Staley 16-57, Haynes 7-34, Randle El 1-1, Maddox 1-1. Baltimore, J. Lewis 24-62, C. Taylor 9-76, Boller 8-34.

PASSING—Pittsburgh, Roethlisberger 12-20-2-176, Maddox 4-13-0-67. Baltimore, Boller 10-18-0-98.

RECEIVING—Pittsburgh, Ward 6-151, Randle El 3-29, Burress 2-30, Haynes 2-6, Riemersma 1-10, Staley 1-9, Mays 1-8. Baltimore, Heap 3-27, Hymes 3-24, K. Johnson 2-32, T. Jones 1-11, Wilcox 1-4.

MISSED FIELD GOAL ATTEMPTS—Pittsburgh, Reed 48.

INTERCEPTIONS—Baltimore, McAlister 1-51, A. Thomas 1-8.

KICKOFF RETURNS—Pittsburgh, Colclough 5-97, Randle El 2-42. Baltimore, Sams 3-46.

PUNT RETURNS—Pittsburgh, Randle El 3-11. Baltimore, Sams 5-59, Sanders 1-23.

SACKS—Pittsburgh, Townsend 1, A. Smith 1. Baltimore, Williams 1, Demps 1, Suggs 1, Baxter 1.

LIONS 28, TEXANS 16
Sunday, September 19

Houston	0	3	7	6—16
Detroit	0	7	14	7—28

Second Quarter
Det.—Schlesinger 1 pass from Harrington (Hanson kick), 8:04.
Hou.—FG, K. Brown 34, 13:54.
Third Quarter
Det.—Williams 31 pass from Harrington (Hanson kick), 8:22.
Hou.—An. Johnson 54 pass from Carr (K. Brown kick), 12:29.
Det.—Drummond 99 kickoff return (Hanson kick), 12:44.
Fourth Quarter
Hou.—Bradford 27 pass from Carr (pass failed), 2:40.
Det.—Williams 14 pass from Harrington (Hanson kick), 10:19.
Attendance—61,465.

	Houston	Detroit
First downs	24	18
Rushes-yards	32-112	23-94
Passing	274	172
Punt returns	3-15	0-0
Kickoff returns	4-54	4-157

	Houston	Detroit
Interception returns	1-23	1-2
Comp.-att.-int.	23-34-1	18-25-1
Sacked-yards lost	5-39	2-4
Punts	2-42	3-48
Fumbles-lost	4-2	0-0
Penalties-yards	9-74	8-65
Time of possession	31:50	28:10

INDIVIDUAL STATISTICS

RUSHING—Houston, D. Davis 25-78, Carr 5-30, Wells 1-3, An. Johnson 1-1. Detroit, Jones 12-57, Pinner 6-19, Harrington 4-17, Bryson 1-1.

PASSING—Houston, Carr 23-34-1-313. Detroit, Harrington 18-25-1-176.

RECEIVING—Houston, D. Davis 11-95, Armstrong 4-49, An. Johnson 3-86, Bradford 3-52, Gaffney 1-25, Bruener 1-6. Detroit, Williams 4-73, Streets 4-32, Hakim 2-26, Alexander 2-13, Schlesinger 2-13, Jones 1-13, Pinner 1-7, FitzSimmons 1-6, Bryson 1-(minus 7).

MISSED FIELD GOAL ATTEMPTS—Detroit, Hanson 47.

INTERCEPTIONS—Houston, Glenn 1-23. Detroit, K. Smith 1-2.

KICKOFF RETURNS—Houston, Moses 4-54. Detroit, Drummond 4-157.

PUNT RETURNS—Houston, Moses 3-15.

SACKS—Houston, Wong 1, Babin 1. Detroit, Hall 2.5, Bell 1, Davis 1, S. Rogers 0.5.

FALCONS 34, RAMS 17
Sunday, September 19

St. Louis	0	7	10	0	—17
Atlanta	7	10	0	17	—34

First Quarter
Atl.—Griffith 3 pass from Vick (Feely kick), 9:32.
Second Quarter
Atl.—Dunn 2 run (Feely kick), 5:18.
St.L.—M. Faulk 1 run (J. Wilkins kick), 13:48.
Atl.—FG, Feely 35, 14:58.
Third Quarter
St.L.—Holt 33 pass from Bulger (J. Wilkins kick), 6:02.
St.L.—FG, J. Wilkins 46, 12:19.
Fourth Quarter
Atl.—Dunn 2 run (Feely kick), 2:24.
Atl.—B. Smith 0 fumble return (Feely kick), 3:12.
Atl.—FG, Feely 25, 10:19.
Attendance—70,882.

	St. Louis	Atlanta
First downs	14	22
Rushes-yards	15-30	38-242
Passing	250	174
Punt returns	1-(-2)	3-35
Kickoff returns	4-58	4-89
Interception returns	0-0	1-0
Comp.-att.-int.	24-31-1	14-19-0
Sacked-yards lost	5-35	1-5
Punts	4-50	4-46
Fumbles-lost	1-1	0-0
Penalties-yards	10-75	6-51
Time of possession	30:09	29:51

INDIVIDUAL STATISTICS

RUSHING—St. Louis, M. Faulk 12-20, S. Jackson 3-10. Atlanta, Dunn 14-43, Vick 12-109, Duckett 9-52, White 1-26, P. Price 1-9, Griffith 1-3.

PASSING—St. Louis, Bulger 24-31-1-285. Atlanta, Vick 14-19-0-179.

RECEIVING—St. Louis, Holt 9-121, Bruce 8-102, M. Faulk 5-21, Looker 2-41. Atlanta, Griffith 4-78, Crumpler 3-49, White 3-24, P. Price 2-18, Finneran 1-9, Dunn 1-1.

MISSED FIELD GOAL ATTEMPTS—None.

INTERCEPTIONS—Atlanta, Beasley 1-0.

KICKOFF RETURNS—St. Louis, S. Jackson 3-59, Coady 1-(minus 1). Atlanta, Rossum 4-89.

PUNT RETURNS—St. Louis, McDonald 1-(minus 2). Atlanta, Rossum 3-35.

SACKS—St. Louis, Tinoisamoa 1. Atlanta, Kerney 2, Scott 1, Jasper 1, B. Smith 1.

COLTS 31, TITANS 17
Sunday, September 19

Indianapolis	3	0	7	21	—31
Tennessee	7	3	7	0	—17

First Quarter
Ten.—Brown 20 run (Anderson kick), 5:37.
Ind.—FG, Vanderjagt 28, 10:30.

Second Quarter
Ten.—FG, Anderson 39, 7:50.
Third Quarter
Ind.—Wayne 5 pass from Manning (Vanderjagt kick), 3:42.
Ten.—McNair 1 run (Anderson kick), 7:24.
Fourth Quarter
Ind.—Pollard 1 pass from Manning (Vanderjagt kick), :04.
Ind.—James 4 run (Vanderjagt kick), 7:29.
Ind.—James 30 run (Vanderjagt kick), 12:31.
Attendance—68,932.

	Indianapolis	Tennessee
First downs	27	25
Rushes-yards	23-129	30-153
Passing	244	236
Punt returns	1-3	1-4
Kickoff returns	3-65	6-95
Interception returns	1-0	0-0
Comp.-att.-int.	24-33-0	26-40-1
Sacked-yards lost	1-10	3-41
Punts	3-49	2-51
Fumbles-lost	1-1	1-1
Penalties-yards	2-21	8-71
Time of possession	25:05	34:55

INDIVIDUAL STATISTICS

RUSHING—Indianapolis, James 21-124, Manning 2-5. Tennessee, Brown 26-152, McNair 2-2, Holcombe 1-2, Mason 1-(minus 3).

PASSING—Indianapolis, Manning 24-33-0-254. Tennessee, McNair 25-39-1-273, Hentrich 1-1-0-4.

RECEIVING—Indianapolis, Harrison 10-98, Wayne 7-119, Pollard 3-7, Stokley 2-27, James 2-3. Tennessee, Mason 8-104, Bennett 7-85, Kinney 6-45, Troupe 2-12, Berlin 1-19, Brown 1-8, Fleming 1-4.

MISSED FIELD GOAL ATTEMPTS—None.

INTERCEPTIONS—Indianapolis, Harper 1-0.

KICKOFF RETURNS—Indianapolis, Rhodes 3-65. Tennessee, Waddell 5-81, Holcombe 1-14.

PUNT RETURNS—Indianapolis, Pyatt 1-3. Tennessee, Mason 1-4.

SACKS—Indianapolis, Scioli 1, Freeney 1, Mathis 1. Tennessee, Carter 0.5, Hall 0.5.

BEARS 21, PACKERS 10
Sunday, September 19

Chicago	0	14	7	0	—21
Green Bay	3	0	7	0	—10

First Quarter
G.B.—FG, Longwell 25, 5:58.
Second Quarter
Chi.—B. Johnson 11 pass from Grossman (Edinger kick), 7:20.
Chi.—M. Brown 95 fumble return (Edinger kick), 13:16.
Third Quarter
Chi.—T. Jones 1 run (Edinger kick), 3:29.
G.B.—Ferguson 18 pass from Favre (Longwell kick), 13:14.
Attendance—70,688.

	Chicago	Green Bay
First downs	18	23
Rushes-yards	35-182	31-152
Passing	125	252
Punt returns	1-6	3-34
Kickoff returns	3-65	4-74
Interception returns	2-31	1-0
Comp.-att.-int.	10-18-1	24-42-2
Sacked-yards lost	1-7	0-0
Punts	4-44	4-48
Fumbles-lost	2-1	1-1
Penalties-yards	2-15	6-50
Time of possession	27:30	32:30

INDIVIDUAL STATISTICS

RUSHING—Chicago, T. Jones 23-152, Thomas 5-15, Grossman 4-7, Wade 2-23, Terrell 1-(minus 15). Green Bay, Green 24-128, Fisher 6-15, Favre 1-9.

PASSING—Chicago, Grossman 10-18-1-132. Green Bay, Favre 24-42-2-252.

RECEIVING—Chicago, Wade 3-42, Clark 2-43, B. Johnson 2-25, Lyman 2-15, T. Jones 1-7. Green Bay, J. Walker 7-102, Driver 5-49, Ferguson 4-50, Fisher 4-22, Green 2-7, Henderson 1-13, Franks 1-9.

MISSED FIELD GOAL ATTEMPTS—Chicago, Edinger 45. Green Bay, Longwell 45.

INTERCEPTIONS—Chicago, Gray 1-31, Green 1-0. Green Bay, Sharper 1-0.

KICKOFF RETURNS—Chicago, Da. Jones 2-42, Berrian 1-23. Green Bay, Carroll 2-31, Ferguson 1-25, Chatman 1-18.

PUNT RETURNS—Chicago, McQuarters 1-6. Green Bay, Chatman 2-25, Sharper 1-9.

SACKS—Green Bay, Diggs 1.

GIANTS 20, REDSKINS 14
Sunday, September 19

Washington	7	0	0	7—14
N.Y. Giants	0	20	0	0—20

First Quarter
Was.—Cooley 2 pass from Brunell (Hall kick), 7:36.

Second Quarter
NYG—T. Carter 38 pass from Warner (Christie kick), 2:07.
NYG—B. Green 16 fumble return (Christie kick), 8:39.
NYG—FG, Christie 38, 10:26.
NYG—FG, Christie 22, 14:23.

Fourth Quarter
Was.—Portis 13 pass from Ramsey (Hall kick), 2:59.
Attendance—78,767.

	Washington	N.Y. Giants
First downs	20	15
Rushes-yards	28-108	28-62
Passing	214	215
Punt returns	3-26	2-22
Kickoff returns	5-112	3-67
Interception returns	0-0	4-14
Comp.-att.-int.	19-36-4	22-33-0
Sacked-yards lost	4-20	2-17
Punts	4-41	6-39
Fumbles-lost	5-3	2-1
Penalties-yards	7-50	8-50
Time of possession	30:05	29:55

INDIVIDUAL STATISTICS
RUSHING—Washington, Portis 20-69, Betts 3-11, Brunell 2-27, Ramsey 2-17, Coles 1-(minus 16). New York, Barber 18-42, Dayne 9-12, T. Carter 1-8.

PASSING—Washington, Ramsey 9-18-3-142, Brunell 10-18-1-92. New York, Warner 22-33-0-232.

RECEIVING—Washington, Coles 9-100, Gardner 3-66, Cooley 3-14, Portis 2-29, Sellers 1-14, Rasby 1-11. New York, Toomer 6-54, Shockey 5-36, I. Hilliard 4-37, T. Carter 3-63, Barber 2-27, Finn 2-15.

MISSED FIELD GOAL ATTEMPTS—Washington, Hall 41. New York, Christie 47, 51.

INTERCEPTIONS—New York, Alexander 2-1, Robbins 1-13, Wilson 1-0.

KICKOFF RETURNS—Washington, Morton 5-112. New York, Ponder 2-59, Shiancoe 1-8.

PUNT RETURNS—Washington, Morton 3-26. New York, Jones 2-22.

SACKS—Washington, Springs 1, Salave'a 1. New York, Robbins 2, Joseph 1, Washington 1.

SAINTS 30, 49ERS 27
Sunday, September 19

San Francisco	3	14	3	7—27
New Orleans	10	10	3	7—30

First Quarter
S.F.—FG, T. Peterson 30, 6:56.
N.O.—Horn 8 pass from Brooks (Carney kick), 8:05.
N.O.—FG, Carney 32, 12:12.

Second Quarter
S.F.—Barlow 10 run (T. Peterson kick), 3:14.
N.O.—Pathon 37 pass from Brooks (Carney kick), 5:18.
N.O.—FG, Carney 36, 11:25.
S.F.—Barlow 1 run (T. Peterson kick), 14:32.

Third Quarter
N.O.—FG, Carney 37, 3:42.
S.F.—FG, T. Peterson 33, 8:33.

Fourth Quarter
S.F.—Robertson 1 run (T. Peterson kick), 7:53.
N.O.—Stallworth 16 pass from Brooks (Carney kick), 13:59.
Attendance—64,900.

	San Francisco	New Orleans
First downs	22	17
Rushes-yards	34-180	24-46
Passing	190	256
Punt returns	1-6	2-34
Kickoff returns	7-183	6-94
Interception returns	0-0	1-19
Comp.-att.-int.	18-32-1	25-34-0

	San Francisco	New Orleans
Sacked-yards lost	2-15	3-23
Punts	4-42	4-39
Fumbles-lost	4-2	4-1
Penalties-yards	10-125	9-86
Time of possession	31:51	28:09

INDIVIDUAL STATISTICS
RUSHING—San Francisco, Barlow 20-114, Robertson 9-38, Jackson 5-28. New Orleans, Stecker 15-41, Brooks 6-4, McAllister 3-1.

PASSING—San Francisco, Dorsey 18-32-1-205. New Orleans, Brooks 25-34-0-279.

RECEIVING—San Francisco, Conway 8-112, E. Johnson 5-60, Barlow 2-9, Robertson 1-10, Beasley 1-7, Lloyd 1-7. New Orleans, Stallworth 9-113, Horn 8-94, Stecker 6-19, Pathon 2-53.

MISSED FIELD GOAL ATTEMPTS—None.

INTERCEPTIONS—New Orleans, Ambrose 1-19.

KICKOFF RETURNS—San Francisco, Robertson 7-183. New Orleans, M. Lewis 4-80, L. Hall 2-14.

PUNT RETURNS—San Francisco, J. Peterson 1-6. New Orleans, M. Lewis 2-34.

SACKS—San Francisco, J. Peterson 1, Leverette 1, Engelberger 1. New Orleans, Ch. Grant 1, W. Smith 1.

SEAHAWKS 10, BUCCANEERS 6
Sunday, September 19

Seattle	3	7	0	0—10
Tampa Bay	0	3	0	3— 6

First Quarter
Sea.—FG, J. Brown 44, 12:36.

Second Quarter
Sea.—K. Robinson 27 pass from Hasselbeck (J. Brown kick), :35.
T.B.—FG, Gramatica 24, 14:11.

Fourth Quarter
T.B.—FG, Gramatica 27, 10:25.
Attendance—65,089.

	Seattle	Tampa Bay
First downs	9	17
Rushes-yards	22-58	24-92
Passing	124	179
Punt returns	3-25	3-15
Kickoff returns	3-73	3-63
Interception returns	2-47	1-3
Comp.-att.-int.	12-26-1	25-39-2
Sacked-yards lost	5-23	5-30
Punts	10-48	8-46
Fumbles-lost	1-0	3-1
Penalties-yards	7-59	1-5
Time of possession	26:17	33:43

INDIVIDUAL STATISTICS
RUSHING—Seattle, Alexander 17-45, Morris 3-2, Strong 2-11. Tampa Bay, Garner 13-75, Simms 4-13, J. White 4-(minus 5), Alstott 2-6, B. Johnson 1-3.

PASSING—Seattle, Hasselbeck 12-26-1-147. Tampa Bay, Simms 21-32-1-175, B. Johnson 4-7-1-34.

RECEIVING—Seattle, Jackson 5-50, K. Robinson 4-66, Stevens 1-16, Engram 1-13, Morris 1-2. Tampa Bay, Brown 7-49, Clayton 6-61, Garner 6-24, Lee 1-35, Dudley 1-17, Dilger 1-12, Alstott 1-6, Schroeder 1-4, J. White 1-1.

MISSED FIELD GOAL ATTEMPTS—None.

INTERCEPTIONS—Seattle, Trufant 1-41, Boulware 1-6. Tampa Bay, Brooks 1-3.

KICKOFF RETURNS—Seattle, Morris 3-73. Tampa Bay, Murphy 3-63.

PUNT RETURNS—Seattle, Engram 3-25. Tampa Bay, Brown 2-15, Schroeder 1-0.

SACKS—Seattle, Wistrom 2, Huff 1, R. Bernard 1, Cochran 1. Tampa Bay, McFarland 2, Phillips 1, Spires 1, Quarles 1.

JETS 34, CHARGERS 28
Sunday, September 19

N.Y. Jets	14	3	10	7—34
San Diego	0	7	7	14—28

First Quarter
NYJ—C. Martin 1 run (Brien kick), 7:10.
NYJ—C. Martin 2 run (Brien kick), 11:18.

Second Quarter
NYJ—FG, Brien 28, 5:20.
S.D.—Dwight 87 kickoff return (Kaeding kick), 5:32.

Third Quarter

NYJ—FG, Brien 23, 3:44.
NYJ—Sowell 4 pass from Pennington (Brien kick), 11:29.
S.D.—Tomlinson 4 run (Kaeding kick), 12:48.

Fourth Quarter

S.D.—Caldwell 33 pass from Brees (Kaeding kick), 7:22.
NYJ—Baker 1 pass from Pennington (Brien kick), 11:04.
S.D.—Flutie 6 run (Kaeding kick), 14:30.
Attendance—57,310.

	N.Y. Jets	San Diego
First downs	22	21
Rushes-yards	35-122	25-111
Passing	258	216
Punt returns	1-2	4-30
Kickoff returns	4-71	7-209
Interception returns	2-1	0-0
Comp.-att.-int.	22-29-0	15-35-2
Sacked-yards lost	0-0	1-7
Punts	5-42	4-39
Fumbles-lost	1-0	4-2
Penalties-yards	4-22	5-44
Time of possession	36:47	23:13

INDIVIDUAL STATISTICS

RUSHING—New York, C. Martin 32-119, Pennington 2-1, Jordan 1-2. San Diego, Tomlinson 19-87, Chatman 3-10, Flutie 2-14, Brees 1-0.

PASSING—New York, Pennington 22-29-0-258. San Diego, Brees 8-19-2-46, Flutie 7-16-0-77.

RECEIVING—New York, C. Martin 6-25, Sowell 5-56, Moss 4-97, Baker 3-20, McCareins 2-9, J. Carter 1-46, Jordan 1-5. San Diego, Caldwell 4-67, Gates 4-9, Tomlinson 3-76, E. Parker 2-19, Osgood 1-14, Neal 1-8.

MISSED FIELD GOAL ATTEMPTS—None.

INTERCEPTIONS—New York, Coleman 1-1, McGraw 1-0.

KICKOFF RETURNS—New York, Jordan 4-71. San Diego, Dwight 7-209.

PUNT RETURNS—New York, Moss 1-2. San Diego, E. Parker 4-30.

SACKS—New York, Robertson 0.5, Ellis 0.5.

RAIDERS 13, BILLS 10
Sunday, September 19

Buffalo	0	3	0	7—10
Oakland	0	7	3	3—13

Second Quarter

Oak.—Curry 43 pass from Gannon (Janikowski kick), :14.
Buf.—FG, Lindell 32, 11:37.

Third Quarter

Oak.—FG, Janikowski 21, 2:52.

Fourth Quarter

Oak.—FG, Janikowski 33, 12:33.
Buf.—Moulds 5 pass from Bledsoe (Lindell kick), 13:40.
Attendance—53,610.

	Buffalo	Oakland
First downs	14	12
Rushes-yards	24-67	26-73
Passing	176	200
Punt returns	2-9	1-15
Kickoff returns	4-90	3-23
Interception returns	0-0	1-27
Comp.-att.-int.	14-25-1	19-27-0
Sacked-yards lost	7-46	2-9
Punts	5-40	5-50
Fumbles-lost	0-0	0-0
Penalties-yards	7-55	10-96
Time of possession	30:19	29:41

INDIVIDUAL STATISTICS

RUSHING—Buffalo, Henry 21-67, McGahee 2-(minus 3), Moulds 1-3. Oakland, Wheatley 10-21, Zereoue 9-24, Gannon 4-24, Redmond 2-8, Porter 1-(minus 4).

PASSING—Buffalo, Bledsoe 13-24-1-198, Moorman 1-1-0-24. Oakland, Gannon 19-27-0-209.

RECEIVING—Buffalo, Moulds 2-41, Reed 2-29, Shaw 2-22, Campbell 2-20, Shelton 2-11, Henry 2-10, Evans 1-65, Thomas 1-24. Oakland, Curry 5-89, Jolley 4-31, Porter 3-45, Zereoue 3-25, Redmond 2-15, Crockett 1-4, Wheatley 1-0.

MISSED FIELD GOAL ATTEMPTS—None.

INTERCEPTIONS—Oakland, Buchanan 1-27.

KICKOFF RETURNS—Buffalo, McGee 2-48, Fletcher 2-42. Oakland, Curry 1-0, Francis 1-7, Porter 1-6.

PUNT RETURNS—Buffalo, Clements 2-9. Oakland, Buchanon 1-15.

SACKS—Buffalo, P. Williams 1, McGee 1. Oakland, Grant 2, Brayton 1.5, Clark 1, C. Woodson 1, Hamilton 0.5, Asomugha 0.5, Sapp 0.5.

COWBOYS 19, BROWNS 12
Sunday, September 19

Cleveland	0	9	0	3—12
Dallas	7	3	7	2—19

First Quarter

Dal.—Robinson 1 pass from Testaverde (Cundiff kick), 7:11.

Second Quarter

Cle.—FG, Dawson 45, :04.
Cle.—FG, Dawson 23, 7:43.
Dal.—FG, Cundiff 30, 13:17.
Cle.—FG, Dawson 49, 15:00.

Third Quarter

Dal.—George 3 run (Cundiff kick), 11:42.

Fourth Quarter

Cle.—FG, Dawson 22, :35.
Dal.—Safety, 14:52.
Attendance—63,119.

	Cleveland	Dallas
First downs	12	20
Rushes-yards	26-136	28-126
Passing	66	315
Punt returns	1-11	3-16
Kickoff returns	3-21	3-62
Interception returns	3-71	3-42
Comp.-att.-int.	8-28-3	23-35-3
Sacked-yards lost	1-5	1-7
Punts	4-45	3-40
Fumbles-lost	1-0	1-1
Penalties-yards	6-31	11-120
Time of possession	23:52	36:08

INDIVIDUAL STATISTICS

RUSHING—Cleveland, Green 19-52, Garcia 4-34, J. Jackson 3-50. Dallas, George 18-62, J. Jones 5-16, Lee 4-15, Coakley 1-33.

PASSING—Cleveland, Garcia 8-27-3-71, McCown 0-1-0-0. Dallas, Testaverde 23-35-3-322.

RECEIVING—Cleveland, Andre. Davis 3-39, Winslow 1-11, Morgan 1-11, Northcutt 1-7, Green 1-2, J. Jackson 1-1. Dallas, Glenn 6-90, Witten 6-82, Bryant 3-54, K. Johnson 2-57, George 2-17, J. Jones 2-14, Campbell 1-7, Robinson 1-1.

MISSED FIELD GOAL ATTEMPTS—Dallas, Cundiff 49.

INTERCEPTIONS—Cleveland, Henry 1-51, Griffith 1-18, McCutcheon 1-2. Dallas, Newman 1-21, Nguyen 1-19, Hunter 1-2.

KICKOFF RETURNS—Cleveland, De. Brown 2-15, Shea 1-6. Dallas, Lee 2-40, Reeves 1-22.

PUNT RETURNS—Cleveland, Northcutt 1-11. Dallas, Ward 2-9, Newman 1-7.

SACKS—Cleveland, Ekuban 1. Dallas, Ellis 1.

PATRIOTS 23, CARDINALS 12
Sunday, September 19

New England	7	7	3	6—23
Arizona	0	6	6	0—12

First Quarter

N.E.—Graham 2 pass from Brady (Vinatieri kick), 12:49.

Second Quarter

N.E.—Graham 19 pass from Brady (Vinatieri kick), 1:44.
Ariz.—FG, Rackers 51, 6:52.
Ariz.—FG, Rackers 52, 9:47.

Third Quarter

N.E.—FG, Vinatieri 29, 5:39.
Ariz.—E. Smith 1 run (pass failed), 13:27.

Fourth Quarter

N.E.—FG, Vinatieri 28, 2:58.
N.E.—FG, Vinatieri 24, 8:38.
Attendance—51,557.

	New England	Arizona
First downs	24	14
Rushes-yards	42-172	16-50
Passing	207	117
Punt returns	4-27	0-0
Kickoff returns	1-23	5-108
Interception returns	2-27	2-65
Comp.-att.-int.	15-26-2	13-29-2
Sacked-yards lost	2-12	5-43
Punts	3-46	4-45
Fumbles-lost	2-1	3-0

	New England	Arizona
Penalties-yards	12-79	6-43
Time of possession	35:16	24:44

INDIVIDUAL STATISTICS

RUSHING—New England, Dillon 32-158, Brady 5-3, Pass 4-7, Abdullah 1-4. Arizona, E. Smith 13-31, McCown 3-19.

PASSING—New England, Brady 15-26-2-219. Arizona, McCown 13-29-2-160.

RECEIVING—New England, Givens 6-120, Patten 2-39, Pass 2-27, Graham 2-21, Branch 1-7, T. Brown 1-6, Dillon 1-(minus 1). Arizona, Fitzgerald 5-36, F. Jones 4-43, B. Johnson 3-39, Scobey 1-42.

MISSED FIELD GOAL ATTEMPTS—Arizona, Rackers 58.

INTERCEPTIONS—New England, Wilson 2-27. Arizona, Darling 1-65, Macklin 1-0.

KICKOFF RETURNS—New England, B. Johnson 1-23. Arizona, Scobey 5-108.

PUNT RETURNS—New England, T. Brown 4-27.

SACKS—New England, Harrison 2, McGinest 2, Vrabel 1. Arizona, Berry 1, Kolodziej 1.

BENGALS 16, DOLPHINS 13
Sunday, September 19

Miami	0	3	0	10—13
Cincinnati	0	0	13	3—16

Second Quarter
Mia.—FG, Mare 43, 2:21.

Third Quarter
Cin.—Simmons 50 interception return (Graham kick), 2:59.
Cin.—FG, Graham 48, 9:49.
Cin.—FG, Graham 36, 14:47.

Fourth Quarter
Mia.—Chambers 4 pass from Feeley (Mare kick), 11:21.
Mia.—FG, Mare 47, 13:07.
Cin.—FG, Graham 39, 14:58.
Attendance—65,705.

	Miami	Cincinnati
First downs	11	12
Rushes-yards	20-25	29-94
Passing	201	116
Punt returns	7-78	2-27
Kickoff returns	4-47	1-19
Interception returns	1-(-3)	2-50
Comp.-att.-int.	21-39-2	21-38-1
Sacked-yards lost	2-17	5-31
Punts	10-40	10-42
Fumbles-lost	4-1	0-0
Penalties-yards	8-69	3-19
Time of possession	28:33	31:27

INDIVIDUAL STATISTICS

RUSHING—Miami, Gordon 19-22, Feeley 1-3. Cincinnati, Ru. Johnson 22-67, Watson 4-9, Houshmandzadeh 1-11, Warrick 1-6, J. Johnson 1-1.

PASSING—Miami, Feeley 21-39-2-218. Cincinnati, Palmer 21-38-1-147.

RECEIVING—Miami, Gordon 8-44, McMichael 6-93, Chambers 5-69, Thompson 1-7, Booker 1-5. Cincinnati, Warrick 6-51, Schobel 4-12, C. Johnson 3-45, Watson 3-6, Stewart 2-17, Houshmandzadeh 1-13, Ru. Johnson 1-4, R. Kelly 1-(minus 1).

MISSED FIELD GOAL ATTEMPTS—Cincinnati, Graham 38.

INTERCEPTIONS—Miami, Taylor 1-(minus 3). Cincinnati, Simmons 1-50, James 1-0.

KICKOFF RETURNS—Miami, Brightful 2-49, Gilmore 2-(minus 2). Cincinnati, Houshmandzadeh 1-19.

PUNT RETURNS—Miami, Brightful 7-78. Cincinnati, Houshmandzadeh 2-27.

SACKS—Miami, Thomas 1, Edwards 1, Taylor 1, Ahanotu 1, Romero 1. Cincinnati, Webster 1, J. Smith 1.

EAGLES 27, VIKINGS 16
Monday, September 20

Minnesota	3	3	3	7—16
Philadelphia	7	3	7	10—27

First Quarter
Min.—FG, M. Andersen 42, 3:40.
Phi.—Smith 11 pass from McNabb (Akers kick), 9:17.

Second Quarter
Min.—FG, M. Andersen 19, 2:54.
Phi.—FG, Akers 37, 8:24.

Third Quarter
Phi.—McNabb 20 run (Akers kick), 3:38.
Min.—FG, M. Andersen 39, 10:23.

Fourth Quarter
Phi.—Owens 45 pass from McNabb (Akers kick), 7:20.
Min.—Moss 4 pass from Culpepper (M. Andersen kick), 11:28.
Phi.—FG, Akers 47, 13:49.
Attendance—67,676.

	Minnesota	Philadelphia
First downs	25	19
Rushes-yards	19-78	17-91
Passing	332	226
Punt returns	0-0	1-2
Kickoff returns	6-123	5-140
Interception returns	0-0	1-15
Comp.-att.-int.	37-47-1	19-28-0
Sacked-yards lost	4-11	2-19
Punts	1-39	1-49
Fumbles-lost	3-1	1-1
Penalties-yards	10-70	3-25
Time of possession	37:53	22:07

INDIVIDUAL STATISTICS

RUSHING—Minnesota, O. Smith 10-28, Culpepper 8-41, Burleson 1-9. Philadelphia, Westbrook 12-69, McNabb 3-24, Levens 1-1, Owens 1-(minus 3).

PASSING—Minnesota, Culpepper 37-47-1-343. Philadelphia, McNabb 19-28-0-245.

RECEIVING—Minnesota, Moss 8-69, Wiggins 8-65, O. Smith 8-56, Burleson 5-67, Owens 3-36, Campbell 2-30, M. Robinson 2-14, Moore 1-6. Philadelphia, Westbrook 5-69, Owens 4-79, Smith 3-26, C. Lewis 2-24, Ritchie 2-22, G. Lewis 2-11, F. Mitchell 1-14.

MISSED FIELD GOAL ATTEMPTS—Minnesota, M. Andersen 44.

INTERCEPTIONS—Philadelphia, Reese 1-15.

KICKOFF RETURNS—Minnesota, Moore 6-123. Philadelphia, Reed 4-126, Mahe 1-14.

PUNT RETURNS—Philadelphia, Mahe 1-2.

SACKS—Minnesota, Henderson 1, Udeze 1. Philadelphia, Brown 1, Wayne 1, Rayburn 1, Walker 1.

WEEK 3

AMERICAN FOOTBALL CONFERENCE

EAST DIVISION

	W	L	T	Pct.	PF	PA
New England	2	0	0	1.000	50	36
N.Y. Jets	2	0	0	1.000	65	52
Buffalo	0	2	0	.000	20	26
Miami	0	3	0	.000	23	46

NORTH DIVISION

	W	L	T	Pct.	PF	PA
Baltimore	2	1	0	.667	56	42
Pittsburgh	2	1	0	.667	50	54
Cincinnati	1	2	0	.333	49	67
Cleveland	1	2	0	.333	42	49

SOUTH DIVISION

	W	L	T	Pct.	PF	PA
Jacksonville	3	0	0	1.000	35	28
Indianapolis	2	1	0	.667	100	75
Houston	1	2	0	.333	60	76
Tennessee	1	2	0	.333	46	53

WEST DIVISION

	W	L	T	Pct.	PF	PA
Denver	2	1	0	.667	63	44
Oakland	2	1	0	.667	64	54
San Diego	1	2	0	.333	68	77
Kansas City	0	3	0	.000	62	86

NATIONAL FOOTBALL CONFERENCE

EAST DIVISION

	W	L	T	Pct.	PF	PA
Philadelphia	3	0	0	1.000	88	46
Dallas	2	1	0	.667	57	65
N.Y. Giants	2	1	0	.667	64	55
Washington	1	2	0	.333	48	51

NORTH DIVISION

	W	L	T	Pct.	PF	PA
Detroit	2	1	0	.667	61	62
Minnesota	2	1	0	.667	78	66
Chicago	1	2	0	.333	59	57
Green Bay	1	2	0	.333	65	80

SOUTH DIVISION

	W	L	T	Pct.	PF	PA
Atlanta	3	0	0	1.000	61	39
New Orleans	2	1	0	.667	65	73
Carolina	1	1	0	.500	42	41
Tampa Bay	0	3	0	.000	36	56

WEST DIVISION

	W	L	T	Pct.	PF	PA
Seattle	3	0	0	1.000	65	13
St. Louis	1	2	0	.333	59	72
Arizona	0	3	0	.000	25	46
San Francisco	0	3	0	.000	46	85

TOP PERFORMANCES

100-YARD RUSHING GAMES

Player, Team & Opponent	Att.	Yds.	TD
Jamal Lewis, Bal. at Cin.	18	186	1
Priest Holmes, K.C. vs. Hou.	32	134	0
Warrick Dunn, Atl. vs. Ariz.	20	117	0
Thomas Jones, Chi. at Min.	22	110	1
Tiki Barber, NYG vs. Cle.	23	106	1
Aaron Stecker, N.O. at St.L.*	18	106	1
Tyrone Wheatley, Oak. vs. T.B.	18	102	1
Chris Brown, Ten. vs. Jac.	23	101	1
Duce Staley, Pit. at Mia.	22	101	0

300-YARD PASSING GAMES

Player, Team & Opponent	Att.	Cmp.	Yds.	TD	Int.
Peyton Manning, Ind. vs. G.B.	40	28	393	5	0
Daunte Culpepper, Min. vs. Chi.	30	19	360	2	0
Brett Favre, G.B. at Ind.	44	30	360	4	0
Marc Bulger, St.L. vs. N.O.*	49	32	358	1	0
Donovan McNabb, Phi. at Det.	42	29	356	2	0
Mark Brunell, Was. vs. Dal.	43	25	325	2	0
Aaron Brooks, N.O. at St.L.*	41	24	316	1	0
Carson Palmer, Cin. vs. Bal.	52	25	316	0	3
Brad Johnson, T.B. at Oak.	36	22	309	2	1

100-YARD RECEIVING GAMES

Player, Team & Opponent	Rec.	Yds.	TD
Javon Walker, G.B. at Ind.	11	200	3
Reggie Wayne, Ind. vs. G.B.	11	184	1
Rod Gardner, Was. vs. Dal.	10	167	2
Roy Williams, Det. vs. Phi.	9	135	2
Isaac Bruce, St.L. vs. N.O.*	8	134	0
Bill Schroeder, T.B. at Oak.	4	126	1
Amani Toomer, NYG vs. Cle.	5	126	0
Randy Moss, Min. vs. Chi.	7	119	2
T.J. Houshmandzadeh, Cin. vs. Bal.	7	116	0

Player, Team & Opponent	Rec.	Yds.	TD
Brandon Stokley, Ind. vs. G.B.	8	110	2
Terrell Owens, Phi. at Det.	6	107	1
Tony Gonzalez, K.C. vs. Hou.	8	106	1
Onterrio Smith, Min. vs. Chi.	6	104	0

*Overtime game.

RESULTS

SUNDAY, SEPTEMBER 26
Jacksonville 15, TENNESSEE 12
ATLANTA 6, Arizona 3
N.Y. GIANTS 27, Cleveland 10
Baltimore 23, CINCINNATI 9
Philadelphia 30, DETROIT 13
New Orleans 28, ST. LOUIS 25 (OT)
MINNESOTA 27, Chicago 22
Houston 24, KANSAS CITY 21
DENVER 23, San Diego 13
SEATTLE 34, San Francisco 0
INDIANAPOLIS 45, Green Bay 31
Pittsburgh 13, MIAMI 3
OAKLAND 30, Tampa Bay 20

MONDAY, SEPTEMBER 27
Dallas 21, WASHINGTON 18
Open Date: Buffalo, Carolina, New England, N.Y. Jets

2004 REVIEW Week 3

JAGUARS 15, TITANS 12
Sunday, September 26

Jacksonville	0	0	7	8—15
Tennessee	0	6	0	6—12

Second Quarter
Ten.—FG, Anderson 26, 5:07.
Ten.—FG, Anderson 40, 11:40.
Third Quarter
Jac.—Wrighster 7 pass from Leftwich (Scobee kick), 11:45.
Fourth Quarter
Ten.—Brown 26 run (pass failed), 9:23.
Jac.—F. Taylor 1 run (R. Williams pass from Leftwich), 14:51.
Attendance—68,932.

	Jacksonville	Tennessee
First downs	15	13
Rushes-yards	29-136	26-119
Passing	117	130
Punt returns	2-16	4-21
Kickoff returns	3-50	3-25
Interception returns	1-21	0-0
Comp.-att.-int.	14-20-0	16-27-1
Sacked-yards lost	2-7	3-13
Punts	7-39	4-52
Fumbles-lost	3-0	2-0
Penalties-yards	9-87	6-56
Time of possession	28:46	31:14

INDIVIDUAL STATISTICS
RUSHING—Jacksonville, F. Taylor 17-81, Toefield 7-43, Leftwich 3-5, G. Jones 2-7. Tennessee, Brown 23-101, McNair 3-18.
PASSING—Jacksonville, Leftwich 14-20-0-124. Tennessee, McNair 16-26-1-143, Volek 0-1-0-0.
RECEIVING—Jacksonville, Wrighster 5-30, J. Smith 3-58, T. Edwards 2-11, F. Taylor 1-11, Wilford 1-6, Lewis 1-4, R. Williams 1-4. Tennessee, Bennett 6-55, Mason 4-43, Brown 3-30, Kinney 2-11, Holcombe 1-4.
MISSED FIELD GOAL ATTEMPTS—None.INTERCEPTIONS—Jacksonville, Mathis 1-21.
KICKOFF RETURNS—Jacksonville, Toefield 2-24, Lewis 1-26. Tennessee, Kinney 1-21, Fleming 1-12, Bennett 1-(minus 8).
PUNT RETURNS—Jacksonville, Lewis 2-16. Tennessee, Mason 4-21.
SACKS—Jacksonville, Peterson 1, Stroud 1, Henderson 0.5, Meier 0.5. Tennessee, Carter 1, Schulters 1.

FALCONS 6, CARDINALS 3
Sunday, September 26

Arizona	0	0	0	3—3
Atlanta	3	3	0	0—6

First Quarter
Atl.—FG, Feely 25, 7:48.
Second Quarter
Atl.—FG, Feely 23, 2:59.
Fourth Quarter
Ariz.—FG, Rackers 30, 5:36.
Attendance—70,534.

	Arizona	Atlanta
First downs	13	15
Rushes-yards	26-61	29-194
Passing	179	89
Punt returns	3-6	2-28
Kickoff returns	3-56	2-62
Interception returns	1-11	0-0
Comp.-att.-int.	25-32-0	10-20-1
Sacked-yards lost	6-59	6-26
Punts	6-43	5-48
Fumbles-lost	4-4	5-3
Penalties-yards	8-66	3-15
Time of possession	34:37	25:23

INDIVIDUAL STATISTICS
RUSHING—Arizona, E. Smith 18-45, McCown 6-10, K. Williams 1-3, Hambrick 1-3. Atlanta, Dunn 20-117, Vick 8-68, P. Price 1-9.
PASSING—Arizona, McCown 20-26-0-198, S. King 5-6-0-40. Atlanta, Vick 10-20-1-115.
RECEIVING—Arizona, K. Williams 6-90, B. Johnson 6-53, Fitzgerald 5-37, Poole 2-24, E. Smith 2-11, F. Jones 2-11, Scobey 1-7, Diamond 1-5. Atlanta, Griffith 3-25, Crumpler 2-34, Dunn 2-20, P. Price 2-16, White 1-20.

MISSED FIELD GOAL ATTEMPTS—None.
INTERCEPTIONS—Arizona, Wilson 1-11.
KICKOFF RETURNS—Arizona, Scobey 3-56. Atlanta, Rossum 2-62.
PUNT RETURNS—Arizona, K. Williams 3-6. Atlanta, Rossum 2-28.
SACKS—Arizona, Zellner 2, Starks 1, Berry 1, Dansby 1, Pace 1. Atlanta, Kerney 3, R. Coleman 2, B. Smith 1.

GIANTS 27, BROWNS 10
Sunday, September 26

Cleveland	0	0	0	10—10
N.Y. Giants	7	3	7	10—27

First Quarter
NYG—Barber 8 run (Christie kick), 5:59.
Second Quarter
NYG—FG, Christie 43, 7:09.
Third Quarter
NYG—Warner 1 run (Christie kick), 12:06.
Fourth Quarter
Cle.—FG, Dawson 49, 2:07.
NYG—FG, Christie 25, 8:15.
Cle.—Morgan 3 pass from Garcia (Dawson kick), 11:24.
NYG—Cloud 5 run (Christie kick), 12:58.
Attendance—78,521.

	Cleveland	N.Y. Giants
First downs	18	25
Rushes-yards	23-124	32-116
Passing	161	274
Punt returns	1-0	3-28
Kickoff returns	6-105	2-56
Interception returns	0-0	1-0
Comp.-att.-int.	21-31-1	19-27-0
Sacked-yards lost	4-19	2-12
Punts	5-45	4-35
Fumbles-lost	2-2	0-0
Penalties-yards	8-80	8-59
Time of possession	27:58	32:02

INDIVIDUAL STATISTICS
RUSHING—Cleveland, Green 15-91, J. Jackson 5-24, Garcia 3-9. New York, Barber 23-106, Cloud 6-12, Warner 3-(minus 2).
PASSING—Cleveland, Garcia 21-31-1-180. New York, Warner 19-27-0-286.
RECEIVING—Cleveland, Northcutt 9-50, Morgan 3-44, Andre. Davis 3-33, J. Jackson 3-16, King 2-38, Mustard 1-9. New York, Toomer 5-126, Shockey 5-41, Barber 3-48, T. Carter 3-45, I. Hilliard 3-26.
MISSED FIELD GOAL ATTEMPTS—None.
INTERCEPTIONS—New York, Wilson 1-0.
KICKOFF RETURNS—Cleveland, Alston 5-91, King 1-14. New York, Ponder 2-56.
PUNT RETURNS—Cleveland, Northcutt 1-0. New York, Jones 3-28.
SACKS—Cleveland, Ekuban 1, Lang 1. New York, Strahan 2, W. Allen 1, Emmons 1.

RAVENS 23, BENGALS 9
Sunday, September 26

Baltimore	10	7	0	6—23
Cincinnati	0	3	3	3—9

First Quarter
Bal.—FG, Stover 21, 5:17.
Bal.—Boller 7 run (Stover kick), 13:08.
Second Quarter
Bal.—Hymes 38 pass from Boller (Stover kick), 11:54.
Cin.—FG, Graham 29, 15:00.
Third Quarter
Cin.—FG, Graham 47, 8:52.
Fourth Quarter
Cin.—FG, Graham 26, 5:57.
Bal.—J. Lewis 75 run (pass failed), 6:15.
Attendance—65,575.

	Baltimore	Cincinnati
First downs	14	26
Rushes-yards	34-254	26-109
Passing	126	289
Punt returns	4-84	1-9
Kickoff returns	3-55	3-45

	Baltimore	Cincinnati
Interception returns	3-108	0-0
Comp.-att.-int.	11-18-0	25-52-3
Sacked-yards lost	2-0	4-27
Punts	6-39	5-41
Fumbles-lost	5-2	1-1
Penalties-yards	9-71	5-25
Time of possession	26:48	33:12

INDIVIDUAL STATISTICS

RUSHING—Baltimore, J. Lewis 18-186, C. Taylor 8-27, Boller 4-24, Ricard 3-9, Sams 1-8. Cincinnati, Ru. Johnson 23-98, Watson 1-10, Palmer 1-2, Washington 1-(minus 1).

PASSING—Baltimore, Boller 11-18-0-126. Cincinnati, Palmer 25-52-3-316.

RECEIVING—Baltimore, Hymes 4-61, Darling 2-5, J. Lewis 1-46, Ricard 1-8, T. Jones 1-7, Moore 1-6, C. Taylor 1-(minus 7). Cincinnati, C. Johnson 8-99, Houshmandzadeh 7-116, Washington 5-58, Schobel 3-28, Watson 2-15.

MISSED FIELD GOAL ATTEMPTS—None.

INTERCEPTIONS—Baltimore, Reed 2-90, Williams 1-18.

KICKOFF RETURNS—Baltimore, Sams 3-55. Cincinnati, Houshmandzadeh 2-39, Watson 1-6.

PUNT RETURNS—Baltimore, Sams 4-84. Cincinnati, Ratliff 1-9.

SACKS—Baltimore, Suggs 2, Douglas 1, A. Thomas 1. Cincinnati, Thornton 1, Team 1.

EAGLES 30, LIONS 13
Sunday, September 26

Philadelphia	14	7	6	3—30
Detroit	0	7	0	6—13

First Quarter
Phi.—McNabb 1 run (Akers kick), 12:52.
Phi.—Owens 29 pass from McNabb (Akers kick), 13:32.

Second Quarter
Phi.—Bartrum 1 pass from McNabb (Akers kick), 9:01.
Det.—Williams 12 pass from Harrington (Hanson kick), 14:40.

Third Quarter
Phi.—FG, Akers 26, 5:19.
Phi.—FG, Akers 47, 8:18.

Fourth Quarter
Phi.—FG, Akers 39, 4:38.
Det.—Williams 29 pass from Harrington (pass failed), 6:26.
Attendance—62,472.

	Philadelphia	Detroit
First downs	19	15
Rushes-yards	19-59	18-77
Passing	343	179
Punt returns	4-26	2-9
Kickoff returns	3-64	7-192
Interception returns	0-0	0-0
Comp.-att.-int.	29-42-0	21-39-0
Sacked-yards lost	2-13	5-20
Punts	4-52	7-49
Fumbles-lost	2-1	2-1
Penalties-yards	7-54	6-39
Time of possession	32:58	27:02

INDIVIDUAL STATISTICS

RUSHING—Philadelphia, Westbrook 13-44, McNabb 5-(minus 2), Mahe 1-17. Detroit, Pinner 6-16, Bryson 5-43, Jones 4-8, Harrington 3-10.

PASSING—Philadelphia, McNabb 29-42-0-356. Detroit, Harrington 21-38-0-199, Williams 0-1-0-0.

RECEIVING—Philadelphia, Westbrook 7-32, Owens 6-107, Smith 4-74, F. Mitchell 3-71, Pinkston 3-22, C. Lewis 3-19, Bartrum 2-18, G. Lewis 1-13. Detroit, Williams 9-135, Pinner 4-14, Streets 3-23, Alexander 3-15, Hakim 1-13, Bryson 1-(minus 1).

MISSED FIELD GOAL ATTEMPTS—None.

INTERCEPTIONS—None.

KICKOFF RETURNS—Philadelphia, Reed 2-42, Mahe 1-22. Detroit, Drummond 7-192.

PUNT RETURNS—Philadelphia, Mahe 4-8. Detroit, Drummond 2-9.

SACKS—Philadelphia, Kearse 3, Dawkins 1, Team 1. Detroit, Davis 1, Wilkinson 1.

SAINTS 28, RAMS 25
Sunday, September 26

New Orleans	0	13	3	9	3—28
St. Louis	7	3	0	15	0—25

First Quarter
St.L.—Holt 32 pass from Bulger (J. Wilkins kick), 7:02.

Second Quarter
N.O.—FG, Carney 52, :10.
St.L.—FG, J. Wilkins 53, 3:52.
N.O.—Stecker 42 run (Carney kick), 7:14.
N.O.—FG, Carney 53, 13:59.

Third Quarter
N.O.—FG, Carney 39, 9:44.

Fourth Quarter
St.L.—M. Faulk 3 run (J. Wilkins kick), 1:26.
N.O.—Horn 9 pass from Brooks (pass failed), 6:37.
St.L.—Bulger 19 run (Curtis pass from Bulger), 14:32.
N.O.—FG, Carney 38, 14:57.

Overtime
N.O.—FG, Carney 31, 7:04.
Attendance—65,856.

	New Orleans	St. Louis
First downs	27	25
Rushes-yards	32-146	15-78
Passing	316	325
Punt returns	5-66	0-0
Kickoff returns	4-82	8-178
Interception returns	0-0	0-0
Comp.-att.-int.	24-41-0	32-49-0
Sacked-yards lost	1-0	5-33
Punts	1-45	5-42
Fumbles-lost	0-0	1-1
Penalties-yards	5-25	12-85
Time of possession	33:27	33:37

INDIVIDUAL STATISTICS

RUSHING—New Orleans, Stecker 18-106, K. Carter 7-12, Brooks 6-24, Stallworth 1-4. St. Louis, M. Faulk 12-44, S. Jackson 2-15, Bulger 1-19.

PASSING—New Orleans, Brooks 24-41-0-316. St. Louis, Bulger 32-49-0-358.

RECEIVING—New Orleans, Horn 7-91, Stallworth 5-65, Stecker 4-20, B. Williams 3-38, Pathon 2-49, M. Lewis 1-25, Gardner 1-23, Karney 1-5. St. Louis, Bruce 8-134, M. Faulk 8-46, Holt 6-65, Looker 5-69, Manumaleuna 2-8, Curtis 1-13, Goodspeed 1-13, McDonald 1-10.

MISSED FIELD GOAL ATTEMPTS—New Orleans, Carney 51.

INTERCEPTIONS—None.

KICKOFF RETURNS—New Orleans, M. Lewis 3-65, W. Smith 1-17. St. Louis, Harris 4-96, Furrey 4-82.

PUNT RETURNS—New Orleans, M. Lewis 5-66.

SACKS—New Orleans, Ch. Grant 3, Watson 1, Howard 1. St. Louis, Little 1.

VIKINGS 27, BEARS 22
Sunday, September 26

Chicago	3	3	0	16—22
Minnesota	0	10	7	10—27

First Quarter
Chi.—FG, Edinger 34, 6:52.

Second Quarter
Chi.—FG, Edinger 23, 1:19.
Min.—Moss 3 pass from Culpepper (M. Andersen kick), 6:03.
Min.—FG, M. Andersen 42, 9:51.

Third Quarter
Min.—Culpepper 1 run (M. Andersen kick), 4:02.

Fourth Quarter
Chi.—FG, Edinger 32, :14.
Min.—FG, M. Andersen 24, 3:40.
Chi.—T. Jones 1 run (pass failed), 8:40.
Min.—Moss 2 pass from Culpepper (M. Andersen kick), 9:21.
Chi.—Grossman 6 run (Edinger kick), 13:00.
Attendance—64,163.

	Chicago	Minnesota
First downs	24	24
Rushes-yards	28-146	23-93
Passing	239	350
Punt returns	0-0	2-33
Kickoff returns	6-139	5-111
Interception returns	0-0	0-0
Comp.-att.-int.	21-34-0	19-31-0
Sacked-yards lost	2-9	4-10
Punts	2-42	1-29
Fumbles-lost	2-1	4-2
Penalties-yards	14-101	11-70
Time of possession	32:01	27:59

RUSHING—Chicago, T. Jones 22-110, Grossman 3-20, Thomas 2-2, Wade 1-14. Minnesota, O. Smith 17-94, Culpepper 5-13, Campbell 1-(minus 14).

PASSING—Chicago, Grossman 21-31-0-248, Quinn 0-3-0-0. Minnesota, Culpepper 19-30-0-360, Frerotte 0-1-0-0.

RECEIVING—Chicago, T. Jones 8-71, Wade 4-71, Terrell 2-25, Lyman 2-16, Berrian 2-12, Gage 1-32, Gilmore 1-11, B. Johnson 1-10. Minnesota, Moss 7-119, O. Smith 6-104, Burleson 2-71, Campbell 2-50, Owens 2-16.

MISSED FIELD GOAL ATTEMPTS—Chicago, Edinger 39. Minnesota, M. Andersen 46.

INTERCEPTIONS—None.

KICKOFF RETURNS—Chicago, Berrian 5-120, McKie 1-19. Minnesota, Campbell 3-66, Howry 2-45.

PUNT RETURNS—Minnesota, Howry 2-33.

SACKS—Chicago, Harris 1, Ogunleye 1, Worrell 1, Scott 1. Minnesota, K. Williams 1, Johnstone 1.

TEXANS 24, CHIEFS 21
Sunday, September 26

Houston	0	6	8	10—24
Kansas City	7	0	7	7—21

First Quarter
K.C.—Gonzalez 14 pass from Green (Tynes kick), 9:25.

Second Quarter
Hou.—FG, K. Brown 28, 8:45.
Hou.—FG, K. Brown 49, 14:50.

Third Quarter
K.C.—Horn 6 pass from Green (Tynes kick), 3:50.
Hou.—Coleman 102 interception return (Wells run), 11:09.

Fourth Quarter
K.C.—Dunn 5 pass from Green (Tynes kick), 4:05.
Hou.—Gaffney 9 pass from Carr (K. Brown kick), 9:40.
Hou.—FG, K. Brown 49, 14:58.
Attendance—77,433.

	Houston	Kansas City
First downs	18	25
Rushes-yards	26-76	36-168
Passing	220	198
Punt returns	2-31	1-11
Kickoff returns	4-102	6-155
Interception returns	1-102	1-0
Comp.-att.-int.	13-25-1	21-30-1
Sacked-yards lost	3-13	3-28
Punts	4-38	4-40
Fumbles-lost	2-0	0-0
Penalties-yards	7-60	9-87
Time of possession	24:53	35:07

INDIVIDUAL STATISTICS
RUSHING—Houston, Wells 10-37, D. Davis 10-12, Carr 5-26, Simmons 1-1. Kansas City, Holmes 32-134, Hall 3-22, Morton 1-12.

PASSING—Houston, Carr 13-25-1-233. Kansas City, Green 21-30-1-226.

RECEIVING—Houston, An. Johnson 4-96, Miller 3-39, Armstrong 2-55, D. Davis 1-15, Wells 1-10, Gaffney 1-9, Bradford 1-9. Kansas City, Gonzalez 8-106, Hall 5-32, Morton 4-55, Horn 2-16, Blaylock 1-12, Dunn 1-5.

MISSED FIELD GOAL ATTEMPTS—None.

INTERCEPTIONS—Houston, Coleman 1-102. Kansas City, Warfield 1-0.

KICKOFF RETURNS—Houston, Moses 4-102. Kansas City, Hall 4-133, Blaylock 1-22, Stills 1-0.

PUNT RETURNS—Houston, Moses 2-31. Kansas City, Hall 1-11.

SACKS—Houston, Peek 1, Wright 1, Wong 0.5, G. Walker 0.5. Kansas City, Fujita 1, Barber 1, Allen 1.

BRONCOS 23, CHARGERS 13
Sunday, September 26

San Diego	3	0	7	3—13
Denver	7	6	7	3—23

First Quarter
Den.—Smith 16 pass from Plummer (Elam kick), 6:45.
S.D.—FG, Kaeding 23, 12:42.

Second Quarter
Den.—FG, Elam 22, 2:36.
Den.—FG, Elam 23, 7:17.

Third Quarter
S.D.—Brees 1 run (Kaeding kick), 7:23.
Den.—Lelie 33 pass from Plummer (Elam kick), 11:31.

Fourth Quarter
S.D.—FG, Kaeding 51, :54.
Den.—FG, Elam 43, 3:48.
Attendance—74,533.

	San Diego	Denver
First downs	16	18
Rushes-yards	30-85	21-37
Passing	129	291
Punt returns	3-36	0-0
Kickoff returns	6-156	4-137
Interception returns	0-0	0-0
Comp.-att.-int.	15-30-0	25-36-0
Sacked-yards lost	4-30	1-3
Punts	6-49	4-53
Fumbles-lost	2-1	2-1
Penalties-yards	6-61	3-25
Time of possession	30:45	29:15

INDIVIDUAL STATISTICS
RUSHING—San Diego, Tomlinson 22-60, Brees 5-16, Dwight 1-4, E. Parker 1-3, Neal 1-2. Denver, Griffin 12-7, Hearst 3-13, Droughns 2-10, Lelie 2-6, Plummer 2-1.

PASSING—San Diego, Brees 14-29-0-121, Tomlinson 1-1-0-38. Denver, Plummer 25-36-0-294.

RECEIVING—San Diego, Gates 4-30, Caldwell 3-39, Tomlinson 3-10, Brees 1-38, Osgood 1-17, E. Parker 1-17, Dwight 1-8, Chatman 1-0. Denver, Smith 5-75, Putzier 5-66, Lelie 4-67, Watts 4-42, Griffin 3-23, Droughns 3-17, Carswell 1-4.

MISSED FIELD GOAL ATTEMPTS—None.

INTERCEPTIONS—None.

KICKOFF RETURNS—San Diego, Dwight 6-156. Denver, Droughns 4-137.

PUNT RETURNS—San Diego, E. Parker 3-36.

SACKS—San Diego, J. Williams 1. Denver, Kennedy 1, R. Johnson 1, Pope 1, Hayward 1.

SEAHAWKS 34, 49ERS 0
Sunday, September 26

San Francisco	0	0	0	0— 0
Seattle	17	7	10	0—34

First Quarter
Sea.—FG, J. Brown 35, 6:36.
Sea.—Alexander 1 run (J. Brown kick), 10:23.
Sea.—Alexander 3 pass from Hasselbeck (J. Brown kick), 12:32.

Second Quarter
Sea.—Alexander 1 run (J. Brown kick), 13:58.

Third Quarter
Sea.—Mili 1 pass from Hasselbeck (J. Brown kick), 4:19.
Sea.—FG, J. Brown 28, 12:51.
Attendance—66,709.

	San Francisco	Seattle
First downs	9	24
Rushes-yards	18-48	37-117
Passing	127	257
Punt returns	2-13	0-0
Kickoff returns	7-139	1-17
Interception returns	0-0	2-25
Comp.-att.-int.	19-32-2	22-32-0
Sacked-yards lost	3-26	1-6
Punts	7-42	5-41
Fumbles-lost	2-2	1-0
Penalties-yards	6-50	3-19
Time of possession	25:34	34:26

INDIVIDUAL STATISTICS
RUSHING—San Francisco, Barlow 10-22, Robertson 5-24, Jackson 2-2, Isom 1-0. Seattle, Alexander 19-52, Morris 8-42, H. Evans 6-21, K. Robinson 1-3, Strong 1-1, Dilfer 1-(minus 1), Hasselbeck 1-(minus 1).

PASSING—San Francisco, Dorsey 19-32-2-153. Seattle, Hasselbeck 21-30-0-254, Dilfer 1-2-0-9.

RECEIVING—San Francisco, Wilson 6-57, E. Johnson 5-39, Conway 3-14, Walker 2-26, Barlow 2-14, Jackson 1-3. Seattle, Jackson 7-97, Engram 4-95, Alexander 4-22, Stevens 3-22, K. Robinson 1-12, H. Evans 1-9, Morris 1-5, Mili 1-1.

MISSED FIELD GOAL ATTEMPTS—San Francisco, T. Peterson 46.

INTERCEPTIONS—Seattle, Lucas 1-25, Hamlin 1-0.

KICKOFF RETURNS—San Francisco, Robertson 4-91, Battle 2-40, Jackson 1-8. Seattle, Morris 1-17.

PUNT RETURNS—San Francisco, Battle 2-13.

SACKS—San Francisco, J. Peterson 0.5, Engelberger 0.5. Seattle, Okeafor 1, Woodard 1, R. Bernard 1.

COLTS 45, PACKERS 31
Sunday, September 26

Green Bay	14	3	7	7—31
Indianapolis	21	14	0	10—45

First Quarter
Ind.—Wayne 36 pass from Manning (Vanderjagt kick), 1:45.
G.B.—J. Walker 36 pass from Favre (Longwell kick), 6:21.
Ind.—Harrison 28 pass from Manning (Vanderjagt kick), 8:01.
G.B.—J. Walker 79 pass from Favre (Longwell kick), 8:17.
Ind.—Stokley 34 pass from Manning (Vanderjagt kick), 10:49.
Second Quarter
Ind.—Stokley 27 pass from Manning (Vanderjagt kick), 1:17.
G.B.—FG, Longwell 38, 5:26.
Ind.—Mungro 1 pass from Manning (Vanderjagt kick), 14:03.
Third Quarter
G.B.—J. Walker 12 pass from Favre (Longwell kick), 5:01.
Fourth Quarter
Ind.—FG, Vanderjagt 45, 1:26.
G.B.—Driver 27 pass from Favre (Longwell kick), 1:48.
Ind.—James 1 run (Vanderjagt kick), 13:11.
Attendance—57,280.

	Green Bay	Indianapolis
First downs	24	26
Rushes-yards	19-74	24-60
Passing	385	393
Punt returns	2-14	2-10
Kickoff returns	8-209	6-141
Interception returns	0-0	1-5
Comp.-att.-int.	34-50-1	28-40-0
Sacked-yards lost	1-9	0-0
Punts	4-42	4-43
Fumbles-lost	1-1	0-0
Penalties-yards	11-84	9-70
Time of possession	31:08	28:52

INDIVIDUAL STATISTICS
RUSHING—Green Bay, Green 17-67, Fisher 1-5, Luchey 1-2. Indianapolis, James 21-62, Manning 2-(minus 2), Rhodes 1-0.
PASSING—Green Bay, Favre 30-44-0-360, Pederson 4-6-1-34. Indianapolis, Manning 28-40-0-393.
RECEIVING—Green Bay, J. Walker 11-200, Driver 6-64, Franks 4-35, Green 4-34, Fisher 4-16, Henderson 2-20, Chatman 2-14, Ferguson 1-11. Indianapolis, Wayne 11-184, Stokley 8-110, Harrison 5-65, Pollard 2-16, James 1-17, Mungro 1-1.
MISSED FIELD GOAL ATTEMPTS—Green Bay, Longwell 52.
INTERCEPTIONS—Indianapolis, Thornton 1-5.
KICKOFF RETURNS—Green Bay, Chatman 3-89, Whitley 2-33, Henderson 2-16, Ferguson 1-71. Indianapolis, Pyatt 4-110, Mungro 2-31.
PUNT RETURNS—Green Bay, Chatman 2-14. Indianapolis, Pyatt 2-10.
SACKS—Indianapolis, Morris 1.

STEELERS 13, DOLPHINS 3
Sunday, September 26

Pittsburgh	3	0	3	7—13
Miami	0	0	0	3— 3

First Quarter
Pit.—FG, Reed 40, 6:51.
Third Quarter
Pit.—FG, Reed 51, 6:58.
Fourth Quarter
Mia.—FG, Mare 34, 1:35.
Pit.—Ward 7 pass from Roethlisberger (Reed kick), 8:44.
Attendance—72,225.

	Pittsburgh	Miami
First downs	15	13
Rushes-yards	38-153	29-52
Passing	161	117
Punt returns	2-1	2-20
Kickoff returns	2-74	3-66
Interception returns	2-10	1-0
Comp.-att.-int.	12-22-1	13-27-2
Sacked-yards lost	1-2	3-20
Punts	6-45	6-38
Fumbles-lost	0-0	5-2
Penalties-yards	11-103	6-33
Time of possession	34:11	25:49

INDIVIDUAL STATISTICS
RUSHING—Pittsburgh, Staley 22-101, Haynes 7-34, Bettis 7-12, Randle El 1-4, Roethlisberger 1-2. Miami, Henry 21-41, Gordon 4-10, Feeley 4-1.
PASSING—Pittsburgh, Roethlisberger 12-22-1-163. Miami, Feeley 13-27-2-137.
RECEIVING—Pittsburgh, Ward 9-96, Burress 2-60, Randle El 1-7. Miami, McMichael 5-51, Lee 3-16, Thompson 2-47, Chambers 2-15, Booker 1-8.
MISSED FIELD GOAL ATTEMPTS—Pittsburgh, Reed 44, 45.
INTERCEPTIONS—Pittsburgh, Polamalu 1-10, Townsend 1-0. Miami, Surtain 1-0.
KICKOFF RETURNS—Pittsburgh, Randle El 2-74. Miami, Welker 3-66.
PUNT RETURNS—Pittsburgh, Randle El 2-1. Miami, Welker 2-20.
SACKS—Pittsburgh, Porter 1, Townsend 1, Team 1. Miami, Zgonina 1.

RAIDERS 30, BUCCANEERS 20
Sunday, September 26

Tampa Bay	3	3	0	14—20
Oakland	3	10	17	0—30

First Quarter
T.B.—FG, Gramatica 36, 3:59.
Oak.—FG, Janikowski 23, 9:24.
Second Quarter
Oak.—FG, Janikowski 40, 3:12.
T.B.—FG, Gramatica 30, 5:07.
Oak.—Curry 19 pass from Collins (Janikowski kick), 13:44.
Third Quarter
Oak.—FG, Janikowski 39, 3:55.
Oak.—Buchanon 32 interception return (Janikowski kick), 5:12.
Oak.—Wheatley 2 run (Janikowski kick), 11:18.
Fourth Quarter
T.B.—Brown 16 pass from B. Johnson (pass failed), 4:15.
T.B.—Schroeder 41 pass from B. Johnson (Dilger pass from B. Johnson), 13:08.
Attendance—60,874.

	Tampa Bay	Oakland
First downs	19	23
Rushes-yards	22-92	31-173
Passing	297	226
Punt returns	0-0	2-4
Kickoff returns	6-144	4-145
Interception returns	1-16	1-32
Comp.-att.-int.	22-36-1	18-31-1
Sacked-yards lost	2-12	1-12
Punts	4-44	2-50
Fumbles-lost	1-0	1-1
Penalties-yards	8-56	11-74
Time of possession	29:25	30:35

INDIVIDUAL STATISTICS
RUSHING—Tampa Bay, Alstott 12-65, Garner 6-11, B. Johnson 3-13, J. White 1-3. Oakland, Wheatley 18-102, Zereoue 6-41, Fargas 6-28, Gannon 1-2.
PASSING—Tampa Bay, B. Johnson 22-36-1-309. Oakland, Collins 16-27-1-228, Gannon 2-4-0-10.
RECEIVING—Tampa Bay, Schroeder 4-126, Brown 4-41, Alstott 4-30, Clayton 2-35, Garner 2-34, Dilger 2-14, J. White 1-12, Lee 1-11, Coleman 1-4, Moore 1-2. Oakland, Porter 5-84, Whitted 2-35, Rice 2-27, Redmond 2-18, Gabriel 1-30, Curry 1-19, Zereoue 1-9, C. Anderson 1-8, Jolley 1-4, Wheatley 1-3, Crockett 1-1.
MISSED FIELD GOAL ATTEMPTS—Tampa Bay, Gramatica 44. Oakland, Janikowski 46.
INTERCEPTIONS—Tampa Bay, Kelly 1-16. Oakland, Buchanon 1-32.
KICKOFF RETURNS—Tampa Bay, Cox 5-128, Schroeder 1-16. Oakland, Gabriel 4-145.
PUNT RETURNS—Oakland, Buchanon 2-4.
SACKS—Tampa Bay, Rice 1. Oakland, C. Woodson 1, Gbaja-Biamila 1.

COWBOYS 21, REDSKINS 18
Monday, September 27

Dallas	7	0	7	7—21
Washington	0	3	7	8—18

First Quarter
Dal.—George 1 run (Cundiff kick), 10:59.
Second Quarter
Was.—FG, Hall 19, 14:53.
Third Quarter
Dal.—Witten 10 pass from Testaverde (Cundiff kick), 6:13.
Was.—Gardner 1 pass from Brunell (Hall kick), 14:15.

Fourth Quarter

Dal.—Glenn 26 pass from Anderson (Cundiff kick), 2:00.

Was.—Gardner 15 pass from Brunell (Jacobs pass from Brunell), 10:30.

Attendance—90,367.

	Dallas	Washington
First downs	14	21
Rushes-yards	21-50	24-94
Passing	237	290
Punt returns	8-67	3-18
Kickoff returns	4-65	3-70
Interception returns	0-0	0-0
Comp.-att.-int.	15-30-0	25-43-0
Sacked-yards lost	1-3	5-35
Punts	8-39	8-45
Fumbles-lost	1-0	2-0

	Dallas	Washington
Penalties-yards	5-40	7-87
Time of possession	24:51	35:09

INDIVIDUAL STATISTICS

RUSHING—Dallas, George 11-19, Anderson 4-20, Lee 4-10, Barnes 1-2, Testaverde 1-(minus 1). Washington, Portis 23-94, Brunell 1-0.

PASSING—Dallas, Testaverde 14-29-0-214, Anderson 1-1-0-26. Washington, Brunell 25-43-0-325.

RECEIVING—Dallas, Bryant 3-63, Glenn 3-56, Witten 3-22, Anderson 2-41, Barnes 2-26, K. Johnson 1-23, Campbell 1-9. Washington, Gardner 10-167, Coles 5-42, Thrash 4-47, Portis 3-37, Cooley 2-22, Royal 1-10.

MISSED FIELD GOAL ATTEMPTS—None.

INTERCEPTIONS—None.

KICKOFF RETURNS—Dallas, Reeves 2-41, Lee 2-24. Washington, Morton 3-70.

PUNT RETURNS—Dallas, Ward 8-67. Washington, Morton 3-18.

SACKS—Dallas, Dixon 2, Ellis 2, Glover 1. Washington, Wynn 1.

WEEK 4

AMERICAN FOOTBALL CONFERENCE

EAST DIVISION

	W	L	T	Pct.	PF	PA
New England	3	0	0	1.000	81	53
N.Y. Jets	3	0	0	1.000	82	61
Buffalo	0	3	0	.000	37	57
Miami	0	4	0	.000	32	63

NORTH DIVISION

	W	L	T	Pct.	PF	PA
Pittsburgh	3	1	0	.750	78	71
Baltimore	2	2	0	.500	80	69
Cleveland	2	2	0	.500	59	62
Cincinnati	1	3	0	.250	66	95

SOUTH DIVISION

	W	L	T	Pct.	PF	PA
Indianapolis	3	1	0	.750	124	92
Jacksonville	3	1	0	.750	52	52
Houston	2	2	0	.500	90	93
Tennessee	1	3	0	.250	63	91

WEST DIVISION

	W	L	T	Pct.	PF	PA
Denver	3	1	0	.750	79	57
Oakland	2	2	0	.500	81	84
San Diego	2	2	0	.500	106	94
Kansas City	1	3	0	.250	89	110

NATIONAL FOOTBALL CONFERENCE

EAST DIVISION

	W	L	T	Pct.	PF	PA
Philadelphia	4	0	0	1.000	107	55
N.Y. Giants	3	1	0	.750	78	62
Dallas	2	1	0	.667	57	65
Washington	1	3	0	.250	61	68

NORTH DIVISION

	W	L	T	Pct.	PF	PA
Detroit	2	1	0	.667	61	62
Minnesota	2	1	0	.667	78	66
Chicago	1	3	0	.250	68	76
Green Bay	1	3	0	.250	72	94

SOUTH DIVISION

	W	L	T	Pct.	PF	PA
Atlanta	4	0	0	1.000	88	49
New Orleans	2	2	0	.500	75	107
Carolina	1	2	0	.333	52	68
Tampa Bay	0	4	0	.000	49	72

WEST DIVISION

	W	L	T	Pct.	PF	PA
Seattle	3	0	0	1.000	65	13
St. Louis	2	2	0	.500	83	86
Arizona	1	3	0	.250	59	56
San Francisco	0	4	0	.000	60	109

TOP PERFORMANCES

100-YARD RUSHING GAMES

Player, Team & Opponent	Att.	Yds.	TD
Tiki Barber, NYG at G.B.	23	182	1
LaDainian Tomlinson, S.D. vs. Ten.	17	147	1
Emmitt Smith, Ariz. vs. N.O.	21	127	1
Priest Holmes, K.C. at Bal.	33	125	2
Rudi Johnson, Cin. at Pit.	24	123	1
Duce Staley, Pit. vs. Cin.	25	123	1
Marshall Faulk, St.L. at S.F.	23	121	0
Brian Westbrook, Phi. at Chi.	22	119	0
Amos Zereoue, Oak. at Hou.	14	117	2
Curtis Martin, NYJ at Mia.	24	110	1
Jonathan Wells, Hou. vs. Oak.	26	105	1

300-YARD PASSING GAMES

Player, Team & Opponent	Att.	Cmp.	Yds.	TD	Int.
Byron Leftwich, Jac. vs. Ind.	41	29	318	1	0
Jake Delhomme, Car. vs. Atl.	38	23	308	0	2

100-YARD RECEIVING GAMES

Player, Team & Opponent	Rec.	Yds.	TD
Eric Moulds, Buf. vs. N.E.	10	126	1
Laveranues Coles, Was. at Cle.	7	122	0
David Terrell, Chi. vs. Phi.	9	116	0
Andre Johnson, Hou. vs. Oak.	6	115	1
Muhsin Muhammad, Car. vs. Atl.	7	114	0
Eric Johnson, S.F. vs. St.L.	10	113	0
David Patten, N.E. at Buf.	5	113	1
Reche Caldwell, S.D. vs. Ten.	3	110	1
Terrell Owens, Phi. at Chi.	8	110	1
Drew Bennett, Ten. at S.D.	9	109	0
Isaac Bruce, St.L. at S.F.	7	100	0

RESULTS

SUNDAY, OCTOBER 3
CLEVELAND 17, Washington 13
N.Y. Giants 14, GREEN BAY 7
Philadelphia 19, CHICAGO 9
PITTSBURGH 28, Cincinnati 17
Indianapolis 24, JACKSONVILLE 17
New England 31, BUFFALO 17
HOUSTON 30, Oakland 17
N.Y. Jets 17, MIAMI 9
Atlanta 27, CAROLINA 10
Denver 16, TAMPA BAY 13
ARIZONA 34, New Orleans 10
SAN DIEGO 38, Tennessee 17
St. Louis 24, SAN FRANCISCO 14

MONDAY, OCTOBER 4
Kansas City 27, BALTIMORE 24
Open Date: Dallas, Detroit, Minnesota, Seattle

BROWNS 17, REDSKINS 13
Sunday, October 3

Washington	3	7	0	3—13
Cleveland	3	0	7	7—17

First Quarter
Was.—FG, Hall 31, 12:10.
Cle.—FG, Dawson 30, 14:42.

Second Quarter
Was.—Portis 1 run (Hall kick), 10:12.

Third Quarter
Cle.—Shea 15 pass from Garcia (Dawson kick), 2:30.

Fourth Quarter
Was.—FG, Hall 26, :08.
Cle.—Suggs 3 run (Dawson kick), 8:09.
Attendance—73,348.

	Washington	Cleveland
First downs	13	14
Rushes-yards	25-73	32-96
Passing	192	184
Punt returns	3-21	5-74
Kickoff returns	4-67	3-65
Interception returns	0-0	0-0
Comp.-att.-int.	17-32-0	14-21-0
Sacked-yards lost	0-0	3-11
Punts	7-49	7-41
Fumbles-lost	2-2	2-1
Penalties-yards	7-58	8-66
Time of possession	29:56	30:04

INDIVIDUAL STATISTICS
RUSHING—Washington, Portis 20-58, Brunell 3-9, Betts 2-6. Cleveland, Suggs 22-82, Green 4-17, Garcia 3-(minus 5), T. Smith 1-4, Frost 1-1, Andre. Davis 1-(minus 3).
PASSING—Washington, Brunell 17-32-0-192. Cleveland, Garcia 14-21-0-195.
RECEIVING—Washington, Coles 7-122, Rasby 3-29, Gardner 3-19, Portis 2-15, Thrash 2-7. Cleveland, Andre. Davis 3-93, Shea 2-28, T. Smith 2-20, Heiden 2-19, Morgan 2-18, Northcutt 2-11, Suggs 1-6.
MISSED FIELD GOAL ATTEMPTS—None.
INTERCEPTIONS—None.
KICKOFF RETURNS—Washington, Thrash 2-31, Betts 1-24, Sellers 1-12. Cleveland, De. Brown 2-55, L. Sanders 1-10.
PUNT RETURNS—Washington, Thrash 3-21. Cleveland, Northcutt 5-74.
SACKS—Washington, Evans 1, R. Warner 1, Washington 0.5, Wynn 0.5.

GIANTS 14, PACKERS 7
Sunday, October 3

N.Y. Giants	0	0	7	7—14
Green Bay	0	0	7	0— 7

Third Quarter
G.B.—J. Walker 28 pass from Favre (Longwell kick), 4:57.
NYG—Barber 52 run (Christie kick), 5:47.

Fourth Quarter
NYG—Shockey 4 pass from Warner (Christie kick), 2:53.
Attendance—70,623.

	N.Y. Giants	Green Bay
First downs	21	15
Rushes-yards	35-245	19-81
Passing	158	220
Punt returns	4-16	1-1
Kickoff returns	2-39	2-41
Interception returns	2-6	1-18
Comp.-att.-int.	20-26-1	20-36-2
Sacked-yards lost	4-29	0-0
Punts	4-49	6-38
Fumbles-lost	0-0	1-1
Penalties-yards	8-76	7-72
Time of possession	35:53	24:07

INDIVIDUAL STATISTICS
RUSHING—New York, Barber 23-182, Dayne 9-26, Warner 2-22, T. Carter 1-15. Green Bay, Green 15-58, Pederson 2-15, Chatman 1-4, Luchey 1-4.
PASSING—New York, Warner 20-26-1-187. Green Bay, Favre 12-18-1-110, Pederson 7-17-1-86, Nall 1-1-0-24.

RECEIVING—New York, Shockey 5-74, I. Hilliard 5-36, Barber 4-14, Toome 3-34, T. Carter 2-23, Finn 1-6. Green Bay, Driver 4-31, Green 3-48, J. Walker 3 37, Franks 3-21, Henderson 2-28, Fisher 2-13, Ferguson 1-24, Martin 1-9 Chatman 1-9.
MISSED FIELD GOAL ATTEMPTS—New York, Christie 49, 30, 33.
INTERCEPTIONS—New York, Cousin 1-6, Peterson 1-0. Green Bay, Sharpe 1-18.
KICKOFF RETURNS—New York, Cloud 1-23, Finn 1-16. Green Bay, Chatma 2-41.
PUNT RETURNS—New York, Jones 4-16. Green Bay, Chatman 1-1.
SACKS—Green Bay, Gbaja-Biamila 1.5, Kampman 1, Roman 1, Trulluck 0.5

EAGLES 19, BEARS 9
Sunday, October 3

Philadelphia	3	13	3	0—19
Chicago	0	3	0	6— 9

First Quarter
Phi.—FG, Akers 51, 10:00.

Second Quarter
Phi.—FG, Akers 42, 4:01.
Phi.—Owens 11 pass from McNabb (Akers kick), 8:57.
Phi.—FG, Akers 42, 13:03.
Chi.—FG, Edinger 25, 14:54.

Third Quarter
Phi.—FG, Akers 40, 10:19.

Fourth Quarter
Chi.—B. Johnson 2 pass from Quinn (run failed), 11:03.
Attendance—61,894.

	Philadelphia	Chicago
First downs	24	14
Rushes-yards	32-158	13-32
Passing	218	192
Punt returns	5-19	1-0
Kickoff returns	2-37	4-107
Interception returns	0-0	1-(-3)
Comp.-att.-int.	24-38-1	26-43-0
Sacked-yards lost	3-19	4-23
Punts	3-36	8-44
Fumbles-lost	0-0	1-1
Penalties-yards	10-73	4-36
Time of possession	37:21	22:39

INDIVIDUAL STATISTICS
RUSHING—Philadelphia, Westbrook 22-119, Levens 8-26, G. Lewis 1-1 McNabb 1-2. Chicago, T. Jones 13-32.
PASSING—Philadelphia, McNabb 24-38-1-237. Chicago, Quinn 26-43-0-21
RECEIVING—Philadelphia, Westbrook 9-63, Owens 8-110, Pinkston 2-25, Mitchell 2-21, C. Lewis 1-9, Mahe 1-6, Levens 1-3. Chicago, Terrell 9-116, Jones 6-40, Wade 4-36, B. Johnson 4-11, Clark 2-11, Lyman 1-1.
MISSED FIELD GOAL ATTEMPTS—Philadelphia, Akers 39, 45.
INTERCEPTIONS—Chicago, Vasher 1-(minus 3).
KICKOFF RETURNS—Philadelphia, Reed 2-37. Chicago, Berrian 4-107.
PUNT RETURNS—Philadelphia, Mahe 5-19. Chicago, McQuarters 1-0.
SACKS—Philadelphia, Sheppard 1, Burgess 1, H. Douglas 1, Rayburn Chicago, Green 1, A. Brown 1, Harris 0.5, T. Johnson 0.5.

STEELERS 28, BENGALS 17
Sunday, October 3

Cincinnati	7	3	7	0—17
Pittsburgh	7	7	0	14—28

First Quarter
Cin.—J. Johnson 2 pass from Palmer (Graham kick), 6:24.
Pit.—Bettis 2 run (Reed kick), 9:07.

Second Quarter
Pit.—Haynes 11 pass from Roethlisberger (Reed kick), :47.
Cin.—FG, Graham 34, 8:09.

Third Quarter
Cin.—Ru. Johnson 2 run (Graham kick), 6:25.

Fourth Quarter
Pit.—Bettis 1 run (Reed kick), 5:57.
Pit.—Polamalu 26 interception return (Reed kick), 12:57.
Attendance—62,402.

	Cincinnati	Pittsburgh
First downs	22	23
Rushes-yards	27-137	40-165
Passing	156	168
Punt returns	4-28	2-6
Kickoff returns	4-87	4-119
Interception returns	0-0	2-49
Comp.-att.-int.	20-37-2	17-25-0
Sacked-yards lost	1-8	1-6
Punts	6-36	5-45
Fumbles-lost	1-1	4-2
Penalties-yards	5-46	7-90
Time of possession	28:08	31:52

INDIVIDUAL STATISTICS

RUSHING—Cincinnati, Ru. Johnson 24-123, C. Russell 1-13, Palmer 1-1, Watson 1-0. Pittsburgh, Staley 25-123, Bettis 6-9, Roethlisberger 4-2, Haynes -15, Randle El 2-6, Ward 1-10.

PASSING—Cincinnati, Palmer 20-37-2-164. Pittsburgh, Roethlisberger 17-25-0-174.

RECEIVING—Cincinnati, Houshmandzadeh 6-53, C. Johnson 4-54, J. Johnson 3-6, Perry 2-24, Watson 2-17, Washington 1-6, R. Kelly 1-4, Stewart 1-0. Pittsburgh, Ward 6-48, Burress 4-69, Haynes 4-25, Randle El 2-24, Riemersma 1-8.

MISSED FIELD GOAL ATTEMPTS—None.

INTERCEPTIONS—Pittsburgh, Polamalu 1-26, Scott 1-23.

KICKOFF RETURNS—Cincinnati, C. Russell 2-42, Houshmandzadeh 1-25, Watson 1-20. Pittsburgh, Randle El 2-65, Colclough 2-54.

PUNT RETURNS—Cincinnati, Houshmandzadeh 4-28. Pittsburgh, Randle El 2-6.

SACKS—Cincinnati, Clemons 1. Pittsburgh, Foote 1.

COLTS 24, JAGUARS 17
Sunday, October 3

Indianapolis	7	3	7	7—24
Jacksonville	0	3	3	11—17

First Quarter
Ind.—Harrison 15 pass from Manning (Vanderjagt kick), 9:05.

Second Quarter
Ind.—FG, Vanderjagt 46, 14:20.
Jac.—FG, Scobee 48, 15:00.

Third Quarter
Jac.—FG, Scobee 42, 6:14.
Ind.—Pollard 16 pass from Manning (Vanderjagt kick), 12:06.

Fourth Quarter
Jac.—FG, Scobee 22, 2:57.
Jac.—J. Smith 40 pass from Leftwich (B. Jones pass from Leftwich), 4:23.
Ind.—James 3 run (Vanderjagt kick), 11:27.
Attendance—73,114.

	Indianapolis	Jacksonville
First downs	23	23
Rushes-yards	27-117	31-97
Passing	220	311
Punt returns	0-0	2-25
Kickoff returns	3-69	2-22
Interception returns	0-0	1-0
Comp.-att.-int.	20-29-1	29-41-0
Sacked-yards lost	0-0	1-7
Punts	3-48	1-33
Fumbles-lost	0-0	2-1
Penalties-yards	3-26	5-28
Time of possession	24:27	35:33

INDIVIDUAL STATISTICS

RUSHING—Indianapolis, James 19-83, Rhodes 5-37, Manning 3-(minus 3). Jacksonville, F. Taylor 21-68, Toefield 6-14, G. Jones 4-15.

PASSING—Indianapolis, Manning 20-29-1-220. Jacksonville, Leftwich 29-41-0-318.

RECEIVING—Indianapolis, Stokley 8-97, Harrison 4-45, Pollard 3-33, James 3-25, Wayne 2-20. Jacksonville, Wilford 6-56, Toefield 6-34, T. Edwards 4-54, J. Smith 3-59, R. Williams 3-40, F. Taylor 3-31, Wrighster 3-27, B. Jones 1-17.

MISSED FIELD GOAL ATTEMPTS—Jacksonville, Scobee 35.

INTERCEPTIONS—Jacksonville, D. Smith 1-0.

KICKOFF RETURNS—Indianapolis, Pyatt 3-69. Jacksonville, T. Edwards 1-12, Lewis 1-10.

PUNT RETURNS—Jacksonville, Lewis 2-25.

SACKS—Indianapolis, Mathis 1.

PATRIOTS 31, BILLS 17
Sunday, October 3

New England	10	7	0	14—31
Buffalo	10	7	0	0—17

First Quarter
N.E.—Dillon 15 run (Vinatieri kick), 4:49.
Buf.—FG, Lindell 33, 8:41.
N.E.—FG, Vinatieri 42, 13:20.
Buf.—McGee 98 kickoff return (Lindell kick), 13:34.

Second Quarter
Buf.—Moulds 41 pass from Bledsoe (Lindell kick), 12:17.
N.E.—Patten 30 pass from Brady (Vinatieri kick), 13:32.

Fourth Quarter
N.E.—Graham 2 pass from Brady (Vinatieri kick), 3:43.
N.E.—Seymour 68 fumble return (Vinatieri kick), 12:16.
Attendance—72,698.

	New England	Buffalo
First downs	21	18
Rushes-yards	26-99	27-123
Passing	298	214
Punt returns	1-0	2-22
Kickoff returns	4-96	5-191
Interception returns	1-21	0-0
Comp.-att.-int.	17-30-0	18-30-1
Sacked-yards lost	0-0	6-33
Punts	4-50	5-51
Fumbles-lost	2-1	2-1
Penalties-yards	10-77	11-94
Time of possession	28:43	31:17

INDIVIDUAL STATISTICS

RUSHING—New England, Dillon 19-79, Pass 5-18, Brady 2-2. Buffalo, Henry 24-98, Moorman 1-34, Reed 1-6, Bledsoe 1-(minus 15).

PASSING—New England, Brady 17-30-0-298. Buffalo, Bledsoe 18-30-1-247.

RECEIVING—New England, Patten 5-113, Givens 4-86, Dillon 3-23, Graham 2-35, Fauria 2-24, B. Johnson 1-17. Buffalo, Moulds 10-126, Evans 4-93, Aiken 2-12, Henry 1-10, Neufeld 1-6.

MISSED FIELD GOAL ATTEMPTS—None.

INTERCEPTIONS—New England, Poole 1-21.

KICKOFF RETURNS—New England, B. Johnson 4-96. Buffalo, McGee 4-176, Shelton 1-15.

PUNT RETURNS—New England, Poole 1-0. Buffalo, Clements 2-22.

SACKS—New England, Colvin 1.5, Vrabel 1, Seymour 1, Phifer 1, Wilfork 1, Bruschi 0.5.

TEXANS 30, RAIDERS 17
Sunday, October 3

Oakland	3	14	0	0—17
Houston	3	14	3	10—30

First Quarter
Hou.—FG, K. Brown 46, 11:51.
Oak.—FG, Janikowski 50, 14:18.

Second Quarter
Hou.—Sharper 16 fumble return (K. Brown kick), 3:19.
Oak.—Zereoue 55 run (Janikowski kick), 7:58.
Hou.—Wells 1 run (K. Brown kick), 11:35.
Oak.—Zereoue 3 run (Janikowski kick), 14:13.

Third Quarter
Hou.—FG, K. Brown 21, 11:57.

Fourth Quarter
Hou.—An. Johnson 15 pass from Carr (K. Brown kick), :12.
Hou.—FG, K. Brown 44, 11:41.
Attendance—70,741.

	Oakland	Houston
First downs	18	20
Rushes-yards	20-151	41-158
Passing	224	228
Punt returns	2-11	3-41
Kickoff returns	7-199	4-77
Interception returns	0-0	3-86
Comp.-att.-int.	21-38-3	14-24-0
Sacked-yards lost	1-13	0-0
Punts	3-49	3-40
Fumbles-lost	2-2	2-1
Penalties-yards	13-75	4-25
Time of possession	27:11	32:49

INDIVIDUAL STATISTICS

RUSHING—Oakland, Zereoue 14-117, Wheatley 3-27, Gabriel 1-4, Fargas 1-3, Collins 1-0. Houston, Wells 26-105, Carr 9-31, Hollings 6-22.

PASSING—Oakland, Collins 21-38-3-237. Houston, Carr 14-23-0-228, Gaffney 0-1-0-0.

RECEIVING—Oakland, Curry 5-69, C. Anderson 3-37, Porter 2-40, Gabriel 2-20, Zereoue 2-17, Jolley 2-12, Wheatley 2-2, Whitted 1-19, Rice 1-18, Crockett 1-3. Houston, An. Johnson 6-115, Gaffney 4-48, Wells 1-28, Miller 1-27, Armstrong 1-7, Hollings 1-3.

MISSED FIELD GOAL ATTEMPTS—Oakland, Janikowski 35. Houston, K. Brown 57.

INTERCEPTIONS—Houston, Robinson 2-86, Faggins 1-0.

KICKOFF RETURNS—Oakland, Gabriel 7-199. Houston, Moses 3-62, Norris 1-15.

PUNT RETURNS—Oakland, Buchanon 1-7, C. Woodson 1-4. Houston, Moses 3-41.

SACKS—Houston, Sharper 1.

JETS 17, DOLPHINS 9
Sunday, October 3

N.Y. Jets	7	3	7	0—17
Miami	0	9	0	0— 9

First Quarter
NYJ—C. Martin 1 run (Brien kick), 11:05.

Second Quarter
Mia.—FG, Mare 36, 2:07.
Mia.—FG, Mare 37, 7:20.
NYJ—FG, Brien 53, 12:50.
Mia.—FG, Mare 23, 14:55.

Third Quarter
NYJ—D. Abraham 66 interception return (Brien kick), 2:50.
Attendance—73,157.

	N.Y. Jets	Miami
First downs	16	13
Rushes-yards	31-110	21-97
Passing	125	196
Punt returns	3-26	1-8
Kickoff returns	2-52	4-90
Interception returns	2-68	1-47
Comp.-att.-int.	14-24-1	18-33-2
Sacked-yards lost	3-18	4-10
Punts	8-39	5-45
Fumbles-lost	1-0	2-2
Penalties-yards	4-35	4-30
Time of possession	32:17	27:43

INDIVIDUAL STATISTICS

RUSHING—New York, C. Martin 24-110, Pennington 6-3, McCareins 1-(minus 3). Miami, Henry 18-85, Fiedler 2-13, Morris 1-(minus 1).

PASSING—New York, Pennington 14-24-1-143. Miami, Fiedler 18-33-2-206.

RECEIVING—New York, C. Martin 4-31, Chrebet 3-48, Sowell 3-18, Moss 1-17, Baker 1-15, McCareins 1-14, Becht 1-0. Miami, McMichael 5-51, Booker 4-46, Gilmore 3-57, Henry 3-12, Lee 2-15, Thompson 1-25.

MISSED FIELD GOAL ATTEMPTS—None.

INTERCEPTIONS—New York, D. Abraham 1-66, Hobson 1-2. Miami, Freeman 1-47.

KICKOFF RETURNS—New York, Jordan 2-52. Miami, Welker 4-90.

PUNT RETURNS—New York, Moss 3-26. Miami, Welker 1-8.

SACKS—New York, J. Abraham 2, J. Ferguson 1, Barton 1. Miami, D. Bowens 1, Taylor 1, Zgonina 1.

FALCONS 27, PANTHERS 10
Sunday, October 3

Atlanta	10	3	0	14—27
Carolina	7	3	0	0—10

First Quarter
Atl.—Dunn 38 run (Feely kick), 6:32.
Car.—Foster 1 run (Kasay kick), 8:25.
Atl.—FG, Feely 47, 14:28.

Second Quarter
Atl.—FG, Feely 30, 4:50.
Car.—FG, Kasay 26, 14:22.

Fourth Quarter
Atl.—Mathis 35 interception return (Feely kick), 3:00.
Atl.—Duckett 4 run (Feely kick), 10:47.
Attendance—73,461.

	Atlanta	Carolina
First downs	20	19
Rushes-yards	40-165	21-67
Passing	148	293
Punt returns	5-59	2-1
Kickoff returns	3-43	5-76
Interception returns	2-57	0-0
Comp.-att.-int.	10-18-0	23-38-2
Sacked-yards lost	0-0	2-15
Punts	5-38	5-52
Fumbles-lost	1-0	2-1
Penalties-yards	11-106	10-91
Time of possession	32:20	27:40

INDIVIDUAL STATISTICS

RUSHING—Atlanta, Dunn 16-76, Duckett 13-63, Vick 7-35, Schaub 2-(minus 2), Griffith 1-3, White 1-(minus 10). Carolina, Foster 19-51, Delhomme 1-13, Muhammad 1-3.

PASSING—Atlanta, Vick 10-18-0-148. Carolina, Delhomme 23-38-2-308.

RECEIVING—Atlanta, Crumpler 5-85, White 2-23, P. Price 2-22, Griffith 1-18, Carolina, Muhammad 7-114, Colbert 4-40, Foster 3-54, Mangum 3-29, Hoover 2-38, Proehl 2-27, Seidman 1-6, Goings 1-0.

MISSED FIELD GOAL ATTEMPTS—None.

INTERCEPTIONS—Atlanta, Mathis 1-35, Scott 1-22.

KICKOFF RETURNS—Atlanta, Rossum 3-43. Carolina, Smart 3-34, Baker 1-23, Colbert 1-19.

PUNT RETURNS—Atlanta, Rossum 5-59. Carolina, Baker 2-1.

SACKS—Atlanta, Kerney 2.

BRONCOS 16, BUCCANEERS 13
Sunday, October 3

Denver	7	6	0	3—16
Tampa Bay	0	10	3	0—13

First Quarter
Den.—Hape 5 pass from Plummer (Elam kick), 11:59.

Second Quarter
Den.—FG, Elam 49, 1:46.
T.B.—Clayton 51 pass from B. Johnson (Gramatica kick), 4:10.
Den.—FG, Elam 50, 9:28.
T.B.—FG, Gramatica 28, 15:00.

Third Quarter
T.B.—FG, Gramatica 30, 6:45.

Fourth Quarter
Den.—FG, Elam 23, 5:57.
Attendance—65,341.

	Denver	Tampa Bay
First downs	19	12
Rushes-yards	35-111	24-110
Passing	138	159
Punt returns	2-19	1-2
Kickoff returns	2-45	5-119
Interception returns	0-0	0-0
Comp.-att.-int.	13-30-0	15-24-0
Sacked-yards lost	0-0	1-3
Punts	5-38	5-44
Fumbles-lost	1-0	2-1
Penalties-yards	7-50	9-97
Time of possession	32:49	27:11

INDIVIDUAL STATISTICS

RUSHING—Denver, Griffin 21-66, Droughns 8-20, Plummer 5-18, Watts 1-7. Tampa Bay, Pittman 15-72, J. White 4-17, Alstott 3-7, Clayton 1-7, B. Johnson 1-7.

PASSING—Denver, Plummer 13-30-0-138. Tampa Bay, B. Johnson 15-23-0-162, Simms 0-1-0-0.

RECEIVING—Denver, Smith 4-32, Putzier 2-42, Watts 2-20, Griffin 1-15, Droughns 1-12, N. Jackson 1-9, Hape 1-5, Lelie 1-3. Tampa Bay, Lee 5-47, Clayton 4-91, Alstott 3-9, Dilger 1-7, Heller 1-5, Brown 1-3.

MISSED FIELD GOAL ATTEMPTS—None.

INTERCEPTIONS—None.

KICKOFF RETURNS—Denver, Droughns 2-45. Tampa Bay, J. White 4-99, Murphy 1-20.

PUNT RETURNS—Denver, Luke 2-19. Tampa Bay, Clayton 1-2.

SACKS—Denver, Middlebrooks 1.

CARDINALS 34, SAINTS 10
Sunday, October 3

New Orleans	0	3	7	0—10
Arizona	7	7	3	17—34

First Quarter
riz.—Wilson 35 fumble return (Rackers kick), 10:44.
Second Quarter
.O.—FG, Carney 20, :04.
riz.—O. Ayanbadejo 21 pass from E. Smith (Rackers kick), 13:48.
Third Quarter
.O.—Mitchell 0 blocked punt return (Carney kick), 1:58.
riz.—FG, Rackers 26, 13:31.
Fourth Quarter
riz.—FG, Rackers 33, 5:16.
riz.—E. Smith 29 run (Rackers kick), 9:58.
riz.—Hambrick 11 run (Rackers kick), 13:06.
Attendance—28,109.

	New Orleans	Arizona
First downs	14	19
Rushes-yards	14-41	40-211
Passing	238	162
Punt returns	1-7	5-26
Kickoff returns	5-96	3-67
Interception returns	0-0	0-0
Comp.-att.-int.	24-40-0	13-19-0
Sacked-yards lost	1-4	2-16
Punts	7-48	5-34
Fumbles-lost	3-2	1-1
Penalties-yards	12-104	7-65
Time of possession	25:50	34:10

INDIVIDUAL STATISTICS
RUSHING—New Orleans, Stecker 8-23, Brooks 3-13, K. Carter 3-5. Arizona, E. Smith 21-127, Hambrick 16-79, O. Ayanbadejo 2-4, McCown 1-1.

PASSING—New Orleans, Brooks 24-40-0-242. Arizona, McCown 12-18-0-157, E. Smith 1-1-0-21.

RECEIVING—New Orleans, Stecker 6-71, Horn 6-47, Stallworth 5-45, B. Williams 4-41, M. Lewis 3-38. Arizona, Fitzgerald 3-61, F. Jones 3-36, Poole 2-22, O. Ayanbadejo 1-21, E. Smith 1-18, B. Johnson 1-7, K. Williams 1-7, Diamond 1-6.

MISSED FIELD GOAL ATTEMPTS—None.
INTERCEPTIONS—None.KICKOFF RETURNS—New Orleans, M. Lewis 5-96. Arizona, Scobey 2-52, O. Ayanbadejo 1-15.

PUNT RETURNS—New Orleans, M. Lewis 1-7. Arizona, K. Williams 5-26.
SACKS—New Orleans, Howard 1, Ch. Grant 1. Arizona, Pace 1.

CHARGERS 38, TITANS 17
Sunday, October 3

Tennessee	0	7	0	10—17
San Diego	7	14	3	14—38

First Quarter
S.D.—Tomlinson 15 run (Kaeding kick), 9:04.
Second Quarter
Ten.—Mason 4 pass from Volek (Anderson kick), :50.
S.D.—Gates 11 pass from Brees (Kaeding kick), 9:44.
S.D.—Peelle 10 pass from Brees (Kaeding kick), 14:22.
Third Quarter
S.D.—FG, Kaeding 31, 10:42.
Fourth Quarter
Ten.—FG, Anderson 24, 2:34.
Ten.—Meier 3 pass from Volek (Anderson kick), 7:56.
S.D.—Caldwell 58 pass from Brees (Kaeding kick), 8:18.
S.D.—Chatman 21 run (Kaeding kick), 11:42.
Attendance—54,006.

	Tennessee	San Diego
First downs	21	16
Rushes-yards	18-72	24-195
Passing	258	198
Punt returns	2-0	3-10
Kickoff returns	6-101	3-61
Interception returns	0-0	0-0
Comp.-att.-int.	39-58-0	16-20-0
Sacked-yards lost	3-21	1-8
Punts	6-39	4-44
Fumbles-lost	2-0	1-0
Penalties-yards	4-25	7-41
Time of possession	37:13	22:47

INDIVIDUAL STATISTICS
RUSHING—Tennessee, Brown 15-55, Volek 3-17. San Diego, Tomlinson 17-147, Chatman 3-23, Brees 3-5, Caldwell 1-20.

PASSING—Tennessee, Volek 39-58-0-279. San Diego, Brees 16-20-0-206.

RECEIVING—Tennessee, Mason 12-94, Bennett 9-109, Meier 9-31, Brown 2-15, Calico 2-13, Holcombe 2-5, Troupe 1-8, Fleming 1-4, Volek 1-0. San Diego, Gates 7-57, Caldwell 3-110, Neal 3-16, Tomlinson 2-13, Peelle 1-10.

MISSED FIELD GOAL ATTEMPTS—None.
INTERCEPTIONS—None.
KICKOFF RETURNS—Tennessee, Fleming 6-101. San Diego, Dwight 2-42, Chatman 1-19.

PUNT RETURNS—Tennessee, Mason 2-0. San Diego, E. Parker 2-4, Dwight 1-6.
SACKS—Tennessee, Long 1. San Diego, Foley 1.5, Phillips 1, Cesaire 0.5.

RAMS 24, 49ERS 14
Sunday, October 3

St. Louis	14	10	0	0—24
San Francisco	0	0	0	14—14

First Quarter
St.L.—Goodspeed 2 run (J. Wilkins kick), 13:09.
St.L.—McDonald 6 pass from Bulger (J. Wilkins kick), 13:47.
Second Quarter
St.L.—FG, J. Wilkins 20, 7:28.
St.L.—S. Jackson 2 run (J. Wilkins kick), 14:31.
Fourth Quarter
S.F.—Conway 9 pass from Rattay (pass failed), 1:27.
S.F.—Woods 18 pass from Rattay (Conway pass from Rattay), 14:44.
Attendance—66,696.

	St. Louis	San Francisco
First downs	24	26
Rushes-yards	36-174	19-58
Passing	186	274
Punt returns	1-3	2-23
Kickoff returns	3-44	5-96
Interception returns	1-10	0-0
Comp.-att.-int.	17-25-0	31-47-1
Sacked-yards lost	0-0	3-25
Punts	3-46	3-36
Fumbles-lost	0-0	2-1
Penalties-yards	5-43	5-30
Time of possession	34:22	25:38

INDIVIDUAL STATISTICS
RUSHING—St. Louis, M. Faulk 23-121, S. Jackson 10-46, Bulger 2-5, Goodspeed 1-2. San Francisco, Barlow 15-42, Jackson 3-12, Beasley 1-4.

PASSING—St. Louis, Bulger 17-25-0-186. San Francisco, Rattay 31-47-1-299.

RECEIVING—St. Louis, Bruce 7-100, Holt 3-28, Curtis 3-22, M. Faulk 1-25, McDonald 1-6, Manumaleuna 1-3, S. Jackson 1-2. San Francisco, E. Johnson 10-113, Conway 6-55, Barlow 6-48, Jackson 4-19, Wilson 3-29, Woods 2-35.

MISSED FIELD GOAL ATTEMPTS—St. Louis, J. Wilkins 33.
INTERCEPTIONS—St. Louis, Butler 1-10.
KICKOFF RETURNS—St. Louis, Furrey 2-44, M. Faulk 1-0. San Francisco, Robertson 4-78, Battle 1-18.

PUNT RETURNS—St. Louis, McDonald 1-3. San Francisco, Battle 2-23.
SACKS—St. Louis, Little 1, Polley 1, Tinoisamoa 0.5, B. Fisher 0.5.

CHIEFS 27, RAVENS 24
Monday, October 4

Kansas City	10	7	3	7—27
Baltimore	3	14	0	7—24

First Quarter
Bal.—FG, Stover 50, 3:51.
K.C.—Dunn 3 pass from Green (Tynes kick), 8:47.
K.C.—FG, Tynes 42, 14:45.
Second Quarter
Bal.—Hymes 57 pass from Boller (Stover kick), 3:10.
K.C.—Holmes 4 run (Tynes kick), 11:18.
Bal.—Sams 58 punt return (Stover kick), 13:30.
Third Quarter
K.C.—FG, Tynes 38, 6:41.
Fourth Quarter
K.C.—Holmes 1 run (Tynes kick), :03.
Bal.—J. Lewis 1 run (Stover kick), 5:46.
Attendance—69,827.

	Kansas City	Baltimore
First downs	25	13
Rushes-yards	46-178	20-80
Passing	220	127
Punt returns	0-0	2-67
Kickoff returns	2-44	6-183
Interception returns	0-0	0-0
Comp.-att.-int.	21-31-0	10-17-0
Sacked-yards lost	1-3	4-27
Punts	5-36	5-42
Fumbles-lost	0-0	1-0
Penalties-yards	10-72	6-54
Time of possession	39:43	20:17

INDIVIDUAL STATISTICS

RUSHING—Kansas City, Holmes 33-125, Blaylock 6-28, Green 5-17, Morton 1-4, Richardson 1-4. Baltimore, J. Lewis 15-73, Boller 3-3, C. Taylo 1-4, K. Johnson 1-0.

PASSING—Kansas City, Green 21-31-0-223. Baltimore, Boller 10-17-0-154

RECEIVING—Kansas City, Morton 5-64, Horn 5-60, Gonzalez 4-42, Dunn 3-23, Hall 2-24, Richardson 2-10. Baltimore, T. Jones 3-38, Hymes 2-68, K Johnson 2-28, C. Taylor 2-9, Moore 1-11.

MISSED FIELD GOAL ATTEMPTS—None.

INTERCEPTIONS—None.

KICKOFF RETURNS—Kansas City, Hall 2-44. Baltimore, Sams 6-183.

PUNT RETURNS—Baltimore, Sams 2-67.

SACKS—Kansas City, Hicks 1, Dalton 1, Sims 1, Stills 1. Baltimore Weaver 1.

WEEK 5

STANDINGS

AMERICAN FOOTBALL CONFERENCE

EAST DIVISION

	W	L	T	Pct.	PF	PA
New England	4	0	0	1.000	105	63
N.Y. Jets	4	0	0	1.000	98	75
Buffalo	0	4	0	.000	51	73
Miami	0	5	0	.000	42	87

NORTH DIVISION

	W	L	T	Pct.	PF	PA
Pittsburgh	4	1	0	.800	112	94
Baltimore	3	2	0	.600	97	79
Cleveland	2	3	0	.400	82	96
Cincinnati	1	3	0	.250	66	95

SOUTH DIVISION

	W	L	T	Pct.	PF	PA
Indianapolis	4	1	0	.800	159	106
Jacksonville	3	2	0	.600	73	86
Houston	2	3	0	.400	118	127
Tennessee	2	3	0	.400	111	118

WEST DIVISION

	W	L	T	Pct.	PF	PA
Denver	4	1	0	.800	99	74
San Diego	3	2	0	.600	140	115
Oakland	2	3	0	.400	95	119
Kansas City	1	3	0	.250	89	110

NATIONAL FOOTBALL CONFERENCE

EAST DIVISION

	W	L	T	Pct.	PF	PA
Philadelphia	4	0	0	1.000	107	55
N.Y. Giants	4	1	0	.800	104	72
Dallas	2	2	0	.500	67	91
Washington	1	4	0	.200	71	85

NORTH DIVISION

	W	L	T	Pct.	PF	PA
Detroit	3	1	0	.750	78	72
Minnesota	3	1	0	.750	112	94
Chicago	1	3	0	.250	68	76
Green Bay	1	4	0	.200	99	142

SOUTH DIVISION

	W	L	T	Pct.	PF	PA
Atlanta	4	1	0	.800	98	66
New Orleans	2	3	0	.400	92	127
Carolina	1	3	0	.250	69	88
Tampa Bay	1	4	0	.200	69	89

WEST DIVISION

	W	L	T	Pct.	PF	PA
Seattle	3	1	0	.750	92	46
St. Louis	3	2	0	.600	116	113
Arizona	1	4	0	.200	87	87
San Francisco	1	4	0	.200	91	137

TOP PERFORMANCES

100-YARD RUSHING GAMES

Player, Team & Opponent	Att.	Yds.	TD
Reuben Droughns, Den. vs. Car.	30	193	0
Shaun Alexander, Sea. vs. St.L.*	23	150	1
Chris Brown, Ten. at G.B.	27	148	2
Edgerrin James, Ind. vs. Oak.	32	136	1
Tiki Barber, NYG at Dal.	23	122	1
Duce Staley, Pit. vs. Cle.	21	117	1
Jamal Lewis, Bal. at Was.	28	116	0
Jesse Chatman, S.D. vs. Jac.	11	103	1
Deuce McAllister, N.O. vs. T.B.	21	102	0

300-YARD PASSING GAMES

Player, Team & Opponent	Att.	Cmp.	Yds.	TD	Int.
Tim Rattay, S.F. vs. Ariz.*	57	38	417	2	0
Daunte Culpepper, Min. at Hou.*	50	36	396	5	0
David Carr, Hou. vs. Min.*	42	27	372	3	0
Byron Leftwich, Jac. at S.D.	54	36	357	1	2
Brett Favre, G.B. vs. Ten.	44	24	338	2	3
Marc Bulger, St.L. at Sea.*	42	24	325	3	3
Chad Pennington, NYJ vs. Buf.	42	31	304	1	1

100-YARD RECEIVING GAMES

Player, Team & Opponent	Rec.	Yds.	TD
Andre Johnson, Hou. vs. Min.*	12	170	2
Eric Johnson, S.F. vs. Ariz.*	13	162	1
Javon Walker, G.B. vs. Ten.	8	159	1
Donald Driver, G.B. vs. Ten.	10	150	0
Marcus Robinson, Min. at Hou.*	9	150	2
Plaxico Burress, Pit. vs. Cle.	6	136	1
Marty Booker, Mia. at N.E.	7	123	0
Keary Colbert, Car. at Den.	4	115	1
Jimmy Smith, Jac. at S.D.	8	113	0
Derick Armstrong, Hou. vs. Min.*	6	101	1
Andre' Davis, Cle. at Pit.	5	101	1

*Overtime game.

RESULTS

SUNDAY, OCTOBER 10
N.Y. Giants 26, DALLAS 10
INDIANAPOLIS 35, Oakland 14
NEW ENGLAND 24, Miami 10
PITTSBURGH 34, Cleveland 23
Detroit 17, ATLANTA 10
Tampa Bay 20, NEW ORLEANS 17
Minnesota 34, HOUSTON 28 (OT)
SAN DIEGO 34, Jacksonville 21
DENVER 20, Carolina 17
N.Y. JETS 16, Buffalo 14
St. Louis 33, SEATTLE 27 (OT)
SAN FRANCISCO 31, Arizona 28 (OT)
Baltimore 17, WASHINGTON 10

MONDAY, OCTOBER 11
Tennessee 48, GREEN BAY 27
Open Date: Chicago, Cincinnati, Kansas City, Philadelphia

GIANTS 26, COWBOYS 10

Sunday, October 10

N.Y. Giants	3	3	7	13—26
Dallas	0	10	0	0—10

First Quarter
NYG—FG, Christie 31, 9:58.

Second Quarter
Dal.—K. Johnson 7 pass from Testaverde (Cundiff kick), 5:36.
Dal.—FG, Cundiff 41, 13:04.
NYG—FG, Christie 51, 14:58.

Third Quarter
NYG—Shockey 1 pass from Warner (Christie kick), 10:02.

Fourth Quarter
NYG—FG, Christie 47, 2:58.
NYG—FG, Christie 26, 8:44.
NYG—Barber 3 run (Christie kick), 12:46.
Attendance—64,018.

	N.Y. Giants	Dallas
First downs	19	16
Rushes-yards	26-125	30-166
Passing	211	112
Punt returns	2-4	2-17
Kickoff returns	3-68	7-144
Interception returns	1-9	0-0
Comp.-att.-int.	18-33-0	15-25-1
Sacked-yards lost	3-6	2-14
Punts	3-43	3-37
Fumbles-lost	2-1	2-1
Penalties-yards	9-60	11-74
Time of possession	32:12	27:48

INDIVIDUAL STATISTICS

RUSHING—New York, Barber 23-122, Cloud 2-4, Warner 1-(minus 1). Dallas, George 15-75, Anderson 9-56, Lee 4-28, Barnes 2-7.

PASSING—New York, Warner 18-33-0-217. Dallas, Testaverde 15-24-1-126, K. Johnson 0-1-0-0.

RECEIVING—New York, Toomer 6-66, Barber 5-76, Shockey 5-44, I. Hilliard 2-31. Dallas, Witten 5-35, K. Johnson 4-43, Glenn 2-24, Anderson 2-9, Bryant 1-15, Barnes 1-0.

MISSED FIELD GOAL ATTEMPTS—Dallas, Cundiff 52.

INTERCEPTIONS—New York, Peterson 1-9.

KICKOFF RETURNS—New York, Cloud 3-68. Dallas, Lee 3-58, B. Thornton 2-43, N. Jones 2-43.

PUNT RETURNS—New York, Jones 2-4. Dallas, Ward 1-11, Newman 1-6.

SACKS—New York, Wilson 1, Umenyiora 1. Dallas, Ellis 2, Glover 1.

COLTS 35, RAIDERS 14

Sunday, October 10

Oakland	0	7	0	7—14
Indianapolis	7	14	0	14—35

First Quarter
Ind.—Mungro 1 pass from Manning (Bryant kick), 6:03.

Second Quarter
Ind.—Wayne 35 pass from Manning (Bryant kick), 1:36.
Oak.—Fargas 1 run (Janikowski kick), 6:04.
Ind.—Clark 4 pass from Manning (Bryant kick), 12:30.

Fourth Quarter
Ind.—James 1 run (Bryant kick), 1:31.
Oak.—C. Anderson 21 pass from Collins (Janikowski kick), 8:46.
Ind.—David 34 interception return (Bryant kick), 13:12.
Attendance—57,230.

	Oakland	Indianapolis
First downs	18	25
Rushes-yards	13-53	40-150
Passing	216	188
Punt returns	2-13	2-21
Kickoff returns	6-120	2-56
Interception returns	1-0	3-34
Comp.-att.-int.	28-44-3	16-26-1
Sacked-yards lost	4-29	1-10
Punts	4-56	3-52
Fumbles-lost	2-0	0-0
Penalties-yards	9-59	2-20
Time of possession	24:59	35:01

INDIVIDUAL STATISTICS

RUSHING—Oakland, Zereoue 10-41, Collins 1-6, Redmond 1-5, Fargas 1-1. Indianapolis, James 32-136, Rhodes 6-14, Manning 2-0.

PASSING—Oakland, Collins 28-44-3-245. Indianapolis, Manning 16-26-1-198.

RECEIVING—Oakland, Curry 10-72, Zereoue 7-53, Porter 4-35, C. Anderson 3-38, Redmond 2-11, Gabriel 1-24, Jolley 1-12. Indianapolis, Wayne 5-69, Harrison 3-44, Stokley 3-41, James 2-19, Rhodes 1-20, Clark 1-4, Mungro 1-1.

MISSED FIELD GOAL ATTEMPTS—Indianapolis, Bryant 44.

INTERCEPTIONS—Oakland, Buchanon 1-0. Indianapolis, David 1-34, June 1-0, Harper 1-0.

KICKOFF RETURNS—Oakland, Gabriel 4-78, Curry 1-25, Francis 1-17. Indianapolis, Rhodes 1-35, Mungro 1-21.

PUNT RETURNS—Oakland, Buchanon 2-13. Indianapolis, David 2-21.

SACKS—Oakland, Washington 1. Indianapolis, Mathis 2, Reagor 1, Scioli 1.

PATRIOTS 24, DOLPHINS 10

Sunday, October 10

Miami	0	7	3	0—10
New England	7	10	7	0—24

First Quarter
N.E.—Graham 1 pass from Brady (Vinatieri kick), 8:29.

Second Quarter
N.E.—FG, Vinatieri 40, 1:27.
Mia.—Chambers 10 pass from Fiedler (Welker kick), 9:44.
N.E.—Givens 5 pass from Brady (Vinatieri kick), 14:24.

Third Quarter
N.E.—Abdullah 1 run (Vinatieri kick), 6:34.
Mia.—FG, Welker 29, 13:02.
Attendance—68,756.

	Miami	New England
First downs	18	14
Rushes-yards	26-67	38-135
Passing	228	69
Punt returns	5-41	2-13
Kickoff returns	5-101	2-40
Interception returns	1-0	1-10
Comp.-att.-int.	21-43-1	7-19-1
Sacked-yards lost	3-29	1-7
Punts	3-40	5-43
Fumbles-lost	3-1	0-0
Penalties-yards	12-86	7-55
Time of possession	31:02	28:58

INDIVIDUAL STATISTICS

RUSHING—Miami, Forsey 13-44, Henry 5-10, Morris 3-7, Fiedler 3-6, Turk 1-3, Chambers 1-(minus 3). New England, Dillon 18-94, Pass 10-37, Abdullah 5-4, Brady 4-(minus 1), Faulk 1-1.

PASSING—Miami, Fiedler 20-41-1-251, Feeley 1-2-0-6. New England, Brady 7-19-1-76.

RECEIVING—Miami, Booker 7-123, Chambers 6-37, McMichael 4-62, Thompson 2-23, Gilmore 1-11, Konrad 1-1. New England, Givens 4-33, Patten 1-28, Faulk 1-14, Graham 1-1.

MISSED FIELD GOAL ATTEMPTS—New England, Vinatieri 47.

INTERCEPTIONS—Miami, Surtain 1-0. New England, Gay 1-10.

KICKOFF RETURNS—Miami, Welker 5-101. New England, Kasper 2-40.

PUNT RETURNS—Miami, Welker 5-41. New England, Faulk 2-13.

SACKS—Miami, Romero 1. New England, Harrison 1, Wilfork 1, Seymour 1.

STEELERS 34, BROWNS 23

Sunday, October 10

Cleveland	10	3	3	7—23
Pittsburgh	14	13	7	0—34

First Quarter
Pit.—Staley 25 run (Reed kick), 1:20.
Cle.—Crocker 20 interception return (Dawson kick), 3:30.
Pit.—Roethlisberger 6 run (Reed kick), 7:21.
Cle.—FG, Dawson 24, 11:11.

Second Quarter
Pit.—FG, Reed 47, 1:30.
Pit.—Burress 37 pass from Roethlisberger (Reed kick), 7:21.
Cle.—FG, Dawson 34, 12:21.
Pit.—FG, Reed 26, 15:00.

Third Quarter
Pit.—Bettis 3 run (Reed kick), 6:34.
Cle.—FG, Dawson 46, 10:18.

Fourth Quarter

Cle.—Andre. Davis 7 pass from Garcia (Dawson kick), 6:16.
Attendance—63,609.

	Cleveland	Pittsburgh
First downs	17	21
Rushes-yards	21-98	43-170
Passing	207	231
Punt returns	2-12	4-12
Kickoff returns	6-91	6-135
Interception returns	1-20	0-0
Comp.-att.-int.	16-34-0	16-21-1
Sacked-yards lost	2-3	0-0
Punts	5-41	4-45
Fumbles-lost	1-1	1-0
Penalties-yards	8-54	6-63
Time of possession	24:17	35:43

INDIVIDUAL STATISTICS

RUSHING—Cleveland, Suggs 11-30, Garcia 6-41, Green 3-27, Northcutt 1-0. Pittsburgh, Staley 21-117, Bettis 14-34, Roethlisberger 6-13, Haynes 2-6.

PASSING—Cleveland, Garcia 16-34-0-210. Pittsburgh, Roethlisberger 16-21-1-231.

RECEIVING—Cleveland, Andre. Davis 5-101, Northcutt 4-33, Suggs 3-20, Shea 1-35, Morgan 1-15, T. Smith 1-3, Green 1-3. Pittsburgh, Burress 6-136, Ward 6-61, Randle El 2-29, Mays 1-6, Haynes 1-(minus 1).

MISSED FIELD GOAL ATTEMPTS—None.

INTERCEPTIONS—Cleveland, Crocker 1-20.

KICKOFF RETURNS—Cleveland, De. Brown 5-76, King 1-15. Pittsburgh, Colclough 4-99, Randle El 2-36.

PUNT RETURNS—Cleveland, Northcutt 2-12. Pittsburgh, Randle El 4-12.

SACKS—Pittsburgh, A. Smith 1, Kirschke 1.

LIONS 17, FALCONS 10
Sunday, October 10

Detroit	0	14	3	0—17
Atlanta	0	7	0	3—10

Second Quarter

Atl.—Dunn 2 run (Feely kick), 8:34.
Det.—Hakim 39 pass from Harrington (Hanson kick), 11:40.
Det.—Pinner 1 run (Hanson kick), 13:03.

Third Quarter

Det.—FG, Hanson 23, 14:37.

Fourth Quarter

Atl.—FG, Feely 27, 3:37.
Attendance—70,434.

	Detroit	Atlanta
First downs	15	17
Rushes-yards	33-101	27-94
Passing	126	185
Punt returns	2-2	4-66
Kickoff returns	2-34	3-55
Interception returns	1-33	0-0
Comp.-att.-int.	16-24-0	20-31-1
Sacked-yards lost	3-20	6-35
Punts	7-44	5-45
Fumbles-lost	0-0	4-3
Penalties-yards	12-80	8-74
Time of possession	32:55	27:05

INDIVIDUAL STATISTICS

RUSHING—Detroit, Pinner 23-68, Bryson 5-31, Harrington 5-2. Atlanta, Dunn 18-44, Vick 5-29, Griffith 3-21, Rossum 1-0.

PASSING—Detroit, Harrington 16-24-0-146. Atlanta, Vick 18-29-1-196, Mohr 2-2-0-24.

RECEIVING—Detroit, Hakim 3-64, Williams 3-18, Bryson 3-13, Alexander 2-15, Streets 2-7, Trejo 1-11, Pinner 1-11, FitzSimmons 1-7. Atlanta, P. Price 5-84, Dunn 5-31, Finneran 3-45, White 3-26, Crumpler 1-24, Blakley 1-13, Griffith 1-(minus 1), Feely 1-(minus 2).

MISSED FIELD GOAL ATTEMPTS—Detroit, Hanson 48.

INTERCEPTIONS—Detroit, Lewis 1-33.

KICKOFF RETURNS—Detroit, Drummond 2-34. Atlanta, Rossum 3-55.

PUNT RETURNS—Detroit, Drummond 2-2. Atlanta, Rossum 4-66.

SACKS—Detroit, S. Rogers 2, Lewis 1, Edwards 1, Hall 1, DeVries 1. Atlanta, R. Coleman 1, Beasley 1, B. Smith 1.

BUCCANEERS 20, SAINTS 17
Sunday, October 10

Tampa Bay	3	10	7	0—20
New Orleans	0	7	7	3—17

First Quarter

T.B.—FG, Gramatica 23, 7:55.

Second Quarter

N.O.—B. Williams 17 pass from Brooks (Carney kick), 7:42.
T.B.—FG, Gramatica 53, 9:52.
T.B.—Barber 18 fumble return (Gramatica kick), 10:10.

Third Quarter

T.B.—Dilger 45 pass from Griese (Gramatica kick), 3:04.
N.O.—Horn 3 pass from Brooks (Carney kick), 12:14.

Fourth Quarter

N.O.—FG, Carney 47, 11:17.
Attendance—64,900.

	Tampa Bay	New Orleans
First downs	16	16
Rushes-yards	26-81	29-145
Passing	238	106
Punt returns	1-5	3-25
Kickoff returns	4-108	5-57
Interception returns	1-10	0-0
Comp.-att.-int.	21-27-0	11-23-1
Sacked-yards lost	4-24	0-0
Punts	3-46	5-44
Fumbles-lost	2-1	2-1
Penalties-yards	11-65	8-60
Time of possession	32:13	27:47

INDIVIDUAL STATISTICS

RUSHING—Tampa Bay, Pittman 15-51, Griese 5-(minus 2), Alstott 4-8, Clayton 2-24. New Orleans, McAllister 21-102, Stecker 4-27, Brooks 3-15, Karney 1-1.

PASSING—Tampa Bay, Griese 16-19-0-194, Simms 5-8-0-68. New Orleans, Brooks 11-23-1-106.

RECEIVING—Tampa Bay, Pittman 5-29, Lee 4-76, Clayton 4-61, Dilger 3-60, Alstott 2-7, Cornella 1-12, Heller 1-11, Brown 1-6. New Orleans, Horn 4-40, Stecker 4-15, B. Williams 2-24, Stallworth 1-27.

MISSED FIELD GOAL ATTEMPTS—Tampa Bay, Gramatica 41.

INTERCEPTIONS—Tampa Bay, Kelly 1-10.

KICKOFF RETURNS—Tampa Bay, Cox 4-108. New Orleans, M. Lewis 3-37, Stecker 1-14, L. Hall 1-6.

PUNT RETURNS—Tampa Bay, Brown 1-5. New Orleans, M. Lewis 3-25.

SACKS—New Orleans, Ch. Grant 2, W. Smith 1, Howard 0.5, Sullivan 0.5.

VIKINGS 34, TEXANS 28
Sunday, October 10

Minnesota	0	14	7	7	6—34
Houston	0	0	7	21	0—28

Second Quarter

Min.—Moss 1 pass from Culpepper (M. Andersen kick), :49.
Min.—Burleson 5 pass from Culpepper (M. Andersen kick), 14:24.

Third Quarter

Min.—M. Robinson 10 pass from Culpepper (M. Andersen kick), 3:10.
Hou.—An. Johnson 2 pass from Carr (K. Brown kick), 8:08.

Fourth Quarter

Hou.—D. Davis 1 run (K. Brown kick), 3:29.
Min.—Moss 50 pass from Culpepper (M. Andersen kick), 8:11.
Hou.—Armstrong 11 pass from Carr (K. Brown kick), 11:49.
Hou.—An. Johnson 22 pass from Carr (K. Brown kick), 13:07.

Overtime

Min.—M. Robinson 50 pass from Culpepper, 7:55.
Attendance—70,718.

	Minnesota	Houston
First downs	27	19
Rushes-yards	26-122	17-52
Passing	388	358
Punt returns	2-17	4-46
Kickoff returns	5-95	5-123
Interception returns	0-0	0-0
Comp.-att.-int.	36-50-0	27-42-0
Sacked-yards lost	3-8	4-14
Punts	8-41	7-47
Fumbles-lost	0-0	0-0
Penalties-yards	10-75	11-88
Time of possession	38:27	29:28

INDIVIDUAL STATISTICS

RUSHING—Minnesota, Moore 20-92, Culpepper 6-30. Houston, D. Davis 14-31, Carr 3-21.

PASSING—Minnesota, Culpepper 36-50-0-396. Houston, Carr 27-42-0-372.

RECEIVING—Minnesota, Moore 12-90, M. Robinson 9-150, Moss 5-90, Owens 3-17, Burleson 3-16, Campbell 2-21, Ned 1-9, Howry 1-3. Houston, An. Johnson 12-170, Armstrong 6-101, D. Davis 4-31, Gaffney 2-30, Bradford 2-13, Bruener 1-27.

MISSED FIELD GOAL ATTEMPTS—None

INTERCEPTIONS—None.KICKOFF RETURNS—Minnesota, Burleson 2-51, Campbell 2-41, Moore 1-3. Houston, Moses 5-123.

PUNT RETURNS—Minnesota, Burleson 2-17. Houston, Moses 4-46.

SACKS—Minnesota, K. Williams 1, Johnstone 1, Hovan 1, S. Martin 0.5, Mixon 0.5. Houston, Smith 1, Wong 1, Babin 1.

CHARGERS 34, JAGUARS 21
Sunday, October 10

Jacksonville	0	7	0	14	—21
San Diego	14	7	6	7	—34

First Quarter
S.D.—Gates 1 pass from Brees (Kaeding kick), 4:46.
S.D.—Tomlinson 1 run (Kaeding kick), 10:57.

Second Quarter
S.D.—Gates 11 pass from Brees (Kaeding kick), 5:37.
Jac.—Fuamatu-Ma'afala 1 run (Scobee kick), 13:27.

Third Quarter
S.D.—FG, Kaeding 21, 7:45.
S.D.—FG, Kaeding 28, 14:14.

Fourth Quarter
Jac.—Leftwich 2 run (Scobee kick), 4:18.
S.D.—Chatman 41 run (Kaeding kick), 5:06.
Jac.—Hankton 7 pass from Leftwich (Scobee kick), 7:39.
Attendance—52,101.

	Jacksonville	San Diego
First downs	28	18
Rushes-yards	18-80	35-176
Passing	349	210
Punt returns	1-1	0-0
Kickoff returns	7-122	4-93
Interception returns	0-0	2-40
Comp.-att.-int.	36-54-2	17-26-0
Sacked-yards lost	3-8	1-1
Punts	3-39	4-42
Fumbles-lost	1-1	0-0
Penalties-yards	5-33	4-44
Time of possession	30:02	29:58

INDIVIDUAL STATISTICS

RUSHING—Jacksonville, F. Taylor 11-64, Fuamatu-Ma'afala 4-6, Leftwich 3-10. San Diego, Tomlinson 19-56, Chatman 11-103, Caldwell 2-13, Brees 2-1, Neal 1-3.

PASSING—Jacksonville, Leftwich 36-54-2-357. San Diego, Brees 17-26-0-211.

RECEIVING—Jacksonville, J. Smith 8-113, F. Taylor 7-44, T. Edwards 4-46, R. Williams 3-24, Toefield 3-22, Yoder 3-21, Fuamatu-Ma'afala 3-20, Wilford 2-49, B. Jones 1-10, Hankton 1-7, G. Jones 1-1. San Diego, Gates 8-93, Tomlinson 4-78, Caldwell 3-20, Chatman 1-3, Neal 1-3.

MISSED FIELD GOAL ATTEMPTS—None.

INTERCEPTIONS—San Diego, Florence 1-40, Fletcher 1-0.

KICKOFF RETURNS—Jacksonville, Lewis 7-122. San Diego, Dwight 4-93.

PUNT RETURNS—Jacksonville, Lewis 1-1.

SACKS—Jacksonville, McCray 1. San Diego, J. Williams 2, Foley 1.

BRONCOS 20, PANTHERS 17
Sunday, October 10

Carolina	0	10	7	0	—17
Denver	6	7	0	7	—20

First Quarter
Den.—FG, Elam 32, 4:17.
Den.—FG, Elam 33, 9:05.

Second Quarter
Car.—Colbert 26 pass from Delhomme (Kasay kick), 9:34.
Car.—FG, Kasay 53, 12:43.
Den.—Droughns 5 run (Elam kick), 14:08.

Third Quarter
Car.—Delhomme 1 run (Kasay kick), 9:57.

Fourth Quarter
Den.—Lelie 39 pass from Plummer (Elam kick), 5:18.
Attendance—75,072.

	Carolina	Denver
First downs	12	23
Rushes-yards	26-64	37-210
Passing	163	224
Punt returns	3-30	2-10
Kickoff returns	1-16	2-21
Interception returns	2-97	0-0
Comp.-att.-int.	13-20-0	17-29-2
Sacked-yards lost	1-10	1-2
Punts	5-48	3-51
Fumbles-lost	1-0	0-0
Penalties-yards	9-88	4-37
Time of possession	26:51	33:09

INDIVIDUAL STATISTICS

RUSHING—Carolina, Goings 12-22, Hoover 5-21, Foster 5-18, Delhomme 4-3. Denver, Droughns 30-193, Plummer 4-8, Bell 2-5, Watts 1-4.

PASSING—Carolina, Delhomme 13-20-0-173. Denver, Plummer 17-29-2-226.

RECEIVING—Carolina, Colbert 4-115, Proehl 3-35, Gaines 2-18, Foster 2-0, Muhammad 1-9, Goings 1-(minus 4). Denver, Smith 4-60, Carswell 4-45, Droughns 4-18, Lelie 2-52, K. Johnson 1-31, Watts 1-14, N. Jackson 1-6.

MISSED FIELD GOAL ATTEMPTS—Carolina, Kasay 52.

INTERCEPTIONS—Carolina, Peppers 1-97, Manning Jr. 1-0.

KICKOFF RETURNS—Carolina, Baker 1-16. Denver, Droughns 2-21.

PUNT RETURNS—Carolina, Baker 3-30. Denver, Luke 2-10.

SACKS—Carolina, Jordan 1. Denver, E. Johnson 1.

JETS 16, BILLS 14
Sunday, October 10

Buffalo	0	0	0	14	—14
N.Y. Jets	0	10	3	3	—16

Second Quarter
NYJ—Baker 1 pass from Pennington (Brien kick), 7:05.
NYJ—FG, Brien 37, 15:00.

Third Quarter
NYJ—FG, Brien 36, 9:37.

Fourth Quarter
Buf.—Campbell 16 pass from Bledsoe (Lindell kick), 6:03.
Buf.—Evans 46 pass from Bledsoe (Lindell kick), 9:02.
NYJ—FG, Brien 38, 14:02.
Attendance—77,976.

	Buffalo	N.Y. Jets
First downs	17	24
Rushes-yards	22-80	23-85
Passing	172	298
Punt returns	1-6	3-40
Kickoff returns	3-69	2-43
Interception returns	1-3	1-12
Comp.-att.-int.	16-29-1	31-42-1
Sacked-yards lost	4-25	2-6
Punts	7-37	3-30
Fumbles-lost	1-0	2-1
Penalties-yards	7-83	8-45
Time of possession	26:21	33:39

INDIVIDUAL STATISTICS

RUSHING—Buffalo, Henry 12-33, McGahee 8-42, Bledsoe 2-5. New York, C. Martin 22-77, Moss 1-8.

PASSING—Buffalo, Bledsoe 16-29-1-197. New York, Pennington 31-42-1-304.

RECEIVING—Buffalo, Moulds 6-54, Shaw 3-37, Shelton 2-22, Euhus 2-20, Evans 1-46, Campbell 1-16, McGahee 1-2. New York, Chrebet 8-90, Sowell 7-31, C. Martin 6-23, Baker 3-33, Moss 2-62, McCareins 2-32, Becht 2-20, J. Carter 1-13.

MISSED FIELD GOAL ATTEMPTS—New York, Brien 29.

INTERCEPTIONS—Buffalo, Posey 1-3. New York, Buckley 1-12.

KICKOFF RETURNS—Buffalo, McGee 3-69. New York, Jordan 2-43.

PUNT RETURNS—Buffalo, Clements 1-6. New York, Moss 2-39, McCareins 1-1.

SACKS—Buffalo, Schobel 1, Kelsay 1. New York, J. Abraham 3, Vilma 1.

RAMS 33, SEAHAWKS 27
Sunday, October 10

St. Louis	0	7	3	17	6	—33
Seattle	7	17	0	3	0	—27

First Quarter
Sea.—Alexander 1 run (J. Brown kick), 5:08.

Second Quarter

Sea.—FG, J. Brown 48, :43.
St.L.—Bulger 9 run (J. Wilkins kick), 3:31.
Sea.—Stevens 24 pass from Hasselbeck (J. Brown kick), 6:06.
Sea.—Jackson 56 pass from Hasselbeck (J. Brown kick), 14:10.

Third Quarter

St.L.—FG, J. Wilkins 39, 14:04.

Fourth Quarter

Sea.—FG, J. Brown 34, 6:18.
St.L.—Manumaleuna 8 pass from Bulger (J. Wilkins kick), 9:26.
St.L.—Curtis 41 pass from Bulger (J. Wilkins kick), 11:30.
St.L.—FG, J. Wilkins 36, 14:52.

Overtime

St.L.—McDonald 52 pass from Bulger, 3:02.
Attendance—66,940.

	St. Louis	Seattle
First downs	21	20
Rushes-yards	24-124	30-187
Passing	317	204
Punt returns	2-39	1-6
Kickoff returns	7-122	6-113
Interception returns	0-0	3-5
Comp.-att.-int.	24-42-3	20-35-0
Sacked-yards lost	2-8	1-12
Punts	4-40	5-35
Fumbles-lost	0-0	1-0
Penalties-yards	5-45	5-40
Time of possession	31:24	31:38

INDIVIDUAL STATISTIC

RUSHING—St. Louis, M. Faulk 15-51, S. Jackson 5-64, Bulger 4-9. Seattle, Alexander 23-150, Strong 3-19, Hasselbeck 2-13, Morris 2-5.

PASSING—St. Louis, Bulger 24-42-3-325. Seattle, Hasselbeck 20-35-0-216.

RECEIVING—St. Louis, Bruce 6-78, Holt 5-53, Manumaleuna 3-33, McDonald 2-76, Curtis 2-45, S. Jackson 2-11, Looker 1-16, Cleeland 1-5, M. Faulk 1-4, Goodspeed 1-4. Seattle, Jackson 5-91, K. Robinson 5-59, Stevens 3-35, Strong 3-5, Mili 2-20, Alexander 1-4, Engram 1-2.

MISSED FIELD GOAL ATTEMPTS—Seattle, J. Brown 43.

INTERCEPTIONS—Seattle, Lucas 2-0, Trufant 1-5.

KICKOFF RETURNS—St. Louis, Harris 7-122. Seattle, Morris 5-95, Carter 1-18.

PUNT RETURNS—St. Louis, McDonald 2-39. Seattle, Engram 1-6.

SACKS—St. Louis, Little 1. Seattle, Okeafor 2.

49ERS 31, CARDINALS 28

Sunday, October 10

Arizona	0	14	0	14	0—28
San Francisco	0	6	6	16	3—31

Second Quarter

Ariz.—F. Jones 16 pass from McCown (Rackers kick), :06.
S.F.—FG, T. Peterson 37, 6:03.
Ariz.—Hambrick 2 pass from McCown (Rackers kick), 13:04.
S.F.—FG, T. Peterson 42, 14:44.

Third Quarter

S.F.—Battle 71 punt return (pass failed), 3:28.

Fourth Quarter

Ariz.—E. Smith 10 run (Rackers kick), 3:13.
Ariz.—Fitzgerald 24 pass from McCown (Rackers kick), 6:41.
S.F.—E. Johnson 6 pass from Rattay (Rattay run), 10:25.
S.F.—Lloyd 23 pass from Rattay (Lloyd pass from Rattay), 13:53.

Overtime

S.F.—FG, T. Peterson 32, 3:23.
Attendance—62,836.

	Arizona	San Francisco
First downs	19	28
Rushes-yards	29-103	19-57
Passing	217	391
Punt returns	4-36	4-88
Kickoff returns	6-100	5-63
Interception returns	0-0	1-1
Comp.-att.-int.	19-34-1	38-57-0
Sacked-yards lost	2-14	5-26
Punts	8-43	6-42
Fumbles-lost	1-0	4-2
Penalties-yards	8-60	11-85
Time of possession	30:49	32:34

INDIVIDUAL STATISTICS

RUSHING—Arizona, E. Smith 16-63, Hambrick 10-29, McCown 3-11. San Francisco, Barlow 14-34, Rattay 3-14, Robertson 2-9.

PASSING—Arizona, McCown 19-34-1-231. San Francisco, Rattay 38-57-0-417.

RECEIVING—Arizona, Fitzgerald 5-94, K. Williams 4-38, B. Johnson 3-45, F. Jones 2-20, Hambrick 2-11, Croom 1-8, Diamond 1-8, O. Ayanbadejo 1-7. San Francisco, E. Johnson 13-162, Lloyd 5-56, Conway 5-56, Wilson 4-45, Walker 3-41, Robertson 3-24, Barlow 3-23, Jackson 1-8, Battle 1-2.

MISSED FIELD GOAL ATTEMPTS—None.

INTERCEPTIONS—San Francisco, Winborn 1-1.

KICKOFF RETURNS—Arizona, Croom 3-60, O. Ayanbadejo 1-21, Edwards 1-13, Hayes 1-6. San Francisco, Wilson 4-49, Jackson 1-14.

PUNT RETURNS—Arizona, K. Williams 4-36. San Francisco, Battle 4-88.

SACKS—Arizona, Berry 2, Pace 2, Dockett 1. San Francisco, Ulbrich 1, Carpenter 1.

RAVENS 17, REDSKINS 10

Sunday, October 10

Baltimore	0	0	14	3—17
Washington	0	10	0	0—10

Second Quarter

Was.—FG, Hall 26, 9:18.
Was.—Cooley 7 pass from Brunell (Hall kick), 14:34.

Third Quarter

Bal.—Reed 22 fumble return (Stover kick), 6:08.
Bal.—Sams 78 punt return (Stover kick), 8:20.

Fourth Quarter

Bal.—FG, Stover 33, 3:11.
Attendance—90,287.

	Baltimore	Washington
First downs	15	9
Rushes-yards	43-156	26-52
Passing	76	55
Punt returns	5-101	2-17
Kickoff returns	3-51	2-29
Interception returns	1-23	3-51
Comp.-att.-int.	9-18-3	13-29-1
Sacked-yards lost	2-5	3-28
Punts	6-41	9-38
Fumbles-lost	0-0	2-1
Penalties-yards	5-53	2-22
Time of possession	32:05	27:55

INDIVIDUAL STATISTICS

RUSHING—Baltimore, J. Lewis 28-116, C. Taylor 7-43, Boller 7-(minus 6), Ricard 1-3. Washington, Portis 25-53, Betts 1-(minus 1).

PASSING—Baltimore, Boller 9-18-3-81. Washington, Brunell 13-29-1-83.

RECEIVING—Baltimore, Hymes 2-8, Wilcox 2-9, Moore 2-9, T. Jones 2-8, K. Johnson 1-21. Washington, Portis 4-16, Coles 3-25, Jacobs 2-18, Cooley 2-12, Gardner 1-9, Betts 1-3.

MISSED FIELD GOAL ATTEMPTS—None.

INTERCEPTIONS—Baltimore, Sanders 1-23. Washington, Franz 1-22, Smoot 1-17, Springs 1-12.

KICKOFF RETURNS—Baltimore, Sams 3-51. Washington, Morton 1-24, Molinaro 1-5.

PUNT RETURNS—Baltimore, Sams 5-101. Washington, Morton 2-17.

SACKS—Baltimore, Suggs 2, Reed 1. Washington, Pierce 1, Springs 1.

TITANS 48, PACKERS 27

Monday, October 11

Tennessee	17	10	7	14—48
Green Bay	3	10	0	14—27

First Quarter

Ten.—Brown 37 run (Anderson kick), 1:29.
Ten.—Brown 29 run (Anderson kick), 5:15.
Ten.—FG, Anderson 36, 8:55.
G.B.—FG, Longwell 39, 13:47.

Second Quarter

Ten.—Fleming 14 pass from McNair (Anderson kick), 5:33.
G.B.—Franks 1 pass from Favre (Longwell kick), 8:33.
Ten.—FG, Anderson 38, 13:14.
G.B.—FG, Longwell 53, 14:58.

Third Quarter

Ten.—Berlin 11 pass from McNair (Anderson kick), 7:00.

Fourth Quarter

Ten.—Mason 26 pass from Bennett (Anderson kick), 1:18.

G.B.—Franks 11 pass from Favre (Longwell kick), 9:16.

Ten.—A. Smith 15 run (Anderson kick), 12:26.

G.B.—J. Walker 1 pass from Nall (Longwell kick), 13:59.

Attendance—70,420.

	Tennessee	Green Bay
First downs	23	22
Rushes-yards	44-224	11-35
Passing	232	402
Punt returns	1-7	2-1
Kickoff returns	5-76	9-172
Interception returns	3-44	0-0
Comp.-att.-int.	16-27-0	31-52-3
Sacked-yards lost	0-0	0-0
Punts	4-38	2-34
Fumbles-lost	1-0	4-3
Penalties-yards	12-105	3-15
Time of possession	38:00	22:00

INDIVIDUAL STATISTICS

RUSHING—Tennessee, Brown 27-148, A. Smith 9-28, McNair 7-36, Bennett 1-12. Green Bay, Green 10-33, Favre 1-2.

PASSING—Tennessee, McNair 15-26-0-206, Bennett 1-1-0-26. Green Bay, Favre 24-44-3-338, Nall 7-8-0-64.

RECEIVING—Tennessee, Mason 4-63, Berlin 3-53, Fleming 3-38, Brown 3-24, Bennett 2-47, Holcombe 1-7. Green Bay, Driver 10-150, J. Walker 8-159, Fisher 3-22, Henderson 3-11, Chatman 2-32, Franks 2-12, Green 2-5, Ferguson 1-11.

MISSED FIELD GOAL ATTEMPTS—Tennessee, Anderson 42.

INTERCEPTIONS—Tennessee, Thompson 2-31, Ta. Williams 1-13.

KICKOFF RETURNS—Tennessee, Fleming 3-62, Holcombe 1-11, Waddell 1-3. Green Bay, Chatman 8-163, Ferguson 1-9.

PUNT RETURNS—Tennessee, Mason 1-7. Green Bay, Chatman 2-1.

SACKS—None.

WEEK 6

STANDINGS

AMERICAN FOOTBALL CONFERENCE

EAST DIVISION
	W	L	T	Pct.	PF	PA
New England	5	0	0	1.000	135	83
N.Y. Jets	5	0	0	1.000	120	89
Buffalo	1	4	0	.200	71	86
Miami	0	6	0	.000	55	107

NORTH DIVISION
	W	L	T	Pct.	PF	PA
Pittsburgh	5	1	0	.833	136	114
Baltimore	3	2	0	.600	97	79
Cleveland	3	3	0	.500	116	113
Cincinnati	1	4	0	.200	83	129

SOUTH DIVISION
	W	L	T	Pct.	PF	PA
Indianapolis	4	1	0	.800	159	106
Jacksonville	4	2	0	.667	95	102
Houston	3	3	0	.500	138	137
Tennessee	2	4	0	.333	121	138

WEST DIVISION
	W	L	T	Pct.	PF	PA
Denver	5	1	0	.833	130	77
San Diego	3	3	0	.500	160	136
Oakland	2	4	0	.333	98	150
Kansas City	1	4	0	.200	105	132

NATIONAL FOOTBALL CONFERENCE

EAST DIVISION
	W	L	T	Pct.	PF	PA
Philadelphia	5	0	0	1.000	137	63
N.Y. Giants	4	1	0	.800	104	72
Dallas	2	3	0	.400	87	115
Washington	2	4	0	.333	84	95

NORTH DIVISION
	W	L	T	Pct.	PF	PA
Minnesota	4	1	0	.800	150	125
Detroit	3	2	0	.600	88	110
Green Bay	2	4	0	.333	137	152
Chicago	1	4	0	.200	78	89

SOUTH DIVISION
	W	L	T	Pct.	PF	PA
Atlanta	5	1	0	.833	119	86
New Orleans	2	4	0	.333	123	165
Carolina	1	4	0	.200	77	118
Tampa Bay	1	5	0	.167	90	117

WEST DIVISION
	W	L	T	Pct.	PF	PA
St. Louis	4	2	0	.667	144	134
Seattle	3	2	0	.600	112	76
Arizona	1	4	0	.200	87	87
San Francisco	1	5	0	.167	105	159

TOP PERFORMANCES

100-YARD RUSHING GAMES
Player, Team & Opponent	Att.	Yds.	TD
Reuben Droughns, Den. at Oak.	38	176	1
Clinton Portis, Was. at Chi.	36	171	0
William Green, Cle. vs. Cin.	25	115	0
Curtis Martin, NYJ vs. S.F.	25	111	2
Willis McGahee, Buf. vs. Mia.	26	111	0
Mewelde Moore, Min. at N.O.	15	109	0
Corey Dillon, N.E. vs. Sea.	23	105	2

300-YARD PASSING GAMES
Player, Team & Opponent	Att.	Cmp.	Yds.	TD	Int.
Daunte Culpepper, Min. at N.O.	37	26	425	5	2
Matt Hasselbeck, Sea. at N.E.	50	27	349	0	2
Trent Green, K.C. at Jac.	33	23	315	2	1
Jeff Garcia, Cle. vs. Cin.	23	16	310	4	2

100-YARD RECEIVING GAMES
Player, Team & Opponent	Rec.	Yds.	TD
Koren Robinson, Sea. at N.E.	9	150	0
Michael Clayton, T.B. at St.L.	8	142	0
Terry Glenn, Dal. vs. Pit.	7	140	0
Nate Burleson, Min. at N.O.	6	134	0
Torry Holt, St.L. vs. T.B.	6	124	2
Terrell Owens, Phi. vs. Car.	4	123	0
Johnnie Morton, K.C. at Jac.	7	111	0
Donald Driver, G.B. at Det.	9	110	2
Lee Suggs, Cle. vs. Cin.	5	100	1

RESULTS

SUNDAY, OCTOBER 17
Green Bay 38, DETROIT 10
BUFFALO 20, Miami 13
PHILADELPHIA 30, Carolina 8
ATLANTA 21, San Diego 20
CLEVELAND 34, Cincinnati 17
Washington 13, CHICAGO 10
N.Y. JETS 22, San Francisco 14
NEW ENGLAND 30, Seattle 20
JACKSONVILLE 22, Kansas City 16
Houston 20, TENNESSEE 10
Pittsburgh 24, DALLAS 20
Denver 31, OAKLAND 3
Minnesota 38, NEW ORLEANS 31

MONDAY, OCTOBER 18
ST. LOUIS 28, Tampa Bay 21
Open Date: Arizona, Baltimore, Indianapolis, N.Y. Giants

PACKERS 38, LIONS 10
Sunday, October 17

Green Bay	7	10	14	7—38
Detroit	7	3	0	0—10

First Quarter
G.B.—Driver 7 pass from Favre (Longwell kick), 8:12.
Det.—Hakim 28 pass from Harrington (Hanson kick), 11:13.

Second Quarter
G.B.—Fisher 13 pass from Favre (Longwell kick), 5:50.
Det.—FG, Hanson 48, 10:19.
G.B.—FG, Longwell 50, 15:00.

Third Quarter
G.B.—Sharper 36 interception return (Longwell kick), 4:08.
G.B.—Davenport 13 run (Longwell kick), 11:32.

Fourth Quarter
G.B.—Driver 20 pass from Green (Longwell kick), 4:59.
Attendance—62,938.

	Green Bay	Detroit
First downs	28	5
Rushes-yards	39-157	16-33
Passing	277	92
Punt returns	3-32	2-48
Kickoff returns	1-16	6-182
Interception returns	1-36	
Comp.-att.-int.	26-39-0	12-23-1
Sacked-yards lost	0-0	1-9
Punts	5-43	7-43
Fumbles-lost	0-0	1-0
Penalties-yards	3-15	2-20
Time of possession	39:41	20:19

INDIVIDUAL STATISTICS
RUSHING—Green Bay, Green 21-81, Davenport 10-62, Fisher 4-11, Luchey 2-5, Favre 2-(minus 2). Detroit, Pinner 6-7, Harrington 4-12, Bryson 3-6, Jones 2-5, Swinton 1-3.
PASSING—Green Bay, Favre 25-38-0-257, Green 1-1-0-20. Detroit, Harrington 12-23-1-101.
RECEIVING—Green Bay, Driver 9-110, Chatman 5-50, Franks 3-19, Green 3-3, J. Walker 2-62, Fisher 2-30, Henderson 2-3. Detroit, Hakim 4-49, Bryson 3-4, Pinner 2-29, Streets 2-15, Alexander 1-4.
MISSED FIELD GOAL ATTEMPTS—None.
INTERCEPTIONS—Green Bay, Sharper 1-36.
KICKOFF RETURNS—Green Bay, Davenport 1-16. Detroit, Drummond 6-182.
PUNT RETURNS—Green Bay, Chatman 3-32. Detroit, Drummond 2-48.
SACKS—Green Bay, Barnett 1.

BILLS 20, DOLPHINS 13
Sunday, October 17

Miami	0	10	0	3—13
Buffalo	7	0	10	3—20

First Quarter
Buf.—Spikes 11 interception return (Lindell kick), 6:45.

Second Quarter
Mia.—FG, Bryant 47, 2:11.
Mia.—Thompson 24 pass from Fiedler (Bryant kick), 14:08.

Third Quarter
Buf.—FG, Lindell 43, 3:42.
Buf.—Campbell 5 pass from Bledsoe (Lindell kick), 7:17.

Fourth Quarter
Mia.—FG, Bryant 28, :03.
Buf.—FG, Lindell 20, 7:03.
Attendance—72,714.

	Miami	Buffalo
First downs	14	18
Rushes-yards	25-111	31-137
Passing	101	204
Punt returns	1-5	1-7
Kickoff returns	4-80	4-73
Interception returns	0-0	1-11
Comp.-att.-int.	12-23-1	15-28-0
Sacked-yards lost	5-35	1-8
Punts	5-37	3-53
Fumbles-lost	4-0	0-0
Penalties-yards	3-21	7-60
Time of possession	28:00	32:00

INDIVIDUAL STATISTICS
RUSHING—Miami, Morris 18-91, Forsey 5-7, Fiedler 1-10, Chambers 1-3. Buffalo, McGahee 26-111, Burns 4-22, Moulds 1-4. PASSING—Miami, Fiedler 12-23-1-136. Buffalo, Bledsoe 15-28-0-212.
RECEIVING—Miami, McMichael 3-34, Chambers 3-23, Morris 2-28, Thompson 1-24, Lee 1-14, Booker 1-10, Konrad 1-3. Buffalo, Moulds 5-99, Campbell 4-36, McGahee 3-31, Evans 2-32, Reed 1-14.
MISSED FIELD GOAL ATTEMPTS—Buffalo, Lindell 43.
INTERCEPTIONS—Buffalo, Spikes 1-11.
KICKOFF RETURNS—Miami, Welker 4-80. Buffalo, McGee 2-47, Fletcher 1-23, Neufeld 1-3.
PUNT RETURNS—Miami, Welker 1-5. Buffalo, Clements 1-7.
SACKS—Miami, D. Bowens 1. Buffalo, Schobel 2.5, Edwards 2, P. Williams 0.5.

EAGLES 30, PANTHERS 8
Sunday, October 17

Carolina	0	0	0	8—8
Philadelphia	10	3	10	7—30

First Quarter
Phi.—FG, Akers 48, 2:35.
Phi.—Levens 1 run (Akers kick), 11:20.

Second Quarter
Phi.—FG, Akers 34, 10:45.

Third Quarter
Phi.—FG, Akers 43, 6:34.
Phi.—Sheppard 64 interception return (Akers kick), 10:28.

Fourth Quarter
Car.—Muhammad 2 pass from Delhomme (Colbert pass from Delhomme), 12:12.
Phi.—Westbrook 42 run (Akers kick), 12:52.
Attendance—67,707.

	Carolina	Philadelphia
First downs	21	10
Rushes-yards	31-158	20-81
Passing	186	202
Punt returns	1-0	0-0
Kickoff returns	5-92	1-66
Interception returns	1-0	4-84
Comp.-att.-int.	24-42-4	14-26-1
Sacked-yards lost	2-19	1-7
Punts	6-35	4-41
Fumbles-lost	0-0	0-0
Penalties-yards	8-45	4-38
Time of possession	38:30	21:30

INDIVIDUAL STATISTICS
RUSHING—Carolina, Davis 15-66, Hoover 11-63, Goings 4-27, Delhomme 1-2. Philadelphia, Westbrook 13-64, Levens 4-11, McNabb 3-6.
PASSING—Carolina, Delhomme 24-42-4-205. Philadelphia, McNabb 14-26-1-209.
RECEIVING—Carolina, Muhammad 6-48, Goings 5-40, Mangum 4-28, Colbert 2-39, Proehl 2-17, Hoover 2-7, Seidman 1-14, Davis 1-10, Gaines 1-2. Philadelphia, Owens 4-123, Westbrook 4-26, Pinkston 3-22, Mahe 1-24, G. Lewis 1-9, C. Lewis 1-5.
MISSED FIELD GOAL ATTEMPTS—None.
INTERCEPTIONS—Carolina, Manning Jr. 1-0. Philadelphia, Sheppard 2-64, Hood 1-20, Dh. Jones 1-0.
KICKOFF RETURNS—Carolina, Broussard 3-54, Proehl 1-26, Seidman 1-12. Philadelphia, Reed 1-66.
PUNT RETURNS—Carolina, Broussard 1-0.
SACKS—Carolina, Buckner 0.5, Rucker 0.5. Philadelphia, Dawkins 1, Rayburn 1.

FALCONS 21, CHARGERS 20
Sunday, October 17

San Diego	0	14	3	3—20
Atlanta	0	7	0	14—21

Second Quarter
Atl.—Crumpler 19 pass from Vick (Feely kick), 4:36.
S.D.—Tomlinson 1 run (Kaeding kick), 13:42.
S.D.—E. Parker 17 pass from Brees (Kaeding kick), 14:42.

Third Quarter
S.D.—FG, Kaeding 53, 9:50.

Fourth Quarter
Atl.—Vick 14 run (Feely kick), 1:51.
Atl.—White 32 pass from Vick (Feely kick), 4:48.
S.D.—FG, Kaeding 28, 8:59.
Attendance—70,187.

	San Diego	Atlanta
First downs	18	15
Rushes-yards	31-95	25-93
Passing	223	206
Punt returns	0-0	1-17
Kickoff returns	4-103	4-58
Interception returns	1-3	1-2
Comp.-att.-int.	23-31-1	12-21-1
Sacked-yards lost	1-4	3-12
Punts	5-43	5-39
Fumbles-lost	1-0	1-1
Penalties-yards	11-69	4-26
Time of possession	36:51	23:09

INDIVIDUAL STATISTICS
RUSHING—San Diego, Tomlinson 23-64, Chatman 3-12, Dwight 2-2, Caldwell 1-12, Brees 1-4, Neal 1-1. Atlanta, Duckett 11-45, Vick 9-35, Dunn 5-13.

PASSING—San Diego, Brees 23-31-1-227. Atlanta, Vick 12-21-1-218.

RECEIVING—San Diego, Gates 6-80, E. Parker 6-76, Tomlinson 4-16, Osgood 3-37, Neal 2-1, Caldwell 1-9, Peelle 1-8. Atlanta, Crumpler 4-54, P. Price 2-67, Griffith 2-31, Finneran 2-30, White 1-32, Blakley 1-4.

MISSED FIELD GOAL ATTEMPTS—None.

INTERCEPTIONS—San Diego, Florence 1-3. Atlanta, Brooking 1-2.

KICKOFF RETURNS—San Diego, Dwight 4-103. Atlanta, Rossum 4-58.

PUNT RETURNS—Atlanta, Rossum 1-17.

SACKS—San Diego, Foley 2, Olshansky 1. Atlanta, Glymph 1.

BROWNS 34, BENGALS 17
Sunday, October 17

Cincinnati ....0 17 0 0—17
Cleveland ....7 14 3 10—34

First Quarter
Cle.—Andre. Davis 99 pass from Garcia (Dawson kick), 7:21.

Second Quarter
Cle.—Morgan 10 pass from Garcia (Dawson kick), :09.
Cin.—Kaesviharn 3 fumble return (Graham kick), 1:41.
Cin.—Schobel 6 pass from Palmer (Graham kick), 5:32.
Cin.—FG, Graham 32, 8:50.
Cle.—Shea 5 pass from Garcia (Dawson kick), 15:00.

Third Quarter
Cle.—FG, Dawson 23, 14:02.

Fourth Quarter
Cle.—Suggs 59 pass from Garcia (Dawson kick), 4:45.
Cle.—FG, Dawson 33, 12:11.
Attendance—73,263.

	Cincinnati	Cleveland
First downs	11	21
Rushes-yards	18-58	46-139
Passing	131	310
Punt returns	2-2	4-28
Kickoff returns	3-79	4-76
Interception returns	2-23	1-0
Comp.-att.-int.	20-36-1	16-23-2
Sacked-yards lost	3-17	1-0
Punts	8-42	4-36
Fumbles-lost	0-0	2-2
Penalties-yards	10-75	6-50
Time of possession	23:41	36:19

INDIVIDUAL STATISTICS
RUSHING—Cincinnati, Ru. Johnson 16-57, Perry 2-1. Cleveland, Green 25-115, Suggs 13-19, Garcia 6-1, Northcutt 1-2, T. Smith 1-2.

PASSING—Cincinnati, Palmer 20-36-1-148. Cleveland, Garcia 16-23-2-310.

RECEIVING—Cincinnati, Watson 5-28, C. Johnson 3-37, Schobel 3-17, Washington 2-18, Stewart 2-12, J. Johnson 2-6, C. Russell 1-21, Perry 1-9, Ru. Johnson 1-0. Cleveland, Suggs 5-100, Shea 3-25, Northcutt 2-59, King 2-13, Andre. Davis 1-99, Morgan 1-10, T. Smith 1-4, Green 1-0.

MISSED FIELD GOAL ATTEMPTS—Cincinnati, Graham 44.

INTERCEPTIONS—Cincinnati, James 2-23. Cleveland, Henry 1-0.

KICKOFF RETURNS—Cincinnati, C. Russell 3-79. Cleveland, De. Brown 3-67, Mustard 1-9.

PUNT RETURNS—Cincinnati, Houshmandzadeh 2-2. Cleveland, Northcutt 4-28.

SACKS—Cincinnati, Hardy 1. Cleveland, Ekuban 1, Roye 1, Warren 0.5, Rogers 0.5.

REDSKINS 13, BEARS 10
Sunday, October 17

Washington ....3 7 0 3—13
Chicago ....0 7 0 3—10

First Quarter
Was.—FG, Kimrin 41, 9:19.

Second Quarter
Was.—Gardner 18 pass from Brunell (Kimrin kick), :07.
Chi.—Azumah 70 interception return (Edinger kick), 9:24.

Fourth Quarter
Was.—FG, Kimrin 26, 3:47.
Chi.—FG, Edinger 46, 9:50.
Attendance—61,945.

	Washington	Chicago
First downs	18	9
Rushes-yards	47-218	28-126
Passing	93	34
Punt returns	2-1	7-67
Kickoff returns	3-58	4-90
Interception returns	1-45	1-70
Comp.-att.-int.	8-22-1	10-22-1
Sacked-yards lost	1-2	4-31
Punts	9-43	10-45
Fumbles-lost	0-0	0-0
Penalties-yards	5-39	7-65
Time of possession	34:01	25:59

INDIVIDUAL STATISTICS
RUSHING—Washington, Portis 36-171, Betts 6-30, Brunell 5-17. Chicago, T. Jones 24-97, Quinn 2-32, Thomas 1-1, Wade 1-(minus 4).

PASSING—Washington, Brunell 8-22-1-95. Chicago, Quinn 10-22-1-65.

RECEIVING—Washington, Coles 4-52, Gardner 2-20, Rasby 1-12, Portis 1-11. Chicago, Wade 4-17, T. Jones 2-22, Terrell 1-10, Gage 1-9, Berrian 1-6, B. Johnson 1-1.

MISSED FIELD GOAL ATTEMPTS—None.

INTERCEPTIONS—Washington, Taylor 1-45. Chicago, Azumah 1-70.

KICKOFF RETURNS—Washington, Morton 3-58. Chicago, Berrian 2-49, Azumah 2-41.

PUNT RETURNS—Washington, Morton 2-1. Chicago, McQuarters 7-58.

SACKS—Washington, Griffin 2, Springs 1, Taylor 1. Chicago, Urlacher 1.

JETS 22, 49ERS 14
Sunday, October 17

San Francisco...7 7 0 0—14
N.Y. Jets ....0 3 6 13—22

First Quarter
S.F.—Lloyd 33 pass from Rattay (T. Peterson kick), 14:35.

Second Quarter
S.F.—Barlow 2 run (T. Peterson kick), 7:37.
NYJ—FG, Brien 43, 12:48.

Third Quarter
NYJ—Jordan 17 run (run failed), 11:45.

Fourth Quarter
NYJ—C. Martin 1 run (pass failed), 3:19.
NYJ—C. Martin 9 run (Brien kick), 14:35.
Attendance—78,189.

	San Francisco	N.Y. Jets
First downs	19	22
Rushes-yards	27-99	32-152
Passing	272	222
Punt returns	1-6	4-44
Kickoff returns	4-73	3-82
Interception returns	0-0	1-14
Comp.-att.-int.	18-28-1	20-30-0
Sacked-yards lost	3-14	0-0
Punts	7-40	6-39
Fumbles-lost	3-1	0-0
Penalties-yards	7-61	4-29
Time of possession	27:44	32:16

INDIVIDUAL STATISTICS

RUSHING—San Francisco, Barlow 21-79, Beasley 3-7, Rattay 2-11, Jackson 1-2. New York, C. Martin 25-111, Pennington 4-18, Jordan 2-25, McCareins 1-(minus 2).

PASSING—San Francisco, Rattay 18-28-1-286. New York, Pennington 20-30-0-222.

RECEIVING—San Francisco, Lloyd 6-93, E. Johnson 4-24, Wilson 3-56, Battle 2-87, Beasley 1-9, Barlow 1-9, Conway 1-5, Jackson 0-3. New York, Sowell 5-31, Becht 4-47, McCareins 3-56, C. Martin 3-20, Chrebet 1-25, J. Carter 1-19, Baker 1-11, Cotchery 1-7, Jordan 1-6.

MISSED FIELD GOAL ATTEMPTS—None.

INTERCEPTIONS—New York, Vilma 1-14.

KICKOFF RETURNS—San Francisco, Robertson 4-73. New York, J. Carter 3-82.

PUNT RETURNS—San Francisco, Battle 1-6. New York, McCareins 4-44.

SACKS—New York, Ellis 1.5, J. Abraham 1, J. Ferguson 0.5.

PATRIOTS 30, SEAHAWKS 20
Sunday, October 17

Seattle	0	6	3	11—20
New England	10	10	0	10—30

First Quarter
N.E.—Dillon 1 run (Vinatieri kick), 7:16.
N.E.—FG, Vinatieri 40, 12:46.

Second Quarter
N.E.—Patten 6 pass from Brady (Vinatieri kick), 2:28.
Sea.—FG, J. Brown 33, 5:25.
N.E.—FG, Vinatieri 39, 11:53.
Sea.—FG, J. Brown 40, 14:26.

Third Quarter
Sea.—FG, J. Brown 28, 5:59.

Fourth Quarter
Sea.—Alexander 9 run (Stevens pass from Hasselbeck), 3:55.
N.E.—FG, Vinatieri 30, 8:17.
Sea.—FG, J. Brown 31, 11:59.
N.E.—Dillon 9 run (Vinatieri kick), 13:05.
Attendance—68,756.

	Seattle	New England
First downs	23	20
Rushes-yards	21-102	33-138
Passing	341	224
Punt returns	1-0	2-15
Kickoff returns	7-171	5-118
Interception returns	1-0	2-27
Comp.-att.-int.	27-50-2	19-30-1
Sacked-yards lost	3-8	1-7
Punts	3-38	2-41
Fumbles-lost	1-0	1-1
Penalties-yards	6-50	6-46
Time of possession	28:23	31:37

INDIVIDUAL STATISTICS

RUSHING—Seattle, Alexander 16-77, Strong 3-9, Morris 2-16. New England, Dillon 23-105, Faulk 6-21, Brady 3-7, Patten 1-5.

PASSING—Seattle, Hasselbeck 27-50-2-349. New England, Brady 19-30-1-231.

RECEIVING—Seattle, K. Robinson 9-150, Stevens 4-50, Engram 3-35, Strong 3-10, Jackson 2-40, Alexander 2-30, Bannister 2-10, Mili 1-17, Morris 1-7. New England, Patten 5-58, Graham 4-45, Faulk 4-37, Dillon 2-6, B. Johnson 1-48, Givens 1-17, Klecko 1-11, Abdullah 1-9.

MISSED FIELD GOAL ATTEMPTS—None.

INTERCEPTIONS—Seattle, Boulware 1-0. New England, McGinest 1-27, Law 1-0.

KICKOFF RETURNS—Seattle, Morris 7-171. New England, B. Johnson 5-118.

PUNT RETURNS—Seattle, Morris 1-0. New England, Faulk 2-15.

SACKS—Seattle, Okeafor 1. New England, Vrabel 1, J. Green 1, McGinest 0.5, Warren 0.5.

JAGUARS 22, CHIEFS 16
Sunday, October 17

Kansas City	3	0	7	6—16
Jacksonville	7	7	0	8—22

First Quarter
Jac.—Leftwich 7 run (Scobee kick), 6:26.
K.C.—FG, Tynes 31, 12:58.

Second Quarter
Jac.—F. Taylor 64 pass from Leftwich (Scobee kick), :52.

Third Quarter
K.C.—Gonzalez 24 pass from Green (Tynes kick), 4:14.

Fourth Quarter
K.C.—Holmes 28 pass from Green (kick failed), 10:15.
Jac.—Hankton 14 pass from Leftwich (R. Williams pass from Leftwich), 14:15.
Attendance—66,413.

	Kansas City	Jacksonville
First downs	19	19
Rushes-yards	21-77	23-101
Passing	273	277
Punt returns	3-6	2-27
Kickoff returns	4-60	4-67
Interception returns	0-0	1-0
Comp.-att.-int.	23-33-1	24-36-0
Sacked-yards lost	6-42	4-21
Punts	5-42	5-46
Fumbles-lost	3-0	0-0
Penalties-yards	5-30	5-46
Time of possession	30:00	30:00

INDIVIDUAL STATISTICS

RUSHING—Kansas City, Holmes 19-75, Richardson 1-1, Blaylock 1-1. Jacksonville, F. Taylor 19-66, Leftwich 3-25, G. Jones 1-10.

PASSING—Kansas City, Green 23-33-1-315. Jacksonville, Leftwich 24-36-0-298.

RECEIVING—Kansas City, Morton 7-111, Gonzalez 6-81, Holmes 4-47, Kennison 3-61, Hall 1-7, Richardson 1-6, Blaylock 1-2. Jacksonville, J. Smith 7-91, F. Taylor 3-71, T. Edwards 3-41, Hankton 3-28, Brady 3-18, Wilford 2-22, Yoder 1-25, M. Edwards 1-3, Fuamatu-Ma'afala 1-(minus 1).

MISSED FIELD GOAL ATTEMPTS—Kansas City, Tynes 42. Jacksonville, Scobee 51.

INTERCEPTIONS—Jacksonville, D. Cooper 1-0.

KICKOFF RETURNS—Kansas City, Hall 4-60. Jacksonville, Lewis 4-67.

PUNT RETURNS—Kansas City, Hall 2-6, Harts 1-0. Jacksonville, Lewis 2-27.

SACKS—Kansas City, Browning 1, Hicks 1, Dalton 1, Allen 1. Jacksonville, Stroud 2, Ayodele 1, Favors 1, Peterson 1.

TEXANS 20, TITANS 10
Sunday, October 17

Houston	3	10	0	7—20
Tennessee	0	10	0	0—10

First Quarter
Hou.—FG, K. Brown 21, 5:18.

Second Quarter
Ten.—Bennett 10 pass from McNair (Anderson kick), 2:11.
Hou.—Gaffney 20 pass from Carr (K. Brown kick), 5:48.
Ten.—FG, Anderson 40, 8:58.
Hou.—FG, K. Brown 50, 12:22.

Fourth Quarter
Hou.—Wells 4 run (K. Brown kick), 10:18.
Attendance—68,932.

	Houston	Tennessee
First downs	19	19
Rushes-yards	37-98	22-101
Passing	247	204
Punt returns	4-28	2-16
Kickoff returns	3-61	4-70
Interception returns	4-14	1-25
Comp.-att.-int.	16-26-1	19-41-4
Sacked-yards lost	2-19	1-6
Punts	5-39	6-47
Fumbles-lost	2-1	1-0
Penalties-yards	4-19	4-35
Time of possession	32:38	27:22

INDIVIDUAL STATISTICS

RUSHING—Houston, Wells 22-73, D. Davis 10-25, Carr 5-0. Tennessee, Brown 13-52, McNair 4-33, A. Smith 4-16, Holcombe 1-0.

PASSING—Houston, Carr 16-26-1-266. Tennessee, McNair 19-41-4-210.

RECEIVING—Houston, Gaffney 5-85, An. Johnson 4-66, Armstrong 3-37, Bradford 2-65, Miller 1-9, Wells 1-4. Tennessee, Mason 5-74, Bennett 5-59, Berlin 4-50, Troupe 2-12, Holcombe 1-5, Brown 1-5, A. Smith 1-5.

MISSED FIELD GOAL ATTEMPTS—None.

INTERCEPTIONS—Houston, Coleman 1-14, Robinson 1-0, Glenn 1-0, Wong 1-0. Tennessee, Woolfolk 1-25.

KICKOFF RETURNS—Houston, Moses 3-61. Tennessee, Fleming 4-70.

PUNT RETURNS—Houston, Moses 4-28. Tennessee, Mason 2-16.

SACKS—Houston, Sharper 1. Tennessee, Ta. Williams 1, Hall 1.

STEELERS 24, COWBOYS 20
Sunday, October 17

Pittsburgh	7	3	0	14—24
Dallas	7	3	10	0—20

First Quarter
Dal.—Anderson 21 run (Cundiff kick); 5:46.
Pit.—Burress 5 pass from Roethlisberger (Reed kick); 9:38.

Second Quarter
Pit.—FG, Reed 51, 10:23.
Dal.—FG, Cundiff 47, 14:45.

Third Quarter
Dal.—FG, Cundiff 39, 9:22.
Dal.—K. Johnson 22 pass from Testaverde (Cundiff kick); 12:03.

Fourth Quarter
Pit.—Tuman 7 pass from Roethlisberger (Reed kick); 3:12.
Pit.—Bettis 2 run (Reed kick); 14:30.
Attendance—64,162.

	Pittsburgh	Dallas
First downs	21	20
Rushes-yards	29-125	21-100
Passing	172	248
Punt returns	2-21	2-15
Kickoff returns	5-68	4-72
Interception returns	0-0	0-0
Comp.-att.-int.	21-25-0	23-36-0
Sacked-yards lost	3-21	5-36
Punts	5-43	4-50
Fumbles-lost	1-0	3-1
Penalties-yards	6-45	5-30
Time of possession	32:44	27:16

INDIVIDUAL STATISTICS
RUSHING—Pittsburgh, Staley 18-93, Bettis 5-8, Randle El 3-11, Roethlisberger 2-8, Kreider 1-5. Dallas, George 10-28, Anderson 6-54, Lee 2-(minus 3), K. Johnson 1-13, Ward 1-11, Glenn 1-(minus 3).
PASSING—Pittsburgh, Roethlisberger 21-25-0-193. Dallas, Testaverde 23-36-0-284.
RECEIVING—Pittsburgh, Ward 9-76, Tuman 4-21, Burress 3-48, Riemersma 2-24, Staley 2-13, Randle El 1-11. Dallas, Glenn 7-140, K. Johnson 6-61, Witten 5-39, Anderson 3-18, Bryant 1-22, George 1-4.
MISSED FIELD GOAL ATTEMPTS—None.
INTERCEPTIONS—None
KICKOFF RETURNS—Pittsburgh, I. Taylor 2-28, Randle El 2-23, Colclough 1-17. Dallas, Lee 2-37, Reeves 2-35.
PUNT RETURNS—Pittsburgh, Randle El 2-21. Dallas, Ward 2-15.
SACKS—Pittsburgh, Farrior 2, Townsend 1, Foote 1, A. Smith 1. Dallas, T. Williams 1, Glover 1, Ellis 1.

BRONCOS 31, RAIDERS 3
Sunday, October 17

Denver	7	14	10	0—31
Oakland	3	0	0	0— 3

First Quarter
Oak.—FG, Janikowski 35, 8:00.
Den.—Putzier 12 pass from Plummer (Elam kick); 14:02.

Second Quarter
Den.—Carswell 10 pass from Plummer (Elam kick); 6:34.
Den.—Lelie 31 pass from Plummer (Elam kick); 10:57.

Third Quarter
Den.—FG, Elam 33, 3:55.
Den.—Droughns 4 run (Elam kick); 12:50.
Attendance—62,507.

	Denver	Oakland
First downs	25	9
Rushes-yards	51-254	16-31
Passing	190	114
Punt returns	4-59	0-0
Kickoff returns	1-19	6-103
Interception returns	1-2	1-23
Comp.-att.-int.	11-20-1	15-31-1
Sacked-yards lost	0-0	4-22
Punts	2-32	7-48
Fumbles-lost	0-0	1-1
Penalties-yards	9-85	9-81
Time of possession	36:58	23:02

INDIVIDUAL STATISTICS
RUSHING—Denver, Droughns 38-176, Bell 6-25, Griffin 4-16, Smith 2-22, Plummer 1-15. Oakland, Zereoue 15-34, Curry 1-(minus 3).
PASSING—Denver, Plummer 11-20-1-190. Oakland, Collins 15-31-1-136.
RECEIVING—Denver, Putzier 3-52, Lelie 2-45, Carswell 2-30, Watts 1-28, Smith 1-24, Hape 1-7, Droughns 1-4. Oakland, Zereoue 4-17, Porter 3-21, C. Anderson 2-34, Curry 2-25, Gabriel 1-17, Jolley 1-14, Redmond 1-8, Crockett 1-0.
MISSED FIELD GOAL ATTEMPTS—None.
INTERCEPTIONS—Denver, K. Herndon 1-2. Oakland, M. Anderson 1-23.
KICKOFF RETURNS—Denver, Griffin 1-19. Oakland, Francis 3-59, Gabriel 3-44.
PUNT RETURNS—Denver, Luke 4-59.
SACKS—Denver, Palepoi 2, Spragan 1, Elliss 1.

VIKINGS 38, SAINTS 31
Sunday, October 17

Minnesota	7	14	10	7—38
New Orleans	0	14	7	10—31

First Quarter
Min.—Wiggins 1 pass from Culpepper (M. Andersen kick); 7:07.

Second Quarter
Min.—Moss 43 pass from Culpepper (M. Andersen kick); :57.
N.O.—McAllister 2 run (Carney kick); 8:31.
Min.—M. Robinson 16 pass from Culpepper (M. Andersen kick); 13:07.
N.O.—Horn 7 pass from Brooks (Carney kick); 14:39.

Third Quarter
Min.—Wiggins 9 pass from Culpepper (M. Andersen kick); 4:12.
N.O.—McAllister 1 run (Carney kick); 8:47.
Min.—FG, M. Andersen 39, 12:34.

Fourth Quarter
N.O.—FG, Carney 45, 1:52.
Min.—M. Robinson 1 pass from Culpepper (M. Andersen kick); 7:56.
N.O.—Brooks 5 run (Carney kick); 12:09.
Attendance—64,900.

	Minnesota	New Orleans
First downs	29	25
Rushes-yards	28-188	23-159
Passing	417	226
Punt returns	2-11	0-0
Kickoff returns	6-97	7-146
Interception returns	1-56	2-0
Comp.-att.-int.	26-38-2	22-38-1
Sacked-yards lost	2-8	3-23
Punts	0-0	4-46
Fumbles-lost	4-1	1-0
Penalties-yards	5-35	4-21
Time of possession	30:41	29:19

INDIVIDUAL STATISTICS
RUSHING—Minnesota, Moore 15-109, Culpepper 7-13, M. Williams 6-66. New Orleans, McAllister 18-78, Brooks 3-25, McAfee 1-53, Stecker 1-3.
PASSING—Minnesota, Culpepper 26-37-2-425, Moore 0-1-0-0. New Orleans, Brooks 22-38-1-249.
RECEIVING—Minnesota, Moore 7-78, Burleson 6-134, Wiggins 5-56, M. Robinson 4-32, Moss 2-89, Campbell 1-23, M. Williams 1-13. New Orleans, Horn 7-65, Pathon 4-92, Stallworth 4-34, McAllister 3-15, Conwell 2-11, M. Lewis 1-23, Stecker 1-9.
MISSED FIELD GOAL ATTEMPTS—None.
INTERCEPTIONS—Minnesota, Winfield 1-56. New Orleans, Ambrose 1-0, Brown 1-0.
KICKOFF RETURNS—Minnesota, Moore 3-51, Campbell 2-32, Ross 1-14. New Orleans, M. Lewis 7-146.
PUNT RETURNS—Minnesota, Burleson 2-11.
SACKS—Minnesota, Udeze 1, Newman 1, Johnstone 1. New Orleans, Howard 1, Young 0.5, Ch. Grant 0.5.

RAMS 28, BUCCANEERS 21
Monday, October 18

Tampa Bay	7	7	7	0—21
St. Louis	7	7	7	7—28

First Quarter
St.L.—Holt 52 pass from Bulger (J. Wilkins kick); 2:20.
T.B.—Alstott 1 run (Gramatica kick); 5:46.

Second Quarter
T.B.—Pittman 5 pass from Griese (Gramatica kick); 1:58.
St.L.—M. Faulk 1 run (J. Wilkins kick); 13:18.

Third Quarter
St.L.—Archuleta 93 fumble return (J. Wilkins kick); 7:36.
T.B.—Heller 1 pass from Griese (Gramatica kick); 14:23.

Fourth Quarter

St.L.—Holt 36 pass from Bulger (J. Wilkins kick), 4:14.
Attendance—66,040.

	Tampa Bay	St. Louis
First downs	17	14
Rushes-yards	22-55	30-94
Passing	277	230
Punt returns	1-14	2-(-5)
Kickoff returns	4-152	4-84
Interception returns	1-31	1-0
Comp.-att.-int.	27-40-1	18-30-1
Sacked-yards lost	2-9	4-34
Punts	4-43	5-50
Fumbles-lost	3-3	1-1
Penalties-yards	3-12	7-50
Time of possession	27:52	32:08

INDIVIDUAL STATISTICS

RUSHING—Tampa Bay, Pittman 13-37, Alstott 5-17, Griese 4-1. St. Louis, M. Faulk 15-40, S. Jackson 13-48, Curtis 1-7, Bulger 1-(minus 1).

PASSING—Tampa Bay, Griese 27-40-1-286. St. Louis, Bulger 18-30-1-264.

RECEIVING—Tampa Bay, Clayton 8-142, Dilger 4-30, Pittman 4-16, Lee 3-31, Heller 3-21, Alstott 3-20, Brown 2-26. St. Louis, Holt 6-124, McDonald 3-30, S. Jackson 3-30, M. Faulk 3-29, Curtis 1-32, Bruce 1-11, Goodspeed 1-8.

MISSED FIELD GOAL ATTEMPTS—Tampa Bay, Gramatica 35, 48. St. Louis, J. Wilkins 56, 44.

INTERCEPTIONS—Tampa Bay, Gold 1-31. St. Louis, Butler 1-0.

KICKOFF RETURNS—Tampa Bay, Cox 4-152. St. Louis, Harris 4-84.

PUNT RETURNS—Tampa Bay, Brown 1-14. St. Louis, McDonald 2-(minus 5).

SACKS—Tampa Bay, Spires 2, Rice 1, McFarland 1. St. Louis, Polley 1, Flowers 1.

WEEK 7

AMERICAN FOOTBALL CONFERENCE

EAST DIVISION

	W	L	T	Pct.	PF	PA
New England	6	0	0	1.000	148	90
N.Y. Jets	5	1	0	.833	127	102
Buffalo	1	5	0	.167	77	106
Miami	1	6	0	.143	86	121

NORTH DIVISION

	W	L	T	Pct.	PF	PA
Pittsburgh	5	1	0	.833	136	114
Baltimore	4	2	0	.667	117	85
Cleveland	3	4	0	.429	147	147
Cincinnati	2	4	0	.333	106	139

SOUTH DIVISION

	W	L	T	Pct.	PF	PA
Jacksonville	5	2	0	.714	122	126
Indianapolis	4	2	0	.667	183	133
Houston	3	3	0	.500	138	137
Tennessee	2	5	0	.286	124	158

WEST DIVISION

	W	L	T	Pct.	PF	PA
Denver	5	2	0	.714	140	100
San Diego	4	3	0	.571	177	142
Kansas City	2	4	0	.333	161	142
Oakland	2	5	0	.286	124	181

NATIONAL FOOTBALL CONFERENCE

EAST DIVISION

	W	L	T	Pct.	PF	PA
Philadelphia	6	0	0	1.000	171	94
N.Y. Giants	4	2	0	.667	117	100
Dallas	2	4	0	.333	107	156
Washington	2	4	0	.333	84	95

NORTH DIVISION

	W	L	T	Pct.	PF	PA
Minnesota	5	1	0	.833	170	128
Detroit	4	2	0	.667	116	123
Green Bay	3	4	0	.429	178	172
Chicago	1	5	0	.167	85	108

SOUTH DIVISION

	W	L	T	Pct.	PF	PA
Atlanta	5	2	0	.714	129	142
New Orleans	3	4	0	.429	154	191
Tampa Bay	2	5	0	.286	109	124
Carolina	1	5	0	.167	83	135

WEST DIVISION

	W	L	T	Pct.	PF	PA
St. Louis	4	3	0	.571	158	165
Seattle	3	3	0	.500	129	101
Arizona	2	4	0	.333	112	104
San Francisco	1	5	0	.167	105	159

TOP PERFORMANCES

100-YARD RUSHING GAMES

Player, Team & Opponent	Att.	Yds.	TD
Ahman Green, G.B. vs. Dal.	15	163	2
Priest Holmes, K.C. vs. Atl.	22	139	4
Mewelde Moore, Min. vs. Ten.	20	138	0
Rudi Johnson, Cin. vs. Den.	24	119	1
Corey Dillon, N.E. vs. NYJ.	22	115	0
Reuben Droughns, Den. at Cin.	24	110	0
Michael Pittman, T.B. vs. Chi.	23	109	1
Fred Taylor, Jac. at Ind.	20	107	0
Emmitt Smith, Ariz. vs. Sea.	26	106	1

300-YARD PASSING GAMES

Player, Team & Opponent	Att.	Cmp.	Yds.	TD	Int.
Donovan McNabb, Phi. at Cle.*	43	28	376	4	1
Peyton Manning, Ind. vs. Jac.	39	27	368	3	0
Kerry Collins, Oak. vs. N.O.	45	26	350	2	1
Vinny Testaverde, Dal. at G.B.	35	23	308	1	0
Byron Leftwich, Jac. at Ind.	30	23	300	2	1

100-YARD RECEIVING GAMES

Player, Team & Opponent	Rec.	Yds.	TD
Chad Johnson, Cin. vs. Den.	7	149	1
Javon Walker, G.B. vs. Dal.	8	129	1
Chris Chambers, Mia. vs. St.L.	3	128	1
Joe Horn, N.O. at Oak.	9	123	0
Jerry Porter, Oak. vs. N.O.	6	113	1
Jimmy Smith, Jac. at Ind.	5	113	1
Brandon Stokley, Ind. vs. Jac.	7	112	0
Jason Witten, Dal. at G.B.	8	112	1
Darrell Jackson, Sea. at Ariz.	8	109	1
Terrell Owens, Phi. at Cle.*	4	109	2
David Givens, N.E. vs. NYJ.	5	107	0
Tiki Barber, NYG vs. Det.	7	102	1
Todd Pinkston, Phi. at Cle.*	6	100	0

*Overtime game.

RESULTS

SUNDAY, OCTOBER 24
BALTIMORE 20, Buffalo 6
San Diego 17, CAROLINA 6
TAMPA BAY 19, Chicago 7
Detroit 28, N.Y. GIANTS 13
MIAMI 31, St. Louis 14
MINNESOTA 20, Tennessee 3
KANSAS CITY 56, Atlanta 10
Philadelphia 34, CLEVELAND 31 (OT)
Jacksonville 27, INDIANAPOLIS 24
NEW ENGLAND 13, N.Y. Jets 7
ARIZONA 25, Seattle 17
GREEN BAY 41, Dallas 20
New Orleans 31, OAKLAND 26

MONDAY, OCTOBER 25
CINCINNATI 23, Denver 10
Open Date: Houston, Pittsburgh, San Francisco, Washington

RAVENS 20, BILLS 6
Sunday, October 24

Buffalo	3	0	3	0— 6
Baltimore	10	7	0	3—20

First Quarter
Buf.—FG, Lindell 24, 3:49.
Bal.—FG, Stover 24, 10:37.
Bal.—Sanders 48 interception return (Stover kick), 13:35.

Second Quarter
Bal.—Sams 5 run (Stover kick), 4:47.

Third Quarter
Buf.—FG, Lindell 21, 7:17.

Fourth Quarter
Bal.—FG, Stover 19, 10:18.
Attendance—69,809.

	Buffalo	Baltimore
First downs	15	12
Rushes-yards	23-85	33-100
Passing	185	60
Punt returns	4-21	2-6
Kickoff returns	5-90	3-61
Interception returns	0-0	4-156
Comp.-att.-int.	20-37-4	10-19-0
Sacked-yards lost	4-18	4-26
Punts	4-39	6-38
Fumbles-lost	1-1	1-1
Penalties-yards	5-40	4-25
Time of possession	30:52	29:08

INDIVIDUAL STATISTICS
RUSHING—Buffalo, McGahee 16-58, Henry 7-27. Baltimore, C. Taylor 21-89, Smith 6-11, Boller 4-5, Sams 1-5, Sanders 1-(minus 10).
PASSING—Buffalo, Bledsoe 20-37-4-203. Baltimore, Boller 10-19-0-86.
RECEIVING—Buffalo, Moulds 6-96, Reed 4-32, Shelton 4-26, Campbell 2-36, Henry 2-6, Aiken 1-6, McGahee 1-1. Baltimore, T. Taylor 2-52, C. Taylor 2-11, T. Jones 2-8, Wilcox 1-7, K. Johnson 1-5, Hymes 1-3, Ricard 1-0.
MISSED FIELD GOAL ATTEMPTS—Baltimore, Stover 50.
INTERCEPTIONS—Baltimore, Sanders 2-48, Williams 1-94, Reed 1-14.
KICKOFF RETURNS—Buffalo, McGee 5-90. Baltimore, Sams 3-61.
PUNT RETURNS—Buffalo, Clements 4-21. Baltimore, Sanders 1-4, Sams 1-2.
SACKS—Buffalo, Schobel 2, Spikes 1, Fletcher 1. Baltimore, Suggs 2, A. Thomas 1, Weaver 1.

CHARGERS 17, PANTHERS 6
Sunday, October 24

San Diego	0	0	10	7—17
Carolina	6	0	0	0— 6

First Quarter
Car.—FG, Kasay 28, 6:39.
Car.—FG, Kasay 21, 11:32.

Third Quarter
S.D.—Tomlinson 8 run (Kaeding kick), 6:47.
S.D.—FG, Kaeding 44, 12:24.

Fourth Quarter
S.D.—Chatman 5 run (Kaeding kick), 13:18.
Attendance—73,096.

	San Diego	Carolina
First downs	19	20
Rushes-yards	27-114	30-116
Passing	188	147
Punt returns	3-18	1-0
Kickoff returns	3-80	4-75
Interception returns	1-0	0-0
Comp.-att.-int.	21-32-0	17-36-1
Sacked-yards lost	1-8	1-8
Punts	5-35	4-44
Fumbles-lost	1-1	0-0
Penalties-yards	7-83	8-94
Time of possession	29:07	30:53

INDIVIDUAL STATISTICS
RUSHING—San Diego, Tomlinson 17-47, Chatman 8-69, Brees 2-(minus 2). Carolina, Hoover 24-99, Goings 4-11, Harris 2-6.

PASSING—San Diego, Brees 21-32-0-196. Carolina, Delhomme 17-36-1-155.
RECEIVING—San Diego, Gates 7-61, McCardell 5-65, E. Parker 4-47, Tomlinson 3-13, Peelle 1-6, Neal 1-4. Carolina, Colbert 7-71, Muhammad 3-28, Goings 2-11, Hoover 2-6, Mangum 1-15, Gaines 1-14, Seidman 1-10.
MISSED FIELD GOAL ATTEMPTS—San Diego, Kaeding 29. Carolina, Kasay 46.
INTERCEPTIONS—San Diego, Kiel 1-0.
KICKOFF RETURNS—San Diego, Dwight 3-80. Carolina, Broussard 3-64, Proehl 1-11.
PUNT RETURNS—San Diego, E. Parker 3-18. Carolina, Broussard 1-0.
SACKS—San Diego, Phillips 1. Carolina, Morgan 1.

BUCCANEERS 19, BEARS 7
Sunday, October 24

Chicago	0	0	7	0— 7
Tampa Bay	0	10	3	6—19

Second Quarter
T.B.—FG, Gramatica 22, 1:35.
T.B.—Clayton 6 pass from Griese (Gramatica kick), 14:12.

Third Quarter
T.B.—FG, Gramatica 22, 2:37.
Chi.—T. Jones 1 run (Edinger kick), 11:15.

Fourth Quarter
T.B.—Pittman 3 run (pass failed), 6:08.
Attendance—65,550.

	Chicago	Tampa Bay
First downs	11	17
Rushes-yards	20-76	37-138
Passing	91	155
Punt returns	1-3	2-14
Kickoff returns	5-91	2-45
Interception returns	0-0	1-23
Comp.-att.-int.	14-28-1	15-23-0
Sacked-yards lost	4-25	1-8
Punts	7-41	5-43
Fumbles-lost	1-1	2-2
Penalties-yards	10-78	6-41
Time of possession	27:49	32:11

INDIVIDUAL STATISTICS
RUSHING—Chicago, T. Jones 13-52, Thomas 5-17, Krenzel 1-4, Quinn 1-3. Tampa Bay, Pittman 23-109, Alstott 7-29, J. White 4-5, Griese 2-(minus 1), Clayton 1-(minus 4).
PASSING—Chicago, Krenzel 9-19-1-69, Quinn 5-9-0-47. Tampa Bay, Griese 15-23-0-163.
RECEIVING—Chicago, Gage 4-43, Clark 3-31, T. Jones 3-13, Thomas 2-4, Berrian 1-14, Wade 1-11. Tampa Bay, Clayton 6-62, Pittman 2-55, Jurevicius 2-21, Alstott 2-8, Brown 1-13, Heller 1-3, J. White 1-1.
MISSED FIELD GOAL ATTEMPTS—None.
INTERCEPTIONS—Tampa Bay, Barber 1-23.
KICKOFF RETURNS—Chicago, Azumah 4-70, McKie 1-21. Tampa Bay, Cox 2-45.
PUNT RETURNS—Chicago, McQuarters 1-3. Tampa Bay, Brown 2-14.
SACKS—Chicago, Harris 1. Tampa Bay, Rice 2, Quarles 1, D. White 1.

LIONS 28, GIANTS 13
Sunday, October 24

Detroit	7	0	7	14—28
N.Y. Giants	7	3	0	3—13

First Quarter
Det.—Williams 18 pass from Harrington (Hanson kick), 5:35.
NYG—Barber 62 pass from Warner (Christie kick), 14:44.

Second Quarter
NYG—FG, Christie 19, 7:53.

Third Quarter
Det.—Jones 2 run (Hanson kick), 5:26.

Fourth Quarter
NYG—FG, Christie 25, 6:42.
Det.—Swinton 2 pass from Harrington (Hanson kick), 12:08.
Det.—Pinner 8 run (Hanson kick), 13:14.
Attendance—78,841.

	Detroit	N.Y. Giants
First downs	22	22
Rushes-yards	29-115	26-75
Passing	210	250
Punt returns	1-(-2)	1-9

2004 REVIEW Week 7

	Detroit	N.Y. Giants
Kickoff returns	4-62	4-84
Interception returns	1-0	0-0
Comp.-att.-int.	18-22-0	23-34-1
Sacked-yards lost	3-20	6-20
Punts	4-36	2-38
Fumbles-lost	1-0	5-1
Penalties-yards	7-65	4-25
Time of possession	27:44	32:16

INDIVIDUAL STATISTICS

RUSHING—Detroit, Jones 13-65, Pinner 9-36, Bryson 5-16, Harrington 2-(minus 2). New York, Barber 22-70, Dayne 3-2, Cloud 1-3.

PASSING—Detroit, Harrington 18-22-0-230. New York, Warner 23-34-1-270.

RECEIVING—Detroit, Alexander 5-52, Williams 4-67, Swinton 3-32, Bryson 2-32, Trejo 2-19, Streets 1-22, Pinner 1-6. New York, Barber 7-102, I. Hilliard 5-42, Toomer 2-50, Shockey 2-25, Finn 2-18, Taylor 2-16, Shiancoe 2-14, Cloud 1-3.

MISSED FIELD GOAL ATTEMPTS—None.

INTERCEPTIONS—Detroit, Cash 1-0.

KICKOFF RETURNS—Detroit, Drummond 2-39, Bryson 1-13, Trejo 1-10. New York, Cloud 4-84.

PUNT RETURNS—Detroit, Drummond 1-(minus 2). New York, Jones 1-9.

SACKS—Detroit, Edwards 2, S. Rogers 1, Hall 1, Bell 1, Redding 1. New York, Wilson 1, Umenyiora 1, Hand 1.

DOLPHINS 31, RAMS 14
Sunday, October 24

St. Louis	0	7	0	7—14
Miami	7	7	0	17—31

First Quarter
Mia.—Morris 8 run (Bryant kick), 7:31.

Second Quarter
St.L.—Bulger 15 run (J. Wilkins kick), 9:41.
Mia.—McMichael 42 pass from Fiedler (Bryant kick), 14:38.

Fourth Quarter
Mia.—Minor 13 run (Bryant kick), :39.
Mia.—FG, Bryant 43, 6:13.
St.L.—McDonald 15 pass from Bulger (J. Wilkins kick), 10:09.
Mia.—Chambers 71 pass from Fiedler (Bryant kick), 10:36.
Attendance—72,945.

	St. Louis	Miami
First downs	20	19
Rushes-yards	19-103	34-117
Passing	269	206
Punt returns	2-(-1)	4-31
Kickoff returns	6-102	3-93
Interception returns	0-0	1-0
Comp.-att.-int.	23-40-1	14-18-0
Sacked-yards lost	3-26	6-45
Punts	5-38	4-45
Fumbles-lost	0-0	1-0
Penalties-yards	7-63	4-37
Time of possession	29:01	30:59

INDIVIDUAL STATISTICS

RUSHING—St. Louis, M. Faulk 12-61, S. Jackson 6-27, Bulger 1-15. Miami, Morris 28-83, Minor 3-21, Fiedler 2-(minus 2), Chambers 1-15.

PASSING—St. Louis, Bulger 23-39-1-295, Bruce 0-1-0-0. Miami, Fiedler 13-17-0-203, Booker 1-1-0-48.

RECEIVING—St. Louis, M. Faulk 8-74, Bruce 5-98, McDonald 4-77, S. Jackson 2-18, Goodspeed 1-10, Looker 1-9, Cleeland 1-5, Holt 1-4. Miami, McMichael 4-78, Chambers 3-128, Booker 3-35, Morris 3-8, Konrad 1-2.

MISSED FIELD GOAL ATTEMPTS—None.

INTERCEPTIONS—Miami, S. Knight 1-0.

KICKOFF RETURNS—St. Louis, Anderson 4-71, Furrey 2-31. Miami, Welker 3-40.

PUNT RETURNS—St. Louis, McDonald 2-(minus 1). Miami, Welker 4-31.

SACKS—St. Louis, B. Fisher 2, Archuleta 1, Little 1, Lewis 1, Pickett 1. Miami, Thomas 1, Taylor 1, Zgonina 1.

VIKINGS 20, TITANS 3
Sunday, October 24

Tennessee	3	0	0	0—3
Minnesota	3	14	0	3—20

First Quarter
Ten.—FG, Anderson 40, 6:41.
Min.—FG, M. Andersen 29, 14:22.

Second Quarter
Min.—M. Williams 1 run (M. Andersen kick), 3:26.
Min.—M. Robinson 2 pass from Culpepper (M. Andersen kick), 14:37.

Fourth Quarter
Min.—FG, M. Andersen 29, 4:43.
Attendance—64,108.

	Tennessee	Minnesota
First downs	16	20
Rushes-yards	14-55	27-152
Passing	188	161
Punt returns	3-12	1-2
Kickoff returns	5-109	2-37
Interception returns	0-0	3-71
Comp.-att.-int.	20-42-3	24-30-0
Sacked-yards lost	2-10	3-22
Punts	5-40	5-41
Fumbles-lost	3-1	0-0
Penalties-yards	12-85	8-66
Time of possession	27:17	32:43

INDIVIDUAL STATISTICS

RUSHING—Tennessee, Brown 14-55. Minnesota, Moore 20-138, M. Williams 3-10, Culpepper 3-4, M. Bennett 1-0.

PASSING—Tennessee, Volek 17-36-3-190, McNair 2-5-0-2, Hentrich 1-1-0-6. Minnesota, Culpepper 24-30-0-183.

RECEIVING—Tennessee, Mason 8-85, Troupe 6-57, Brown 2-18, Bennett 1-18, Fleming 1-12, Berlin 1-6, McAddley 1-(-6). Minnesota, Burleson 6-53, Wiggins 6-36, Moore 5-30, M. Robinson 3-33, Campbell 2-16, Berton 1-14, M. Williams 1-1.

MISSED FIELD GOAL ATTEMPTS—None.

INTERCEPTIONS—Minnesota, Winfield 1-30, Shaw 1-22, R. Smith 1-19.

KICKOFF RETURNS—Tennessee, Fleming 3-56, Waddell 2-53. Minnesota, Moore 1-19, Campbell 1-18.

PUNT RETURNS—Tennessee, Mason 3-12. Minnesota, Burleson 1-2.

SACKS—Tennessee, LaBoy 2, Bulluck 1. Minnesota, K. Williams 1, Hovan 0.5, Thomas 0.5.

CHIEFS 56, FALCONS 10
Sunday, October 24

Atlanta	3	0	7	0—10
Kansas City	14	21	7	14—56

First Quarter
Atl.—FG, Feely 19, 2:47.
K.C.—Holmes 15 run (Tynes kick), 6:57.
K.C.—Blaylock 7 run (Tynes kick), 13:52.

Second Quarter
K.C.—Holmes 2 run (Tynes kick), 7:35.
K.C.—Holmes 2 run (Tynes kick), 11:43.
K.C.—Holmes 1 run (Tynes kick), 15:00.

Third Quarter
Atl.—Rossum 75 punt return (Feely kick), 2:32.
K.C.—Blaylock 1 run (Tynes kick), 8:20.

Fourth Quarter
K.C.—Blaylock 3 run (Tynes kick), :53.
K.C.—Blaylock 2 run (Tynes kick), 13:01.
Attendance—78,260.

	Atlanta	Kansas City
First downs	9	36
Rushes-yards	21-119	49-271
Passing	103	269
Punt returns	1-75	1-11
Kickoff returns	5-119	2-31
Interception returns	0-0	2-6
Comp.-att.-int.	9-25-2	20-28-0
Sacked-yards lost	4-25	0-0
Punts	4-43	4-42
Fumbles-lost	0-0	2-1
Penalties-yards	3-41	5-45
Time of possession	21:06	38:54

INDIVIDUAL STATISTICS

RUSHING—Atlanta, Dunn 11-49, Vick 6-62, Duckett 4-8. Kansas City, Holmes 22-139, Blaylock 19-90, Richardson 6-29, Hall 2-13.

PASSING—Atlanta, Vick 7-21-2-119, Schaub 2-4-0-9. Kansas City, Green 20-27-0-269, Collins 0-1-0-0.

RECEIVING—Atlanta, Crumpler 3-27, Dunn 2-72, P. Price 2-21, Griffith 2-8. Kansas City, Morton 4-48, Kennison 3-52, Blaylock 3-46, Holmes 3-41, Richardson 3-36, Hall 2-27, Gonzalez 2-19.

MISSED FIELD GOAL ATTEMPTS—None.

INTERCEPTIONS—Kansas City, Warfield 1-6, Wesley 1-0.

KICKOFF RETURNS—Atlanta, Rossum 5-119. Kansas City, Hall 2-31.

PUNT RETURNS—Atlanta, Rossum 1-75. Kansas City, Hall 1-11.

SACKS—Kansas City, Allen 2, Bartee 1, Beisel 0.5, Browning 0.5.

EAGLES 34, BROWNS 31
Sunday, October 24

Philadelphia	14	7	0	10	3—	34
Cleveland	7	10	7	7	0—	31

First Quarter
Phi.—C. Lewis 10 pass from McNabb (Akers kick), :43.

Cle.—Green 11 run (Dawson kick), 5:34.

Phi.—Owens 39 pass from McNabb (Akers kick), 7:27.

Second Quarter
Cle.—FG, Dawson 38, 4:21.

Phi.—Owens 40 pass from McNabb (Akers kick), 6:29.

Cle.—Suggs 13 run (Dawson kick), 11:49.

Third Quarter
Cle.—Heiden 21 pass from Garcia (Dawson kick), 7:29.

Fourth Quarter
Phi.—Smith 2 pass from McNabb (Akers kick), :47.

Phi.—FG, Akers 38, 4:13.

Cle.—Garcia 4 run (Dawson kick), 14:30.

Overtime
Phi.—FG, Akers 50, 9:58.

Attendance—73,394.

	Philadelphia	Cleveland
First downs	23	27
Rushes-yards	23-121	34-165
Passing	367	229
Punt returns	1-1	2-34
Kickoff returns	7-154	6-103
Interception returns	1-0	1-3
Comp.-att.-int.	28-43-1	21-32-1
Sacked-yards lost	2-9	3-7
Punts	5-45	5-40
Fumbles-lost	0-0	3-2
Penalties-yards	11-101	10-80
Time of possession	34:33	35:25

INDIVIDUAL STATISTICS
RUSHING—Philadelphia, Westbrook 13-43, Levens 7-48, McNabb 2-28, G. Lewis 1-2. Cleveland, Suggs 15-78, Green 14-64, Garcia 4-21, T. Smith 1-2.

PASSING—Philadelphia, McNabb 28-43-1-376. Cleveland, Garcia 21-32-1-236.

RECEIVING—Philadelphia, Pinkston 6-100, C. Lewis 5-37, Owens 4-109, Westbrook 3-17, F. Mitchell 2-31, Parry 2-22, Mahe 2-18, Smith 2-6, G. Lewis 1-24, Levens 1-12. Cleveland, Shea 6-45, Northcutt 4-70, F. Jackson 3-45, Heiden 3-42, Bryant 2-26, Suggs 2-5, Green 1-3.

MISSED FIELD GOAL ATTEMPTS—None.

INTERCEPTIONS—Philadelphia, Sheppard 1-0. Cleveland, Andra. Davis 1-3.

KICKOFF RETURNS—Philadelphia, Reed 7-154. Cleveland, King 2-42, J. Jackson 2-39, F. Jackson 1-18, Mustard 1-4.

PUNT RETURNS—Philadelphia, Mahe 1-1. Cleveland, Northcutt 2-34.

SACKS—Philadelphia, Dawkins 1, Kearse 1, Burgess 1. Cleveland, Ekuban 1, Warren 1.

JAGUARS 27, COLTS 24
Sunday, October 24

Jacksonville	0	10	3	14—	27
Indianapolis	0	14	0	10—	24

Second Quarter
Jac.—Brady 4 pass from Leftwich (Scobee kick), 1:33.

Ind.—Harrison 7 pass from Manning (Vanderjagt kick), 5:37.

Jac.—FG, Scobee 26, 13:08.

Ind.—Clark 17 pass from Manning (Vanderjagt kick), 14:48.

Third Quarter
Jac.—FG, Scobee 32, 11:49.

Fourth Quarter
Jac.—FG, Scobee 26, :08.

Ind.—FG, Vanderjagt 34, 5:28.

Jac.—J. Smith 25 pass from Leftwich (Wilford pass from Leftwich), 8:46.

Ind.—Harrison 39 pass from Manning (Vanderjagt kick), 11:08.

Jac.—FG, Scobee 53, 14:22.

Attendance—56,615.

	Jacksonville	Indianapolis
First downs	20	23
Rushes-yards	27-128	18-87
Passing	286	359
Punt returns	1-12	0-0
Kickoff returns	5-88	6-79
Interception returns	0-0	1-0
Comp.-att.-int.	23-30-1	27-40-0
Sacked-yards lost	3-14	1-9
Punts	1-36	3-48
Fumbles-lost	2-1	2-2
Penalties-yards	6-48	12-62
Time of possession	34:34	25:26

INDIVIDUAL STATISTICS
RUSHING—Jacksonville, F. Taylor 20-107, G. Jones 3-10, Toefield 2-8, Leftwich 2-3. Indianapolis, James 18-87.

PASSING—Jacksonville, Leftwich 23-30-1-300. Indianapolis, Manning 27-39-0-368, Saturday 0-1-0-0.

RECEIVING—Jacksonville, J. Smith 5-113, F. Taylor 5-67, T. Edwards 3-32, Yoder 3-26, Brady 2-25, R. Williams 2-19, Wilford 1-9, Toefield 1-5, M. Edwards 1-4. Indianapolis, Stokley 7-112, James 6-54, Harrison 5-70, Pollard 3-52, Clark 3-36, Wayne 2-28, Mungro 1-16.

MISSED FIELD GOAL ATTEMPTS—None.

INTERCEPTIONS—Indianapolis, David 1-0.

KICKOFF RETURNS—Jacksonville, T. Edwards 3-65, Brady 1-15, M. Edwards 1-8. Indianapolis, Rhodes 4-64, Mungro 2-15.

PUNT RETURNS—Jacksonville, T. Edwards 1-12.

SACKS—Jacksonville, Favors 1. Indianapolis, Freeney 2, Mathis 1.

PATRIOTS 13, JETS 7
Sunday, October 24

N.Y. Jets	0	7	0	0—	7
New England	3	10	0	0—	13

First Quarter
N.E.—FG, Vinatieri 41, 6:27.

Second Quarter
N.E.—FG, Vinatieri 27, 5:29.

NYJ—Pennington 1 run (Brien kick), 13:05.

N.E.—Patten 7 pass from Brady (Vinatieri kick), 14:55.

Attendance—68,756.

	N.Y. Jets	New England
First downs	15	21
Rushes-yards	27-106	29-133
Passing	162	210
Punt returns	1-5	2-3
Kickoff returns	4-66	2-46
Interception returns	0-0	0-0
Comp.-att.-int.	19-30-0	20-29-0
Sacked-yards lost	0-0	3-20
Punts	4-34	3-37
Fumbles-lost	2-1	1-1
Penalties-yards	6-37	6-53
Time of possession	31:01	28:59

INDIVIDUAL STATISTICS
RUSHING—New York, C. Martin 20-70, Jordan 3-21, Pennington 3-15, Moss 1-0. New England, Dillon 22-115, Faulk 4-21, Brady 3-(minus 3).

PASSING—New York, Pennington 19-30-0-162. New England, Brady 20-29-0-230.

RECEIVING—New York, McCareins 6-83, Baker 3-26, Sowell 2-13, Moss 2-12, Becht 2-8, C. Martin 2-0, Chrebet 1-18, Jordan 1-2. New England, Faulk 6-44, Givens 5-107, Patten 3-33, Graham 2-21, B. Johnson 2-18, Klecko 2-7.

MISSED FIELD GOAL ATTEMPTS—None.

INTERCEPTIONS—None.

KICKOFF RETURNS—New York, J. Carter 3-53, Askew 1-13. New England, B. Johnson 2-46.

PUNT RETURNS—New York, McCareins 1-5. New England, Faulk 2-3.

SACKS—New York, Ellis 1.5, Robertson 1, J. Abraham 0.5.

CARDINALS 25, SEAHAWKS 17
Sunday, October 24

Seattle	0	3	7	7—	17
Arizona	7	6	3	9—	25

First Quarter
Ariz.—Fitzgerald 25 pass from McCown (Rackers kick), 6:37.

Second Quarter
Sea.—FG, J. Brown 54, 8:32.

Ariz.—FG, Rackers 55, 11:59.

Ariz.—FG, Rackers 55, 13:59.

Third Quarter
Ariz.—FG, Rackers 50, 12:10.
Sea.—Jackson 1 pass from Hasselbeck (J. Brown kick), 14:55.

Fourth Quarter
Sea.—Lucas 21 interception return (J. Brown kick), 1:53.
Ariz.—Safety, 6:10.
Ariz.—E. Smith 23 run (Rackers kick), 13:07.
  Attendance—35,695.

	Seattle	Arizona
First downs	12	16
Rushes-yards	14-77	37-127
Passing	180	189
Punt returns	4-7	2-(-2)
Kickoff returns	4-92	5-107
Interception returns	1-21	4-11
Comp.-att.-int.	14-41-4	22-36-1
Sacked-yards lost	1-7	3-23
Punts	7-35	6-41
Fumbles-lost	0-0	2-1
Penalties-yards	4-35	6-45
Time of possession	20:09	39:51

INDIVIDUAL STATISTICS
RUSHING—Seattle, Alexander 12-65, Hasselbeck 1-9, Strong 1-3. Arizona, E. Smith 26-106, Hambrick 7-16, McCown 3-3, Croom 1-2.
PASSING—Seattle, Hasselbeck 14-41-4-187. Arizona, McCown 22-36-1-212.
RECEIVING—Seattle, Jackson 8-109, K. Robinson 2-32, Strong 2-19, Stevens 1-17, Rice 1-10. Arizona, B. Johnson 7-54, Fitzgerald 4-73, F. Jones 4-35, E. Smith 4-30, O. Ayanbadejo 2-14, K. Williams 1-6.
MISSED FIELD GOAL ATTEMPTS—None.
INTERCEPTIONS—Seattle, Lucas 1-21. Arizona, Starks 1-5, Hill 1-2, Macklin 1-2, Dansby 1-2.
KICKOFF RETURNS—Seattle, Morris 3-80, Stevens 1-12. Arizona, Croom 4-89, K. Williams 1-18.
PUNT RETURNS—Seattle, Morris 4-7. Arizona, K. Williams 2-(minus 2).
SACKS—Seattle, White 1, Cochran 1, Okeafor 1. Arizona, Thompson 1.

PACKERS 41, COWBOYS 20
Sunday, October 24

Dallas	6	0	7	7—20
Green Bay	3	17	21	0—41

First Quarter
Dal.—FG, Cundiff 46, 6:28.
G.B.—FG, Longwell 26, 9:43.
Dal.—FG, Cundiff 24, 14:05.

Second Quarter
G.B.—Green 1 run (Longwell kick), 1:44.
G.B.—J. Walker 5 pass from Favre (Longwell kick), 13:05.
G.B.—FG, Longwell 40, 15:00.

Third Quarter
G.B.—Franks 8 pass from Fisher (Longwell kick), 3:58.
Dal.—Witten 42 pass from Testaverde (Cundiff kick), 7:06.
G.B.—Driver 33 pass from Favre (Longwell kick), 11:44.
G.B.—Green 90 run (Longwell kick), 13:35.

Fourth Quarter
Dal.—George 5 run (Cundiff kick), 6:41.
  Attendance—70,679.

	Dallas	Green Bay
First downs	18	23
Rushes-yards	16-66	31-220
Passing	296	260
Punt returns	1-9	0-0
Kickoff returns	6-68	5-119
Interception returns	0-0	0-0
Comp.-att.-int.	23-36-0	24-30-0
Sacked-yards lost	2-12	1-6
Punts	5-36	2-39
Fumbles-lost	2-0	1-0
Penalties-yards	6-37	6-40
Time of possession	26:41	33:19

INDIVIDUAL STATISTICS
RUSHING—Dallas, George 10-41, Anderson 5-25, Testaverde 1-0. Green Bay, Green 15-163, Davenport 12-37, Nall 2-(minus 2), Chatman 1-18, Favre 1-4.
PASSING—Dallas, Testaverde 23-35-0-308, Glenn 0-1-0-0. Green Bay, Favre 23-29-0-258, Fisher 1-1-0-8.

RECEIVING—Dallas, Witten 8-112, K. Johnson 5-73, Morgan 4-76, Anderson 2-22, George 1-10, Glenn 1-6, Ward 1-5, Lee 1-4. Green Bay, J. Walker 8-129, Driver 3-52, Henderson 3-23, Green 3-4, Davenport 2-20, Chatman 1-12, Franks 1-8, Ferguson 1-8, Martin 1-6, Fisher 1-4.
MISSED FIELD GOAL ATTEMPTS—None.
INTERCEPTIONS—None.
KICKOFF RETURNS—Dallas, Lee 2-32, Morgan 2-25, Reeves 2-11. Green Bay, Ferguson 2-57, Davenport 2-51, Chatman 1-11.
PUNT RETURNS—Dallas, Frazier 1-9.
SACKS—Dallas, Ogbogu 1. Green Bay, Roman 1, Kampman 0.5, Jenkins 0.5.

SAINTS 31, RAIDERS 26
Sunday, October 24

New Orleans	0	7	14	10—31
Oakland	6	3	0	17—26

First Quarter
Oak.—FG, Janikowski 28, 8:07.
Oak.—FG, Janikowski 42, 14:52.

Second Quarter
Oak.—FG, Janikowski 44, 8:07.
N.O.—L. Hall 4 pass from Brooks (Carney kick), 13:59.

Third Quarter
N.O.—McAllister 3 run (Carney kick), 6:29.
N.O.—McAllister 1 run (Carney kick), 13:28.

Fourth Quarter
Oak.—Jolley 34 pass from Collins (Janikowski kick), :26.
Oak.—FG, Janikowski 40, 5:09.
N.O.—Carney 41, 10:29.
N.O.—Bockwoldt 6 fumble return (Carney kick), 10:40.
Oak.—Porter 13 pass from Collins (Janikowski kick), 12:26.
  Attendance—45,337.

	New Orleans	Oakland
First downs	20	20
Rushes-yards	28-42	24-82
Passing	280	350
Punt returns	2-20	5-26
Kickoff returns	5-114	6-118
Interception returns	1-55	0-0
Comp.-att.-int.	23-39-0	26-45-1
Sacked-yards lost	1-2	0-0
Punts	7-42	5-39
Fumbles-lost	0-0	1-1
Penalties-yards	5-30	6-46
Time of possession	29:39	30:21

INDIVIDUAL STATISTICS
RUSHING—New Orleans, McAllister 24-42, Brooks 3-0, Stecker 1-0. Oakland, Zereoue 21-70, Crockett 2-9, Collins 1-3.
PASSING—New Orleans, Brooks 23-39-0-282. Oakland, Collins 26-45-1-350.
RECEIVING—New Orleans, Horn 9-123, Pathon 6-79, McAllister 3-17, M. Lewis 2-36, Stallworth 1-15, B. Williams 1-8, L. Hall 1-4. Oakland, Porter 6-113, Jolley 4-72, Gabriel 4-59, Curry 3-21, Redmond 3-10, C. Anderson 2-17, Crockett 2-17, Whitted 1-32, Zereoue 1-9.
MISSED FIELD GOAL ATTEMPTS—None.
INTERCEPTIONS—New Orleans, T. Jones 1-55.
KICKOFF RETURNS—New Orleans, M. Lewis 3-89, McAfee 1-16, Ruff 1-9. Oakland, Francis 5-82, Whitted 1-36.
PUNT RETURNS—New Orleans, M. Lewis 2-20. Oakland, Buchanon 5-26.
SACKS—Oakland, Kelly 1.

BENGALS 23, BRONCOS 10
Monday, October 25

Denver	0	7	3	0—10
Cincinnati	7	6	7	3—23

First Quarter
Cin.—C. Johnson 50 pass from Palmer (Graham kick), 6:34.

Second Quarter
Cin.—FG, Graham 53, 9:25.
Den.—Smith 3 pass from Plummer (Elam kick), 13:07.
Cin.—FG, Graham 34, 15:00.

Third Quarter
Den.—FG, Elam 29, 8:12.
Cin.—Ru. Johnson 36 run (Graham kick), 14:58.

Fourth Quarter
Cin.—FG, Graham 35, 7:29.
  Attendance—65,806.

	Denver	Cincinnati
First downs	22	13
Rushes-yards	26-123	33-133
Passing	195	188
Punt returns	1-2	3-25
Kickoff returns	5-68	3-64
Interception returns	1-0	2-48
Comp.-att.-int.	23-40-2	12-21-1
Sacked-yards lost	3-26	1-10
Punts	5-41	5-38
Fumbles-lost	2-1	1-0
Penalties-yards	8-88	9-65
Time of possession	32:29	27:31

INDIVIDUAL STATISTICS

RUSHING—Denver, Droughns 24-110, Watts 1-10, Plummer 1-3. Cincinnati, Ru. Johnson 24-119, Watson 4-22, Palmer 4-0, C. Russell 1-(minus 8).

PASSING—Denver, Plummer 23-40-2-221. Cincinnati, Palmer 12-21-1-198.

RECEIVING—Denver, Lelie 6-82, Smith 5-50, Watts 4-36, N. Jackson 4-33, Droughns 4-20. Cincinnati, C. Johnson 7-149, Watson 2-6, Washington 1-16, R. Kelly 1-14, Houshmandzadeh 1-13.

MISSED FIELD GOAL ATTEMPTS—Denver, Elam 49.

INTERCEPTIONS—Denver, Bailey 1-0. Cincinnati, O'Neal 1-29, James 1-19.

KICKOFF RETURNS—Denver, Griffin 3-33, Luke 2-35. Cincinnati, C. Russell 2-39, Watson 1-25.

PUNT RETURNS—Denver, Luke 1-2. Cincinnati, O'Neal 3-25.

SACKS—Denver, Wilson 1. Cincinnati, J. Smith 2, Simmons 1.

WEEK 8

AMERICAN FOOTBALL CONFERENCE

EAST DIVISION

	W	L	T	Pct.	PF	PA
New England	6	1	0	.857	168	124
N.Y. Jets	6	1	0	.857	168	116
Buffalo	2	5	0	.286	115	120
Miami	1	7	0	.125	100	162

NORTH DIVISION

	W	L	T	Pct.	PF	PA
Pittsburgh	6	1	0	.857	170	134
Baltimore	4	3	0	.571	127	100
Cleveland	3	4	0	.429	147	147
Cincinnati	2	5	0	.286	126	166

SOUTH DIVISION

	W	L	T	Pct.	PF	PA
Jacksonville	5	3	0	.625	128	146
Houston	4	3	0	.571	158	143
Indianapolis	4	3	0	.571	218	178
Tennessee	3	5	0	.375	151	178

WEST DIVISION

	W	L	T	Pct.	PF	PA
Denver	5	3	0	.625	168	141
San Diego	5	3	0	.625	219	156
Kansas City	3	4	0	.429	206	177
Oakland	2	6	0	.250	138	223

NATIONAL FOOTBALL CONFERENCE

EAST DIVISION

	W	L	T	Pct.	PF	PA
Philadelphia	7	0	0	1.000	186	104
N.Y. Giants	5	2	0	.714	151	113
Dallas	3	4	0	.429	138	177
Washington	2	5	0	.286	98	123

NORTH DIVISION

	W	L	T	Pct.	PF	PA
Minnesota	5	2	0	.714	183	162
Detroit	4	3	0	.571	137	154
Green Bay	4	4	0	.500	206	186
Chicago	2	5	0	.286	108	121

SOUTH DIVISION

	W	L	T	Pct.	PF	PA
Atlanta	6	2	0	.750	170	170
New Orleans	3	4	0	.429	154	191
Tampa Bay	2	5	0	.286	109	124
Carolina	1	6	0	.143	100	158

WEST DIVISION

	W	L	T	Pct.	PF	PA
Seattle	4	3	0	.571	152	118
St. Louis	4	3	0	.571	158	165
Arizona	2	5	0	.286	126	142
San Francisco	1	6	0	.143	118	182

TOP PERFORMANCES

100-YARD RUSHING GAMES

Player, Team & Opponent	Att.	Yds.	TD
Shaun Alexander, Sea. vs. Car.	32	195	1
Chris Brown, Ten. vs. Cin.	32	147	1
Priest Holmes, K.C. vs. Ind.	32	143	3
Duce Staley, Pit. vs. N.E.	25	125	0
LaMont Jordan, NYJ vs. Mia.	14	115	1
Curtis Martin, NYJ vs. Mia.	19	115	1
Michael Vick, Atl. at Den.	12	115	0
Willis McGahee, Buf. vs. Ariz.	30	102	2
Tiki Barber, NYG at Min.	24	101	2

300-YARD PASSING GAMES

Player, Team & Opponent	Att.	Cmp.	Yds.	TD	Int.
Jake Plummer, Den. vs. Atl.	55	31	499	4	3
Peyton Manning, Ind. at K.C.	44	25	472	5	1
Trent Green, K.C. vs. Ind.	34	27	389	3	0

100-YARD RECEIVING GAMES

Player, Team & Opponent	Rec.	Yds.	TD
Rod Smith, Den. vs. Atl.	9	208	1
Tony Gonzalez, K.C. vs. Ind.	8	125	2
Marvin Harrison, Ind. at K.C.	5	119	2
Reggie Wayne, Ind. at K.C.	6	119	2.
Jimmy Smith, Jac. at Hou.	9	117	0
Muhsin Muhammad, Car. at Sea.	8	106	2
David Givens, N.E. at Pit.	8	101	2
Terrell Owens, Phi. vs. Bal.	8	101	1
Keary Colbert, Car. at Sea.	4	100	0

RESULTS

SUNDAY, OCTOBER 31
DALLAS 31, Detroit 21
PHILADELPHIA 15, Baltimore 10
TENNESSEE 27, Cincinnati 20
N.Y. Giants 34, MINNESOTA 13
Green Bay 28, WASHINGTON 14
BUFFALO 38, Arizona 14
HOUSTON 20, Jacksonville 6
KANSAS CITY 45, Indianapolis 35
SEATTLE 23, Carolina 17
SAN DIEGO 42, Oakland 14
PITTSBURGH 34, New England 20
Atlanta 41, DENVER 28
CHICAGO 23, San Francisco 13

MONDAY, NOVEMBER 1
N.Y. JETS 41, Miami 14
Open Date: Cleveland, New Orleans, St. Louis, Tampa Bay

COWBOYS 31, LIONS 21
Sunday, October 31

Detroit	7	7	0	7—21
Dallas	7	7	7	10—31

First Quarter
Det.—Jones 1 pass from Harrington (Hanson kick), 3:58.
Dal.—Witten 17 pass from Testaverde (Cundiff kick), 13:53.

Second Quarter
Det.—Bly 55 interception return (Hanson kick), 6:42.
Dal.—K. Johnson 26 pass from Testaverde (Cundiff kick), 13:06.

Third Quarter
Dal.—Testaverde 3 run (Cundiff kick), :23.

Fourth Quarter
Dal.—FG, Cundiff 40, 8:01.
Det.—Kircus 50 pass from Harrington (Hanson kick), 9:31.
Dal.—K. Johnson 38 pass from Testaverde (Cundiff kick), 13:06.
Attendance—63,616.

	Detroit	Dallas
First downs	15	22
Rushes-yards	14-39	41-127
Passing	245	230
Punt returns	1-25	2-55
Kickoff returns	5-86	4-106
Interception returns	3-97	1-0
Comp.-att.-int.	19-32-1	19-24-3
Sacked-yards lost	1-10	1-5
Punts	5-40	2-50
Fumbles-lost	0-0	0-0
Penalties-yards	10-112	5-35
Time of possession	21:17	38:43

INDIVIDUAL STATISTICS
RUSHING—Detroit, Jones 11-36, Bryson 2-4, Harrington 1-(minus 1). Dallas, George 31-99, Anderson 7-5, Testaverde 2-10, Ra. Williams 1-13.
PASSING—Detroit, Harrington 19-32-1-255. Dallas, Testaverde 19-24-3-235.
RECEIVING—Detroit, Hakim 4-90, Jones 4-11, Swinton 2-33, Alexander 2-25, Streets 2-16, Bryson 2-14, Kircus 1-50, FitzSimmons 1-9, Trejo 1-7. Dallas, Witten 9-84, K. Johnson 3-80, Anderson 2-21, George 2-14, Barnes 2-6, Crayton 1-30.
MISSED FIELD GOAL ATTEMPTS—None.
INTERCEPTIONS—Detroit, Bly 2-85, Marion 1-12. Dallas, Frazier 1-0.
KICKOFF RETURNS—Detroit, Drummond 5-86. Dallas, Lee 3-85, Copper 1-21.
PUNT RETURNS—Detroit, Drummond 1-25. Dallas, Frazier 1-55, Crayton 1-0.
SACKS—Detroit, Lewis 1. Dallas, N. Jones 1.

EAGLES 15, RAVENS 10
Sunday, October 31

Baltimore	3	0	0	7—10
Philadelphia	3	3	0	9—15

First Quarter
Phi.—FG, Akers 20, 2:44.
Bal.—FG, Stover 44, 12:42.

Second Quarter
Phi.—FG, Akers 41, 10:08.

Fourth Quarter
Phi.—FG, Akers 43, :04.
Phi.—Owens 11 pass from McNabb (pass failed), 5:48.
Bal.—Wilcox 7 pass from Boller (Stover kick), 9:08.
Attendance—67,715.

	Baltimore	Philadelphia
First downs	19	19
Rushes-yards	27-113	23-98
Passing	214	200
Punt returns	5-27	3-16
Kickoff returns	2-42	2-39
Interception returns	0-0	1-0
Comp.-att.-int.	24-38-1	18-34-0
Sacked-yards lost	2-9	2-19
Punts	7-44	6-47
Fumbles-lost	2-1	2-1
Penalties-yards	6-91	8-72
Time of possession	33:50	26:10

INDIVIDUAL STATISTICS
RUSHING—Baltimore, C. Taylor 18-78, Smith 5-25, Ricard 2-1, Boller 1-?. Sams 1-2. Philadelphia, Levens 12-40, McNabb 6-36, Mahe 5-22.
PASSING—Baltimore, Boller 24-38-1-223. Philadelphia, McNabb 18-33-0-219, Bartrum 0-1-0-0.
RECEIVING—Baltimore, T. Taylor 6-80, Wilcox 5-26, C. Taylor 4-18, Moore 3-82, T. Jones 3-10, Smith 1-6, Sams 1-2, Ricard 1-(minus 1). Philadelphia, Owens 8-101, C. Lewis 3-34, Smith 2-28, Levens 2-10, Parry 1-22, Pinkston 1-16, Mahe 1-8.
MISSED FIELD GOAL ATTEMPTS—None.
INTERCEPTIONS—Philadelphia, M. Lewis 1-0.
KICKOFF RETURNS—Baltimore, Sams 2-42. Philadelphia, Hood 1-22, Reed 1-17.
PUNT RETURNS—Baltimore, Sams 3-18, Sanders 2-9. Philadelphia, Mahe 3-16.
SACKS—Baltimore, Reed 1, Weaver 1. Philadelphia, Kearse 2.

TITANS 27, BENGALS 20
Sunday, October 31

Cincinnati	3	0	10	7—20
Tennessee	0	13	14	0—27

First Quarter
Cin.—FG, Graham 28, 6:31.

Second Quarter
Ten.—FG, Anderson 23, :33.
Ten.—FG, Anderson 45, 6:27.
Ten.—Meier 1 pass from Volek (Anderson kick), 15:00.

Third Quarter
Cin.—M. Williams 51 interception return (Graham kick), 2:44.
Cin.—FG, Graham 50, 10:11.
Ten.—Fleming 13 pass from Volek (Anderson kick), 12:50.
Ten.—Brown 1 run (Anderson kick), 14:51.

Fourth Quarter
Cin.—Ru. Johnson 6 run (Graham kick), 1:13.
Attendance—68,932.

	Cincinnati	Tennessee
First downs	16	22
Rushes-yards	17-57	37-163
Passing	217	195
Punt returns	0-0	3-3
Kickoff returns	5-92	5-97
Interception returns	1-51	1-16
Comp.-att.-int.	20-36-1	21-32-1
Sacked-yards lost	4-30	2-15
Punts	5-53	5-44
Fumbles-lost	1-1	1-0
Penalties-yards	10-64	7-58
Time of possession	23:25	36:35

INDIVIDUAL STATISTICS
RUSHING—Cincinnati, Ru. Johnson 17-57. Tennessee, Brown 32-147, Volek 3-4, Hentrich 1-8, Holcombe 1-4.
PASSING—Cincinnati, Palmer 20-36-1-247. Tennessee, Volek 21-32-1-214.
RECEIVING—Cincinnati, C. Johnson 6-67, Houshmandzadeh 4-8, Washington 3-55, Watson 2-13, Ru. Johnson 2-4, Schobel 1-10, Stewart 1-5, R. Kelly 1-8. Tennessee, Mason 8-85, Brown 4-23, Meier 3-6, Fleming 2-5, Troupe 2-33, Holcombe 1-9, Berlin 1-4.
MISSED FIELD GOAL ATTEMPTS—None.
INTERCEPTIONS—Cincinnati, M. Williams 1-51. Tennessee, A. Dyson 1-16.
KICKOFF RETURNS—Cincinnati, C. Russell 4-87, Stewart 1-5. Tennessee, Waddell 4-96, Holcombe 1-1. PUNT RETURNS—Tennessee, Waddell 3-3.
SACKS—Cincinnati, Hardy 1, Clemons 1. Tennessee, Bulluck 1, Haynesworth 1, Carter 1, Starks 0.5, LaBoy 0.5.

GIANTS 34, VIKINGS 13
Sunday, October 31

N.Y. Giants	10	10	7	7—34
Minnesota	0	0	0	13—13

First Quarter
NYG—FG, Christie 50, 3:44.
NYG—Barber 2 run (Christie kick), 6:45.

Second Quarter
NYG—Barber 5 run (Christie kick), 1:40.
NYG—FG, Christie 30, 14:55. Third Quarter
NYG—Cloud 1 run (Christie kick), 9:21.

– 158 –

Fourth Quarter
G—Cloud 2 run (Christie kick), 2:52.
in.—M. Bennett 10 run (M. Andersen kick), 5:59.
in.—Burleson 1 pass from Culpepper (pass failed), 12:16.
Attendance—64,012.

	N.Y. Giants	Minnesota
rst downs	22	15
ushes-yards	39-168	20-93
assing	115	231
unt returns	3-15	2-6
ckoff returns	2-48	7-119
terception returns	2-50	0-0
omp.-att.-int.	13-21-0	24-41-2
acked-yards lost	5-29	0-0
unts	6-41	5-34
umbles-lost	3-0	1-1
enalties-yards	7-87	9-83
me of possession	32:28	27:32

INDIVIDUAL STATISTICS
RUSHING—New York, Barber 24-101, Cloud 9-55, Finn 3-7, Warner 2-0, I. lliard 1-5. Minnesota, Moore 8-29, Culpepper 5-32, M. Bennett 5-20, Burleson 8, M. Williams 1-4.
PASSING—New York, Warner 13-21-0-144. Minnesota, Culpepper 24-41-2-231.
RECEIVING—New York, Shockey 3-60, Toomer 3-31, I. Hilliard 2-8, Taylor 1-9, Barber 1-10, Finn 1-8, Shiancoe 1-5, Ponder 1-3. Minnesota, Burleson 6-43, . Bennett 6-18, M. Robinson 4-91, Wiggins 3-27, Campbell 3-18, Moore 1-26, erton 1-8.
MISSED FIELD GOAL ATTEMPTS—Minnesota, M. Andersen 38.
INTERCEPTIONS—New York, Wilson 1-39, W. Allen 1-11.
KICKOFF RETURNS—New York, Ponder 1-28, Jones 1-20. Minnesota, ampbell 5-101, Davis 1-15, Berton 1-3.
PUNT RETURNS—New York, Jones 3-15. Minnesota, Burleson 2-6.
SACKS—Minnesota, Johnstone 2, Mixon 1, K. Williams 1, Udeze 1.

PACKERS 28, REDSKINS 14
Sunday, October 31

reen Bay	3	14	3	8—28
ashington	0	7	0	7—14

First Quarter
.B.—FG, Longwell 37, 9:05.

Second Quarter
.B.—Green 1 run (Longwell kick), 1:19.
.B.—J. Walker 9 pass from Favre (Longwell kick), 8:32.
/as.—Gardner 12 pass from Brunell (Kimrin kick), 13:10.

Third Quarter
.B.—FG, Longwell 39, 2:11.

Fourth Quarter
/as.—Gardner 12 pass from Brunell (Kimrin kick), 10:14.
.B.—Green 11 run (Ferguson pass from Favre), 13:16.
Attendance—89,295.

	Green Bay	Washington
irst downs	20	20
ushes-yards	28-88	19-81
assing	273	191
unt returns	3-30	2-17
ickoff returns	2-49	5-125
terception returns	2-52	3-57
omp.-att.-int.	20-32-3	25-45-2
acked-yards lost	1-16	4-27
unts	3-44	6-39
umbles-lost	2-1	0-0
enalties-yards	9-73	10-82
me of possession	29:43	30:17

INDIVIDUAL STATISTICS
RUSHING—Green Bay, Green 24-70, Davenport 4-18. Washington, Portis 7-70, Gardner 1-6, Brunell 1-5.
PASSING—Green Bay, Favre 20-32-3-289. Washington, Brunell 25-44-2-18, Gardner 0-1-0-0.
RECEIVING—Green Bay, J. Walker 5-57, Green 4-73, Henderson 4-17, Driver -48, Ferguson 1-48, Martin 1-25, Luchey 1-11, Franks 1-7, Fisher 1-3. Washington, Coles 7-84, Portis 7-17, Jacobs 5-30, Gardner 3-41, Cooley 2-23, oyal 1-23.
MISSED FIELD GOAL ATTEMPTS—Washington, Kimrin 35.
INTERCEPTIONS—Green Bay, Harris 1-29, Jue 1-23. Washington, Springs 2-7, Smoot 1-0.
KICKOFF RETURNS—Green Bay, Davenport 2-49. Washington, Betts 2-57, Morton 2-46, Thrash 1-22.

PUNT RETURNS—Green Bay, Chatman 3-30. Washington, Thrash 2-17.
SACKS—Green Bay, Kampman 1, Gbaja-Biamila 1, Carroll 1, Jenkins 1. Washington, Washington 1.

BILLS 38, CARDINALS 14
Sunday, October 31

Arizona	0	7	0	7—14
Buffalo	10	7	0	21—38

First Quarter
Buf.—FG, Lindell 25, 5:28.
Buf.—McGahee 5 run (Lindell kick), 10:29.

Second Quarter
Ariz.—O. Ayanbadejo 4 run (Rackers kick), 6:35.
Buf.—McGee 87 kickoff return (Lindell kick), 6:48.

Fourth Quarter
Buf.—Moulds 8 pass from Bledsoe (Lindell kick), :05.
Buf.—Euhus 12 pass from Bledsoe (Lindell kick), 2:55.
Buf.—McGahee 1 run (Lindell kick), 8:03.
Ariz.—B. Johnson 28 pass from McCown (Rackers kick), 11:06.
Attendance—65,887.

	Arizona	Buffalo
First downs	14	11
Rushes-yards	38-128	38-128
Passing	85	81
Punt returns	2-16	6-89
Kickoff returns	6-69	3-115
Interception returns	0-0	0-0
Comp.-att.-int.	9-24-0	8-17-0
Sacked-yards lost	3-16	0-0
Punts	10-37	7-44
Fumbles-lost	3-0	2-0
Penalties-yards	14-101	7-55
Time of possession	31:42	28:18

INDIVIDUAL STATISTICS
RUSHING—Arizona, E. Smith 22-64, Hambrick 13-53, O. Ayanbadejo 1-4, Fitzgerald 1-4, McCown 1-3. Buffalo, McGahee 30-102, Burns 4-27, Matthews 2-(minus 3), Henry 1-2, Bledsoe 1-0.
PASSING—Arizona, McCown 9-24-0-101. Buffalo, Bledsoe 8-17-0-81.
RECEIVING—Arizona, Boldin 4-50, B. Johnson 3-38, F. Jones 1-8, E. Smith 1-5. Buffalo, Moulds 3-40, Euhus 2-21, McGahee 1-9, Evans 1-9, Shelton 1-2.
MISSED FIELD GOAL ATTEMPTS—Arizona, Rackers 64.
INTERCEPTIONS—None.
KICKOFF RETURNS—Arizona, Croom 4-69, Hayes 2-0. Buffalo, McGee 3-115.
PUNT RETURNS—Arizona, K. Williams 2-16. Buffalo, Clements 5-82, Reed 1-7.
SACKS—Buffalo, Edwards 1, Wire 1, Fletcher 0.5, Clements 0.5.

TEXANS 20, JAGUARS 6
Sunday, October 31

Jacksonville	0	3	0	3— 6
Houston	7	3	0	10—20

First Quarter
Hou.—Bradford 15 pass from Carr (K. Brown kick), 11:40.

Second Quarter
Jac.—FG, Scobee 44, 8:27.
Hou.—FG, K. Brown 38, 15:00.

Fourth Quarter
Hou.—FG, K. Brown 21, 8:15.
Jac.—FG, Scobee 36, 11:08.
Hou.—Faggins 43 interception return (K. Brown kick), 14:18.
Attendance—70,502.

	Jacksonville	Houston
First downs	14	24
Rushes-yards	12-39	32-93
Passing	248	276
Punt returns	2-14	2-34
Kickoff returns	4-105	3-63
Interception returns	0-0	2-43
Comp.-att.-int.	27-42-2	26-35-0
Sacked-yards lost	1-7	0-0
Punts	4-47	4-39
Fumbles-lost	1-0	2-2
Penalties-yards	11-80	8-75
Time of possession	24:54	35:06

INDIVIDUAL STATISTICS

RUSHING—Jacksonville, Toefield 5-22, F. Taylor 3-9, Leftwich 2-5, G. Jones 2-3. Houston, D. Davis 22-56, Wells 4-2, Carr 3-15, Gaffney 2-15, Stanley 1-5.

PASSING—Jacksonville, Leftwich 25-40-2-227, Garrard 2-2-0-28. Houston, Carr 26-34-0-276, Banks 0-1-0-0.

RECEIVING—Jacksonville, J. Smith 9-117, T. Edwards 5-43, R. Williams 5-27, Toefield 4-28, B. Jones 1-18, F. Taylor 1-10, M. Edwards 1-9, G. Jones 1-3. Houston, An. Johnson 9-74, Gaffney 5-88, D. Davis 5-39, Bradford 3-52, Wells 2-7, Armstrong 1-11, Miller 1-5.

MISSED FIELD GOAL ATTEMPTS—Jacksonville, Scobee 49.

INTERCEPTIONS—Houston, Faggins 1-43, Wong 1-0.

KICKOFF RETURNS—Jacksonville, T. Edwards 4-105. Houston, Moses 2-54, Wells 1-9.

PUNT RETURNS—Jacksonville, T. Edwards 2-14. Houston, Moses 2-34.

SACKS—Houston, Payne 1.

CHIEFS 45, COLTS 35
Sunday, October 31

Indianapolis	7	7	14	7—35
Kansas City	7	24	0	14—45

First Quarter
Ind.—Harrison 52 pass from Manning (Vanderjagt kick), 10:42.
K.C.—Gonzalez 21 pass from Green (Tynes kick), 13:33.

Second Quarter
K.C.—Morton 7 pass from Green (Tynes kick), :40.
K.C.—Holmes 21 run (Tynes kick), 5:52.
Ind.—Pollard 5 pass from Manning (Vanderjagt kick), 8:57.
K.C.—Holmes 11 run (Tynes kick), 10:01.
K.C.—FG, Tynes 32, 14:13.

Third Quarter
Ind.—Harrison 22 pass from Manning (Vanderjagt kick), 3:17.
Ind.—Wayne 41 pass from Manning (Vanderjagt kick), 10:44.

Fourth Quarter
K.C.—Holmes 1 run (Tynes kick), 2:02.
Ind.—Wayne 6 pass from Manning (Vanderjagt kick), 9:33.
K.C.—Gonzalez 14 pass from Green (Tynes kick), 12:43.
Attendance—78,312.

	Indianapolis	Kansas City
First downs	23	33
Rushes-yards	12-33	42-203
Passing	472	387
Punt returns	1-7	1-46
Kickoff returns	8-182	6-122
Interception returns	0-0	1-65
Comp.-att.-int.	25-44-1	27-34-0
Sacked-yards lost	0-0	1-2
Punts	4-45	2-39
Fumbles-lost	1-0	4-2
Penalties-yards	7-40	5-46
Time of possession	22:27	37:33

INDIVIDUAL STATISTICS

RUSHING—Indianapolis, James 10-34, H. Smith 1-2, Rhodes 1-(minus 3). Kansas City, Holmes 32-143, Blaylock 3-18, Green 3-(minus 3), Morton 2-26, L. Johnson 1-19, Cheek 1-0.

PASSING—Indianapolis, Manning 25-44-1-472. Kansas City, Green 27-34-0-389.

RECEIVING—Indianapolis, Wayne 6-119, James 6-90, Harrison 5-119, Clark 3-88, Pollard 3-21, Stokley 2-35. Kansas City, Gonzalez 8-125, Morton 5-69, Kennison 5-50, Holmes 3-82, Hall 3-43, Blaylock 2-19, Richardson 1-1.

MISSED FIELD GOAL ATTEMPTS—Indianapolis, Vanderjagt 54.

INTERCEPTIONS—Kansas City, Wesley 1-65.

KICKOFF RETURNS—Indianapolis, Rhodes 8-182. Kansas City, Hall 6-122.

PUNT RETURNS—Indianapolis, David 1-7. Kansas City, Hall 1-46.

SACKS—Indianapolis, Doss 1.

SEAHAWKS 23, PANTHERS 17
Sunday, October 31

Carolina	0	7	3	7—17
Seattle	7	7	3	6—23

First Quarter
Sea.—Alexander 3 pass from Hasselbeck (J. Brown kick), 5:48.

Second Quarter
Sea.—Alexander 4 run (J. Brown kick), 5:53.
Car.—Muhammad 15 pass from Delhomme (Kasay kick), 9:46.

Third Quarter
Car.—FG, Kasay 30, 2:56.
Sea.—FG, J. Brown 27, 8:16.

Fourth Quarter
Sea.—FG, J. Brown 45, 1:33.
Sea.—FG, J. Brown 22, 9:18.
Car.—Muhammad 7 pass from Delhomme (Kasay kick), 13:21.
Attendance—66,214.

	Carolina	Seattle
First downs	16	24
Rushes-yards	20-94	43-237
Passing	248	199
Punt returns	0-0	1-10
Kickoff returns	6-157	3-57
Interception returns	1-21	1-58
Comp.-att.-int.	19-36-1	21-30-1
Sacked-yards lost	0-0	1-7
Punts	6-42	1-56
Fumbles-lost	0-0	3-2
Penalties-yards	10-79	2-13
Time of possession	24:22	35:38

INDIVIDUAL STATISTICS

RUSHING—Carolina, Harris 9-45, Hoover 7-20, Delhomme 3-18, Goings 11. Seattle, Alexander 32-195, Hasselbeck 7-24, Strong 4-18.

PASSING—Carolina, Delhomme 19-36-1-248. Seattle, Hasselbeck 21-30-1-206.

RECEIVING—Carolina, Muhammad 8-106, Colbert 4-100, Mangum 4-29, Goings 2-14, Hoover 1-7. Seattle, Jackson 6-71, K. Robinson 3-52, Strong 3-29, Stevens 3-16, Alexander 3-13, Mili 2-22, Rice 1-6.

MISSED FIELD GOAL ATTEMPTS—None.

INTERCEPTIONS—Carolina, Allen 1-21. Seattle, Trufant 1-58.

KICKOFF RETURNS—Carolina, Broussard 6-157. Seattle, Morris 1-21, Carter 1-20, Mili 1-12.

PUNT RETURNS—Seattle, Richard 1-10.

SACKS—Carolina, Buckner 1.

CHARGERS 42, RAIDERS 14
Sunday, October 31

Oakland	0	7	7	0—14
San Diego	14	14	14	0—42

First Quarter
S.D.—Peelle 17 pass from Brees (Kaeding kick), 3:46.
S.D.—Tomlinson 1 run (Kaeding kick), 14:52.

Second Quarter
Oak.—Wheatley 5 run (Janikowski kick), 4:58.
S.D.—McCardell 13 pass from Brees (Kaeding kick), 10:04.
S.D.—Dwight 23 pass from Brees (Kaeding kick), 14:24.

Third Quarter
S.D.—Gates 5 pass from Brees (Kaeding kick), 2:55.
S.D.—Gates 1 pass from Brees (Kaeding kick), 11:52.
Oak.—Jolley 13 pass from Collins (Janikowski kick), 14:58.
Attendance—66,210.

	Oakland	San Diego
First downs	15	33
Rushes-yards	11-22	38-175
Passing	259	273
Punt returns	1-18	4-62
Kickoff returns	5-94	2-71
Interception returns	0-0	2-17
Comp.-att.-int.	24-39-2	22-25-0
Sacked-yards lost	1-4	1-8
Punts	5-50	3-49
Fumbles-lost	1-1	1-1
Penalties-yards	10-75	7-46
Time of possession	24:30	35:30

INDIVIDUAL STATISTICS

RUSHING—Oakland, Zereoue 6-(minus 1), Wheatley 4-23, Redmond 1-0. San Diego, Tomlinson 19-71, Chatman 12-69, Neal 5-14, Brees 2-21.

PASSING—Oakland, Collins 24-39-2-263. San Diego, Brees 22-25-0-281.

RECEIVING—Oakland, Zereoue 5-42, Porter 4-50, Wheatley 4-22, Gabriel 3-50, Redmond 3-29, Jolley 3-22, C. Anderson 1-28, Morant 1-20. San Diego, Parker 6-91, Gates 5-63, McCardell 4-55, Peelle 3-28, Neal 2-14, Dwight 1-23, Tomlinson 1-7.

MISSED FIELD GOAL ATTEMPTS—None.

INTERCEPTIONS—San Diego, Hart 1-13, Davis 1-4.

KICKOFF RETURNS—Oakland, Gabriel 5-94. San Diego, Dwight 2-71.

PUNT RETURNS—Oakland, Buchanon 1-18. San Diego, E. Parker 4-62.

SACKS—Oakland, Kelly 1. San Diego, Scott 1.

STEELERS 34, PATRIOTS 20
Sunday, October 31

New England	3	7	3	7—20
Pittsburgh	21	3	10	0—34

First Quarter
N.E.—FG, Vinatieri 43, 3:21.
Pit.—Burress 47 pass from Roethlisberger (Reed kick), 11:14.
Pit.—Burress 4 pass from Roethlisberger (Reed kick), 14:31.
Pit.—Townsend 39 interception return (Reed kick), 14:47.

Second Quarter
Pit.—FG, Reed 19, 12:54.
N.E.—Givens 2 pass from Brady (Vinatieri kick), 14:18.

Third Quarter
Pit.—Bettis 2 run (Reed kick), 1:54.
N.E.—FG, Vinatieri 25, 4:19.
Pit.—FG, Reed 29, 12:54.

Fourth Quarter
N.E.—Givens 23 pass from Brady (Vinatieri kick), 8:27.
Attendance—64,737.

	New England	Pittsburgh
First downs	19	25
Rushes-yards	6-5	49-221
Passing	243	196
Punt returns	3-15	2-10
Kickoff returns	6-158	5-136
Interception returns	0-0	2-39
Comp.-att.-int.	25-43-2	18-24-0
Sacked-yards lost	4-28	0-0
Punts	3-52	4-44
Fumbles-lost	3-2	1-0
Penalties-yards	6-55	9-90
Time of possession	17:02	42:58

INDIVIDUAL STATISTICS
RUSHING—New England, Faulk 5-4, Cobbs 1-1. Pittsburgh, Staley 25-125, Bettis 15-65, Roethlisberger 5-3, Haynes 3-17, Ward 1-11.
PASSING—New England, Brady 25-43-2-271. Pittsburgh, Roethlisberger 18-24-0-196.
RECEIVING—New England, Givens 8-101, Faulk 8-72, T. Brown 5-59, Patten 4-39. Pittsburgh, Ward 6-58, Randle El 6-44, Burress 3-63, Haynes 2-18, Kreider 1-13.
MISSED FIELD GOAL ATTEMPTS—None.
INTERCEPTIONS—Pittsburgh, Townsend 1-39, I. Taylor 1-0.
KICKOFF RETURNS—New England, B. Johnson 6-158. Pittsburgh, Randle El 4-113, Colclough 1-23.
PUNT RETURNS—New England, Faulk 3-15. Pittsburgh, Randle El 2-10.
SACKS—Pittsburgh, Porter 3, A. Smith 1.

FALCONS 41, BRONCOS 28
Sunday, October 31

Atlanta	3	17	7	14—41
Denver	14	0	0	14—28

First Quarter
Den.—Hape 1 pass from Plummer (Elam kick), 5:35.
Atl.—FG, Feely 24, 11:22.
Den.—Smith 80 pass from Plummer (Elam kick), 11:34.

Second Quarter
Atl.—Duckett 21 run (Feely kick), 3:58.
Atl.—P. Price 34 pass from Vick (Feely kick), 11:05.
Atl.—FG, Feely 43, 14:41.

Third Quarter
Atl.—Dunn 5 run (Feely kick), 4:24.

Fourth Quarter
Atl.—P. Price 25 pass from Vick (Feely kick), :43.
Den.—Watts 7 pass from Plummer (Elam kick), 5:32.
Atl.—Mathis 66 interception return (Feely kick), 12:40.
Den.—Lelie 35 pass from Plummer (Elam kick), 14:03.
Attendance—75,083.

	Atlanta	Denver
First downs	22	27
Rushes-yards	36-195	19-68
Passing	272	499
Punt returns	1-12	2-23
Kickoff returns	3-97	4-79
Interception returns	3-78	0-0
Comp.-att.-int.	19-25-0	31-55-3
Sacked-yards lost	1-5	0-0
Punts	3-40	3-37
Fumbles-lost	2-1	2-0
Penalties-yards	7-56	9-70
Time of possession	30:41	29:19

INDIVIDUAL STATISTICS
RUSHING—Atlanta, Dunn 15-33, Vick 12-115, Duckett 8-45, Jenkins 1-2. Denver, Droughns 15-49, Plummer 2-5, Watts 1-8, Smith 1-6.
PASSING—Atlanta, Vick 18-24-0-252, P. Price 1-1-0-25. Denver, Plummer 31-55-3-499.
RECEIVING—Atlanta, Crumpler 7-86, White 3-46, Finneran 3-19, P. Price 2-59, Griffith 2-14, Jenkins 1-46, Dunn 1-7. Denver, Smith 9-208, Watts 7-86, Lelie 6-94, Droughns 6-63, Putzier 2-47, Hape 1-1.
MISSED FIELD GOAL ATTEMPTS—Atlanta, Feely 49.
INTERCEPTIONS—Atlanta, Mathis 1-66, Brooking 1-12, Kerney 1-0.
KICKOFF RETURNS—Atlanta, Rossum 3-97. Denver, R. Alexander 4-79.
PUNT RETURNS—Atlanta, Rossum 1-12. Denver, Smith 2-23.
SACKS—Denver, Fatafehi 1.

BEARS 23, 49ERS 13
Sunday, October 31

San Francisco	10	3	0	0—13
Chicago	7	6	0	10—23

First Quarter
Chi.—Berrian 49 pass from Krenzel (Edinger kick), 1:59.
S.F.—Carpenter 80 fumble return (T. Peterson kick), 9:34.
S.F.—FG, T. Peterson 48, 14:20.

Second Quarter
Chi.—FG, Edinger 52, 1:33.
S.F.—FG, T. Peterson 51, 8:40.
Chi.—FG, Edinger 45, 10:25.

Fourth Quarter
Chi.—FG, Edinger 27, 1:01.
Chi.—Vasher 71 interception return (Edinger kick), 11:08.
Attendance—62,054.

	San Francisco	Chicago
First downs	10	14
Rushes-yards	23-62	33-120
Passing	100	134
Punt returns	3-20	6-84
Kickoff returns	6-135	4-159
Interception returns	1-14	1-71
Comp.-att.-int.	16-36-1	13-25-1
Sacked-yards lost	3-22	5-34
Punts	8-41	6-37
Fumbles-lost	2-1	2-2
Penalties-yards	5-30	8-58
Time of possession	26:55	33:05

INDIVIDUAL STATISTICS
RUSHING—San Francisco, Barlow 18-56, Beasley 3-1, Dorsey 2-5. Chicago, Thomas 25-98, Krenzel 4-9, Wade 2-5, Berrian 1-7, T. Jones 1-1.
PASSING—San Francisco, Dorsey 16-36-1-122. Chicago, Krenzel 13-25-1-168.
RECEIVING—San Francisco, Lloyd 5-63, Barlow 3-16, Jackson 2-7, Beasley 2-(minus 1), Battle 1-20, E. Johnson 1-9, Conway 1-4, Walker 1-4. Chicago, Thomas 4-46, Wade 3-33, B. Johnson 3-5, Berrian 1-49, Clark 1-21, Terrell 1-14.
MISSED FIELD GOAL ATTEMPTS—San Francisco, T. Peterson 50. Chicago, Edinger 53.
INTERCEPTIONS—San Francisco, Heard 1-14. Chicago, Vasher 1-71.
KICKOFF RETURNS—San Francisco, Robertson 6-135. Chicago, Azumah 4-159.
PUNT RETURNS—San Francisco, Battle 3-20. Chicago, McQuarters 6-84.
SACKS—San Francisco, Young 2, Winborn 1.5, B. Moore 1, Engelberger 0.5. Chicago, Urlacher 2, Idonije 1.

JETS 41, DOLPHINS 14
Monday, November 1

Miami	0	7	0	7—14
N.Y. Jets	7	10	14	10—41

First Quarter
NYJ—Chrebet 35 pass from Pennington (Brien kick), 7:34.

Second Quarter
Mia.—McMichael 21 pass from Fiedler (Bryant kick), 10:25.
NYJ—McCareins 27 pass from Pennington (Brien kick), 13:53.
NYJ—FG, Brien 49, 15:00.

Third Quarter
NYJ—C. Martin 25 run (Brien kick), 4:31.
NYJ—Baker 1 pass from Pennington (Brien kick), 12:50.

Fourth Quarter
NYJ—FG, Brien 43, 2:10.
NYJ—Jordan 25 run (Brien kick), 3:46.
Mia.—Thompson 29 pass from Fiedler (Bryant kick), 15:00.
Attendance—78,216.

	Miami	N.Y. Jets
First downs	16	22
Rushes-yards	16-78	41-275
Passing	181	197
Punt returns	2-9	4-(-4)
Kickoff returns	7-135	2-52
Interception returns	0-0	2-0
Comp.-att.-int.	20-41-2	12-20-0
Sacked-yards lost	4-37	1-0
Punts	8-40	5-38
Fumbles-lost	2-1	0-0
Penalties-yards	3-20	6-45
Time of possession	26:19	33:41

INDIVIDUAL STATISTICS

RUSHING—Miami, Morris 11-48, Minor 4-4, Fiedler 1-26. New York, C. Martin 19-115, Jordan 14-115, Askew 6-23, Pennington 2-22.

PASSING—Miami, Fiedler 20-41-2-218. New York, Pennington 11-19-0-189, Q. Carter 1-1-0-8.

RECEIVING—Miami, McMichael 7-87, Booker 3-37, Chambers 3-29, Morris 3-12, Thompson 1-29, Konrad 1-15, Lee 1-6, Gilmore 1-3. New York, McCareins 3-56, Chrebet 2-41, Moss 1-47, Jordan 1-21, C. Martin 1-13, Sowell 1-8, Cotchery 1-5, Becht 1-5, Baker 1-1.

MISSED FIELD GOAL ATTEMPTS—None.

INTERCEPTIONS—New York, McGraw 1-0, Buckley 1-0.

KICKOFF RETURNS—Miami, Welker 6-117, Gilmore 1-18. New York, J. Carter 2-52.

PUNT RETURNS—Miami, Welker 2-9. New York, Moss 4-(minus 4).

SACKS—Miami, D. Bowens 1. New York, J. Ferguson 2, J. Abraham 1, Robertson 0.5, Barton 0.5.

WEEK 9

STANDINGS

AMERICAN FOOTBALL CONFERENCE

EAST DIVISION

	W	L	T	Pct.	PF	PA
New England	7	1	0	.875	208	146
N.Y. Jets	6	2	0	.750	185	138
Buffalo	3	5	0	.375	137	137
Miami	1	8	0	.111	123	186

NORTH DIVISION

	W	L	T	Pct.	PF	PA
Pittsburgh	7	1	0	.875	197	137
Baltimore	5	3	0	.625	154	113
Cincinnati	3	5	0	.375	152	169
Cleveland	3	5	0	.375	160	174

SOUTH DIVISION

	W	L	T	Pct.	PF	PA
Indianapolis	5	3	0	.625	249	206
Jacksonville	5	3	0	.625	128	146
Houston	4	4	0	.500	171	174
Tennessee	3	5	0	.375	151	178

WEST DIVISION

	W	L	T	Pct.	PF	PA
Denver	6	3	0	.667	199	154
San Diego	6	3	0	.667	262	173
Kansas City	3	5	0	.375	237	211
Oakland	3	6	0	.333	165	247

NATIONAL FOOTBALL CONFERENCE

EAST DIVISION

	W	L	T	Pct.	PF	PA
Philadelphia	7	1	0	.875	189	131
N.Y. Giants	5	3	0	.625	172	141
Dallas	3	5	0	.375	141	203
Washington	3	5	0	.375	115	133

NORTH DIVISION

	W	L	T	Pct.	PF	PA
Minnesota	5	3	0	.625	211	193
Detroit	4	4	0	.500	147	171
Green Bay	4	4	0	.500	206	186
Chicago	3	5	0	.375	136	142

SOUTH DIVISION

	W	L	T	Pct.	PF	PA
Atlanta	6	2	0	.750	170	170
New Orleans	3	5	0	.375	171	234
Tampa Bay	3	5	0	.375	143	155
Carolina	1	7	0	.125	124	185

WEST DIVISION

	W	L	T	Pct.	PF	PA
Seattle	5	3	0	.625	194	145
St. Louis	4	4	0	.500	180	205
Arizona	3	5	0	.375	150	165
San Francisco	1	7	0	.125	145	224

TOP PERFORMANCES

100-YARD RUSHING GAMES

Player, Team & Opponent	Att.	Yds.	TD
Shaun Alexander, Sea. at S.F.	26	160	2
Jerome Bettis, Pit. vs. Phi.	33	149	0
Clinton Portis, Was. at Det.	34	147	0
Willis McGahee, Buf. vs. NYJ	37	132	1
Michael Pittman, T.B. vs. K.C.	15	128	3
Edgerrin James, Ind. vs. Min.	26	123	0
Reuben Droughns, Den. vs. Hou.	29	120	0
Corey Dillon, N.E. at St.L.	25	112	1
Anthony Thomas, Chi. at NYG	28	110	2

300-YARD PASSING GAMES

Player, Team & Opponent	Att.	Cmp.	Yds.	TD	Int.
Trent Green, K.C. at T.B.	42	32	369	3	2

100-YARD RECEIVING GAMES

Player, Team & Opponent	Rec.	Yds.	TD
Santana Moss, NYJ at Buf.	6	157	1
Tony Gonzalez, K.C. at T.B.	9	123	1
Az-Zahir Hakim, Det. vs. Was.	7	120	0
Darrell Jackson, Sea. at S.F.	5	114	2
Torry Holt, St.L. vs. N.E.	6	111	1
Chris Chambers, Mia. vs. Ariz.	7	104	0
Eddie Kennison, K.C. at T.B.	6	104	0
David Givens, N.E. at St.L.	5	100	0

RESULTS

SUNDAY, NOVEMBER 7
CINCINNATI 26, Dallas 3
PITTSBURGH 27, Philadelphia 3
TAMPA BAY 34, Kansas City 31
Arizona 24, MIAMI 23
Oakland 27, CAROLINA 24
BUFFALO 22, N.Y. Jets 17
Washington 17, DETROIT 10
Seattle 42, SAN FRANCISCO 27
SAN DIEGO 43, New Orleans 17
Chicago 28, N.Y. GIANTS 21
New England 40, ST. LOUIS 22
DENVER 31, Houston 13
BALTIMORE 27, Cleveland 13

MONDAY, NOVEMBER 8
INDIANAPOLIS 31, Minnesota 28
Open Date: Atlanta, Green Bay, Jacksonville, Tennessee

2004 REVIEW *Week 9*

BENGALS 26, COWBOYS 3
Sunday, November 7

Dallas	0	3	0	0— 3
Cincinnati	3	6	7	10—26

First Quarter
Cin.—FG, Graham 35, 10:54.

Second Quarter
Cin.—FG, Graham 47, 1:58.
Cin.—FG, Graham 45, 5:03.
Dal.—FG, Cundiff 24, 14:42.

Third Quarter
Cin.—Schobel 76 pass from Palmer (Graham kick), 5:24.

Fourth Quarter
Cin.—FG, Graham 30, 2:39.
Cin.—Palmer 2 run (Graham kick), 12:40.
Attendance—65,721.

	Dallas	Cincinnati
First downs	13	15
Rushes-yards	27-109	31-116
Passing	202	212
Punt returns	2-21	2-29
Kickoff returns	7-140	2-37
Interception returns	0-0	3-0
Comp.-att.-int.	18-30-3	21-32-0
Sacked-yards lost	1-5	0-0
Punts	4-48	5-40
Fumbles-lost	2-2	0-0
Penalties-yards	7-46	4-20
Time of possession	26:43	33:17

INDIVIDUAL STATISTICS
RUSHING—Dallas, Anderson 10-29, George 8-23, Lee 6-39, Testaverde 3-18. Cincinnati, Ru. Johnson 26-95, Watson 2-10, Palmer 2-1, C. Russell 1-10.
PASSING—Dallas, Testaverde 18-30-3-207. Cincinnati, Palmer 21-32-0-212.
RECEIVING—Dallas, Witten 6-97, K. Johnson 4-58, Anderson 4-21, Crayton 2-14, Ra. Williams 1-14, George 1-3. Cincinnati, C. Johnson 8-74, Ru. Johnson 4-19, J. Johnson 3-11, Schobel 2-84, R. Kelly 2-9, Houshmandzadeh 1-8, Walter 1-7.
MISSED FIELD GOAL ATTEMPTS—None.
INTERCEPTIONS—Cincinnati, M. Williams 1-0, O'Neal 1-0, James 1-0.
KICKOFF RETURNS—Dallas, Lee 4-90, Copper 2-37, Pierce 1-13. Cincinnati, C. Russell 2-37.
PUNT RETURNS—Dallas, Frazier 2-21. Cincinnati, Houshmandzadeh 2-29.
SACKS—Cincinnati, Geathers 1.

STEELERS 27, EAGLES 3
Sunday, November 7

Philadelphia	0	3	0	0— 3
Pittsburgh	14	7	3	3—27

First Quarter
Pit.—Ward 16 run (Reed kick), 6:04.
Pit.—Ward 20 pass from Roethlisberger (Reed kick), 12:33.

Second Quarter
Pit.—Riemersma 2 pass from Roethlisberger (Reed kick), 4:09.
Phi.—FG, Akers 33, 8:46.

Third Quarter
Pit.—FG, Reed 42, 12:24.

Fourth Quarter
Pit.—FG, Reed 31, 7:02.
Attendance—64,975.

	Philadelphia	Pittsburgh
First downs	7	25
Rushes-yards	9-23	56-252
Passing	90	168
Punt returns	0-0	6-26
Kickoff returns	3-95	1-22
Interception returns	1-32	1-41
Comp.-att.-int.	15-24-1	11-18-1
Sacked-yards lost	4-19	2-15
Punts	6-42	0-0
Fumbles-lost	0-0	2-1
Penalties-yards	5-25	4-20
Time of possession	18:11	41:49

INDIVIDUAL STATISTICS
RUSHING—Philadelphia, Westbrook 6-17, Levens 2-4, Mahe 1-2. Pittsburgh, Bettis 33-149, Haynes 12-51, Roethlisberger 6-10, Parker 3-14, Ward 1-16, Randle El 1-12.
PASSING—Philadelphia, McNabb 15-24-1-109. Pittsburgh, Roethlisberger 11-18-1-183.
RECEIVING—Philadelphia, Owens 7-53, C. Lewis 3-32, Westbrook 3-4, Pinkston 1-10, Smith 1-10. Pittsburgh, Burress 3-70, Haynes 2-44, Ward 2-32, Cushing 1-17, Kreider 1-12, Randle El 1-6, Riemersma 1-2.
MISSED FIELD GOAL ATTEMPTS—Pittsburgh, Reed 33.
INTERCEPTIONS—Philadelphia, Dawkins 1-32. Pittsburgh, Farrior 1-41.
KICKOFF RETURNS—Philadelphia, Hood 2-74, Wynn 1-21. Pittsburgh, Colclough 1-22.
PUNT RETURNS—Pittsburgh, Randle El 5-21, Haynes 1-5.
SACKS—Philadelphia, Rayburn 2. Pittsburgh, W. Williams 1, Farrior 1, Haggans 1, Foote 1.

BUCCANEERS 34, CHIEFS 31
Sunday, November 7

Kansas City	7	17	7	0—31
Tampa Bay	7	14	7	6—34

First Quarter
K.C.—Morton 25 pass from Green (Tynes kick), 5:18.
T.B.—Cook 8 pass from Griese (Gramatica kick), 7:21.

Second Quarter
T.B.—Pittman 1 run (Gramatica kick), 1:11.
K.C.—Holmes 2 run (Tynes kick), 5:55.
K.C.—FG, Tynes 31, 8:35.
T.B.—Dilger 3 pass from Griese (Gramatica kick), 13:05.
K.C.—Gonzalez 23 pass from Green (Tynes kick), 14:25.

Third Quarter
T.B.—Pittman 78 run (Gramatica kick), 1:00.
K.C.—Dunn 1 pass from Green (Tynes kick), 12:47.

Fourth Quarter
T.B.—Pittman 3 run (kick failed), 3:10.
Attendance—65,495.

	Kansas City	Tampa Bay
First downs	27	23
Rushes-yards	30-105	20-130
Passing	354	288
Punt returns	2-42	1-2
Kickoff returns	5-92	5-108
Interception returns	0-0	2-0
Comp.-att.-int.	32-42-2	22-34-0
Sacked-yards lost	2-15	1-8
Punts	1-44	4-45
Fumbles-lost	2-1	0-0
Penalties-yards	10-97	10-95
Time of possession	33:39	26:21

INDIVIDUAL STATISTICS
RUSHING—Kansas City, Holmes 16-59, L. Johnson 10-21, Green 2-4, Kennison 1-15, Morton 1-6. Tampa Bay, Pittman 15-128, Griese 4-1, Graham 1-1.
PASSING—Kansas City, Green 32-42-2-369. Tampa Bay, Griese 22-34-0-296.
RECEIVING—Kansas City, Gonzalez 9-123, Kennison 6-104, Morton 6-69, L. Johnson 4-38, Holmes 4-3, Horn 1-30, Richardson 1-1, Dunn 1-1. Tampa Bay, Clayton 5-90, Dilger 5-47, Jurevicius 3-43, Cook 3-17, Galloway 2-40, Pittman 2-30, Heller 1-22, Lee 1-7.
MISSED FIELD GOAL ATTEMPTS—Tampa Bay, Gramatica 46.
INTERCEPTIONS—Tampa Bay, D. Smith 1-0, Phillips 1-0.
KICKOFF RETURNS—Kansas City, Hall 3-76, Horn 2-16. Tampa Bay, Cox 4-88, Comella 1-20.
PUNT RETURNS—Kansas City, Hall 2-42. Tampa Bay, Galloway 1-2.
SACKS—Kansas City, Fujita 1. Tampa Bay, Barber 1, D. White 1.

CARDINALS 24, DOLPHINS 23
Sunday, November 7

Arizona	3	0	7	14—24
Miami	9	3	0	11—23

First Quarter
Mia.—FG, Gramatica 30, 2:58.
Ariz.—FG, Rackers 29, 5:58.
Mia.—Konrad 20 pass from Fiedler (kick failed), 14:02.

Second Quarter
Mia.—FG, Gramatica 29, 6:53.

Third Quarter
riz.—Starks 41 interception return (Rackers kick), 11:42.

Fourth Quarter
riz.—E. Smith 5 run (Rackers kick), 5:16.
Mia.—FG, Gramatica 28, 7:07.
Mia.—Morris 1 run (McMichael pass from Feeley), 13:04.
riz.—Fitzgerald 2 pass from McCown (Rackers kick), 14:41.
Attendance—72,612.

	Arizona	Miami
rst downs	17	22
ushes-yards	27-121	31-168
assing	149	235
unt returns	1-9	4-44
ckoff returns	5-96	4-90
terception returns	1-41	0-0
omp.-att.-int.	18-31-0	18-36-1
acked-yards lost	1-13	3-23
unts	7-44	5-46
umbles-lost	2-1	2-1
enalties-yards	9-45	12-99
me of possession	27:34	32:26

INDIVIDUAL STATISTICS
RUSHING—Arizona, E. Smith 19-42, Hambrick 4-70, O. Ayanbadejo 2-7, cCown 1-9, B. Johnson 1-(minus 7). Miami, Morris 16-56, Minor 11-90, edler 2-6, Chambers 1-24, Booker 1-(minus 8).
PASSING—Arizona, McCown 18-31-0-162. Miami, Fiedler 12-21-0-129, eeley 6-15-1-129.
RECEIVING—Arizona, Fitzgerald 5-92, Boldin 5-37, B. Johnson 3-20, ambrick 2-5, F. Jones 1-5, E. Smith 1-3, O. Ayanbadejo 1-0. Miami, Chambers -104, Booker 4-91, Morris 3-6, Konrad 1-20, McMichael 1-16, Thompson 1-4, Gilmore 1-7.
MISSED FIELD GOAL ATTEMPTS—None.
INTERCEPTIONS—Arizona, Starks 1-41.
KICKOFF RETURNS—Arizona, Croom 5-96. Miami, Gilmore 2-45, Welker 2-45.
PUNT RETURNS—Arizona, K. Williams 1-9. Miami, Welker 4-33.
SACKS—Arizona, Berry 1, Dockett 1, Dansby 1. Miami, Taylor 1.

RAIDERS 27, PANTHERS 24
Sunday, November 70

akland	3	14	0	10—27
arolina	0	7	7	10—24

First Quarter
ak.—FG, Janikowski 26, 6:16.

Second Quarter
ak.—Wheatley 1 run (Janikowski kick), :54.
ar.—Mangum 1 pass from Delhomme (Kasay kick), 8:23.
ak.—Wheatley 1 run (Janikowski kick), 13:51.

Third Quarter
ar.—Hoover 16 pass from Delhomme (Kasay kick), 7:57.

Fourth Quarter
ak.—Zereoue 7 run (Janikowski kick), 5:44.
ar.—FG, Kasay 38, 11:03.
ar.—Goings 3 pass from Delhomme (Kasay kick), 12:35.
ak.—FG, Janikowski 19, 14:54.
Attendance—73,518.

	Oakland	Carolina
rst downs	21	24
ushes-yards	28-69	18-37
assing	228	267
unt returns	2-8	1-13
ickoff returns	5-93	5-83
terception returns	0-0	1-0
omp.-att.-int.	20-32-1	25-45-0
acked-yards lost	2-3	2-32
unts	3-56	5-35
umbles-lost	1-0	1-0
enalties-yards	8-53	8-83
me of possession	30:33	29:27

INDIVIDUAL STATISTICS
RUSHING—Oakland, Wheatley 19-54, Zereoue 7-7, Redmond 1-9, Collins 1-minus 1). Carolina, Hoover 8-17, Goings 4-11, Harris 4-2, Delhomme 2-7.
PASSING—Oakland, Collins 20-32-1-231. Carolina, Delhomme 25-45-0-299.
RECEIVING—Oakland, Curry 4-63, Gabriel 4-60, Wheatley 3-10, Jolley 2-41, orter 2-28, Collins 2-14, Redmond 1-4. Carolina, Muhammad -94, Proehl 6-91, Goings 4-36, Colbert 3-42, Hoover 2-21, Mangum 2-15.
MISSED FIELD GOAL ATTEMPTS—None.
INTERCEPTIONS—Carolina, Witherspoon 1-0.

KICKOFF RETURNS—Oakland, Gabriel 5-93. Carolina, Broussard 2-36, Bennett 1-24, Wesley 1-15, Seidman 1-8.
PUNT RETURNS—Oakland, Buchanon 2-8. Carolina, Broussard 1-13.
SACKS—Oakland, J. Cooper 1, Kelly 1. Carolina, Peppers 2.

BILLS 22, JETS 17
Sunday, November 7

N.Y. Jets	0	10	0	7—17
Buffalo	7	3	7	5—22

First Quarter
Buf.—McGahee 12 run (Lindell kick), 9:42.

Second Quarter
NYJ—FG, Brien 41, 4:39.
NYJ—McCareins 6 pass from Pennington (Brien kick), 10:25.
Buf.—FG, Lindell 20, 15:00.

Third Quarter
Buf.—Evans 4 pass from Bledsoe (Lindell kick), 6:52.

Fourth Quarter
Buf.—FG, Lindell 30, 4:22.
Buf.—Safety, 8:56.
NYJ—Moss 51 pass from Q. Carter (Brien kick), 10:54.
Attendance—72,574.

	N.Y. Jets	Buffalo
First downs	12	19
Rushes-yards	25-88	46-157
Passing	194	184
Punt returns	3-34	2-5
Kickoff returns	3-50	5-108
Interception returns	0-0	1-11
Comp.-att.-int.	9-18-1	18-30-0
Sacked-yards lost	1-13	0-0
Punts	4-42	8-41
Fumbles-lost	1-1	1-0
Penalties-yards	7-40	8-66
Time of possession	22:32	37:28

INDIVIDUAL STATISTICS
RUSHING—New York, C. Martin 19-67, Pennington 2-14, Jordan 2-2, Moss 1-3, Q. Carter 1-2. Buffalo, McGahee 37-132, Bledsoe 4-16, Henry 4-15, Greer 1-(minus 6).
PASSING—New York, Pennington 7-15-1-141, Q. Carter 2-3-0-66. Buffalo, Bledsoe 18-30-0-184.
RECEIVING—New York, Moss 6-157, McCareins 2-27, Baker 1-23. Buffalo, Moulds 7-85, Evans 5-64, Shelton 2-11, McGahee 2-11, Burns 1-7, Aiken 1-6.
MISSED FIELD GOAL ATTEMPTS—New York, Brien 36.
INTERCEPTIONS—Buffalo, Milloy 1-11.
KICKOFF RETURNS—New York, Jordan 3-50. Buffalo, McGee 4-94, Clements 1-14.
PUNT RETURNS—New York, Moss 2-27, McCareins 1-7. Buffalo, Clements 1-5, J. Smith 1-0.
SACKS—Buffalo, Kelsay 1.

REDSKINS 17, LIONS 10
Sunday, November 7

Washington	0	3	14	0—17
Detroit	0	3	0	7—10

Second Quarter
Was.—FG, Kimrin 24, 10:25.
Det.—FG, Hanson 40, 14:57.

Third Quarter
Was.—Coles 15 pass from Portis (Kimrin kick), 4:35.
Was.—Harris 13 blocked punt return (Kimrin kick), 10:28.

Fourth Quarter
Det.—Schlesinger 1 pass from Harrington (Hanson kick), 12:52.
Attendance—62,657.

	Washington	Detroit
First downs	15	21
Rushes-yards	40-156	24-64
Passing	73	258
Punt returns	2-46	5-21
Kickoff returns	2-24	3-57
Interception returns	1-0	0-0
Comp.-att.-int.	7-18-0	26-52-1
Sacked-yards lost	0-0	2-11
Punts	9-48	10-35
Fumbles-lost	0-0	0-0
Penalties-yards	7-75	4-40
Time of possession	30:31	29:29

INDIVIDUAL STATISTICS

RUSHING—Washington, Portis 34-147, Betts 5-19, Gardner 1-(minus 10). Detroit, Jones 12-20, Bryson 6-21, Harrington 2-14, Pinner 2-7, Schlesinger 1-2, Hakim 1-0.

PASSING—Washington, Brunell 6-17-0-58, Portis 1-1-0-15. Detroit, Harrington 26-52-1-269.

RECEIVING—Washington, Coles 4-46, Kozlowski 1-13, Portis 1-11, Betts 1-3. Detroit, Hakim 7-120, Swinton 5-45, Bryson 4-28, Williams 3-33, Alexander 2-19, Schlesinger 2-7, FitzSimmons 1-14, Jones 1-3, Pinner 1-0.

MISSED FIELD GOAL ATTEMPTS—Washington, Kimrin 51.

INTERCEPTIONS—Washington, Smoot 1-0.

KICKOFF RETURNS—Washington, Thrash 1-20, Kozlowski 1-4. Detroit, Drummond 3-57.

PUNT RETURNS—Washington, Thrash 2-46. Detroit, Drummond 5-21.

SACKS—Washington, Griffin 2.

SEAHAWKS 42, 49ERS 27
Sunday, November 7

Seattle	7	14	14	7—42
San Francisco	14	3	7	3—27

First Quarter
S.F.—Barlow 3 run (T. Peterson kick), 2:52.
Sea.—Jackson 33 pass from Hasselbeck (J. Brown kick), 9:45.
S.F.—Conway 28 pass from Rattay (T. Peterson kick), 13:38.

Second Quarter
Sea.—Alexander 1 run (J. Brown kick), 8:23.
Sea.—Alexander 4 run (J. Brown kick), 13:03.
S.F.—FG, T. Peterson 27, 14:57.

Third Quarter
S.F.—Lloyd 39 pass from Rattay (T. Peterson kick), 2:19.
Sea.—K. Robinson 25 pass from Hasselbeck (J. Brown kick), 3:44.
Sea.—Jackson 39 pass from Hasselbeck (J. Brown kick), 13:28.

Fourth Quarter
S.F.—FG, T. Peterson 30, 3:51.
Sea.—Simmons 23 interception return (J. Brown kick), 6:33.
Attendance—64,423.

	Seattle	San Francisco
First downs	26	19
Rushes-yards	37-184	21-74
Passing	269	243
Punt returns	3-21	4-33
Kickoff returns	6-105	7-139
Interception returns	1-23	0-0
Comp.-att.-int.	17-28-0	23-35-1
Sacked-yards lost	3-16	3-16
Punts	5-36	6-43
Fumbles-lost	0-0	1-0
Penalties-yards	7-55	3-29
Time of possession	32:37	27:23

INDIVIDUAL STATISTICS

RUSHING—Seattle, Alexander 26-160, Carter 4-15, Strong 3-11, Hasselbeck 3-(minus 1), H. Evans 1-(minus 1). San Francisco, Barlow 18-61, Battle 1-7, Rattay 1-5, Beasley 1-1.

PASSING—Seattle, Hasselbeck 17-28-0-285. San Francisco, Rattay 23-35-1-259.

RECEIVING—Seattle, Jackson 5-114, Stevens 4-44, Urban 2-50, K. Robinson 2-39, Hannam 1-17, Mili 1-13, Rice 1-5, Strong 1-3. San Francisco, E. Johnson 5-54, Lloyd 4-75, Conway 3-48, Wilson 3-44, Barlow 2-18, Beasley 2-8, Jackson 2-(minus 3), Battle 1-12, Walker 1-3.

MISSED FIELD GOAL ATTEMPTS—None.

INTERCEPTIONS—Seattle, Simmons 1-23.

KICKOFF RETURNS—Seattle, Carter 5-88, H. Evans 1-17. San Francisco, Hicks 6-127, Battle 1-12.

PUNT RETURNS—Seattle, Richard 3-21. San Francisco, Battle 4-33.

SACKS—Seattle, Trufant 1, Moore 1, Cochran 1. San Francisco, Winborn 1, Engelberger 1, D. Smith 0.5, Brown 0.5.

CHARGERS 43, SAINTS 17
Sunday, November 7

New Orleans	0	7	0	10—17
San Diego	14	6	16	7—43

First Quarter
S.D.—Gates 12 pass from Brees (Kaeding kick), 5:10.
S.D.—Tomlinson 1 run (Kaeding kick), 9:31.

Second Quarter
S.D.—FG, Kaeding 40, 1:58.
N.O.—McAllister 2 run (Carney kick), 6:48.
S.D.—FG, Kaeding 27, 11:44.

Third Quarter
S.D.—Safety, 6:24.
S.D.—Gates 7 pass from Brees (Kaeding kick), 11:45.
S.D.—Gates 2 pass from Brees (Kaeding kick), 12:56.

Fourth Quarter
N.O.—FG, Carney 37, 1:07.
S.D.—Osgood 12 pass from Brees (Kaeding kick), 7:54.
N.O.—B. Williams 6 run from Brooks (Carney kick), 10:56.
Attendance—59,662.

	New Orleans	San Diego
First downs	18	28
Rushes-yards	18-55	35-152
Passing	165	250
Punt returns	0-0	2-6
Kickoff returns	7-170	4-77
Interception returns	0-0	1-12
Comp.-att.-int.	16-29-1	22-37-0
Sacked-yards lost	3-8	1-7
Punts	2-51	1-31
Fumbles-lost	2-1	2-0
Penalties-yards	10-117	5-32
Time of possession	23:10	36:50

INDIVIDUAL STATISTICS

RUSHING—New Orleans, McAllister 16-63, Brooks 2-(minus 8). San Diego, Tomlinson 17-36, Chatman 7-51, Turner 5-17, Rivers 3-(minus 4), Brees 2-4, Dwight 1-48.

PASSING—New Orleans, Brooks 16-29-1-173. San Diego, Brees 22-36-0-257, McCardell 0-1-0-0.

RECEIVING—New Orleans, B. Williams 5-71, McAllister 4-18, Pathon 3-34, Horn 2-21, Conwell 1-28, Brooks 1-1. San Diego, McCardell 6-89, Gates 5-56, Tomlinson 4-40, E. Parker 3-36, Osgood 2-23, Neal 2-13.

MISSED FIELD GOAL ATTEMPTS—New Orleans, Carney 46.

INTERCEPTIONS—San Diego, Wilson 1-12.

KICKOFF RETURNS—New Orleans, M. Lewis 6-144, McAfee 1-26. San Diego, Dwight 4-77.

PUNT RETURNS—San Diego, E. Parker 2-6.

SACKS—New Orleans, Howard 1. San Diego, Foley 1.5, Dingle 1, Scott 0.5.

BEARS 28, GIANTS 21
Sunday, November 7

Chicago	0	20	0	8—28
N.Y. Giants	14	0	0	7—21

First Quarter
NYG—Barber 3 run (Christie kick), 6:57.
NYG—Barber 1 run (Christie kick), 11:06.

Second Quarter
Chi.—Berrian 35 pass from Krenzel (Edinger kick), 9:47.
Chi.—Thomas 4 run (Edinger kick), 12:25.
Chi.—FG, Edinger 22, 13:51.
Chi.—FG, Edinger 21, 15:00.

Fourth Quarter
Chi.—Thomas 41 run (Krenzel run), 7:16.
NYG—Shockey 1 pass from Warner (Christie kick), 13:04.
Attendance—78,786.

	Chicago	N.Y. Giants
First downs	13	15
Rushes-yards	34-122	25-91
Passing	109	167
Punt returns	3-43	3-45
Kickoff returns	2-27	5-155
Interception returns	2-46	0-0
Comp.-att.-int.	8-21-0	18-36-2
Sacked-yards lost	5-35	7-28
Punts	10-37	7-39
Fumbles-lost	2-2	4-3
Penalties-yards	11-70	14-109
Time of possession	30:03	29:57

INDIVIDUAL STATISTICS

RUSHING—Chicago, Thomas 28-110, Krenzel 6-12. New York, Barber 21-72, Cloud 3-16, Warner 1-3.

PASSING—Chicago, Krenzel 8-21-0-144. New York, Warner 18-36-2-195.

RECEIVING—Chicago, Terrell 4-70, Berrian 1-35, Wade 1-33, Thomas 1-5, B. Johnson 1-1. New York, Shockey 6-64, I. Hilliard 6-38, Barber 4-59, Toomer 2-34.

MISSED FIELD GOAL ATTEMPTS—None.

INTERCEPTIONS—Chicago, Vasher 1-41, Azumah 1-5.

KICKOFF RETURNS—Chicago, Azumah 2-27. New York, Ponder 5-155.

PUNT RETURNS—Chicago, McQuarters 3-43. New York, Jones 3-45.

SACKS—Chicago, A. Brown 4, Azumah 1, Ogunleye 1, Harris 1. New York, Robbins 2, Wilson 1, Strahan 1, Umenyiora 1.

PATRIOTS 40, RAMS 22
Sunday, November 7

New England	6	13	14	7—40
St. Louis	0	14	0	8—22

First Quarter
N.E.—FG, Vinatieri 43, 3:35.
N.E.—FG, Vinatieri 31, 9:18.

Second Quarter
St.L.—Little 0 fumble return (J. Wilkins kick), :14.
N.E.—Vrabel 2 pass from Brady (Vinatieri kick), 5:56.
St.L.—Bruce 11 pass from Bulger (J. Wilkins kick), 9:41.
N.E.—FG, Vinatieri 45, 11:57.
N.E.—FG, Vinatieri 36, 15:00.

Third Quarter
N.E.—T. Brown 4 pass from Vinatieri (Vinatieri kick), 7:45.
N.E.—Dillon 5 run (Vinatieri kick), 11:24.

Fourth Quarter
St.L.—Holt 16 pass from Bulger (M. Faulk run), :47.
N.E.—B. Johnson 4 pass from Brady (Vinatieri kick), 9:37.
Attendance—66,107.

	New England	St. Louis
First downs	22	21
Rushes-yards	32-147	19-81
Passing	229	259
Punt returns	2-22	2-3
Kickoff returns	4-85	7-159
Interception returns	1-26	0-0
Comp.-att.-int.	19-32-0	23-33-1
Sacked-yards lost	2-9	5-26
Punts	2-46	4-43
Fumbles-lost	1-1	2-2
Penalties-yards	7-48	10-80
Time of possession	31:45	28:15

INDIVIDUAL STATISTICS
RUSHING—New England, Dillon 25-112, Pass 3-25, Brady 3-1, Faulk 1-9. St. Louis, M. Faulk 12-66, S. Jackson 3-1, Bulger 2-14, McDonald 2-0.

PASSING—New England, Brady 18-31-0-234, Vinatieri 1-1-0-4. St. Louis, Bulger 23-33-1-285.

RECEIVING—New England, Givens 5-100, Pass 3-32, T. Brown 3-30, Patten 2-34, Dillon 2-19, Faulk 2-17, B. Johnson 1-4, Vrabel 1-2. St. Louis, Holt 6-111, M. Faulk 6-22, Bruce 4-59, Manumaleuna 3-53, McDonald 3-33, Curtis 1-7.

MISSED FIELD GOAL ATTEMPTS—None.

INTERCEPTIONS—New England, Phifer 1-26.

KICKOFF RETURNS—New England, B. Johnson 2-43, Pass 2-42. St. Louis, Harris 7-159.

PUNT RETURNS—New England, Faulk 2-22. St. Louis, McDonald 2-3.

SACKS—New England, Bruschi 1, McGinest 1, Warren 1, Seymour 1, J. Green 1. St. Louis, Lewis 1, T. Jackson 1.

BRONCOS 31, TEXANS 13
Sunday, November 7

Houston	0	7	0	6—13
Denver	7	17	7	0—31

First Quarter
Den.—Putzier 34 pass from Plummer (Elam kick), 13:09.

Second Quarter
Den.—FG, Elam 52, 5:08.
Hou.—D. Davis 1 run (K. Brown kick), 9:48.
Den.—Lelie 40 pass from Plummer (Elam kick), 13:08.
Den.—Smith 13 pass from Plummer (Elam kick), 14:28.

Third Quarter
Den.—K. Johnson 23 pass from Plummer (Elam kick), 3:53.

Fourth Quarter
Hou.—D. Davis 1 run (pass failed), 8:07.
Attendance—74,292.

	Houston	Denver
First downs	22	21
Rushes-yards	27-103	36-139
Passing	228	225
Punt returns	3-(-6)	2-18

	Houston	Denver
Kickoff returns	3-59	1-17
Interception returns	0-0	0-0

Comp.-att.-int.	22-41-0	16-24-0
Sacked-yards lost	4-17	1-9
Punts	6-47	6-35
Fumbles-lost	0-0	0-0
Penalties-yards	9-109	4-50
Time of possession	27:55	32:05

INDIVIDUAL STATISTICS
RUSHING—Houston, D. Davis 19-71, Carr 5-10, Hollings 2-15, Wells 1-7. Denver, Droughns 29-120, Hearst 5-13, Watts 1-4, Plummer 1-2.

PASSING—Houston, Carr 22-41-0-245. Denver, Plummer 16-24-0-234.

RECEIVING—Houston, Gaffney 6-86, Armstrong 6-84, An. Johnson 3-28, Hollings 3-16, D. Davis 2-19, Norris 1-7, Bradford 1-5. Denver, Lelie 4-81, K. Johnson 3-46, Smith 3-29, Putzier 2-48, Carswell 2-19, Droughns 1-6, Watts 1-5.

MISSED FIELD GOAL ATTEMPTS—Houston, K. Brown 37.

INTERCEPTIONS—None.

KICKOFF RETURNS—Houston, Moses 3-59. Denver, Droughns 1-17.

PUNT RETURNS—Houston, Moses 3-(minus 4). Denver, Smith 2-18.

SACKS—Houston, Payne 1. Denver, K. Herndon 1, Hayward 1, Elliss 1, Coleman 1.

RAVENS 27, BROWNS 13
Sunday, November 7

Cleveland	10	0	0	3—13
Baltimore	3	9	0	15—27

First Quarter
Cle.—Alston 93 kickoff return (Dawson kick), :14.
Bal.—FG, Stover 44, 5:23.
Cle.—FG, Dawson 50, 13:38.

Second Quarter
Bal.—FG, Stover 39, 4:15.
Bal.—FG, Stover 43, 11:51.
Bal.—FG, Stover 36, 15:00.

Fourth Quarter
Cle.—FG, Dawson 29, :46.
Bal.—J. Lewis 2 run (Moore pass from Boller), 7:57.
Bal.—Reed 106 interception return (Stover kick), 14:34.
Attendance—69,781.

	Cleveland	Baltimore
First downs	13	15
Rushes-yards	28-91	28-106
Passing	126	134
Punt returns	2-24	4-33
Kickoff returns	6-197	4-61
Interception returns	0-0	1-106
Comp.-att.-int.	15-26-1	17-30-0
Sacked-yards lost	3-20	1-8
Punts	6-36	5-47
Fumbles-lost	3-1	1-1
Penalties-yards	9-55	3-25
Time of possession	32:10	27:50

INDIVIDUAL STATISTICS
RUSHING—Cleveland, Suggs 18-56, Green 8-10, Garcia 2-25. Baltimore, J. Lewis 22-81, Ricard 2-18, C. Taylor 2-6, Boller 2-1.

PASSING—Cleveland, Garcia 15-26-1-146. Baltimore, Boller 17-30-0-142.

RECEIVING—Cleveland, Bryant 4-43, Heiden 4-31, F. Jackson 2-26, Shea 2-20, Green 1-10, Northcutt 1-9, Suggs 1-7. Baltimore, T. Taylor 7-58, K. Johnson 3-24, Moore 2-24, Wilcox 2-9, J. Lewis 1-14, Ricard 1-7, Hymes 1-6.

MISSED FIELD GOAL ATTEMPTS—None.

INTERCEPTIONS—Baltimore, Reed 1-106.

KICKOFF RETURNS—Cleveland, Alston 6-197. Baltimore, Sams 4-61.

PUNT RETURNS—Cleveland, Northcutt 2-24. Baltimore, Sams 4-33.

SACKS—Cleveland, Ekuban 1. Baltimore, Demps 1.5, A. Thomas 1, Suggs 0.5.

COLTS 31, VIKINGS 28
Monday, November 8

Minnesota	0	6	8	14—28
Indianapolis	7	7	7	10—31

First Quarter
Ind.—Wayne 5 pass from Manning (Vanderjagt kick), 5:51.

Second Quarter
Ind.—Pollard 10 pass from Manning (Vanderjagt kick), :06.
Min.—FG, M. Andersen 42, 2:17.
Min.—FG, M. Andersen 23, 15:00.

Third Quarter
Min.—Burleson 91 punt return (Culpepper run), 4:11.

Ind.—Clark 4 pass from Manning (Vanderjagt kick), 12:53.

Fourth Quarter

Min.—Burleson 8 pass from Culpepper (M. Andersen kick), 3:33.
Ind.—Pollard 19 pass from Manning (Vanderjagt kick), 7:36.
Min.—O. Smith 24 run (M. Andersen kick), 12:06.
Ind.—FG, Vanderjagt 35, 14:58.
Attendance—57,307.

	Minnesota	Indianapolis
First downs	15	26
Rushes-yards	24-138	31-144
Passing	154	264
Punt returns	2-96	1-(-2)
Kickoff returns	6-134	5-108
Interception returns	0-0	0-0
Comp.-att.-int.	16-19-0	23-29-0
Sacked-yards lost	2-15	1-4
Punts	3-37	3-41
Fumbles-lost	2-1	0-0
Penalties-yards	6-53	8-65
Time of possession	25:48	34:12

INDIVIDUAL STATISTICS

RUSHING—Minnesota, O. Smith 13-80, Culpepper 5-27, M. Bennett 5-18, M. Williams 1-13. Indianapolis, James 26-123, Manning 4-20, Rhodes 1-1.

PASSING—Minnesota, Culpepper 16-19-0-169. Indianapolis, Manning 23-29-0-268.

RECEIVING—Minnesota, Wiggins 5-63, M. Robinson 3-23, O. Smith 2-15, M. Williams 2-15, M. Bennett 2-15, Campbell 1-30, Burleson 1-8. Indianapolis, Harrison 6-81, James 5-56, Clark 3-38, Wayne 3-22, Stokley 2-34, Pollard 2-29, Mungro 1-4, Rhodes 1-4.

MISSED FIELD GOAL ATTEMPTS—None.

INTERCEPTIONS—None.

KICKOFF RETURNS—Minnesota, Campbell 4-115, Ross 1-19, Johnson 1-0. Indianapolis, Pyatt 3-51, Rhodes 2-57.

PUNT RETURNS—Minnesota, Burleson 2-96. Indianapolis, Pyatt 1-(minus 2).

SACKS—Minnesota, K. Williams 1. Indianapolis, Freeney 2.

WEEK 10

AMERICAN FOOTBALL CONFERENCE

EAST DIVISION

	W	L	T	Pct.	PF	PA
New England	8	1	0	.889	237	152
J.Y. Jets	6	3	0	.667	202	158
Buffalo	3	6	0	.333	143	166
Miami	1	8	0	.111	123	186

NORTH DIVISION

	W	L	T	Pct.	PF	PA
Pittsburgh	8	1	0	.889	221	147
Baltimore	6	3	0	.667	174	130
Cincinnati	4	5	0	.444	169	179
Cleveland	3	6	0	.333	170	198

SOUTH DIVISION

	W	L	T	Pct.	PF	PA
Indianapolis	6	3	0	.667	298	220
Jacksonville	6	3	0	.667	151	163
Houston	4	5	0	.444	185	223
Tennessee	3	6	0	.333	168	197

WEST DIVISION

	W	L	T	Pct.	PF	PA
Denver	6	3	0	.667	199	154
San Diego	6	3	0	.667	262	173
Kansas City	3	6	0	.333	257	238
Oakland	3	6	0	.333	165	247

NATIONAL FOOTBALL CONFERENCE

EAST DIVISION

	W	L	T	Pct.	PF	PA
Philadelphia	8	1	0	.889	238	152
N.Y. Giants	5	4	0	.556	186	158
Dallas	3	6	0	.333	162	252
Washington	3	6	0	.333	125	150

NORTH DIVISION

	W	L	T	Pct.	PF	PA
Green Bay	5	4	0	.556	240	217
Minnesota	5	4	0	.556	242	227
Chicago	4	5	0	.444	155	159
Detroit	4	5	0	.444	164	194

SOUTH DIVISION

	W	L	T	Pct.	PF	PA
Atlanta	7	2	0	.778	194	184
New Orleans	4	5	0	.444	198	254
Tampa Bay	3	6	0	.333	157	179
Carolina	2	7	0	.222	161	212

WEST DIVISION

	W	L	T	Pct.	PF	PA
Seattle	5	4	0	.556	206	168
St. Louis	5	4	0	.556	203	217
Arizona	4	5	0	.444	167	179
San Francisco	1	8	0	.111	172	261

TOP PERFORMANCES

100-YARD RUSHING GAMES

Player, Team & Opponent	Att.	Yds.	TD
Derrick Blaylock, K.C. at N.O.	33	186	1
Shaun Alexander, Sea. at St.L.	22	176	0
Corey Dillon, N.E. vs. Buf.	26	151	0
Ahman Green, G.B. vs. Min.	21	145	0
Fred Taylor, Jac. vs. Det.*	23	144	0
Marshall Faulk, St.L. vs. Sea.	18	139	0
Deuce McAllister, N.O. vs. K.C.	16	127	1
Curtis Martin, NYJ vs. Bal.*	28	119	2
Tiki Barber, NYG at Ariz.	21	108	1
Jerome Bettis, Pit. at Cle.	29	103	2
Rudi Johnson, Cin. at Was.	31	102	1

300-YARD PASSING GAMES

Player, Team & Opponent	Att.	Cmp.	Yds.	TD	Int.
Daunte Culpepper, Min. at G.B.	44	27	363	4	0
Donovan McNabb, Phi. at Dal.	27	15	345	4	0
Billy Volek, Ten. vs. Chi.*	44	27	334	2	1
Peyton Manning, Ind. vs. Hou.	27	18	320	5	2
Trent Green, K.C. at N.O.	33	22	311	1	2
Jake Delhomme, Car. at S.F.	34	19	303	3	0

100-YARD RECEIVING GAMES

Player, Team & Opponent	Rec.	Yds.	TD
Joe Horn, N.O. vs. K.C.	5	167	1
Drew Bennett, Ten. vs. Chi.*	6	148	1
Nate Burleson, Min. at G.B.	11	141	1
Terrell Owens, Phi. at Dal.	6	134	3
Jason Witten, Dal. vs. Phi.	9	133	2
Brandon Stokley, Ind. vs. Hou.	5	132	2
Muhsin Muhammad, Car. at S.F.	6	123	3
Eddie Kennison, K.C. at N.O.	7	121	1
Alge Crumpler, Atl. vs. T.B.	4	118	1
Jimmy Smith, Jac. vs. Det.*	7	109	1

Player, Team & Opponent	Rec.	Yds.	TD
Isaac Bruce, St.L. vs. Sea.	7	104	0
Dallas Clark, Ind. vs. Hou.	3	102	2
Cedrick Wilson, S.F. vs. Car.	5	101	0
Amani Toomer, NYG at Ariz.	8	100	0
*Overtime game.			

RESULTS

SUNDAY, NOVEMBER 14
ST. LOUIS 23, Seattle 12
Pittsburgh 24, CLEVELAND 10
ATLANTA 24, Tampa Bay 14
NEW ORLEANS 27, Kansas City 20
Baltimore 20, N.Y. JETS 17 (OT)
Chicago 19, TENNESSEE 17 (OT)
INDIANAPOLIS 49, Houston 14
JACKSONVILLE 23, Detroit 17 (OT)
ARIZONA 17, N.Y. Giants 14
GREEN BAY 34, Minnesota 31
Cincinnati 17, WASHINGTON 10
Carolina 37, SAN FRANCISCO 27
NEW ENGLAND 29, Buffalo 6

MONDAY, NOVEMBER 15
Philadelphia 49, DALLAS 21
Open Date: Denver, Miami, Oakland, San Diego

– 169 –

RAMS 23, SEAHAWKS 12
Sunday, November 14

Seattle	0	6	6	0—12
St. Louis	14	3	3	3—23

First Quarter
St.L.—Curtis 15 pass from Bulger (J. Wilkins kick), 2:37.
St.L.—S. Jackson 4 run (J. Wilkins kick), 8:09.

Second Quarter
St.L.—FG, J. Wilkins 36, 2:42.
Sea.—FG, J. Brown 28, 8:10.
Sea.—FG, J. Brown 30, 9:57.

Third Quarter
St.L.—FG, J. Wilkins 47, 5:28.
Sea.—FG, J. Brown 45, 9:06.
Sea.—FG, J. Brown 41, 11:06.

Fourth Quarter
St.L.—FG, J. Wilkins 23, 14:34.
Attendance—66,044.

	Seattle	St. Louis
First downs	20	24
Rushes-yards	29-200	31-202
Passing	172	260
Punt returns	2-20	0-0
Kickoff returns	6-168	5-110
Interception returns	0-0	1-0
Comp.-att.-int.	15-36-1	23-34-0
Sacked-yards lost	0-0	1-2
Punts	3-49	3-46
Fumbles-lost	1-1	2-2
Penalties-yards	4-20	7-55
Time of possession	25:33	34:27

INDIVIDUAL STATISTICS
RUSHING—Seattle, Alexander 22-176, Strong 3-10, Hasselbeck 2-11, Morris 2-3. St. Louis, M. Faulk 18-139, S. Jackson 10-47, Bulger 2-1, Curtis 1-15.
PASSING—Seattle, Hasselbeck 15-36-1-172. St. Louis, Bulger 23-34-0-262.
RECEIVING—Seattle, Stevens 3-34, Jackson 3-33, Engram 3-28, K. Robinson 2-50, Rice 1-9, Morris 1-8, Strong 1-7, Alexander 1-3. St. Louis, Bruce 7-104, M. Faulk 5-21, Curtis 3-39, Holt 2-32, McDonald 1-21, Cleeland 1-15, S. Jackson 1-9, Furrey 1-8, Goodspeed 1-7, Manumaleuna 1-6.
MISSED FIELD GOAL ATTEMPTS—None.
INTERCEPTIONS—St. Louis, Butler 1-0.
KICKOFF RETURNS—Seattle, Carter 5-155, H. Evans 1-13. St. Louis, Harris 4-95, Groce 1-15. ....
PUNT RETURNS—Seattle, Morris 2-20.
SACKS—Seattle, Mitchell 1.

STEELERS 24, BROWNS 10
Sunday, November 14

Pittsburgh	7	7	0	10—24
Cleveland	3	0	0	7—10

First Quarter
Cle.—FG, Dawson 31, 2:26.
Pit.—Bettis 5 run (Reed kick), 14:19.

Second Quarter
Pit.—Bettis 1 run (Reed kick), 10:31.

Fourth Quarter
Pit.—FG, Reed 20, 2:35.
Pit.—Stuvaints 24 fumble return (Reed kick), 5:46.
Cle.—Shea 7 pass from Holcomb (Dawson kick), 8:37.
Attendance—73,703.

	Pittsburgh	Cleveland
First downs	18	12
Rushes-yards	47-180	22-68
Passing	120	160
Punt returns	2-29	1-14
Kickoff returns	2-48	5-105
Interception returns	2-0	1-(-2)
Comp.-att.-int.	10-16-1	12-25-2
Sacked-yards lost	2-14	4-14
Punts	4-43	5-38
Fumbles-lost	0-0	3-2
Penalties-yards	5-38	3-11
Time of possession	36:00	24:00

INDIVIDUAL STATISTICS
RUSHING—Pittsburgh, Bettis 29-103, Parker 8-44, Roethlisberger 7-38, Ward 2-(minus 7), Da. Brown 1-2. Cleveland, Suggs 18-38, Garcia 4-30.
PASSING—Pittsburgh, Roethlisberger 10-16-1-134. Cleveland, Garcia 7-16-1-110, Holcomb 5-9-1-64.
RECEIVING—Pittsburgh, Burress 5-66, Ward 3-42, Randle El 1-19, Bettis 1-7. Cleveland, F. Jackson 5-61, Northcutt 2-69, Bryant 2-26, T. Smith 1-8, Shea 1-7, Heiden 1-3.
MISSED FIELD GOAL ATTEMPTS—Pittsburgh, Reed 24.
INTERCEPTIONS—Pittsburgh, Polamalu 2-0. Cleveland, McCutcheon 1 (minus 2).
KICKOFF RETURNS—Pittsburgh, Randle El 2-48. Cleveland, Alston 4-90, Jackson 1-16.
PUNT RETURNS—Pittsburgh, Randle El 2-29. Cleveland, Northcutt 1-14.
SACKS—Pittsburgh, Harrison 1, Hoke 1, Townsend 1, A. Smith 1. Cleveland, Thompson 1, Crocker 1.

FALCONS 24, BUCCANEERS 14
Sunday, November 14

Tampa Bay	0	7	7	0—14
Atlanta	10	7	0	7—24

First Quarter
Atl.—FG, Feely 33, 3:36.
Atl.—Duckett 2 run (Feely kick), 9:38.

Second Quarter
Atl.—Duckett 1 run (Feely kick), 4:35.
T.B.—Clayton 25 pass from Griese (Gramatica kick), 9:17.

Third Quarter
T.B.—Dilger 22 pass from Griese (Gramatica kick), 5:25.

Fourth Quarter
Atl.—Crumpler 49 pass from Vick (Feely kick), 5:11.
Attendance—70,810.

	Tampa Bay	Atlanta
First downs	14	18
Rushes-yards	23-68	39-205
Passing	125	120
Punt returns	2-24	2-0
Kickoff returns	5-118	3-74
Interception returns	1-0	1-8
Comp.-att.-int.	19-26-1	8-16-1
Sacked-yards lost	7-49	5-27
Punts	7-39	6-42
Fumbles-lost	0-0	0-0
Penalties-yards	13-83	6-45
Time of possession	29:31	30:29

INDIVIDUAL STATISTICS
RUSHING—Tampa Bay, Pittman 20-62, Clayton 1-3, Graham 1-2, Griese 1-1. Atlanta, Dunn 17-76, Duckett 12-53, Vick 9-73, Griffith 1-3.
PASSING—Tampa Bay, Griese 19-26-1-174. Atlanta, Vick 8-16-1-147.
RECEIVING—Tampa Bay, Clayton 6-90, Dilger 5-51, Pittman 4-16, Cook 2-10, Galloway 1-4, Jurevicius 1-3. Atlanta, Crumpler 4-118, P. Price 2-20, Dunn 1-5, White 1-4.
MISSED FIELD GOAL ATTEMPTS—None.
INTERCEPTIONS—Tampa Bay, Barber 1-0. Atlanta, Rossum 1-8.
KICKOFF RETURNS—Tampa Bay, Cox 4-101, Graham 1-17. Atlanta, Rossum 3-74.
PUNT RETURNS—Tampa Bay, Galloway 2-24. Atlanta, Rossum 2-0.
SACKS—Tampa Bay, Quarles 1.5, Rice 1, D. White 1, Spires 0.5, Gold 0.5, Ahanotu 0.5. Atlanta, R. Coleman 2, Stewart 1.5, Kerney 1, Williams 1, Brooking 1, T. Hall 0.5.

SAINTS 27, CHIEFS 20
Sunday, November 14

Kansas City	10	3	0	7—20
New Orleans	0	14	3	10—27

First Quarter
K.C.—Kennison 21 pass from Green (Tynes kick), 2:11.
K.C.—FG, Tynes 24, 12:33.

Second Quarter
N.O.—Brooks 1 run (Carney kick), :06.
N.O.—McAllister 13 run (Carney kick), 5:19.
K.C.—FG, Tynes 44, 8:56.

Third Quarter
N.O.—FG, Carney 39, 4:55.

Fourth Quarter

N.O.—FG, Carney 38, 1:19.
K.C.—Blaylock 3 run (Tynes kick), 6:53.
N.O.—Horn 42 pass from Brooks (Carney kick), 9:32.
Attendance—64,900.

	Kansas City	New Orleans
First downs	28	20
Rushes-yards	36-200	23-134
Passing	297	240
Punt returns	4-22	1-10
Kickoff returns	6-164	5-108
Interception returns	1-2	2-14
Comp.-att.-int.	22-33-2	15-27-1
Sacked-yards lost	2-14	4-19
Punts	3-38	5-41
Fumbles-lost	2-2	2-0
Penalties-yards	12-94	8-57
Time of possession	35:44	24:16

INDIVIDUAL STATISTICS

RUSHING—Kansas City, Blaylock 33-186, Green 1-13, Richardson 1-1, Kennison 1-0. New Orleans, McAllister 16-127, Brooks 4-1, Stecker 2-0, Stallworth 1-6.

PASSING—Kansas City, Green 22-33-2-311. New Orleans, Brooks 15-27-1-259.

RECEIVING—Kansas City, Kennison 7-121, Gonzalez 6-71, Morton 4-59, Blaylock 3-38, Dunn 1-11, Hall 1-11. New Orleans, Horn 5-167, B. Williams 3-49, Stallworth 3-11, Pathon 2-33, Karney 1-17, Stecker 1-2.

MISSED FIELD GOAL ATTEMPTS—None.

INTERCEPTIONS—Kansas City, Wesley 1-2. New Orleans, M. McKenzie 1-14, Ruff 1-0.

KICKOFF RETURNS—Kansas City, Hall 6-164. New Orleans, M. Lewis 5-108.

PUNT RETURNS—Kansas City, Hall 4-22. New Orleans, M. Lewis 1-10.

SACKS—Kansas City, Fujita 2, Woods 1, Hicks 1. New Orleans, Howard 1, W. Smith 1.

RAVENS 20, JETS 17
Sunday, November 14

Baltimore	0	7	3	7	3—20
N.Y. Jets	0	14	0	3	0—17

Second Quarter

NYJ—C. Martin 1 run (Brien kick), 1:25.
NYJ—C. Martin 9 run (Brien kick), 11:17.
Bal.—Moore 6 pass from Boller (Stover kick), 14:20.

Third Quarter

Bal.—FG, Stover 24, 6:26.

Fourth Quarter

Bal.—Moore 16 pass from Boller (Stover kick), 10:47.
NYJ—FG, Brien 20, 14:55.

Overtime

Bal.—FG, Stover 42, 7:25.
Attendance—77,826.

	Baltimore	N.Y. Jets
First downs	18	16
Rushes-yards	32-76	36-156
Passing	186	149
Punt returns	7-45	4-21
Kickoff returns	4-101	3-62
Interception returns	1-78	0-0
Comp.-att.-int.	19-33-0	13-23-1
Sacked-yards lost	3-27	5-26
Punts	7-39	9-41
Fumbles-lost	2-1	1-0
Penalties-yards	5-39	6-55
Time of possession	33:56	33:29

INDIVIDUAL STATISTICS

RUSHING—Baltimore, J. Lewis 30-71, Boller 2-5. New York, C. Martin 28-119, Q. Carter 5-22, Jordan 3-15.

PASSING—Baltimore, Boller 19-33-0-213. New York, Q. Carter 13-22-0-175, Jordan 0-1-1-0.

RECEIVING—Baltimore, Moore 5-45, T. Taylor 4-42, J. Lewis 3-20, K. Johnson 2-23, Wilcox 2-21, Smith 1-25, C. Taylor 1-23, Hymes 1-14. New York, Moss 3-75, Chrebet 3-19, McCareins 2-30, C. Martin 2-5, Jordan 1-25, Baker 1-19, Sowell 1-2.

MISSED FIELD GOAL ATTEMPTS—None.

INTERCEPTIONS—Baltimore, Reed 1-78.

KICKOFF RETURNS—Baltimore, Sams 4-101. New York, Jordan 2-57, Askew 1-5.

PUNT RETURNS—Baltimore, Sams 7-45. New York, Moss 3-21, McCareins 1-0.

SACKS—Baltimore, Douglas 1.5, Gregg 1.5, A. Thomas 1, Williams 1. New York, B. Thomas 1.5, J. Abraham 1, Robertson 0.5.

BEARS 19, TITANS 17
Sunday, November 14

Chicago	0	7	7	3	2—19
Tennessee	7	0	0	10	0—17

First Quarter

Ten.—Mason 29 pass from Volek (Anderson kick), 12:43.

Second Quarter

Chi.—Haynes 45 interception return (Edinger kick), 14:42.

Third Quarter

Chi.—McQuarters 75 punt return (Edinger kick), 3:56.

Fourth Quarter

Ten.—FG, Anderson 33, 2:05.
Ten.—Bennett 47 pass from Volek (Anderson kick), 9:00.
Chi.—FG, Edinger 29, 14:08.

Overtime

Chi.—Safety, 3:17.
Attendance—68,932.

	Chicago	Tennessee
First downs	10	14
Rushes-yards	34-101	24-72
Passing	75	318
Punt returns	6-100	7-34
Kickoff returns	5-108	4-108
Interception returns	1-45	2-21
Comp.-att.-int.	10-28-2	27-44-1
Sacked-yards lost	5-41	3-16
Punts	11-46	9-44
Fumbles-lost	2-1	4-2
Penalties-yards	6-50	4-25
Time of possession	33:09	30:08

INDIVIDUAL STATISTICS

RUSHING—Chicago, Thomas 29-72, Wade 3-21, Krenzel 1-9, Berrian 1-(minus 1). Tennessee, Brown 20-62, A. Smith 2-4, Volek 1-5, Holcombe 1-1.

PASSING—Chicago, Krenzel 10-28-2-116. Tennessee, Volek 27-44-1-334.

RECEIVING—Chicago, Wade 4-63, Thomas 3-10, Clark 1-24, Terrell 1-11, Berrian 1-8. Tennessee, Mason 7-91, Bennett 6-148, Meier 4-18, Kinney 2-14, Holcombe 2-14, Brown 2-6, Berlin 1-26, A. Smith 1-12, Troupe 1-3, Fleming 1-2.

MISSED FIELD GOAL ATTEMPTS—Chicago, Edinger 39. Tennessee, Hentrich 58, 52.

INTERCEPTIONS—Chicago, Haynes 1-45. Tennessee, A. Dyson 2-21.

KICKOFF RETURNS—Chicago, Azumah 4-98, Berrian 1-10. Tennessee, McAddley 2-57, Waddell 2-51.

PUNT RETURNS—Chicago, McQuarters 5-102, Berrian 1-(minus 2). Tennessee, Waddell 4-25, Mason 3-9.

SACKS—Chicago, Ogunleye 1.5, Hillenmeyer 1, A. Brown 0.5. Tennessee, Carter 3, Bulluck 1, Starks 1.

COLTS 49, TEXANS 14
Sunday, November 14

Houston	0	0	7	7—14
Indianapolis	7	14	21	7—49

First Quarter

Ind.—Stokley 4 pass from Manning (Vanderjagt kick), 7:08.

Second Quarter

Ind.—Wayne 5 pass from Manning (Vanderjagt kick), 3:05.
Ind.—Clark 1 pass from Manning (Vanderjagt kick), 10:58.

Third Quarter

Ind.—Stokley 69 pass from Manning (Vanderjagt kick), :59.
Ind.—Sanders 37 fumble return (Vanderjagt kick), 1:59.
Hou.—D. Davis 1 run (K. Brown kick), 12:31.
Ind.—Clark 80 pass from Manning (Vanderjagt kick), 13:24.

Fourth Quarter

Hou.—D. Davis 1 run (K. Brown kick), 7:13.
Ind.—Hutchins 77 interception return (Vanderjagt kick), 13:25.
Attendance—56,511.

	Houston	Indianapolis
First downs	20	17
Rushes-yards	37-132	20-86
Passing	170	312
Punt returns	2-19	2-42
Kickoff returns	7-166	3-70
Interception returns	2-34	3-77
Comp.-att.-int.	22-41-3	18-27-2
Sacked-yards lost	5-45	1-8

	Houston	Indianapolis
Punts	4-34	3-41
Fumbles-lost	3-1	1-0
Penalties-yards	8-65	11-85
Time of possession	35:41	24:19

INDIVIDUAL STATISTICS

RUSHING—Houston, D. Davis 31-98, Carr 3-10, Wells 2-10, An. Johnson 1-14. Indianapolis, James 20-86.

PASSING—Houston, Carr 22-41-3-215. Indianapolis, Manning 18-27-2-320.

RECEIVING—Houston, D. Davis 7-54, An. Johnson 6-59, Gaffney 3-41, Bradford 2-38, Armstrong 1-14, Miller 1-6, Norris 1-4, Wells 1-(minus 1). Indianapolis, Stokley 5-132, Wayne 4-33, Clark 3-102, Harrison 2-22, Pollard 2-17, James 2-14.

MISSED FIELD GOAL ATTEMPTS—Houston, K. Brown 55. Indianapolis, Vanderjagt 39.

INTERCEPTIONS—Houston, Peek 1-20, Glenn 1-14. Indianapolis, Hutchins 1-77, Nelson 1-0, Brackett 1-0.

KICKOFF RETURNS—Houston, Moses 7-166. Indianapolis, Rhodes 3-70.

PUNT RETURNS—Houston, Moses 2-19. Indianapolis, Moorehead 1-34, David 1-8.

SACKS—Houston, Wong 1. Indianapolis, Mathis 3, Brock 1, Thomas 1.

JAGUARS 23, LIONS 17
Sunday, November 14

Detroit	0	0	0	17	0—17
Jacksonville	7	3	7	0	6—23

First Quarter
Jac.—Toefield 12 pass from Garrard (Scobee kick), 6:42.

Second Quarter
Jac.—FG, Scobee 31, 15:00.

Third Quarter
Jac.—G. Jones 1 run (Scobee kick), 9:11.

Fourth Quarter
Det.—Drummond 55 punt return (Hanson kick), 1:53.
Det.—FG, Hanson 21, 8:30.
Det.—Drummond 83 punt return (Hanson kick), 14:14.

Overtime
Jac.—J. Smith 36 pass from Garrard, 5:28.
Attendance—66,431.

	Detroit	Jacksonville
First downs	10	22
Rushes-yards	19-81	50-239
Passing	109	176
Punt returns	6-199	4-35
Kickoff returns	2-58	3-58
Interception returns	0-0	1-21
Comp.-att.-int.	11-33-1	19-36-0
Sacked-yards lost	2-12	3-22
Punts	6-44	8-39
Fumbles-lost	0-0	0-0
Penalties-yards	8-45	10-99
Time of possession	23:44	41:44

INDIVIDUAL STATISTICS

RUSHING—Detroit, Jones 19-81. Jacksonville, F. Taylor 23-144, Toefield 12-41, G. Jones 8-12, Garrard 7-42.

PASSING—Detroit, Harrington 11-33-1-121. Jacksonville, Garrard 19-36-0-198.

RECEIVING—Detroit, Alexander 3-24, Williams 2-64, Swinton 2-13, Bryson 2-13, Jones 2-7. Jacksonville, J. Smith 7-109, Brady 3-27, F. Taylor 3-21, Toefield 2-18, G. Jones 1-9, R. Williams 1-8, M. Edwards 1-4, Yoder 1-2.

MISSED FIELD GOAL ATTEMPTS—Detroit, Hanson 32.

INTERCEPTIONS—Jacksonville, Mathis 1-21.

KICKOFF RETURNS—Detroit, Drummond 2-58. Jacksonville, Lewis 3-58.

PUNT RETURNS—Detroit, Drummond 6-199. Jacksonville, Lewis 4-35.

SACKS—Detroit, Bra. Walker 1, Hall 1, Davis 0.5, Wilkinson 0.5. Jacksonville, Peterson 1, Henderson 1.

CARDINALS 17, GIANTS 14
Sunday, November 14

N.Y. Giants	7	7	0	0—14	
Arizona	0	10	7	0—17	

First Quarter
NYG—Shockey 2 pass from Warner (Christie kick), 11:22.

Second Quarter
Ariz.—FG, Rackers 41, 1:24.
NYG—Barber 2 run (Christie kick), 5:57.
Ariz.—E. Smith 2 run (Rackers kick), 14:21.

Third Quarter
Ariz.—E. Smith 3 run (Rackers kick), 13:51.
Attendance—42,297.

	N.Y. Giants	Arizona
First downs	19	18
Rushes-yards	28-147	32-104
Passing	161	74
Punt returns	4-17	5-65
Kickoff returns	2-39	3-62
Interception returns	0-0	0-0
Comp.-att.-int.	19-31-0	12-24-0
Sacked-yards lost	6-32	2-16
Punts	5-47	6-46
Fumbles-lost	0-0	2-0
Penalties-yards	10-97	3-15
Time of possession	33:27	26:33

INDIVIDUAL STATISTICS

RUSHING—New York, Barber 21-108, Dayne 3-19, Warner 3-8, I. Hilliard 1-12. Arizona, E. Smith 19-67, Hambrick 7-22, O. Ayanbadejo 3-12, McCown 3-3.

PASSING—New York, Warner 19-30-0-193, Feagles 0-1-0-0. Arizona, McCown 12-24-0-90.

RECEIVING—New York, Toomer 8-100, Barber 5-52, Shockey 4-24, Taylor 1-9, I. Hilliard 1-8. Arizona, Boldin 5-31, B. Johnson 3-32, O. Ayanbadejo 1-16, K. Williams 1-5, F. Jones 1-4, Fitzgerald 1-2.

MISSED FIELD GOAL ATTEMPTS—New York, Christie 44.

INTERCEPTIONS—None.

KICKOFF RETURNS—New York, Ward 1-28, Dayne 1-11. Arizona, Scobey 3-62.

PUNT RETURNS—New York, Jones 4-17. Arizona, K. Williams 5-65.

SACKS—New York, Umenyiora 1, Legree 1. Arizona, Berry 4, Dansby 2.

PACKERS 34, VIKINGS 31
Sunday, November 14

Minnesota	7	3	7	14—31	
Green Bay	7	17	0	10—34	

First Quarter
G.B.—J. Walker 50 pass from Favre (Longwell kick), 3:52.
Min.—Wiggins 13 pass from Culpepper (M. Andersen kick), 8:35.

Second Quarter
G.B.—Fisher 2 pass from Favre (Longwell kick), :51.
Min.—FG, M. Andersen 21, 6:13.
G.B.—Franks 17 pass from Favre (Longwell kick), 7:33.
G.B.—FG, Longwell 43, 15:00.

Third Quarter
Min.—Burleson 8 pass from Culpepper (M. Andersen kick), 12:21.

Fourth Quarter
G.B.—Henderson 6 pass from Favre (Longwell kick), 1:36.
Min.—O. Smith 2 pass from Culpepper (M. Andersen kick), 12:07.
Min.—M. Williams 17 pass from Culpepper (M. Andersen kick), 13:40.
G.B.—FG, Longwell 33, 15:00.
Attendance—70,671.

	Minnesota	Green Bay
First downs	22	24
Rushes-yards	16-71	35-206
Passing	345	236
Punt returns	1-(-1)	2-17
Kickoff returns	5-98	6-163
Interception returns	0-0	0-0
Comp.-att.-int.	27-44-0	20-29-0
Sacked-yards lost	4-18	0-0
Punts	5-35	3-30
Fumbles-lost	0-0	3-1
Penalties-yards	6-37	4-25
Time of possession	29:49	30:11

INDIVIDUAL STATISTICS

RUSHING—Minnesota, O. Smith 5-21, M. Bennett 5-21, Culpepper 3-19, Burleson 1-11, Campbell 1-2, M. Williams 1-(minus 3). Green Bay, Green 21-145, Fisher 8-31, Davenport 2-5, Luchey 2-3, Driver 1-14, Chatman 1-8.

PASSING—Minnesota, Culpepper 27-44-0-363. Green Bay, Favre 20-29-0-236.

RECEIVING—Minnesota, Burleson 11-141, Wiggins 6-94, M. Williams 4-57, M. Robinson 2-39, O. Smith 2-13, Campbell 1-10, Berton 1-9. Green Bay, Henderson 4-16, J. Walker 3-74, Fisher 3-36, Driver 3-28, Franks 2-24, Green 2-7, Martin 1-35, Chatman 1-14, Ferguson 1-2.

MISSED FIELD GOAL ATTEMPTS—None.

INTERCEPTIONS—None. . .

KICKOFF RETURNS—Minnesota, Campbell 5-98. Green Bay, Ferguson 3-109, Chatman 2-27, Davenport 1-27.

PUNT RETURNS—Minnesota, Burleson 1-(minus 1). Green Bay, Chatman 2-17.

SACKS—Green Bay, Gbaja-Biamila 2, Jenkins 1, Lee 1.

BENGALS 17, REDSKINS 10.
Sunday, November 14

Cincinnati 7	10	0	0—17
Washington 0	0	0	10—10

First Quarter
Cin.—Ru. Johnson 1 run (Graham kick), 9:23.

Second Quarter
Cin.—Stewart 1 pass from Palmer (Graham kick), 2:34.
Cin.—FG, Graham 41, 7:32.

Fourth Quarter
Was.—FG, Kimrin 33, 9:14.
Was.—Cooley 9 pass from Ramsey (Kimrin kick), 12:38.
Attendance—87,786.

	Cincinnati	Washington
First downs	19	17
Rushes-yards......................................	34-99	20-87
Passing	217	181
Punt returns	4-8	4-35
Kickoff returns	2-29	4-64
Interception returns	3-12	2-31
Comp.-att.-int.	24-39-2	19-46-3
Sacked-yards lost	0-0	5-35
Punts	6-40	6-43
Fumbles-lost.....................................	1-1	1-0
Penalties-yards	5-50	7-50
Time of possession...........................	32:50	27:10

INDIVIDUAL STATISTICS
RUSHING—Cincinnati, Ru. Johnson 31-102, Palmer 2-(minus 3), Houshmandzadeh 1-0. Washington, Portis 17-81, Brunell 2-3, Ramsey 1-3.

PASSING—Cincinnati, Palmer 24-39-2-217. Washington, Ramsey 18-37-2-210, Brunell 1-8-1-6, Gardner 0-1-0-0.

RECEIVING—Cincinnati, Houshmandzadeh 7-59, C. Johnson 6-89, Washington 4-23, Walter 2-23, Watson 2-19, Stewart 2-4, J. Johnson 1-0. Washington, Coles 6-74, Jacobs 4-37, Portis 4-32, McCants 2-46, Gardner 2-18, Cooley 1-9.

MISSED FIELD GOAL ATTEMPTS—Washington, Kimrin 47.

INTERCEPTIONS—Cincinnati, Simmons 1-11, James 1-1, Herring 1-0. Washington, Harris 1-31, Taylor 1-0.

KICKOFF RETURNS—Cincinnati, O'Neal 1-15, Watson 1-14. Washington, Thrash 3-46, Betts 1-18.

PUNT RETURNS—Cincinnati, O'Neal 4-8. Washington, Thrash 4-35.

SACKS—Cincinnati, L. Johnson 1, J. Smith 1, Lan. Moore 1, Clemons 1, Geathers 1.

PANTHERS 37, 49ERS 27
Sunday, November 14

Carolina 0	3	17	17—37
San Francisco.................................10	7	3	7—27

First Quarter
S.F.—Barlow 1 run (T. Peterson kick), 5:51.
S.F.—FG, T. Peterson 28, 11:04.

Second Quarter
S.F.—Barlow 3 run (T. Peterson kick), 12:00.
Car.—FG, Kasay 37, 13:42.

Third Quarter
Car.—FG, Kasay 25, 4:58.
Car.—Bennett 1 run (Sauerbrun kick), 5:36.
Car.—Muhammad 40 pass from Delhomme (Sauerbrun kick), 11:14.
S.F.—FG, T. Peterson 46, 14:14.

Fourth Quarter
S.F.—Lloyd 30 pass from Rattay (T. Peterson kick), 4:19.
Car.—Muhammad 4 pass from Delhomme (Sauerbrun kick), 7:48.
Car.—FG, Sauerbrun 34, 10:35.
Car.—Muhammad 26 pass from Delhomme (Sauerbrun kick), 12:22.
Attendance—63,618.

	Carolina	San Francisco
First downs	17	23
Rushes-yards......................................	18-57	33-110
Passing	301	247
Punt returns	1-5	3-22
Kickoff returns	6-125	8-178
Interception returns	4-22	0-0
Comp.-att.-int.	19-34-0	22-37-4
Sacked-yards lost	1-2	4-37

	Carolina	San Francisco
Punts	4-41	3-41
Fumbles-lost.....................................	2-2	2-1
Penalties-yards	7-49	7-60
Time of possession...........................	23:19	36:41

INDIVIDUAL STATISTICS
RUSHING—Carolina, Goings 8-42, Hoover 5-12, Bennett 4-5, Delhomme 1-(minus 2). San Francisco, Barlow 21-47, Hicks 8-46, Rattay 2-9, Jackson 2-8.

PASSING—Carolina, Delhomme 19-34-0-303. San Francisco, Rattay 22-37-4-284.

RECEIVING—Carolina, Muhammad 6-123, Proehl 5-69, Colbert 4-57, Goings 3-50, Hoover 1-4. San Francisco, E. Johnson 6-71, Wilson 5-101, Lloyd 5-62, Jackson 2-16, Barlow 2-14, Hicks 1-12, Beasley 1-8.

MISSED FIELD GOAL ATTEMPTS—None.

INTERCEPTIONS—Carolina, Fields 1-14, Buckner 1-8, Witherspoon 1-0, Gamble 1-0.

KICKOFF RETURNS—Carolina, Broussard 5-113, Rasmussen 1-12. San Francisco, Hicks 5-103, Battle 3-75.

PUNT RETURNS—Carolina, Broussard 1-5. San Francisco, Battle 2-14, Wilson 1-8.

SACKS—Carolina, Peppers 2, Minter 1, Witherspoon 1. San Francisco, Carter 1.

PATRIOTS 29, BILLS 6
Sunday, November 14

Buffalo..0	0	6	0— 6
New England 3	17	3	6—29

First Quarter
N.E.—FG, Vinatieri 27, 10:40.

Second Quarter
N.E.—FG, Vinatieri 24, 4:25.
N.E.—Patten 13 pass from Brady (Vinatieri kick), 11:04.
N.E.—Fauria 5 pass from Brady (Vinatieri kick), 14:25.

Third Quarter
N.E.—FG, Vinatieri 20, 5:52.
Buf.—J. Smith 70 punt return (run failed), 12:27.

Fourth Quarter
N.E.—FG, Vinatieri 45, :05.
N.E.—FG, Vinatieri 37, 10:20.
Attendance—68,756.

	Buffalo	New England
First downs	8	25
Rushes-yards......................................	17-50	45-208
Passing	75	220
Punt returns	2-70	3-34
Kickoff returns	7-142	2-48
Interception returns	1-35	4-50
Comp.-att.-int.	9-21-4	19-35-1
Sacked-yards lost	3-6	2-13
Punts	5-48	3-47
Fumbles-lost.....................................	1-1	0-0
Penalties-yards	2-48	5-44
Time of possession...........................	18:38	41:22

INDIVIDUAL STATISTICS
RUSHING—Buffalo, McGahee 14-37, Bledsoe 1-8, Losman 1-5, Burns 1-0. New England, Dillon 26-151, Faulk 13-61, Abdullah 4-(minus 5), Brady 1-2, Davey 1-(minus 1).

PASSING—Buffalo, Bledsoe 8-19-3-76, Losman 1-2-1-5. New England, Brady 19-35-1-233.

RECEIVING—Buffalo, Moulds 5-46, Evans 1-15, McGahee 1-12, Shelton 1-5, Euhus 1-3. New England, Givens 5-66, Patten 3-43, T. Brown 2-23, Faulk 2-16, Pass 2-9, B. Johnson 1-47, Weaver 1-10, Graham 1-9, Dillon 1-5, Fauria 1-5.

MISSED FIELD GOAL ATTEMPTS—None.

INTERCEPTIONS—Buffalo, Clements 1-35. New England, Bruschi 1-29, T. Brown 1-17, Banta-Cain 1-4, Wilson 1-0.

KICKOFF RETURNS—Buffalo, McGee 6-132, Shelton 1-10. New England, B. Johnson 1-32, Pass 1-16.

PUNT RETURNS—Buffalo, J. Smith 1-70, Clements 1-0. New England, Faulk 3-34.

SACKS—Buffalo, Adams 1, Kelsay 1. New England, Banta-Cain 1.5, McGinest 1, Colvin 0.5.

EAGLES 49, COWBOYS 21
Monday, November 15

Philadelphia 7	28	7	7—49
Dallas 0	14	7	0—21

First Quarter
Phi.—Owens 59 pass from McNabb (Akers kick), 8:50.

Second Quarter
Phi.—Levens 4 run (Akers kick), :07.
Dal.—Witten 29 pass from Testaverde (Cundiff kick), 1:45.
Phi.—Owens 27 pass from McNabb (Akers kick), 5:15.
Phi.—Pinkston 59 pass from McNabb (Akers kick), 6:58.
Dal.—Witten 24 pass from Testaverde (Cundiff kick), 11:37.
Phi.—Westbrook 1 run (Akers kick), 14:32.

Third Quarter
Dal.—George 15 run (Cundiff kick), 3:45.
Phi.—Owens 16 pass from McNabb (Akers kick), 8:56.

Fourth Quarter
Phi.—Sheppard 101 interception return (Akers kick), 10:41.
Attendance—64,190.

	Philadelphia	Dallas
First downs	20	14
Rushes-yards	33-149	24-71
Passing	336	246
Punt returns	2-9	5-34
Kickoff returns	4-70	7-195
Interception returns	1-101	0-0
Comp.-att.-int.	15-27-0	21-30-1
Sacked-yards lost	1-9	1-8
Punts	6-41	7-44
Fumbles-lost	0-0	3-2
Penalties-yards	9-59	7-50
Time of possession	30:10	29:50

INDIVIDUAL STATISTICS
RUSHING—Philadelphia, Westbrook 15-56, Levens 12-73, McNabb 2-14, Blake 2-(minus 2), Owens 1-6, G. Lewis 1-2. Dallas, George 11-39, Anderson 6-28, Testaverde 3-1, Lee 2-4, K. Johnson 1-0, Morgan 1-(minus 1).

PASSING—Philadelphia, McNabb 15-27-0-345. Dallas, Testaverde 21-30-1-254.

RECEIVING—Philadelphia, Owens 6-134, Westbrook 4-62, F. Mitchell 1-60, Pinkston 1-59, G. Lewis 1-13, C. Lewis 1-12, Parry 1-5. Dallas, Witten 9-133, K. Johnson 4-53, George 2-35, Anderson 2-6, Crayton 2-6, Morgan 1-21, Barnes 1-0.

MISSED FIELD GOAL ATTEMPTS—None.

INTERCEPTIONS—Philadelphia, Sheppard 1-101.

KICKOFF RETURNS—Philadelphia, Hood 3-55, G. Lewis 1-15. Dallas, Lee 5-153, Copper 2-42.

PUNT RETURNS—Philadelphia, Mahe 1-6, Sheppard 1-3. Dallas, Crayton 3-34, Frazier 2-0.

SACKS—Philadelphia, Trotter 1. Dallas, Ellis 0.5, Carson 0.5.

WEEK 11

STANDINGS

AMERICAN FOOTBALL CONFERENCE

EAST DIVISION
	W	L	T	Pct.	PF	PA
New England	9	1	0	.900	264	171
N.Y. Jets	7	3	0	.700	212	165
Buffalo	4	6	0	.400	180	183
Miami	1	9	0	.100	140	210

NORTH DIVISION
	W	L	T	Pct.	PF	PA
Pittsburgh	9	1	0	.900	240	161
Baltimore	7	3	0	.700	204	140
Cincinnati	4	6	0	.400	183	198
Cleveland	3	7	0	.300	177	208

SOUTH DIVISION
	W	L	T	Pct.	PF	PA
Indianapolis	7	3	0	.700	339	230
Jacksonville	6	4	0	.600	166	181
Houston	4	6	0	.400	198	239
Tennessee	4	6	0	.400	186	212

WEST DIVISION
	W	L	T	Pct.	PF	PA
Denver	7	3	0	.700	233	167
San Diego	7	3	0	.700	285	190
Kansas City	3	7	0	.300	276	265
Oakland	3	7	0	.300	182	270

NATIONAL FOOTBALL CONFERENCE

EAST DIVISION
	W	L	T	Pct.	PF	PA
Philadelphia	9	1	0	.900	266	158
N.Y. Giants	5	5	0	.500	196	172
Dallas	3	7	0	.300	172	282
Washington	3	7	0	.300	131	178

NORTH DIVISION
	W	L	T	Pct.	PF	PA
Green Bay	6	4	0	.600	256	230
Minnesota	6	4	0	.600	264	246
Chicago	4	6	0	.400	165	200
Detroit	4	6	0	.400	183	216

SOUTH DIVISION
	W	L	T	Pct.	PF	PA
Atlanta	8	2	0	.800	208	194
New Orleans	4	6	0	.400	211	288
Tampa Bay	4	6	0	.400	192	182
Carolina	3	7	0	.300	196	222

WEST DIVISION
	W	L	T	Pct.	PF	PA
Seattle	6	4	0	.600	230	185
St. Louis	5	5	0	.500	220	254
Arizona	4	6	0	.400	177	214
San Francisco	1	9	0	.100	175	296

TOP PERFORMANCES

100-YARD RUSHING GAMES
Player, Team & Opponent	Att.	Yds.	TD
Edgerrin James, Ind. at Chi.	23	204	1
Reuben Droughns, Den. at N.O.	28	166	1
LaDainian Tomlinson, S.D. at Oak.	37	164	1
Jerome Bettis, Pit. at Cin.	29	129	0
Nick Goings, Car. vs. Ariz.	22	121	3
Tiki Barber, NYG vs. Atl.	21	107	0
Michael Pittman, T.B. vs. S.F.	21	106	2
Michael Vick, Atl. at NYG	15	104	0
Fred Taylor, Jac. vs. Ten.	21	103	0
Kevin Jones, Det. at Min.	19	100	0
Willis McGahee, Buf. vs. St.L.	20	100	0

300-YARD PASSING GAMES
Player, Team & Opponent	Att.	Cmp.	Yds.	TD	Int.
Brett Favre, G.B. at Hou.	50	33	383	1	2
Trent Green, K.C. vs. N.E.	42	27	381	2	1
Aaron Brooks, N.O. vs. Den.	60	34	377	1	3
Shaun King, Ariz. at Car.	52	28	343	1	3
Tom Brady, N.E. at K.C.	26	17	315	1	0

100-YARD RECEIVING GAMES
Player, Team & Opponent	Rec.	Yds.	TD
Donald Driver, G.B. at Hou.	10	148	1
Donte' Stallworth, N.O. vs. Den.	10	122	1
Muhsin Muhammad, Car. vs. Ariz.	6	118	2
Andre Johnson, Hou. vs. G.B.	6	107	0
Johnnie Morton, K.C. vs. N.E.	5	107	0
Todd Pinkston, Phi. vs. Was.	5	106	0
Reggie Wayne, Ind. at Chi.	6	106	2
Deion Branch, N.E. at K.C.	6	105	1
Chris Chambers, Mia. at Sea.	9	103	1
Antonio Gates, S.D. at Oak.	8	101	1

RESULTS

SUNDAY, NOVEMBER 21
TAMPA BAY 35, San Francisco 3
BALTIMORE 30, Dallas 10
N.Y. Jets 10, CLEVELAND 7
MINNESOTA 22, Detroit 19
Indianapolis 41, CHICAGO 10
Tennessee 18, JACKSONVILLE 15
Pittsburgh 19, CINCINNATI 14
Denver 34, NEW ORLEANS 13
BUFFALO 37, St. Louis 17
CAROLINA 35, Arizona 10
PHILADELPHIA 28, Washington 6
Atlanta 14, N.Y. GIANTS 10
San Diego 23, OAKLAND 17
SEATTLE 24, Miami 17
Green Bay 16, HOUSTON 13

MONDAY, NOVEMBER 22
New England 27, KANSAS CITY 19

– 175 –

BUCCANEERS 35, 49ERS 3
Sunday, November 21

San Francisco	0	0	3	0— 3
Tampa Bay	7	14	7	7—35

First Quarter
T.B.—Pittman 14 run (Gramatica kick), 3:17.

Second Quarter
T.B.—Jurevicius 9 pass from Griese (Gramatica kick), 6:12.
T.B.—Jurevicius 42 pass from Griese (Gramatica kick), 14:43.

Third Quarter
T.B.—Pittman 6 run (Gramatica kick), 5:05.
S.F.—FG, T. Peterson 47, 12:47.

Fourth Quarter
T.B.—Cox 55 interception return (Gramatica kick), 6:47.
Attendance—65,234.

	San Francisco	Tampa Bay
First downs	13	1
Rushes-yards	23-72	35-15
Passing	125	193
Punt returns	2-11	3-16
Kickoff returns	2-50	2-36
Interception returns	2-39	1-55
Comp.-att.-int.	15-31-1	15-21-2
Sacked-yards lost	5-22	2-17
Punts	7-48	5-49
Fumbles-lost	1-1	2-0
Penalties-yards	4-30	5-50
Time of possession	26:27	33:33

INDIVIDUAL STATISTICS

RUSHING—San Francisco, Barlow 14-30, Hicks 7-36, Rattay 2-6. Tampa Bay, Pittman 21-106, Alstott 7-21, Graham 4-27, Griese 3-5.

PASSING—San Francisco, Rattay 15-31-1-147. Tampa Bay, Griese 15-21-2-210.

RECEIVING—San Francisco, Barlow 5-14, Hicks 3-37, Jackson 2-31, Woods 1-32, E. Johnson 1-9, Ware 1-9, Wilson 1-8, Lloyd 1-7. Tampa Bay, Jurevicius 5-82, Clayton 4-66, Galloway 3-33, Heller 1-13, Cook 1-9, Dilger 1-7.

MISSED FIELD GOAL ATTEMPTS—San Francisco, T. Peterson 50.

INTERCEPTIONS—San Francisco, Parrish 2-39. Tampa Bay, Cox 1-55.

KICKOFF RETURNS—San Francisco, Hicks 2-50. Tampa Bay, Cox 1-18, Graham 1-18.

PUNT RETURNS—San Francisco, Battle 2-11. Tampa Bay, Galloway 3-16.

SACKS—San Francisco, Carpenter 1, C. Cooper 1. Tampa Bay, Brooks 1, Barber 1, Ahanotu 1, Bradley 1, D. White 0.5, Gooch 0.5.

RAVENS 30, COWBOYS 10
Sunday, November 21

Dallas	3	0	0	7—10
Baltimore	0	0	14	16—30

First Quarter
Dal.—FG, Cundiff 19, 11:07.

Third Quarter
Bal.—Dinkins 17 pass from Boller (Stover kick), 8:07.
Bal.—K. Johnson 31 pass from Boller (Stover kick), 10:30.

Fourth Quarter
Bal.—FG, Stover 50, 3:38.
Bal.—Williams 44 interception return (Stover kick), 4:18.
Bal.—C. Taylor 1 run (run failed), 5:14.
Dal.—Robinson 1 pass from Henson (Cundiff kick), 14:20.
Attendance—69,924.

	Dallas	Baltimore
First downs	16	15
Rushes-yards	35-94	21-59
Passing	128	228
Punt returns	2-33	4-25
Kickoff returns	6-141	3-42
Interception returns	0-0	2-46
Comp.-att.-int.	15-28-2	23-35-0
Sacked-yards lost	2-28	1-4
Punts	6-42	5-40
Fumbles-lost	1-1	2-2
Penalties-yards	4-20	4-30
Time of possession	33:49	26:11

INDIVIDUAL STATISTICS

RUSHING—Dallas, J. Jones 30-81, George 3-5, Henson 1-7, Testaverde 1-1. Baltimore, C. Taylor 15-33, Boller 3-9, J. Lewis 2-5, Smith 1-12.

PASSING—Dallas, Testaverde 9-22-2-109, Henson 6-6-0-47. Baltimore, Boller 23-34-0-232, Hymes 0-1-0-0.

RECEIVING—Dallas, Morgan 4-42, Copper 3-44, K. Johnson 3-40, Witten 3-29, Robinson 1-1, Barnes 1-0. Baltimore, T. Taylor 6-68, K. Johnson 4-51, C. Taylor 4-18, Dinkins 3-40, Wilcox 2-23, Ricard 2-5, Moore 1-24, J. Lewis 1-3.

MISSED FIELD GOAL ATTEMPTS—Dallas, Cundiff 41.

INTERCEPTIONS—Baltimore, Williams 1-44, Reed 1-2.

KICKOFF RETURNS—Dallas, Lee 5-102, Copper 1-39. Baltimore, Sams 3-42.

PUNT RETURNS—Dallas, Frazier 2-33. Baltimore, Sams 4-25.

SACKS—Dallas, K. Coleman 1. Baltimore, Suggs 1, Douglas 1.

JETS 10, BROWNS 7
Sunday, November 21

N.Y. Jets	0	0	3	7—10
Cleveland	0	7	0	0— 7

Second Quarter
Cle.—Shea 3 pass from Garcia (Dawson kick), 3:56.

Third Quarter
NYJ—FG, Brien 41, 5:54.

Fourth Quarter
NYJ—McCareins 11 pass from Q. Carter (Brien kick), 9:28.
Attendance—72,547.

	N.Y. Jets	Cleveland
First downs	17	13
Rushes-yards	39-157	27-99
Passing	78	117
Punt returns	4-31	5-81
Kickoff returns	1-30	3-77
Interception returns	0-0	1-28
Comp.-att.-int.	11-20-1	14-27-0
Sacked-yards lost	6-38	1-3
Punts	8-42	9-41
Fumbles-lost	0-0	1-1
Penalties-yards	5-50	7-40
Time of possession	32:56	27:04

INDIVIDUAL STATISTICS

RUSHING—New York, Jordan 18-73, C. Martin 17-88, Q. Carter 4-(minus 4). Cleveland, Suggs 17-62, Green 8-32, Northcutt 2-5.

PASSING—New York, Q. Carter 11-20-1-116. Cleveland, Garcia 10-17-0-88, Holcomb 4-10-0-32.

RECEIVING—New York, McCareins 6-71, Moss 2-25, Sowell 2-9, Jordan 1-11. Cleveland, Bryant 3-36, Heiden 3-19, Suggs 3-15, Northcutt 2-40, Shea 2-7, T. Smith 1-3.

MISSED FIELD GOAL ATTEMPTS—New York, Brien 43. Cleveland, Dawson 42, 34.

INTERCEPTIONS—Cleveland, Little 1-28.

KICKOFF RETURNS—New York, Cotchery 1-30. Cleveland, Alston 3-77.

PUNT RETURNS—New York, Moss 4-31. Cleveland, Northcutt 5-81.

SACKS—New York, Coleman 1. Cleveland, Thompson 1.5, Warren 1.5, Crocker 1, Lang 1, Holdman 0.5, Andra. Davis 0.5.

VIKINGS 22, LIONS 19
Sunday, November 21

Detroit	14	3	2	0—19
Minnesota	7	0	0	15—22

First Quarter
Det.—Drummond 92 kickoff return (Hanson kick), :12.
Min.—Wiggins 8 pass from Culpepper (M. Andersen kick), 1:42.
Det.—Alexander 1 pass from Harrington (Hanson kick), 9:07.

Second Quarter
Det.—FG, Hanson 48, 11:27.

Third Quarter
Det.—Safety, 5:31.

Fourth Quarter
Min.—Burleson 6 pass from Culpepper (Burleson pass from Culpepper), :43.
Min.—M. Williams 1 run (M. Andersen kick), 9:33.
Attendance—64,156.

	Detroit	Minnesota
First downs	13	22
Rushes-yards	27-146	34-107
Passing	67	212
Punt returns	3-12	4-13
Kickoff returns	5-170	3-57
Interception returns	1-7	1-3
Comp.-att.-int.	12-19-1	22-32-1
Sacked-yards lost	3-24	3-21
Punts	6-42	4-41
Fumbles-lost	0-0	0-0
Penalties-yards	9-116	7-51
Time of possession	27:36	32:24

INDIVIDUAL STATISTICS

RUSHING—Detroit, Jones 19-100, Harrington 4-17, Bryson 2-19, Drummond 1-9, Schlesinger 1-1. Minnesota, Culpepper 11-35, M. Bennett 11-30, O. Smith 8-27, M. Williams 4-15.

PASSING—Detroit, Harrington 12-19-1-91. Minnesota, Culpepper 22-32-1-233.

RECEIVING—Detroit, Alexander 4-27, Jones 3-0, Williams 2-19, Streets 1-21, FitzSimmons 1-15, Bryson 1-9. Minnesota, Wiggins 8-51, Burleson 5-52, M. Bennett 3-27, M. Williams 2-21, O. Smith 2-14, Campbell 1-61, M. Robinson 1-7.

MISSED FIELD GOAL ATTEMPTS—None.

INTERCEPTIONS—Detroit, Marion 1-7. Minnesota, Winfield 1-3.

KICKOFF RETURNS—Detroit, Drummond 4-156, Bryson 1-14. Minnesota, O. Smith 2-40, Campbell 1-17.

PUNT RETURNS—Detroit, Drummond 3-12. Minnesota, Burleson 4-13.

SACKS—Detroit, Hall 2, Davis 1. Minnesota, Johnstone 3.

COLTS 41, BEARS 10
Sunday, November 21

Indianapolis	7	20	14	0—41
Chicago	3	0	0	7—10

First Quarter
Ind.—Pollard 14 pass from Manning (Vanderjagt kick), 5:55.
Chi.—FG, Edinger 51, 12:48.

Second Quarter
Ind.—Wayne 35 pass from Manning (Vanderjagt kick), :56.
Ind.—FG, Vanderjagt 34, 4:04.
Ind.—Harrison 10 pass from Manning (Vanderjagt kick), 9:19.
Ind.—FG, Vanderjagt 20, 14:01.

Third Quarter
Ind.—Wayne 27 pass from Manning (Vanderjagt kick), 6:34.
Ind.—James 11 run (Vanderjagt kick), 14:18.

Fourth Quarter
Chi.—Lyman 2 pass from Krenzel (Edinger kick), 13:23
Attendance—61,908.

	Indianapolis	Chicago
First downs	31	14
Rushes-yards	39-275	26-79
Passing	211	145
Punt returns	2-9	0-0
Kickoff returns	3-57	8-158
Interception returns	2-0	1-30
Comp.-att.-int.	17-28-1	14-24-2
Sacked-yards lost	0-0	4-30
Punts	2-35	4-41
Fumbles-lost	1-0	5-3
Penalties-yards	10-91	9-50
Time of possession	35:37	24:23

INDIVIDUAL STATISTICS

RUSHING—Indianapolis, James 23-204, Rhodes 9-54, Mungro 3-15, Sorgi 3-(minus 3), Manning 1-5. Chicago, T. Jones 18-59, Peterson 4-15, Krenzel 4-5.

PASSING—Indianapolis, Manning 17-28-1-211. Chicago, Krenzel 14-24-2-175.

RECEIVING—Indianapolis, Wayne 6-106, Harrison 4-49, Clark 3-19, Pollard 2-19, James 1-11, Stokley 1-7. Chicago, T. Jones 4-23, Terrell 3-76, Wade 2-6, Peterson 1-30, Berrian 1-17, Clark 1-14, Gage 1-7, Lyman 1-2.

MISSED FIELD GOAL ATTEMPTS—None.

INTERCEPTIONS—Indianapolis, Jefferson 1-0, Doss 1-0. Chicago, Vasher 1-30.

KICKOFF RETURNS—Indianapolis, Rhodes 3-57. Chicago, Azumah 6-111, Berrian 2-47.

PUNT RETURNS—Indianapolis, David 2-9.

SACKS—Indianapolis, Reagor 2, Mathis 1, Freeney 1.

TITANS 18, JAGUARS 15
Sunday, November 21

Tennessee	3	7	0	8—18
Jacksonville	0	6	7	2—15

First Quarter
Ten.—FG, Anderson 41, 14:02.

Second Quarter
Jac.—FG, Scobee 35, 4:46.
Ten.—Mason 37 pass from McNair (Anderson kick), 8:12.
Jac.—FG, Scobee 48, 13:54.

Third Quarter
Jac.—Garrard 5 run (Scobee kick), 13:58.

Fourth Quarter
Jac.—Safety, 5:48.
Ten.—A. Smith 2 run (McNair run), 11:29.
Attendance—69,703.

	Tennessee	Jacksonville
First downs	14	18
Rushes-yards	27-103	32-151
Passing	192	123
Punt returns	3-18	1-0
Kickoff returns	2-36	5-12
Interception returns	1-(-1)	2-7
Comp.-att.-int.	18-30-2	13-27-1
Sacked-yards lost	3-17	2-6
Punts	5-43	6-41
Fumbles-lost	1-0	1-1
Penalties-yards	4-49	3-22
Time of possession	28:28	31:32

INDIVIDUAL STATISTICS

RUSHING—Tennessee, A. Smith 24-95, McNair 2-4, Fleming 1-4. Jacksonville, F. Taylor 21-103, Garrard 5-34, Fuamatu-Ma'afala 3-12, G. Jones 2-2, Toefield 1-0.

PASSING—Tennessee, McNair 18-30-2-209. Jacksonville, Garrard 13-27-1-129.

RECEIVING—Tennessee, Bennett 4-64, Mason 3-56, Fleming 3-17, A. Smith 3-14, Kinney 2-31, Berlin 1-12, Meier 1-8, Troupe 1-7. Jacksonville, Hankton 3-27, F. Taylor 3-20, J. Smith 2-29, T. Edwards 2-24, R. Williams 1-13, Brady 1-12, Toefield 1-4.

MISSED FIELD GOAL ATTEMPTS—Jacksonville, Scobee 44.

INTERCEPTIONS—Tennessee, Gardner 1-(minus 1). Jacksonville, Darius 1-7, Washington 1-0.

KICKOFF RETURNS—Tennessee, McAddley 2-36. Jacksonville, T. Edwards 5-121.

PUNT RETURNS—Tennessee, Mason 2-10, Waddell 1-8. Jacksonville, Lewis 1-0.

SACKS—Tennessee, Long 1, LaBoy 1. Jacksonville, Favors 2, Stroud 1.
Steelers 19, Bengals 14.

STEELERS 19, BENGALS 14
Sunday, November 21

Pittsburgh	3	7	7	2—19
Cincinnati	7	7	0	0—14

First Quarter
Pit.—FG, Reed 32, 11:04.
Cin.—C. Johnson 36 pass from Palmer (Graham kick), 13:55.

Second Quarter
Pit.—Farrior 14 interception return (Reed kick), 7:57.
Cin.—Washington 19 pass from Palmer (Graham kick), 11:04.

Third Quarter
Pit.—Kreider 8 pass from Roethlisberger (Reed kick), 12:14.

Fourth Quarter
Pit.—Safety, 12:22.
Attendance—65,780.

	Pittsburgh	Cincinnati
First downs	21	10
Rushes-yards	40-151	16-62
Passing	84	147
Punt returns	7-83	3-11
Kickoff returns	4-84	4-79
Interception returns	1-14	0-0
Comp.-att.-int.	15-21-0	13-25-1
Sacked-yards lost	7-54	3-18
Punts	7-40	7-47
Fumbles-lost	2-1	1-0
Penalties-yards	8-56	10-97
Time of possession	38:56	21:04

INDIVIDUAL STATISTICS

RUSHING—Pittsburgh, Bettis 29-129, Roethlisberger 9-16, Haynes 2-6. Cincinnati, Ru. Johnson 16-62.

PASSING—Pittsburgh, Roethlisberger 15-21-0-138. Cincinnati, Palmer 13-25-1-165.

RECEIVING—Pittsburgh, Kreider 4-22, Burress 3-46, Ward 3-15, Randle El 2-17, Tuman 1-26, Mays 1-9, Bettis 1-3. Cincinnati, C. Johnson 5-80, Washington 3-47, Houshmandzadeh 2-24, J. Johnson 1-9, Walter 1-4, Ru. Johnson 1-1.

MISSED FIELD GOAL ATTEMPTS—None.

INTERCEPTIONS—Pittsburgh, Farrior 1-14.

KICKOFF RETURNS—Pittsburgh, Randle El 2-50, Colclough 1-21, Cushing 1-13. Cincinnati, C. Russell 2-41, Watson 2-38.

PUNT RETURNS—Pittsburgh, Randle El 7-83. Cincinnati, Ratliff 2-9, Houshmandzadeh 1-2.

SACKS—Pittsburgh, A. Smith 1, Porter 1, von Oelhoffen 1. Cincinnati, Clemons 2.5, J. Smith 1.5, L. Johnson 1, M. Williams 1, Hardy 1.

BRONCOS 34, SAINTS 13
Sunday, November 21

Denver	20	7	0	7—34
New Orleans	0	13	0	0—13

First Quarter
Den.—Droughns 51 run (Elam kick), 1:46.
Den.—Lelie 37 pass from Plummer (Elam kick), 5:27.
Den.—FG, Elam 48, 11:34.
Den.—FG, Elam 34, 13:57.

Second Quarter
N.O.—FG, Carney 24, 4:02.
Den.—Wilson 7 interception return (Elam kick), 7:52.
N.O.—Stallworth 30 pass from Brooks (Carney kick), 11:33.
N.O.—FG, Carney 36, 13:34.

Fourth Quarter
Den.—K. Johnson 19 pass from Plummer (Elam kick), :14.
Attendance—64,900.

	Denver	New Orleans
First downs	18	20
Rushes-yards	31-165	14-49
Passing	224	362
Punt returns	3-36	2-8
Kickoff returns	4-87	7-174
Interception returns	3-83	0-0
Comp.-att.-int.	19-29-0	34-60-3
Sacked-yards lost	0-0	2-15
Punts	6-41	4-47
Fumbles-lost	0-0	1-1
Penalties-yards	6-82	10-79
Time of possession	30:25	29:35

INDIVIDUAL STATISTICS

RUSHING—Denver, Droughns 28-166, Plummer 3-(minus 1). New Orleans, McAllister 13-42, Brooks 1-7.

PASSING—Denver, Plummer 19-29-0-224. New Orleans, Brooks 34-60-3-377.

RECEIVING—Denver, Carswell 5-27, Putzier 4-36, Lelie 3-79, Smith 3-26, Droughns 2-25, K. Johnson 1-19, Watts 1-12. New Orleans, McAllister 11-87, Stallworth 10-122, Horn 5-81, Pathon 3-44, B. Williams 3-35, M. Lewis 1-5, Stecker 1-3.

MISSED FIELD GOAL ATTEMPTS—None.

INTERCEPTIONS—Denver, Hayward 1-76, Wilson 1-7, Bailey 1-0.

KICKOFF RETURNS—Denver, R. Alexander 4-87. New Orleans, M. Lewis 6-158, McAfee 1-16.

PUNT RETURNS—Denver, Smith 3-36. New Orleans, M. Lewis 2-8.

SACKS—Denver, Hayward 1, Chukwurah 1.

BILLS 37, RAMS 17
Sunday, November 21

St. Louis	10	7	0	0—17
Buffalo	0	17	20	0—37

First Quarter
St.L.—FG, J. Wilkins 41, 10:10.
St.L.—Bruce 18 pass from Bulger (J. Wilkins kick), 12:12.

Second Quarter
Buf.—Campbell 10 pass from Bledsoe (Lindell kick), 1:04.
Buf.—Campbell 19 pass from Bledsoe (Lindell kick), 3:59.
St.L.—Holt 11 pass from Bulger (J. Wilkins kick), 11:55.
Buf.—FG, Lindell 21, 14:26.

Third Quarter
Buf.—Campbell 5 pass from Bledsoe (Lindell kick), 1:17.
Buf.—Clements 86 punt return (Lindell kick), 3:48.
Buf.—FG, Lindell 35, 6:57.
Buf.—FG, Lindell 33, 13:35.
Attendance—72,393.

	St. Louis	Buffalo
First downs	19	16
Rushes-yards	20-35	26-119
Passing	235	175
Punt returns	3-20	3-148
Kickoff returns	8-118	4-93
Interception returns	1-30	3-0
Comp.-att.-int.	27-45-3	15-24-1
Sacked-yards lost	6-52	1-10
Punts	4-40	4-41
Fumbles-lost	2-1	1-0
Penalties-yards	11-84	15-123
Time of possession	35:24	24:36

INDIVIDUAL STATISTICS

RUSHING—St. Louis, M. Faulk 13-6, S. Jackson 7-29. Buffalo, McGahee 20-100, Bledsoe 3-(minus 2), Henry 2-9, Moulds 1-12.

PASSING—St. Louis, Bulger 27-45-3-287. Buffalo, Bledsoe 15-24-1-185.

RECEIVING—St. Louis, Holt 8-90, McDonald 6-72, Curtis 5-51, M. Faulk 4-13, Bruce 3-58, S. Jackson 1-3. Buffalo, Campbell 4-37, McGahee 3-27, Moulds 3-17, Aiken 2-61, Evans 2-38, Henry 1-5.

MISSED FIELD GOAL ATTEMPTS—None.

INTERCEPTIONS—St. Louis, T. Fisher 1-30. Buffalo, McGee 1-0, Spikes 1-0, Adams 1-0.

KICKOFF RETURNS—St. Louis, Harris 6-109, Goodspeed 1-9, Flowers 1-0. Buffalo, McGee 4-93.

PUNT RETURNS—St. Louis, McDonald 3-20. Buffalo, J. Smith 2-62, Clements 1-86.

SACKS—St. Louis, Little 1. Buffalo, Milloy 3, McGee 1, Greer 1, Denney 1. Panthers 35, Cardinals 10.

PANTHERS 35, CARDINALS 10
Sunday, November 21

Arizona	0	0	10	0—10
Carolina	14	14	0	7—35

First Quarter
Car.—Goings 2 run (J. Chandler kick), 8:05.
Car.—Goings 57 run (J. Chandler kick), 13:07.

Second Quarter
Car.—Goings 1 run (J. Chandler kick), 10:29.
Car.—Muhammad 28 pass from Delhomme (J. Chandler kick), 14:58.

Third Quarter
Ariz.—Fitzgerald 21 pass from S. King (Rackers kick), 5:40.
Ariz.—FG, Rackers 28, 10:20.

Fourth Quarter
Car.—Muhammad 17 pass from Delhomme (J. Chandler kick), 3:22.
Attendance—72,796.

	Arizona	Carolina
First downs	23	16
Rushes-yards	28-85	27-157
Passing	314	160
Punt returns	3-26	1-7
Kickoff returns	6-110	2-47
Interception returns	1-27	3-79
Comp.-att.-int.	28-52-3	13-27-1
Sacked-yards lost	4-29	0-0
Punts	3-40	5-48
Fumbles-lost	5-1	0-0
Penalties-yards	12-105	12-85
Time of possession	33:44	26:16

INDIVIDUAL STATISTICS

RUSHING—Arizona, E. Smith 11-26, S. King 6-22, Scobey 4-19, Hambrick 3-9, Fitzgerald 2-0, O. Ayanbadejo 1-6, K. Williams 1-3. Carolina, Goings 22-121, Muhammad 1-13, Bennett 1-11, Proehl 1-4, Delhomme 1-4, Peete 1-(minus 1).

PASSING—Arizona, S. King 28-52-3-343. Carolina, Delhomme 12-25-1-157, Proehl 0-1-0-0, Peete 1-1-0-3.

RECEIVING—Arizona, Fitzgerald 7-92, Boldin 6-75, F. Jones 5-73, K. Williams 3-37, Scobey 2-35, O. Ayanbadejo 2-15, Edwards 2-12, E. Smith 1-4. Carolina, Muhammad 6-118, Goings 3-21, Colbert 3-18, Mangum 1-3.

MISSED FIELD GOAL ATTEMPTS—Arizona, Rackers 50.

INTERCEPTIONS—Arizona, Wilson 1-27. Carolina, Branch 2-79, Gamble 1-0.

KICKOFF RETURNS—Arizona, Scobey 4-89, Edwards 1-14, Vanden Bosch 1-7. Carolina, Broussard 2-47.

PUNT RETURNS—Arizona, K. Williams 3-26. Carolina, Broussard 1-7.

SACKS—Carolina, Peppers 2, Witherspoon 1, Fields 1.

EAGLES 28, REDSKINS 6
Sunday, November 21

Washington	3	3	0	0— 6
Philadelphia	7	0	7	14—28

First Quarter
Was.—FG, Kimrin 35, 7:01.
Phi.—C. Lewis 2 pass from McNabb (Akers kick), 14:24.

Second Quarter
Was.—FG, Kimrin 24, 14:18.

Third Quarter
Phi.—Owens 10 pass from McNabb (Akers kick), 11:54.

Fourth Quarter
Phi.—Westbrook 1 pass from McNabb (Akers kick), 6:04.
Phi.—Westbrook 14 pass from McNabb (Akers kick), 8:06.
Attendance—67,720.

	Washington	Philadelphia
First downs	15	20
Rushes-yards	23-51	30-125
Passing	162	208
Punt returns	0-0	2-53
Kickoff returns	5-115	2-35
Interception returns	1-10	1-7
Comp.-att.-int.	21-34-1	18-27-1
Sacked-yards lost	1-0	4-14
Punts	5-54	3-44
Fumbles-lost	0-0	1-1
Penalties-yards	12-115	9-69
Time of possession	28:29	31:31

INDIVIDUAL STATISTICS
RUSHING—Washington, Portis 17-37, Betts 5-14, Ramsey 1-0. Philadelphia, Westbrook 12-63, Levens 7-19, McNabb 4-33, Tapeh 4-14, Detmer 3-(minus 4).
PASSING—Washington, Ramsey 21-34-1-162. Philadelphia, McNabb 18-26-1-222, Detmer 0-1-0-0.
RECEIVING—Washington, Betts 6-39, Gardner 4-35, Coles 4-34, Cooley 2-22, Thrash 2-19, McCants 2-17, Portis 1-(minus 4). Philadelphia, Pinkston 5-106, Westbrook 5-42, Smith 3-20, Owens 2-24, C. Lewis 2-17, F. Mitchell 1-13.
MISSED FIELD GOAL ATTEMPTS—Washington, Kimrin 48.
INTERCEPTIONS—Washington, Taylor 1-10. Philadelphia, Reese 1-7.
KICKOFF RETURNS—Washington, Betts 4-98, Sellers 1-17. Philadelphia, Hood 2-35.
PUNT RETURNS—Philadelphia, Sheppard 1-39, Westbrook 1-14.
SACKS—Washington, Wynn 1, Haley 1, Noble 1, Salave'a 1. Philadelphia, Kearse 1.

FALCONS 14, GIANTS 10
Sunday, November 21

Atlanta	7	7	0	0—14
N.Y. Giants	0	0	7	3—10

First Quarter
Atl.—Crumpler 6 pass from Vick (Feely kick), 7:58.

Second Quarter
Atl.—Crumpler 2 pass from Vick (Feely kick), 5:51.

Third Quarter
NYG—Shockey 6 pass from Manning (Christie kick), 10:23.

Fourth Quarter
NYG—FG, Christie 24, 8:32.
Attendance—78,793.

	Atlanta	N.Y. Giants
First downs	16	20
Rushes-yards	34-201	26-119
Passing	97	158
Punt returns	3-11	4-1
Kickoff returns	3-54	2-36
Interception returns	2-19	0-0
Comp.-att.-int.	12-20-0	17-37-2
Sacked-yards lost	2-18	1-4
Punts	7-35	5-42
Fumbles-lost	2-0	1-0
Penalties-yards	12-94	6-50
Time of possession	31:43	28:17

INDIVIDUAL STATISTICS
RUSHING—Atlanta, Vick 15-104, Dunn 12-69, Duckett 6-30, White 1-(minus 2). New York, Barber 21-107, Dayne 4-13, Manning 1-(minus 1).
PASSING—Atlanta, Vick 12-20-0-115. New York, Manning 17-37-2-162.

RECEIVING—Atlanta, Crumpler 4-47, White 4-35, Griffith 2-22, Dunn 2-11. New York, Shockey 5-45, I. Hilliard 4-28, Barber 3-24, Finn 2-30, Toomer 2-24, Rivers 1-11.
MISSED FIELD GOAL ATTEMPTS—Atlanta, Feely 46.
INTERCEPTIONS—Atlanta, Webster 1-18, B. Smith 1-1.
KICKOFF RETURNS—Atlanta, Rossum 3-54. New York, Ponder 2-36.
PUNT RETURNS—Atlanta, Rossum 3-11. New York, Jones 4-1.
SACKS—Atlanta, Kerney 0.5, Jasper 0.5. New York, Umenyiora 0.5, Legree 0.5, Wiley 0.5, Robbins 0.5.

CHARGERS 23, RAIDERS 17
Sunday, November 21

San Diego	6	7	3	7—23
Oakland	0	7	7	3—17

First Quarter
S.D.—Gates 11 pass from Brees (kick blocked), 5:55.

Second Quarter
S.D.—Brees 6 run (Kaeding kick), 4:53.
Oak.—Curry 22 pass from Collins (Janikowski kick), 8:20.

Third Quarter
S.D.—FG, Kaeding 19, 9:39.
Oak.—T. Johnson 8 pass from Collins (Janikowski kick), 13:02.

Fourth Quarter
S.D.—Tomlinson 6 run (Kaeding kick), 3:54.
Oak.—FG, Janikowski 31, 7:49.
Attendance—46,905.

	San Diego	Oakland
First downs	26	14
Rushes-yards	44-176	14-53
Passing	226	220
Punt returns	1-15	2-9
Kickoff returns	3-64	5-70
Interception returns	0-0	0-0
Comp.-att.-int.	18-35-0	18-31-0
Sacked-yards lost	0-0	1-7
Punts	4-43	6-45
Fumbles-lost	1-1	1-1
Penalties-yards	9-80	8-76
Time of possession	38:26	21:34

INDIVIDUAL STATISTICS
RUSHING—San Diego, Tomlinson 37-164, Brees 5-5, Neal 1-4, McCardell 1-3. Oakland, Wheatley 12-42, Collins 2-11.
PASSING—San Diego, Brees 18-34-0-226, Tomlinson 0-1-0-0. Oakland, Collins 18-30-0-227, Curry 0-1-0-0.
RECEIVING—San Diego, Gates 8-101, McCardell 7-91, E. Parker 2-25, Tomlinson 1-9. Oakland, Porter 5-63, Curry 4-58, Gabriel 2-36, Jolley 2-22, Redmond 2-20, Zereoue 1-11, Wheatley 1-9, T. Johnson 1-8.
MISSED FIELD GOAL ATTEMPTS—San Diego, Kaeding 42.
INTERCEPTIONS—None.
KICKOFF RETURNS—San Diego, Dwight 3-64. Oakland, Gabriel 3-42, Curry 2-28.
PUNT RETURNS—San Diego, E. Parker 1-15. Oakland, Buchanon 2-9.
SACKS—San Diego, Leber 1.

SEAHAWKS 24, DOLPHINS 17
Sunday, November 21

Miami	7	0	7	3—17
Seattle	10	7	0	7—24

First Quarter
Sea.—Rice 21 pass from Dilfer (J. Brown kick), 5:41.
Mia.—Feeley 7 run (Mare kick), 10:35.
Sea.—FG, J. Brown 33, 13:47.

Second Quarter
Sea.—Alexander 4 run (J. Brown kick), 10:22.

Third Quarter
Mia.—Chambers 16 pass from Feeley (Mare kick), 4:27.

Fourth Quarter
Mia.—FG, Mare 39, 12:40.
Sea.—Boulware 63 interception return (J. Brown kick), 14:04.
Attendance—66,644.

	Miami	Seattle
First downs	19	17
Rushes-yards	23-69	38-116
Passing	219	177
Punt returns	3-33	5-27

	Miami	Seattle
Kickoff returns	4-91	4-72
Interception returns	2-0	2-63
Comp.-att.-int.	24-46-2	14-28-2
Sacked-yards lost	4-11	3-19
Punts	8-42	8-32
Fumbles-lost	3-2	1-1
Penalties-yards	8-98	9-70
Time of possession	27:29	32:31

INDIVIDUAL STATISTICS

RUSHING—Miami, Minor 13-37, Morris 7-16, Chambers 1-7, Feeley 1-7, Forsey 1-2. Seattle, Alexander 29-96, Dilfer 5-11, Strong 3-6, Morris 1-3.

PASSING—Miami, Feeley 23-45-2-229, Fiedler 1-1-0-1. Seattle, Dilfer 14-28-2-196.

RECEIVING—Miami, Chambers 9-103, McMichael 6-43, Minor 4-13, Thompson 3-51, Booker 2-20. Seattle, Mili 4-24, Rice 3-86, Jackson 3-39, Engram 2-41, Stevens 1-5, Strong 1-1.

MISSED FIELD GOAL ATTEMPTS—Miami, Mare 34.

INTERCEPTIONS—Miami, Surtain 1-0, Freeman 1-0. Seattle, Boulware 1-63, Cochran 1-0.

KICKOFF RETURNS—Miami, Welker 4-91. Seattle, Carter 3-60, Locklear 1-12.

PUNT RETURNS—Miami, Welker 3-33. Seattle, Morris 4-21, Hannam 1-6.

SACKS—Miami, Surtain 1, Poole 1, Taylor 0.5, Romero 0.5. Seattle, Kacyvenski 1, Koutouvides 1, Cochran 1, Tubbs 1.

PACKERS 16, TEXANS 13
Sunday, November 21

Green Bay	0	3	0	13—16
Houston	0	13	0	0—13

Second Quarter
G.B.—FG, Longwell 23, 5:39.
Hou.—D. Davis 6 pass from Carr (K. Brown kick), 7:37.
Hou.—FG, K. Brown 46, 13:12.
Hou.—FG, K. Brown 40, 14:43.

Fourth Quarter
G.B.—Driver 24 pass from Favre (Longwell kick), 2:32.
G.B.—FG, Longwell 39, 7:05.
G.B.—FG, Longwell 46, 15:00.
Attendance—70,769.

	Green Bay	Houston
First downs	22	13
Rushes-yards	21-90	27-107
Passing	383	144
Punt returns	4-23	3-38
Kickoff returns	4-60	4-73
Interception returns	0-0	2-0
Comp.-att.-int.	33-50-2	13-27-0
Sacked-yards lost	0-0	2-20
Punts	3-40	7-44
Fumbles-lost	0-0	0-0
Penalties-yards	10-90	3-25
Time of possession	32:06	27:54

INDIVIDUAL STATISTICS

RUSHING—Green Bay, Fisher 7-14, W. Williams 6-42, Green 5-15, Favre 2-16, Luchey 1-3. Houston, D. Davis 21-65, Carr 3-36, Gaffney 2-15, An. Johnson 1-(minus 9).

PASSING—Green Bay, Favre 33-50-2-383. Houston, Carr 13-26-0-164, Gaffney 0-1-0-0.

RECEIVING—Green Bay, Driver 10-148, J. Walker 9-88, Ferguson 4-44, Fisher 4-18, Franks 2-43, Chatman 2-17, Henderson 1-20, Steele 1-5. Houston, An. Johnson 6-107, D. Davis 6-41, Armstrong 1-16.

MISSED FIELD GOAL ATTEMPTS—Green Bay, Longwell 49. Houston, K. Brown 40.

INTERCEPTIONS—Houston, Robinson 1-0, Glenn 1-0.

KICKOFF RETURNS—Green Bay, Chatman 2-39, Ferguson 2-21. Houston, Moses 4-73.

PUNT RETURNS—Green Bay, Chatman 4-23. Houston, Moses 3-38.

SACKS—Green Bay, Gbaja-Biamila 2.

PATRIOTS 27, CHIEFS 19
Monday, November 22

New England	7	10	7	3—27
Kansas City	10	0	3	6—19

First Quarter
N.E.—Dillon 5 run (Vinatieri kick), 4:31.
K.C.—FG, Tynes 44, 7:13.
K.C.—Kennison 65 pass from Green (Tynes kick), 11:19.

Second Quarter
N.E.—Dillon 1 run (Vinatieri kick), 6:33.
N.E.—FG, Vinatieri 37, 11:08.

Third Quarter
K.C.—FG, Tynes 24, 8:15.
N.E.—Branch 26 pass from Brady (Vinatieri kick), 10:06.

Fourth Quarter
K.C.—Kennison 26 pass from Green (pass failed), 8:47.
N.E.—FG, Vinatieri 28, 13:14.
Attendance—78,431.

	New England	Kansas City
First downs	21	20
Rushes-yards	32-98	20-64
Passing	309	353
Punt returns	1-4	1-0
Kickoff returns	5-94	6-156
Interception returns	1-12	0-0
Comp.-att.-int.	17-26-0	27-42-1
Sacked-yards lost	1-6	4-28
Punts	2-44	3-32
Fumbles-lost	1-1	1-0
Penalties-yards	4-25	7-50
Time of possession	27:59	32:01

INDIVIDUAL STATISTICS

RUSHING—New England, Dillon 26-98, Brady 5-(minus 1), Faulk 1-1. Kansas City, Blaylock 19-58, Green 1-6.

PASSING—New England, Brady 17-26-0-315. Kansas City, Green 27-42-1-381.

RECEIVING—New England, Branch 6-105, Graham 3-83, T. Brown 2-27, Pass 2-17, Patten 1-46, Dillon 1-20, Fauria 1-14, Givens 1-3. Kansas City, Gonzalez 7-86, Morton 5-107, Blaylock 5-33, Kennison 3-99, Hall 3-32, Dunn 3-17, Richardson 1-7.

MISSED FIELD GOAL ATTEMPTS—None.

INTERCEPTIONS—New England, Harrison 1-12.

KICKOFF RETURNS—New England, B. Johnson 4-73, Banta-Cain 1-21. Kansas City, Hall 6-156.

PUNT RETURNS—New England, Faulk 1-4. Kansas City, Hall 1-0.

SACKS—New England, Warren 2, McGinest 1, Colvin 1. Kansas City, Allen 1.

WEEK 12

AMERICAN FOOTBALL CONFERENCE

EAST DIVISION

	W	L	T	Pct.	PF	PA
New England	10	1	0	.909	288	174
N.Y. Jets	8	3	0	.727	225	168
Buffalo	5	6	0	.455	218	192
Miami	2	9	0	.182	164	227

NORTH DIVISION

	W	L	T	Pct.	PF	PA
Pittsburgh	10	1	0	.909	256	168
Baltimore	7	4	0	.636	207	164
Cincinnati	5	6	0	.455	241	246
Cleveland	3	8	0	.273	225	266

SOUTH DIVISION

	W	L	T	Pct.	PF	PA
Indianapolis	8	3	0	.727	380	239
Jacksonville	6	5	0	.545	182	208
Houston	5	6	0	.455	229	260
Tennessee	4	7	0	.364	207	243

WEST DIVISION

	W	L	T	Pct.	PF	PA
San Diego	8	3	0	.727	319	221
Denver	7	4	0	.636	257	192
Oakland	4	7	0	.364	207	294
Kansas City	3	8	0	.273	307	299

NATIONAL FOOTBALL CONFERENCE

EAST DIVISION

	W	L	T	Pct.	PF	PA
Philadelphia	10	1	0	.909	293	164
N.Y. Giants	5	6	0	.455	202	199
Dallas	4	7	0	.364	193	289
Washington	3	8	0	.273	138	194

NORTH DIVISION

	W	L	T	Pct.	PF	PA
Green Bay	7	4	0	.636	301	247
Minnesota	7	4	0	.636	291	262
Chicago	4	7	0	.364	172	221
Detroit	4	7	0	.364	192	257

SOUTH DIVISION

	W	L	T	Pct.	PF	PA
Atlanta	9	2	0	.818	232	215
Carolina	4	7	0	.364	217	236
New Orleans	4	7	0	.364	232	312
Tampa Bay	4	7	0	.364	206	203

WEST DIVISION

	W	L	T	Pct.	PF	PA
Seattle	6	5	0	.545	239	223
St. Louis	5	6	0	.455	237	299
Arizona	4	7	0	.364	180	227
San Francisco	1	10	0	.091	192	320

TOP PERFORMANCES

100-YARD RUSHING GAMES

Player, Team & Opponent	Att.	Yds.	TD
Rudi Johnson, Cin. vs. Cle.	26	202	2
Najeh Davenport, G.B. vs. St.L.	19	178	1
Julius Jones, Dal. vs. Chi.	33	150	2
Fred Taylor, Jac. at Min.	22	147	0
Domanick Davis, Hou. vs. Ten.	16	129	1
Corey Dillon, N.E. vs. Bal.	30	123	1
Willis McGahee, Buf. at Sea.	28	116	4
Tiki Barber, NYG vs. Phi.	19	110	0
Nick Goings, Car. vs. T.B.	23	106	0
Edgerrin James, Ind. at Det.	23	105	0
Reuben Droughns, Den. vs. Oak.	28	102	1
Jerome Bettis, Pit. vs. Was.	31	100	1
Deuce McAllister, N.O. at Atl.	23	100	0

300-YARD PASSING GAMES

Player, Team & Opponent	Att.	Cmp.	Yds.	TD	Int.
Marc Bulger, St.L. at G.B.	53	35	448	2	1
Kelly Holcomb, Cle. at Cin.	39	30	413	5	2
Drew Brees, S.D. at K.C.	37	28	378	2	0
Brian Griese, T.B. at Car.	39	27	347	2	1
Kerry Collins, Oak. at Den.	45	26	339	4	2

100-YARD RECEIVING GAMES

Player, Team & Opponent	Rec.	Yds.	TD
Isaac Bruce, St.L. at G.B.	9	170	1
Jerry Porter, Oak. at Den.	6	135	3
Michael Pittman, T.B. at Car.	8	134	2
Antonio Bryant, Cle. at Cin.	8	131	2
Marvin Harrison, Ind. at Det.	12	127	3
Chad Johnson, Cin. vs. Cle.	10	117	1
Ronald Curry, Oak. at Den.	6	110	1
Santana Moss, NYJ at Ariz.	5	109	1
Tony Gonzalez, K.C. vs. S.D.	8	105	0

Player, Team & Opponent	Rec.	Yds.	TD
Alge Crumpler, Atl. vs. N.O.	4	103	1
Jamaar Taylor, NYG vs. Phi.	2	102	0
Joe Horn, N.O. at Atl.	9	101	1

RESULTS

THURSDAY, NOVEMBER 25
Indianapolis 41, DETROIT 9
DALLAS 21, Chicago 7
SUNDAY, NOVEMBER 28
PITTSBURGH 16, Washington 7
MINNESOTA 27, Jacksonville 16
Philadelphia 27, N.Y. GIANTS 6
CAROLINA 21, Tampa Bay 14
HOUSTON 31, Tennessee 21
San Diego 34, KANSAS CITY 31
CINCINNATI 58, Cleveland 48
N.Y. Jets 13, ARIZONA 3
Buffalo 38, SEATTLE 9
ATLANTA 24, New Orleans 21
Miami 24, SAN FRANCISCO 17
NEW ENGLAND 24, Baltimore 3
Oakland 25, DENVER 24
MONDAY, NOVEMBER 29
GREEN BAY 45, St. Louis 17

COLTS 41, LIONS 9
Thursday, November 25

Indianapolis	13	14	14	0—41
Detroit	6	3	0	0— 9

First Quarter
Ind.—Stokley 4 pass from Manning (Vanderjagt kick), 4:44.
Det.—FG, Hanson 20, 7:44.
Ind.—Stokley 12 pass from Manning (kick blocked), 10:40.
Det.—FG, Hanson 34, 14:11.

Second Quarter
Ind.—Stokley 25 pass from Manning (Vanderjagt kick), 12:40.
Ind.—Harrison 13 pass from Manning (Vanderjagt kick), 14:10.
Det.—FG, Hanson 32, 15:00.

Third Quarter
Ind.—Harrison 10 pass from Manning (Vanderjagt kick), 5:42.
Ind.—Harrison 5 pass from Manning (Vanderjagt kick), 12:49.
Attendance—63,107.

	Indianapolis	Detroit
First downs	24	19
Rushes-yards	29-113	21-168
Passing	243	218
Punt returns	2-5	3-29
Kickoff returns	2-48	5-102
Interception returns	1-0	0-0
Comp.-att.-int.	24-31-0	25-38-1
Sacked-yards lost	0-0	3-15
Punts	5-42	3-41
Fumbles-lost	0-0	5-4
Penalties-yards	5-40	10-60
Time of possession	31:12	28:48

INDIVIDUAL STATISTICS
RUSHING—Indianapolis, James 23-105, Mungro 2-4, Rhodes 2-4, Manning 1-4, Wayne 1-(minus 4). Detroit, Jones 12-99, Bryson 7-51, McMahon 2-18.
PASSING—Indianapolis, Manning 23-28-0-236, Sorgi 1-3-0-7. Detroit, Harrington 14-23-0-156, McMahon 11-15-1-77.
RECEIVING—Indianapolis, Harrison 12-127, Stokley 5-57, Wayne 3-37, James 3-16, Clark 1-6. Detroit, Bryson 6-44, Alexander 5-58, Williams 4-51, Streets 3-26, Jones 3-3, Swinton 1-23, Vines 1-11, Schlesinger 1-10, FitzSimmons 1-7.
MISSED FIELD GOAL ATTEMPTS—Detroit, Hanson 48.
INTERCEPTIONS—Indianapolis, Bacon 1-0.
KICKOFF RETURNS—Indianapolis, Rhodes 2-48. Detroit, Drummond 3-57, Swinton 2-45.
PUNT RETURNS—Indianapolis, David 2-5. Detroit, Swinton 2-29, Drummond 1-0.
SACKS—Indianapolis, Morris 1, Reagor 1, Brock 0.5, Mathis 0.5.

COWBOYS 21, BEARS 7
Thursday, November 25

Chicago	0	7	0	0— 7
Dallas	7	0	0	14—21

First Quarter
Dal.—J. Jones 33 run (Cundiff kick), 4:17.

Second Quarter
Chi.—McQuarters 45 interception return (Edinger kick), 9:03.

Fourth Quarter
Dal.—Barnes 5 pass from Testaverde (Cundiff kick), 3:53.
Dal.—J. Jones 4 run (Cundiff kick), 8:00.
Attendance—64,026.

	Chicago	Dallas
First downs	10	18
Rushes-yards	20-49	40-154
Passing	91	113
Punt returns	6-68	5-37
Kickoff returns	4-62	1-22
Interception returns	2-85	2-13
Comp.-att.-int.	15-31-2	13-26-2
Sacked-yards lost	6-41	2-10
Punts	10-41	9-43
Fumbles-lost	4-2	0-0
Penalties-yards	7-45	5-30
Time of possession	24:23	35:37

INDIVIDUAL STATISTICS
RUSHING—Chicago, T. Jones 14-46, Thomas 3-0, Krenzel 2-2, Wade 1-1. Dallas, J. Jones 33-150, George 3-8, Testaverde 3-(minus 3), Copper 1-(minus 1).
PASSING—Chicago, Quinn 10-21-2-86, Krenzel 5-10-0-46. Dallas, Testaverde 9-14-1-92, Henson 4-12-1-31.
RECEIVING—Chicago, T. Jones 6-48, Terrell 2-34, Wade 2-23, Thomas 2-20, Clark 1-6, Berrian 1-3, B. Johnson 1-(minus 2). Dallas, K. Johnson 6-58, Morgan 2-22, Copper 2-22, Witten 1-17, Barnes 1-5, J. Jones 1-(minus 1).
MISSED FIELD GOAL ATTEMPTS—Chicago, Edinger 48. Dallas, Cundiff 52.
INTERCEPTIONS—Chicago, McQuarters 2-85. Dallas, Newman 1-11, Nguyen 1-2.
KICKOFF RETURNS—Chicago, Azumah 2-26, Peterson 1-18, B. Johnson 1-18. Dallas, Copper 1-22.
PUNT RETURNS—Chicago, McQuarters 6-68. Dallas, Frazier 5-37.
SACKS—Chicago, Haynes 1, Ogunleye 1. Dallas, Ogbogu 3.5, Ellis 1.5, Wiley 1.

STEELERS 16, REDSKINS 7
Sunday, November 28

Washington	0	0	7	0— 7
Pittsburgh	3	10	0	3—16

First Quarter
Pit.—FG, Reed 33, 12:55.

Second Quarter
Pit.—Bettis 4 run (Reed kick), 3:09.
Pit.—FG, Reed 36, 10:52.

Third Quarter
Was.—Cooley 2 pass from Ramsey (Hall kick), 11:37.

Fourth Quarter
Pit.—FG, Reed 32, 5:06.
Attendance—63,707.

	Washington	Pittsburgh
First downs	10	15
Rushes-yards	14-51	38-107
Passing	105	100
Punt returns	4-22	6-111
Kickoff returns	5-74	2-43
Interception returns	0-0	1-15
Comp.-att.-int.	19-35-1	9-20-0
Sacked-yards lost	5-33	4-31
Punts	7-46	6-39
Fumbles-lost	1-0	0-0
Penalties-yards	6-68	6-39
Time of possession	25:44	34:16

INDIVIDUAL STATISTICS
RUSHING—Washington, Betts 8-34, Portis 6-17. Pittsburgh, Bettis 31-100, Roethlisberger 6-4, Haynes 1-3.
PASSING—Washington, Ramsey 19-34-1-138, Gardner 0-1-0-0. Pittsburgh, Roethlisberger 9-20-0-131.
RECEIVING—Washington, Cooley 7-31, Coles 6-55, Betts 3-35, Gardner 1-11, Royal 1-6, Portis 1-0. Pittsburgh, Ward 3-42, Randle El 2-37, Haynes 2-24, Bettis 1-20, Morey 1-8.
MISSED FIELD GOAL ATTEMPTS—None.
INTERCEPTIONS—Pittsburgh, Townsend 1-15.
KICKOFF RETURNS—Washington, Betts 5-74. Pittsburgh, Colclough 1-22, I. Taylor 1-21.
PUNT RETURNS—Washington, Thrash 4-22. Pittsburgh, Randle El 6-111.
SACKS—Washington, Washington 2, Marshall 1, Clemons 1. Pittsburgh, Porter 2, Haggans 2, A. Smith 1.

VIKINGS 27, JAGUARS 16
Sunday, November 28

Jacksonville	0	13	0	3—16
Minnesota	3	10	7	7—27

First Quarter
Min.—FG, M. Andersen 25, 8:28.

Second Quarter
Jac.—B. Jones 26 pass from Leftwich (Scobee kick), 1:21.
Jac.—FG, Scobee 33, 3:37.
Min.—Culpepper 1 run (M. Andersen kick), 8:45.
Jac.—FG, Scobee 32, 13:51.
Min.—FG, M. Andersen 33, 15:00.

Third Quarter
Min.—Moss 2 pass from Culpepper (M. Andersen kick), 9:26.

Fourth Quarter

Jac.—FG, Scobee 42, 1:32.
Min.—K. Williams 77 fumble return (M. Andersen kick), 13:01.
Attendance—64,004.

	Jacksonville	Minnesota
First downs	18	24
Rushes-yards	27-154	30-112
Passing	225	218
Punt returns	2-11	2-32
Kickoff returns	3-52	1-21
Interception returns	1-16	0-0
Comp.-att.-int.	19-34-0	19-27-1
Sacked-yards lost	2-10	4-17
Punts	2-54	2-49
Fumbles-lost	3-2	1-1
Penalties-yards	6-45	4-35
Time of possession	31:17	28:43

INDIVIDUAL STATISTICS

RUSHING—Jacksonville, F. Taylor 22-147, Toefield 2-5, Fuamatu-Ma'afala 2-2, T. Edwards 1-0. Minnesota, O. Smith 20-72, Culpepper 8-18, Campbell 1-16, M. Williams 1-6.
PASSING—Jacksonville, Leftwich 19-34-0-235. Minnesota, Culpepper 19-27-1-235.
RECEIVING—Jacksonville, J. Smith 4-68, T. Edwards 3-55, R. Williams 3-32, B. Jones 2-28, Hankton 2-19, Toefield 2-11, F. Taylor 1-13, Yoder 1-5, Brady 1-4. Minnesota, Wiggins 4-55, M. Robinson 4-48, Moss 4-40, O. Smith 3-18, Burleson 2-21, Campbell 1-48, M. Bennett 1-5.
MISSED FIELD GOAL ATTEMPTS—None
INTERCEPTIONS—Jacksonville, Darius 1-16.
KICKOFF RETURNS—Jacksonville, T. Edwards 2-32, Lewis 1-20. Minnesota, O. Smith 1-21.
PUNT RETURNS—Jacksonville, Lewis 2-11. Minnesota, Burleson 2-32.
SACKS—Jacksonville, Henderson 2, McCray 1, Gildon 1. Minnesota, Udeze 1, K. Williams 1.

EAGLES 27, GIANTS 6
Sunday, November 28

Philadelphia	0	7	13	7—27
N.Y. Giants	3	3	0	0— 6

First Quarter
NYG—FG, Christie 22, 11:34.

Second Quarter
Phi.—McNabb 4 run (Akers kick), :07.
NYG—FG, Christie 31, 5:52.

Third Quarter
Phi.—FG, Akers 47, 3:34.
Phi.—FG, Akers 42, 6:02.
Phi.—Westbrook 1 run (Akers kick), 13:19.

Fourth Quarter
Phi.—Westbrook 34 pass from McNabb (Akers kick), 5:08.
Attendance—78,830.

	Philadelphia	N.Y. Giants
First downs	22	12
Rushes-yards	38-152	26-161
Passing	238	111
Punt returns	1-0	3-16
Kickoff returns	3-65	5-116
Interception returns	2-0	0-0
Comp.-att.-int.	18-27-0	6-21-2
Sacked-yards lost	2-6	5-37
Punts	5-39	6-37
Fumbles-lost	2-1	2-0
Penalties-yards	12-75	6-64
Time of possession	33:48	26:12

INDIVIDUAL STATISTICS

RUSHING—Philadelphia, Westbrook 18-74, Levens 9-38, McNabb 5-30, Tapeh 3-12, Detmer 3-(minus 2). New York, Barber 19-110, Dayne 3-24, Manning 2-18, I. Hilliard 1-17, Taylor 1-(minus 8).
PASSING—Philadelphia, McNabb 18-27-0-244. New York, Manning 6-21-2-148.
RECEIVING—Philadelphia, Westbrook 5-53, Owens 4-61, Smith 4-31, Pinkston 3-75, Parry 1-15, F. Mitchell 1-9. New York, Taylor 2-102, Shockey 2-31, Barber 1-9, Toomer 1-6.
MISSED FIELD GOAL ATTEMPTS—None.
INTERCEPTIONS—Philadelphia, Dawkins 1-0, Mikell 1-0.
KICKOFF RETURNS—Philadelphia, Hood 2-47, Reed 1-18. New York, Ponder 4-99, Jones 1-17.
PUNT RETURNS—Philadelphia, Westbrook 1-0. New York, Jones 3-16.
SACKS—Philadelphia, Simon 2, Simoneau 1, Walker 0.5, Kearse 0.5, Team 1. New York, K. Allen 1, Team 1.

PANTHERS 21, BUCCANEERS 14
Sunday, November 28

Tampa Bay	0	7	0	7—14
Carolina	7	0	7	7—21

First Quarter
Car.—Colbert 24 pass from Delhomme (J. Chandler kick), 5:37.

Second Quarter
T.B.—Pittman 6 pass from Griese (Gramatica kick), 13:05.

Third Quarter
Car.—Peppers 46 interception return (J. Chandler kick), 6:23.

Fourth Quarter
T.B.—Pittman 8 pass from Griese (Gramatica kick), 8:18.
Car.—Colbert 40 pass from Delhomme (J. Chandler kick), 14:40.
Attendance—73,124.

	Tampa Bay	Carolina
First downs	20	15
Rushes-yards	28-62	25-112
Passing	336	188
Punt returns	2-12	1-16
Kickoff returns	2-35	2-45
Interception returns	1-0	1-46
Comp.-att.-int.	27-39-1	14-21-1
Sacked-yards lost	2-11	4-25
Punts	2-47	4-48
Fumbles-lost	4-2	0-0
Penalties-yards	7-40	5-50
Time of possession	33:43	26:17

INDIVIDUAL STATISTICS

RUSHING—Tampa Bay, Pittman 18-29, Alstott 6-15, Griese 2-9, Graham 2-9. Carolina, Goings 23-106, Delhomme 1-5, Bennett 1-1.
PASSING—Tampa Bay, Griese 27-39-1-347. Carolina, Delhomme 14-21-1-213.
RECEIVING—Tampa Bay, Pittman 8-134, Clayton 8-77, Jurevicius 4-60, Galloway 3-34, Alstott 2-19, Dilger 1-19, Heller 1-4. Carolina, Colbert 3-72, Mangum 3-44, Goings 3-17, Muhammad 2-52, Proehl 2-22, Seidman 1-6.
MISSED FIELD GOAL ATTEMPTS—Tampa Bay, Gramatica 39, 26, 37. Carolina, J. Chandler 38, 38.
INTERCEPTIONS—Tampa Bay, Kelly 1-0. Carolina, Peppers 1-46.
KICKOFF RETURNS—Tampa Bay, Cox 2-35. Carolina, Robertson 2-45.
PUNT RETURNS—Tampa Bay, Galloway 2-12. Carolina, Gamble 1-16.
SACKS—Tampa Bay, D. White 1, Rice 1, Ahanotu 1, Spires 1. Carolina, Minter 1, Peppers 1.

TEXANS 31, TITANS 21
Sunday, November 28

Tennessee	14	7	0	0—21
Houston	3	7	14	7—31

First Quarter
Ten.—Kinney 12 pass from McNair (Anderson kick), 4:47.
Ten.—Kinney 11 pass from McNair (Anderson kick), 9:16.
Hou.—FG, K. Brown 29, 14:25.

Second Quarter
Ten.—Mason 4 pass from McNair (Anderson kick), 4:22.
Hou.—Wells 7 run (K. Brown kick), 8:14.

Third Quarter
Hou.—Miller 14 pass from Carr (K. Brown kick), 5:40.
Hou.—An. Johnson 11 pass from Carr (K. Brown kick), 12:25.

Fourth Quarter
Hou.—D. Davis 41 run (K. Brown kick), 13:26.
Attendance—70,721.

	Tennessee	Houston
First downs	23	19
Rushes-yards	25-134	21-149
Passing	221	179
Punt returns	2-6	1-0
Kickoff returns	5-91	4-93
Interception returns	1-11	1-24
Comp.-att.-int.	25-34-1	21-30-1
Sacked-yards lost	1-6	3-22
Punts	3-42	3-45
Fumbles-lost	4-2	0-0
Penalties-yards	5-37	3-36
Time of possession	32:55	27:05

RUSHING—Tennessee, A. Smith 21-90, McNair 3-24, Holcombe 1-20. Houston, D. Davis 16-129, Wells 3-10, Carr 2-10.

PASSING—Tennessee, McNair 25-34-1-227. Houston, Carr 21-30-1-201.

RECEIVING—Tennessee, Mason 8-87, Kinney 6-53, Bennett 5-54, Meier 2-12, A. Smith 2-11, Troupe 1-6, Holcombe 1-4. Houston, D. Davis 7-52, Miller 4-42, An. Johnson 4-34, Bradford 3-32, Armstrong 1-20, Bruener 1-12, Wells 1-9.

MISSED FIELD GOAL ATTEMPTS—Houston, K. Brown 41.

INTERCEPTIONS—Tennessee, McGarrahan 1-11. Houston, McCree 1-24.

KICKOFF RETURNS—Tennessee, McAddley 3-53, Waddell 2-38. Houston, Moses 3-70, Hollings 1-23.

PUNT RETURNS—Tennessee, Mason 2-6. Houston, Moses 1-0.

SACKS—Tennessee, Starks 2, Bulluck 1. Houston, Peek 1.

CHARGERS 34, CHIEFS 31

Sunday, November 28

San Diego	7	7	3	17—34
Kansas City	7	10	0	14—31

First Quarter

S.D.—Tomlinson 1 run (Kaeding kick), 7:59.
K.C.—Blaylock 5 run (Tynes kick), 10:34.

Second Quarter

K.C.—L. Johnson 6 run (Tynes kick), 5:55.
S.D.—Tomlinson 3 run (Kaeding kick), 11:49.
K.C.—FG, Tynes 28, 14:15.

Third Quarter

S.D.—FG, Kaeding 25, 7:36.

Fourth Quarter

K.C.—Blaylock 22 run (kick failed), :43.
S.D.—Gates 18 pass from Brees (Kaeding kick), 4:47.
K.C.—Hall 96 kickoff return (Kennison pass from Green), 5:00.
S.D.—Gates 11 pass from Brees (Kaeding kick), 8:38.
S.D.—FG, Kaeding 43, 12:36.
Attendance—77,447.

	San Diego	Kansas City
First downs	25	20
Rushes-yards	31-127	20-110
Passing	371	200
Punt returns	1-(-1)	1-1
Kickoff returns	6-135	6-233
Interception returns	1-13	0-0
Comp.-att.-int.	28-37-0	21-34-1
Sacked-yards lost	1-7	1-8
Punts	3-45	3-33
Fumbles-lost	1-0	1-1
Penalties-yards	9-60	5-26
Time of possession	36:46	23:14

INDIVIDUAL STATISTICS

RUSHING—San Diego, Tomlinson 21-46, Brees 8-23, E. Parker 2-58. Kansas City, L. Johnson 10-43, Blaylock 8-57, Green 1-7, Morton 1-3.

PASSING—San Diego, Brees 28-37-0-378. Kansas City, Green 21-34-1-208.

RECEIVING—San Diego, Tomlinson 10-57, Gates 7-92, McCardell 4-48, E. Parker 3-78, Osgood 2-92, Neal 1-7, Peelle 1-4. Kansas City, Gonzalez 8-105, Morton 4-39, Blaylock 3-21, Dunn 2-16, Kennison 1-9, Hall 1-8, L. Johnson 1-7, Richardson 1-3.

MISSED FIELD GOAL ATTEMPTS—San Diego, Kaeding 29, 52.

INTERCEPTIONS—San Diego, Edwards 1-13.

KICKOFF RETURNS—San Diego, Dwight 6-135. Kansas City, Hall 6-233.

PUNT RETURNS—San Diego, E. Parker 1-(minus 1). Kansas City, Hall 1-1.

SACKS—San Diego, Godfrey 1. Kansas City, Fujita 0.5, Bartee 0.5.

BENGALS 58, BROWNS 48

Sunday, November 28

Cleveland	10	3	21	14—48
Cincinnati	14	13	14	17—58

First Quarter

Cle.—Heiden 7 pass from Holcomb (Dawson kick), :33.
Cin.—Washington 18 pass from Palmer (Graham kick), 2:02.
Cin.—C. Johnson 46 pass from Palmer (Graham kick), 4:53.
Cle.—FG, Dawson 23, 9:46.

Second Quarter

Cle.—FG, Dawson 29, :04.
Cin.—Houshmandzadeh 3 pass from Palmer (Graham kick), 8:41.
Cin.—FG, Graham 21, 13:43.
Cin.—FG, Graham 32, 14:58.

Third Quarter

Cle.—Heiden 20 pass from Holcomb (Dawson kick), 1:26.
Cin.—Houshmandzadeh 53 pass from Palmer (Graham kick), 2:55.
Cle.—Bryant 9 pass from Holcomb (Dawson kick), 6:25.
Cin.—Ru. Johnson 7 run (Graham kick), 10:26.
Cle.—Bryant 55 pass from Holcomb (Dawson kick), 11:21.

Fourth Quarter

Cin.—FG, Graham 36, :45.
Cle.—Green 1 run (Dawson kick), 4:09.
Cle.—Heiden 1 pass from Holcomb (Dawson kick), 4:38.
Cin.—Ru. Johnson 7 run (Graham kick), 8:31.
Cin.—O'Neal 31 interception return (Graham kick), 13:17.
Attendance—65,677.

	Cleveland	Cincinnati
First downs	23	26
Rushes-yards	17-76	32-253
Passing	386	251
Punt returns	2-6	2-60
Kickoff returns	10-212	9-200
Interception returns	3-92	2-44
Comp.-att.-int.	30-39-2	22-29-3
Sacked-yards lost	3-27	0-0
Punts	4-44	2-53
Fumbles-lost	3-0	0-0
Penalties-yards	12-87	8-63
Time of possession	28:41	31:19

INDIVIDUAL STATISTICS

RUSHING—Cleveland, Green 15-75, T. Smith 1-1, Holcomb 1-0. Cincinnati, Ru. Johnson 26-202, Houshmandzadeh 2-17, Palmer 2-10, Watson 1-15, C. Johnson 1-9.

PASSING—Cleveland, Holcomb 30-39-2-413. Cincinnati, Palmer 22-29-3-251.

RECEIVING—Cleveland, Bryant 8-131, Heiden 7-82, Northcutt 5-87, Shea 5-67, F. Jackson 2-30, Green 2-15, T. Smith 1-1. Cincinnati, C. Johnson 10-117, Houshmandzadeh 4-79, Washington 3-35, Walter 2-12, J. Johnson 2-3, Ru. Johnson 1-5.

MISSED FIELD GOAL ATTEMPTS—None.

INTERCEPTIONS—Cleveland, Henry 1-32, Gardner 1-30, Andra. Davis 1-30. Cincinnati, O'Neal 1-31, James 1-13.

KICKOFF RETURNS—Cleveland, Alston 10-212. Cincinnati, C. Russell 5-114, Watson 2-54, Houshmandzadeh 1-17, Lan. Moore 1-15.

PUNT RETURNS—Cleveland, Northcutt 2-6. Cincinnati, Ratliff 2-60.

SACKS—Cincinnati, Geathers 1.5, Thornton 1, J. Smith 0.5.

JETS 13, CARDINALS 3

Sunday, November 28

N.Y. Jets	0	3	10	0—13
Arizona	0	3	0	0— 3

Second Quarter

NYJ—FG, Brien 28, 11:32.
Ariz.—FG, Rackers 20, 15:00.

Third Quarter

NYJ—FG, Brien 46, 10:07.
NYJ—Moss 69 pass from Q. Carter (Brien kick), 12:19.
Attendance—35,820.

	N.Y. Jets	Arizona
First downs	16	17
Rushes-yards	38-146	24-71
Passing	179	174
Punt returns	3-10	2-4
Kickoff returns	0-0	1-21
Interception returns	3-38	0-0
Comp.-att.-int.	13-21-0	19-36-3
Sacked-yards lost	2-14	1-7
Punts	7-31	6-42
Fumbles-lost	3-0	2-1
Penalties-yards	9-85	6-51
Time of possession	34:07	25:53

INDIVIDUAL STATISTICS

RUSHING—New York, C. Martin 24-99, Jordan 12-43, Q. Carter 1-2, Bollinger 1-2. Arizona, Croom 10-25, Scobey 5-5, E. Smith 3-21, O. Ayanbadejo 3-12, S. King 3-8.

PASSING—New York, Q. Carter 8-12-0-133, Bollinger 5-9-0-60. Arizona, S. King 14-26-1-119, McCown 5-10-2-62.

RECEIVING—New York, Moss 5-109, McCareins 2-23, J. Carter 2-18, Chrebet 1-26, Askew 1-11, Jordan 1-3, Sowell 1-3. Arizona, Boldin 8-87, F. Jones 4-37, Scobey 3-14, Fitzgerald 2-21, O. Ayanbadejo 1-14, Croom 1-8.

MISSED FIELD GOAL ATTEMPTS—None.
INTERCEPTIONS—New York, Buckley 1-18, Barrett 1-14, Vilma 1-6.
KICKOFF RETURNS—Arizona, Scobey 1-21.
PUNT RETURNS—New York, Moss 3-10. Arizona, K. Williams 2-4.
SACKS—New York, Ellis 1. Arizona, Berry 1, Dockett 0.5, Pace 0.5.

BILLS 38, SEAHAWKS 9
Sunday, November 28

Buffalo	7	10	7	14—38
Seattle	0	3	0	6— 9

First Quarter
Buf.—McGahee 2 run (Lindell kick), 4:22.

Second Quarter
Buf.—FG, Lindell 25, 1:30.
Sea.—FG, J. Brown 19, 7:09.
Buf.—Evans 3 pass from Bledsoe (Lindell kick), 14:54.

Third Quarter
Buf.—McGahee 2 run (Lindell kick), 8:16.

Fourth Quarter
Buf.—McGahee 30 run (Lindell kick), 4:22.
Buf.—McGahee 1 run (Lindell kick), 7:46.
Sea.—Engram 8 pass from Hasselbeck (pass failed), 11:19.
Attendance—66,271.

	Buffalo	Seattle
First downs	25	17
Rushes-yards	37-148	17-55
Passing	286	175
Punt returns	2-7	1-0
Kickoff returns	2-25	6-107
Interception returns	1-0	3-36
Comp.-att.-int.	26-38-3	19-38-1
Sacked-yards lost	1-6	2-10
Punts	1-36	4-37
Fumbles-lost	0-0	1-1
Penalties-yards	6-44	7-64
Time of possession	36:24	23:36

INDIVIDUAL STATISTICS
RUSHING—Buffalo, McGahee 28-116, Burns 7-14, Evans 1-15, J. Smith 1-3. Seattle, Alexander 13-39, Morris 2-10, Hasselbeck 2-6.
PASSING—Buffalo, Bledsoe 25-37-3-275, Losman 1-1-0-17. Seattle, Hasselbeck 19-38-1-185.
RECEIVING—Buffalo, Moulds 8-93, Evans 6-70, Campbell 3-31, McGahee 2-26, Euhus 2-22, J. Smith 2-10, Shelton 1-24, Aiken 1-11, Henry 1-5. Seattle, Jackson 4-45, Urban 2-31, Stevens 2-29, Rice 2-24, Engram 2-19, Mili 2-18, Morris 2-10, Strong 2-9, Hannam 1-0.
MISSED FIELD GOAL ATTEMPTS—None.
INTERCEPTIONS—Buffalo, McGee 1-0. Seattle, Hamlin 2-36, Lucas 1-0.
KICKOFF RETURNS—Buffalo, McGee 1-23, Moulds 1-2. Seattle, Carter 6-107.
PUNT RETURNS—Buffalo, Clements 2-7. Seattle, Morris 1-0.
SACKS—Buffalo, Spikes 1, Denney 1. Seattle, Cochran 1.

FALCONS 24, SAINTS 21
Sunday, November 28

New Orleans	0	6	8	7—21
Atlanta	7	10	0	7—24

First Quarter
Atl.—Vick 16 run (Feely kick), 7:24.

Second Quarter
Atl.—Pritchett 1 pass from Vick (Feely kick), 2:34.
N.O.—FG, Carney 48, 5:39.
N.O.—FG, Carney 38, 8:38.
Atl.—FG, Feely 31, 15:00.

Third Quarter
N.O.—Brooks 1 run (Horn pass from Brooks), 12:42.

Fourth Quarter
N.O.—Horn 7 pass from Brooks (Carney kick), 3:04.
Atl.—Crumpler 20 pass from Vick (Feely kick), 13:38
Attendance—70,521.

	New Orleans	Atlanta
First downs	19	21
Rushes-yards	28-141	33-186
Passing	165	210
Punt returns	4-2	2-13
Kickoff returns	3-56	4-99

	New Orleans	Atlanta
Interception returns	1-8	2-16
Comp.-att.-int.	19-34-2	16-29-1
Sacked-yards lost	4-24	2-2
Punts	5-44	5-42
Fumbles-lost	1-0	1-1
Penalties-yards	5-25	6-46
Time of possession	32:00	28:00

INDIVIDUAL STATISTICS
RUSHING—New Orleans, McAllister 23-100, Brooks 3-10, Stallworth 1-26, Stecker 1-5. Atlanta, Duckett 12-58, Dunn 11-59, Vick 10-69.
PASSING—New Orleans, Brooks 19-34-2-189. Atlanta, Vick 16-29-1-212.
RECEIVING—New Orleans, Horn 9-101, McAllister 4-10, Pathon 2-43, Stallworth 2-20, B. Williams 1-14, Karney 1-1. Atlanta, Crumpler 4-103, P. Price 4-59, Dunn 3-22, Finneran 2-16, Pritchett 2-5, White 1-7.
MISSED FIELD GOAL ATTEMPTS—New Orleans, Carney 37. Atlanta, Feely 37.
INTERCEPTIONS—New Orleans, Ch. Grant 1-8. Atlanta, Rossum 1-14, D. Hall 1-2.
KICKOFF RETURNS—New Orleans, Stecker 3-56. Atlanta, Rossum 4-99.
PUNT RETURNS—New Orleans, Stallworth 4-2. Atlanta, Rossum 2-13.
SACKS—New Orleans, Bockwoldt 1, W. Smith 1. Atlanta, R. Coleman 2, B. Smith 1, Jasper 0.5, Williams 0.5.

DOLPHINS 24, 49ERS 17
Sunday, November 28

Miami	7	0	0	17—24
San Francisco	0	3	0	14—17

First Quarter
Mia.—Chambers 25 pass from Feeley (Mare kick), 6:06.

Second Quarter
S.F.—FG, T. Peterson 19, 11:59.

Fourth Quarter
S.F.—D. Smith 46 fumble return (T. Peterson kick), :15.
Mia.—McMichael 15 pass from Feeley (Mare kick), 4:25.
Mia.—FG, Mare 50, 7:43.
Mia.—Pope 1 fumble return (Mare kick), 11:50.
S.F.—Hicks 1 run (T. Peterson kick), 14:23.
Attendance—66,156.

	Miami	San Francisco
First downs	15	16
Rushes-yards	26-49	24-77
Passing	151	147
Punt returns	5-72	3-11
Kickoff returns	2-31	4-104
Interception returns	0-0	1-0
Comp.-att.-int.	17-33-1	23-38-0
Sacked-yards lost	1-8	8-34
Punts	7-43	9-37
Fumbles-lost	1-1	5-3
Penalties-yards	7-50	6-58
Time of possession	27:28	32:32

INDIVIDUAL STATISTICS
RUSHING—Miami, Minor 22-47, Feeley 4-2. San Francisco, Hicks 13-46, Barlow 9-20, Rattay 1-9, Beasley 1-2.
PASSING—Miami, Feeley 17-33-1-159. San Francisco, Rattay 23-38-0-181.
RECEIVING—Miami, Chambers 5-64, Booker 3-20, Thompson 3-19, McMichael 2-28, Minor 2-15, Konrad 1-11, Martin 1-2. San Francisco, E. Johnson 7-57, Wilson 5-59, Barlow 3-0, Hicks 2-33, Lloyd 2-15, Beasley 2-5, Jackson 1-6, Battle 1-6.
MISSED FIELD GOAL ATTEMPTS—Miami, Mare 22.
INTERCEPTIONS—San Francisco, M. Adams 1-0.
KICKOFF RETURNS—Miami, Welker 2-31. San Francisco, Hicks 4-104.
PUNT RETURNS—Miami, Welker 5-72. San Francisco, Battle 3-11.
SACKS—Miami, Taylor 3, D. Bowens 1, Pope 1, Zgonina 1, Romero 1, J. Williams 1. San Francisco, D. Smith 1.

PATRIOTS 24, RAVENS 3
Sunday, November 28

Baltimore	0	3	0	0— 3
New England	0	3	6	15—24

Second Quarter
N.E.—FG, Vinatieri 28, :29.
Bal.—FG, Stover 24, 14:58.

Third Quarter
N.E.—FG, Vinatieri 40, 3:38.
N.E.—FG, Vinatieri 48, 9:21.

Fourth Quarter
N.E.—Dillon 1 run (Dillon run), :03.
N.E.—J. Green 0 fumble return (Vinatieri kick), :45.
Attendance—68,756.

	Baltimore	New England
First downs	8	18
Rushes-yards	20-77	41-144
Passing	47	170
Punt returns	3-32	6-38
Kickoff returns	6-106	2-45
Interception returns	0-0	1-13
Comp.-att.-int.	15-35-1	15-30-0
Sacked-yards lost	4-46	1-2
Punts	10-44	8-32
Fumbles-lost	2-1	2-0
Penalties-yards	10-106	10-97
Time of possession	24:06	35:54

INDIVIDUAL STATISTICS

RUSHING—Baltimore, C. Taylor 16-61, Boller 2-10, J. White 2-6. New England, Dillon 30-123, Pass 4-12, Faulk 3-7, Brady 3-3, Davey 1-(minus 1).

PASSING—Baltimore, Boller 15-35-1-93. New England, Brady 15-30-0-172.

RECEIVING—Baltimore, C. Taylor 5-24, K. Johnson 3-20, Wilcox 2-30, Moore 2-15, T. Taylor 1-4, Ricard 1-0, Hymes 1-0. New England, Givens 6-42, Branch 4-51, Graham 2-24, Pass 2-18, Patten 1-37.

MISSED FIELD GOAL ATTEMPTS—None.

INTERCEPTIONS—New England, Gay 1-13.

KICKOFF RETURNS—Baltimore, Sams 6-106. New England, B. Johnson 1-27, Pass 1-18.

PUNT RETURNS—Baltimore, Sams 3-32. New England, T. Brown 3-28, Faulk 3-10.

SACKS—Baltimore, Douglas 1. New England, T. Johnson 1, Bruschi 1, Colvin 1, Seymour 1.

RAIDERS 25, BRONCOS 24
Sunday, November 28

Oakland	0	7	6	12—25
Denver	0	10	0	14—24

Second Quarter
Den.—FG, Elam 32, 13:05.
Den.—Smith 85 pass from Plummer (Elam kick), 14:16.
Oak.—Porter 42 pass from Collins (Janikowski kick), 14:44.

Third Quarter
Oak.—Porter 14 pass from Collins (kick blocked), 2:10.

Fourth Quarter
Den.—Droughns 3 run (Elam kick), :34.
Den.—E. Johnson 32 interception return (Elam kick), 1:34.
Oak.—Curry 6 pass from Collins (pass failed), 8:49.
Oak.—Porter 5 pass from Collins (pass failed), 13:11.
Attendance—75,936.

	Oakland	Denver
First downs	19	16
Rushes-yards	18-61	34-122
Passing	334	245
Punt returns	3-10	1-2
Kickoff returns	5-132	4-85
Interception returns	1-37	2-34
Comp.-att.-int.	26-45-2	14-23-1
Sacked-yards lost	1-5	0-0
Punts	6-44	7-36
Fumbles-lost	3-1	3-2
Penalties-yards	5-38	5-31
Time of possession	29:19	30:41

INDIVIDUAL STATISTICS

RUSHING—Oakland, Wheatley 8-34, Redmond 3-16, Collins 3-7, Fargas 3-0, Zereoue 1-4. Denver, Droughns 28-102, Plummer 5-18, Hearst 1-2.

PASSING—Oakland, Collins 26-45-2-339. Denver, Plummer 14-23-1-245.

RECEIVING—Oakland, Porter 6-135, Curry 6-110, Gabriel 4-51, Fargas 4-15, Wheatley 2-12, Redmond 2-2, Jolley 1-9, Zereoue 1-5. Denver, Lelie 4-80, Smith 2-99, Watts 2-27, K. Johnson 2-8, Putzier 1-18, Luke 1-12, Carswell 1-6, Droughns 1-(minus 5).

MISSED FIELD GOAL ATTEMPTS—Oakland, Janikowski 48. Denver, Elam 43.

INTERCEPTIONS—Oakland, Buchanon 1-37. Denver, E. Johnson 1-32, Lynch 1-2.

KICKOFF RETURNS—Oakland, Gabriel 3-82, Redmond 2-50. Denver, R. Alexander 4-85.

PUNT RETURNS—Oakland, Buchanon 3-10. Denver, Smith 1-2.

SACKS—Denver, Hayward 1.

PACKERS 45, RAMS 17
Monday, November 29

St. Louis	0	10	0	7—17
Green Bay	7	14	7	17—45

First Quarter
G.B.—Carroll 40 fumble return (Longwell kick), 2:37.

Second Quarter
St.L.—FG, J. Wilkins 34, 2:13.
G.B.—Franks 7 pass from Favre (Longwell kick), 7:35.
G.B.—J. Walker 10 pass from Favre (Longwell kick), 12:10.
St.L.—Bruce 4 pass from Bulger (J. Wilkins kick), 14:30.

Third Quarter
G.B.—Driver 16 pass from Favre (Longwell kick), 13:16.

Fourth Quarter
St.L.—M. Faulk 8 pass from Bulger (J. Wilkins kick), :41.
G.B.—FG, Longwell 27, 6:31.
G.B.—Davenport 40 run (Longwell kick), 13:08.
G.B.—Hawthorne 34 fumble return (Longwell kick), 14:14.
Attendance—70,385.

	St. Louis	Green Bay
First downs	25	22
Rushes-yards	17-47	28-231
Passing	405	215
Punt returns	1-4	0-0
Kickoff returns	8-149	4-72
Interception returns	0-0	1-0
Comp.-att.-int.	35-53-1	18-27-0
Sacked-yards lost	4-43	0-0
Punts	2-30	3-40
Fumbles-lost	3-2	1-0
Penalties-yards	7-50	7-55
Time of possession	33:20	26:40

INDIVIDUAL STATISTICS

RUSHING—St. Louis, S. Jackson 8-40, M. Faulk 7-7, Bulger 1-5, J. Wilkins 1-(minus 5). Green Bay, Davenport 19-178, Fisher 6-42, Favre 2-5, Chatman 1-6.

PASSING—St. Louis, Bulger 35-53-1-448. Green Bay, Favre 18-27-0-215.

RECEIVING—St. Louis, Bruce 9-170, McDonald 6-79, Curtis 6-67, Holt 5-51, M. Faulk 5-14, S. Jackson 2-35, Manumaleuna 1-25, Cleeland 1-7. Green Bay, Driver 6-85, Ferguson 4-53, Franks 2-36, J. Walker 2-15, Henderson 2-7, Fisher 1-11, Davenport 1-8.

MISSED FIELD GOAL ATTEMPTS—St. Louis, J. Wilkins 42.

INTERCEPTIONS—Green Bay, Carroll 1-0.

KICKOFF RETURNS—St. Louis, Harris 7-136, Manumaleuna 1-13. Green Bay, Chatman 2-40, Ferguson 1-26, Peterson 1-6.

PUNT RETURNS—St. Louis, McDonald 1-4.

SACKS—Green Bay, Kampman 1, Hunt 1, Gbaja-Biamila 1, Truluck 1.

WEEK 13

STANDINGS

AMERICAN FOOTBALL CONFERENCE

EAST DIVISION

	W	L	T	Pct.	PF	PA
New England	11	1	0	.917	330	189
N.Y. Jets	9	3	0	.750	254	175
Buffalo	6	6	0	.500	260	224
Miami	2	10	0	.167	196	269

NORTH DIVISION

	W	L	T	Pct.	PF	PA
Pittsburgh	11	1	0	.917	273	184
Baltimore	7	5	0	.583	233	191
Cincinnati	6	6	0	.500	268	272
Cleveland	3	9	0	.250	240	308

SOUTH DIVISION

	W	L	T	Pct.	PF	PA
Indianapolis	9	3	0	.750	431	263
Jacksonville	6	6	0	.500	198	225
Houston	5	7	0	.417	236	289
Tennessee	4	8	0	.333	231	294

WEST DIVISION

	W	L	T	Pct.	PF	PA
San Diego	9	3	0	.750	339	238
Denver	7	5	0	.583	274	212
Kansas City	4	8	0	.333	341	326
Oakland	4	8	0	.333	234	328

NATIONAL FOOTBALL CONFERENCE

EAST DIVISION

	W	L	T	Pct.	PF	PA
Philadelphia	11	1	0	.917	340	181
Dallas	5	7	0	.417	236	328
N.Y. Giants	5	7	0	.417	209	230
Washington	4	8	0	.333	169	201

NORTH DIVISION

	W	L	T	Pct.	PF	PA
Green Bay	7	5	0	.583	318	294
Minnesota	7	5	0	.583	305	286
Chicago	5	7	0	.417	196	235
Detroit	5	7	0	.417	218	269

SOUTH DIVISION

	W	L	T	Pct.	PF	PA
Atlanta	9	3	0	.750	232	242
Carolina	5	7	0	.417	249	257
Tampa Bay	5	7	0	.417	233	203
New Orleans	4	8	0	.333	253	344

WEST DIVISION

	W	L	T	Pct.	PF	PA
Seattle	6	6	0	.500	278	266
St. Louis	6	6	0	.500	253	305
Arizona	4	8	0	.333	192	253
San Francisco	1	11	0	.083	198	336

TOP PERFORMANCES

100-YARD RUSHING GAMES

Player, Team & Opponent	Att.	Yds.	TD
Julius Jones, Dal. at Sea.	30	198	3
Kevin Jones, Det. vs. Ariz.	26	196	1
Clinton Portis, Was. vs. NYG	31	148	1
Chester Taylor, Bal. vs. Cin.	23	139	1
Curtis Martin, NYJ vs. Hou.	23	134	1
Nick Goings, Car. at N.O.	36	122	1
Steven Jackson, St.L. vs. S.F.	26	119	0
Larry Johnson, K.C. at Oak.	20	118	1
LaDainian Tomlinson, S.D. vs. Den.	30	113	2
Edgerrin James, Ind. vs. Ten.	18	105	2
Chris Brown, Ten. at Ind.	19	104	0
Corey Dillon, N.E. at Cle.	18	100	2

300-YARD PASSING GAMES

Player, Team & Opponent	Att.	Cmp.	Yds.	TD	Int.
Donovan McNabb, Phi. vs. G.B.	43	32	464	5	0
Peyton Manning, Ind. vs. Ten.	33	25	425	3	2
Matt Hasselbeck, Sea. vs. Dal.	40	28	414	3	0
Carson Palmer, Cin. at Bal.	36	29	382	3	1
Kerry Collins, Oak. vs. K.C.	41	27	343	3	0
Trent Green, K.C. at Oak.	35	23	340	3	1
A.J. Feeley, Mia. vs. Buf.	51	25	303	3	5

100-YARD RECEIVING GAMES

Player, Team & Opponent	Rec.	Yds.	TD
Muhsin Muhammad, Car. at N.O.	10	179	1
T.J. Houshmandzadeh, Cin. at Bal.	10	171	1
Chad Johnson, Cin. at Bal.	10	161	2
Terrell Owens, Phi. vs. G.B.	8	161	1
Torry Holt, St.L. vs. S.F.	10	160	1
Joe Horn, N.O. vs. Car.	8	160	2
Brian Westbrook, Phi. vs. G.B.	11	156	3
Brandon Stokley, Ind. vs. Ten.	8	153	1
Eddie Kennison, K.C. at Oak.	8	149	1
Jerry Rice, Sea. vs. Dal.	8	145	1
Ronald Curry, Oak. vs. K.C.	9	141	2
Andre Johnson, Hou. at NYJ	7	125	0
Drew Bennett, Ten. at Ind.	3	124	3
Keyshawn Johnson, Dal. at Sea.	6	116	1
Antonio Bryant, Cle. vs. N.E.	7	115	2
Darrell Jackson, Sea. vs. Dal.	9	113	1
Lee Evans, Buf. at Mia.	4	110	2
Marvin Harrison, Ind. vs. Ten.	4	106	1
Ashley Lelie, Den. at S.D.	4	105	0

RESULTS

SUNDAY, DECEMBER 5

Cincinnati 27, BALTIMORE 26
TAMPA BAY 27, Atlanta 0
Carolina 32, NEW ORLEANS 21
ST. LOUIS 16, San Francisco 6
CHICAGO 24, Minnesota 14
DETROIT 26, Arizona 12
N.Y. JETS 29, Houston 7
Buffalo 42, MIAMI 32
New England 42, CLEVELAND 15
INDIANAPOLIS 51, Tennessee 24
WASHINGTON 31, N.Y. Giants 7
Kansas City 34, OAKLAND 27
SAN DIEGO 20, Denver 17
PHILADELPHIA 47, Green Bay 17
Pittsburgh 17, JACKSONVILLE 16

MONDAY, DECEMBER 6

Dallas 43, SEATTLE 39

BENGALS 27, RAVENS 26
Sunday, December 5

Cincinnati	0	3	0	24—27
Baltimore	3	3	14	6—26

First Quarter
Bal.—FG, Stover 20, 5:44.

Second Quarter
Cin.—FG, Graham 41, 12:35.
Bal.—FG, Stover 22, 14:56.

Third Quarter
Bal.—C. Taylor 1 run (Stover kick), 6:47.
Bal.—McAlister 64 fumble return (Stover kick), 12:31.

Fourth Quarter
Cin.—C. Johnson 13 pass from Palmer (Graham kick), :05.
Cin.—C. Johnson 12 pass from Palmer (Graham kick), 4:21.
Bal.—FG, Stover 38, 6:26.
Cin.—Houshmandzadeh 9 pass from Palmer (Graham kick), 9:22.
Bal.—FG, Stover 45, 13:18.
Cin.—FG, Graham 24, 15:00.
Attendance—69,695.

	Cincinnati	Baltimore
First downs	23	21
Rushes-yards	24-98	31-192
Passing	355	164
Punt returns	1-8	2-(-4)
Kickoff returns	7-148	5-104
Interception returns	1-0	1-21
Comp.-att.-int.	29-36-1	19-33-1
Sacked-yards lost	3-27	1-8
Punts	4-38	4-42
Fumbles-lost	1-1	2-1
Penalties-yards	5-45	4-30
Time of possession	31:20	28:40

INDIVIDUAL STATISTICS
RUSHING—Cincinnati, Ru. Johnson 19-56, Palmer 2-7, Watson 1-19, Houshmandzadeh 1-16, J. Johnson 1-0. Baltimore, C. Taylor 23-139, J. White 6-43, Boller 2-10.
PASSING—Cincinnati, Palmer 29-36-1-382. Baltimore, Boller 19-33-1-172.
RECEIVING—Cincinnati, Houshmandzadeh 10-171, C. Johnson 10-161, R. Kelly 4-25, Schobel 2-11, Watson 1-7, Stewart 1-4, Ru. Johnson 1-3. Baltimore, T. Jones 3-38, K. Johnson 3-27, C. Taylor 3-25, Heap 3-22, T. Taylor 2-40, Moore 2-9, Dinkins 1-9, Ricard 1-4, J. White 1-(minus 2).
MISSED FIELD GOAL ATTEMPTS—Cincinnati, Graham 53.
INTERCEPTIONS—Cincinnati, M. Williams 1-0. Baltimore, Reed 1-21.
KICKOFF RETURNS—Cincinnati, C. Russell 7-148. Baltimore, Sams 5-104.
PUNT RETURNS—Cincinnati, Ratliff 1-8. Baltimore, Sams 2-(minus 4).
SACKS—Cincinnati, O'Neal 1. Baltimore, Suggs 1, A. Thomas 1, Weaver 1.

BUCCANEERS 27, FALCONS 0
Sunday, December 5

Atlanta	0	0	0	0— 0
Tampa Bay	7	6	7	7—27

First Quarter
T.B.—Pittman 4 run (Taylor kick), 7:55.

Second Quarter
T.B.—FG, Taylor 50, 4:04.
T.B.—FG, Taylor 30, 13:54.

Third Quarter
T.B.—Galloway 36 pass from Griese (Taylor kick), 4:58.

Fourth Quarter
T.B.—Alstott 5 run (Taylor kick), 13:05.
Attendance—65,556.

	Atlanta	Tampa Bay
First downs	13	16
Rushes-yards	28-163	31-132
Passing	92	115
Punt returns	2-13	2-14
Kickoff returns	6-135	1-17
Interception returns	1-33	3-88
Comp.-att.-int.	13-30-3	13-21-1
Sacked-yards lost	5-23	3-16
Punts	5-34	5-42

	Atlanta	Tampa Bay
Fumbles-lost	2-2	1-0
Penalties-yards	7-50	3-32
Time of possession	30:28	29:32

INDIVIDUAL STATISTICS
RUSHING—Atlanta, Dunn 11-43, Vick 8-81, Duckett 7-32, Griffith 2-7. Tampa Bay, Pittman 17-68, Alstott 9-42, Griese 4-(minus 3), Smart 1-25.
PASSING—Atlanta, Vick 13-27-2-115, Schaub 0-2-1-0, Mohr 0-1-0-0. Tampa Bay, Griese 13-21-1-131.
RECEIVING—Atlanta, White 3-37, P. Price 2-30, Dunn 2-9, Griffith 2-2, Jenkins 1-3, Blakley 1-6, Crumpler 1-5, Duckett 1-3. Tampa Bay, Galloway 4-63, Dilger 4-27, Pittman 2-12, Clayton 1-15, Cook 1-8, Alstott 1-6.
MISSED FIELD GOAL ATTEMPTS—None.
INTERCEPTIONS—Atlanta, Draft 1-33. Tampa Bay, Kelly 1-75, Nece 1-2, D. Smith 1-0.
KICKOFF RETURNS—Atlanta, Rossum 5-104, Griffith 1-31. Tampa Bay, Smart 1-17.
PUNT RETURNS—Atlanta, Rossum 2-13. Tampa Bay, Galloway 2-14.
SACKS—Atlanta, Kerney 1.5, Brooking 0.5, R. Coleman 0.5, T. Hall 0.5. Tampa Bay, Brooks 2, Rice 2, D. White 1.

PANTHERS 32, SAINTS 21
Sunday, December 5

Carolina	13	13	0	6—32
New Orleans	0	7	7	7—21

First Quarter
Car.—FG, Kasay 30, 3:28.
Car.—FG, Kasay 50, 9:35.
Car.—Muhammad 10 pass from Delhomme (Kasay kick), 14:08.

Second Quarter
Car.—Goings 6 run (Kasay kick), 2:59.
Car.—FG, Kasay 46, 12:00.
N.O.—Horn 13 pass from Brooks (Carney kick), 13:22.
Car.—FG, Kasay 25, 14:27.

Third Quarter
N.O.—Horn 24 pass from Brooks (Carney kick), 8:27.

Fourth Quarter
Car.—FG, Kasay 21, 7:29.
Car.—FG, Kasay 21, 12:51.
N.O.—Stallworth 25 pass from Brooks (Carney kick), 14:21.
Attendance—58,878.

	Carolina	New Orleans
First downs	25	15
Rushes-yards	42-132	11-30
Passing	269	250
Punt returns	3-10	2-4
Kickoff returns	3-87	9-237
Interception returns	2-32	0-0
Comp.-att.-int.	22-29-0	20-40-2
Sacked-yards lost	4-25	1-1
Punts	3-44	5-48
Fumbles-lost	1-0	2-1
Penalties-yards	6-44	10-104
Time of possession	41:51	18:09

INDIVIDUAL STATISTICS
RUSHING—Carolina, Goings 36-122, Hoover 4-10, Delhomme 2-0. New Orleans, McAllister 7-22, Brooks 4-8.
PASSING—Carolina, Delhomme 22-29-0-294. New Orleans, Brooks 20-40-2-251.
RECEIVING—Carolina, Muhammad 10-179, Goings 6-46, Mangum 2-21, Hoover 2-5, Colbert 1-22, Proehl 1-21. New Orleans, Horn 8-160, Stallworth 3-44, B. Williams 3-24, Pathon 2-12, Conwell 1-8, Karney 1-3, McAllister 1-1, Stecker 1-(minus 1).
MISSED FIELD GOAL ATTEMPTS—None.
INTERCEPTIONS—Carolina, Witherspoon 1-23, Hawkins 1-9.
KICKOFF RETURNS—Carolina, Broussard 2-68, Bennett 1-19. New Orleans, Stecker 8-214, McAfee 1-23.
PUNT RETURNS—Carolina, Broussard 3-10. New Orleans, Stallworth 2-4.
SACKS—Carolina, Rucker 1. New Orleans, Howard 2, Young 1, W. Smith 1.

RAMS 16, 49ERS 6
Sunday, December 5

San Francisco	3	0	3	0— 6
St. Louis	3	10	0	3—16

First Quarter
t.L.—FG, J. Wilkins 29, 10:17.
.F.—FG, T. Peterson 51, 12:37.

Second Quarter
.L.—Holt 22 pass from C. Chandler (J. Wilkins kick), 5:31.
t.L.—FG, J. Wilkins 52, 14:15.

Third Quarter
.F.—FG, T. Peterson 40, 7:05.

Fourth Quarter
t.L.—FG, J. Wilkins 52, 8:16.
Attendance—65,793.

	San Francisco	St. Louis
rst downs	9	19
ushes-yards	27-63	31-136
assing	97	214
unt returns	1-9	3-8
ckoff returns	3-71	3-50
terception returns	1-0	1-(-1)
omp.-att.-int.	10-21-1	21-31-1
acked-yards lost	4-24	3-24
unts	6-41	4-35
umbles-lost	0-0	2-1
enalties-yards	6-35	8-59
me of possession	26:40	33:20

INDIVIDUAL STATISTICS
RUSHING—San Francisco, Barlow 19-48, Hicks 3-16, Jackson 3-(minus 8), Wilson 1-6, Rattay 1-1. St. Louis, S. Jackson 26-119, Goodspeed 2-4, Bulger 1-Harris 1-2, Curtis 1-2.
PASSING—San Francisco, Rattay 10-21-1-121. St. Louis, C. Chandler 18-27--216, Bulger 3-4-0-22.
RECEIVING—San Francisco, Barlow 3-21, Lloyd 2-64, E. Johnson 2-15, Walker 1-8, Beasley 1-8, Conway 1-5. St. Louis, Holt 10-160, S. Jackson 3-30, oodspeed 3-11, Bruce 2-18, McDonald 2-10, Cleeland 1-9.
MISSED FIELD GOAL ATTEMPTS—None.
INTERCEPTIONS—San Francisco, Parrish 1-0. St. Louis, Butler 1-(minus 1).
KICKOFF RETURNS—San Francisco, Hicks 3-71. St. Louis, Harris 3-50.
PUNT RETURNS—San Francisco, Battle 1-9. St. Louis, McDonald 3-8.
SACKS—San Francisco, Engelberger 2, Young 1. St. Louis, T. Jackson 2, ittle 1, Lewis 1.

BEARS 24, VIKINGS 14
Sunday, December 5

Minnesota	7	7	0	0—14
hicago	7	10	0	7—24

First Quarter
hi.—Clark 6 pass from Hutchinson (Edinger kick), 10:13.
lin.—Burleson 4 pass from Culpepper (M. Andersen kick), 13:41.

Second Quarter
hi.—FG, Edinger 53, 3:38.
lin.—M. Robinson 40 pass from Culpepper (M. Andersen kick), 12:37.
hi.—Terrell 15 pass from Hutchinson (Edinger kick), 14:38.

Fourth Quarter
hi.—McKie 5 pass from Hutchinson (Edinger kick), 4:37.
Attendance—62,051.

	Minnesota	Chicago
irst downs	24	21
ushes-yards	22-146	35-144
assing	245	174
unt returns	3-3	0-0
ckoff returns	5-64	3-50
terception returns	0-0	3-95
omp.-att.-int.	23-33-3	18-30-0
acked-yards lost	5-34	5-39
unts	1-34	3-49
umbles-lost	1-1	2-1
enalties-yards	6-30	7-55
ime of possession	29:01	30:59

INDIVIDUAL STATISTICS
RUSHING—Minnesota, O. Smith 13-79, Culpepper 6-50, Burleson 1-10, Russell 1-4, M. Williams 1-3. Chicago, Thomas 15-55, T. Jones 15-49, utchinson 3-14, Berrian 2-26.
PASSING—Minnesota, Culpepper 23-33-3-279. Chicago, Hutchinson 18-30--213.
RECEIVING—Minnesota, M. Robinson 6-90, Wiggins 4-73, M. Williams 4-5, Moss 4-31, Burleson 3-31, O. Smith 2-9. Chicago, Clark 6-58, Terrell 3-44, Jones 3-22, Wade 2-43, Gage 2-31, Thomas 1-10, McKie 1-5.

MISSED FIELD GOAL ATTEMPTS—Minnesota, M. Andersen 38. Chicago, Edinger 52.
INTERCEPTIONS—Chicago, Azumah 2-53, Urlacher 1-42.
KICKOFF RETURNS—Minnesota, O. Smith 3-40, Campbell 2-24. Chicago, Azumah 2-36, Berrian 1-14.
PUNT RETURNS—Minnesota, Burleson 3-3.
SACKS—Minnesota, K. Williams 2, Johnson 1, Mixon 1, Johnstone 1. Chicago, Urlacher 1.5, Boone 1.5, Azumah 0.5, Hillenmeyer 0.5, A. Brown 0.5, Ogunleye 0.5.

LIONS 26, CARDINALS 12
Sunday, December 5

Arizona	3	9	0	0—12
Detroit	7	7	6	6—26

First Quarter
Ariz.—FG, Rackers 42, 3:51.
Det.—Streets 17 pass from Harrington (Hanson kick), 11:55.

Second Quarter
Ariz.—FG, Rackers 33, :47.
Det.—Jones 2 run (Hanson kick), 6:47.
Ariz.—F. Jones 33 pass from Navarre (pass failed), 11:20.

Third Quarter
Det.—FG, Hanson 45, 7:28.
Det.—FG, Hanson 22, 11:43.

Fourth Quarter
Det.—FG, Hanson 31, 5:00.
Det.—FG, Hanson 36, 9:47.
Attendance—62,262.

	Arizona	Detroit
First downs	15	16
Rushes-yards	26-94	32-215
Passing	160	183
Punt returns	4-15	3-13
Kickoff returns	5-108	4-67
Interception returns	1-16	4-53
Comp.-att.-int.	18-40-4	15-27-1
Sacked-yards lost	1-8	2-13
Punts	5-48	5-39
Fumbles-lost	0-0	0-0
Penalties-yards	7-70	10-69
Time of possession	29:41	30:19

INDIVIDUAL STATISTICS
RUSHING—Arizona, Croom 18-49, Scobey 5-23, O. Ayanbadejo 3-22. Detroit, Jones 26-196, Harrington 6-19.
PASSING—Arizona, Navarre 18-40-4-168. Detroit, Harrington 15-27-1-196.
RECEIVING—Arizona, Boldin 5-48, B. Johnson 4-34, F. Jones 3-46, Scobey 3-23, Fitzgerald 2-12, Newhouse 1-5. Detroit, Williams 4-76, Jones 4-22, Streets 3-54, Bryson 2-38, Alexander 1-5, Schlesinger 1-1.
MISSED FIELD GOAL ATTEMPTS—None.
INTERCEPTIONS—Arizona, Macklin 1-16. Detroit, Bly 2-22, Hall 1-30, Lehman 1-1.
KICKOFF RETURNS—Arizona, B. Johnson 3-77, Scobey 2-31. Detroit, Swinton 4-67.
PUNT RETURNS—Arizona, K. Williams 4-15. Detroit, Swinton 3-13.
SACKS—Arizona, Darling 1, Berry 1. Detroit, Hall 1.

JETS 29, TEXANS 7
Sunday, December 5

Houston	0	7	0	0— 7
N.Y. Jets	3	3	7	16—29

First Quarter
NYJ—FG, Brien 41, 10:30.

Second Quarter
NYJ—FG, Brien 26, 4:47.
Hou.—D. Davis 2 run (K. Brown kick), 10:15.

Third Quarter
NYJ—C. Martin 4 run (Brien kick), 7:01.

Fourth Quarter
NYJ—C. Martin 5 pass from Pennington (pass failed), 1:30.
NYJ—Becht 2 pass from Pennington (Brien kick), 5:55.
NYJ—FG, Brien 25, 12:51.
Attendance—77,875.

	Houston	N.Y. Jets
First downs	13	26
Rushes-yards	25-83	36-210
Passing	147	150

	Houston	N.Y. Jets
Punt returns	1-2	1-46
Kickoff returns	7-129	1-29
Interception returns	1-20	2-37
Comp.-att.-int.	12-25-2	20-27-1
Sacked-yards lost	2-10	1-5
Punts	3-39	2-40
Fumbles-lost	1-0	0-0
Penalties-yards	5-48	6-49
Time of possession	25:17	34:43

INDIVIDUAL STATISTICS

RUSHING—Houston, D. Davis 17-52, Carr 4-16, Wells 2-9, An. Johnson 1-6, Norris 1-0. New York, C. Martin 23-134, Jordan 11-60, Pennington 2-16.

PASSING—Houston, Carr 12-25-2-157. New York, Pennington 20-27-1-155.

RECEIVING—Houston, An. Johnson 7-125, Gaffney 2-21, Armstrong 1-7, D. Davis 1-4, Norris 1-0. New York, Sowell 5-38, McCareins 4-47, C. Martin 4-20, Chrebet 2-25, J. Carter 2-18, Moss 1-6, Becht 1-2, Jordan 1-(minus 1).

MISSED FIELD GOAL ATTEMPTS—None.

INTERCEPTIONS—Houston, Robinson 1-20. New York, Coleman 1-37, Barrett 1-0.

KICKOFF RETURNS—Houston, Moses 4-87, Wells 1-18, Starling 1-14, Norris 1-10. New York, J. Carter 1-29.

PUNT RETURNS—Houston, Moses 1-2. New York, Moss 1-46.

SACKS—Houston, Babin 1. New York, Reed 2.

BILLS 42, DOLPHINS 32
Sunday, December 5

Buffalo	14	7	7	14—42
Miami	21	3	0	8—32

First Quarter

Buf.—McGee 104 kickoff return (Lindell kick), :13.
Mia.—Gilmore 27 pass from Feeley (Mare kick), 2:44.
Buf.—Euhus 15 pass from Bledsoe (Lindell kick), 7:07.
Mia.—Chambers 2 pass from Feeley (Mare kick), 9:06.
Mia.—Lee 15 pass from Feeley (Mare kick), 12:25.

Second Quarter

Mia.—FG, Mare 47, 1:39.
Buf.—Evans 21 pass from Bledsoe (Lindell kick), 6:21.

Third Quarter

Buf.—Evans 69 pass from Bledsoe (Lindell kick), 15:00.

Fourth Quarter

Buf.—Moulds 30 pass from Bledsoe (Lindell kick), 2:19.
Mia.—Minor 3 run (Chambers pass from Feeley), 7:46.
Buf.—P. Williams 20 interception return (Lindell kick), 13:05.
Attendance—73,084.

	Buffalo	Miami
First downs	16	25
Rushes-yards	28-105	26-106
Passing	257	297
Punt returns	4-0	6-51
Kickoff returns	5-173	7-216
Interception returns	5-105	0-0
Comp.-att.-int.	19-30-0	25-51-5
Sacked-yards lost	3-20	1-6
Punts	9-44	5-45
Fumbles-lost	1-1	3-2
Penalties-yards	11-73	7-46
Time of possession	29:41	30:19

INDIVIDUAL STATISTICS

RUSHING—Buffalo, McGahee 23-91, Burns 3-8, Bledsoe 1-7, Moulds 1-(minus 1). Miami, Minor 19-75, King 3-8, Konrad 2-18, Henry 2-5.

PASSING—Buffalo, Bledsoe 19-30-0-277. Miami, Feeley 25-51-5-303.

RECEIVING—Buffalo, Moulds 5-68, Evans 4-110, Euhus 4-32, Neufeld 2-40, Reed 2-14, Shelton 1-4, McGahee 1-4. Miami, Booker 5-96, Chambers 5-49, Gilmore 3-44, Thompson 3-42, Minor 2-14, McMichael 2-14, Martin 2-8, Lee 1-15, Konrad 1-13, King 1-8.

MISSED FIELD GOAL ATTEMPTS—Buffalo, Lindell 38.

INTERCEPTIONS—Buffalo, Spikes 1-33, Baker 1-26, McGee 1-21, P. Williams 1-20, Clements 1-5.

KICKOFF RETURNS—Buffalo, McGee 5-173. Miami, Welker 6-158, Wyrick 1-58.

PUNT RETURNS—Buffalo, Clements 4-0. Miami, Welker 6-51.

SACKS—Buffalo, Schobel 0.5, Kelsay 0.5. Miami, Pope 1, Zgonina 1, D. Bowens 1.

PATRIOTS 42, BROWNS 15
Sunday, December 5

New England	14	7	21	0—42
Cleveland	0	7	0	8—15

First Quarter

N.E.—B. Johnson 93 kickoff return (Vinatieri kick), :14.
N.E.—Dillon 4 run (Vinatieri kick), 14:44.

Second Quarter

N.E.—Dillon 1 run (Vinatieri kick), 8:06.
Cle.—Bryant 16 pass from McCown (Dawson kick), 14:10.

Third Quarter

N.E.—Gay 41 fumble return (Vinatieri kick), 1:33.
N.E.—Faulk 10 run (Vinatieri kick), 7:32.
N.E.—Patten 44 pass from Brady (Vinatieri kick), 9:00.

Fourth Quarter

Cle.—Bryant 40 pass from McCown (Heiden pass from McCown), 4:58.
Attendance—73,028.

	New England	Cleveland
First downs	27	16
Rushes-yards	50-225	17-46
Passing	187	241
Punt returns	3-5	1-12
Kickoff returns	3-134	6-137
Interception returns	2-0	1-12
Comp.-att.-int.	14-26-1	20-35-2
Sacked-yards lost	2-14	3-36
Punts	3-34	4-37
Fumbles-lost	4-2	2-2
Penalties-yards	7-60	7-84
Time of possession	39:08	20:52

INDIVIDUAL STATISTICS

RUSHING—New England, Dillon 18-100, Cobbs 16-29, Faulk 13-87, Brady 1-10, Pass 1-1, Davey 1-(minus 2). Cleveland, Green 12-15, Echemandu 3-12, McCown 1-11, Northcutt 1-8.

PASSING—New England, Brady 11-20-1-157, Davey 3-6-0-44. Cleveland, McCown 20-34-2-277, F. Jackson 0-1-0-0.

RECEIVING—New England, Givens 3-25, Pass 2-19, Fauria 1-25, B. Johnson 1-20, Graham 1-14, Branch 1-13, Weaver 1-7, Faulk 1-4. Cleveland, Bryant 7-115, Northcutt 5-93, Echemandu 3-25, Green 3-24, Heiden 2-20.

MISSED FIELD GOAL ATTEMPTS—None.

INTERCEPTIONS—New England, Harrison 1-0, T. Brown 1-0. Cleveland, L. Sanders 1-12.

KICKOFF RETURNS—New England, B. Johnson 3-134. Cleveland, Alston 6-137.

PUNT RETURNS—New England, T. Brown 2-5, Gay 1-0. Cleveland, Northcutt 1-12.

SACKS—New England, Bruschi 1, McGinest 1, Vrabel 1. Cleveland, Lang 2.

COLTS 51, TITANS 24
Sunday, December 5

Tennessee	24	0	0	0—24
Indianapolis	17	14	10	10—51

First Quarter

Ind.—FG, Vanderjagt 47, 3:27.
Ten.—Bennett 48 pass from Volek (Anderson kick), 4:23.
Ten.—FG, Anderson 45, 6:52.
Ind.—Harrison 24 pass from Manning (Vanderjagt kick), 9:50.
Ten.—Bennett 28 pass from Volek (Anderson kick), 11:06.
Ind.—James 4 run (Vanderjagt kick), 13:27.
Ten.—Bennett 48 pass from Volek (Anderson kick), 15:00.

Second Quarter

Ind.—Stokley 28 pass from Manning (Vanderjagt kick), 5:58.
Ind.—Morris 68 blocked FG return (Vanderjagt kick), 9:55.

Third Quarter

Ind.—FG, Vanderjagt 20, 3:03.
Ind.—James 12 run (Vanderjagt kick), 10:23.

Fourth Quarter

Ind.—Wayne 10 pass from Manning (Vanderjagt kick), 2:04.
Ind.—FG, Vanderjagt 37, 8:03.
Attendance—57,278.

	Tennessee	Indianapolis
First downs	17	29
Rushes-yards	25-115	28-150
Passing	225	417
Punt returns	0-0	3-11
Kickoff returns	9-216	3-49
Interception returns	2-53	2-3
Comp.-att.-int.	21-36-2	25-34-2
Sacked-yards lost	7-44	1-8
Punts	4-47	0-0
Fumbles-lost	2-0	2-1
Penalties-yards	9-105	7-88
Time of possession	33:05	26:55

INDIVIDUAL STATISTICS

RUSHING—Tennessee, Brown 19-104, A. Smith 5-12, Volek 1-(minus 1). Iianapolis, James 18-105, Rhodes 4-52, Manning 3-(minus 3), Sorgi 3-(minus 4).

PASSING—Tennessee, Volek 21-35-2-269, Hentrich 0-1-0-0. Indianapolis, nning 25-33-2-425, Sorgi 0-1-0-0.

RECEIVING—Tennessee, Mason 6-79, A. Smith 4-31, Bennett 3-124, Kinney 23, Troupe 3-1, Holcombe 1-6, Berlin 1-5. Indianapolis, Stokley 8-153, Wayne 96, Harrison 4-106, James 4-31, Pollard 3-39.

MISSED FIELD GOAL ATTEMPTS—Tennessee, Anderson 43.

INTERCEPTIONS—Tennessee, A. Dyson 1-44, Thompson 1-9. Indianapolis, ackett 1-2, David 1-1.

KICKOFF RETURNS—Tennessee, McAddley 7-184, Waddell 1-20, Schobel 1-, Indianapolis, Rhodes 3-49.

PUNT RETURNS—Indianapolis, Walters 3-11.

SACKS—Tennessee, Odom 0.5, Carter 0.5. Indianapolis, Freeney 3, Brock 2, orris 1, Reagor 1.

REDSKINS 31, GIANTS 7
Sunday, December 5

Y. Giants	.0	0	7	0—	7
ashington	.7	14	3	7—	31

First Quarter
as.—Portis 1 run (Hall kick), 9:13.

Second Quarter
as.—Portis 4 pass from Ramsey (Hall kick), 10:16.
as.—Royal 9 pass from Ramsey (Hall kick), 14:19.

Third Quarter
as.—FG, Hall 46, 9:22.
'G—Ward 92 kickoff return (Christie kick), 9:35.

Fourth Quarter
as.—Cooley 6 pass from Ramsey (Hall kick), 3:18.
Attendance—87,872.

	N.Y. Giants	Washington
st downs	7	27
shes-yards	15-38	45-211
ssing	107	168
nt returns	2-24	1-5
ckoff returns	6-194	2-51
erception returns	0-0	0-0
mp.-att.-int.	12-25-0	19-22-0
cked-yards lost	1-6	1-6
nts	5-31	4-43
mbles-lost	1-0	0-0
nalties-yards	7-40	8-66
ne of possession	19:31	40:29

INDIVIDUAL STATISTICS

RUSHING—New York, Barber 15-38. Washington, Portis 31-148, Betts 11-, Ramsey 3-(minus 1).

PASSING—New York, Manning 12-25-0-113. Washington, Ramsey 19-22-0-174.

RECEIVING—New York, Shockey 3-23, I. Hilliard 3-13, Finn 3-11, Toomer 2-, Dayne 1-7. Washington, Coles 6-60, Cooley 3-21, Portis 3-14, Thrash 2-27, rdner 2-27, Royal 1-9, Kozlowski 1-8, McCants 1-8.

MISSED FIELD GOAL ATTEMPTS—None.

INTERCEPTIONS—None.

KICKOFF RETURNS—New York, Ward 6-194. Washington, Thrash 1-31, tts 1-20.

PUNT RETURNS—New York, Jones 2-24. Washington, Thrash 1-5.

SACKS—New York, Joseph 1. Washington, Daniels 1.

CHIEFS 34, RAIDERS 27
Sunday, December 5

nsas City	.7	3	14	10—	34
kland	.6	14	0	7—	27

First Quarter
k.—FG, Janikowski 27, 3:57.
C.—Blaylock 20 pass from Green (Tynes kick), 10:42.
k.—FG, Janikowski 36, 13:54.

Second Quarter
k.—Curry 34 pass from Collins (Janikowski kick), 6:00.
k.—Porter 51 pass from Collins (Janikowski kick), 9:02.
C.—FG, Tynes 28, 14:46.

Third Quarter
C.—L. Johnson 5 run (Tynes kick), 4:37.
C.—L. Johnson 10 pass from Green (Tynes kick), 10:44.

Fourth Quarter
Oak.—Curry 26 pass from Collins (Janikowski kick), :47.
K.C.—FG, Tynes 22, 8:01.
K.C.—Kennison 70 pass from Green (Tynes kick), 12:56.
Attendance—51,292.

	Kansas City	Oakland
First downs	29	16
Rushes-yards	36-160	9-31
Passing	340	333
Punt returns	1-8	0-0
Kickoff returns	5-136	7-152
Interception returns	0-0	1-25
Comp.-att.-int.	23-35-1	27-41-0
Sacked-yards lost	0-0	3-10
Punts	2-32	3-43
Fumbles-lost	0-0	0-0
Penalties-yards	7-45	6-49
Time of possession	36:35	23:25

INDIVIDUAL STATISTICS

RUSHING—Kansas City, L. Johnson 20-118, Blaylock 12-37, Green 4-5. Oakland, Zereoue 4-15, Fargas 2-14, Collins 2-0, Redmond 1-2.

PASSING—Kansas City, Green 23-35-1-340. Oakland, Collins 27-41-0-343.

RECEIVING—Kansas City, Kennison 8-149, L. Johnson 3-56, Blaylock 3-37, Gonzalez 3-32, Richardson 3-21, Dunn 2-22, Morton 1-23. Oakland, Curry 9-141, Redmond 5-49, Porter 3-67, Fargas 3-17, Zereoue 2-18, Crockett 2-13, J. Stone 1-18, Gabriel 1-11, T. Johnson 1-9.

MISSED FIELD GOAL ATTEMPTS—None.

INTERCEPTIONS—Oakland, C. Woodson 1-25.

KICKOFF RETURNS—Kansas City, Hall 5-136. Oakland, Gabriel 7-152.

PUNT RETURNS—Kansas City, Hall 1-8.

SACKS—Kansas City, Allen 2, Stills 1.

CHARGERS 20, BRONCOS 17
Sunday, December 5

Denver	.0	7	0	10—	17
San Diego	.7	10	3	0—	20

First Quarter
S.D.—Tomlinson 5 run (Kaeding kick), 2:59.

Second Quarter
Den.—Bell 16 run (Elam kick), 1:33.
S.D.—Tomlinson 1 run (Kaeding kick), 7:55.
S.D.—FG, Kaeding 23, 15:00.

Third Quarter
S.D.—FG, Kaeding 23, 9:48.

Fourth Quarter
Den.—Droughns 4 run (Elam kick), :42.
Den.—FG, Elam 31, 5:34.
Attendance—65,395.

	Denver	San Diego
First downs	21	14
Rushes-yards	24-74	35-122
Passing	263	86
Punt returns	4-33	1-19
Kickoff returns	4-62	4-88
Interception returns	1-21	4-4
Comp.-att.-int.	16-40-4	14-27-1
Sacked-yards lost	2-15	2-20
Punts	5-40	8-47
Fumbles-lost	0-0	3-1
Penalties-yards	8-57	11-94
Time of possession	28:25	31:35

INDIVIDUAL STATISTICS

RUSHING—Denver, Droughns 14-38, Bell 7-31, Plummer 2-6, Lelie 1-(minus 1). San Diego, Tomlinson 30-113, Chatman 2-7, Neal 1-8, Brees 1-2, E. Parker 1-(minus 8).

PASSING—Denver, Plummer 16-40-4-278. San Diego, Brees 14-27-1-106.

RECEIVING—Denver, Lelie 4-105, Smith 4-76, Droughns 4-35, Putzier 1-39, Carswell 1-0. San Diego, Tomlinson 5-17, E. Parker 3-37, Gates 3-31, McCardell 2-15, Peelle 1-6.

MISSED FIELD GOAL ATTEMPTS—Denver, Elam 43.

INTERCEPTIONS—Denver, Kennedy 1-21. San Diego, Foley 1-4, Florence 1-0, Wilson 1-0, Phillips 1-0.

KICKOFF RETURNS—Denver, R. Alexander 4-62. San Diego, Dwight 4-88.

PUNT RETURNS—Denver, Smith 4-33. San Diego, E. Parker 1-19.

SACKS—Denver, Lynch 1, Hayward 1. San Diego, Godfrey 1, J. Williams 1.

2004 REVIEW   Week 13

EAGLES 47, PACKERS 17
Sunday, December 5

Green Bay	0	3	0	14—17
Philadelphia	7	28	9	3—47

First Quarter
Phi.—Owens 41 pass from McNabb (Akers kick), 9:03.

Second Quarter
Phi.—Westbrook 9 pass from McNabb (Akers kick), 4:33.
Phi.—Westbrook 41 pass from McNabb (Akers kick), 9:23.
Phi.—Smith 6 pass from McNabb (Akers kick), 11:56.
Phi.—Westbrook 12 pass from McNabb (Akers kick), 13:12.
G.B.—FG, Longwell 40, 14:58.

Third Quarter
Phi.—FG, Akers 22, 3:22.
Phi.—FG, Akers 45, 7:51.
Phi.—FG, Akers 47, 12:26.

Fourth Quarter
Phi.—FG, Akers 22, 3:44.
G.B.—Henderson 1 pass from Nall (Longwell kick), 6:34.
G.B.—J. Walker 17 pass from Nall (Longwell kick), 12:39.
Attendance—67,723.

	Green Bay	Philadelphia
First downs	20	29
Rushes-yards	18-50	21-93
Passing	199	449
Punt returns	1-11	6-69
Kickoff returns	8-174	4-60
Interception returns	0-0	2-8
Comp.-att.-int.	22-40-2	32-45-0
Sacked-yards lost	5-27	4-15
Punts	8-45	3-42
Fumbles-lost	2-0	2-1
Penalties-yards	12-99	8-89
Time of possession	26:13	33:47

INDIVIDUAL STATISTICS
RUSHING—Green Bay, Green 11-37, Davenport 4-4, Fisher 2-10, Driver 1-(minus 1). Philadelphia, Westbrook 12-37, Levens 7-63, G. Lewis 1-1, Owens 1-(minus 8).
PASSING—Green Bay, Favre 14-29-2-131, Nall 8-11-0-95. Philadelphia, McNabb 32-43-0-464, Detmer 0-2-0-0.
RECEIVING—Green Bay, J. Walker 7-72, Ferguson 3-68, Driver 3-33, Green 3-17, Henderson 3-7, Fisher 2-10, Chatman 1-19. Philadelphia, Westbrook 11-156, Owens 8-161, Smith 4-42, Pinkston 3-32, G. Lewis 2-25, Levens 2-14, F. Mitchell 1-30, Parry 1-4.
MISSED FIELD GOAL ATTEMPTS—None.
INTERCEPTIONS—Philadelphia, Dawkins 1-8, Brown 1-0.
KICKOFF RETURNS—Green Bay, Ferguson 5-115, Davenport 3-59. Philadelphia, Reed 3-47, G. Lewis 1-13.
PUNT RETURNS—Green Bay, Chatman 1-11. Philadelphia, Wynn 6-69.
SACKS—Green Bay, Kampman 1, Carroll 1, G. Jackson 1, Jenkins 1. Philadelphia, Walker 2, Simon 2, Wynn 1.

STEELERS 17, JAGUARS 16
Sunday, December 5

Pittsburgh	7	7	0	3—17
Jacksonville	7	0	6	3—16

First Quarter
Pit.—Ward 37 pass from Roethlisberger (Reed kick), 5:15.
Jac.—T. Edwards 22 pass from Leftwich (Scobee kick), 12:57.

Second Quarter
Pit.—Riemersma 26 pass from Roethlisberger (Reed kick), 3:13.

Third Quarter
Jac.—FG, Scobee 20, 6:13.
Jac.—FG, Scobee 29, 14:52.

Fourth Quarter
Jac.—FG, Scobee 36, 13:05.
Pit.—FG, Reed 37, 14:42.
Attendance—76,877.

	Pittsburgh	Jacksonville
First downs	15	20
Rushes-yards	25-120	34-100
Passing	196	259
Punt returns	1-10	2-3
Kickoff returns	4-88	4-78
Interception returns	0-0	0-0
Comp.-att.-int.	14-17-0	16-27-0
Sacked-yards lost	3-25	2-9
Punts	5-46	3-50
Fumbles-lost	2-0	1-0
Penalties-yards	11-82	3-28
Time of possession	25:23	34:37

INDIVIDUAL STATISTICS
RUSHING—Pittsburgh, Staley 17-51, Roethlisberger 3-40, Bettis 3-1, Parker 1-12, Ward 1-0. Jacksonville, F. Taylor 27-76, Fuamatu-Ma'afala 6-2, Leftwich 1-4.
PASSING—Pittsburgh, Roethlisberger 14-17-0-221. Jacksonville, Leftwich 16-27-0-268.
RECEIVING—Pittsburgh, Randle El 5-71, Ward 4-80, Mays 3-32, Riemersma 1-26, Parker 1-12. Jacksonville, T. Edwards 5-90, F. Taylor 5-34, J. Smith 4-5, Yoder 1-56, Wilford 1-36.
MISSED FIELD GOAL ATTEMPTS—Jacksonville, Scobee 32, 60.
INTERCEPTIONS—None.
KICKOFF RETURNS—Pittsburgh, Colclough 3-69, I. Taylor 1-1, Jacksonville, G. Jones 2-43, Allen 2-35.
PUNT RETURNS—Pittsburgh, Randle El 1-10. Jacksonville, Allen 2-3.
SACKS—Pittsburgh, Haggans 1, Team 1. Jacksonville, Grant 1, Gildon 1, Ransom 0.5, Patterson 0.5.

COWBOYS 43, SEAHAWKS 39
Monday, December 6

Dallas	3	16	10	14—43
Seattle	14	0	3	22—39

First Quarter
Sea.—Rice 27 pass from Hasselbeck (J. Brown kick), 4:18.
Dal.—FG, Cundiff 39, 6:11.
Sea.—Jackson 2 pass from Hasselbeck (J. Brown kick), 11:13.

Second Quarter
Dal.—FG, Cundiff 49, 2:48.
Dal.—Copper 9 pass from Testaverde (run failed), 8:52.
Dal.—J. Jones 8 run (Cundiff kick), 14:28.

Third Quarter
Dal.—J. Jones 10 run (Cundiff kick), 1:15.
Dal.—FG, Cundiff 47, 4:50.
Sea.—FG, J. Brown 21, 11:59.

Fourth Quarter
Sea.—Alexander 1 run (J. Brown kick), 5:30.
Sea.—Urban 19 pass from Hasselbeck (Jackson pass from Hasselbeck), 9:31.
Sea.—Alexander 32 run (J. Brown kick), 12:14.
Dal.—K. Johnson 34 pass from Testaverde (Cundiff kick), 13:15.
Dal.—J. Jones 17 run (Cundiff kick), 14:28.
Attendance—68,093.

	Dallas	Seattle
First downs	24	22
Rushes-yards	31-198	27-102
Passing	207	396
Punt returns	1-12	2-24
Kickoff returns	7-156	7-127
Interception returns	0-0	2-22
Comp.-att.-int.	18-34-2	28-40-0
Sacked-yards lost	3-18	2-10
Punts	3-37	2-36
Fumbles-lost	1-0	3-
Penalties-yards	6-49	6-41
Time of possession	28:43	31:17

INDIVIDUAL STATISTICS
RUSHING—Dallas, J. Jones 30-198, Testaverde 1-0. Seattle, Alexander 24-183, Hasselbeck 3-16, Strong 2-4, Morris 1-6.
PASSING—Dallas, Testaverde 18-34-2-225. Seattle, Hasselbeck 28-40-0-416.
RECEIVING—Dallas, K. Johnson 6-116, Witten 5-61, J. Jones 3-11, Morgan 2-19, Copper 2-18. Seattle, Jackson 9-113, Rice 8-145, Alexander 3-21, Stevens 2-58, Urban 2-36, Mili 2-30, Engram 2-11.
MISSED FIELD GOAL ATTEMPTS—None.
INTERCEPTIONS—Seattle, Hamlin 1-12, Bierria 1-10.
KICKOFF RETURNS—Dallas, Lee 6-143, Copper 1-13. Seattle, Morris 7-127.
PUNT RETURNS—Dallas, Frazier 1-12. Seattle, Morris 2-24.
SACKS—Dallas, Glover 2. Seattle, Wistrom 1, Moore 1, Okeafor 1.

WEEK 14

STANDINGS

AMERICAN FOOTBALL CONFERENCE

EAST DIVISION

	W	L	T	Pct.	PF	PA
New England	12	1	0	.923	365	217
N.Y. Jets	9	4	0	.692	260	192
Buffalo	7	6	0	.538	297	231
Miami	2	11	0	.154	213	289

NORTH DIVISION

	W	L	T	Pct.	PF	PA
Pittsburgh	12	1	0	.923	290	190
Baltimore	8	5	0	.615	270	205
Cincinnati	6	7	0	.462	296	307
Cleveland	3	10	0	.231	247	345

SOUTH DIVISION

	W	L	T	Pct.	PF	PA
Indianapolis	10	3	0	.769	454	277
Jacksonville	7	6	0	.538	220	228
Houston	5	8	0	.385	250	312
Tennessee	4	9	0	.308	269	343

WEST DIVISION

	W	L	T	Pct.	PF	PA
San Diego	10	3	0	.769	370	262
Denver	8	5	0	.615	294	229
Kansas City	5	8	0	.385	390	364
Oakland	4	9	0	.308	244	363

NATIONAL FOOTBALL CONFERENCE

EAST DIVISION

	W	L	T	Pct.	PF	PA
Philadelphia	12	1	0	.923	357	195
Dallas	5	8	0	.385	249	355
N.Y. Giants	5	8	0	.385	223	267
Washington	4	9	0	.308	183	218

NORTH DIVISION

	W	L	T	Pct.	PF	PA
Green Bay	8	5	0	.615	334	307
Minnesota	7	6	0	.538	328	313
Chicago	5	8	0	.385	199	257
Detroit	5	8	0	.385	231	285

SOUTH DIVISION

	W	L	T	Pct.	PF	PA
Atlanta	10	3	0	.769	267	252
Carolina	6	7	0	.462	269	264
New Orleans	5	8	0	.385	280	357
Tampa Bay	5	8	0	.385	257	234

WEST DIVISION

	W	L	T	Pct.	PF	PA
Seattle	7	6	0	.538	305	289
St. Louis	6	7	0	.462	260	325
Arizona	4	9	0	.308	220	284
San Francisco	2	11	0	.154	229	364

TOP PERFORMANCES

100-YARD RUSHING GAMES

Player, Team & Opponent	Att.	Yds.	TD
Kevin Jones, Det. at G.B.	33	156	1
Maurice Hicks, S.F. at Ariz.*	34	139	1
LaDainian Tomlinson, S.D. vs. T.B.	25	131	1
Domanick Davis, Hou. vs. Ind.	23	128	1
Tatum Bell, Den. vs. Mia.	17	123	2
Shaun Alexander, Sea. at Min.	27	112	0
Nick Goings, Car. vs. St.L.	31	108	1
Willis McGahee, Buf. vs. Cle.	27	105	2
Edgerrin James, Ind. at Hou.	28	104	0
Larry Johnson, K.C. at Ten.	7	104	2
Chester Taylor, Bal. vs. NYG	25	104	0
Warrick Dunn, Atl. vs. Oak.	25	103	0

300-YARD PASSING GAMES

Player, Team & Opponent	Att.	Cmp.	Yds.	TD	Int.
Billy Volek, Ten. vs. K.C.	43	29	426	4	0
Brian Griese, T.B. at S.D.	50	36	392	3	3
Matt Hasselbeck, Sea. at Min.	34	23	334	3	2
Josh McCown, Ariz. vs. S.F.*	44	26	307	0	1

100-YARD RECEIVING GAMES

Player, Team & Opponent	Rec.	Yds.	TD
Drew Bennett, Ten. vs. K.C.	12	233	3
Torry Holt, St.L. at Car.	6	151	1
Michael Clayton, T.B. at S.D.	9	145	1
T.J. Houshmandzadeh, Cin. at N.E.	12	145	0
Darrell Jackson, Sea. at Min.	10	135	1
Eric Parker, S.D. vs. T.B.	6	118	1
Donte' Stallworth, N.O. at Dal.	5	113	0
Anquan Boldin, Ariz. vs. S.F.*	9	109	0
David Patten, N.E. vs. Cin.	5	107	1
Randy Moss, Min. vs. Sea.	4	104	1
Laveranues Coles, Was. vs. Phi.	12	100	0

*Overtime game.

RESULTS

SUNDAY, DECEMBER 12
ATLANTA 35, Oakland 10
Indianapolis 23, HOUSTON 14
Seattle 27, MINNESOTA 23
NEW ENGLAND 35, Cincinnati 28
BALTIMORE 37, N.Y. Giants 14
New Orleans 27, DALLAS 13
JACKSONVILLE 22, Chicago 3
BUFFALO 37, Cleveland 7
PITTSBURGH 17, N.Y. Jets 6
DENVER 20, Miami 17
CAROLINA 20, St. Louis 7
GREEN BAY 16, Detroit 13
SAN DIEGO 31, Tampa Bay 24
San Francisco 31, ARIZONA 28 (OT)
Philadelphia 17, WASHINGTON 14

MONDAY, DECEMBER 13
Kansas City 49, TENNESSEE 38

FALCONS 35, RAIDERS 10
Sunday, December 12

Oakland	3	0	0	7—10
Atlanta	0	21	7	7—35

First Quarter
Oak.—FG, Janikowski 52, 10:01.

Second Quarter
Atl.—Duckett 28 run (Feely kick), 6:13.
Atl.—Duckett 2 run (Feely kick), 12:49.
Atl.—R. Coleman 39 interception return (Feely kick), 13:46.

Third Quarter
Atl.—Duckett 4 run (Feely kick), 9:29.

Fourth Quarter
Atl.—Duckett 1 run (Feely kick), 6:00.
Oak.—Crockett 1 run (Janikowski kick), 11:33.
Attendance—70,616.

	Oakland	Atlanta
First downs	18	23
Rushes-yards	23-131	46-219
Passing	165	135
Punt returns	0-0	2-54
Kickoff returns	5-89	2-24
Interception returns	0-0	1-39
Comp.-att.-int.	14-28-1	13-21-0
Sacked-yards lost	1-1	1-10
Punts	4-49	4-37
Fumbles-lost	2-2	0-0
Penalties-yards	9-59	9-75
Time of possession	23:27	36:33

INDIVIDUAL STATISTICS
RUSHING—Oakland, Zereoue 10-50, Redmond 6-50, Crockett 5-20, Fargas 1-7, Hetherington 1-4. Atlanta, Dunn 25-103, Duckett 12-65, Pritchett 6-18, Vick 2-31, Griffith 1-2.
PASSING—Oakland, Collins 14-28-1-166. Atlanta, Vick 13-20-0-145, Schaub 0-1-0-0.
RECEIVING—Oakland, J. Stone 2-62, Porter 2-33, Gabriel 2-19, Hetherington 2-14, Zereoue 2-7, T. Johnson 1-13, Jolley 1-9, Redmond 1-5, Crockett 1-4. Atlanta, White 3-34, Griffith 2-21, Finneran 2-21, Jenkins 2-20, P. Price 2-18, Crumpler 1-22, Dunn 1-9.
MISSED FIELD GOAL ATTEMPTS—None.
INTERCEPTIONS—Atlanta, R. Coleman 1-39.
KICKOFF RETURNS—Oakland, Redmond 4-69, J. Stone 1-20. Atlanta, Rossum 1-22, Pritchett 1-2.
PUNT RETURNS—Atlanta, Rossum 2-54.
SACKS—Oakland, T. Johnson 0.5, C. Woodson 0.5. Atlanta, Williams 0.5, D. Hall 0.5.

COLTS 23, TEXANS 14
Sunday, December 12

Indianapolis	14	0	3	6—23
Houston	0	7	7	0—14

First Quarter
Ind.—Harrison 3 pass from Manning (Vanderjagt kick), 4:20.
Ind.—Wayne 12 pass from Manning (Vanderjagt kick), 11:23.

Second Quarter
Hou.—Wells 3 pass from Carr (K. Brown kick), 6:34.

Third Quarter
Ind.—FG, Vanderjagt 30, 3:24.
Hou.—D. Davis 15 run (K. Brown kick), 8:42.

Fourth Quarter
Ind.—FG, Vanderjagt 43, 7:22.
Ind.—FG, Vanderjagt 44, 13:04.
Attendance—70,762.

	Indianapolis	Houston
First downs	22	17
Rushes-yards	30-101	28-148
Passing	281	125
Punt returns	2-8	1-9
Kickoff returns	2-41	5-98
Interception returns	1-1	0-0
Comp.-att.-int.	26-33-0	16-21-1
Sacked-yards lost	2-17	5-42

	Indianapolis	Houston
Punts	3-38	4-43
Fumbles-lost	3-0	1-1
Penalties-yards	8-50	6-30
Time of possession	32:19	27:41

INDIVIDUAL STATISTICS
RUSHING—Indianapolis, James 28-104, Manning 2-(minus 3). Houston, D. Davis 23-128, Carr 4-19, Wells 1-1.
PASSING—Indianapolis, Manning 26-33-0-298. Houston, Carr 16-21-1-167.
RECEIVING—Indianapolis, Wayne 7-96, James 7-54, Pollard 4-42, Stokley 3-54, Harrison 3-26, Clark 2-26. Houston, D. Davis 6-73, An. Johnson 3-34, Bradford 2-27, Miller 2-23, Wells 2-8, Norris 1-2.
MISSED FIELD GOAL ATTEMPTS—None.
INTERCEPTIONS—Indianapolis, David 1-1.
KICKOFF RETURNS—Indianapolis, Rhodes 1-21, Mungro 1-20. Houston, Moses 3-71, Washington 2-27.
PUNT RETURNS—Indianapolis, Walters 2-8. Houston, Moses 1-9.
SACKS—Indianapolis, Freeney 3, Brock 1, Mathis 1. Houston, Robinson 2.

SEAHAWKS 27, VIKINGS 23
Sunday, December 12

Seattle	7	14	3	3—27
Minnesota	10	10	3	0—23

First Quarter
Min.—FG, M. Andersen 48, 4:18.
Min.—O. Smith 5 run (M. Andersen kick), 11:18.
Sea.—Engram 35 pass from Hasselbeck (J. Brown kick), 13:48.

Second Quarter
Sea.—Alexander 12 pass from Hasselbeck (J. Brown kick), 2:47.
Min.—FG, M. Andersen 32, 5:12.
Min.—Moss 3 pass from Culpepper (M. Andersen kick), 9:54.
Sea.—Jackson 19 pass from Hasselbeck (J. Brown kick), 11:55.

Third Quarter
Min.—FG, M. Andersen 31, 3:02.
Sea.—FG, J. Brown 33, 8:18.

Fourth Quarter
Sea.—FG, J. Brown 28, 11:20.
Attendance—64,110.

	Seattle	Minnesota
First downs	26	22
Rushes-yards	31-138	25-113
Passing	317	261
Punt returns	0-0	1-18
Kickoff returns	5-122	4-90
Interception returns	1-0	2-41
Comp.-att.-int.	23-34-2	21-34-1
Sacked-yards lost	3-17	1-9
Punts	4-41	4-46
Fumbles-lost	0-0	2-1
Penalties-yards	5-79	5-42
Time of possession	32:43	27:17

INDIVIDUAL STATISTICS
RUSHING—Seattle, Alexander 27-112, Morris 3-13, Hasselbeck 1-13. Minnesota, O. Smith 14-56, Culpepper 6-32, M. Bennett 5-25.
PASSING—Seattle, Hasselbeck 23-34-2-334. Minnesota, Culpepper 21-33-0-270, Moss 0-1-1-0.
RECEIVING—Seattle, Jackson 10-135, Rice 5-52, Engram 4-79, Hannam 2-44, Alexander 1-12, Morris 1-12. Minnesota, Moss 4-104, Burleson 4-42, O. Smith 4-41, Wiggins 3-33, M. Williams 3-23, Campbell 2-14, M. Robinson 1-13.
MISSED FIELD GOAL ATTEMPTS—Seattle, J. Brown 38.
INTERCEPTIONS—Seattle, Boulware 1-0. Minnesota, Russell 1-41, B. Williams 1-0.
KICKOFF RETURNS—Seattle, Morris 5-122. Minnesota, Campbell 3-60, Moore 1-30.
PUNT RETURNS—Minnesota, Burleson 1-18.
SACKS—Seattle, Boulware 1. Minnesota, Claiborne 1, K. Williams 1, Johnstone 1.

PATRIOTS 35, BENGALS 28
Sunday, December 12

Cincinnati	0	14	7	7—28
New England	7	21	7	0—35

First Quarter
N.E.—Dillon 1 run (Vinatieri kick), 9:52.

in.—Schobel 2 pass from Palmer (Graham kick), 4:57.
.E.—Patten 48 pass from Brady (Vinatieri kick), 6:29.
.E.—Samuel 34 interception return (Vinatieri kick), 6:41.
in.—C. Johnson 5 pass from Palmer (Graham kick), 12:29.
.E.—Faulk 4 run (Vinatieri kick), 14:38.

Third Quarter
.E.—Fauria 17 pass from Brady (Vinatieri kick), 5:46.
in.—Larson 11 run (Graham kick), 11:50.

Fourth Quarter
in.—Washington 27 pass from Kitna (Graham kick), 11:10.
Attendance—68,756.

	Cincinnati	New England
rst downs	26	22
ushes-yards	31-150	29-94
assing	328	257
unt returns	3-35	0-0
ickoff returns	5-108	5-109
terception returns	0-0	2-39
omp.-att.-int.	27-37-2	18-26-0
acked-yards lost	0-0	1-3
unts	2-31	3-54
umbles-lost	2-1	0-0
enalties-yards	9-75	2-13
ime of possession	33:11	26:49

INDIVIDUAL STATISTICS
RUSHING—Cincinnati, Ru. Johnson 24-89, Palmer 2-19, Watson 2-12, arson 1-11, C. Johnson 1-10, Kitna 1-9. New England, Dillon 22-88, Brady 5-Faulk 1-4, Izzo 1-0.
PASSING—Cincinnati, Palmer 18-24-1-202, Kitna 9-13-1-126. New England, rady 18-26-0-260.
RECEIVING—Cincinnati, Houshmandzadeh 12-145, C. Johnson 5-80, Ru. ohnson 2-35, Washington 2-35, Watson 2-15, Walter 1-11, R. Kelly 1-5, chobel 1-2, J. Johnson 1-0. New England, Patten 5-107, Branch 3-44, Fauria -33, T. Brown 2-27, Pass 2-22, Weaver 2-14, Faulk 1-13.
MISSED FIELD GOAL ATTEMPTS—None.
INTERCEPTIONS—New England, Samuel 1-34, T. Brown 1-5.
KICKOFF RETURNS—Cincinnati, C. Russell 4-94, Watson 1-14. New ngland, B. Johnson 5-109.
PUNT RETURNS—Cincinnati, Ratliff 3-35.
SACKS—Cincinnati, Clemons 1.

RAVENS 37, GIANTS 14
Sunday, December 12

Y. Giants	0	7	0	7—14
altimore	10	17	10	0—37

First Quarter
al.—Moore 12 pass from Boller (Stover kick), 2:56.
al.—FG, Stover 46, 5:59.

Second Quarter
al.—Heap 6 pass from Boller (Stover kick), 7:55.
YG—Umenyiora 50 fumble return (Christie kick), 12:17.
al.—Moore 8 pass from Boller (Stover kick), 14:39.
al.—FG, Stover 44, 15:00.

Third Quarter
al.—FG, Stover 27, 7:10.
al.—Heap 1 pass from Boller (Stover kick), 13:18.

Fourth Quarter
YG—Barber 1 run (Christie kick), 11:11.
Attendance—69,856.

	N.Y. Giants	Baltimore
rst downs	11	23
ushes-yards	21-51	44-169
assing	145	184
unt returns	2-22	5-54
ickoff returns	7-177	2-45
terception returns	0-0	2-55
omp.-att.-int.	10-27-2	18-34-0
acked-yards lost	2-9	4-35
unts	7-41	8-37
umbles-lost	4-4	3-1
enalties-yards	9-65	6-86
me of possession	20:19	39:41

INDIVIDUAL STATISTICS
RUSHING—New York, Barber 19-55, Manning 1-0, Ponder 1-(minus 4). Baltimore, C. Taylor 25-104, J. Lewis 8-32, Boller 4-19, J. White 4-7, Sams 1-4, Ricard 1-4, Stewart 1-(minus 1).
PASSING—New York, Manning 4-18-2-27, Warner 6-9-0-127. Baltimore, Boller 18-34-0-219.
RECEIVING—New York, Shockey 5-83, Toomer 2-53, Barber 2-9, I. Hilliard 1-9. Baltimore, Heap 5-76, C. Taylor 4-27, Moore 3-37, T. Taylor 3-33, K. Johnson 2-41, Dinkins 1-5.
MISSED FIELD GOAL ATTEMPTS—None.
INTERCEPTIONS—Baltimore, Baxter 1-33, Reed 1-6.
KICKOFF RETURNS—New York, Ward 7-177. Baltimore, Sams 2-45.
PUNT RETURNS—New York, Jones 2-22. Baltimore, Sams 5-54.
SACKS—New York, Alexander 1, Maxwell 1, Torbor 1, Umenyiora 0.5, Legree 0.5. Baltimore, Douglas 1, A. Thomas 1.

SAINTS 27, COWBOYS 13
Sunday, December 12

New Orleans	0	10	3	14—27
Dallas	10	0	3	0—13

First Quarter
Dal.—FG, Cundiff 34, 11:41.
Dal.—J. Jones 1 run (Cundiff kick), 14:39.

Second Quarter
N.O.—McAllister 5 run (Carney kick), 9:04.
N.O.—FG, Carney 39, 14:24.

Third Quarter
Dal.—FG, Cundiff 41, 4:27.
N.O.—FG, Carney 44, 8:53.

Fourth Quarter
N.O.—McAllister 4 run (Carney kick), 9:39.
N.O.—Horn 31 pass from Brooks (Carney kick), 12:13.
Attendance—64,056.

	New Orleans	Dallas
First downs	21	18
Rushes-yards	37-105	27-121
Passing	239	148
Punt returns	4-58	3-6
Kickoff returns	4-66	5-115
Interception returns	2-5	2-22
Comp.-att.-int.	18-31-2	14-36-2
Sacked-yards lost	2-13	3-12
Punts	5-46	5-49
Fumbles-lost	0-0	3-2
Penalties-yards	9-136	11-76
Time of possession	31:35	28:25

INDIVIDUAL STATISTICS
RUSHING—New Orleans, McAllister 30-83, Brooks 5-18, Stecker 1-3, McAfee 1-1. Dallas, J. Jones 23-88, Anderson 2-7, Morgan 1-24, Testaverde 1-2.
PASSING—New Orleans, Brooks 18-31-2-252. Dallas, Testaverde 14-35-1-160, K. Johnson 0-1-1-0.
RECEIVING—New Orleans, Stallworth 5-113, Horn 5-84, McAllister 4-37, Stecker 2-10, B. Williams 1-4, Conwell 1-4. Dallas, Witten 4-59, Morgan 3-26, Anderson 3-22, K. Johnson 2-45, J. Jones 2-8.
MISSED FIELD GOAL ATTEMPTS—Dallas, Cundiff 42.
INTERCEPTIONS—New Orleans, M. McKenzie 1-5, Brown 1-0. Dallas, Ro. Williams 1-20, Frazier 1-2.
KICKOFF RETURNS—New Orleans, Stecker 3-55, McAfee 1-11. Dallas, Lee 4-103, Copper 1-12.
PUNT RETURNS—New Orleans, M. Lewis 4-58. Dallas, Frazier 3-6.
SACKS—New Orleans, Ch. Grant 1, Watson 1, W. Smith 1. Dallas, L. Scott 1, Wiley 1.

JAGUARS 22, BEARS 3
Sunday, December 12

Chicago	0	3	0	0—3
Jacksonville	7	3	3	9—22

First Quarter
Jac.—R. Williams 6 pass from Leftwich (Scobee kick), 11:42.

Second Quarter
Chi.—FG, Edinger 42, 13:16.
Jac.—FG, Scobee 30, 14:29.

Third Quarter
Jac.—FG, Scobee 25, 9:24.

Fourth Quarter
Jac.—Safety, 1:12.
Jac.—J. Smith 31 pass from Leftwich (Scobee kick), 5:34.
Attendance—67,572.

	Chicago	Jacksonville
First downs	10	22
Rushes-yards	14-31	28-90
Passing	179	242
Punt returns	4-14	6-63
Kickoff returns	5-140	3-51
Interception returns	1-38	1-20
Comp.-att.-int.	17-33-1	25-45-1
Sacked-yards lost	5-33	0-0
Punts	7-48	8-43
Fumbles-lost	2-1	1-0
Penalties-yards	13-104	8-75
Time of possession	24:17	35:43

INDIVIDUAL STATISTICS

RUSHING—Chicago, T. Jones 13-26, Terrell 1-5. Jacksonville, F. Taylor 21-79, Leftwich 4-8, G. Jones 3-3.

PASSING—Chicago, Hutchinson 17-33-1-212. Jacksonville, Leftwich 25-45-1-242.

RECEIVING—Chicago, T. Jones 3-68, Thomas 3-18, McKie 3-17, Berrian 2-46, Terrell 2-23, Lyman 2-19, Wade 1-14, Gage 1-7. Jacksonville, J. Smith 6-85, R. Williams 4-62, T. Edwards 4-30, F. Taylor 4-23, Toefield 2-10, B. Jones 1-14, Wilford 1-9, Yoder 1-4, Allen 1-3, Brady 1-2.

MISSED FIELD GOAL ATTEMPTS—Chicago, Edinger 47.

INTERCEPTIONS—Chicago, Vasher 1-38. Jacksonville, Darius 1-20.

KICKOFF RETURNS—Chicago, Azumah 5-140. Jacksonville, Allen 3-51.

PUNT RETURNS—Chicago, McQuarters 4-14. Jacksonville, Allen 5-55, Mathis 1-8.

SACKS—Jacksonville, Henderson 1, D. Smith 1, Peterson 1, Gildon 1, Patterson 0.5, Favors 0.5.

BILLS 37, BROWNS 7
Sunday, December 12

Cleveland	7	0	0	0— 7
Buffalo	3	14	3	17—37

First Quarter
Buf.—FG, Lindell 23, 5:49.
Cle.—Northcutt 3 pass from McCown (Dawson kick), 13:15.

Second Quarter
Buf.—Evans 7 pass from Bledsoe (Lindell kick), 5:21.
Buf.—McGahee 13 run (Lindell kick), 12:03.

Third Quarter
Buf.—FG, Lindell 21, 10:55.

Fourth Quarter
Buf.—McGahee 6 run (Lindell kick), :11.
Buf.—FG, Lindell 37, 4:07.
Buf.—S. Williams 4 run (Lindell kick), 12:59.
Attendance—72,330.

	Cleveland	Buffalo
First downs	6	22
Rushes-yards	18-29	42-215
Passing	-3	106
Punt returns	1-8	6-34
Kickoff returns	8-154	2-36
Interception returns	1-24	2-13
Comp.-att.-int.	9-21-2	13-30-1
Sacked-yards lost	7-70	1-4
Punts	6-38	3-38
Fumbles-lost	5-3	4-2
Penalties-yards	7-40	7-37
Time of possession	23:05	36:55

INDIVIDUAL STATISTICS

RUSHING—Cleveland, Green 11-5, Echemandu 5-13, McCown 2-11. Buffalo, McGahee 27-105, S. Williams 10-42, Evans 1-48, Losman 1-10, J. Smith 1-8, Burns 1-2, Bledsoe 1-0.

PASSING—Cleveland, McCown 8-20-2-62, Garcia 1-1-0-5. Buffalo, Bledsoe 12-27-1-100, Losman 1-2-0-10, Moorman 0-1-0-0.

RECEIVING—Cleveland, Bryant 4-37, Heiden 2-19, Northcutt 2-6, Shea 1-5. Buffalo, Evans 4-33, Moulds 3-38, McGahee 2-12, Trafford 1-10, S. Williams 1-10, Reed 1-6, Shelton 1-1.

MISSED FIELD GOAL ATTEMPTS—Cleveland, Dawson 45.

INTERCEPTIONS—Cleveland, L. Sanders 1-24. Buffalo, Vincent 1-8, Clements 1-5.

KICKOFF RETURNS—Cleveland, Alston 6-119, F. Jackson 1-22, Shea 1-13. Buffalo, McGee 2-36.

PUNT RETURNS—Cleveland, Northcutt 1-8. Buffalo, J. Smith 3-26, Clements 3-8.

SACKS—Cleveland, McKinley 1. Buffalo, Adams 2, Schobel 1, Milloy 1, Kelsay 1, Vincent 1, Posey 1.

STEELERS 17, JETS 6
Sunday, December 12

N.Y. Jets	0	0	3	3— 6
Pittsburgh	3	0	0	14—17

First Quarter
Pit.—FG, Reed 34, 12:36.

Third Quarter
NYJ—FG, Brien 43, 7:56.

Fourth Quarter
Pit.—Tuman 10 pass from Bettis (Reed kick), 2:09.
NYJ—FG, Brien 41, 8:44.
Pit.—Bettis 12 run (Reed kick), 12:00.
Attendance—63,581.

	N.Y. Jets	Pittsburgh
First downs	15	15
Rushes-yards	32-107	31-120
Passing	189	142
Punt returns	2-14	2-(-6)
Kickoff returns	3-58	3-39
Interception returns	2-23	3-85
Comp.-att.-int.	17-31-3	10-20-2
Sacked-yards lost	0-0	2-12
Punts	5-44	5-42
Fumbles-lost	1-0	1-0
Penalties-yards	12-84	2-15
Time of possession	30:48	29:12

INDIVIDUAL STATISTICS

RUSHING—New York, C. Martin 24-72, Pennington 4-16, Jordan 3-10 Sowell 1-9. Pittsburgh, Staley 16-51, Bettis 10-57, Roethlisberger 4-(minus 2 Parker 1-7.

PASSING—New York, Pennington 17-31-3-189. Pittsburgh, Roethlisberge 9-19-2-144, Bettis 1-1-0-10.

RECEIVING—New York, McCareins 4-78, Moss 3-37, C. Martin 3-35, Chrebe 2-15, J. Carter 2-13, Baker 1-5, Becht 1-4, Sowell 1-2. Pittsburgh, Kreider 3-19 Ward 2-38, Staley 2-30, Mays 1-46, Randle El 1-11, Tuman 1-10.

MISSED FIELD GOAL ATTEMPTS—None.

INTERCEPTIONS—New York, Tongue 1-23, D. Abraham 1-0. Pittsburgh Hope 1-41, Farrior 1-22, Polamalu 1-22.

KICKOFF RETURNS—New York, J. Carter 3-58. Pittsburgh, Colclough 2-2 I. Taylor 1-12.

PUNT RETURNS—New York, Moss 2-14. Pittsburgh, Randle El 2-(minus 6 SACKS—New York, Ellis 1.5, Robertson 0.5.

BRONCOS 20, DOLPHINS 17
Sunday, December 12

Miami	7	7	3	0—17
Denver	0	14	3	3—20

First Quarter
Mia.—Booker 8 pass from Feeley (Mare kick), 11:59.

Second Quarter
Den.—Bell 7 run (Elam kick), 1:52.
Mia.—Morris 11 run (Mare kick), 6:22.
Den.—Bell 11 run (Elam kick), 13:39.

Third Quarter
Den.—FG, Elam 20, 2:16.
Mia.—FG, Mare 32, 10:26.

Fourth Quarter
Den.—FG, Elam 50, 12:10.
Attendance—75,027.

	Miami	Denver
First downs	13	24
Rushes-yards	22-70	40-196
Passing	144	219
Punt returns	2-9	7-36
Kickoff returns	4-97	1-17
Interception returns	2-0	1-10
Comp.-att.-int.	17-35-1	16-30-2
Sacked-yards lost	4-26	0-0
Punts	8-45	5-40
Fumbles-lost	2-0	2-1
Penalties-yards	4-40	5-43
Time of possession	26:16	33:44

INDIVIDUAL STATISTICS

RUSHING—Miami, Minor 10-24, Morris 9-36, Feeley 2-2, Chambers 1- Denver, Droughns 18-62, Bell 17-123, Plummer 5-11.

PASSING—Miami, Feeley 17-35-1-170. Denver, Plummer 16-30-2-219.

RECEIVING—Miami, McMichael 5-62, Chambers 5-47, Booker 4-45, Lee 1-0, Konrad 1-4, Minor 1-2. Denver, Smith 8-97, Lelie 2-60, Putzier 2-30, K. Johnson 2-22, Watts 1-16, Bell 1-(minus 6).

MISSED FIELD GOAL ATTEMPTS—None.

INTERCEPTIONS—Miami, J. Williams 1-0, S. Knight 1-0. Denver, Wilson 1-10.

KICKOFF RETURNS—Miami, Welker 4-97. Denver, Droughns 1-17.

PUNT RETURNS—Miami, Welker 2-9. Denver, Luke 5-23, Smith 2-13.

SACKS—Denver, Kennedy 1, Lynch 1, E. Johnson 1, Coleman 1.

PANTHERS 20, RAMS 7
Sunday, December 12

St. Louis	7	0	0	0— 7
Carolina	14	6	0	0—20

First Quarter
Car.—Muhammad 14 pass from Delhomme (Kasay kick), 7:47.
Car.—Goings 1 run (Kasay kick), 13:56.
St.L.—Holt 75 pass from C. Chandler (J. Wilkins kick), 14:54.

Second Quarter
Car.—FG, Kasay 27, 8:48.
Car.—FG, Kasay 20, 14:21.
Attendance—73,306.

	St. Louis	Carolina
First downs	11	18
Rushes-yards	21-66	38-119
Passing	226	189
Punt returns	3-7	3-9
Kickoff returns	5-93	2-62
Interception returns	1-6	6-91
Comp.-att.-int.	16-29-6	16-30-1
Sacked-yards lost	3-20	2-17
Punts	4-40	5-44
Fumbles-lost	2-1	3-1
Penalties-yards	5-44	7-55
Time of possession	24:24	35:36

INDIVIDUAL STATISTICS
RUSHING—St. Louis, Harris 19-61, McDonald 1-3, C. Chandler 1-2. Carolina, Goings 31-108, Delhomme 5-9, Hoover 2-2.

PASSING—St. Louis, C. Chandler 16-29-6-246. Carolina, Delhomme 16-30-1-206.

RECEIVING—St. Louis, Holt 6-151, Harris 4-44, Bruce 3-27, McDonald 1-9, Goodspeed 1-8, Curtis 1-7. Carolina, Muhammad 6-98, Colbert 5-46, Proehl 2-30, Seidman 2-7, Hoover 1-15.

MISSED FIELD GOAL ATTEMPTS—None.

INTERCEPTIONS—St. Louis, Butler 1-6. Carolina, Manning Jr. 2-46, Morgan 2-20, Witherspoon 1-25, Gamble 1-0.

KICKOFF RETURNS—St. Louis, Cason 5-93. Carolina, Bennett 2-62.

PUNT RETURNS—St. Louis, McDonald 3-7. Carolina, Gamble 2-5, Hawkins 1-4.

SACKS—St. Louis, B. Fisher 2. Carolina, Moorehead 2, Peppers 1.

PACKERS 16, LIONS 13
Sunday, December 12

Detroit	3	10	0	0—13
Green Bay	0	0	10	6—16

First Quarter
Det.—FG, Hanson 31, 7:45.

Second Quarter
Det.—Jones 24 run (Hanson kick), :40.
Det.—FG, Hanson 36, 14:03.

Third Quarter
G.B.—FG, Longwell 36, 4:24.
G.B.—Driver 23 pass from Favre (Longwell kick), 11:50.

Fourth Quarter
G.B.—FG, Longwell 28, 4:14.
G.B.—FG, Longwell 23, 14:58.
Attendance—70,497.

	Detroit	Green Bay
First downs	17	20
Rushes-yards	39-193	29-116
Passing	35	185
Punt returns	3-24	0-0
Kickoff returns	5-86	2-27
Interception returns	0-0	0-0
Comp.-att.-int.	5-22-0	19-36-0
Sacked-yards lost	2-12	1-3
Punts	8-31	7-40

	Detroit	Green Bay
Fumbles-lost	0-0	0-0
Penalties-yards	10-85	9-94
Time of possession	30:31	29:29

INDIVIDUAL STATISTICS
RUSHING—Detroit, Jones 33-156, Harrington 4-29, Bryson 2-8. Green Bay, Green 23-76, Davenport 3-12, Fisher 2-20, Favre 1-8.

PASSING—Detroit, Harrington 5-22-0-47. Green Bay, Favre 19-36-0-188.

RECEIVING—Detroit, Hakim 1-18, Williams 1-13, Streets 1-10, FitzSimmons 1-9, Bryson 1-(minus 3). Green Bay, Green 5-20, Driver 4-87, Franks 4-29, J. Walker 3-26, Henderson 1-11, Fisher 1-10, Davenport 1-5.

MISSED FIELD GOAL ATTEMPTS—None.

INTERCEPTIONS—None.

KICKOFF RETURNS—Detroit, Swinton 3-82, DeVries 1-5, D. Curry 1-(minus 1). Green Bay, Ferguson 1-15, Davenport 1-12.

PUNT RETURNS—Detroit, Swinton 3-24. SACKS—Detroit, DeVries 1. Green Bay, Barnett 1, Gbaja-Biamila 1.

CHARGERS 31, BUCCANEERS 24
Sunday, December 12

Tampa Bay	0	7	7	10—24
San Diego	0	14	7	10—31

Second Quarter
S.D.—E. Parker 79 pass from Brees (Kaeding kick), 3:11.
T.B.—Galloway 36 pass from Griese (Taylor kick), 5:58.
S.D.—Osgood 19 pass from Brees (Kaeding kick), 14:11.

Third Quarter
T.B.—Galloway 4 pass from Griese (Taylor kick), 10:04.
S.D.—Tomlinson 7 run (Kaeding kick), 14:30.

Fourth Quarter
T.B.—Clayton 20 pass from Griese (Taylor kick), 8:07.
S.D.—Edwards 30 interception return (Kaeding kick), 10:51.
S.D.—FG, Kaeding 40, 12:54.
T.B.—FG, Taylor 41, 14:44.
Attendance—65,858.

	Tampa Bay	San Diego
First downs	21	18
Rushes-yards	18-63	30-130
Passing	373	206
Punt returns	3-5	2-10
Kickoff returns	5-106	4-82
Interception returns	2-0	3-46
Comp.-att.-int.	36-50-3	17-23-2
Sacked-yards lost	3-19	2-14
Punts	5-40	4-47
Fumbles-lost	2-1	2-1
Penalties-yards	12-111	4-40
Time of possession	32:30	27:30

INDIVIDUAL STATISTICS
RUSHING—Tampa Bay, Pittman 12-42, Alstott 4-12, Graham 1-6, Griese 1-3. San Diego, Tomlinson 25-131, Brees 4-(minus 3), Neal 1-2.

PASSING—Tampa Bay, Griese 36-50-3-392. San Diego, Brees 17-23-2-220.

RECEIVING—Tampa Bay, Clayton 9-145, Pittman 6-46, Galloway 5-78, Dilger 4-28, Heller 3-19, Jurevicius 2-33, Alstott 2-23, Brown 2-14, Smart 2-10, Griese 1-(minus 4). San Diego, E. Parker 6-118, Tomlinson 4-19, McCardell 3-30, Osgood 2-27, Gates 1-17, Peelle 1-9.

MISSED FIELD GOAL ATTEMPTS—Tampa Bay, Taylor 30. San Diego, Kaeding 51.

INTERCEPTIONS—Tampa Bay, Barber 1-0, Allen 1-0. San Diego, Edwards 2-34, Jammer 1-12.

KICKOFF RETURNS—Tampa Bay, Smart 5-106. San Diego, Chatman 3-70, Neal 1-12.

PUNT RETURNS—Tampa Bay, Galloway 3-5. San Diego, E. Parker 2-10.

SACKS—Tampa Bay, Rice 1, Spires 1. San Diego, Foley 1, Leber 1, Fisk 1.

49ERS 31, CARDINALS 28
Sunday, December 12

San Francisco	7	14	7	0	3—31
Arizona	0	3	7	18	0—28

First Quarter
S.F.—Lloyd 5 pass from Dorsey (T. Peterson kick), 5:12.

Second Quarter
S.F.—Wilson 19 pass from Dorsey (T. Peterson kick), 1:24.
S.F.—Hicks 1 run (T. Peterson kick), 6:41.
Ariz.—FG, Rackers 44, 11:45.

Third Quarter
S.F.—Wilson 27 pass from Dorsey (T. Peterson kick), 5:03.
Ariz.—O. Ayanbadejo 4 run (Rackers kick), 13:01.

Fourth Quarter
Ariz.—O. Ayanbadejo 1 run (Rackers kick), 3:07.
Ariz.—E. Smith 8 run (McCown run), 12:20.
Ariz.—FG, Rackers 22, 14:01.

Overtime
S.F.—FG, T. Peterson 31, 6:22.
Attendance—35,069.

	San Francisco	Arizona
First downs	23	25
Rushes-yards	41-168	25-75
Passing	184	299
Punt returns	4-34	5-26
Kickoff returns	3-60	4-71
Interception returns	1-25	0-0
Comp.-att.-int.	18-34-0	26-44-1
Sacked-yards lost	1-7	1-8
Punts	7-46	5-51
Fumbles-lost	1-1	2-1
Penalties-yards	7-70	9-61
Time of possession	36:23	29:59

INDIVIDUAL STATISTICS
RUSHING—San Francisco, Hicks 34-139, Jackson 5-27, Dorsey 2-2. Arizona, E. Smith 18-53, O. Ayanbadejo 5-13, McCown 1-7, Scobey 1-2.

PASSING—San Francisco, Dorsey 18-34-0-191. Arizona, McCown 26-44-1-307.

RECEIVING—San Francisco, Wilson 5-83, Hicks 5-29, Lloyd 2-18, Jackson 2-13, E. Johnson 2-8, Walker 1-30, Battle 1-10. Arizona, Boldin 9-109, B. Johnson 4-77, Fitzgerald 4-47, F. Jones 4-34, Edwards 3-39, Scobey 1-4, E. Smith 1-(minus 3).

MISSED FIELD GOAL ATTEMPTS—Arizona, Rackers 34.

INTERCEPTIONS—San Francisco, Parrish 1-25.

KICKOFF RETURNS—San Francisco, J. Williams 2-43, Battle 1-17. Arizona, B. Johnson 3-58, Edwards 1-13.

PUNT RETURNS—San Francisco, Battle 4-34. Arizona, K. Williams 3-4, Starks 2-22.

SACKS—San Francisco, Carter 1. Arizona, Berry 1.

EAGLES 17, REDSKINS 14
Sunday, December 12

Philadelphia	7	0	10	0	17
Washington	7	0	0	7	14

First Quarter
Was.—Portis 5 run (Hall kick), :46.
Phi.—Smith 2 pass from McNabb (Akers kick), 2:11.

Third Quarter
Phi.—FG, Akers 38, 4:17.
Phi.—Levens 1 run (Akers kick), 14:35.

Fourth Quarter
Was.—Portis 2 run (Hall kick), 2:56.
Attendance—90,089.

	Philadelphia	Washington
First downs	15	19
Rushes-yards	17-67	25-88
Passing	245	224
Punt returns	5-81	3-16
Kickoff returns	3-45	4-137
Interception returns	1-0	1-10
Comp.-att.-int.	21-38-1	29-46-1
Sacked-yards lost	2-15	3-27
Punts	7-43	9-41
Fumbles-lost	2-1	1-0
Penalties-yards	5-41	12-137
Time of possession	26:03	33:57

INDIVIDUAL STATISTICS
RUSHING—Philadelphia, Westbrook 12-59, Levens 3-0, McNabb 2-8 Washington, Portis 23-80, Betts 2-8.

PASSING—Philadelphia, McNabb 21-38-1-260. Washington, Ramsey 29-45 1-251, Portis 0-1-0-0.

RECEIVING—Philadelphia, Westbrook 6-59, Owens 6-46, Pinkston 3-99, (Lewis 2-29, Smith 2-12, Levens 1-13, F. Mitchell 1-2. Washington, Coles 12 100, Cooley 5-75, Gardner 4-25, Portis 4-22, Thrash 2-22, Betts 1-6, Royal 1-1

MISSED FIELD GOAL ATTEMPTS—Philadelphia, Akers 48. Washington, Hall 4:

INTERCEPTIONS—Philadelphia, Dawkins 1-0. Washington, Springs 1-10.

KICKOFF RETURNS—Philadelphia, Reed 3-45. Washington, Betts 4-137.

PUNT RETURNS—Philadelphia, Wynn 5-81. Washington, Thrash 3-16.

SACKS—Philadelphia, Rayburn 1, H. Douglas 1, Walker 1. Washington Clemons 1, R. Warner 1.

CHIEFS 49, TITANS 38
Monday, December 13

Kansas City	0	14	14	21	49
Tennessee	7	14	7	10	38

First Quarter
Ten.—Brown 1 run (Anderson kick), 7:41.

Second Quarter
Ten.—Bennett 42 pass from Volek (Anderson kick), 1:33.
K.C.—Kennison 58 pass from Green (Tynes kick), 2:32.
K.C.—Morton 30 pass from Green (Tynes kick), 13:43.
Ten.—Bennett 22 pass from Volek (Anderson kick), 14:51.

Third Quarter
K.C.—Blaylock 1 run (Tynes kick), 4:34.
Ten.—Bennett 7 pass from Volek (Anderson kick), 7:38.
K.C.—L. Johnson 46 run (Tynes kick), 8:31.

Fourth Quarter
K.C.—L. Johnson 41 run (Tynes kick), 10:11.
Ten.—Mason 4 pass from Volek (Anderson kick), 12:34.
Ten.—FG, Anderson 27, 13:21.
K.C.—Kennison 9 pass from Green (Tynes kick), 14:28.
K.C.—Mitchell 39 fumble return (Tynes kick), 14:52.
Attendance—68,932.

	Kansas City	Tennessee
First downs	24	30
Rushes-yards	24-146	33-163
Passing	237	379
Punt returns	1-4	2-0
Kickoff returns	7-144	8-148
Interception returns	0-0	1-0
Comp.-att.-int.	18-32-1	29-43-0
Sacked-yards lost	1-7	5-47
Punts	5-38	4-37
Fumbles-lost	1-1	5-4
Penalties-yards	7-58	13-104
Time of possession	22:01	37:59

INDIVIDUAL STATISTICS
RUSHING—Kansas City, Blaylock 14-51, L. Johnson 7-104, Green 2-(minu 1), Morton 1-(minus 8). Tennessee, Brown 15-91, A. Smith 10-31, Holcombe 5 4, Volek 2-24, Fleming 1-13.

PASSING—Kansas City, Green 18-32-1-244. Tennessee, Volek 29-43-0-42€

RECEIVING—Kansas City, Gonzalez 7-76, Kennison 2-67, Morton 2-45 Blaylock 2-22, L. Johnson 2-19, Horn 1-17, Dunn 1-0, Hall 1-(minus 2' Tennessee, Bennett 12-233, Meier 4-50, Mason 3-22, A. Smith 2-38, Kinney 2 10, Fleming 2-4, McAddley 1-36, Troupe 1-16, Brown 1-13, Berlin 1-4.

MISSED FIELD GOAL ATTEMPTS—Tennessee, Anderson 50.

INTERCEPTIONS—Tennessee, Waddell 1-0.

KICKOFF RETURNS—Kansas City, Hall 5-116, Horn 2-28. Tennessee McAddley 7-133, Fleming 1-15.

PUNT RETURNS—Kansas City, Hall 1-4. Tennessee, Mason 1-0, Waddell 1-0

SACKS—Kansas City, Beisel 1, Browning 1, Allen 1, Dalton 1, Sims 1 Tennessee, McGarrahan 0.5, Odom 0.5.

WEEK 15

STANDINGS

AMERICAN FOOTBALL CONFERENCE

EAST DIVISION
	W	L	T	Pct.	PF	PA
w England	12	2	0	.857	393	246
Y. Jets	10	4	0	.714	297	206
ffalo	8	6	0	.571	330	248
ami	3	11	0	.214	242	317

NORTH DIVISION
	W	L	T	Pct.	PF	PA
tsburgh	13	1	0	.929	323	220
ltimore	8	6	0	.571	280	225
cinnati	6	8	0	.429	313	340
eveland	3	11	0	.214	247	366

SOUTH DIVISION
	W	L	T	Pct.	PF	PA
dianapolis	11	3	0	.786	474	287
cksonville	8	6	0	.571	248	253
uston	6	8	0	.429	274	317
nnessee	4	10	0	.286	304	383

WEST DIVISION
	W	L	T	Pct.	PF	PA
n Diego	11	3	0	.786	391	262
enver	8	6	0	.571	311	274
nsas City	6	8	0	.429	435	381
akland	5	9	0	.357	284	398

NATIONAL FOOTBALL CONFERENCE

EAST DIVISION
	W	L	T	Pct.	PF	PA
Philadelphia	13	1	0	.929	369	202
Dallas	5	9	0	.357	256	367
N.Y. Giants	5	9	0	.357	253	300
Washington	5	9	0	.357	209	234

NORTH DIVISION
	W	L	T	Pct.	PF	PA
Green Bay	8	6	0	.571	359	335
Minnesota	8	6	0	.571	356	340
Chicago	5	9	0	.357	204	281
Detroit	5	9	0	.357	258	313

SOUTH DIVISION
	W	L	T	Pct.	PF	PA
Atlanta	11	3	0	.786	301	283
Carolina	6	8	0	.429	300	298
New Orleans	6	8	0	.429	301	374
Tampa Bay	5	9	0	.357	274	255

WEST DIVISION
	W	L	T	Pct.	PF	PA
Seattle	7	7	0	.500	319	326
St. Louis	6	8	0	.429	267	356
Arizona	5	9	0	.357	251	291
San Francisco	2	12	0	.143	245	390

TOP PERFORMANCES

100-YARD RUSHING GAMES
ayer, Team & Opponent	Att.	Yds.	TD
ed Taylor, Jac. at G.B.	22	165	1
rry Johnson, K.C. vs. Den.	30	151	2
rome Bettis, Pit. at NYG	36	140	1
arrick Dunn, Atl. vs. Car.*	28	134	1
rtis Martin, NYJ vs. Sea.	24	134	2
chael Pittman, T.B. vs. N.O.	24	131	0
di Johnson, Cin. vs. Buf.	23	130	1
mal Lewis, Bal. at Ind.	20	130	0
rey Dillon, N.E. at Mia.	26	121	1
Dainian Tomlinson, S.D. at Cle.	26	111	2
nton Portis, Was. at S.F.	35	110	0
e Suggs, Cle. vs. S.D.	21	105	0

300-YARD PASSING GAMES
ayer, Team & Opponent	Att.	Cmp.	Yds.	TD	Int.
lly Volek, Ten. at Oak.	60	40	492	4	1
unte Culpepper, Min. at Det.	35	25	404	3	1
rry Collins, Oak. vs. Ten.	37	21	371	5	1
ett Favre, G.B. vs. Jac.	44	30	367	2	3
ey Harrington, Det. vs. Min.	44	25	361	2	2
ke Delhomme, Car. at Atl.*	35	24	340	2	1
n Roethlisberger, Pit. at NYG	28	18	316	1	2

100-YARD RECEIVING GAMES
ayer, Team & Opponent	Rec.	Yds.	TD
ew Bennett, Ten. at Oak.	13	160	2
von Walker, G.B. vs. Jac.	11	152	0
twaan Randle El, Pit. at NYG	5	149	1
rry Porter, Oak. vs. Ten.	8	148	3
hsin Muhammad, Car. at Atl.*	10	135	1
ate Burleson, Min. at Det.	5	134	2
nes Ward, Pit. at NYG	9	134	0
rrick Mason, Ten. at Oak.	9	121	1

Player, Team & Opponent	Rec.	Yds.	TD
Rod Gardner, Was. at S.F.	6	111	0
Jabar Gaffney, Hou. at Chi.	4	109	0
Az-Zahir Hakim, Det. vs. Min.	4	108	0
Roy Williams, Det. vs. Min.	7	104	2
Randy Moss, Min. at Det.	4	102	1
Lee Evans, Buf. at Cin.	5	101	1
Eddie Kennison, K.C. vs. Den.	7	101	2

*Overtime game.

RESULTS

SATURDAY, DECEMBER 18
Pittsburgh 33, N.Y. GIANTS 30
Washington 26, SAN FRANCISCO 16
ATLANTA 34, Carolina 31 (OT)

SUNDAY, DECEMBER 19
N.Y. JETS 37, Seattle 14
PHILADELPHIA 12, Dallas 7
San Diego 21, CLEVELAND 0
Minnesota 28, DETROIT 27
Buffalo 33, CINCINNATI 17
KANSAS CITY 45, Denver 17
Houston 24, CHICAGO 5
New Orleans 21, TAMPA BAY 17
ARIZONA 31, St. Louis 7
Jacksonville 28, GREEN BAY 25
OAKLAND 40, Tennessee 35
INDIANAPOLIS 20, Baltimore 10

MONDAY, DECEMBER 20
MIAMI 29, New England 28

STEELERS 33, GIANTS 30
Saturday, December 18

Pittsburgh 10   10   3   10—33
N.Y. Giants 14   0   10   6—30

First Quarter
NYG—Ponder 91 kickoff return (Christie kick), :15.
Pit.—Haynes 10 pass from Randle El (Reed kick), 7:34.
NYG—Shockey 2 pass from Manning (Christie kick), 10:58.
Pit.—FG, Reed 33, 14:41.

Second Quarter
Pit.—Randle El 35 pass from Roethlisberger (Reed kick), 9:24.
Pit.—FG, Reed 21, 14:46.

Third Quarter
NYG—FG, Christie 22, 6:25.
Pit.—FG, Reed 36, 10:45.
NYG—Rivers 1 pass from Manning (Christie kick), 14:31.

Fourth Quarter
Pit.—FG, Reed 28, 3:25.
NYG—Barber 1 run (sack), 6:45.
Pit.—Bettis 1 run (Reed kick), 10:03.
Attendance—78,836.

	Pittsburgh	N.Y. Giants
First downs	27	18
Rushes-yards	39-160	21-96
Passing	309	182
Punt returns	1-(-2)	0-0
Kickoff returns	6-127	8-259
Interception returns	1-0	2-12
Comp.-att.-int.	19-29-2	16-23-1
Sacked-yards lost	3-17	0-0
Punts	0-0	3-34
Fumbles-lost	0-0	0-0
Penalties-yards	2-14	5-55
Time of possession	35:43	24:17

INDIVIDUAL STATISTICS
RUSHING—Pittsburgh, Bettis 36-140, Haynes 2-21, Roethlisberger 1-(minus 1). New York, Barber 18-76, Manning 2-18, Dayne 1-2.
PASSING—Pittsburgh, Roethlisberger 18-28-2-316, Randle El 1-1-0-10. New York, Manning 16-23-1-182.
RECEIVING—Pittsburgh, Ward 9-134, Randle El 5-149, Haynes 3-28, Mays 1-12, Bettis 1-3. New York, Barber 5-38, I. Hilliard 3-34, Shockey 3-13, Toomer 2-34, Tyree 1-49, Finn 1-13, Rivers 1-1.
MISSED FIELD GOAL ATTEMPTS—None.
INTERCEPTIONS—Pittsburgh, W. Williams 1-0. New York, F. Walker 1-10, Alexander 1-2.
KICKOFF RETURNS—Pittsburgh, Colclough 3-67, I. Taylor 3-60. New York, Ponder 8-259.
PUNT RETURNS—Pittsburgh, Randle El 1-(minus 2).
SACKS—New York, Greisen 1, Umenyiora 1, Alexander 1.

REDSKINS 26, 49ERS 16
Saturday, December 18

Washington 7   16   3   0—26
San Francisco.....................................7   2   0   7—16

First Quarter
Was.—Royal 12 pass from Ramsey (J. Chandler kick), 5:46.
S.F.—Lloyd 17 pass from Dorsey (T. Peterson kick), 10:10.

Second Quarter
Was.—FG, J. Chandler 49, :15.
Was.—FG, J. Chandler 25, 6:32.
Was.—FG, J. Chandler 20, 9:43.
S.F.—Safety, 12:52.
Was.—Pierce 78 interception return (J. Chandler kick), 14:12.

Third Quarter
Was.—FG, J. Chandler 26, 11:28.

Fourth Quarter
S.F.—Conway 11 pass from Dorsey (T. Peterson kick), 10:34.
Attendance—65,710.

	Washington	San Francisco
First downs	17	12
Rushes-yards	40-128	18-55
Passing	209	199
Punt returns	3-8	1-13
Kickoff returns	2-42	8-166
Interception returns	4-147	0-0
Comp.-att.-int.	18-27-0	20-38-4
Sacked-yards lost	1-5	1-2
Punts	5-37	7-39
Fumbles-lost	1-1	1-0
Penalties-yards	11-93	5-45
Time of possession	36:59	23:01

INDIVIDUAL STATISTICS
RUSHING—Washington, Portis 35-110, Betts 3-8, Gardner 1-11, Ramsey (minus 1). San Francisco, Hicks 11-37, Barlow 6-18, Dorsey 1-0.
PASSING—Washington, Ramsey 18-27-0-214. San Francisco, Dorsey 2 38-4-206.
RECEIVING—Washington, Gardner 6-111, Coles 4-39, Cooley 3-21, Portis 20, Royal 1-12, Betts 1-11. San Francisco, E. Johnson 8-73, Lloyd 4-51, Wilson 3-40, Conway 3-24, Hicks 2-18.
MISSED FIELD GOAL ATTEMPTS—None.
INTERCEPTIONS—Washington, Pierce 1-78, R. Warner 1-39, Taylor 1-30, Harris 1-0.
KICKOFF RETURNS—Washington, Betts 2-42. San Francisco, Wilson 4-100, Battle 3-80, J. Williams 1-15, Hicks 1-10.
PUNT RETURNS—Washington, A. Brown 3-8. San Francisco, Wilson 1-13.
SACKS—Washington, Griffin 1. San Francisco, Parrish 0.5, Brown 0.5.

FALCONS 34, PANTHERS 31
Saturday, December 18

Carolina.....................................0   10   0   21   0—31
Atlanta.....................................7   3   14   7   3—34

First Quarter
Atl.—Finneran 3 pass from Vick (Feely kick), 7:44.

Second Quarter
Atl.—FG, Feely 37, :49.
Car.—Muhammad 6 pass from Delhomme (Kasay kick), 7:37.
Car.—FG, Kasay 21, 14:39.

Third Quarter
Atl.—Dunn 6 run (Feely kick), 8:12.
Atl.—White 12 pass from Vick (Feely kick), 12:13.

Fourth Quarter
Car.—Mangum 11 pass from Delhomme (Kasay kick), 2:39.
Car.—Peppers 60 fumble return (Kasay kick), 4:51.
Car.—Goings 5 run (Kasay kick), 11:23.
Atl.—Vick 12 run (Feely kick), 13:23.

Overtime
Atl.—FG, Feely 38, 2:25.
Attendance—70,845.

	Carolina	Atlanta
First downs	22	22
Rushes-yards	25-61	38-204
Passing	314	125
Punt returns	2-8	3-45
Kickoff returns	5-88	6-184
Interception returns	2-2	1-30
Comp.-att.-int.	24-35-1	11-28-2
Sacked-yards lost	4-26	4-25
Punts	3-48	2-47
Fumbles-lost	6-3	3-1
Penalties-yards	7-50	6-66
Time of possession	29:48	32:37

INDIVIDUAL STATISTICS
RUSHING—Carolina, Goings 24-61, Delhomme 1-0. Atlanta, Dunn 28-131, Vick 8-68, Wright 2-2.
PASSING—Carolina, Delhomme 24-35-1-340. Atlanta, Vick 11-28-2-154.
RECEIVING—Carolina, Muhammad 10-135, Mangum 4-53, Goings 3-2, Proehl 2-40, Seidman 2-29, Hoover 2-11, Colbert 1-43. Atlanta, White 3-7, Crumpler 3-38, Finneran 3-19, Jenkins 1-22, P. Price 1-4.
MISSED FIELD GOAL ATTEMPTS—Atlanta, Feely 45.
INTERCEPTIONS—Carolina, Gamble 2-2. Atlanta, Beasley 1-30.
KICKOFF RETURNS—Carolina, Bennett 4-72, Broussard 1-16. Atlanta, Rossum 5-140, D. Hall 1-48.

PUNT RETURNS—Carolina, Broussard 2-8. Atlanta, Rossum 3-45.
SACKS—Carolina, Buckner 1, Fields 1, Wallace 1, Rucker 1. Atlanta, B. Smith Brooking 1, Kerney 1, R. Coleman 1.

JETS 37, SEAHAWKS 14
Sunday, December 19

Seattle	7	7	0	0—14
N.Y. Jets	3	21	6	7—37

First Quarter
NYJ—FG, Brien 21, 5:06.
Sea.—Rice 12 pass from Hasselbeck (J. Brown kick), 9:33.
Second Quarter
NYJ—C. Martin 1 run (Brien kick), :03.
NYJ—C. Martin 3 run (Brien kick), 7:16.
NYJ—Moss 32 pass from Pennington (Brien kick), 13:12.
Sea.—Stevens 6 pass from Hasselbeck (J. Brown kick), 14:57.
Third Quarter
NYJ—Moss 7 pass from Pennington (kick failed), 5:38.
Fourth Quarter
NYJ—McCareins 5 pass from Pennington (Brien kick), 6:46.
Attendance—77,894.

	Seattle	N.Y. Jets
First downs	19	27
Rushes-yards	22-88	41-229
Passing	187	253
Punt returns	0-0	1-8
Kickoff returns	7-131	3-50
Interception returns	0-0	1-7
Comp.-att.-int.	22-32-1	18-24-0
Sacked-yards lost	4-14	0-0
Punts	3-36	0-0
Fumbles-lost	3-2	1-0
Penalties-yards	2-20	2-15
Time of possession	24:34	35:26

INDIVIDUAL STATISTICS
RUSHING—Seattle, Alexander 19-77, Strong 2-5, Morris 1-6. New York, C. Martin 24-134, Jordan 15-84, Moss 1-12, Pennington 1-(minus 1).
PASSING—Seattle, Hasselbeck 22-30-1-201, Dilfer 0-2-0-0. New York, Pennington 18-24-0-253.
RECEIVING—Seattle, Jackson 4-45, Mili 4-43, Engram 4-39, Alexander 4-19, Rice 3-25, Hannam 1-17, Strong 1-7, Stevens 1-6. New York, Sowell 5-83, Moss 4-79, McCareins 3-40, Jordan 2-18, Baker 1-17, Cotchery 1-15, Askew 1-1.
MISSED FIELD GOAL ATTEMPTS—New York, Brien 30.
INTERCEPTIONS—New York, Barton 1-7.
KICKOFF RETURNS—Seattle, Morris 7-131. New York, Cotchery 2-39, Jordan 1-11.
PUNT RETURNS—New York, McCareins 1-8.
SACKS—New York, Ellis 2, Barton 1, Coleman 1.

EAGLES 12, COWBOYS 7
Sunday, December 19

Dallas	0	7	0	0— 7
Philadelphia	0	6	0	6—12

Second Quarter
Phi.—C. Lewis 2 pass from McNabb (kick blocked), 4:53.
Dal.—K. Johnson 7 pass from Testaverde (Cundiff kick), 11:38.
Fourth Quarter
Phi.—Levens 2 run (pass failed), 13:03.
Attendance—67,723.

	Dallas	Philadelphia
First downs	14	24
Rushes-yards	26-80	28-120
Passing	157	208
Punt returns	1-15	3-35
Kickoff returns	3-55	2-44
Interception returns	2-33	2-40
Comp.-att.-int.	16-28-2	20-35-2
Sacked-yards lost	3-19	2-15
Punts	6-39	5-39
Fumbles-lost	1-0	1-1
Penalties-yards	6-35	5-36
Time of possession	29:28	30:32

INDIVIDUAL STATISTICS
RUSHING—Dallas, J. Jones 25-80, Barnes 1-0. Philadelphia, Westbrook 12-48, Levens 12-43, McNabb 4-29.
PASSING—Dallas, Testaverde 16-28-2-176. Philadelphia, McNabb 20-35-2-223.

RECEIVING—Dallas, Witten 6-66, K. Johnson 5-61, J. Jones 2-21, Morgan 2-19, Anderson 1-9. Philadelphia, Westbrook 8-78, Smith 4-41, Pinkston 2-34, Owens 2-24, C. Lewis 2-20, Levens 1-17, Parry 1-9.
MISSED FIELD GOAL ATTEMPTS—Dallas, Cundiff 46.
INTERCEPTIONS—Dallas, Ro. Williams 1-33, Newman 1-0. Philadelphia, Brown 1-33, Sheppard 1-7.
KICKOFF RETURNS—Dallas, Copper 3-55. Philadelphia, Reed 2-44.
PUNT RETURNS—Dallas, Frazier 1-15. Philadelphia, Wynn 3-35.
SACKS—Dallas, Nguyen 1, Ellis 1. Philadelphia, Brown 1, Reese 1, Simon 1.

CHARGERS 21, BROWNS 0
Sunday, December 19

San Diego	7	7	7	0—21
Cleveland	0	0	0	0— 0

First Quarter
S.D.—Tomlinson 1 run (Kaeding kick), 12:51.
Second Quarter
S.D.—Gates 72 pass from Brees (Kaeding kick), 12:49.
Third Quarter
S.D.—Tomlinson 1 run (Kaeding kick), 6:28.
Attendance—72,489.

	San Diego	Cleveland
First downs	16	11
Rushes-yards	50-174	29-126
Passing	83	105
Punt returns	1-0	2-45
Kickoff returns	0-0	4-56
Interception returns	1-0	0-0
Comp.-att.-int.	4-6-0	11-28-1
Sacked-yards lost	1-2	1-3
Punts	6-39	5-35
Fumbles-lost	1-1	0-0
Penalties-yards	1-8	7-55
Time of possession	33:51	26:09

INDIVIDUAL STATISTICS
RUSHING—San Diego, Tomlinson 26-111, Chatman 14-48, Brees 6-(minus 1), Neal 4-16. Cleveland, Suggs 21-105, Green 5-17, Northcutt 2-0, McCown 1-4.
PASSING—San Diego, Brees 4-6-0-85. Cleveland, McCown 11-27-1-108, Echemandu 0-1-0-0.
RECEIVING—San Diego, E. Parker 2-18, Gates 1-72, Tomlinson 1-(minus 5). Cleveland, Northcutt 4-61, Bryant 3-30, Shea 1-8, F. Jackson 1-6, Heiden 1-5, Suggs 1-(minus 2).
MISSED FIELD GOAL ATTEMPTS—Cleveland, Dawson 39.
INTERCEPTIONS—San Diego, Edwards 1-0.
KICKOFF RETURNS—Cleveland, Alston 3-42, F. Jackson 1-14.
PUNT RETURNS—San Diego, Florence 1-0. Cleveland, Northcutt 2-45.
SACKS—San Diego, Phillips 1. Cleveland, Ekuban 1.

VIKINGS 28, LIONS 27
Sunday, December 19

Minnesota	7	7	0	14—28
Detroit	3	10	0	14—27

First Quarter
Det.—FG, Hanson 32, 6:26.
Min.—Burleson 36 pass from Culpepper (M. Andersen kick), 13:02.
Second Quarter
Min.—Moss 82 pass from Culpepper (M. Andersen kick), 5:07.
Det.—Jones 16 run (Hanson kick), 11:39.
Det.—FG, Hanson 23, 14:30.
Fourth Quarter
Min.—Burleson 37 pass from Culpepper (M. Andersen kick), 6:16.
Det.—Williams 9 pass from Harrington (Streets pass from Harrington), 8:49.
Min.—M. Williams 11 run (M. Andersen kick), 13:23.
Det.—Williams 1 pass from Harrington (run failed), 14:52.
Attendance—62,337.

	Minnesota	Detroit
First downs	21	24
Rushes-yards	23-91	25-113
Passing	370	350
Punt returns	3-27	2-15
Kickoff returns	5-94	4-83
Interception returns	2-14	1-24
Comp.-att.-int.	25-35-1	25-44-2
Sacked-yards lost	5-34	2-11
Punts	5-41	3-45

2004 REVIEW Week 15

	Minnesota	Detroit
Fumbles-lost	1-0	1-1
Penalties-yards	9-70	4-25
Time of possession	30:27	29:33

INDIVIDUAL STATISTICS

RUSHING—Minnesota, M. Bennett 13-51, Culpepper 4-22, O. Smith 4-6, M. Williams 2-12. Detroit, Jones 19-79, Harrington 3-13, Bryson 2-19, Schlesinger 1-2.

PASSING—Minnesota, Culpepper 25-35-1-404. Detroit, Harrington 25-44-2-361.

RECEIVING—Minnesota, Wiggins 6-39, Burleson 5-134, Moss 4-102, M. Bennett 3-51, Berton 3-23, O. Smith 2-18, M. Williams 1-28, M. Robinson 1-9. Detroit, Williams 7-104, Hakim 4-108, Jones 4-35, Streets 4-30, Bryson 3-51, Alexander 2-26, Schlesinger 1-7.

MISSED FIELD GOAL ATTEMPTS—None.

INTERCEPTIONS—Minnesota, B. Williams 1-14, Chavous 1-0. Detroit, Marion 1-24.

KICKOFF RETURNS—Minnesota, Moore 3-59, Campbell 2-35. Detroit, Swinton 4-83.

PUNT RETURNS—Minnesota, Moore 3-27. Detroit, Swinton 2-15.

SACKS—Minnesota, Udeze 1, Newman 1. Detroit, Hall 2, Lehman 1, Edwards 1, Redding 1.

BILLS 33, BENGALS 17
Sunday, December 19

Buffalo	14	13	0	6	33
Cincinnati	7	3	0	7	17

First Quarter
Cin.—Ru. Johnson 3 run (Graham kick), 10:12.
Buf.—Evans 5 pass from Bledsoe (Lindell kick), 10:53.
Buf.—Peters 0 blocked punt return (Lindell kick), 11:23.

Second Quarter
Buf.—Spikes 62 interception return (Lindell kick), 2:24.
Cin.—FG, Graham 24, 8:07.
Buf.—FG, Lindell 23, 13:47.
Buf.—FG, Lindell 39, 15:00.

Fourth Quarter
Buf.—FG, Lindell 21, 2:02.
Buf.—FG, Lindell 33, 9:29.
Cin.—Schobel 4 pass from Kitna (Graham kick), 11:51.
Attendance—65,378.

	Buffalo	Cincinnati
First downs	13	16
Rushes-yards	29-43	31-149
Passing	169	126
Punt returns	4-4	4-21
Kickoff returns	3-81	6-109
Interception returns	2-65	0-0
Comp.-att.-int.	15-30-0	16-32-2
Sacked-yards lost	2-14	3-25
Punts	5-45	6-34
Fumbles-lost	5-1	3-2
Penalties-yards	4-37	7-62
Time of possession	28:57	31:03

INDIVIDUAL STATISTICS

RUSHING—Buffalo, S. Williams 14-30, McGahee 11-25, Bledsoe 2-13, Moorman 1-(minus 11), Evans 1-(minus 14). Cincinnati, Ru. Johnson 23-130, Kitna 4-8, Watson 3-9, C. Johnson 1-2.

PASSING—Buffalo, Bledsoe 15-30-0-183. Cincinnati, Kitna 16-32-2-151.

RECEIVING—Buffalo, Evans 5-101, Moulds 5-47, Reed 2-24, McGahee 2-1, S. Williams 1-10. Cincinnati, Washington 4-60, Houshmandzadeh 4-43, Schobel 3-20, R. Kelly 3-18, C. Johnson 2-10.

MISSED FIELD GOAL ATTEMPTS—None.

INTERCEPTIONS—Buffalo, Spikes 1-62, Kelsay 1-3.

KICKOFF RETURNS—Buffalo, McGee 2-60, Fletcher 1-21. Cincinnati, C. Russell 3-56, Watson 3-53.

PUNT RETURNS—Buffalo, Clements 2-5, S. Williams 1-0, J. Smith 1-(minus 1). Cincinnati, Ratliff 4-21.

SACKS—Buffalo, Fletcher 1, Schobel 1, Adams 1. Cincinnati, Powell 2.

CHIEFS 45, BRONCOS 17
Sunday, December 19

Denver	7	3	0	7	17
Kansas City	14	14	7	10	45

First Quarter
K.C.—Hall 97 kickoff return (Tynes kick), :13.
K.C.—L. Johnson 5 run (Tynes kick), 10:11.
Den.—Smith 22 pass from Plummer (Elam kick), 14:58.

Second Quarter
K.C.—Kennison 7 pass from Green (Tynes kick), 5:24.
K.C.—L. Johnson 32 run (Tynes kick), 10:54.
Den.—FG, Elam 27, 14:56.

Third Quarter
K.C.—Parker 48 pass from Green (Tynes kick), 6:49.

Fourth Quarter
K.C.—Kennison 18 pass from Green (Tynes kick), :47.
K.C.—FG, Tynes 39, 9:29.
Den.—Hearst 4 run (Elam kick), 10:47.
Attendance—77,702.

	Denver	Kansas City
First downs	24	22
Rushes-yards	21-129	36-162
Passing	273	248
Punt returns	1-0	2-30
Kickoff returns	8-155	4-147
Interception returns	0-0	2-23
Comp.-att.-int.	23-41-2	17-23-0
Sacked-yards lost	5-19	3-18
Punts	4-39	4-33
Fumbles-lost	2-1	2-0
Penalties-yards	10-100	6-58
Time of possession	26:49	33:11

INDIVIDUAL STATISTICS

RUSHING—Denver, Bell 9-50, Hearst 5-26, Droughns 4-27, Plummer 3-26, Kansas City, L. Johnson 30-151, Easy 4-1, Hall 1-6, Collins 1-4.

PASSING—Denver, Plummer 23-41-2-292. Kansas City, Green 16-19-0-224, Collins 1-4-0-42.

RECEIVING—Denver, Smith 6-75, Luke 5-40, Lelie 3-37, Putzier 3-30, Droughns 2-14, Bell 1-58, Hearst 1-15, Watts 1-14, Carswell 1-9. Kansas City, Kennison 7-101, Parker 3-84, Gonzalez 3-44, Hall 2-17, Richardson 1-11, Dunn 1-9.

MISSED FIELD GOAL ATTEMPTS—None.

INTERCEPTIONS—Kansas City, McCleon 2-23.

KICKOFF RETURNS—Denver, Luke 8-155. Kansas City, Hall 3-111, Kennison 1-36.

PUNT RETURNS—Denver, Luke 1-0. Kansas City, Hall 2-30.

SACKS—Denver, Williams 1, Wilson 1, Fatafehi 0.5, Coleman 0.5. Kansas City, Mitchell 1, Hicks 1, Dalton 1, Browning 1, Wilkerson 0.5, Stills 0.5.

TEXANS 24, BEARS 5
Sunday, December 19

Houston	0	7	0	17	24
Chicago	0	0	2	3	5

Second Quarter
Hou.—Bradford 37 pass from Carr (K. Brown kick), 14:33.

Third Quarter
Chi.—Safety, 10:54.

Fourth Quarter
Chi.—FG, Edinger 43, :51.
Hou.—FG, K. Brown 20, 3:23.
Hou.—D. Davis 11 run (K. Brown kick), 10:37.
Hou.—Anderson 60 fumble return (K. Brown kick), 12:23.
Attendance—62,122.

	Houston	Chicago
First downs	15	11
Rushes-yards	34-106	26-54
Passing	208	149
Punt returns	5-44	3-3
Kickoff returns	2-23	6-107
Interception returns	2-43	0-0
Comp.-att.-int.	13-29-0	17-35-2
Sacked-yards lost	2-12	2-19
Punts	7-31	7-42
Fumbles-lost	0-0	5-2
Penalties-yards	10-89	5-50
Time of possession	31:34	28:26

INDIVIDUAL STATISTICS

RUSHING—Houston, D. Davis 25-95, Carr 6-8, Wells 3-3. Chicago, T. Jones 15-40, Thomas 6-21, Hutchinson 3-0, Berrian 2-(minus 7).

PASSING—Houston, Carr 13-29-0-220. Chicago, Hutchinson 17-34-1-168, Edinger 0-1-1-0.

RECEIVING—Houston, Gaffney 4-109, D. Davis 4-22, Bradford 3-58, An. Johnson 2-31. Chicago, T. Jones 7-37, Terrell 3-41, Wade 2-23, Thomas 1-19, Gage 1-18, Clark 1-14, Berrian 1-9, McKie 1-7.

MISSED FIELD GOAL ATTEMPTS—Houston, K. Brown 42. Chicago, Edinger 39.

INTERCEPTIONS—Houston, Robinson 1-40, Glenn 1-3.

KICKOFF RETURNS—Houston, Moses 1-19, Gaffney 1-4. Chicago, Azumah
-59, Peterson 2-39, McQuarters 1-9.
PUNT RETURNS—Houston, Moses 4-26, Glenn 1-18. Chicago, McQuarters 3-3.
SACKS—Houston, Robinson 1, Smith 1. Chicago, Hillenmeyer 1, Boone 1.

SAINTS 21, BUCCANEERS 17
Sunday, December 19

ew Orleans	.7	0	0	14—21
ımpa Bay	.7	0	7	3—17

First Quarter
.O.—Stecker 98 kickoff return (Carney kick), :20.
B.—Galloway 3 pass from Griese (Taylor kick), 3:35.

Third Quarter
B.—Galloway 59 punt return (Taylor kick), 6:03.

Fourth Quarter
B.—FG, Taylor 37, 3:43.
.O.—Horn 4 pass from Brooks (Carney kick), 11:27.
.O.—Stallworth 7 pass from Brooks (Carney kick), 14:28.
Attendance—65,075.

	New Orleans	Tampa Bay
ırst downs	15	17
ushes-yards	29-115	34-169
assing	132	114
unt returns	1-53	2-59
ickoff returns	4-148	3-61
nterception returns	1-0	0-0
omp.-att.-int.	14-21-0	13-22-1
acked-yards lost	7-37	1-4
unts	7-42	5-37
umbles-lost	2-1	3-3
enalties-yards	8-69	5-45
ime of possession	30:05	29:55

INDIVIDUAL STATISTICS
RUSHING—New Orleans, McAllister 25-89, Brooks 3-17, Stecker 1-9. Tampa
ay, Pittman 24-131, Graham 3-16, Galloway 2-19, Alstott 2-2, Griese 2-0,
mart 1-1.
PASSING—New Orleans, Brooks 14-21-0-169. Tampa Bay, Griese 13-22-1-118.
RECEIVING—New Orleans, Horn 4-64, Stecker 3-26, Stallworth 2-29, B.
Villiams 2-22, Pathon 1-15, McAllister 1-9, Karney 1-4. Tampa Bay, Clayton 4-
3, Galloway 2-18, Pittman 2-10, Brown 1-17, Moore 1-5, Dilger 1-5, Alstott 1-
, Jurevicius 1-5.
MISSED FIELD GOAL ATTEMPTS—New Orleans, Carney 38.
INTERCEPTIONS—New Orleans, M. McKenzie 1-0.
KICKOFF RETURNS—New Orleans, Stecker 1-98, M. Lewis 1-22, McAfee 1-
6, Whitehead 1-12. Tampa Bay, Smart 2-44, Graham 1-17.
PUNT RETURNS—New Orleans, M. Lewis 1-53. Tampa Bay, Galloway 2-59.
SACKS—New Orleans, Howard 1. Tampa Bay, Rice 3, Spires 1.5, Barber 1,
hanotu 1, D. White 0.5.

CARDINALS 31, RAMS 7
Sunday, December 19

St. Louis	.0	7	0	0— 7
ırizona	.10	7	7	7—31

First Quarter
Ariz.—McCown 1 run (Rackers kick), 9:36.
ıriz.—FG, Rackers 48, 13:16.

Second Quarter
ıriz.—Fitzgerald 8 pass from McCown (Rackers kick), 2:36.
t.L.—Little 61 fumble return (J. Wilkins kick), 14:53.

Third Quarter
Ariz.—Fitzgerald 4 pass from McCown (Rackers kick), 7:58.

Fourth Quarter
Ariz.—McCown 9 run (Rackers kick), 4:06.
Attendance—40,070.

	St. Louis	Arizona
ïrst downs	12	26
₹ushes-yards	10-22	40-131
²assing	163	271
²unt returns	5-28	5-21
(ickoff returns	4-86	2-33
nterception returns	0-0	1-0
℃omp.-att.-int.	17-36-1	22-34-0
§acked-yards lost	4-26	2-16
²unts	9-45	6-50
℉umbles-lost	4-1	2-1
²enalties-yards	9-74	7-67
ℸime of possession	22:31	37:29

INDIVIDUAL STATISTICS
RUSHING—St. Louis, M. Faulk 10-22. Arizona, E. Smith 19-71, McCown 9-
33, Scobey 9-23, O. Ayanbadejo 2-2, Anderson 1-2.
PASSING—St. Louis, J. Martin 16-30-0-188, C. Chandler 1-6-1-1. Arizona,
McCown 22-34-0-287.
RECEIVING—St. Louis, Holt 6-95, Bruce 4-37, Cleeland 2-16, McDonald 2-
14, M. Faulk 1-13, Manumaleuna 1-10, Curtis 1-4. Arizona, Boldin 4-48, O.
Ayanbadejo 4-45, Fitzgerald 4-37, B. Johnson 3-69, Scobey 3-52, E. Smith 2-24,
F. Jones 2-12.
MISSED FIELD GOAL ATTEMPTS—None.
INTERCEPTIONS—Arizona, Macklin 1-0.
KICKOFF RETURNS—St. Louis, Harris 4-86. Arizona, Scobey 1-19, O.
Ayanbadejo 1-14.
PUNT RETURNS—St. Louis, McDonald 5-28. Arizona, Starks 5-21.
SACKS—St. Louis, Hargrove 1, Archuleta 1. Arizona, Dansby 1, Hill 1, Wilson
1, Macklin 0.5, Berry 0.5.

JAGUARS 28, PACKERS 25
Sunday, December 19

Jacksonville	.7	7	7	7—28
Green Bay	.0	10	7	8—25

First Quarter
Jac.—J. Smith 31 pass from Leftwich (Scobee kick), 2:04.

Second Quarter
G.B.—FG, Longwell 35, 1:25.
G.B.—Sharper 15 fumble return (Longwell kick), 10:16.
Jac.—J. Smith 16 pass from Leftwich (Scobee kick), 12:32.

Third Quarter
G.B.—Driver 32 pass from Favre (Longwell kick), 3:16.
Jac.—F. Taylor 37 run (Scobee kick), 4:45.

Fourth Quarter
Jac.—G. Jones 1 run (Scobee kick), 5:11.
G.B.—Chatman 6 pass from Favre (Driver pass from Favre), 13:52.
Attendance—70,437.

	Jacksonville	Green Bay
First downs	19	26
Rushes-yards	36-197	21-94
Passing	115	350
Punt returns	2-20	5-54
Kickoff returns	4-69	5-94
Interception returns	3-0	0-0
Comp.-att.-int.	9-20-0	30-44-3
Sacked-yards lost	1-6	2-17
Punts	7-37	3-38
Fumbles-lost	3-2	4-2
Penalties-yards	7-85	12-101
Time of possession	30:42	29:18

INDIVIDUAL STATISTICS
RUSHING—Jacksonville, F. Taylor 22-165, G. Jones 9-20, Leftwich 3-9, T.
Edwards 1-2, Toefield 1-1. Green Bay, Green 17-94, Davenport 2-1, Favre 2-
(minus 1).
PASSING—Jacksonville, Leftwich 9-20-0-121. Green Bay, Favre 30-44-3-367.
RECEIVING—Jacksonville, J. Smith 4-87, T. Edwards 2-10, R. Williams 1-11,
Yoder 1-10, Brady 1-3. Green Bay, J. Walker 11-152, Driver 4-74, Chatman 4-
48, Ferguson 2-43, Green 2-11, Steele 2-10, Franks 2-10, Fisher 1-10, Luchey
1-9, Henderson 1-0.
MISSED FIELD GOAL ATTEMPTS—Green Bay, Longwell 31.
INTERCEPTIONS—Jacksonville, Mathis 2-0, Grant 1-0.
KICKOFF RETURNS—Jacksonville, G. Jones 3-47, Allen 1-22. Green Bay,
Ferguson 4-78, Davenport 1-16.
PUNT RETURNS—Jacksonville, Allen 2-20. Green Bay, Chatman 5-54.
SACKS—Jacksonville, D. Smith 1, McCray 1. Green Bay, Gbaja-Biamila 1.

RAIDERS 40, TITANS 35
Sunday, December 19

Tennessee	.7	14	0	14—35
Oakland	.14	7	14	5—40

First Quarter
Oak.—T. Johnson 18 pass from Collins (Janikowski kick), 5:48.
Ten.—Bennett 17 pass from Volek (Anderson kick), 11:52.
Oak.—Porter 32 pass from Collins (Janikowski kick), 13:56.

Second Quarter
Ten.—Bennett 23 pass from Volek (Anderson kick), 6:18.
Oak.—Jordan 1 run from Collins (Janikowski kick), 13:05.
Ten.—Troupe 7 pass from Volek (Anderson kick), 13:31.

Third Quarter
Oak.—Gabriel 45 pass from Collins (Janikowski kick), 7:32.
Oak.—Porter 3 pass from Collins (Janikowski kick), 10:30.

Fourth Quarter
Ten.—Mason 3 pass from Volek (Anderson kick), 3:07.
Oak.—FG, Janikowski 42, 11:21.
Ten.—Volek 1 run (Anderson kick), 13:39.
Oak.—Safety, 14:52.
Attendance—44,299.

	Tennessee	Oakland
First downs	31	20
Rushes-yards	19-61	22-57
Passing	466	358
Punt returns	4-37	1-(-2)
Kickoff returns	5-152	5-70
Interception returns	1-0	1-45
Comp.-att.-int.	40-61-1	21-37-1
Sacked-yards lost	3-26	2-13
Punts	4-41	6-50
Fumbles-lost	1-1	0-0
Penalties-yards	5-47	5-39
Time of possession	35:03	24:57

INDIVIDUAL STATISTICS
RUSHING—Tennessee, A. Smith 16-45, Fleming 2-15, Volek 1-1. Oakland, Crockett 8-27, Fargas 7-17, Collins 4-10, Redmond 2-(minus 1), Zereoue 1-4.
PASSING—Tennessee, Volek 40-60-1-492, Hentrich 0-1-0-0. Oakland, Collins 21-37-1-371.
RECEIVING—Tennessee, Bennett 13-160, Mason 9-121, Troupe 6-75, A. Smith 4-38, Berlin 3-69, Fleming 2-21, Meier 2-2, Holcombe 1-6. Oakland, Porter 8-148, T. Johnson 3-49, Whitted 2-61, Gabriel 2-52, Zereoue 2-11, Fargas 1-21, Hetherington 1-14, Crockett 1-11, Jolley 1-4.
MISSED FIELD GOAL ATTEMPTS—Tennessee, Anderson 41.
INTERCEPTIONS—Tennessee, Bulluck 1-0. Oakland, D. Walker 1-45.
KICKOFF RETURNS—Tennessee, McAddley 5-152. Oakland, Gabriel 3-36, Redmond 2-34.
PUNT RETURNS—Tennessee, Berlin 3-20, Mason 1-(minus 1). Oakland, Buchanon 1-(minus 2).
SACKS—Tennessee, Long 2. Oakland, Clark 1, Sapp 1, Kelly 1.

COLTS 20, RAVENS 10
Sunday, December 19

Baltimore	0	3	0	7—10
Indianapolis	3	3	14	0—20

First Quarter
Ind.—FG, Vanderjagt 24, 3:43.

Second Quarter
Bal.—FG, Stover 42, 1:56.
Ind.—FG, Vanderjagt 33, 14:59.

Third Quarter
Ind.—Harrison 29 pass from Manning (Vanderjagt kick), 9:06.
Ind.—James 3 run (Vanderjagt kick), 14:32.

Fourth Quarter
Bal.—Heap 13 pass from Boller (Stover kick), 2:10.
Attendance—57,240.

	Baltimore	Indianapolis
First downs	19	17
Rushes-yards	29-160	24-67
Passing	194	249
Punt returns	3-27	1-14
Kickoff returns	5-129	2-51
Interception returns	0-0	2-103
Comp.-att.-int.	19-40-2	20-33-0
Sacked-yards lost	2-16	0-0
Punts	5-39	6-49
Fumbles-lost	1-0	1-0
Penalties-yards	7-35	5-28
Time of possession	31:22	28:38

INDIVIDUAL STATISTICS
RUSHING—Baltimore, J. Lewis 20-130, C. Taylor 7-22, J. White 1-6, Bolle 1-2. Indianapolis, James 22-69, Manning 2-(minus 2).
PASSING—Baltimore, Boller 19-40-2-210. Indianapolis, Manning 20-33-0-249
RECEIVING—Baltimore, Heap 4-58, K. Johnson 4-33, T. Taylor 2-39, C. Taylc 2-20, J. Lewis 2-17, Moore 1-17, Dinkins 1-10, T. Jones 1-7, J. White 1-€ Ricard 1-3. Indianapolis, Wayne 8-88, Harrison 5-73, Stokley 3-18, Pollard 2-34 James 1-23, Clark 1-13.
MISSED FIELD GOAL ATTEMPTS—Baltimore, Stover 31. Indianapolis Vanderjagt 33.
INTERCEPTIONS—Indianapolis, June 1-71, Doss 1-32.
KICKOFF RETURNS—Baltimore, Sams 4-123, J. Johnson 1-6. Indianapolis Rhodes 2-51.
PUNT RETURNS—Baltimore, Sams 3-27. Indianapolis, Walters 1-14.
SACKS—Indianapolis, Freeney 2.

DOLPHINS 29, PATRIOTS 28
Monday, December 20

New England	7	7	7	7—28
Miami	7	3	7	12—29

First Quarter
N.E.—Faulk 31 pass from Brady (Vinatieri kick), 5:01.
Mia.—Morris 2 run (Mare kick), 8:30.

Second Quarter
N.E.—Dillon 3 run (Vinatieri kick), 7:59.
Mia.—FG, Mare 30, 13:08.

Third Quarter
Mia.—Minor 1 run (Mare kick), 8:10.
N.E.—Dillon 2 pass from Brady (Vinatieri kick), 12:53.

Fourth Quarter
N.E.—Graham 2 pass from Brady (Vinatieri kick), 11:01.
Mia.—Morris 1 run (pass failed), 12:53.
Mia.—Thompson 21 pass from Feeley (pass failed), 13:37.
Attendance—73,629.

	New England	Miami
First downs	24	18
Rushes-yards	38-166	20-52
Passing	156	179
Punt returns	2-17	2-87
Kickoff returns	6-111	5-139
Interception returns	0-0	4-48
Comp.-att.-int.	18-29-4	22-35-0
Sacked-yards lost	2-15	4-19
Punts	4-43	6-46
Fumbles-lost	0-0	3-1
Penalties-yards	4-53	9-67
Time of possession	35:06	24:54

INDIVIDUAL STATISTICS
RUSHING—New England, Dillon 26-121, Faulk 6-39, Pass 4-8, Brady 2- (minus 2). Miami, Morris 9-27, Minor 8-27, Feeley 2-(minus 2), Chambers 1-0.
PASSING—New England, Brady 18-29-4-171. Miami, Feeley 22-35-0-198.
RECEIVING—New England, Patten 4-40, Branch 3-44, Graham 3-24, Pass 3-17, Dillon 2-1, Faulk 1-31, Fauria 1-8, T. Brown 1-6. Miami, Morris 6-46, Booker 4-35, McMichael 4-29, Chambers 3-24, Thompson 2-31, Gilmore 2-24, Lee 1-9.
MISSED FIELD GOAL ATTEMPTS—None.
INTERCEPTIONS—Miami, S. Knight 2-32, Freeman 1-14, B. Ayanbadejo 1-2.
KICKOFF RETURNS—New England, Faulk 4-73, Pass 1-22, Patten 1-16. Miami, Welker 5-139.
PUNT RETURNS—New England, Faulk 2-17. Miami, Welker 2-87.
SACKS—New England, McGinest 1, Seymour 1, J. Green 1, Phifer 0.5, Vrabel 0.5. Miami, Taylor 1, D. Bowens 1.

WEEK 16

STANDINGS

AMERICAN FOOTBALL CONFERENCE

EAST DIVISION
	W	L	T	Pct.	PF	PA
New England	13	2	0	.867	416	253
N.Y. Jets	10	5	0	.667	304	229
Buffalo	9	6	0	.600	371	255
Miami	4	11	0	.267	252	324

NORTH DIVISION
	W	L	T	Pct.	PF	PA
Pittsburgh	14	1	0	.933	343	227
Baltimore	8	7	0	.533	287	245
Cincinnati	7	8	0	.467	336	362
Cleveland	3	12	0	.200	254	376

SOUTH DIVISION
	W	L	T	Pct.	PF	PA
Indianapolis	12	3	0	.800	508	318
Jacksonville	8	7	0	.533	248	274
Houston	7	8	0	.467	295	317
Tennessee	4	11	0	.267	320	420

WEST DIVISION
	W	L	T	Pct.	PF	PA
San Diego	11	4	0	.733	422	296
Denver	9	6	0	.600	348	290
Kansas City	7	8	0	.467	466	411
Oakland	5	10	0	.333	314	429

NATIONAL FOOTBALL CONFERENCE

EAST DIVISION
	W	L	T	Pct.	PF	PA
Philadelphia	13	2	0	.867	376	222
Dallas	6	9	0	.400	269	377
N.Y. Giants	5	10	0	.333	275	323
Washington	5	10	0	.333	219	247

NORTH DIVISION
	W	L	T	Pct.	PF	PA
Green Bay	9	6	0	.600	393	366
Minnesota	8	7	0	.533	387	374
Detroit	6	9	0	.400	277	326
Chicago	5	10	0	.333	217	300

SOUTH DIVISION
	W	L	T	Pct.	PF	PA
Atlanta	11	4	0	.733	314	309
Carolina	7	8	0	.467	337	318
New Orleans	7	8	0	.467	327	387
Tampa Bay	5	10	0	.333	294	292

WEST DIVISION
	W	L	T	Pct.	PF	PA
Seattle	8	7	0	.533	343	347
St. Louis	7	8	0	.467	287	363
Arizona	5	10	0	.333	272	315
San Francisco	2	13	0	.133	252	431

TOP PERFORMANCES

100-YARD RUSHING GAMES
Player, Team & Opponent	Att.	Yds.	TD
Domanick Davis, Hou. at Jac.	31	158	1
Shaun Alexander, Sea. vs. Ariz.	30	154	3
Steven Jackson, St.L. vs. Phi.	24	148	1
Lee Suggs, Cle. at Mia.	38	143	0
Deuce McAllister, N.O. vs. Atl.	29	128	0
Nick Goings, Car. at T.B.	33	127	0
Kevin Jones, Det. vs. Chi.	25	123	1
Jerome Bettis, Pit. vs. Bal.	27	117	0
Tiki Barber, NYG at Cin.	22	109	1
Thomas Jones, Chi. at Det.	22	109	0
Willis McGahee, Buf. at S.F.	15	102	2

300-YARD PASSING GAMES
Player, Team & Opponent	Att.	Cmp.	Yds.	TD	Int.
Peyton Manning, Ind. vs. S.D.*	44	27	383	2	1
Brett Favre, G.B. at Min.	43	30	365	3	1
Trent Green, K.C. vs. Oak.	45	32	358	2	1
Brian Griese, T.B. vs. Car.	41	30	321	3	2
Jake Plummer, Den. at Ten.	26	21	303	2	1

100-YARD RECEIVING GAMES
Player, Team & Opponent	Rec.	Yds.	TD
Donald Driver, G.B. at Min.	11	162	1
Tony Gonzalez, K.C. vs. Oak.	11	124	2
Brandon Stokley, Ind. vs. S.D.*	7	123	1
Muhsin Muhammad, Car. at T.B.	8	115	2
Dennis Northcutt, Cle. at Mia.	4	114	1
Marvin Harrison, Ind. vs. S.D.*	6	111	0
Nate Burleson, Min. vs. G.B.	2	110	1
Anquan Boldin, Ariz. at Sea.	7	107	1
Eric Parker, S.D. at Ind.*	7	103	1
Darrell Jackson, Sea. vs. Ariz.	6	101	0
*Overtime game.			

RESULTS

FRIDAY, DECEMBER 24
Green Bay 34, MINNESOTA 31

SATURDAY, DECEMBER 25
KANSAS CITY 31, Oakland 30
Denver 37, TENNESSEE 16

SUNDAY, DECEMBER 26
PITTSBURGH 20, Baltimore 7
Houston 21, JACKSONVILLE 0
DETROIT 19, Chicago 13
CINCINNATI 23, N.Y. Giants 22
NEW ORLEANS 26, Atlanta 13
INDIANAPOLIS 34, San Diego 31 (OT)
New England 23, N.Y. JETS 7
Buffalo 41, SAN FRANCISCO 7
DALLAS 13, Washington 10
Carolina 37, TAMPA BAY 20
SEATTLE 24, Arizona 21
MIAMI 10, Cleveland 7

MONDAY, DECEMBER 27
ST. LOUIS 20, Philadelphia 7

PACKERS 34, VIKINGS 31
Friday, December 24

Green Bay	0	17	7	10—34
Minnesota	0	21	0	10—31

Second Quarter
Min.—Moss 12 pass from Culpepper (M. Andersen kick), :11.
G.B.—Green 1 run (Longwell kick), 8:23.
Min.—Burleson 68 pass from Culpepper (M. Andersen kick), 8:45.
G.B.—Franks 22 pass from Favre (Longwell kick), 13:43.
Min.—M. Bennett 38 pass from Culpepper (M. Andersen kick), 14:02.
G.B.—FG, Longwell 42, 15:00.

Third Quarter
G.B.—J. Walker 9 pass from Favre (Longwell kick), 7:19.

Fourth Quarter
Min.—FG, M. Andersen 29, :03.
Min.—Claiborne 15 interception return (M. Andersen kick), 6:42.
G.B.—Driver 3 pass from Favre (Longwell kick), 11:26.
G.B.—FG, Longwell 29, 15:00.
Attendance—64,311.

	Green Bay	Minnesota
First downs	26	17
Rushes-yards	34-102	24-131
Passing	358	285
Punt returns	1-7	3-3
Kickoff returns	5-150	5-152
Interception returns	0-0	1-15
Comp.-att.-int.	30-43-1	16-23-0
Sacked-yards lost	1-7	0-0
Punts	3-44	4-39
Fumbles-lost	1-0	0-0
Penalties-yards	4-25	9-78
Time of possession	34:13	25:47

INDIVIDUAL STATISTICS
RUSHING—Green Bay, Green 19-64, Davenport 11-40, Favre 3-(minus 4), Fisher 1-2. Minnesota, M. Bennett 17-92, Culpepper 3-21, Burleson 2-11, M. Williams 1-4, Moore 1-3.
PASSING—Green Bay, Favre 30-43-1-365. Minnesota, Culpepper 16-23-0-285.
RECEIVING—Green Bay, Driver 11-162, J. Walker 5-90, Fisher 4-31, Green 4-26, Chatman 2-19, Thurman 2-12, Franks 1-22, Henderson 1-3. Minnesota, Wiggins 4-37, M. Bennett 3-67, Berton 3-24, Burleson 2-110, Moss 2-30, M. Williams 1-14, M. Robinson 1-3.
MISSED FIELD GOAL ATTEMPTS—None.
INTERCEPTIONS—Minnesota, Claiborne 1-15.
KICKOFF RETURNS—Green Bay, Chatman 4-137, Davenport 1-13. Minnesota, Campbell 3-110, Moore 2-42.
PUNT RETURNS—Green Bay, Chatman 1-7. Minnesota, Burleson 3-3.
SACKS—Minnesota, Johnstone 1.

CHIEFS 31, RAIDERS 30
Saturday, December 25

Oakland	7	14	3	6—30
Kansas City	7	14	0	10—31

First Quarter
Oak.—Porter 5 pass from Collins (Janikowski kick), 1:35.
K.C.—L. Johnson 6 run (Tynes kick), 12:46.

Second Quarter
Oak.—Crockett 3 run (Janikowski kick), 3:20.
K.C.—Gonzalez 2 pass from Green (Tynes kick), 8:16.
K.C.—Gonzalez 26 pass from Green (Tynes kick), 13:06.
Oak.—Whitted 32 pass from Collins (Janikowski kick), 14:36.

Third Quarter
Oak.—FG, Janikowski 40, 14:51.

Fourth Quarter
K.C.—L. Johnson 4 run (Tynes kick), 8:49.
Oak.—FG, Janikowski 45, 11:11.
Oak.—FG, Janikowski 46, 13:57.
K.C.—FG, Tynes 38, 14:38.
Attendance—77,289.

	Oakland	Kansas City
First downs	18	32
Rushes-yards	22-100	29-99
Passing	200	334
Punt returns	1-7	2-5
Kickoff returns	6-146	6-175
Interception returns	1-24	1-0
Comp.-att.-int.	18-37-1	32-45-1
Sacked-yards lost	2-17	4-24
Punts	5-43	2-56
Fumbles-lost	0-0	1-1
Penalties-yards	12-90	7-52
Time of possession	25:14	34:46

INDIVIDUAL STATISTICS
RUSHING—Oakland, Crockett 10-32, Fargas 6-38, Zereoue 4-14, Redmond 2-16. Kansas City, L. Johnson 25-79, Green 2-15, Richardson 2-8.
PASSING—Oakland, Collins 18-37-1-217. Kansas City, Green 32-45-1-358.
RECEIVING—Oakland, Porter 4-57, Zereoue 4-38, T. Johnson 3-52 Redmond 3-23, Whitted 1-32, Gabriel 1-11, Jolley 1-5, Fargas 1-(minus 4) Kansas City, Gonzalez 11-124, Kennison 6-79, L. Johnson 4-43, Horn 4-43 Parker 3-35, Hall 2-14, Dunn 1-13, Richardson 1-7.
MISSED FIELD GOAL ATTEMPTS—Kansas City, Tynes 43, 50.
INTERCEPTIONS—Oakland, Brayton 1-24. Kansas City, Sapp 1-0.
KICKOFF RETURNS—Oakland, Gabriel 5-123, Hetherington 1-23. Kansas City, Hall 6-175.
PUNT RETURNS—Oakland, Gabriel 1-7. Kansas City, Hall 2-5.
SACKS—Oakland, Irons 1, Washington 1, Sapp 1, Asomugha 0.5, Hamilton 0.5. Kansas City, Beisel 1, Allen 1.

BRONCOS 37, TITANS 16
Saturday, December 25

Denver	17	7	3	10—37
Tennessee	10	6	0	0—16

First Quarter
Den.—Droughns 23 pass from Plummer (Elam kick), 2:57.
Den.—FG, Elam 22, 6:18.
Ten.—FG, Anderson 44, 8:15.
Den.—Droughns 8 run (Elam kick), 10:34.
Ten.—A. Smith 13 run (Anderson kick), 13:15.

Second Quarter
Den.—Smith 7 pass from Plummer (Elam kick), 11:04.
Ten.—FG, Anderson 43, 14:17.
Ten.—FG, Hentrich 50, 15:00.

Third Quarter
Den.—FG, Elam 22, 11:10.

Fourth Quarter
Den.—FG, Elam 30, 3:41.
Den.—Droughns 23 run (Elam kick), 8:05.
Attendance—68,809.

	Denver	Tennessee
First downs	26	10
Rushes-yards	46-193	14-59
Passing	303	94
Punt returns	2-6	0-0
Kickoff returns	4-96	8-154
Interception returns	2-25	1-25
Comp.-att.-int.	21-26-1	12-27-2
Sacked-yards lost	0-0	6-43
Punts	2-44	6-40
Fumbles-lost	1-1	1-0
Penalties-yards	2-45	3-16
Time of possession	39:24	20:36

INDIVIDUAL STATISTICS
RUSHING—Denver, Droughns 22-91, Bell 12-44, Plummer 7-28, Hearst 4-22, Smith 1-8. Tennessee, A. Smith 14-59.
PASSING—Denver, Plummer 21-26-1-303. Tennessee, Volek 8-20-2-111, D. Johnson 4-7-0-26.
RECEIVING—Denver, Smith 6-58, Putzier 4-60, Lelie 3-88, Droughns 2-30, Watts 2-29, Hape 2-12, Carswell 1-14, Bell 1-12. Tennessee, Mason 4-65, Troupe 3-24, Bennett 2-26, Berlin 2-19, A. Smith 1-3.
MISSED FIELD GOAL ATTEMPTS—Denver, Elam 34.
INTERCEPTIONS—Denver, K. Herndon 1-15, Williams 1-10. Tennessee, Bulluck 1-25.
KICKOFF RETURNS—Denver, Luke 4-96. Tennessee, McAddley 8-154.
PUNT RETURNS—Denver, Luke 2-6.
SACKS—Denver, Hayward 3, Palepoi 1, E. Johnson 1, Wilson 0.5, Fatafehi 0.5.

STEELERS 20, RAVENS 7

Sunday, December 26

Baltimore	7	0	0	0— 7
Pittsburgh	7	3	7	3—20

First Quarter
Pit.—Burress 36 pass from Roethlisberger (Reed kick), 4:36.
Bal.—J. Lewis 5 run (Stover kick), 10:33.

Second Quarter
Pit.—FG, Reed 23, 1:58.

Third Quarter
Pit.—Tuman 2 pass from Roethlisberger (Reed kick), 8:34.

Fourth Quarter
Pit.—FG, Reed 40, 2:07.
Attendance—64,227.

	Baltimore	Pittsburgh
First downs	16	20
Rushes-yards	21-71	42-183
Passing	177	221
Punt returns	0-0	0-0
Kickoff returns	4-82	2-35
Interception returns	1-0	1-3
Comp.-att.-int.	18-32-1	15-20-1
Sacked-yards lost	0-0	0-0
Punts	3-38	0-0
Fumbles-lost	0-0	1-1
Penalties-yards	3-30	3-25
Time of possession	26:07	33:53

INDIVIDUAL STATISTICS
RUSHING—Baltimore, J. Lewis 14-26, Boller 4-28, C. Taylor 3-17. Pittsburgh, Bettis 27-117, Haynes 8-61, Maddox 4-(minus 1), Roethlisberger 2-11, Ward 1-(minus 5).
PASSING—Baltimore, Boller 18-32-1-177. Pittsburgh, Roethlisberger 14-19-1-221, Maddox 1-1-0-0.
RECEIVING—Baltimore, Hymes 4-55, Heap 3-34, T. Jones 3-24, J. Lewis 2-16, C. Taylor 2-16, Ricard 2-13, K. Johnson 1-14, Dinkins 1-5. Pittsburgh, Burress 3-97, Randle El 3-55, Ward 3-21, Tuman 2-26, Bettis 2-13, Kreider 1-9, Haynes 1-0.
MISSED FIELD GOAL ATTEMPTS—Baltimore, Stover 44.
INTERCEPTIONS—Baltimore, Demps 1-0. Pittsburgh, Porter 1-3.
KICKOFF RETURNS—Baltimore, Sams 3-75, Dinkins 1-7. Pittsburgh, Colclough 1-25, I. Taylor 1-10.
PUNT RETURNS—None.
SACKS—None.

TEXANS 21, JAGUARS 0

Sunday, December 26

Houston	7	7	0	7—21
Jacksonville	0	0	0	0— 0

First Quarter
Hou.—D. Davis 1 run (K. Brown kick), 6:27.

Second Quarter
Hou.—An. Johnson 10 pass from Carr (K. Brown kick), 8:14.

Fourth Quarter
Hou.—Peek 66 fumble return (K. Brown kick), 11:49.
Attendance—66,227.

	Houston	Jacksonville
First downs	19	6
Rushes-yards	44-219	20-95
Passing	114	31
Punt returns	3-4	2-21
Kickoff returns	1-27	3-64
Interception returns	1-0	2-4
Comp.-att.-int.	13-19-2	10-21-1
Sacked-yards lost	4-17	3-23
Punts	5-44	7-45
Fumbles-lost	2-0	3-2
Penalties-yards	6-50	5-45
Time of possession	38:58	21:02

INDIVIDUAL STATISTICS
RUSHING—Houston, D. Davis 31-158, Carr 8-27, Wells 5-34. Jacksonville, G. Jones 9-38, Fuamatu-Ma'afala 4-25, Leftwich 4-19, Toefield 3-13.
PASSING—Houston, Carr 13-19-2-131. Jacksonville, Leftwich 6-14-1-35, Garrard 4-7-0-19.

RECEIVING—Houston, An. Johnson 4-46, D. Davis 4-31, Gaffney 3-39, Armstrong 1-8, Miller 1-7. Jacksonville, T. Edwards 3-24, J. Smith 2-17, Toefield 2-(minus 5), Wilford 1-9, Allen 1-5, Brady 1-4.
MISSED FIELD GOAL ATTEMPTS—Houston, K. Brown 34. Jacksonville, Scobee 31.
INTERCEPTIONS—Houston, Wong 1-0. Jacksonville, Grant 1-4, Washington 1-0.
KICKOFF RETURNS—Houston, Gaffney 1-27. Jacksonville, Allen 2-45, Toefield 1-19.
PUNT RETURNS—Houston, Glenn 3-4. Jacksonville, Allen 2-21.
SACKS—Houston, Wong 1, Babin 1, Team 1. Jacksonville, Peterson 1, Henderson 1, Favors 1, Stroud 0.5, McCray 0.5.

LIONS 19, BEARS 13

Sunday, December 26

Chicago	0	0	6	7—13
Detroit	3	13	0	3—19

First Quarter
Det.—FG, Hanson 31, 11:54.

Second Quarter
Det.—Jones 1 run (Hanson kick), 3:30.
Det.—FG, Hanson 39, 9:10.
Det.—FG, Hanson 34, 15:00.

Third Quarter
Chi.—Briggs 38 interception return (pass failed), 11:20.

Fourth Quarter
Det.—FG, Hanson 40, 3:31.
Chi.—McKie 15 pass from Hutchinson (Edinger kick), 7:56.
Attendance—61,924.

	Chicago	Detroit
First downs	16	17
Rushes-yards	25-124	32-158
Passing	105	156
Punt returns	2-11	5-18
Kickoff returns	3-51	3-87
Interception returns	1-38	0-0
Comp.-att.-int.	20-35-0	15-30-1
Sacked-yards lost	2-9	2-10
Punts	8-43	6-42
Fumbles-lost	1-1	1-0
Penalties-yards	8-55	6-47
Time of possession	28:38	31:22

INDIVIDUAL STATISTICS
RUSHING—Chicago, T. Jones 22-109, Peterson 2-4, Wade 1-11. Detroit, Jones 25-123, Harrington 5-26, Bryson 2-9.
PASSING—Chicago, Hutchinson 20-35-0-114. Detroit, Harrington 15-30-1-166.
RECEIVING—Chicago, McKie 5-21, T. Jones 4-34, Wade 4-27, Clark 2-12, Terrell 2-10, Lyman 1-7, Berrian 1-5, Peterson 1-0. Detroit, Bryson 4-24, Williams 3-33, Swinton 2-42, Hakim 2-16, FitzSimmons 1-27, Alexander 1-13, Jones 1-8, Streets 1-3.
MISSED FIELD GOAL ATTEMPTS—None.
INTERCEPTIONS—Chicago, Briggs 1-38.
KICKOFF RETURNS—Chicago, Azumah 3-51. Detroit, Swinton 2-64, Schlesinger 1-23.
PUNT RETURNS—Chicago, McQuarters 2-11. Detroit, Swinton 5-18.
SACKS—Chicago, Scott 1, Green 0.5, Briggs 0.5. Detroit, DeVries 1, Redding 1.

BENGALS 23, GIANTS 22

Sunday, December 26

N.Y. Giants	0	13	3	6—22
Cincinnati	7	3	7	6—23

First Quarter
Cin.—C. Johnson 5 pass from Kitna (Graham kick), 9:34.

Second Quarter
NYG—Barber 1 run (Christie kick), 2:11.
Cin.—FG, Graham 42, 5:14.
NYG—FG, Christie 31, 9:38.
NYG—FG, Christie 36, 15:00.

Third Quarter
NYG—FG, Christie 44, 7:24.
Cin.—Ru. Johnson 1 run (Graham kick), 13:39.

Fourth Quarter
NYG—FG, Christie 41, 2:22.
NYG—FG, Christie 28, 9:45.
Cin.—C. Johnson 4 pass from Kitna (pass failed), 14:16.
Attendance—64,606.

	N.Y. Giants	Cincinnati
First downs	18	16
Rushes-yards	28-142	25-63
Passing	184	170
Punt returns	2-3	3-61
Kickoff returns	5-121	6-132
Interception returns	1-10	1-(-2)
Comp.-att.-int.	19-37-1	20-32-1
Sacked-yards lost	2-17	3-16
Punts	4-38	3-47
Fumbles-lost	1-0	3-1
Penalties-yards	9-85	3-20
Time of possession	30:46	29:14

INDIVIDUAL STATISTICS

RUSHING—New York, Barber 22-109, Dayne 6-33. Cincinnati, Ru. Johnson 19-31, Kitna 2-14, Watson 2-7, Houshmandzadeh 1-7, J. Johnson 1-4.

PASSING—New York, Manning 19-37-1-201. Cincinnati, Kitna 20-32-1-186.

RECEIVING—New York, Shockey 6-64, I. Hilliard 4-46, Toomer 3-35, Tyree 2-35, Barber 2-14, Finn 2-7. Cincinnati, C. Johnson 8-46, Houshmandzadeh 5-64, Ru. Johnson 2-13, Watson 1-21, Schobel 1-13, Washington 1-13, Walter 1-10, J. Johnson 1-6.

MISSED FIELD GOAL ATTEMPTS—None.

INTERCEPTIONS—New York, F. Walker 1-10. Cincinnati, Powell 1-(minus 2).

KICKOFF RETURNS—New York, Ponder 5-121. Cincinnati, C. Russell 4-113, R. Kelly 1-14, Stewart 1-5.

PUNT RETURNS—New York, I. Hilliard 2-3. Cincinnati, Ratliff 3-61.

SACKS—New York, Torbor 1.5, Greisen 1, Robbins 0.5. Cincinnati, M. Williams 1, J. Smith 1.

SAINTS 26, FALCONS 13
Sunday, December 26

Atlanta	0	6	7	0—13
New Orleans	5	7	14	0—26

First Quarter
N.O.—Safety, 9:00.
N.O.—FG, Carney 22, 14:49.

Second Quarter
Atl.—FG, Feely 25, 1:42.
Atl.—FG, Feely 20, 5:20.
N.O.—Brooks 1 run (Carney kick), 11:35.

Third Quarter
N.O.—Stallworth 39 pass from Brooks (Carney kick), 3:08.
Atl.—Dunn 16 run (Feely kick), 9:15.
N.O.—M. Lewis 96 kickoff return (Carney kick), 9:28.
Attendance—64,900.

	Atlanta	New Orleans
First downs	15	17
Rushes-yards	24-93	40-160
Passing	174	209
Punt returns	1-10	5-40
Kickoff returns	5-110	4-144
Interception returns	2-27	2-0
Comp.-att.-int.	17-41-2	12-24-2
Sacked-yards lost	3-14	4-18
Punts	6-43	7-44
Fumbles-lost	2-1	0-0
Penalties-yards	6-35	10-73
Time of possession	26:55	33:05

INDIVIDUAL STATISTICS

RUSHING—Atlanta, Dunn 18-52, Schaub 4-21, Layne 1-12, Wright 1-8. New Orleans, McAllister 29-128, Stecker 5-20, Brooks 5-12, Stallworth 1-0.

PASSING—Atlanta, Schaub 17-41-2-188. New Orleans, Brooks 12-24-2-227.

RECEIVING—Atlanta, Dunn 6-87, P. Price 6-49, Finneran 3-38, Blakley 1-12, White 1-2. New Orleans, Horn 5-76, Pathon 3-49, Stallworth 2-62, B. Williams 1-21, Conwell 1-19.

MISSED FIELD GOAL ATTEMPTS—None.

INTERCEPTIONS—Atlanta, Brooking 1-27, Beasley 1-0. New Orleans, M. McKenzie 2-0.

KICKOFF RETURNS—Atlanta, Rossum 5-110. New Orleans, M. Lewis 3-122, McAfee 1-22.

PUNT RETURNS—Atlanta, Rossum 1-10. New Orleans, M. Lewis 5-40.

SACKS—Atlanta, T. Hall 2, Kerney 1, Scott 0.5, Williams 0.5. New Orleans, Young 1, Howard 1, Bryant 1.

COLTS 34, CHARGERS 31
Sunday, December 26

San Diego	7	10	7	7	0—31	
Indianapolis	0	9	7	15	3—34	

First Quarter
S.D.—Tomlinson 74 pass from Brees (Kaeding kick), 10:12.

Second Quarter
Ind.—FG, Vanderjagt 36, :42.
S.D.—FG, Kaeding 50, 2:14.
S.D.—E. Parker 19 pass from Brees (Kaeding kick), 7:51.
Ind.—FG, Vanderjagt 26, 10:30.
Ind.—FG, Vanderjagt 23, 14:42.

Third Quarter
S.D.—Gates 4 pass from Brees (Kaeding kick), 5:36.
Ind.—Mungro 3 run from Manning (Vanderjagt kick), 8:49.

Fourth Quarter
S.D.—Tomlinson 16 run (Kaeding kick), :05.
Ind.—Rhodes 88 kickoff return (Vanderjagt kick), :18.
Ind.—Stokley 21 pass from Manning (James run), 14:04.

Overtime
Ind.—FG, Vanderjagt 30, 2:47.
Attendance—57,330.

	San Diego	Indianapolis
First downs	22	30
Rushes-yards	29-93	25-104
Passing	281	360
Punt returns	2-26	1-7
Kickoff returns	6-122	7-252
Interception returns	1-4	1-17
Comp.-att.-int.	21-31-1	27-44-1
Sacked-yards lost	1-9	4-23
Punts	4-50	2-49
Fumbles-lost	1-0	3-0
Penalties-yards	7-63	10-70
Time of possession	31:13	31:34

INDIVIDUAL STATISTICS

RUSHING—San Diego, Tomlinson 21-81, Brees 6-12, Chatman 2-0. Indianapolis, James 22-86, Rhodes 2-19, Manning 1-(minus 1).

PASSING—San Diego, Brees 21-31-1-290. Indianapolis, Manning 27-44-1-383.

RECEIVING—San Diego, E. Parker 7-103, Gates 7-49, Tomlinson 5-95, Osgood 2-43. Indianapolis, Stokley 7-123, Harrison 6-111, James 5-41, Wayne 3-61, Clark 3-23, Hartsock 2-21, Mungro 1-3.

MISSED FIELD GOAL ATTEMPTS—Indianapolis, Vanderjagt 47.

INTERCEPTIONS—San Diego, Edwards 1-2. Indianapolis, Morris 1-17.

KICKOFF RETURNS—San Diego, Dwight 5-104, Turner 1-18. Indianapolis, Rhodes 6-236, Walters 1-16.

PUNT RETURNS—San Diego, E. Parker 2-26. Indianapolis, Walters 1-7.

SACKS—San Diego, Foley 3, Edwards 1. Indianapolis, Freeney 1.

PATRIOTS 23, JETS 7
Sunday, December 26

New England	0	13	3	7—23	
N.Y. Jets	0	0	0	7— 7	

Second Quarter
N.E.—FG, Vinatieri 28, 7:13.
N.E.—Graham 16 pass from Brady (Vinatieri kick), 13:10.
N.E.—FG, Vinatieri 29, 14:53.

Third Quarter
N.E.—FG, Vinatieri 26, 14:23.

Fourth Quarter
N.E.—Branch 6 pass from Brady (Vinatieri kick), 2:24.
NYJ—Moss 15 pass from Pennington (Brien kick), 5:28.
Attendance—77,975.

	New England	N.Y. Jets
First downs	21	17
Rushes-yards	38-114	18-46
Passing	258	233
Punt returns	3-23	3-18
Kickoff returns	2-38	5-97
Interception returns	2-60	0-0

	New England	N.Y. Jets
omp.-att.-int.	21-32-0	22-36-2
Sacked-yards lost	1-6	3-19
Punts	4-37	5-31
Fumbles-lost	2-0	2-1
Penalties-yards	3-25	4-20
Time of possession	35:48	24:12

INDIVIDUAL STATISTICS

RUSHING—New England, Dillon 29-89,'Pass 4-17, Brady 4-3, Abdullah 1-5. New York, C. Martin 13-33, Pennington 3-7, Jordan 2-6.

PASSING—New England, Brady 21-32-0-264. New York, Pennington 22-36-2-252.

RECEIVING—New England, Branch 7-82, Pass 5-32, Fauria 3-44, Givens 2-34, Graham 2-30, Dillon 2-12. New York, McCareins 5-76, C. Martin 5-44, Chrebet 4-51, Jordan 3-16, Moss 2-32, Sowell 2-15, Cotchery 1-18.

MISSED FIELD GOAL ATTEMPTS—New England, Vinatieri 50.

INTERCEPTIONS—New England, Bruschi 1-36, Wilson 1-24.

KICKOFF RETURNS—New England, Kasper 1-21, Pass 1-17. New York, Cotchery 5-97.

PUNT RETURNS—New England, T. Brown 3-23. New York, McCareins 3-18.

SACKS—New England, Vrabel 1, Colvin 1, J. Green 1. New York, Vilma 1.

BILLS 41, 49ERS 7
Sunday, December 26

Buffalo	0	17	10	14—41
San Francisco	0	0	0	7— 7

Second Quarter
Buf.—McGahee 3 run (Lindell kick), 3:41.
Buf.—FG, Lindell 23, 8:13.
Buf.—Evans 8 pass from Bledsoe (Lindell kick), 14:35.

Third Quarter
Buf.—FG, Lindell 31, 2:58.
Buf.—McGahee 1 run (Lindell kick), 10:40.

Fourth Quarter
Buf.—Evans 33 pass from Matthews (Lindell kick), 1:34.
Buf.—S. Williams 27 run (Lindell kick), 2:21.
S.F.—Barlow 1 run (T. Peterson kick), 8:41.
Attendance—63,248.

	Buffalo	San Francisco
First downs	27	12
Rushes-yards	36-226	28-98
Passing	215	91
Punt returns	4-61	0-0
Kickoff returns	2-64	8-106
Interception returns	3-9	0-0
Comp.-att.-int.	23-36-0	9-20-3
Sacked-yards lost	1-1	3-18
Punts	1-36	5-43
Fumbles-lost	1-1	2-1
Penalties-yards	5-46	4-30
Time of possession	34:57	25:03

INDIVIDUAL STATISTICS

RUSHING—Buffalo, S. Williams 17-93, McGahee 15-102, Bledsoe 2-9, Evans 1-21, Moulds 1-1. San Francisco, Barlow 15-72, Hicks 10-10, Jackson 2-11, Pickett 1-5.

PASSING—Buffalo, Bledsoe 21-32-0-172, Matthews 2-3-0-44, Moorman 0-1-0-0. San Francisco, Dorsey 5-10-1-54, Pickett 4-10-2-55.

RECEIVING—Buffalo, Evans 8-92, Moulds 8-81, Reed 2-11, McGahee 1-14, J. Smith 1-11, Shelton 1-5. San Francisco, Lloyd 2-25, E. Johnson 2-17, Wilson 1-18, Woods 1-17, Hicks 1-15, Conway 1-12, Jackson 1-5.

MISSED FIELD GOAL ATTEMPTS—None.

INTERCEPTIONS—Buffalo, Milloy 1-9, Stamer 1-0, Clements 1-0.

KICKOFF RETURNS—Buffalo, McGee 1-36, J. Smith 1-28. San Francisco, Hicks 7-91, Wilson 1-15.

PUNT RETURNS—Buffalo, Clements 4-61.

SACKS—Buffalo, Spikes 1, Thomas 1, Adams 1. San Francisco, Hanson 1.

COWBOYS 13, REDSKINS 10
Sunday, December 26

Washington	3	0	0	7—10
Dallas	0	6	0	7—13

First Quarter
Was.—FG, J. Chandler 25, 11:59.

Second Quarter
Dal.—FG, Cundiff 26, 5:09.
Dal.—FG, Cundiff 23, 15:00.

Fourth Quarter
Was.—Royal 5 pass from Ramsey (J. Chandler kick), 8:16.
Dal.—Crayton 39 pass from Testaverde (Cundiff kick), 14:30.
Attendance—63,705.

	Washington	Dallas
First downs	15	21
Rushes-yards	25-84	30-89
Passing	149	217
Punt returns	4-59	3-20
Kickoff returns	3-58	3-45
Interception returns	1-38	2-1
Comp.-att.-int.	19-29-2	23-39-1
Sacked-yards lost	2-9	5-17
Punts	5-44	5-47
Fumbles-lost	1-1	1-1
Penalties-yards	8-69	1-13
Time of possession	27:18	32:42

INDIVIDUAL STATISTICS

RUSHING—Washington, Betts 13-43, Portis 10-32, Coles 1-7, Ramsey 1-2. Dallas, J. Jones 22-57, Testaverde 3-14, George 3-6, Anderson 2-12.

PASSING—Washington, Ramsey 19-29-2-158. Dallas, Testaverde 23-39-1-234.

RECEIVING—Washington, Coles 7-53, Gardner 5-31, Cooley 3-24, Jacobs 2-37, Kozlowski 1-8, Royal 1-5. Dallas, K. Johnson 9-84, Witten 6-50, Crayton 2-54, Barnes 2-22, J. Jones 2-10, Morgan 1-7, Anderson 1-7.

MISSED FIELD GOAL ATTEMPTS—Washington, J. Chandler 57.

INTERCEPTIONS—Washington, Springs 1-38. Dallas, L. Scott 1-2, Newman 1-(minus 1).

KICKOFF RETURNS—Washington, Betts 3-58. Dallas, Copper 2-26, Reeves 1-19.

PUNT RETURNS—Washington, A. Brown 4-59. Dallas, Frazier 3-20.

SACKS—Washington, Springs 2, Washington 1, Clemons 1, R. Warner 1. Dallas, Glover 2.

PANTHERS 37, BUCCANEERS 20
Sunday, December 26

Carolina	7	10	7	13—37
Tampa Bay	7	0	7	6—20

First Quarter
Car.—Muhammad 15 pass from Delhomme (Kasay kick), 7:41.
T.B.—Clayton 22 pass from Griese (Taylor kick), 13:12.

Second Quarter
Car.—Muhammad 6 pass from Delhomme (Kasay kick), 3:47.
Car.—FG, Kasay 26, 15:00.

Third Quarter
Car.—Colbert 4 pass from Delhomme (Kasay kick), 5:55.
T.B.—Clayton 6 pass from Griese (Taylor kick), 8:35.

Fourth Quarter
Car.—Seidman 2 pass from Delhomme (kick failed), 2:46.
T.B.—Galloway 14 pass from Griese (pass failed), 6:43.
Car.—Moorehead 17 interception return (Kasay kick), 10:19.
Attendance—65,380.

	Carolina	Tampa Bay
First downs	22	22
Rushes-yards	36-141	13-46
Passing	207	299
Punt returns	0-0	0-0
Kickoff returns	4-90	6-12
OInterception returns	2-17	0-0
Comp.-att.-int.	19-24-0	30-41-2
Sacked-yards lost	1-7	2-22
Punts	5-45	4-33
Fumbles-lost	1-0	2-1
Penalties-yards	5-52	10-77
Time of possession	35:34	24:26

INDIVIDUAL STATISTICS

RUSHING—Carolina, Goings 33-127, Delhomme 1-12, Hoover 1-3, Muhammad 1-(minus 1). Tampa Bay, Pittman 10-41, Griese 2-3, Alstott 1-2.

PASSING—Carolina, Delhomme 19-24-0-214. Tampa Bay, Griese 30-41-2-321.

RECEIVING—Carolina, Muhammad 8-115, Goings 4-39, Mangum 2-25, Seidman 2-16, Hoover 1-9, Proehl 1-6, Colbert 1-4. Tampa Bay, Galloway 9-98, Jurevicius 6-66, Clayton 4-66, Alstott 3-37, Dilger 3-23, Pittman 3-13, Moore 1-10, Brown 1-8.

MISSED FIELD GOAL ATTEMPTS—None.

INTERCEPTIONS—Carolina, Moorehead 1-17, Branch 1-0.

KICKOFF RETURNS—Carolina, Robertson 1-36, Proehl 1-27, Hoover 1-16, Colbert 1-11. Tampa Bay, Cox 5-111, D. White 1-9.

PUNT RETURNS—None.

SACKS—Carolina, Fields 1, Rucker 1. Tampa Bay, Spires 1.

SEAHAWKS 24, CARDINALS 21

Sunday, December 26

Arizona	7	0	0	14	21
Seattle	0	10	7	7	24

First Quarter
Ariz.—Boldin 31 pass from McCown (Rackers kick), 10:37.

Second Quarter
Sea.—Alexander 1 run (J. Brown kick), 10:16.
Sea.—FG, J. Brown 34, 15:00.

Third Quarter
Sea.—Alexander 17 run (J. Brown kick), 11:54.

Fourth Quarter
Sea.—Alexander 23 run (J. Brown kick), :10.
Ariz.—Fitzgerald 29 pass from McCown (Rackers kick), 3:28.
Ariz.—Fitzgerald 29 pass from McCown (Rackers kick), 12:30.
Attendance—65,825.

	Arizona	Seattle
First downs	18	16
Rushes-yards	30-97	36-175
Passing	220	126
Punt returns	4-29	4-64
Kickoff returns	4-106	3-63
Interception returns	1-0	2-6
Comp.-att.-int.	21-33-2	10-26-1
Sacked-yards lost	4-28	1-2
Punts	7-39	8-37
Fumbles-lost	4-0	2-0
Penalties-yards	4-25	6-51
Time of possession	32:32	27:28

INDIVIDUAL STATISTICS

RUSHING—Arizona, E. Smith 23-65, Fitzgerald 2-10, McCown 2-10, O. Ayanbadejo 2-9, Boldin 1-3. Seattle, Alexander 30-154, Dilfer 4-4, Morris 1-10, Strong 1-7.

PASSING—Arizona, McCown 21-33-2-248. Seattle, Dilfer 10-26-1-128.

RECEIVING—Arizona, Boldin 7-107, Fitzgerald 4-70, B. Johnson 4-41, O. Ayanbadejo 4-34, F. Jones 1-5, Scobey 1-(minus 9). Seattle, Jackson 6-101, Hannam 1-18, Morris 1-3, Stevens 1-3, Engram 1-3.

MISSED FIELD GOAL ATTEMPTS—Arizona, Rackers 52.

INTERCEPTIONS—Arizona, Starks 1-0. Seattle, Trufant 1-6, Lucas 1-0.

KICKOFF RETURNS—Arizona, Scobey 4-106. Seattle, Morris 3-63.

PUNT RETURNS—Arizona, K. Williams 4-29. Seattle, Engram 3-61, Morris 1-3.

SACKS—Arizona, Harris 1. Seattle, Okeafor 2, Hamlin 1, Cochran 1.

DOLPHINS 10, BROWNS 7

Sunday, December 26

Cleveland	7	0	0	0	7
Miami	7	0	0	3	10

First Quarter
Mia.—Thompson 18 pass from Feeley (Mare kick), 6:00.
Cle.—Northcutt 58 pass from McCown (Dawson kick), 7:28.

Fourth Quarter
Mia.—FG, Mare 51, 14:53.
Attendance—73,169.

	Cleveland	Miami
First downs	14	19
Rushes-yards	40-142	25-116
Passing	143	164
Punt returns	3-48	3-37
Kickoff returns	3-51	2-48
Interception returns	0-0	2-0
Comp.-att.-int.	9-16-2	25-44-0
Sacked-yards lost	2-18	2-12
Punts	6-42	9-37
Fumbles-lost	4-2	3-2
Penalties-yards	5-25	7-35
Time of possession	30:26	29:34

INDIVIDUAL STATISTICS

RUSHING—Cleveland, Suggs 38-143, McCown 2-(minus 1). Miami, Morris 17-69, Minor 6-30, Chambers 1-16, King 1-1.

PASSING—Cleveland, McCown 9-16-2-161. Miami, Feeley 25-43-0-176, Rosenfels 0-1-0-0.

RECEIVING—Cleveland, Northcutt 4-114, Bryant 2-15, Heiden 1-27, Suggs 1-4, Heinrich 1-1. Miami, McMichael 9-59, Booker 4-31, Chambers 3-25, Morris 3-5, Thompson 2-34, Minor 2-4, Gilmore 1-13, Martin 1-5.

MISSED FIELD GOAL ATTEMPTS—Cleveland, Dawson 43.

INTERCEPTIONS—Miami, Surtain 1-2, Freeman 1-(minus 2).

KICKOFF RETURNS—Cleveland, Alston 3-51. Miami, Welker 2-48.

PUNT RETURNS—Cleveland, Northcutt 3-48. Miami, Welker 3-37.

SACKS—Cleveland, Griffith 1, Warren 1. Miami, Taylor 1, D. Bowens 1.

RAMS 20, EAGLES 7

Monday, December 27

Philadelphia	7	0	0	0	7
St. Louis	7	3	7	3	20

First Quarter
St.L.—S. Jackson 5 run (J. Wilkins kick), 5:57.
Phi.—F. Mitchell 7 pass from McNabb (Akers kick), 13:22.

Second Quarter
St.L.—FG, J. Wilkins 28, 14:18.

Third Quarter
St.L.—Bruce 7 pass from Bulger (J. Wilkins kick), 7:22.

Fourth Quarter
St.L.—FG, J. Wilkins 29, 9:36.
Attendance—66,129.

	Philadelphia	St. Louis
First downs	11	24
Rushes-yards	23-81	44-209
Passing	74	210
Punt returns	0-0	2-21
Kickoff returns	5-137	2-53
Interception returns	0-0	0-0
Comp.-att.-int.	8-23-0	20-28-0
Sacked-yards lost	1-8	2-15
Punts	6-42	2-36
Fumbles-lost	1-1	3-1
Penalties-yards	13-95	7-55
Time of possession	18:16	41:44

INDIVIDUAL STATISTICS

RUSHING—Philadelphia, Levens 10-44, Mahe 6-17, Detmer 4-(minus 1), Tapeh 2-13, Blake 1-8. St. Louis, S. Jackson 24-148, M. Faulk 17-54, Bulger 3-7.

PASSING—Philadelphia, Blake 4-14-0-41, Detmer 1-6-0-5, McNabb 3-3-0-36. St. Louis, Bulger 20-27-0-225, J. Wilkins 0-1-0-0.

RECEIVING—Philadelphia, F. Mitchell 2-28, Tapeh 2-15, Levens 1-23, G. Lewis 1-6, McMullen 1-5, Mahe 1-5. St. Louis, Bruce 8-98, Holt 7-75, Curtis 2-35, McDonald 1-9, Goodspeed 1-4, Manumaleuna 1-4.

MISSED FIELD GOAL ATTEMPTS—St. Louis, J. Wilkins 44.

INTERCEPTIONS—None.

KICKOFF RETURNS—Philadelphia, Hood 3-84, Reed 2-53. St. Louis, Cason 2-53.

PUNT RETURNS—St. Louis, McDonald 2-21.

SACKS—Philadelphia, McDougle 1, Green 1. St. Louis, B. Fisher 1.

WEEK 17

STANDINGS

AMERICAN FOOTBALL CONFERENCE

EAST DIVISION

	W	L	T	Pct.	PF	PA
New England	14	2	0	.875	437	260
N.Y. Jets	10	6	0	.625	333	261
Buffalo	9	7	0	.563	395	284
Miami	4	12	0	.250	275	354

NORTH DIVISION

	W	L	T	Pct.	PF	PA
Pittsburgh	15	1	0	.938	372	251
Baltimore	9	7	0	.563	317	268
Cincinnati	8	8	0	.500	374	372
Cleveland	4	12	0	.250	276	390

SOUTH DIVISION

	W	L	T	Pct.	PF	PA
Indianapolis	12	4	0	.750	522	351
Jacksonville	9	7	0	.563	261	280
Houston	7	9	0	.438	309	339
Tennessee	5	11	0	.313	344	439

WEST DIVISION

	W	L	T	Pct.	PF	PA
San Diego	12	4	0	.750	446	313
Denver	10	6	0	.625	381	304
Kansas City	7	9	0	.438	483	435
Oakland	5	11	0	.313	320	442

NATIONAL FOOTBALL CONFERENCE

EAST DIVISION

	W	L	T	Pct.	PF	PA
Philadelphia	13	3	0	.813	386	260
N.Y. Giants	6	10	0	.375	303	347
Dallas	6	10	0	.375	293	405
Washington	6	10	0	.375	240	265

NORTH DIVISION

	W	L	T	Pct.	PF	PA
Green Bay	10	6	0	.625	424	380
Minnesota	8	8	0	.500	405	395
Detroit	6	10	0	.375	296	350
Chicago	5	11	0	.313	231	331

SOUTH DIVISION

	W	L	T	Pct.	PF	PA
Atlanta	11	5	0	.688	340	337
New Orleans	8	8	0	.500	348	405
Carolina	7	9	0	.438	355	339
Tampa Bay	5	11	0	.313	301	304

WEST DIVISION

	W	L	T	Pct.	PF	PA
Seattle	9	7	0	.563	371	373
St. Louis	8	8	0	.500	319	392
Arizona	6	10	0	.375	284	322
San Francisco	2	14	0	.125	259	452

TOP PERFORMANCES

100-YARD RUSHING GAMES

Player, Team & Opponent	Att.	Yds.	TD
Jamal Lewis, Bal. vs. Mia.	34	167	1
Curtis Martin, NYJ at St.L.*	28	153	0
Julius Jones, Dal. at NYG	29	149	1
Deuce McAllister, N.O. at Car.	28	140	1
Zack Crockett, Oak. vs. Jac.	21	134	0
Warrick Dunn, Atl. at Sea.	25	132	0
Lee Suggs, Cle. at Hou.	26	131	0
Ladell Betts, Was. vs. Min.	26	118	1
Corey Dillon, N.E. vs. S.F.	14	116	1
Thomas Jones, Chi. vs. G.B.	26	108	2
Kevan Barlow, S.F. at N.E.	25	103	0
Domanick Davis, Hou. vs. Cle.	17	103	1
Willie Parker, Pit. at Buf.	19	102	0

300-YARD PASSING GAMES

Player, Team & Opponent	Att.	Cmp.	Yds.	TD	Int.
Marc Bulger, St.L. vs. NYJ*	39	29	450	3	2
Trent Green, K.C. at S.D.	53	33	373	1	4
Joey Harrington, Det. at Ten.	49	33	346	2	1
Jake Delhomme, Car. vs. N.O.	50	24	307	2	0

100-YARD RECEIVING GAMES

Player, Team & Opponent	Rec.	Yds.	TD
Chris Chambers, Mia. at Bal.	4	146	1
Tony Gonzalez, K.C. at S.D.	14	144	0
Torry Holt, St.L. vs. NYJ*	7	116	2
Larry Johnson, K.C. at S.D.	8	115	1

*Overtime game.

RESULTS

SUNDAY, JANUARY 2
NEW ENGLAND 21, San Francisco 7
WASHINGTON 21, Minnesota 18
Cleveland 22, HOUSTON 14
BALTIMORE 30, Miami 23
TENNESSEE 24, Detroit 19
Green Bay 31, CHICAGO 14
New Orleans 21, CAROLINA 18
Cincinnati 38, PHILADELPHIA 10
Pittsburgh 29, BUFFALO 24
ST. LOUIS 32, N.Y. Jets 29 (OT)
SEATTLE 28, Atlanta 26
ARIZONA 12, Tampa Bay 7
SAN DIEGO 24, Kansas City 17
DENVER 33, Indianapolis 14
Jacksonville 13, OAKLAND 6
N.Y. GIANTS 28, Dallas 24

PATRIOTS 21, 49ERS 7

Sunday, January 2

San Francisco	7	0	0	0— 7
New England	0	7	7	7—21

First Quarter

S.F.—Bush 4 pass from Dorsey (T. Peterson kick), 12:12.

Second Quarter

N.E.—Vrabel 1 pass from Brady (Vinatieri kick), 9:03.

Third Quarter

N.E.—Branch 8 pass from Brady (Vinatieri kick), 6:10.

Fourth Quarter

N.E.—Dillon 6 run (Vinatieri kick), :36.
Attendance—68,756.

	San Francisco	New England
First downs	15	23
Rushes-yards	35-135	28-174
Passing	183	231
Punt returns	1-10	4-8
Kickoff returns	4-97	2-50
Interception returns	1-31	0-0
Comp.-att.-int.	18-29-0	23-34-1
Sacked-yards lost	1-6	1-5
Punts	5-43	4-38
Fumbles-lost	2-2	3-2
Penalties-yards	7-64	4-37
Time of possession	30:48	29:12

INDIVIDUAL STATISTICS

RUSHING—San Francisco, Barlow 25-103, Hicks 10-32. New England, Dillon 14-116, Cobbs 5-20, Pass 4-16, Abdullah 2-5, B. Johnson 1-11, Davey 1-3, Brady 1-3.

PASSING—San Francisco, Dorsey 18-29-0-189. New England, Brady 22-30-1-226, Davey 1-4-0-10.

RECEIVING—San Francisco, Conway 4-44, Woods 3-76, E. Johnson 3-28, Barlow 2-11, Bush 2-10, Hicks 2-10, Wilson 1-7, Walker 1-3. New England, Pass 5-22, Weaver 4-62, Fauria 3-37, Branch 3-22, Givens 2-30, B. Johnson 2-15, Patten 1-23, Dillon 1-18, T. Brown 1-6, Vrabel 1-1.

MISSED FIELD GOAL ATTEMPTS—San Francisco, T. Peterson 39.

INTERCEPTIONS—San Francisco, Carpenter 1-31.

KICKOFF RETURNS—San Francisco, Hicks 3-67, Wilson 1-30. New England, B. Johnson 2-50.

PUNT RETURNS—San Francisco, Fleck 1-10. New England, B. Johnson 4-8.

SACKS—San Francisco, Engelberger 1. New England, McGinest 1.

REDSKINS 21, VIKINGS 18

Sunday, January 2

Minnesota	0	3	7	8—18
Washington	7	7	0	7—21

First Quarter

Was.—Cooley 6 pass from Ramsey (J. Chandler kick), 4:19.

Second Quarter

Min.—FG, M. Andersen 23, 3:28.
Was.—Royal 4 pass from Ramsey (J. Chandler kick), 13:43.

Third Quarter

Min.—Moss 28 pass from Culpepper (M. Andersen kick), 9:19.

Fourth Quarter

Was.—Betts 1 run (J. Chandler kick), 4:19.
Min.—M. Robinson 38 pass from Culpepper (O. Smith pass from Culpepper), 14:58.
Attendance—76,876.

	Minnesota	Washington
First downs	21	20
Rushes-yards	18-52	31-117
Passing	268	201
Punt returns	2-14	3-22
Kickoff returns	4-85	3-114
Interception returns	1-7	0-0
Comp.-att.-int.	27-44-0	17-26-1
Sacked-yards lost	4-31	3-15
Punts	6-42	4-38
Fumbles-lost	0-0	1-1
Penalties-yards	7-49	3-13
Time of possession	29:44	30:16

INDIVIDUAL STATISTICS

RUSHING—Minnesota, M. Bennett 8-19, O. Smith 5-5, M. Williams 3-4, Culpepper 2-24. Washington, Betts 26-118, Cartwright 2-0, Coles 1-6, Ramsey 1-(minus 1), Jacobs 1-(minus 6).

PASSING—Minnesota, Culpepper 27-44-0-299. Washington, Ramsey 17-26-1-216.

RECEIVING—Minnesota, Wiggins 7-58, Moss 5-66, Burleson 4-49, O. Smith 4-43, M. Robinson 3-51, M. Bennett 3-24, M. Williams 1-8. Washington, Thrash 5-81, Jacobs 3-56, Coles 3-37, Cooley 3-24, Gardner 1-9, Betts 1-5, Royal 1-4.

MISSED FIELD GOAL ATTEMPTS—None.

INTERCEPTIONS—Minnesota, K. Williams 1-7.

KICKOFF RETURNS—Minnesota, Campbell 2-43, Moore 2-42. Washington, A. Brown 1-66, Thrash 1-36, Sellers 1-12.

PUNT RETURNS—Minnesota, Burleson 2-14. Washington, A. Brown 3-22.

SACKS—Minnesota, K. Williams 1.5, Newman 1.5. Washington, Evans 1.5, Griffin 1, Springs 1, Marshall 0.5.

BROWNS 22, TEXANS 14

Sunday, January 2

Cleveland	3	6	7	6—22
Houston	7	0	0	7—14

First Quarter

Cle.—FG, Dawson 45, 5:09.
Hou.—Wells 6 pass from Carr (K. Brown kick), 10:12.

Second Quarter

Cle.—FG, Dawson 22, 3:32.
Cle.—FG, Dawson 29, 13:00.

Third Quarter

Cle.—Heiden 9 pass from Holcomb (Dawson kick), 9:36.

Fourth Quarter

Cle.—FG, Dawson 45, :51.
Cle.—FG, Dawson 22, 10:59.
Hou.—D. Davis 1 run (K. Brown kick), 13:37.
Attendance—70,724.

	Cleveland	Houston
First downs	18	18
Rushes-yards	32-137	24-136
Passing	227	102
Punt returns	2-16	1-(-1)
Kickoff returns	1-24	7-148
Interception returns	0-0	2-4
Comp.-att.-int.	20-29-2	16-27-0
Sacked-yards lost	1-1	6-28
Punts	3-33	7-43
Fumbles-lost	0-0	1-1
Penalties-yards	6-46	7-52
Time of possession	34:05	25:55

INDIVIDUAL STATISTICS

RUSHING—Cleveland, Suggs 26-131, Green 2-0, Holcomb 2-(minus 2), Northcutt 1-4, F. Jackson 1-4. Houston, D. Davis 17-103, Carr 5-28, Wells 2-5.

PASSING—Cleveland, Holcomb 20-29-2-228. Houston, Carr 15-25-0-114, Gaffney 0-1-0-0, Banks 1-1-0-16.

RECEIVING—Cleveland, Bryant 7-87, Northcutt 5-85, Suggs 3-23, Heiden 2-20, Shea 2-5, King 1-8. Houston, D. Davis 5-42, Miller 3-20, Bradford 2-24, Wells 2-14, An. Johnson 2-13, Gaffney 1-11, Armstrong 1-6.

MISSED FIELD GOAL ATTEMPTS—None.

INTERCEPTIONS—Houston, Faggins 1-4, Simmons 1-0.

KICKOFF RETURNS—Cleveland, King 1-24. Houston, Moses 7-148.

PUNT RETURNS—Cleveland, Northcutt 2-16. Houston, Moses 1-(minus 1).

SACKS—Cleveland, McKinley 2, Ekuban 2, Rogers 1, Myers 1. Houston, Polk 1.

RAVENS 30, DOLPHINS 23

Sunday, January 2

Miami	7	0	14	2—23
Baltimore	7	13	10	0—30

First Quarter

Mia.—Chambers 76 pass from Rosenfels (Mare kick), :16.
Bal.—T. Jones 1 pass from Boller (Stover kick), 3:34.

Second Quarter

Bal.—FG, Stover 25, 7:03.
Bal.—J. Johnson 6 interception return (Stover kick), 7:52.
Bal.—FG, Stover 19, 14:52.

Third Quarter
Bal.—J. Lewis 2 run (Stover kick), 3:36.
Mia.—Welker 95 kickoff return (Mare kick), 3:50.
Mia.—Morris 35 run (Mare kick), 9:50.
Bal.—FG, Stover 33, 14:58.

Fourth Quarter
Mia.—Safety, 4:47.
Attendance—69,843.

	Miami	Baltimore
First downs	18	21
Rushes-yards	20-97	41-190
Passing	248	142
Punt returns	3-28	2-32
Kickoff returns	8-237	4-78
Interception returns	0-0	3-48
Comp.-att.-int.	16-38-3	14-27-0
Sacked-yards lost	3-16	0-0
Punts	5-35	6-39
Fumbles-lost	2-0	2-0
Penalties-yards	5-50	6-50
Time of possession	26:55	33:05

INDIVIDUAL STATISTICS

RUSHING—Miami, Morris 12-89, Minor 8-8. Baltimore, J. Lewis 34-167, Boller 4-22, C. Taylor 2-1, J. White 1-0.

PASSING—Miami, Rosenfels 16-38-3-264. Baltimore, Boller 14-27-0-142.

RECEIVING—Miami, Chambers 4-146, Gilmore 3-47, Lee 3-25, McMichael 2-5, Thompson 1-13, Morris 1-13, Bellamy 1-8, Minor 1-7. Baltimore, Wilcox 6-72, Dinkins 2-25, Hymes 2-19, K. Johnson 2-11, Moore 1-14, T. Jones 1-1.

MISSED FIELD GOAL ATTEMPTS—Miami, Mare 53.

INTERCEPTIONS—Baltimore, Reed 1-41, J. Johnson 1-6, Weaver 1-1.

KICKOFF RETURNS—Miami, Welker 7-210, Morris 1-27. Baltimore, Sams 4-78.

PUNT RETURNS—Miami, Welker 3-28. Baltimore, Sams 2-32.

SACKS—Baltimore, A. Thomas 2, Suggs 1.

TITANS 24, LIONS 19
Sunday, January 2

Detroit	3	7	3	6—19
Tennessee	7	7	7	3—24

First Quarter
Ten.—Bulluck 39 fumble return (Anderson kick), 5:00.
Det.—FG, Hanson 26, 11:44.

Second Quarter
Det.—Schlesinger 21 pass from Harrington (Hanson kick), 9:18.
Ten.—Bennett 32 pass from Volek (Anderson kick), 13:54.

Third Quarter
Det.—FG, Hanson 26, 11:35.
Ten.—A. Smith 2 run (Anderson kick), 14:00.

Fourth Quarter
Ten.—FG, Anderson 40, 4:35.
Det.—Williams 17 pass from Harrington (pass failed), 10:54.
Attendance—68,809.

	Detroit	Tennessee
First downs	23	15
Rushes-yards	26-103	26-95
Passing	331	217
Punt returns	1-5	4-6
Kickoff returns	4-71	4-80
Interception returns	0-0	1-43
Comp.-att.-int.	33-49-1	18-33-0
Sacked-yards lost	2-15	0-0
Punts	5-43	6-40
Fumbles-lost	1-1	0-0
Penalties-yards	6-52	7-50
Time of possession	32:58	27:02

INDIVIDUAL STATISTICS

RUSHING—Detroit, Jones 19-72, Bryson 5-18, Harrington 2-13. Tennessee, A. Smith 21-89, Fleming 3-8, D. Johnson 2-(minus 2).

PASSING—Detroit, Harrington 33-49-1-346. Tennessee, Volek 16-28-0-175, D. Johnson 2-5-0-42.

RECEIVING—Detroit, Bryson 9-63, Alexander 6-66, Williams 4-62, Jones 4-44, Swinton 3-25, Vines 2-40, Schlesinger 2-23, Kircus 2-18, FitzSimmons 1-5. Tennessee, Troupe 4-75, Mason 4-48, A. Smith 3-16, Fleming 3-12, Bennett 2-50, Berlin 1-11, Kinney 1-5.

MISSED FIELD GOAL ATTEMPTS—Tennessee, Anderson 27.

INTERCEPTIONS—Tennessee, A. Dyson 1-43.

KICKOFF RETURNS—Detroit, Swinton 3-69, Trejo 1-2. Tennessee, McAddley 4-80.

PUNT RETURNS—Detroit, Swinton 1-5. Tennessee, Berlin 4-6.
SACKS—Tennessee, Bulluck 1, Hall 1.

PACKERS 31, BEARS 14
Sunday, January 2

Green Bay	7	21	3	0—31
Chicago	7	0	7	0—14

First Quarter
Chi.—T. Jones 2 run (Edinger kick), 2:06.
G.B.—Franks 17 pass from Favre (Longwell kick), 11:38.

Second Quarter
G.B.—Henderson 38 pass from Favre (Longwell kick), 1:44.
G.B.—Sharper 43 interception return (Longwell kick), 3:08.
G.B.—J. Walker 25 pass from Nall (Longwell kick), 8:46.

Third Quarter
Chi.—T. Jones 1 run (Edinger kick), 9:12.
G.B.—FG, Longwell 20, 14:19.
Attendance—62,197.

	Green Bay	Chicago
First downs	17	17
Rushes-yards	30-60	27-110
Passing	327	136
Punt returns	3-4	2-31
Kickoff returns	3-59	6-121
Interception returns	1-43	0-0C
Comp.-att.-int.	16-26-0	20-29-1
Sacked-yards lost	0-0	9-60
Punts	5-37	6-38
Fumbles-lost	0-0	1-0
Penalties-yards	5-35	4-29
Time of possession	28:51	31:09

INDIVIDUAL STATISTICS

RUSHING—Green Bay, Fisher 19-42, Green 4-13, Luchey 3-7, O'Sullivan 2-(minus 2), Nall 1-0, Driver 1-(minus 9). Chicago, T. Jones 26-108, Berrian 1-2.

PASSING—Green Bay, Favre 9-13-0-196, Nall 7-13-0-131. Chicago, Hutchinson 20-29-1-196.

RECEIVING—Green Bay, Franks 4-59, J. Walker 3-82, Fisher 3-23, Henderson 2-53, Driver 1-48, Steele 1-27, Green 1-23, Chatman 1-12. Chicago, Terrell 4-99, Wade 4-27, Clark 3-20, T. Jones 3-4, Berrian 2-23, Lyman 2-13, McKie 2-10.

MISSED FIELD GOAL ATTEMPTS—None.

INTERCEPTIONS—Green Bay, Sharper 1-43.

KICKOFF RETURNS—Green Bay, Thurman 3-59. Chicago, Azumah 5-106, Berrian 1-15.

PUNT RETURNS—Green Bay, Chatman 3-4. Chicago, McQuarters 2-31.

SACKS—Green Bay, Gbaja-Biamila 4, Roman 1, Hunt 1, C. Williams 1, Jenkins 1, Truluck 1.

SAINTS 21, PANTHERS 18
Sunday, January 2

New Orleans	7	7	7	0—21
Carolina	3	0	7	8—18

First Quarter
Car.—FG, Kasay 54, 5:36.
N.O.—Stecker 7 run (Carney kick), 14:34.

Second Quarter
N.O.—McAllister 1 run (Carney kick), 13:54.

Third Quarter
Car.—Muhammad 9 pass from Delhomme (Kasay kick), 10:27.
N.O.—Horn 44 pass from Brooks (Carney kick), 11:50.

Fourth Quarter
Car.—Muhammad 9 pass from Delhomme (Seidman pass from Delhomme), 9:52.
Attendance—73,302.

	New Orleans	Carolina
First downs	15	21
Rushes-yards	37-164	13-46
Passing	196	274
Punt returns	4-37	6-48
Kickoff returns	4-58	4-113
Interception returns	0-0	0-0
Comp.-att.-int.	14-24-0	24-50-0
Sacked-yards lost	3-20	6-33
Punts	10-40	8-40
Fumbles-lost	1-0	3-3
Penalties-yards	8-87	6-45
Time of possession	33:32	26:28

INDIVIDUAL STATISTICS

RUSHING—New Orleans, McAllister 28-140, Brooks 5-11, Karney 2-6, Stecker 1-7, Stallworth 1-0. Carolina, Goings 13-46.

PASSING—New Orleans, Brooks 14-24-0-216. Carolina, Delhomme 24-50-0-307.

RECEIVING—New Orleans, Pathon 4-78, Horn 4-75, Stallworth 3-31, B. Williams 1-18, McAllister 1-14, Conwell 1-0. Carolina, Muhammad 6-95, Goings 6-63, Mangum 6-51, Colbert 2-39, Seidman 2-34, Proehl 2-25.

MISSED FIELD GOAL ATTEMPTS—New Orleans, Carney 38. Carolina, Kasay 60.

INTERCEPTIONS—None.

KICKOFF RETURNS—New Orleans, Stecker 2-32, M. Lewis 1-19, McAfee 1-7. Carolina, Robertson 3-99, Hoover 1-14.

PUNT RETURNS—New Orleans, M. Lewis 4-37. Carolina, Gamble 6-48.

SACKS—New Orleans, Ch. Grant 2, W. Smith 1.5, Howard 1.5, Bryant 1. Carolina, Fields 1, Witherspoon 1, Peppers 1.

BENGALS 38, EAGLES 10

Sunday, January 2

Cincinnati	0	17	14	7	38
Philadelphia	0	3	0	7	10

Second Quarter

Cin.—Ru. Johnson 5 run (Graham kick), :42.

Cin.—Houshmandzadeh 20 pass from Kitna (Graham kick), 6:58.

Cin.—FG, Graham 50, 13:50.

Phi.—FG, Akers 46, 14:57.

Third Quarter

Cin.—Geathers 36 interception return (Graham kick), 8:40.

Cin.—Ru. Johnson 6 run (Graham kick), 10:01.

Fourth Quarter

Cin.—Ru. Johnson 3 run (Graham kick), 4:46.

Phi.—F. Mitchell 3 pass from Blake (Akers kick), 8:46.

Attendance—67,074.

	Cincinnati	Philadelphia
First downs	16	18
Rushes-yards	35-148	16-80
Passing	160	262
Punt returns	1-4	5-16
Kickoff returns	3-48	7-96
Interception returns	3-46	0-0
Comp.-att.-int.	16-27-0	31-54-3
Sacked-yards lost	0-0	3-25
Punts	7-42	5-39
Fumbles-lost	1-0	3-2
Penalties-yards	4-35	7-50
Time of possession	29:32	30:28

INDIVIDUAL STATISTICS

RUSHING—Cincinnati, Ru. Johnson 28-99, Watson 3-20, Kitna 3-11, C. Johnson 1-18. Philadelphia, McCoo 9-54, Mahe 7-26.

PASSING—Cincinnati, Kitna 16-27-0-160. Philadelphia, Detmer 17-31-2-202, Blake 14-23-1-85.

RECEIVING—Cincinnati, Houshmandzadeh 6-71, C. Johnson 5-67, Watson 1-9, J. Johnson 1-4, Schobel 1-4, Washington 1-3, Stewart 1-2. Philadelphia, Mahe 8-62, F. Mitchell 6-76, G. Lewis 6-53, Bartrum 3-27, Smith 2-37, McMullen 2-19, McCoo 2-15, Parry 2-(minus 2).

MISSED FIELD GOAL ATTEMPTS—Cincinnati, Graham 37. Philadelphia, Akers 45.

INTERCEPTIONS—Cincinnati, Geathers 1-36, James 1-10, O'Neal 1-0.

KICKOFF RETURNS—Cincinnati, C. Russell 1-22, Watson 1-16, Stewart 1-10. Philadelphia, Reed 2-45, Parry 2-24, Hood 2-19, Mahe 1-8.

PUNT RETURNS—Cincinnati, Ratliff 1-4. Philadelphia, Wynn 4-9, Mahe 1-7.

SACKS—Cincinnati, Thornton 1, J. Smith 1, Hardy 1.

STEELERS 29, BILLS 24

Sunday, January 2

Pittsburgh	10	6	0	13	29
Buffalo	7	3	7	7	24

First Quarter

Pit.—FG, Reed 22, 4:16.

Buf.—McGahee 3 run (Lindell kick), 8:46.

Pit.—Randle El 16 pass from Maddox (Reed kick), 11:32.

Second Quarter

Pit.—FG, Reed 21, 1:21.

Pit.—FG, Reed 31, 10:38.

Buf.—FG, Lindell 37, 14:57.

Third Quarter

Buf.—Clements 30 interception return (Lindell kick), 2:29.

Fourth Quarter

Pit.—FG, Reed 37, :11.

Pit.—Harrison 18 fumble return (Reed kick), 1:36.

Pit.—FG, Reed 33, 12:37.

Buf.—McGahee 1 run (Lindell kick), 13:42.

Attendance—73,414.

	Pittsburgh	Buffalo
First downs	15	16
Rushes-yards	43-157	21-96
Passing	105	171
Punt returns	2-31	2-3
Kickoff returns	4-67	7-149
Interception returns	1-1	2-46
Comp.-att.-int.	12-25-2	16-30-1
Sacked-yards lost	2-15	3-18
Punts	3-46	6-45
Fumbles-lost	2-1	3-2
Penalties-yards	7-40	12-108
Time of possession	35:03	24:57

INDIVIDUAL STATISTICS

RUSHING—Pittsburgh, Parker 19-102, Haynes 8-22, Staley 8-21, St. Pierre 4-(minus 3), Kreider 3-13, Maddox 1-2. Buffalo, McGahee 18-79, Evans 1-15, S. Williams 1-2, Bledsoe 1-0.

PASSING—Pittsburgh, Maddox 12-24-2-120, St. Pierre 0-1-0-0. Buffalo, Bledsoe 16-30-1-189.

RECEIVING—Pittsburgh, Randle El 7-81, Ward 2-11, Parker 2-4, Mays 1-24. Buffalo, Aiken 4-52, Moulds 4-37, Neufeld 3-15, Evans 2-63, Trafford 1-10, McGahee 1-7, Shelton 1-5.

MISSED FIELD GOAL ATTEMPTS—Buffalo, Lindell 28.

INTERCEPTIONS—Pittsburgh, Foote 1-1. Buffalo, Clements 1-30, Spikes 1-16.

KICKOFF RETURNS—Pittsburgh, I. Taylor 2-34, Cushing 1-20, Kirschke 1-13. Buffalo, McGee 6-135, Kelsay 1-14.

PUNT RETURNS—Pittsburgh, Randle El 1-18, Colclough 1-13. Buffalo, Clements 1-3, J. Smith 1-0.

SACKS—Pittsburgh, Colclough 1.5, Polamalu 1, Kriewaldt 0.5. Buffalo, P. Williams 1, Denney 1.

RAMS 32, JETS 29

Sunday, January 2

N.Y. Jets	3	7	16	3	0	29
St. Louis	0	14	7	8	3	32

First Quarter

NYJ—FG, Brien 47, 13:47.

Second Quarter

St.L.—Bruce 27 pass from Bulger (J. Wilkins kick), 7:06.

NYJ—Baker 8 pass from Pennington (Brien kick), 10:46.

St.L.—Holt 44 pass from Bulger (J. Wilkins kick), 14:00.

Third Quarter

St.L.—S. Jackson 20 run (J. Wilkins kick), 1:30.

NYJ—Cotchery 94 kickoff return (Brien kick), 1:41.

NYJ—FG, Brien 33, 5:04.

NYJ—Vilma 38 interception return (pass failed), 13:48.

Fourth Quarter

St.L.—Holt 19 pass from Bulger (S. Jackson run), 9:54.

NYJ—FG, Brien 27, 14:57.

Overtime

St.L.—FG, J. Wilkins 31, 11:58.

Attendance—65,877.

	N.Y. Jets	St. Louis
First downs	22	21
Rushes-yards	39-180	19-47
Passing	144	432
Punt returns	2-5	1-5
Kickoff returns	5-196	8-164
Interception returns	2-39	0-0
Comp.-att.-int.	21-36-0	29-40-2
Sacked-yards lost	6-37	3-18
Punts	7-37	7-40
Fumbles-lost	1-0	2-1
Penalties-yards	7-75	10-76
Time of possession	41:08	30:50

INDIVIDUAL STATISTICS

RUSHING—New York, C. Martin 28-153, Jordan 7-23, Pennington 3-17, Moss 1-(minus 13). St. Louis, S. Jackson 10-29, M. Faulk 7-15, Bulger 1-6, McDonald 1-(minus 3).

PASSING—New York, Pennington 21-36-0-181. St. Louis, Bulger 29-39-2-450, Bruce 0-1-0-0.

RECEIVING—New York, McCareins 6-62, Moss 4-28, C. Martin 2-22, Chrebet 2-18, Cotchery 2-15, Sowell 2-13, Becht 1-14, Baker 1-8, Jordan 1-1. St. Louis, Holt 7-116, Curtis 6-99, Bruce 5-86, S. Jackson 4-51, McDonald 2-35, Manumaleuna 2-32, Looker 1-14, M. Faulk 1-11, Goodspeed 1-6.

MISSED FIELD GOAL ATTEMPTS—New York, Brien 53.

INTERCEPTIONS—New York, Vilma 1-38, Coleman 1-1.

KICKOFF RETURNS—New York, Cotchery 5-196. St. Louis, Cason 7-164, Manumaleuna 1-0.

PUNT RETURNS—New York, McCareins 2-5. St. Louis, McDonald 1-5.

SACKS—New York, Ellis 3. St. Louis, B. Fisher 2, Pickett 1, T. Jackson 1, Little 1, Lewis 1.

SEAHAWKS 28, FALCONS 26
Sunday, January 2

Atlanta	7	10	0	9	26
Seattle	7	7	7	7	28

First Quarter
Atl.—P. Price 2 pass from Vick (Feely kick), 8:41.
Sea.—Alexander 1 run (J. Brown kick), 11:54.

Second Quarter
Atl.—FG, Feely 33, 6:28.
Atl.—D. Hall 48 interception return (Feely kick), 8:04.
Sea.—Jackson 3 pass from Hasselbeck (J. Brown kick), 11:35.

Third Quarter
Sea.—Stevens 3 pass from Hasselbeck (J. Brown kick), 7:25.

Fourth Quarter
Atl.—FG, Feely 40, 4:48.
Sea.—Hasselbeck 1 run (J. Brown kick), 10:32.
Atl.—Finneran 3 pass from Schaub (run failed), 15:00.
Attendance—66,740.

	Atlanta	Seattle
First downs	22	21
Rushes-yards	38-204	21-83
Passing	150	170
Punt returns	2-0	0-0
Kickoff returns	4-75	4-75
Interception returns	1-48	1-31
Comp.-att.-int.	20-29-1	21-27-1
Sacked-yards lost	3-18	4-21
Punts	2-31	4-34
Fumbles-lost	1-0	0-0
Penalties-yards	8-53	1-5
Time of possession	34:54	25:06

INDIVIDUAL STATISTICS
RUSHING—Atlanta, Dunn 25-132, Duckett 8-52, Vick 3-13, Schaub 2-7. Seattle, Alexander 19-80, Strong 1-2, Hasselbeck 1-1.

PASSING—Atlanta, Schaub 14-22-1-133, Vick 6-7-0-35. Seattle, Hasselbeck 21-27-1-191.

RECEIVING—Atlanta, P. Price 7-46, Finneran 3-45, Dunn 3-20, McCrary 2-23, Jenkins 2-8, Duckett 1-11, White 1-9, Layne 1-6. Seattle, Engram 6-79, Mili 3-37, Jackson 3-18, Alexander 2-15, Stevens 2-14, Hannam 2-14, Strong 2-8, Morris 1-6.

MISSED FIELD GOAL ATTEMPTS—Atlanta, Feely 39.

INTERCEPTIONS—Atlanta, D. Hall 1-48. Seattle, Trufant 1-31.

KICKOFF RETURNS—Atlanta, Rossum 4-75. Seattle, Morris 3-54, H. Evans 1-21.

PUNT RETURNS—Atlanta, Rossum 2-0.

SACKS—Atlanta, R. Coleman 2, Rossum 1, Kerney 1. Seattle, C. Brown 1, Hamlin 1, R. Bernard 0.5, Cochran 0.5.

CARDINALS 12, BUCCANEERS 7
Sunday, January 2

Tampa Bay	0	0	7	0	7
Arizona	3	3	0	6	12

First Quarter
Ariz.—FG, Rackers 40, 5:54.

Second Quarter
Ariz.—FG, Rackers 45, 14:57.

Third Quarter
T.B.—Clayton 75 pass from Simms (Taylor kick), 13:36.

Fourth Quarter
Ariz.—FG, Rackers 39, 3:53.
Ariz.—FG, Rackers 31, 8:48.
Attendance—31,650.

	Tampa Bay	Arizona
First downs	11	12
Rushes-yards	21-62	34-107
Passing	187	115
Punt returns	5-10	3-45
Kickoff returns	2-80	2-41
Interception returns	1-13	2-44
Comp.-att.-int.	16-32-2	16-36-1
Sacked-yards lost	4-37	0-0
Punts	8-37	7-43
Fumbles-lost	2-2	1-0
Penalties-yards	8-63	10-70
Time of possession	26:11	33:49

INDIVIDUAL STATISTICS
RUSHING—Tampa Bay, Pittman 16-50, Simms 3-1, Graham 1-12, Alstott 1-(minus 1). Arizona, E. Smith 23-69, O. Ayanbadejo 6-31, Fitzgerald 2-1, McCown 2-(minus 2), Scobey 1-8.

PASSING—Tampa Bay, Simms 16-32-2-224. Arizona, McCown 16-36-1-115.

RECEIVING—Tampa Bay, Galloway 3-48, Pittman 3-30, Jurevicius 3-20, Clayton 2-86, Alstott 2-15, Lawrie 1-15, Baber 1-7, Dilger 1-3. Arizona, Fitzgerald 3-36, Boldin 3-31, F. Jones 2-18, E. Smith 2-13, B. Johnson 2-9, O. Ayanbadejo 2-5, K. Williams 1-8, McCown 1-(minus 5).

MISSED FIELD GOAL ATTEMPTS—Arizona, Rackers 35, 47.

INTERCEPTIONS—Tampa Bay, D. Smith 1-13. Arizona, Wilson 1-24, Dockett 1-20.

KICKOFF RETURNS—Tampa Bay, Cox 2-80. Arizona, Scobey 2-41.

PUNT RETURNS—Tampa Bay, Galloway 5-10. Arizona, K. Williams 3-45.

SACKS—Arizona, Berry 2, R. Davis 1, Dockett 1.

CHARGERS 24, CHIEFS 17
Sunday, January 2

Kansas City	0	3	0	14	17
San Diego	3	14	0	7	24

First Quarter
S.D.—FG, Kaeding 34, 4:04.

Second Quarter
K.C.—FG, Tynes 50, 7:52.
S.D.—Flutie 1 run (Kaeding kick), 12:36.
S.D.—Krause 10 pass from Flutie (Kaeding kick), 14:48.

Fourth Quarter
S.D.—Floyd 13 pass from Rivers (Kaeding kick), 7:49.
K.C.—L. Johnson 2 run (Tynes kick), 10:50.
K.C.—L. Johnson 14 pass from Green (Tynes kick), 12:50.
Attendance—64,920.

	Kansas City	San Diego
First downs	26	21
Rushes-yards	20-70	29-138
Passing	373	215
Punt returns	1-1	1-(-1)
Kickoff returns	5-85	2-35
Interception returns	1-25	4-41
Comp.-att.-int.	33-53-4	18-31-1
Sacked-yards lost	0-0	2-17
Punts	2-39	4-39
Fumbles-lost	0-0	4-1
Penalties-yards	5-45	7-50
Time of possession	30:11	29:49

INDIVIDUAL STATISTICS
RUSHING—Kansas City, L. Johnson 17-46, Horn 1-12, Green 1-7, Gonzalez 1-5. San Diego, Turner 15-87, Pinnock 9-26, Flutie 3-25, Shaw 1-1, Rivers 1-(minus 1).

PASSING—Kansas City, Green 33-53-4-373. San Diego, Flutie 13-22-0-199, Rivers 5-8-0-33, Scifres 0-1-1-0.

RECEIVING—Kansas City, Gonzalez 14-144, L. Johnson 8-115, Kennison 4-73, Parker 3-18, Horn 2-12, Richardson 1-8, Dunn 1-3. San Diego, Krause 5-81, Turner 4-8, Floyd 3-49, Pinnock 3-26, Osgood 2-55, Peelle 1-13.

MISSED FIELD GOAL ATTEMPTS—Kansas City, Tynes 33.

INTERCEPTIONS—Kansas City, Wesley 1-25. San Diego, Kiel 1-31, Florence 1-9, Dingle 1-1, Wilhelm 1-0.

KICKOFF RETURNS—Kansas City, Hall 5-85. San Diego, Butler 2-35.

PUNT RETURNS—Kansas City, Hall 1-1. San Diego, E. Parker 1-(minus 1).

SACKS—Kansas City, Hicks 1, Team 1.

BRONCOS 33, COLTS 14
Sunday, January 2

Indianapolis	7	7	0	0—14
Denver	7	13	10	3—33

First Quarter
Ind.—Harrison 7 pass from Sorgi (Vanderjagt kick), 7:43.
Den.—Lelie 38 pass from Plummer (Elam kick), 10:46.

Second Quarter
Den.—FG, Elam 45, 2:48.
Den.—Hape 2 pass from Plummer (Elam kick), 9:11.
Ind.—Wayne 71 pass from Sorgi (Vanderjagt kick), 10:13.
Den.—FG, Elam 23, 14:11.

Third Quarter
Den.—Plummer 5 run (Elam kick), 7:57.
Den.—FG, Elam 40, 12:40.

Fourth Quarter
Den.—FG, Elam 40, 9:20.
Attendance—75,149.

	Indianapolis	Denver
First downs	8	23
Rushes-yards	15-34	42-214
Passing	166	239
Punt returns	2-16	5-69
Kickoff returns	7-188	3-72
Interception returns	0-0	0-0
Comp.-att.-int.	17-27-0	17-30-0
Sacked-yards lost	1-8	1-7
Punts	8-49	4-38
Fumbles-lost	2-1	2-0
Penalties-yards	4-25	2-25
Time of possession	22:16	37:44

INDIVIDUAL STATISTICS
RUSHING—Indianapolis, Rhodes 12-34, Sorgi 2-2, James 1-(minus 2). Denver, Bell 16-91, Droughns 15-76, Plummer 7-15, Sapp 4-32.
PASSING—Indianapolis, Sorgi 16-25-0-168, Manning 1-2-0-6. Denver, Plummer 17-30-0-246.
RECEIVING—Indianapolis, Harrison 5-33, Wayne 3-90, Pyatt 2-12, Hartsock 2-12, Mungro 2-11, Moorehead 1-7, Walters 1-5, Clark 1-4. Denver, Smith 6-76, Lelie 3-70, Putzier 3-67, Bell 2-16, Hape 2-8, Carswell 1-9.
MISSED FIELD GOAL ATTEMPTS—None.
INTERCEPTIONS—None.
KICKOFF RETURNS—Indianapolis, Rhodes 6-164, Mungro 1-24. Denver, Sapp 1-34, Luke 1-20, R. Alexander 1-18.
PUNT RETURNS—Indianapolis, Pyatt 2-16. Denver, Adams 2-42, Luke 2-16, Smith 1-11.
SACKS—Indianapolis, Brock 1. Denver, Hayward 1.

JAGUARS 13, RAIDERS 6
Sunday, January 2

Jacksonville	0	3	10	0—13
Oakland	3	3	0	0— 6

First Quarter
Oak.—FG, Janikowski 35, 5:33.

Second Quarter
Jac.—FG, Scobee 26, 4:45.
Oak.—FG, Janikowski 27, 14:58.

Third Quarter
Jac.—FG, Scobee 22, 7:50.
Jac.—G. Jones 1 run (Scobee kick), 11:19.
Attendance—41,112.

	Jacksonville	Oakland
First downs	13	16
Rushes-yards	34-93	28-147
Passing	149	134
Punt returns	4-45	1-0
Kickoff returns	3-57	3-50
Interception returns	3-37	1-8

	Jacksonville	Oakland
Comp.-att.-int.	15-28-1	15-39-3
Sacked-yards lost	1-0	2-8
Punts	7-44	6-40
Fumbles-lost	1-1	3-1
Penalties-yards	7-87	8-72
Time of possession	30:53	29:07

INDIVIDUAL STATISTICS
RUSHING—Jacksonville, G. Jones 16-30, Leftwich 10-41, Toefield 7-18, Fuamatu-Ma'afala 1-4. Oakland, Crockett 21-134, Zereoue 4-5, Redmond 1-7, Fargas 1-1, Collins 1-0.
PASSING—Jacksonville, Leftwich 15-28-1-149. Oakland, Collins 15-39-3-142
RECEIVING—Jacksonville, J. Smith 3-22, T. Edwards 3-21, Wilford 2-56, Toefield 2-26, Yoder 2-8, M. Edwards 1-15, Brady 1-8, Leftwich 1-(minus 7). Oakland, Porter 3-35, Zereoue 3-18, Crockett 3-12, Jolley 2-34, Gabriel 2-30, Whitted 1-10, Redmond 1-3.
MISSED FIELD GOAL ATTEMPTS—None.
INTERCEPTIONS—Jacksonville, Darius 2-37, Mathis 1-0. Oakland, T. Johnson 1-8.
KICKOFF RETURNS—Jacksonville, Allen 3-57. Oakland, Gabriel 3-50.
PUNT RETURNS—Jacksonville, Allen 4-45. Oakland, Gabriel 1-0.
SACKS—Jacksonville, D. Cooper 1, Team 1. Oakland, Washington 1.

GIANTS 28, COWBOYS 24
Sunday, January 2

Dallas	3	6	7	8—24
N.Y. Giants	0	7	0	21—28

First Quarter
Dal.—FG, Cundiff 40, 10:45.

Second Quarter
NYG—Shiancoe 2 pass from Manning (Christie kick), 2:12.
Dal.—FG, Cundiff 24, 13:06.
Dal.—FG, Cundiff 45, 15:00.

Third Quarter
Dal.—Witten 7 pass from Testaverde (Cundiff kick), 14:15.

Fourth Quarter
NYG—Tyree 15 pass from Manning (Christie kick), :05.
NYG—Barber 3 pass from Manning (Christie kick), 3:09.
Dal.—J. Jones 1 run (Witten pass from Testaverde), 13:11.
NYG—Barber 3 run (Christie kick), 14:49.
Attendance—78,500.

	Dallas	N.Y. Giants
First downs	21	18
Rushes-yards	31-147	25-98
Passing	220	137
Punt returns	3-21	2-23
Kickoff returns	5-65	5-80
Interception returns	1-(-2)	1-12
Comp.-att.-int.	23-31-1	18-27-1
Sacked-yards lost	3-11	1-7
Punts	3-43	5-44
Fumbles-lost	1-1	1-0
Penalties-yards	6-93	3-25
Time of possession	33:28	26:32

INDIVIDUAL STATISTICS
RUSHING—Dallas, J. Jones 29-149, George 1-2, Testaverde 1-(minus 4). New York, Barber 24-95, Dayne 1-3.
PASSING—Dallas, Testaverde 23-30-0-231, Crayton 0-1-1-0. New York, Manning 18-27-1-144.
RECEIVING—Dallas, Witten 8-77, Crayton 5-58, J. Jones 5-46, Morgan 3-28, K. Johnson 1-18, Polite 1-4. New York, Tyree 7-71, Rivers 3-24, I. Hilliard 3-22, Barber 3-21, Shiancoe 2-6.
MISSED FIELD GOAL ATTEMPTS—None.
INTERCEPTIONS—Dallas, Nguyen 1-(minus 2). New York, Burns 1-12.
KICKOFF RETURNS—Dallas, Reeves 3-25, Copper 2-40. New York, Ward 2-37, Ponder 2-35, Rivers 1-8.
PUNT RETURNS—Dallas, Frazier 3-21. New York, I. Hilliard 2-23.
SACKS—Dallas, Wiley 1. New York, Umenyiora 1, Duckett 1, Williams 0.5, Torbor 0.5.

WILD-CARD GAMES

RAMS 27, SEAHAWKS 20

Saturday, January 8

St. Louis	7	7	3	10—27
Seattle	3	7	3	7—20

First Quarter

St.L.—Holt 15 pass from Bulger (J. Wilkins kick), 3:27.
Sea.—FG, J. Brown 47, 12:55.

Second Quarter

St.L.—M. Faulk 1 run (J. Wilkins kick), 1:28.
Sea.—Engram 19 pass from Hasselbeck (J. Brown kick), 6:42.

Third Quarter

Sea.—FG, J. Brown 30, 6:08.
St.L.—FG, J. Wilkins 38, 12:25.

Fourth Quarter

Sea.—Jackson 23 pass from Hasselbeck (J. Brown kick), 1:17.
St.L.—FG, J. Wilkins 27, 6:53.
St.L.—Cleeland 17 pass from Bulger (J. Wilkins kick), 12:49.
Attendance—65,397.

	St. Louis	Seattle
First downs	22	24
Rushes-yards	27-102	20-81
Passing	294	332
Punt returns	3-14	1-9
Kickoff returns	5-101	6-109
Interception returns	1-0	1-0
Comp.-att.-int.	18-32-1	27-43-1
Sacked-yards lost	5-19	3-9
Punts	3-29	3-44
Fumbles-lost	0-0	2-0
Penalties-yards	4-30	9-61
Time of possession	31:06	28:54

INDIVIDUAL STATISTICS

RUSHING—St. Louis, M. Faulk 13-55, S. Jackson 10-36, Bulger 3-10, Bruce 1-1. Seattle, Alexander 15-40, Hasselbeck 2-26, Morris 2-9, Strong 1-6.

PASSING—St. Louis, Bulger 18-32-1-313. Seattle, Hasselbeck 27-43-1-341.

RECEIVING—St. Louis, Holt 6-108, Curtis 4-107, Bruce 3-40, M. Faulk 2-12, McDonald 1-31, Cleeland 1-17, S. Jackson 1-(minus 2). Seattle, Jackson 12-128, Mili 6-98, K. Robinson 4-40, Engram 3-34, Alexander 1-25, Stevens 1-16.

MISSED FIELD GOAL ATTEMPTS—None.

INTERCEPTIONS—St. Louis, T. Fisher 1-0. Seattle, Hamlin 1-0.

KICKOFF RETURNS—St. Louis, Cason 5-101. Seattle, Morris 6-109.

PUNT RETURNS—St. Louis, McDonald 3-14. Seattle, Engram 1-9.

SACKS—St. Louis, Kennedy 1, Lewis 1, B. Fisher 0.5, Thomas 0.5. Seattle, Okeafor 2, C. Brown 1, R. Bernard 1, Woodard 0.5, Terrill 0.5.

JETS 20, CHARGERS 17

Saturday, January 8

N.Y. Jets	0	7	10	0	3—20
San Diego	0	7	0	10	0—17

Second Quarter

S.D.—McCardell 26 pass from Brees (Kaeding kick), 5:34.
NYJ—Becht 13 pass from Pennington (Brien kick), 12:06.

Third Quarter

NYJ—Moss 47 pass from Pennington (Brien kick), 4:31.
NYJ—FG, Brien 42, 13:37.

Fourth Quarter

S.D.—FG, Kaeding 35, 4:17.
S.D.—Gates 1 pass from Brees (Kaeding kick), 14:49.

Overtime

NYJ—FG, Brien 28, 14:55.
Attendance—67,536.

	N.Y. Jets	San Diego
First downs	20	24
Rushes-yards	28-126	33-100
Passing	270	308
Punt returns	0-0	2-11
Kickoff returns	3-66	5-85
Interception returns	1-22	0-0
Comp.-att.-int.	23-33-0	31-42-1
Sacked-yards lost	2-9	2-11
Punts	5-40	5-36
Fumbles-lost	0-0	1-0
Penalties-yards	8-49	9-75
Time of possession	35:39	39:16

INDIVIDUAL STATISTICS

RUSHING—New York, C. Martin 18-66, Jordan 7-50, Pennington 3-10. San Diego, Tomlinson 26-80, Brees 5-17, Neal 1-3, E. Parker 1-0.

PASSING—New York, Pennington 23-33-0-279. San Diego, Brees 31-42-1-319.

RECEIVING—New York, McCareins 8-87, Moss 4-100, C. Martin 4-47, Jordan 3-18, Baker 2-7, Becht 1-13, J. Carter 1-7. San Diego, E. Parker 9-93, Tomlinson 9-53, Gates 6-89, McCardell 4-50, Peelle 3-34.

MISSED FIELD GOAL ATTEMPTS—New York, Brien 33. San Diego, Kaeding 40.

INTERCEPTIONS—New York, Tongue 1-22.

KICKOFF RETURNS—New York, Cotchery 3-66. San Diego, Dwight 5-85.

PUNT RETURNS—San Diego, E. Parker 2-11.

SACKS—New York, Vilma 1, J. Ferguson 1. San Diego, Foley 1.5, Phillips 1.5.

2004 REVIEW *Wild-card games*

COLTS 49, BRONCOS 24

Sunday, January 9

Denver	0	3	14	7—24
Indianapolis	14	21	0	14—49

First Quarter
Ind.—Mungro 2 pass from Manning (Vanderjagt kick), 7:37.
Ind.—James 1 run (Vanderjagt kick), 14:22.

Second Quarter
Ind.—Clark 19 pass from Manning (Vanderjagt kick), 6:49.
Den.—FG, Elam 33, 9:41.
Ind.—Wayne 35 pass from Manning (Vanderjagt kick), 10:31.
Ind.—Manning 1 run (Vanderjagt kick), 14:54.

Third Quarter
Den.—Smith 9 pass from Plummer (Elam kick), 5:59.
Den.—Putzier 35 pass from Plummer (Elam kick), 13:50.

Fourth Quarter
Ind.—Wayne 43 pass from Manning (Vanderjagt kick), 2:12.
Den.—Bell 1 run (Elam kick), 7:15.
Ind.—Rhodes 2 run (Vanderjagt kick), 12:58.
    Attendance—56,609.

	Denver	Indianapolis
First downs	18	27
Rushes-yards	21-78	24-76
Passing	260	454
Punt returns	1-(-1)	1-9
Kickoff returns	8-188	2-54
Interception returns	1-0	1-0
Comp.-att.-int.	24-34-1	27-33-1
Sacked-yards lost	3-24	1-4
Punts	4-38	2-38
Fumbles-lost	1-0	0-0
Penalties-yards	5-24	4-26
Time of possession	30:42	29:18

INDIVIDUAL STATISTICS
RUSHING—Denver, Bell 12-49, Droughns 8-29, Plummer 1-0. Indianapolis, James 18-63, Rhodes 5-12, Manning 1-1.

PASSING—Denver, Plummer 24-34-1-284. Indianapolis, Manning 27-33-1-458.

RECEIVING—Denver, Smith 7-99, Bell 4-32, Droughns 4-28, Putzier 3-67, Lelie 2-27, Hape 2-8, Carswell 1-15, Watts 1-8. Indianapolis, Wayne 10-221, Clark 6-112, Harrison 4-51, Stokley 2-33, Pollard 2-28, James 2-11, Mungro 1-2.

MISSED FIELD GOAL ATTEMPTS—None.

INTERCEPTIONS—Denver, K. Herndon 1-0. Indianapolis, Doss 1-0.

KICKOFF RETURNS—Denver, Sapp 4-86, Droughns 2-36, Luke 1-41, Adams 1-25. Indianapolis, Rhodes 1-36, Mungro 1-18.

PUNT RETURNS—Denver, Adams 1-(minus 1). Indianapolis, Walters 1-9.

SACKS—Denver, Hayward 1. Indianapolis, Brock 1, Tripplett 1, Scioli 1.

VIKINGS 31, PACKERS 17

Sunday, January 9

Minnesota	17	7	0	7—31
Green Bay...	3	7	0	7—17

First Quarter
Min.—M. Williams 68 pass from Culpepper (M. Andersen kick), 1:40.
Min.—Moss 20 pass from Culpepper (M. Andersen kick), 5:10.
Min.—FG, M. Andersen 35, 8:54.
G.B.—FG, Longwell 43, 12:18.

Second Quarter
G.B.—Franks 4 pass from Favre (Longwell kick), 4:36.
Min.—Burleson 19 pass from Culpepper (M. Andersen kick), 8:27.

Fourth Quarter
G.B.—Davenport 1 run (Longwell kick), 1:23.
Min.—Moss 34 pass from Culpepper (M. Andersen kick), 4:42.
    Attendance—71,075.

	Minnesota	Green Bay
First downs	18	24
Rushes-yards	27-116	29-105
Passing	268	201
Punt returns	3-7	1-(-4)
Kickoff returns	4-71	5-96
Interception returns	4-44	0-0
Comp.-att.-int.	19-29-0	22-33-4
Sacked-yards lost	3-16	2-15
Punts	4-32	3-41
Fumbles-lost	2-0	3-0
Penalties-yards	7-56	8-55
Time of possession	29:48	30:12

INDIVIDUAL STATISTICS
RUSHING—Minnesota, O. Smith 11-38, M. Bennett 9-31, Culpepper 7-47. Green Bay, Green 20-80, Davenport 5-14, Favre 3-7, Fisher 1-4.

PASSING—Minnesota, Culpepper 19-29-0-284. Green Bay, Favre 22-33-4-216.

RECEIVING—Minnesota, Moss 4-70, Burleson 4-60, Wiggins 3-32, M. Williams 2-72, O. Smith 2-22, M. Bennett 2-12, Campbell 1-12, M. Robinson 1-4. Green Bay, Driver 7-78, Henderson 3-27, Franks 2-32, J. Walker 2-27, Chatman 2-25, Green 2-16, Luchey 2-10, Fisher 2-1.

MISSED FIELD GOAL ATTEMPTS—Minnesota, M. Andersen 27. Green Bay, Longwell 28.

INTERCEPTIONS—Minnesota, Brown 1-27, Russell 1-14, Winfield 1-3, B. Williams 1-0.

KICKOFF RETURNS—Minnesota, Moore 2-36, O. Smith 2-35. Green Bay, Davenport 3-69, Thurman 1-17, Fisher 1-10.

PUNT RETURNS—Minnesota, Burleson 3-7. Green Bay, Chatman 1-(minus 4).

SACKS—Minnesota, Scott 1, Claiborne 1. Green Bay, Peterson 1, Truluck 1, Hawthorne 1.

Daunte Culpepper threw four TD passes in the Vikings' win over their division rivals.

DIVISIONAL PLAYOFFS

STEELERS 20, JETS 17
Saturday, January 15

N.Y. Jets	0	10	7	0	0—17
Pittsburgh	10	0	0	7	3—20

First Quarter
Pit.—FG, Reed 45, 9:42.
Pit.—Bettis 3 run (Reed kick), 13:02.

Second Quarter
NYJ—FG, Brien 42, 4:27.
NYJ—Moss 75 punt return (Brien kick), 12:00.

Third Quarter
NYJ—Tongue 86 interception return (Brien kick), 11:08.

Fourth Quarter
Pit.—Ward 4 pass from Roethlisberger (Reed kick), 9:00.

Overtime
Pit.—FG, Reed 33, 11:04.
Attendance—64,915.

	N.Y. Jets	Pittsburgh
First downs	17	23
Rushes-yards	27-110	43-193
Passing	165	171
Punt returns	5-83	4-25
Kickoff returns	5-113	4-78
Interception returns	2-110	1-14
Comp.-att.-int.	21-33-1	17-30-2
Sacked-yards lost	3-17	1-10
Punts	6-39	5-40
Fumbles-lost	0-0	1-1
Penalties-yards	4-35	6-45
Time of possession	31:22	39:42

INDIVIDUAL STATISTICS

RUSHING—New York, C. Martin 19-77, Jordan 5-30, Pennington 2-3, Cotchery 1-0. Pittsburgh, Bettis 27-101, Staley 11-54, Roethlisberger 4-30, Haynes 1-8.

PASSING—New York, Pennington 21-33-1-182. Pittsburgh, Roethlisberger 17-30-2-181.

RECEIVING—New York, McCareins 5-82, Moss 4-31, C. Martin 4-29, Sowell 3-11, Becht 2-15, Baker 2-8, Jordan 1-6. Pittsburgh, Ward 10-105, Burress 2-8, Mays 2-19, Bettis 1-21, Randle El 1-6, Haynes 1-2.

MISSED FIELD GOAL ATTEMPTS—New York, Brien 47, 43.

INTERCEPTIONS—New York, Tongue 1-86, Barrett 1-24. Pittsburgh, Polamalu 1-14.

KICKOFF RETURNS—New York, Cotchery 5-113. Pittsburgh, I. Taylor 3-58, Randle El 1-20.

PUNT RETURNS—New York, Moss 5-83. Pittsburgh, Randle El 4-25.

SACKS—New York, J. Ferguson 1. Pittsburgh, Haggans 1, Hoke 1, A. Smith 1.

In a matchup of two of the NFL's all-time leading rushers, Jerome Bettis outgained Curtis Martin.

FALCONS 47, RAMS 17
Saturday, January 15

St. Louis	7	10	0	0—17
Atlanta	14	14	10	9—47

First Quarter
Atl.—Crumpler 18 pass from Vick (Feely kick), 3:00.
St.L.—Curtis 57 pass from Bulger (J. Wilkins kick), 5:46.
Atl.—Dunn 62 run (Feely kick), 7:08.

Second Quarter
Atl.—Dunn 19 run (Feely kick), 5:02.
St.L.—Holt 28 pass from Bulger (J. Wilkins kick), 9:34.
Atl.—Rossum 68 punt return (Feely kick), 14:01.
St.L.—FG, J. Wilkins 55, 15:00.

Third Quarter
Atl.—P. Price 6 pass from Vick (Feely kick), 4:55.
Atl.—FG, Feely 38, 9:06.

Fourth Quarter
Atl.—Safety, 3:21.
Atl.—Duckett 4 run (Feely kick), 13:06.
Attendance—70,709.

	St. Louis	Atlanta
First downs	19	18
Rushes-yards	18-77	40-327
Passing	262	70
Punt returns	0-0	3-152
Kickoff returns	7-122	4-80
Interception returns	0-0	1-0
Comp.-att.-int.	23-35-1	13-17-0
Sacked-yards lost	4-37	1-14
Punts	4-46	2-42
Fumbles-lost	1-1	1-1
Penalties-yards	4-26	4-32
Time of possession	24:25	35:35

INDIVIDUAL STATISTICS

RUSHING—St. Louis, S. Jackson 9-32, M. Faulk 7-30, Looker 1-11, Bulger 1-4. Atlanta, Dunn 17-142, Duckett 15-66, Vick 8-119.

PASSING—St. Louis, Bulger 23-35-1-299. Atlanta, Vick 12-16-0-82, Dunn 1-1-0-2.

RECEIVING—St. Louis, Curtis 7-128, McDonald 4-37, M. Faulk 4-31, Looker 3-38, Holt 2-42, S. Jackson 2-5, Manumaleuna 1-18. Atlanta, P. Price 3-22, Crumpler 2-22, Jenkins 2-19, Finneran 2-8, D. Hall 1-6, White 1-3, Vick 1-2, Dunn 1-2.

MISSED FIELD GOAL ATTEMPTS—None.

INTERCEPTIONS—Atlanta, Webster 1-0.

KICKOFF RETURNS—St. Louis, Cason 6-122, Manumaleuna 1-0. Atlanta, Rossum 4-80.

PUNT RETURNS—Atlanta, Rossum 3-152.

SACKS—St. Louis, Little 1. Atlanta, Brooking 1, T. Hall 1, B. Smith 1, R. Coleman 1.

2004 REVIEW Divisional playoffs

- 219 -

EAGLES 27, VIKINGS 14

Sunday, January 16

Minnesota	0	7	0	7—14
Philadelphia	7	14	0	6—27

First Quarter

Phi.—F. Mitchell 2 pass from McNabb (Akers kick), 8:42.

Second Quarter

Phi.—Westbrook 7 pass from McNabb (Akers kick), :44.
Min.—Culpepper 7 run (M. Andersen kick), 4:23.
Phi.—F. Mitchell 0 fumble return (Akers kick), 4:52.

Fourth Quarter

Phi.—FG, Akers 21, 1:40.
Phi.—FG, Akers 23, 8:21.
Min.—M. Robinson 32 pass from Culpepper (M. Andersen kick), 13:01.
Attendance—67,722.

	Minnesota	Philadelphia
First downs	21	23
Rushes-yards	21-97	25-109
Passing	288	286
Punt returns	2-7	2-7
Kickoff returns	4-111	2-74
Interception returns	0-0	2-38
Comp.-att.-int.	24-47-2	21-33-0
Sacked-yards lost	3-28	1-0
Punts	4-35	3-37
Fumbles-lost	1-0	3-1
Penalties-yards	7-108	4-20
Time of possession	32:25	27:35

INDIVIDUAL STATISTICS

RUSHING—Minnesota, M. Bennett 8-37, O. Smith 7-35, Culpepper 5-25, Moore 1-0. Philadelphia, Westbrook 12-70, Levens 10-36, McNabb 3-3.

PASSING—Minnesota, Culpepper 24-46-2-316, Frerotte 0-1-0-0. Philadelphia, McNabb 21-33-0-286.

RECEIVING—Minnesota, M. Robinson 5-119, Burleson 4-50, O. Smith 4-28, Moss 3-51, Wiggins 2-26, Moore 2-20, M. Bennett 2-(minus 1), Berton 1-16, Campbell 1-7. Philadelphia, F. Mitchell 5-65, Westbrook 5-47, Smith 4-52, Pinkston 3-46, G. Lewis 2-64, Parry 1-7, Levens 1-5.

MISSED FIELD GOAL ATTEMPTS—None.

INTERCEPTIONS—Philadelphia, Trotter 1-35, Reese 1-3.

KICKOFF RETURNS—Minnesota, Moore 2-71, O. Smith 2-40. Philadelphia, Reed 2-74.

PUNT RETURNS—Minnesota, Burleson 2-7. Philadelphia, Wynn 2-7.

SACKS—Minnesota, Winfield 1. Philadelphia, Dawkins 1, Kearse 1, Trotter 0.5, Wayne 0.5.

Todd Pinkston was one of five Eagles with at least three catches and 45 yards receiving.

PATRIOTS 20, COLTS 3

Sunday, January 16

Indianapolis	0	3	0	0—3
New England	0	6	7	7—20

Second Quarter

N.E.—FG, Vinatieri 24, 4:20.
N.E.—FG, Vinatieri 31, 7:04.
Ind.—FG, Vanderjagt 23, 15:00.

Third Quarter

N.E.—Givens 5 pass from Brady (Vinatieri kick), 13:30.

Fourth Quarter

N.E.—Brady 1 run (Vinatieri kick), 7:50.
Attendance—68,756.

	Indianapolis	New England
First downs	18	21
Rushes-yards	15-46	39-210
Passing	230	115
Punt returns	0-0	2-28
Kickoff returns	4-58	1-15
Interception returns	0-0	1-9
Comp.-att.-int.	27-42-1	18-27-0
Sacked-yards lost	1-8	3-29
Punts	6-41	5-39
Fumbles-lost	3-2	0-0
Penalties-yards	4-44	5-35
Time of possession	22:17	37:43

INDIVIDUAL STATISTICS

RUSHING—Indianapolis, James 14-39, Manning 1-7. New England, Dillon 23-144, Faulk 11-56, Brady 4-6, Branch 1-4.

PASSING—Indianapolis, Manning 27-42-1-238. New England, Brady 18-27-0-144.

RECEIVING—Indianapolis, Stokley 8-64, James 7-69, Harrison 5-44, Wayne 3-35, Clark 2-26, Pollard 1-2, Rhodes 1-(minus 2). New England, Dillon 5-17, Givens 4-26, T. Brown 2-13, Fauria 1-17, Branch 1-15, Pass 1-14, Patten 1-12, Faulk 1-11, Graham 1-10, B. Johnson 1-9.

MISSED FIELD GOAL ATTEMPTS—None.

INTERCEPTIONS—New England, Harrison 1-9.

KICKOFF RETURNS—Indianapolis, Rhodes 2-48, Mungro 2-10. New England, Bruschi 1-15.

PUNT RETURNS—New England, T. Brown 2-28.

SACKS—Indianapolis, Reagor 1, Tripplett 1, Freeney 1. New England, Vrabel 1

CONFERENCE CHAMPIONSHIPS

EAGLES 27, FALCONS 10
Sunday, January 23

lanta	.0	10	0	0—10
hiladelphia	.7	7	6	7—27

First Quarter
hi.—Levens 4 run (Akers kick), 10:44.

Second Quarter
tl.—FG, Feely 23, 4:41.
ni.—C. Lewis 3 pass from McNabb (Akers kick), 10:02.
.l.—Dunn 10 run (Feely kick), 12:58.

Third Quarter
hi.—FG, Akers 31, 6:05.
hi.—FG, Akers 34, 13:00.

Fourth Quarter
hi.—C. Lewis 2 pass from McNabb (Akers kick), 11:39.
Attendance—67,717.

	Atlanta	Philadelphia
rst downs	14	22
ushes-yards	26-99	33-156
assing	103	170
unt returns	2-20	1-(-4)
ickoff returns	5-117	3-54
terception returns	0-0	1-19
omp.-att.-int.	11-24-1	18-27-0
acked-yards lost	4-33	2-13
unts	5-26	3-38
umbles-lost	1-0	2-0
enalties-yards	5-24	6-59
me of possession	26:45	33:15

INDIVIDUAL STATISTICS
RUSHING—Atlanta, Dunn 15-59, Duckett 7-14, Vick 4-26. Philadelphia, Westbrook 16-96, McNabb 10-32, Levens 6-18, G. Lewis 1-10.
PASSING—Atlanta, Vick 11-24-1-136. Philadelphia, McNabb 17-26-0-180, etmer 1-1-0-3.
RECEIVING—Atlanta, Crumpler 4-49, P. Price 2-37, Finneran 1-29, White 1-, Jenkins 1-7, Dunn 1-4, McCrary 1-3. Philadelphia, Westbrook 5-39, C. Lewis -20, G. Lewis 2-65, F. Mitchell 2-20, Levens 2-2, Smith 1-21, Pinkston 1-13, arry 1-3.
MISSED FIELD GOAL ATTEMPTS—None.
INTERCEPTIONS—Philadelphia, Dawkins 1-19.
KICKOFF RETURNS—Atlanta, Rossum 4-102, D. Hall 1-15. Philadelphia, ood 2-33, Reed 1-21.
PUNT RETURNS—Atlanta, Rossum 2-20. Philadelphia, Mahe 1-(minus 4).
SACKS—Atlanta, B. Smith 1, Kerney 1. Philadelphia, Burgess 2, H. Thomas, Kearse 1.

The stingy Patriots' defense shut down Staley and ended the Steelers' storybook season.

PATRIOTS 41, STEELERS 27
Sunday, January 23

New England	.10	14	7	10—41
Pittsburgh	.3	0	14	10—27

First Quarter
N.E.—FG, Vinatieri 48, 3:40.
N.E.—Branch 60 pass from Brady (Vinatieri kick), 8:11.
Pit.—FG, Reed 43, 13:38.

Second Quarter
N.E.—Givens 9 pass from Brady (Vinatieri kick), 7:52.
N.E.—Harrison 87 interception return (Vinatieri kick), 12:46.

Third Quarter
Pit.—Bettis 5 run (Reed kick), 4:06.
N.E.—Dillon 25 run (Vinatieri kick), 7:33.
Pit.—Ward 30 pass from Roethlisberger (Reed kick), 12:25.

Fourth Quarter
Pit.—FG, Reed 20, 1:31.
N.E.—FG, Vinatieri 31, 6:57.
N.E.—Branch 23 run (Vinatieri kick), 12:37.
Pit.—Burress 7 pass from Roethlisberger (Reed kick), 14:08.
Attendance—65,242.

	New England	Pittsburgh
First downs	18	19
Rushes-yards	32-126	37-163
Passing	196	225
Punt returns	2-6	3-40
Kickoff returns	5-107	8-115
Interception returns	3-87	0-0
Comp.-att.-int.	14-21-0	14-24-3
Sacked-yards lost	2-11	1-1
Punts	4-40	3-43
Fumbles-lost	1-0	2-1
Penalties-yards	1-5	2-20
Time of possession	28:29	31:31

INDIVIDUAL STATISTICS
RUSHING—New England, Dillon 24-73, Faulk 3-20, Branch 2-37, Brady 2-(minus 2), Givens 1-(minus 2). Pittsburgh, Bettis 17-64, Staley 10-26, Roethlisberger 5-45, Haynes 5-28.
PASSING—New England, Brady 14-21-0-207. Pittsburgh, Roethlisberger 14-24-3-226.
RECEIVING—New England, Givens 5-59, Branch 4-116, T. Brown 1-11, Fauria 1-9, Patten 1-8, Dillon 1-5, Graham 1-(minus 1). Pittsburgh, Ward 5-109, Randle El 3-52, Burress 3-37, Haynes 1-14, Tuman 1-8, Rasby 1-6.
MISSED FIELD GOAL ATTEMPTS—None.
INTERCEPTIONS—New England, Wilson 2-0, Harrison 1-87.
KICKOFF RETURNS—New England, B. Johnson 4-90, Pass 1-17. Pittsburgh, Randle El 4-75, I. Taylor 3-29, Cushing 1-11.
PUNT RETURNS—New England, T. Brown 2-6. Pittsburgh, Randle El 3-40.
SACKS—New England, J. Green 1. Pittsburgh, Porter 1, Haggans 1.

2004 REVIEW Conference championships

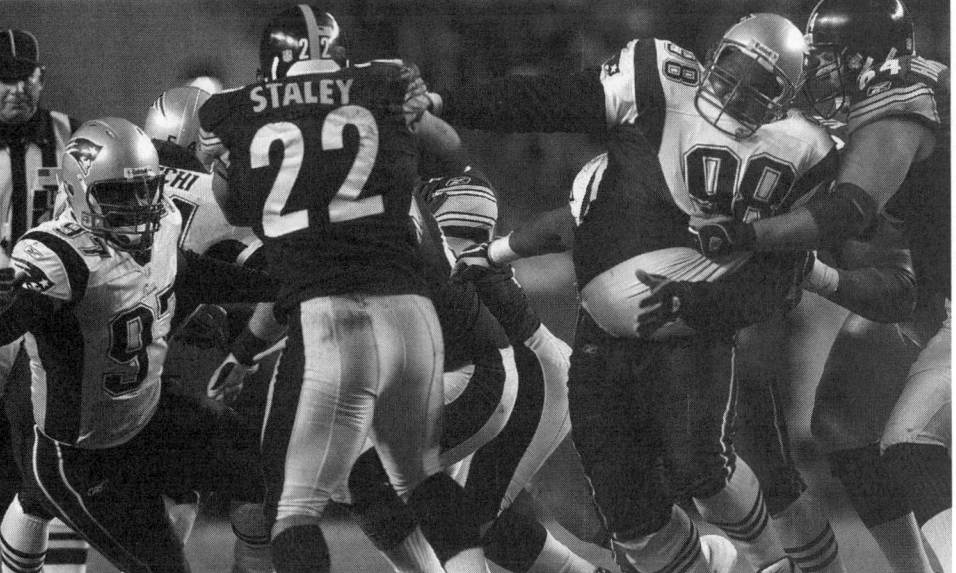

By PAUL ATTNER

Reprinted from the February 18, 2005 issue of *Sporting News.*

THREE OF A KIND

The Patriots' winning hand comes with power-ful preparation, incomparable teamwork—and a little Belichick magic

The wonder of the Patriots isn't just how they keep winning and winning and winning these Super Bowls. It is more than the blinding glitter from all those rings and their secured place among the dominant teams in history. It's their astonishing consistency, their unflappable composure, the almost matter-of-fact approach they employ to make the difficulty of what they have achieved seem so unremarkable.

Amid all the praise and admiration generated by their continued romp through the NFL, these Patriots leave you with the impression that not only did they expect to win Super Bowl 39 but that they expect to win a lot more before this incredible run is over.

"We are not necessarily done," linebacker Mike Vrabel says. "This team is set up for championships, and I don't think we are necessarily finished." That's the chilling part of what we are witnessing. This is not a team at its peak but a team built for continuity and stability. So we better not be surprised if we again see Bill Belichick being doused with water, the signal for his players to begin celebration of yet another title.

New England already is in the same elite territory shared by wondrous clubs from the past: the Bears of the '40s, the Browns of the '50s, the Packers of the '60s, the Steelers of the '70s, the 49ers of the '80s and the Cowboys of the '90s. "For them to win all these titles in this current environment is incredible," Ravens general manager Ozzie Newsome says. "This is a team game, and they show all of us how you win as a team. You've got to put them right up there with these other great teams from the past."

That's what makes them so unique. This era of free agents and a salary cap wasn't supposed to allow any franchise to dominate—"All of us thought it couldn't be done," Falcons General Manager Rich McKay says—yet the Patriots, lacking as they are in abundant superstars, have created a rare blend of intelligence, sacrifice, savvy and coaching to produce this picture of excellence.

How the Patriots hate all these comparisons. They just want to do their jobs and get on with business as soon as possible; after No. 3, they barely mounted a proper postgame celebration. Belichick has convinced them that even a hint of outward satisfaction with their body of work will somehow destroy what they've constructed. "This just means we started at the bottom of the mountain in August

Like many Patriots, Troy Brown—a receiver, nickel back and punt returner—is used at a variety of positions.

and we are now at the top of that mountain," Belichick says.

But they can't dismiss what they've done so easily, not with all this mounting evidence. Now they are the second team to win three Super Bowls in four years—matching the Cowboys of Troy Aikman and Emmitt Smith. Belichick is the the fourth coach to produce as many as three Super Bowl titles, joining Chuck Noll (four), Bill Walsh (three) and Joe Gibbs (three). And Tom Brady is the fourth quarterback with at least three Super Bowl rings, joining Terry Bradshaw, Aikman and Joe Montana. And at 27, Brady won his third at the youngest age.

The Patriots' latest Super Bowl victory, a 24-21 test of nerves over the Eagles, was no easier than

the previous two. It took another exceptional effort by Brady, who passed for two touchdowns and nary an interception, a record-tying 11 catches by Super Bowl MVP Deion Branch and an opportune defense that yielded 357 passing yards to Donovan McNabb but created four turnovers. And that still was barely enough to subdue Philadelphia. But there was no reason to suspect it would be simple; these Eagles are almost as solid and competent as the Patriots, and together they represent the best the NFL has to offer. And that, for the rest of the league, should be very, very scary.

The problem for the remaining 30 teams is this: How do they close this gap of success the Eagles and Patriots have created between themselves and everyone else? It is the crucial competitive question facing the NFL, one that once seemed outlandish to raise given the constant upheaval created by a parity-pushing system the past decade-plus. Yet the presence of these two franchises—the most successful and consistent of any over the past five years—in this Super Bowl highlights the change we are seeing. That is, at least these two clubs have shown you can maintain dominant rosters in an era in which that seemed impossible.

"These two teams are almost mirror images of each other as to how they go about trying to win," says Aikman, now a FOX analyst. "You walk through the door at both places, and it doesn't take long to figure out why they are successful. You just feel it.

llon (right) is rarity on the atriots—a guy ho was a star omewhere lse.

They have a chain of command, lines are clearly defined as to what people do, there is tremendous respect for everyone within those buildings, and they get good, quality people. And they do sacrifice individual for the team. There is a culture right now where players want it to be about them. But not with these two teams. That is the bottom line."

This is how bullies bludgeon the competition. Over the past five years, the Eagles are the only team to make the playoffs each season— and the only one to play in four conference championship games. And their record (59-21) exceeds anyone else's. Once the playoffs start, it is the Patriots who excel.

There seems little reason both franchises can't maintain such splendor. The Eagles are $17 million under the cap and have five picks in the first three rounds of this year's draft. New England, which traditionally spends to the cap limit, is methodically adding younger players to its roster, stockpiling quality reserve talent to cushion the aging process in some spots. Neither should lose any quality player in the free-agent market this offseason. Plus, their quarterbacks are young enough to still improve, and who would not want Belichick or Andy Reid as their coach?

Even the usually stoic Belichick celebrated when Rodney Harrison's interception sealed the Patriots' second consecutive Super Bowl victory.

OK, maybe there is one possible crack, at least in New England. Belichick will lose both of his coordinators, Charlie Weis and Romeo Crennel. Weis is the new head coach at Notre Dame, and Crennel will be named coach of the Browns this week. Both have been with Belichick at every Super Bowl, and their expertise has drawn leaguewide admiration. For the first time in his New England tenure, Belichick will be faced with a major staff shakeup, which might be enough to help the pretenders close the gap. Yet, as long as Belichick keeps showing up on game days in that ugly sweatshirt of his, you have to believe the Patriots still will be more than OK.

As soon as this Super Bowl was over, "30 other teams suddenly had a lot of hope," Newsome says. Certainly, the pattern created by the free-agent system and the salary cap reinforces Newsome's optimism. Every new season, we have teams moving from last place to ring challengers. But the new reality of the league should start to dampen this kind of enthusiasm. You likely will still see examples of the dramatic ascent every season, but now such improvement might not be sufficient to dislodge the Patriots and Eagles. So instead of the free-for-all scramble we have been witnessing for Super Bowl berths, the NFL now is more about bullies against 98-pound weaklings.

Look how difficult it is to overcome New England. The Eagles couldn't do it despite a truly inspirational effort from receiver Terrell Owens, who returned from a broken ankle weeks ahead of his original prognosis and caught nine passes for 122 yards. The Patriots limited the Philadelphia running game to 45 yards and forced 51 passes by McNabb, who wasn't quite sharp enough against a surprising 4-3 scheme—New England primarily had been a 3-4 club all season—that contained his scrambling. And he wasn't good enough in a puzzlingly slow hurry-up offense late in the game to help the Eagles win their first title in 44 years.

The Patriots also have Brady, who grows more impressive with every championship. His coolness and accuracy under the greatest of pressure separate him from his peers. On this night, he overcame a slow start with a scintillating second half in which he led the Patriots on two long scoring drives to break away from a 7-all halftime tie and gain control of the contest.

He is now 9-0 in the playoffs and never was more professional than in this latest playoff run, when the Patriots toppled the Colts, Steelers and Eagles, all momentous achievements. "He is just an amazing young man," Weis says. "He kept calling me during the week late at night to talk about the game plan. I just wanted to sleep." No wonder the Eagles had problems with him.

"The gap can be eliminated, no doubt about it," says ESPN analyst Randy Mueller, a top candidate t take over the Seahawks' front office. "But it's different than it used to be when I was the Saints' general manager (2000-02). These two have taken talent evaluation to the next level. They have shown that i is not necessarily the most talented teams that win. It is more the way their head coaches and staff brin them together as a team; how they use the chem-

Tedy Bruschi and the Pats' defense limited McNabb's effectiveness by containing—and sacking—him and kept the powerful Philadelphia offense in check.

stry, the IQ of the players and fit the players' strengths into the team's schemes. You need to pay special attention to 'team' and chemistry now when putting together your roster."

Certainly, the model used by the Patriots and Eagles is influencing the shaping of front offices and rosters throughout the league. Both franchises have head coaches who also are in charge of personnel. A similar alignment has been adopted this offseason by the Dolphins, who have handed over all power to Nick Saban, and the 49ers, who have done likewise with Mike Nolan. John York, owner of the 49ers, admits he is attempting to revitalize his once-proud franchise by copying the New England blueprint. But playing copycat is easy; actually constructing rosters good enough to knock off these bullies is something else.

Because of this new league order, no more than half the teams—if that—can realistically overcome the Eagles and Patriots. At the moment, no one else has the proper combination of elements it would take to kick them off the top.

"To catch them, you need a new stadium to give you the proper cash flow, a new practice facility to attract free agents, a franchise quarterback who can be the face of the organization, a head coach who has command of his situation and a front office that has a blueprint for success and can work in concert with the head coach," FOX analyst Brian Baldinger says. "And you need a philosophy about how to go about winning games, a sound philosophy that cuts through an entire organization."

Franchises that constantly change head coaches,

assistant coaches and front office personnel have no chance against the stability of the Pats and Eagles. Just consider the past two offseasons; there have been 14 head coaching changes and double that in offensive and defensive coordinator changes. The Packers alone are on their third defensive coordinator in three years. Just as important, franchises with clueless ownership can't compete with these two teams. "I think some owners are more committed to winning than others," Patriots owner Robert Kraft says. "Some just want to make as much money as they can." Kraft and Eagles owner Jeffrey Lurie have demonstrated the proper mentality to produce a winner. They are willing to provide the financial resources for free agents (to acquire needed talent) and assistant coaching salaries (to maintain staff stability) along with allowing their football people to make all the football decisions. There hardly has been any turnover among the staff or front office of either team the past five years. Owners can be educated, too. Lurie once was considered a bumbler who was messing up the Eagles. Then he hired Reid.

"They have done a good job of dealing with the hard decisions, letting name players go because of salary cap problems, things like that," the Falcons' McKay says. "That takes understanding by the owner. He has to realize not everything is going to work out and you have to ride out the downs. Not every owner can handle that."

The quick turnarounds of so many teams from season to season have created a leaguewide quest for the quick fix, a mentality that contradicts the approach by these Super Bowl clubs. "It is so hard to be disciplined right now," Mueller says. "But you have to be. That is what I have learned, too. You have to stick with what you think is right and not chase talent for talent's sake. The Eagles and Patriots have figured out the players they need to make their systems work, and they are willing to confine their talent search to these players."

Nor can the wannabes hope to become dominant by adopting a fantasy football approach to roster building. The Patriots and Eagles don't believe in wild spending sprees for available players. Instead, they are incredibly selective, using offseason pickups such as Corey Dillon, Jevon Kearse and Owens to fill major needs. "It is tempting to want to use free agents to make everything better," McKay says. "But I am firmly convinced that is just the wrong way to go about it. We feel we can close the gap by identifying our core players, keeping them on the team, be smart in the draft and have continuity in the scheme and staff. I tell my people I want our offseason grade (for free agents) to be a C. If we get an A, we should be scared. Too many offseason A's boomerang."

McKay's gap-closing ability is enhanced by a decision he made almost a year ago, when he hired Jim Mora as his coach. The importance of the head coach has grown during this era; just consider the way Belichick and Reid dominate their organizations, how their players reflect their demeanor and respond to their party lines. "I think having a coaching staff comprised of great teachers, starting with the head coach, is paramount if you want to get to the top now," Texans G.M. Charley Casserly says. "There's something like 15 new guys on a roster every year, so you are assimilating new people into your system constantly. So your coaches need to be able to get their methods across quickly." Reid puts it this way: "It's like we are college coaches."

So you can close the gap by hiring a special head coach. But no one has developed an accurate measure that identifies who will succeed. Belichick had been mediocre in Cleveland; Kraft still gave him total control. Reid had been a position coach with the Packers when Lurie hired him; only later did he give him G.M. duties. Now York in San Francisco hopes the untested Nolan, who never has been an NFL head coach or G.M., can duplicate the triumphs of Belichick and Reid. As much as anything, you have to get lucky in this coach search.

The bullies also keep demonstrating that it is now the smarter teams, and not necessarily the most gifted ones, that win. Everyone raves about the Patriots' IQs. The Patriots didn't get that way by accident. New England refuses to employ players who lack ability to absorb its schemes. "You have to have players who are not going to lose games for you, who

Branch is small in stature but came up with big plays to win the MVP trophy.

don't do dumb things at the wrong times," Newsome says. "You rarely see the Patriots do things in games that hurt them. So you have to beat them; they won't beat themselves. The bottom line to me right now is to add impact players, rid yourself of guys who do things to lose games and manage the cap. If we do that, we can overcome the Patriots."

Character matters, too. "When I hired Bill," Kraft says, "I said, 'Just don't bring thugs or hoodlums to New England.'" And he hasn't.

What he has brought is glory. "We all want what he has now," Casserly says. "Nothing lasts forever. The league keeps getting better, and we'll catch these teams. Otherwise, we shouldn't be in this business."

Still, you wonder. These bullies are really, really good. Don't look for them to be trampled any time soon. **TSN**

PATRIOTS 24, EAGLES 21
Sunday, February 6

New England	0	7	7	10—24
Philadelphia	0	7	7	7—21

Second Quarter
Phi.—Smith 6 pass from McNabb (Akers kick), 5:05.
N.E.—Givens 4 pass from Brady (Vinatieri kick), 13:50.

Third Quarter
N.E.—Vrabel 2 pass from Brady (Vinatieri kick), 3:56.
Phi.—Westbrook 10 pass from McNabb (Akers kick), 11:25.

Fourth Quarter
N.E.—Dillon 2 run (Vinatieri kick), 1:16.
N.E.—FG, Vinatieri 22, 6:20.
Phi.—G. Lewis 30 pass from McNabb (Akers kick), 13:12.
Attendance—78,125.

	New England	Philadelphia
First downs	21	24
Rushes-yards	28-112	17-45
Passing	219	324
Punt returns	4-26	3-19
Kickoff returns	3-61	5-114
Interception returns	3-5	0-0
Comp.-att.-int.	23-33-0	30-51-3
Sacked-yards lost	2-17	4-33
Punts	7-45	5-43
Fumbles-lost	1-1	2-1
Penalties-yards	7-47	3-3
Time of possession	31:37	28:23

INDIVIDUAL STATISTICS
RUSHING—New England, Dillon 18-75, Faulk 8-38, Pass 1-0, Brady 1 (minus 1). Philadelphia, Westbrook 15-44, Levens 1-1, McNabb 1-0.
PASSING—New England, Brady 23-33-0-236. Philadelphia, McNabb 30-51-3-35?
RECEIVING—New England, Branch 11-133, Dillon 3-31, Givens 3-19, Fau 2-27, T. Brown 2-17, Graham 1-7, Vrabel 1-2. Philadelphia, Owens 9-12 Westbrook 7-60, Pinkston 4-82, G. Lewis 4-53, Smith 4-27, F. Mitchell 1-1 Parry 1-2.
MISSED FIELD GOAL ATTEMPTS—None.
INTERCEPTIONS—New England, Harrison 2-5, Bruschi 1-0.
KICKOFF RETURNS—New England, B. Johnson 2-44, Pass 1-17 Philadelphia, Reed 4-82, Hood 1-32.
PUNT RETURNS—New England, T. Brown 3-12, B. Johnson 1-1 Philadelphia, Westbrook 3-19.
SACKS—New England, Harrison 1, Bruschi 1, Vrabel 1, Seymour Philadelphia, Burgess 1, Team 1.

PRO BOWL

NFC SQUAD

OFFENSE

WR— Muhsin Muhammad, Carolina*
Joe Horn, New Orleans*
Javon Walker, Green Bay
Torry Holt, St. Louis
Terrell Owens, Philadelphia*
T— Walter Jones, Seattle*
Orlando Pace, St. Louis*
Flozell Adams, Dallas
Tra Thomas, Philadelphia*
G— Larry Allen, Dallas*
Marco Rivera, Green Bay*
Steve Hutchinson, Seattle
C— Olin Kreutz, Chicago*
Matt Birk, Minnesota
TE— Alge Crumpler, Atlanta*
Jason Witten, Dallas
QB— Donovan McNabb, Philadelphia*
Daunte Culpepper, Minnesota
Michael Vick, Atlanta
RB— Tiki Barber, N.Y. Giants*
Ahman Green, Green Bay
Brian Westbrook, Philadelphia
Shaun Alexander, Seattle
FB— William Henderson, GB*
NOTE: WR Owens was replaced due to injury by Holt; T Thomas was replaced due to injury by Adams; RB Alexander was replaced due to injury by Westbrook.

DEFENSE

DE— Bertrand Berry, Arizona*
Julius Peppers, Carolina*
Patrick Kerney, Atlanta*
DT— La'Roi Glover, Dallas*
Shaun Rogers, Detroit
Kevin Williams, Minnesota
OLB—Keith Brooking, Atlanta*
Marcus Washington, Washington*
Mark Fields, Carolina
Derrick Brooks, Tampa Bay
ILB— Dan Morgan, Carolina*
Jeremiah Trotter, Philadelphia
CB— Ronde Barber, Tampa Bay*
Lito Sheppard, Philadelphia*
Dre Bly, Detroit

SS— Michael Lewis, Philadelphia*
FS— Brian Dawkins, Philadelphia*
Roy Williams, Dallas
NOTE: OLB Brooks was replaced due to injury by Fields.

SPECIALISTS

P— Mitch Berger, New Orleans
PK— David Akers, Philadelphia
KR— Allen Rossum, Atlanta
Eddie Drummond, Detroit
ST— Ike Reese, Philadelphia
LS— Brian Jennings, San Francisco
NOTE: KR Drummond was replaced due to injury by Rossum.

AFC SQUAD

OFFENSE

WR— Marvin Harrison, Indianapolis*
Chad Johnson, Cincinnati*
Andre Johnson, Houston
Hines Ward, Pittsburgh
T— Jonathan Ogden, Baltimore*
Tarik Glenn, Indianapolis
Marvel Smith, Pittsburgh
Willie Roaf, Kansas City*
Willie Anderson, Cincinnati
G— Alan Faneca, Pittsburgh*
Will Shields, Kansas City*
Brian Waters, Kansas City
C— Kevin Mawae, N.Y. Jets*
Jeff Hartings, Pittsburgh
TE— Antonio Gates, San Diego*
Tony Gonzalez, Kansas City
QB— Peyton Manning, Indianapolis*
Tom Brady, New England
Drew Brees, San Diego
RB— LaDainian Tomlinson, San Diego*
Jerome Bettis, Pittsburgh
Rudi Johnson, Cincinnati
Corey Dillon, New England
Edgerrin James, Indianapolis
Curtis Martin, N.Y. Jets
FB— Tony Richardson, Kansas City*
NOTE: G Roaf was replaced due to injury by Glenn; G Anderson was replaced due to injury by M. Smith; RB James was replaced due to injury by Dillon; RB Dillon was replaced due to injury by Bettis; RB Martin was replaced due to injury by Johnson.

DEFENSE

DE— Jason Taylor, Miami*
Dwight Freeney, Indiana*
Aaron Smith, Pittsburgh
John Abraham, N.Y. Jets
IL— Marcus Stroud, Jacksonville*
Sam Adams, Buffalo*
John Henderson, Jacksonville
Richard Seymour, New England
OLB—Takeo Spikes, Buffalo*
Terrell Suggs, Baltimore*
Joey Porter, Pittsburgh
ILB— James Farrior, Pittsburgh*
Tedy Bruschi, New England
Ray Lewis, Baltimore
CB— Champ Bailey, Denver*
Tory James, Cincinnati*
Nate Clements, Buffalo
Chris McAlister, Baltimore
SS— Ed Reed, Baltimore*
Troy Polamalu, Pittsburgh
FS— John Lynch, Denver*
NOTE: DE Abraham was replaced due to injury by Smith; IL Seymour was replaced due to injury by Henderson; ILB Lewis was replaced due to injury by Bruschi; CB McAlister was replaced due to injury by Clements.

SPECIALISTS

P— Shane Lechler, Oakland
PK— Adam Vinatieri, New England
KR— Terrence McGee, Buffalo
ST— Larry Izzo, New England
LS— Kendall Gammon, Kansas City

*Elected starter.

Pro Bowl

2004 REVIEW

AT ALOHA STADIUM, HONOLULU, FEBRUARY 13, 2005

Sunday, February 13

AFC 0   10   14   3—27
NFC 14   14   0   10—38

First Quarter

AFC—Harrison 62 pass from Manning (Vinatieri kick), 8:44.
NFC—Ward 41 pass from Manning (Vinatieri kick), 2:57.

Second Quarter

NFC—Westbrook 12 run (Akers kick), 12:15.
NFC—Ward 39 onside kick return (Vinatieri kick), 12:09.
AFC—Gates 12 pass from Manning (Vinatieri kick), 6:01.
NFC—FG Akers 33, 1:45.

Third Quarter

NFC—Holt 27 pass from Vick (Akers kick), 11:19.
NFC—Vick 3 run (Akers kick), 4:10.

Fourth Quarter

NFC—FG Vinatieri 44, 14:19.
NFC—FG Akers 29, 9:07.
AFC—Tomlinson 4 run (Vinatieri kick), 8:56.
Attendance—50,225.

Individual Statistics

RUSHING—NFC, T. Barber 9-70, B. Westbrook 7-39, A. Green 5-25, M. Vick 6-10, D. Culpepper 2-8, D. McNabb 1-3. AFC, R. Johnson 6-33, L. Tomlinson 7-8, L. Izzo 1-27, J. Bettis 5-23, T. Richardson 3-6, H. Ward 1-4, T. Brady 1-2, D. Brees 3--3.

PASSING—NFC, M. Vick 14-24-1-205, D. Culpepper 9-15-0-124, D. McNabb 1-8-0-24, J. Horn 0-1-0-0. AFC, P. Manning 6-10-3-130, T. Brady 4-9-0-48, D. Brees 2-2-0-58, L. Tomlinson 0-1-0-0.

RECEIVING—NFC, T. Holt 5-99. J. Horn 4-60, M. Muhammad 4-54, J. Walker 4-53, J. Witten 3-50, B. Westbrook 2-7, A. Crumpler 1-24, T. Barber 1-6. AFC, H. Ward 3-63, A. Gates 3-51, M. Harrison 2-66, T. Richardson 2-7, T. Gonzalez 1-25, A. Johnson 1-24.

FIELD GOALS—NFC, Akers 2-3. AFC, Vinatieri 1-2.

INTERCEPTIONS—NFC, L. Sheppard 1. AFC, J. Porter 1, N. Clements 1, T. Spikes 1.

KICKOFF RETURNS—NFC, A. Rossum 5-27.2. AFC, T. McGee 5-25.2, H. Ward 1-39.0.

PUNT RETURNS—AFC, N. Clements 1-7.0.

SACKS—NFC, K. Williams 1.0, B. Berry 1.0. AFC, J. Henderson 1.0.

	AFC	NFC
First Downs	15	26
Rushes-yards	27-120	27-155
Passes complete-yards	12-223	24-337
Punt returns-yards	1-7	0-0
Kickoff returns-yards	6-165	5-136
Interception returns-yards	3-51	0-0
Comp.-Att.-Int.	12-22-1	24-48-3
Sacked-yds. lost	2-13	2-16
Punts-avg.	2-42.5	1-59.0
Penalties-Yards	3-28	2-10
Fumbles-Lost	1-1	1-0
Time Of Possession	24:26	35:34

PLAYER PARTICIPATION

COMPLETE LIST

Player, Team	GP	GS
Abdullah, Rabih, N.E.	9	0
Abraham, Donnie, N.Y. Jets	16	16
Abraham, John, N.Y. Jets	12	12
Adams, Anthony, S.F.	14	12
Adams, Charlie, Denver	4	0
Adams, Flozell, Dallas	16	16
Adams, Keith, Philadelphia	16	2
Adams, Mike, San Francisco	8	0
Adams, Sam, Buffalo	16	16
Ahanotu, Chidi, Miami-T.B.	13	5
Aiken, Sam, Buffalo	16	0
Akers, David, Philadelphia	16	0
Albright, Ethan, Washington	16	0
Alexander, Brent, N.Y. Giants	16	16
Alexander, Eric, New England	3	0
Alexander, P.J., Denver	5	0
Alexander, Roc, Denver	16	1
Alexander, Shaun, Seattle	16	16
Alexander, Stephen, Detroit	16	15
Allen, Brian, Carolina	14	0
Allen, David, Jacksonville	5	0
Allen, Ian, Philadelphia	4	0
Allen, James, New Orleans	16	10
Allen, Jared, Kansas City	15	10
Allen, Kenderick, N.Y. Giants	5	2
Allen, Larry, Dallas	16	16
Allen, Will, N.Y. Giants	16	16
Allen, Will, Tampa Bay	16	0
Alston, Richard, Cleveland	9	0
Alstott, Mike, Tampa Bay	14	11
Amano, Eugene, Tennessee	15	2
Amato, Ken, Tennessee	16	0
Ambrose, Ashley, N.O.	9	6
Andersen, Morten, Minnesota	16	0
Anderson, Bennie, Baltimore	16	12
Anderson, Bryan, Chicago	4	0
Anderson, Charlie, Houston	15	0
Anderson, Courtney, Oakland	9	4
Anderson, Damien, Arizona	4	0
Anderson, Dwight, St. Louis	12	0
Anderson, Gary, Tennessee	15	0
Anderson, Marques, Oakland	14	10
Anderson, Richie, Dallas	12	4
Anderson, Tim, Buffalo	3	0
Anderson, Willie, Cincinnati	16	16
Andrews, Shawn, Philadelphia	1	1
Andrews, Stacy, Cincinnati	1	0
Andruzzi, Joe, New England	16	16
Archuleta, Adam, St. Louis	16	14
Armstrong, Derick, Houston	14	1
Arrington, LaVar, Washington	4	2
Ashworth, Tom, New England	6	6
Askew, B.J., N.Y. Jets	16	0
Askew, Matthias, Cincinnati	5	0
Asomugha, Nnamdi, Oakland	16	7
Atkins, James, San Francisco	3	0
Ayanbadejo, Brendon, Miami	16	2
Ayanbadejo, Obafemi, Arizona	16	5
Ayodele, Akin, Jacksonville	16	16
Azumah, Jerry, Chicago	12	8
Baber, Billy, Tampa Bay	1	0
Babers, Roderick, Detroit	2	0
Babin, Jason, Houston	16	16
Babineaux, Jordan, Seattle	6	0
Backus, Jeff, Detroit	16	16
Bacon, Waine, Indianapolis	11	0
Badger, Brad, Oakland	16	12
Bailey, Champ, Denver	16	16
Baker, Chris, N.Y. Jets	16	0
Baker, Eugene, Carolina	3	0
Baker, Jason, K.C.-Ind.-Den.	10	0
Baker, Rashad, Buffalo	14	3
Ball, Dave, San Diego	6	0
Ball, Jason, San Diego	3	2
Banks, Tony, Houston	5	0
Bannan, Justin, Buffalo	10	0
Bannister, Alex, Seattle	7	1
Banta, Bradford, Buffalo	3	0
Banta-Cain, Tully, N.E.	16	0
Barber, Ronde, Tampa Bay	16	16
Barber, Shawn, Kansas City	8	8
Barber, Tiki, N.Y. Giants	16	14
Barker, Bryan, Green Bay	16	0
Barlow, Kevan, San Francisco	15	14
Barnes, Brandon, Washington	12	0
Barnes, Darian, Dallas	16	10
Barnes, Lionel, Jacksonville	3	3
Barnett, Nick, Green Bay	16	16
Barrett, David, N.Y. Jets	16	16
Barry, Kevin, Green Bay	13	3
Bartee, William, Kansas City	14	9
Barton, Eric, N.Y. Jets	16	15
Bartrum, Mike, Philadelphia	16	0
Bashir, Idrees, Indianapolis	13	13
Bates, Solomon, Seattle	10	3
Battle, Arnaz, San Francisco	14	0
Battle, Julian, Kansas City	12	1
Battles, Ainsley, Pittsburgh	1	0
Bauman, Rashad, Cincinnati	4	0
Baxter, Gary, Baltimore	16	16
Baxter, Jarrod, Houston	8	1
Beasley, Aaron, Atlanta	14	3
Beasley, Fred, San Francisco	14	10
Becht, Anthony, N.Y. Jets	16	16
Beckett, Rogers, Cincinnati	7	5
Beckham, Tony, Tennessee	5	1
Bedell, Brad, Green Bay	4	0
Beisel, Monty, Kansas City	11	9
Bell, Jacob, Tennessee	15	14
Bell, Jason, Houston	9	0
Bell, Kendrell, Pittsburgh	3	0
Bell, Marcus, Detroit	16	0
Bell, Tatum, Denver	14	0
Bell, Yeremiah, Miami	13	0
Bellamy, Jay, New Orleans	16	16
Bellamy, Ronald, Miami	2	0
Bennett, Brandon, Carolina	8	0
Bennett, Darren, Minnesota	15	0
Bennett, Drew, Tennessee	16	16
Bennett, Michael, Minnesota	11	7
Bentley, Kevin, Cleveland	16	3
Bentley, LeCharles, N. O.	16	16
Berger, Mitch, New Orleans	16	0
Berlin, Eddie, Tennessee	16	1
Bernard, Rocky, Seattle	14	1
Berrian, Bernard, Chicago	16	1
Berry, Bertrand, Arizona	16	16
Berton, Sean, Minnesota	14	7
Bettis, Jerome, Pittsburgh	15	6
Betts, Ladell, Washington	16	1
Beverly, Eric, Atlanta	13	3
Bibla, Martin, Atlanta	11	0
Bidwell, Josh, Tampa Bay	16	0
Bierria, Terreal, Seattle	15	12
Binn, David, San Diego	16	0
Bird, Cory, Indianapolis	13	4
Birk, Matt, Minnesota	12	11
Black, Jordan, Kansas City	16	4
Blade, Willie, Jacksonville	5	1
Blake, Jeff, Philadelphia	3	0
Blakley, Dwayne, Atlanta	15	1
Blaylock, Derrick, Kansas City	12	5
Bledsoe, Drew, Buffalo	16	16
Bly, Dre', Detroit	13	13
Bober, Chris, Kansas City	12	2
Bockwoldt, Colby, N.O.	16	7
Bodden, Leigh, Cleveland	8	1
Boiman, Rocky, Tennessee	7	0
Bolden, Juran, Jacksonville	13	0
Boldin, Anquan, Arizona	10	9
Boller, Kyle, Baltimore	16	16
Bollinger, Brooks, N.Y. Jets	1	0
Booker, Marty, Miami	15	15
Boone, Alfonso, Chicago	12	2
Boschetti, Ryan, Washington	3	1
Boulware, Michael, Seattle	16	6
Bouman, Todd, New Orleans	16	0
Bowen, Matt, Washington	5	5
Bowens, David, Miami	16	15
Bowens, Tim, Miami	2	0
Brackett, Gary, Indianapolis	15	0
Bradford, Corey, Houston	15	16
Bradley, Jon, Tampa Bay	6	0
Brady, Kyle, Jacksonville	11	8
Brady, Tom, New England	16	16
Braham, Rich, Cincinnati	10	10
Branch, Colin, Carolina	16	15
Branch, Deion, New England	9	7
Brandon, Sam, Denver	9	0
Brandt, David, San Diego	3	0
Brayton, Tyler, Oakland	15	15
Brees, Drew, San Diego	15	15
Brewer, Jack, N.Y. Giants	13	0
Bridges, Jeremy, Arizona	14	8
Brien, Doug, N.Y. Jets	16	0
Briggs, Lance, Chicago	16	16
Brightful, Lamont, Miami	2	0
Brock, Raheem, Indianapolis	16	6
Bromell, Lorenzo, N.Y. Giants	2	0
Brooking, Keith, Atlanta	16	16
Brooks, Aaron, New Orleans	16	16
Brooks, Barrett, Pittsburgh	5	0
Brooks, Derrick, Tampa Bay	16	16
Brooks, Ethan, Baltimore	14	0
Broussard, Jamall, Carolina	8	0
Brown, Alex, Chicago	16	16

Player, Team	GP	GS	Player, Team	GP	GS	Player, Team	GP	GS
rown, Antonio, Washington	3	0	Carson, Leonardo, Dallas	15	15	Colombo, Marc, Chicago	8	2
rown, Chad, Seattle	7	7	Carstens, Jordan, Carolina	12	1	Colvin, Rosevelt, N.E.	16	1
rown, Chris, Tennessee	11	11	Carswell, Dwayne, Denver	15	14	Comella, Greg, Tampa Bay	7	0
rown, Cornell, Baltimore	13	0	Carter, Andre, San Francisco	7	6	Compton, Mike, Jacksonville.....	13	0
rown, Courtney, Cleveland	2	2	Carter, Dyshod, Ariz.-Clev.	11	0	Conaty, Bill, Minnesota	8	0
rown, Dante, Pittsburgh	1	0	Carter, Jonathan, N.Y. Jets.......	13	1	Connot, Scott, Kansas City	2	0
rown, Dee, Cleveland	5	0	Carter, Kerry, Seattle	16	0	Conway, Curtis, S.F.	16	5
rown, Eric, Houston	13	4	Carter, Kevin, Tennessee	16	16	Conwell, Ernie, New Orleans	16	10
rown, Fakhir, New Orleans	16	10	Carter, Ki-Jana, New Orleans.....	2	0	Cook, Damion, Balt.-Clev.	15	6
rown, Josh, Seattle.................	16	0	Carter, Quincy, N.Y. Jets...........	7	3	Cook, Jameel, Tampa Bay	12	5
rown, Kris, Houston	16	0	Carter, Tim, N.Y. Giants	5	0	Cooley, Chris, Washington	16	9
rown, Mark, N.Y. Jets	12	6	Carter, Tyrone, Pittsburgh.........	9	0	Cooper, Chris, Dal.-S.F.	10	2
rown, Michael, Washington	2	0	Cartwright, Rock, Wash.	13	0	Cooper, Deke, Jacksonville........	16	0
rown, Mike, Chicago...............	2	2	Cash, Chris, Detroit..................	11	5	Cooper, Jarrod, Car.-Oak.	15	0
rown, Milford, Houston	2	2	Cason, Aveion, St. Louis............	3	0	Cooper, Josh, San Francisco	1	0
rown, Orlando, Baltimore	14	13	Caver, Quinton, Kansas City	16	4	Cooper, Marquis, Tampa Bay	14	0
rown, Ralph, Minnesota	12	0	Celestin, Oliver, N.Y. Jets	8	0	Cooper, Stephen, San Diego......	16	2
rown, Ray, Washington	16	14	Cesaire, Jacques, San Diego	16	12	Copper, Terrance, Dallas	10	0
rown, Ruben, Chicago.............	9	9	Chambers, Chris, Miami	15	15	Cortez, Jose, Minnesota	8	0
rown, Rufus, Washington	1	0	Chambers, Kirk, Cleveland........	6	0	Cotchery, Jerricho, N.Y. Jets	12	0
rown, Sheldon, Philadelphia....	16	16	Chandler, Chris, St. Louis	5	2	Cousin, Terry, N.Y. Giants	16	5
rown, Tim, Tampa Bay	15	4	Chandler, Jeff, Car.-Wash.	5	0	Cowart, Sam, N.Y. Jets	9	2
rown, Tony, San Francisco	16	4	Chatham, Matt, New England....	5	0	Cox, Torrie, Tampa Bay	10	0
rown, Troy, New England	12	0	Chatman, Antonio, Green Bay ...	16	2	Craft, Jason, New Orleans	14	0
rowning, John, Kansas City	16	7	Chatman, Jesse, San Diego.......	15	0	Cramer, Casey, Carolina	6	1
ruce, Isaac, St. Louis..............	16	16	Chavous, Corey, Minnesota	16	16	Crayton, Patrick, Dallas............	8	0
ruener, Mark, Houston	16	11	Cheek, Steve, Kansas City	12	0	Crecion, Gabriel, S.F.	1	0
runell, Mark, Washington	9	9	Cherry, Je'Rod, New England	12	0	Crocker, Chris, Cleveland..........	12	5
ruschi, Tedy, New England	16	16	Chester, Larry, Miami...............	2	2	Crockett, Zack, Oakland	16	9
ryant, Antonio, Dal.-Clev.	15	8	Chillar, Brandon, St. Louis	16	5	Croom, Larry, Arizona	6	1
ryant, Fernando, Detroit	10	10	Chrebet, Wayne, N.Y. Jets	16	1	Crowell, Angelo, Buffalo	16	0
ryant, Matt, Ind.-Mia.	4	0	Christie, Steve, N.Y. Giants	16	0	Crumpler, Alge, Atlanta	14	14
ryant, Roderick, N.Y. Jets........	13	0	Chukwurah, Patrick, Denver	14	0	Culpepper, Daunte, Minn.	16	16
ryant, Tony, New Orleans	16	0	Ciurciu, Vinny, Carolina............	16	4	Cundiff, Billy, Dallas	16	0
ryant, Wendell, Arizona	3	0	Claiborne, Chris, Minnesota	12	12	Curry, Clarence, Arizona	1	0
ryson, Shawn, Detroit..............	16	1	Clancy, Kendrick, Pittsburgh	8	0	Curry, Donte', Detroit...............	12	0
rzezinski, Doug, Carolina........	8	8	Clark, Dallas, Indianapolis	15	13	Curry, Ronald, Oakland	12	3
ua, Tony, Miami	7	0	Clark, Danny, Oakland..............	16	16	Curtis, Kevin, St. Louis	15	0
uchanan, Ray, Oakland	16	16	Clark, Desmond, Chicago	15	13	Cushing, Matt, Pittsburgh.........	16	0
uchanon, Phillip, Oakland.......	14	14	Clark, Ryan, Washington	15	11	Dalton, Lional, Kansas City.......	16	13
uckley, Terrell, N.Y. Jets	16	0	Clauss, Jared, Tennessee..........	14	1	Daniels, Phillip, Washington	5	5
uckner, Brentson, Carolina	15	15	Claybrooks, DeVone, Dallas.......	8	0	Dansby, Karlos, Arizona	15	11
ulger, Marc, St. Louis..............	14	14	Clayton, Michael, Tampa Bay	16	13	Darby, Chartric, Tampa Bay	16	16
ulluck, Keith, Tennessee	16	16	Cleeland, Cam, St. Louis...........	16	9	Darche, Jean-Philippe, Seattle...	16	0
urgess, Derrick, Phil.	12	11	Clement, Anthony, Arizona	16	7	Darilek, Trey, Philadelphia	3	0
urleson, Nate, Minnesota	16	15	Clements, Nate, Buffalo	16	16	Darius, Donovin, Jacksonville	16	16
urns, Curry, N.Y. Giants..........	8	2	Clemons, Chris, Washington	6	0	Darling, Devard, Baltimore	3	0
urns, Joe, Buffalo	16	0	Clemons, Duane, Cincinnati	14	14	Darling, James, Arizona	15	15
urns, Keith, Tampa Bay	16	0	Clifton, Chad, Green Bay..........	16	16	Davenport, Najeh, Green Bay	11	1
urress, Plaxico, Pittsburgh	11	11	Cloud, Michael, N.Y. Giants	10	0	Davey, Rohan, New England	4	0
ush, Steve, San Francisco	5	2	Coady, Rich, St. Louis	16	5	David, Jason, Indianapolis.........	16	11
utler, Jerametrius, St. Louis ...	16	16	Coakley, Dexter, Dallas	16	16	Davis, Andra, Cleveland	11	11
utler, Robb, San Diego	5	0	Coates, Sherrod, Cleveland	5	0	Davis, Andre', Cleveland	7	7
ain, Jeremy, Chicago...............	5	0	Cobbs, Cedric, New England	3	0	Davis, Anthony, Tampa Bay	2	0
aldwell, Reche, San Diego	6	6	Cochran, Antonio, Seattle	16	7	Davis, Carey, Indianapolis.........	1	0
alico, Tyrone, Tennessee	1	0	Colbert, Keary, Carolina	15	15	Davis, Domanick, Houston........	15	15
almus, Rocky, Tennessee	4	3	Colclough, Ricardo, Pitts.	16	0	Davis, Don, New England	16	2
ampbell, Dan, Dallas..............	3	2	Cole, Colin, Green Bay.............	3	1	Davis, James, Detroit...............	16	15
ampbell, Kelly, Minnesota	16	3	Coleman, Cosey, Tampa Bay	16	16	Davis, Jerome, San Francisco ...	2	0
ampbell, Khary, Washington ...	9	0	Coleman, Erik, N.Y. Jets...........	16	16	Davis, Keith, Dallas	15	0
ampbell, Mark, Buffalo	12	12	Coleman, Kenyon, Dallas	12	0	Davis, Leonard, Arizona	15	15
arey, Vernon, Miami	14	2	Coleman, Marco, Denver	16	16	Davis, Rob, Green Bay	16	0
arlisle, Cooper, Denver	16	4	Coleman, Marcus, Houston	12	12	Davis, Rod, Minnesota	14	0
arney, John, New Orleans	16	0	Coleman, Rod, Atlanta	13	13	Davis, Russell, Arizona	16	16
arpenter, Dwaine, S.F.	15	6	Coles, Laveranues, Wash.	16	16	Davis, Sammy, San Diego	12	10
arr, David, Houston.................	16	16	Collins, Kerry, Oakland.............	14	13	Davis, Stephen, Carolina	2	2
arroll, Ahmad, Green Bay	14	11	Collins, Todd, Kansas City	2	0	Dawkins, Brian, Philadelphia	15	15

Player, Team	GP	GS	Player, Team	GP	GS	Player, Team	GP	G
Dawson, Phil, Cleveland	16	0	Edwards, Steve, Chicago	15	8	Foreman, Jay, Houston	11	1
Dayne, Ron, N.Y. Giants	14	2	Edwards, Troy, Jacksonville	16	4	Forney, Kynan, Atlanta	16	1
Dearth, James, N.Y. Jets	16	0	Ekuban, Ebenezer, Cleveland	16	11	Forsey, Brock, Miami	7	
Deese, Derrick, Tampa Bay	16	16	Elam, Jason, Denver	16	0	Foster, DeShaun, Carolina	4	
Delhomme, Jake, Carolina	16	16	Elling, Aaron, Tenn.-Minn.	8	0	Foster, George, Denver	16	1
DeLoach, Jerry, Houston	15	3	Ellis, Greg, Dallas	16	16	Fowler, Melvin, Cleveland	15	
DeLoatch, Curtis, N.Y. Giants	16	0	Ellis, Shaun, N.Y. Jets	15	15	Fowler, Ryan, Dallas	2	
DeMar, Enoch, Cleveland	15	11	Elliss, Luther, Denver	8	0	Fox, Keyaron, Kansas City	12	
Demps, Will, Baltimore	16	16	Emmons, Carlos, N.Y. Giants	15	15	Fox, Vernon, Detroit	14	
DeMulling, Rick, Indianapolis	11	11	Ena, Justin, Tennessee	16	5	Fraley, Hank, Philadelphia	16	1
Denney, Ryan, Buffalo	16	5	Engelberger, John, S.F.	16	15	Francis, Carlos, Oakland	5	
Dennis, Pat, Washington	11	0	Engram, Bobby, Seattle	13	7	Franklin, Aubrayo, Baltimore	6	
Detmer, Koy, Philadelphia	16	1	Ephraim, Alonzo, Philadelphia	14	2	Franks, Bubba, Green Bay	16	1
DeVries, Jared, Detroit	15	0	Euhus, Tim, Buffalo	12	5	Franz, Todd, Washington	16	
Diamond, Lorenzo, Arizona	5	4	Evans, Demetric, Washington	12	8	Frazier, Lance, Dallas	12	
Diedrick, Dahrran, Wash.	1	0	Evans, Heath, Seattle	15	0	Freeman, Arturo, Miami	16	
Diehl, David, N.Y. Giants	16	16	Evans, Josh, N.Y. Jets	1	0	Freeney, Dwight, Indianapolis	16	1
Dielman, Kris, San Diego	15	0	Evans, Lee, Buffalo	16	11	Freitas, Makoa, Indianapolis	16	
Diem, Ryan, Indianapolis	16	16	Evans, Troy, Houston	13	0	Frerotte, Gus, Minnesota	16	
Diggs, Na'il, Green Bay	14	14	Fabini, Jason, N.Y. Jets	16	16	Friedman, Lennie, Wash.	5	
Dilfer, Trent, Seattle	5	2	Faggins, DeMarcus, Houston	16	2	Frost, Derrick, Cleveland	16	
Dilger, Ken, Tampa Bay	16	14	Faine, Jeff, Cleveland	13	13	Fuamatu-Ma'afala, Chris, Jack.	7	
Dillon, Corey, New England	15	14	Faneca, Alan, Pittsburgh	16	16	Fujita, Scott, Kansas City	16	1
Dingle, Adrian, San Diego	10	2	Fargas, Justin, Oakland	12	0	Fuller, Corey, Baltimore	14	
Dinkins, Darnell, Baltimore	10	4	Farrior, James, Pittsburgh	16	16	Fuller, Curtis, G.B.-Car.	7	
Dishman, Chris, St. Louis	7	5	Farris, Jimmy, Atlanta	14	0	Furrey, Mike, St. Louis	8	
Dixon, David, Minnesota	16	16	Fatafehi, Mario, Denver	16	16	Gabriel, Doug, Oakland	16	
Dixon, Tony, Dallas	16	7	Faulk, Kevin, New England	11	1	Gaffney, Jabar, Houston	16	1
Dockery, Derrick, Washington	16	16	Faulk, Marshall, St. Louis	14	14	Gage, Justin, Chicago	16	
Dockett, Darnell, Arizona	16	15	Faulk, Trev, St. Louis	13	2	Gaines, Michael, Carolina	15	
Doering, Chris, Pittsburgh	3	0	Fauria, Christian, N.E.	16	10	Gallery, Robert, Oakland	16	1
Doering, Jason, Washington	6	0	Favors, Greg, Jacksonville	15	11	Galloway, Joey, Tampa Bay	10	
Dorenbos, Jon, Buffalo	13	0	Favre, Brett, Green Bay	16	16	Gamble, Chris, Carolina	16	
Dorsey, Ken, San Francisco	9	7	Feagles, Jeff, N.Y. Giants	16	0	Gammon, Kendall, K.C.	16	
Dorsey, Nat, Minnesota	13	7	Feeley, A.J., Miami	11	8	Gandy, Mike, Chicago	5	
Doss, Mike, Indianapolis	10	9	Feely, Jay, Atlanta	16	0	Gandy, Wayne, New Orleans	16	1
Douglas, Hugh, Philadelphia	16	3	Ferguson, Jason, N.Y. Jets	16	14	Gannon, Rich, Oakland	3	
Douglas, Marques, Baltimore	16	15	Ferguson, Nick, Denver	16	1	Garcia, Jeff, Cleveland	11	1
Downing, Eric, San Diego	3	0	Ferguson, Robert, Green Bay	13	5	Gardner, Barry, Cleveland	14	
Draft, Chris, Atlanta	14	13	Fiedler, Jay, Miami	8	7	Gardner, Gilbert, Indianapolis	11	
Driver, Donald, Green Bay	16	11	Fields, Mark, Carolina	14	10	Gardner, Rich, Tennessee	15	
Droughns, Reuben, Denver	16	15	Finn, Jim, N.Y. Giants	16	9	Gardner, Rod, Washington	16	1
Drummond, Eddie, Detroit	11	1	Finneran, Brian, Atlanta	12	1	Gardner, Talman, N.O.	11	
Duckett, Damane, Car.-N.Y. G.	6	1	Fisher, Bryce, St. Louis	16	14	Gardocki, Chris, Pittsburgh	16	
Duckett, T.J., Atlanta	13	0	Fisher, Tony, Green Bay	16	0	Garmon, Kelvin, Cleveland	8	
Dudley, Rickey, Tampa Bay	3	0	Fisher, Travis, St. Louis	10	10	Garner, Charlie, Tampa Bay	3	
Dugan, Jeff, Minnesota	14	2	Fisk, Jason, San Diego	15	1	Garrard, David, Jacksonville	4	
Duncan, Jamie, Atlanta	4	2	Fitzgerald, Larry, Arizona	16	16	Garrett, Kevin, St. Louis	14	
Dunn, Jason, Kansas City	16	0	FitzSimmons, Casey, Detroit	16	2	Garza, Roberto, Atlanta	16	1
Dunn, Warrick, Atlanta	16	16	Flanagan, Mike, Green Bay	3	3	Gates, Antonio, San Diego	15	1
Dwight, Tim, San Diego	12	0	Fleck, P.J., San Francisco	1	0	Gay, Randall, New England	15	
Dyson, Andre, Tennessee	16	16	Fleming, Troy, Tennessee	16	0	Gbaja-Biamila, Akbar, Oak.	14	
Earl, Glenn, Houston	12	9	Flemons, Ronald, Miami	1	0	Gbaja-Biamila, Kabeer, G.B.	16	1
Easlick, Doug, Miami	3	1	Fletcher, Jamar, San Diego	16	0	Geathers, Robert, Cincinnati	14	
Eason, Nicholas, Cleveland	1	0	Fletcher, London, Buffalo	16	16	George, Eddie, Dallas	13	
Easy, Omar, Kansas City	15	0	Florence, Drayton, San Diego	13	5	Gibson, Aaron, Chicago	4	
Eaton, Chad, Dallas	6	1	Flowers, Erik, St. Louis	9	0	Gilbert, Tony, Jacksonville	16	
Echemandu, Adimchinobe, Clev.	4	0	Floyd, Anthony, Indianapolis	11	2	Gildon, Jason, Jacksonville	9	
Edinger, Paul, Chicago	16	0	Floyd, Malcom, San Diego	4	2	Gilmore, Bryan, Miami	16	
Edwards, Antuan, Mia.-St. L.	14	13	Flutie, Doug, San Diego	2	1	Gilmore, John, Chicago	16	
Edwards, Donnie, San Diego	16	16	Flynn, Mike, Baltimore	9	5	Givens, David, New England	15	1
Edwards, Dwan, Baltimore	4	0	Folau, Spencer, New Orleans	16	3	Gleason, Steve, New Orleans	15	
Edwards, Eric, Arizona	16	1	Foley, Steve, San Diego	16	16	Glenn, Aaron, Houston	16	1
Edwards, Kalimba, Detroit	16	0	Fonoti, Toniu, San Diego	16	16	Glenn, Jason, N.Y. Jets	10	
Edwards, Marc, Jacksonville	13	5	Fontenot, Jerry, Cincinnati	11	6	Glenn, Tarik, Indianapolis	16	
Edwards, Mario, Tampa Bay	15	3	Foote, Larry, Pittsburgh	16	16	Glenn, Terry, Dallas	6	
Edwards, Ron, Buffalo	16	2	Fordham, Todd, Carolina	15	7	Glover, La'Roi, Dallas	16	1

Player, Team	GP	GS	Player, Team	GP	GS	Player, Team	GP	GS
ymph, Junior, Atlanta	3	0	Hall, John, Washington	8	0	Henry, Travis, Buffalo	10	5
odfrey, Randall, San Diego	15	15	Hall, Lamont, New Orleans	16	2	Henson, Drew, Dallas	7	1
off, Mike, San Diego	16	16	Hall, Travis, Atlanta	15	0	Hentrich, Craig, Tennessee	16	0
ings, Nick, Carolina	16	8	Hallen, Bob, San Diego	2	0	Herndon, Kelly, Denver	16	16
old, Ian, Tampa Bay	16	13	Hambrick, Troy, Arizona	10	0	Herndon, Steve, Atlanta	15	1
aldberg, Adam, Minnesota	13	6	Hamilton, Ben, Denver	16	16	Herring, Kim, Cincinnati	12	10
onzalez, Joaquin, Cleveland	16	11	Hamilton, Bobby, Oakland	16	15	Hetherington, Chris, Oakland	5	2
onzalez, Tony, Kansas City	16	16	Hamilton, Derrick, S.F.	2	0	Hicks, Artis, Philadelphia	14	13
ooch, Jeff, Tampa Bay	16	1	Hamilton, Lawrence, Arizona	1	0	Hicks, Eric, Kansas City	16	16
oodman, Andre', Detroit	11	4	Hamlin, Ken, Seattle	16	16	Hicks, Maurice, S.F.	9	2
oodspeed, Joey, St. Louis	16	5	Hampton, Casey, Pittsburgh	6	6	Hill, Darrell, Tennessee	14	0
oodwin, Jonathan, N.Y. Jets	15	3	Hampton, William, Carolina	4	0	Hill, Marquise, New England	1	0
ordon, Amon, Cleveland	6	0	Hand, Norman, N.Y. Giants	11	11	Hill, Renaldo, Arizona	13	10
ordon, Lamar, Miami	3	2	Hankton, Cortez, Jacksonville	12	0	Hillenmeyer, Hunter, Chicago	16	11
orin, Brandon, New England	14	10	Hankton, Karl, Carolina	15	0	Hilliard, Ike, N.Y. Giants	16	15
owin, Toby, N.Y. Jets	16	0	Hannam, Ryan, Seattle	16	0	Hilliard, Jason, N.Y. Giants	2	0
agg, Scott, San Francisco	16	16	Hanson, Chris, Jacksonville	16	0	Hobson, Victor, N.Y. Jets	12	10
aham, Daniel, New England	14	14	Hanson, Jason, Detroit	16	0	Hochstein, Russ, N.E.	16	2
aham, Earnest, Tampa Bay	9	0	Hanson, Joselio, S.F.	13	3	Hodel, Nathan, Arizona	16	0
aham, Shayne, Cincinnati	16	0	Hape, Patrick, Denver	16	5	Hodge, Sedrick, New Orleans	9	6
amatica, Bill, Miami	1	0	Hardwick, Nick, San Diego	14	14	Hoke, Chris, Pittsburgh	14	10
amatica, Martin, T.B.-Ind.	15	0	Hardy, Kevin, Cincinnati	16	14	Holcomb, Kelly, Cleveland	4	2
ant, Charles, New Orleans	16	16	Hargrove, Anthony, St. Louis	15	2	Holcombe, Robert, Tennessee	16	8
ant, DeLawrence, Oakland	9	9	Harper, Alan, N.Y. Jets	11	0	Holdman, Warrick, Cleveland	16	14
ant, Deon, Jacksonville	16	16	Harper, Deveron, N.O.	5	0	Holland, Darius, Denver	2	0
asmanis, Paul, Philadelphia	4	0	Harper, Nick, Indianapolis	14	14	Holland, Montrae, N.O.	13	13
ay, Bobby, Chicago	10	4	Harrington, Joey, Detroit	16	16	Holliday, Vonnie, Kansas City	9	3
ay, Chris, Seattle	16	16	Harris, Al, Green Bay	16	16	Hollings, Tony, Houston	7	0
een, Ahman, Green Bay	15	15	Harris, Arlen, St. Louis	14	1	Hollowell, T.J., N.Y. Giants	4	0
een, Barrett, N.Y. Giants	10	9	Harris, Joey, Carolina	4	0	Holmes, Earl, Detroit	16	14
een, Brandon, Jacksonville	3	0	Harris, Kwame, S.F.	14	7	Holmes, Priest, Kansas City	8	8
een, Howard, New Orleans	14	12	Harris, Napoleon, Oakland	14	9	Holt, Terrence, Detroit	16	0
een, Jamaal, Philadelphia	8	0	Harris, Nick, Detroit	16	0	Holt, Torry, St. Louis	16	16
een, Jarvis, New England	16	1	Harris, Quentin, Arizona	16	4	Hood, Roderick, Philadelphia	16	2
een, Louis, Denver	6	0	Harris, Tommie, Chicago	16	16	Hoover, Brad, Carolina	14	9
een, Mike, Chicago	16	16	Harris, Walt, Washington	16	2	Hope, Chris, Pittsburgh	16	16
een, Roderick, Baltimore	9	0	Harrison, James, Pittsburgh	16	4	Hopkins, Brad, Tennessee	11	11
een, Trent, Kansas City	16	16	Harrison, Marvin, Ind.	16	16	Hopson, Tyrone, Detroit	11	0
een, William, Cleveland	15	12	Harrison, Rodney, N.E.	16	16	Horn, Chris, Kansas City	14	0
eenwood, Morlon, Miami	16	15	Hart, Clinton, San Diego	14	0	Horn, Joe, New Orleans	16	16
eer, Jabari, Buffalo	12	1	Hartings, Jeff, Pittsburgh	16	16	Horton, Jason, Green Bay	14	0
egg, Kelly, Baltimore	14	14	Harts, Shaunard, Kansas City	16	6	Houser, Kevin, New Orleans	16	0
egory, Damian, Tampa Bay	6	0	Hartsock, Ben, Indianapolis	16	3	Houshmandzadeh, T.J., Cin.	16	13
eisen, Nick, N.Y. Giants	15	7	Hartwell, Edgerton, Baltimore	16	15	Hovan, Chris, Minnesota	13	9
iese, Brian, Tampa Bay	11	10	Hartwig, Justin, Tennessee	15	15	Howard, Brian, St. Louis	15	1
iffin, Cornelius, Wash.	15	15	Hasselbeck, Matt, Seattle	14	14	Howard, Darren, New Orleans	13	12
iffin, Quentin, Denver	6	4	Hawkins, Artrell, Carolina	14	4	Howard, Reggie, Miami	15	3
iffith, Justin, Atlanta	12	11	Hawthorne, Michael, G.B.	16	5	Howell, John, Tampa Bay	16	6
iffith, Robert, Cleveland	16	16	Hayes, Gerald, Arizona	16	1	Howry, Keenan, Minnesota	6	0
oce, DeJuan, St. Louis	11	4	Haynes, Michael, Chicago	16	4	Huff, Orlando, Seattle	16	14
oss, Jordan, Carolina	16	16	Haynes, Verron, Pittsburgh	13	0	Hulsey, Corey, Oakland	3	0
ossman, Rex, Chicago	3	3	Haynesworth, Albert, Tenn.	10	10	Hunt, Cletidus, Green Bay	16	14
ove, Jake, Oakland	9	8	Hayward, Reggie, Denver	16	15	Hunter, Pete, Dallas	3	3
urode, Andre, Dallas	14	13	Heap, Todd, Baltimore	6	6	Hunter, Wayne, Seattle	1	0
utierrez, Brock, S.F.	16	15	Heard, Ronnie, S.F.	16	14	Hutchins, Von, Indianapolis	16	1
aayer, Adam, Minnesota	4	1	Hearst, Garrison, Denver	7	0	Hutchinson, Chad, Chicago	5	5
addad, Drew, Buffalo	1	0	Heiden, Steve, Cleveland	13	13	Hutchinson, Steve, Seattle	16	16
adnot, Rex, Miami	14	7	Heinrich, Keith, Cleveland	7	0	Hutton, Trevor, Indianapolis	4	0
aggan, Mario, Buffalo	16	0	Heitmann, Eric, S.F.	16	16	Hymes, Randy, Baltimore	14	7
aggans, Clark, Pittsburgh	13	13	Heller, Will, Tampa Bay	10	2	Idonije, Israel, Chicago	15	0
akim, Az-Zahir, Detroit	12	5	Henderson, Devery, N.O.	1	0	Ioane, Junior, Houston	3	0
aley, Jermaine, Washington	13	1	Henderson, E.J., Minnesota	14	14	Irons, Grant, Oakland	8	2
all, Carlos, Tennessee	14	14	Henderson, John, Jack.	16	16	Isom, Jasen, San Francisco	5	1
all, Cory, Atlanta	14	13	Henderson, William, G.B.	16	8	Ivy, Corey, Tampa Bay	16	0
all, Dante, Kansas City	16	6	Hendricks, Tommy, Jack.	15	1	Iwuoma, Chidi, Pittsburgh	14	0
all, DeAngelo, Atlanta	10	9	Henry, Anthony, Cleveland	15	14	Izzo, Larry, New England	16	0
all, James, Detroit	16	16	Henry, Leonard, Miami	6	2	Jackson, Alonzo, Pittsburgh	7	0

Player, Team	GP	GS	Player, Team	GP	GS	Player, Team	GP	G
Jackson, Corey, Cleveland	1	0	Jones, Fred, Kansas City	16	0	Kooistra, Scott, Cincinnati	16	
Jackson, Darrell, Seattle	16	16	Jones, Freddie, Arizona	16	15	Koppen, Daniel, New England	16	1
Jackson, Dexter, Tampa Bay	6	1	Jones, Greg, Jacksonville	16	3	Kosier, Kyle, San Francisco	16	1
Jackson, Eddie, Carolina	10	0	Jones, Julius, Dallas	8	7	Koutouvides, Niko, Seattle	16	
Jackson, Frisman, Cleveland	10	0	Jones, Kenyatta, Washington	3	2	Kozlowski, Brian, Washington	11	
Jackson, Grady, Green Bay	10	10	Jones, Kevin, Detroit	15	14	Kramer, Jordan, Tennessee	4	
Jackson, James, Clev.-G.B.	5	0	Jones, Levi, Cincinnati	16	16	Kranchick, Matt, Pittsburgh	2	
Jackson, Nate, Denver	12	0	Jones, Mark, N.Y. Giants	14	0	Krause, Ryan, San Diego	1	
Jackson, Steven, St. Louis	14	3	Jones, Nathan, Dallas	16	1	Kreider, Dan, Pittsburgh	16	
Jackson, Terry, San Francisco	16	0	Jones, Rushen, Minnesota	5	0	Krenzel, Craig, Chicago	6	
Jackson, Tyoka, St. Louis	14	0	Jones, Tebucky, New Orleans	16	16	Kreutz, Olin, Chicago	16	1
Jacobs, Taylor, Washington	15	4	Jones, Terry, Baltimore	15	10	Kriewaldt, Clint, Pittsburgh	15	
Jacox, Kendyl, New Orleans	13	13	Jones, Thomas, Chicago	14	14	Kuehl, Ryan, N.Y. Giants	16	
James, Bradie, Dallas	16	2	Jones, Walter, Seattle	16	16	Kurpeikis, Justin, N.E.	5	
James, Edgerrin, Indianapolis	16	16	Jordan, LaMont, N.Y. Jets	16	0	Kyle, Jason, Carolina	16	
James, Jeno, Miami	14	14	Jordan, Leander, San Diego	5	0	Labinjo, Mike, Philadelphia	3	
James, Tory, Cincinnati	16	16	Jordan, Omari, Carolina	4	0	LaBoy, Travis, Tennessee	13	
Jameson, Michael, Cleveland	16	0	Joseph, William, N.Y. Giants	15	4	Lake, Antwan, Atlanta	16	
Jammer, Quentin, San Diego	16	16	Josue, Steve, Green Bay	4	0	Landeta, Sean, St. Louis	10	
Janikowski, Sebastian, Oak.	16	0	Joyce, Matt, Detroit	12	3	Lang, Kenard, Cleveland	16	1
Jasper, Ed, Atlanta	12	12	Jue, Bhawoh, Green Bay	16	4	Larson, Kyle, Cincinnati	16	
Jefferson, Joseph, Ind.	9	3	June, Cato, Indianapolis	16	16	Lassiter, Kwamie, St. Louis	4	
Jenkins, Corey, Chi.-Mia.	7	0	Jurevicius, Joe, Tampa Bay	10	3	Lavalais, Chad, Atlanta	16	
Jenkins, Cullen, Green Bay	16	6	Kacyvenski, Isaiah, Seattle	16	13	Law, Ty, New England	7	
Jenkins, Kris, Carolina	4	4	Kadela, Dave, Carolina	1	0	Lawrie, Nate, Tampa Bay	2	
Jenkins, Michael, Atlanta	16	0	Kaeding, Nate, San Diego	16	0	Layne, George, S.D.-Atl.	4	
Jennings, Brian, S.F.	16	0	Kaesviharn, Kevin, Cincinnati	15	6	Leach, Mike, Denver	16	
Jennings, Jonas, Buffalo	14	14	Kampman, Aaron, Green Bay	16	16	Leach, Vonta, Green Bay	6	
Jerman, Greg, Miami	1	0	Karney, Mike, New Orleans	16	8	Leber, Ben, San Diego	16	1
Jimoh, Ade, Washington	15	0	Kasay, John, Carolina	14	0	Lechler, Shane, Oakland	16	
Joe, Leon, Chicago-Arizona	5	0	Kashama, Alain, Chicago	3	0	Leckey, Nick, Arizona	16	
Johnson, Al, Dallas	16	15	Kasper, Kevin, New England	8	0	Lee, Andy, San Francisco	16	
Johnson, Andre, Houston	16	16	Kassell, Brad, Tennessee	15	14	Lee, Charles, Tampa Bay	7	
Johnson, Bethel, N.E.	13	1	Kearse, Jevon, Philadelphia	14	14	Lee, Donald, Miami	16	
Johnson, Brad, Tampa Bay	4	4	Keisel, Brett, Pittsburgh	13	0	Lee, James, Green Bay	9	
Johnson, Bryan, Chicago	12	6	Kelley, Ethan, New England	1	0	Lee, ReShard, Dallas	14	
Johnson, Bryant, Arizona	16	11	Kelly, Brian, Tampa Bay	16	16	Leftwich, Byron, Jacksonville	14	1
Johnson, Chad, Cincinnati	16	16	Kelly, Reggie, Cincinnati	16	15	Legree, Lance, N.Y. Giants	15	
Johnson, Dennis, S.F.	1	0	Kelly, Tommy, Oakland	10	3	Lehan, Michael, Cleveland	10	
Johnson, Dirk, Philadelphia	16	0	Kelsay, Chris, Buffalo	16	10	Lehman, Teddy, Detroit	16	1
Johnson, Doug, Tennessee	2	0	Kemoeatu, Maake, Baltimore	14	3	Lehr, Matt, Dallas	7	
Johnson, Ellis, Denver	13	0	Kendall, Pete, N.Y. Jets	15	15	Leisle, Rodney, New Orleans	2	
Johnson, Eric, Atlanta	16	0	Kennedy, Jimmy, St. Louis	9	5	Lelie, Ashley, Denver	16	1
Johnson, Eric, San Francisco	16	14	Kennedy, Kenoy, Denver	16	16	Lemons, Devin, Washington	1	
Johnson, Jarret, Baltimore	16	0	Kennison, Eddie, Kansas City	14	14	Lenon, Paris, Green Bay	16	
Johnson, Jeremi, Cincinnati	16	6	Kern, Chris, Detroit	2	0	Lepsis, Matt, Denver	16	1
Johnson, Kevin, Baltimore	16	5	Kerney, Patrick, Atlanta	16	15	Levens, Dorsey, Philadelphia	15	
Johnson, Keyshawn, Dallas	16	16	Keys, Isaac, Arizona	3	0	Leverette, Otis, San Francisco	5	
Johnson, Kyle, Denver	14	3	Kiel, Terrence, San Diego	16	16	Lewis, Alex, Detroit	15	
Johnson, Landon, Cincinnati	16	11	Kight, Kelvin, Green Bay	1	0	Lewis, Chad, Philadelphia	15	
Johnson, Larry, Kansas City	10	3	Kimrin, Ola, Washington	5	0	Lewis, Damione, St. Louis	16	1
Johnson, Raylee, Denver	14	1	King, Andre, Cleveland	9	2	Lewis, Greg, Philadelphia	16	
Johnson, Rudi, Cincinnati	16	16	King, Austin, Atlanta	4	0	Lewis, Jamal, Baltimore	12	1
Johnson, Spencer, Minnesota	9	7	King, Shaun, Arizona	3	2	Lewis, Jermaine, Jacksonville	9	
Johnson, Tank, Chicago	16	1	King, Vick, Miami	2	0	Lewis, Keith, San Francisco	16	
Johnson, Ted, New England	16	15	Kinney, Erron, Tennessee	9	9	Lewis, Kevin, N.Y. Giants	16	1
Johnson, Teyo, Oakland	8	1	Kircus, David, Detroit	7	0	Lewis, Michael, New Orleans	14	
Johnson, Tim, Oakland	16	0	Kirschke, Travis, Pittsburgh	16	1	Lewis, Michael, Philadelphia	16	1
Johnson, Todd, Chicago	16	10	Kitna, Jon, Cincinnati	4	3	Lewis, Ray, Baltimore	15	1
Johnstone, Lance, Minnesota	16	1	Klecko, Dan, New England	6	2	Light, Matt, New England	16	1
Jolley, Doug, Oakland	16	13	Kleinsasser, Jim, Minnesota	1	1	Lilja, Ryan, Indianapolis	7	
Jones, Adrian, N.Y. Jets	12	0	Klemm, Adrian, New England	2	0	Lindell, Rian, Buffalo	16	
Jones, Brian, Jacksonville	16	0	Knight, Roger, New Orleans	15	0	Little, Earl, Cleveland	16	1
Jones, Daryl, Chicago	2	0	Knight, Sammy, Miami	16	16	Little, Leonard, St. Louis	16	1
Jones, Dhani, Philadelphia	16	15	Knorr, Micah, Denver	12	0	Littleton, Jody, Detroit	8	
Jones, Donnie, Seattle	7	0	Kolodziej, Ross, Arizona	13	4	Liwienski, Chris, Minnesota	16	1
			Konrad, Rob, Miami	10	1	Lloyd, Brandon, S.F.	13	1

Player, Team	GP	GS	Player, Team	GP	GS	Player, Team	GP	GS
cklear, Sean, Seattle	16	0	McCadam, Kevin, Atlanta	16	2	Mitchell, Qasim, Chicago	16	14
effler, Cullen, Minnesota	16	0	McCants, Darnerien, Wash.	5	1	Mixon, Kenny, Minnesota	14	14
gan, Mike, Pittsburgh	3	0	McCardell, Keenan, S. D.	7	6	Mohr, Chris, Atlanta	16	0
ng, Rien, Tennessee	15	3	McCareins, Justin, N.Y. Jets	16	16	Molinaro, Jim, Washington	11	0
ngwell, Ryan, Green Bay	16	0	McClain, Jimmy, Jacksonville	1	0	Monds, Mario, Miami	5	0
oker, Dane, St. Louis	14	0	McCleon, Dexter, Kansas City	13	6	Monk, Quincy, Houston	2	0
pienski, Tom, Indianapolis	2	0	McClover, Darrell, N.Y. Jets	16	0	Montgomery, Monty, N.O.	5	0
rd, Jammal, Houston	1	0	McClure, Todd, Atlanta	16	16	Moore, Brandon, S.F.	12	1
sman, J.P., Buffalo	4	0	McCollum, Andy, St. Louis	16	16	Moore, Brandon, N.Y. Jets	13	13
tt, Andre, Washington	4	3	McCoo, Eric, Philadelphia	1	0	Moore, Clarence, Baltimore	15	6
verne, David, Detroit	15	13	McCown, Josh, Arizona	14	13	Moore, Dave, Tampa Bay	15	0
we, Omare, New England	3	0	McCown, Luke, Cleveland	5	4	Moore, Eddie, Miami	13	3
cas, Justin, St. Louis	7	0	McCrary, Fred, Atlanta	3	2	Moore, Langston, Cincinnati	15	8
cas, Ken, Seattle	16	16	McCray, Bobby, Jacksonville	16	7	Moore, Larry, Cincinnati	13	1
chey, Nick, Green Bay	16	6	McCree, Marlon, Houston	16	1	Moore, Mewelde, Minnesota	10	3
cier, Wayne, N.Y. Giants	15	9	McCutcheon, Daylon, Clev.	12	10	Moore, Michael, Atlanta	1	1
ke, Triandos, Denver	10	0	McDonald, Shaun, St. Louis	16	0	Moore, Rashad, Seattle	16	12
man, Dustin, Chicago	16	10	McDougle, Jerome, Phil.	11	0	Moorehead, Aaron, Ind.	7	0
nch, James, Cincinnati	1	0	McDougle, Stockar, Detroit	16	16	Moorehead, Kindal, Carolina	14	12
nch, John, Denver	15	15	McFarland, Anthony, T.B.	8	8	Moorman, Brian, Buffalo	16	0
acklin, David, Arizona	16	16	McFarland, Dylan, Buffalo	2	0	Morant, Johnnie, Oakland	4	0
addox, Anthony, Jack.	2	0	McGahee, Willis, Buffalo	16	11	Moreland, Earthwind, N.E.	9	2
addox, Tommy, Pittsburgh	4	3	McGarrahan, Scott, Tenn.	16	1	Moreno, Zeke, San Diego	9	0
adison, Sam, Miami	16	16	McGee, Terrence, Buffalo	16	13	Morey, Sean, Pittsburgh	16	0
aese, Joe, Baltimore	15	0	McGinest, Willie, N.E.	16	16	Morgan, Dan, Carolina	12	12
ahan, Sean, Tampa Bay	16	8	McGraw, Jon, N.Y. Jets	12	1	Morgan, Quincy, Clev.-Dal.	15	12
ahe, Reno, Philadelphia	11	0	McGrorty, Dusty, St. Louis	1	0	Morris, Maurice, Seattle	15	0
allard, Wesly, N.Y. Giants	4	0	McHugh, Sean, Green Bay	1	0	Morris, Rob, Indianapolis	15	14
angum, Kris, Carolina	15	10	McIntosh, Damion, Miami	14	14	Morris, Sammy, Miami	13	8
annelly, Patrick, Chicago	16	0	McKenzie, Kareem, N.Y. Jets	16	16	Morrow, Harold, Baltimore	15	0
anning, Eli, N.Y. Giants	9	7	McKenzie, Mike, G.B.-N.O.	11	10	Morton, Chad, Washington	6	0
anning, Peyton, Ind.	16	16	McKie, Jason, Chicago	15	2	Morton, Christian, Atlanta	2	0
anning Jr., Ricky, Carolina	16	16	McKinley, Alvin, Cleveland	16	2	Morton, Johnnie, Kansas City	13	12
anuel, Marquand, Seattle	15	0	McKinney, Seth, Miami	16	16	Moses, J.J., Houston	15	0
anumaleuna, Brandon, St.L.	16	16	McKinney, Steve, Houston	16	16	Moss, Randy, Minnesota	13	13
anuwai, Vince, Jacksonville	16	16	McKinnie, Bryant, Minnesota	16	16	Moss, Santana, N.Y. Jets	15	14
are, Olindo, Miami	11	0	McKinnon, Ronald, Arizona	16	10	Moulds, Eric, Buffalo	16	16
arion, Brock, Detroit	16	16	McMahon, Mike, Detroit	1	0	Mruczkowski, Gene, N.E.	10	0
arshall, Alfonso, Chicago	7	0	McMichael, Randy, Miami	16	16	Mughelli, Ovie, Baltimore	3	0
arshall, Lemar, Washington	16	14	McMillon, Todd, Chicago	14	1	Muhammad, Muhsin, Car.	16	16
arshall, Torrance, G. B.	9	0	McMullen, Billy, Philadelphia	8	0	Muhlbach, Don, Detroit	8	0
artin, Curtis, N.Y. Jets	16	16	McNabb, Donovan, Phil.	15	15	Mulitalo, Edwin, Baltimore	15	15
artin, David, Green Bay	9	3	McNair, Steve, Tennessee	8	8	Mungro, James, Indianapolis	15	0
artin, Jamar, Miami	9	1	McQuarters, R.W., Chicago	16	14	Murphy, Frank, Tampa Bay	3	0
artin, Jamie, St. Louis	1	0	Meester, Brad, Jacksonville	16	16	Murphy, Matt, Houston	11	1
artin, Steve, Minnesota	12	0	Meier, Rob, Jacksonville	11	8	Murphy, Nick, Balt.-K.C.	5	0
artin, Terrance, Cincinnati	2	0	Meier, Shad, Tennessee	14	7	Murphy, Rob, San Francisco	15	0
ason, Derrick, Tennessee	16	16	Melton, Terrence, Atl.-N.O.	3	0	Mustard, Chad, Cleveland	7	0
assey, Chris, St. Louis	16	0	Metcalf, Terrence, Chicago	13	5	Myers, Michael, Cleveland	16	7
athews, Jason, Tennessee	15	7	Middlebrooks, Willie, Denver	12	2	Myles, Reggie, Cincinnati	16	0
athis, Kevin, Atlanta	15	12	Middleton, Frank, Oakland	7	7	Naeole, Chris, Jacksonville	16	16
athis, Rashean, Jack.	16	16	Mikell, Quintin, Philadelphia	14	0	Nalen, Tom, Denver	16	16
athis, Robert, Indianapolis	16	1	Mili, Itula, Seattle	15	4	Nall, Craig, Green Bay	5	0
atthews, Shane, Buffalo	3	0	Miller, Billy, Houston	16	8	Nash, Keyon, Oakland	2	0
awae, Kevin, N.Y. Jets	16	16	Miller, Caleb, Cincinnati	13	3	Nattiel, Michael, Minnesota	16	0
axwell, James, N.Y. Giants	14	0	Miller, Fred, Tennessee	16	16	Navarre, John, Arizona	1	1
ayberry, Jermane, Phil.	12	12	Miller, Josh, New England	16	0	Navies, Hannibal, Green Bay	15	14
ayer, Shawn, New England	3	0	Milligan, Hanik, San Diego	14	0	Neal, Lorenzo, San Diego	16	10
ayes, Adrian, Arizona	4	0	Milloy, Lawyer, Buffalo	11	11	Neal, Stephen, New England	16	14
aynard, Brad, Chicago	16	0	Minor, Travis, Miami	11	4	Nece, Ryan, Tampa Bay	16	0
ays, Lee, Pittsburgh	16	1	Minter, Mike, Carolina	16	16	Ned, Larry, Minnesota	16	0
cAddley, Jason, Tennessee	11	1	Mitchell, Anthony, Cincinnati	12	0	Neil, Dan, Denver	13	12
cAfee, Fred, New Orleans	11	0	Mitchell, Brandon, Seattle	15	0	Nelson, Ben, Minnesota	3	0
cAlister, Chris, Baltimore	15	14	Mitchell, Freddie, Philadelphia	16	9	Nelson, Jim, Indianapolis	15	1
cAllister, Deuce, N.O.	14	14	Mitchell, Jeff, Carolina	16	16	Nelson, Rhett, Minnesota	4	0
cBriar, Mat, Dallas	16	0	Mitchell, Kawika, Kansas City	15	12	Nesbit, Jamar, New Orleans	16	4
cBride, Tod, St. Louis	2	0	Mitchell, Mel, New Orleans	15	0	Neufeld, Ryan, Buffalo	16	5

Player, Team	GP	GS
Newberry, Jeremy, S.F.	2	1
Newhouse, Reggie, Arizona	3	0
Newman, Keith, Minnesota	15	14
Newman, Terence, Dallas	16	16
Newson, Tony, St. Louis	3	0
Nguyen, Dat, Dallas	16	16
Nickey, Donnie, Tennessee	15	6
Nix, John, Arizona	1	0
Noble, Brandon, Washington	16	7
Noll, Ben, Dallas	1	1
Norris, Moran, Houston	12	4
Northcutt, Dennis, Cleveland	16	11
Nutten, Tom, St. Louis	8	6
Oben, Roman, San Diego	16	16
Odom, Antwan, Tennessee	16	8
Odom, Joe, Chicago	16	5
O'Dwyer, Matt, Tampa Bay	4	0
Offord, Willie, Minnesota	16	0
Ogbogu, Eric, Dallas	15	1
Ogden, Jonathan, Baltimore	12	12
Ogunleye, Adewale, Chicago	12	12
Ohalete, Ifeanyi, Arizona	16	13
O'Hara, Shaun, N.Y. Giants	12	12
Okeafor, Chike, Seattle	16	16
Okobi, Chukky, Pittsburgh	16	0
Olivea, Shane, San Diego	16	16
Olshansky, Igor, San Diego	16	16
Olson, Benji, Tennessee	15	15
O'Neal, Deltha, Cincinnati	12	10
O'Neil, Keith, Dallas	16	0
Orr, Raheem, N.Y. Giants	2	0
Orr, Shantee, Houston	4	0
Osgood, Kassim, San Diego	16	7
O'Sullivan, J.T., Green Bay	1	0
Owens, John, Chicago	2	0
Owens, Richard, Minnesota	7	2
Owens, Terrell, Philadelphia	14	14
Pace, Calvin, Arizona	14	0
Pace, Orlando, St. Louis	16	16
Pagel, Derek, N.Y. Jets	5	0
Palepoi, Anton, Sea.-Den.	12	0
Palmer, Carson, Cincinnati	13	13
Parker, Eric, San Diego	15	13
Parker, Samie, Kansas City	4	0
Parker, Vaughn, Washington	1	0
Parker, Willie, Pittsburgh	8	0
Parrella, John, Oakland	16	0
Parrish, Tony, San Francisco	16	16
Parry, Josh, Philadelphia	13	4
Pashos, Tony, Baltimore	6	0
Pass, Patrick, New England	14	4
Pathon, Jerome, New Orleans	15	7
Patten, David, New England	16	11
Patterson, Elton, Cin.-Jack.	8	0
Paxton, Lonie, New England	16	0
Payne, Seth, Houston	16	12
Pears, Morgan, N.Y. Giants	2	0
Pearson, Mike, Jacksonville	4	4
Pederson, Doug, Green Bay	4	0
Peek, Antwan, Houston	14	1
Peelle, Justin, San Diego	16	4
Peete, Rodney, Carolina	1	0
Peko, Tupe, Indianapolis	11	8
Pennington, Chad, N.Y. Jets	13	13
Peppers, Julius, Carolina	16	16
Perry, Chris, Cincinnati	2	0
Perry, Ed, Miami	16	0

Player, Team	GP	GS
Perryman, Ray, Jacksonville	4	0
Peters, Jason, Buffalo	5	1
Peterson, Adrian, Chicago	14	0
Peterson, Julian, S.F.	5	5
Peterson, Kenny, Green Bay	9	0
Peterson, Mike, Jacksonville	16	16
Peterson, Todd, S.F.	16	0
Peterson, Will, N.Y. Giants	16	15
Petitgout, Luke, N.Y. Giants	16	16
Phifer, Roman, New England	13	1
Phillips, Jermaine, T.B.	9	9
Phillips, Shaun, San Diego	16	0
Pickett, Cody, San Francisco	2	0
Pickett, Ryan, St. Louis	16	16
Pierce, Antonio, Washington	16	16
Pierce, Brett, Dallas	8	1
Pierce, Terry, Denver	15	0
Pierson, Shurron, Chicago	6	0
Pile, Willie, Kansas City	16	5
Piller, Zach, Tennessee	1	1
Pinkney, Cleveland, Atl.-Car.	5	0
Pinkston, Todd, Philadelphia	16	16
Pinner, Artose, Detroit	9	2
Pinnock, Andrew, San Diego	1	0
Pippens, Jerrell, S.D.-Chi.	9	0
Pittman, Bryan, Houston	16	0
Pittman, Michael, Tampa Bay	13	13
Pitts, Chester, Houston	16	16
Player, Scott, Arizona	16	0
Plummer, Ahmed, S.F.	6	6
Plummer, Jake, Denver	16	16
Polamalu, Troy, Pittsburgh	16	16
Polite, Lousaka, Dallas	1	0
Polk, Carlos, San Diego	1	0
Polk, DaShon, Houston	16	4
Pollard, Marcus, Indianapolis	13	13
Pollard, Robert, San Diego	1	0
Polley, Tommy, St. Louis	15	13
Ponder, Willie, N.Y. Giants	11	0
Poole, Nathan, Arizona	9	1
Poole, Tyrone, New England	5	4
Poole, Will, Miami	15	1
Pope, Derrick, Miami	16	3
Pope, Kendyll, Indianapolis	2	0
Pope, Monsanto, Denver	16	15
Porter, Jerry, Oakland	16	16
Porter, Joey, Pittsburgh	15	15
Portis, Clinton, Washington	15	15
Portis, Marico, Tennessee	1	0
Posey, Jeff, Buffalo	16	15
Powell, Carl, Cincinnati	10	2
Price, Marcus, Buffalo	14	3
Price, Peerless, Atlanta	16	15
Prioleau, Pierson, Buffalo	16	2
Pritchett, Kelvin, Detroit	16	0
Pritchett, Stanley, Atlanta	14	2
Proehl, Ricky, Carolina	16	3
Pruitt, Etric, Atlanta	3	0
Pryce, Trevor, Denver	2	1
Pucillo, Mike, Buffalo	2	0
Putzier, Jeb, Denver	16	5
Pyatt, Brad, Indianapolis	8	0
Quarles, Shelton, Tampa Bay	15	15
Quinn, Jonathan, Chicago	5	3
Rabach, Casey, Baltimore	16	16
Rackers, Neil, Arizona	16	0

Player, Team	GP	GS
Rackley, Derek, Atlanta	16	
Rainer, Wali, Detroit	16	
Raiola, Dominic, Detroit	16	16
Ramsey, Patrick, Washington	9	
Randall, Curtis, Seattle	4	
Randle El, Antwaan, Pitts.	16	
Ransom, Derrick, Jack.	10	
Rasby, Walter, Wash.-Pitts.	10	
Rasheed, Saleem, S.F.	14	
Rasmussen, Kemp, Carolina	12	
Ratliff, Keiwan, Cincinnati	16	
Rattay, Tim, San Francisco	9	
Rayburn, Sam, Philadelphia	16	
Raymer, Cory, Washington	15	1
Reagor, Montae, Indianapolis	16	16
Redding, Cory, Detroit	16	16
Redmond, J.R., Oakland	16	
Reed, Ed, Baltimore	16	16
Reed, J.R., Philadelphia	14	
Reed, James, N.Y. Jets	16	
Reed, Jeff, Pittsburgh	16	
Reed, Josh, Buffalo	12	
Reed, Rayshun, S.F.	7	
Reese, Ike, Philadelphia	16	
Reese, Izell, Buffalo	9	
Reese, Marcus, Chicago	11	
Reeves, Jacques, Dallas	15	
Reid, Dexter, New England	13	
Reuber, Alan, Arizona	3	
Reyes, Tutan, Carolina	14	12
Reynolds, Robert, Tennessee	14	
Rhodes, Dominic, Ind.	16	
Ricard, Alan, Baltimore	16	
Rice, Jerry, Oakland-Seattle	17	1
Rice, Simeon, Tampa Bay	16	16
Richard, Kris, Seattle	16	
Richardson, David, Jack.	2	
Richardson, Tony, K.C.	16	16
Richey, Wade, Baltimore	12	
Riemersma, Jay, Pittsburgh	11	2
Riley, Karon, Atlanta	1	
Riley, Victor, New Orleans	16	13
Rimpf, Brian, Baltimore	1	
Ritchie, Jon, Philadelphia	3	
Rivera, Marco, Green Bay	16	16
Rivers, Marcellus, N.Y. Giants	16	
Rivers, Philip, San Diego	2	0
Roaf, Willie, Kansas City	16	16
Robbins, Fred, N.Y. Giants	15	15
Roberts, Terrell, Cincinnati	11	1
Robertson, Dewayne, N.Y. J.	16	16
Robertson, Jamal, S.F.-Car.	12	0
Robinson, Bryan, Miami	16	13
Robinson, Dunta, Houston	16	16
Robinson, Jeff, Dallas	16	0
Robinson, Koren, Seattle	10	8
Robinson, Marcus, Minn.	16	7
Rodgers, Derrick, N.O.	8	8
Roethlisberger, Ben, Pitts.	14	13
Rogers, Charles, Detroit	1	1
Rogers, Jacob, Dallas	2	0
Rogers, Nick, G.B.-Ind.	11	0
Rogers, Shaun, Detroit	16	16
Rogers, Tyrone, Cleveland	14	0
Rogers, Victor, Detroit	1	0
Rolle, Samari, Tennessee	12	11
Roman, Mark, Green Bay	16	15

Player, Team	GP	GS
ᴏmero, Dario, Miami	14	1
ᴏmo, Tony, Dallas	6	0
ᴏsenfels, Sage, Miami	3	1
ᴪsenthal, Mike, Minnesota	2	2
ᴏss, Derek, Minnesota	9	0
ᴏss, Micah, S.D.-Car.	17	0
ᴏss, Oliver, Pittsburgh	16	16
ᴏssum, Allen, Atlanta	16	1
ᴏuen, Tom, Seattle	4	0
ᴏyal, Robert, Washington	14	9
ᴏye, Orpheus, Cleveland	15	14
ᴊcker, Mike, Carolina	16	16
ᴊegamer, Grey, Green Bay	15	11
ᴊff, Orlando, New Orleans	14	8
ᴊmph, Mike, San Francisco	2	2
ᴊnyan, Jon, Philadelphia	16	16
ᴊssell, Brian, Minnesota	16	16
ᴊssell, Cliff, Cincinnati	13	1
ᴗan, Sean, Dallas	6	1
ᴀipaia, Blaine, St. Louis	8	5
ᴀlaam, Ephraim, Jack.	15	12
ᴀlave'a, Joe, Washington	15	9
ᴀm, P.K., New England	2	0
ᴀmpson, Kevin, Kansas City	6	0
ᴀms, B.J., Baltimore	16	1
ᴀmuel, Asante, N.E.	13	8
ᴀmuels, Chris, Washington	16	16
ᴀnders, Bob, Indianapolis	6	4
ᴀnders, Darnell, Atlanta	2	0
ᴀnders, Deion, Baltimore	9	2
ᴀnders, Lewis, Cleveland	16	5
ᴀnds, Terdell, Oakland	15	0
ᴀndy, Justin, Tennessee	1	0
ᴀpp, Benny, Kansas City	15	1
ᴀpp, Cecil, Denver	5	0
ᴀpp, Gerome, Indianapolis	13	0
ᴀpp, Warren, Oakland	16	16
ᴀturday, Jeff, Indianapolis	14	14
ᴀuerbrun, Todd, Carolina	16	0
ᴀvage, Josh, Tampa Bay	6	0
ᴄanlon, Rich, Kansas City	6	0
ᴄhaub, Matt, Atlanta	6	1
ᴄhifino, Jake, Tennessee	1	0
ᴄhlesinger, Cory, Detroit	13	11
ᴄhneck, Mike, Pittsburgh	16	0
ᴄhobel, Aaron, Buffalo	16	16
ᴄhobel, Bo, Tennessee	5	2
ᴄhobel, Matt, Cincinnati	16	1
ᴄhroeder, Bill, Tampa Bay	7	2
ᴄhulters, Lance, Tennessee	3	3
ᴄhweigert, Stuart, Oakland	16	3
ᴄifres, Mike, San Diego	16	0
ᴄcioli, Brad, Indianapolis	9	0
ᴄciullo, Steve, Philadelphia	15	5
ᴄcobee, Josh, Jacksonville	16	0
ᴄcobey, Josh, Arizona	12	0
ᴄcott, Bart, Baltimore	13	0
ᴄcott, Bryan, Atlanta	16	16
ᴄcott, Chad, Pittsburgh	7	7
ᴄcott, Darrion, Minnesota	12	0
ᴄcott, DeQuincy, San Diego	14	2
ᴄcott, Greg, Cincinnati	1	0
ᴄcott, Ian, Chicago	14	13
ᴄcott, Jake, Indianapolis	12	9
ᴄcott, Lynn, Dallas	16	9
ᴇears, Corey, Houston	15	0
ᴇeau, Junior, Miami	8	8
Seidman, Mike, Carolina	16	6
Seigler, Richard, S.F.	7	0
Sellers, Mike, Washington	16	1
Seymour, Richard, N.E.	15	15
Shabazz, Siddeeq, Atlanta	15	0
Shaffer, Kevin, Atlanta	15	15
Shanle, Scott, Dallas	16	3
Sharper, Darren, Green Bay	15	13
Sharper, Jamie, Houston	16	16
Shaw, Bobby, Buffalo-S.D.	11	0
Shaw, Josh, Miami	5	0
Shaw, Terrance, Minnesota	15	4
Shea, Aaron, Cleveland	15	8
Shelton, Daimon, Buffalo	16	12
Shelton, L.J., Arizona	12	9
Sheppard, Lito, Philadelphia	15	15
Shiancoe, Visanthe, N.Y. G.	16	7
Shields, Will, Kansas City	16	16
Shivers, Jason, Chicago	1	0
Shoate, Jeff, Denver	7	0
Shockey, Jeremy, N.Y. Giants	15	15
Short, Brandon, Carolina	16	2
Short, Jason, Philadelphia	11	0
Siavii, Junior, Kansas City	12	0
Simmons, Anthony, Seattle	7	7
Simmons, Brian, Cincinnati	15	15
Simmons, Jason, Houston	10	6
Simms, Chris, Tampa Bay	5	2
Simon, Corey, Philadelphia	16	16
Simoneau, Mark, Philadelphia	14	13
Sims, Barry, Oakland	16	16
Sims, Ryan, Kansas City	15	13
Singleton, Al, Dallas	13	12
Slaughter, Chad, Oakland	10	0
Slaughter, T.J., Baltimore	14	1
Smart, Ian, Tampa Bay	4	0
Smart, Rod, Carolina	3	0
Smiley, Justin, San Francisco	16	9
Smith, Aaron, Pittsburgh	16	15
Smith, Antonio, Arizona	2	0
Smith, Antowain, Tennessee	13	4
Smith, Brady, Atlanta	16	16
Smith, Brent, N.Y. Jets	4	1
Smith, Corey, T.B.-S.F.	5	0
Smith, Darrin, New Orleans	3	0
Smith, Daryl, Jacksonville	15	13
Smith, Derek, San Francisco	14	14
Smith, Dwight, Tampa Bay	16	16
Smith, Emmitt, Arizona	15	15
Smith, Hunter, Indianapolis	16	0
Smith, Jimmy, Jacksonville	16	16
Smith, Jonathan, Buffalo	9	0
Smith, Justin, Cincinnati	16	16
Smith, Keith, Detroit	15	2
Smith, L.J., Philadelphia	16	8
Smith, Larry, Green Bay	3	0
Smith, Lawrence, Buffalo	16	8
Smith, Marvel, Pittsburgh	16	16
Smith, Musa, Baltimore	9	0
Smith, Onterrio, Minnesota	11	6
Smith, Raonall, Minnesota	7	3
Smith, Richard, Kansas City	4	0
Smith, Robaire, Houston	16	16
Smith, Rod, Denver	16	16
Smith, Shaun, N.O.-Cin.	8	2
Smith, Steve, Carolina	1	1
Smith, Terrelle, Cleveland	16	9
Smith, Travian, Oakland	8	4
Smith, Wade, Miami	6	2
Smith, Will, New Orleans	16	4
Smoot, Fred, Washington	15	15
Snee, Chris, N.Y. Giants	11	11
Snow, Justin, Indianapolis	16	0
Solwold, Mike, Baltimore	1	0
Sorensen, Nick, Jacksonville	16	0
Sorgi, Jim, Indianapolis	4	0
Sowell, Jerald, N.Y. Jets	16	16
Spears, Marcus, Houston	16	3
Spencer, Cody, Tennessee	7	0
Spencer, Shawntae, S.F.	16	12
Spicer, Paul, Jacksonville	2	2
Spikes, Cameron, Arizona	16	9
Spikes, Takeo, Buffalo	16	16
Spires, Greg, Tampa Bay	16	16
Spragan, Donnie, Denver	16	14
Springs, Shawn, Washington	15	15
St. Clair, John, Miami	14	14
St. Louis, Brad, Cincinnati	16	0
St. Pierre, Brian, Pittsburgh	1	0
Staley, Duce, Pittsburgh	10	10
Stallworth, Donte', N.O.	16	10
Stamer, Josh, Buffalo	16	0
Stanley, Chad, Houston	16	0
Stanley, Matt, San Francisco	1	0
Starks, Duane, Arizona	15	8
Starks, Max, Pittsburgh	10	0
Starks, Randy, Tennessee	14	8
Starling, Kendrick, Houston	8	0
Stecker, Aaron, New Orleans	16	3
Steele, Ben, Green Bay	15	0
Steinbach, Eric, Cincinnati	16	15
Stemke, Kevin, St. Louis	6	0
Stepanovich, Alex, Arizona	16	16
Steussie, Todd, Tampa Bay	16	5
Stevens, Jerramy, Seattle	16	5
Stevens, Larry, Cincinnati	9	0
Stevenson, Dominique, Wash.	1	0
Stewart, Daleroy, Dal.-N.Y. J.-S.F.	11	0
Stewart, Kordell, Baltimore	2	0
Stewart, Matt, Atlanta	16	15
Stewart, Tony, Cincinnati	16	9
Stills, Gary, Kansas City	16	0
Stinchcomb, Jon, N.O.	4	0
Stinchcomb, Matt, T.B.	16	16
Stokley, Brandon, Ind.	16	3
Stone, John, Oakland	4	0
Stone, Michael, Arizona	14	0
Stone, Ron, Oakland	5	5
Stoutmire, Omar, N.Y. Giants	1	0
Stover, Matt, Baltimore	16	0
Strahan, Michael, N.Y. Giants	8	8
Strait, Derrick, N.Y. Jets	5	1
Streets, Tai, Detroit	13	12
Strickland, Donald, Ind.	4	4
Strong, Mack, Seattle	16	13
Strother, Billy, Wash.-Mia.	3	0
Stroud, Marcus, Jack.	16	16
Stuvaints, Russell, Pitts.	15	0
Suggs, Lee, Cleveland	10	4
Suggs, Terrell, Baltimore	16	16
Sulfsted, Alex, Cincinnati	3	0
Sullivan, Johnathan, N.O.	7	4
Surtain, Patrick, Miami	15	15
Swinton, Reggie, Detroit	13	1

2004 REVIEW Player participation

Player, Team	GP	GS
Sykes, Jashon, Denver	3	0
Tait, John, Chicago	13	13
Tapeh, Thomas, Philadelphia	7	0
Tate, Robert, Arizona	14	0
Tauscher, Mark, Green Bay	16	16
Taylor, Ben, Cleveland	3	2
Taylor, Bobby, Seattle	10	0
Taylor, Chester, Baltimore	16	4
Taylor, Fred, Jacksonville	14	14
Taylor, Ike, Pittsburgh	13	1
Taylor, Jamaar, N.Y. Giants	8	0
Taylor, Jason, Miami	16	16
Taylor, Jay, Tampa Bay	5	0
Taylor, Sean, Washington	15	13
Taylor, Travis, Baltimore	10	9
Teague, Trey, Buffalo	12	12
Tercero, Scott, St. Louis	8	4
Terrell, David, Oakland	16	0
Terrell, David, Chicago	16	15
Terrill, Craig, Seattle	4	0
Terry, Chris, Seattle	8	8
Terry, Jeb, Tampa Bay	4	0
Testaverde, Vinny, Dallas	16	15
Thomas, Adalius, Baltimore	16	16
Thomas, Anthony, Chicago	12	2
Thomas, Bryan, N.Y. Jets	14	6
Thomas, Dontarrious, Minn.	16	5
Thomas, Fred, New Orleans	15	7
Thomas, Hollis, Philadelphia	13	2
Thomas, Joey, Green Bay	14	0
Thomas, Josh, Indianapolis	11	0
Thomas, Juqua, Tennessee	10	0
Thomas, Kevin, Buffalo	16	1
Thomas, Kiwaukee, Jack.	16	2
Thomas, Randy, Washington	15	15
Thomas, Robert, St. Louis	14	11
Thomas, Tra, Philadelphia	15	15
Thomas, Zach, Miami	13	13
Thompson, Chaun, Cleveland	16	13
Thompson, Derrius, Miami	16	3
Thompson, Lamont, Tenn.	16	13
Thompson, Ray, Arizona	11	3
Thornton, Bruce, Dallas	1	0
Thornton, David, Indianapolis	16	15
Thornton, John, Cincinnati	16	16
Thornton, Kalen, Dallas	16	0
Thrash, James, Washington	16	3
Thurman, Andrae, Green Bay	2	0
Tillman, Charles, Chicago	8	7
Tillman, Travares, Carolina	6	1
Timmerman, Adam, St. L.	16	16
Tinoisamoa, Pisa, St. Louis	16	16
Tobeck, Robbie, Seattle	16	16
Toefield, LaBrandon, Jack.	14	0
Tomlinson, LaDainian, S.D.	15	15
Tongue, Reggie, N.Y. Jets	16	16
Toomer, Amani, N.Y. Giants	15	14
Torbor, Reggie, N.Y. Giants	16	1
Townsend, Deshea, Pitts.	15	15
Trafford, Rodney, Buffalo	4	0
Traylor, Keith, New England	16	10
Trejo, Stephen, St. L.-Det.	13	2
Treu, Adam, Oakland	16	16
Tripplett, Larry, Indianapolis	16	0
Trotter, Jeremiah, Phil.	16	9
Troupe, Ben, Tennessee	14	6
Trufant, Marcus, Seattle	16	16

Player, Team	GP	GS
Truluck, R-Kal, Green Bay	14	1
Tubbs, Marcus, Seattle	11	3
Tucker, Rex, Chicago	6	5
Tucker, Ross, Buffalo	16	12
Tucker, Ryan, Cleveland	7	7
Tucker, Torrin, Dallas	13	13
Tufts, Sean, Carolina	3	0
Tuitele, Maugaula, Oakland	1	0
Tuman, Jerame, Pittsburgh	16	16
Tupa, Tom, Washington	16	0
Turk, Matt, Miami	16	0
Turner, Larry, St. Louis	14	1
Turner, Michael, San Diego	14	1
Tylski, Rich, Carolina	16	1
Tynes, Lawrence, Kansas City	16	0
Tyree, David, N.Y. Giants	16	1
Udeze, Kenechi, Minnesota	16	15
Ulbrich, Jeff, San Francisco	16	14
Ulmer, Artie, Atlanta	16	0
Umenyiora, Osi, N.Y. Giants	16	7
Unck, Mason, Cleveland	11	0
Upshaw, Regan, N.Y. Giants	3	0
Urban, Jerheme, Seattle	7	1
Urlacher, Brian, Chicago	9	9
Van Buren, Courtney, S.D.	1	0
Vanden Bosch, Kyle, Arizona	16	1
Vanderjagt, Mike, Ind.	15	0
Vasher, Nathan, Chicago	16	7
Vaughn, Khaleed, Atlanta	3	0
Verba, Ross, Cleveland	16	16
Vick, Michael, Atlanta	15	15
Villarrial, Chris, Buffalo	16	16
Vilma, Jonathan, N.Y. Jets	16	14
Vinatieri, Adam, New England	16	0
Vincent, Keydrick, Pittsburgh	16	16
Vincent, Troy, Buffalo	7	7
Vines, Scottie, Detroit	6	1
Volek, Billy, Tennessee	10	8
Vollers, Kurt, Dallas	13	3
von Oelhoffen, Kimo, Pitts.	16	15
Vrabel, Mike, New England	16	15
Waddell, Michael, Tennessee	16	4
Wade, Bobby, Chicago	16	14
Wade, John, Tampa Bay	8	8
Wade, Todd, Houston	14	13
Wahle, Mike, Green Bay	16	16
Wahlroos, Drew, St. Louis	6	0
Walker, Aaron, San Francisco	16	4
Walker, Bracy, Detroit	16	16
Walker, Darwin, Philadelphia	16	16
Walker, Denard, Oakland	16	5
Walker, Frank, N.Y. Giants	13	1
Walker, Gary, Houston	15	15
Walker, Greg, N.Y. Giants	7	0
Walker, Javon, Green Bay	16	12
Walker, Kenyatta, Tampa Bay	13	11
Walker, Langston, Oakland	16	1
Wallace, Al, Carolina	16	0
Wallace, Taco, Seattle	2	0
Walls, Lenny, Denver	7	1
Walls, Raymond, Baltimore	16	1
Walter, Ken, Seattle	6	0
Walter, Kevin, Cincinnati	16	0
Walter, Tyson, Dallas	13	1
Walters, Troy, Indianapolis	5	0
Wand, Seth, Houston	16	16
Ward, Dedric, Dallas	8	0

Player, Team	GP	GS
Ward, Derrick, N.Y. Giants	5	0
Ward, Hines, Pittsburgh	16	16
Ware, Kevin, San Francisco	5	0
Ware, Matt, Philadelphia	12	0
Warfield, Eric, Kansas City	16	16
Warner, Kurt, N.Y. Giants	10	9
Warner, Ron, Washington	14	2
Warren, Gerard, Cleveland	13	13
Warren, Ty, New England	16	16
Warrick, Peter, Cincinnati	4	1
Washington, Dewayne, Jack.	16	16
Washington, Keith, N.Y. G.	8	8
Washington, Kelley, Cin.	16	2
Washington, Marcus, Wash.	16	16
Washington, Rashad, N.Y. J.	16	0
Washington, Ted, Oakland	16	16
Washington, Todd, Houston	15	0
Waters, Brian, Kansas City	16	16
Watson, Ben, New England	1	1
Watson, Courtney, N.O.	12	8
Watson, Kenny, Cincinnati	16	0
Watts, Darius, Denver	16	2
Wayne, Nate, Philadelphia	9	7
Wayne, Reggie, Indianapolis	16	16
Weary, Fred, Houston	2	1
Weaver, Anthony, Baltimore	16	15
Weaver, Jed, New England	10	1
Webster, Jason, Atlanta	10	9
Webster, Nate, Cincinnati	3	3
Weiner, Todd, Atlanta	16	16
Welbourn, John, Kansas City	10	10
Welker, Wesley, S.D.-Mia.	15	0
Wells, Jonathan, Houston	16	1
Wells, Ray, San Francisco	6	0
Wells, Reggie, Arizona	16	16
Wells, Scott, Green Bay	5	5
Wesley, Dante, Carolina	13	0
Wesley, Greg, Kansas City	12	11
Westbrook, Brian, Phil.	13	12
Westmoreland, Eric, Clev.	16	0
Wharton, Travelle, Carolina	11	11
Wheatley, Tyrone, Oakland	8	7
White, Dewayne, T.B.	16	3
White, Dez, Atlanta	16	15
White, Jamel, T.B.-Balt.	13	0
White, Tracy, Seattle	10	2
Whitehead, Willie, N.O.	8	0
Whiteside, Keyon, Ind.	7	0
Whitfield, Bob, Jack.	10	0
Whiting, Brandon, S.F.	5	5
Whitley, James, G.B.	6	0
Whitley, Taylor, Miami	16	11
Whitted, Alvis, Oakland	11	5
Whittle, Jason, N.Y. Giants	16	16
Wiegert, Zach, Houston	13	13
Wiegmann, Casey, K.C.	16	16
Wiggins, Jermaine, Minn.	14	13
Wilcox, Daniel, Baltimore	16	5
Wilds, Garnell, Washington	2	0
Wiley, Chuck, Minn.-N.Y. G.	8	2
Wiley, Marcellus, Dallas	16	15
Wilford, Ernest, Jacksonville	15	3
Wilfork, Vince, New England	16	6
Wilhelm, Matt, San Diego	7	0
Wilkerson, Jimmy, K.C.	15	0
Wilkins, Jeff, St. Louis	16	0
Wilkins, Marcus, Cincinnati	16	0

Player, Team	GP	GS
Wilkinson, Dan, Detroit	16	16
Williams, Aeneas, St. Louis	13	10
Williams, Andrew, S.F.	7	3
Williams, Bobbie, Cincinnati	16	16
Williams, Boo, New Orleans	16	8
Williams, Brett, Kansas City	5	0
Williams, Brian, Minnesota	16	16
Williams, Brock, Oakland	2	0
Williams, Chad, Baltimore	16	1
Williams, Corey, Green Bay	12	0
Williams, D.J., Denver	16	14
Williams, Davern, N.Y. Giants	3	1
Williams, Demorrio, Atlanta	16	1
Williams, Grant, St. Louis	16	11
Williams, Jamal, San Diego	15	15
Williams, Jay, Miami	16	1
Williams, Jimmy, S.F.	12	6
Williams, Josh, Indianapolis	16	15
Williams, Karl, Arizona	15	2
Williams, Kevin, Minnesota	16	16
Williams, Madieu, Cincinnati	16	13
Williams, Maurice, Jack.	16	16
Williams, Melvin, S.F.	3	0
Williams, Mike, Buffalo	15	15
Williams, Moe, Minnesota	14	1
Williams, Pat, Buffalo	16	15
Williams, Quintin, Miami	6	0
Williams, Randal, Dallas	2	2
Williams, Reggie, Jack.	16	15
Williams, Renauld, Miami	2	0
Williams, Roland, Oakland	12	3
Williams, Roy, Dallas	16	16
Williams, Roy, Detroit	14	12
Williams, Sam, Oakland	9	4
Williams, Shaud, Buffalo	4	0
Williams, Shaun, N.Y. Giants	2	2
Williams, Tank, Tennessee	9	9
Williams, Todd, Tennessee	6	0
Williams, Tony, Cincinnati	6	6
Williams, Tyrone, Dallas	3	2
Williams, Walter, Green Bay	1	0
Williams, Willie, Pittsburgh	16	10
Willig, Matt, Carolina	16	9
Willis, Jason, Seattle	1	0
Wilson, Adrian, Arizona	16	16
Wilson, Al, Denver	16	16
Wilson, Cedrick, S.F.	15	15
Wilson, Eugene, N.E.	15	14
Wilson, Gibril, N.Y. Giants	8	7
Wilson, Jerry, San Diego	16	16
Wilson, Kris, Kansas City	3	0
Wilson, Mark, Washington	2	1
Winborn, Jamie, S.F.	14	10
Winey, Brandon, N.Y. Giants	13	0
Winfield, Antoine, Minnesota	14	12
Winslow, Kellen, Cleveland	2	2
Wire, Coy, Buffalo	12	3
Wistrom, Grant, Seattle	9	9
Witherspoon, Will, Carolina	16	16
Withrow, Cory, Minnesota	12	5
Witten, Jason, Dallas	16	15
Womack, Floyd, Seattle	15	8
Wong, Kailee, Houston	16	16
Woodard, Cedric, Seattle	16	16
Woods, Jerome, Kansas City	10	10
Woods, LeVar, Arizona	14	3
Woods, Rashaun, S.F.	14	0
Woodson, Charles, Oakland	13	12
Woody, Damien, Detroit	16	16
Woolfolk, Andre, Tennessee	10	2
Worrell, Cameron, Chicago	13	0
Wrighster, George, Jack.	4	3
Wright, Jason, Atlanta	2	0
Wright, Kenny, Houston	16	0
Wright, Kenyatta, N.Y. Jets	16	0
Wunsch, Jerry, Seattle	5	0
Wyms, Ellis, Tampa Bay	6	0
Wynn, Dexter, Philadelphia	12	0
Wynn, Renaldo, Washington	16	16
Wyrick, Jimmy, Miami	14	0
Yates, Max, Minnesota	1	0
Yoder, Todd, Jacksonville	16	8
Young, Brian, New Orleans	15	15
Young, Bryant, San Francisco	16	16
Young, Chris, Denver	10	0
Yovanovits, Dave, N.Y. Jets	4	0
Zastudil, Dave, Baltimore	13	0
Zelenka, Joe, Jacksonville	16	0
Zellner, Peppi, Arizona	16	14
Zereoue, Amos, Oakland	15	6
Zgonina, Jeff, Miami	16	14
Zukauskas, Paul, Cleveland	14	5

PLAYERS WITH TWO OR MORE CLUBS

Player, Team	GP	GS
Ahanotu, Chidi, Miami	5	0
Ahanotu, Chidi, Tampa Bay	8	5
Baker, Jason, Kansas City	2	0
Baker, Jason, Indianapolis	4	0
Baker, Jason, Denver	4	0
Bryant, Antonio, Dallas	5	1
Bryant, Antonio, Cleveland	10	7
Bryant, Matt, Indianapolis	1	0
Bryant, Matt, Miami	3	0
Carter, Dyshod, Arizona	6	0
Carter, Dyshod, Cleveland	5	0
Chandler, Jeff, Carolina	2	0
Chandler, Jeff, Washington	3	0
Cook, Damion, Baltimore	9	0
Cook, Damion, Cleveland	6	6
Cooper, Chris, Dallas	2	0
Cooper, Chris, San Francisco	8	2
Cooper, Jarrod, Carolina	6	0
Cooper, Jarrod, Oakland	9	0
Duckett, Damane, Carolina	2	0
Duckett, Damane, N.Y. Giants	4	1
Edwards, Antuan, Miami	8	8
Edwards, Antuan, St. Louis	6	5
Elling, Aaron, Tennessee	1	0
Elling, Aaron, Minnesota	7	0
Fuller, Curtis, Green Bay	1	0
Fuller, Curtis, Carolina	6	0
Gramatica, Martin, T.B.	11	0
Gramatica, Martin, Ind.	4	0
Jackson, James, Cleveland	4	0
Jackson, James, Green Bay	1	0
Jenkins, Corey, Chicago	4	0
Jenkins, Corey, Miami	3	0
Joe, Leon, Chicago	1	0
Joe, Leon, Arizona	4	0
Layne, George, San Diego	2	0
Layne, George, Atlanta	2	0
McKenzie, Mike, Green Bay	1	0
McKenzie, Mike, New Orleans	10	10
Melton, Terrence, Atlanta	1	0
Melton, Terrence, N.O.	2	0
Morgan, Quincy, Cleveland	6	5
Morgan, Quincy, Dallas	9	7
Murphy, Nick, Baltimore	3	0
Murphy, Nick, Kansas City	2	0
Palepoi, Anton, Seattle	1	0
Palepoi, Anton, Denver	11	0
Patterson, Elton, Cincinnati	2	0
Patterson, Elton, Jacksonville	6	0
Pinkney, Cleveland, Atlanta	3	0
Pinkney, Cleveland, Carolina	2	0
Pippens, Jerrell, San Diego	7	0
Pippens, Jerrell, Chicago	2	0
Rasby, Walter, Washington	6	6
Rasby, Walter, Pittsburgh	4	2
Rice, Jerry, Oakland	6	5
Rice, Jerry, Seattle	11	9
Robertson, Jamal, S.F.	7	0
Robertson, Jamal, Carolina	5	0
Rogers, Nick, Green Bay	10	0
Rogers, Nick, Indianapolis	1	0
Ross, Micah, San Diego	7	0
Ross, Micah, Carolina	10	0
Shaw, Bobby, Buffalo	4	0
Shaw, Bobby, San Diego	7	0
Smith, Corey, Tampa Bay	4	0
Smith, Corey, San Francisco	1	0
Smith, Shaun, New Orleans	5	1
Smith, Shaun, Cincinnati	3	1
Stewart, Daleroy, Dallas	1	0
Stewart, Daleroy, N.Y. Jets	1	0
Stewart, Daleroy, S.F.	9	0
Strother, Billy, Washington	2	0
Strother, Billy, Miami	1	0
Trejo, Stephen, St. Louis	2	0
Trejo, Stephen, Detroit	11	2
Welker, Wesley, San Diego	1	0
Welker, Wesley, Miami	14	0
White, Jamel, Tampa Bay	7	0
White, Jamel, Baltimore	6	0
Wiley, Chuck, Minnesota	5	2
Wiley, Chuck, N.Y. Giants	3	0

ATTENDANCE

REGULAR SEASON

Team	Home Attendance	Average	NFL Rank	Road Attendance	Average	NFL Rank
Arizona	300,267	37,533	32	538,290	67,286	19
Atlanta	564,829	70,604	11	568,377	71,047	4
Baltimore	558,594	69,824	13	564,694	70,587	5
Buffalo	574,399	71,800	9	538,132	67,267	20
Carolina	586,259	73,282	6	545,850	68,231	13
Chicago	495,706	61,963	28	541,641	67,705	17
Cincinnati	524,248	65,531	18	575,138	71,892	1
Cleveland	584,840	73,105	7	556,930	69,616	10
Dallas	510,892	63,862	25	575,112	71,889	2
Denver	601,031	75,129	5	539,587	67,448	18
Detroit	499,162	62,395	27	544,319	68,040	15
Green Bay	564,400	70,550	12	548,169	68,521	12
Houston	565,192	70,649	10	544,857	68,107	14
Indianapolis	456,791	57,099	30	560,040	70,005	8
Jacksonville	555,464	69,433	14	496,092	62,012	31
Kansas City	623,010	77,876	4	527,718	65,965	25
Miami	580,808	72,601	8	563,061	70,383	6
Minnesota	512,969	64,121	24	532,536	66,567	23
New England	550,048	68,756	16	558,162	69,770	9
New Orleans	513,178	64,147	23	471,918	58,990	32
N.Y. Giants	629,874	78,734	2	530,816	66,352	24
N.Y. Jets	623,181	77,898	3	509,622	63,703	27
Oakland	405,936	50,742	31	551,687	68,961	11
Philadelphia	540,870	67,609	17	561,973	70,247	7
Pittsburgh	507,385	63,423	26	574,856	71,857	3
St. Louis	527,384	65,923	20	533,617	66,702	22
San Diego	485,462	60,683	29	542,242	67,780	16
San Francisco	518,271	64,784	22	506,704	63,338	29
Seattle	533,436	66,680	19	506,911	63,364	28
Tampa Bay	522,720	65,340	21	523,354	65,419	26
Tennessee	551,210	68,901	15	500,522	62,565	30
Washington	702,670	87,834	1	537,559	67,195	21
NFL total	17,270,486	67,463		17,270,486	67,463	

Note: Attendance figures are unofficial and are based on box scores of games.

HISTORICAL

TOP REGULAR-SEASON HOME CROWDS

Team	Attendance	Date	Site	Opponent
Arizona	73,400	October 30, 1994	Sun Devil Stadium	Pittsburgh
Atlanta	71,253	November 21, 1993	Georgia Dome	Dallas
Baltimore	70,001	December 28, 2003	M&T Bank Stadium	Pittsburgh
Buffalo	80,368	October 4, 1992	Rich Stadium	Miami
Carolina	76,136	December 10, 1995	Clemson Memorial Stadium	San Francisco
Chicago	66,944	Occurred many times. Last time: January 6, 2002	Soldier Field	Jacksonville
Cincinnati	65,806	October 25, 2004	Paul Brown Stadium	Denver
Cleveland	85,703	September 21, 1970	Cleveland Stadium	N.Y. Jets
Dallas	80,259	November 24, 1966	Cotton Bowl	Cleveland
Denver	76,753	September 22, 2003	Invesco Field at Mile High	Oakland
Detroit	80,444	December 20, 1981	Pontiac Silverdome	Tampa Bay
Green Bay	70,688	September 19, 2004	Lambeau Field	Chicago
Houston	70,769	November 21, 2004	Reliant Stadium	Green Bay
Indianapolis	61,282	December 14, 1997	RCA Dome	Miami
Jacksonville	76,877	December 5, 2004	ALLTEL Stadium	Pittsburgh
Kansas City	82,893	October 2, 2000	Arrowhead Stadium	Seattle
Miami	78,914	November 19, 1972	Orange Bowl	N.Y. Jets
Minnesota	64,482	November 2, 2003	Metrodome	Green Bay
New England	68,756	Occurred many times. Last time: January 1, 2005	Gillette Stadium	San Francisco
New Orleans	83,437	November 12, 1967	Tulane Stadium	Dallas
		November 26, 1967	Tulane Stadium	Atlanta

Team	Attendance	Date	Site	Opponent
New York Giants	78,907	September 15, 2003	Giants Stadium	Dallas
New York Jets	79,469	September 20, 1998	Giants Stadium	Indianapolis
Oakland	74,121	September 23, 1973	Memorial Stadium; Berkeley, Cal.	Miami
Philadelphia	72,977	November 20, 2003	Lincoln Financial Field	Carolina
Pittsburgh	64,975	November 7, 2004	Heinz Field	Philadelphia
St. Louis	66,273	December 10, 2000	Trans World Dome	Minnesota
San Diego	68,274	October 24, 1999	Qualcomm Stadium	Green Bay
San Francisco	69,014	November 13, 1994	Candlestick Park	Dallas
Seattle	68,681	December 16, 2000	Husky Stadium	Oakland
Tampa Bay	73,523	December 7, 1997	Houlihan's Stadium	Green Bay
Tennessee	68,932	December 13, 2004	The Coliseum	Kansas City
Washington	90,367	September 27, 2004	FedEx Field	Dallas

YEAR BY YEAR

NATIONAL FOOTBALL LEAGUE

Year	Regular season*		Average	Postseason†	
1934	492,684	(60)	8,211	35,059	(1)
1935	638,178	(53)	12,041	15,000	(1)
1936	816,007	(54)	15,111	29,545	(1)
1937	963,039	(55)	17,510	15,878	(1)
1938	937,197	(55)	17,040	48,120	(1)
1939	1,071,200	(55)	19,476	32,279	(1)
1940	1,063,025	(55)	19,328	36,034	(1)
1941	1,108,615	(55)	20,157	55,870	(2)
1942	887,920	(55)	16,144	36,006	(1)
1943	969,128	(40)	24,228	71,315	(2)
1944	1,019,649	(50)	20,393	46,016	(1)
1945	1,270,401	(50)	25,408	32,178	(1)
1946	1,732,135	(55)	31,493	58,346	(1)
1947	1,837,437	(60)	30,624	66,268	(2)
1948	1,525,243	(60)	25,421	36,309	(1)
1949	1,391,735	(60)	23,196	27,980	(1)
1950	1,977,753	(78)	25,356	136,647	(3)
1951	1,913,019	(72)	26,570	57,522	(1)
1952	2,052,126	(72)	28,502	97,507	(2)
1953	2,164,585	(72)	30,064	54,577	(1)
1954	2,190,571	(72)	30,425	43,827	(1)
1955	2,521,836	(72)	35,026	85,693	(1)
1956	2,551,263	(72)	35,434	56,836	(1)
1957	2,836,318	(72)	39,393	119,579	(2)
1958	3,006,124	(72)	41,752	123,659	(2)
1959	3,140,000	(72)	43,617	57,545	(1)
1960	3,128,296	(78)	40,106	67,325	(1)
1961	3,986,159	(98)	40,675	39,029	(1)
1962	4,003,421	(98)	40,851	64,892	(1)
1963	4,163,643	(98)	42,486	45,801	(1)
1964	4,563,049	(98)	46,562	79,544	(1)
1965	4,634,021	(98)	47,286	100,304	(2)
1966	5,337,044	(105)	50,829	135,098	(2)
1967	5,938,924	(112)	53,026	241,754	(4)
1968	5,882,313	(112)	52,521	291,279	(4)
1969	6,096,127	(112)	54,430	242,841	(4)
1970	9,533,333	(182)	52,381	410,371	(7)
1971	10,076,035	(182)	55,363	430,244	(7)
1972	10,445,827	(182)	57,395	435,466	(7)
1973	10,730,933	(182)	58,961	458,515	(7)
1974	10,236,322	(182)	56,244	412,180	(7)
1975	10,213,193	(182)	56,116	443,811	(7)
1976	11,070,543	(196)	56,482	428,733	(7)
1977	11,018,632	(196)	56,218	483,588	(7)
1978	12,771,800	(224)	57,017	578,107	(9)
1979	13,182,039	(224)	58,848	582,266	(9)
1980	13,392,230	(224)	59,787	577,186	(9)
1981	13,606,990	(224)	60,745	587,361	(9)
1982‡	7,367,438	(126)	58,472	985,952	(15)
1983	13,277,222	(224)	59,273	625,068	(9)
1984	13,398,112	(224)	59,813	614,809	(9)
1985	13,345,047	(224)	59,567	660,667	(9)
1986	13,588,551	(224)	60,663	683,901	(9)
1987§	10,032,493	(168)	59,717	606,864	(9)
1988	13,539,848	(224)	60,446	608,204	(9)
1989	13,625,662	(224)	60,829	635,326	(9)
1990	14,266,240	(224)	63,689	797,198	(11)
1991	13,187,478	(224)	58,873	758,186	(11)
1992	13,159,387	(224)	58,747	756,005	(11)
1993	13,328,760	(224)	59,503	755,625	(11)
1994	13,479,680	(224)	60,177	719,143	(11)
1995	14,196,205	(240)	59,151	733,729	(11)
1996	13,695,748	(240)	57,066	711,601	(11)
1997	14,691,416	(240)	61,214	751,884	(11)
1998	14,977,358	(240)	62,406	776,225	(11)
1999	16,105,716	(248)	64,942	758,045	(11)
2000	16,346,740	(248)	65,914	760,710	(11)
2001	16,314,003	(248)	65,782	721,104	(11)
2002	16,979,369	(256)	66,326	732,722	(11)
2003	17,105,267	(256)	66,817	805,546	(11)
2004	17,270,486	(256)	67,463	743,803	(11)

*Number of tickets sold, including no-shows; number of regular-season games in parentheses.

†Includes conference, league championship and Super Bowl games, but not Pro Bowl; number of postseason games in parentheses.

‡A 57-day players strike reduced 224-game schedule to 126 games.

§A 24-day players strike reduced 224-game schedule to 168 nonstrike games.

AMERICAN FOOTBALL LEAGUE

Year	Regular season*	Average	AFL Champ. Game
1960	926,156 (56)	16,538	32,183
1961	1,002,657 (56)	17,904	29,556
1962	1,147,302 (56)	20,487	37,981
1963	1,208,697 (56)	21,584	30,127
1964	1,447,875 (56)	25,855	40,242
1965	1,782,384 (56)	31,828	30,361
1966	2,160,369 (63)	34,291	42,080
1967	2,295,697 (63)	36,439	53,330
1968	2,635,004 (70)	37,643	62,627
1969	2,843,373 (70)	40,620	53,564

*Number of regular-season games in parentheses.

TRADES

(Covering May 2004 through April 2005)

JUNE 9

Tampa Bay traded OT Roman Oben to **San Diego** for the Chargers' 2005 fifth-round draft choice. Buccaneers traded the pick to the **New York Giants**.

AUGUST 17

New England traded LB Quinn Dorsey to **Chicago** for a 2006 conditional draft choice.

AUGUST 21

Miami traded DE Adewale Ogunleye to **Chicago** for WR Marty Booker and the Bears' 2005 third-round draft choice. Dolphins selected LB Channing Crowder (Florida).

AUGUST 24

Dallas traded OT Javiar Collins to **Carolina** for a 2005 conditional draft choice.

AUGUST 30

Oakland traded DE/LB Shurron Pierson to **Chicago** for an undisclosed draft choice.

AUGUST 31

Oakland traded DE Peppi Zellner and RB Troy Hambrick to **Arizona** for an undisclosed draft choice.

Tampa Bay traded G Jason Whittle to the **New York Giants** for a 2005 undisclosed draft choice. Buccaneers selected WR Paris Warren (Utah) in the seventh round.

SEPTEMBER 1

Houston traded P Steve Cheek to **Kansas City** for future considerations.

SEPTEMBER 3

Green Bay traded S Marques Anderson to **Oakland** for the Raiders' 2005 fifth- and sixth-round draft choices. Packers selected C Junius Coston (North Carolina A&T) and DE Mike Montgomery (Texas A&M).

SEPTEMBER 5

Pittsburgh traded OT Todd Fordham to **Carolina** for the Panthers' 2005 seventh-round draft choice. Steelers selected DE Shaun Nua (Brigham Young).

Kansas City traded DE R-Kal Truluck to **Green Bay** for the Packers' 2005 fifth- and sixth-round draft choices. Chiefs traded the fifth-round pick to **Miami** and selected DE Khari Long (Baylor).

Miami traded OT Brad Bedell to **Green Bay** for a 2006 undisclosed draft choice.

SEPTEMBER 8

St. Louis traded RB Lamar Gordon to **Miami** for the Dolphins'

2005 third-round draft choice. Rams selected S Oshiomogho Atogwe (Stanford).

SEPTEMBER 11

Oakland traded DE Chris Cooper to **Dallas** for a 2006 conditional draft choice.

SEPTEMBER 20

Atlanta traded DT Ellis Johnson to **Denver** for a 2005 conditional draft choice. Falcons selected LB Michael Boley (Southern Mississippi) in the fifth round.

OCTOBER 4

Green Bay traded CB Mike McKenzie and a future conditional draft choice to **New Orleans** for QB J.T. O'Sullivan and the Saints' 2005 second-round draft choice. Packers selected S Nick Collins (Bethune-Cookman).

OCTOBER 19

Cleveland traded WR Quincy Morgan to **Dallas** for WR Antonio Bryant.

Oakland traded WR Jerry Rice to **Seattle** for the Seahawks' 2005 seventh-round draft choice.

Tampa Bay traded WR Keenan McCardell to **San Diego** for the Chargers' 2005 third- and sixth-round draft choices. Buccaneers selected OT Chris Colmer (North Carolina State) and traded the sixth-round pick to **Cleveland**.

MARCH 2

Cleveland traded DT Gerard Warren to **Denver** for the Broncos' 2005 fourth-round draft choice. Browns traded the pick to **Seattle**.

Minnesota traded WR Randy Moss to **Oakland** for LB Napoleon Harris and the Raiders' 2005 first- and seventh-round draft choices. Vikings selected WR Troy Williamson (South Carolina) and CB Adrian Ward (Texas-El Paso).

MARCH 3

Arizona traded CB Duane Starks and a 2005 fifth-round draft choice to **New England** for the Patriots' 2005 third- and fifth-round draft choices. Patriots traded the fifth-round pick to **Detroit**. Cardinals selected LB Darryl Blackstock (Virginia) and LB Lance Mitchell (Oklahoma).

MARCH 7

Seattle traded QB Trent Dilfer to **Cleveland** for a the Browns' 2005 fourth-round draft choice. Seattle traded the pick to **Carolina**.

MARCH 9

Washington traded WR Lavernues Coles to the **New York Jets** for WR Santana Moss.

2004 REVIEW *Trades*

MARCH 18

New York Jets traded LB Sam Cowart to Minnesota for the Vikings' 2005 seventh-round draft choice. Jets traded the pick to New England.

MARCH 30

Cleveland traded DE Ebenezer Ekuban and DT Michael Myers to Denver for RB Reuben Droughns.

APRIL 5

Tennessee traded DE Carlos Hall to Kansas City for a 2005 undisclosed draft choice. Titans selected OT Daniel Loper (Texas Tech) in the fifth round.

APRIL 19

Washington traded its 2005 third-round draft choice and its 2006 first- and fourth-round draft choices to Denver for the Broncos' 2005 first-round draft choice. Washington selected QB Jason Campbell (Auburn). Denver selected CB Karl Paymah (Washington State).

APRIL 20

Oakland traded CB Phillip Buchanon to Houston for the Texans' 2005 second- and third-round draft choices. Raiders traded the second-round pick to New York Jets and selected LB Kirk Morrison (San Diego State).

APRIL 21

Oakland traded TE Doug Jolley and a 2005 second-round draft choice and two 2005 sixth-round draft choices to New York Jets for the Jets' 2005 first- and seventh-round draft choices. Jets selected K Mike Nugent (Ohio State) and RB Cedric Houston (Tennessee) and traded the second sixth-round pick to Jacksonville. Raiders traded the first-round pick to Seattle and the seventh-round pick to New England.

APRIL 22

Miami traded CB Patrick Surtain and a 2005 fifth-round draft choice to Kansas City for the Chiefs' 2005 second- and fifth-round draft choices. Dolphins selected DE Matt Roth (Iowa) and OT Anthony Alabi (Texas Christian). Kansas City selected LB Boomer Grigsby (Illinois State).

APRIL 23

Houston traded its 2005 first-round draft choice to New Orleans for the Saints' 2005 first-round draft choice and a 2006 third-round draft choice. New Orleans selected OT Jammal Brown (Oklahoma). Houston selected DT Travis Johnson (Florida State).

Seattle traded its 2005 first-round draft choice to Oakland for the Raiders' 2005 first- and fourth-round draft choices. Oakland selected CB Fabian Washington (Nebraska). Seattle selected C Chris Spencer (Mississippi) and OT Ray Willis (Florida State).

Tennessee traded its 2005 second-round draft choice to Detroit for the Lions' 2005 second-round and fourth-round draft choices. Detroit selected DT Shaun Cody (Southern California). Tennessee selected OT Michael Roos (Eastern Washington) and OT David Stewart (Mississippi State).

Carolina traded its 2005 second-round draft choice to Seattle for the Seahawks' 2005 second-round draft choice and two

fourth-round draft choices. Seattle selected LB Lofa Tatupu (Southern California). Carolina selected RB Eric Shelton (Louisville) and QB Stefan LeFors (Louisville) and traded the other fourth-round pick to Green Bay.

New England traded its 2005 second-round draft choice to Baltimore for the Ravens' 2005 third-round, sixth-round and 2006 third-round draft choices. Baltimore selected OT Adam Terry (Syracuse). New England selected CB Ellis Hobbs (Iowa State) and traded No. 125 to Green Bay.

Green Bay traded its 2005 third-round draft choice to Carolina for the Panthers' 2005 fourth-round draft choice. Carolina selected DT Atiyyah Ellison (Missouri). The Packers selected DB Marviel Underwood (San Diego State) and traded No. 126 to Philadelphia.

Philadelphia traded its 2005 third-round draft choice to San Francisco for the 49ers' 2005 fourth-round and sixth-round draft choices. San Francisco selected G Adam Snyder (Oregon). Philadelphia selected S Sean Considine (Iowa) and traded No. 175 to New England.

APRIL 24

Washington traded its 2005 fourth-round draft choice to Minnesota for the Vikings' 2005 fourth-round and fifth-round draft choices. Minnesota selected RB Ciatrick Fason (Florida). Washington selected RB Manuel White (UCLA) and LB Robert McCune (Louisville).

Jacksonville traded its 2005 fourth-round draft choice to the New York Jets for the Jets' 2005 fourth-round and sixth-round draft choices. New York selected FS Kerry Rhodes (Louisville). Jacksonville selected RB Alvin Pearman (Virginia) and WR Chad Owens (Hawaii).

Cleveland traded QB Luke McCown to Tampa Bay for the Buccaneers' 2005 sixth-round draft choice. Cleveland selected DT Andrew Hoffman (Virginia).

Green Bay traded its 2005 fourth-round draft choice to Philadelphia for the Eagles' 2005 fifth-, sixth- and seventh-round picks. Eagles selected OT Todd Herremans (Saginaw Valley State). Packers selected CB Michael Hawkins (Oklahoma), traded the sixth-round pick to New England and selected CB Kurt Campbell (Albany).

Philadelphia traded its 2005 fourth-round and 2006 sixth-round draft choices to Dallas for the Cowboys' 2005 fifth-round and 2006 fourth-round picks. Cowboys selected DE Chris Canty (Virginia). Eagles traded the fifth-round pick to Indianapolis.

Tampa Bay traded its 2005 fifth-round draft choice to St. Louis for the Rams' 2005 fifth-round and seventh-round draft choices. Rams selected TE Jerome Collins (Notre Dame). Buccaneers selected WR Larry Brackins (Pearl River CC) and CB Hamza Abdullah (Washington State).

New England traded its 2005 fifth- and sixth-round draft choices to Detroit for the Lions' 2006 fourth-round draft choice. Lions selected QB Dan Orlovsky (Connecticut) and DE Jonathan Goddard (Marshall).

Philadelphia traded its 2005 fifth-round draft choice to Indianapolis for the Colts' 2006 fourth-round draft choice. Colts selected DE Jonathan Welsh (Wisconsin).

Green Bay traded its 2005 sixth-round draft choice to New England for the Patriots' 2005 sixth- and seventh-round draft choices. Patriots traded the sixth-round pick to Oakland. Packers selected WR Craig Bragg (UCLA) and G Will Whitticker (Michigan State).

New England traded its 2005 sixth-round draft choice to Oakland for the Raiders' 2005 seventh-round and 2006 fifth-round draft choices. Raiders selected DT Anttaj Hawthorne (Wisconsin). Patriots selected QB Matt Cassel (Southern California).

2004 STATISTICS

Rushing

Passing

Receiving

Scoring

Interceptions

Sacks

Fumbles

Field goals

Punting

Punt returns

Kickoff returns

Tackles

Miscellaneous

RUSHING

TEAM

AFC

Team	Att.	Yds.	Avg.	Long	TD
Pittsburgh	618	2464	4.0	58	16
N.Y. Jets	527	2388	4.5	33	15
Denver	534	2333	4.4	t51	13
Kansas City	496	2289	4.6	t46	31
San Diego	525	2185	4.2	52	24
New England	524	2134	4.1	44	15
Baltimore	491	2063	4.2	t75	11
Houston	481	1882	3.9	44	16
Buffalo	483	1874	3.9	48	15
Tennessee	420	1871	4.5	52	12
Indianapolis	427	1852	4.3	55	10
Jacksonville	446	1850	4.1	46	9
Cincinnati	437	1839	4.2	52	14
Cleveland	441	1657	3.8	46	6
Miami	384	1339	3.5	53	10
Oakland	327	1295	4.0	60	10
AFC total	7561	31315	...	t75	227
AFC average	472.6	1957.2	4.1	...	14.2

t—touchdown.

NFC

Team	Att.	Yds.	Avg.	Long	TD
Atlanta	524	2672	5.1	60	20
Seattle	468	2095	4.5	44	17
Green Bay	441	1908	4.3	t90	9
N.Y. Giants	424	1904	4.5	t72	18
Minnesota	387	1823	4.7	49	8
Detroit	407	1777	4.4	74	7
Dallas	449	1769	3.9	53	14
Washington	471	1765	3.7	t64	6
Arizona	475	1668	3.5	62	15
Philadelphia	376	1639	4.4	50	10
Chicago	430	1624	3.8	54	10
St. Louis	381	1624	4.3	48	11
New Orleans	406	1606	4.0	71	15
Carolina	422	1582	3.7	71	10
Tampa Bay	393	1489	3.8	t78	9
San Francisco	413	1449	3.5	60	10
NFC total	6867	28394	...	t90	189
NFC average	429.2	1774.6	4.1	...	11.8
NFL total	14428	59709	...	t90	416
NFL average	450.9	1865.9	4.1	...	13.0

INDIVIDUAL

BESTS OF THE SEASON

Yards, season
AFC: 1697—Curtis Martin, N.Y. Jets.
NFC: 1696—Shaun Alexander, Seattle.

Yards, game
AFC: 204—Edgerrin James, Indianapolis at Chicago, Nov. 21 (23 attempts, 1 TD).
NFC: 198—Julius Jones, Dallas at Seattle, Dec. 6 (30 attempts, (3 TDs).

Longest gain
NFC: 90—Ahman Green, Green Bay vs. Dallas, Oct. 24 (TD).
AFC: 75—Jamal Lewis, Baltimore at Cincinnati, Sep. 26 (TD).

Attempts, season
AFC: 371—Curtis Martin, N.Y. Jets.
NFC: 353—Shaun Alexander, Seattle.

Attempts, game
AFC: 38—Reuben Droughns, Denver at Oakland, Oct. 17 (176 yards, 1 TD); Lee Suggs, Cleveland at Miami, Dec. 26 (143 yards).
NFC: 36—Clinton Portis, Washington at Chicago, Oct. 17 (171 yards); Nick Goings, Carolina at New Orleans, Dec. 5 (122 yards, 1 TD).

Yards per attempt, season
NFC: 7.5—Michael Vick, Atlanta.
AFC: 4.9—Chris Brown, Tennessee.

Touchdowns, season
AFC: 17—LaDainian Tomlinson, San Diego.
NFC: 16—Shaun Alexander, Seattle.

Team leaders, yards
AFC:

Team	Yds	Player
Baltimore	1006	Jamal Lewis
Buffalo	1128	Willis McGahee
Cincinnati	1454	Rudi Johnson
Cleveland	744	Lee Suggs
Denver	1240	Reuben Droughns
Houston	1188	Domanick Davis
Indianapolis	1548	Edgerrin James
Jacksonville	1224	Fred Taylor
Kansas City	892	Priest Holmes
Miami	523	Sammy Morris
N.Y. Jets	1697	Curtis Martin
New England	1635	Corey Dillon
Oakland	425	Amos Zereoue
Pittsburgh	941	Jerome Bettis
San Diego	1335	LaDainian Tomlinson
Tennessee	1067	Chris Brown

NFC:

Team	Yds	Player
Arizona	937	Emmitt Smith
Atlanta	1106	Warrick Dunn
Carolina	821	Nick Goings
Chicago	948	Thomas Jones
Dallas	819	Julius Jones
Detroit	1133	Kevin Jones
Green Bay	1163	Ahman Green
Minnesota	544	Onterrio Smith
N.Y. Giants	1518	Tiki Barber
New Orleans	1074	Deuce McAllister
Philadelphia	812	Brian Westbrook
San Francisco	822	Kevan Barlow
Seattle	1696	Shaun Alexander
St. Louis	774	Marshall Faulk
Tampa Bay	926	Michael Pittman
Washington	1315	Clinton Portis

NFL LEADERS

Player, Team	Att.	Yds.	Avg.	Long	TD
Martin, Curtis, N.Y. Jets*	371	1697	4.6	t25	12
Alexander, Shaun, Seattle	353	1696	4.8	44	16
Dillon, Corey, New England*	345	1635	4.7	44	12
James, Edgerrin, Indianapolis*	334	1548	4.6	40	9
Barber, Tiki, N.Y. Giants*	322	1518	4.7	t72	13
Johnson, Rudi, Cincinnati*	361	1454	4.0	52	12
Tomlinson, LaDainian, S.D. *	339	1335	3.9	42	17
Portis, Clinton, Washington	343	1315	3.8	t64	5
Droughns, Reuben, Denver*	275	1240	4.5	t51	6
Taylor, Fred, Jacksonville*	260	1224	4.7	46	2
Davis, Domanick, Houston*	302	1188	3.9	44	13
Green, Ahman, Green Bay	259	1163	4.5	t90	7
Jones, Kevin, Detroit	241	1133	4.7	74	5
McGahee, Willis, Buffalo*	284	1128	4.0	41	13
Dunn, Warrick, Atlanta	265	1106	4.2	60	9

Player, Team	Att.	Yds.	Avg.	Long	TD
McAllister, Deuce, New Orleans....	269	1074	4.0	71	9
Brown, Chris, Tennessee*	220	1067	4.9	52	6
Lewis, Jamal, Baltimore*	235	1006	4.3	t75	7
Jones, Thomas, Chicago	240	948	4.0	54	7
Bettis, Jerome, Pittsburgh*	250	941	3.8	29	13
Smith, Emmitt, Arizona	267	937	3.5	t29	9
Pittman, Michael, Tampa Bay	219	926	4.2	t78	7
Vick, Michael, Atlanta	120	902	7.5	58	3
Holmes, Priest, Kansas City*	196	892	4.6	t33	14

Player, Team	Att.	Yds.	Avg.	Long	TD
Staley, Duce, Pittsburgh*	192	830	4.3	38	1
Barlow, Kevan, San Francisco	244	822	3.4	60	7
Goings, Nick, Carolina	217	821	3.8	t57	6
Jones, Julius, Dallas	197	819	4.2	53	7
Westbrook, Brian, Philadelphia	177	812	4.6	50	3
Faulk, Marshall, St. Louis	195	774	4.0	40	3

*AFC.
t—touchdown.
Leaders based on yards gained.

AFC

Player, Team	Att.	Yds.	Avg.	Long	TD
Abdullah, Rabih, New England	13	13	1.0	5	1
Askew, B.J., N.Y. Jets	6	23	3.8	14	0
Baxter, Jarrod, Houston	2	1	0.5	1	0
Bell, Tatum, Denver	75	396	5.3	29	3
Bennett, Drew, Tennessee	1	12	12.0	12	0
Bettis, Jerome, Pittsburgh	250	941	3.8	29	13
Blaylock, Derrick, Kansas City	118	539	4.6	24	8
Bledsoe, Drew, Buffalo	22	37	1.7	17	0
Boller, Kyle, Baltimore	53	189	3.6	19	1
Bollinger, Brooks, N.Y. Jets	1	2	2.0	2	0
Booker, Marty, Miami	1	-8	-8.0	-8	0
Brady, Tom, New England	43	28	0.7	10	0
Brees, Drew, San Diego	53	85	1.6	22	2
Brown, Chris, Tennessee	220	1067	4.9	52	6
Brown, Dante, Pittsburgh	1	2	2.0	2	0
Burns, Joe, Buffalo	20	73	3.7	21	0
Caldwell, Reche, San Diego	4	45	11.3	20	0
Carr, David, Houston	73	299	4.1	24	0
Carter, Quincy, N.Y. Jets	12	20	1.7	9	0
Chambers, Chris, Miami	9	76	8.4	24	0
Chatman, Jesse, San Diego	65	392	6.0	52	3
Cheek, Steve, Kansas City	1	0	0.0	0	0
Cobbs, Cedric, New England	22	50	2.3	13	0
Collins, Kerry, Oakland	16	36	2.3	8	0
Collins, Todd, Kansas City	1	4	4.0	4	0
Crockett, Zack, Oakland	48	232	4.8	47	2
Curry, Ronald, Oakland	1	-3	-3.0	-3	0
Davey, Rohan, New England	4	-1	-.3	3	0
Davis, Andre', Cleveland	1	-3	-3.0	-3	0
Davis, Domanick, Houston	302	1188	3.9	44	13
Dillon, Corey, New England	345	1635	4.7	44	12
Droughns, Reuben, Denver	275	1240	4.5	t51	6
Dwight, Tim, San Diego	4	54	13.5	48	0
Easy, Omar, Kansas City	4	1	0.3	4	0
Echemandu, Adimchinobe, Clev. ..	8	25	3.1	6	0
Edwards, Troy, Jacksonville	2	2	1.0	2	0
Evans, Lee, Buffalo	5	85	17.0	48	0
Fargas, Justin, Oakland	35	126	3.6	15	1
Faulk, Kevin, New England	54	255	4.7	20	2
Feeley, A.J., Miami	14	13	0.9	t7	1
Fiedler, Jay, Miami	12	59	4.9	26	0
Fleming, Troy, Tennessee	7	40	5.7	13	0
Flutie, Doug, San Diego	5	39	7.8	20	2
Forsey, Brock, Miami	19	53	2.8	15	0
Frost, Derrick, Cleveland	1	1	1.0	1	0
Fuamatu-Ma'afala, Chris, Jack. ...	20	69	3.5	10	1
Gabriel, Doug, Oakland	2	7	3.5	4	0
Gaffney, Jabar, Houston	4	30	7.5	10	0
Gannon, Rich, Oakland	5	26	5.2	20	0
Garcia, Jeff, Cleveland	35	169	4.8	21	2
Garrard, David, Jacksonville	12	76	6.3	12	1
Gonzalez, Tony, Kansas City	1	5	5.0	5	0
Gordon, Lamar, Miami	35	64	1.8	11	0
Green, Trent, Kansas City	25	85	3.4	13	0
Green, William, Cleveland	163	585	3.6	46	2
Greer, Jabari, Buffalo	1	-6	-6.0	-6	0
Griffin, Quentin, Denver	85	311	3.7	t47	2
Hall, Dante, Kansas City	8	56	7.0	17	0
Haynes, Verron, Pittsburgh	55	272	4.9	18	0
Hearst, Garrison, Denver	20	81	4.1	11	1
Henry, Leonard, Miami	46	141	3.1	53	0
Henry, Travis, Buffalo	94	326	3.5	19	0
Hentrich, Craig, Tennessee	1	8	8.0	8	0
Hetherington, Chris, Oakland	1	4	4.0	4	0
Holcomb, Kelly, Cleveland	3	-2	-.7	0	0
Holcomb, Robert, Tennessee	17	62	3.6	20	0
Hollings, Tony, Houston	11	47	4.3	13	0
Holmes, Priest, Kansas City	196	892	4.6	t33	14
Horn, Chris, Kansas City	1	12	12.0	12	0
Houshmandzadeh, T.J., Cin.	6	51	8.5	16	0
Izzo, Larry, New England	1	0	0.0	0	0
Jackson, Frisman, Cleveland	1	4	4.0	4	0
Jackson, James, Cleveland	12	81	6.8	38	0
James, Edgerrin, Indianapolis	334	1548	4.6	40	9
Johnson, Andre, Houston	4	12	3.0	14	0
Johnson, Bethel, New England	2	8	4.0	11	0
Johnson, Chad, Cincinnati	4	39	9.8	18	0
Johnson, Doug, Tennessee	2	-2	-1.0	-1	0
Johnson, Jeremi, Cincinnati	3	5	1.7	4	0
Johnson, Kevin, Baltimore	1	0	0.0	0	0
Johnson, Larry, Kansas City	120	581	4.8	t46	9
Johnson, Rudi, Cincinnati	361	1454	4.0	52	12
Jones, Greg, Jacksonville	62	162	2.6	12	3
Jordan, LaMont, N.Y. Jets	93	479	5.2	33	2
Kennison, Eddie, Kansas City	2	15	7.5	15	0
King, Vick, Miami	4	9	2.3	3	0
Kitna, Jon, Cincinnati	10	42	4.2	15	0
Konrad, Rob, Miami	2	18	9.0	15	0
Kreider, Dan, Pittsburgh	4	18	4.5	6	0
Larson, Kyle, Cincinnati	1	11	11.0	t11	1
Leftwich, Byron, Jacksonville	39	148	3.8	17	2
Lelie, Ashley, Denver	3	5	1.7	8	0
Lewis, Jamal, Baltimore	235	1006	4.3	t75	7
Losman, J.P., Buffalo	2	15	7.5	10	0
Maddox, Tommy, Pittsburgh	9	15	1.7	10	0
Manning, Peyton, Indianapolis	25	38	1.5	19	0
Martin, Curtis, N.Y. Jets	371	1697	4.6	t25	12
Mason, Derrick, Tennessee	1	-3	-3.0	-3	0
Matthews, Shane, Buffalo	2	-3	-1.5	-1	0
McCardell, Keenan, San Diego	1	3	3.0	3	0
McCareins, Justin, N.Y. Jets	2	-5	-2.5	-2	0
McCown, Luke, Cleveland	6	25	4.2	11	0
McGahee, Willis, Buffalo	284	1128	4.0	41	13
McNair, Steve, Tennessee	23	128	5.6	23	1
Minor, Travis, Miami	109	388	3.6	34	3
Moorman, Brian, Buffalo	2	23	11.5	34	0
Morris, Sammy, Miami	132	523	4.0	t35	6
Morton, Johnnie, Kansas City	7	43	6.1	14	0
Moss, Santana, N.Y. Jets	6	18	3.0	12	0
Moulds, Eric, Buffalo	5	19	3.8	12	0
Mungro, James, Indianapolis	5	19	3.8	8	0
Neal, Lorenzo, San Diego	16	53	3.3	8	0
Norris, Moran, Houston	1	0	0.0	0	0
Northcutt, Dennis, Cleveland	8	19	2.4	8	0
Palmer, Carson, Cincinnati	18	47	2.6	14	1
Parker, Eric, San Diego	4	53	13.3	38	0

AFC (continued)

Player, Team	Att.	Yds.	Avg.	Long	TD
Parker, Willie, Pittsburgh	32	186	5.8	58	0
Pass, Patrick, New England	39	141	3.6	19	0
Patten, David, New England	1	5	5.0	5	0
Pennington, Chad, N.Y. Jets	34	126	3.7	16	1
Perry, Chris, Cincinnati	2	1	0.5	1	0
Pinnock, Andrew, San Diego	9	26	2.9	11	0
Plummer, Jake, Denver	62	202	3.3	22	1
Porter, Jerry, Oakland	1	-4	-4.0	-4	0
Randle El, Antwaan, Pittsburgh	8	34	4.3	12	0
Redmond, J.R., Oakland	21	119	5.7	18	0
Reed, Josh, Buffalo	2	-1	-.5	6	0
Rhodes, Dominic, Indianapolis	53	254	4.8	55	1
Ricard, Alan, Baltimore	10	36	3.6	14	0
Richardson, Tony, Kansas City	12	56	4.7	13	0
Rivers, Philip, San Diego	4	-5	-1.3	-1	0
Roethlisberger, Ben, Pittsburgh	56	144	2.6	20	1
Russell, Cliff, Cincinnati	3	15	5.0	13	0
Sams, B.J., Baltimore	4	19	4.8	8	1
Sanders, Deion, Baltimore	1	-10	-10.0	-10	0
Sapp, Cecil, Denver	4	32	8.0	18	0
Shaw, Bobby, San Diego	1	1	1.0	1	0
Simmons, Jason, Houston	1	1	1.0	1	0
Smith, Antowain, Tennessee	137	509	3.7	43	4
Smith, Hunter, Indianapolis	1	2	2.0	2	0
Smith, Jonathan, Buffalo	2	11	5.5	8	0
Smith, Musa, Baltimore	12	48	4.0	13	0
Smith, Rod, Denver	5	33	6.6	14	0
Smith, Terrelle, Cleveland	4	9	2.3	4	0
Sorgi, Jim, Indianapolis	8	-5	-.6	2	0
Sowell, Jerald, N.Y. Jets	2	28	14.0	19	0
St. Pierre, Brian, Pittsburgh	4	-3	-.8	2	0
Staley, Duce, Pittsburgh	192	830	4.3	38	1
Stanley, Chad, Houston	1	5	5.0	5	0
Stewart, Kordell, Baltimore	1	-1	-1.0	-1	0
Suggs, Lee, Cleveland	199	744	3.7	39	2
Taylor, Chester, Baltimore	160	714	4.5	47	2
Taylor, Fred, Jacksonville	260	1224	4.7	46	2
Toefield, LaBrandon, Jack.	51	169	3.3	16	0
Tomlinson, LaDainian, S.D.	339	1335	3.9	42	17
Turk, Matt, Miami	1	3	3.0	3	0
Turner, Michael, San Diego	20	104	5.2	30	0
Volek, Billy, Tennessee	11	50	4.5	14	1
Ward, Hines, Pittsburgh	7	25	3.6	t16	1
Warrick, Peter, Cincinnati	2	14	7.0	8	0
Washington, Kelley, Cincinnati	1	-1	-1.0	-1	0
Watson, Kenny, Cincinnati	26	161	6.2	25	0
Watts, Darius, Denver	5	33	6.6	10	0
Wayne, Reggie, Indianapolis	1	-4	-4.0	-4	0
Wells, Jonathan, Houston	82	299	3.6	14	3
Wheatley, Tyrone, Oakland	85	327	3.8	60	4
White, Jamel, T.B.-Bal.*	27	82	3.0	16	0
Williams, Shaud, Buffalo	42	167	4.0	t27	2
Zereoue, Amos, Oakland	112	425	3.8	t55	3

*Includes both NFC and AFC statistics.
t—touchdown.

NFC

Player, Team	Att.	Yds.	Avg.	Long	TD
Alexander, Shaun, Seattle	353	1696	4.8	44	16
Alstott, Mike, Tampa Bay	67	230	3.4	32	2
Anderson, Damien, Arizona	1	2	2.0	2	0
Anderson, Richie, Dallas	57	246	4.3	27	1
Ayanbadejo, Obafemi, Arizona	30	122	4.1	23	3
Barber, Tiki, N.Y. Giants	322	1518	4.7	t72	13
Barlow, Kevan, San Francisco	244	822	3.4	60	7
Barnes, Darian, Dallas	5	10	2.0	8	0
Battle, Arnaz, San Francisco	2	5	2.5	7	0
Beasley, Fred, San Francisco	9	15	1.7	4	0
Bennett, Brandon, Carolina	6	17	2.8	11	1
Bennett, Michael, Minnesota	70	276	3.9	25	1
Berrian, Bernard, Chicago	8	28	3.5	25	0
Betts, Ladell, Washington	90	371	4.1	27	1
Blake, Jeff, Philadelphia	3	6	2.0	8	0
Boldin, Anquan, Arizona	1	3	3.0	3	0
Brooks, Aaron, New Orleans	58	173	3.0	15	4
Brunell, Mark, Washington	19	62	3.3	21	0
Bryson, Shawn, Detroit	50	264	5.3	28	0
Bulger, Marc, St. Louis	19	89	4.7	t19	3
Burleson, Nate, Minnesota	6	49	8.2	11	0
Campbell, Kelly, Minnesota	3	4	1.3	16	0
Carter, Kerry, Seattle	4	15	3.8	6	0
Carter, Ki-Jana, New Orleans	10	17	1.7	8	0
Carter, Tim, N.Y. Giants	2	23	11.5	15	0
Cartwright, Rock, Washington	2	0	0.0	2	0
Chandler, Chris, St. Louis	1	2	2.0	2	0
Chatman, Antonio, Green Bay	4	36	9.0	18	0
Clayton, Michael, Tampa Bay	5	30	6.0	15	0
Cleeland, Cam, St. Louis	1	-2	-2.0	-2	0
Cloud, Michael, N.Y. Giants	21	90	4.3	26	3
Coakley, Dexter, Dallas	1	33	33.0	33	0
Coles, Laveranues, Washington	3	-3	-1.0	7	0
Copper, Terrance, Dallas	1	-1	-1.0	-1	0
Croom, Larry, Arizona	29	76	2.6	20	0
Culpepper, Daunte, Minnesota	88	406	4.6	16	2
Curtis, Kevin, St. Louis	3	24	8.0	15	0
Davenport, Najeh, Green Bay	71	359	5.1	t40	2
Davis, Stephen, Carolina	24	92	3.8	12	0
Dayne, Ron, N.Y. Giants	52	179	3.4	15	1
Delhomme, Jake, Carolina	25	71	2.8	13	1
Detmer, Koy, Philadelphia	10	-7	-.7	2	0
Dilfer, Trent, Seattle	10	14	1.4	11	0
Dorsey, Ken, San Francisco	5	7	1.4	3	0
Driver, Donald, Green Bay	3	4	1.3	14	0
Drummond, Eddie, Detroit	1	9	9.0	9	0
Duckett, T.J., Atlanta	104	509	4.9	35	8
Dunn, Warrick, Atlanta	265	1106	4.2	60	9
Evans, Heath, Seattle	7	20	2.9	7	0
Faulk, Marshall, St. Louis	195	774	4.0	40	3
Favre, Brett, Green Bay	16	36	2.3	17	0
Finn, Jim, N.Y. Giants	3	7	2.3	5	0
Fisher, Tony, Green Bay	65	224	3.4	24	0
Fitzgerald, Larry, Arizona	8	14	1.8	10	0
Foster, DeShaun, Carolina	59	255	4.3	71	2
Galloway, Joey, Tampa Bay	2	19	9.5	14	0
Gardner, Rod, Washington	3	7	2.3	11	0
Garner, Charlie, Tampa Bay	30	111	3.7	25	0
George, Eddie, Dallas	132	432	3.3	24	4
Glenn, Terry, Dallas	1	-3	-3.0	-3	0
Goings, Nick, Carolina	217	821	3.8	t57	6
Goodspeed, Joey, St. Louis	3	6	2.0	t2	1
Graham, Earnest, Tampa Bay	13	73	5.6	13	0
Green, Ahman, Green Bay	259	1163	4.5	t90	7
Griese, Brian, Tampa Bay	30	17	0.6	7	0
Griffith, Justin, Atlanta	9	39	4.3	10	0
Grossman, Rex, Chicago	11	48	4.4	8	1
Hakim, Az-Zahir, Detroit	1	0	0.0	0	0
Hambrick, Troy, Arizona	63	283	4.5	62	1
Harrington, Joey, Detroit	48	175	3.6	17	0
Harris, Arlen, St. Louis	20	63	3.2	14	0
Harris, Joey, Carolina	15	53	3.5	19	0
Harris, Nick, Detroit	1	-7	-7.0	-7	0
Hasselbeck, Matt, Seattle	27	90	3.3	19	1
Henson, Drew, Dallas	1	7	7.0	7	0
Hicks, Maurice, San Francisco	96	362	3.8	35	2
Hilliard, Ike, N.Y. Giants	3	34	11.3	17	0
Hoover, Brad, Carolina	68	246	3.6	16	0
Hutchinson, Chad, Chicago	6	14	2.3	11	0
Isom, Jasen, San Francisco	1	0	0.0	0	0

Player, Team	Att.	Yds.	Avg.	Long	TD
Jackson, Steven, St. Louis	134	673	5.0	48	4
Jackson, Terry, San Francisco	26	101	3.9	13	0
Jacobs, Taylor, Washington..........	1	-6	-6.0	-6	0
Jenkins, Michael, Atlanta..............	1	2	2.0	2	0
Johnson, Brad, Tampa Bay..........	5	23	4.6	7	0
Johnson, Bryant, Arizona	2	-6	-3.0	1	0
Johnson, Keyshawn, Dallas..........	2	13	6.5	13	0
Jones, Julius, Dallas....................	197	819	4.2	53	7
Jones, Kevin, Detroit	241	1133	4.7	74	5
Jones, Thomas, Chicago	240	948	4.0	54	7
Karney, Mike, New Orleans...........	3	7	2.3	4	0
King, Shaun, Arizona....................	9	30	3.3	16	0
Krenzel, Craig, Chicago	18	41	2.3	12	0
Layne, George, Atlanta.................	1	12	12.0	12	0
Lee, ReShard, Dallas	27	128	4.7	14	1
Levens, Dorsey, Philadelphia........	94	410	4.4	45	4
Lewis, Greg, Philadelphia	4	16	4.0	11	0
Luchey, Nick, Green Bay	10	24	2.4	4	0
Mahe, Reno, Philadelphia.............	23	91	4.0	22	0
Manning, Eli, N.Y. Giants	6	35	5.8	15	0
McAfee, Fred, New Orleans	2	54	27.0	53	0
McAllister, Deuce, New Orleans.....	269	1074	4.0	71	9
McCoo, Eric, Philadelphia.............	9	54	6.0	12	0
McCown, Josh, Arizona................	36	112	3.1	12	2
McDonald, Shaun, St. Louis.........	4	0	0.0	7	0
McKie, Jason, Chicago	1	1	1.0	1	0
McMahon, Mike, Detroit...............	2	18	9.0	14	0
McNabb, Donovan, Philadelphia....	41	220	5.4	28	3
Moore, Mewelde, Minnesota	65	379	5.8	33	0
Morgan, Quincy, Dallas	2	23	11.5	24	0
Morris, Maurice, Seattle	30	126	4.2	12	0
Muhammad, Muhsin, Carolina	3	15	5.0	13	0
Nall, Craig, Green Bay	3	7	2.3	9	0
O'Sullivan, J.T., Green Bay...........	2	-2	-1.0	-1	0
Owens, Terrell, Philadelphia	3	-5	-1.7	6	0
Pederson, Doug, Green Bay	2	15	7.5	9	0
Peete, Rodney, Carolina...............	1	-1	-1.0	-1	0
Peterson, Adrian, Chicago	6	19	3.2	13	0
Pickett, Cody, San Francisco	1	5	5.0	5	0
Pinner, Artose, Detroit	57	174	3.1	14	2
Pittman, Michael, Tampa Bay	219	926	4.2	t78	7
Ponder, Willie, N.Y. Giants............	1	-4	-4.0	-4	0
Portis, Clinton, Washington..........	343	1315	3.8	t64	5
Price, Peerless, Atlanta.................	3	34	11.3	16	0
Pritchett, Stanley, Atlanta	6	18	3.0	8	0

Player, Team	Att.	Yds.	Avg.	Long	TD
Proehl, Ricky, Carolina	1	9	9.0	9	0
Quinn, Jonathan, Chicago	3	35	11.7	23	0
Ramsey, Patrick, Washington........	10	19	1.9	17	0
Rattay, Tim, San Francisco	12	55	4.6	15	0
Robertson, Jamal, S.F.	16	71	4.4	16	1
Robinson, Koren, Seattle..............	1	3	3.0	3	0
Rossum, Allen, Atlanta	1	0	0.0	0	0
Russell, Brian, Minnesota.............	1	4	4.0	4	0
Schaub, Matt, Atlanta	8	26	3.3	11	0
Schlesinger, Cory, Detroit	4	7	1.8	2	0
Scobey, Josh, Arizona	27	89	3.3	10	0
Simms, Chris, Tampa Bay	7	14	2.0	12	0
Smart, Ian, Tampa Bay	2	26	13.0	25	0
Smart, Rod, Carolina	3	4	1.3	3	0
Smith, Emmitt, Arizona	267	937	3.5	t29	9
Smith, Onterrio, Minnesota	124	544	4.4	38	2
Stallworth, Donte', New Orleans....	6	37	6.2	26	0
Stecker, Aaron, New Orleans	58	244	4.2	t42	2
Strong, Mack, Seattle	36	131	3.6	11	0
Swinton, Reggie, Detroit	1	3	3.0	3	0
Tapeh, Thomas, Philadelphia........	12	42	3.5	10	0
Taylor, Jamaar, N.Y. Giants	1	-8	-8.0	-8	0
Terrell, David, Chicago.................	3	10	3.3	20	0
Testaverde, Vinny, Dallas	21	38	1.8	10	1
Thomas, Anthony, Chicago...........	122	404	3.3	t41	2
Vick, Michael, Atlanta	120	902	7.5	58	3
Wade, Bobby, Chicago	12	76	6.3	14	0
Ward, Dedric, Dallas....................	1	11	11.0	11	0
Warner, Kurt, N.Y. Giants..............	13	30	2.3	13	1
Westbrook, Brian, Philadelphia......	177	812	4.6	50	3
White, Dez, Atlanta	3	14	4.7	26	0
Wilkins, Jeff, St. Louis	1	-5	-5.0	-5	0
Williams, Karl, Arizona	2	6	3.0	3	0
Williams, Moe, Minnesota	30	161	5.4	49	3
Williams, Randal, Dallas...............	1	13	13.0	13	0
Williams, Roy, Detroit...................	1	1	1.0	1	0
Williams, Walter, Green Bay	6	42	7.0	28	0
Wilson, Cedrick, San Francisco	1	6	6.0	6	0
Wright, Jason, Atlanta	3	10	3.3	8	0
t—touchdown.					

PLAYERS WITH TWO CLUBS

Player, Team	Att.	Yds.	Avg.	Long	TD
White, Jamel, Tampa Bay	13	20	1.5	10	0
White, Jamel, Baltimore	14	62	4.4	16	0

2004 STATISTICS Rushing

PASSING

TEAM

TEAM

AFC

Team	Att.	Cmp.	Pct.	Gross Yds.	Sack	Yds. Lost	Net Yds.	Yds./ Att.	Yds./ Cmp.	TD	Pct. TD	Long	Int.	Pct. Int.	Rat.
Indianapolis	527	353	67.0	4732	14	109	4623	8.98	13.4	51	9.7	t80	10	1.9	119.7
Kansas City	561	370	66.0	4633	32	227	4406	8.26	12.5	27	4.8	t70	17	3.0	94.9
Denver	521	303	58.2	4089	15	90	3999	7.85	13.5	27	5.2	t85	20	3.8	84.5
Oakland	582	330	56.7	4019	30	161	3858	6.91	12.2	24	4.1	63	22	3.8	76.1
Tennessee	589	356	60.4	3933	44	317	3616	6.68	11.1	27	4.6	t48	19	3.2	82.1
New England	485	293	60.4	3750	26	162	3588	7.73	12.2	29	6.0	50	14	2.9	92.5
Houston	471	286	60.7	3547	49	301	3246	7.53	12.4	16	3.4	69	14	3.0	83.0
Cincinnati	536	324	60.4	3520	31	219	3301	6.57	10.9	23	4.3	t76	22	4.1	77.0
San Diego	450	288	64.0	3506	21	149	3357	7.79	12.2	29	6.4	t79	8	1.8	102.0
Miami	586	309	52.7	3391	62	326	3065	5.79	11.0	19	3.2	t76	26	4.4	62.5
Jacksonville	513	305	59.5	3315	32	156	3159	6.46	10.9	17	3.3	65	11	2.1	80.7
N.Y. Jets...............	438	282	64.4	3231	31	181	3050	7.38	11.5	19	4.3	t69	11	2.5	90.5
Cleveland	439	251	57.2	3076	41	252	2824	7.01	12.3	21	4.8	t99	21	4.8	74.9
Buffalo	461	262	56.8	3032	38	215	2817	6.58	11.8	21	4.6	t69	17	3.7	76.7
Pittsburgh	358	228	63.7	2970	36	250	2720	8.30	13.0	20	5.6	58	13	3.6	93.2
Baltimore	465	258	55.5	2559	35	247	2312	5.50	9.9	13	2.8	t57	11	2.4	70.7
AFC total	7982	4798	...	57303	527	3362	53941	...	...	383	...	t99	256	...	...
AFC average........	498.9	299.9	60.1	3581.4	32.9	210.1	3371.3	7.18	11.9	23.9	4.8	...	16.0	3.2	84.7

t—touchdown.

NFC

Team	Att.	Cmp.	Pct.	Gross Yds.	Sack	Yds. Lost	Net Yds.	Yds./ Att.	Yds./ Cmp.	TD	Pct. TD	Long	Int.	Pct. Int.	Rat.
Minnesota	552	380	68.8	4754	46	238	4516	8.61	12.51	39	7.07	t82	12	2.2	109.8
St. Louis...............	580	372	64.1	4615	50	362	4253	7.96	12.41	23	3.97	t75	22	3.8	86.1
Green Bay..............	598	382	63.9	4550	14	101	4449	7.61	11.91	36	6.02	t79	19	3.2	93.8
Philadelphia..........	547	336	61.4	4208	37	229	3979	7.69	12.52	32	5.85	80	11	2.0	96.4
Carolina	536	311	58.0	3889	33	246	3643	7.26	12.50	29	5.41	63	15	2.8	87.0
New Orleans	542	309	57.0	3810	41	223	3587	7.03	12.33	21	3.87	t76	16	3.0	79.5
Tampa Bay.............	512	340	66.4	3773	44	299	3474	7.37	11.10	24	4.69	t75	18	3.5	89.1
Seattle	532	304	57.1	3715	34	176	3539	6.98	12.22	23	4.32	60	18	3.4	79.1
Dallas	519	308	59.3	3636	36	208	3428	7.01	11.81	19	3.66	53	23	4.4	74.5
San Francisco........	561	325	57.9	3455	52	319	3136	6.16	10.63	16	2.85	65	21	3.7	69.9
Arizona	533	299	56.1	3202	39	320	2882	6.01	10.71	14	2.63	48	18	3.4	68.5
Detroit	505	285	56.4	3124	37	208	2916	6.19	10.96	19	3.76	62	13	2.6	76.7
N.Y. Giants............	475	269	56.6	3097	52	279	2818	6.52	11.51	12	2.53	t62	13	2.7	73.5
Washington	514	288	56.0	2874	38	242	2632	5.59	9.98	18	3.50	51	17	3.3	70.0
Atlanta	395	217	54.9	2692	50	280	2412	6.82	12.41	15	3.80	62	16	4.1	72.0
Chicago	471	249	52.9	2641	66	449	2192	5.61	10.61	9	1.91	63	16	3.4	61.7
NFC total............	8372	4974	...	58035	669	4179	53856	...	...	349	...	t82	268	...	...
NFC average......	523.3	310.9	59.4	3627.2	41.8	261.2	3366.0	6.93	11.67	21.8	4.2	...	16.8	3.2	81.0
NFL total............	16354	9772	...	115338	1196	7541	107797	...	...	732	...	t99	524	...	...
NFL average......	511.1	305.4	59.8	3604.3	37.4	235.7	3368.7	7.05	11.80	22.9	4.5	...	16.4	3.2	82.8

INDIVIDUAL

BESTS OF THE SEASON

Highest rating, season
AFC: 121.1—Peyton Manning, Indianapolis.
NFC: 110.9—Daunte Culpepper, Minnesota.

Completion percentage, season
NFC: 69.3—Brian Griese, Tampa Bay.
AFC: 67.6—Peyton Manning, Indianapolis.

Attempts, season
AFC: 556—Trent Green, Kansas City.
NFC: 548—Daunte Culpepper, Minnesota.

Completions, season
NFC: 379—Daunte Culpepper, Minnesota.
AFC: 369—Trent Green, Kansas City.

Yards, season
NFC: 4717—Daunte Culpepper, Minnesota.
AFC: 4591—Trent Green, Kansas City.

Yards, game
AFC: 499—Jake Plummer, Denver vs. Atlanta, Oct. 31 (31-55, 4 TDs).
NFC: 464—Donovan McNabb, Philadelphia vs. Green Bay, Dec. 5 (32-43, 5 TDs).

Longest gain
AFC: 99—Jeff Garcia, (to Andre' Davis), Cleveland vs. Cincinnati, Oct. 17 (TD).
NFC: 82—Daunte Culpepper, (to Randy Moss), Minnesota at Detroit, Dec. 19 (TD).

Yards per attempt, season
AFC: 9.17—Peyton Manning, Indianapolis.
NFC: 8.61—Daunte Culpepper, Minnesota.

Touchdown passes, season
AFC: 49—Peyton Manning, Indianapolis.
NFC: 39—Daunte Culpepper, Minnesota.

2004 STATISTICS · Passing

Touchdown passes, game
AFC: 6—Peyton Manning, Indianapolis at Detroit, Nov. 25 (23-28, 236 yards).
NFC: 5—Daunte Culpepper, Minnesota at New Orleans, Oct. 17 (26-37, 425 yards); Daunte Culpepper, Minnesota at Houston, Oct. 10 (OT; 36-50, 396 yards); Daunte Culpepper, Minnesota vs. Dallas, Sep. 12 (17-23, 242 yards); Donovan McNabb, Philadelphia vs. Green Bay, Dec. 5 (32-43, 464 yards).

Lowest interception percentage, season
AFC: 1.8—Drew Brees, San Diego.
NFC: 1.4—Kurt Warner, N.Y. Giants.

NFL LEADERS

Player, Team	Att.	Cmp.	Pct.	Yds.	Avg. Gain	TD	Pct. TD	Long	Int.	Pct. Int.	Sack	Yds. Lost	Rat.
Manning, Peyton, Indianapolis*	497	336	67.6	4557	9.17	49	9.9	t80	10	2.0	13	101	121.1
Culpepper, Daunte, Minnesota	548	379	69.2	4717	8.61	39	7.1	t82	11	2.0	46	238	110.9
Brees, Drew, San Diego*	400	262	65.5	3159	7.90	27	6.8	t79	7	1.8	18	131	104.8
McNabb, Donovan, Philadelphia	469	300	64.0	3875	8.26	31	6.6	80	8	1.7	32	192	104.7
Roethlisberger, Ben, Pittsburgh*	295	196	66.4	2621	8.88	17	5.8	58	11	3.7	30	213	98.1
Griese, Brian, Tampa Bay	336	233	69.3	2632	7.83	20	6.0	68	12	3.6	26	169	97.5
Green, Trent, Kansas City*	556	369	66.4	4591	8.26	27	4.9	t70	17	3.1	32	227	95.2
Bulger, Marc, St. Louis	485	321	66.2	3964	8.17	21	4.3	56	14	2.9	41	302	93.7
Brady, Tom, New England*	474	288	60.8	3692	7.79	28	5.9	50	14	3.0	26	162	92.6
Favre, Brett, Green Bay	540	346	64.1	4088	7.57	30	5.6	t79	17	3.1	12	93	92.4
Pennington, Chad, N.Y. Jets*	370	242	65.4	2673	7.22	16	4.3	48	9	2.4	18	103	91.0
Delhomme, Jake, Carolina	533	310	58.2	3886	7.29	29	5.4	63	15	2.8	33	246	87.3
Volek, Billy, Tennessee*	357	218	61.1	2486	6.96	18	5.0	t48	10	2.8	30	216	87.1
Warner, Kurt, N.Y. Giants	277	174	62.8	2054	7.42	6	2.2	t62	4	1.4	39	196	86.5
Plummer, Jake, Denver*	521	303	58.2	4089	7.85	27	5.2	t85	20	3.8	15	90	84.5
Carr, David, Houston*	466	285	61.2	3531	7.58	16	3.4	69	14	3.0	49	301	83.5
Hasselbeck, Matt, Seattle	474	279	58.9	3382	7.14	22	4.6	60	15	3.2	30	155	83.1
Leftwich, Byron, Jacksonville*	441	267	60.5	2941	6.67	15	3.4	65	10	2.3	25	114	82.2
Brooks, Aaron, New Orleans	542	309	57.0	3810	7.03	21	3.9	57	16	3.0	41	223	79.5
Rattay, Tim, San Francisco	325	198	60.9	2169	6.67	10	3.1	65	10	3.1	37	211	78.1
Vick, Michael, Atlanta	321	181	56.4	2313	7.21	14	4.4	62	12	3.7	46	266	78.1
Harrington, Joey, Detroit	489	274	56.0	3047	6.23	19	3.9	62	12	2.5	36	196	77.5
Palmer, Carson, Cincinnati*	432	263	60.9	2897	6.71	18	4.2	t76	18	4.2	25	178	77.3
Garcia, Jeff, Cleveland*	252	144	57.1	1731	6.87	10	4.0	t99	9	3.6	24	99	76.7
Bledsoe, Drew, Buffalo*	450	256	56.9	2932	6.52	20	4.4	t69	16	3.6	37	215	76.6
Testaverde, Vinny, Dallas	495	297	60.0	3532	7.14	17	3.4	53	20	4.0	34	182	76.4
Collins, Kerry, Oakland*	513	289	56.3	3495	6.81	21	4.1	63	20	3.9	25	144	74.8
Ramsey, Patrick, Washington	272	169	62.1	1665	6.12	10	3.7	51	11	4.0	23	137	74.8
McCown, Josh, Arizona	408	233	57.1	2511	6.15	11	2.7	48	10	2.5	31	263	74.1
Boller, Kyle, Baltimore*	464	258	55.6	2559	5.52	13	2.8	t57	11	2.4	35	247	70.9

*AFC.
t—touchdown.
Leader based on rating points, minimum 224 attempts.

AFC

Player, Team	Att.	Cmp.	Pct.	Yds.	Avg. Gain	TD	Pct. TD	Long	Int.	Pct. Int.	Sack	Yds. Lost	Rat.
Banks, Tony, Houston	2	1	50.0	16	8.00	0	0.0	16	0	0.0	0	0	77.1
Bennett, Drew, Tennessee	1	1	100.0	26	26.00	1	100.0	t26	0	0.0	0	0	158.3
Bettis, Jerome, Pittsburgh	1	1	100.0	10	10.00	1	100.0	t10	0	0.0	0	0	147.9
Bledsoe, Drew, Buffalo	450	256	56.9	2932	6.52	20	4.4	t69	16	3.6	37	215	76.6
Boller, Kyle, Baltimore	464	258	55.6	2559	5.52	13	2.8	t57	11	2.4	35	247	70.9
Bollinger, Brooks, N.Y. Jets	9	5	55.6	60	6.67	0	0.0	26	0	0.0	1	8	76.2
Booker, Marty, Miami	1	1	100.0	48	48.00	0	0.0	48	0	0.0	0	0	118.8
Brady, Tom, New England	474	288	60.8	3692	7.79	28	5.9	50	14	3.0	26	162	92.6
Brees, Drew, San Diego	400	262	65.5	3159	7.90	27	6.8	t79	7	1.8	18	131	104.8
Carr, David, Houston	466	285	61.2	3531	7.58	16	3.4	69	14	3.0	49	301	83.5
Carter, Quincy, N.Y. Jets	58	35	60.3	498	8.59	3	5.2	t69	1	1.7	12	70	98.2
Collins, Kerry, Oakland	513	289	56.3	3495	6.81	21	4.1	63	20	3.9	25	144	74.8
Collins, Todd, Kansas City	5	1	20.0	42	8.40	0	0.0	42	0	0.0	0	0	62.1
Curry, Ronald, Oakland	1	0	0.0	0	0.00	0	0.0	0	0	0.0	0	0	39.6
Davey, Rohan, New England	10	4	40.0	54	5.40	0	0.0	20	0	0.0	0	0	57.9
Echemandu, Adimchinobe, Cleveland	1	0	0.0	0	0.00	0	0.0	0	0	0.0	0	0	39.6
Feeley, A.J., Miami	356	191	53.7	1893	5.32	11	3.1	38	15	4.2	23	136	61.7
Fiedler, Jay, Miami	190	101	53.2	1186	6.24	7	3.7	t71	8	4.2	25	165	67.1
Flutie, Doug, San Diego	38	20	52.6	276	7.26	1	2.6	29	0	0.0	1	7	85.0
Gaffney, Jabar, Houston	3	0	0.0	0	0.00	0	0.0	0	0	0.0	0	0	39.6
Gannon, Rich, Oakland	68	41	60.3	524	7.71	3	4.4	t58	2	2.9	5	17	86.9
Garcia, Jeff, Cleveland	252	144	57.1	1731	6.87	10	4.0	t99	9	3.6	24	99	76.7
Garrard, David, Jacksonville	72	38	52.8	374	5.19	2	2.8	t36	1	1.4	6	35	71.2
Green, Trent, Kansas City	556	369	66.4	4591	8.26	27	4.9	t70	17	3.1	32	227	95.2

2004 STATISTICS Passing

Player, Team	Att.	Cmp.	Pct.	Yds.	Avg. Gain	TD	Pct. TD	Long	Int.	Pct. Int.	Sack	Yds. Lost	Rat.
Hentrich, Craig, Tennessee	4	2	50.0	10	2.50	0	0.0	6	0	0.0	0	0	56.3
Holcomb, Kelly, Cleveland	87	59	67.8	737	8.47	7	8.0	t55	5	5.7	5	31	96.8
Hymes, Randy, Baltimore	1	0	0.0	0	0.00	0	0.0	0	0	0.0	0	0	39.6
Jackson, Frisman, Cleveland	1	0	0.0	0	0.00	0	0.0	0	0	0.0	0	0	39.6
Johnson, Doug, Tennessee	12	6	50.0	68	5.67	0	0.0	33	0	0.0	1	6	67.4
Jordan, LaMont, N.Y. Jets	1	0	0.0	0	0.00	0	0.0	0	1	100.0	0	0	0.0
Kitna, Jon, Cincinnati	104	61	58.7	623	5.99	5	4.8	30	4	3.8	6	41	75.9
Leftwich, Byron, Jacksonville	441	267	60.5	2941	6.67	15	3.4	65	10	2.3	25	114	82.2
Losman, J.P., Buffalo	5	3	60.0	32	6.40	0	0.0	17	1	20.0	1	0	39.2
Maddox, Tommy, Pittsburgh	60	30	50.0	329	5.48	1	1.7	39	2	3.3	6	37	58.3
Manning, Peyton, Indianapolis	497	336	67.6	4557	9.17	49	9.9	t80	10	2.0	13	101	121.1
Matthews, Shane, Buffalo	3	2	66.7	44	14.67	1	33.3	t33	0	0.0	0	0	149.3
McCardell, Keenan, San Diego	1	0	0.0	0	0.00	0	0.0	0	0	0.0	0	0	39.6
McCown, Luke, Cleveland	98	48	49.0	608	6.20	4	4.1	t58	7	7.1	12	122	52.6
McNair, Steve, Tennessee	215	129	60.0	1343	6.25	8	3.7	t37	9	4.2	13	95	73.1
Moorman, Brian, Buffalo	3	1	33.3	24	8.00	0	0.0	24	0	0.0	0	0	63.2
Morris, Sammy, Miami	0	0		0	...	0	...	...	0	...	1	9	...
Palmer, Carson, Cincinnati	432	263	60.9	2897	6.71	18	4.2	t76	18	4.2	25	178	77.3
Pennington, Chad, N.Y. Jets	370	242	65.4	2673	7.22	16	4.3	48	9	2.4	18	103	91.0
Plummer, Jake, Denver	521	303	58.2	4089	7.85	27	5.2	t85	20	3.8	15	90	84.5
Randle El, Antwaan, Pittsburgh	1	1	100.0	10	10.00	1	100.0	t10	0	0.0	0	0	147.9
Rivers, Philip, San Diego	8	5	62.5	33	4.13	1	12.5	t13	0	0.0	1	10	110.9
Roethlisberger, Ben, Pittsburgh	295	196	66.4	2621	8.88	17	5.8	58	11	3.7	30	213	98.1
Rosenfels, Sage, Miami	39	16	41.0	264	6.77	1	2.6	t76	3	7.7	3	16	41.0
Saturday, Jeff, Indianapolis	1	0	0.0	0	0.00	0	0.0	0	0	0.0	0	0	39.6
Scifres, Mike, San Diego	1	0	0.0	0	0.00	0	0.0	0	1	100.0	0	0	0.0
Sorgi, Jim, Indianapolis	29	17	58.6	175	6.03	2	6.9	t71	0	0.0	1	8	99.1
St. Pierre, Brian, Pittsburgh	1	0	0.0	0	0.00	0	0.0	0	0	0.0	0	0	39.6
Toefield, LaBrandon, Jacksonville	0	0	...	0	...	0	...	...	0	...	1	7	...
Tomlinson, LaDainian, San Diego	2	1	50.0	38	19.00	0	0.0	38	0	0.0	1	1	95.8
Vinatieri, Adam, New England	1	1	100.0	4	4.00	1	100.0	t4	0	0.0	0	0	122.9
Volek, Billy, Tennessee	357	218	61.1	2486	6.96	18	5.0	t48	10	2.8	30	216	87.1

t—touchdown.

NFC

Player, Team	Att.	Cmp.	Pct.	Yds.	Avg. Gain	TD	Pct. TD	Long	Int.	Pct. Int.	Sack	Yds. Lost	Rat.
Anderson, Richie, Dallas	1	1	100.0	26	26.00	1	100.0	t26	0	0.0	0	0	158.3
Bartrum, Mike, Philadelphia	1	0	0.0	0	0.00	0	0.0	0	0	0.0	0	0	39.6
Blake, Jeff, Philadelphia	37	18	48.6	126	3.41	1	2.7	21	1	2.7	2	17	54.6
Brooks, Aaron, New Orleans	542	309	57.0	3810	7.03	21	3.9	57	16	3.0	41	223	79.5
Bruce, Isaac, St. Louis	2	0	0.0	0	0.00	0	0.0	0	0	0.0	0	0	39.6
Brunell, Mark, Washington	237	118	49.8	1194	5.04	7	3.0	49	6	2.5	15	105	63.9
Bulger, Marc, St. Louis	485	321	66.2	3964	8.17	21	4.3	56	14	2.9	41	302	93.7
Chandler, Chris, St. Louis	62	35	56.5	463	7.47	2	3.2	t75	8	12.9	7	54	51.4
Crayton, Patrick, Dallas	1	0	0.0	0	0.00	0	0.0	0	1	100.0	0	0	0.0
Culpepper, Daunte, Minnesota	548	379	69.2	4717	8.61	39	7.1	t82	11	2.0	46	238	110.9
Delhomme, Jake, Carolina	533	310	58.2	3886	7.29	29	5.4	63	15	2.8	33	246	87.3
Detmer, Koy, Philadelphia	40	18	45.0	207	5.18	0	0.0	31	2	5.0	2	16	40.3
Dilfer, Trent, Seattle	58	25	43.1	333	5.74	1	1.7	56	3	5.2	4	21	46.1
Dorsey, Ken, San Francisco	226	123	54.4	1231	5.45	6	2.7	59	9	4.0	13	94	62.4
Edinger, Paul, Chicago	1	0	0.0	0	0.00	0	0.0	0	1	100.0	0	0	0.0
Favre, Brett, Green Bay	540	346	64.1	4088	7.57	30	5.6	t79	17	3.1	12	93	92.4
Feagles, Jeff, N.Y. Giants	1	0	0.0	0	0.00	0	0.0	0	0	0.0	0	0	39.6
Fisher, Tony, Green Bay	1	1	100.0	8	8.00	1	100.0	t8	0	0.0	0	0	139.6
Fitzgerald, Larry, Arizona	0	0	...	0	...	0	...	...	0	...	1	7	...
Frerotte, Gus, Minnesota	1	0	0.0	0	0.00	0	0.0	0	0	0.0	0	0	39.6
Gardner, Rod, Washington	3	0	0.0	0	0.00	0	0.0	0	0	0.0	0	0	39.6
Glenn, Terry, Dallas	1	0	0.0	0	0.00	0	0.0	0	0	0.0	0	0	39.6
Green, Ahman, Green Bay	1	1	100.0	20	20.00	1	100.0	t20	0	0.0	0	0	158.3
Griese, Brian, Tampa Bay	336	233	69.3	2632	7.83	20	6.0	68	12	3.6	26	169	97.5
Grossman, Rex, Chicago	84	47	56.0	607	7.23	1	1.2	40	3	3.6	5	22	67.9
Harrington, Joey, Detroit	489	274	56.0	3047	6.23	19	3.9	62	12	2.5	36	196	77.5
Hasselbeck, Matt, Seattle	474	279	58.9	3382	7.14	22	4.6	60	15	3.2	30	155	83.1
Henson, Drew, Dallas	18	10	55.6	78	4.33	1	5.6	16	1	5.6	2	26	61.8
Hutchinson, Chad, Chicago	161	92	57.1	903	5.61	4	2.5	63	3	1.9	23	160	73.6
Johnson, Brad, Tampa Bay	103	65	63.1	674	6.54	3	2.9	54	3	2.9	8	55	79.5
Johnson, Keyshawn, Dallas	2	0	0.0	0	0.00	0	0.0	0	1	50.0	0	0	0.0

Player, Team	Att.	Cmp.	Pct.	Yds.	Avg. Gain	TD	Pct. TD	Long	Int.	Pct. Int.	Sack	Yds. Lost	Rat.
King, Shaun, Arizona	84	47	56.0	502	5.98	1	1.2	40	4	4.8	6	42	57.7
Krenzel, Craig, Chicago	127	59	46.5	718	5.65	3	2.4	t49	6	4.7	23	158	52.5
Manning, Eli, N.Y. Giants	197	95	48.2	1043	5.29	6	3.0	52	9	4.6	13	83	55.4
Martin, Jamie, St. Louis	30	16	53.3	188	6.27	0	0.0	26	0	0.0	2	6	72.6
McBriar, Mat, Dallas	1	0	0.0	0	0.00	0	0.0	0	0	0.0	0	0	39.6
McCown, Josh, Arizona	408	233	57.1	2511	6.15	11	2.7	48	10	2.5	31	263	74.1
McMahon, Mike, Detroit	15	11	73.3	77	5.13	0	0.0	19	1	6.7	1	12	56.8
McNabb, Donovan, Philadelphia	469	300	64.0	3875	8.26	31	6.6	80	8	1.7	32	192	104.7
Mohr, Chris, Atlanta	3	2	66.7	24	8.00	0	0.0	26	0	0.0	0	0	91.0
Moore, Mewelde, Minnesota	1	0	0.0	0	0.00	0	0.0	0	0	0.0	0	0	39.6
Moss, Randy, Minnesota	2	1	50.0	37	18.50	0	0.0	37	1	50.0	0	0	56.3
Nall, Craig, Green Bay	33	23	69.7	314	9.52	4	12.1	43	0	0.0	2	8	139.4
Navarre, John, Arizona	40	18	45.0	168	4.20	1	2.5	t33	4	10.0	1	8	25.8
Pederson, Doug, Green Bay	23	11	47.8	120	5.22	0	0.0	24	2	8.7	0	0	27.4
Peete, Rodney, Carolina	1	1	100.0	3	3.00	0	0.0	3	0	0.0	0	0	79.2
Pickett, Cody, San Francisco	10	4	40.0	55	5.50	0	0.0	18	2	20.0	2	14	18.8
Portis, Clinton, Washington	2	1	50.0	15	7.50	1	50.0	t15	0	0.0	0	0	114.6
Price, Peerless, Atlanta	1	1	100.0	25	25.00	0	0.0	25	0	0.0	0	0	118.8
Proehl, Ricky, Carolina	1	0	0.0	0	0.00	0	0.0	0	0	0.0	0	0	39.6
Quinn, Jonathan, Chicago	98	51	52.0	413	4.21	1	1.0	32	3	3.1	15	109	53.7
Ramsey, Patrick, Washington	272	169	62.1	1665	6.12	10	3.7	51	11	4.0	23	137	74.8
Rattay, Tim, San Francisco	325	198	60.9	2169	6.67	10	3.1	65	10	3.1	37	211	78.1
Schaub, Matt, Atlanta	70	33	47.1	330	4.71	1	1.4	59	4	5.7	4	14	42.0
Simms, Chris, Tampa Bay	73	42	57.5	467	6.40	1	1.4	t75	3	4.1	10	75	64.1
Smith, Emmitt, Arizona	1	1	100.0	21	21.00	1	100.0	t21	0	0.0	0	0	158.3
Smith, Steve, Carolina	1	0	0.0	0	0.00	0	0.0	0	0	0.0	0	0	39.6
Testaverde, Vinny, Dallas	495	297	60.0	3532	7.14	17	3.4	53	20	4.0	34	182	76.4
Vick, Michael, Atlanta	321	181	56.4	2313	7.21	14	4.4	62	12	3.7	46	266	78.1
Warner, Kurt, N.Y. Giants	277	174	62.8	2054	7.42	6	2.2	t62	4	1.4	39	196	86.5
Westbrook, Brian, Philadelphia	0	0	...	0	0.00	0	...	...	0	...	1	4	...
Wilkins, Jeff, St. Louis	1	0	0.0	0	0.00	0	0.0	0	0	0.0	0	0	39.6
Williams, Roy, Detroit	1	0	0.0	0	0.00	0	0.0	0	0	0.0	0	0	39.6

t—touchdown.

RECEIVING

BESTS OF THE SEASON

Receptions, season
AFC: 102—Tony Gonzalez, Kansas City.
NFC: 94—Torry Holt, St. Louis; Joe Horn, New Orleans.

Receptions, game
AFC: 14—Tony Gonzalez, Kansas City at San Diego, Jan. 2 (144 yards).
NFC: 13—Eric Johnson, San Francisco vs. Arizona, Oct. 10 (OT; 162 yards, 1 TD).

Yards, season
NFC: 1405—Muhsin Muhammad, Carolina.
AFC: 1274—Chad Johnson, Cincinnati.

Yards, game
AFC: 233—Drew Bennett, Tennessee vs. Kansas City, Dec. 13 (12 receptions, 3 TDs).
NFC: 200—Javon Walker, Green Bay at Indianapolis, Sep. 26 (11 receptions, 3 TDs).

Longest gain
AFC: 99—Andre' Davis, (from Jeff Garcia), Cleveland vs. Cincinnati, Oct. 17 (TD).
NFC: 82—Randy Moss, (from Daunte Culpepper), Minnesota at Detroit, Dec. 19 (TD).

Yards per reception, season
AFC: 20.1—Ashley Lelie, Denver.
NFC: 18.8—Todd Pinkston, Philadelphia.

Touchdowns, season
NFC: 16—Muhsin Muhammad, Carolina.
AFC: 15—Marvin Harrison, Indianapolis.

Team leaders, receptions

AFC:

Baltimore	35	Kevin Johnson
Buffalo	88	Eric Moulds
Cincinnati	95	Chad Johnson
Cleveland	55	Dennis Northcutt
Denver	79	Rod Smith
Houston	79	Andre Johnson
Indianapolis	86	Marvin Harrison
Jacksonville	74	Jimmy Smith
Kansas City	102	Tony Gonzalez
Miami	73	Randy McMichael
N.Y. Jets	56	Justin McCareins
New England	56	David Givens
Oakland	64	Jerry Porter
Pittsburgh	80	Hines Ward
San Diego	81	Antonio Gates
Tennessee	96	Derrick Mason

NFC:

Arizona	58	Larry Fitzgerald
Atlanta	48	Alge Crumpler
Carolina	93	Muhsin
Muhammad		
Chicago	56	Thomas Jones
Dallas	87	Jason Witten
Detroit	54	Roy Williams
Green Bay	89	Javon Walker
Minnesota	71	Jermaine Wiggins
N.Y. Giants	61	Jeremy Shockey
New Orleans	94	Joe Horn
Philadelphia	77	Terrell Owens
San Francisco	82	Eric Johnson
Seattle	87	Darrell Jackson
St. Louis	94	Torry Holt
Tampa Bay	80	Michael Clayton
Washington	90	Laveranues Coles

NFL LEADERS

Player, Team	No.	Yds.	Avg.	Long	TD
Gonzalez, Tony, Kansas City*	102	1258	12.3	32	7
Mason, Derrick, Tennessee*	96	1168	12.2	t37	7
Johnson, Chad, Cincinnati*	95	1274	13.4	t53	9
Horn, Joe, New Orleans	94	1399	14.9	57	11
Holt, Torry, St. Louis	94	1372	14.6	t75	10
Muhammad, Muhsin, Carolina	93	1405	15.1	51	16
Coles, Laveranues, Washington	90	950	10.6	45	1
Walker, Javon, Green Bay	89	1382	15.5	t79	12
Bruce, Isaac, St. Louis	89	1292	14.5	56	6
Moulds, Eric, Buffalo*	88	1043	11.9	49	5
Jackson, Darrell, Seattle	87	1199	13.8	t56	7
Witten, Jason, Dallas	87	980	11.3	t42	6
Harrison, Marvin, Indianapolis*	86	1113	12.9	59	15
Driver, Donald, Green Bay	84	1208	14.4	50	9
Johnson, Eric, San Francisco	82	825	10.1	25	2
Gates, Antonio, San Diego*	81	964	11.9	t72	13
Bennett, Drew, Tennessee*	80	1247	15.6	t48	11
Clayton, Michael, Tampa Bay	80	1193	14.9	t75	7
Ward, Hines, Pittsburgh*	80	1004	12.6	58	4
Smith, Rod, Denver*	79	1144	14.5	t85	7
Johnson, Andre, Houston*	79	1142	14.5	t54	6
Wayne, Reggie, Indianapolis*	77	1210	15.7	t71	12
Owens, Terrell, Philadelphia	77	1200	15.6	t59	14
Smith, Jimmy, Jacksonville*	74	1172	15.8	65	6
Houshmandzadeh, T.J., Cincinnati*	73	978	13.4	62	4
McMichael, Randy, Miami*	73	791	10.8	t42	4
Westbrook, Brian, Philadelphia	73	703	9.6	50	6
Wiggins, Jermaine, Minnesota	71	705	9.9	39	4
Johnson, Keyshawn, Dallas	70	981	14.0	39	6
Chambers, Chris, Miami*	69	898	13.0	t76	7

*AFC
t—touchdown
Leader based on most passes caught

AFC

Player, Team	No.	Yds.	Avg.	Long	TD
Abdullah, Rabih, New England	1	9	9.0	9	0
Aiken, Sam, Buffalo	11	148	13.5	54	0
Allen, David, Jacksonville	2	8	4.0	5	0
Anderson, Courtney, Oakland	13	175	13.5	28	1
Armstrong, Derrick, Houston	29	415	14.3	44	1
Askew, B.J., N.Y. Jets	2	12	6.0	11	0
Bailey, Champ, Denver	1	11	11.0	11	0
Baker, Chris, N.Y. Jets	18	182	10.1	23	4
Baxter, Jarrod, Houston	1	3	3.0	3	0
Becht, Anthony, N.Y. Jets	13	100	7.7	19	1
Bell, Tatum, Denver	5	80	16.0	58	0
Bellamy, Ronald, Miami	1	8	8.0	8	0
Bennett, Drew, Tennessee	80	1247	15.6	t48	11
Berlin, Eddie, Tennessee	20	278	13.9	31	1
Bettis, Jerome, Pittsburgh	6	46	7.7	20	0
Blaylock, Derrick, Kansas City	25	246	9.8	30	1
Booker, Marty, Miami	50	638	12.8	45	1
Bradford, Corey, Houston	27	399	14.8	47	3
Brady, Kyle, Jacksonville	14	103	7.4	21	1
Branch, Deion, New England	35	454	13.0	t26	4
Brees, Drew, San Diego	1	38	38.0	38	0
Brown, Chris, Tennessee	20	147	7.4	21	0
Brown, Troy, New England	17	184	10.8	22	1
Bruener, Mark, Houston	4	52	13.0	27	0
Bryant, Antonio, Dal.-Cle.*	58	812	14.0	t55	4
Burns, Joe, Buffalo	1	7	7.0	7	0
Burress, Plaxico, Pittsburgh	35	698	19.9	48	5

Player, Team	No.	Yds.	Avg.	Long	TD
aldwell, Reche, San Diego	18	310	17.2	t58	3
alico, Tyrone, Tennessee	2	13	6.5	9	0
ampbell, Mark, Buffalo	17	203	11.9	27	5
arswell, Dwayne, Denver	22	198	9.0	20	1
arter, Jonathan, N.Y. Jets	10	173	17.3	t46	1
hambers, Chris, Miami	69	898	13.0	t76	7
hatman, Jesse, San Diego	2	17	8.5	17	0
hrebet, Wayne, N.Y. Jets	31	397	12.8	t35	1
lark, Dallas, Indianapolis	25	423	16.9	t80	5
otchery, Jerricho, N.Y. Jets	6	60	10.0	18	0
rockett, Zack, Oakland	16	87	5.4	11	0
urry, Ronald, Denver	50	679	13.6	63	6
ushing, Matt, Pittsburgh	1	17	17.0	17	0
arling, Devard, Baltimore	2	5	2.5	4	0
avis, Andre', Cleveland	16	416	26.0	t99	2
avis, Domanick, Houston	68	588	8.6	38	1
illon, Corey, New England	15	103	6.9	20	1
inkins, Darnell, Baltimore	9	94	10.4	18	1
roughns, Reuben, Denver	32	241	7.5	t23	2
unn, Jason, Kansas City	17	120	7.1	17	3
wight, Tim, San Diego	2	31	15.5	t23	1
aslick, Doug, Miami	1	4	4.0	4	0
chemandu, Adimchinobe, Cleveland	3	25	8.3	19	0
dwards, Marc, Jacksonville	7	41	5.9	15	0
dwards, Troy, Jacksonville	50	533	10.7	36	1
uhus, Tim, Buffalo	11	98	8.9	17	2
vans, Lee, Buffalo	48	843	17.6	t69	9
argas, Justin, Oakland	11	68	6.2	21	0
aulk, Kevin, New England	26	248	9.5	t31	1
auria, Christian, New England	16	195	12.2	25	2
leming, Troy, Tennessee	19	164	8.6	37	2
loyd, Malcom, San Diego	3	49	16.3	27	1
uamatu-Ma'afala, Chris, Jacksonville	4	19	4.8	8	0
abriel, Doug, Oakland	33	551	16.7	t58	2
affney, Jabar, Houston	41	632	15.4	69	2
ates, Antonio, San Diego	81	964	11.9	t72	13
ilmore, Bryan, Miami	15	206	13.7	37	1
ivens, David, New England	56	874	15.6	50	3
onzalez, Tony, Kansas City	102	1258	12.3	32	7
ordon, Lamar, Miami	13	74	5.7	20	0
raham, Daniel, New England	30	364	12.1	48	7
reen, William, Cleveland	14	84	6.0	17	0
riffin, Quentin, Denver	10	68	6.8	22	1
all, Dante, Kansas City	25	230	9.2	22	0
ankton, Cortez, Jacksonville	9	81	9.0	t14	2
ape, Patrick, Denver	8	35	4.4	11	4
arrison, Marvin, Indianapolis	86	1113	12.9	59	15
artsock, Ben, Indianapolis	4	33	8.3	17	0
aynes, Verron, Pittsburgh	18	142	7.9	26	2
eap, Todd, Baltimore	27	303	11.2	37	3
earst, Garrison, Denver	2	20	10.0	15	0
eiden, Steve, Cleveland	28	287	10.3	30	5
einrich, Keith, Cleveland	1	1	1.0	1	0
enry, Leonard, Miami	3	12	4.0	7	0
enry, Travis, Buffalo	10	45	4.5	10	0
etherington, Chris, Oakland	3	28	9.3	14	0
olcombe, Robert, Tennessee	11	60	5.5	9	0
ollings, Tony, Houston	5	46	9.2	27	0
olmes, Priest, Kansas City	19	187	9.8	52	1
orn, Chris, Kansas City	15	178	11.9	30	1
oushmandzadeh, T.J., Cincinnati	73	978	13.4	62	4
ymes, Randy, Baltimore	26	323	12.4	t57	2
ackson, Frisman, Cleveland	13	168	12.9	24	0
ackson, James, Cleveland	6	22	3.7	13	0
ackson, Nate, Denver	8	73	9.1	20	0
ames, Edgerrin, Indianapolis	51	483	9.5	56	0
ohnson, Andre, Houston	79	1142	14.5	t54	6
ohnson, Bethel, New England	10	174	17.4	48	1
ohnson, Chad, Cincinnati	95	1274	13.4	t53	9
ohnson, Jeremi, Cincinnati	16	53	3.3	9	1
ohnson, Kevin, Baltimore	35	373	10.7	35	1
ohnson, Kyle, Denver	9	126	14.0	31	2

Player, Team	No.	Yds.	Avg.	Long	TD
Johnson, Larry, Kansas City	22	278	12.6	40	2
Johnson, Rudi, Cincinnati	15	84	5.6	30	0
Johnson, Teyo, Oakland	9	131	14.6	25	2
Jolley, Doug, Oakland	27	313	11.6	t34	2
Jones, Brian, Jacksonville	6	87	14.5	t26	1
Jones, Greg, Jacksonville	3	13	4.3	9	0
Jones, Terry, Baltimore	20	152	7.6	19	1
Jordan, LaMont, N.Y. Jets	15	112	7.5	25	0
Kelly, Reggie, Cincinnati	15	85	5.7	14	0
Kennison, Eddie, Kansas City	62	1086	17.5	t70	8
King, Andre, Cleveland	5	49	9.8	16	0
King, Vick, Miami	1	8	8.0	8	0
Kinney, Erron, Tennessee	25	193	7.7	21	3
Klecko, Dan, New England	3	18	6.0	11	0
Konrad, Rob, Miami	8	69	8.6	t20	1
Krause, Ryan, San Diego	5	81	16.2	29	1
Kreider, Dan, Pittsburgh	10	75	7.5	13	1
Lee, Donald, Miami	13	110	8.5	t15	1
Leftwich, Byron, Jacksonville	1	-7	-7.0	-7	0
Lelie, Ashley, Denver	54	1084	20.1	58	7
Lewis, Jamal, Baltimore	10	116	11.6	46	0
Lewis, Jermaine, Jacksonville	1	4	4.0	4	0
Luke, Triandos, Denver	6	52	8.7	12	0
Martin, Curtis, N.Y. Jets	41	245	6.0	22	2
Martin, Jamar, Miami	4	15	3.8	9	0
Mason, Derrick, Tennessee	96	1168	12.2	t37	7
Mays, Lee, Pittsburgh	9	137	15.2	46	0
McAddley, Jason, Tennessee	2	38	19.0	36	0
McCardell, Keenan, San Diego	31	393	12.7	31	1
McCareins, Justin, N.Y. Jets	56	770	13.8	43	4
McGahee, Willis, Buffalo	22	169	7.7	16	0
McMichael, Randy, Miami	73	791	10.8	t42	4
Meier, Shad, Tennessee	25	127	5.1	29	2
Miller, Billy, Houston	17	178	10.5	27	1
Minor, Travis, Miami	13	75	5.8	20	0
Moore, Clarence, Baltimore	24	293	12.2	52	4
Moorehead, Aaron, Indianapolis	1	7	7.0	7	0
Morant, Johnnie, Oakland	1	20	20.0	20	0
Morey, Sean, Pittsburgh	1	8	8.0	8	0
Morris, Sammy, Miami	22	124	5.6	24	0
Morton, Johnnie, Kansas City	55	795	14.5	52	3
Moss, Santana, N.Y. Jets	45	838	18.6	t69	5
Moulds, Eric, Buffalo	88	1043	11.9	49	5
Mungro, James, Indianapolis	7	36	5.1	16	3
Mustard, Chad, Cleveland	1	9	9.0	9	0
Neal, Lorenzo, San Diego	13	66	5.1	12	0
Neufeld, Ryan, Buffalo	6	61	10.2	29	0
Norris, Moran, Houston	4	13	3.3	7	0
Northcutt, Dennis, Cleveland	55	806	14.7	t58	2
Osgood, Kassim, San Diego	15	308	20.5	65	2
Parker, Eric, San Diego	47	690	14.7	t79	4
Parker, Samie, Kansas City	9	137	15.2	t48	1
Parker, Willie, Pittsburgh	3	16	5.3	12	0
Pass, Patrick, New England	28	215	7.7	22	0
Patten, David, New England	44	800	18.2	t48	7
Peelle, Justin, San Diego	10	84	8.4	t17	2
Perry, Chris, Cincinnati	3	33	11.0	13	0
Pinnock, Andrew, San Diego	3	26	8.7	14	0
Pollard, Marcus, Indianapolis	29	309	10.7	31	6
Porter, Jerry, Oakland	64	998	15.6	52	9
Putzier, Jeb, Denver	36	572	15.9	39	2
Pyatt, Brad, Indianapolis	2	12	6.0	7	0
Randle El, Antwaan, Pittsburgh	43	601	14.0	39	3
Redmond, J.R., Oakland	32	233	7.3	22	0
Reed, Josh, Buffalo	16	153	9.6	20	0
Rhodes, Dominic, Indianapolis	2	24	12.0	20	0
Ricard, Alan, Baltimore	11	39	3.5	8	0
Richardson, Tony, Kansas City	19	118	6.2	22	0
Riemersma, Jay, Pittsburgh	7	82	11.7	t26	1
Russell, Cliff, Cincinnati	1	21	21.0	21	0
Sams, B.J., Baltimore	1	2	2.0	2	0
Schobel, Matt, Cincinnati	21	201	9.6	t76	4

Player, Team	No.	Yds.	Avg.	Long	TD
Shaw, Bobby, Buffalo	5	59	11.8	20	0
Shea, Aaron, Cleveland	26	252	9.7	35	4
Shelton, Daimon, Buffalo	17	114	6.7	24	0
Smith, Antowain, Tennessee	22	169	7.7	31	0
Smith, Jimmy, Jacksonville	74	1172	15.8	65	6
Smith, Jonathan, Buffalo	3	21	7.0	11	0
Smith, Musa, Baltimore	2	31	15.5	25	0
Smith, Rod, Denver	79	1144	14.5	t85	7
Smith, Terrelle, Cleveland	7	39	5.6	16	0
Sowell, Jerald, N.Y. Jets	45	342	7.6	34	1
Staley, Duce, Pittsburgh	6	55	9.2	21	0
Stewart, Tony, Cincinnati	10	48	4.8	9	1
Stokley, Brandon, Indianapolis	68	1077	15.8	t69	10
Stone, John, Oakland	3	80	26.7	55	0
Suggs, Lee, Cleveland	20	178	8.9	t59	1
Taylor, Chester, Baltimore	30	184	6.1	23	0
Taylor, Fred, Jacksonville	36	345	9.6	t64	1
Taylor, Travis, Baltimore	34	421	12.4	47	0
Thomas, Kevin, Buffalo	1	24	24.0	24	0
Thompson, Derrius, Miami	23	359	15.6	36	4
Toefield, LaBrandon, Jacksonville	28	151	5.4	16	1
Tomlinson, LaDainian, San Diego	53	441	8.3	t74	1
Trafford, Rodney, Buffalo	3	25	8.3	10	0
Troupe, Ben, Tennessee	33	329	10.0	33	1
Tuman, Jerame, Pittsburgh	9	89	9.9	26	3
Turner, Michael, San Diego	4	8	2.0	7	0
Volek, Billy, Tennessee	1	0	0.0	0	0
Vrabel, Mike, New England	2	3	1.5	t2	2
Walter, Kevin, Cincinnati	8	67	8.4	18	0
Walters, Troy, Indianapolis	1	5	5.0	5	0
Ward, Hines, Pittsburgh	80	1004	12.6	58	4
Warrick, Peter, Cincinnati	11	127	11.5	30	0
Washington, Kelley, Cincinnati	31	378	12.2	28	3
Watson, Ben, New England	2	16	8.0	14	0
Watson, Kenny, Cincinnati	25	171	6.8	21	1
Watts, Darius, Denver	31	385	12.4	28	1
Wayne, Reggie, Indianapolis	77	1210	15.7	t71	12
Weaver, Jed, New England	8	93	11.6	25	0
Wells, Jonathan, Houston	11	79	7.2	28	2
Wheatley, Tyrone, Oakland	15	78	5.2	20	0
White, Jamel, T.B.-Bal.*	6	21	3.5	12	0
Whitted, Alvis, Oakland	9	227	25.2	57	2
Wilcox, Daniel, Baltimore	25	219	8.8	20	1
Wilford, Ernest, Jacksonville	19	271	14.3	46	2
Williams, Reggie, Jacksonville	27	268	9.9	26	1
Williams, Shaud, Buffalo	3	19	6.3	10	0
Winslow, Kellen, Cleveland	5	50	10.0	21	0
Wrighster, George, Jacksonville	10	69	6.9	12	1
Yoder, Todd, Jacksonville	14	157	11.2	56	0
Zereoue, Amos, Oakland	39	284	7.3	13	0

*Includes both NFC and AFC statistics.
t—touchdown.

NFC

Player, Team	No.	Yds.	Avg.	Long	TD
Alexander, Shaun, Seattle	23	170	7.4	24	4
Alexander, Stephen, Detroit	41	377	9.2	30	1
Alstott, Mike, Tampa Bay	29	202	7.0	20	0
Anderson, Richie, Dallas	26	207	8.0	28	0
Ayanbadejo, Obafemi, Arizona	19	171	9.0	t21	1
Baber, Billy, Tampa Bay	1	7	7.0	7	0
Bannister, Alex, Seattle	2	10	5.0	8	0
Barber, Tiki, N.Y. Giants	52	578	11.1	t62	2
Barlow, Kevan, San Francisco	35	212	6.1	15	0
Barnes, Darian, Dallas	10	59	5.9	14	1
Bartrum, Mike, Philadelphia	5	45	9.0	17	1
Battle, Arnaz, San Francisco	8	143	17.9	65	1
Beasley, Fred, San Francisco	10	44	4.4	9	0
Bennett, Michael, Minnesota	21	207	9.9	t38	1
Berrian, Bernard, Chicago	15	225	15.0	t49	2
Berton, Sean, Minnesota	9	78	8.7	14	0

Player, Team	No.	Yds.	Avg.	Long	TD
Betts, Ladell, Washington	15	108	7.2	20	1
Blakley, Dwayne, Atlanta	4	35	8.8	13	1
Boldin, Anquan, Arizona	56	623	11.1	t31	1
Brooks, Aaron, New Orleans	1	1	1.0	1	1
Brown, Tim, Tampa Bay	24	200	8.3	21	1
Bruce, Isaac, St. Louis	89	1292	14.5	56	6
Bryson, Shawn, Detroit	44	322	7.3	30	1
Burleson, Nate, Minnesota	68	1006	14.8	t68	9
Bush, Steve, San Francisco	2	10	5.0	6	0
Campbell, Dan, Dallas	2	16	8.0	9	1
Campbell, Kelly, Minnesota	19	364	19.2	61	0
Carter, Tim, N.Y. Giants	12	182	15.2	t38	1
Chatman, Antonio, Green Bay	22	246	11.2	21	0
Clark, Desmond, Chicago	24	282	11.8	31	0
Clayton, Michael, Tampa Bay	80	1193	14.9	t75	7
Cleeland, Cam, St. Louis	7	57	8.1	15	0
Cloud, Michael, N.Y. Giants	1	3	3.0	3	0
Colbert, Keary, Carolina	47	754	16.0	63	5
Coleman, Cosey, Tampa Bay	1	4	4.0	4	0
Coles, Laveranues, Washington	90	950	10.6	45	1
Comella, Greg, Tampa Bay	1	12	12.0	12	0
Conway, Curtis, San Francisco	38	403	10.6	37	3
Conwell, Ernie, New Orleans	10	102	10.2	28	1
Cook, Jameel, Tampa Bay	7	44	6.3	9	0
Cooley, Chris, Washington	37	314	8.5	31	6
Copper, Terrance, Dallas	7	84	12.0	22	0
Crayton, Patrick, Dallas	12	162	13.5	t39	1
Croom, Larry, Arizona	2	16	8.0	8	0
Crumpler, Alge, Atlanta	48	774	16.1	t49	6
Curtis, Kevin, St. Louis	32	421	13.2	t41	6
Davenport, Najeh, Green Bay	4	33	8.3	12	0
Davis, Stephen, Carolina	2	32	16.0	22	1
Dayne, Ron, N.Y. Giants	1	7	7.0	7	1
Diamond, Lorenzo, Arizona	3	19	6.3	8	1
Dilger, Ken, Tampa Bay	39	345	8.8	t45	4
Driver, Donald, Green Bay	84	1208	14.4	50	9
Duckett, T.J., Atlanta	3	15	5.0	11	0
Dudley, Rickey, Tampa Bay	3	48	16.0	24	0
Dunn, Warrick, Atlanta	29	294	10.1	59	1
Edwards, Eric, Arizona	5	51	10.2	19	0
Engram, Bobby, Seattle	36	499	13.9	60	1
Evans, Heath, Seattle	2	12	6.0	9	0
Faulk, Marshall, St. Louis	50	310	6.2	25	0
Feely, Jay, Atlanta	1	-2	-2.0	-2	0
Ferguson, Robert, Green Bay	24	367	15.3	48	3
Finn, Jim, N.Y. Giants	15	112	7.5	15	0
Finneran, Brian, Atlanta	23	258	11.2	26	0
Fisher, Tony, Green Bay	38	277	7.3	25	0
Fitzgerald, Larry, Arizona	58	780	13.4	48	8
FitzSimmons, Casey, Detroit	10	103	10.3	27	2
Foster, DeShaun, Carolina	9	76	8.4	42	1
Franks, Bubba, Green Bay	34	361	10.6	29	1
Furrey, Mike, St. Louis	1	8	8.0	8	0
Gage, Justin, Chicago	12	156	13.0	32	0
Gaines, Michael, Carolina	4	34	8.5	14	0
Galloway, Joey, Tampa Bay	33	416	12.6	t36	5
Gardner, Rod, Washington	51	650	12.7	51	0
Gardner, Talman, New Orleans	1	23	23.0	23	0
Garner, Charlie, Tampa Bay	9	62	6.9	31	0
George, Eddie, Dallas	9	83	9.2	28	0
Gilmore, John, Chicago	1	11	11.0	11	0
Glenn, Terry, Dallas	24	400	16.7	48	5
Goings, Nick, Carolina	45	394	8.8	37	1
Goodspeed, Joey, St. Louis	11	71	6.5	13	0
Green, Ahman, Green Bay	40	275	6.9	48	1
Griese, Brian, Tampa Bay	1	-4	-4.0	-4	0
Griffith, Justin, Atlanta	22	220	10.0	62	2
Hakim, Az-Zahir, Detroit	31	533	17.2	t39	4
Hall, Lamont, New Orleans	1	4	4.0	t4	1
Hambrick, Troy, Arizona	4	16	4.0	9	0
Hankton, Karl, Carolina	2	25	12.5	20	0
Hannam, Ryan, Seattle	8	110	13.8	36	0

ayer, Team	No.	Yds.	Avg.	Long	TD
rris, Arlen, St. Louis	4	44	11.0	21	0
ller, Will, Tampa Bay	12	98	8.2	22	1
nderson, William, Green Bay	34	239	7.0	t38	3
cks, Maurice, San Francisco	16	154	9.6	19	0
liard, Ike, N.Y. Giants	49	437	8.9	43	0
lt, Torry, St. Louis	94	1372	14.6	t75	10
oover, Brad, Carolina	21	161	7.7	34	2
rn, Joe, New Orleans	94	1399	14.9	57	11
wry, Keenan, Minnesota	1	3	3.0	3	0
m, Jasen, San Francisco	1	1	1.0	1	0
ckson, Darrell, Seattle	87	1199	13.8	t56	7
ckson, Steven, St. Louis	19	189	9.9	28	0
ckson, Terry, San Francisco	21	139	6.6	22	0
cobs, Taylor, Washington	16	178	11.1	45	0
nkins, Michael, Atlanta	7	119	17.0	46	0
hnson, Bryan, Chicago	14	55	3.9	14	2
hnson, Bryant, Arizona	49	537	11.0	40	1
hnson, Eric, San Francisco	82	825	10.1	25	2
hnson, Keyshawn, Dallas	70	981	14.0	39	6
nes, Freddie, Arizona	45	426	9.5	40	2
nes, Julius, Dallas	17	109	6.4	37	0
nes, Kevin, Detroit	28	180	6.4	34	1
nes, Thomas, Chicago	56	427	7.6	45	0
revicius, Joe, Tampa Bay	27	333	12.3	t42	2
rney, Mike, New Orleans	6	42	7.0	17	0
rcus, David, Detroit	3	68	22.7	t50	1
einsasser, Jim, Minnesota	2	24	12.0	18	0
zlowski, Brian, Washington	3	29	9.7	13	0
wrie, Nate, Tampa Bay	1	15	15.0	15	0
yne, George, Atlanta	1	6	6.0	6	0
e, Charles, Tampa Bay	15	207	13.8	35	0
e, ReShard, Dallas	1	4	4.0	4	0
vens, Dorsey, Philadelphia	9	92	10.2	23	0
wis, Chad, Philadelphia	29	267	9.2	21	3
wis, Greg, Philadelphia	17	183	10.8	25	0
wis, Michael, New Orleans	8	127	15.9	30	0
yd, Brandon, San Francisco	43	565	13.1	52	6
oker, Dane, St. Louis	13	183	14.1	29	0
chey, Nick, Green Bay	2	20	10.0	11	0
man, Dustin, Chicago	11	73	6.6	13	1
ahe, Reno, Philadelphia	14	123	8.8	30	0
angum, Kris, Carolina	34	323	9.5	26	3
anumaleuna, Brandon, St. Louis	15	174	11.6	48	1
artin, David, Green Bay	5	88	17.6	35	0
cAllister, Deuce, New Orleans	34	228	6.7	20	0
cCants, Darnerien, Washington	5	71	14.2	27	0
cCoo, Eric, Philadelphia	2	15	7.5	8	0
cCown, Josh, Arizona	1	-5	-5.0	-5	0
cCrary, Fred, Atlanta	2	23	11.5	14	0
cDonald, Shaun, St. Louis	37	494	13.4	t52	3
cKie, Jason, Chicago	13	70	5.4	t15	2
cMullen, Billy, Philadelphia	3	24	8.0	15	0
li, Itula, Seattle	23	240	10.4	20	1
tchell, Freddie, Philadelphia	22	377	17.1	60	2
oore, Dave, Tampa Bay	3	17	5.7	10	0
oore, Mewelde, Minnesota	27	238	8.8	26	0
organ, Quincy, Cle.-Dal.*	31	404	13.0	53	3
orris, Maurice, Seattle	9	53	5.9	12	0
oss, Randy, Minnesota	49	767	15.7	t82	13
uhammad, Muhsin, Carolina	93	1405	15.1	51	16
d, Larry, Minnesota	1	9	9.0	9	0
whouse, Reggie, Arizona	1	5	5.0	5	0
vens, Richard, Minnesota	8	69	8.6	18	0
vens, Terrell, Philadelphia	77	1200	15.6	t59	14
rry, Josh, Philadelphia	9	75	8.3	22	0
thon, Jerome, New Orleans	34	581	17.1	38	1
terson, Adrian, Chicago	2	30	15.0	30	0
nkston, Todd, Philadelphia	36	676	18.8	80	1
nner, Artose, Detroit	11	72	6.5	26	0
tman, Michael, Tampa Bay	41	391	9.5	68	3
lite, Lousaka, Seattle	1	4	4.0	4	0
nder, Willie, N.Y. Giants	1	3	3.0	3	0
ole, Nathan, Arizona	5	70	14.0	24	0

Player, Team	No.	Yds.	Avg.	Long	TD
Portis, Clinton, Washington	40	235	5.9	18	2
Price, Peerless, Atlanta	45	575	12.8	50	3
Pritchett, Stanley, Atlanta	2	5	2.5	4	1
Proehl, Ricky, Carolina	34	497	14.6	34	0
Rasby, Walter, Washington	5	52	10.4	13	0
Rice, Jerry, Oak.-Sea.*	30	429	14.3	56	3
Ritchie, Jon, Philadelphia	4	36	9.0	11	0
Rivers, Marcellus, N.Y. Giants	5	36	7.2	13	1
Robertson, Jamal, San Francisco	4	34	8.5	14	0
Robinson, Jeff, Dallas	2	2	1.0	t1	2
Robinson, Koren, Seattle	31	495	16.0	33	2
Robinson, Marcus, Minnesota	47	657	14.0	t50	8
Royal, Robert, Washington	8	70	8.8	23	4
Schlesinger, Cory, Detroit	10	91	9.1	30	3
Schroeder, Bill, Tampa Bay	7	156	22.3	54	1
Scobey, Josh, Arizona	18	191	10.6	42	0
Seidman, Mike, Carolina	13	123	9.5	27	2
Sellers, Mike, Washington	1	14	14.0	14	0
Shiancoe, Visanthe, N.Y. Giants	5	25	5.0	9	1
Shockey, Jeremy, N.Y. Giants	61	666	10.9	38	6
Smart, Ian, Tampa Bay	2	10	5.0	5	0
Smart, Rod, Carolina	1	5	5.0	5	0
Smith, Emmitt, Arizona	15	105	7.0	18	0
Smith, L.J., Philadelphia	34	377	11.1	31	5
Smith, Onterrio, Minnesota	36	394	10.9	t63	2
Smith, Steve, Carolina	6	60	10.0	15	0
Stallworth, Donte', New Orleans	58	767	13.2	45	5
Stecker, Aaron, New Orleans	29	174	6.0	26	0
Steele, Ben, Green Bay	4	42	10.5	27	0
Stevens, Jerramy, Seattle	31	349	11.3	32	3
Streets, Tai, Detroit	28	260	9.3	22	1
Strong, Mack, Seattle	21	99	4.7	13	0
Swinton, Reggie, Detroit	18	213	11.8	28	1
Tapeh, Thomas, Philadelphia	2	15	7.5	13	0
Taylor, Jamaar, N.Y. Giants	6	146	24.3	52	0
Terrell, David, Chicago	42	699	16.6	63	1
Thomas, Anthony, Chicago	17	132	7.8	30	0
Thrash, James, Washington	17	203	11.9	31	0
Thurman, Andrae, Green Bay	2	12	6.0	9	0
Toomer, Amani, N.Y. Giants	51	747	14.6	48	0
Trejo, Stephen, Detroit	4	37	9.3	18	0
Tyree, David, N.Y. Giants	10	155	15.5	49	1
Urban, Jerheme, Seattle	6	117	19.5	33	1
Vines, Scottie, Detroit	3	51	17.0	26	0
Wade, Bobby, Chicago	42	481	11.5	40	0
Walker, Aaron, San Francisco	10	115	11.5	30	0
Walker, Javon, Green Bay	89	1382	15.5	t79	12
Ward, Dedric, Dallas	1	5	5.0	5	0
Ware, Kevin, San Francisco	1	9	9.0	9	0
Westbrook, Brian, Philadelphia	73	703	9.6	50	6
White, Dez, Atlanta	30	370	12.3	54	2
Wiggins, Jermaine, Minnesota	71	705	9.9	39	4
Williams, Boo, New Orleans	33	362	11.0	22	2
Williams, Karl, Arizona	18	197	10.9	33	0
Williams, Moe, Minnesota	21	233	11.1	28	1
Williams, Randal, Dallas	1	14	14.0	14	0
Williams, Roy, Detroit	54	817	15.1	46	8
Wilson, Cedrick, San Francisco	47	641	13.6	39	3
Witten, Jason, Dallas	87	980	11.3	t42	6
Woods, Rashaun, San Francisco	7	160	22.9	59	1

*Includes both NFC and AFC statistics
t—touchdown

PLAYERS WITH TWO CLUBS

Player, Team	No.	Yds.	Avg.	Long	TD
Bryant, Antonio, Dallas	16	266	16.6	48	0
Bryant, Antonio, Cleveland	42	546	13.0	t55	4
Morgan, Quincy, Cleveland	9	144	16.0	t46	3
Morgan, Quincy, Dallas	22	260	11.8	53	0
Rice, Jerry, Oakland	5	67	13.4	18	0
Rice, Jerry, Seattle	25	362	14.5	56	3
White, Jamel, Tampa Bay	4	17	4.3	12	0
White, Jamel, Baltimore	2	4	2.0	6	0

2004 STATISTICS Receiving

SCORING

TEAM

AFC

Team	Total TD	TD Rush	TD Pass	TD Misc.	XP	XPA	FG	FGA	2Pt.	Safeties	Total Pts
Indianapolis	66	10	51	5	64	65	20	26	1	0	52
Kansas City	62	31	27	4	58	60	17	23	1	0	48
San Diego	55	24	29	2	54	55	20	25	0	1	44
New England	49	15	29	5	48	48	31	33	1	0	43
Buffalo	46	15	21	10	45	45	24	28	0	1	39
Denver	42	13	27	2	42	42	29	34	0	0	38
Cincinnati	42	14	23	5	41	41	27	31	0	0	37
Pittsburgh	41	16	20	5	40	40	28	33	0	1	37
Tennessee	41	12	27	2	39	39	19	27	1	0	34
N.Y. Jets	38	15	19	4	33	34	24	29	0	0	33
Oakland	35	10	24	1	31	32	25	28	1	1	32
Baltimore	33	11	13	9	30	30	29	32	1	0	31
Houston	37	16	16	5	34	34	17	24	1	0	30
Cleveland	29	6	21	2	28	28	24	29	1	0	27
Miami	31	10	19	2	26	27	19	23	2	1	27
Jacksonville	26	9	17	0	21	21	24	31	4	2	26
AFC total	673	227	383	63	634	641	377	456	14	7	584
AFC average	42.1	14.2	23.9	3.9	39.6	40.1	23.6	28.5	0.9	0.4	365.

NFC

Team	Total TD	TD Rush	TD Pass	TD Misc.	XP	XPA	FG	FGA	2Pt.	Safeties	Total Pts
Green Bay	50	9	36	5	48	48	24	28	2	0	42
Minnesota	50	8	39	3	45	45	18	22	3	0	40
Philadelphia	44	10	32	2	41	42	27	32	0	0	38
Seattle	43	17	23	3	40	40	23	25	2	0	37
Carolina	42	10	29	3	39	40	20	25	2	0	35
New Orleans	40	15	21	4	38	38	22	27	1	1	34
Atlanta	41	20	15	6	40	40	18	23	0	0	34
St. Louis	37	11	23	3	32	32	19	24	4	0	31
N.Y. Giants	34	18	12	4	33	33	22	28	0	0	30
Tampa Bay	37	9	24	4	32	33	15	24	1	0	30
Detroit	32	7	19	6	28	28	24	28	1	1	29
Dallas	33	14	19	0	31	31	20	26	1	1	29
Arizona	31	15	14	2	28	28	22	29	1	1	28
San Francisco	29	10	16	3	23	23	18	22	3	1	25
Washington	26	6	18	2	25	25	19	27	1	0	24
Chicago	26	10	9	7	22	22	15	24	1	3	23
NFC total	595	189	349	57	545	548	326	414	23	8	515
NFC average	37.2	11.8	21.8	3.6	34.1	34.3	20.4	25.9	1.4	0.5	322.
NFL total	1268	416	732	120	1179	1189	703	870	37	15	1100
NFL average	39.6	13.0	22.9	3.8	36.8	37.2	22.0	27.2	1.2	0.5	343.

INDIVIDUAL

BESTS OF THE SEASON

Points, season
AFC: 141—Adam Vinatieri, New England.
NFC: 122—David Akers, Philadelphia.
Touchdowns, season
NFC: 20—Shaun Alexander, Seattle.
AFC: 18—LaDainian Tomlinson, San Diego.
Extra points, season
AFC: 59—Mike Vanderjagt, Indianapolis.
NFC: 48—Ryan Longwell, Green Bay.
Field goals, season
AFC: 31—Adam Vinatieri, New England.
NFC: 27—David Akers, Philadelphia.
Field goal attempts, season
AFC: 34—Jason Elam, Denver.
NFC: 32—David Akers, Philadelphia.

Longest field goal
NFC: 55—Neil Rackers, Arizona vs. Seattle, Oct. 24; Neil Rackers, Arizona vs. Seattle, Oct. 24.
AFC: 53—Held by 5 players.
Most points, game
AFC: 24—Priest Holmes, Kansas City vs. Atlanta, Oct. 24; Derrick Blaylock, Kansas City vs. Atlanta, Oct. 24; Willis McGahee, Buffalo at Seattle, Nov. 28.
NFC: 24—T.J. Duckett, Atlanta vs. Oakland, Dec. 1
Team leaders, points
AFC:

Baltimore	117	Matt Stover
Buffalo	117	Rian Lindell
Cincinnati	122	Shayne Graham
Cleveland	100	Phil Dawson
Denver	129	Jason Elam
Houston	85	Kris Brown

Indianapolis	119
Jacksonville	93
Kansas City	109
Miami	54
N.Y. Jets	105
New England	141
Oakland	106
Pittsburgh	124
San Diego	114
Tennessee	88
NFC:	
Arizona	94
Atlanta	94
Carolina	96
Chicago	67
Dallas	91
Detroit	100
Green Bay	120
Minnesota	99
N.Y. Giants	99
New Orleans	104
Philadelphia	122
San Francisco	77
Seattle	120
St. Louis	89
Tampa Bay	60
Washington	42

Mike Vanderjagt
Josh Scobee
Lawrence Tynes
Olindo Mare
Doug Brien
Adam Vinatieri
Sebastian Janikowski
Jeff Reed
Nate Kaeding
Gary Anderson
Neil Rackers
Jay Feely
Muhsin Muhammad
Paul Edinger
Billy Cundiff
Jason Hanson
Ryan Longwell
Morten Andersen
Steve Christie
John Carney
David Akers
Todd Peterson
Shaun Alexander
Jeff Wilkins
Michael Pittman
Clinton Portis

Player, Team	XPM	XPA	FGM	FGA	Tot. Pts.
Janikowski, Sebastian, Oak.*	31	32	25	28	106
Brien, Doug, N.Y. Jets*	33	34	24	29	105
Carney, John, New Orleans	38	38	22	27	104
Hanson, Jason, Detroit	28	28	24	28	100
Dawson, Phil, Cleveland*	28	28	24	29	100
Andersen, Morten, Minnesota	45	45	18	22	99
Christie, Steve, N.Y. Giants	33	33	22	28	99
Rackers, Neil, Arizona	28	28	22	29	94

*AFC.

NON-KICKERS

Player, Team	TD	RTD	PTD	MTD	2Pt.	Tot. Pts.
Alexander, Shaun, Seattle	20	16	4	0	0	120
Tomlinson, LaDainian, S.D.*	18	17	1	0	0	108
Muhammad, Muhsin, Car.	16	0	16	0	0	96
Harrison, Marvin, Ind.*	15	0	15	0	0	90
Barber, Tiki, N.Y. Giants	15	13	2	0	0	90
Holmes, Priest, K.C.*	15	14	1	0	0	90
Martin, Curtis, N.Y. Jets*	14	12	2	0	0	84
Owens, Terrell, Philadelphia	14	0	14	0	0	84
Davis, Domanick, Houston*	14	13	1	0	0	84
Dillon, Corey, New England*	13	12	1	0	1	80
Bettis, Jerome, Pittsburgh*	13	13	0	0	0	78
Moss, Randy, Minnesota	13	0	13	0	0	78
McGahee, Willis, Buffalo*	13	13	0	0	0	78
Gates, Antonio, San Diego*	13	0	13	0	0	78
Wayne, Reggie, Ind.*	12	0	12	0	0	72
Johnson, Rudi, Cincinnati*	12	12	0	0	0	72
Walker, Javon, Green Bay	12	0	12	0	0	72
Horn, Joe, New Orleans	11	0	11	0	1	68
Bennett, Drew, Tennessee*	11	0	11	0	0	66
Johnson, Larry, K.C.*	11	9	2	0	0	66
Burleson, Nate, Minnesota	10	0	9	1	1	62
Pittman, Michael, T.B.	10	7	3	0	0	60
Holt, Torry, St. Louis	10	0	10	0	0	60
Stokley, Brandon, Ind.*	10	0	10	0	0	60
James, Edgerrin, Ind.*	9	9	0	0	1	56
Driver, Donald, Green Bay	9	0	9	0	1	56
Smith, Emmitt, Arizona	9	9	0	0	0	54
Dunn, Warrick, Atlanta	9	9	0	0	0	54
Porter, Jerry, Oakland*	9	0	9	0	0	54
McAllister, Deuce, N.O.	9	9	0	0	0	54

*AFC.

NFL LEADERS

KICKERS

Player, Team	XPM	XPA	FGM	FGA	Tot. Pts.
Vinatieri, Adam, New England*	48	48	31	33	141
Elam, Jason, Denver*	42	42	29	34	129
Reed, Jeff, Pittsburgh*	40	40	28	33	124
Akers, David, Philadelphia	41	42	27	32	122
Graham, Shayne, Cincinnati*	41	41	27	31	122
Longwell, Ryan, Green Bay	48	48	24	28	120
Vanderjagt, Mike, Indianapolis*	59	60	20	25	119
Stover, Matt, Baltimore*	30	30	29	32	117
Lindell, Rian, Buffalo*	45	45	24	28	117
Kaeding, Nate, San Diego*	54	55	20	25	114
Brown, Josh, Seattle	40	40	23	25	109
Tynes, Lawrence, Kansas City*	58	60	17	23	109

AFC

KICKERS

Player, Team	XPM	XPA	FGM	FGA	Tot. Pts.
Anderson, Gary, Tennessee	37	37	17	22	88
Brien, Doug, N.Y. Jets	33	34	24	29	105
Brown, Kris, Houston	34	34	17	24	85
Bryant, Matt, Ind.-Mia.*	12	12	3	4	21
Dawson, Phil, Cleveland	28	28	24	29	100
Elam, Jason, Denver	42	42	29	34	129
Elling, Aaron, Tennessee	2	2	1	2	5
Graham, Shayne, Cincinnati	41	41	27	31	122
Gramatica, Bill, Miami	0	1	3	3	9
Hentrich, Craig, Tennessee	0	0	1	3	3
Janikowski, Sebastian, Oakland	31	32	25	28	106
Kaeding, Nate, San Diego	54	55	20	25	114
Lindell, Rian, Buffalo	45	45	24	28	117
Mare, Olindo, Miami	18	18	12	16	54
Reed, Jeff, Pittsburgh	40	40	28	33	124
Scobee, Josh, Jacksonville	21	21	24	31	93
Stover, Matt, Baltimore	30	30	29	32	117
Tynes, Lawrence, Kansas City	58	60	17	23	109
Vanderjagt, Mike, Indianapolis	59	60	20	25	119
Vinatieri, Adam, New England	48	48	31	33	141
Welker, Wesley, Miami	1	1	1	1	4

NON-KICKERS

Player, Team	TD	RTD	PTD	MTD	2Pt.	Tot. Pts.
Abdullah, Rabih, N.E.	1	1	0	0	0	6
Abraham, Donnie, N.Y. Jets	2	0	0	2	0	12
Alston, Richard, Cleveland	1	0	0	1	0	6
Anderson, Charlie, Houston	1	0	0	1	0	6
Anderson, Courtney, Oak.	1	0	1	0	0	6
Armstrong, Derick, Houston	1	0	1	0	0	6
Baker, Chris, N.Y. Jets	4	0	4	0	0	24
Becht, Anthony, N.Y. Jets	1	0	1	0	0	6
Bell, Tatum, Denver	3	3	0	0	0	18
Bennett, Drew, Tennessee	11	0	11	0	0	66
Berlin, Eddie, Tennessee	1	0	1	0	0	6
Bettis, Jerome, Pittsburgh	13	13	0	0	0	78
Blaylock, Derrick, K.C.	9	8	1	0	0	54
Boller, Kyle, Baltimore	1	1	0	0	0	6
Booker, Marty, Miami	1	0	1	0	0	6
Bradford, Corey, Houston	3	0	3	0	0	18
Brady, Kyle, Jacksonville	1	0	1	0	0	6
Branch, Deion, N.E.	4	0	4	0	0	24
Brees, Drew, San Diego	2	2	0	0	0	12
Brown, Chris, Tennessee	6	6	0	0	0	36
Brown, Troy, New England	1	0	1	0	0	6

2004 STATISTICS Scoring

Player, Team	Tot. TD	RTD	PTD	MTD	2Pt.	Tot. Pts.
Bryant, Antonio, Cleveland	4	0	4	0	0	24
Buchanon, Phillip, Oakland	1	0	0	1	0	6
Bulluck, Keith, Tennessee	1	0	0	1	0	6
Burress, Plaxico, Pittsburgh	5	0	5	0	0	30
Caldwell, Reche, San Diego	3	0	3	0	0	18
Campbell, Mark, Buffalo	5	0	5	0	0	30
Carswell, Dwayne, Denver	1	0	1	0	0	6
Carter, Jonathan, N.Y. Jets	1	0	1	0	0	6
Chambers, Chris, Miami	7	0	7	0	1	44
Chatman, Jesse, San Diego	3	3	0	0	0	18
Chrebet, Wayne, N.Y. Jets	1	0	1	0	0	6
Clark, Dallas, Indianapolis	5	0	5	0	0	30
Clements, Nate, Buffalo	2	0	0	2	0	12
Coleman, Marcus, Houston	1	0	0	1	0	6
Cotchery, Jerricho, N.Y. Jets	1	0	0	1	0	6
Crocker, Chris, Cleveland	1	0	0	1	0	6
Crockett, Zack, Oakland	2	2	0	0	0	12
Curry, Ronald, Oakland	6	0	6	0	0	36
David, Jason, Indianapolis	1	0	0	1	0	6
Davis, Andre', Cleveland	2	0	2	0	0	12
Davis, Domanick, Houston	14	13	1	0	0	84
Dillon, Corey, New England	13	12	1	0	1	80
Dinkins, Darnell, Baltimore	1	0	1	0	0	6
Droughns, Reuben, Denver	8	6	2	0	0	48
Dunn, Jason, Kansas City	3	0	3	0	0	18
Dwight, Tim, San Diego	2	0	1	1	0	12
Edwards, Donnie, S.D.	1	0	0	1	0	6
Edwards, Troy, Jacksonville	1	0	1	0	0	6
Euhus, Tim, Buffalo	2	0	2	0	0	12
Evans, Lee, Buffalo	9	0	9	0	0	54
Faggins, DeMarcus, Hou.	1	0	0	1	0	6
Fargas, Justin, Oakland	1	1	0	0	0	6
Farrior, James, Pittsburgh	1	0	0	1	0	6
Faulk, Kevin, New England	3	2	1	0	0	18
Fauria, Christian, N.E.	2	0	2	0	0	12
Favors, Greg, Jacksonville	0	0	0	0	0	*2
Feeley, A.J., Miami	1	1	0	0	0	6
Fleming, Troy, Tennessee	2	0	2	0	0	12
Floyd, Malcom, San Diego	1	0	1	0	0	6
Flutie, Doug, San Diego	2	2	0	0	0	12
Fuamatu-Ma'afal, Chris, Jack.	1	1	0	0	0	6
Gabriel, Doug, Oakland	2	0	2	0	0	12
Gaffney, Jabar, Houston	2	0	2	0	0	12
Garcia, Jeff, Cleveland	2	2	0	0	0	12
Garrard, David, Jacksonville	1	1	0	0	0	6
Gates, Antonio, San Diego	13	0	13	0	0	78
Gay, Randall, New England	1	0	0	1	0	6
Geathers, Robert, Cincinnati	1	0	0	1	0	6
Gilmore, Bryan, Miami	1	0	1	0	0	6
Givens, David, New England	3	0	3	0	0	18
Gonzalez, Tony, Kansas City	7	0	7	0	0	42
Graham, Daniel, N.E.	7	0	7	0	0	42
Green, Jarvis, New England	1	0	0	1	0	6
Green, William, Cleveland	2	2	0	0	0	12
Griffin, Quentin, Denver	3	2	1	0	0	18
Hall, Dante, Kansas City	2	0	0	2	0	12
Hankton, Cortez, Jack.	2	0	2	0	0	12
Hape, Patrick, Denver	4	0	4	0	0	24
Harrison, James, Pittsburgh	1	0	0	1	0	6
Harrison, Marvin, Ind.	15	0	15	0	0	90
Haynes, Verron, Pittsburgh	2	0	2	0	0	12
Heap, Todd, Baltimore	3	0	3	0	0	18
Hearst, Garrison, Denver	1	1	0	0	0	6
Heiden, Steve, Cleveland	5	0	5	0	1	32
Holmes, Priest, Kansas City	15	14	1	0	0	90
Horn, Chris, Kansas City	1	0	1	0	0	6
Houshmandzadeh, T.J., Cin.	4	0	4	0	0	24
Hutchins, Von, Indianapolis	1	0	0	1	0	6
Hymes, Randy, Baltimore	2	0	2	0	0	12
James, Edgerrin, Ind.	9	9	0	0	1	56
Johnson, Andre, Houston	6	0	6	0	0	36
Johnson, Bethel, N.E.	2	0	1	1	0	12
Johnson, Chad, Cincinnati	9	0	9	0	0	54
Johnson, Ellis, Denver	1	0	0	1	0	6
Johnson, Jarret, Baltimore	1	0	0	1	0	6
Johnson, Jeremi, Cincinnati	1	0	1	0	0	6
Johnson, Kevin, Baltimore	1	0	1	0	0	6
Johnson, Kyle, Denver	2	0	2	0	0	12
Johnson, Larry, Kansas City	11	9	2	0	0	66
Johnson, Rudi, Cincinnati	12	12	0	0	0	72
Johnson, Teyo, Oakland	2	0	2	0	0	12
Jolley, Doug, Oakland	2	0	2	0	0	12
Jones, Brian, Jacksonville	1	0	1	0	1	8
Jones, Greg, Jacksonville	3	3	0	0	0	18
Jones, Terry, Baltimore	1	0	1	0	0	6
Jordan, LaMont, N.Y. Jets	2	2	0	0	0	12
Kaesviharn, Kevin, Cin.	1	0	0	1	0	6
Kennison, Eddie, K.C.	8	0	8	0	1	50
Kinney, Erron, Tennessee	3	0	3	0	0	18
Knight, Sammy, Miami	0	0	0	0	0	*2
Konrad, Rob, Miami	1	0	1	0	0	6
Krause, Ryan, San Diego	1	0	1	0	0	6
Kreider, Dan, Pittsburgh	1	0	1	0	0	6
Larson, Kyle, Cincinnati	1	1	0	0	0	6
Lee, Donald, Miami	1	0	1	0	0	6
Leftwich, Byron, Jack.	2	2	0	0	0	12
Lelie, Ashley, Denver	7	0	7	0	0	42
Lewis, Jamal, Baltimore	7	7	0	0	0	42
Martin, Curtis, N.Y. Jets	14	12	2	0	0	84
Mason, Derrick, Tennessee	7	0	7	0	0	42
McAlister, Chris, Baltimore	2	0	0	2	0	12
McCardell, Keenan, S.D.	1	0	1	0	0	6
McCareins, Justin, N.Y. Jets	4	0	4	0	0	24
McGahee, Willis, Buffalo	13	13	0	0	0	78
McGee, Terrence, Buffalo	3	0	0	3	0	18
McMichael, Randy, Miami	4	0	4	0	1	26
McNair, Steve, Tennessee	1	1	0	0	1	8
Meier, Shad, Tennessee	2	0	2	0	0	12
Miller, Billy, Houston	1	0	1	0	0	6
Minor, Travis, Miami	3	3	0	0	0	18
Mitchell, Kawika, K.C.	1	0	0	1	0	6
Moore, Clarence, Baltimore	4	0	4	0	1	26
Morgan, Quincy, Cleveland	3	0	3	0	0	18
Morris, Rob, Indianapolis	1	0	0	1	0	6
Morris, Sammy, Miami	6	6	0	0	0	36
Morton, Johnnie, K.C.	3	0	3	0	0	18
Moss, Santana, N.Y. Jets	5	0	5	0	0	30
Moulds, Eric, Buffalo	5	0	5	0	0	30
Mungro, James, Ind.	3	0	3	0	0	18
Northcutt, Dennis, Clev.	2	0	2	0	0	12
O'Neal, Deltha, Cincinnati	1	0	0	1	0	6
Osgood, Kassim, San Diego	2	0	2	0	0	12
Palmer, Carson, Cincinnati	1	1	0	0	0	6
Parker, Eric, San Diego	4	0	4	0	0	24
Parker, Samie, Kansas City	1	0	1	0	0	6
Patten, David, New England	7	0	7	0	0	42
Peek, Antwan, Houston	1	0	0	1	0	6
Peelle, Justin, San Diego	2	0	2	0	0	12
Pennington, Chad, N.Y. Jets	1	1	0	0	0	6
Peters, Jason, Buffalo	1	0	0	1	0	6
Plummer, Jake, Denver	1	1	0	0	0	6
Polamalu, Troy, Pittsburgh	1	0	0	1	0	6
Pollard, Marcus, Ind.	6	0	6	0	0	36
Pope, Derrick, Miami	1	0	0	1	0	6
Porter, Jerry, Oakland	9	0	9	0	0	54
Putzier, Jeb, Denver	2	0	2	0	0	12
Randle El, Antwaan, Pitts.	3	0	3	0	0	18
Reed, Ed, Baltimore	2	0	0	2	0	12
Rhodes, Dominic, Ind.	2	1	0	1	0	12
Riemersma, Jay, Pittsburgh	2	0	2	0	0	12
Roethlisberger, Ben, Pitts.	1	1	0	0	0	6
Sams, B.J., Baltimore	3	1	0	2	0	18

Player, Team	Tot. TD	RTD	PTD	MTD	2Pt.	Tot. Pts.
amuel, Asante, N.E.	1	0	0	1	0	6
anders, Bob, Indianapolis.....	1	0	0	1	0	6
anders, Deion, Baltimore	1	0	0	1	0	6
chobel, Matt, Cincinnati	4	0	4	0	0	24
eymour, Richard, N.E.	1	0	0	1	0	6
harper, Jamie, Houston	1	0	0	1	0	6
hea, Aaron, Cleveland	4	0	4	0	0	24
immons, Brian, Cincinnati	1	0	0	1	0	6
mith, Antowain, Tennessee...	4	4	0	0	0	24
mith, Daryl, Jacksonville	0	0	0	0	0	*2
mith, Jimmy, Jacksonville	6	0	6	0	0	36
mith, Jonathan, Buffalo	1	0	0	1	0	6
mith, Rod, Denver	7	0	7	0	0	42
owell, Jerald, N.Y. Jets	1	0	1	0	0	6
pikes, Takeo, Buffalo	2	0	0	2	0	12
taley, Duce, Pittsburgh	1	1	0	0	0	6
tewart, Tony, Cincinnati	1	0	1	0	0	6
tokley, Brandon, Ind.	10	0	10	0	0	60
tuvaints, Russell, Pitts.	1	0	0	1	0	6
uggs, Lee, Cleveland	3	2	1	0	0	18
aylor, Chester, Baltimore	2	2	0	0	0	12
aylor, Fred, Jacksonville	3	2	1	0	0	18
hompson, Derrius, Miami.....	4	0	4	0	0	24
hompson, Lamont, Tenn.	1	0	0	1	0	6
oefield, LaBrandon, Jack.	1	0	1	0	0	6
omlinson, LaDainian, S.D. ...	18	17	1	0	0	108
ownsend, Deshea, Pitts.	1	0	0	1	0	6
roupe, Ben, Tennessee	1	0	1	0	0	6
uman, Jerame, Pittsburgh.....	3	0	3	0	0	18
ilma, Jonathan, N.Y. Jets	1	0	0	1	0	6
olek, Billy, Tennessee...........	1	1	0	0	0	6
rabel, Mike, New England	2	0	2	0	0	12
ard, Hines, Pittsburgh	5	1	4	0	0	30
Varfield, Eric, Kansas City.....	1	0	0	1	0	6
Vashington, Kelley, Cin.	3	0	3	0	0	18
Vatson, Kenny, Cincinnati	1	0	1	0	0	6
Vatts, Darius, Denver...........	1	0	1	0	0	6
ayne, Reggie, Indianapolis...	12	0	12	0	0	72
Velker, Wesley, Miami...........	1	0	0	1	0	6
ells, Jonathan, Houston........	5	3	2	0	1	32
Vheatley, Tyrone, Oakland.....	4	4	0	0	0	24
Vhitted, Alvis, Oakland	2	0	2	0	1	14
Vilcox, Daniel, Baltimore........	1	0	1	0	0	6
Vilford, Ernest, Jacksonville...	2	0	2	0	1	14
Villiams, Chad, Baltimore.......	1	0	0	1	0	6
Villiams, Madieu, Cincinnati...	1	0	1	0	0	6
Villiams, Pat, Buffalo	1	0	0	1	0	*8
Villiams, Reggie, Jack.	1	0	1	0	2	10
Villiams, Shaud, Buffalo	2	2	0	0	0	12
Vilson, Al, Denver	1	0	0	1	0	6
Vrighster, George, Jack.	1	0	1	0	0	6
ereoue, Amos, Oakland........	3	3	0	0	0	18

*Includes safety.

NOTE: Team safeties credited to Oakland; Pittsburgh; San Diego.

NFC

KICKERS

Player, Team	XPM	XPA	FGM	FGA	Tot. Pts
kers, David, Philadelphia............	41	42	27	32	122
ndersen, Morten, Minnesota......	45	45	18	22	99
own, Josh, Seattle	40	40	23	25	109
arney, John, New Orleans	38	38	22	27	104
handler, Jeff, Car.-Was.*	14	14	5	8	29
hristie, Steve, N.Y. Giants..........	33	33	22	28	99
undiff, Billy, Dallas.................	31	31	20	26	91
dinger, Paul, Chicago	22	22	15	24	67
eely, Jay, Atlanta....................	40	40	18	23	94

Player, Team	XPM	XPA	FGM	FGA	Tot. Pts
Gramatica, Martin, Tampa Bay	21	22	11	19	54
Hall, John, Washington	13	13	8	11	37
Hanson, Jason, Detroit................	28	28	24	28	100
Kasay, John, Carolina.................	27	28	19	22	84
Kimrin, Ola, Washington	6	6	6	10	24
Longwell, Ryan, Green Bay	48	48	24	28	120
Peterson, Todd, San Francisco....	23	23	18	22	77
Rackers, Neil, Arizona	28	28	22	29	94
Sauerbrun, Todd, Carolina..........	4	4	1	1	7
Taylor, Jay, Tampa Bay	11	11	4	5	23
Wilkins, Jeff, St. Louis	32	32	19	24	89

NON-KICKERS

Player, Team	Tot. TD	RTD	PTD	MTD	2Pt.	Tot. Pts.
Alexander, Shaun, Seattle	20	16	4	0	0	120
Alexander, Stephen, Detroit	1	0	1	0	0	6
Alstott, Mike, Tampa Bay	2	2	0	0	0	12
Anderson, Richie, Dallas.........	1	1	0	0	0	6
Archuleta, Adam, St. Louis	1	0	0	1	0	6
Ayanbadejo, Obafemi, Ar........	4	3	1	0	0	24
Azumah, Jerry, Chicago...........	1	0	0	1	0	6
Barber, Ronde, Tampa Bay.......	2	0	0	2	0	12
Barber, Tiki, N.Y. Giants	15	13	2	0	0	90
Barlow, Kevan, S.F.	7	7	0	0	0	42
Barnes, Darian, Dallas.............	1	0	1	0	0	6
Bartrum, Mike, Philadelphia......	1	0	1	0	0	6
Battle, Arnaz, San Francisco	1	0	1	0	0	6
Bennett, Brandon, Carolina	1	1	0	0	0	6
Bennett, Michael, Minn.	2	1	1	0	0	12
Berrian, Bernard, Chicago........	2	0	2	0	0	12
Betts, Ladell, Washington	1	1	0	0	0	6
Bly, Dre', Detroit	1	0	0	1	0	6
Bockwoldt, Colby, N.O.	1	0	0	1	0	6
Boldin, Anquan, Arizona	1	0	1	0	0	6
Boulware, Michael, Seattle.......	1	0	0	1	0	6
Briggs, Lance, Chicago............	1	0	0	1	0	6
Brooks, Aaron, New Orleans ...	4	4	0	0	0	24
Brown, Mike, Chicago..............	1	0	0	1	0	6
Brown, Tim, Tampa Bay...........	1	0	1	0	0	6
Bruce, Isaac, St. Louis	6	0	6	0	0	36
Bryant, Tony, New Orleans.......	0	0	0	0	0	*2
Bulger, Marc, St. Louis	3	3	0	0	0	18
Burleson, Nate, Minnesota.......	10	0	9	1	1	62
Bush, Steve, San Francisco	1	0	1	0	0	6
Campbell, Kelly, Minnesota......	1	0	1	0	0	6
Carpenter, Dwaine, S.F.	1	0	0	1	0	6
Carroll, Ahmad, Green Bay	1	0	0	1	0	6
Carter, Tim, N.Y. Giants...........	1	0	1	0	0	6
Chatman, Antonio, G.B.	1	0	1	0	0	6
Claiborne, Chris, Minnesota.....	1	0	0	1	0	6
Clark, Desmond, Chicago	1	0	1	0	0	6
Clayton, Michael, T.B.	7	0	7	0	0	42
Cloud, Michael, N.Y. Giants.....	3	3	0	0	0	18
Colbert, Keary, Carolina	5	0	5	0	1	32
Coleman, Rod, Atlanta.............	1	0	0	1	0	6
Coles, Laveranues, Wash.	1	0	1	0	0	6
Conway, Curtis, S.F.	3	0	3	0	1	20
Conwell, Ernie, New Orleans...	1	0	1	0	0	6
Cook, Jameel, Tampa Bay	1	0	1	0	0	6
Cooley, Chris, Washington.......	6	0	6	0	0	36
Copper, Terrance, Dallas.........	1	0	1	0	0	6
Cox, Torrie, Tampa Bay...........	1	0	0	1	0	6
Crayton, Patrick, Dallas...........	1	0	1	0	0	6
Crumpler, Alge, Atlanta............	6	0	6	0	0	36
Culpepper, Daunte, Minn.	2	2	0	0	1	14
Curtis, Kevin, St. Louis	2	0	2	0	1	14
Davenport, Najeh, G.B.	2	2	0	0	0	12
Dayne, Ron, N.Y. Giants..........	1	1	0	0	0	6
Delhomme, Jake, Carolina	1	1	0	0	0	6
Dilger, Ken, Tampa Bay	3	0	3	0	1	20

– 259 –

Player, Team	Tot. TD	RTD	PTD	MTD	2Pt.	Tot. Pts.
Driver, Donald, Green Bay	9	0	9	0	1	56
Drummond, Eddie, Detroit	4	0	0	4	0	24
Duckett, T.J., Atlanta	8	8	0	0	0	48
Dunn, Warrick, Atlanta	9	9	0	0	0	54
Engram, Bobby, Seattle	2	0	2	0	0	12
Faulk, Marshall, St. Louis	4	3	1	0	2	28
Ferguson, Robert, G.B.	1	0	1	0	1	8
Finneran, Brian, Atlanta	2	0	2	0	0	12
Fisher, Tony, Green Bay	2	0	2	0	0	12
Fitzgerald, Larry, Arizona	8	0	8	0	0	48
Foster, DeShaun, Carolina	2	2	0	0	0	12
Franks, Bubba, Green Bay	7	0	7	0	0	42
Galloway, Joey, Tampa Bay	6	0	5	1	0	36
Gardner, Rod, Washington	5	0	5	0	0	30
George, Eddie, Dallas	4	4	0	0	0	24
Glenn, Terry, Dallas	2	0	2	0	0	12
Goings, Nick, Carolina	7	6	1	0	0	42
Goodspeed, Joey, St. Louis	1	1	0	0	0	6
Green, Ahman, Green Bay	8	7	1	0	0	48
Green, Barrett, N.Y. Giants	1	0	0	1	0	6
Griffith, Justin, Atlanta	1	0	1	0	0	6
Grossman, Rex, Chicago	1	1	0	0	0	6
Hakim, Az-Zahir, Detroit	3	0	3	0	0	18
Hall, DeAngelo, Atlanta	1	0	0	1	0	6
Hall, Lamont, New Orleans	1	0	1	0	0	6
Hambrick, Troy, Arizona	2	1	1	0	0	12
Harris, Walt, Washington	1	0	0	1	0	6
Hasselbeck, Matt, Seattle	1	1	0	0	0	6
Hawthorne, Michael, G.B.	1	0	0	1	0	6
Haynes, Michael, Chicago	1	0	0	1	0	6
Heller, Will, Tampa Bay	1	0	1	0	0	6
Henderson, William, G.B.	3	0	3	0	0	18
Hicks, Maurice, S.F.	2	2	0	0	0	12
Holt, Torry, St. Louis	10	0	10	0	0	60
Hoover, Brad, Carolina	2	0	2	0	0	12
Horn, Joe, New Orleans	11	0	11	0	1	68
Jackson, Darrell, Seattle	7	0	7	0	1	44
Jackson, Steven, St. Louis	4	4	0	0	1	26
Jacobs, Taylor, Washington	0	0	0	0	1	2
Johnson, Bryan, Chicago	2	0	2	0	0	12
Johnson, Bryant, Arizona	1	0	1	0	0	6
Johnson, Eric, S.F.	2	0	2	0	0	12
Johnson, Keyshawn, Dallas	6	0	6	0	0	36
Jones, Freddie, Arizona	2	0	2	0	0	12
Jones, Julius, Dallas	7	7	0	0	0	42
Jones, Kevin, Detroit	6	5	1	0	0	36
Jones, Thomas, Chicago	7	7	0	0	0	42
Jurevicius, Joe, Tampa Bay	2	0	2	0	0	12
Kircus, David, Detroit	1	0	1	0	0	6
Krenzel, Craig, Chicago	0	0	0	0	1	2
Lee, ReShard, Dallas	1	1	0	0	0	6
Levens, Dorsey, Phil.	4	4	0	0	0	24
Lewis, Chad, Philadelphia	3	0	3	0	0	18
Lewis, Michael, N.O.	1	0	0	1	0	6
Little, Leonard, St. Louis	2	0	0	2	0	12
Lloyd, Brandon, S.F.	6	0	6	0	1	38
Lucas, Ken, Seattle	1	0	0	1	0	6
Lyman, Dustin, Chicago	1	0	1	0	0	6
Mangum, Kris, Carolina	3	0	3	0	0	18
Manumaleuna, Brandon, St. L.	1	0	1	0	0	6
Mathis, Kevin, Atlanta	2	0	0	2	0	12
McAllister, Deuce, N.O.	9	9	0	0	0	54
McCown, Josh, Arizona	2	2	0	0	1	14
McDonald, Shaun, St. Louis	3	0	3	0	0	18
McKie, Jason, Chicago	2	0	2	0	0	12
McNabb, Donovan, Phil.	3	3	0	0	0	18
McQuarters, R.W., Chicago	2	0	0	2	0	12
Mili, Itula, Seattle	1	0	1	0	0	6
Mitchell, Freddie, Phil.	2	0	2	0	0	12
Mitchell, Mel, New Orleans	1	0	0	1	0	6
Moorehead, Kindal, Carolina	1	0	0	1	0	6
Moss, Randy, Minnesota	13	0	13	0	0	78
Muhammad, Muhsin, Car.	16	0	16	0	0	96
Ogunleye, Adewale, Chicago	0	0	0	0	0	*2
Owens, Terrell, Philadelphia	14	0	14	0	0	84
Pathon, Jerome, N.O.	1	0	1	0	0	6
Peppers, Julius, Carolina	2	0	0	2	0	12
Pierce, Antonio, Wash.	1	0	0	1	0	6
Pinkston, Todd, Philadelphia	1	0	1	0	0	6
Pinner, Artose, Detroit	2	2	0	0	0	12
Pittman, Michael, T.B.	10	7	3	0	0	60
Ponder, Willie, N.Y. Giants	1	0	0	1	0	6
Portis, Clinton, Washington	7	5	2	0	0	42
Price, Peerless, Atlanta	3	0	3	0	0	18
Pritchett, Stanley, Atlanta	1	0	1	0	0	6
Rattay, Tim, San Francisco	0	0	0	0	1	2
Redding, Cory, Detroit	0	0	0	0	0	*2
Rice, Jerry, Seattle	3	0	3	0	0	18
Rivers, Marcellus, N.Y. G.	1	0	1	0	0	6
Robertson, Jamal, S.F.	1	1	0	0	0	6
Robinson, Jeff, Dallas	2	0	2	0	0	12
Robinson, Koren, Seattle	2	0	2	0	0	12
Robinson, Marcus, Minn.	8	0	8	0	0	48
Rossum, Allen, Atlanta	1	0	0	1	0	6
Royal, Robert, Washington	4	0	4	0	0	24
Schlesinger, Cory, Detroit	3	0	3	0	0	18
Schroeder, Bill, Tampa Bay	1	0	1	0	0	6
Seidman, Mike, Carolina	2	0	2	0	1	14
Sharper, Darren, Green Bay	3	0	0	3	0	18
Sheppard, Lito, Philadelphia	2	0	0	2	0	12
Shiancoe, Visanthe, N.Y. G.	1	0	1	0	0	6
Shockey, Jeremy, N.Y. G.	6	0	6	0	0	36
Simmons, Anthony, Seattle	1	0	0	1	0	6
Smith, Brady, Atlanta	1	0	0	1	0	6
Smith, Derek, San Francisco	1	0	0	1	0	6
Smith, Emmitt, Arizona	9	9	0	0	0	54
Smith, L.J., Philadelphia	5	0	5	0	0	30
Smith, Onterrio, Minnesota	4	2	2	0	1	26
Stallworth, Donte', N.O.	5	0	5	0	0	30
Starks, Duane, Arizona	1	0	0	1	0	6
Stecker, Aaron, N.O.	3	2	0	1	0	18
Stevens, Jerramy, Seattle	3	0	3	0	1	20
Streets, Tai, Detroit	1	0	1	0	1	8
Swinton, Reggie, Detroit	1	0	1	0	0	6
Terrell, David, Chicago	1	0	1	0	0	6
Testaverde, Vinny, Dallas	1	1	0	0	0	6
Thomas, Anthony, Chicago	2	2	0	0	0	12
Tyree, David, N.Y. Giants	1	0	1	0	0	6
Umenyiora, Osi, N.Y. Giants	1	0	0	1	0	6
Urban, Jerheme, Seattle	1	0	1	0	0	6
Vasher, Nathan, Chicago	1	0	0	1	0	6
Vick, Michael, Atlanta	3	3	0	0	0	18
Walker, Bracy, Detroit	1	0	0	1	0	6
Walker, Javon, Green Bay	12	0	12	0	0	72
Ward, Derrick, N.Y. Giants	1	0	0	1	0	6
Warner, Kurt, N.Y. Giants	1	1	0	0	0	6
Westbrook, Brian, Phil.	9	3	6	0	0	54
White, Dez, Atlanta	2	0	2	0	0	12
Wiggins, Jermaine, Minn.	4	0	4	0	0	24
Williams, Boo, New Orleans	2	0	2	0	0	12
Williams, Kevin, Minnesota	1	0	0	1	0	6
Williams, Moe, Minnesota	4	3	1	0	0	24
Williams, Roy, Detroit	8	0	8	0	0	48
Wilson, Adrian, Arizona	1	0	0	1	0	6
Wilson, Cedrick, S.F.	3	0	3	0	0	18
Witten, Jason, Dallas	6	0	6	0	1	38
Woods, Rashaun, S.F.	1	0	1	0	0	6

*Includes safety.

NOTE: Team safeties credited to Chicago(2); Dallas; Arizona; San Francisco.

INTERCEPTIONS

TEAM

AFC

am	No.	Yds.	Avg.	Long	TD
ıffalo	24	333	13.9	t62	4
ın Diego	23	180	7.8	40	1
ɔuston	22	393	17.9	t102	2
altimore	21	700	33.3	t106	5
ɛw England	20	290	14.5	36	1
ncinnati	20	272	13.6	t51	4
ttsburgh	19	293	15.4	41	3
dianapolis	19	252	13.3	t77	2
Y. Jets	19	243	12.8	t66	2
ınnessee	18	285	15.8	44	1
ıcksonville	16	126	7.9	37	0
eveland	15	250	16.7	51	1
iami	15	92	6.1	47	0
ansas City	13	173	13.3	65	1
ɛnver	12	175	14.6	76	2
akland	9	221	24.6	45	1
AFC total	285	4278	...	t106	30
AFC average	17.8	267.4	15.0	...	1.9

—touchdown.

NFC

Team	No.	Yds.	Avg.	Long	TD
Carolina	26	420	16.2	97	2
Seattle	23	337	14.7	t63	3
Atlanta	19	442	23.3	85	4
Washington	18	405	22.5	t78	1
Chicago	17	546	32.1	t71	5
Philadelphia	17	287	16.9	t101	2
Tampa Bay	16	239	14.9	75	1
Arizona	15	214	14.3	65	1
Detroit	14	216	15.4	t55	1
N.Y. Giants	14	113	8.1	39	0
Dallas	13	109	8.4	33	0
New Orleans	13	101	7.8	55	0
Minnesota	11	207	18.8	56	1
San Francisco	9	129	14.3	31	0
Green Bay	8	165	20.6	t43	2
St. Louis	6	45	7.5	30	0
NFC total	239	3975	...	t101	23
NFC average	14.9	248.4	16.6	...	1.4
NFL total	524	8253	...	t106	53
NFL average	16.4	257.9	15.8	...	1.7

INDIVIDUAL

BESTS OF THE SEASON

ıterceptions, season
ʳC: 9—Ed Reed, Baltimore.
ꟻC: 6—Chris Gamble, Carolina; Ken Lucas, Seattle.

ıterceptions, game
ꟻC: 2—Held by 14 players.
ꟻC: 2—Held by 15 players.

ırds, season
ꟻC: 358—Ed Reed, Baltimore.
ꟻC: 177—Nathan Vasher, Chicago.

ıngest
ꟻC: 106—Ed Reed, Baltimore vs. Cleveland, Nov. 7 (TD).
ꟻC: 101—Lito Sheppard, Philadelphia at Dallas, Nov. 15 (TD).

ıuchdowns, season
ꟻC: 2—Takeo Spikes, Buffalo..
ꟻC: 2—Kevin Mathis, Atlanta; Darren Sharper, Green Bay; Lito ıeppard, Philadelphia.

ıam leaders, interceptions
ꟻC:

Team	No.	Player
altimore	9	Ed Reed
ıffalo	6	Nate Clements
ncinnati	8	Tory James
eveland	4	Anthony Henry
ɛnver	3	Champ Bailey
ɔuston	6	Dunta Robinson
dianapolis	4	Jason David
cksonville	5	Donovin Darius, Rashean Mathis
ınsas City	4	Greg Wesley, Eric Warfield
iami	4	Arturo Freeman, Sammy Knight, Patrick Surtain
Y. Jets	4	Erik Coleman
ɛw England	4	Eugene Wilson
akland	3	Phillip Buchanon
ttsburgh	5	Troy Polamalu
ın Diego	5	Donnie Edwards
nnessee	6	Andre Dyson

NFC:

Team	No.	Player
Arizona	4	David Macklin
Atlanta	4	Aaron Beasley
Carolina	6	Chris Gamble
Chicago	5	Nathan Vasher
Dallas	4	Terence Newman
Detroit	4	Dre' Bly
Green Bay	4	Darren Sharper
Minnesota	3	Antoine Winfield
N.Y. Giants	3	Gibril Wilson, Brent Alexander
New Orleans	5	Mike McKenzie
Philadelphia	5	Lito Sheppard
San Francisco	4	Tony Parrish
Seattle	6	Ken Lucas
St. Louis	5	Jerametrius Butler
Tampa Bay	4	Brian Kelly
Washington	5	Shawn Springs

NFL LEADERS

Player, Team	No.	Yds.	Avg.	Long	TD
Reed, Ed, Baltimore*	9	358	39.8	t106	1
James, Tory, Cincinnati*	8	66	8.3	23	0
Robinson, Dunta, Houston*	6	146	24.3	61	0
Dyson, Andre, Tennessee*	6	135	22.5	40	0
Clements, Nate, Buffalo*	6	77	12.8	35	1
Lucas, Ken, Seattle	6	46	7.7	25	1
Gamble, Chris, Carolina	6	15	2.5	13	0

*AFC.
t—touchdown.
Leader based on most interceptions.

2004 STATISTICS Interceptions

AFC

Player, Team	No.	Yds.	Avg.	Long	TD
Abraham, Donnie, N.Y. Jets	2	66	33.0	t66	1
Adams, Sam, Buffalo	1	0	0.0	0	0
Anderson, Marques, Oakland	1	23	23.0	23	0
Ayanbadejo, Brendon, Miami	1	2	2.0	2	0
Bacon, Waine, Indianapolis	1	0	0.0	0	0
Bailey, Champ, Denver	3	0	0.0	0	0
Baker, Rashad, Buffalo	1	26	26.0	26	0
Banta-Cain, Tully, New England	1	4	4.0	4	0
Barber, Shawn, Kansas City	1	10	10.0	10	0
Barrett, David, N.Y. Jets	2	14	7.0	14	0
Barton, Eric, N.Y. Jets	1	7	7.0	7	0
Baxter, Gary, Baltimore	1	33	33.0	33	0
Beisel, Monty, Kansas City	1	-1	-1.0	-1	0
Brackett, Gary, Indianapolis	2	2	1.0	2	0
Brayton, Tyler, Oakland	1	24	24.0	24	0
Brown, Troy, New England	3	22	7.3	17	0
Bruschi, Tedy, New England	3	70	23.3	36	0
Buchanan, Ray, Oakland	1	27	27.0	27	0
Buchanon, Phillip, Oakland	3	69	23.0	37	1
Buckley, Terrell, N.Y. Jets	3	30	10.0	18	0
Bulluck, Keith, Tennessee	2	25	12.5	25	0
Clements, Nate, Buffalo	6	77	12.8	35	1
Coleman, Erik, N.Y. Jets	4	43	10.8	37	0
Coleman, Marcus, Houston	2	116	58.0	t102	1
Cooper, Deke, Jacksonville	1	0	0.0	0	0
Crocker, Chris, Cleveland	1	20	20.0	t20	1
Darius, Donovin, Jacksonville	5	80	16.0	37	0
David, Jason, Indianapolis	4	36	9.0	t34	1
Davis, Andra, Cleveland	3	35	11.7	30	0
Davis, Sammy, San Diego	1	4	4.0	4	0
Demps, Will, Baltimore	1	0	0.0	0	0
Dingle, Adrian, San Diego	1	1	1.0	1	0
Doss, Mike, Indianapolis	2	32	16.0	32	0
Dyson, Andre, Tennessee	6	135	22.5	44	0
Edwards, Donnie, San Diego	5	49	9.8	t30	1
Faggins, DeMarcus, Houston	3	47	15.7	t43	1
Farrior, James, Pittsburgh	4	113	28.3	41	1
Fletcher, Jamar, San Diego	1	0	0.0	0	0
Florence, Drayton, San Diego	4	54	13.5	40	0
Foley, Steve, San Diego	2	4	2.0	4	0
Foote, Larry, Pittsburgh	1	1	1.0	1	0
Freeman, Arturo, Miami	4	59	14.8	47	0
Gardner, Barry, Cleveland	1	30	30.0	30	0
Gardner, Rich, Tennessee	1	-1	-1.0	-1	0
Gay, Randall, New England	2	23	11.5	13	0
Geathers, Robert, Cincinnati	1	36	36.0	t36	1
Glenn, Aaron, Houston	5	40	8.0	23	0
Grant, Deon, Jacksonville	2	4	2.0	4	0
Griffith, Robert, Cleveland	1	18	18.0	18	0
Harper, Nick, Indianapolis	3	12	4.0	12	0
Harrison, Rodney, New England	2	12	6.0	12	0
Hart, Clinton, San Diego	1	13	13.0	13	0
Hayward, Reggie, Denver	1	76	76.0	76	0
Henry, Anthony, Cleveland	4	83	20.8	51	0
Herndon, Kelly, Denver	2	17	8.5	15	0
Herring, Kim, Cincinnati	1	0	0.0	0	0
Hobson, Victor, N.Y. Jets	1	2	2.0	2	0
Hope, Chris, Pittsburgh	1	41	41.0	41	0
Hutchins, Von, Indianapolis	1	77	77.0	t77	1
James, Tory, Cincinnati	8	66	8.3	23	0
Jammer, Quentin, San Diego	1	12	12.0	12	0
Jefferson, Joseph, Indianapolis	1	0	0.0	0	0
Johnson, Ellis, Denver	1	32	32.0	t32	1
Johnson, Jarret, Baltimore	1	6	6.0	t6	1
Johnson, Tim, Oakland	1	8	8.0	8	0
June, Cato, Indianapolis	2	71	35.5	71	0
Kelsay, Chris, Buffalo	1	3	3.0	3	0
Kennedy, Kenoy, Denver	1	21	21.0	21	0
Kiel, Terrence, San Diego	2	31	15.5	31	0
Knight, Sammy, Miami	4	32	8.0	32	
Law, Ty, New England	1	0	0.0	0	
Little, Earl, Cleveland	1	28	28.0	28	
Lynch, John, Denver	1	2	2.0	2	
Mathis, Rashean, Jacksonville	5	42	8.4	21	
McAlister, Chris, Baltimore	1	51	51.0	t51	
McCleon, Dexter, Kansas City	2	23	11.5	23	
McCree, Marlon, Houston	1	24	24.0	24	
McCutcheon, Daylon, Cleveland	2	0	0.0	2	
McGarrahan, Scott, Tennessee	1	11	11.0	11	
McGee, Terrence, Buffalo	3	21	7.0	21	
McGinest, Willie, New England	1	27	27.0	27	
McGraw, Jon, N.Y. Jets	2	0	0.0	0	
Milloy, Lawyer, Buffalo	2	20	10.0	11	
Morris, Rob, Indianapolis	1	17	17.0	17	
Nelson, Jim, Indianapolis	1	0	0.0	0	
O'Neal, Deltha, Cincinnati	4	60	15.0	t31	
Peek, Antwan, Houston	1	20	20.0	20	
Phifer, Roman, New England	1	26	26.0	26	
Phillips, Shaun, San Diego	1	0	0.0	0	
Polamalu, Troy, Pittsburgh	5	58	11.6	t26	
Poole, Tyrone, New England	1	21	21.0	21	
Porter, Joey, Pittsburgh	1	3	3.0	3	
Posey, Jeff, Buffalo	1	3	3.0	3	
Powell, Carl, Cincinnati	1	-2	-2.0	-2	
Reed, Ed, Baltimore	9	358	39.8	t106	
Reese, Izell, Buffalo	1	33	33.0	33	
Robinson, Dunta, Houston	6	146	24.3	61	
Rolle, Samari, Tennessee	1	0	0.0	0	
Samuel, Asante, New England	1	34	34.0	t34	
Sanders, Deion, Baltimore	3	87	29.0	t48	
Sanders, Lewis, Cleveland	2	36	18.0	24	
Sapp, Benny, Kansas City	1	0	0.0	0	
Scott, Chad, Pittsburgh	1	23	23.0	23	
Simmons, Brian, Cincinnati	2	61	30.5	t50	
Simmons, Jason, Houston	1	0	0.0	0	
Smith, Daryl, Jacksonville	1	0	0.0	0	
Spikes, Takeo, Buffalo	5	122	24.4	t62	
Stamer, Josh, Buffalo	1	0	0.0	0	
Surtain, Patrick, Miami	4	2	0.5	2	
Taylor, Ike, Pittsburgh	1	0	0.0	0	
Taylor, Jason, Miami	1	-3	-3.0	-3	
Thomas, Adalius, Baltimore	1	8	8.0	8	
Thompson, Lamont, Tennessee	4	77	19.3	t37	
Thornton, David, Indianapolis	1	5	5.0	5	
Tongue, Reggie, N.Y. Jets	1	23	23.0	23	
Townsend, Deshea, Pittsburgh	4	54	13.5	t39	
Vilma, Jonathan, N.Y. Jets	3	58	19.3	t38	
Vincent, Troy, Buffalo	1	8	8.0	8	
Waddell, Michael, Tennessee	1	0	0.0	0	
Walker, Denard, Oakland	1	45	45.0	45	
Warfield, Eric, Kansas City	4	49	12.3	t43	
Washington, Dewayne, Jack.	2	0	0.0	0	
Weaver, Anthony, Baltimore	1	1	1.0	1	
Wesley, Greg, Kansas City	4	92	23.0	65	
Wilhelm, Matt, San Diego	1	0	0.0	0	
Williams, Chad, Baltimore	3	156	52.0	94	
Williams, D.J., Denver	1	10	10.0	10	
Williams, Jay, Miami	1	0	0.0	0	
Williams, Madieu, Cincinnati	3	51	17.0	t51	
Williams, Pat, Buffalo	1	20	20.0	t20	
Williams, Tank, Tennessee	1	13	13.0	13	
Williams, Willie, Pittsburgh	1	0	0.0	0	
Wilson, Al, Denver	2	17	8.5	10	
Wilson, Eugene, New England	4	51	12.8	24	
Wilson, Jerry, San Diego	3	12	4.0	12	
Wong, Kailee, Houston	3	0	0.0	0	
Woodson, Charles, Oakland	1	25	25.0	25	
Woolfolk, Andre, Tennessee	1	25	25.0	25	

t—touchdown.

NFC

ayer, Team	No.	Yds.	Avg.	Long	TD
ams, Mike, San Francisco	1	0	0.0	0	0
xander, Brent, N.Y. Giants	3	3	1.0	2	0
en, Brian, Carolina	1	21	21.0	21	0
en, Will, N.Y. Giants	1	11	11.0	11	0
en, Will, Tampa Bay	1	0	0.0	0	0
brose, Ashley, New Orleans	3	19	6.3	19	0
umah, Jerry, Chicago	4	128	32.0	t70	1
rber, Ronde, Tampa Bay	3	23	7.7	23	0
rnett, Nick, Green Bay	1	16	16.0	16	0
asley, Aaron, Atlanta	4	115	28.8	85	0
rria, Terreal, Seattle	1	10	10.0	10	0
, Dre', Detroit	4	107	26.8	t55	1
ulware, Michael, Seattle	5	69	13.8	t63	1
anch, Colin, Carolina	3	79	26.3	76	0
iggs, Lance, Chicago	1	38	38.0	t38	1
ooking, Keith, Atlanta	3	41	13.7	27	0
ooks, Derrick, Tampa Bay	1	3	3.0	3	0
own, Fakhir, New Orleans	2	0	0.0	0	0
own, Sheldon, Philadelphia	2	33	16.5	33	0
ckner, Brentson, Carolina	1	8	8.0	8	0
rns, Curry, N.Y. Giants	1	12	12.0	12	0
tler, Jerametrius, St. Louis	5	15	3.0	10	0
rpenter, Dwaine, S.F.	1	31	31.0	31	0
rroll, Ahmad, Green Bay	1	0	0.0	0	0
sh, Chris, Detroit	1	0	0.0	0	0
avous, Corey, Minnesota	1	0	0.0	0	0
aiborne, Chris, Minnesota	1	15	15.0	t15	1
chran, Antonio, Seattle	1	0	0.0	0	0
leman, Rod, Atlanta	1	39	39.0	t39	1
usin, Terry, N.Y. Giants	1	6	6.0	6	0
x, Torrie, Tampa Bay	1	55	55.0	t55	1
nsby, Karlos, Arizona	1	2	2.0	2	0
rling, James, Arizona	1	65	65.0	65	0
wkins, Brian, Philadelphia	4	40	10.0	32	0
ckett, Darnell, Arizona	1	20	20.0	20	0
aft, Chris, Atlanta	1	33	33.0	33	0
lds, Mark, Carolina	1	14	14.0	14	0
her, Travis, St. Louis	1	30	30.0	30	0
anz, Todd, Washington	1	22	22.0	22	0
azier, Lance, Dallas	2	2	1.0	2	0
mble, Chris, Carolina	6	15	2.5	13	0
ld, Ian, Tampa Bay	1	31	31.0	31	0
odman, Andre', Detroit	1	0	0.0	?	0
ant, Charles, New Orleans	1	8	8.0	8	0
ay, Bobby, Chicago	1	31	31.0	31	0
een, Mike, Chicago	2	0	0.0	0	0
ll, DeAngelo, Atlanta	2	50	25.0	t48	1
ll, James, Detroit	1	30	30.0	30	0
mlin, Ken, Seattle	4	48	12.0	24	0
rris, Al, Green Bay	1	29	29.0	29	0
rris, Quentin, Arizona	1	-1	-1.0	-1	0
rris, Walt, Washington	2	31	15.5	31	0
wkins, Artrell, Carolina	1	9	9.0	9	0
ynes, Michael, Chicago	1	45	45.0	t45	1
ard, Ronnie, San Francisco	1	14	14.0	14	0
l, Renaldo, Arizona	1	2	2.0	2	0
od, Roderick, Philadelphia	1	20	20.0	20	0
nter, Pete, Dallas	1	2	2.0	2	0
, Corey, Tampa Bay	0	11	...	11	0

Player, Team	No.	Yds.	Avg.	Long	TD
Jones, Dhani, Philadelphia	1	0	0.0	0	0
Jones, Tebucky, New Orleans	1	55	55.0	55	0
Jue, Bhawoh, Green Bay	1	23	23.0	23	0
Kelly, Brian, Tampa Bay	4	101	25.3	75	0
Kerney, Patrick, Atlanta	1	0	0.0	0	0
Lehman, Teddy, Detroit	1	1	1.0	1	0
Lewis, Alex, Detroit	1	33	33.0	33	0
Lewis, Michael, Philadelphia	1	0	0.0	0	0
Lucas, Ken, Seattle	6	46	7.7	25	1
Macklin, David, Arizona	4	18	4.5	16	0
Manning Jr., Ricky, Carolina	4	46	11.5	30	0
Marion, Brock, Detroit	3	43	14.3	24	0
Mathis, Kevin, Atlanta	2	101	50.5	t66	2
McKenzie, Mike, New Orleans	5	19	3.8	14	0
McQuarters, R.W., Chicago	2	85	42.5	t45	1
Mikell, Quintin, Philadelphia	1	0	0.0	0	0
Moorehead, Kindal, Carolina	1	17	17.0	t17	0
Morgan, Dan, Carolina	2	20	10.0	11	0
Nece, Ryan, Tampa Bay	1	2	2.0	2	0
Newman, Terence, Dallas	4	31	7.8	21	0
Nguyen, Dat, Dallas	3	19	6.3	19	0
Parrish, Tony, San Francisco	4	64	16.0	26	0
Peppers, Julius, Carolina	2	143	71.5	97	1
Peterson, Will, N.Y. Giants	2	9	4.5	9	0
Phillips, Jermaine, Tampa Bay	1	0	0.0	0	0
Pierce, Antonio, Washington	2	94	47.0	t78	1
Reese, Ike, Philadelphia	2	22	11.0	15	0
Robbins, Fred, N.Y. Giants	1	13	13.0	13	0
Rossum, Allen, Atlanta	2	22	11.0	14	0
Ruff, Orlando, New Orleans	1	0	0.0	0	0
Russell, Brian, Minnesota	1	41	41.0	41	0
Scott, Bryan, Atlanta	1	22	22.0	22	0
Scott, Lynn, Dallas	1	2	2.0	2	0
Sharper, Darren, Green Bay	4	97	24.3	t43	2
Shaw, Terrance, Minnesota	1	22	22.0	22	0
Sheppard, Lito, Philadelphia	5	172	34.4	t101	2
Simmons, Anthony, Seattle	1	23	23.0	t23	1
Smith, Brady, Atlanta	1	1	1.0	1	0
Smith, Dwight, Tampa Bay,	3	13	4.3	13	0
Smith, Keith, Detroit	1	2	2.0	2	0
Smith, Raonall, Minnesota	1	19	19.0	19	0
Smoot, Fred, Washington	3	17	5.7	17	0
Springs, Shawn, Washington	5	117	23.4	38	0
Starks, Duane, Arizona	3	46	15.3	t41	1
Taylor, Sean, Washington	4	85	21.3	45	0
Trufant, Marcus, Seattle	5	141	28.2	58	0
Ulbrich, Jeff, San Francisco	1	19	19.0	19	0
Urlacher, Brian, Chicago	1	42	42.0	42	0
Vasher, Nathan, Chicago	5	177	35.4	t71	1
Walker, Bracy, Detroit	1	0	0.0	0	0
Walker, Frank, N.Y. Giants	2	20	10.0	10	0
Warner, Ron, Washington	1	39	39.0	39	0
Webster, Jason, Atlanta	1	18	18.0	18	0
Williams, Brian, Minnesota	2	14	7.0	14	0
Williams, Kevin, Minnesota	1	7	7.0	7	0
Williams, Roy, Dallas	2	53	26.5	33	0
Wilson, Adrian, Arizona	3	62	20.7	27	0
Wilson, Gibril, N.Y. Giants	3	39	13.0	39	0
Winborn, Jamie, San Francisco	1	1	1.0	1	0
Winfield, Antoine, Minnesota	3	89	29.7	56	0
Witherspoon, Will, Carolina	4	48	12.0	25	0

t—touchdown.

2004 STATISTICS Interceptions

SACKS

AFC

Team	Sacks	Yards
Indianapolis	45	340
Buffalo	45	319
New England	45	311
Kansas City	41	250
Pittsburgh	41	225
Baltimore	39	264
Denver	38	266
Cincinnati	37	257
N.Y. Jets	37	220
Jacksonville	37	217
Miami	36	223
Tennessee	32	220
Cleveland	32	190
San Diego	29	142
Oakland	25	182
Houston	24	161
AFC total	583	3787
AFC average	36.4	236.7

NFC

Team	Sacks	Yard
Atlanta	48	31
Philadelphia	47	26
Tampa Bay	45	26
Green Bay	40	28
N.Y. Giants	40	25
Washington	40	24
Minnesota	39	23
Arizona	38	22
Detroit	38	22
New Orleans	37	20
Seattle	36	21
Chicago	35	17
St. Louis	34	24
Carolina	34	22
Dallas	33	19
San Francisco	29	19
NFC total	613	375
NFC average	38.3	234.
NFL total	1196	754
NFL average	37.4	235.

INDIVIDUAL

BESTS OF THE SEASON

Sacks, season
AFC: 16.0—Dwight Freeney, Indianapolis.
NFC: 14.5—Bertrand Berry, Arizona.

Sacks, game
NFC: 4.0—Kabeer Gbaja-Biamila, Green Bay at Chicago, Jan. 2
Bertrand Berry, Arizona vs. N.Y. Giants, Nov. 14; Alex Brown,
Chicago at N.Y. Giants, Nov. 7
AFC: 3.0—Held by 12 players.

NFL LEADERS

Player, Team	No.
Freeney, Dwight, Indianapolis*	16.0
Berry, Bertrand, Arizona	14.5
Gbaja-Biamila, Kabeer, Green Bay	13.5
Kerney, Patrick, Atlanta	13.0
Rice, Simeon, Tampa Bay	12.0
Coleman, Rod, Atlanta	11.5
Hall, James, Detroit	11.5
Williams, Kevin, Minnesota	11.5
Peppers, Julius, Carolina	11.0
Johnstone, Lance, Minnesota	11.0

Player, Team	No
Howard, Darren, New Orleans	11.
Ellis, Shaun, N.Y. Jets*	11.
Mathis, Robert, Indianapolis*	10.
Suggs, Terrell, Baltimore*	10.
Hayward, Reggie, Denver*	10.
Grant, Charles, New Orleans	10.
Foley, Steve, San Diego*	10.
Taylor, Jason, Miami*	9.
Abraham, John, N.Y. Jets*	9.
McGinest, Willie, New England*	9.
*AFC.	

AFC

Player, Team	No.
Abraham, John, N.Y. Jets	9.5
Adams, Sam, Buffalo	5.0
Allen, Jared, Kansas City	9.0
Asomugha, Nnamdi, Oakland	1.0
Ayodele, Akin, Jacksonville	2.0
Babin, Jason, Houston	4.0
Banta-Cain, Tully, New England	1.5
Barber, Shawn, Kansas City	1.0
Barnes, Lionel, Jacksonville	1.0
Bartee, William, Kansas City	1.5
Barton, Eric, N.Y. Jets	2.5
Baxter, Gary, Baltimore	2.0
Beisel, Monty, Kansas City	2.5
Bowens, David, Miami	7.0
Brayton, Tyler, Oakland	2.5
Brock, Raheem, Indianapolis	6.5
Browning, John, Kansas City	4.5

Player, Team	No.
Bruschi, Tedy, New England	3.5
Bulluck, Keith, Tennessee	5.0
Carter, Kevin, Tennessee	6.0
Cesaire, Jacques, San Diego	0.5
Chukwurah, Patrick, Denver	1.0
Clark, Danny, Oakland	2.0
Clements, Nate, Buffalo	0.5
Clemons, Duane, Cincinnati	6.5
Colclough, Ricardo, Pittsburgh	1.5
Coleman, Erik, N.Y. Jets	2.0
Coleman, Marco, Denver	2.5
Colvin, Rosevelt, New England	5.0
Cooper, Deke, Jacksonville	1.0
Cooper, Jarrod, Oakland	1.0
Crocker, Chris, Cleveland	2.0
Dalton, Lional, Kansas City	4.0
Davis, Andra, Cleveland	0.5
Demps, Will, Baltimore	2.5
Denney, Ryan, Buffalo	3.0

Player, Team	N
Dingle, Adrian, San Diego	1
Doss, Mike, Indianapolis	1
Douglas, Marques, Baltimore	5
Edwards, Antuan, Miami	1
Edwards, Donnie, San Diego	1
Edwards, Ron, Buffalo	4
Ekuban, Ebenezer, Cleveland	8
Ellis, Shaun, N.Y. Jets	11
Elliss, Luther, Denver	2
Farrior, James, Pittsburgh	3
Fatafehi, Mario, Denver	2
Favors, Greg, Jacksonville	5
Ferguson, Jason, N.Y. Jets	3
Fisk, Jason, San Diego	1
Fletcher, London, Buffalo	3
Foley, Steve, San Diego	10
Foote, Larry, Pittsburgh	3
Freeney, Dwight, Indianapolis	16
Fujita, Scott, Kansas City	4

ayer, Team	No.	Player, Team	No.		
aja-Biamila, Akbar, Oakland	1.0	Porter, Joey, Pittsburgh	7.0		

Player, Team	No.

Left Column		Middle Column		Right Column (NFC)	
aja-Biamila, Akbar, Oakland	1.0	Porter, Joey, Pittsburgh	7.0		
athers, Robert, Cincinnati	3.5	Posey, Jeff, Buffalo	1.0	Ahanotu, Chidi, Mia.-T.B.*	4.5
don, Jason, Jacksonville	3.0	Powell, Carl, Cincinnati	2.0	Alexander, Brent, N.Y. Giants	2.0
dfrey, Randall, San Diego	2.0	Ransom, Derrick, Jacksonville	0.5	Allen, Kenderick, N.Y. Giants	1.0
ant, DeLawrence, Oakland	2.0	Reagor, Montae, Indianapolis	5.0	Allen, Will, N.Y. Giants	1.0
ant, Deon, Jacksonville	1.0	Reed, Ed, Baltimore	2.0	Archuleta, Adam, St. Louis	2.0
een, Jarvis, New England	4.0	Reed, James, N.Y. Jets	2.0	Arrington, LaVar, Washington	1.0
eer, Jabari, Buffalo	1.0	Robertson, Dewayne, N.Y. Jets	3.0	Azumah, Jerry, Chicago	1.5
egg, Kelly, Baltimore	1.5	Robinson, Dunta, Houston	3.0	Barber, Ronde, Tampa Bay	3.0
iffith, Robert, Cleveland	1.0	Rogers, Tyrone, Cleveland	1.5	Barnett, Nick, Green Bay	3.0
iggans, Clark, Pittsburgh	6.0	Romero, Dario, Miami	3.5	Beasley, Aaron, Atlanta	1.0
ill, Carlos, Tennessee	2.5	Roye, Orpheus, Cleveland	1.0	Bell, Marcus, Detroit	2.0
milton, Bobby, Oakland	1.0	Sapp, Warren, Oakland	2.5	Bernard, Rocky, Seattle	3.5
rdy, Kevin, Cincinnati	4.0	Schobel, Aaron, Buffalo	8.0	Berry, Bertrand, Arizona	14.5
rrison, James, Pittsburgh	1.0	Schulters, Lance, Tennessee	1.0	Bockwoldt, Colby, New Orleans	1.0
rrison, Rodney, New England	3.0	Scioli, Brad, Indianapolis	2.0	Boone, Alfonso, Chicago	2.5
ynesworth, Albert, Tennessee	1.0	Scott, DeQuincy, San Diego	1.5	Boulware, Michael, Seattle	1.0
yward, Reggie, Denver	10.5	Seau, Junior, Miami	1.0	Bowen, Matt, Washington	2.0
enderson, John, Jacksonville	5.5	Seymour, Richard, New England	5.0	Bradley, Jon, Tampa Bay	1.0
rndon, Kelly, Denver	1.0	Sharper, Jamie, Houston	2.0	Briggs, Lance, Chicago	0.5
cks, Eric, Kansas City	5.0	Siavii, Junior, Kansas City	1.0	Brooking, Keith, Atlanta	2.5
ke, Chris, Pittsburgh	1.0	Simmons, Brian, Cincinnati	1.0	Brooks, Derrick, Tampa Bay	3.0
oldman, Warrick, Cleveland	0.5	Sims, Ryan, Kansas City	2.0	Brown, Alex, Chicago	6.0
ons, Grant, Oakland	1.0	Smith, Aaron, Pittsburgh	8.0	Brown, Chad, Seattle	1.0
hnson, Ellis, Denver	3.0	Smith, Daryl, Jacksonville	2.0	Brown, Sheldon, Philadelphia	3.0
hnson, Landon, Cincinnati	2.0	Smith, Justin, Cincinnati	8.0	Brown, Tony, San Francisco	1.0
hnson, Raylee, Denver	1.0	Smith, Robaire, Houston	2.0	Bryant, Tony, New Orleans	2.0
hnson, Ted, New England	1.0	Spikes, Takeo, Buffalo	3.0	Buckner, Brentson, Arizona	3.5
hnson, Tim, Oakland	0.5	Spragan, Donnie, Denver	1.0	Burgess, Derrick, Philadelphia	2.5
lly, Tommy, Oakland	4.0	Starks, Randy, Tennessee	4.5	Carpenter, Dwaine, San Francisco	2.0
lsay, Chris, Buffalo	4.5	Stills, Gary, Kansas City	2.5	Carroll, Ahmad, Green Bay	2.0
nnedy, Kenoy, Denver	2.0	Stroud, Marcus, Jacksonville	4.5	Carson, Leonardo, Dallas	0.5
el, Terrence, San Diego	1.0	Suggs, Terrell, Baltimore	10.5	Carter, Andre, San Francisco	2.0
rschke, Travis, Pittsburgh	1.0	Surtain, Patrick, Miami	1.0	Claiborne, Chris, Minnesota	1.0
iewaldt, Clint, Pittsburgh	0.5	Taylor, Jason, Miami	9.5	Clemons, Chris, Washington	3.0
aBoy, Travis, Tennessee	3.5	Thomas, Adalius, Baltimore	8.0	Cochran, Antonio, Seattle	6.5
ang, Kenard, Cleveland	7.0	Thomas, Bryan, N.Y. Jets	1.5	Coleman, Kenyon, Dallas	1.0
eber, Ben, San Diego	2.0	Thomas, Josh, Indianapolis	1.0	Coleman, Rod, Atlanta	11.5
ewis, Ray, Baltimore	1.0	Thomas, Kevin, Buffalo	1.0	Cooper, Chris, San Francisco	1.0
ong, Rien, Tennessee	5.0	Thomas, Zach, Miami	2.0	Daniels, Phillip, Washington	1.0
nch, John, Denver	2.0	Thompson, Chaun, Cleveland	2.5	Dansby, Karlos, Arizona	5.0
athis, Robert, Indianapolis	10.5	Thornton, John, Cincinnati	3.0	Darling, James, Arizona	1.0
cCray, Bobby, Jacksonville	3.5	Townsend, Deshea, Pittsburgh	4.0	Davis, James, Detroit	3.5
cGarrahan, Scott, Tennessee	0.5	Vilma, Jonathan, N.Y. Jets	2.0	Davis, Russell, Arizona	1.0
cGee, Terrence, Buffalo	2.0	Vincent, Troy, Buffalo	1.0	Dawkins, Brian, Philadelphia	3.0
cGinest, Willie, New England	9.5	von Oelhoffen, Kimo, Pittsburgh	1.0	DeVries, Jared, Detroit	3.0
cKinley, Alvin, Cleveland	3.0	Vrabel, Mike, New England	5.5	Diggs, Na'il, Green Bay	1.0
eier, Rob, Jacksonville	0.5	Walker, Gary, Houston	0.5	Dixon, Tony, Dallas	3.0
iddlebrooks, Willie, Denver	1.0	Warren, Gerard, Cleveland	4.0	Dockett, Darnell, Arizona	3.5
illoy, Lawyer, Buffalo	4.0	Warren, Ty, New England	3.5	Douglas, Hugh, Philadelphia	3.0
itchell, Kawika, Kansas City	1.0	Washington, Ted, Oakland	3.0	Duckett, Damane, N.Y. Giants	1.0
oore, Langston, Cincinnati	1.0	Weaver, Anthony, Baltimore	4.0	Edwards, Kalimba, Detroit	4.5
orris, Rob, Indianapolis	3.0	Webster, Nate, Cincinnati	1.0	Ellis, Greg, Dallas	9.0
yers, Michael, Cleveland	1.0	Wilfork, Vince, New England	2.0	Emmons, Carlos, N.Y. Giants	1.0
'Neal, Deltha, Cincinnati	1.0	Wilkerson, Jimmy, Kansas City	0.5	Engelberger, John, San Francisco	6.0
dom, Antwan, Tennessee	2.0	Williams, Chad, Baltimore	2.0	Evans, Demetric, Washington	2.5
lshansky, Igor, San Diego	1.0	Williams, D.J., Denver	2.0	Fields, Mark, Carolina	4.0
alepoi, Anton, Denver	3.0	Williams, Jamal, San Diego	4.0	Fisher, Bryce, St. Louis	8.5
atterson, Elton, Jacksonville	1.0	Williams, Jay, Miami	2.0	Flowers, Erik, St. Louis	1.0
ayne, Seth, Houston	2.0	Williams, Madieu, Cincinnati	2.0	Gbaja-Biamila, Kabeer, Green Bay	13.5
eek, Antwan, Houston	2.0	Williams, Pat, Buffalo	2.5	Glover, La'Roi, Dallas	7.0
eterson, Mike, Jacksonville	5.0	Williams, Tank, Tennessee	1.0	Glymph, Junior, Atlanta	1.0
hifer, Roman, New England	1.5	Williams, Willie, Pittsburgh	1.0	Gold, Ian, Tampa Bay	0.5
hillips, Shaun, San Diego	4.0	Wilson, Al, Denver	2.5	Gooch, Jeff, Tampa Bay	0.5
olamalu, Troy, Pittsburgh	1.0	Wire, Coy, Buffalo	1.0	Grant, Charles, New Orleans	10.5
olk, DaShon, Houston	1.0	Wong, Kailee, Houston	5.5	Green, Jamaal, Philadelphia	1.0
oole, Will, Miami	1.0	Woods, Jerome, Kansas City	1.0	Green, Mike, Chicago	1.5
ope, Derrick, Miami	2.0	Woodson, Charles, Oakland	2.5	Greisen, Nick, N.Y. Giants	2.0
ope, Monsanto, Denver	1.0	Wright, Kenny, Houston	1.0		
		Zgonina, Jeff, Miami	5.0		

Player, Team	No.	Player, Team	No.	Player, Team	No
Griffin, Cornelius, Washington	6.0	McDougle, Jerome, Philadelphia	2.0	Taylor, Sean, Washington	1
Haley, Jermaine, Washington	1.0	McFarland, Anthony, Tampa Bay	3.0	Thomas, Dontarrious, Minnesota	0.
Hall, DeAngelo, Atlanta	0.5	Minter, Mike, Carolina	2.0	Thompson, Ray, Arizona	1.
Hall, James, Detroit	11.5	Mitchell, Brandon, Seattle	1.0	Tinoisamoa, Pisa, St. Louis	1.
Hall, Travis, Atlanta	3.0	Mixon, Kenny, Minnesota	2.5	Torbor, Reggie, N.Y. Giants	3.
Hamlin, Ken, Seattle	2.0	Moore, Brandon, San Francisco	1.0	Trotter, Jeremiah, Philadelphia	1.
Hand, Norman, N.Y. Giants	1.0	Moore, Rashad, Seattle	2.0	Trufant, Marcus, Seattle	1.
Hanson, Joselio, San Francisco	1.0	Moorehead, Kindal, Carolina	2.0	Truluck, R-Kal, Green Bay	2.
Hargrove, Anthony, St. Louis	1.0	Morgan, Dan, Carolina	2.0	Tubbs, Marcus, Seattle	1.
Harris, Quentin, Arizona	1.0	Navies, Hannibal, Green Bay	0.5	Udeze, Kenechi, Minnesota	5.
Harris, Tommie, Chicago	3.5	Newman, Keith, Minnesota	3.5	Ulbrich, Jeff, San Francisco	1.
Haynes, Michael, Chicago	2.0	Nguyen, Dat, Dallas	1.0	Umenyiora, Osi, N.Y. Giants	7.
Henderson, E.J., Minnesota	1.0	Noble, Brandon, Washington	1.0	Urlacher, Brian, Chicago	5.
Hill, Renaldo, Arizona	1.0	Ogbogu, Eric, Dallas	4.5	Walker, Bracy, Detroit	1.
Hillenmeyer, Hunter, Chicago	2.5	Ogunleye, Adewale, Chicago	5.0	Walker, Darwin, Philadelphia	4.
Hovan, Chris, Minnesota	1.5	Okeafor, Chike, Seattle	8.5	Wallace, Al, Carolina	1.
Howard, Darren, New Orleans	11.0	Pace, Calvin, Arizona	4.5	Warner, Ron, Washington	3.
Huff, Orlando, Seattle	1.0	Parrish, Tony, San Francisco	0.5	Washington, Keith, N.Y. Giants	1.
Hunt, Cletidus, Green Bay	2.0	Peppers, Julius, Carolina	11.0	Washington, Marcus, Washington	4.
Hunter, Pete, Dallas	1.0	Peterson, Julian, San Francisco	2.5	Watson, Courtney, New Orleans	2.
Idonije, Israel, Chicago	1.0	Phillips, Jermaine, Tampa Bay	1.0	Wayne, Nate, Philadelphia	1.
Jackson, Grady, Green Bay	1.0	Pickett, Ryan, St. Louis	2.0	White, Dewayne, Tampa Bay	6.
Jackson, Tyoka, St. Louis	4.0	Pierce, Antonio, Washington	1.0	White, Tracy, Seattle	1.
Jasper, Ed, Atlanta	2.0	Polley, Tommy, St. Louis	2.0	Wiley, Chuck, N.Y. Giants	0.
Jenkins, Cullen, Green Bay	4.5	Pritchett, Kelvin, Detroit	1.0	Wiley, Marcellus, Dallas	3.
Jenkins, Kris, Carolina	1.0	Quarles, Shelton, Tampa Bay	3.5	Wilkinson, Dan, Detroit	1.
Johnson, Spencer, Minnesota	1.0	Rayburn, Sam, Philadelphia	6.0	Williams, Corey, Green Bay	1.
Johnson, Tank, Chicago	0.5	Redding, Cory, Detroit	3.0	Williams, Davern, N.Y. Giants	0.
Johnstone, Lance, Minnesota	11.0	Reese, Ike, Philadelphia	1.0	Williams, Demorrio, Atlanta	2.
Jones, Dhani, Philadelphia	0.5	Rice, Simeon, Tampa Bay	12.0	Williams, Jimmy, San Francisco	1.
Jones, Nathan, Dallas	1.0	Robbins, Fred, N.Y. Giants	5.0	Williams, Kevin, Minnesota	11.
Jordan, Omari, Carolina	1.0	Rogers, Shaun, Detroit	4.0	Williams, Tyrone, Dallas	1.
Joseph, William, N.Y. Giants	2.0	Roman, Mark, Green Bay	3.5	Wilson, Adrian, Arizona	1.
Kacyvenski, Isaiah, Seattle	1.0	Rossum, Allen, Atlanta	1.0	Wilson, Gibril, N.Y. Giants	3.
Kampman, Aaron, Green Bay	4.5	Rucker, Mike, Carolina	3.5	Winborn, Jamie, San Francisco	4.
Kearse, Jevon, Philadelphia	7.5	Salave'a, Joe, Washington	2.0	Wistrom, Grant, Seattle	3.
Kerney, Patrick, Atlanta	13.0	Scott, Bryan, Atlanta	2.5	Witherspoon, Will, Carolina	3.
Kolodziej, Ross, Arizona	1.0	Scott, Ian, Chicago	2.0	Woodard, Cedric, Seattle	1.
Koutouvides, Niko, Seattle	1.0	Scott, Lynn, Dallas	1.0	Worrell, Cameron, Chicago	1.
Lee, James, Green Bay	1.0	Sheppard, Lito, Philadelphia	1.0	Wynn, Dexter, Philadelphia	1.
Legree, Lance, N.Y. Giants	2.0	Simon, Corey, Philadelphia	5.5	Wynn, Renaldo, Washington	3.
Lehman, Teddy, Detroit	1.0	Simoneau, Mark, Philadelphia	1.5	Young, Brian, New Orleans	2.
Leverette, Otis, San Francisco	1.0	Smith, Brady, Atlanta	6.0	Young, Bryant, San Francisco	3.
Lewis, Alex, Detroit	2.0	Smith, Derek, San Francisco	1.5	Zellner, Peppi, Arizona	2.
Lewis, Damione, St. Louis	5.0	Smith, Will, New Orleans	7.5	*Includes both NFC and AFC statistics.	
Lewis, Kevin, N.Y. Giants	1.0	Spires, Greg, Tampa Bay	8.0		
Little, Leonard, St. Louis	7.0	Springs, Shawn, Washington	6.0		
Macklin, David, Arizona	0.5	Starks, Duane, Arizona	1.0		
Marshall, Lemar, Washington	1.5	Stewart, Matt, Atlanta	1.5		
Martin, Steve, Minnesota	0.5	Strahan, Michael, N.Y. Giants	4.0		
Maxwell, James, N.Y. Giants	1.0	Sullivan, Johnathan, New Orleans	0.5		

PLAYERS WITH TWO CLUBS

Player, Team	No
Ahanotu, Chidi, Miami	1.
Ahanotu, Chidi, Tampa Bay	3.

FUMBLES

TEAM

AFC

Team	Fum.	Own Fum. Rec.	Own Fum. *O.B.	Own Fum. Lost	TD	Opp Fum. Rec.	TD	†Yards	Total Rec.
N.Y. Jets	19	13	1	5	0	14	1	31	27
Indianapolis	19	10	2	7	0	17	1	67	27
Denver	23	11	4	8	0	8	0	3	19
Pittsburgh	20	8	4	8	0	13	2	113	21
Cincinnati	17	6	1	10	0	16	1	17	22
Kansas City	20	10	0	10	0	7	1	35	17
San Diego	27	15	2	10	0	10	0	20	25
Houston	22	10	2	10	0	8	3	155	18
Jacksonville	23	9	3	11	0	11	0	-41	20
Buffalo	26	13	1	12	0	15	0	-11	28
Tennessee	33	19	2	12	0	12	1	105	31
Baltimore	26	13	1	12	1	13	1	127	26
New England	24	9	2	13	0	16	3	85	25
Oakland	23	9	1	13	0	9	0	7	18
Miami	42	23	3	16	0	10	1	24	33
Cleveland	32	10	3	19	0	13	0	-55	23
AFC total	396	188	32	176	1	192	15	682	380
AFC average	24.8	11.8	2.0	11.0	0.1	12.0	0.9	42.6	23.8

*Fumbled out of bounds.
†Includes all fumble yardage (aborted plays and recoveries of own and opponents' fumbles).

NFC

Team	Fum.	Own Fum. Rec.	Own Fum. *O.B.	Own Fum. Lost	TD	Opp Fum. Rec.	TD	†Yards	Total Rec.
Detroit	12	5	0	7	0	10	0	-4	15
Minnesota	20	10	1	9	0	11	1	35	21
Seattle	19	8	2	9	0	12	0	10	20
Green Bay	22	10	2	10	0	7	3	118	17
New Orleans	23	13	0	10	0	20	1	34	33
Washington	20	10	0	10	0	8	0	-24	18
N.Y. Giants	29	17	1	11	0	14	2	137	31
Philadelphia	17	5	1	11	0	11	0	11	16
Arizona	34	18	5	11	0	15	1	40	33
Carolina	23	11	1	11	0	12	1	48	23
Atlanta	26	11	1	14	0	13	1	0	24
Dallas	26	11	1	14	0	9	0	25	20
St. Louis	27	8	2	17	0	9	3	172	17
Tampa Bay	32	11	3	18	0	11	2	50	22
San Francisco	33	14	0	19	0	12	2	130	26
Chicago	35	13	1	21	0	12	1	135	25
NFC total	398	175	21	202	0	186	18	917	361
NFC average	24.9	10.9	1.3	12.6	0.0	11.6	1.1	57.3	22.6
NFL total	794	363	53	378	1	378	33	1599	741
NFL average	24.8	11.3	1.7	11.8	0.0	11.8	1.0	50.0	23.2

INDIVIDUAL

BESTS OF THE SEASON

Fumbles, season
NFC: 16—Michael Vick, Atlanta.
AFC: 11—Kyle Boller, Baltimore; Trent Green, Kansas City.

Fumbles, game
NFC: 4—Shaun King, Arizona at Carolina, Nov. 21; Jake Delhomme, Carolina at Atlanta, Dec. 18 (OT); Chad Hutchinson, Chicago vs. Houston, Dec. 19.
AFC: 3—Held by 6 players.

Own fumbles recovered, season
AFC: 6—Jake Plummer, Denver.
NFC: 6—Aaron Brooks, New Orleans.

Own fumbles recovered, game
AFC: 3—Lamont Brightful, Miami at Cincinnati, Sep. 19.
NFC: 2—Held by 6 players.

Opponents' fumbles recovered, season
AFC: 4—Eric Barton, N.Y. Jets; Donovin Darius, Jacksonville.
NFC: 4—Mike Green, Chicago; Leonard Little, St. Louis; Osi Umenyiora, N.Y. Giants.

Opponents' fumbles recovered, game
AFC: 2—Donovin Darius, Jacksonville at Buffalo, Sep. 12; James Farrior, Pittsburgh at Miami, Sep. 26; Kawika Mitchell, Kansas City at Tennessee, Dec. 13.
NFC: 2—Greg Spires, Tampa Bay vs. Atlanta, Dec. 5; Michael Strahan, N.Y. Giants vs. Cleveland, Sep. 26.

Yards returning fumbles, season
NFC: 95—Mike Brown, Chicago.
AFC: 68—Richard Seymour, New England.

Longest fumble return
NFC: 95—Mike Brown, Chicago at Green Bay, Sep. 19 (TD).
AFC: 68—Richard Seymour, New England at Buffalo, Oct. 3 (TD).

AFC

Player, Team	Fum.	Own Rec.	Opp. Rec.	Yds.	Tot. Rec.	TD
Abraham, Donnie, N.Y. Jets	0	0	2	39	2	1
Abraham, John, N.Y. Jets	0	0	1	0	1	0
Alexander, Roc, Denver..........	0	0	1	0	1	0
Allen, David, Jacksonville	2	0	0	0	0	0
Alston, Richard, Cleveland.....	2	0	0	0	0	0
Anderson, Charlie, Houston....	0	0	1	60	1	1
Anderson, Marques, Oak.	0	0	2	0	2	0
Askew, B.J., N.Y. Jets	0	0	1	0	1	0
Ayodele, Akin, Jacksonville.....	0	0	1	0	1	0
Babin, Jason, Houston..........	0	0	2	22	2	0
Badger, Brad, Oakland	0	1	0	0	1	0
Baker, Chris, N.Y. Jets.........	1	1	0	0	1	0
Banta-Cain, Tully, N.E.	0	0	1	0	1	0
Barton, Eric, N.Y. Jets	0	0	4	2	4	0
Bashir, Idrees, Indianapolis....	0	0	1	0	1	0
Baxter, Gary, Baltimore	1	0	0	0	0	0
Beisel, Monty, Kansas City.....	0	0	1	9	1	0
Bell, Tatum, Denver.............	1	0	0	0	0	0
Bennett, Drew, Tennessee......	3	2	0	0	2	0
Bettis, Jerome, Pittsburgh	1	1	0	0	1	0
Bledsoe, Drew, Buffalo..........	9	2	0	-56	2	0
Boller, Kyle, Baltimore...........	11	4	0	-5	4	0
Brady, Tom, New England......	7	1	0	-17	1	0
Branch, Deion, N.E.	1	1	0	-1	1	0
Brees, Drew, San Diego	7	3	0	-9	3	0
Brightful, Lamont, Miami........	3	3	0	11	3	0
Brock, Raheem, Ind.	0	0	2	0	2	0
Brown, Chris, Tennessee	6	0	0	0	0	0
Brown, Orlando, Baltimore	0	1	0	0	1	0
Brown, Troy, New England......	1	2	0	0	2	0
Buchanon, Phillip, Oakland.....	2	1	1	0	2	0
Bulluck, Keith, Tennessee	0	0	1	39	1	1
Burress, Plaxico, Pitts.	1	1	0	0	1	0
Caldwell, Reche, San Diego	1	0	0	0	0	0
Calmus, Rocky, Tennessee	0	0	1	0	1	0
Campbell, Mark, Buffalo	1	0	0	0	0	0
Carey, Vernon, Miami	0	1	0	0	1	0
Carr, David, Houston...........	10	4	0	-8	4	0
Carswell, Dwayne, Denver	0	1	0	0	1	0
Carter, Dyshod, Cleveland......	0	0	1	0	1	0
Carter, Jonathan, N.Y. Jets......	2	0	0	0	0	0
Carter, Kevin, Tennessee	0	0	1	0	1	0
Carter, Quincy, N.Y. Jets	2	0	0	0	0	0
Celestin, Oliver, N.Y. Jets	0	1	0	0	1	0
Chambers, Chris, Miami	1	0	0	-5	0	0
Chatman, Jesse, San Diego	1	0	0	0	0	0
Cheek, Steve, Kansas City	1	0	0	-7	0	0
Clark, Dallas, Indianapolis......	2	1	0	0	1	0
Clements, Nate, Buffalo	3	1	1	0	2	0
Cobbs, Cedric, New England...	1	0	0	0	0	0
Colclough, Ricardo, Pitts.	3	0	0	0	0	0
Coleman, Erik, N.Y. Jets........	0	0	1	0	1	0
Coleman, Marco, Denver	0	0	1	-2	1	0
Collins, Kerry, Oakland..........	7	3	0	-21	3	0
Cooper, Jarrod, Oakland	0	1	0	0	1	0
Cooper, Stephen, San Diego ...	0	0	1	0	1	0
Curry, Ronald, Oakland	1	1	0	0	1	0
Dalton, Lional, Kansas City.....	0	0	1	0	1	0
Darius, Donovin, Jack.	0	0	4	0	4	0
Darling, Devard, Baltimore	1	0	0	0	0	0
Davis, Andra, Cleveland	0	0	1	0	1	0
Davis, Domanick, Houston	4	0	0	0	0	0
Demps, Will, Baltimore..........	0	0	2	2	2	0
DeMulling, Rick, Ind.	1	0	0	-2	0	0
Dillon, Corey, New England.....	5	1	0	0	1	0
Droughns, Reuben, Denver.....	5	0	0	0	0	0
Echemandu, Adimchinobe, Clev.	1	0	0	0	0	0
Edwards, Troy, Jacksonville.....	3	0	0	-24	0	0
Ekuban, Ebenezer, Cleveland...	0	0	2	4	2	
Ellis, Shaun, N.Y. Jets...........	0	0	1	0	1	
Evans, Lee, Buffalo	1	1	0	0	1	
Faine, Jeff, Cleveland	2	1	0	-47	1	
Fargas, Justin, Oakland	1	0	0	0	0	
Farrior, James, Pittsburgh	0	0	3	0	3	
Fatafehi, Mario, Denver..........	0	0	1	8	1	
Faulk, Kevin, New England......	2	1	0	0	1	
Fauria, Christian, N.E.	0	1	0	0	1	
Feeley, A.J., Miami..............	10	1	0	-4	1	
Fiedler, Jay, Miami	9	1	0	0	1	
Fleming, Troy, Tennessee.......	0	1	0	0	1	
Fletcher, Jamar, San Diego	0	0	1	7	1	
Fletcher, London, Buffalo	0	0	1	0	1	
Florence, Drayton, S.D.	1	0	0	0	0	
Foley, Steve, San Diego	0	0	2	0	2	
Foote, Larry, Pittsburgh.........	0	0	1	0	1	
Foreman, Jay, Houston.........	0	0	1	3	1	
Forsey, Brock, Miami	1	0	0	0	0	
Fowler, Melvin, Cleveland	0	0	1	0	1	
Francis, Carlos, Oakland	1	0	0	0	0	
Freeman, Arturo, Miami	1	0	0	0	0	
Gabriel, Doug, Oakland	2	0	0	0	0	
Gaffney, Jabar, Houston........	1	0	0	0	0	
Gallery, Robert, Oakland	0	1	0	0	1	
Gannon, Rich, Oakland	3	1	0	0	1	
Garcia, Jeff, Cleveland	9	0	0	0	0	
Gardner, Barry, Cleveland	0	0	1	0	1	
Gardner, Rich, Tennessee	2	0	0	0	0	
Gay, Randall, New England.....	1	0	2	41	2	1
Gilmore, Bryan, Miami...........	1	0	0	0	0	
Glenn, Aaron, Houston	2	1	0	0	1	
Glenn, Jason, N.Y. Jets..........	0	1	1	2	2	
Godfrey, Randall, San Diego...	0	0	1	0	1	
Goff, Mike, San Diego...........	0	2	0	11	2	
Gonzalez, Joaquin, Clev.	0	1	0	0	1	
Gonzalez, Tony, Kansas City ...	0	1	0	0	1	
Gordon, Lamar, Miami..........	1	1	0	0	1	
Grant, Deon, Jacksonville	0	0	1	0	1	
Green, Jarvis, New England....	0	0	3	0	3	1
Green, Trent, Kansas City	11	3	0	-6	3	
Green, William, Cleveland.......	3	0	0	0	0	
Gregg, Kelly, Baltimore	0	0	1	0	1	
Griffin, Quentin, Denver.........	3	0	0	0	0	
Hadnot, Rex, Miami	0	1	0	0	1	
Haggan, Mario, Buffalo	0	2	0	0	2	
Haggans, Clark, Pittsburgh	0	0	1	0	1	
Hall, Carlos, Tennessee.........	0	0	1	0	1	
Hall, Dante, Kansas City........	1	0	0	0	0	
Hamilton, Ben, Denver..........	0	1	0	0	1	
Hardwick, Nick, San Diego	0	1	0	0	1	
Harper, Nick, Indianapolis.......	0	0	1	15	1	
Harrison, James, Pittsburgh.....	0	0	1	18	1	
Harrison, Marvin, Ind.	1	0	0	0	0	
Hartwell, Edgerton, Balt.	0	0	1	-1	1	
Hartwig, Justin, Tennessee.....	0	1	0	0	1	
Haynes, Verron, Pittsburgh.....	0	1	0	2	1	
Hayward, Reggie, Denver	0	1	0	1	1	
Heiden, Steve, Cleveland.......	1	2	0	0	2	
Henderson, John, Jack.	0	0	1	0	1	
Henry, Leonard, Miami	1	0	0	0	0	
Herndon, Kelly, Denver	0	0	1	0	1	
Hetherington, Chris, Oak.	1	0	0	0	0	
Hill, Darrell, Tennessee	0	0	1	0	1	
Holcomb, Kelly, Cleveland	1	2	0	-5	2	
Hollings, Tony, Houston.........	1	0	0	0	0	
Holmes, Priest, Kansas City.....	4	0	0	0	0	
Howard, Reggie, Miami	0	0	1	0	1	
Jackson, Frisman, Cleveland...	1	0	0	0	0	
Jackson, James, Cleveland.....	1	0	0	0	0	
James, Edgerrin, Ind.	6	1	0	0	1	

Player, Team	Fum.	Own Rec.	Opp. Rec.	Yds.	Tot. Rec.	TD
James, Jeno, Miami	0	3	0	0	3	0
James, Tory, Cincinnati	0	0	1	0	1	0
Jameson, Michael, Clev.	0	0	1	0	1	0
Johnson, Andre, Houston	1	1	0	0	1	0
Johnson, Bethel, N.E.	2	1	0	0	1	0
Johnson, Chad, Cincinnati	1	0	0	0	0	0
Johnson, Jarret, Baltimore	0	0	1	0	1	0
Johnson, Jeremi, Cincinnati	1	0	0	0	0	0
Johnson, Kevin, Baltimore	1	2	0	0	2	0
Johnson, Landon, Cin.	0	0	1	0	1	0
Johnson, Rudi, Cincinnati	4	0	0	0	0	0
Jones, Greg, Jacksonville	1	0	0	0	0	0
Jordan, LaMont, N.Y. Jets	1	0	0	0	0	0
June, Cato, Indianapolis	0	0	2	-1	2	0
Kaesviharn, Kevin, Cin.	0	0	1	3	1	1
Kassell, Brad, Tennessee	0	1	0	0	1	0
Kelly, Tommy, Oakland	0	0	1	0	1	0
Kelsay, Chris, Buffalo	0	0	2	0	2	0
Kennedy, Kenoy, Denver	0	0	1	5	1	0
Kennison, Eddie, K.C.	1	0	0	0	0	0
Kiel, Terrence, San Diego	0	0	1	0	1	0
Kitna, Jon, Cincinnati	2	1	0	-1	1	0
Klecko, Dan, New England	1	0	0	0	0	0
Knight, Sammy, Miami	1	0	1	0	1	0
Koppen, Daniel, N.E.	1	1	0	-6	1	0
Kramer, Jordan, Tennessee	0	0	1	0	1	0
Kreider, Dan, Pittsburgh	0	2	0	0	2	0
LaBoy, Travis, Tennessee	0	0	1	0	1	0
Leber, Ben, San Diego	0	0	1	25	1	0
Lee, Donald, Miami	2	1	0	8	1	0
Leftwich, Byron, Jack.	5	3	0	0	3	0
Lewis, Jamal, Baltimore	2	1	0	-2	1	0
Lewis, Jermaine, Jack.	1	1	0	0	1	0
Lewis, Ray, Baltimore	0	0	2	0	2	0
Little, Earl, Cleveland	0	0	1	14	1	0
Losman, J.P., Buffalo	1	0	0	0	0	0
Luke, Triandos, Denver	2	0	0	0	0	0
Maddox, Tommy, Pittsburgh	3	0	0	0	0	0
Madison, Sam, Miami	1	0	0	4	0	0
Manning, Peyton, Ind.	5	3	0	-3	3	0
Manuwai, Vince, Jack.	1	2	0	-3	2	0
Martin, Curtis, N.Y. Jets	2	2	0	-9	2	0
Martin, Jamar, Miami	1	0	0	0	0	0
Mason, Derrick, Tennessee	2	2	0	0	2	0
Mathis, Robert, Indianapolis	0	0	3	26	3	0
Mays, Lee, Pittsburgh	0	0	1	0	1	0
McAddley, Jason, Tenn.	1	0	0	0	0	0
McAlister, Chris, Baltimore	0	1	1	65	2	1
McCareins, Justin, N.Y. Jets	3	4	0	0	4	0
McCleon, Dexter, K.C.	0	0	1	0	1	0
McCown, Luke, Cleveland	2	1	0	-12	1	0
McGahee, Willis, Buffalo	4	0	0	0	0	0
McGee, Terrence, Buffalo	2	0	1	38	1	0
McGinest, Willie, N.E.	0	0	1	0	1	0
McIntosh, Damion, Miami	0	2	0	0	2	0
McKenzie, Kareem, N.Y. J.	0	2	0	0	2	0
McKinley, Alvin, Cleveland	0	0	2	0	2	0
McKinney, Seth, Miami	0	2	0	0	2	0
McKinney, Steve, Houston	1	0	0	-7	0	0
McMichael, Randy, Miami	2	2	0	0	2	0
McNair, Steve, Tennessee	5	1	0	0	1	0
Meester, Brad, Jacksonville	1	1	0	-14	1	0
Meier, Shad, Tennessee	1	1	0	0	1	0
Middlebrooks, Willie, Den.	0	0	1	0	1	0
Miller, Billy, Houston	1	0	0	0	0	0
Miller, Caleb, Cincinnati	0	0	1	0	1	0
Miller, Fred, Tennessee	0	1	0	0	1	0
Minor, Travis, Miami	0	1	0	0	1	0
Mitchell, Anthony, Cin.	0	0	1	0	1	0
Mitchell, Kawika, K.C.	0	0	2	39	2	1
Moore, Eddie, Miami	0	0	2	0	2	0
Moorman, Brian, Buffalo	2	2	0	0	2	0
Moreland, Earthwind, N.E.	0	0	1	0	1	0
Morgan, Quincy, Cleveland	1	0	0	0	0	0
Morris, Sammy, Miami	1	0	0	0	0	0
Morton, Johnnie, K.C.	2	1	0	0	1	0
Moses, J.J., Houston	1	0	0	0	0	0
Moss, Santana, N.Y. Jets	2	2	0	0	2	0
Moulds, Eric, Buffalo	1	0	0	0	0	0
Myers, Michael, Cleveland	0	0	1	0	1	0
Myles, Reggie, Cincinnati	0	0	1	0	1	0
Naeole, Chris, Jacksonville	1	1	0	0	1	0
Nalen, Tom, Denver	1	0	0	0	0	0
Neal, Lorenzo, San Diego	1	0	0	0	0	0
Nelson, Jim, Indianapolis	0	0	2	0	2	0
Northcutt, Dennis, Clev.	2	1	0	0	1	0
Ogden, Jonathan, Baltimore	0	1	0	0	1	0
Olivea, Shane, San Diego	0	1	0	0	1	0
Orr, Shantee, Houston	0	1	0	3	1	0
Palmer, Carson, Cincinnati	2	0	0	0	0	0
Parker, Eric, San Diego	5	4	0	-14	4	0
Pass, Patrick, New England	1	0	0	0	0	0
Patterson, Elton, Jack.	0	0	1	0	1	0
Paxton, Lonie, New England	0	0	1	0	1	0
Peek, Antwan, Houston	0	0	1	66	1	1
Peelle, Justin, San Diego	1	0	0	0	0	0
Pennington, Chad, N.Y. Jets	5	1	0	-3	0	0
Peters, Jason, Buffalo	0	0	1	0	1	0
Peterson, Mike, Jacksonville	0	0	1	0	1	0
Phifer, Roman, N.E.	0	0	1	0	1	0
Phillips, Shaun, San Diego	0	0	2	0	2	0
Pinnock, Andrew, S.D.	1	0	0	0	0	0
Pippens, Jerrell, San Diego	0	0	1	0	1	0
Plummer, Jake, Denver	6	6	0	-8	6	0
Polk, DaShon, Houston	0	0	1	0	1	0
Poole, Tyrone, New England	1	0	0	0	0	0
Pope, Derrick, Miami	0	0	1	1	1	1
Porter, Jerry, Oakland	2	0	0	0	0	0
Posey, Jeff, Buffalo	0	0	1	0	1	0
Prioleau, Pierson, Buffalo	0	0	1	12	1	0
Rabach, Casey, Baltimore	1	0	0	0	0	0
Randle El, Antwaan, Pitts.	5	2	0	0	2	0
Ratliff, Keiwan, Cincinnati	2	2	1	0	3	0
Reagor, Montae, Ind.	0	0	1	0	1	0
Redmond, J.R., Oakland	2	0	0	0	0	0
Reed, Ed, Baltimore	1	0	2	44	2	1
Reid, Dexter, New England	0	0	1	0	1	0
Rhodes, Dominic, Ind.	2	0	0	0	0	0
Richardson, Tony, K.C.	0	2	0	0	2	0
Rivers, Philip, San Diego	1	1	0	0	1	0
Roaf, Willie, Kansas City	0	1	0	0	1	0
Roethlisberger, Ben, Pitts.	2	0	0	-6	0	0
Rolle, Samari, Tennessee	0	1	1	5	2	0
Rosenfels, Sage, Miami	2	0	0	0	0	0
Russell, Cliff, Cincinnati	2	1	0	0	1	0
Sams, B.J., Baltimore	5	1	0	0	1	0
Sanders, Bob, Indianapolis	0	0	2	37	2	1
Sapp, Warren, Oakland	0	0	2	0	2	0
Saturday, Jeff, Indianapolis	0	1	0	0	1	0
Schobel, Aaron, Buffalo	0	0	3	0	3	0
Schobel, Matt, Cincinnati	1	0	1	0	1	0
Scifres, Mike, San Diego	1	1	0	0	1	0
Scott, Bart, Baltimore	0	0	1	0	1	0
Scott, Jake, Indianapolis	0	0	1	0	1	0
Seau, Junior, Miami	0	0	1	0	1	0
Seymour, Richard, N.E.	0	0	1	68	1	1
Sharper, Jamie, Houston	0	0	1	16	1	1
Shields, Will, Kansas City	0	1	0	0	1	0
Simmons, Brian, Cincinnati	0	0	1	18	1	0
Smith, Aaron, Pittsburgh	0	0	2	54	2	0
Smith, Antowain, Tennessee	2	1	0	0	1	0
Smith, Daryl, Jacksonville	0	0	1	0	1	0

Player, Team	Fum.	Own Rec.	Opp. Rec.	Yds.	Tot. Rec.	TD
Smith, Hunter, Indianapolis	0	0	1	0	1	0
Smith, Jimmy, Jacksonville	2	0	0	0	0	0
Smith, Justin, Cincinnati........	0	0	2	0	2	0
Smith, Rod, Denver	4	3	0	0	3	0
Smith, Travian, Oakland	0	0	1	0	1	0
Sorgi, Jim, Indianapolis.........	1	1	0	-5	1	0
Sowell, Jerald, N.Y. Jets	1	0	0	0	0	0
Spears, Marcus, Houston	0	1	0	0	1	0
Spencer, Cody, Tennessee	0	1	0	0	1	0
Spikes, Takeo, Buffalo............	0	0	1	0	1	0
Spragan, Donnie, Denver........	0	0	1	0	1	0
St. Clair, John, Miami	0	1	0	0	1	0
Staley, Duce, Pittsburgh	3	1	0	0	1	0
Starks, Randy, Tennessee	0	0	2	0	2	0
Stevens, Larry, Cincinnati	0	1	0	0	1	0
Stills, Gary, Kansas City.........	0	0	2	0	2	0
Stokley, Brandon, Ind.	1	2	0	0	2	0
Stroud, Marcus, Jack.............	0	0	1	0	1	0
Stuvaints, Russell, Pitts.	0	0	1	24	1	1
Suggs, Lee, Cleveland	6	1	0	0	1	0
Suggs, Terrell, Baltimore	0	0	2	24	2	0
Surtain, Patrick, Miami	0	1	1	8	2	0
Taylor, Chester, Baltimore.......	1	0	0	0	0	0
Taylor, Fred, Jacksonville	3	0	0	0	0	0
Taylor, Ike, Pittsburgh............	1	0	0	0	0	0
Taylor, Jason, Miami..............	0	0	3	1	3	0
Taylor, Travis, Baltimore.........	1	0	0	0	0	0
Teague, Trey, Buffalo.............	0	1	0	0	1	0
Thomas, Juqua, Tennessee.....	0	0	1	0	1	0
Thompson, Chaun, Clev.	0	0	1	0	1	0
Toefield, LaBrandon, Jack.	1	0	0	0	0	0
Tomlinson, LaDainian, S. D. ..	6	2	0	0	2	0
Tongue, Reggie, N.Y. Jets.......	0	0	1	0	1	0
Townsend, Deshea, Pitts.	0	0	1	0	1	0
Trafford, Rodney, Buffalo........	0	1	0	0	1	0
Troupe, Ben, Tennessee	2	1	0	0	1	0
Tucker, Ross, Buffalo.............	1	0	0	-5	0	0
Tucker, Ryan, Cleveland	0	1	0	0	1	0
Turner, Michael, San Diego.....	1	0	0	0	0	0
Villarrial, Chris, Buffalo...........	0	1	0	0	1	0
Vilma, Jonathan, N.Y. Jets	0	0	1	0	1	0
Vincent, Troy, Buffalo.............	0	0	1	0	1	0
Volek, Billy, Tennessee...........	6	3	0	0	3	0
von Oelhoffen, Kimo, Pitts.	0	0	2	21	2	0
Waddell, Michael, Tenn.	3	2	0	33	2	0
Walker, Denard, Oakland........	0	0	1	28	1	0
Walls, Raymond, Baltimore......	0	1	0	0	1	0
Wand, Seth, Houston.............	0	1	0	0	1	0
Ward, Hines, Pittsburgh	1	0	0	0	0	0
Watson, Kenny, Cincinnati	2	1	0	0	1	0
Watts, Darius, Denver............	1	0	0	0	0	0
Weaver, Anthony, Baltimore.....	0	0	1	0	1	0
Webster, Nate, Cincinnati.......	0	0	1	0	1	0
Welker, Wesley, Miami...........	4	1	0	0	1	0
Wells, Jonathan, Houston.......	1	0	0	0	0	0
Westmoreland, Eric, Clev.	0	0	1	0	1	0
Whitley, Taylor, Miami............	0	1	0	0	1	0
Wiegmann, Casey, K.C.	0	1	0	0	1	0
Wilcox, Daniel, Baltimore........	1	0	0	0	0	0
Wilfork, Vince, New England...	0	0	2	0	2	0
Wilkins, Marcus, Cincinnati	0	0	2	0	2	0
Williams, Josh, Indianapolis...	0	0	2	0	2	0
Williams, Madieu, Cincinnati...	0	0	2	-3	2	0
Williams, Maurice, Jack.	0	1	0	0	1	0
Williams, Pat, Buffalo.............	0	0	1	0	1	0
Williams, Reggie, Jack.	1	0	0	0	0	0
Williams, Shaud, Buffalo	1	2	0	0	2	0
Williams, Tank, Tennessee......	0	0	1	28	1	0
Wilson, Eugene, N.E.	0	0	2	0	2	0
Wire, Coy, Buffalo..................	0	0	1	0	1	0
Wong, Kailee, Houston	0	0	1	0	1	0
Woodson, Charles, Oakland....	0	0	1	0	1	0
Wrighster, George, Jack.	1	0	0	0	0	0
Wright, Kenyatta, N.Y. Jets	0	0	1	0	1	0
Zereoue, Amos, Oakland........	1	0	0	0	0	0

NFC

Player, Team	Fum.	Own Rec.	Opp. Rec.	Yds.	Tot. Rec.	TD
Adams, Flozell, Dallas	0	0	1	0	1	0
Adams, Mike, San Francisco...	0	0	1	0	1	0
Alexander, Brent, N.Y. G.	0	0	2	29	2	0
Alexander, Shaun, Seattle	5	2	0	0	2	0
Allen, James, New Orleans	0	0	2	1	2	0
Alstott, Mike, Tampa Bay	2	0	0	0	0	0
Ambrose, Ashley, N.O.	0	0	1	40	1	0
Anderson, Richie, Dallas.........	1	0	0	0	0	0
Archuleta, Adam, St. Louis	0	0	1	93	1	1
Ayanbadejo, Obafemi, Ariz.	1	0	0	0	0	0
Azumah, Jerry, Chicago..........	1	0	0	0	0	0
Backus, Jeff, Detroit...............	0	1	0	0	1	0
Barber, Ronde, Tampa Bay.....	0	0	2	27	2	2
Barber, Tiki, N.Y. Giants	5	2	0	0	2	0
Barlow, Kevan, S.F.	2	0	0	0	0	0
Barnes, Darian, Dallas............	1	1	0	0	1	0
Barnett, Nick, Green Bay........	0	0	1	7	1	0
Bartrum, Mike, Philadelphia....	1	1	0	0	1	0
Battle, Arnaz, San Francisco ..	2	3	0	0	3	0
Bellamy, Jay, New Orleans......	0	0	3	12	3	0
Bennett, Michael, Minnesota...	1	1	0	0	1	0
Bernard, Rocky, Seattle..........	0	0	1	0	1	0
Berry, Bertrand, Arizona..........	0	0	2	9	2	0
Bidwell, Josh, Tampa Bay	1	1	0	0	1	0
Birk, Matt, Minnesota.............	2	0	0	-31	0	0
Blake, Jeff, Philadelphia..........	1	0	0	0	0	0
Bockwoldt, Colby, N.O.	0	0	1	6	1	1
Boldin, Anquan, Arizona	1	0	0	0	0	0
Briggs, Lance, Chicago...........	0	0	1	11	1	0
Brooking, Keith, Atlanta..........	0	0	1	4	1	0
Brooks, Aaron, New Orleans...	13	6	0	-12	6	0
Broussard, Jamall, Carolina....	2	0	0	0	0	0
Brown, Alex, Chicago.............	0	0	1	0	1	0
Brown, Antonio, Wash.	1	0	0	0	0	0
Brown, Chad, Seattle	0	0	1	15	1	0
Brown, Fakhir, New Orleans....	0	0	3	2	3	0
Brown, Mike, Chicago.............	0	0	1	95	1	1
Brown, Tim, Tampa Bay..........	2	0	0	0	0	0
Bruce, Isaac, St. Louis...........	5	0	1	0	1	0
Brunell, Mark, Washington	6	2	0	-6	2	0
Bryant, Antonio, Dallas	1	0	0	0	0	0
Bryson, Shawn, Detroit...........	1	0	0	0	0	0
Bulger, Marc, St. Louis	5	0	0	0	0	0
Burleson, Nate, Minnesota.....	1	1	0	0	1	0
Butler, Jerametrius, St. L.	0	0	1	2	1	0
Campbell, Kelly, Minnesota.....	1	0	0	0	0	0
Carpenter, Dwaine, S.F.	0	0	1	80	1	1
Carroll, Ahmad, Green Bay	0	0	1	40	1	0
Carson, Leonardo, Dallas.......	0	0	1	0	1	0
Carstens, Jordan, Carolina......	0	0	1	1	1	0
Chandler, Chris, St. Louis	1	0	0	0	0	0
Chatman, Antonio, G.B.	3	0	0	0	0	0
Claiborne, Chris, Minnesota....	0	0	1	0	1	0
Clark, Desmond, Chicago	1	0	0	0	0	0
Clayton, Michael, T.B.	1	1	0	0	1	0
Clement, Anthony, Arizona......	0	1	0	0	1	0
Cloud, Michael, N.Y. Giants....	0	1	0	0	1	0
Coady, Rich, St. Louis	0	0	1	0	1	0
Coakley, Dexter, Dallas...........	0	0	1	0	1	0
Cochran, Antonio, Seattle.......	0	0	1	0	1	0
Colbert, Keary, Carolina..........	1	0	0	0	0	0
Coleman, Rod, Atlanta............	0	0	1	0	1	0
Coles, Laveranues, Wash.	1	0	0	0	0	0
Colombo, Marc, Chicago	0	1	0	0	1	0
Conwell, Ernie, N. O.	0	1	0	0	1	0
Cox, Torrie, Tampa Bay...........	0	0	1	0	1	0
Croom, Larry, Arizona.............	2	1	0	0	1	0
Crumpler, Alge, Atlanta	1	0	0	0	0	0
Culpepper, Daunte, Minn.	9	0	0	-11	0	0

Player, Team	Fum.	Own Rec.	Opp. Rec.	Yds.	Tot. Rec.	TD
Curry, Donte', Detroit	0	0	1	0	1	0
Curtis, Kevin, St. Louis	1	1	0	1	1	0
Daniels, Phillip, Washington	0	0	1	0	1	0
Dansby, Karlos, Arizona	0	0	3	0	3	0
Darby, Chartric, Tampa Bay	0	0	1	0	1	0
Darling, James, Arizona	1	0	0	0	0	0
Davenport, Najeh, G.B.	1	0	0	0	0	0
Davis, James, Detroit	0	0	1	0	1	0
Davis, Leonard, Arizona	0	2	0	0	2	0
Dawkins, Brian, Philadelphia	0	0	1	0	1	0
Dayne, Ron, N.Y. Giants	0	1	0	0	1	0
Delhomme, Jake, Carolina	12	5	0	-13	5	0
Detmer, Koy, Philadelphia	1	0	0	0	0	0
Diehl, David, N.Y. Giants	0	2	0	0	2	0
Dilfer, Trent, Seattle	1	0	0	0	0	0
Dockett, Darnell, Arizona	0	0	1	-4	1	0
Dorsey, Ken, San Francisco	5	1	0	-3	1	0
Driver, Donald, Green Bay	2	1	0	0	1	0
Drummond, Eddie, Detroit	0	0	1	0	1	0
Duckett, T.J., Atlanta	2	0	0	0	0	0
Dunn, Warrick, Atlanta	3	1	0	0	1	0
Edwards, Kalimba, Detroit	0	0	1	0	1	0
Edwards, Mario, Tampa Bay	0	0	1	0	1	0
Edwards, Steve, Chicago	0	2	0	0	2	0
Engelberger, John, S.F.	0	0	1	0	1	0
Engram, Bobby, Seattle	1	0	0	0	0	0
Evans, Heath, Seattle	1	1	0	0	1	0
Faulk, Marshall, St. Louis	2	0	0	0	0	0
Favre, Brett, Green Bay	4	1	0	-8	1	0
Ferguson, Robert, G.B.	1	1	0	16	1	0
Fields, Mark, Carolina	0	0	1	0	1	0
Finneran, Brian, Atlanta	1	0	0	0	0	0
Fisher, Tony, Green Bay	1	1	0	1	1	0
Fitzgerald, Larry, Arizona	1	1	0	0	1	0
Flowers, Erik, St. Louis	1	0	0	0	0	0
Franz, Todd, Washington	0	0	1	0	1	0
Frazier, Lance, Dallas	2	1	1	0	2	0
Friedman, Lennie, Wash.	1	1	0	-11	1	0
Galloway, Joey, Tampa Bay	3	2	0	0	2	0
Gamble, Chris, Carolina	1	1	0	0	1	0
Garza, Roberto, Atlanta	0	1	0	0	1	0
George, Eddie, Dallas	3	1	0	0	1	0
Goings, Nick, Carolina	1	1	0	0	1	0
Goodspeed, Joey, St. Louis	1	0	0	0	0	0
Grant, Charles, New Orleans	0	0	1	0	1	0
Green, Ahman, Green Bay	7	2	0	0	2	0
Green, Barrett, N.Y. Giants	0	0	2	16	2	1
Green, Mike, Chicago	0	0	4	3	4	0
Greisen, Nick, N.Y. Giants	0	0	1	0	1	0
Griese, Brian, Tampa Bay	6	2	0	-7	2	0
Griffin, Cornelius, Wash.	0	0	1	0	1	0
Grossman, Rex, Chicago	2	0	0	0	0	0
Gutierrez, Brock, S.F.	1	1	0	-7	1	0
Haayer, Adam, Minnesota	0	1	0	0	1	0
Haley, Jermaine, Wash.	0	0	1	0	1	0
Hall, Cory, Atlanta	0	0	1	0	1	0
Hall, James, Detroit	0	0	1	0	1	0
Hall, Travis, Atlanta	0	0	1	0	1	0
Harper, Deveron, N.O.	0	0	1	0	1	0
Harrington, Joey, Detroit	6	0	0	-6	0	0
Harris, Arlen, St. Louis	1	0	0	0	0	0
Harris, Quentin, Arizona	0	0	1	0	1	0
Hasselbeck, Matt, Seattle	5	2	0	-8	2	0
Hawkins, Artrell, Carolina	1	0	0	0	0	0
Hawthorne, Michael, G. B.	0	0	2	34	2	1
Hayes, Gerald, Arizona	1	0	1	0	1	0
Heard, Ronnie, S.F.	0	0	1	0	1	0
Heitmann, Eric, S.F.	0	1	0	0	1	0
Heller, Will, Tampa Bay	1	1	0	0	1	0
Henson, Drew, Dallas	1	0	0	0	0	0
Hicks, Maurice, S.F.	3	2	0	0	2	0
Hillenmeyer, Hunter, Chi.	0	0	1	13	1	0
Hilliard, Ike, N.Y. Giants	3	1	0	0	1	0
Holt, Torry, St. Louis	3	3	0	0	3	0
Hood, Roderick, Phil.	1	0	3	1	3	0
Hoover, Brad, Carolina	0	1	1	0	2	0
Hovan, Chris, Minnesota	0	0	1	0	2	0
Howard, Darren, N. O.	0	0	3	0	3	0
Huff, Orlando, Seattle	0	0	2	0	2	0
Hutchinson, Chad, Chicago	8	2	0	-11	2	0
Hutchinson, Steve, Seattle	1	2	0	0	2	0
Ivy, Corey, Tampa Bay	0	1	0	0	1	0
Jackson, Darrell, Seattle	2	0	0	0	0	0
Jackson, Steven, St. Louis	1	0	0	0	0	0
Jackson, Terry, S.F.	3	1	0	0	1	0
Jasper, Ed, Atlanta	0	0	2	0	2	0
Jenkins, Cullen, Green Bay	0	0	1	0	1	0
Jenkins, Michael, Atlanta	0	1	0	0	1	0
Johnson, Al, Dallas	1	0	0	-8	0	0
Johnson, Brad, Tampa Bay	2	0	0	0	0	0
Johnson, Bryant, Arizona	1	0	0	0	0	0
Johnson, Eric, S.F.	1	1	0	0	1	0
Johnson, Keyshawn, Dallas	1	1	0	0	1	0
Johnson, Spencer, Minn.	1	0	0	0	0	0
Johnson, Todd, Chicago	0	0	1	0	1	0
Jones, Dhani, Philadelphia	0	0	1	0	1	0
Jones, Freddie, Arizona	0	1	0	0	1	0
Jones, Julius, Dallas	3	0	0	0	0	0
Jones, Kevin, Detroit	2	1	0	0	1	0
Jones, Mark, N.Y. Giants	1	1	0	0	1	0
Jones, Tebucky, N.O.	0	0	1	0	1	0
Jones, Thomas, Chicago	2	0	0	0	0	0
Kampman, Aaron, G.B.	0	0	1	3	1	0
Kearse, Jevon, Philadelphia	0	0	1	0	1	0
Kelly, Brian, Tampa Bay	0	0	1	32	1	0
Kerney, Patrick, Atlanta	0	0	1	0	1	0
King, Shaun, Arizona	4	1	0	-3	1	0
Krenzel, Craig, Chicago	8	1	0	-11	1	0
Kreutz, Olin, Chicago	1	1	0	0	1	0
Lavalais, Chad, Atlanta	0	0	2	0	2	0
Lee, Charles, Tampa Bay	1	0	0	0	0	0
Lewis, Keith, San Francisco	0	0	1	0	1	0
Lewis, Kevin, N.Y. Giants	0	0	1	16	1	0
Lewis, Michael, N.O.	1	0	0	0	0	0
Lewis, Michael, Phil.	0	0	1	0	1	0
Little, Leonard, St. Louis	0	0	4	66	4	2
Liwienski, Chris, Minnesota	0	1	0	0	1	0
Looker, Dane, St. Louis	1	0	0	0	0	0
Lucas, Ken, Seattle	0	0	2	3	2	0
Lucier, Wayne, N.Y. Giants	0	1	0	0	1	0
Macklin, David, Arizona	0	0	1	1	1	0
Mahan, Sean, Tampa Bay	1	0	0	0	0	0
Mahe, Reno, Philadelphia	1	1	0	0	1	0
Manning, Eli, N.Y. Giants	3	0	0	-9	0	0
Manning, Ricky, Carolina	1	0	0	0	0	0
Marshall, Torrance, G.B.	0	1	0	0	1	0
Martin, Jamie, St. Louis	1	0	0	0	0	0
McAllister, Deuce, N.O.	5	2	0	0	2	0
McBriar, Mat, Dallas	1	1	0	0	1	0
McCadam, Kevin, Atlanta	0	0	1	0	1	0
McClure, Todd, Atlanta	0	1	0	0	1	0
McCollum, Andy, St. Louis	0	1	0	0	1	0
McCown, Josh, Arizona	12	2	0	0	2	0
McDonald, Shaun, St. Louis	4	1	0	0	1	0
McFarland, Anthony, T.B.	0	0	1	0	1	0
McKie, Jason, Chicago	1	0	0	0	0	0
McKinnie, Bryant, Minn.	0	1	0	0	1	0
McMahon, Mike, Detroit	1	1	0	0	1	0
McMillon, Todd, Chicago	0	2	0	0	2	0
McNabb, Donovan, Phil.	8	1	0	-6	1	0
McQuarters, R.W., Chicago	5	1	1	3	2	0
Mikell, Quintin, Philadelphia	0	0	1	0	1	0

Player, Team	Fum.	Own Rec.	Opp. Rec.	Yds.	Tot. Rec.	TD
Minter, Mike, Carolina	0	0	2	0	2	0
Mitchell, Qasim, Chicago	0	1	0	0	1	0
Moore, Mewelde, Minn.	0	1	0	0	1	0
Moore, Rashad, Seattle	0	0	3	0	3	0
Moorehead, Kindal, Carolina	0	0	1	0	1	0
Morgan, Dan, Carolina	0	0	2	0	2	0
Morton, Chad, Washington	0	1	0	0	1	0
Moss, Randy, Minnesota	1	0	0	0	0	0
Muhammad, Muhsin, Car.	3	1	0	0	1	0
Nall, Craig, Green Bay	1	0	0	0	0	0
Nece, Ryan, Tampa Bay	0	0	1	0	1	0
Nesbit, Jamar, New Orleans	0	1	0	0	1	0
Nguyen, Dat, Dallas	0	0	1	9	1	0
Nutten, Tom, St. Louis	0	1	0	0	1	0
O'Neil, Keith, Dallas	0	0	1	0	1	0
Ogbogu, Eric, Dallas	0	0	1	0	1	0
Ogunleye, Adewale, Chicago	0	0	1	7	1	0
Ohalete, Ifeanyi, Arizona	0	1	1	0	2	0
Owens, Terrell, Philadelphia	2	0	0	0	0	0
Parrish, Tony, S.F.	0	0	1	8	1	0
Pathon, Jerome, N.O.	1	0	0	0	0	0
Peppers, Julius, Carolina	0	0	1	60	1	1
Peterson, Julian, S.F.	1	0	0	0	0	0
Petitgout, Luke, N.Y. Giants	0	1	0	0	1	0
Pickett, Cody, San Francisco	1	0	0	0	0	0
Pierce, Antonio, Wash.	0	0	2	2	2	0
Pinner, Artose, Detroit	0	1	0	0	1	0
Pittman, Michael, T.B.	6	0	0	0	0	0
Player, Scott, Arizona	1	1	0	0	1	0
Ponder, Willie, N.Y. Giants	1	0	0	0	0	0
Portis, Clinton, Washington	5	2	0	0	2	0
Quinn, Jonathan, Chicago	2	0	0	0	0	0
Raiola, Dominic, Detroit	0	1	0	0	1	0
Ramsey, Patrick, Wash.	6	1	0	-5	1	0
Rasheed, Saleem, S.F.	0	0	1	0	1	0
Rattay, Tim, San Francisco	11	2	0	-8	2	0
Redding, Cory, Detroit	0	0	2	0	2	0
Reeves, Jacques, Dallas	0	0	1	0	1	0
Riley, Victor, New Orleans	0	1	0	0	1	0
Rivers, Marcellus, N.Y. G.	1	2	0	0	2	0
Robertson, Jamal, S.F.	3	0	0	0	0	0
Robinson, Marcus, Minn.	1	0	0	0	0	0
Rogers, Shaun, Detroit	0	0	1	0	1	0
Rossum, Allen, Atlanta	2	1	0	0	1	0
Royal, Robert, Washington	0	1	0	0	1	0
Rucker, Mike, Carolina	0	0	1	0	1	0
Runyan, Jon, Philadelphia	0	1	0	0	1	0
Russell, Brian, Minnesota	0	0	1	0	1	0
Ryan, Sean, Dallas	0	1	0	1	1	0
Saipaia, Blaine, St. Louis	0	1	0	0	1	0
Samuels, Chris, Washington	0	2	0	0	2	0
Schaub, Matt, Atlanta	1	0	0	0	0	0
Schroeder, Bill, Tampa Bay	2	1	0	0	1	0
Scobey, Josh, Arizona	1	1	0	0	1	0
Scott, Bryan, Atlanta	0	0	1	1	1	0
Scott, Darrion, Minnesota	0	0	2	0	2	0
Scott, Ian, Chicago	0	0	1	9	1	0
Scott, Lynn, Dallas	0	0	1	26	1	0
Shaffer, Kevin, Atlanta	0	1	0	0	1	0
Sharper, Darren, Green Bay	0	0	1	15	1	1
Shiancoe, Visanthe, N.Y. G.	0	1	0	0	1	0
Shockey, Jeremy, N.Y. G.	1	0	0	0	0	0
Short, Brandon, Carolina	0	1	0	0	1	0
Simms, Chris, Tampa Bay	3	1	0	0	1	0
Simoneau, Mark, Phil.	0	0	1	7	1	0
Smart, Rod, Carolina	1	0	0	0	0	0
Smith, Brady, Atlanta	0	0	2	0	2	1
Smith, Derek, San Francisco	0	0	2	46	2	1
Smith, Emmitt, Arizona	4	2	0	4	2	0
Smith, Onterrio, Minnesota	2	1	0	0	1	0
Smith, Will, New Orleans	0	0	1	-1	1	0
Smoot, Fred, Washington	0	0	1	0	1	0
Snee, Chris, N.Y. Giants	0	3	0	0	3	0
Spires, Greg, Tampa Bay	0	0	2	0	2	0
Stallworth, Donte', N.O.	0	1	0	0	1	0
Starks, Duane, Arizona	0	0	2	2	2	0
Stecker, Aaron, N.O.	1	0	0	-14	0	0
Steele, Ben, Green Bay	0	1	0	0	1	0
Stepanovich, Alex, Arizona	0	2	0	-4	2	0
Steussie, Todd, Tampa Bay	0	1	0	0	1	0
Strahan, Michael, N.Y. G.	0	0	3	0	3	0
Strong, Mack, Seattle	2	0	0	0	0	0
Swinton, Reggie, Detroit	1	0	0	0	0	0
Terrell, David, Chicago	1	0	0	0	0	0
Testaverde, Vinny, Dallas	8	4	0	-3	4	0
Thomas, Anthony, Chicago	1	1	0	0	1	0
Thomas, Dontarrious, Minn.	0	0	1	2	1	0
Thomas, Fred, New Orleans	0	0	2	0	2	0
Thomas, Hollis, Philadelphia	0	0	1	0	1	0
Tillman, Charles, Chicago	0	1	0	4	1	0
Tinoisamoa, Pisa, St. Louis	0	0	1	10	1	0
Tobeck, Robbie, Seattle	0	1	0	0	1	0
Toomer, Amani, N.Y. Giants	1	0	0	0	0	0
Torbor, Reggie, N.Y. Giants	0	0	1	0	1	0
Udeze, Kenechi, Minnesota	0	0	1	-2	1	0
Umenyiora, Osi, N.Y. Giants	0	0	4	88	4	1
Urban, Jerheme, Seattle	1	0	0	0	0	0
Vasher, Nathan, Chicago	0	0	1	12	1	0
Vick, Michael, Atlanta	16	4	0	-5	4	0
Wade, Bobby, Chicago	2	0	0	0	0	0
Wade, John, Tampa Bay	1	0	0	-2	0	0
Wahle, Mike, Green Bay	0	1	0	0	1	0
Walker, Bracy, Detroit	0	0	2	2	2	0
Walker, Javon, Green Bay	2	1	0	11	1	0
Wallace, Al, Carolina	0	0	1	0	1	0
Ward, Dedric, Dallas	1	1	0	0	1	0
Ward, Derrick, N.Y. Giants	1	0	0	0	0	0
Ware, Kevin, San Francisco	0	1	0	0	1	0
Ware, Matt, Philadelphia	0	0	1	9	1	0
Warner, Kurt, N.Y. Giants	12	1	0	-3	1	0
Washington, Marcus, Wash.	0	0	1	-4	1	0
Weiner, Todd, Atlanta	0	1	0	0	1	0
Westbrook, Brian, Phil.	1	0	0	0	0	0
White, Dewayne, Tampa Bay	0	0	1	0	1	0
Wiggins, Jermaine, Minn.	1	1	0	0	1	0
Williams, Boo, New Orleans	2	1	0	0	1	0
Williams, Jimmy, S.F.	0	0	1	0	1	0
Williams, Karl, Arizona	4	1	0	0	1	0
Williams, Kevin, Minnesota	0	0	3	77	3	1
Williams, Moe, Minnesota	1	0	0	0	1	0
Williams, Roy, Detroit	1	0	0	0	0	0
Willig, Matt, Carolina	0	1	0	0	1	0
Wilson, Adrian, Arizona	0	0	2	35	2	0
Winborn, Jamie, S.F.	0	1	1	10	2	0
Winfield, Antoine, Minn.	0	0	1	0	1	0
Wistrom, Grant, Seattle	0	0	1	0	1	0
Witherspoon, Will, Carolina	0	0	1	0	1	0
Withrow, Cory, Minnesota	0	1	0	0	1	0
Witten, Jason, Dallas	2	0	0	0	0	0
Woodard, Cedric, Seattle	0	0	1	0	1	0
Woods, LeVar, Arizona	0	1	0	0	1	0
Wynn, Dexter, Philadelphia	1	1	0	0	1	0
Young, Brian, New Orleans	0	0	1	0	1	0
Young, Bryant, S.F.	0	0	1	4	1	0
Zellner, Peppi, Arizona	0	0	1	0	1	0

FIELD GOALS

TEAM

AFC

Team	Made	Att.	Pct.	Long
ndianapolis	37	37	1.000	50
ew England	31	33	.939	48
altimore	29	32	.906	50
akland	25	28	.893	52
incinnati	27	31	.871	53
uffalo	24	28	.857	43
enver	29	34	.853	52
ittsburgh	28	33	.848	51
.Y. Jets	24	29	.828	53
leveland	24	29	.828	50
iami	19	23	.826	51
an Diego	20	25	.800	53
acksonville	24	31	.774	53
ndianapolis	20	26	.769	47
ansas City	17	23	.739	50
ouston	17	24	.708	50
ennessee	19	27	.704	50
AFC total	337	456	...	53
AFC average	23.6	28.5	.827	...

NFC

Team	Made	Att.	Pct.	Long
Seattle	23	25	.920	54
Green Bay	24	28	.857	53
Detroit	24	28	.857	48
Philadelphia	27	32	.844	51
San Francisco	18	22	.818	51
Minnesota	18	22	.818	48
New Orleans	22	27	.815	53
Carolina	20	25	.800	54
St. Louis	19	24	.792	53
N.Y. Giants	22	28	.786	53
Atlanta	18	23	.783	47
Dallas	20	26	.769	49
Arizona	22	29	.759	55
Washington	19	27	.704	49
Chicago	15	24	.625	53
Tampa Bay	15	24	.625	53
NFC total	326	414	...	55
NFC average	20.4	25.9	.787	...
NFL total	703	870	...	55
NFL average	22.0	27.2	.808	...

INDIVIDUAL

BESTS OF THE SEASON

Field goal percentage, season
AFC: .939—Adam Vinatieri, New England.
NFC: .920—Josh Brown, Seattle.

Field goals, season
AFC: 31—Adam Vinatieri, New England.
NFC: 27—David Akers, Philadelphia.

Field goal attempts, season
AFC: 34—Jason Elam, Denver.
NFC: 32—David Akers, Philadelphia.

Longest field goal
NFC: 55—Neil Rackers, Arizona vs. Seattle, Oct. 24; Neil Rackers, Arizona vs. Seattle, Oct. 24.
AFC: 53—Held by 5 players.

Average yards made, season
NFC: 39.8—David Akers, Philadelphia.
AFC: 39.1—Olindo Mare, Miami.

NFL LEADERS

Team	Made	Att.	Pct.	Long
Vinatieri, Adam, New England*	31	33	.939	48
Brown, Josh, Seattle	23	25	.920	54
Stover, Matt, Baltimore*	29	32	.906	50
Janikowski, Sebastian, Oakland*	25	28	.893	52
Graham, Shayne, Cincinnati*	27	31	.871	53
Kasay, John, Carolina	19	22	.864	54
Hanson, Jason, Detroit	24	28	.857	48
Longwell, Ryan, Green Bay	24	28	.857	53
Lindell, Rian, Buffalo*	24	28	.857	43
Elam, Jason, Denver*	29	34	.853	52

*AFC.

Leader based on percentage, minimum 16 attempts.

AFC

Player, Team	1-19	20-29	30-39	40-49	50 & Over	Totals	Avg. Yds. Att.	Avg. Yds. Made	Avg. Yds. Miss	Long
Anderson, Gary	0-0	4-5	4-4	9-12	0-1	17-22	37.6	36.7	40.6	45
Tennessee	...	.800	1.000	.750	.000	.773				
Brien, Doug	0-0	9-10	4-6	10-11	1-2	24-29	35.9	35.5	38.2	53
N.Y. Jets	...	.900	.667	.909	.500	.828				
Brown, Kris	0-0	7-7	3-5	6-9	1-3	17-24	37.5	34.9	43.7	50
Houston	...	1.000	.600	.667	.333	.708				
Bryant, Matt	0-0	1-1	0-0	2-3	0-0	3-4	40.5	39.3	44.0	47
Ind.-Mia.	...	1.000		.667		.750				
Dawson, Phil	0-0	11-11	6-8	6-9	1-1	24-29	34.7	33.5	40.6	50
Cleveland	...	1.000	.750	.667	1.000	.828				
Elam, Jason	0-0	10-10	7-8	9-12	3-4	29-34	36.1	34.7	44.0	52
Denver	...	1.000	.875	.750	.750	.853				
Elling, Aaron	0-0	1-1	0-1	0-0	0-0	1-2	27.5	22.0	33.0	22
Tennessee	...	1.000	.000			.500				
Graham, Shayne	0-0	7-7	10-12	7-8	3-4	27-31	37.2	36.3	43.0	53
Cincinnati	...	1.000	.833	.875	.750	.871				
Gramatica, Bill	0-0	2-2	1-1	0-0	0-0	3-3	29.0	29.0	-	30
Miami	...	1.000	1.000			1.000				
Hentrich, Craig	0-0	0-0	0-0	0-0	1-3	1-3	53.3	50.0	55.0	50
Tennessee	...	...	...	...	.333	.333				
Janikowski, Sebastian	1-1	7-7	7-8	8-10	2-2	25-28	36.3	35.5	43.0	52
Oakland	1.000	1.000	.875	.800	1.000	.893				

Player, Team	1-19	20-29	30-39	40-49	50 & Over	Totals	Avg. Yds. Att.	Avg. Yds. Made	Avg. Yds. Miss	Long
Kaeding, Nate	1-1	9-11	2-2	5-6	3-5	20-25	35.3	34.0	40.6	5
San Diego	1.000	.818	1.000	.833	.600	.800				
Lindell, Rian	0-0	13-14	10-11	1-3	0-0	24-28	29.5	28.1	37.8	4
Buffalo	...	.929	.909	.333	...	.857				
Mare, Olindo	0-0	1-2	6-7	3-4	2-3	12-16	39.0	39.1	38.8	5
Miami	...	.500	.857	.750	.667	.750				
Reed, Jeff	1-1	8-9	12-13	5-8	2-2	28-33	34.0	33.1	38.8	5
Pittsburgh	1.000	.889	.923	.625	1.000	.848				
Scobee, Josh	0-0	10-10	8-11	5-7	1-3	24-31	35.2	32.9	43.1	5
Jacksonville	...	1.000	.727	.714	.333	.774				
Stover, Matt	2-2	9-9	7-8	9-10	2-3	29-32	34.8	34.1	41.7	5
Baltimore	1.000	1.000	.875	.900	.667	.906				
Tynes, Lawrence	0-0	5-5	7-8	3-6	2-4	17-23	37.9	35.2	45.5	5
Kansas City	...	1.000	.875	.500	.500	.739				
Vanderjagt, Mike	0-0	6-6	9-11	5-7	0-1	20-25	35.5	33.4	44.2	4
Indianapolis	...	1.000	.818	.714	.000	.800				
Vinatieri, Adam	0-0	13-13	7-7	11-12	0-1	31-33	34.9	34.0	48.5	4
New England	...	1.000	1.000	.917	.000	.939				
Welker, Wesley	0-0	1-1	0-0	0-0	0-0	1-1	29.0	29.0	...	2
Miami	...	1.000	...	...	...	1.000				

NFC

Player, Team	1-19	20-29	30-39	40-49	50 & Over	Totals	Avg. Yds. Att.	Avg. Yds. Made	Avg. Yds. Miss	Long
Akers, David	0-0	4-4	6-7	15-18	2-3	27-32	40.8	39.8	46.0	5
Philadelphia	...	1.000	.857	.833	.667	.844				
Andersen, Morten	1-1	8-8	5-7	4-6	0-0	18-22	33.5	31.7	41.5	48
Minnesota	1.000	1.000	.714	.667	...	.818				
Brown, Josh	1-1	7-7	8-9	6-7	1-1	23-25	34.5	34.0	40.5	54
Seattle	1.000	1.000	.889	.857	1.000	.920				
Carney, John	0-0	3-3	12-15	5-6	2-3	22-27	38.7	38.0	42.0	53
New Orleans	...	1.000	.800	.833	.667	.815				
Chandler, Jeff	0-0	4-4	0-2	1-1	0-1	5-8	34.8	29.0	44.3	49
Car.-Was.	...	1.000	.000	1.000	.000	.625				
Christie, Steve	1-1	8-8	6-8	4-7	3-4	22-28	35.5	33.6	42.3	5
N.Y. Giants	1.000	1.000	.750	.571	.750	.786				
Cundiff, Billy	1-1	6-6	4-4	9-13	0-2	20-26	38.0	35.3	47.0	49
Dallas	1.000	1.000	1.000	.692	.000	.769				
Edinger, Paul	0-0	6-7	2-5	4-7	3-5	15-24	38.9	36.3	43.2	53
Chicago	...	.857	.400	.571	.600	.625				
Feely, Jay	1-1	7-7	7-9	3-6	0-0	18-23	33.5	30.8	43.2	47
Atlanta	1.000	1.000	.778	.500	...	.783				
Gramatica, Martin	0-0	6-7	3-6	1-5	1-1	11-19	34.6	31.1	39.5	53
Tampa Bay	...	.857	.500	.200	1.000	.579				
Hall, John	1-1	3-3	3-3	1-3	0-1	8-11	33.3	29.0	44.7	46
Washington	1.000	1.000	1.000	.333	.000	.727				
Hanson, Jason	0-0	9-9	10-11	5-8	0-0	24-28	33.6	31.9	43.8	48
Detroit	...	1.000	.909	.625	...	.857				
Kasay, John	0-0	11-11	4-4	1-2	3-5	19-22	34.4	31.5	52.7	54
Carolina	...	1.000	1.000	.500	.600	.864				
Kimrin, Ola	0-0	3-3	2-3	1-3	0-1	6-10	36.4	30.5	45.3	41
Washington	...	1.000	.667	.333	.000	.600				
Longwell, Ryan	0-0	8-8	8-9	6-8	2-3	24-28	36.8	35.5	44.3	53
Green Bay	...	1.000	.889	.750	.667	.857				
Peterson, Todd	1-1	3-3	7-8	5-6	2-4	18-22	37.8	35.9	46.3	5
San Francisco	1.000	1.000	.875	.833	.500	.818				
Rackers, Neil	0-0	6-6	5-7	6-7	5-9	22-29	40.6	38.0	48.6	55
Arizona	...	1.000	.714	.857	.556	.759				
Sauerbrun, Todd	0-0	0-0	1-1	0-0	0-0	1-1	34.0	34.0	-	34
Carolina	...	...	1.000	...	...	1.000				
Taylor, Jay	0-0	0-0	2-3	1-1	1-1	4-5	37.6	39.5	30.0	50
Tampa Bay	...	...	.667	1.000	1.000	.800				
Wilkins, Jeff	0-0	7-7	5-6	3-6	4-5	19-24	38.1	36.6	43.8	53
St. Louis	...	1.000	.833	.500	.800	.792				

PLAYERS WITH TWO CLUBS

Player, Team	1-19	20-29	30-39	40-49	50 & Over	Totals	Avg. Yds. Att.	Avg. Yds. Made	Avg. Yds. Miss	Long
Bryant, Matt	0-0	0-0	0-0	0-1	0-0	0-1	44.0	...	44.0	...
Indianapolis	...	...	.000	...		.000				
Bryant, Matt	0-0	1-1	0-0	2-2	0-0	3-3	39.3	39.3	...	47
Miami	1.000	...	1.000	...		1.000				
Chandler, Jeff	0-0	0-0	0-2	0-0	0-0	0-2	19.0	...	19.0	...
Carolina	...	.000	...	...		.000				
Chandler, Jeff	0-0	4-4	0-0	1-1	0-1	5-6	33.7	29.0	57.0	49
Washington	1.000	...	1.000	.000		.833				

PUNTING

TEAM

AFC

Team	Total Punts	Yards	Long	Avg.	TB	Blk.	Opp. Ret.	Ret. Yards	In. 20	Net Avg.
Oakland	73	3409	67	46.7	14	0	35	413	22	37.2
Indianapolis	54	2443	62	45.2	3	0	29	395	21	36.8
Buffalo	78	3362	80	43.1	10	0	37	315	17	36.5
San Diego	69	2974	60	43.1	8	0	23	164	29	38.4
Pittsburgh	67	2879	61	43.0	6	0	34	252	24	37.4
Tennessee	79	3389	64	42.9	9	0	31	195	21	38.2
Jacksonville	84	3592	69	42.8	9	0	38	429	28	35.5
New England	56	2350	69	42.0	5	0	31	365	19	33.7
Cincinnati	84	3499	66	41.7	7	1	51	378	21	35.5
Miami	99	4107	67	41.5	10	0	45	258	29	36.9
Houston	73	3009	57	41.2	7	0	30	265	19	35.7
Baltimore	97	3935	61	40.6	15	0	36	281	34	34.6
Denver	70	2834	66	40.5	7	1	32	295	19	34.3
Cleveland	85	3404	54	40.0	4	0	48	313	24	35.4
Kansas City	55	2172	58	39.5	7	0	24	301	12	31.5
N.Y. Jets	80	3057	58	38.2	8	0	34	221	22	33.5
AFC total	1203	50415	80	...	129	2	558	4840	361	...
AFC average	75.2	3150.9	...	41.9	8.1	0.1	34.9	302.5	22.6	35.7

Leader based on average.

NFC

Team	Total Punts	Yards	Long	Avg.	TB	Blk.	Opp. Ret.	Ret. Yards	In. 20	Net Avg.
Washington	104	4544	61	43.7	8	1	65	727	30	35.2
New Orleans	85	3704	63	43.6	4	0	43	310	28	39.0
Carolina	79	3402	65	43.1	9	1	38	303	25	36.9
Arizona	99	4230	57	42.7	7	1	56	486	32	36.4
Chicago	110	4691	58	42.6	5	0	57	380	35	38.3
Dallas	76	3216	68	42.3	7	0	39	410	23	35.1
Philadelphia	73	3068	62	42.0	7	0	34	221	20	37.1
St. Louis	68	2848	63	41.9	6	0	35	416	21	34.0
Tampa Bay	83	3472	60	41.8	7	1	31	279	23	36.8
San Francisco	96	3990	81	41.6	8	0	51	445	25	35.3
Atlanta	76	3082	56	40.6	7	0	33	134	19	36.9
Detroit	93	3765	60	40.5	7	1	46	441	32	34.2
N.Y. Giants	77	3088	55	40.1	4	2	38	356	24	34.4
Green Bay	66	2644	64	40.1	7	0	34	301	16	33.4
Minnesota	57	2240	61	39.3	3	0	26	169	18	35.3
Seattle	79	3036	60	38.4	4	2	33	244	20	34.3
NFC total	1321	55020	81	...	100	9	659	5622	391	...
NFC average	82.6	3438.8	...	41.7	6.3	0.6	41.2	351.4	24.4	35.9
NFL total	2524	105435	81	...	229	11	1217	10462	752	...
NFL average	78.9	3294.8	...	41.8	7.2	0.3	38.0	326.9	23.5	35.8

INDIVIDUAL

BESTS OF THE SEASON

Average yards per punt, season
AFC: 46.7—Shane Lechler, Oakland.
NFC: 44.1—Tom Tupa, Washington.

Net average yards per punt, season
NFC: 39.0—Mitch Berger, New Orleans.
AFC: 38.4—Mike Scifres, San Diego.

Longest
NFC: 81—Andy Lee, San Francisco at Tampa Bay, Nov. 21.
AFC: 80—Brian Moorman, Buffalo vs. Jacksonville, Sep. 12.

Punts, season
NFC: 108—Brad Maynard, Chicago.
AFC: 98—Matt Turk, Miami.

Punts, game
NFC: 11—Brad Maynard, Chicago at Tennessee, Nov. 14 (OT).
AFC: 10—Nick Murphy, Baltimore at New England, Nov. 28; Matt Turk, Miami at Cincinnati, Sep. 19; Kyle Larson, Cincinnati vs. Miami, Sep. 19.

2004 STATISTICS Punting

AFC

Player, Team	Net Punts	Yards	Long	Avg.	Total Punts	TB	Blk.	Opp. Ret.	Ret. Yds.	In. 20	Net Avg.
Baker, Jason, K.C.-Den.	24	931	52	38.8	24	1	0	10	153	10	31.6
Cheek, Steve, Kansas City	42	1643	55	39.1	42	6	0	18	197	8	31.6
Elling, Aaron, Tennessee	6	272	58	45.3	6	1	0	2	11	1	40.2
Frost, Derrick, Cleveland	85	3404	54	40.0	85	4	0	48	313	24	35.4
Gardocki, Chris, Pittsburgh	67	2879	61	43.0	67	6	0	34	252	24	37.4
Gowin, Toby, N.Y. Jets	80	3057	58	38.2	80	- 8	0	34	221	22	33.5
Hanson, Chris, Jacksonville	84	3592	69	42.8	84	9	0	38	429	28	35.5
Hentrich, Craig, Tennessee	73	3117	64	42.7	73	8	0	29	184	20	38.0
Knorr, Micah, Denver	54	2243	66	41.5	55	6	1	26	240	12	34.2
Larson, Kyle, Cincinnati	83	3499	66	42.2	84	7	1	51	378	21	35.5
Lechler, Shane, Oakland	73	3409	67	46.7	73	14	0	35	413	22	37.2
Lindell, Rian, Buffalo	1	37	37	37.0	1	1	0	0	0	0	17.0
Mare, Olindo, Miami	1	19	19	19.0	1	0	0	1	17	0	2.0
Miller, Josh, New England	56	2350	69	42.0	56	5	0	31	365	19	33.7
Moorman, Brian, Buffalo	77	3325	80	43.2	77	9	0	37	315	17	36.8
Murphy, Nick, Bal.-K.C.	22	966	58	43.9	22	3	0	11	85	7	37.3
Scifres, Mike, San Diego	69	2974	60	43.1	69	8	0	23	164	29	38.4
Smith, Hunter, Indianapolis	54	2443	62	45.2	54	3	0	29	395	21	36.8
Stanley, Chad, Houston	73	3009	57	41.2	73	7	0	30	265	19	35.7
Stewart, Kordell, Baltimore	5	177	42	35.4	5	0	0	3	21	2	31.2
Stover, Matt, Baltimore	1	33	33	33.0	1	1	0	0	0	0	13.0
Turk, Matt, Miami	98	4088	67	41.7	98	10	0	44	241	29	37.2
Zastudil, Dave, Baltimore	73	2948	61	40.4	73	12	0	24	181	26	34.6

NFC

Player, Team	Net Punts	Yards	Long	Avg.	Total Punts	TB	Blk.	Opp. Ret.	Ret. Yds.	In. 20	Net Avg.
Akers, David, Philadelphia	1	36	36	36.0	1	1	0	0	0	0	16.0
Barker, Bryan, Green Bay	66	2644	64	40.1	66	7	0	34	301	16	33.4
Bennett, Darren, Minnesota	57	2240	61	39.3	57	3	0	26	169	18	35.3
Berger, Mitch, New Orleans	85	3704	63	43.6	85	4	0	43	310	28	39.0
Bidwell, Josh, Tampa Bay	82	3472	60	42.3	83	7	1	31	279	23	36.8
Brown, Josh, Seattle	1	35	35	35.0	1	0	0	1	0	0	35.0
Christie, Steve, N.Y. Giants	1	19	19	19.0	1	0	0	0	0	1	19.0
Cundiff, Billy, Dallas	1	34	34	34.0	1	0	0	0	0	1	34.0
Edinger, Paul, Chicago	2	53	30	26.5	2	0	0	2	17	1	18.0
Feagles, Jeff, N.Y. Giants	74	3069	55	41.5	76	4	2	38	356	23	34.6
Harris, Nick, Detroit	92	3765	60	40.9	93	7	1	46	441	32	34.2
Johnson, Dirk, Philadelphia	72	3032	62	42.1	72	6	0	34	221	20	37.4
Jones, Donnie, Seattle	26	988	51	38.0	27	2	1	11	79	6	32.2
Kasay, John, Carolina	2	51	34	25.5	2	1	0	0	0	0	15.5
Landeta, Sean, St. Louis	40	1733	63	43.3	40	3	0	24	372	9	32.5
Lee, Andy, San Francisco	96	3990	81	41.6	96	8	0	51	445	25	35.3
Maynard, Brad, Chicago	108	4638	58	42.9	108	5	0	55	363	34	38.7
McBriar, Mat, Dallas	75	3182	68	42.4	75	7	0	39	410	22	35.1
Mohr, Chris, Atlanta	76	3082	56	40.6	76	7	0	33	134	19	36.9
Player, Scott, Arizona	98	4230	57	43.2	99	7	1	56	486	32	36.4
Rouen, Tom, Seattle	26	1093	60	42.0	26	1	0	10	91	10	37.8
Sauerbrun, Todd, Carolina	76	3351	65	44.1	77	8	1	38	303	25	37.5
Stemke, Kevin, St. Louis	28	1115	56	39.8	28	3	0	11	44	12	36.1
Tupa, Tom, Washington	103	4544	61	44.1	104	8	1	65	727	30	35.2
Walter, Ken, Seattle	24	920	50	38.3	25	1	1	11	74	4	33.0

PLAYERS WITH TWO CLUBS

Player, Team	Net Punts	Yards	Long	Avg.	Total Punts	TB	Blk.	Opp. Ret.	Ret. Yds.	In. 20	Net Avg.
Baker, Jason, Kansas City	9	340	52	37.8	9	0	0	4	98	3	26.9
Baker, Jason, Denver	15	591	48	39.4	15	1	0	6	55	7	34.4
Murphy, Nick, Baltimore	18	777	54	43.2	18	2	0	9	79	6	36.6
Murphy, Nick, Kansas City	4	189	58	47.3	4	1	0	2	6	1	40.8

PUNT RETURNS

TEAM

AFC

Team	No.	FC	Yds.	Avg.	Long	TD
Cleveland	36	12	432	12.0	44	0
Miami	52	14	564	10.8	71	0
Buffalo	46	10	491	10.7	t86	2
Baltimore	60	12	616	10.3	t78	2
Kansas City	24	17	232	9.7	46	0
Jacksonville	42	10	405	9.6	50	0
Cincinnati	35	18	328	9.4	49	0
Denver	43	17	400	9.3	39	0
San Diego	29	15	243	8.4	32	0
Pittsburgh	44	13	365	8.3	60	0
Houston	40	13	329	8.2	27	0
N.Y. Jets	41	13	313	7.6	46	0
Indianapolis	24	15	171	7.1	34	0
New England	40	15	230	5.8	23	0
Oakland	24	9	132	5.5	18	0
Tennessee	40	16	173	4.3	18	0
AFC total	620	219	5424	...	t86	4
AFC average	38.8	13.7	339.0	8.7	...	0.3

t—touchdown.

NFC

Team	No.	FC	Yds.	Avg.	Long	TD
Atlanta	37	17	457	12.4	t75	1
Chicago	46	15	510	11.1	t75	1
Detroit	40	17	420	10.5	t83	2
New Orleans	40	12	388	9.7	53	0
Philadelphia	41	20	377	9.2	40	0
Minnesota	31	14	275	8.9	t91	1
Dallas	44	16	390	8.9	55	0
San Francisco	35	21	303	8.7	t71	1
Washington	42	23	331	7.9	43	0
Green Bay	33	27	254	7.7	28	0
Seattle	30	26	230	7.7	48	0
Arizona	49	14	329	6.7	38	0
N.Y. Giants	38	11	253	6.7	29	0
Tampa Bay	33	22	213	6.5	t59	1
Carolina	28	14	165	5.9	18	0
St. Louis	30	18	143	4.8	39	0
NFC total	597	287	5038	...	t91	7
NFC average	37.3	17.9	314.9	8.4	...	0.4
NFL total	1217	506	10462	...	t91	11
NFL average	38.0	15.8	326.9	8.6	...	0.3

INDIVIDUAL

BESTS OF THE SEASON

Yards per attempt, season
NFC: 13.2—Eddie Drummond, Detroit.
AFC: 12.0—Dennis Northcutt, Cleveland.

Yards, season
AFC: 575—B.J. Sams, Baltimore.
NFC: 457—Allen Rossum, Atlanta.

Yards, game
NFC: 199—Eddie Drummond, Detroit at Jacksonville, Nov. 14 (OT; 6 returns, 2 TDs).
AFC: 111—Antwaan Randle El, Pittsburgh vs. Washington, Nov. 28 (6 returns).

Longest
NFC: 91—Nate Burleson, Minnesota at Indianapolis, Nov. 8 (TD).
AFC: 86—Nate Clements, Buffalo vs. St. Louis, Nov. 21 (TD).

Returns, season
AFC: 55—B.J. Sams, Baltimore.
NFC: 44—R.W. McQuarters, Chicago.

Returns, game
NFC: 8—Dedric Ward, Dallas at Washington, Sep. 27 (67 yards).
AFC: 7—Lamont Brightful, Miami at Cincinnati, Sep. 19 (78 yards); Antwaan Randle El, Pittsburgh at Cincinnati, Nov. 21 (83 yards); B.J. Sams, Baltimore at N.Y. Jets, Nov. 14 (OT; 45 yards).

Fair catches, season
NFC: 27—Antonio Chatman, Green Bay.
AFC: 17—Dante Hall, Kansas City.

Touchdowns, season
AFC: 2—B.J. Sams, Baltimore.
NFC: 2—Eddie Drummond, Detroit.

NFL LEADERS

Player, Team	No.	FC	Yds.	Avg.	Lg.	TD
Drummond, Eddie, Detroit	24	8	316	13.2	t83	2
Rossum, Allen, Atlanta	37	14	457	12.4	t75	1
Northcutt, Dennis, Clev.*	36	12	432	12.0	44	0

Player, Team	No.	FC	Yds.	Avg.	Lg.	TD
Lewis, Michael, N.O.	34	11	382	11.2	53	0
Welker, Wesley, Miami*	43	12	464	10.8	71	0
Sams, B.J., Baltimore*	55	12	575	10.5	t78	2
Smith, Rod, Denver*	22	8	223	10.1	30	0
Hall, Dante, Kansas City*	23	17	232	10.1	46	0
McQuarters, R.W., Chicago	44	13	435	9.9	t75	1
Lewis, Jermaine, Jacks.*	23	7	227	9.9	50	0
Frazier, Lance, Dallas	24	9	229	9.5	55	0
Clements, Nate, Buffalo*	35	10	327	9.3	t86	1
Parker, Eric, San Diego*	27	10	237	8.8	32	0
Moses, J.J., Houston*	36	13	309	8.6	27	0
Battle, Arnaz, San Francisco	31	20	266	8.6	t71	0

*AFC.
t—touchdown.
Leader based on average return, minimum 20.

AFC

Player, Team	No.	FC	Yds.	Avg.	Lg.	TD
Allen, David, Jacksonville	27	15	324	12.0	52	0
Adams, Charlie, Denver	2	1	42	21.0	39	0
Allen, David, Jacksonville	15	2	144	9.6	32	0
Berlin, Eddie, Tennessee	7	1	26	3.7	13	0
Branch, Deion, N.E.	1	0	0	0.0	0	0
Brightful, Lamont, Miami	9	2	89	9.9	36	0
Brown, Troy, New England	12	3	83	6.9	23	0
Buchanon, Phillip, Oakland	21	7	121	5.8	18	0
Clements, Nate, Buffalo	35	10	327	9.3	t86	1
Colclough, Ricardo, Pitts.	1	0	13	13.0	13	0
David, Jason, Indianapolis	8	4	50	6.3	13	0
Dwight, Tim, San Diego	1	5	6	6.0	6	0
Edwards, Troy, Jacksonville	3	1	26	8.7	14	0
Faulk, Kevin, New England	20	11	133	6.7	16	0
Florence, Drayton, S.D.	1	0	0	0.0	0	0
Gabriel, Doug, Oakland	2	2	7	3.5	7	0
Gay, Randall, New England	1	0	0	0.0	0	0
Gilmore, Bryan, Miami	0	0	11	...	11	0
Glenn, Aaron, Houston	4	0	22	5.5	18	0
Hall, Dante, Kansas City	23	17	232	10.1	46	0
Harts, Shaunard, K.C.	1	0	0	0.0	0	0
Haynes, Verron, Pitts.	1	0	5	5.0	5	0

Player, Team	No.	FC	Yds.	Avg.	Lg.	TD
Houshmandzadeh, T.J., Cin.	11	7	88	8.0	28	0
Johnson, Bethel, N.E.	4	1	8	2.0	6	0
Lewis, Jermaine, Jack.	23	7	227	9.9	50	0
Luke, Triandos, Denver	19	8	135	7.1	21	0
Mason, Derrick, Tenn.	24	12	93	3.9	13	0
Mathis, Rashean, Jack.	1	0	8	8.0	8	0
McCareins, Justin, N.Y. J.	14	6	88	6.3	26	0
Moorehead, Aaron, Ind.	1	0	34	34.0	34	0
Moses, J.J., Houston	36	13	309	8.6	27	0
Moss, Santana, N.Y. Jets	27	7	225	8.3	46	0
Northcutt, Dennis, Clev.	36	12	432	12.0	44	0
O'Neal, Deltha, Cin.	7	6	33	4.7	17	0
Parker, Eric, San Diego	27	10	237	8.8	32	0
Poole, Tyrone, N.E.	2	0	6	3.0	6	0
Pyatt, Brad, Indianapolis	8	5	47	5.9	13	0
Randle El, Antwaan, Pitts.	42	13	347	8.3	60	0
Ratliff, Keiwan, Cin.	17	5	207	12.2	49	0
Reed, Josh, Buffalo	1	0	7	7.0	7	0
Robinson, Dunta, Hou.	0	0	-2	...	-2	0
Sams, B.J., Baltimore	55	12	575	10.5	t78	2
Sanders, Deion, Balt.	5	0	41	8.2	23	0
Smith, Jonathan, Buffalo	9	0	157	17.4	t70	1
Smith, Rod, Denver	22	8	223	10.1	30	0
Waddell, Michael, Tenn.	9	3	54	6.0	18	0
Walters, Troy, Ind.	7	6	40	5.7	14	0
Welker, Wesley, Miami	43	12	464	10.8	71	0
Williams, Shaud, Buffalo	1	0	0	0.0	0	0
Woodson, Charles, Oak.	1	0	4	4.0	4	0

t—touchdown.

NFC

Player, Team	No.	FC	Yds.	Avg.	Lg.	TD
Baker, Eugene, Carolina	8	3	49	6.1	18	0
Battle, Arnaz, San Francisco	31	20	266	8.6	t71	1
Berrian, Bernard, Chicago	2	2	10	5.0	12	0
Boldin, Anquan, Arizona	0	1	0	...	...	0
Broussard, Jamall, Carolina	10	8	43	4.3	13	0
Brown, Antonio, Wash.	10	2	89	8.9	39	0
Brown, Tim, Tampa Bay	6	12	48	8.0	14	0
Burleson, Nate, Minnesota	25	9	214	8.6	t91	1
Chatman, Antonio, G.B.	32	27	245	7.7	28	0
Clayton, Michael, T. B.	1	1	2	2.0	2	0
Crayton, Patrick, Dallas	4	1	34	8.5	17	0
Drummond, Eddie, Detroit	24	8	316	13.2	t83	2
Engram, Bobby, Seattle	10	19	118	11.8	48	0
Finneran, Brian, Atlanta	0	3	0	...	...	0
Fleck, P.J., San Francisco	1	0	10	10.0	10	0
Frazier, Lance, Dallas	24	9	229	9.5	55	0
Gage, Justin, Chicago	0	0	56	...	56	0
Galloway, Joey, Tampa Bay	20	8	142	7.1	t59	1
Gamble, Chris, Carolina	9	2	69	7.7	16	0
Gray, Bobby, Chicago	0	0	9	...	9	0
Hannam, Ryan, Seattle	1	0	6	6.0	6	0
Hawkins, Artrell, Carolina	1	0	4	4.0	4	0
Hilliard, Ike, N.Y. Giants	4	0	26	6.5	15	0
Howry, Keenan, Minnesota	2	3	33	16.5	21	0
Jones, Mark, N.Y. Giants	34	11	227	6.7	29	0
Lewis, Michael, N.O.	34	11	382	11.2	53	0
Mahe, Reno, Philadelphia	19	8	109	5.7	25	0
Marshall, Lemar, Wash.	0	1	0	...	...	0
McDonald, Shaun, St. Louis	30	18	143	4.8	39	0
McQuarters, R.W., Chicago	44	13	435	9.9	t75	1
Moore, Mewelde, Minn.	4	1	28	7.0	17	0
Morris, Maurice, Seattle	15	4	75	5.0	22	0
Morton, Chad, Washington	13	12	80	6.2	14	0
Moss, Randy, Minnesota	0	1	0	...	...	0
Newman, Terence, Dallas	2	0	13	6.5	7	0
Peterson, Julian, S.F.	1	0	6	6.0	6	0
Reed, J.R., Philadelphia	0	0	18	...	18	0
Richard, Kris, Seattle	4	3	31	7.8	14	0
Rossum, Allen, Atlanta	37	14	457	12.4	t75	0
Schroeder, Bill, Tampa Bay	6	1	21	3.5	12	0
Sharper, Darren, Green Bay	1	0	9	9.0	9	0
Sheppard, Lito, Philadelphia	2	5	42	21.0	39	0
Smith, Steve, Carolina	0	1	0	...	...	0
Stallworth, Donte', N.O.	6	1	6	1.0	4	0
Starks, Duane, Arizona	7	1	43	6.1	15	0
Swinton, Reggie, Detroit	16	9	104	6.5	18	0
Thrash, James, Washington	19	8	162	8.5	43	0
Ward, Dedric, Dallas	14	6	114	8.1	13	0
Westbrook, Brian, Phil.	2	0	14	7.0	14	0
Williams, Karl, Arizona	42	12	286	6.8	38	0
Wilson, Cedrick, S.F.	2	1	21	10.5	13	0
Wynn, Dexter, Philadelphia	18	7	194	10.8	40	0

t—touchdown.

KICKOFF RETURNS

TEAM

AFC

Team	No.	Yds.	Avg.	Long	TD
Buffalo	63	1542	24.5	t104	3
Kansas City	75	1820	24.3	t97	2
San Diego	62	1478	23.8	t87	1
Miami	70	1660	23.7	t95	1
Indianapolis	66	1545	23.4	t88	1
New England	56	1302	23.3	t93	1
N.Y. Jets	46	1038	22.6	t94	1
Pittsburgh	62	1335	21.5	48	0
Denver	53	1122	21.2	48	0
Houston	69	1450	21.0	49	0
Baltimore	61	1264	20.7	64	0
Cincinnati	68	1403	20.6	40	0
Oakland	83	1700	20.5	64	0
Cleveland	75	1504	20.1	t93	1
Tennessee	79	1558	19.7	45	0
Jacksonville	57	1087	19.1	45	0
AFC total	1045	22808	...	t104	11
AFC average	65.3	1425.5	21.8	...	0.7

t—touchdown.

NFC

Team	No.	Yds.	Avg.	Long	TD
N.Y. Giants	66	1658	25.1	t92	2
Tampa Bay	60	1450	24.2	59	0
Detroit	66	1568	23.8	t99	2
New Orleans	83	1879	22.6	t98	2
Washington	55	1203	21.9	70	0
Atlanta	61	1331	21.8	49	0
Green Bay	70	1522	21.7	71	0
Chicago	74	1607	21.7	73	0
Philadelphia	56	1214	21.7	66	0
Carolina	61	1307	21.4	49	0
Seattle	74	1529	20.7	36	0
Dallas	78	1603	20.6	62	0
San Francisco	84	1716	20.4	40	0
Arizona	65	1293	19.9	71	0
Minnesota	73	1448	19.8	55	0
St. Louis	84	1604	19.1	31	0
NFC total	1110	23932	...	t99	6
NFC average	69.4	1495.8	21.6	...	0.4
NFL total	2155	46740	...	t104	17
NFL average	67.3	1460.6	21.7	...	0.5

INDIVIDUAL

BESTS OF THE SEASON

Yards per attempt, season
NFC: 26.9—Willie Ponder, N.Y. Giants.
AFC: 26.3—Terrence McGee, Buffalo.

Yards, season
AFC: 1718—Dante Hall, Kansas City.
NFC: 1250—Allen Rossum, Atlanta.

Yards, game
NFC: 259—Willie Ponder, N.Y. Giants vs. Pittsburgh, Dec. 18 (8 returns, 1 TD).
AFC: 236—Dominic Rhodes, Indianapolis vs. San Diego, Dec. 26 (OT; 6 returns, 1 TD).

Longest
AFC: 104—Terrence McGee, Buffalo at Miami, Dec. 5 (TD).
NFC: 99—Eddie Drummond, Detroit vs. Houston, Sep. 19 (TD).

Returns, season
AFC: 68—Dante Hall, Kansas City.
NFC: 58—Allen Rossum, Atlanta.

Returns, game
AFC: 10—Richard Alston, Cleveland at Cincinnati, Nov. 28 (212 yards).
NFC: 8—Aaron Stecker, New Orleans vs. Carolina, Dec. 5 (214 yards); Willie Ponder, N.Y. Giants vs. Pittsburgh, Dec. 18 (259 yards, 1 TD); Antonio Chatman, Green Bay vs. Tennessee, Oct. 11 (163 yards).

Touchdowns, season
AFC: 3—Terrence McGee, Buffalo.
NFC: 2—Eddie Drummond, Detroit.

NFL LEADERS

Player, Team	No.	Yds.	Avg.	Long	TD
Ponder, Willie, N.Y. Giants	36	967	26.9	t91	1
Drummond, Eddie, Detroit	41	1092	26.6	t99	2
McGee, Terrence, Buffalo*	52	1370	26.3	t104	3
Cox, Torrie, Tampa Bay	33	866	26.2	59	0
Hall, Dante, Kansas City*	68	1718	25.3	t97	2
Randle El, Antwaan, Pittsburgh*	21	527	25.1	41	0
Ferguson, Robert, Green Bay	21	526	25.0	71	0

Player, Team	No.	Yds.	Avg.	Long	TD
Johnson, Bethel, New England*	41	1016	24.8	t93	1
Rhodes, Dominic, Indianapolis*	48	1188	24.8	t88	1
Dwight, Tim, San Diego*	50	1222	24.4	t87	1
Robertson, Jamal, S.F.-Car.	31	740	23.9	49	0
Lewis, Michael, New Orleans	51	1215	23.8	t96	1
Lee, ReShard, Dallas	41	964	23.5	62	0
Welker, Wesley, S.D.-Mia.*	61	1415	23.2	t95	1
Broussard, Jamall, Carolina	24	555	23.1	49	0

*AFC.
t—touchdown.
Leader based on average return, minimum 20.

AFC

Player, Team	No.	Yds.	Avg.	Long	TD
Alexander, Roc, Denver	19	386	20.3	32	0
Allen, David, Jacksonville	11	210	19.1	25	0
Alston, Richard, Cleveland	46	1016	22.1	t93	1
Askew, B.J., N.Y. Jets	2	18	9.0	13	0
Banta-Cain, Tully, New England	1	21	21.0	21	0
Bennett, Drew, Tennessee	1	-8	-8.0	-8	0
Blaylock, Derrick, Kansas City	1	22	22.0	22	0
Brady, Kyle, Jacksonville	1	15	15.0	15	0
Brightful, Lamont, Miami	5	126	25.2	32	0
Brown, Dee, Cleveland	13	243	18.7	30	0
Butler, Robb, San Diego	2	35	17.5	24	0
Carter, Jonathan, N.Y. Jets	17	374	22.0	40	0
Chatman, Jesse, San Diego	4	89	22.3	35	0
Clements, Nate, Buffalo	1	14	14.0	14	0
Colclough, Ricardo, Pittsburgh	26	566	21.8	48	0
Cotchery, Jerricho, N.Y. Jets	13	362	27.8	t94	1
Curry, Ronald, Oakland	4	63	15.8	25	0
Cushing, Matt, Pittsburgh	3	45	15.0	20	0
Dinkins, Darnell, Baltimore	1	7	7.0	7	0
Droughns, Reuben, Denver	14	344	24.6	48	0
Dwight, Tim, San Diego	50	1222	24.4	t87	1
Edwards, Marc, Jacksonville	1	8	8.0	8	0
Edwards, Troy, Jacksonville	15	335	22.3	45	0
Faulk, Kevin, New England	4	73	18.3	24	0
Fleming, Troy, Tennessee	18	316	17.6	30	0
Fletcher, London, Buffalo	4	86	21.5	23	0

Player, Team	No.	Yds.	Avg.	Long	TD
Francis, Carlos, Oakland	14	259	18.5	33	0
Gabriel, Doug, Oakland	53	1140	21.5	64	0
Gaffney, Jabar, Houston	2	31	15.5	27	0
Gilmore, Bryan, Miami	5	114	22.8	53	0
Griffin, Quentin, Denver	4	52	13.0	21	0
Hall, Dante, Kansas City	68	1718	25.3	t97	2
Hetherington, Chris, Oakland	1	23	23.0	23	0
Holcombe, Robert, Tennessee	3	26	8.7	14	0
Hollings, Tony, Houston	1	23	23.0	23	0
Horn, Chris, Kansas City	4	44	11.0	17	0
Houshmandzadeh, T.J., Cin.	10	227	22.7	32	0
Jackson, Frisman, Cleveland	4	70	17.5	22	0
Jackson, James, Cleveland	2	39	19.5	23	0
Johnson, Bethel, New England	41	1016	24.8	t93	1
Johnson, Jarret, Baltimore	1	6	6.0	6	0
Jones, Greg, Jacksonville	5	90	18.0	23	0
Jordan, LaMont, N.Y. Jets	14	284	20.3	40	0
Kasper, Kevin, New England	3	61	20.3	21	0
Kelly, Reggie, Cincinnati	1	14	14.0	14	0
Kelsay, Chris, Buffalo	1	14	14.0	14	0
Kennison, Eddie, Kansas City	1	36	36.0	36	0
King, Andre, Cleveland	5	95	19.0	24	0
Kinney, Erron, Tennessee	1	21	21.0	21	0
Kirschke, Travis, Pittsburgh	1	13	13.0	13	0
Klecko, Dan, New England	f0	0	...	...	0
Lewis, Jermaine, Jacksonville	21	386	18.4	26	0
Luke, Triandos, Denver	15	306	20.4	32	0
McAddley, Jason, Tennessee	38	849	22.3	45	0
McGee, Terrence, Buffalo	52	1370	26.3	t104	3
Moore, Langston, Cincinnati	1	15	15.0	15	0
Morris, Sammy, Miami	1	27	27.0	27	0
Moses, J.J., Houston	59	1303	22.1	49	0
Moulds, Eric, Buffalo	1	2	2.0	2	0
Mungro, James, Indianapolis	7	111	15.9	24	0
Mustard, Chad, Cleveland	2	13	6.5	9	0
Neal, Lorenzo, San Diego	1	12	12.0	12	0
Neufeld, Ryan, Buffalo	1	3	3.0	3	0
Norris, Moran, Houston	2	25	12.5	15	0
O'Neal, Deltha, Cincinnati	1	15	15.0	15	0
Pass, Patrick, New England	6	115	19.2	24	0
Patten, David, New England	1	16	16.0	16	0
Peko, Tupe, Indianapolis	f0	0	...	...	0
Poole, Will, Miami	1	22	22.0	22	0
Porter, Jerry, Oakland	1	6	6.0	6	0
Pyatt, Brad, Indianapolis	10	230	23.0	32	0
Randle El, Antwaan, Pittsburgh	21	527	25.1	41	0
Redmond, J.R., Oakland	8	153	19.1	31	0
Rhodes, Dominic, Indianapolis	48	1188	24.8	t88	1
Russell, Cliff, Cincinnati	39	872	22.4	40	0
Sams, B.J., Baltimore	59	1251	21.2	64	0
Sanders, Lewis, Cleveland	1	9	9.0	10	0
Sapp, Cecil, Denver	1	34	34.0	34	0
Schobel, Bo, Tennessee	1	12	12.0	12	0
Shea, Aaron, Cleveland	2	19	9.5	13	0
Shelton, Daimon, Buffalo	2	25	12.5	15	0
Smith, Jonathan, Buffalo	1	28	28.0	28	0
Starling, Kendrick, Houston	1	14	14.0	14	0
Stewart, Tony, Cincinnati	3	20	6.7	10	0
Stills, Gary, Kansas City	1	0	0.0	0	0
Stone, John, Oakland	1	20	20.0	20	0
Taylor, Ike, Pittsburgh	11	184	16.7	22	0
Toefield, LaBrandon, Jack.	3	43	14.3	19	0
Turner, Michael, San Diego	1	18	18.0	18	0
Waddell, Michael, Tennessee	17	342	20.1	33	0
Walters, Troy, Indianapolis	1	16	16.0	16	0
Washington, Todd, Houston	2	27	13.5	16	0
Watson, Kenny, Cincinnati	13	240	18.5	32	0
Welker, Wesley, S.D.-Mia.	61	1415	23.2	t95	1
Wells, Jonathan, Houston	2	27	13.5	18	0
Whitted, Alvis, Oakland	1	36	36.0	36	0
Wyrick, Jimmy, Miami	1	58	58.0	58	0

t—touchdown.
f—includes at least one fair catch.

NFC

Player, Team	No.	Yds.	Avg.	Long	TD
Anderson, Dwight, St. Louis	4	71	17.8	25	0
Ayanbadejo, Obafemi, Arizona	3	50	16.7	21	0
Azumah, Jerry, Chicago	42	924	22.0	73	0
Baker, Eugene, Carolina	2	39	19.5	23	0
Battle, Arnaz, San Francisco	13	257	19.8	40	0
Bennett, Brandon, Carolina	8	177	22.1	43	0
Berrian, Bernard, Chicago	17	385	22.6	41	0
Berton, Sean, Minnesota	1	3	3.0	3	0
Betts, Ladell, Washington	23	528	23.0	70	0
Broussard, Jamall, Carolina	24	555	23.1	49	0
Brown, Antonio, Washington	1	66	66.0	66	0
Bryson, Shawn, Detroit	2	27	13.5	14	0
Burleson, Nate, Minnesota	2	51	25.5	29	0
Campbell, Kelly, Minnesota	35	760	21.7	55	0
Carroll, Ahmad, Green Bay	2	31	15.5	16	0
Carter, Kerry, Seattle	21	448	21.3	36	0
Cason, Aveion, St. Louis	14	310	22.1	31	0
Chatman, Antonio, Green Bay	25	565	22.6	59	0
Cloud, Michael, N.Y. Giants	8	175	21.9	38	0
Coady, Rich, St. Louis	1	-1	-1.0	-1	0
Colbert, Keary, Carolina	2	30	15.0	19	0
Comella, Greg, Tampa Bay	1	20	20.0	20	0
Copper, Terrance, Dallas	16	307	19.2	39	0
Cox, Torrie, Tampa Bay	33	866	26.2	59	0
Croom, Larry, Arizona	16	314	19.6	35	0
Curry, Donte', Detroit	1	-1	-1.0	-1	0
Davenport, Najeh, Green Bay	14	286	20.4	27	0
Davis, Rod, Minnesota	1	15	15.0	15	0
Dayne, Ron, N.Y. Giants	1	11	11.0	11	0
DeVries, Jared, Detroit	1	5	5.0	5	0
Drummond, Eddie, Detroit	41	1092	26.6	t99	2
Edwards, Eric, Arizona	3	40	13.3	14	0
Evans, Heath, Seattle	3	51	17.0	21	0
Faulk, Marshall, St. Louis	1	0	0.0	0	0
Ferguson, Robert, Green Bay	21	526	25.0	71	0
Finn, Jim, N.Y. Giants	1	16	16.0	16	0
Flowers, Erik, St. Louis	1	0	0.0	0	0
Foster, DeShaun, Carolina	2	16	8.0	14	0
Furrey, Mike, St. Louis	8	157	19.6	23	0
Goodspeed, Joey, St. Louis	1	9	9.0	9	0
Graham, Earnest, Tampa Bay	3	52	17.3	18	0
Griffith, Justin, Atlanta	1	31	31.0	31	0
Groce, DeJuan, St. Louis	1	15	15.0	15	0
Hall, DeAngelo, Atlanta	1	48	48.0	48	0
Hall, Lamont, New Orleans	3	20	6.7	8	0
Harris, Arlen, St. Louis	47	951	20.2	29	0
Hayes, Gerald, Arizona	3	6	2.0	6	0
Henderson, William, Green Bay	2	16	8.0	10	0
Hicks, Maurice, San Francisco	31	623	20.1	35	0
Hood, Roderick, Philadelphia	15	336	22.4	45	0
Hoover, Brad, Carolina	2	30	15.0	16	0
Howry, Keenan, Minnesota	2	45	22.5	24	0
Jackson, Steven, St. Louis	4	79	19.8	23	0
Jackson, Terry, San Francisco	2	22	11.0	14	0
Johnson, Bryan, Chicago	1	18	18.0	18	0
Johnson, Bryant, Arizona	6	135	22.5	47	0
Johnson, Spencer, Minnesota	1	0	0.0	0	0
Jones, Daryl, Chicago	6	112	18.7	23	0
Jones, Mark, N.Y. Giants	2	37	18.5	20	0
Jones, Nathan, Dallas	2	43	21.5	25	0
Kozlowski, Brian, Washington	1	4	4.0	4	0
Lee, ReShard, Dallas	41	964	23.5	62	0
Lehr, Matt, Dallas	1	9	9.0	9	0
Lewis, Greg, Philadelphia	2	28	14.0	15	0
Lewis, Michael, New Orleans	51	1215	23.8	t96	1
Locklear, Sean, Seattle	1	12	12.0	12	0
Mahe, Reno, Philadelphia	3	44	14.7	22	0
Manumaleuna, Brandon, St. Louis	2	13	6.5	13	0
McAfee, Fred, New Orleans	8	137	17.1	26	0
McKie, Jason, Chicago	3	65	21.7	25	0

Player, Team	No.	Yds.	Avg.	Long	TD
McQuarters, R.W., Chicago	2	46	23.0	37	0
Mili, Itula, Seattle	1	12	12.0	12	0
Molinaro, Jim, Washington	1	5	5.0	5	0
Moore, Mewelde, Minnesota	20	386	19.3	33	0
Morgan, Quincy, Dallas	2	25	12.5	19	0
Morris, Maurice, Seattle	47	994	21.1	34	0
Morton, Chad, Washington	16	358	22.4	49	0
Murphy, Frank, Tampa Bay	8	208	26.0	54	0
Parry, Josh, Philadelphia	2	24	12.0	14	0
Peterson, Adrian, Chicago	3	57	19.0	22	0
Peterson, Kenny, Green Bay	1	6	6.0	6	0
Pierce, Brett, Dallas	1	13	13.0	13	0
Ponder, Willie, N.Y. Giants	36	967	26.9	t91	1
Pritchett, Stanley, Atlanta	1	2	2.0	2	0
Proehl, Ricky, Carolina	3	64	21.3	27	0
Rasmussen, Kemp, Carolina	1	12	12.0	12	0
Reed, J.R., Philadelphia	33	761	23.1	66	0
Reeves, Jacques, Dallas	13	199	15.3	27	0
Rivers, Marcellus, N.Y. Giants	1	8	8.0	8	0
Robertson, Jamal, S.F.-Car.	31	740	23.9	49	0
Ross, Derek, Minnesota	2	33	16.5	19	0
Rossum, Allen, Atlanta	58	1250	21.6	49	0
Ruff, Orlando, New Orleans	1	9	9.0	9	0
Schlesinger, Cory, Detroit	1	23	23.0	23	0
Schroeder, Bill, Tampa Bay	2	29	14.5	16	0
Scobey, Josh, Arizona	32	723	22.6	71	0
Seidman, Mike, Carolina	f2	20	10.0	12	0
Sellers, Mike, Washington	4	56	14.0	17	0
Shiancoe, Visanthe, N.Y. Giants	1	8	8.0	8	0
Smart, Ian, Tampa Bay	8	167	20.9	27	0
Smart, Rod, Carolina	8	169	21.1	33	0
Smith, Onterrio, Minnesota	9	155	17.2	24	0
Smith, Will, New Orleans	1	17	17.0	17	0
Stecker, Aaron, New Orleans	18	469	26.1	t98	1
Stevens, Jerramy, Seattle	1	12	12.0	12	0
Swinton, Reggie, Detroit	18	410	22.8	43	0
Thornton, Bruce, Dallas	2	43	21.5	24	0
Thrash, James, Washington	9	186	20.7	36	0
Thurman, Andrae, Green Bay	3	59	19.7	28	0
Trejo, Stephen, Detroit	2	12	6.0	10	0
Vanden Bosch, Kyle, Arizona	1	7	7.0	7	0
Ward, Derrick, N.Y. Giants	16	436	27.3	t92	1
Wesley, Dante, Carolina	1	15	15.0	15	0
White, Dewayne, Tampa Bay	1	9	9.0	9	0
White, Jamel, Tampa Bay	4	99	24.8	44	0
Whitehead, Willie, New Orleans	1	12	12.0	12	0
Whitley, James, Green Bay	2	33	16.5	20	0
Williams, Jimmy, San Francisco	3	58	19.3	23	0
Williams, Karl, Arizona	1	18	18.0	18	0
Wilson, Cedrick, San Francisco	10	196	19.6	36	0
Wynn, Dexter, Philadelphia	1	21	21.0	21	0

t—touchdown.
f—includes at least one fair catch.

PLAYERS WITH TWO CLUBS

Player, Team	No.	Yds.	Avg.	Lg.	TD
Robertson, Jamal, San Francisco	25	560	22.4	37	0
Robertson, Jamal, Carolina	6	180	30.0	49	0
Welker, Wesley, San Diego	4	102	25.5	33	0
Welker, Wesley, Miami	57	1313	23.0	t95	1

2004 STATISTICS Kickoff returns

TACKLES

BESTS OF THE SEASON

Tackles, season
AFC: 105—Donnie Edwards, San Diego.
NFC: 109—Derrick Brooks, Tampa Bay.

Tackles, game
AFC: 15—London Fletcher, Buffalo at N.Y. Jets, Oct. 10.
NFC: 14—Lance Briggs, Chicago at Jacksonville, Dec. 12.

NFL LEADERS

Player, Team	Tk.	Ast.
Brooks, Derrick, Tampa Bay ...	109	28
Edwards, Donnie, S.D.*	105	46
Briggs, Lance, Chicago	102	24
Lewis, Ray, Baltimore*	101	46
Bulluck, Keith, Tennessee*	99	53
Clark, Danny, Oakland*	99	31
Sharper, Jamie, Houston*	98	41
Fletcher, London, Buffalo*	94	50
Peterson, Mike, Jack.*	93	33
Griffith, Robert, Cleveland*....	92	26
Barnett, Nick, Green Bay	91	30
Harrison, Rodney, N.E.*	89	40
Brooking, Keith, Atlanta	86	16
Thomas, Zach, Miami*	85	60
Pierce, Antonio, Washington ..	84	26
Green, Mike, Chicago	84	23
Witherspoon, Will, Carolina ...	84	18
Washington, Marcus, Wash. ..	83	19
Trufant, Marcus, Seattle	83	10
Smith, Derek, San Francisco...	80	29
*AFC.

AFC

Player, Team	Tk.	Ast.
Abraham, Donnie, N.Y. Jets	38	15
Abraham, John, N.Y. Jets	35	14
Adams, Sam, Buffalo	26	14
Alexander, Roc, Denver..........	5	1
Allen, Jared, Kansas City	29	2
Amato, Ken, Tennessee..........	4	0
Anderson, Charlie, Houston	1	1
Anderson, Marques, Oak.	54	18
Askew, Matthias, Cincinnati	0	2
Asomugha, Nnamdi, Oak.	33	6
Ayanbadejo, Brendon, Mia.	9	8
Ayodele, Akin, Jacksonville.....	76	17
Babin, Jason, Houston...........	51	12
Bacon, Waine, Indianapolis.....	6	0
Bailey, Champ, Denver	68	13
Baker, Rashad, Buffalo	13	6
Ball, Dave, San Diego	2	1
Bannan, Justin, Buffalo..........	1	1
Banta-Cain, Tully, N. E.	6	4
Barber, Shawn, Kansas City	29	5
Barnes, Lionel, Jacksonville....	5	1
Barrett, David, N.Y. Jets	64	14
Bartee, William, Kansas City ...	33	5
Barton, Eric, N.Y. Jets	77	30
Bashir, Idrees, Indianapolis.....	41	17
Battle, Julian, Kansas City......	10	0
Battles, Ainsley, Pittsburgh	1	0
Bauman, Rashad, Cincinnati	2	1
Baxter, Gary, Baltimore	72	16
Beckett, Rogers, Cincinnati	14	5
Beckham, Tony, Tennessee	5	0
Bell, Kendrell, Pittsburgh	6	2
Bell, Yeremiah, Miami	3	0
Bentley, Kevin, Cleveland	35	16
Bird, Cory, Indianapolis	21	8
Blade, Willie, Jacksonville.......	1	1
Blaylock, Derrick, K.C.	1	0
Bodden, Leigh, Cleveland	11	0
Boiman, Rocky, Tennessee	8	11
Bolden, Juran, Jacksonville	17	4

Player, Team	Tk.	Ast.
Bowens, David, Miami	26	14
Bowens, Tim, Miami	2	1
Brackett, Gary, Indianapolis	12	9
Brayton, Tyler, Oakland	37	8
Brock, Raheem, Ind.	36	11
Brown, Cornell, Baltimore......	4	3
Brown, Courtney, Cleveland....	2	0
Brown, Eric, Houston............	3	3
Brown, Mark, N.Y. Jets	8	5
Brown, Troy, New England.....	14	3
Browning, John, K.C.	32	7
Bruschi, Tedy, New England....	75	45
Bryant, Roderick, N.Y. Jets	2	0
Buchanan, Ray, Oakland	63	24
Buchanon, Phillip, Oakland.....	50	9
Buckley, Terrell, N.Y. Jets.......	8	2
Bulluck, Keith, Tennessee	99	53
Butler, Robb, San Diego	3	1
Calmus, Rocky, Tennessee	12	3
Carter, Dyshod, Ariz.-Clev.*	5	0
Carter, Kevin, Tennessee........	26	23
Carter, Tyrone, Pittsburgh.......	4	0
Caver, Quinton, Kansas City....	24	4
Celestin, Oliver, N.Y. Jets.......	5	0
Cesaire, Jacques, San Diego...	18	6
Cherry, Je'Rod, N.E.	1	1
Chester, Larry, Miami............	7	0
Chukwurah, Patrick, Denver ...	2	2
Clancy, Kendrick, Pittsburgh...	7	1
Clark, Danny, Oakland	99	31
Clauss, Jared, Tennessee	4	3
Clements, Nate, Buffalo	58	20
Clemons, Duane, Cincinnati	32	18
Colclough, Ricardo, Pitts.	13	4
Coleman, Erik, N.Y. Jets.........	67	21
Coleman, Marco, Denver	21	7
Coleman, Marcus, Houston	45	11
Colvin, Rosevelt, N.E.	18	14
Cooper, Deke, Jacksonville......	21	3
Cooper, Jarrod, Car.-Oak.*	13	0
Cooper, Stephen, San Diego....	25	8
Cowart, Sam, N.Y. Jets	21	5
Crocker, Chris, Cleveland	37	10
Crowell, Angelo, Buffalo	0	1
Dalton, Lional, Kansas City	19	2
Darius, Donovin, Jack.	61	28
David, Jason, Indianapolis	47	4
Davis, Andra, Cleveland	54	16
Davis, Don, New England	10	6
Davis, Sammy, San Diego	32	6
DeLoach, Jerry, Houston	17	8
Demps, Will, Baltimore	64	19
Denney, Ryan, Buffalo............	12	20
Diem, Ryan, Indianapolis........	0	1
Dingle, Adrian, San Diego.......	3	3
Doss, Mike, Indianapolis.........	41	7
Douglas, Marques, Balt.	49	23
Downing, Eric, San Diego........	1	0
Dyson, Andre, Tennessee........	35	6
Earl, Glenn, Houston	35	9
Eason, Nicholas, Cleveland	1	1
Edwards, Donnie, S.D.............	105	46
Edwards, Dwan, Baltimore.......	1	0
Edwards, Ron, Buffalo	12	9
Ekuban, Ebenezer, Cleveland...	29	10
Ellis, Shaun, N.Y. Jets	39	18
Elliss, Luther, Denver.............	6	1
Ena, Justin, Tennessee	17	4

Player, Team	Tk.	Ast.
Evans, Josh, N.Y. Jets...........	0	1
Evans, Troy, Houston	0	1
Faggins, DeMarcus, Hou.	35	4
Fargas, Justin, Oakland..........	1	0
Farrior, James, Pittsburgh	67	28
Fatafehi, Mario, Denver..........	14	7
Favors, Greg, Jacksonville	25	11
Ferguson, Jason, N.Y. Jets	38	21
Ferguson, Nick, Denver..........	10	5
Fisk, Jason, San Diego	19	11
Flemons, Ronald, Miami........	1	0
Fletcher, Jamar, San Diego	24	3
Fletcher, London, Buffalo........	94	50
Florence, Drayton, S.D.	28	4
Floyd, Anthony, Indianapolis....	23	12
Foley, Steve, San Diego	48	17
Foote, Larry, Pittsburgh	53	16
Foreman, Jay, Houston	53	26
Franklin, Aubrayo, Baltimore....	2	0
Freeman, Arturo, Miami	19	9
Freeney, Dwight, Ind.	33	3
Fujita, Scott, Kansas City	67	23
Fuller, Corey, Baltimore..........	10	3
Gardner, Barry, Cleveland	17	10
Gardner, Gilbert, Ind.	4	2
Gardner, Rich, Tennessee	8	1
Gay, Randall, New England......	29	5
Gbaja-Biamila, Akbar, Oak.	10	3
Geathers, Robert, Cincinnati ...	7	6
Gildon, Jason, Jacksonville......	11	1
Glenn, Aaron, Houston	55	8
Glenn, Jason, N.Y. Jets	3	0
Godfrey, Randall, San Diego....	68	19
Gordon, Amon, Cleveland	5	2
Grant, DeLawrence, Oakland...	14	6
Grant, Deon, Jacksonville	50	15
Green, Brandon, Jack.	14	6
Green, Jarvis, New England.....	15	6
Green, Roderick, Baltimore	1	0
Green, William, Cleveland	0	1
Greenwood, Morlon, Miami	61	40
Greer, Jabari, Buffalo	12	0
Gregg, Kelly, Baltimore	44	17
Griffith, Robert, Cleveland	92	26
Haggan, Mario, Buffalo	1	1
Haggans, Clark, Pittsburgh	30	8
Hall, Carlos, Tennessee..........	26	15
Hamilton, Bobby, Oakland.......	35	22
Hampton, Casey, Pittsburgh	8	7
Hardy, Kevin, Cincinnati	42	7
Harper, Alan, N.Y. Jets	3	2
Harper, Nick, Indianapolis	58	19
Harris, Napoleon, Oakland	46	14
Harrison, James, Pittsburgh	20	2
Harrison, Rodney, N.E.............	89	40
Hart, Clinton, San Diego	5	4
Harts, Shaunard, K.C.	37	7
Hartsock, Ben, Indianapolis.....	1	0
Hartwell, Edgerton, Balt.	56	41
Haynesworth, Albert, Tenn.	26	14
Hayward, Reggie, Denver	31	12
Henderson, John, Jack.	62	13
Hendricks, Tommy, Jack.	11	5
Henry, Anthony, Cleveland	67	9
Herndon, Kelly, Denver	56	13
Herring, Kim, Cincinnati	49	13
Hicks, Eric, Kansas City	27	6
Hobson, Victor, N.Y. Jets	30	15

Player, Team	Tk.	Ast.	Player, Team	Tk.	Ast.	Player, Team	Tk.	Ast.
Hoke, Chris, Pittsburgh	13	11	Nelson, Jim, Indianapolis	40	12	Smith, Travian, Oakland	29	11
Holcombe, Robert, Tenn.	0	1	Nickey, Donnie, Tennessee	28	4	Spencer, Cody, Tennessee	1	0
Holdman, Warrick, Cleve.	49	27	O'Neal, Deltha, Cincinnati	35	5	Spicer, Paul, Jacksonville	4	1
Holland, Darius, Denver	2	0	Odom, Antwan, Tennessee	15	6	Spikes, Takeo, Buffalo	64	35
Holliday, Vonnie, K.C.	12	1	Olshansky, Igor, San Diego	24	15	Spragan, Donnie, Denver	44	22
Hope, Chris, Pittsburgh	59	31	Pagel, Derek, N.Y. Jets	1	0	Stamer, Josh, Buffalo	5	4
Howard, Reggie, Miami	16	7	Palepoi, Anton, Sea.-Den.*	15	4	Starks, Randy, Tennessee	17	11
Hutchins, Von, Indianapolis	29	11	Palmer, Carson, Cincinnati	1	0	Stevens, Larry, Cincinnati	2	3
Ioane, Junior, Houston	1	0	Parrella, John, Oakland	20	2	Stills, Gary, Kansas City	8	1
Irons, Grant, Oakland	10	2	Pass, Patrick, New England	2	0	Strait, Derrick, N.Y. Jets	3	2
Izzo, Larry, New England	1	0	Patterson, Elton, Cin.-Jack.	3	4	Strickland, Donald, Ind.	15	5
Jackson, Alonzo, Pittsburgh	2	1	Payne, Seth, Houston	36	15	Stroud, Marcus, Jack.	38	16
James, Tory, Cincinnati	58	5	Peek, Antwan, Houston	8	5	Stuvaints, Russell, Pitts.	14	3
Jameson, Michael, Clev.	8	5	Peterson, Mike, Jacksonville	93	33	Suggs, Terrell, Baltimore	46	14
Jammer, Quentin, S.D.	53	9	Phifer, Roman, N.E.	30	10	Surtain, Patrick, Miami	40	18
Jefferson, Joseph, Ind.	19	4	Phillips, Shaun, San Diego	14	4	Taylor, Ben, Cleveland	2	6
Johnson, Ellis, Denver	15	1	Pierce, Terry, Denver	3	0	Taylor, Ike, Pittsburgh	9	2
Johnson, Jarret, Baltimore	9	8	Pile, Willie, Kansas City	23	5	Taylor, Jason, Miami	41	27
Johnson, Landon, Cin.	57	27	Polamalu, Troy, Pittsburgh	66	28	Terrell, David, Oakland	6	1
Johnson, Raylee, Denver	6	6	Polk, DaShon, Houston	18	12	Thomas, Adalius, Baltimore	49	15
Johnson, Ted, New England	56	22	Poole, Tyrone, New England	12	1	Thomas, Bryan, N.Y. Jets	28	15
Johnson, Tim, Oakland	12	10	Poole, Will, Miami	26	5	Thomas, Josh, Indianapolis	7	1
Johnson, Trevor, N.Y. Jets	9	4	Pope, Derrick, Miami	22	15	Thomas, Juqua, Tennessee	5	1
Jones, Fred, Kansas City	2	0	Pope, Monsanto, Denver	19	5	Thomas, Kevin, Buffalo	30	10
June, Cato, Indianapolis	79	25	Porter, Joey, Pittsburgh	37	17	Thomas, Kiwaukee, Jack.	9	3
Kaesviharn, Kevin, Cin.	44	14	Posey, Jeff, Buffalo	39	27	Thomas, Zach, Miami	85	60
Kassell, Brad, Tennessee	75	27	Powell, Carl, Cincinnati	16	6	Thompson, Chaun, Clev.	39	19
Keisel, Brett, Pittsburgh	3	3	Prioleau, Pierson, Buffalo	15	7	Thompson, Lamont, Tenn.	55	10
Kelley, Ethan, New England	1	0	Pryce, Trevor, Denver	1	1	Thornton, David, Ind.	66	19
Kelly, Tommy, Oakland	16	4	Ransom, Derrick, Jack.	4	4	Thornton, John, Cincinnati	37	20
Kelsay, Chris, Buffalo	22	15	Ratliff, Keiwan, Cincinnati	27	8	Tongue, Reggie, N.Y. Jets	55	17
Kemoeatu, Maake, Balt.	19	8	Reagor, Montae, Ind.	35	8	Townsend, Deshea, Pitts.	47	9
Kendall, Pete, N.Y. Jets	1	0	Reed, Ed, Baltimore	64	14	Traylor, Keith, New England	23	5
Kennedy, Kenoy, Denver	66	16	Reed, James, N.Y. Jets	13	6	Tripplett, Larry, Indianapolis	26	3
Kiel, Terrence, San Diego	71	25	Reese, Izell, Buffalo	18	18	Unck, Mason, Cleveland	4	1
Kirschke, Travis, Pittsburgh	6	6	Reid, Dexter, New England	4	6	Vilma, Jonathan, N.Y. Jets	75	30
Klecko, Dan, New England	0	1	Reynolds, Robert, Tennessee	2	3	Vincent, Troy, Buffalo	18	9
Knight, Sammy, Miami	52	44	Roberts, Terrell, Cincinnati	8	1	von Oelhoffen, Kimo, Pitts.	16	8
Kriewaldt, Clint, Pittsburgh	3	1	Robertson, Dewayne, N.Y. J.	39	14	Vrabel, Mike, New England	52	15
LaBoy, Travis, Tennessee	13	8	Robinson, Bryan, Miami	24	17	Waddell, Michael, Tenn.	30	2
Lang, Kenard, Cleveland	49	13	Robinson, Dunta, Houston	74	14	Walker, Denard, Oakland	42	2
Law, Ty, New England	23	5	Rogers, Nick, G.B.-Ind.*	3	1	Walker, Gary, Houston	20	10
Leber, Ben, San Diego	47	11	Rogers, Tyrone, Cleveland	17	5	Walls, Lenny, Denver	20	1
Lehan, Michael, Cleveland	10	4	Rolle, Samari, Tennessee	27	1	Walls, Raymond, Baltimore	8	4
Lewis, Ray, Baltimore	101	46	Romero, Dario, Miami	15	6	Walter, Kevin, Cincinnati	1	0
Little, Earl, Cleveland	37	11	Roye, Orpheus, Cleveland	30	8	Warfield, Eric, Kansas City	50	8
Logan, Mike, Pittsburgh	1	2	Samuel, Asante, N.E.	37	2	Warren, Gerard, Cleveland	14	5
Long, Rien, Tennessee	21	5	Sanders, Bob, Indianapolis	25	4	Warren, Ty, New England	40	9
Lynch, John, Denver	48	17	Sanders, Deion, Baltimore	7	1	Washington, Dewayne, Jack.	68	9
Maddox, Anthony, Jack.	0	1	Sanders, Lewis, Cleveland	19	4	Washington, Ted, Oakland	33	8
Madison, Sam, Miami	34	13	Sands, Terdell, Oakland	17	5	Watson, Kenny, Cincinnati	1	0
Martin, Terrance, Cincinnati	1	0	Sandy, Justin, Tennessee	1	0	Watts, Darius, Denver	0	0
Mathis, Rashean, Jack.	52	10	Sapp, Benny, Kansas City	8	1	Weaver, Anthony, Baltimore	35	4
Mathis, Robert, Indianapolis	22	1	Sapp, Gerome, Indianapolis	13	2	Webster, Nate, Cincinnati	16	5
McAlister, Chris, Baltimore	38	4	Sapp, Warren, Oakland	31	11	Wesley, Greg, Kansas City	60	9
McCleon, Dexter, K.C.	30	6	Schobel, Aaron, Buffalo	46	27	Westmoreland, Eric, Clev.	6	2
McClover, Darrell, N.Y. Jets	1	0	Schobel, Bo, Tennessee	14	1	Wilfork, Vince, New England.	27	15
McCray, Bobby, Jacksonville	19	5	Schulters, Lance, Tennessee	12	2	Wilhelm, Matt, San Diego	5	0
McCree, Marlon, Houston	22	2	Schweigert, Stuart, Oakland	29	7	Wilkerson, Jimmy, K.C.	8	1
McCutcheon, Daylon, Clev.	45	5	Scioli, Brad, Indianapolis	7	5	Wilkins, Marcus, Cincinnati	0	3
McGarrahan, Scott, Tenn.	21	6	Scott, Bart, Baltimore	5	7	Williams, Brock, Oakland	5	1
McGee, Terrence, Buffalo	71	16	Scott, Chad, Pittsburgh	27	2	Williams, Chad, Baltimore	24	4
McGinest, Willie, N.E.	35	16	Scott, DeQuincy, San Diego	14	5	Williams, D.J., Denver	75	31
McGraw, Jon, N.Y. Jets	22	6	Sears, Corey, Houston	5	5	Williams, Jamal, San Diego	25	7
McKinley, Alvin, Cleveland	29	20	Seau, Junior, Miami	31	26	Williams, Jay, Miami	21	17
Meier, Rob, Jacksonville	15	7	Seymour, Richard, N.E.	25	15	Williams, Josh, Indianapolis	28	7
Middlebrooks, Willie, Den.	17	3	Sharper, Jamie, Houston	98	41	Williams, Madieu, Cincinnati.	76	15
Miller, Caleb, Cincinnati	17	11	Shaw, Josh, Miami	3	1	Williams, Pat, Buffalo	37	16
Milligan, Hanik, San Diego	3	1	Siavii, Junior, Kansas City	8	1	Williams, Sam, Oakland	21	5
Milloy, Lawyer, Buffalo	39	23	Simmons, Brian, Cincinnati	76	31	Williams, Tank, Tennessee	41	11
Mitchell, Anthony, Cin.	4	1	Simmons, Jason, Houston	32	6	Williams, Tony, Cincinnati	10	6
Mitchell, Kawika, K.C.	57	14	Sims, Ryan, Kansas City	13	2	Williams, Willie, Pittsburgh	40	14
Monds, Mario, Miami	3	2	Slaughter, T.J., Baltimore	2	1	Wilson, Al, Denver	72	33
Moore, Eddie, Miami	18	7	Smith, Aaron, Pittsburgh	31	13	Wilson, Eugene, N.E.	56	9
Moore, Langston, Cincinnati	22	9	Smith, Daryl, Jacksonville	41	7	Wilson, Jerry, San Diego	52	23
Moreland, Earthwind, N.E.	14	1	Smith, Justin, Cincinnati	42	29	Wire, Coy, Buffalo	10	8
Moreno, Zeke, San Diego	6	2	Smith, Musa, Baltimore	1	0	Wong, Kailee, Houston	51	20
Morris, Rob, Indianapolis	53	23	Smith, Robaire, Houston	33	19	Woods, Jerome, K.C.	36	6
Morris, Sammy, Miami	1	0	Smith, Rod, Denver	1	0	Woodson, Charles, Oakland	59	15
Myers, Michael, Cleveland	22	12	Smith, Shaun, N.O.-Cin.*	8	3	Woolfolk, Andre, Tennessee	36	5

Player, Team	Tk.	Ast.
Wright, Kenny, Houston	5	2
Wright, Kenyatta, N.Y. Jets	2	0
Wyrick, Jimmy, Miami	5	0
Zgonina, Jeff, Miami	32	31

*Includes both NFC and AFC statistics.

NFC

Player, Team	Tk.	Ast.
Adams, Anthony, S.F.	41	7
Adams, Flozell, Dallas	0	1
Adams, Keith, Philadelphia	30	4
Adams, Mike, San Francisco	4	1
Ahanotu, Chidi, Mia.-T B.*	14	5
Alexander, Brent, N.Y. G.	56	24
Allen, Brian, Carolina	11	4
Allen, James, New Orleans	30	16
Allen, Kenderick, N.Y. Giants	17	3
Allen, Will, N.Y. Giants	75	6
Allen, Will, Tampa Bay	3	1
Ambrose, Ashley, N.O.	23	3
Anderson, Dwight, St. Louis	4	1
Archuleta, Adam, St. Louis	69	14
Arrington, LaVar, Wash.	11	4
Atkins, James, S.F.	1	0
Azumah, Jerry, Chicago	39	11
Babers, Roderick, Detroit	0	1
Babineaux, Jordan, Seattle	2	1
Barber, Ronde, Tampa Bay	77	15
Barnes, Brandon, Wash.	1	0
Barnett, Nick, Green Bay	91	30
Bates, Solomon, Seattle	16	10
Beasley, Aaron, Atlanta	16	2
Bell, Marcus, Detroit	19	8
Bellamy, Jay, New Orleans	74	18
Bernard, Rocky, Seattle	26	13
Berry, Bertrand, Arizona	40	8
Bierria, Terreal, Seattle	47	22
Bly, Dre', Detroit	32	6
Bockwoldt, Colby, N.O.	31	6
Boone, Alfonso, Chicago	8	3
Boschetti, Ryan, Wash.	3	3
Boulware, Michael, Seattle	40	13
Bowen, Matt, Washington	17	4
Bradley, Jon, Tampa Bay	5	0
Branch, Colin, Carolina	40	14
Briggs, Lance, Chicago	102	24
Bromell, Lorenzo, N.Y. G.	3	0
Brooking, Keith, Atlanta	86	16
Brooks, Derrick, Tampa Bay	109	28
Brown, Alex, Chicago	41	10
Brown, Chad, Seattle	26	11
Brown, Fakhir, New Orleans	53	1
Brown, Mike, Chicago	9	1
Brown, Ralph, Minnesota	6	1
Brown, Sheldon, Phil.	66	23
Brown, Tony, San Francisco	19	3
Bryant, Fernando, Detroit	42	8
Bryant, Tony, New Orleans	7	4
Bryant, Wendell, Arizona	1	0
Buckner, Brentson, Carolina	28	13
Burgess, Derrick, Phil.	20	4
Burleson, Nate, Minnesota	1	0
Burns, Curry, N.Y. Giants	17	3
Butler, Jerametrius, St. L.	73	5
Cain, Jeremy, Chicago	0	2
Campbell, Khary, Wash.	2	0
Carpenter, Dwaine, S.F.	43	5
Carroll, Ahmad, Green Bay	43	3
Carson, Leonardo, Dallas	29	14
Carstens, Jordan, Carolina	10	3
Carter, Andre, S.F.	7	3
Cash, Chris, Detroit	25	4
Chavous, Corey, Minnesota	59	20
Chillar, Brandon, St. Louis	14	5
Ciurciu, Vinny, Carolina	23	8
Claiborne, Chris, Minnesota	39	18
Clark, Ryan, Washington	61	14
Claybrooks, DeVone, Dallas	0	1
Clemons, Chris, Wash.	6	0
Coady, Rich, St. Louis	34	6

Player, Team	Tk.	Ast.
Coakley, Dexter, Dallas	51	17
Cochran, Antonio, Seattle	27	9
Cole, Colin, Green Bay	6	1
Coleman, Kenyon, Dallas	9	0
Coleman, Rod, Atlanta	32	9
Cooper, Chris, Dal.-S.F.	11	4
Cooper, Marquis, T.B.	1	0
Cousin, Terry, N.Y. Giants	32	7
Cox, Torrie, Tampa Bay	8	1
Craft, Jason, New Orleans	14	2
Curry, Donte', Detroit	5	2
Daniels, Phillip, Washington	4	0
Dansby, Karlos, Arizona	38	16
Darby, Chartric, Tampa Bay	40	10
Darling, James, Arizona	73	15
Davis, James, Detroit	54	25
Davis, Rod, Minnesota	1	0
Davis, Russell, Arizona	39	11
Dawkins, Brian, Phil.	62	8
DeLoatch, Curtis, N.Y. G.	15	2
Dennis, Pat, Washington	1	0
DeVries, Jared, Detroit	16	9
Diggs, Na'il, Green Bay	61	19
Dixon, Tony, Dallas	28	2
Dockett, Darnell, Arizona	35	5
Douglas, Hugh, Philadelphia	15	0
Draft, Chris, Atlanta	42	15
Duckett, Damane, Car. -N.Y. G.	2	3
Duncan, Jamie, Atlanta	6	0
Eaton, Chad, Dallas	5	4
Edwards, Antuan, Mia.-St. L.	47	18
Edwards, Kalimba, Detroit	18	4
Edwards, Mario, Tampa Bay	19	1
Ellis, Greg, Dallas	44	15
Emmons, Carlos, N.Y. G.	62	35
Engelberger, John, S.F.	25	20
Evans, Demetric, Wash.	17	9
Evans, Heath, Seattle	1	0
Faulk, Trev, St. Louis	15	8
Fields, Mark, Carolina	50	12
Fisher, Bryce, St. Louis	35	11
Fisher, Travis, St. Louis	32	3
Flowers, Erik, St. Louis	5	2
Franz, Todd, Washington	3	1
Frazier, Lance, Dallas	34	6
Gamble, Chris, Carolina	60	6
Garrett, Kevin, St. Louis	8	2
Gbaja-Biamila, Kabeer, G.B.	33	14
Gleason, Steve, N.O.	0	2
Glover, La'Roi, Dallas	31	10
Glymph, Junior, Atlanta	4	0
Gold, Ian, Tampa Bay	54	17
Gooch, Jeff, Tampa Bay	18	6
Goodman, Andre', Detroit	19	5
Grant, Charles, New Orleans	67	13
Grasmanis, Paul, Phil.	10	0
Gray, Bobby, Chicago	16	4
Green, Barrett, N.Y. Giants	26	12
Green, Howard, N.O.	18	10
Green, Jamaal, Philadelphia	2	0
Green, Mike, Chicago	84	23
Gregory, Damian, T.B.	3	0
Greisen, Nick, N.Y. Giants	53	19
Griffin, Cornelius, Wash.	55	15
Groce, DeJuan, St. Louis	27	0
Haley, Jermaine, Wash.	7	1
Hall, Cory, Atlanta	42	11
Hall, DeAngelo, Atlanta	30	6
Hall, James, Detroit	38	10
Hall, Travis, Atlanta	23	6
Hamlin, Ken, Seattle	63	16
Hand, Norman, N.Y. Giants	11	4
Hanson, Joselio, S.F.	18	2
Hargrove, Anthony, St. L.	21	6
Harper, Deveron, N.O.	2	0
Harris, Al, Green Bay	56	6
Harris, Quentin, Arizona	21	2
Harris, Tommie, Chicago	29	15
Harris, Walt, Washington	16	2
Hawkins, Artrell, Carolina	24	5

Player, Team	Tk.	Ast.
Hawthorne, Michael, G.B.	26	8
Hayes, Gerald, Arizona	12	3
Haynes, Michael, Chicago	25	6
Heard, Ronnie, S.F.	56	12
Henderson, E.J., Minnesota	66	28
Hill, Renaldo, Arizona	38	7
Hillenmeyer, Hunter, Chi.	51	20
Hodge, Sedrick, N.O.	17	7
Holmes, Earl, Detroit	78	33
Holt, Terrence, Detroit	15	5
Hood, Roderick, Phil.	33	2
Horton, Jason, Green Bay	3	2
Hovan, Chris, Minnesota	11	9
Howard, Brian, St. Louis	2	5
Howard, Darren, N.O.	37	9
Howell, John, Tampa Bay	15	2
Huff, Orlando, Seattle	41	10
Hunt, Cletidus, Green Bay	18	14
Hunter, Pete, Dallas	6	0
Idonije, Israel, Chicago	10	3
Jackson, Dexter, Tampa Bay	14	2
Jackson, Eddie, Carolina	7	1
Jackson, Grady, Green Bay	17	6
Jackson, Tyoka, St. Louis	21	3
James, Bradie, Dallas	24	7
Jasper, Ed, Atlanta	27	7
Jenkins, Cullen, Green Bay	13	5
Jenkins, Kris, Carolina	8	3
Jimoh, Ade, Washington	6	0
Johnson, Bryant, Arizona	1	0
Johnson, Spencer, Minn.	27	11
Johnson, Tank, Chicago	10	2
Johnson, Todd, Chicago	56	12
Johnstone, Lance, Minn.	25	6
Jones, Dhani, Philadelphia	45	22
Jones, Nathan, Dallas	29	2
Jones, Rushen, Minnesota	1	0
Jones, Tebucky, N.O.	79	23
Jordan, Omari, Carolina	1	2
Joseph, William, N.Y. Giants	20	5
Josue, Steve, Green Bay	5	0
Jue, Bhawoh, Green Bay	29	3
Kacyvenski, Isaiah, Seattle	62	19
Kampman, Aaron, G.B.	48	20
Kashama, Alain, Chicago	0	1
Kearse, Jevon, Philadelphia	27	4
Kelly, Brian, Tampa Bay	51	7
Kennedy, Jimmy, St. Louis	13	3
Kerney, Patrick, Atlanta	55	11
Knight, Roger, New Orleans	6	2
Kolodziej, Ross, Arizona	7	0
Koutouvides, Niko, Seattle	38	8
Labinjo, Mike, Philadelphia	10	0
Lake, Antwan, Atlanta	3	2
Lassiter, Kwamie, St. Louis	6	1
Lavalais, Chad, Atlanta	24	4
Lee, James, Green Bay	7	2
Legree, Lance, N.Y. Giants	22	14
Lehman, Teddy, Detroit	73	24
Leisle, Rodney, New Orleans	1	0
Lenon, Paris, Green Bay	15	6
Leverette, Otis, S.F.	7	0
Lewis, Alex, Detroit	35	14
Lewis, Damione, St. Louis	26	10
Lewis, Keith, San Francisco	0	1
Lewis, Kevin, N.Y. Giants	62	26
Lewis, Michael, Philadelphia	76	14
Little, Leonard, St. Louis	36	10
Lott, Andre, Washington	7	1
Lucas, Justin, St. Louis	1	0
Lucas, Ken, Seattle	60	7
Luchey, Nick, Green Bay	1	0
Macklin, David, Arizona	59	12
Mallard, Wesly, N.Y. Giants	3	0
Manning Jr., Ricky, Carolina	50	10
Manuel, Marquand, Seattle	7	3
Marion, Brock, Detroit	66	22
Marshall, Alfonso, Chicago	1	0
Marshall, Lemar, Wash.	45	20
Marshall, Torrance, G.B.	3	0

Player, Team	Tk.	Ast.
artin, Steve, Minnesota	11	9
athis, Kevin, Atlanta	59	5
axwell, James, N.Y. Giants	4	3
aynard, Brad, Chicago	0	1
cAfee, Fred, New Orleans	1	0
cBride, Tod, St. Louis	1	0
cCadam, Kevin, Atlanta	12	2
cDougle, Jerome, Phil.	13	0
cFarland, Anthony, T. B.	10	2
cKenzie, Mike, G.B.-N.O.	31	2
cKinnon, Ronald, Arizona	49	25
cMillon, Todd, Chicago	1	2
cQuarters, R.W., Chicago	55	12
ikell, Quintin, Philadelphia	6	0
inter, Mike, Carolina	63	20
itchell, Brandon, Seattle	13	3
itchell, Mel, New Orleans	3	0
ixon, Kenny, Minnesota	28	18
ontgomery, Monty, N.O.	1	0
oore, Brandon, S.F.	11	2
oore, Mewelde, Minn.	1	0
oore, Rashad, Seattle	34	12
oorehead, Kindal, Carolina	31	7
organ, Dan, Carolina	79	23
orton, Christian, Atlanta	2	0
attiel, Michael, Minnesota	11	3
avies, Hannibal, Green Bay	37	10
ece, Ryan, Tampa Bay	0	1
ed, Larry, Minnesota	1	0
elson, Rhett, Minnesota	2	0
ewman, Keith, Minnesota	36	12
ewman, Terence, Dallas	66	4
guyen, Dat, Dallas	75	32
oble, Brandon, Wash.	9	5
dom, Joe, Chicago	12	6
fford, Willie, Minnesota	12	6
gbogu, Eric, Dallas	10	4
gunleye, Adewale, Chicago	28	9
halete, Ifeanyi, Arizona	51	13
keafor, Chike, Seattle	41	12
ace, Calvin, Arizona	6	4
arrish, Tony, S.F.	54	28
eppers, Julius, Carolina	53	12
eterson, Julian, S.F.	24	3
eterson, Kenny, Green Bay	9	2
eterson, Will, N.Y. Giants	61	8
hillips, Jermaine, T.B.	31	11
ckett, Ryan, St. Louis	42	4
ierce, Antonio, Wash.	84	26
erson, Shurron, Chicago	1	1
nkney, Cleveland, Atl.-Car.	5	0
ummer, Ahmed, S.F.	15	7
olley, Tommy, St. Louis	65	13
ritchett, Kelvin, Detroit	10	7
uarles, Shelton, T.B.	72	32
ainer, Wali, Detroit	3	4
asheed, Saleem, S.F.	13	5
asmussen, Kemp, Carolina	1	1
ayburn, Sam, Philadelphia	28	2
edding, Cory, Detroit	34	6
eed, J.R., Philadelphia	12	0
eed, Rayshun, S.F.	4	0
eese, Ike, Philadelphia	33	3
eese, Marcus, Chicago	6	2
eeves, Jacques, Dallas	12	1
ce, Simeon, Tampa Bay	35	5
obbins, Fred, N.Y. Giants	31	9
odgers, Derrick, N.O.	44	11
oman, Mark, Green Bay	49	19
oss, Derek, Minnesota	52	19
ossum, Allen, Atlanta	9	0
ossum, Allen, Atlanta	19	1
ucker, Mike, Carolina	35	3
uff, Orlando, New Orleans	53	21

Player, Team	Tk.	Ast.
Rumph, Mike, S.F.	4	1
Russell, Brian, Minnesota	58	20
Salave'a, Joe, Washington	17	3
Savage, Josh, Tampa Bay	0	1
Scott, Bryan, Atlanta	76	11
Scott, Darrion, Minnesota	12	11
Scott, Ian, Chicago	34	10
Scott, Lynn, Dallas	28	9
Seigler, Richard, S.F.	0	1
Shabazz, Siddeeq, Atlanta	1	0
Shanle, Scott, Dallas	17	6
Sharper, Darren, Green Bay	59	13
Shaw, Terrance, Minnesota	27	4
Sheppard, Lito, Philadelphia	52	4
Short, Brandon, Carolina	29	11
Simmons, Anthony, Seattle	30	12
Simon, Corey, Philadelphia	26	6
Simoneau, Mark, Phil.	35	14
Singleton, Al, Dallas	31	14
Smith, Brady, Atlanta	25	5
Smith, Corey, T.B.-S.F.	2	0
Smith, Derek, San Francisco	80	29
Smith, Dwight, Tampa Bay	72	11
Smith, Keith, Detroit	22	7
Smith, Larry, Green Bay	3	1
Smith, Raonall, Minnesota	12	5
Smith, Will, New Orleans	32	10
Smoot, Fred, Washington	55	6
Spencer, Shawntae, S.F.	59	8
Spires, Greg, Tampa Bay	47	14
Springs, Shawn, Wash.	52	12
Starks, Duane, Arizona	53	5
Stewart, Daleroy, Dal.-N.Y. J.-S. F.*	5	4
Stewart, Matt, Atlanta	56	11
Stone, Michael, Arizona	1	1
Stoutmire, Omar, N.Y. G.	1	1
Strahan, Michael, N.Y. G.	25	10
Sullivan, Johnathan, N.O.	11	4
Tate, Robert, Arizona	12	0
Taylor, Bobby, Seattle	11	2
Taylor, Sean, Washington	59	17
Terrill, Craig, Seattle	1	3
Thomas, Dontarrious, Minn.	36	15
Thomas, Fred, New Orleans	43	2
Thomas, Hollis, Philadelphia	17	4
Thomas, Joey, Green Bay	14	1
Thomas, Robert, St. Louis	39	15
Thompson, Ray, Arizona	21	13
Thornton, Kalen, Dallas	6	0
Tillman, Charles, Chicago	32	7
Tillman, Travares, Carolina	3	1
Tinoisamoa, Pisa, St. Louis	73	19
Torbor, Reggie, N.Y. Giants	15	6
Trotter, Jeremiah, Phil.	55	6
Trufant, Marcus, Seattle	83	10
Truluck, R-Kal, Green Bay	12	1
Tubbs, Marcus, Seattle	6	7
Udeze, Kenechi, Minnesota	25	11
Ulbrich, Jeff, San Francisco	71	19
Umenyiora, Osi, N.Y. Giants	42	16
Urlacher, Brian, Chicago	54	18
Vanden Bosch, Kyle, Ariz.	11	2
Vasher, Nathan, Chicago	22	1
Vaughn, Khaleed, Atlanta	3	0
Walker, Bracy, Detroit	52	22
Walker, Darwin, Phil.	22	7
Walker, Frank, N.Y. Giants	10	2
Wallace, Al, Carolina	20	2
Ware, Matt, Philadelphia	8	0
Warner, Ron, Washington	9	3
Washington, Keith, N.Y. G.	12	5
Washington, Marcus, Wash.	83	19
Watson, Courtney, N.O.	38	17
Wayne, Nate, Philadelphia	23	7
Webster, Jason, Atlanta	39	2

Player, Team	Tk.	Ast.
Wesley, Dante, Carolina	4	0
White, Dewayne, Tampa Bay	23	7
White, Tracy, Seattle	19	7
Whitehead, Willie, N.O.	6	4
Whiting, Brandon, S.F.	8	3
Whitley, James, Green Bay	1	0
Wilds, Garnell, Washington	5	0
Wiley, Chuck, Minn.-N.Y. G.	3	4
Wiley, Marcellus, Dallas	31	7
Wilkinson, Dan, Detroit	18	5
Williams, Aeneas, St. Louis	40	8
Williams, Andrew, S.F.	9	2
Williams, Brian, Minnesota	59	12
Williams, Corey, Green Bay	12	9
Williams, Davern, N.Y. G.	3	4
Williams, Demorrio, Atlanta	38	7
Williams, Jimmy, S.F.	35	8
Williams, Kevin, Minnesota	53	17
Williams, Melvin, S.F.	3	1
Williams, Roy, Dallas	70	18
Williams, Shaun, N.Y. G.	11	0
Williams, Tyrone, Dallas	7	0
Wilson, Adrian, Arizona	78	22
Wilson, Gibril, N.Y. Giants	49	6
Winborn, Jamie, S.F.	55	8
Winfield, Antoine, Minn.	64	14
Wistrom, Grant, Seattle	27	11
Witherspoon, Will, Carolina	84	18
Woodard, Cedric, Seattle	28	21
Woods, LeVar, Arizona	13	5
Worrell, Cameron, Chicago	7	0
Wyms, Ellis, Tampa Bay	7	4
Wynn, Dexter, Philadelphia	11	0
Wynn, Renaldo, Wash.	31	7
Yates, Max, Minnesota	1	1
Young, Brian, New Orleans	40	19
Young, Bryant, S. F.	37	11
Zellner, Peppi, Arizona	16	6

*Includes both NFC and AFC statistics.

PLAYERS WITH TWO CLUBS

Player, Team	Tk.	Ast.
Ahanotu, Chidi, Miami	2	1
Ahanotu, Chidi, Tampa Bay	12	4
Carter, Dyshod, Arizona	3	0
Carter, Dyshod, Cleveland	2	0
Cooper, Chris, Dallas	0	0
Cooper, Chris, S.F.	11	4
Cooper, Jarrod, Carolina	0	0
Cooper, Jarrod, Oakland	13	0
Duckett, Damane, Carolina	0	0
Duckett, Damane, N.Y. G.	2	3
Edwards, Antuan, Miami	24	12
Edwards, Antuan, St. Louis	23	6
McKenzie, Mike, Green Bay	0	0
McKenzie, Mike, New O.	31	2
Palepoi, Anton, Seattle	0	0
Palepoi, Anton, Denver	15	4
Patterson, Elton, Cincinnati	0	0
Patterson, Elton, Jack.	3	4
Pinkney, Cleveland, Atlanta	5	0
Pinkney, Cleveland, Carolina	0	0
Rogers, Nick, Green Bay	0	0
Rogers, Nick, Indianapolis	3	1
Smith, Corey, Tampa Bay	2	0
Smith, Corey, San Francisco	0	0
Smith, Shaun, New Orleans	6	3
Smith, Shaun, Cincinnati	2	0
Stewart, Daleroy, Dallas	0	1
Stewart, Daleroy, N.Y. Jets	0	0
Stewart, Daleroy, S.F.	5	3
Wiley, Chuck, Minnesota	2	1
Wiley, Chuck, N.Y. Giants	1	3

2004 STATISTICS Tackles

CLUB RANKINGS BY YARDS

Team	OFFENSE			DEFENSE		
	Total	Rush	Pass	Total	Rush	Pass
Arizona	27	22	24	12	27	9
Atlanta	20	*1	30	14	T8	22
Baltimore	31	9	31	6	T8	10
Buffalo	25	13	27	2	7	3
Carolina	13	28	9	20	17	18
Chicago	32	T25	32	21	25	15
Cincinnati	18	17	17	19	26	13
Cleveland	28	23	25	15	32	5
Dallas	14	20	15	16	10	21
Denver	5	4	6	4	4	6
Detroit	24	19	23	22	15	20
Green Bay	3	10	3	25	14	25
Houston	19	12	18	23	13	24
Indianapolis	2	15	*1	29	24	28
Jacksonville	21	16	19	11	11	16
Kansas City	*1	5	4	31	12	32
Miami	29	31	21	8	31	2
Minnesota	4	18	2	28	21	29
New England	7	7	11	9	6	17
New Orleans	15	27	12	32	30	27
N.Y. Giants	23	11	26	13	28	8
N.Y. Jets	12	3	22	7	5	14
Oakland	17	32	8	30	22	30
Philadelphia	9	24	7	10	16	12
Pittsburgh	16	2	28	*1	*1	4
San Diego	10	6	16	18	3	31
San Francisco	26	30	20	24	20	19
Seattle	8	8	13	26	23	23
St. Louis	6	T25	5	17	29	11
Tampa Bay	22	29	14	5	19	*1
Tennessee	11	14	10	27	18	26
Washington	30	21	29	3	2	7

*NFL leader.
T-Tied for position.

TAKEAWAYS/GIVEAWAYS

AFC

	TAKEAWAYS			GIVEAWAYS			
	Int.	Fum.	Tot.	Int.	Fum.	Tot.	Net Diff.
Indianapolis	19	17	36	10	7	17	19
N.Y. Jets	19	14	33	11	5	16	17
San Diego	23	10	33	8	10	18	15
Pittsburgh	19	13	32	13	8	21	11
Baltimore	21	13	34	11	12	23	11
Buffalo	24	15	39	17	12	29	10
New England	20	16	36	14	13	27	9
Jacksonville	16	12	28	11	11	22	6
Houston	22	8	30	14	11	25	5
Cincinnati	20	16	36	22	10	32	4
Tennessee	18	12	30	19	12	31	-1
Kansas City	13	8	21	17	10	27	-6
Denver	12	8	20	20	9	29	-9
Cleveland	15	13	28	21	19	40	-12
Miami	15	10	25	26	16	42	-17
Oakland	9	9	18	22	13	35	-17

NFC

	TAKEAWAYS			GIVEAWAYS			
	Int.	Fum.	Tot.	Int.	Fum.	Tot.	Net Diff.
Carolina	26	12	38	15	11	26	12
Seattle	23	12	35	18	9	27	8
New Orleans	13	20	33	16	10	26	7
Philadelphia	17	11	28	11	11	22	6
Detroit	14	10	24	13	7	20	4
N.Y. Giants	14	14	28	13	11	24	4
Atlanta	19	13	32	16	14	30	2
Minnesota	11	11	22	12	9	21	1
Arizona	15	15	30	18	11	29	1
Washington	18	8	26	17	10	27	-1
Chicago	17	12	29	16	21	37	-8
Tampa Bay	16	11	27	18	18	36	-9
Green Bay	8	7	15	19	10	29	-14
Dallas	13	9	22	23	14	37	-15
San Francisco	9	12	21	21	19	40	-19
St. Louis	6	9	15	22	17	39	-24

CLUB LEADERS

	Offense	Defense
First downs	K.C. 398	Den. 235
Rushing	K.C. 138	Was. 67
Passing	Ind. 238	Den. 130
Penalty	Ind. 47	Sea. 18
Rushes	Pit. 618	S.D. 355
Net yards gained	Atl. 2672	Pit. 1299
Average gain	Atl. 5.1	Was. 3.1
Passes attempted	G.B. 598	Mia. 434
Completed	G.B. 382	Mia. 244
Percent completed	Min. 68.8	Ariz. 53.7
Total yards gained	Min. 4754	Mia. 2815
Times sacked	G.B.,Ind. 14	Atl. 48
Yards lost	Den. 90	Ind. 340
Net yards gained	Ind. 4623	T.B. 2579
Net yards per pass play	Ind. 8.55	Buf. 4.94
Yards gained per completion	Den. 13.5	Phi. 10.4
Combined net yards gained	K.C. 6695	Pit. 4134
Percent total yards rushing	Atl. 52.6	S.D. 24.4
Percent total yards passing	Oak. 74.9	Mia. 53.0
Ball-control plays	K.C. 1089	Pit. 882
Average yards per play	Ind. 6.69	Buf. 4.32
Avg. time of possession	Pit. 34:00	—
Third-down efficiency	Min.52.3	Chi. 30.5
Interceptions	—	Car. 26
Yards returned	—	Bal. 700
Returned for TD	—	Chi., Bal. 5
Punts	Chi. 110	—
Yards punted	Chi. 4691	—
Average yards per punt	Oak. 46.7	—
Punt returns	Bal. 60	S.D. 23
Yards returned	Bal. 616	Atl. 134
Average yds. per return	Atl. 12.4	Atl. 4.1
Returned for TD	3 tied with 2	—
Kickoff returns	S.F., St.L. 84	Ariz. 46
Yards returned	N.O. 1879	Jac. 995
Average yards per return	NYG 25.1	Dal. 17.5
Returned for TD	Buf. 3	—
Total Points Scored	Ind. 522	Pit. 251
Total TDs	Ind. 66	Pit. 26
TDs rushing	K.C. 31	Hou.4
TDs passing	Ind. 51	Pit., Bal. 14
TDs on ret. and recov.	Buf. 10	NYG 9
Extra point kicks	Ind. 64	N.E. 23
2-Pt. conversions	Jac., St.L. 4	9 tied with 0
Safeties	Chi. 3	—
Field goals made	N.E. 31	N.E. 18
Field goals attempted	Den. 34	Atl., N.E. 18
Percent successful	N.E. 93.9	T.B. 64.5
Extra points	Ind. 65	Pit., Bal. 25

2004 STATISTICS Miscellanceous

OFFENSE

	Bal.	Buf.	Cin.	Cle.	Den.	Hou.	Ind.	Jac.	K.C.	Mia.	N.E.	NYJ	Oak.	Pit.	S.D.	Ten.
st downs	260	271	286	245	351	300	379	279	398	267	344	313	275	310	328	308
Rushing	103	102	93	94	127	103	94	88	138	71	120	135	75	134	131	85
Passing	135	149	172	125	184	174	238	161	228	165	193	163	176	147	160	200
Penalty	22	20	21	26	40	23	47	30	32	31	31	15	24	29	37	23
shes	491	483	437	441	534	481	427	446	496	384	524	527	327	618	525	420
Net yards gained	2063	1874	1839	1657	2333	1882	1852	1850	2289	1339	2134	2388	1295	2464	2185	1871
Average gain	4.2	3.9	4.2	3.8	4.4	3.9	4.3	4.1	4.6	3.5	4.1	4.5	4.0	4.0	4.2	4.5
Average yards per game	128.9	117.1	114.9	103.6	145.8	117.6	115.8	115.6	143.1	83.7	133.4	149.3	80.9	154.0	136.6	116.9
sses attempted	465	461	536	439	521	471	527	513	561	586	485	438	582	358	450	589
Completed	258	262	324	251	303	286	353	305	370	309	293	282	330	228	288	356
Percent completed	55.5	56.8	60.4	57.2	58.2	60.7	67.0	59.5	66.0	52.7	60.4	64.4	56.7	63.7	64.0	60.4
Total yards gained	2559	3032	3520	3076	4089	3547	4732	3315	4633	3391	3750	3231	4019	2970	3506	3933
Times sacked	35	38	31	41	15	49	14	32	32	52	26	31	30	36	21	44
Yards lost	247	215	219	252	90	301	109	156	227	326	162	181	161	250	149	317
Net yards gained	2312	2817	3301	2824	3999	3246	4623	3159	4406	3065	3588	3050	3858	2720	3357	3616
Average yards per game	144.5	176.1	206.3	176.5	249.9	202.9	288.9	197.4	275.4	191.6	224.3	190.6	241.1	170.0	209.8	226.0
Net yards per pass play	4.62	5.65	5.82	5.88	7.46	6.24	8.55	5.80	7.43	4.80	7.02	6.50	6.30	6.90	7.13	5.71
Yards gained per completion	9.92	11.57	10.86	12.25	13.50	12.40	13.41	10.87	12.52	10.97	12.80	11.46	12.18	13.03	12.17	11.05
mbined net yards gained	4375	4691	5140	4481	6332	5128	6475	5009	6695	4404	5722	5438	5153	5184	5542	5487
Percent total yards rushing	47.2	39.9	35.8	37.0	36.8	36.7	28.6	36.9	34.2	30.4	37.3	43.9	25.1	47.5	39.4	34.1
Percent total yards passing	52.8	60.1	64.2	63.0	63.2	63.3	71.4	63.1	65.8	69.6	62.7	56.1	74.9	52.5	60.6	65.9
Average yards per game	273.4	293.2	321.3	280.1	395.8	320.5	404.7	313.1	418.4	275.3	357.6	339.9	322.1	324.0	346.4	342.9
ll-control plays	991	982	1004	921	1070	1001	968	991	1089	1022	1035	996	939	1012	996	1053
Average yards per play	4.4	4.8	5.1	4.9	5.9	5.1	6.7	5.1	6.1	4.3	5.5	5.5	5.5	5.1	5.6	5.2
Average time of possession	29:36	30:21	29:20	28:03	32:38	29:59	28:40	30:28	32:14	28:20	31:22	31:51	26:47	34:00	31:30	31:40
ird-down efficiency	35.1	35.8	40.2	29.1	37.9	38.4	42.7	36.9	47.2	34.5	45.1	42.5	35.5	42.9	46.6	34.1
d intercepted	11	17	22	21	20	14	10	11	17	26	14	11	22	13	8	19
Yards opponents returned	172	357	446	232	344	157	191	163	244	464	242	332	356	190	66	306
Returned by oppponents for TD	0	1	4	2	1	1	0	1	1	8	1	0	3	3	0	2
nts	97	78	84	85	70	73	54	84	55	99	56	80	73	67	69	79
Yards punted	3935	3362	3499	3404	2834	3009	2443	3592	2172	4107	2350	3057	3409	2879	2974	3389
Average yards per punt	40.6	43.1	41.7	40.0	40.5	41.2	45.2	42.8	39.5	41.5	42.0	38.2	46.7	43.0	43.1	42.9
nt returns	60	46	35	36	43	40	24	42	24	52	40	41	24	44	29	40
Yards returned	616	491	328	432	400	329	171	405	232	564	230	313	132	365	243	173
Average yards per return	10.3	10.7	9.4	12.0	9.3	8.2	7.1	9.6	9.7	10.8	5.8	7.6	5.5	8.3	8.4	4.3
Returned for TD	2	2	0	0	0	0	0	0	0	0	0	0	0	0	0	0
koff returns	61	63	68	75	53	69	66	57	75	70	56	46	83	62	62	79
Yards returned	1264	1542	1403	1504	1122	1450	1545	1087	1820	1660	1302	1038	1700	1335	1478	1558
Average yards per return	20.7	24.5	20.6	20.1	21.2	21.0	23.4	19.1	24.3	23.7	23.3	22.6	20.5	21.5	23.8	19.7
Returned for TD	0	3	0	1	0	0	1	0	2	1	1	1	0	0	1	0
mbles	26	26	17	32	23	22	19	23	20	42	24	19	23	20	27	33
Lost	12	12	10	19	9	11	7	11	10	16	13	5	13	8	10	12
Out of bounds	1	1	1	3	4	2	2	3	0	3	2	1	1	4	2	2
Recovered for TD	1	0	0	0	0	0	0	0	0	0	0	0	1	1	0	0
nalties	94	121	103	115	93	106	106	109	117	112	101	91	134	99	108	110
Yards penalized	894	1047	810	854	880	928	801	940	963	852	822	693	1013	837	875	923
tal Points Scored	317	395	374	276	381	309	522	261	483	275	437	333	320	372	446	344
Total TDs	33	46	42	29	42	37	66	26	62	31	49	38	35	41	55	41
TDs rushing	11	15	14	6	13	16	10	9	31	10	15	10	10	16	24	12
TDs passing	13	21	23	21	27	16	51	17	27	19	29	19	24	20	29	27
TDs on returns and recoveries	9	10	5	2	2	5	5	0	4	2	5	4	1	5	2	2
Extra point kicks	30	45	41	28	42	34	64	21	58	26	48	33	31	40	54	39
Extra point kick att	30	45	41	28	42	34	65	21	60	27	48	34	32	40	55	39
2-Pt. conversions	1	0	0	1	0	1	1	4	1	2	1	0	1	0	1	1
2-Pt. conversions att.	3	1	1	1	0	3	1	4	2	4	1	4	3	1	2	2
Safeties	0	1	0	0	0	0	0	2	0	1	0	0	1	1	1	0
Field goals made	29	24	27	24	29	17	20	24	17	19	31	24	25	28	20	19
Field goals attempted	32	28	31	29	34	24	26	31	23	23	33	29	28	33	25	27
Percent successful	90.6	85.7	87.1	82.8	85.3	70.8	76.9	77.4	73.9	82.6	93.9	82.8	89.3	84.8	80.0	70.4
Extra points	31	45	41	29	42	35	65	25	59	28	49	33	32	40	54	40
Field goals blocked	1	0	0	1	0	2	0	0	1	0	0	1	0	0	0	4

	Bal.	Buf.	Cin.	Cle.	Den.	Hou.	Ind.	Jac.	K.C.	Mia.	N.E.	NYJ	Oak.	Pit.	S.D.	T
First downs	273	258	303	307	235	304	331	290	327	281	290	282	367	248	320	3
Rushing	88	79	123	141	83	89	103	83	97	107	83	87	115	79	79	
Passing	158	150	158	144	130	194	209	181	190	139	177	169	210	146	200	1
Penalty	27	29	22	22	22	21	19	26	40	35	30	26	42	23	41	
Rushes	469	447	474	532	396	417	440	438	397	539	405	432	537	357	355	4
Net yards gained	1681	1604	2062	2314	1512	1843	2037	1777	1834	2302	1572	1566	2012	1299	1307	19
Average gain	3.6	3.6	4.4	4.3	3.8	4.4	4.6	4.1	4.6	4.3	3.9	3.6	3.7	3.6	3.7	
Average yards per game	105.1	100.3	128.9	144.6	94.5	115.2	127.3	111.1	114.6	143.9	98.3	97.9	125.8	81.2	81.7	11
Passes attempted	501	486	520	460	484	530	557	497	522	434	538	497	510	484	607	5
Completed	276	261	313	277	272	344	364	306	312	244	315	289	315	269	372	3
Percent completed	55.1	53.7	60.2	60.2	56.2	64.9	65.4	61.6	59.8	56.2	58.6	58.1	61.8	55.6	61.3	6
Total yards gained	3386	2943	3560	3091	3213	3776	4232	3574	4453	2815	3711	3532	4106	3060	4195	4C
Times sacked	39	45	37	32	38	24	45	37	41	36	45	37	25	41	29	
Yards lost	264	319	257	190	266	161	340	217	250	223	311	220	182	225	142	2
Net yards gained	3122	2624	3303	2901	2947	3615	3892	3357	4203	2592	3400	3312	3924	2835	4053	38
Average yards per game	195.1	164.0	206.4	181.3	184.2	225.9	243.3	209.8	262.7	162.0	212.5	207.0	245.3	177.2	253.3	23
Net yards per pass play	5.78	4.94	5.93	5.90	5.65	6.53	6.47	6.29	7.47	5.51	5.83	6.20	7.33	5.40	6.37	6
Yards gained per completion	12.27	11.28	11.37	11.16	11.81	10.98	11.63	11.68	14.27	11.54	11.78	12.22	13.03	11.38	11.28	12
Combined net yards gained	4803	4228	5365	5215	4459	5458	5929	5134	6037	4894	4972	4878	5936	4134	5360	57
Percent total yards rushing	35.0	37.9	38.4	44.4	33.9	33.8	34.4	34.6	30.4	47.0	31.6	32.1	33.9	31.4	24.4	3
Percent total yards passing	65.0	62.1	61.6	55.6	66.1	66.2	65.6	65.4	69.6	53.0	68.4	67.9	66.1	68.6	75.6	6
Average yards per game	300.2	264.3	335.3	325.9	278.7	341.1	370.6	320.9	377.3	305.9	310.8	304.9	371.0	258.4	335.0	35
Ball-control plays	1009	978	1031	1024	918	971	1042	972	960	1009	988	966	1072	882	991	9
Average yards per play	4.8	4.3	5.2	5.1	4.9	5.6	5.7	5.3	6.3	4.9	5.0	5.0	5.5	4.7	5.4	
Average time of possession	30:24	29:39	30:40	31:57	27:23	30:01	31:20	29:32	27:46	31:40	28:38	28:09	33:13	26:01	28:30	28
Third-down efficiency	34.4	36.0	36.7	36.1	31.1	43.4	41.9	41.0	38.4	32.3	38.8	38.0	47.4	32.6	35.2	3
Intercepted by	21	24	20	15	12	22	19	16	13	15	20	19	9	19	23	
Yards returned by	700	333	272	250	175	393	252	126	173	92	290	243	221	293	180	2
Returned for TD	5	4	4	1	2	2	2	0	1	0	1	2	1	3	1	
Punts	94	79	79	85	95	69	52	74	64	102	69	89	68	79	64	
Yards punted	3767	3218	3309	3537	4250	2880	2220	3265	2703	4177	2866	3571	2808	3375	2713	32
Average yards per punt	40.1	40.7	41.9	41.6	44.7	41.7	42.7	44.1	42.2	41.0	41.5	40.1	41.3	42.7	42.4	4
Punt returns	36	37	51	48	32	30	29	38	24	45	31	34	58	34	23	
Yards returned	281	315	378	313	295	265	395	429	301	258	365	221	413	252	164	1
Average yards per return	7.8	8.5	7.4	6.5	9.2	8.8	13.6	11.3	12.5	5.7	11.8	6.5	11.8	7.4	7.1	
Returned for TD	0	0	0	0	0	0	1	2	2	0	1	0	0	0	0	
Kickoff returns	65	77	80	59	68	60	92	50	85	51	86	72	62	74	83	
Yards returned	1509	1406	1573	1336	1635	1386	1960	995	1908	1114	2003	1557	1458	1595	1846	13
Average yards per return	23.2	18.3	19.7	22.6	24.0	23.1	21.3	19.9	22.4	21.8	23.3	21.6	23.5	21.6	22.2	2
Returned for TD	2	0	0	1	1	1	0	0	0	1	1	1	0	1	2	
Fumbles	23	31	40	20	24	22	36	30	23	22	31	29	14	28	19	
Recovered by	13	15	16	13	8	8	17	12	8	10	16	14	9	13	10	
Out of bounds	0	4	3	1	0	1	0	2	6	3	3	2	0	3	0	
Recovered for TD	0	0	1	0	0	0	0	0	0	0	0	0	0	0	0	
Penalties	101	120	106	109	120	123	116	118	117	107	118	86	102	104	109	
Yards penalized	798	865	887	890	1062	979	877	966	957	852	1014	720	837	875	940	7
Total points scored	268	284	372	390	304	339	351	280	435	354	260	261	442	251	313	4
Total TDs	27	29	41	45	35	39	39	31	53	42	31	30	56	26	36	
TDs rushing	9	6	11	22	16	4	12	7	18	12	9	8	21	8	15	
TDs passing	14	20	23	17	17	32	26	18	32	20	18	21	30	14	19	
TDs on returns and recoveries	4	3	7	6	2	3	1	6	3	10	4	1	5	4	2	
Extra point kicks	24	27	40	44	31	37	36	27	50	42	23	29	53	24	33	
Extra point kick att.	24	27	40	44	32	37	36	28	51	42	23	29	54	24	34	
2-Pt. conversions	1	1	0	1	0	0	3	2	2	0	3	1	1	1	2	
2-Pt. conversions att.	3	2	1	1	3	1	3	3	2	0	8	1	2	2	2	
Safeties	1	0	1	1	0	1	0	0	0	0	0	1	0	0	0	
Field goals made	26	27	28	24	21	22	25	21	21	20	15	16	17	23	20	
Field goals attempted	31	32	31	28	26	29	31	28	27	28	18	19	25	27	27	
Percent successful	83.9	84.4	90.3	85.7	80.8	75.9	80.6	75.0	77.8	71.4	83.3	84.2	68.0	85.2	74.1	8
Extra points	25	28	40	45	31	37	39	29	52	42	26	30	54	25	35	
Field goals blocked	0	0	0	1	0	0	2	1	0	0	0	0	0	2	0	

OFFENSE

	Ariz.	Atl.	Car.	Chi.	Dal.	Det.	G.B.	Min.	N.O.	NYG	Phi.	St.L.	S.F.	Sea.	T.B.	Was.
First downs	280	284	308	230	296	263	354	351	291	281	301	321	280	320	271	269
Rushing	86	133	85	84	101	92	98	98	82	105	87	96	83	110	74	91
Passing	152	120	192	121	171	142	228	225	177	143	188	203	172	189	175	156
Penalty	42	31	31	25	24	29	28	28	32	33	26	22	25	21	22	22
Rushes	475	524	422	430	449	407	441	387	406	424	376	381	413	468	393	471
Net yards gained	1668	2672	1582	1624	1769	1777	1908	1823	1606	1904	1639	1624	1449	2095	1489	1765
Average gain	3.5	5.1	3.7	3.8	3.9	4.4	4.3	4.7	4.0	4.5	4.4	4.3	3.5	4.5	3.8	3.7
Average yards per game	104.3	167.0	98.9	101.5	110.6	111.1	119.3	113.9	100.4	119.0	102.4	101.5	90.6	130.9	93.1	110.3
Passes attempted	533	395	536	471	519	505	598	552	542	475	547	580	561	532	512	514
Completed	299	217	311	249	308	285	382	380	309	269	336	372	325	304	340	288
Percent completed	56.1	54.9	58.0	52.9	59.3	56.4	63.9	68.8	57.0	56.6	61.4	64.1	57.9	57.1	66.4	56.0
Total yards gained	3202	2692	3889	2641	3636	3124	4550	4754	3810	3097	4208	4615	3455	3715	3773	2874
Times sacked	39	50	33	66	36	37	14	46	41	52	37	50	52	34	44	38
Yards lost	320	280	246	449	208	208	101	238	223	279	229	362	319	176	299	242
Net yards gained	2882	2412	3643	2192	3428	2916	4449	4516	3587	2818	3979	4253	3136	3539	3474	2632
Average yards per game	180.1	150.8	227.7	137.0	214.3	182.3	278.1	282.3	224.2	176.1	248.7	265.8	196.0	221.2	217.1	164.5
Net yards per pass play	5.04	5.42	6.40	4.08	6.18	5.38	7.27	7.55	6.15	5.35	6.81	6.75	5.12	6.25	6.25	4.77
Yards gained per completion	10.71	12.41	12.50	10.61	11.81	10.96	11.91	12.51	12.33	11.51	12.52	12.41	10.63	12.22	11.10	9.98
Combined net yards gained	4550	5084	5225	3816	5197	4693	6357	6339	5193	4722	5618	5877	4585	5634	4963	4397
Percent total yards rushing	36.7	52.6	30.3	42.6	34.0	37.9	30.0	28.8	30.9	40.3	29.2	27.6	31.6	37.2	30.0	40.1
Percent total yards passing	63.3	47.4	69.7	57.4	66.0	62.1	70.0	71.2	69.1	59.7	70.8	72.4	68.4	62.8	70.0	59.9
Average yards per game	284.4	317.8	326.6	238.5	324.8	293.3	397.3	396.2	324.6	295.1	351.1	367.3	286.6	352.1	310.2	274.8
Ball-control plays	1047	969	991	967	1004	949	1053	985	989	951	960	1011	1026	1034	949	1023
Average yards per play	4.3	5.2	5.3	3.9	5.2	4.9	6.0	6.4	5.3	5.0	5.9	5.8	4.5	5.4	5.2	4.3
Average time of possession	30:53	29:10	29:56	28:20	30:37	28:03	30:28	30:02	28:18	28:52	28:26	31:05	29:00	29:00	29:43	31:19
Third-down efficiency	34.9	36.3	40.3	25.1	36.4	31.4	47.3	52.3	33.3	29.5	36.9	42.2	32.4	36.2	37.7	31.7
Had intercepted	18	16	15	16	23	13	19	12	16	13	11	22	21	18	18	17
Yards opponents returned	263	201	321	222	526	194	166	207	260	134	140	191	479	158	328	201
Returned by opponents for TD	1	0	3	1	4	2	1	0	1	0	1	4	1	4	1	1
Punts	99	76	79	110	76	93	66	57	85	77	73	68	96	79	83	104
Yards punted	4230	3082	3402	4691	3216	3765	2644	2240	3704	3088	3068	2848	3990	3036	3472	4544
Average yards per punt	42.7	40.6	43.1	42.6	42.3	40.5	40.1	39.3	43.6	40.1	42.0	41.9	41.6	38.4	41.8	43.7
Punt returns	49	37	28	46	44	40	33	31	40	38	41	30	35	30	33	42
Yards returned	329	457	165	510	390	420	254	275	388	253	377	143	303	230	213	331
Average yards per return	6.7	12.4	5.9	11.1	8.9	10.5	7.7	8.9	9.7	6.7	9.2	4.8	8.7	7.7	6.5	7.9
Returned for TD	0	1	0	1	0	2	0	1	0	0	0	0	0	1	0	0
Kickoff returns	65	61	61	74	78	66	70	73	83	66	56	84	84	74	60	55
Yards returned	1293	1331	1307	1607	1603	1568	1522	1448	1879	1658	1214	1604	1716	1529	1450	1203
Average yards per return	19.9	21.8	21.4	21.7	20.6	23.8	21.7	19.8	22.6	25.1	21.7	19.1	20.4	20.7	24.2	21.9
Returned for TD	0	0	0	0	0	0	0	0	2	2	0	0	0	0	0	0
Fumbles	34	26	23	35	26	12	22	20	23	29	17	27	33	19	32	20
Lost	11	14	11	21	14	7	10	9	10	11	11	17	19	9	18	10
Out of bounds	5	1	1	1	1	0	2	1	0	1	1	2	0	2	3	0
Recovered for TD	0	0	0	0	0	0	0	0	0	0	0	0	0	0	0	0
Penalties	124	109	123	124	105	121	116	117	129	118	124	127	103	79	117	115
Yards penalized	948	905	1020	956	867	1000	950	884	1141	977	952	993	859	669	916	1047
Total points scored	284	340	355	231	293	296	424	405	348	303	386	319	259	371	301	240
Total TDs	31	41	42	26	33	32	50	50	40	34	44	37	29	43	37	26
TDs rushing	15	20	10	10	14	7	9	8	15	18	10	11	10	17	9	6
TDs passing	14	15	29	9	19	19	36	39	21	12	32	23	16	23	24	18
TDs on returns and recoveries	2	6	3	7	0	6	5	3	4	4	2	3	3	3	4	2
Extra point kicks	28	40	39	22	31	28	48	45	38	33	41	32	23	40	32	25
Extra point kick att.	28	40	40	22	31	28	48	45	38	33	42	32	23	40	33	25
2-Pt. conversions	1	0	2	1	1	1	2	3	1	0	0	4	3	2	1	0
2-Pt. conversions att.	3	1	2	4	2	4	2	4	2	1	2	4	6	3	4	1
Safeties	1	0	0	3	1	1	0	1	0	0	0	1	0	0	0	0
Field goals made	22	18	20	15	20	24	24	18	22	22	27	19	18	23	15	19
Field goals attempted	29	23	25	24	26	28	28	22	27	28	32	24	22	25	24	27
Percent successful	75.9	78.3	80.0	62.5	76.9	85.7	85.7	81.8	81.5	78.6	84.4	79.2	81.8	92.0	62.5	70.4
2-Pt. conversions	1	0	2	1	1	1	2	3	1	0	0	4	3	2	1	1
Extra points	29	40	41	23	32	29	50	48	39	33	41	36	26	42	33	26
Field goals blocked	0	0	2	1	0	0	0	0	1	2	0	0	0	0	1	0

DEFENSE

	Ariz.	Atl.	Car.	Chi.	Dal.	Det.	G.B.	Min.	N.O.	NYG	Phi.	St.L.	S.F.	Sea.	T.B.	Was.
First downs	282	310	307	302	297	320	307	350	343	310	299	311	322	311	258	251
Rushing	101	107	98	109	88	118	92	110	118	112	101	118	121	102	101	67
Passing	153	183	177	165	180	167	181	220	193	170	165	172	179	191	131	153
Penalty	28	20	32	28	29	35	34	20	32	28	33	21	22	18	26	31
Rushes	450	434	474	496	425	498	409	435	485	498	442	480	495	452	480	419
Net yards gained	2105	1681	1904	2050	1764	1887	1878	2006	2253	2157	1903	2179	1995	2031	1973	1304
Average gain	4.7	3.9	4.0	4.1	4.2	3.8	4.6	4.6	4.3	4.3	4.3	4.5	4.0	4.5	4.1	3.1
Average yards per game	131.6	105.1	119.0	128.1	110.3	117.9	117.4	125.4	140.8	134.8	118.9	136.2	124.7	126.9	123.3	81.5
Passes attempted	505	517	513	515	502	535	518	544	545	467	550	492	490	559	436	515
Completed	271	328	303	287	310	328	314	338	324	292	334	292	308	340	247	294
Percent completed	53.7	63.4	59.1	55.7	61.8	61.3	60.6	62.1	59.4	62.5	60.7	59.3	62.9	60.8	56.7	57.1
Total yards gained	3265	3838	3703	3513	3718	3736	3943	4130	4095	3280	3475	3415	3680	3808	2843	3222
Times sacked	38	48	34	35	33	38	40	39	37	40	47	34	29	36	45	40
Yards lost	229	312	225	173	197	222	280	234	207	250	263	241	194	218	264	245
Net yards gained	3036	3526	3478	3340	3521	3514	3663	3896	3888	3030	3212	3174	3486	3590	2579	2977
Average yards per game	189.8	220.4	217.4	208.8	220.1	219.6	228.9	243.5	243.0	189.4	200.8	198.4	217.9	224.4	161.2	186.1
Net yards per pass play	5.59	6.24	6.36	6.07	6.58	6.13	6.56	6.68	6.68	5.98	5.38	6.03	6.72	6.03	5.36	5.38
Yards gained per completion	12.05	11.70	12.22	12.24	11.99	11.39	12.56	12.22	12.64	11.23	10.40	11.70	11.95	11.20	11.51	10.96
Combined net yards gained	5141	5207	5382	5390	5285	5401	5541	5902	6141	5187	5115	5353	5481	5621	4552	4281
Percent total yards rushing	40.9	32.3	35.4	38.0	33.4	34.9	33.9	34.0	36.7	41.6	37.2	40.7	36.4	36.1	43.3	30.5
Percent total yards passing	59.1	67.7	64.6	62.0	66.6	65.1	66.1	66.0	63.3	58.4	62.8	59.3	63.6	63.9	56.7	69.5
Average yards per game	321.3	325.4	336.4	336.9	330.3	337.6	346.3	368.9	383.8	324.2	319.7	334.6	342.6	351.3	284.5	267.6
Ball-control plays	993	999	1021	1046	960	1071	967	1018	1067	1005	1039	1006	1014	1047	961	974
Average yards per play	5.2	5.2	5.3	5.2	5.5	5.0	5.7	5.8	5.8	5.2	4.9	5.3	5.4	5.4	4.7	4.4
Average time of possession	29:07	30:50	30:04	31:40	29:23	31:57	29:32	29:58	31:42	31:08	31:34	28:55	31:00	31:00	30:17	28:41
Third-down efficiency	31.6	36.0	46.0	30.5	39.1	42.4	35.0	45.9	38.1	41.8	35.8	36.4	40.3	42.4	35.3	31.0
Intercepted by	15	19	26	17	13	14	8	11	13	14	17	6	9	23	16	18
Yards returned by	214	442	420	546	109	216	165	207	101	113	287	45	129	337	239	405
Returned for TD	1	4	2	5	0	1	2	1	0	0	2	0	0	3	1	1
Punts	97	80	64	92	78	84	81	59	71	77	89	71	80	74	87	104
Yards punted	4064	3466	2630	3713	3260	3658	3176	2488	2896	2997	3785	3014	3268	3091	3867	4180
Average yards per punt	41.9	43.3	41.1	40.4	41.8	43.5	39.2	42.2	40.8	38.9	42.5	42.5	40.9	41.8	44.4	40.1
Punt returns	56	33	38	57	39	46	34	26	43	38	34	35	51	33	31	65
Yards returned	486	134	303	380	410	441	301	169	310	356	221	416	445	244	279	72
Average yards per return	8.7	4.1	8.0	6.7	10.5	9.6	8.9	6.5	7.2	9.4	6.5	11.9	8.7	7.4	9.0	11.2
Returned for TD	1	0	0	0	0	0	0	0	1	0	0	1	0	0	0	0
Kickoff returns	46	56	69	54	62	54	79	75	74	66	73	66	56	77	58	5
Yards returned	1017	1117	1477	1160	1083	1058	1594	1869	1710	1278	1693	1680	1119	1677	1315	122
Average yards per return	22.1	19.9	21.4	21.5	17.5	19.6	20.2	24.9	23.1	19.4	23.2	25.5	20.0	21.8	22.7	21.
Returned for TD	1	1	0	0	0	0	0	1	0	0	0	1	0	0	1	
Fumbles	32	24	29	21	20	20	17	25	31	27	29	18	24	25	21	1
Recovered	15	13	12	12	9	10	7	11	20	14	11	9	12	12	11	
Out of bounds	2	1	3	2	1	1	1	1	2	4	0	3	1	0	1	
Recovered for TD	0	0	0	0	0	0	0	0	0	0	0	0	0	0	0	
Penalties	139	129	117	120	104	114	112	110	119	120	119	109	107	91	112	9
Yards penalized	1121	930	1078	914	879	976	942	974	965	1007	1001	827	867	748	897	79
Total points scored	322	337	339	331	405	350	380	395	405	347	260	392	452	373	304	26
Total TDs	35	41	40	36	49	43	47	46	44	41	30	43	54	42	35	3
TDs rushing	12	20	19	9	14	10	12	15	16	13	13	13	22	17	8	
TDs passing	18	19	18	23	31	29	33	30	24	28	16	24	27	24	21	1
TDs on returns and recoveries	5	2	3	4	4	4	2	1	0	1	6	5	1	6		
Extra point kicks	29	39	39	35	44	37	47	43	42	37	27	39	51	38	34	2
Extra point kick att.	30	39	39	35	45	38	47	43	42	37	27	39	51	39	35	2
2-Pt. conversions	4	1	0	0	2	1	0	1	2	2	1	1	1	0	0	
2-Pt. conversions att.	5	2	1	1	4	4	0	3	2	4	3	4	3	2	0	
Safeties	0	1	0	1	0	1	0	1	1	0	0	0	0	1	0	
Field goals made	25	16	20	26	21	17	17	24	31	20	17	31	25	27	20	1
Field goals attempted	26	18	28	36	23	20	25	27	35	25	24	36	29	32	31	2
Percent successful	96.2	88.9	71.4	72.2	91.3	85.0	68.0	88.9	88.6	80.0	70.8	86.1	86.2	84.4	64.5	85.
Extra points	33	40	39	35	46	38	47	44	44	39	28	40	52	38	34	3
Field goals blocked	1	1	1	1	0	2	1	0	1	0	0	0	0	0	1	

	AFC Offense Total	AFC Offense Average	AFC Defense Total	AFC Defense Average	NFC Offense Total	NFC Offense Average	NFC Defense Total	NFC Defense Average	NFL Total	NFL Average
First downs	4914	307.1	4734	295.9	4700	293.8	4880	305.0	9614	300.4
Rushing	1693	105.8	1535	95.9	1505	94.1	1663	103.9	3198	99.9
Passing	2770	173.1	2744	171.5	2754	172.1	2780	173.8	5524	172.6
Penalty	451	28.2	455	28.4	441	27.6	437	27.3	892	27.9
Rushes	7561	472.6	7056	441.0	6867	429.2	7372	460.8	14428	450.9
Net yards gained	31315	1957.2	28639	1789.9	28394	1774.6	31070	1941.9	59709	1865.9
Average gain	....	4.1	....	4.1	....	4.1	....	4.2	....	4.1
Average yards per game	....	122.3	....	111.9	....	110.9	....	121.4	....	116.6
Passes attempted	7982	498.9	8151	509.4	8372	523.3	8203	512.7	16354	511.1
Completed	4798	299.9	4862	303.9	4974	310.9	4910	306.9	9772	305.4
Percent completed	....	60.1	....	59.6	....	59.4	....	59.9	....	59.8
Total yards gained	57303	3581.4	57674	3604.6	58035	3627.2	57664	3604.0	115338	3604.3
Times sacked	527	32.9	583	36.4	669	41.8	613	38.3	1196	37.4
Yards lost	3362	210.1	3787	236.7	4179	261.2	3754	234.6	7541	235.7
Net yards gained	53941	3371.3	53887	3367.9	53856	3366.0	53910	3369.4	107797	3368.7
Average yards per game	....	210.7	....	210.5	....	210.4	....	210.6	....	210.5
Net yards per pass play	....	6.34	....	6.17	....	5.96	....	6.12	....	6.14
Yards gained per completion	....	11.94	....	11.86	....	11.67	....	11.74	....	11.80
Combined net yards gained	85256	5328.5	82526	5157.9	82250	5140.6	84980	5311.3	167506	5234.6
Percent total yards rushing	....	36.7	....	34.7	....	34.5	....	36.6	....	35.6
Percent total yards passing	....	63.3	....	65.3	....	65.5	....	63.4	....	64.4
Average yards per game	....	333.0	....	322.4	....	321.3	....	332.0	....	327.2
Ball-control plays	16070	1004.4	15790	986.9	15908	994.3	16188	1011.8	31978	999.3
Average yards per play	....	5.3	....	5.2	....	5.2	....	5.2	....	5.2
Third-down efficiency	....	38.9	....	37.3	....	36.4	....	37.9	....	37.6
Interceptions	256	16.0	285	17.8	268	16.8	239	14.9	524	16.4
Yards returned	4262	266.4	4278	267.4	3991	249.4	3975	248.4	8253	257.9
Returned for TD	28	1.8	30	1.9	25	1.6	23	1.4	53	1.7
Punts	1203	75.2	1236	77.3	1321	82.6	1288	80.5	2524	78.9
Yards punted	50415	3150.9	51882	3242.6	55020	3438.8	53553	3347.1	105435	3294.8
Average yards per punt	....	41.9	....	42.0	....	41.7	....	41.6	....	41.8
Punt returns	620	38.8	558	34.9	597	37.3	659	41.2	1217	38.0
Yards returned	5424	339.0	4840	302.5	5038	314.9	5622	351.4	10462	326.9
Average yards per return	....	8.7	....	8.7	....	8.4	....	8.5	....	8.6
Returned for TD	4	0.3	7	0.4	7	0.4	4	0.3	11	0.3
Kickoff returns	1045	65.3	1133	70.8	1110	69.4	1022	63.9	2155	67.3
Yards returned	22808	1425.5	24670	1541.9	23932	1495.8	22070	1379.4	46740	1460.6
Average yards per return	....	21.8	....	21.8	....	21.6	....	21.6	....	21.7
Returned for TD	11	0.7	11	0.7	6	0.4	6	0.4	17	0.5
Fumbles	396	24.8	414	25.9	398	24.9	380	23.8	794	24.8
Lost	178	11.1	194	12.1	202	12.6	186	11.6	380	11.9
Out of bounds	32	2.0	29	1.8	21	1.3	24	1.5	53	1.7
Own recovered for TD	1	0.1	1	0.1	0	0.0	0	0.0	1	0.0
Opponents recovered by	192	12.0	176	11.0	186	11.6	202	12.6	378	11.8
Opponents recovered for TD	15	0.9	17	1.1	18	1.1	16	1.0	33	1.0
Penalties	1719	107.4	1751	109.4	1851	115.7	1819	113.7	3570	111.6
Yards penalized	14132	883.3	14293	893.3	15084	942.8	14923	932.7	29216	913.0
Total points scored	5845	365.3	5343	333.9	5155	322.2	5657	353.6	11000	343.8
Total TDs	673	42.1	612	38.3	595	37.2	656	41.0	1268	39.6
TDs rushing	227	14.2	196	12.3	189	11.8	220	13.8	416	13.0
TDs passing	383	23.9	350	21.9	349	21.8	382	23.9	732	22.9
TDs on returns and recoveries	63	3.9	66	4.1	57	3.6	54	3.4	120	3.8
Extra point kicks	634	39.6	570	35.6	545	34.1	609	38.1	1179	36.8
Extra point kick att.	641	40.1	575	35.9	548	34.3	614	38.4	1189	37.2
2-Pt. conversions	14	0.9	19	1.2	23	1.4	18	1.1	37	1.2
2-Pt. conversion att.	31	1.9	36	2.3	45	2.8	40	2.5	76	2.4
Safeties	7	0.4	8	0.5	8	0.5	7	0.4	15	0.5
Field goals made	377	23.6	349	21.8	326	20.4	354	22.1	703	22.0
Field goals attempted	456	28.5	435	27.2	414	25.9	435	27.2	870	27.2
Percent successful	....	82.7	....	80.2	....	78.7	....	81.4	....	80.8
Extra points	648	40.5	589	36.8	568	35.5	627	39.2	1216	38.0
Field goals blocked	10	0.6	7	0.4	7	0.4	10	0.6	17	0.5

2004 STATISTICS *Miscellaneous*

Player, Team	Opponent	Date	Att.	Yds.	TD
Edgerrin James, Indianapolis	at Chicago	November 21	23	204	
Rudi Johnson, Cincinnati	vs. Cleveland	November 28	26	202	
Julius Jones, Dallas	at Seattle	December 6	30	198	
Kevin Jones, Detroit	vs. Arizona	December 5	26	196	
Curtis Martin, N.Y. Jets	vs. Cincinnati	September 12	29	196	
Shaun Alexander, Seattle	vs. Carolina	October 31	32	195	
Reuben Droughns, Denver	vs. Carolina	October 10	30	193	
Jamal Lewis, Baltimore	at Cincinnati	September 26	18	186	
Derrick Blaylock, Kansas City	at New Orleans	November 14	33	186	
Tiki Barber, N.Y. Giants	at Green Bay	October 3	23	182	
Najeh Davenport, Green Bay	vs. St. Louis	November 29	19	178	
Shaun Alexander, Seattle	at St. Louis	November 14	22	176	
Reuben Droughns, Denver	at Oakland	October 17	38	176	
DeShaun Foster, Carolina	at Kansas City	September 19	32	174	
Clinton Portis, Washington	at Chicago	October 17	36	171	
Jamal Lewis, Baltimore	vs. Miami	January 2	34	167	
Reuben Droughns, Denver	at New Orleans	November 21	28	166	
Fred Taylor, Jacksonville	at Green Bay	December 19	22	165	
LaDainian Tomlinson, San Diego	at Oakland	November 21	37	164	
Ahman Green, Green Bay	vs. Dallas	October 24	15	163	
Shaun Alexander, Seattle	at San Francisco	November 7	26	160	
Domanick Davis, Houston	at Jacksonville	December 26	31	158	
Corey Dillon, New England	at Arizona	September 19	32	158	
Quentin Griffin, Denver	vs. Kansas City	September 12	23	156	
Kevin Jones, Detroit	at Green Bay	December 12	33	156	
Shaun Alexander, Seattle	vs. Arizona	December 26	30	154	
Curtis Martin, N.Y. Jets	at St. Louis	January 2*	28	153	
Thomas Jones, Chicago	at Green Bay	September 19	23	152	
Chris Brown, Tennessee	vs. Indianapolis	September 19	26	152	
Priest Holmes, Kansas City	at Denver	September 12	26	151	
Corey Dillon, New England	vs. Buffalo	November 14	26	151	
Larry Johnson, Kansas City	vs. Denver	December 19	30	151	
Shaun Alexander, Seattle	vs. St. Louis	October 10*	23	150	
Julius Jones, Dallas	vs. Chicago	November 25	33	150	
Julius Jones, Dallas	at N.Y. Giants	January 2	29	149	
Jerome Bettis, Pittsburgh	vs. Philadelphia	November 7	33	149	
Steven Jackson, St. Louis	vs. Philadelphia	December 27	24	148	
Chris Brown, Tennessee	at Green Bay	October 11	27	148	
Clinton Portis, Washington	vs. Tampa Bay	September 12	29	148	
Clinton Portis, Washington	vs. N.Y. Giants	December 5	31	148	
LaDainian Tomlinson, San Diego	vs. Tennessee	October 3	17	147	
Fred Taylor, Jacksonville	at Minnesota	November 28	22	147	
Chris Brown, Tennessee	vs. Cincinnati	October 31	32	147	
Clinton Portis, Washington	at Detroit	November 7	34	147	
Ahman Green, Green Bay	vs. Minnesota	November 14	21	145	
Fred Taylor, Jacksonville	vs. Detroit	November 14*	23	144	
Priest Holmes, Kansas City	vs. Indianapolis	October 31	32	143	
Lee Suggs, Cleveland	at Miami	December 26	38	143	
Edgerrin James, Indianapolis	at New England	September 9	30	142	
Deuce McAllister, New Orleans	at Carolina	January 2	28	140	
Jerome Bettis, Pittsburgh	at N.Y. Giants	December 18	36	140	
Marshall Faulk, St. Louis	vs. Seattle	November 14	18	139	
Priest Holmes, Kansas City	vs. Atlanta	October 24	22	139	
Chester Taylor, Baltimore	vs. Cincinnati	December 5	23	139	
Maurice Hicks, San Francisco	at Arizona	December 12*	34	139	
Mewelde Moore, Minnesota	vs. Tennessee	October 24	20	138	
Edgerrin James, Indianapolis	vs. Oakland	October 10	32	136	
Shaun Alexander, Seattle	at New Orleans	September 12	28	135	
Zack Crockett, Oakland	vs. Jacksonville	January 2	21	134	
Curtis Martin, N.Y. Jets	vs. Houston	December 5	23	134	
Curtis Martin, N.Y. Jets	vs. Seattle	December 19	24	134	
Warrick Dunn, Atlanta	vs. Carolina	December 18*	28	134	
Priest Holmes, Kansas City	vs. Houston	September 26	32	134	
Warrick Dunn, Atlanta	at Seattle	January 2	25	132	
Willis McGahee, Buffalo	vs. N.Y. Jets	November 7	37	132	
Michael Pittman, Tampa Bay	vs. New Orleans	December 19	24	131	
LaDainian Tomlinson, San Diego	vs. Tampa Bay	December 12	25	131	
Lee Suggs, Cleveland	at Houston	January 2	26	131	
Jamal Lewis, Baltimore	at Indianapolis	December 19	20	130	
Rudi Johnson, Cincinnati	vs. Buffalo	December 19	23	130	
Domanick Davis, Houston	vs. Tennessee	November 28	16	129	
Jerome Bettis, Pittsburgh	at Cincinnati	November 21	29	129	
Michael Pittman, Tampa Bay	vs. Kansas City	November 7	15	128	
Marshall Faulk, St. Louis	vs. Arizona	September 12	22	128	
Domanick Davis, Houston	vs. Indianapolis	December 12	23	128	
Ahman Green, Green Bay	vs. Chicago	September 19	24	128	
Deuce McAllister, New Orleans	vs. Atlanta	December 26	29	128	
Deuce McAllister, New Orleans	vs. Kansas City	November 14	16	127	
Emmitt Smith, Arizona	vs. New Orleans	October 3	21	127	
Nick Goings, Carolina	at Tampa Bay	December 26	33	127	
Tiki Barber, N.Y. Giants	at Philadelphia	September 12	9	125	
Duce Staley, Pittsburgh	vs. New England	October 31	25	125	
Priest Holmes, Kansas City	at Baltimore	October 4	33	125	
Edgerrin James, Indianapolis	at Tennessee	September 19	21	124	
Tatum Bell, Denver	vs. Miami	December 12	17	123	
Rudi Johnson, Cincinnati	at Pittsburgh	October 3	24	123	
Duce Staley, Pittsburgh	vs. Cincinnati	October 3	25	123	
Kevin Jones, Detroit	vs. Chicago	December 26	25	123	

ayer, Team	Opponent	Date	Att.	Yds.	TD
gerrin James, Indianapolis	vs. Minnesota	November 8	26	123	0
rey Dillon, New England	vs. Baltimore	November 28	30	123	1
ki Barber, N.Y. Giants	at Dallas	October 10	23	122	1
ck Goings, Carolina	at New Orleans	December 5	36	122	1
ck Goings, Carolina	vs. Arizona	November 21	22	121	3
arshall Faulk, St. Louis	at San Francisco	October 3	23	121	0
Dainian Tomlinson, San Diego	at Houston	September 12	26	121	1
rey Dillon, New England	at Miami	December 20	26	121	1
euben Droughns, Denver	vs. Houston	November 7	29	120	0
ian Westbrook, Philadelphia	vs. N.Y. Giants	September 12	17	119	0
ian Westbrook, Philadelphia	at Chicago	October 3	22	119	0
idi Johnson, Cincinnati	vs. Denver	October 25	24	119	1
even Jackson, St. Louis	vs. San Francisco	December 5	26	119	0
irtis Martin, N.Y. Jets	vs. Baltimore	November 14*	28	119	2
irtis Martin, N.Y. Jets	at San Diego	September 19	32	119	2
iman Green, Green Bay	at Carolina	September 13	33	119	2
rry Johnson, Kansas City	at Oakland	December 5	20	118	1
dell Betts, Washington	vs. Minnesota	January 2	26	118	1
nos Zereoue, Oakland	at Houston	October 3	14	117	2
arrick Dunn, Atlanta	vs. Arizona	September 26	20	117	0
ice Staley, Pittsburgh	vs. Cleveland	October 10	21	117	1
rome Bettis, Pittsburgh	vs. Baltimore	December 26	27	117	0
rey Dillon, New England	vs. San Francisco	January 2	14	116	1
mal Lewis, Baltimore	at Washington	October 10	28	116	0
ichael Vick, Atlanta	at Denver	October 31	12	115	0
illis McGahee, Buffalo	at Seattle	November 28	28	116	4
Mont Jordan, N.Y. Jets	vs. Miami	November 1	14	115	1
irtis Martin, N.Y. Jets	vs. Miami	November 1	19	115	1
rey Dillon, New England	vs. N.Y. Jets	October 24	22	115	0
illiam Green, Cleveland	vs. Cincinnati	October 17	25	115	0
van Barlow, San Francisco	at New Orleans	September 19	20	114	2
Dainian Tomlinson, San Diego	vs. Denver	December 5	30	113	2
rey Dillon, New England	at St. Louis	November 7	25	112	1
aun Alexander, Seattle	at Minnesota	December 12	27	112	0
irtis Martin, N.Y. Jets	vs. San Francisco	October 17	25	111	2
illis McGahee, Buffalo	vs. Miami	October 17	26	111	0
Dainian Tomlinson, San Diego	at Cleveland	December 19	26	111	2
ki Barber, N.Y. Giants	vs. Philadelphia	November 28	19	110	0
omas Jones, Chicago	at Minnesota	September 26	22	110	1
irtis Martin, N.Y. Jets	at Miami	October 3	24	110	1
euben Droughns, Denver	at Cincinnati	October 25	24	110	0
thony Thomas, Chicago	at N.Y. Giants	November 7	28	110	2
nton Portis, Washington	at San Francisco	December 18	35	110	0
ichael Vick, Atlanta	vs. St. Louis	September 19	12	109	0
ewelde Moore, Minnesota	at New Orleans	October 17	15	109	0
ki Barber, N.Y. Giants	at Cincinnati	December 26	22	109	1
omas Jones, Chicago	at Detroit	December 26	22	109	0
ichael Pittman, Tampa Bay	vs. Chicago	October 24	23	109	1
ki Barber, N.Y. Giants	at Arizona	November 14	21	108	1
omas Jones, Chicago	vs. Green Bay	January 2	26	108	2
ck Goings, Carolina	vs. St. Louis	December 12	31	108	1
ed Taylor, Jacksonville	at Indianapolis	October 24	20	107	0
ki Barber, N.Y. Giants	vs. Atlanta	November 21	21	107	0
iron Stecker, New Orleans	at St. Louis	September 26*	18	106	1
ichael Pittman, Tampa Bay	vs. San Francisco	November 21	21	106	2
ki Barber, N.Y. Giants	vs. Cleveland	September 26	23	106	1
ck Goings, Carolina	vs. Tampa Bay	November 28	23	106	0
nmitt Smith, Arizona	vs. Seattle	October 24	26	106	1
gerrin James, Indianapolis	vs. Tennessee	December 5	18	105	2
e Suggs, Cleveland	vs. San Diego	December 19	21	105	0
rey Dillon, New England	vs. Seattle	October 17	23	105	2
gerrin James, Indianapolis	at Detroit	November 25	23	105	0
nathan Wells, Houston	vs. Oakland	October 3	26	105	1
illis McGahee, Buffalo	vs. Cleveland	December 12	27	105	2
rry Johnson, Kansas City	at Tennessee	December 13	7	104	2
ichael Vick, Atlanta	at N.Y. Giants	November 21	15	104	0
iris Brown, Tennessee	at Indianapolis	December 5	19	104	0
ester Taylor, Baltimore	vs. N.Y. Giants	December 12	25	104	0
gerrin James, Indianapolis	at Houston	December 12	28	104	0
sse Chatman, San Diego	vs. Jacksonville	October 10	11	103	1
omanick Davis, Houston	vs. Cleveland	January 2	17	103	1
ed Taylor, Jacksonville	vs. Tennessee	November 21	21	103	0
arrick Dunn, Atlanta	vs. Oakland	December 12	25	103	0
van Barlow, San Francisco	at New England	January 2	25	103	0
rome Bettis, Pittsburgh	at Cleveland	November 14	29	103	2
illis McGahee, Buffalo	at San Francisco	December 26	15	102	2
rone Wheatley, Oakland	vs. Tampa Bay	September 26	18	102	1
illie Parker, Pittsburgh	at Buffalo	January 2	19	102	0
euce McAllister, New Orleans	vs. Tampa Bay	October 10	21	102	0
euben Droughns, Denver	vs. Oakland	November 28	28	102	1
illis McGahee, Buffalo	vs. Arizona	October 31	30	102	2
idi Johnson, Cincinnati	at Washington	November 14	31	102	1
ice Staley, Pittsburgh	at Miami	September 26	22	101	0
iris Brown, Tennessee	vs. Jacksonville	September 26	23	101	1
ki Barber, N.Y. Giants	at Minnesota	October 31	24	101	2
iris Brown, Tennessee	at Miami	September 11	16	100	0
rey Dillon, New England	at Cleveland	December 5	18	100	2
evin Jones, Detroit	at Minnesota	November 21	19	100	0
illis McGahee, Buffalo	vs. St. Louis	November 21	20	100	0
euce McAllister, New Orleans	at Atlanta	November 28	23	100	0
rome Bettis, Pittsburgh	vs. Washington	November 28	31	100	1

*Overtime game.

2004 STATISTICS *Miscellaneous*

PASSING

Player, Team	Opponent	Date	Att.	Cmp.	Yds.	TD	Int.
Jake Plummer, Denver	vs. Atlanta	October 31	55	31	499	4	3
Billy Volek, Tennessee	at Oakland	December 19	60	40	492	4	1
Peyton Manning, Indianapolis	at Kansas City	October 31	44	25	472	5	1
Donovan McNabb, Philadelphia	vs. Green Bay	December 5	43	32	464	5	0
Marc Bulger, St. Louis	vs. N.Y. Jets	January 2*	39	29	450	3	2
Marc Bulger, St. Louis	at Green Bay	November 29	53	35	448	2	1
Billy Volek, Tennessee	vs. Kansas City	December 13	43	29	426	4	0
Daunte Culpepper, Minnesota	at New Orleans	October 17	37	26	425	5	2
Peyton Manning, Indianapolis	vs. Tennessee	December 5	33	25	425	3	2
Tim Rattay, San Francisco	vs. Arizona	October 10*	57	38	417	2	0
Matt Hasselbeck, Seattle	vs. Dallas	December 6	40	28	414	3	0
Kelly Holcomb, Cleveland	at Cincinnati	November 28	39	30	413	5	2
Daunte Culpepper, Minnesota	at Detroit	December 19	35	25	404	3	1
Daunte Culpepper, Minnesota	at Houston	October 10*	50	36	396	5	0
Peyton Manning, Indianapolis	vs. Green Bay	September 26	40	28	393	5	0
Brian Griese, Tampa Bay	at San Diego	December 12	50	36	392	3	3
Trent Green, Kansas City	vs. Indianapolis	October 31	34	27	389	3	0
Brett Favre, Green Bay	at Houston	November 21	50	33	383	1	2
Peyton Manning, Indianapolis	vs. San Diego	December 26*	44	27	383	2	1
Carson Palmer, Cincinnati	at Baltimore	December 5	36	29	382	3	1
Trent Green, Kansas City	vs. New England	November 22	42	27	381	2	1
Drew Brees, San Diego	at Kansas City	November 28	37	28	378	2	0
Aaron Brooks, New Orleans	vs. Denver	November 21	60	34	377	1	3
Donovan McNabb, Philadelphia	at Cleveland	October 24*	43	28	376	4	1
Trent Green, Kansas City	at San Diego	January 2	53	33	373	1	4
David Carr, Houston	vs. Minnesota	October 10*	42	27	372	3	0
Kerry Collins, Oakland	vs. Tennessee	December 19	37	21	371	5	1
Trent Green, Kansas City	at Tampa Bay	November 7	42	32	369	3	2
Peyton Manning, Indianapolis	vs. Jacksonville	October 24	39	27	368	3	0
Brett Favre, Green Bay	vs. Jacksonville	December 19	44	30	367	2	3
Brett Favre, Green Bay	at Minnesota	December 24	43	30	365	3	1
Daunte Culpepper, Minnesota	at Green Bay	November 14	44	27	363	4	0
Joey Harrington, Detroit	vs. Minnesota	December 19	44	25	361	2	2
Brett Favre, Green Bay	at Indianapolis	September 26	44	30	360	4	0
Daunte Culpepper, Minnesota	vs. Chicago	September 26	30	19	360	2	0
Marc Bulger, St. Louis	vs. New Orleans	September 26*	49	32	358	1	0
Trent Green, Kansas City	vs. Oakland	December 25	45	32	358	2	1
Byron Leftwich, Jacksonville	at San Diego	October 10	54	36	357	1	2
Donovan McNabb, Philadelphia	at Detroit	September 26	42	29	356	2	0
Vinny Testaverde, Dallas	at Minnesota	September 12	50	29	355	1	0
Kerry Collins, Oakland	vs. New Orleans	October 24	45	26	350	2	1
Matt Hasselbeck, Seattle	at New England	October 17	50	27	349	0	2
Brian Griese, Tampa Bay	at Carolina	November 28	39	27	347	2	1
Joey Harrington, Detroit	at Tennessee	January 2	49	33	346	2	1
Donovan McNabb, Philadelphia	at Dallas	November 15	27	15	345	4	0
Daunte Culpepper, Minnesota	at Philadelphia	September 20	47	37	343	1	1
Shaun King, Arizona	at Carolina	November 21	52	28	343	1	3
Kerry Collins, Oakland	vs. Kansas City	December 5	41	27	343	3	0
Jake Delhomme, Carolina	at Atlanta	December 18*	35	24	340	2	1
Trent Green, Kansas City	at Oakland	December 5	35	23	340	3	1
Kerry Collins, Oakland	at Denver	November 28	45	26	339	4	2
Brett Favre, Green Bay	vs. Tennessee	October 11	44	24	338	2	1
Tom Brady, New England	vs. Indianapolis	September 9	38	26	335	3	1
Billy Volek, Tennessee	vs. Chicago	November 14*	44	27	334	2	2
Matt Hasselbeck, Seattle	at Minnesota	December 12	34	23	334	3	2
Donovan McNabb, Philadelphia	vs. N.Y. Giants	September 12	36	26	330	4	0
Mark Brunell, Washington	vs. Dallas	September 27	43	25	325	2	0
Marc Bulger, St. Louis	at Seattle	October 10*	42	24	325	3	3
Vinny Testaverde, Dallas	vs. Cleveland	September 19	35	23	322	1	3
Brian Griese, Tampa Bay	vs. Carolina	December 26	41	30	321	3	2
Peyton Manning, Indianapolis	vs. Houston	November 14	27	18	320	5	2
Byron Leftwich, Jacksonville	vs. Indianapolis	October 3	41	29	318	1	0
Carson Palmer, Cincinnati	vs. Baltimore	September 26	52	25	316	0	3
Aaron Brooks, New Orleans	at St. Louis	September 26*	41	24	316	1	0
Ben Roethlisberger, Pittsburgh	at N.Y. Giants	December 18	28	18	316	1	2
Trent Green, Kansas City	at Jacksonville	October 17	33	23	315	2	1
Tom Brady, New England	at Kansas City	November 22	26	17	315	1	0
David Carr, Houston	at Detroit	September 19	34	23	313	2	1
Trent Green, Kansas City	at New Orleans	November 14	33	22	311	1	0
Jeff Garcia, Cleveland	at Cincinnati	October 17	23	16	310	4	2
Brad Johnson, Tampa Bay	at Oakland	September 26	36	22	309	2	1
Jake Delhomme, Carolina	vs. Atlanta	October 3	38	23	308	0	2
Vinny Testaverde, Dallas	at Green Bay	October 24	35	23	308	1	0
Josh McCown, Arizona	vs. San Francisco	December 12*	44	26	307	0	1
Jake Delhomme, Carolina	vs. New Orleans	January 2	50	24	307	2	2
Rich Gannon, Oakland	at Pittsburgh	September 12	37	20	305	2	2
Chad Pennington, N.Y. Jets	vs. Buffalo	October 10	42	31	304	1	1
A.J. Feeley, Miami	vs. Buffalo	December 5	51	25	303	3	5
Jake Plummer, Denver	at Tennessee	December 25	26	21	303	2	1
Jake Delhomme, Carolina	at San Francisco	November 14	34	19	303	3	0
Byron Leftwich, Jacksonville	at Indianapolis	October 24	30	23	300	2	1

*Overtime game.

RECEIVING

Player, Team	Opponent	Date	No.	Yds.	T
Drew Bennett, Tennessee	vs. Kansas City	December 13	12	233	
Rod Smith, Denver	vs. Atlanta	October 31	9	208	
Javon Walker, Green Bay	at Indianapolis	September 26	11	200	

yer, Team	Opponent	Date	No.	Yds.	TD
ggie Wayne, Indianapolis	vs. Green Bay	September 26	11	184	1
hsin Muhammad, Carolina	at New Orleans	December 5	10	179	1
Houshmandzadeh, Cincinnati	at Baltimore	December 5	10	171	1
dre Johnson, Houston	vs. Minnesota	October 10*	12	170	2
ac Bruce, St. Louis	at Green Bay	November 29	9	170	1
d Gardner, Washington	vs. Dallas	September 27	10	167	2
Horn, New Orleans	vs. Kansas City	November 14	5	167	1
c Johnson, San Francisco	vs. Arizona	October 10*	13	162	1
nald Driver, Green Bay	at Minnesota	December 24	11	162	1
ad Johnson, Cincinnati	at Baltimore	December 5	10	161	2
rell Owens, Philadelphia	vs. Green Bay	December 5	8	161	1
ew Bennett, Tennessee	at Oakland	December 19	13	160	2
ry Holt, St. Louis	vs. San Francisco	December 5	10	160	1
Horn, New Orleans	vs. Carolina	December 5	8	160	2
on Walker, Green Bay	vs. Tennessee	October 11	8	159	1
ntana Moss, N.Y. Jets	at Buffalo	November 7	6	157	1
an Westbrook, Philadelphia	vs. Green Bay	December 5	11	156	3
andon Stokley, Indianapolis	vs. Tennessee	December 5	8	153	1
on Walker, Green Bay	vs. Jacksonville	December 19	11	152	0
es Ward, Pittsburgh	at Baltimore	September 19	6	151	1
ry Holt, St. Louis	at Carolina	December 12	6	151	1
nald Driver, Green Bay	vs. Tennessee	October 11	10	150	0
rcus Robinson, Minnesota	at Houston	October 10*	9	150	2
en Robinson, Seattle	at New England	October 17	9	150	0
die Kennison, Kansas City	at Oakland	December 5	8	149	1
ad Johnson, Cincinnati	vs. Denver	October 25	7	149	1
twaan Randle El, Pittsburgh	at N.Y. Giants	December 18	5	149	1
nald Driver, Green Bay	at Houston	November 21	10	148	1
ry Porter, Oakland	vs. Tennessee	December 19	8	148	3
ew Bennett, Tennessee	vs. Chicago	November 14*	6	148	1
ris Chambers, Miami	at Baltimore	January 2	4	146	1
Houshmandzadeh, Cincinnati	at New England	December 12	12	145	0
chael Clayton, Tampa Bay	at San Diego	December 12	9	145	1
rry Rice, Seattle	vs. Dallas	December 6	8	145	1
ny Gonzalez, Kansas City	at San Diego	January 2	14	144	0
chael Clayton, Tampa Bay	at St. Louis	October 18	8	142	0
te Burleson, Minnesota	at Green Bay	November 14	11	141	1
nald Curry, Oakland	vs. Kansas City	December 5	9	141	2
ry Glenn, Dallas	vs. Pittsburgh	October 17	7	140	0
xico Burress, Pittsburgh	vs. Cleveland	October 10	6	136	1
rrell Jackson, Seattle	at Minnesota	December 12	10	135	1
hsin Muhammad, Carolina	at Atlanta	December 18*	10	135	1
y Williams, Detroit	vs. Philadelphia	September 26	9	135	2
ry Porter, Oakland	at Denver	November 28	6	135	3
es Ward, Pittsburgh	at N.Y. Giants	December 18	9	134	0
ac Bruce, St. Louis	vs. New Orleans	September 26*	8	134	0
chael Pittman, Tampa Bay	at Carolina	November 28	8	134	2
te Burleson, Minnesota	at New Orleans	October 17	6	134	0
rell Owens, Philadelphia	at Dallas	November 15	6	134	3
te Burleson, Minnesota	at Detroit	December 19	5	134	2
son Witten, Dallas	vs. Philadelphia	November 15	9	133	2
andon Stokley, Indianapolis	vs. Houston	November 14	5	132	2
tonio Bryant, Cleveland	at Cincinnati	November 28	8	131	2
von Walker, Green Bay	vs. Dallas	October 24	8	129	1
ris Chambers, Miami	vs. St. Louis	October 24	3	128	1
rvin Harrison, Indianapolis	at Detroit	November 25	12	127	3
c Moulds, Buffalo	vs. New England	October 3	10	126	1
vid Terrell, Chicago	vs. Detroit	September 12	5	126	0
ani Toomer, N.Y. Giants	vs. Cleveland	September 26	5	126	0
Schroeder, Tampa Bay	at Oakland	September 26	4	126	1
ny Gonzalez, Kansas City	vs. Indianapolis	October 31	8	125	2
dre Johnson, Houston	at N.Y. Jets	December 5	7	125	0
ny Gonzalez, Kansas City	vs. Oakland	December 25	11	124	2
rry Holt, St. Louis	vs. Tampa Bay	October 18	6	124	2
ew Bennett, Tennessee	at Indianapolis	December 5	3	124	3
Horn, New Orleans	at Oakland	October 24	9	123	0
ny Gonzalez, Kansas City	at Tampa Bay	November 7	9	123	1
tonio Gates, San Diego	at Houston	September 12	8	123	0
rty Booker, Miami	at New England	October 10	7	123	0
andon Stokley, Indianapolis	vs. San Diego	December 26*	7	123	1
hsin Muhammad, Carolina	at San Francisco	November 14	6	123	3
rell Owens, Philadelphia	vs. Carolina	October 17	4	123	0
nte' Stallworth, New Orleans	vs. Denver	November 21	10	122	1
veranues Coles, Washington	at Cleveland	October 3	7	122	0
rry Holt, St. Louis	at Atlanta	September 19	9	121	1
rrick Mason, Tennessee	at Oakland	December 19	9	121	1
die Kennison, Kansas City	at New Orleans	November 14	7	121	1
Zahir Hakim, Detroit	vs. Washington	November 7	7	120	0
vid Givens, New England	at Arizona	September 19	6	120	0
ggie Wayne, Indianapolis	at Tennessee	September 19	7	119	1
ndy Moss, Minnesota	vs. Chicago	September 26	7	119	2
ggie Wayne, Indianapolis	at Kansas City	October 31	6	119	2
rvin Harrison, Indianapolis	at Kansas City	October 31	5	119	2
hsin Muhammad, Carolina	vs. Arizona	November 21	6	118	2
c Parker, San Diego	vs. Tampa Bay	December 12	6	118	1
ge Crumpler, Atlanta	vs. Tampa Bay	November 14	4	118	1
ad Johnson, Cincinnati	vs. Cleveland	November 28	10	117	1
mmy Smith, Jacksonville	at Houston	October 31	9	117	0
vid Terrell, Chicago	vs. Philadelphia	October 3	9	116	0
Houshmandzadeh, Cincinnati	vs. Baltimore	September 26	7	116	0
rry Holt, St. Louis	vs. N.Y. Jets	January 2*	7	116	2

Player, Team	Opponent	Date	No.	Yds.
Keyshawn Johnson, Dallas	at Seattle	December 6	6	116
Muhsin Muhammad, Carolina	at Tampa Bay	December 26	8	115
Larry Johnson, Kansas City	at San Diego	January 2	8	115
Antonio Bryant, Cleveland	vs. New England	December 5	7	115
Andre Johnson, Houston	vs. Oakland	October 3	6	115
Keary Colbert, Carolina	at Denver	October 10	4	115
Muhsin Muhammad, Carolina	vs. Atlanta	October 3	7	114
Darrell Jackson, Seattle	at San Francisco	November 7	5	114
Dennis Northcutt, Cleveland	at Miami	December 26	4	114
Eric Johnson, San Francisco	vs. St. Louis	October 3	10	113
Donte' Stallworth, New Orleans	vs. San Francisco	September 19	9	113
Darrell Jackson, Seattle	vs. Dallas	December 6	9	113
Jimmy Smith, Jacksonville	at San Diego	October 10	8	113
Jerry Porter, Oakland	vs. New Orleans	October 24	6	113
David Patten, New England	at Buffalo	October 3	5	113
Jimmy Smith, Jacksonville	at Indianapolis	October 24	5	113
Donte' Stallworth, New Orleans	at Dallas	December 12	5	113
Isaac Bruce, St. Louis	vs. Arizona	September 12	9	112
Antonio Bryant, Dallas	at Minnesota	September 12	8	112
Curtis Conway, San Francisco	at New Orleans	September 19	8	112
Jason Witten, Dallas	at Green Bay	October 24	8	112
Brandon Stokley, Indianapolis	vs. Jacksonville	October 24	7	112
Keyshawn Johnson, Dallas	at Minnesota	September 12	9	111
Johnnie Morton, Kansas City	at Jacksonville	October 17	7	111
Torry Holt, St. Louis	vs. New England	November 7	6	111
Rod Gardner, Washington	at San Francisco	December 18	6	111
Marvin Harrison, Indianapolis	vs. San Diego	December 26*	6	111
Donald Driver, Green Bay	at Detroit	October 17	9	110
Brandon Stokley, Indianapolis	vs. Green Bay	September 26	8	110
Terrell Owens, Philadelphia	at Chicago	October 3	8	110
Joe Horn, New Orleans	vs. Seattle	September 12	6	110
Ronald Curry, Oakland	at Denver	November 28	6	110
Lee Evans, Buffalo	at Miami	December 5	4	110
Reche Caldwell, San Diego	vs. Tennessee	October 3	3	110
Nate Burleson, Minnesota	vs. Green Bay	December 24	2	110
Drew Bennett, Tennessee	at San Diego	October 3	9	109
Anquan Boldin, Arizona	vs. San Francisco	December 12*	9	109
Darrell Jackson, Seattle	at Arizona	October 24	8	109
Jimmy Smith, Jacksonville	vs. Detroit	November 14*	7	109
Santana Moss, N.Y. Jets	at Arizona	November 28	5	109
Terrell Owens, Philadelphia	at Cleveland	October 24*	4	109
Jabar Gaffney, Houston	at Chicago	December 19	4	109
Az-Zahir Hakim, Detroit	vs. Minnesota	December 19	4	108
Anquan Boldin, Arizona	at Seattle	December 26	7	107
Terrell Owens, Philadelphia	at Detroit	September 26	6	107
Andre Johnson, Houston	vs. Green Bay	November 21	6	107
David Givens, New England	vs. N.Y. Jets	October 24	5	107
Johnnie Morton, Kansas City	vs. New England	November 22	5	107
David Patten, New England	vs. Cincinnati	December 12	5	107
Tony Gonzalez, Kansas City	vs. Houston	September 26	8	106
Muhsin Muhammad, Carolina	at Seattle	October 31	8	106
Reggie Wayne, Indianapolis	at Chicago	November 21	6	106
Todd Pinkston, Philadelphia	vs. Washington	November 21	5	106
Marvin Harrison, Indianapolis	vs. Tennessee	December 5	4	106
Tony Gonzalez, Kansas City	vs. San Diego	November 28	8	105
Deion Branch, New England	at Kansas City	November 22	6	105
Ashley Lelie, Denver	at San Diego	December 5	4	105
Derrick Mason, Tennessee	vs. Indianapolis	September 19	8	104
Chris Chambers, Miami	vs. Arizona	November 7	7	104
Isaac Bruce, St. Louis	vs. Seattle	November 14	7	104
Roy Williams, Detroit	vs. Minnesota	December 19	7	104
Onterrio Smith, Minnesota	vs. Chicago	September 26	6	104
Eddie Kennison, Kansas City	at Tampa Bay	November 7	6	104
Randy Moss, Minnesota	vs. Seattle	December 12	4	104
Chris Chambers, Miami	at Seattle	November 21	9	103
Eric Parker, San Diego	at Indianapolis	December 26*	7	103
Alge Crumpler, Atlanta	vs. New Orleans	November 28	4	103
Isaac Bruce, St. Louis	at Atlanta	September 19	8	102
Javon Walker, Green Bay	vs. Chicago	September 19	7	102
Tiki Barber, N.Y. Giants	vs. Detroit	October 24	7	102
Randy Moss, Minnesota	at Detroit	December 19	4	102
Dallas Clark, Indianapolis	vs. Houston	November 14	3	102
Jamaar Taylor, N.Y. Giants	vs. Philadelphia	November 28	2	102
Joe Horn, New Orleans	at Atlanta	November 28	5	101
David Givens, New England	at Pittsburgh	October 31	8	101
Terrell Owens, Philadelphia	vs. Baltimore	October 31	8	101
Antonio Gates, San Diego	at Oakland	November 21	8	101
Eddie Kennison, Kansas City	vs. Denver	December 19	7	101
Eddie Kennison, Kansas City	at Denver	September 12	6	101
Derick Armstrong, Houston	vs. Minnesota	October 10*	6	101
Darrell Jackson, Seattle	vs. Arizona	December 26	6	101
Andre' Davis, Cleveland	at Pittsburgh	October 10	5	101
Cedrick Wilson, San Francisco	vs. Carolina	November 14	5	101
Lee Evans, Buffalo	at Cincinnati	December 5	5	101
Laveranues Coles, Washington	vs. Philadelphia	December 12	12	100
Laveranues Coles, Washington	at N.Y. Giants	September 19	9	100
Amani Toomer, N.Y. Giants	at Arizona	November 14	8	100
Isaac Bruce, St. Louis	at San Francisco	October 3	7	100
Todd Pinkston, Philadelphia	at Cleveland	October 24*	6	100
Lee Suggs, Cleveland	vs. Cincinnati	October 17	5	100
David Givens, New England	at St. Louis	November 7	5	100
Keary Colbert, Carolina	at Seattle	October 31	4	100

*Overtime game.

OFFENSE

TOTAL SCORES

am	Series	TD Rush	TD Pass	Total TDs	TD Efficiency Pct.	FGM	Total Scores	Scoring Efficiency Pct.
dianapolis	67	9	33	42	62.69	15	57	85.07
w England	63	15	22	37	58.73	20	57	90.48
n Diego	63	22	22	44	69.84	13	57	90.48
ffalo	61	13	15	28	45.90	22	50	81.97
nsas City	59	25	15	40	67.80	9	49	83.05
ttsburgh	61	15	13	28	45.90	21	49	80.33
attle	53	16	15	31	58.49	17	48	90.57
rolina	52	9	22	31	59.62	16	47	90.38
ncinnati	55	13	15	28	50.91	18	46	83.64
nnesota	58	7	26	33	56.90	13	46	79.31
een Bay	52	7	23	30	57.69	14	44	84.62
anta	51	17	10	27	52.94	15	42	82.35
nver	53	9	15	24	45.28	18	42	79.25
Y. Giants	54	16	10	26	48.15	15	41	75.93
iladelphia	47	8	22	30	63.83	9	39	82.98
ashington	44	5	18	23	52.27	16	39	88.64
troit	43	6	13	19	44.19	18	37	86.05
Y. Jets	43	12	13	25	58.14	12	37	86.05
cksonville	45	8	11	19	42.22	18	37	82.22
ltimore	40	10	10	20	50.00	17	37	92.50
nnessee	45	9	16	25	55.56	11	36	80.00
ew Orleans	47	14	13	27	57.45	9	36	76.60
eveland	41	6	13	19	46.34	16	35	85.37
. Louis	42	10	13	23	54.76	12	35	83.33
ouston	44	15	11	26	59.09	9	35	79.55
akland	41	9	11	20	48.78	14	34	82.93
allas	40	12	9	21	52.50	12	33	82.50
an Francisco	41	10	10	20	48.78	13	33	80.49
mpa Bay	40	8	13	21	52.50	11	32	80.00
ami	38	9	9	18	47.37	11	29	76.32
izona	37	13	5	18	48.65	11	29	78.38
icago	38	9	7	16	42.11	9	25	65.79
Total	1558	366	473	839	53.85	454	1293	82.99
Average	48.7	11.4	14.8	26.2	53.85	14.2	40.4	82.99

SCORING EFFICIENCY

eam	Series	TD Rush	TD Pass	Total TDs	TD Efficiency Pct.	FGM	Total Scores	Scoring Efficiency Pct.
altimore	40	10	10	20	50.00	17	37	92.50
eattle	53	16	15	31	58.49	17	48	90.57
ew England	63	15	22	37	58.73	20	57	90.48
an Diego	63	22	22	44	69.84	13	57	90.48
arolina	52	9	22	31	59.62	16	47	90.38
ashington	44	5	18	23	52.27	16	39	88.64
etroit	43	6	13	19	44.19	18	37	86.05
Y. Jets	43	12	13	25	58.14	12	37	86.05
eveland	41	6	13	19	46.34	16	35	85.37
dianapolis	67	9	33	42	62.69	15	57	85.07
een Bay	52	7	23	30	57.69	14	44	84.62
ncinnati	55	13	15	28	50.91	18	46	83.64
t. Louis	42	10	13	23	54.76	12	35	83.33
ansas City	59	25	15	40	67.80	9	49	83.05
hiladelphia	47	8	22	30	63.83	9	39	82.98
akland	41	9	11	20	48.78	14	34	82.93
allas	40	12	9	21	52.50	12	33	82.50
tlanta	51	17	10	27	52.94	15	42	82.35
acksonville	45	8	11	19	42.22	18	37	82.22
uffalo	61	13	15	28	45.90	22	50	81.97
an Francisco	41	10	10	20	48.78	13	33	80.49
ttsburgh	61	15	13	28	45.90	21	49	80.33
ennessee	45	9	16	25	55.56	11	36	80.00
ampa Bay	40	8	13	21	52.50	11	32	80.00
ouston	44	15	11	26	59.09	9	35	79.55
innesota	58	7	26	33	56.90	13	46	79.31
enver	53	9	15	24	45.28	18	42	79.25
rizona	37	13	5	18	48.65	11	29	78.38
ew Orleans	47	14	13	27	57.45	9	36	76.60
iami	38	9	9	18	47.37	11	29	76.32
.Y. Giants	54	16	10	26	48.15	15	41	75.93
hicago	38	9	7	16	42.11	9	25	65.79
Total	1558	366	473	839	53.85	454	1293	82.99
Average	48.7	11.4	14.8	26.2	53.85	14.2	40.4	82.99

2004 STATISTICS Miscellaneous

TOTAL SCORES

Team	Series	TD Rush	TD Pass	Total TDs	TD Efficiency Pct.	FGM	Total Scores	Scoring Efficiency Pct
Tampa Bay	40	7	12	19	47.50	11	30	75.0
Washington	37	7	12	19	51.35	11	30	81.0
Pittsburgh	33	7	9	16	48.48	15	31	93.9
Denver	41	12	8	20	48.78	12	32	78.0
New England	49	9	11	20	40.82	12	32	65.3
Philadelphia	46	12	10	22	47.83	10	32	69.5
Miami	42	10	13	23	54.76	10	33	78.5
N.Y. Jets	41	7	13	20	48.78	14	34	82.9
Baltimore	45	8	10	18	40.00	16	34	75.5
Indianapolis	46	9	13	22	47.83	13	35	76.0
Jacksonville	47	6	12	18	38.30	17	35	74.4
Houston	44	3	22	25	56.82	10	35	79.5
Detroit	45	10	14	24	53.33	13	37	82.2
Green Bay	44	7	21	28	63.64	9	37	84.0
Buffalo	46	6	14	20	43.48	20	40	86.9
Chicago	54	8	15	23	42.59	17	40	74.0
Carolina	50	17	10	27	54.00	13	40	80.0
Atlanta	49	20	11	31	63.27	10	41	83.6
Dallas	45	12	20	32	71.11	11	43	95.5
Arizona	51	11	12	23	45.10	21	44	86.2
San Diego	54	14	13	27	50.00	17	44	81.4
Seattle	51	15	14	29	56.86	16	45	88.2
Cleveland	53	21	10	31	58.49	15	46	86.7
N.Y. Giants	50	12	24	36	72.00	10	46	92.0
Cincinnati	52	9	16	25	48.08	22	47	90.3
Tennessee	54	12	19	31	57.41	16	47	87.0
Kansas City	54	15	19	34	62.96	13	47	87.0
St. Louis	56	11	20	31	55.36	18	49	87.5
New Orleans	60	14	17	31	51.67	19	50	83.3
San Francisco	60	21	15	36	60.00	16	52	86.6
Oakland	56	20	21	41	73.21	11	52	92.8
Minnesota	63	14	23	37	58.73	16	53	84.1
Total	1558	366	473	839	53.85	454	1293	82.9
Average	48.7	11.4	14.8	26.2	53.85	14.2	40.4	82.9

SCORING EFFICIENCY

Team	Series	TD Rush	TD Pass	Total TDs	TD Efficiency Pct.	FGM	Total Scores	Scoring Efficiency Pct
New England	49	9	11	20	40.82	12	32	65.3
Philadelphia	46	12	10	22	47.83	10	32	69.5
Chicago	54	8	15	23	42.59	17	40	74.0
Jacksonville	47	6	12	18	38.30	17	35	74.4
Tampa Bay	40	7	12	19	47.50	11	30	75.0
Baltimore	45	8	10	18	40.00	16	34	75.5
Indianapolis	46	9	13	22	47.83	13	35	76.0
Denver	41	12	8	20	48.78	12	32	78.0
Miami	42	10	13	23	54.76	10	33	78.5
Houston	44	3	22	25	56.82	10	35	79.5
Carolina	50	17	10	27	54.00	13	40	80.0
Washington	37	7	12	19	51.35	11	30	81.0
San Diego	54	14	13	27	50.00	17	44	81.4
Detroit	45	10	14	24	53.33	13	37	82.2
N.Y. Jets	41	7	13	20	48.78	14	34	82.9
New Orleans	60	14	17	31	51.67	19	50	83.3
Atlanta	49	20	11	31	63.27	10	41	83.6
Green Bay	44	7	21	28	63.64	9	37	84.0
Minnesota	63	14	23	37	58.73	16	53	84.1
Arizona	51	11	12	23	45.10	21	44	86.2
San Francisco	60	21	15	36	60.00	16	52	86.6
Cleveland	53	21	10	31	58.49	15	46	86.7
Buffalo	46	6	14	20	43.48	20	40	86.9
Tennessee	54	12	19	31	57.41	16	47	87.0
Kansas City	54	15	19	34	62.96	13	47	87.0
St. Louis	56	11	20	31	55.36	18	49	87.5
Seattle	51	15	14	29	56.86	16	45	88.2
Cincinnati	52	9	16	25	48.08	22	47	90.3
N.Y. Giants	50	12	24	36	72.00	10	46	92.0
Oakland	56	20	21	41	73.21	11	52	92.8
Pittsburgh	33	7	9	16	48.48	15	31	93.9
Dallas	45	12	20	32	71.11	11	43	95.5
Total	1558	366	473	839	53.85	454	1293	82.9
Average	48.7	11.4	14.8	26.2	53.85	14.2	40.4	82.9

2004 STATISTICAL LEADERS

2004 National Football League leaders
2004 NFL active career leaders

2004 NFL LEADERS

PRIMARY STATISTICS

Points

Player, Team	TD	FG	PAT	Pts.
A. Vinatieri, N.E.	0	31	48	141
J. Elam, Den.	0	29	42	129
J. Reed, Pit.	0	28	40	124
D. Akers, Phi.	0	27	41	122
S. Graham, Cin.	0	27	41	122
S. Alexander, Sea.	20	0	0	120
R. Longwell, G.B.	0	24	48	120
M. Vanderjagt, Ind.	0	20	59	119
R. Lindell, Buf.	0	24	45	117
M. Stover, Bal.	0	29	30	117

Touchdowns

Player, Team	Rush.	Rec.	Misc.	Tot.
S. Alexander, Sea.	16	4	0	20
L. Tomlinson, S.D.	17	1	0	18
M. Muhammad, Car.	0	16	0	16
T. Barber, NYG	13	2	0	15
M. Harrison, Ind.	0	15	0	15
P. Holmes, K.C.	14	1	0	15
D. Davis, Hou.	13	1	0	14
C. Martin, NYJ	12	2	0	14
T. Owens, Phi.	0	14	0	14
5 tied with				13

Rushing Yards

Player, Team	Att.	Avg.	Yds
C. Martin, NYJ	371	4.6	1697
S. Alexander, Sea.	353	4.8	1696
C. Dillon, N.E.	345	4.7	1635
E. James, Ind.	334	4.6	1548
T. Barber, NYG	322	4.7	1518
R. Johnson, Cin.	361	4.0	1454
L. Tomlinson, S.D.	339	3.9	1335
C. Portis, Was.	343	3.8	1315
R. Droughns, Den.	275	4.5	1240
F. Taylor, Jac.	260	4.7	1224

Passer Rating†
(minimum 224 attempts)

Player, Team	Att.	Rating
P. Manning, Ind.	497	121.1
D. Culpepper, Min.	548	110.9
D. Brees, S.D.	400	104.8
D. McNabb, Phi	469	104.7
B. Roethlisberger, Pit.	295	98.1
B. Griese, T.B.	336	97.5
T. Green, K.C.	556	95.2
M. Bulger, St.L.	485	93.7
T. Brady, N.E.	474	92.6
B. Favre, G.B.	540	92.4

Passing Yards

Player, Team	Att.	Y/A	Yds.
D. Culpepper, Min.	548	8.61	4717
T. Green, K.C.	556	8.26	4591
P. Manning, Ind.	497	9.17	4557
J. Plummer, Den.	521	7.85	4089
B. Favre, G.B.	540	7.57	4088
M. Bulger, St.L.	485	8.17	3964
J. Delhomme, Car.	533	7.29	3886
D. McNabb, Phi.	469	8.26	3875
A. Brooks, N.O.	542	7.03	3810
T. Brady, N.E.	474	7.79	3692

Receptions

Player, Team	No
T. Gonzalez, K.C.	102
D. Mason, Ten.	96
C. Johnson, Cin.	95
T. Holt, St.L.	94
J. Horn, N.O.	94
M. Muhammad, Car.	93
L. Coles, Was.	90
I. Bruce, St.L.	89
J. Walker, G.B.	89
E. Moulds, Buf.	88

Receiving Yards

Player, Team	No.	Avg.	Yds.
M. Muhammad, Car.	93	15.1	1405
J. Horn, N.O.	94	14.9	1399
J. Walker, G.B.	89	15.5	1382
T. Holt, St.L.	94	14.6	1372
I. Bruce, St.L.	89	14.5	1292
C. Johnson, Cin.	95	13.4	1274
T. Gonzalez, K.C.	102	12.3	1258
D. Bennett, Ten.	80	15.6	1247
R. Wayne, Ind.	77	15.7	1210
D. Driver, G.B.	84	14.4	1208

Fumbles

Player, Team	Lost	Fum.
M. Vick, Atl.	7	16
A. Brooks, N.O.	2	13
J. Delhomme, Car.	5	12
J. McCown, Ariz.	5	12
K. Warner, NYG	4	12
K. Boller, Bal.	7	11
T. Green, K.C.	4	11
T. Rattay, S.F.	6	11
D. Carr, Hou.	2	10
A. Feeley, Mia.	5	10

Interceptions

Player, Team	Ret. Yds.	Int.
E. Reed, Bal.	358	9
T. James, Cin.	66	8
N. Clements, Buf.	77	6
A. Dyson, Ten.	135	6
C. Gamble, Car.	15	6
K. Lucas, Sea.	46	6
D. Robinson, Hou.	146	6
13 tied with		5

Sacks

Player, Team	No.
D. Freeney, Ind.	16.0
B. Berry, Ariz.	14.5
K. Gbaja-Biamila, G.B.	13.5
P. Kerney, Atl.	13.0
S. Rice, T.B.	12.0
R. Coleman, Atl.	11.5
J. Hall, Det.	11.5
K. Williams, Min.	11.5
4 tied with	11.0

Kickoff Return Average
(minimum 20 returns)

Player, Team	No.	Yds.	Avg.
W. Ponder, NYG	36	967	26.9
E. Drummond, Det.	41	1092	26.6
T. McGee, Buf.	52	1370	26.3
T. Cox, T.B.	33	866	26.2
D. Hall, K.C.	68	1718	25.3
A. Randle El, Pit.	21	527	25.1
R. Ferguson, G.B.	21	526	25.0
B. Johnson, N.E.	41	1016	24.8
D. Rhodes, Ind.	48	1188	24.8
T. Dwight, S.D.	50	1222	24.4

Punt Return Average
(minimum 20 returns)

Player, Team	No.	Yds.	Avg
E. Drummond, Det.	24	316	13.1
A. Rossum, Atl.	37	457	12.4
D. Northcutt, Cle.	36	432	12.0
M. Lewis, N.O.	34	382	11.2
W. Welker, S.D., Mia.	43	464	10.8
B. Sams, Bal.	55	575	10.5
R. Smith, Den.	22	223	10.1
D. Hall, K.C.	23	232	10.1
R. McQuarters, Chi.	44	435	9.9
J. Lewis, Jac.	23	227	9.9

†**Passer Rating** denotes the NFL formula used to rate quarterbacks. *Step 1:* Complete passes divided by pass attempts. Subtract 0.3, then divide by 0.2. *Step 2:* Passing yards divided by pass attempts. Subtract 3, then divide by 4. *Step 3:* Touchdown passes divided by pass attempts, then divide by .05. *Step 4:* Start with .095, and subtract interceptions divided by attempts. Divide the difference by .04. *Step 5:* The sum of each step cannot be greater than 2.375 or less than zero. Add the sums of Steps 1 through 4, multiply by 100 and divide by 6.

2004 STATISTICAL LEADERS NFL

Touchdowns

layer, Team	No.
P. Manning, Ind.	49
D. Culpepper, Min.	39
D. McNabb, Phi.	31
B. Favre, G.B.	30
J. Delhomme, Car.	29
T. Brady, N.E.	28
D. Brees, S.D.	27
T. Green, K.C.	27
J. Plummer, Den.	27
M. Hasselbeck, Sea.	22

Yards per Attempt
(minimum 224 attempts)

Player, Team	Att.	Yds.	Y/A
P. Manning, Ind.	497	4557	9.17
B. Roethlisberger, Pit.	295	2621	8.88
D. Culpepper, Min.	548	4717	8.61
D. McNabb, Phi.	469	3875	8.26
T. Green, K.C.	556	4591	8.26
M. Bulger, St.L.	485	3964	8.17
D. Brees, S.D.	400	3159	7.90
J. Plummer, Den.	521	4089	7.85
B. Griese, T.B.	336	2632	7.83
T. Brady, N.E.	474	3692	7.79

Attempts

Player, Team	No.
T. Green, K.C.	556
D. Culpepper, Min.	548
A. Brooks, N.O.	542
B. Favre, G.B.	540
J. Delhomme, Car.	533
J. Plummer, Den.	521
K. Collins, Oak.	513
P. Manning, Ind.	497
V. Testaverde, Dal.	495
J. Harrington, Det.	489

Completions

layer, Team	Att.	Cmp.
D. Culpepper, Min.	548	379
T. Green, K.C.	556	369
B. Favre, G.B.	540	346
P. Manning, Ind.	497	336
M. Bulger, St.L.	485	321
J. Delhomme, Car.	533	310
A. Brooks, N.O.	542	309
J. Plummer, Den.	521	303
D. McNabb, Phi.	469	300
V. Testaverde, Dal.	495	297

Completion Pct.
(minimum 224 attempts)

Player, Team	Att.	Cmp.	Pct.
B. Griese, T.B.	336	233	69.3
D. Culpepper, Min.	548	379	69.2
P. Manning, Ind.	497	336	67.6
B. Roethlisberger, Pit.	295	196	66.4
T. Green, K.C.	556	369	66.4
M. Bulger, St.L.	485	321	66.2
D. Brees, S.D.	400	262	65.5
C. Pennington, NYJ.	370	242	65.4
B. Favre, G.B.	540	346	64.1
D. McNabb, Phi.	469	300	64.0

Interceptions

Player, Team	Att.	Int.
V. Testaverde, Dal.	495	20
K. Collins, Oak.	513	20
J. Plummer, Den.	521	20
C. Palmer, Cin.	432	18
B. Favre, G.B.	540	17
T. Green, K.C.	556	17
D. Bledsoe, Buf.	450	16
A. Brooks, N.O.	542	16
3 tied with		15

Interception Pct.
(minimum 224 attempts)

Player, Team	Att.	Int.	Pct.
K. Warner, NYG	277	4	1.4
D. McNabb, Phi.	469	8	1.7
D. Brees, S.D.	400	7	1.8
D. Culpepper, Min.	548	11	2.0
P. Manning, Ind.	497	10	2.0
B. Leftwich, Jac.	441	10	2.3
K. Boller, Bal.	464	11	2.4
C. Pennington, NYJ	370	9	2.4
J. McCown, Ariz.	408	10	2.5
J. Harrington, Det.	489	12	2.5

Passing Yards per Game
(minimum 7 games)

Player, Team	Yds.	G	Y/G
D. Culpepper, Min.	4717	16	294.8
T. Green, K.C.	4591	16	286.9
P. Manning, Ind.	4557	16	284.8
M. Bulger, St.L.	3964	14	283.1
D. McNabb, Phi.	3875	15	258.3
J. Plummer, Den.	4089	16	255.6
B. Favre, G.B.	4088	16	255.5
K. Collins, Oak.	3495	14	249.6
B. Volek, Ten.	2486	10	248.6
J. Delhomme, Car.	3886	16	242.9

Big Play Passes†

Player, Team	No.
P. Manning, Ind.	41
D. Culpepper, Min.	40
J. Plummer, Den.	38
A. Brooks, N.O.	35
B. Favre, G.B.	34
M. Bulger, St.L.	33
J. Delhomme, Car.	32
D. Carr, Hou.	31
T. Green, K.C.	31
D. McNabb, Phi.	31

Longest Completion

Player, Team	Yds.
J. Garcia, Cle.	99
J. Plummer, Den.	85
D. Culpepper, Min.	82
P. Manning, Ind.	80
D. McNabb, Phi.	80
J. Plummer, Den.	80
D. Brees, S.D.	79
B. Favre, G.B.	79
2 tied with	76

Times Sacked

Player, Team	No.
D. Carr, Hou.	49
D. Culpepper, Min.	46
M. Vick, Atl.	46
A. Brooks, N.O.	41
M. Bulger, St.L.	41
K. Warner, NYG	39
D. Bledsoe, Buf.	37
T. Rattay, S.F.	37
J. Harrington, Det.	36
K. Boller, Bal.	35

Sack Percentage
(minimum 224 attempts; pass plays*)

Player, Team	PP*	Skd.	Pct.
B. Favre, G.B.	552	12	2.2
P. Manning, Ind.	510	13	2.5
J. Plummer, Den.	536	15	2.8
D. Brees, S.D.	418	18	4.3
C. Pennington, NYJ	388	18	4.6
K. Collins, Oak.	538	25	4.6
T. Brady, N.E.	500	26	5.2
B. Leftwich, Jac.	466	25	5.4
K. Dorsey, S.F.	239	13	5.4
T. Green, K.C.	588	32	5.4

†**Big Play Passes** denote pass completions of 25 or more yards. ***Pass Plays** denote passing attempts plus times sacked.

2004 STATISTICAL LEADERS *NFL*

Attempts

Player, Team	No.
C. Martin, NYJ	371
R. Johnson, Cin.	361
S. Alexander, Sea.	353
C. Dillon, N.E.	345
C. Portis, Was.	343
L. Tomlinson, S.D.	339
E. James, Ind.	334
T. Barber, NYG	322
D. Davis, Hou.	302
W. McGahee, Buf.	284

Yards per Attempt
(minimum 100 attempts)

Player, Team	Att.	Yds.	Avg.
M. Vick, Atl.	120	902	7.5
S. Jackson, St.L.	134	673	5.0
T. Duckett, Atl.	104	509	4.9
C. Brown, Ten.	220	1067	4.9
L. Johnson, K.C.	120	581	4.8
S. Alexander, Sea.	353	1696	4.8
C. Dillon, N.E.	345	1635	4.7
T. Barber, NYG	322	1518	4.7
F. Taylor, Jac.	260	1224	4.7
K. Jones, Det.	241	1133	4.7

Touchdowns

Player, Team	No.
L. Tomlinson, S.D.	1
S. Alexander, Sea.	1
P. Holmes, K.C.	1
T. Barber, NYG	1
J. Bettis, Pit.	1
D. Davis, Hou.	1
W. McGahee, Buf.	1
C. Dillon, N.E.	1
R. Johnson, Cin.	1
C. Martin, NYJ	1

Big Running Plays†

Player, Team	No.
C. Martin, NYJ	50
S. Alexander, Sea.	47
C. Dillon, N.E.	42
F. Taylor, Jac.	36
M. Vick, Atl.	36
T. Barber, NYG	35
E. James, Ind.	35
R. Johnson, Cin.	35
K. Jones, Det.	35
3 tied with	32

Longest Run

Player, Team	Yds.
A. Green, G.B.	90
M. Pittman, T.B.	78
J. Lewis, Bal.	75
K. Jones, Det.	74
T. Barber, NYG	72
D. Foster, Car.	71
D. McAllister, N.O.	71
C. Portis, Was.	64
T. Hambrick, Ariz.	62
3 tied with	60

Yards per Attempt, Grass
(minimum 40 attempts)

Player, Team	Att.	Yds.	Avg.
T. Barber, NYG	68	453	6.7
J. Chatman, S.D.	60	380	6.3
T. Bell, Den.	75	396	5.3
E. James, Ind.	132	689	5.2
N. Davenport, G.B.	50	257	5.1
C. Dillon, N.E.	272	1355	5.0
Z. Crockett, Oak.	43	212	4.9
S. Alexander, Sea.	71	347	4.9
B. Westbrook, Phi.	131	638	4.9
C. Brown, Ten.	187	908	4.9

Yards per Attempt, Turf
(minimum 40 attempts)

Player, Team	Att.	Yds.	Avg.
M. Vick, Atl.	81	599	7.4
M. Moore, Min.	45	287	6.4
L. Jordan, NYJ	56	330	5.9
S. Bryson, Det.	40	220	5.5
F. Taylor, Jac.	59	315	5.3
R. Droughns, Den.	52	276	5.3
S. Jackson, St.L.	110	560	5.1
K. Jones, Det.	155	788	5.1
S. Morris, Mia.	48	244	5.1
T. Duckett, Atl.	70	355	5.1

Yards per Attempt, Att 21+†
(minimum 20 attempts)

Player, Team	Att.	Yds.	Avg.
S. Alexander, Sea.	58	334	5.8
R. Johnson, Cin.	54	296	5.5
C. Martin, NYJ	63	318	5.0
C. Brown, Ten.	28	141	5.0
L. Suggs, Cle.	27	128	4.7
E. James, Ind.	48	225	4.7
P. Holmes, K.C.	45	203	4.5
J. Jones, Dal.	52	227	4.4
A. Thomas, Chi.	22	95	4.3
T. Barber, NYG	24	101	4.2

Pct. TD, Inside 3-Yard Line
(minimum 5 attempts)

Player, Team	Att.	TD	TD%
T. Jones, Chi.	8	7	87.5
K. Barlow, S.F.	5	4	80.0
D. Davis, Hou.	13	10	76.9
T. Barber, NYG	8	6	75.0
C. Martin, NYJ	8	6	75.0
P. Holmes, K.C.	11	8	72.7
T. Duckett, Atl.	6	4	66.7
J. Lewis, Bal.	6	4	66.7
J. Bettis, Pit.	14	9	64.3
S. Alexander, Sea.	11	7	63.6

Times Stuffed†

Player, Team	No.
R. Johnson, Cin.	42
W. McGahee, Buf.	38
S. Alexander, Sea.	35
T. Barber, NYG	34
L. Tomlinson, S.D.	34
C. Portis, Was.	33
E. Smith, Ariz.	32
K. Jones, Det.	30
3 tied with	29

Times Stuffed per Attempt†
(minimum 100 attempts)

Player, Team	Att.	Stuffed	Avg.
T. Duckett, Atl.	104	1	.010
C. Taylor, Bal.	160	10	.063
L. Johnson, K.C.	120	8	.067
D. Staley, Pit.	192	13	.068
D. Blaylock, K.C.	118	8	.068
E. George, Dal.	132	10	.076
R. Droughns, Den.	275	21	.076
C. Brown, Ten.	220	17	.077
C. Martin, NYJ	371	29	.078
J. Bettis, Pit.	250	20	.080

4th Qtr. Rushing Yards

Player, Team	Att.	Yds.
S. Alexander, Sea.	84	472
T. Barber, NYG	88	412
C. Martin, NYJ	83	409
C. Dillon, N.E.	88	371
R. Droughns, Den.	77	345
R. Johnson, Cin.	71	343
W. McGahee, Buf.	77	338
J. Bettis, Pit.	86	326
E. James, Ind.	77	322
J. Lewis, Bal.	55	301

†**Big Running Plays** denote running plays gaining 10 or more yards. **Yards per Attempt, Att. 21+** denotes the average yards gained on all rushing attempts a player makes beyond his first 20 attempts in a game. Example: A player with 25 rushing attempts in a game is credited with only the yardage gained on his last five attempts. ***Times Stuffed** denotes the number of times a ball carrier is tackled behind the line of scrimmage on a rushing attempt. Any rush for zero yards is *not* counted as a stuff.

2004 STATISTICAL LEADERS *NFL*

Yards per Reception
(minimum 30 receptions)

Player, Team	No.	Yds.	Avg.
A. Lelie, Den.	54	1084	20.1
P. Burress, Pit.	35	698	19.9
T. Pinkston, Phi.	36	676	18.8
S. Moss, NYJ	45	838	18.6
D. Patten, N.E.	44	800	18.2
L. Evans, Buf.	48	843	17.6
E. Kennison, K.C.	62	1086	17.5
A. Hakim, Det.	31	533	17.2
J. Pathon, N.O.	34	581	17.1
D. Gabriel, Oak.	33	551	16.7

Touchdowns

Player, Team	No.
M. Muhammad, Car.	16
M. Harrison, Ind.	15
T. Owens, Phi.	14
A. Gates, S.D.	13
R. Moss, Min.	13
J. Walker, G.B.	12
R. Wayne, Ind.	12
D. Bennett, Ten.	11
J. Horn, N.O.	11
2 tied with	10

Target†

Player, Team	No.
C. Johnson, Cin.	170
L. Coles, Was.	168
M. Muhammad, Car.	160
D. Mason, Ten.	158
D. Jackson, Sea.	156
J. Horn, N.O.	153
E. Moulds, Buf.	152
I. Bruce, St.L.	148
T. Gonzalez, K.C.	148
2 tied with	144

Yards After Catch (YAC)†

Player, Team	No.	Yds.
B. Westbrook, Phi.	73	640
T. Barber, NYG	52	542
D. Davis, Hou.	68	526
M. Clayton, T.B.	80	521
L. Tomlinson, S.D.	53	509
A. Johnson, Hou.	79	489
N. Burleson, Min.	68	456
T. Gonzalez, K.C.	102	435
E. James, Ind.	51	431
D. Jackson, Sea.	87	425

Average Throw†
(minimum 32 targets)

Player, Team	Tgt.	Yds.	Avg.
B. Berrian, Chi.	44	904	20.5
P. Burress, Pit.	60	1186	19.8
T. Pinkston, Phi.	63	1201	19.1
A. Lelie, Den.	101	1883	18.6
K. Campbell, Min.	32	590	18.4
D. Gabriel, Oak.	79	1367	17.3
C. Moore, Bal.	58	993	17.1
Q. Morgan, Cle., Dal.	68	1124	16.5
K. Osgood, S.D.	33	544	16.5
D. Patten, N.E.	95	1555	16.4

Pct. Receptions per Target†
(minimum 50 targets)

Player, Team	No.	Tgt.	Pct.
E. James, Ind.	51	60	85.0
B. Westbrook, Phi.	73	87	83.9
D. Davis, Hou.	68	84	81.0
L. Tomlinson, S.D.	53	66	80.3
S. Bryson, Det.	44	56	78.6
A. Green, G.B.	40	51	78.4
T. Jones, Chi.	56	72	77.8
J. Wiggins, Min.	71	92	77.2
M. Faulk, St.L.	50	65	76.9
J. Sowell, NYJ	45	59	76.3

1st Down Receptions†

Player, Team	No.
M. Muhammad, Car.	74
J. Horn, N.O.	73
T. Gonzalez, K.C.	69
D. Mason, Ten.	67
I. Bruce, St.L.	64
M. Harrison, Ind.	63
C. Johnson, Cin.	63
J. Walker, G.B.	63
D. Bennett, Ten.	62
3 tied with	59

Longest Reception

Player, Team	Yds.
A. Davis, Cle.	99
R. Smith, Den.	85
R. Moss, Min.	82
D. Clark, Ind.	80
T. Pinkston, Phi.	80
R. Smith, Den.	80
E. Parker, S.D.	79
J. Walker, G.B.	79
2 tied with	76

Big Catches†

Player, Team	No.
A. Lelie, Den.	18
J. Smith, Jac.	16
M. Muhammad, Car.	15
J. Horn, N.O.	14
J. Walker, G.B.	14
D. Bennett, Ten.	13
A. Johnson, Hou.	13
J. Porter, Oak.	13
R. Wayne, Ind.	13
3 tied with	12

4th Qtr TD Receptions†

Player, Team	No.
M. Muhammad, Car.	7
J. Horn, N.O.	5
R. Williams, Det.	5
N. Burleson, Min.	4
D. Driver, G.B.	4
L. Fitzgerald, Ariz.	4
C. Johnson, Cin.	4
E. Kennison, K.C.	4
7 tied with	3

Receptions Lost on Penalty†

Player, Team	No.
C. Chambers, Mia.	6
B. Stokley, Ind.	6
T. Edwards, Jac.	5
C. Johnson, Cin.	5
D. Mason, Ten.	5
A. Randle El, Pit.	5
R. Smith, Den.	5
H. Ward, Pit.	5
7 tied with	4

Passes Dropped†

Player, Team	No.
C. Johnson, Cin.	14
D. Driver, G.B.	11
D. Jackson, Sea.	11
K. Colbert, Car.	10
A. Hakim, Det.	10
K. Robinson, Sea.	10
J. Smith, Jac.	10
F. Taylor, Jac.	10
R. Gardner, Was.	9
R. McMichael, Mia.	9

†**Target** denotes the intended receiver of a pass. **Yards After Catch (YAC)** denotes the number of yards a receiver gains from the spot on the field at which he establishes possession of a thrown football to the play's end. A receiver catching a pass in the end zone receives credit for no yards after the catch, regardless of the length of the entire pass play. Example: With the line of scrimmage on the offensive team's own 15-yard line, a receiver catches a pass on his own 25-yard line and is tackled (or runs out of bounds) at his team's 39-yard line. While he gets credit for a 24-yard reception, the receiver is credited with 14 yards after catch (YAC). **Average Throw** denotes the average distance that all passes intended for a given receiver travel in the air before hitting the ground, being touched by a player, going out of bounds or crossing the goal line. **Pct. Receptions per Target** denotes the percentage of time a pass intended for a receiver was caught by that receiver. **1st Down Receptions** denote the number of receptions resulting in a first down. **Big Catches** denote receptions of 25 or more yards. **Receptions Lost on Penalty** denote the number of receptions nullified by a penalty. **Passes Dropped** denote any incomplete pass which was catchable with normal effort. To determine if a pass was dropped, STATS, Inc. compares and reviews the judgment of multiple reporters.

DEFENSIVE STATISTICS

Tackles

Player, Team	No.
D. Brooks, T.B.	109
D. Edwards, S.D.	105
L. Briggs, Chi.	102
R. Lewis, Bal.	101
K. Bulluck, Ten.	99
D. Clark, Oak.	99
J. Sharper, Hou.	98
L. Fletcher, Buf.	94
M. Peterson, Jac.	93
R. Griffith, Cle.	92

Assists

Player, Team	No.
Z. Thomas, Mia.	60
K. Bulluck, Ten.	53
L. Fletcher, Buf.	50
D. Edwards, S.D.	46
R. Lewis, Bal.	46
T. Bruschi, N.E.	45
S. Knight, Mia.	44
E. Hartwell, Bal.	41
J. Sharper, Hou.	41
2 tied with	40

Sack Yards

Player, Team	Sacks	Yds.
D. Freeney, Ind.	16.01	20.0
K. Gbaja-Biamila, G.B.	13.59	7.0
B. Berry, Ariz.	14.59	5.0
P. Kerney, Atl.	13.09	4.5
R. Mathis, Ind.	10.5	90.0
T. Suggs, Bal.	10.5	83.5
R. Coleman, Atl.	11.5	81.5
J. Hall, Det.	11.5	74.5
R. Hayward, Den.	10.5	73.5
2 tied with		73.0

Interception Return Yards

Player, Team	Int.	Yds.
E. Reed, Bal.	9	358
N. Vasher, Chi.	5	177
L. Sheppard, Phi.	5	172
C. Williams, Bal.	3	156
D. Robinson, Hou.	6	146
J. Peppers, Car.	2	143
M. Trufant, Sea.	5	141
A. Dyson, Ten.	6	135
J. Azumah, Chi.	4	128
T. Spikes, Buf.	5	122

Yards per Int. Return

(minimum 4 interceptions)

Player, Team	Int.	Yds.	Avg.
E. Reed, Bal.	9	358	39.8
N. Vasher, Chi.	5	177	35.4
L. Sheppard, Phi.	5	172	34.4
J. Azumah, Chi.	4	128	32.0
A. Beasley, Atl.	4	115	28.8
J. Farrior, Pit.	4	113	28.3
M. Trufant, Sea.	5	141	28.2
D. Bly, Det.	4	107	26.8
B. Kelly, T.B.	4	101	25.3
T. Spikes, Buf.	5	122	24.4

Passes Defensed†

Player, Team	No.
K. Herndon, Den.	23
B. Kelly, T.B.	22
K. Lucas, Sea.	21
R. Mathis, Jac.	21
A. Harris, G.B.	20
M. Trufant, Sea.	20
W. Allen, NYG	19
D. Bly, Det.	19
J. Butler, St.L.	19
D. Robinson, Hou.	19

Touchdowns

Player, Team	No.
D. Sharper, G.B.	3
D. Abraham, NYJ	2
R. Barber, T.B.	2
L. Little, St.L.	2
K. Mathis, Atl.	2
J. Peppers, Car.	2
E. Reed, Bal.	2
L. Sheppard, Phi.	2
T. Spikes, Buf.	2
67 tied with	1

Stuffs†

Player, Team	No.
C. Griffin, Was.	14.5
C. Grant, N.O.	11.5
M. Washington, Was.	10.5
D. Williams, Den.	10.0
A. Wilson, Ariz.	10.0
K. Lang, Cle.	9.5
J. Trotter, Phi.	9.0
L. Briggs, Chi.	8.5
A. Schobel, Buf.	8.5
B. Young, S.F.	8.5

Stuff Yards†

Player, Team	Stuffs	Yds.
M. Fields, Car.	8.0	31.5
K. Lang, Cle.	9.5	31.5
A. Wilson, Ariz.	10.0	31.5
S. Adams, Buf.	7.5	26.5
C. Grant, N.O.	11.5	26.0
C. Griffin, Was.	14.5	25.5
B. Young, S.F.	8.5	24.0
M. Washington, Was.	10.5	23.0
D. Williams, Den.	10.0	23.0
K. Bulluck, Ten.	7.5	22.0

Forced Fumbles

Player, Team	No.
R. Mathis, Ind.	6
W. Smith, N.O.	6
N. Clements, Buf.	5
S. Foley, S.D.	5
L. Johnstone, Min.	5
A. Schobel, Buf.	5
8 tied with	4

Fumbles Recovered

Player, Team	No.
E. Barton, NYJ	4
D. Darius, Jac.	4
M. Green, Chi.	4
L. Little, St.L.	4
O. Umenyiora, NYG	4
13 tied with	3

Blocked FGs/Punts/PATs

Player, Team	No.
S. Rogers, Det.	3
L. Walker, Oak.	3
26 tied with	1

†**Passes Defensed** denote any passes which a defender, through contact with the football, causes to be incomplete. Interceptions are included in passes defensed. **Stuffs** denote the number of times a ball carrier, including a quarterback on a rushing play, is tackled behind the line of scrimmage on a rushing attempt. Any rush for zero yards is *not* counted as a stuff. **Stuff Yards** denote the number of yards lost as the result of being stuffed (see "Stuffs" explanation).

Return Touchdowns

Player, Team	No.
. Drummond, Det.	4
. McGee, Buf.	3
. Hall, K.C.	2
. Sams, Bal.	2
7 tied with	1

Tackles

Player, Team	No.
R. Myles, Cin.	22
L. Izzo, N.E.	20
M. Mitchell, N.O.	20
G. Stills, K.C.	20
J. Thrash, Was.	20
F. McAfee, N.O.	17
Q. Mikell, Phi.	17
M. Wilkins, Cin.	17
4 tied with	16

Hang Time†

(minimum 40 punts)		
Player, Team	Punts	Seconds
M. Scifres, S.D.	69	4.57
J. Feagles, NYG	73	4.33
M. Turk, Mia.	98	4.31
M. McBriar, Dal.	75	4.30
C. Mohr, Atl.	76	4.29
C. Stanley, Hou.	73	4.29
J. Bidwell, T.B.	82	4.24
S. Lechler, Oak.	73	4.24
S. Cheek, K.C.	42	4.24
D. Bennett, Min.	57	4.23

Field Goals

Player, Team	No.
A. Vinatieri, N.E.	31
. Elam, Den.	29
M. Stover, Bal.	29
. Reed, Pit.	28
D. Akers, Phi.	27
S. Graham, Cin.	27
S. Janikowski, Oak.	25
tied with	24

Field Goal Pct.

(minimum 16 attempts)			
Player, Team	Made	Att.	Pct.
A. Vinatieri, N.E.	31	33	93.9
J. Brown, Sea.	23	25	92.0
M. Stover, Bal.	29	32	90.6
S. Janikowski, Oak.	25	28	89.3
S. Graham, Cin.	27	31	87.1
J. Kasay, Car.	19	22	86.4
J. Hanson, Det.	24	28	85.7
R. Lindell, Buf.	24	28	85.7
R. Longwell, G.B.	24	28	85.7
J. Elam, Den.	29	34	85.3

Inside-40 Yard FG Pct.

(minimum 10 attempts)			
Player, Team	Made	Att.	Pct.
B. Cundiff, Dal.	11	11	100.0
J. Kasay, Car.	15	15	100.0
A. Vinatieri, N.E.	20	20	100.0
J. Hanson, Det.	19	20	95.0
M. Stover, Bal.	18	19	94.7
J. Elam, Den.	17	18	94.4
J. Brown, Sea.	16	17	94.1
R. Longwell, G.B.	16	17	94.1
S. Janikowski, Oak.	15	16	93.8
2 tied with			92.3

40+ Yd FG Pct.

(minimum 10 attempts)			
Player, Team	Made	Att.	Pct.
. Brien, NYJ	11	13	84.6
M. Stover, Bal.	11	13	84.6
A. Vinatieri, N.E.	11	13	84.6
S. Graham, Cin.	10	12	83.3
S. Janikowski, Oak.	10	12	83.3
D. Akers, Phi.	17	21	81.0
J. Elam, Den.	12	16	75.0
N. Kaeding, S.D.	8	11	72.7
R. Longwell, G.B.	8	11	72.7
3 tied with			70.0

Net Kickoff Average†

Player, Team	Avg.
A. Elling, Ten., Min.	64.9
J. Carney, N.O.	64.9
M. Berger, N.O.	64.9
J. Wilkins, St.L.	63.3
D. Akers, Phi.	62.6
M. Bryant, Ind., Mia.	62.3
J. Feely, Atl.	62.1
K. Brown, Hou.	61.9
J. Cortez, Min.	61.8
P. Dawson, Cle.	61.8

Gross Punting Average

(minimum 40 punts)			
Player, Team	Punts	Yds.	Avg.
S. Lechler, Oak.	73	3409	46.7
H. Smith, Ind.	54	2443	45.2
T. Tupa, Was.	103	4544	44.1
T. Sauerbrun, Car.	76	3351	44.1
M. Berger, N.O.	85	3704	43.6
S. Landeta, St.L.	40	1733	43.3
B. Moorman, Buf.	77	3325	43.2
S. Player, Ariz.	98	4230	43.2
M. Scifres, S.D.	69	2974	43.1
C. Gardocki, Pit.	67	2879	43.0

Net Punting Average†

(minimum 40 punts)			
Player, Team	Punts	Yds.	Avg.
M. Berger, N.O.	85	3314	39.0
B. Maynard, Chi.	108	4175	38.7
M. Scifres, S.D.	69	2650	38.4
C. Hentrich, Ten.	73	2773	38.0
T. Sauerbrun, Car.	77	2888	37.5
C. Gardocki, Pit.	67	2507	37.4
D. Johnson, Phi.	72	2691	37.4
M. Turk, Mia.	98	3647	37.2
S. Lechler, Oak.	73	2716	37.2
C. Mohr, Atl.	76	2808	36.9

Inside-20 Pct.†

(minimum 40 punts)			
Player, Team	Punts	In-20	Pct.
M. Scifres, S.D.	69	29	42.0
H. Smith, Ind.	54	21	38.9
C. Gardocki, Pit.	67	24	35.8
D. Zastudil, Bal.	73	26	35.6
N. Harris, Det.	92	32	34.8
J. Miller, N.E.	56	19	33.9
C. Hanson, Jac.	84	28	33.3
M. Berger, N.O.	85	28	32.9
T. Sauerbrun, Car.	76	25	32.9
S. Player, Ariz.	98	32	32.7

Touchback Pct.

(minimum 40 punts)			
Player, Team	Punts	TB	Pct.
B. Maynard, Chi.	108	5	4.6
M. Berger, N.O.	85	4	4.7
D. Frost, Cle.	85	4	4.7
D. Bennett, Min.	57	3	5.3
J. Feagles, NYG	74	4	5.4
H. Smith, Ind.	54	3	5.6
S. Player, Ariz.	98	7	7.1
S. Landeta, St.L.	40	3	7.5
N. Harris, Det.	92	7	7.6
T. Tupa, Was.	103	8	7.8

†**Hang Time** denotes the average time in seconds from when the ball strikes the punter's foot until it is touched by another player or hits the ground. If a punt is deflected at the line of scrimmage, that deflection is ignored. **Net Kickoff Average** denotes kickoff yards, minus return yards, minus 20 yards for every touchback, divided by the number of kickoffs. **Net Punting Average** denotes gross punting yards, minus return yards, minus 20 yards for every touchback, divided by the total number of punts. **Inside-20 Percentage** denotes the percentage of punts which are considered inside-20. According to the NFL, "Credit a player with an inside-20 when his punt is not returned to the receivers' 20-yard line or beyond. Also credit an inside-20 when a punt does not penetrate the 20, but the returner carries the ball back inside the 20 and his return ends there. A touchback is *not* an inside-20."

2004 STATISTICAL LEADERS *Active career*

Points

Player	No.
Gary Anderson	2434
Morten Andersen	2358
John Carney	1537
Matt Stover	1481
Steve Christie	1476
Jason Elam	1442
Jason Hanson	1336
Jerry Rice	1256
John Kasay	1184
Jeff Wilkins	1071

Total Touchdowns

Player	No.
Jerry Rice	208
Marshall Faulk	135
Tim Brown	105
Marvin Harrison	98
Terrell Owens	97
Curtis Martin	95
Randy Moss	91
Priest Holmes	87
Jerome Bettis	85
Eddie George	78

Rushing Yards

Player	Yds.
Curtis Martin	13366
Jerome Bettis	13294
Marshall Faulk	11987
Eddie George	10441
Corey Dillon	9696
Garrison Hearst	7966
Edgerrin James	7720
Priest Holmes	7584
Fred Taylor	7580
Stephen Davis	7326

Rushing Yards per Attempt
(minimum 750 attempts)

Player	Att.	Yds.	Avg.
Clinton Portis	906	4414	4.9
Ahman Green	1528	7177	4.7
Priest Holmes	1615	7584	4.7
Jamal Lewis	1239	5763	4.7
Fred Taylor	1637	7580	4.6
Charlie Garner	1537	7097	4.6
Tiki Barber	1533	6927	4.5
Shaun Alexander	1347	5937	4.4
Corey Dillon	2210	9696	4.4
Deuce McAllister	961	4194	4.4

Rushing Touchdowns

Player	No.
Marshall Faulk	100
Curtis Martin	85
Jerome Bettis	82
Priest Holmes	80
Eddie George	68
Shaun Alexander	62
Corey Dillon	57
LaDainian Tomlinson	54
Stephen Davis	53
Edgerrin James	51

Rushing Attempts

Player	No.
Jerome Bettis	3369
Curtis Martin	3298
Eddie George	2865
Marshall Faulk	2771
Corey Dillon	2210
Garrison Hearst	1831
Edgerrin James	1828
Stephen Davis	1725
Warrick Dunn	1690
Fred Taylor	1637

Receptions

Player	No.
Jerry Rice	1549
Tim Brown	1094
Marvin Harrison	845
Jimmy Smith	792
Isaac Bruce	777
Keenan McCardell	755
Marshall Faulk	723
Rod Smith	712
Keyshawn Johnson	673
Terrell Owens	669

Receiving Yards

Player	Yds.
Jerry Rice	22895
Tim Brown	14934
Isaac Bruce	11753
Jimmy Smith	11264
Marvin Harrison	11185
Terrell Owens	9772
Rod Smith	9772
Keenan McCardell	9763
Randy Moss	9142
Keyshawn Johnson	8917

Receiving Touchdowns

Player	No.
Jerry Rice	197
Tim Brown	100
Marvin Harrison	98
Terrell Owens	95
Randy Moss	90
Isaac Bruce	74
Jimmy Smith	61
Rod Smith	59
3 tied with	54

Yards per Reception
(minimum 200 receptions)

Player	No.	Yds.	Avg.
Randy Moss	574	9142	15.9
Torry Holt	517	8156	15.8
Joey Galloway	467	7214	15.4
Eddie Kennison	414	6282	15.2
Amani Toomer	469	7113	15.2
Isaac Bruce	777	11753	15.1
Bill Schroeder	304	4583	15.1
Chris Chambers	233	3478	14.9
David Patten	236	3519	14.9
Koren Robinson	213	3167	14.9

Fumbles

Player	No.
Brett Favre	120
Kerry Collins	108
Vinny Testaverde	106
Drew Bledsoe	103
Chris Chandler	98
Rich Gannon	79
Steve McNair	77
Daunte Culpepper	76
Jon Kitna	72
Rodney Peete	71

Games Played

Player	No.
Morten Andersen	354
Gary Anderson	353
Jerry Rice	303
Sean Landeta	279
Jeff Feagles	272
Tim Brown	255
Jerry Fontenot	239
Chris Mohr	239
John Carney	239
Steve Christie	229

Passing Yards

Player	Yds.
Brett Favre	49734
Vinny Testaverde	44475
Drew Bledsoe	39808
Kerry Collins	29878
Peyton Manning	29442
Rich Gannon	28743
Chris Chandler	28484
Jeff George	27602
Mark Brunell	26987
Steve McNair	23980

Touchdowns

Player	No.
Brett Favre	376
Vinny Testaverde	268
Drew Bledsoe	221
Peyton Manning	216
Rich Gannon	180
Chris Chandler	170
Jeff George	154
Kerry Collins	153
Mark Brunell	151
Steve McNair	140

Yards per Attempt
(minimum 1500 attempts)

Player	Att.	Yds.	Y/A
Kurt Warner	1965	16501	8.40
Daunte Culpepper	2391	18598	7.78
Trent Green	2822	21607	7.66
Peyton Manning	3880	29442	7.59
Chris Chandler	4005	28484	7.11
Brett Favre	7004	49734	7.10
Matt Hasselbeck	1756	12466	7.10
Brian Griese	2144	15208	7.09
Steve McNair	3395	23980	7.06
Rodney Peete	2346	16338	6.96

Attempts

Player	No.
Brett Favre	7004
Vinny Testaverde	6420
Drew Bledsoe	6049
Kerry Collins	4517
Rich Gannon	4206
Chris Chandler	4005
Jeff George	3967
Mark Brunell	3880
Peyton Manning	3880
Jake Plummer	3577

Completions

Player	No.
Brett Favre	4306
Vinny Testaverde	3631
Drew Bledsoe	3449
Rich Gannon	2533
Kerry Collins	2524
Peyton Manning	2464
Chris Chandler	2328
Mark Brunell	2314
Jeff George	2298
Jake Plummer	2032

Completion Pct.
(minimum 1500 attempts)

Player	Att.	Cmp.	Pct.
Kurt Warner	1965	1295	65.9
Daunte Culpepper	2391	1539	64.4
Peyton Manning	3880	2464	63.5
Brian Griese	2144	1351	63.0
Tom Brady	2018	1243	61.6
Brett Favre	7004	4306	61.5
Trent Green	2822	1705	60.4
Rich Gannon	4206	2533	60.2
Matt Hasselbeck	1756	1048	59.7
Mark Brunell	3880	2314	59.6

Passer Rating†
(minimum 1500 attempts)

Player	Att.	Rating
Kurt Warner	1965	95.7
Daunte Culpepper	2391	93.2
Peyton Manning	3880	92.3
Trent Green	2822	87.9
Tom Brady	2018	87.5
Brett Favre	7004	87.4
Brian Griese	2144	85.3
Rich Gannon	4206	84.7
Donovan McNabb	2586	83.9
Mark Brunell	3880	83.9

Interceptions

Player	No.
Vinny Testaverde	255
Brett Favre	226
Drew Bledsoe	181
Kerry Collins	154
Chris Chandler	146
Jake Plummer	141
Peyton Manning	120
Jeff George	113
Rich Gannon	104
Jon Kitna	102

Interception Pct.
(minimum 1500 attempts)

Player	Att.	Int.	Pct.
Donovan McNabb	2586	57	2.2
Mark Brunell	3880	92	2.4
Rich Gannon	4206	104	2.5
Tom Brady	2018	52	2.6
Steve McNair	3395	92	2.7
Matt Hasselbeck	1756	48	2.7
Jeff George	3967	113	2.8
Aaron Brooks	2340	67	2.9
Trent Green	2822	82	2.9
Drew Bledsoe	6049	181	3.0

Passing Yards per Game
(minimum 1500 attempts)

Player	Yds.	G	Y/G
Peyton Manning	29442	112	262.9
Kurt Warner	16501	63	261.9
Daunte Culpepper	18598	74	251.3
Trent Green	21607	88	245.5
Brett Favre	49734	209	238.0
Drew Bledsoe	39808	172	231.4
Aaron Brooks	16274	72	226.0
Brian Griese	15208	69	220.4
Kerry Collins	29878	137	218.1
Tom Brady	13925	64	217.6

Times Sacked

Player	No.
Drew Bledsoe	402
Vinny Testaverde	396
Chris Chandler	380
Brett Favre	379
Jeff George	358
Mark Brunell	350
Rich Gannon	302
Kerry Collins	257
Jeff Blake	248
2 tied with	244

Sack Percentage
(minimum 1500 attempts; pass plays*)

Player	PP*	Skd.	Pct.
Peyton Manning	4019	139	3.5
Brett Favre	7383	379	5.1
Kerry Collins	4774	257	5.4
Jon Kitna	2979	171	5.7
Steve McNair	3604	209	5.8
Vinny Testaverde	6816	396	5.8
Tom Brady	2148	130	6.1
Drew Bledsoe	6451	402	6.2
Trent Green	3012	190	6.3
Jake Plummer	3821	244	6.4

†**Passer Rating** denotes the NFL formula used to rate quarterbacks. *Step 1:* Complete passes divided by pass attempts. Subtract 0.3, then divide by 0.2. *Step 2:* Passing yards divided by pass attempts. Subtract 3, then divide by 4. *Step 3:* Touchdown passes divided by pass attempts, then divide by .05. *Step 4:* Start with .095, and subtract interceptions divided by attempts. Divide the difference by .04. *Step 5:* The sum of each step cannot be greater than 2.375 or less than zero. Add the sums of Steps 1 through 4, multiply by 100 and divide by 6. ***Pass Plays** denote passing attempts plus times sacked.

SPECIAL TEAMS

Field Goals

Player	No.
Gary Anderson	538
Morten Andersen	520
John Carney	365
Matt Stover	350
Steve Christie	336
Jason Elam	317
Jason Hanson	308
John Kasay	284
Adam Vinatieri	243
Jeff Wilkins	224

Field Goal Pct.
(minimum 100 FG Made)

Player	Made	Att.	Pct.
Mike Vanderjagt	194	223	87.0
David Akers	139	167	83.2
Matt Stover	350	423	82.7
Ryan Longwell	206	250	82.4
Adam Vinatieri	243	296	82.1
Olindo Mare	194	237	81.9
Phil Dawson	108	132	81.8
John Carney	365	448	81.5
Jeff Wilkins	224	275	81.5
Doug Brien	206	254	81.1

Inside-40 Yard FG Pct.
(minimum 50 FG Made)

Player	Made	Att.	Pct.
Jason Hanson	204	213	95.8
Mike Vanderjagt	122	129	94.6
David Akers	87	92	94.6
Matt Stover	242	258	93.8
Sebastian Janikowski	73	78	93.6
Jason Elam	209	224	93.3
Jeff Wilkins	155	168	92.3
Morten Andersen	344	374	92.0
John Kasay	190	208	91.3
Olindo Mare	135	148	91.2

40-49 Yard FG Pct.
(minimum 25 FG Made)

Player	Made	Att.	Pct.
Mike Vanderjagt	58	73	79.5
Doug Brien	67	90	74.4
Ryan Longwell	58	80	72.5
David Akers	43	60	71.7
John Kasay	68	95	71.6
Gary Anderson	160	225	71.1
Adam Vinatieri	66	93	71.0
Paul Edinger	40	57	70.2
Olindo Mare	47	67	70.1
Matt Stover	96	137	70.1

50+ Yard FG Pct.
(minimum 10 FG Made)

Player	Made	Att.	Pct.
Paul Edinger	13	19	68.4
Mike Vanderjagt	14	21	66.7
Jeff Wilkins	16	24	66.7
Jason Elam	34	54	63.0
Martin Gramatica	15	24	62.5
John Carney	19	34	55.9
Olindo Mare	12	22	54.5
Doug Brien	15	28	53.6
Steve Christie	21	40	52.5
John Kasay	26	50	52.0

Gross Punting Average
(minimum 250 punts)

Player	Punts	Yds.	Avg.
Shane Lechler	360	16522	45.9
Todd Sauerbrun	760	33443	44.0
Tom Rouen	749	32650	43.6
Darren Bennett	828	36016	43.5
Chris Hanson	274	11910	43.5
Tom Tupa	873	37862	43.4
Sean Landeta	1367	59224	43.3
Hunter Smith	373	16128	43.2
Mitch Berger	639	27614	43.2
Brian Moorman	308	13219	42.9

Net Punting Average†
(minimum 250 punts)

Player	Punts	Yds.	Avg.
Matt Turk	792	29501	37.2
Craig Hentrich	821	30100	36.7
Darren Bennett	831	30446	36.6
Shane Lechler	362	13163	36.4
Tom Rouen	758	27536	36.3
Chris Hanson	275	9969	36.3
Brad Maynard	745	26966	36.2
Brian Moorman	309	11095	35.9
Todd Sauerbrun	766	27462	35.9
Josh Bidwell	391	13986	35.8

Inside-20 Pct.†
(minimum 250 punts)

Player	Punts	In-20	Pct.
Craig Hentrich	818	292	35.7
Josh Miller	628	213	33.9
Brad Maynard	741	242	32.7
Kyle Richardson	494	160	32.4
Matt Turk	790	252	31.9
Shane Lechler	360	114	31.7
Jeff Feagles	1364	430	31.5
Darren Bennett	828	261	31.5
Mitch Berger	639	199	31.1
Ken Walter	510	158	31.0

Touchback Pct.
(minimum 250 punts)

Player	Punts	TB	Pct.
Ken Walter	510	27	5.3
Chad Stanley	441	33	7.5
Darren Bennett	828	62	7.5
Nick Harris	332	25	7.5
Chris Mohr	1152	87	7.6
Jeff Feagles	1364	109	8.0
Brad Maynard	741	60	8.1
Brian Moorman	308	26	8.4
Chris Gardocki	1045	92	8.8
Josh Bidwell	390	35	9.0

Kickoff Return Average
(minimum 75 returns)

Player	No.	Yds.	Avg.
Eddie Drummond	102	2600	25.5
Dominic Rhodes	78	1955	25.1
Jerry Azumah	87	2180	25.1
Steve Smith	93	2311	24.8
Michael Lewis	198	4852	24.5
Dante Hall	242	5877	24.3
Kevin Kasper	77	1869	24.3
Aaron Stecker	118	2845	24.1
Brock Marion	123	2951	24.0
Chad Morton	174	4172	24.0

Punt Return Average
(minimum 75 returns)

Player	No.	Yds.	Avg.
Az-Zahir Hakim	131	1513	11.5
Dante Hall	119	1366	11.5
Michael Lewis	122	1363	11.2
Jermaine Lewis	295	3282	11.1
Reggie Swinton	90	977	10.9
Brian Mitchell	463	4999	10.8
Troy Brown	237	2524	10.6
Dennis Northcutt	139	1469	10.6
Bobby Engram	100	1044	10.4
Deion Sanders	212	2199	10.4

Return Touchdowns

Player	No.
Brian Mitchell	13
Dante Hall	9
Deion Sanders	9
Eddie Drummond	6
Jermaine Lewis	6
Steve Smith	6
Joey Galloway	5
Tim Brown	4
Michael Lewis	4
Reggie Swinton	4

†**Net Punting Average** denotes gross punting yards, minus return yards, minus 20 yards for every touchback, divided by the total number of punts. **Inside-20 Percentage** denotes the percentage of punts which are considered inside-20. According to the NFL, "Credit a player with an inside-20 when his punt is not returned to the receivers' 20-yard line or beyond. Also credit an inside-20 when a punt does not penetrate the 20, but the returner carries the ball back inside the 20 and his return ends there. A touchback is *not* an inside-20."

Interceptions

Player	No.
Aeneas Williams	55
Deion Sanders	51
Terrell Buckley	50
Ray Buchanan	47
Troy Vincent	43
Ashley Ambrose	42
Donnie Abraham	38
Ty Law	36
Aaron Glenn	35
3 tied with	31

Fumbles Recovered

Player	No.
Aeneas Williams	20
Jason Taylor	19
Junior Seau	17
Chad Brown	15
Willie McGinest	14
Takeo Spikes	14
Michael Strahan	13
Brian Dawkins	11
Warren Sapp	11
Derek Smith	11

Forced Fumbles

Player	No.
Simeon Rice	24
Jason Taylor	23
Mike Barrow	22
Michael Strahan	22
Jevon Kearse	21
Derrick Brooks	20
Robert Porcher	20
Marco Coleman	19
Lance Johnstone	19
Leonard Little	19

Yards per Interception Return
(minimum 20 interceptions)

Player	Int.	Yds.	Avg.
Ed Reed	21	657	31.3
Deion Sanders	51	1274	25.0
Derrick Brooks	20	481	24.0
Tony Parrish	28	636	22.7
Aaron Beasley	24	487	20.3
Greg Wesley	20	397	19.9
Marcus Coleman	24	470	19.6
Dre' Bly	24	443	18.5
Dewayne Washington	31	569	18.4
Ray Lewis	20	359	18.0

Interception Return Yards

Player	Yds.
Deion Sanders	1274
Ray Buchanan	827
Aeneas Williams	807
Terrell Buckley	793
Ed Reed	657
Tony Parrish	636
Troy Vincent	633
Ty Law	583
Dewayne Washington	569
Brock Marion	527

Defensive Touchdowns

Player	No.
Aeneas Williams	12
Deion Sanders	10
Dre' Bly	7
Terrell Buckley	7
Dewayne Washington	7
Ronde Barber	6
Derrick Brooks	6
Donnie Edwards	6
Ty Law	6
4 tied with	5

Sacks

Player	No.
Michael Strahan	118.0
Simeon Rice	105.0
Robert Porcher	95.5
Kevin Carter	86.0
Jason Taylor	80.5
Hugh Douglas	80.0
Jason Gildon	80.0
Warren Sapp	79.5
Chad Brown	78.0
Willie McGinest	72.0

Int. Return TDs

Player	No.
Deion Sanders	9
Aeneas Williams	9
Terrell Buckley	6
Ty Law	6
Dre' Bly	5
Derrick Brooks	5
Aaron Glenn	5
Dewayne Washington	5
11 tied with	4

MILESTONES

100-Yard Rushing Games

Player	No.
Jerome Bettis	60
Curtis Martin	56
Marshall Faulk	41
Edgerrin James	40
Corey Dillon	37
Eddie George	36
Fred Taylor	35
Priest Holmes	31
Ahman Green	29
Jamal Lewis	26

200-Yard Rushing Games

Player	No.
LaDainian Tomlinson	4
Corey Dillon	3
Marshall Faulk	3
Edgerrin James	2
Jamal Lewis	2
Clinton Portis	2
12 tied with	1

300-Yard Passing Games

Player	No.
Brett Favre	41
Drew Bledsoe	34
Peyton Manning	30
Vinny Testaverde	30
Kurt Warner	30
Kerry Collins	27
Trent Green	25
Rich Gannon	24
Mark Brunell	23
2 tied with	18

400-Yard Passing Games

Player	No.
Drew Bledsoe	6
Peyton Manning	6
Vinny Testaverde	4
Marc Bulger	3
Matt Hasselbeck	3
6 tied with	2

100-Yard Receiving Games

Player	No.
Jerry Rice	76
Marvin Harrison	47
Tim Brown	43
Jimmy Smith	43
Randy Moss	41
Isaac Bruce	39
Torry Holt	33
Terrell Owens	32
Rod Smith	28
2 tied with	26

200-Yard Receiving Games

Player	No.
Jerry Rice	4
Isaac Bruce	3
Torry Holt	2
Jimmy Smith	2
12 tied with	1

1,000-Yd. Rushing Seasons

Player	No.
Curtis Martin	10
Jerome Bettis	8
Corey Dillon	7
Marshall Faulk	7
Eddie George	7
Ahman Green	5
Fred Taylor	5
8 tied with	4

1,500-Yd. Rushing Seasons

Player	No.
Edgerrin James	3
Priest Holmes	2
Curtis Martin	2
Clinton Portis	2
LaDainian Tomlinson	2
10 tied with	1

3,000-Yd. Passing Seasons

Player	No.
Brett Favre	13
Drew Bledsoe	8
Peyton Manning	7
Vinny Testaverde	6
Mark Brunell	5
Kerry Collins	5
Trent Green	5
6 tied with	4

4,000-Yd. Passing Seasons

Player	No.
Peyton Manning	6
Brett Favre	4
Drew Bledsoe	3
Trent Green	2
Kurt Warner	2
7 tied with	1

1,000-Yd. Rec. Seasons

Player	No.
Jerry Rice	14
Tim Brown	9
Jimmy Smith	8
Isaac Bruce	7
Rod Smith	7
Marvin Harrison	6
Randy Moss	6
Terrell Owens	6
3 tied with	5

1,500-Yd. Rec. Seasons

Player	No.
Jerry Rice	4
Marvin Harrison	3
Torry Holt	2
David Boston	1
Isaac Bruce	1
Randy Moss	1
Jimmy Smith	1
Rod Smith	1

HISTORY

Championship games

Year-by-year standings

Super Bowls

Pro Bowls

Records

Statistical leaders

Coaching records

Hall of Fame

The Sporting News awards

First-round draft choices

Team by team

CHAMPIONSHIP GAMES

NFL (1933-1969); NFC (1970-2004)

RESULTS

Sea.	Date	Winner	Loser	Score	Site	Attendance
1933	Dec. 17	Chicago Bears	N.Y. Giants	23-21	Chicago	26,000
1934	Dec. 9	N.Y. Giants	Chicago Bears	30-13	N.Y. Giants	35,059
1935	Dec. 15	Detroit	N.Y. Giants	26-7	Detroit	15,000
1936	Dec. 13	Green Bay	Boston Redskins	21-6	N.Y. Giants	29,545
1937	Dec. 12	Washington	Chicago Bears	28-21	Chicago	15,870
1938	Dec. 11	N.Y. Giants	Green Bay	23-17	N.Y. Giants	48,120
1939	Dec. 10	Green Bay	N.Y. Giants	27-0	Milwaukee	32,279
1940	Dec. 8	Chicago Bears	Washington	73-0	Washington	36,034
1941	Dec. 21	Chicago Bears	N.Y. Giants	37-9	Chicago	13,341
1942	Dec. 13	Washington	Chicago Bears	14-6	Washington	36,006
1943	Dec. 26	Chicago Bears	Washington	41-21	Chicago	34,320
1944	Dec. 17	Green Bay	N.Y. Giants	14-7	N.Y. Giants	46,016
1945	Dec. 16	Cleveland Rams	Washington	15-14	Cleveland	32,178
1946	Dec. 15	Chicago Bears	N.Y. Giants	24-14	N.Y. Giants	58,346
1947	Dec. 28	Chicago Cardinals	Philadelphia	28-21	Chicago	30,759
1948	Dec. 19	Philadelphia	Chicago Cardinals	7-0	Philadelphia	36,309
1949	Dec. 18	Philadelphia	L.A. Rams	14-0	L.A. Rams	27,980
1950	Dec. 24	Cleveland Browns	L.A. Rams	30-28	Cleveland	29,751
1951	Dec. 23	L.A. Rams	Cleveland Browns	24-17	L.A. Rams	57,522
1952	Dec. 28	Detroit	Cleveland Browns	17-7	Cleveland	50,934
1953	Dec. 27	Detroit	Cleveland Browns	17-16	Detroit	54,577
1954	Dec. 26	Cleveland Browns	Detroit	56-10	Cleveland	43,827
1955	Dec. 26	Cleveland Browns	L.A. Rams	38-14	L.A. Rams	85,693
1956	Dec. 30	N.Y. Giants	Chicago Bears	47-7	N.Y. Giants	56,836
1957	Dec. 29	Detroit	Cleveland Browns	59-14	Detroit	55,263
1958	Dec. 28	Baltimore	N.Y. Giants	23-17*	N.Y. Giants	64,185
1959	Dec. 27	Baltimore	N.Y. Giants	31-16	Baltimore	57,545
1960	Dec. 26	Philadelphia	Green Bay	17-13	Philadelphia	67,325
1961	Dec. 31	Green Bay	N.Y. Giants	37-0	Green Bay	39,029
1962	Dec. 30	Green Bay	N.Y. Giants	16-7	N.Y. Giants	64,892
1963	Dec. 29	Chicago Bears	N.Y. Giants	14-10	Chicago	45,801
1964	Dec. 27	Cleveland Browns	Baltimore	27-0	Cleveland	79,544
1965	Jan. 2	Green Bay	Cleveland Browns	23-12	Green Bay	50,777
1966	Jan. 1	Green Bay	Dallas	34-27	Dallas	74,152
1967	Dec. 31	Green Bay	Dallas	21-17	Green Bay	50,861
1968	Dec. 29	Baltimore	Cleveland Browns	34-0	Cleveland	78,410
1969	Jan. 4	Minnesota	Cleveland Browns	27-7	Minnesota	46,503
1970	Jan. 3	Dallas	San Francisco	17-10	San Francisco	59,364
1971	Jan. 2	Dallas	San Francisco	14-3	Dallas	63,409
1972	Dec. 31	Washington	Dallas	26-3	Washington	53,129
1973	Dec. 30	Minnesota	Dallas	27-10	Dallas	64,422
1974	Dec. 29	Minnesota	L.A. Rams	14-10	Minnesota	48,444
1975	Jan. 4	Dallas	L.A. Rams	37-7	L.A. Rams	88,919
1976	Dec. 26	Minnesota	L.A. Rams	24-13	Minnesota	48,379
1977	Jan. 1	Dallas	Minnesota	23-6	Dallas	64,293
1978	Jan. 7	Dallas	L.A. Rams	28-0	L.A. Rams	71,086
1979	Jan. 6	L.A. Rams	Tampa Bay	9-0	Tampa Bay	72,033
1980	Jan. 11	Philadelphia	Dallas	20-7	Philadelphia	70,696
1981	Jan. 10	San Francisco	Dallas	28-27	San Francisco	60,525
1982	Jan. 22	Washington	Dallas	31-17	Washington	55,045
1983	Jan. 8	Washington	San Francisco	24-21	Washington	55,363
1984	Jan. 6	San Francisco	Chicago Bears	23-0	San Francisco	61,040
1985	Jan. 12	Chicago Bears	L.A. Rams	24-0	Chicago	63,522
1986	Jan. 11	N.Y. Giants	Washington	17-0	N.Y. Giants	76,633
1987	Jan. 17	Washington	Minnesota	17-10	Washington	55,212
1988	Jan. 8	San Francisco	Chicago Bears	28-3	Chicago	64,830
1989	Jan. 14	San Francisco	L.A. Rams	30-3	San Francisco	64,769
1990	Jan. 20	N.Y. Giants	San Francisco	15-13	San Francisco	65,750
1991	Jan. 12	Washington	Detroit	41-10	Washington	55,585
1992	Jan. 17	Dallas	San Francisco	30-20	San Francisco	64,920
1993	Jan. 23	Dallas	San Francisco	38-21	Dallas	64,902
1994	Jan. 15	San Francisco	Dallas	38-28	San Francisco	69,125
1995	Jan. 14	Dallas	Green Bay	38-27	Dallas	65,135
1996	Jan. 12	Green Bay	Carolina	30-13	Green Bay	60,216
1997	Jan. 11	Green Bay	San Francisco	23-10	San Francisco	68,987

Sea.	Date	Winner	Loser	Score	Site	Attendance
1998	Jan. 17	Atlanta	Minnesota	30-27*	Minnesota	64,060
1999	Jan. 23	St. Louis	Tampa Bay	11-6	St. Louis	66,496
2000	Jan. 14	N.Y. Giants	Minnesota	41-0	New York	79,310
2001	Jan. 27	St. Louis	Philadelphia	29-24	St. Louis	66,502
2002	Jan. 19	Tampa Bay	Philadelphia	27-10	Philadelphia	66,713
2003	Jan. 18	Carolina	Philadelphia	14-3	Philadelphia	65,158
2004	Jan. 23	Philadelphia	Atlanta	27-10	Philadelphia	67,717

*Overtime.

COMPOSITE STANDINGS

	W	L	Pct.	PF	PA		W	L	Pct.	PF	PA
Green Bay Packers	10	3	.769	303	177	Arizona Cardinals*	1	1	.500	28	28
Baltimore Colts	3	1	.750	88	60	Atlanta Falcons	1	1	.500	40	54
Detroit Lions	4	2	.667	139	141	Carolina Panthers	1	1	.500	27	33
Washington Redskins†	7	5	.583	222	255	San Francisco 49ers	5	7	.417	245	222
Philadelphia Eagles	5	4	.556	143	128	Cleveland Browns	4	7	.364	224	253
Chicago Bears	7	6	.538	286	245	St. Louis Rams‡	5	9	.357	163	300
Dallas Cowboys	8	8	.500	361	319	New York Giants	6	11	.353	281	322
Minnesota Vikings	4	4	.500	135	151	Tampa Bay Buccaneers	1	2	.333	33	30

*Both games played when franchise was in Chicago; won 28-21, lost 7-0.
†One game played when franchise was in Boston; lost 21-6.
‡One game played when franchise was in Cleveland; won 15-14. 11 games played when franchise was in Los Angeles, record of 2-9.

AFL (1960-1969); AFC (1970-2004)
RESULTS

Sea.	Date	Winner	Loser	Score	Site	Attendance
1960	Jan. 1	Houston	L.A. Chargers	24-16	Houston	32,183
1961	Dec. 24	Houston	San Diego	10-3	San Diego	29,556
1962	Dec. 23	Dallas Texans	Houston	20-17*	Houston	37,981
1963	Jan. 5	San Diego	Boston Patriots	51-10	San Diego	30,127
1964	Dec. 26	Buffalo	San Diego	20-7	Buffalo	40,242
1965	Dec. 26	Buffalo	San Diego	23-0	San Diego	30,361
1966	Jan. 1	Kansas City	Buffalo	31-7	Buffalo	42,080
1967	Dec. 31	Oakland	Houston	40-7	Oakland	53,330
1968	Dec. 29	N.Y. Jets	Oakland	27-23	New York	62,627
1969	Jan. 4	Kansas City	Oakland	17-7	Oakland	53,564
1970	Jan. 3	Baltimore	Oakland	27-17	Baltimore	54,799
1971	Jan. 2	Miami	Baltimore	21-0	Miami	76,622
1972	Dec. 31	Miami	Pittsburgh	21-17	Pittsburgh	50,845
1973	Dec. 30	Miami	Oakland	27-10	Miami	79,325
1974	Dec. 29	Pittsburgh	Oakland	24-13	Oakland	53,800
1975	Jan. 4	Pittsburgh	Oakland	16-10	Pittsburgh	50,609
1976	Dec. 26	Oakland	Pittsburgh	24-7	Oakland	53,821
1977	Jan. 1	Denver	Oakland	20-17	Denver	75,044
1978	Jan. 7	Pittsburgh	Houston	34-5	Pittsburgh	50,725
1979	Jan. 6	Pittsburgh	Houston	27-13	Pittsburgh	50,475
1980	Jan. 11	Oakland	San Diego	34-27	San Diego	52,428
1981	Jan. 10	Cincinnati	San Diego	27-7	Cincinnati	46,302
1982	Jan. 23	Miami	N.Y. Jets	14-0	Miami	67,396
1983	Jan. 8	L.A. Raiders	Seattle	30-14	Los Angeles	88,734
1984	Jan. 6	Miami	Pittsburgh	45-28	Miami	76,029
1985	Jan. 12	New England	Miami	31-14	Miami	74,978
1986	Jan. 11	Denver	Cleveland	23-20*	Cleveland	79,915
1987	Jan. 17	Denver	Cleveland	38-33	Denver	75,993
1988	Jan. 8	Cincinnati	Buffalo	21-10	Cincinnati	59,747
1989	Jan. 14	Denver	Cleveland	37-21	Denver	76,046
1990	Jan. 20	Buffalo	L.A. Raiders	51-3	Buffalo	80,234
1991	Jan. 12	Buffalo	Denver	10-7	Buffalo	80,272
1992	Jan. 17	Buffalo	Miami	29-10	Miami	72,703
1993	Jan. 23	Buffalo	Kansas City	30-13	Buffalo	76,642
1994	Jan. 15	San Diego	Pittsburgh	17-13	Pittsburgh	61,545
1995	Jan. 14	Pittsburgh	Indianapolis	20-16	Pittsburgh	61,062
1996	Jan. 12	New England	Jacksonville	20-6	New England	60,190
1997	Jan. 11	Denver	Pittsburgh	24-21	Pittsburgh	61,382
1998	Jan. 17	Denver	N.Y. Jets	23-10	Denver	75,482
1999	Jan. 23	Tennessee	Jacksonville	33-14	Jacksonville	75,206
2000	Jan. 14	Baltimore	Oakland	16-3	Oakland	62,784
2001	Jan. 27	New England	Pittsburgh	24-17	Pittsburgh	64,704
2002	Jan. 19	Oakland	Tennessee	41-24	Oakland	62,544
2003	Jan. 18	New England	Indianapolis	24-14	New England	68,436
2004	Jan. 23	New England	Pittsburgh	41-27	New England	65,242

*Overtime.

HISTORY *Championship games*

COMPOSITE STANDINGS

	W	L	Pct.	PF	PA		W	L	Pct.	PF	PA
Cincinnati Bengals	2	0	1.000	48	17	Tennessee Titans▲	3	5	.375	133	195
Baltimore Ravens	1	0	1.000	16	3	Oakland Raiders§	5	9	.357	272	304
Denver Broncos	6	1	.857	172	132	New York Jets	1	2	.333	37	60
New England Patriots‡	5	1	.833	150	129	San Diego Chargers*	2	6	.250	128	161
Buffalo Bills	6	2	.750	180	92	Indianapolis Colts∞	1	3	.250	57	82
Kansas City Chiefs†	3	1	.750	81	61	Seattle Seahawks	0	1	.000	14	30
Miami Dolphins	5	2	.714	152	115	Jacksonville Jaguars	0	2	.000	20	53
Pittsburgh Steelers	5	7	.417	251	253	Cleveland Browns	0	3	.000	74	98

*One game played when franchise was in Los Angeles; lost 24-16.
†One game played when franchise was in Dallas (Texans); won 20-17.
‡One game played when franchise was in Boston; lost 51-10.
§Two games played when franchise was in Los Angeles; record of 1-1.
∞Two games played when franchise was in Baltimore; record of 1-1.
▲Six games played when franchise was in Houston (Oilers); record of 2-4.

POSTSEASON GAME COMPOSITE STANDINGS

	W	L	Pct.	PF	PA		W	L	Pct.	PF	PA
Baltimore Ravens	5	2	.714	142	73	Indianapolis Colts■	13	15	.464	538	581
Carolina Panthers	4	2	.667	140	115	Tampa Bay Buccaneers	6	7	.462	206	238
Green Bay Packers	24	14	.632	888	723	Tennessee Titans▼	14	17	.452	563	732
San Francisco 49ers	25	17	.595	1044	853	New York Jets	8	10	.444	372	352
Washington Redskins‡	22	15	.595	778	642	St. Louis Rams†	19	24	.442	770	944
Dallas Cowboys	32	22	.593	1281	1008	New York Giants	16	21	.432	647	699
Oakland Raiders♦	25	18	.581	1028	797	Minnesota Vikings	18	24	.429	824	957
Pittsburgh Steelers	24	18	.571	959	866	Atlanta Falcons	6	8	.429	298	331
New England Patriots§	16	10	.615	528	512	Cincinnati Bengals	5	7	.417	246	257
Denver Broncos	16	14	.533	650	747	Detroit Lions	7	10	.412	365	404
Miami Dolphins	20	19	.513	780	848	Kansas City Chiefs*	8	12	.400	332	422
Philadelphia Eagles	16	16	.500	606	561	San Diego Chargers▲	7	12	.368	349	448
Jacksonville Jaguars	4	4	.500	208	200	Cleveland Browns	11	20	.355	629	738
Buffalo Bills	14	15	.483	681	658	Seattle Seahawks	3	7	.300	192	219
Chicago Bears	14	15	.483	598	585	Arizona Cardinals∞	2	5	.286	122	182
						New Orleans Saints	1	5	.167	103	185

*One game played when franchise was in Dallas (Texans); won 20-17.
†One game played when franchise was in Cleveland; won 15-14. 32 games played when franchise was in Los Angeles; record of 12-20.
‡One game played when franchise was in Boston; lost 21-6.
§Two games played when franchise was in Boston; won 26-8, lost 51-10.
∞Two games played when franchise was in Chicago; won 28-21, lost 7-0. Three games played when franchise was in St. Louis; lost 35-23, lost 30-14, lost 41-16.
▲One game played when franchise was in Los Angeles; lost 24-16.
♦12 games played when franchise was in Los Angeles; record of 6-6.
■15 games played when franchise was in Baltimore; record of 8-7.
▼22 games played when franchise was in Houston; record of 9-13.

CHAMPIONS OF DEFUNCT PRO FOOTBALL LEAGUES
ALL-AMERICAN FOOTBALL CONFERENCE

Year	Winner	Coach	Loser	Coach	Score, Site
1946	Cleveland Browns	Paul Brown	N.Y. Yankees	Ray Flaherty	14-9, Cleveland
1947	Cleveland Browns	Paul Brown	N.Y. Yankees	Ray Flaherty	14-3, New York
1948	Cleveland Browns	Paul Brown	Buffalo Bills	Red Dawson	49-7, Cleveland
1949	Cleveland Browns	Paul Brown	S.F. 49ers	Buck Shaw	21-7, Cleveland

NOTE: Cleveland Browns and San Francisco 49ers joined the NFL after the AAFC folded in 1949.

WORLD FOOTBALL LEAGUE

Year	Winner	Coach	Loser	Coach	Score, Site
1974	Birmingham Americans	Jack Gotta	Florida Blazers	Jack Pardee	22-21, Birmingham
1975	League folded October 22				

UNITED STATES FOOTBALL LEAGUE

Year	Winner	Coach	Loser	Coach	Score, Site
1983	Michigan Panthers	Jim Stanley	Philadelphia Stars	Jim Mora	24-22, Denver
1984	Philadelphia Stars	Jim Mora	Arizona Wranglers	George Allen	23-3, Tampa
1985	Baltimore Stars	Jim Mora	Oakland Invaders	Charlie Sumner	28-24, E. Rutherford, N.J.

YEAR-BY-YEAR STANDINGS

1920

Team	W	L	T	Pct.
Akron Pros*	8	0	3	1.000
Decatur Staleys	10	1	2	.909
Buffalo All-Americans	9	1	1	.900
Chicago Cardinals	6	2	2	.750
Rock Island Independents	6	2	2	.750
Dayton Triangles	5	2	2	.714
Rochester Jeffersons	6	3	2	.667
Canton Bulldogs	7	4	2	.636
Detroit Heralds	2	3	3	.400
Cleveland Tigers	2	4	2	.333
Chicago Tigers	2	5	1	.286
Hammond Pros	2	5	0	.286
Columbus Panhandles	2	6	2	.250
Muncie Flyers	0	1	0	.000

*No official standings were maintained for the 1920 season, and the championship was awarded to the Akron Pros in a League meeting on April 30, 1921. Clubs played schedules which included games against non-league opponents. Records of clubs against all opponents are listed above.

1921

Team	W	L	T	Pct.
Chicago Staleys	9	1	1	.900
Buffalo All-Americans	9	1	2	.900
Akron Pros	8	3	1	.727
Canton Bulldogs	5	2	3	.714
Rock Island Independents	4	2	1	.667
Evansville Crimson Giants	3	2	0	.600
Green Bay Packers	3	2	1	.600
Dayton Triangles	4	4	1	.500
Chicago Cardinals	3	3	2	.500
Rochester Jeffersons	2	3	0	.400
Cleveland Indians	3	5	0	.375
Washington Senators	1	2	0	.333
Cincinnati Celts	1	3	0	.250
Hammond Pros	1	3	1	.250
Minneapolis Marines	1	3	0	.250
Detroit Heralds	1	5	1	.167
Columbus Panhandles	1	8	0	.111
Tonawanda Kardex	0	1	0	.000
Muncie Flyers	0	2	0	.000
Louisville Brecks	0	2	0	.000
New York Giants	0	2	0	.000

1922

Team	W	L	T	Pct.
Canton Bulldogs	10	0	2	1.000
Chicago Bears	9	3	0	.750
Chicago Cardinals	8	3	0	.727
Toledo Maroons	5	2	2	.714
Rock Island Independents	4	2	1	.667
Racine Legion	6	4	1	.600
Dayton Triangles	4	3	1	.571
Green Bay Packers	4	3	3	.571
Buffalo All-Americans	5	4	1	.556
Akron Pros	3	5	2	.375
Milwaukee Badgers	2	4	3	.333
Oorang Indians	3	6	0	.333
Minneapolis Marines	1	3	0	.250
Louisville Brecks	1	3	0	.250
Evansville Crimson Giants	0	3	0	.000
Rochester Jeffersons	0	4	1	.000
Hammond Pros	0	5	1	.000
Columbus Panhandles	0	8	0	.000

1923

Team	W	L	T	Pct.
Canton Bulldogs	11	0	1	1.000
Chicago Bears	9	2	1	.818
Green Bay Packers	7	2	1	.778
Milwaukee Badgers	7	2	3	.778
Cleveland Indians	3	1	3	.750
Chicago Cardinals	8	4	0	.667
Duluth Kelleys	4	3	0	.571
Buffalo All-Americans	5	4	3	.556
Columbus Tigers	5	4	1	.556
Racine Legion	4	4	2	.500
Toledo Maroons	3	3	2	.500
Rock Island Independents	2	3	3	.400
Minneapolis Marines	2	5	2	.286
St. Louis All-Stars	1	4	2	.200
Hammond Pros	1	5	1	.167
Dayton Triangles	1	6	1	.143
Akron Indians	1	6	0	.143
Oorang Indians	1	10	0	.091
Louisville Brecks	0	3	0	.000
Rochester Jeffersons	0	4	0	.000

1924

Team	W	L	T	Pct.
Cleveland Bulldogs	7	1	1	.875
Chicago Bears	6	1	4	.857
Frankford Yellow Jackets	11	2	1	.846
Duluth Kelleys	5	1	0	.833
Rock Island Independents	5	2	2	.714
Green Bay Packers	7	4	0	.636
Racine Legion	4	3	3	.571
Chicago Cardinals	5	4	1	.556
Buffalo Bisons	6	5	0	.545
Columbus Tigers	4	4	0	.500
Hammond Pros	2	2	1	.500
Milwaukee Badgers	5	8	0	.385
Akron Indians	2	6	0	.250
Dayton Triangles	2	6	0	.250
Kansas City Blues	2	7	0	.222
Kenosha Maroons	0	4	1	.000
Minneapolis Marines	0	6	0	.000
Rochester Jeffersons	0	7	0	.000

1925

Team	W	L	T	Pct.
Chicago Cardinals	11	2	1	.846
Pottsville Maroons	10	2	0	.833
Detroit Panthers	8	2	2	.800
New York Giants	8	4	0	.667
Akron Indians	4	2	2	.667
Frankford Yellow Jackets	13	7	0	.650
Chicago Bears	9	5	3	.643
Rock Island Independents	5	3	3	.625
Green Bay Packers	8	5	0	.615
Providence Steam Roller	6	5	1	.545
Canton Bulldogs	4	4	0	.500
Cleveland Bulldogs	5	8	1	.385
Kansas City Cowboys	2	5	1	.286
Hammond Pros	1	4	0	.200
Buffalo Bisons	1	6	2	.143
Duluth Kelleys	0	3	0	.000
Rochester Jeffersons	0	6	1	.000
Milwaukee Badgers	0	6	0	.000
Dayton Triangles	0	7	1	.000
Columbus Tigers	0	9	0	.000

1926

Team	W	L	T	Pct.
Frankford Yellow Jackets	14	1	2	.933
Chicago Bears	12	1	3	.923
Pottsville Maroons	10	2	2	.833
Kansas City Cowboys	8	3	0	.727
Green Bay Packers	7	3	3	.700
Los Angeles Buccaneers	6	3	1	.667
New York Giants	8	4	1	.667
Duluth Eskimos	6	5	3	.545
Buffalo Rangers	4	4	2	.500
Chicago Cardinals	5	6	1	.455
Providence Steam Roller	5	7	1	.417
Detroit Panthers	4	6	2	.400
Hartford Blues	3	7	0	.300
Brooklyn Lions	3	8	0	.273
Milwaukee Badgers	2	7	0	.222
Akron Pros	1	4	3	.200
Dayton Triangles	1	4	1	.200
Racine Tornadoes	1	4	0	.200
Columbus Tigers	1	6	0	.143
Canton Bulldogs	1	9	3	.100
Hammond Pros	0	4	0	.000
Louisville Colonels	0	4	0	.000

1927

Team	W	L	T	Pct.
New York Giants	11	1	1	.917
Green Bay Packers	7	2	1	.778
Chicago Bears	9	3	2	.750
Cleveland Bulldogs	8	4	1	.667
Providence Steam Roller	8	5	1	.615
New York Yankees	7	8	1	.467
Frankford Yellow Jackets	6	9	3	.400
Pottsville Maroons	5	8	0	.385
Chicago Cardinals	3	7	1	.300
Dayton Triangles	1	6	1	.143
Duluth Eskimos	1	8	0	.111
Buffalo Bisons	0	5	0	.000

1928

Team	W	L	T	Pct.
Providence Steam Roller	8	1	2	.889
Frankford Yellow Jackets	11	3	2	.786
Detroit Wolverines	7	2	1	.778
Green Bay Packers	6	4	3	.600
Chicago Bears	7	5	1	.583
New York Giants	4	7	2	.364
New York Yankees	4	8	1	.333
Pottsville Maroons	2	8	0	.200
Chicago Cardinals	1	5	0	.167
Dayton Triangles	0	7	0	.000

1929

Team	W	L	T	Pct.
Green Bay Packers	12	0	1	1.000
New York Giants	13	1	1	.929
Frankford Yellow Jackets	10	4	5	.714
Chicago Cardinals	6	6	1	.500
Boston Bulldogs	4	4	0	.500
Staten Island Stapletons	3	4	3	.429
Providence Steam Roller	4	6	2	.400
Orange Tornadoes	3	5	4	.375
Chicago Bears	4	9	2	.308
Buffalo Bisons	1	7	1	.125
Minneapolis Red Jackets	1	9	0	.100
Dayton Triangles	0	6	0	.000

1930

Team	W	L	T	Pct.
Green Bay Packers	10	3	1	.769
New York Giants	13	4	0	.765
Chicago Bears	9	4	1	.692
Brooklyn Dodgers	7	4	1	.636
Providence Steam Roller	6	4	1	.600
Staten Island Stapletons	5	5	2	.500
Chicago Cardinals	5	6	2	.455
Portsmouth Spartans	5	6	3	.455
Frankford Yellow Jackets	4	13	1	.222
Minneapolis Red Jackets	1	7	1	.125
Newark Tornadoes	1	10	1	.091

1931

Team	W	L	T	Pct.
Green Bay Packers	12	2	0	.857
Portsmouth Spartans	11	3	0	.786
Chicago Bears	8	5	0	.615
Chicago Cardinals	5	4	0	.556
New York Giants	7	6	1	.538
Providence Steam Roller	4	4	3	.500
Staten Island Stapletons	4	6	1	.400
Cleveland Indians	2	8	0	.200
Brooklyn Dodgers	2	12	0	.143
Frankford Yellow Jackets	1	6	1	.143

1932

Team	W	L	T	Pct.
Chicago Bears	7	1	6	.875
Green Bay Packers	10	3	1	.769
Portsmouth Spartans	6	2	4	.750
Boston Braves	4	4	2	.500
New York Giants	4	6	2	.400
Brooklyn Dodgers	3	9	0	.250
Chicago Cardinals	2	6	2	.250
Staten Island Stapletons	2	7	3	.222

NOTE: Chicago Bears and Portsmouth finished regularly scheduled game tied for first place. Bears won playoff game, which counted in standings, 9-0.

1933

EASTERN DIVISION

Team	W	L	T	Pct.	PF	PA
N.Y. Giants	11	3	0	.786	244	101
Brooklyn	5	4	1	.556	93	54
Boston	5	5	2	.500	103	97
Philadelphia	3	5	1	.375	77	158
Pittsburgh	3	6	2	.333	67	208

WESTERN DIVISION

Team	W	L	T	Pct.	PF	PA
Chicago Bears	10	2	1	.833	133	82
Portsmouth	6	5	0	.545	128	87
Green Bay	5	7	1	.417	170	107
Cincinnati	3	6	1	.333	38	110
Chi. Cardinals	1	9	1	.100	52	101

PLAYOFFS

NFL championship
Chicago Bears 23 vs. N.Y. Giants 21

1934

EASTERN DIVISION	W	L	T	Pct.	PF	PA
Y. Giants	8	5	0	.615	147	107
ston	6	6	0	.500	107	94
ooklyn	4	7	0	.364	61	153
iladelphia	4	7	0	.364	127	85
tsburgh	2	10	0	.167	51	206

WESTERN DIVISION / Team	W	L	T	Pct.	PF	PA
Chicago Bears	13	0	0	1.000	286	86
Detroit	10	3	0	.769	238	59
Green Bay	7	6	0	.538	156	112
Chi. Cardinals	5	6	0	.455	80	84
St. Louis	1	2	0	.333	27	61
Cincinnati	0	8	0	.000	10	243

PLAYOFFS

NFL championship
N.Y. Giants 30 vs. Chicago Bears 13

1935

EASTERN DIVISION	W	L	T	Pct.	PF	PA
Y. Giants	9	3	0	.750	180	96
ooklyn	5	6	1	.455	90	141
tsburgh	4	8	0	.333	100	209
ston	2	8	1	.200	65	123
iladelphia	2	9	0	.182	60	179

WESTERN DIVISION / Team	W	L	T	Pct.	PF	PA
Detroit	7	3	2	.700	191	111
Green Bay	8	4	0	.667	181	96
Chicago Bears	6	4	2	.600	192	106
Chi. Cardinals	6	4	2	.600	99	97

PLAYOFFS

NFL championship
Detroit 26 vs. N.Y. Giants 7

NOTE: One game between Boston and Philadelphia was cancelled.

1936

EASTERN DIVISION	W	L	T	Pct.	PF	PA
ston	7	5	0	.583	149	110
tsburgh	6	6	0	.500	98	187
Y. Giants	5	6	1	.455	115	163
ooklyn	3	8	1	.273	92	161
iladelphia	1	11	0	.083	51	206

WESTERN DIVISION / Team	W	L	T	Pct.	PF	PA
Green Bay	10	1	1	.909	248	118
Chicago Bears	9	3	0	.750	222	94
Detroit	8	4	0	.667	235	102
Chi. Cardinals	3	8	1	.273	74	143

PLAYOFFS

NFL championship
Green Bay 21, Boston 6, at New York.

1937

EASTERN DIVISION	W	L	T	Pct.	PF	PA
ashington	8	3	0	.727	195	120
Y. Giants	6	3	2	.667	128	109
tsburgh	4	7	0	.364	122	145
ooklyn	3	7	1	.300	82	174
iladelphia	2	8	1	.200	86	177

WESTERN DIVISION / Team	W	L	T	Pct.	PF	PA
Chicago Bears	9	1	1	.900	201	100
Green Bay	7	4	0	.636	220	122
Detroit	7	4	0	.636	180	105
Chi. Cardinals	5	5	1	.500	135	165
Cleveland	1	10	0	.091	75	207

PLAYOFFS

NFL championship
Washington 28 at Chicago Bears 21

1938

EASTERN DIVISION	W	L	T	Pct.	PF	PA
Y. Giants	8	2	1	.800	194	79
ashington	6	3	2	.667	148	154
ooklyn	4	4	3	.500	131	161
iladelphia	5	6	0	.455	154	164
tsburgh	2	9	0	.182	79	169

WESTERN DIVISION / Team	W	L	T	Pct.	PF	PA
Green Bay	8	3	0	.727	223	118
Detroit	7	4	0	.636	119	108
Chicago Bears	6	5	0	.545	194	148
Cleveland	4	7	0	.364	131	215
Chi. Cardinals	2	9	0	.182	111	168

PLAYOFFS

NFL championship
N.Y. Giants 23 vs. Green Bay 17

1939

EASTERN DIVISION	W	L	T	Pct.	PF	PA
Y. Giants	9	1	1	.900	168	85
ashington	8	2	1	.800	242	94
ooklyn	4	6	1	.400	108	219
iladelphia	1	9	1	.100	105	200
tsburgh	1	9	1	.100	114	216

WESTERN DIVISION / Team	W	L	T	Pct.	PF	PA
Green Bay	9	2	0	.818	233	153
Chicago Bears	8	3	0	.727	298	157
Detroit	6	5	0	.545	145	150
Cleveland	5	5	1	.500	195	164
Chi. Cardinals	1	10	0	.091	84	254

PLAYOFFS

NFL championship
Green Bay 27 vs. N.Y. Giants 0

1940

EASTERN DIVISION	W	L	T	Pct.	PF	PA
ashington	9	2	0	.818	245	142
ooklyn	8	3	0	.727	186	120
Y. Giants	6	4	1	.600	131	133
tsburgh	2	7	2	.222	60	178
iladelphia	1	10	0	.091	111	211

WESTERN DIVISION / Team	W	L	T	Pct.	PF	PA
Chicago Bears	8	3	0	.727	238	152
Green Bay	6	4	1	.600	238	155
Detroit	5	5	0	.500	138	153
Cleveland	4	6	1	.400	171	191
Chi. Cardinals	2	7	2	.222	139	222

PLAYOFFS

NFL championship
Chicago Bears 73 at Washington 0

1941

EASTERN DIVISION

Team	W	L	T	Pct.	PF	PA
N.Y. Giants	8	3	0	.727	238	114
Brooklyn	7	4	0	.636	158	127
Washington	6	5	0	.545	176	174
Philadelphia	2	8	1	.200	119	218
Pittsburgh	1	9	1	.100	103	276

WESTERN DIVISION

Team	W	L	T	Pct.	PF	PA
Chicago Bears	10	1	0	.909	396	147
Green Bay	10	1	0	.909	258	120
Detroit	4	6	1	.400	121	195
Chi. Cardinals	3	7	1	.300	127	197
Cleveland	2	9	0	.182	116	244

PLAYOFFS

Western Division playoff
Chicago Bears 33 vs. Green Bay 14

NFL championship
Chicago Bears 37 vs. N.Y. Giants 9

1942

EASTERN DIVISION

Team	W	L	T	Pct.	PF	PA
Washington	10	1	0	.909	227	102
Pittsburgh	7	4	0	.636	167	119
N.Y. Giants	5	5	1	.500	155	139
Brooklyn	3	8	0	.273	100	168
Philadelphia	2	9	0	.182	134	239

WESTERN DIVISION

Team	W	L	T	Pct.	PF	PA
Chicago Bears	11	0	0	1.000	376	84
Green Bay	8	2	1	.800	300	215
Cleveland	5	6	0	.455	150	207
Chi. Cardinals	3	8	0	.273	98	209
Detroit	0	11	0	.000	38	263

PLAYOFFS

NFL championship
Washington 14 vs. Chicago Bears 6

1943

EASTERN DIVISION

Team	W	L	T	Pct.	PF	PA
Washington	6	3	1	.667	229	137
N.Y. Giants	6	3	1	.667	197	170
Phil.-Pitt.	5	4	1	.556	225	230
Brooklyn	2	8	0	.200	65	234

NOTE: Cleveland Rams did not play in 1943.

WESTERN DIVISION

Team	W	L	T	Pct.	PF	PA
Chicago Bears	8	1	1	.889	303	157
Green Bay	7	2	1	.778	264	172
Detroit	3	6	1	.333	178	218
Chi. Cardinals	0	10	0	.000	95	238

PLAYOFFS

Eastern Division playoff
Washington 28 at N.Y. Giants 0

NFL championship
Chicago Bears 41 vs. Washington 21

1944

EASTERN DIVISION

Team	W	L	T	Pct.	PF	PA
N.Y. Giants	8	1	1	.889	206	75
Philadelphia	7	1	2	.875	267	131
Washington	6	3	1	.667	169	180
Boston	2	8	0	.200	82	233
Brooklyn	0	10	0	.000	69	166

WESTERN DIVISION

Team	W	L	T	Pct.	PF	PA
Green Bay	8	2	0	.800	238	141
Chicago Bears	6	3	1	.667	258	172
Detroit	6	3	1	.667	216	151
Cleveland	4	6	0	.400	188	224
Card-Pitt	0	10	0	.000	108	328

PLAYOFFS

NFL championship
Green Bay 14 at N.Y. Giants 7

1945

EASTERN DIVISION

Team	W	L	T	Pct.	PF	PA
Washington	8	2	0	.800	209	121
Philadelphia	7	3	0	.700	272	133
N.Y. Giants	3	6	1	.333	179	198
Boston	3	6	1	.333	123	211
Pittsburgh	2	8	0	.200	79	220

WESTERN DIVISION

Team	W	L	T	Pct.	PF	PA
Cleveland	9	1	0	.900	244	136
Detroit	7	3	0	.700	195	194
Green Bay	6	4	0	.600	258	173
Chicago Bears	3	7	0	.300	192	235
Chi. Cardinals	1	9	0	.100	98	228

PLAYOFFS

NFL championship
Cleveland 15 vs. Washington 14

1946

AAFC

EASTERN DIVISION

Team	W	L	T	Pct.	PF	PA
New York	10	3	1	.769	270	192
Brooklyn	3	10	1	.231	226	339
Buffalo	3	10	1	.231	249	370
Miami	3	11	0	.214	167	378

WESTERN DIVISION

Team	W	L	T	Pct.	PF	PA
Cleveland	12	2	0	.857	423	137
San Francisco	9	5	0	.643	307	189
Los Angeles	7	5	2	.583	305	290
Chicago	5	6	3	.455	263	315

PLAYOFFS

AAFC championship
Cleveland 14 vs. New York 9

NFL

EASTERN DIVISION

Team	W	L	T	Pct.	PF	PA
N.Y. Giants	7	3	1	.700	236	162
Philadelphia	6	5	0	.545	231	220
Washington	5	5	1	.500	171	191
Pittsburgh	5	5	1	.500	136	117
Boston	2	8	1	.200	189	273

WESTERN DIVISION

Team	W	L	T	Pct.	PF	PA
Chicago Bears	8	2	1	.800	289	193
Los Angeles	6	4	1	.600	277	257
Green Bay	6	5	0	.545	148	158
Chi. Cardinals	6	5	0	.545	260	198
Detroit	1	10	0	.091	142	310

PLAYOFFS

NFL championship
Chicago Bears 24 at N.Y. Giants 14

1947

AAFC

EASTERN DIVISION

am	W	L	T	Pct.	PF	PA
w York	11	2	1	.846	378	239
ffalo	8	4	2	.667	320	288
ooklyn	3	10	1	.231	181	340
timore	2	11	1	.154	167	377

WESTERN DIVISION

Team	W	L	T	Pct.	PF	PA
Cleveland	12	1	1	.923	410	185
San Francisco	8	4	2	.667	327	264
Los Angeles	7	7	0	.500	328	256
Chicago	1	13	0	.071	263	425

PLAYOFFS

AAFC championship
Cleveland 14 at New York 3

NFL

EASTERN DIVISION

am	W	L	T	Pct.	PF	PA
ladelphia	8	4	0	.667	308	242
sburgh	8	4	0	.667	240	259
ston	4	7	1	.364	168	256
shington	4	8	0	.333	295	367
Y. Giants	2	8	2	.200	190	309

WESTERN DIVISION

Team	W	L	T	Pct.	PF	PA
Chi. Cardinals	9	3	0	.750	306	231
Chicago Bears	8	4	0	.667	363	241
Green Bay	6	5	1	.545	274	210
Los Angeles	6	6	0	.500	259	214
Detroit	3	9	0	.250	231	305

PLAYOFFS

Eastern Division playoff
Philadelphia 21 at Pittsburgh 0

NFL championship
Chicago Cardinals 28 vs. Philadelphia 21

1948

AAFC

EASTERN DIVISION

am	W	L	T	Pct.	PF	PA
ffalo	7	7	0	.500	360	358
timore	7	7	0	.500	333	327
w York	6	8	0	.429	265	301
ooklyn	2	12	0	.143	253	387

WESTERN DIVISION

Team	W	L	T	Pct.	PF	PA
Cleveland	14	0	0	1.000	389	190
San Francisco	12	2	0	.857	495	248
Los Angeles	7	7	0	.500	258	305
Chicago	1	13	0	.071	202	439

PLAYOFFS

Eastern Division playoff
Buffalo 28 vs. Baltimore 17

AAFC championship
Cleveland 49 vs. Buffalo 7

NFL

EASTERN DIVISION

am	W	L	T	Pct.	PF	PA
ladelphia	9	2	1	.818	376	156
shington	7	5	0	.583	291	287
Y. Giants	4	8	0	.333	297	388
tsburgh	4	8	0	.333	200	243
ston	3	9	0	.250	174	372

WESTERN DIVISION

Team	W	L	T	Pct.	PF	PA
Chi. Cardinals	11	1	0	.917	395	226
Chicago Bears	10	2	0	.833	375	151
Los Angeles	6	5	1	.545	327	269
Green Bay	3	9	0	.250	154	290
Detroit	2	10	0	.167	200	407

PLAYOFFS

NFL championship
Philadelphia 7 vs. Chicago Cardinals 0

1949

AAFC

Team	W	L	T	Pct.	PF	PA
Cleveland	9	1	2	.900	339	171
San Francisco	9	3	0	.750	416	227
Brooklyn-N.Y.	8	4	0	.667	196	206
Buffalo	5	5	2	.500	236	256
Chicago	4	8	0	.333	179	268
Los Angeles	4	8	0	.333	253	322
Baltimore	1	11	0	.083	172	341

PLAYOFFS

AAFC Semifinals
Cleveland 31 vs. Buffalo 21
San Francisco 17 vs. Brooklyn-N.Y. 7

AAFC championship
Cleveland 21 vs. San Francisco 7

NFL

EASTERN DIVISION

am	W	L	T	Pct.	PF	PA
ladelphia	11	1	0	.917	364	134
tsburgh	6	5	1	.545	224	214
Y. Giants	6	6	0	.500	287	298
shington	4	7	1	.364	268	339
Y. Bulldogs	1	10	1	.091	153	368

WESTERN DIVISION

Team	W	L	T	Pct.	PF	PA
Los Angeles	8	2	2	.800	360	239
Chicago Bears	9	3	0	.750	332	218
Chi. Cardinals	6	5	1	.545	360	301
Detroit	4	8	0	.333	237	259
Green Bay	2	10	0	.167	114	329

PLAYOFFS

NFL championship
Philadelphia 14 at Los Angeles 0

1950

AMERICAN CONFERENCE

am	W	L	T	Pct.	PF	PA
veland	10	2	0	.833	310	144
Y. Giants	10	2	0	.833	268	150
ladelphia	6	6	0	.500	254	141
tsburgh	6	6	0	.500	180	195
. Cardinals	5	7	0	.417	233	287
shington	3	9	0	.250	232	326

NATIONAL CONFERENCE

Team	W	L	T	Pct.	PF	PA
Los Angeles	9	3	0	.750	466	309
Chicago Bears	9	3	0	.750	279	207
N.Y. Yanks	7	5	0	.583	366	367
Detroit	6	6	0	.500	321	285
Green Bay	3	9	0	.250	244	406
San Francisco	3	9	0	.250	213	300
Baltimore	1	11	0	.083	213	462

PLAYOFFS

American Conference playoff
Cleveland 8 vs. N.Y. Giants 3

National Conference playoff
Los Angeles 24 vs. Chicago Bears 14

NFL championship
Cleveland 30 vs. Los Angeles 28

1951

AMERICAN CONFERENCE

Team	W	L	T	Pct.	PF	PA
Cleveland	11	1	0	.917	331	152
N.Y. Giants	9	2	1	.818	254	161
Washington	5	7	0	.417	183	296
Pittsburgh	4	7	1	.364	183	235
Philadelphia	4	8	0	.333	234	264
Chi. Cardinals	3	9	0	.250	210	287

NATIONAL CONFERENCE

Team	W	L	T	Pct.	PF	PA
Los Angeles	8	4	0	.667	392	261
Detroit	7	4	1	.636	336	259
San Francisco	7	4	1	.636	255	205
Chicago Bears	7	5	0	.583	286	282
Green Bay	3	9	0	.250	254	375
N.Y. Yanks	1	9	2	.100	241	382

PLAYOFFS

NFL championship
Los Angeles 24 vs. Cleveland 17

1952

AMERICAN CONFERENCE

Team	W	L	T	Pct.	PF	PA
Cleveland	8	4	0	.667	310	213
N.Y. Giants	7	5	0	.583	234	231
Philadelphia	7	5	0	.583	252	271
Pittsburgh	5	7	0	.417	300	273
Chi. Cardinals	4	8	0	.333	172	221
Washington	4	8	0	.333	240	287

NATIONAL CONFERENCE

Team	W	L	T	Pct.	PF	PA
Detroit	9	3	0	.750	344	192
Los Angeles	9	3	0	.750	349	234
San Francisco	7	5	0	.583	285	221
Green Bay	6	6	0	.500	295	312
Chicago Bears	5	7	0	.417	245	326
Dallas Texans	1	11	0	.083	182	427

PLAYOFFS

National Conference playoff
Detroit 31 vs. Los Angeles 21

NFL championship
Detroit 17 at Cleveland 7

1953

EASTERN CONFERENCE

Team	W	L	T	Pct.	PF	PA
Cleveland	11	1	0	.917	348	162
Philadelphia	7	4	1	.636	352	215
Washington	6	5	1	.545	208	215
Pittsburgh	6	6	0	.500	211	263
N.Y. Giants	3	9	0	.250	179	277
Chi. Cardinals	1	10	1	.091	190	337

WESTERN CONFERENCE

Team	W	L	T	Pct.	PF	PA
Detroit	10	2	0	.833	271	205
San Francisco	9	3	0	.750	372	237
Los Angeles	8	3	1	.727	366	236
Chicago Bears	3	8	1	.273	218	262
Baltimore	3	9	0	.250	182	350
Green Bay	2	9	1	.182	200	338

PLAYOFFS

NFL championship
Detroit 17 vs. Cleveland 16

1954

EASTERN CONFERENCE

Team	W	L	T	Pct.	PF	PA
Cleveland	9	3	0	.750	336	162
Philadelphia	7	4	1	.636	284	230
N.Y. Giants	7	5	0	.583	293	184
Pittsburgh	5	7	0	.417	219	263
Washington	3	9	0	.250	207	432
Chi. Cardinals	2	10	0	.167	183	347

WESTERN CONFERENCE

Team	W	L	T	Pct.	PF	PA
Detroit	9	2	1	.818	337	189
Chicago Bears	8	4	0	.667	301	279
San Francisco	7	4	1	.636	313	251
Los Angeles	6	5	1	.545	314	285
Green Bay	4	8	0	.333	234	251
Baltimore	3	9	0	.250	131	279

PLAYOFFS

NFL championship
Cleveland 56 vs. Detroit 10

1955

EASTERN CONFERENCE

Team	W	L	T	Pct.	PF	PA
Cleveland	9	2	1	.818	349	218
Washington	8	4	0	.667	246	222
N.Y. Giants	6	5	1	.545	267	223
Chi. Cardinals	4	7	1	.364	224	252
Philadelphia	4	7	1	.364	248	231
Pittsburgh	4	8	0	.333	195	285

WESTERN CONFERENCE

Team	W	L	T	Pct.	PF	PA
Los Angeles	8	3	1	.727	260	231
Chicago Bears	8	4	0	.667	294	251
Green Bay	6	6	0	.500	258	276
Baltimore	5	6	1	.455	214	239
San Francisco	4	8	0	.333	216	298
Detroit	3	9	0	.250	230	275

PLAYOFFS

NFL championship
Cleveland 38 at Los Angeles 14

1956

EASTERN CONFERENCE

Team	W	L	T	Pct.	PF	PA
N.Y. Giants	8	3	1	.727	264	197
Chi. Cardinals	7	5	0	.583	240	182
Washington	6	6	0	.500	183	225
Cleveland	5	7	0	.417	167	177
Pittsburgh	5	7	0	.417	217	250
Philadelphia	3	8	1	.273	143	215

WESTERN CONFERENCE

Team	W	L	T	Pct.	PF	PA
Chicago Bears	9	2	1	.818	363	246
Detroit	9	3	0	.750	300	188
San Francisco	5	6	1	.455	233	284
Baltimore	5	7	0	.417	270	322
Green Bay	4	8	0	.333	264	342
Los Angeles	4	8	0	.333	291	307

PLAYOFFS

NFL championship
N.Y. Giants 47 vs. Chicago Bears 7

1957

EASTERN CONFERENCE

Team	W	L	T	Pct.	PF	PA
Cleveland	9	2	1	.818	269	172
N.Y. Giants	7	5	0	.583	254	211
Pittsburgh	6	6	0	.500	161	178
Washington	5	6	1	.455	251	230
Philadelphia	4	8	0	.333	173	230
Chi. Cardinals	3	9	0	.250	200	299

WESTERN CONFERENCE

Team	W	L	T	Pct.	PF	PA
Detroit	8	4	0	.667	251	231
San Francisco	8	4	0	.667	260	264
Baltimore	7	5	0	.583	303	235
Los Angeles	6	6	0	.500	307	278
Chicago Bears	5	7	0	.417	203	211
Green Bay	3	9	0	.250	218	311

PLAYOFFS

Western Conference playoff
Detroit 31 at San Francisco 27

NFL championship
Detroit 59 vs. Cleveland 14

1958

EASTERN CONFERENCE

Team	W	L	T	Pct.	PF	PA
N.Y. Giants	9	3	0	.750	246	183
Cleveland	9	3	0	.750	302	217
Pittsburgh	7	4	1	.636	261	230
Washington	4	7	1	.364	214	268
Chi. Cardinals	2	9	1	.182	261	356
Philadelphia	2	9	1	.182	235	306

WESTERN CONFERENCE

Team	W	L	T	Pct.	PF	PA
Baltimore	9	3	0	.750	381	203
Chicago Bears	8	4	0	.667	298	230
Los Angeles	8	4	0	.667	344	278
San Francisco	6	6	0	.500	257	324
Detroit	4	7	1	.364	261	276
Green Bay	1	10	1	.091	193	382

PLAYOFFS

Eastern Conference playoff
N.Y. Giants 10 vs. Cleveland 0

NFL championship
Baltimore 23 at N.Y. Giants 17 (OT)

1959

EASTERN CONFERENCE

Team	W	L	T	Pct.	PF	PA
N.Y. Giants	10	2	0	.833	284	170
Cleveland	7	5	0	.583	270	214
Philadelphia	7	5	0	.583	268	278
Pittsburgh	6	5	1	.545	257	216
Washington	3	9	0	.250	185	350
Chi. Cardinals	2	10	0	.167	234	324

WESTERN CONFERENCE

Team	W	L	T	Pct.	PF	PA
Baltimore	9	3	0	.750	374	251
Chicago Bears	8	4	0	.667	252	196
Green Bay	7	5	0	.583	248	246
San Francisco	7	5	0	.583	255	237
Detroit	3	8	1	.273	203	275
Los Angeles	2	10	0	.167	242	315

PLAYOFFS

NFL championship
Baltimore 31 vs. N.Y. Giants 16

1960

AFL

EASTERN DIVISION

Team	W	L	T	Pct.	PF	PA
Houston	10	4	0	.714	379	285
N.Y. Titans	7	7	0	.500	382	399
Buffalo	5	8	1	.385	296	303
Boston Patriots	5	9	0	.357	286	349

WESTERN DIVISION

Team	W	L	T	Pct.	PF	PA
L.A. Chargers	10	4	0	.714	373	336
Dallas Texans	8	6	0	.571	362	253
Oakland	6	8	0	.429	319	388
Denver	4	9	1	.308	309	393

PLAYOFFS

AFL championship
Houston 24 vs. L.A. Chargers 16

NFL

EASTERN CONFERENCE

Team	W	L	T	Pct.	PF	PA
Philadelphia	10	2	0	.833	321	246
Cleveland	8	3	1	.727	362	217
N.Y. Giants	6	4	2	.600	271	261
St. Louis	6	5	1	.545	288	230
Pittsburgh	5	6	1	.455	240	275
Washington	1	9	2	.100	178	309

WESTERN CONFERENCE

Team	W	L	T	Pct.	PF	PA
Green Bay	8	4	0	.667	332	209
Detroit	7	5	0	.583	239	212
San Francisco	7	5	0	.583	208	205
Baltimore	6	6	0	.500	288	234
Chicago	5	6	1	.455	194	299
L.A. Rams	4	7	1	.364	265	297
Dallas Cowboys	0	11	1	.000	177	369

PLAYOFFS

NFL championship
Philadelphia 17 vs. Green Bay 13

1961

AFL

EASTERN DIVISION

Team	W	L	T	Pct.	PF	PA
Houston	10	3	1	.769	513	242
Boston Patriots	9	4	1	.692	413	313
N.Y. Titans	7	7	0	.500	301	390
Buffalo	6	8	0	.429	294	342

WESTERN DIVISION

Team	W	L	T	Pct.	PF	PA
San Diego	12	2	0	.857	396	219
Dallas Texans	6	8	0	.429	334	343
Denver	3	11	0	.214	251	432
Oakland	2	12	0	.143	237	458

PLAYOFFS

AFL championship
Houston 10 at San Diego 3

NFL

EASTERN CONFERENCE

Team	W	L	T	Pct.	PF	PA
N.Y. Giants	10	3	1	.769	368	220
Philadelphia	10	4	0	.714	361	297
Cleveland	8	5	1	.615	319	270
St. Louis	7	7	0	.500	279	267
Pittsburgh	6	8	0	.429	295	287
Dallas Cowboys	4	9	1	.308	236	380
Washington	1	12	1	.077	174	392

WESTERN CONFERENCE

Team	W	L	T	Pct.	PF	PA
Green Bay	11	3	0	.786	391	223
Detroit	8	5	1	.615	270	258
Baltimore	8	6	0	.571	302	307
Chicago	8	6	0	.571	326	302
San Francisco	7	6	1	.538	346	272
Los Angeles	4	10	0	.286	263	333
Minnesota	3	11	0	.214	285	407

PLAYOFFS

NFL championship
Green Bay 37 vs. N.Y. Giants 0

1962

AFL

EASTERN DIVISION

Team	W	L	T	Pct.	PF	PA
Houston	11	3	0	.786	387	270
Boston Patriots	9	4	1	.692	346	295
Buffalo	7	6	1	.538	309	272
N.Y. Titans	5	9	0	.357	278	423

WESTERN DIVISION

Team	W	L	T	Pct.	PF	PA
Dallas Texans	11	3	0	.786	389	233
Denver	7	7	0	.500	353	334
San Diego	4	10	0	.286	314	392
Oakland	1	13	0	.071	213	370

PLAYOFFS

AFL championship
Dallas Texans 20 at Houston 17 (OT)

NFL

EASTERN CONFERENCE

Team	W	L	T	Pct.	PF	PA
N.Y. Giants	12	2	0	.857	398	283
Pittsburgh	9	5	0	.643	312	363
Cleveland	7	6	1	.538	291	257
Washington	5	7	2	.417	305	376
Dallas Cowboys	5	8	1	.385	398	402
St. Louis	4	9	1	.308	287	361
Philadelphia	3	10	1	.231	282	356

WESTERN CONFERENCE

Team	W	L	T	Pct.	PF	PA
Green Bay	13	1	0	.929	415	148
Detroit	11	3	0	.786	315	177
Chicago	9	5	0	.643	321	287
Baltimore	7	7	0	.500	293	288
San Francisco	6	8	0	.429	282	331
Minnesota	2	11	1	.154	254	410
Los Angeles	1	12	1	.077	220	334

PLAYOFFS

NFL championship
Green Bay 16 at N.Y. Giants 7

1963

AFL

EASTERN DIVISION

Team	W	L	T	Pct.	PF	PA
Boston Patriots	7	6	1	.538	327	257
Buffalo	7	6	1	.538	304	291
Houston	6	8	0	.429	302	372
N.Y. Jets	5	8	1	.385	249	399

WESTERN DIVISION

Team	W	L	T	Pct.	PF	PA
San Diego	11	3	0	.786	399	256
Oakland	10	4	0	.714	363	288
Kansas City	5	7	2	.417	347	263
Denver	2	11	1	.154	301	473

PLAYOFFS

Eastern Division playoff
Boston 26 at Buffalo 8

AFL championship
San Diego 51 vs. Boston 10

NFL

EASTERN CONFERENCE

Team	W	L	T	Pct.	PF	PA
N.Y. Giants	11	3	0	.786	448	280
Cleveland	10	4	0	.714	343	262
St. Louis	9	5	0	.643	341	283
Pittsburgh	7	4	3	.636	321	295
Dallas	4	10	0	.286	305	378
Washington	3	11	0	.214	279	398
Philadelphia	2	10	2	.167	242	381

WESTERN CONFERENCE

Team	W	L	T	Pct.	PF	PA
Chicago	11	1	2	.917	301	144
Green Bay	11	2	1	.846	369	206
Baltimore	8	6	0	.571	316	285
Detroit	5	8	1	.385	326	265
Minnesota	5	8	1	.385	309	390
Los Angeles	5	9	0	.357	210	350
San Francisco	2	12	0	.143	198	391

PLAYOFFS

NFL championship
Chicago 14 vs. N.Y. Giants 10

1964

AFL

EASTERN DIVISION

Team	W	L	T	Pct.	PF	PA
Buffalo	12	2	0	.857	400	242
Boston Patriots	10	3	1	.769	365	297
N.Y. Jets	5	8	1	.385	278	315
Houston	4	10	0	.286	310	355

WESTERN DIVISION

Team	W	L	T	Pct.	PF	PA
San Diego	8	5	1	.615	341	300
Kansas City	7	7	0	.500	366	306
Oakland	5	7	2	.417	303	350
Denver	2	11	1	.154	240	438

PLAYOFFS

AFL championship
Buffalo 20 vs. San Diego 7

NFL

EASTERN CONFERENCE

am	W	L	T	Pct.	PF	PA
eveland	10	3	1	.769	415	293
Louis	9	3	2	.750	357	331
iladelphia	6	8	0	.429	312	313
ashington	6	8	0	.429	307	305
llas	5	8	1	.385	250	289
tsburgh	5	9	0	.357	253	315
Y. Giants	2	10	2	.167	241	399

WESTERN CONFERENCE

Team	W	L	T	Pct.	PF	PA
Baltimore	12	2	0	.857	428	225
Green Bay	8	5	1	.615	342	245
Minnesota	8	5	1	.615	355	296
Detroit	7	5	2	.583	280	260
Los Angeles	5	7	2	.417	283	339
Chicago	5	9	0	.357	260	379
San Francisco	4	10	0	.286	236	330

PLAYOFFS

NFL championship
Cleveland 27 vs. Baltimore 0

1965

AFL

EASTERN DIVISION

am	W	L	T	Pct.	PF	PA
ffalo	10	3	1	.769	313	226
Y. Jets	5	8	1	.385	285	303
ston Patriots	4	8	2	.333	244	302
uston	4	10	0	.286	298	429

WESTERN DIVISION

Team	W	L	T	Pct.	PF	PA
San Diego	9	2	3	.818	340	227
Oakland	8	5	1	.615	298	239
Kansas City	7	5	2	.583	322	285
Denver	4	10	0	.286	303	392

PLAYOFFS

AFL championship
Buffalo 23 at San Diego 0

NFL

EASTERN CONFERENCE

am	W	L	T	Pct.	PF	PA
eveland	11	3	0	.786	363	325
llas	7	7	0	.500	325	280
Y. Giants	7	7	0	.500	270	338
ashington	6	8	0	.429	257	301
iladelphia	5	9	0	.357	363	359
Louis	5	9	0	.357	296	309
tsburgh	2	12	0	.143	202	397

WESTERN CONFERENCE

Team	W	L	T	Pct.	PF	PA
Green Bay	10	3	1	.769	316	224
Baltimore	10	3	1	.769	389	284
Chicago	9	5	0	.643	409	275
San Francisco	7	6	1	.538	421	402
Minnesota	7	7	0	.500	383	403
Detroit	6	7	1	.462	257	295
Los Angeles	4	10	0	.286	269	328

PLAYOFFS

Western Conference playoff
Green Bay 13 vs. Baltimore 10 (OT)

NFL championship
Green Bay 23 vs. Cleveland 12

1966

AFL

EASTERN DIVISION

am	W	L	T	Pct.	PF	PA
ffalo	9	4	1	.692	358	255
ston Patriots	8	4	2	.667	315	283
Y. Jets	6	6	2	.500	322	312
uston	3	11	0	.214	335	396
ami	3	11	0	.214	213	362

WESTERN DIVISION

Team	W	L	T	Pct.	PF	PA
Kansas City	11	2	1	.846	448	276
Oakland	8	5	1	.615	315	288
San Diego	7	6	1	.538	335	284
Denver	4	10	0	.286	196	381

PLAYOFFS

AFL championship
Kansas City 31 at Buffalo 7

NFL

EASTERN CONFERENCE

am	W	L	T	Pct.	PF	PA
llas	10	3	1	.769	445	239
eveland	9	5	0	.643	403	259
iladelphia	9	5	0	.643	326	340
Louis	8	5	1	.615	264	265
ashington	7	7	0	.500	351	355
tsburgh	5	8	1	.385	316	347
anta	3	11	0	.214	204	437
Y. Giants	1	12	1	.077	263	501

WESTERN CONFERENCE

Team	W	L	T	Pct.	PF	PA
Green Bay	12	2	0	.857	335	163
Baltimore	9	5	0	.643	314	226
Los Angeles	8	6	0	.571	289	212
San Francisco	6	6	2	.500	320	325
Chicago	5	7	2	.417	234	272
Detroit	4	9	1	.308	206	317
Minnesota	4	9	1	.308	292	304

PLAYOFFS

NFL championship
Green Bay 34 at Dallas 27

Super Bowl 1
Green Bay 35, Kansas City 10, at Los Angeles.

1967

AFL

EASTERN DIVISION

am	W	L	T	Pct.	PF	PA
uston	9	4	1	.692	258	199
Y. Jets	8	5	1	.615	371	329
ffalo	4	10	0	.286	237	285
ami	4	10	0	.286	219	407
ston Patriots	3	10	1	.231	280	389

WESTERN DIVISION

Team	W	L	T	Pct.	PF	PA
Oakland	13	1	0	.929	468	233
Kansas City	9	5	0	.643	408	254
San Diego	8	5	1	.615	360	352
Denver	3	11	0	.214	256	409

PLAYOFFS

AFL championship
Oakland 40 vs. Houston 7

NFL

EASTERN CONFERENCE

CAPITOL DIVISION

Team	W	L	T	Pct.	PF	PA
Dallas	9	5	0	.643	342	268
Philadelphia	6	7	1	.462	351	409
Washington	5	6	3	.455	347	353
New Orleans	3	11	0	.214	233	379

CENTURY DIVISION

Team	W	L	T	Pct.	PF	PA
Cleveland	9	5	0	.643	334	297
N.Y. Giants	7	7	0	.500	369	379
St. Louis	6	7	1	.462	333	356
Pittsburgh	4	9	1	.308	281	320

WESTERN CONFERENCE

COASTAL DIVISION

Team	W	L	T	Pct.	PF	PA
Los Angeles	11	1	2	.917	398	196
Baltimore	11	1	2	.917	394	198
San Francisco	7	7	0	.500	273	337
Atlanta	1	12	1	.077	175	422

CENTRAL DIVISION

Team	W	L	T	Pct.	PF	PA
Green Bay	9	4	1	.692	332	209
Chicago	7	6	1	.538	239	218
Detroit	5	7	2	.417	260	259
Minnesota	3	8	3	.273	233	294

PLAYOFFS

Conference championships
Dallas 52 vs. Cleveland 14
Green Bay 28 vs. Los Angeles 7

NFL championship
Green Bay 21 vs. Dallas 17

Super Bowl 2
Green Bay 33, Oakland 14, at Miami.

1968

AFL

EASTERN DIVISION

Team	W	L	T	Pct.	PF	PA
N.Y. Jets	11	3	0	.786	419	280
Houston	7	7	0	.500	303	248
Miami	5	8	1	.385	276	355
Boston Patriots	4	10	0	.286	229	406
Buffalo	1	12	1	.077	199	367

WESTERN DIVISION

Team	W	L	T	Pct.	PF	PA
Oakland	12	2	0	.857	453	233
Kansas City	12	2	0	.857	371	170
San Diego	9	5	0	.643	382	310
Denver	5	9	0	.357	255	404
Cincinnati	3	11	0	.214	215	329

PLAYOFFS

Western Division playoff
Oakland 41 vs. Kansas City 6

AFL championship
N.Y. Jets 27 vs. Oakland 23

NFL

EASTERN CONFERENCE

CAPITOL DIVISION

Team	W	L	T	Pct.	PF	PA
Dallas	12	2	0	.857	431	186
N.Y. Giants	7	7	0	.500	294	325
Washington	5	9	0	.357	249	358
Philadelphia	2	12	0	.143	202	351

CENTURY DIVISION

Team	W	L	T	Pct.	PF	PA
Cleveland	10	4	0	.714	394	273
St. Louis	9	4	1	.692	325	289
New Orleans	4	9	1	.308	246	327
Pittsburgh	2	11	1	.154	244	397

WESTERN CONFERENCE

COASTAL DIVISION

Team	W	L	T	Pct.	PF	PA
Baltimore	13	1	0	.929	402	144
Los Angeles	10	3	1	.769	312	200
San Francisco	7	6	1	.538	303	310
Atlanta	2	12	0	.143	170	389

CENTRAL DIVISION

Team	W	L	T	Pct.	PF	PA
Minnesota	8	6	0	.571	282	242
Chicago	7	7	0	.500	250	333
Green Bay	6	7	1	.462	281	227
Detroit	4	8	2	.333	207	241

PLAYOFFS

Conference championships
Cleveland 31 vs. Dallas 20
Baltimore 24 vs. Minnesota 14

NFL championship
Baltimore 34 at Cleveland 0

Super Bowl 3
N.Y. Jets 16, Baltimore 7, at Miami.

1969

AFL

EASTERN DIVISION

Team	W	L	T	Pct.	PF	PA
N.Y. Jets	10	4	0	.714	353	269
Houston	6	6	2	.500	278	279
Boston Patriots	4	10	0	.286	266	316
Buffalo	4	10	0	.286	230	359
Miami	3	10	1	.231	233	332

WESTERN DIVISION

Team	W	L	T	Pct.	PF	PA
Oakland	12	1	1	.923	377	242
Kansas City	11	3	0	.786	359	177
San Diego	8	6	0	.571	288	276
Denver	5	8	1	.385	297	344
Cincinnati	4	9	1	.308	280	367

PLAYOFFS

Divisional games
Kansas City 13 at N.Y. Jets 6
Oakland 56 vs. Houston 7

AFL championship
Kansas City 17 at Oakland 7

NFL

EASTERN CONFERENCE

CAPITOL DIVISION

Team	W	L	T	Pct.	PF	PA
Dallas	11	2	1	.846	369	223
Washington	7	5	2	.583	307	319
New Orleans	5	9	0	.357	311	393
Philadelphia	4	9	1	.308	279	377

CENTURY DIVISION

Team	W	L	T	Pct.	PF	PA
Cleveland	10	3	1	.769	351	300
N.Y. Giants	6	8	0	.429	264	298
St. Louis	4	9	1	.308	314	389
Pittsburgh	1	13	0	.071	218	404

WESTERN CONFERENCE

COASTAL DIVISION

Team	W	L	T	Pct.	PF	PA
Los Angeles	11	3	0	.786	320	243
Baltimore	8	5	1	.615	279	268
Atlanta	6	8	0	.429	276	268
San Francisco	4	8	2	.333	277	319

CENTRAL DIVISION

Team	W	L	T	Pct.	PF	PA
Minnesota	12	2	0	.857	379	133
Detroit	9	4	1	.692	259	188
Green Bay	8	6	0	.571	269	221
Chicago	1	13	0	.071	210	339

PLAYOFFS

Conference championships
Cleveland 38 at Dallas 14
Minnesota 23 vs. Los Angeles 20

NFL championship
Minnesota 27 vs. Cleveland 7

Super Bowl 4
Kansas City 23, Minnesota 7, at New Orleans.

AMERICAN CONFERENCE

EASTERN DIVISION

am	W	L	T	Pct.	PF	PA
timore*	11	2	1	.846	321	234
ami†	10	4	0	.714	297	228
. Jets	4	10	0	.286	255	286
ffalo	3	10	1	.231	204	337
ston Patriots	2	12	0	.143	149	361

CENTRAL DIVISION

am	W	L	T	Pct.	PF	PA
cinnati*	8	6	0	.571	312	255
veland	7	7	0	.500	286	265
sburgh	5	9	0	.357	210	272
uston	3	10	1	.231	217	352

WESTERN DIVISION

am	W	L	T	Pct.	PF	PA
kland*	8	4	2	.667	300	293
nsas City	7	5	2	.583	272	244
n Diego	5	6	3	.455	282	278
nver	5	8	1	.385	253	264

*Division champion.
†Wild-card team.

NATIONAL CONFERENCE

EASTERN DIVISION

Team	W	L	T	Pct.	PF	PA
Dallas*	10	4	0	.714	299	221
N.Y. Giants	9	5	0	.643	301	270
St. Louis	8	5	1	.615	325	228
Washington	6	8	0	.429	297	314
Philadelphia	3	10	1	.231	241	332

CENTRAL DIVISION

Team	W	L	T	Pct.	PF	PA
Minnesota*	12	2	0	.857	335	143
Detroit†	10	4	0	.714	347	202
Green Bay	6	8	0	.429	196	293
Chicago	6	8	0	.429	256	261

WESTERN DIVISION

Team	W	L	T	Pct.	PF	PA
San Francisco*	10	3	1	.769	352	267
Los Angeles	9	4	1	.692	325	202
Atlanta	4	8	2	.333	206	261
New Orleans	2	11	1	.154	172	347

PLAYOFFS

AFC divisional games
Baltimore 17 vs. Cincinnati 0
Oakland 21 vs. Miami 14

AFC championship
Baltimore 27 vs. Oakland 17

NFC divisional games
Dallas 5 vs. Detroit 0
San Francisco 17 at Minnesota 14

NFC championship
Dallas 17 at San Francisco 10

Super Bowl 5
Baltimore 16, Dallas 13, at Miami.

AMERICAN CONFERENCE

EASTERN DIVISION

am	W	L	T	Pct.	PF	PA
ami*	10	3	1	.769	315	174
timore†	10	4	0	.714	313	140
w England	6	8	0	.429	238	325
. Jets	6	8	0	.429	212	299
ffalo	1	13	0	.071	184	394

CENTRAL DIVISION

am	W	L	T	Pct.	PF	PA
veland*	9	5	0	.643	285	273
sburgh	6	8	0	.429	246	292
uston	4	9	1	.308	251	330
cinnati	4	10	0	.286	284	265

WESTERN DIVISION

am	W	L	T	Pct.	PF	PA
nsas City*	10	3	1	.769	302	208
kland	8	4	2	.667	344	278
n Diego	6	8	0	.429	311	341
nver	4	9	1	.308	203	275

*Division champion.
†Wild-card team.

NATIONAL CONFERENCE

EASTERN DIVISION

Team	W	L	T	Pct.	PF	PA
Dallas*	11	3	0	.786	406	222
Washington†	9	4	1	.692	276	190
Philadelphia	6	7	1	.462	221	302
St. Louis	4	9	1	.308	231	279
N.Y. Giants	4	10	0	.286	228	362

CENTRAL DIVISION

Team	W	L	T	Pct.	PF	PA
Minnesota*	11	3	0	.786	245	139
Detroit	7	6	1	.538	341	286
Chicago	6	8	0	.429	185	276
Green Bay	4	8	2	.333	274	298

WESTERN DIVISION

Team	W	L	T	Pct.	PF	PA
San Francisco*	9	5	0	.643	300	216
Los Angeles	8	5	1	.615	313	260
Atlanta	7	6	1	.538	274	277
New Orleans	4	8	2	.333	266	347

PLAYOFFS

AFC divisional games
Miami 27 at Kansas City 24 (OT)
Baltimore 20 at Cleveland 3

AFC championship
Miami 21 vs. Baltimore 0

NFC divisional games
Dallas 20 at Minnesota 12
San Francisco 24 vs. Washington 20

NFC championship
Dallas 14 vs. San Francisco 3

Super Bowl 6
Dallas 24, Miami 3, at New Orleans.

HISTORY *Year-by-year standings*

FOOTBALL COMES TO MONDAY NIGHT

Although few people at the time could have guessed at the kind of popularity the show would come to enjoy, ABC's *Monday Night Football* debuted on September 21, 1970 with the telecast of a Jets-Browns game from Cleveland Stadium. With 85,703 fans look-ing on, coach Blanton Collier's Browns beat Weeb Ewbank's Jets, 31-21. Though the game had little of the excitement of future Monday night encounters, it did have a few noteworthy accomplishments. Jets quarterback Joe Namath completed 19 of 32 pass-es for 299 yards and one touchdown, but he also was intercepted three times, turnovers that proved crucial to the Browns' victo-ry. Homer Jones returned a kickoff 94 yards for a Cleveland touchdown.

1972

AMERICAN CONFERENCE

EASTERN DIVISION

Team	W	L	T	Pct.	PF	PA
Miami*	14	0	0	1.000	385	171
N.Y. Jets	7	7	0	.500	367	324
Baltimore	5	9	0	.357	235	252
Buffalo	4	9	1	.321	257	377
New England	3	11	0	.214	192	446

CENTRAL DIVISION

Team	W	L	T	Pct.	PF	PA
Pittsburgh*	11	3	0	.786	343	175
Cleveland†	10	4	0	.714	268	249
Cincinnati	8	6	0	.571	299	229
Houston	1	13	0	.071	164	380

WESTERN DIVISION

Team	W	L	T	Pct.	PF	PA
Oakland*	10	3	1	.750	365	248
Kansas City	8	6	0	.571	287	254
Denver	5	9	0	.357	325	350
San Diego	4	9	1	.321	264	344

*Division champion.
†Wild-card team.

NATIONAL CONFERENCE

EASTERN DIVISION

Team	W	L	T	Pct.	PF	PA
Washington*	11	3	0	.786	336	218
Dallas†	10	4	0	.714	319	240
N.Y. Giants	8	6	0	.571	331	247
St. Louis	4	9	1	.321	193	303
Philadelphia	2	11	1	.179	145	352

CENTRAL DIVISION

Team	W	L	T	Pct.	PF	PA
Green Bay*	10	4	0	.714	304	226
Detroit	8	5	1	.607	339	290
Minnesota	7	7	0	.500	301	252
Chicago	4	9	1	.321	225	275

WESTERN DIVISION

Team	W	L	T	Pct.	PF	PA
San Francisco*	8	5	1	.607	353	249
Atlanta	7	7	0	.500	269	274
Los Angeles	6	7	1	.464	291	286
New Orleans	2	11	1	.179	215	361

PLAYOFFS

AFC divisional games
Pittsburgh 13 vs. Oakland 7
Miami 20 vs. Cleveland 14

AFC championship
Miami 21 at Pittsburgh 17

NFC divisional games
Dallas 30 at San Francisco 28
Washington 16 vs. Green Bay 3

NFC championship
Washington 26 vs. Dallas 3

Super Bowl 7
Miami 14, Washington 7, at Los Angeles.

1973

AMERICAN CONFERENCE

EASTERN DIVISION

Team	W	L	T	Pct.	PF	PA
Miami*	12	2	0	.857	343	150
Buffalo	9	5	0	.643	259	230
New England	5	9	0	.357	258	300
N.Y. Jets	4	10	0	.286	240	306
Baltimore	4	10	0	.286	226	341

CENTRAL DIVISION

Team	W	L	T	Pct.	PF	PA
Cincinnati*	10	4	0	.714	286	231
Pittsburgh†	10	4	0	.714	347	210
Cleveland	7	5	2	.571	234	255
Houston	1	13	0	.071	199	447

WESTERN DIVISION

Team	W	L	T	Pct.	PF	PA
Oakland*	9	4	1	.679	292	175
Kansas City	7	5	2	.571	231	192
Denver	7	5	2	.571	354	296
San Diego	2	11	1	.179	188	386

*Division champion.
†Wild-card team.

NATIONAL CONFERENCE

EASTERN DIVISION

Team	W	L	T	Pct.	PF	PA
Dallas*	10	4	0	.714	382	203
Washington†	10	4	0	.714	325	198
Philadelphia	5	8	1	.393	310	393
St. Louis	4	9	1	.321	286	365
N.Y. Giants	2	11	1	.179	226	362

CENTRAL DIVISION

Team	W	L	T	Pct.	PF	PA
Minnesota*	12	2	0	.857	296	168
Detroit	6	7	1	.464	271	247
Green Bay	5	7	2	.429	202	259
Chicago	3	11	0	.214	195	334

WESTERN DIVISION

Team	W	L	T	Pct.	PF	PA
Los Angeles*	12	2	0	.857	388	178
Atlanta	9	5	0	.643	318	224
San Francisco	5	9	0	.357	262	319
New Orleans	5	9	0	.357	163	312

PLAYOFFS

AFC divisional games
Oakland 33 vs. Pittsburgh 14
Miami 34 vs. Cincinnati 16

AFC championship
Miami 27 vs. Oakland 10

NFC divisional games
Minnesota 27 vs. Washington 20
Dallas 27 vs. Los Angeles 16

NFC championship
Minnesota 27 at Dallas 10

Super Bowl 8
Miami 24, Minnesota 7, at Houston.

1974

AMERICAN CONFERENCE

EASTERN DIVISION

Team	W	L	T	Pct.	PF	PA
Miami*	11	3	0	.786	327	216
Buffalo†	9	5	0	.643	264	244
New England	7	7	0	.500	348	289
N.Y. Jets	7	7	0	.500	279	300
Baltimore	2	12	0	.143	190	329

CENTRAL DIVISION

Team	W	L	T	Pct.	PF	PA
Pittsburgh*	10	3	1	.750	305	189
Houston	7	7	0	.500	236	282
Cincinnati	7	7	0	.500	283	259
Cleveland	4	10	0	.286	251	344

WESTERN DIVISION

Team	W	L	T	Pct.	PF	PA
Oakland*	12	2	0	.857	355	228
Denver	7	6	1	.536	302	294
Kansas City	5	9	0	.357	233	293
San Diego	5	9	0	.357	212	285

*Division champion.
†Wild-card team.

NATIONAL CONFERENCE

EASTERN DIVISION

Team	W	L	T	Pct.	PF	PA
St. Louis*	10	4	0	.714	285	218
Washington†	10	4	0	.714	320	196
Dallas	8	6	0	.571	297	235
Philadelphia	7	7	0	.500	242	217
N.Y. Giants	2	12	0	.143	195	299

CENTRAL DIVISION

Team	W	L	T	Pct.	PF	PA
Minnesota*	10	4	0	.714	310	195
Detroit	7	7	0	.500	256	270
Green Bay	6	8	0	.429	210	206
Chicago	4	10	0	.286	152	279

WESTERN DIVISION

Team	W	L	T	Pct.	PF	PA
Los Angeles*	10	4	0	.714	263	181
San Francisco	6	8	0	.429	226	236
New Orleans	5	9	0	.357	166	263
Atlanta	3	11	0	.214	111	271

PLAYOFFS

AFC divisional games
Oakland 28 vs. Miami 26
Pittsburgh 32 vs. Buffalo 14

AFC championship
Pittsburgh 24 at Oakland 13

NFC divisional games
Minnesota 30 vs. St. Louis 14
Los Angeles 19 vs. Washington 10

NFC championship
Minnesota 14 vs. Los Angeles 10

Super Bowl 9
Pittsburgh 16, Minnesota 6, at New Orleans.

1975

AMERICAN CONFERENCE

EASTERN DIVISION

eam	W	L	T	Pct.	PF	PA
altimore*	10	4	0	.714	395	269
iami	10	4	0	.714	357	222
uffalo	8	6	0	.571	420	355
Y. Jets	3	11	0	.214	258	433
ew England	3	11	0	.214	258	358

CENTRAL DIVISION

eam	W	L	T	Pct.	PF	PA
ttsburgh*	12	2	0	.857	373	162
ncinnati†	11	3	0	.786	340	246
ouston	10	4	0	.714	293	226
eveland	3	11	0	.214	218	372

WESTERN DIVISION

eam	W	L	T	Pct.	PF	PA
akland*	11	3	0	.786	375	255
enver	6	8	0	.429	254	307
ansas City	5	9	0	.357	282	341
an Diego	2	12	0	.143	189	345

*Division champion.
†Wild-card team.

NATIONAL CONFERENCE

EASTERN DIVISION

Team	W	L	T	Pct.	PF	PA
St. Louis*	11	3	0	.786	356	276
Dallas†	10	4	0	.714	350	268
Washington	8	6	0	.571	325	276
N.Y. Giants	5	9	0	.357	216	306
Philadelphia	4	10	0	.286	225	302

CENTRAL DIVISION

Team	W	L	T	Pct.	PF	PA
Minnesota*	12	2	0	.857	377	180
Detroit	7	7	0	.500	245	262
Chicago	4	10	0	.286	191	379
Green Bay	4	10	0	.286	226	285

WESTERN DIVISION

Team	W	L	T	Pct.	PF	PA
Los Angeles*	12	2	0	.857	312	135
San Francisco	5	9	0	.357	255	286
Atlanta	4	10	0	.286	240	289
New Orleans	2	12	0	.143	165	360

PLAYOFFS

AFC divisional games
Pittsburgh 28 vs. Baltimore 10
Oakland 31 vs. Cincinnati 28

AFC championship
Pittsburgh 16 vs. Oakland 10

NFC divisional games
Los Angeles 35 vs. St. Louis 23
Dallas 17 at Minnesota 14

NFC championship
Dallas 37 at Los Angeles 7

Super Bowl 10
Pittsburgh 21, Dallas 17, at Miami.

1976

AMERICAN CONFERENCE

EASTERN DIVISION

eam	W	L	T	Pct.	PF	PA
altimore*	11	3	0	.786	417	246
ew England†	11	3	0	.786	376	236
iami	6	8	0	.429	263	264
Y. Jets	3	11	0	.214	169	383
uffalo	2	12	0	.143	245	363

CENTRAL DIVISION

eam	W	L	T	Pct.	PF	PA
ittsburgh*	10	4	0	.714	342	138
incinnati	10	4	0	.714	335	210
leveland	9	5	0	.643	267	287
ouston	5	9	0	.357	222	273

WESTERN DIVISION

eam	W	L	T	Pct.	PF	PA
akland*	13	1	0	.929	350	237
enver	9	5	0	.643	315	206
an Diego	6	8	0	.429	248	285
ansas City	5	9	0	.357	290	376
ampa Bay	0	14	0	.000	125	412

*Division champion.
†Wild-card team.

NATIONAL CONFERENCE

EASTERN DIVISION

Team	W	L	T	Pct.	PF	PA
Dallas*	11	3	0	.786	296	194
Washington†	10	4	0	.714	291	217
St. Louis	10	4	0	.714	309	267
Philadelphia	4	10	0	.286	165	286
N.Y. Giants	3	11	0	.214	170	250

CENTRAL DIVISION

Team	W	L	T	Pct.	PF	PA
Minnesota*	11	2	1	.821	305	176
Chicago	7	7	0	.500	253	216
Detroit	6	8	0	.429	262	220
Green Bay	5	9	0	.357	218	299

WESTERN DIVISION

Team	W	L	T	Pct.	PF	PA
Los Angeles*	10	3	1	.750	351	190
San Francisco	8	6	0	.571	270	190
Atlanta	4	10	0	.286	172	312
New Orleans	4	10	0	.286	253	346
Seattle	2	12	0	.143	229	429

PLAYOFFS

AFC divisional games
Oakland 24 vs. New England 21
Pittsburgh 40 at Baltimore 14

AFC championship
Oakland 24 vs. Pittsburgh 7

NFC divisional games
Minnesota 35 vs. Washington 20
Los Angeles 14 at Dallas 12

NFC championship
Minnesota 24 vs. Los Angeles 13

Super Bowl 11
Oakland 32, Minnesota 14, at Pasadena, Calif.

THE '76 BUCS: THE WRONG KIND OF FAME

Four seasons after the Miami Dolphins went through an entire season without losing a game, another Florida team also made NFL history, but not the kind it would have preferred. In their inaugural season the Tampa Bay Buccaneers failed to win a game, going 0-14 as a member of the AFC's Western Division. Coach John McKay's Bucs scored a league-low 125 points and allowed 412, a total surpassed only by the league's other 1976 expansion team, the Seattle Seahawks. Tampa Bay failed to score more than 20 points in any game and did not come within three points of winning a game. One of those three-point defeats came in Week 6, when the Seahawks beat the Bucs, 13-10, a victory preserved when veteran linebacker Mike Curtis blocked a 35-yard field goal attempt by Bucs kicker Dave Green with 42 seconds left.

AMERICAN CONFERENCE

EASTERN DIVISION

Team	W	L	T	Pct.	PF	PA
Baltimore*	10	4	0	.714	295	221
Miami	10	4	0	.714	313	197
New England	9	5	0	.643	278	217
Buffalo	3	11	0	.214	160	313
N.Y. Jets	3	11	0	.214	191	300

CENTRAL DIVISION

Team	W	L	T	Pct.	PF	PA
Pittsburgh*	9	5	0	.643	283	243
Cincinnati	8	6	0	.571	238	235
Houston	8	6	0	.571	299	230
Cleveland	6	8	0	.429	269	267

WESTERN DIVISION

Team	W	L	T	Pct.	PF	PA
Denver*	12	2	0	.857	274	148
Oakland†	11	3	0	.786	351	230
San Diego	7	7	0	.500	222	205
Seattle	5	9	0	.357	282	373
Kansas City	2	12	0	.143	225	349

*Division champion.
†Wild-card team.

NATIONAL CONFERENCE

EASTERN DIVISION

Team	W	L	T	Pct.	PF	PA
Dallas*	12	2	0	.857	345	212
Washington	9	5	0	.643	196	189
St. Louis	7	7	0	.500	272	287
Philadelphia	5	9	0	.357	220	207
N.Y. Giants	5	9	0	.357	181	265

CENTRAL DIVISION

Team	W	L	T	Pct.	PF	PA
Minnesota*	9	5	0	.643	231	227
Chicago†	9	5	0	.643	255	253
Detroit	6	8	0	.429	183	252
Green Bay	4	10	0	.286	134	219
Tampa Bay	2	12	0	.143	103	223

WESTERN DIVISION

Team	W	L	T	Pct.	PF	PA
Los Angeles*	10	4	0	.714	302	146
Atlanta	7	7	0	.500	179	129
San Francisco	5	9	0	.357	220	260
New Orleans	3	11	0	.214	232	336

PLAYOFFS

AFC divisional games
Denver 34 vs. Pittsburgh 21
Oakland 37 at Baltimore 31 (OT)
AFC championship
Denver 20 vs. Oakland 17
NFC divisional games
Dallas 37 vs. Chicago 7
Minnesota 14 at Los Angeles 7
NFC championship
Dallas 23 vs. Minnesota 6
Super Bowl 12
Dallas 27, Denver 10, at New Orleans.

AMERICAN CONFERENCE

EASTERN DIVISION

Team	W	L	T	Pct.	PF	PA
New England*	11	5	0	.688	358	286
Miami†	11	5	0	.688	372	254
N.Y. Jets	8	8	0	.500	359	364
Buffalo	5	11	0	.313	302	354
Baltimore	5	11	0	.313	239	421

CENTRAL DIVISION

Team	W	L	T	Pct.	PF	PA
Pittsburgh*	14	2	0	.875	356	195
Houston†	10	6	0	.625	283	298
Cleveland	8	8	0	.500	334	356
Cincinnati	4	12	0	.250	252	284

WESTERN DIVISION

Team	W	L	T	Pct.	PF	PA
Denver*	10	6	0	.625	282	198
Oakland	9	7	0	.563	311	283
Seattle	9	7	0	.563	345	358
San Diego	9	7	0	.563	355	309
Kansas City	4	12	0	.250	243	327

*Division champion.
†Wild-card team.

NATIONAL CONFERENCE

EASTERN DIVISION

Team	W	L	T	Pct.	PF	PA
Dallas*	12	4	0	.750	384	208
Philadelphia†	9	7	0	.563	270	250
Washington	8	8	0	.500	273	283
St. Louis	6	10	0	.375	248	296
N.Y. Giants	6	10	0	.375	264	298

CENTRAL DIVISION

Team	W	L	T	Pct.	PF	PA
Minnesota*	8	7	1	.531	294	306
Green Bay	8	7	1	.531	249	269
Detroit	7	9	0	.438	290	300
Chicago	7	9	0	.438	253	274
Tampa Bay	5	11	0	.313	241	259

WESTERN DIVISION

Team	W	L	T	Pct.	PF	PA
Los Angeles*	12	4	0	.750	316	245
Atlanta†	9	7	0	.563	240	290
New Orleans	7	9	0	.438	281	298
San Francisco	2	14	0	.125	219	350

PLAYOFFS

AFC wild-card game
Houston 17 at Miami 9
AFC divisional games
Houston 31 at New England 14
Pittsburgh 33 vs. Denver 10
AFC championship
Pittsburgh 34 vs. Houston 5
NFC wild-card game
Atlanta 14 vs. Philadelphia 13
NFC divisional games
Dallas 27 vs. Atlanta 20
Los Angeles 34 vs. Minnesota 10
NFC championship
Dallas 28 at Los Angeles 0
Super Bowl 13
Pittsburgh 35, Dallas 31, at Miami.

HISTORY Year-by-year standings

SMASHING '78 DEBUT FOR BIG EARL

Houston running back Earl Campbell, winner of the Heisman Trophy at Texas the year before and the league's top draft pick, gave NFL fans a preview of things to come by rushing for a league-high 1,450 yards and scoring 13 touchdowns in one of the most electrifying rookie seasons in NFL history. Campbell dethroned defending league rushing champ Walter Payton by 55 yards despite carrying the ball 31 fewer times. More important, he took a team that had not been to the playoffs in the eight previous seasons to the AFC championship game. Campbell's best game of 1978 came under the brightest of lights: a 199-yard, four-touchdown performance in a 35-30 victory over Miami on Monday, November 20. He capped his big evening by scoring the Oilers' final touchdown on an 81-yard run in the fourth quarter.

1979

AMERICAN CONFERENCE

EASTERN DIVISION

am	W	L	T	Pct.	PF	PA
ami*	10	6	0	.625	341	257
w England	9	7	0	.563	411	326
Y. Jets	8	8	0	.500	337	383
ffalo	7	9	0	.438	268	279
timore	5	11	0	.313	271	351

CENTRAL DIVISION

am	W	L	T	Pct.	PF	PA
tsburgh*	12	4	0	.750	416	262
uston†	11	5	0	.688	362	331
veland	9	7	0	.563	359	352
ncinnati	4	12	0	.250	337	421

WESTERN DIVISION

am	W	L	T	Pct.	PF	PA
n Diego*	12	4	0	.750	411	246
nver†	10	6	0	.625	289	262
attle	9	7	0	.563	378	372
kland	9	7	0	.563	365	337
nsas City	7	9	0	.438	238	262

*Division champion.
†Wild-card team.

NATIONAL CONFERENCE

EASTERN DIVISION

Team	W	L	T	Pct.	PF	PA
Dallas*	11	5	0	.688	371	313
Philadelphia†	11	5	0	.688	339	282
Washington	10	6	0	.625	348	295
N.Y. Giants	6	10	0	.375	237	323
St. Louis	5	11	0	.313	307	358

CENTRAL DIVISION

Team	W	L	T	Pct.	PF	PA
Tampa Bay*	10	6	0	.625	273	237
Chicago†	10	6	0	.625	306	249
Minnesota	7	9	0	.438	259	337
Green Bay	5	11	0	.313	246	316
Detroit	2	14	0	.125	219	365

WESTERN DIVISION

Team	W	L	T	Pct.	PF	PA
Los Angeles*	9	7	0	.563	323	309
New Orleans	8	8	0	.500	370	360
Atlanta	6	10	0	.375	300	388
San Francisco	2	14	0	.125	308	416

PLAYOFFS

AFC wild-card game
Houston 13 vs. Denver 7

AFC divisional games
Houston 17 at San Diego 14
Pittsburgh 34 vs. Miami 14

AFC championship
Pittsburgh 27 vs. Houston 13

NFC wild-card game
Philadelphia 27 vs. Chicago 17

NFC divisional games
Tampa Bay 24 vs. Philadelphia 17
Los Angeles 21 at Dallas 19

NFC championship
Los Angeles 9 at Tampa Bay 0

Super Bowl 14
Pittsburgh 31, Los Angeles 19, at Pasadena, Calif.

1980

AMERICAN CONFERENCE

EASTERN DIVISION

am	W	L	T	Pct.	PF	PA
ffalo*	11	5	0	.688	320	260
w England	10	6	0	.625	441	325
ami	8	8	0	.500	266	305
ltimore	7	9	0	.438	355	387
Y. Jets	4	12	0	.250	302	395

CENTRAL DIVISION

am	W	L	T	Pct.	PF	PA
eveland*	11	5	0	.688	357	310
uston†	11	5	0	.688	295	251
ttsburgh	9	7	0	.563	352	313
ncinnati	6	10	0	.375	244	312

WESTERN DIVISION

am	W	L	T	Pct.	PF	PA
n Diego*	11	5	0	.688	418	327
akland†	11	5	0	.688	364	306
nsas City	8	8	0	.500	319	336
enver	8	8	0	.500	310	323
attle	4	12	0	.250	291	408

*Division champion.
†Wild-card team.

NATIONAL CONFERENCE

EASTERN DIVISION

Team	W	L	T	Pct.	PF	PA
Philadelphia*	12	4	0	.750	384	222
Dallas†	12	4	0	.750	454	311
Washington	6	10	0	.375	261	293
St. Louis	5	11	0	.313	299	350
N.Y. Giants	4	12	0	.250	249	425

CENTRAL DIVISION

Team	W	L	T	Pct.	PF	PA
Minnesota*	9	7	0	.563	317	308
Detroit	9	7	0	.563	334	272
Chicago	7	9	0	.438	304	264
Tampa Bay	5	10	1	.344	271	341
Green Bay	5	10	1	.344	231	371

WESTERN DIVISION

Team	W	L	T	Pct.	PF	PA
Atlanta*	12	4	0	.750	405	272
Los Angeles†	11	5	0	.688	424	289
San Francisco	6	10	0	.375	320	415
New Orleans	1	15	0	.063	291	487

PLAYOFFS

AFC wild-card game
Oakland 27 vs. Houston 7

AFC divisional games
San Diego 20 vs. Buffalo 14
Oakland 14 at Cleveland 12

AFC championship
Oakland 34 at San Diego 27

NFC wild-card game
Dallas 34 vs. Los Angeles 13

NFC divisional games
Philadelphia 31 vs. Minnesota 16
Dallas 30 at Atlanta 27

NFC championship
Philadelphia 20 vs. Dallas 7

Super Bowl 15
Oakland 27, Philadelphia 10, at New Orleans.

HISTORY *Year-by-year standings*

AIR CORYELL TAKES TO THE SKIES

Although their season would end in disappointment—a loss to Oakland in the AFC championship game—few teams were more exciting to watch in 1980 than coach Don Coryell's San Diego Chargers. Only eight receivers caught passes for 1,000 or more yards that year, but San Diego had three of them: John Jefferson (who led the league with 1,340 yards), Kellen Winslow (1,290) and Charlie Joiner (1,132). It marked the first time in history that three receivers on the same team each topped 1,000 yards in the same season. In addition, Winslow caught 89 passes to set a record for receptions by a tight end and Jefferson became the first player to begin his NFL career with three consecutive 1,000-yard seasons. Not surprisingly, the Chargers won the AFC West title for the second year in a row, the only team to repeat from the 1979 season.

1981

AMERICAN CONFERENCE

EASTERN DIVISION

Team	W	L	T	Pct.	PF	PA
Miami*	11	4	1	.719	345	275
N.Y. Jets†	10	5	1	.656	355	287
Buffalo†	10	6	0	.625	311	276
Baltimore	2	14	0	.125	259	533
New England	2	14	0	.125	322	370

CENTRAL DIVISION

Team	W	L	T	Pct.	PF	PA
Cincinnati*	12	4	0	.750	421	304
Pittsburgh	8	8	0	.500	356	297
Houston	7	9	0	.438	281	355
Cleveland	5	11	0	.313	276	375

WESTERN DIVISION

Team	W	L	T	Pct.	PF	PA
San Diego*	10	6	0	.625	478	390
Denver	10	6	0	.625	321	289
Kansas City	9	7	0	.563	343	290
Oakland	7	9	0	.438	273	343
Seattle	6	10	0	.375	322	388

*Division champion.
†Wild-card team.

NATIONAL CONFERENCE

EASTERN DIVISION

Team	W	L	T	Pct.	PF	PA
Dallas*	12	4	0	.750	367	277
Philadelphia†	10	6	0	.625	368	221
N.Y. Giants†	9	7	0	.563	295	257
Washington	8	8	0	.500	347	349
St. Louis	7	9	0	.438	315	408

CENTRAL DIVISION

Team	W	L	T	Pct.	PF	PA
Tampa Bay*	9	7	0	.563	315	268
Detroit	8	8	0	.500	397	322
Green Bay	8	8	0	.500	324	361
Minnesota	7	9	0	.438	325	369
Chicago	6	10	0	.375	253	324

WESTERN DIVISION

Team	W	L	T	Pct.	PF	PA
San Francisco*	13	3	0	.813	357	250
Atlanta	7	9	0	.438	426	355
Los Angeles	6	10	0	.375	303	351
New Orleans	4	12	0	.250	207	378

PLAYOFFS

AFC wild-card game
Buffalo 31 at New York Jets 27

AFC divisional games
San Diego 41 at Miami 38 (OT)
Cincinnati 28 vs. Buffalo 21

AFC championship
Cincinnati 27 vs. San Diego 7

NFC wild-card game
N.Y. Giants 27 at Philadelphia 21

NFC divisional games
Dallas 38 vs. Tampa Bay 0
San Francisco 38 vs. N.Y. Giants 24

NFC championship
San Francisco 28 vs. Dallas 27

Super Bowl 16
San Francisco 26, Cincinnati 21, at Pontiac, Mich.

1982

AMERICAN CONFERENCE

Team	W	L	T	Pct.	PF	PA
L.A. Raiders	8	1	0	.889	260	200
Miami	7	2	0	.778	198	131
Cincinnati	7	2	0	.778	232	177
Pittsburgh	6	3	0	.667	204	146
San Diego	6	3	0	.667	288	221
N.Y. Jets	6	3	0	.667	245	166
New England	5	4	0	.556	143	157
Cleveland	4	5	0	.444	140	182
Buffalo	4	5	0	.444	150	154
Seattle	4	5	0	.444	127	147
Kansas City	3	6	0	.333	176	184
Denver	2	7	0	.222	148	226
Houston	1	8	0	.111	136	245
Baltimore	0	8	1	.056	113	236

NATIONAL CONFERENCE

Team	W	L	T	Pct.	PF	PA
Washington	8	1	0	.889	190	128
Dallas	6	3	0	.667	226	145
Green Bay	5	3	1	.611	226	169
Minnesota	5	4	0	.556	187	198
Atlanta	5	4	0	.556	183	199
St. Louis	5	4	0	.556	135	170
Tampa Bay	5	4	0	.556	158	178
Detroit	4	5	0	.444	181	176
New Orleans	4	5	0	.444	129	160
N.Y. Giants	4	5	0	.444	164	160
San Francisco	3	6	0	.333	209	206
Chicago	3	6	0	.333	141	174
Philadelphia	3	6	0	.333	191	195
L.A. Rams	2	7	0	.222	200	250

As a result of a 57-day players' strike, the 1982 NFL regular season schedule was reduced from 16 weeks to 9. At the conclusion of the regular season, a 16-team Super Bowl Tournament was held. Eight teams from each conference were seeded 1 through 8 based on their records during regular season play.

Miami finished ahead of Cincinnati based on a better conference record. Pittsburgh won common games tiebreaker with San Diego after New York Jets were eliminated based on conference record. Cleveland finished ahead of Buffalo and Seattle based on a better conference record. Minnesota, Atlanta, St. Louis and Tampa Bay seeds were determined by best won-lost record in conference games. Detroit finished ahead of New Orleans and the New York Giants based on a better conference record.

PLAYOFFS

AFC first round
Miami 28 vs. New England 13
L.A. Raiders 27 vs. Cleveland 10
New York Jets 44 at Cincinnati 17
San Diego 31 at Pittsburgh 28

AFC second round
N.Y. Jets 17 at L.A. Raiders 14
Miami 34 vs. San Diego 13

AFC championship
Miami 14 vs. New York Jets 0

NFC first round
Washington 31 vs. Detroit 7
Green Bay 41 vs. St. Louis 16
Minnesota 30 vs. Atlanta 24
Dallas 30 vs. Tampa Bay 17

NFC second round
Washington 21 vs. Minnesota 7
Dallas 37 vs. Green Bay 26

NFC championship
Washington 31 vs. Dallas 17

Super Bowl 17
Washington 27, Miami 17, at Pasadena, Calif.

LT: A ROOKIE TO REMEMBER

The 1981 season was a big one for rookies (six made the Pro Bowl), but none had more impact than Giants linebacker Lawrence Taylor, who had no problem adjusting to the pro game after an All-American career at North Carolina. The second player drafted in 1981, Taylor was simply marvelous, helping to make a good New York defense with veterans like linebacker Harry Carson and cornerback Mark Haynes great. In 16 games (all starts) Taylor had 133 tackles, 10.5 sacks, recovered a fumble and intercepted a pass. He followed that up with 14 tackles and two sacks in two playoff games, the Giants' first postseason action since 1963. For his efforts Taylor was a unanimous All-NFL first-team selection, a Pro Bowl starter and the Associated Press Defensive Player of the Year.

AMERICAN CONFERENCE

EASTERN DIVISION

Team	W	L	T	Pct.	PF	PA
Miami*	12	4	0	.750	389	250
New England	8	8	0	.500	274	289
Buffalo	8	8	0	.500	283	351
Baltimore	7	9	0	.438	264	354
N.Y. Jets	7	9	0	.438	313	331

CENTRAL DIVISION

Team	W	L	T	Pct.	PF	PA
Pittsburgh*	10	6	0	.625	355	303
Cleveland	9	7	0	.563	356	342
Cincinnati	7	9	0	.438	346	302
Houston	2	14	0	.125	288	460

WESTERN DIVISION

Team	W	L	T	Pct.	PF	PA
L.A. Raiders*	12	4	0	.750	442	338
Seattle†	9	7	0	.563	403	397
Denver†	9	7	0	.563	302	327
San Diego	6	10	0	.375	358	462
Kansas City	6	10	0	.375	386	367

*Division champion.
†Wild-card team.

NATIONAL CONFERENCE

EASTERN DIVISION

Team	W	L	T	Pct.	PF	PA
Washington*	14	2	0	.875	541	332
Dallas†	12	4	0	.750	479	360
St. Louis	8	7	1	.531	374	428
Philadelphia	5	11	0	.313	233	322
N.Y. Giants	3	12	1	.219	267	347

CENTRAL DIVISION

Team	W	L	T	Pct.	PF	PA
Detroit*	9	7	0	.563	347	286
Green Bay	8	8	0	.500	429	439
Chicago	8	8	0	.500	311	301
Minnesota	8	8	0	.500	316	348
Tampa Bay	2	14	0	.125	241	380

WESTERN DIVISION

Team	W	L	T	Pct.	PF	PA
San Francisco*	10	6	0	.625	432	293
L.A. Rams†	9	7	0	.563	361	344
New Orleans	8	8	0	.500	319	337
Atlanta	7	9	0	.438	370	389

PLAYOFFS

AFC wild-card game
Seattle 31 vs. Denver 7

AFC divisional games
Seattle 27 at Miami 20
L.A. Raiders 38 vs. Pittsburgh 10

AFC championship game
L.A. Raiders 30 vs. Seattle 14

NFC wild-card game
Los Angeles Rams 24 at Dallas 17

NFC divisional games
San Francisco 24 vs. Detroit 23
Washington 51 vs. L.A. Rams 7

NFC championship
Washington 24 vs. San Francisco 21

Super Bowl 18
L.A. Raiders 38, Washington 9, at Tampa, Fla.

AMERICAN CONFERENCE

EASTERN DIVISION

Team	W	L	T	Pct.	PF	PA
Miami*	14	2	0	.875	513	298
New England	9	7	0	.563	362	352
N.Y. Jets	7	9	0	.438	332	364
Indianapolis	4	12	0	.250	239	414
Buffalo	2	14	0	.125	250	454

CENTRAL DIVISION

Team	W	L	T	Pct.	PF	PA
Pittsburgh*	9	7	0	.563	387	310
Cincinnati	8	8	0	.500	339	339
Cleveland	5	11	0	.313	250	297
Houston	3	13	0	.188	240	437

WESTERN DIVISION

Team	W	L	T	Pct.	PF	PA
Denver*	13	3	0	.813	353	241
Seattle†	12	4	0	.750	418	282
L.A. Raiders†	11	5	0	.688	368	278
Kansas City	8	8	0	.500	314	324
San Diego	7	9	0	.438	394	413

*Division champion.
†Wild-card team.

NATIONAL CONFERENCE

EASTERN DIVISION

Team	W	L	T	Pct.	PF	PA
Washington*	11	5	0	.688	426	310
N.Y. Giants†	9	7	0	.563	299	301
St. Louis	9	7	0	.563	423	345
Dallas	9	7	0	.563	308	308
Philadelphia	6	9	1	.406	278	320

CENTRAL DIVISION

Team	W	L	T	Pct.	PF	PA
Chicago*	10	6	0	.625	325	248
Green Bay	8	8	0	.500	390	309
Tampa Bay	6	10	0	.375	335	380
Detroit	4	11	1	.281	283	408
Minnesota	3	13	0	.188	276	484

WESTERN DIVISION

Team	W	L	T	Pct.	PF	PA
San Francisco*	15	1	0	.938	475	227
L.A. Rams†	10	6	0	.625	346	316
New Orleans	7	9	0	.438	298	361
Atlanta	4	12	0	.250	281	382

PLAYOFFS

AFC wild-card game
Seattle 13 vs. Los Angeles Raiders 7

AFC divisional games
Miami 31 vs. Seattle 10
Pittsburgh 24 at Denver 17

AFC championship
Miami 45 vs. Pittsburgh 28

NFC wild-card game
N.Y. Giants 16 at L.A. Rams 13

NFC divisional games
San Francisco 21 vs. N.Y. Giants 10
Chicago 23 at Washington 19

NFC championship
San Francisco 23 vs. Chicago 0

Super Bowl 19
San Francisco 38, Miami 16, at Stanford, Calif.

HISTORY *Year-by-year standings*

CAPITAL GAINS FOR THE REDSKINS

Although they failed to successfully defend their Super Bowl championship, the Washington Redskins did just about everything else right in 1983, especially on offense. Washington scored 541 points, the most in NFL history and 62 more than the next highest scoring team that year. Running back John Riggins scored a record 24 touchdowns, rushed for a club-record 1,347 yards and set a league mark over two seasons by rushing for a TD in 13 consecutive games. Mark Moseley's 161 points set a new league standard for kickers. But as good as Riggins and Moseley were, the league's Most Valuable Player, in voting conducted by the Associated Press, was quarterback Joe Theismann, who threw 29 TD passes, compiled a 97.0 passer rating and had streaks of 161 and 104 consecutive passes without an interception.

AMERICAN CONFERENCE

EASTERN DIVISION

Team	W	L	T	Pct.	PF	PA
Miami*	12	4	0	.750	428	320
N.Y. Jets†	11	5	0	.688	393	264
New England†	11	5	0	.688	362	290
Indianapolis	5	11	0	.313	320	386
Buffalo	2	14	0	.125	200	381

CENTRAL DIVISION

Team	W	L	T	Pct.	PF	PA
Cleveland*	8	8	0	.500	287	294
Cincinnati	7	9	0	.438	441	437
Pittsburgh	7	9	0	.438	379	355
Houston	5	11	0	.313	284	412

WESTERN DIVISION

Team	W	L	T	Pct.	PF	PA
L.A. Raiders*	12	4	0	.750	354	308
Denver	11	5	0	.688	380	329
Seattle	8	8	0	.500	349	303
San Diego	8	8	0	.500	467	435
Kansas City	6	10	0	.375	317	360

*Division champion.
†Wild-card team.

NATIONAL CONFERENCE

EASTERN DIVISION

Team	W	L	T	Pct.	PF	PA
Dallas*	10	6	0	.625	357	333
N.Y. Giants†	10	6	0	.625	399	283
Washington	10	6	0	.625	297	312
Philadelphia	7	9	0	.438	286	310
St. Louis	5	11	0	.313	278	414

CENTRAL DIVISION

Team	W	L	T	Pct.	PF	PA
Chicago*	15	1	0	.938	456	198
Green Bay	8	8	0	.500	337	355
Minnesota	7	9	0	.438	346	359
Detroit	7	9	0	.438	307	366
Tampa Bay	2	14	0	.125	294	448

WESTERN DIVISION

Team	W	L	T	Pct.	PF	PA
L.A. Rams*	11	5	0	.688	340	277
San Francisco†	10	6	0	.625	411	263
New Orleans	5	11	0	.313	294	401
Atlanta	4	12	0	.250	282	452

PLAYOFFS

AFC wild-card game
New England 26 at N.Y. Jets 14

AFC divisional games
Miami 24 vs. Cleveland 21
New England 27 at L.A. Raiders 20

AFC championship
New England 31 at Miami 14

NFC wild-card game
N.Y. Giants 17 vs. San Francisco 3

NFC divisional games
Los Angeles Rams 20 vs. Dallas 0
Chicago 21 vs. New York Giants 0

NFC championship
Chicago 24 vs. Los Angeles Rams 0

Super Bowl 20
Chicago 46, New England 10, at New Orleans.

AMERICAN CONFERENCE

EASTERN DIVISION

Team	W	L	T	Pct.	PF	PA
New England*	11	5	0	.688	412	307
N.Y. Jets†	10	6	0	.625	364	386
Miami	8	8	0	.500	430	405
Buffalo	4	12	0	.250	287	348
Indianapolis	3	13	0	.188	229	400

CENTRAL DIVISION

Team	W	L	T	Pct.	PF	PA
Cleveland*	12	4	0	.750	391	310
Cincinnati	10	6	0	.625	409	394
Pittsburgh	6	10	0	.375	307	336
Houston	5	11	0	.313	274	329

WESTERN DIVISION

Team	W	L	T	Pct.	PF	PA
Denver*	11	5	0	.688	378	327
Kansas City†	10	6	0	.625	358	326
Seattle	10	6	0	.625	366	293
L.A. Raiders	8	8	0	.500	323	346
San Diego	4	12	0	.250	335	396

*Division champion.
†Wild-card team.

NATIONAL CONFERENCE

EASTERN DIVISION

Team	W	L	T	Pct.	PF	PA
N.Y. Giants*	14	2	0	.875	371	236
Washington†	12	4	0	.750	368	296
Dallas	7	9	0	.438	346	337
Philadelphia	5	10	1	.344	256	312
St. Louis	4	11	1	.281	218	351

CENTRAL DIVISION

Team	W	L	T	Pct.	PF	PA
Chicago*	14	2	0	.875	352	187
Minnesota	9	7	0	.563	398	273
Detroit	5	11	0	.313	277	326
Green Bay	4	12	0	.250	254	418
Tampa Bay	2	14	0	.125	239	473

WESTERN DIVISION

Team	W	L	T	Pct.	PF	PA
San Francisco*	10	5	1	.656	374	247
L.A. Rams†	10	6	0	.625	309	267
Atlanta	7	8	1	.469	280	280
New Orleans	7	9	0	.438	288	287

PLAYOFFS

AFC wild-card game
N.Y. Jets 35 vs. Kansas City 15

AFC divisional games
Cleveland 23 vs. N.Y. Jets 20 (OT)
Denver 22 vs. New England 17

AFC championship
Denver 23 at Cleveland 20 (OT)

NFC wild-card game
Washington 19 vs. L.A. Rams 7

NFC divisional games
Washington 27 at Chicago 13
N.Y. Giants 49 vs. San Francisco 3

NFC championship
N.Y. Giants 17 vs. Washington 0

Super Bowl 21
New York Giants 39, Denver 20, at Pasadena, Ca

HISTORY Year-by-year standings

DA BEARS

The 1985 Chicago Bears may not have been the best team ever, but they were certainly among the most colorful. Running back Walter Payton suggested his teammates could have stepped right from the pages of "One Flew Over the Cuckoo's Nest." Rookie defensive tackle William Perry, whose girth earned him the nickname "The Refrigerator," said "I was big when I was little" when queried about his weight. The players cut a popular music video "The Super Bowl Shuffle"—while the regular season was still in progress. But there were good reasons for the cockiness: The Bears were good. They scored 456 points and allowed 198, one of the lowest totals ever for a 16-game season. Their final record, including the playoffs, was 18-1, and they outscored their three postseason opponents by a combined 91-10. Chicago's 46-10 rout of New England in the Super Bowl was the most lopsided in the game's first 20 years.

AMERICAN CONFERENCE

EASTERN DIVISION

Team	W	L	T	Pct.	PF	PA
Indianapolis*	9	6	0	.600	300	238
New England	8	7	0	.533	320	293
Miami	8	7	0	.533	362	335
Buffalo	7	8	0	.467	270	305
N.Y. Jets	6	9	0	.400	334	360

CENTRAL DIVISION

Team	W	L	T	Pct.	PF	PA
Cleveland*	10	5	0	.667	390	239
Houston†	9	6	0	.600	345	349
Pittsburgh	8	7	0	.533	285	299
Cincinnati	4	11	0	.267	285	370

WESTERN DIVISION

Team	W	L	T	Pct.	PF	PA
Denver*	10	4	1	.700	379	288
Seattle†	9	6	0	.600	371	314
San Diego	8	7	0	.533	253	317
L.A. Raiders	5	10	0	.333	301	289
Kansas City	4	11	0	.267	273	388

*Division champion.
†Wild-card team.

NOTE: The 1987 NFL regular season was reduced from 224 games to 210 (16 to 15 for each team) due to players' strike.

NATIONAL CONFERENCE

EASTERN DIVISION

Team	W	L	T	Pct.	PF	PA
Washington*	11	4	0	.733	379	285
Dallas	7	8	0	.467	340	348
St. Louis	7	8	0	.467	362	368
Philadelphia	7	8	0	.467	337	380
N.Y. Giants	6	9	0	.400	280	312

CENTRAL DIVISION

Team	W	L	T	Pct.	PF	PA
Chicago*	11	4	0	.733	356	282
Minnesota†	8	7	0	.533	336	335
Green Bay	5	9	1	.367	255	300
Tampa Bay	4	11	0	.267	286	360
Detroit	4	11	0	.267	269	384

WESTERN DIVISION

Team	W	L	T	Pct.	PF	PA
San Francisco*	13	2	0	.867	459	253
New Orleans†	12	3	0	.800	422	283
L.A. Rams	6	9	0	.400	317	361
Atlanta	3	12	0	.200	205	436

PLAYOFFS

AFC wild-card game
Houston 23 vs. Seattle 20 (OT)

AFC divisional games
Cleveland 38 vs. Indianapolis 21
Denver 34 vs. Houston 10

AFC championship
Denver 38 vs. Cleveland 33

NFC wild-card game
Minnesota 44 at New Orleans 10

NFC divisional games
Minnesota 36 at San Francisco 24
Washington 21 at Chicago 17

NFC championship
Washington 17 vs. Minnesota 10

Super Bowl 22
Washington 42, Denver 10, at San Diego.

AMERICAN CONFERENCE

EASTERN DIVISION

Team	W	L	T	Pct.	PF	PA
Buffalo*	12	4	0	.750	329	237
Indianapolis	9	7	0	.563	354	315
New England	9	7	0	.563	250	284
N.Y. Jets	8	7	1	.531	372	354
Miami	6	10	0	.375	319	380

CENTRAL DIVISION

Team	W	L	T	Pct.	PF	PA
Cincinnati*	12	4	0	.750	448	329
Cleveland†	10	6	0	.625	304	288
Houston†	10	6	0	.625	424	365
Pittsburgh	5	11	0	.313	336	421

WESTERN DIVISION

Team	W	L	T	Pct.	PF	PA
Seattle*	9	7	0	.563	339	329
Denver	8	8	0	.500	327	352
L.A. Raiders	7	9	0	.438	325	369
San Diego	6	10	0	.375	231	332
Kansas City	4	11	1	.281	254	320

*Division champion.
†Wild-card team.

NATIONAL CONFERENCE

EASTERN DIVISION

Team	W	L	T	Pct.	PF	PA
Philadelphia*	10	6	0	.625	379	319
N.Y. Giants	10	6	0	.625	359	304
Washington	7	9	0	.438	345	387
Phoenix	7	9	0	.438	344	398
Dallas	3	13	0	.188	265	381

CENTRAL DIVISION

Team	W	L	T	Pct.	PF	PA
Chicago*	12	4	0	.750	312	215
Minnesota†	11	5	0	.688	406	233
Tampa Bay	5	11	0	.313	261	350
Detroit	4	12	0	.250	220	313
Green Bay	4	12	0	.250	240	315

WESTERN DIVISION

Team	W	L	T	Pct.	PF	PA
San Francisco*	10	6	0	.625	369	294
L.A. Rams†	10	6	0	.625	407	293
New Orleans	10	6	0	.625	312	283
Atlanta	5	11	0	.313	244	315

PLAYOFFS

AFC wild-card game
Houston 24 at Cleveland 23

AFC divisional games
Cincinnati 21 vs. Seattle 13
Buffalo 17 vs. Houston 10

AFC championship
Cincinnati 21 vs. Buffalo 10

NFC wild-card game
Minnesota 28 vs. L.A. Rams 17

NFC divisional games
Chicago 20 vs. Philadelphia 12
San Francisco 34 vs. Minnesota 9

NFC championship
San Francisco 28 at Chicago 3

Super Bowl 23
San Francisco 20, Cincinnati 16, at Miami.

REPLACEMENT BALL

Frustrated in their attempts to gain a fairer form of unrestricted free agency, NFL players went on strike for the second time in league history on September 22, 1987. The work stoppage forced the cancellation of all Week 3 games and brought about three subsequent weeks of what came to be called "replacement football." With their regular players on strike, team owners quickly assembled new squads consisting of former NFL and United States Football League players, castoffs and amateur dreamers willing to cross a picket line. The result? There was a wide discrepancy in the quality of the teams, depending largely on how much effort management invested in assembling new rosters. The defending Super Bowl champion Giants, for example, lost all three of their replacement games (which counted in the standings) and never recovered once their regular players returned, finishing the season 6-9 and out of the playoffs. The Redskins, meanwhile, went 3-0 in replacement ball, helping to propel them to an 11-4 regular-season finish en route to the club's second Super Bowl title in six years.

1989

AMERICAN CONFERENCE

EASTERN DIVISION

Team	W	L	T	Pct.	PF	PA
Buffalo*	9	7	0	.563	409	317
Indianapolis	8	8	0	.500	298	301
Miami	8	8	0	.500	331	379
New England	5	11	0	.313	297	391
N.Y. Jets	4	12	0	.250	253	411

CENTRAL DIVISION

Team	W	L	T	Pct.	PF	PA
Cleveland*	9	6	1	.594	334	254
Houston†	9	7	0	.563	365	412
Pittsburgh†	9	7	0	.563	265	326
Cincinnati	8	8	0	.500	404	285

WESTERN DIVISION

Team	W	L	T	Pct.	PF	PA
Denver*	11	5	0	.688	362	226
Kansas City	8	7	1	.531	318	286
L.A. Raiders	8	8	0	.500	315	297
Seattle	7	9	0	.438	241	327
San Diego	6	10	0	.375	266	290

*Division champion.
†Wild-card team.

NATIONAL CONFERENCE

EASTERN DIVISION

Team	W	L	T	Pct.	PF	PA
N.Y. Giants*	12	4	0	.750	348	252
Philadelphia†	11	5	0	.688	342	274
Washington	10	6	0	.625	386	308
Phoenix	5	11	0	.313	258	377
Dallas	1	15	0	.063	204	393

CENTRAL DIVISION

Team	W	L	T	Pct.	PF	PA
Minnesota*	10	6	0	.625	351	275
Green Bay	10	6	0	.625	362	356
Detroit	7	9	0	.438	312	364
Chicago	6	10	0	.375	358	377
Tampa Bay	5	11	0	.313	320	419

WESTERN DIVISION

Team	W	L	T	Pct.	PF	PA
San Francisco*	14	2	0	.875	442	253
L.A. Rams†	11	5	0	.688	426	344
New Orleans	9	7	0	.563	386	301
Atlanta	3	13	0	.188	279	437

PLAYOFFS

AFC wild-card game
Pittsburgh 26 at Houston 23 (OT)

AFC divisional games
Cleveland 34 vs. Buffalo 30
Denver 24 vs. Pittsburgh 23

AFC championship
Denver 37 vs. Cleveland 21

NFC wild-card game
L.A. Rams 21 at Philadelphia 7

NFC divisional games
L.A. Rams 19 at N.Y. Giants 13 (OT)
San Francisco 41 vs. Minnesota 13

NFC championship
San Francisco 30 vs. L.A. Rams 3

Super Bowl 24
San Francisco 55, Denver 10, at New Orleans.

1990

AMERICAN CONFERENCE

EASTERN DIVISION

Team	W	L	T	Pct.	PF	PA
Buffalo*	13	3	0	.813	428	263
Miami†	12	4	0	.750	336	242
Indianapolis	7	9	0	.438	281	353
N.Y. Jets	6	10	0	.375	295	345
New England	1	15	0	.063	181	446

CENTRAL DIVISION

Team	W	L	T	Pct.	PF	PA
Cincinnati*	9	7	0	.563	360	352
Houston†	9	7	0	.563	405	307
Pittsburgh	9	7	0	.563	292	240
Cleveland	3	13	0	.188	228	462

WESTERN DIVISION

Team	W	L	T	Pct.	PF	PA
L.A. Raiders*	12	4	0	.750	337	268
Kansas City†	11	5	0	.688	369	257
Seattle	9	7	0	.563	306	286
San Diego	6	10	0	.375	315	281
Denver	5	11	0	.313	331	374

*Division champion.
†Wild-card team.

NATIONAL CONFERENCE

EASTERN DIVISION

Team	W	L	T	Pct.	PF	PA
N.Y. Giants*	13	3	0	.813	335	211
Philadelphia†	10	6	0	.625	396	299
Washington†	10	6	0	.625	381	301
Dallas	7	9	0	.438	244	308
Phoenix	5	11	0	.313	268	396

CENTRAL DIVISION

Team	W	L	T	Pct.	PF	PA
Chicago*	11	5	0	.688	348	280
Tampa Bay	6	10	0	.375	264	367
Detroit	6	10	0	.375	373	413
Green Bay	6	10	0	.375	271	347
Minnesota	6	10	0	.375	351	326

WESTERN DIVISION

Team	W	L	T	Pct.	PF	PA
San Francisco*	14	2	0	.875	353	239
New Orleans†	8	8	0	.500	274	275
L.A. Rams	5	11	0	.313	345	412
Atlanta	5	11	0	.313	348	365

PLAYOFFS

AFC wild-card playoffs
Miami 17 vs. Kansas City 16
Cincinnati 41 vs. Houston 14

AFC divisional playoffs
Buffalo 44 vs. Miami 34
L.A. Raiders 20 vs. Cincinnati 10

AFC championship
Buffalo 51 vs. L.A. Raiders 3

NFC wild-card playoffs
Washington 20 at Philadelphia 6
Chicago 16 vs. New Orleans 6

NFC divisional playoffs
San Francisco 28 vs. Washington 10
N.Y. Giants 31 vs. Chicago 3

NFC championship
N.Y. Giants 15 at San Francisco 13

Super Bowl 25
N.Y. Giants 20 vs. Buffalo 19, at Tampa, Fla.

GIANTS AND BILLS GO DOWN TO THE WIRE

One year after the most lopsided Super Bowl ever, the Giants and Bills staged the closest, with New York edging Buffalo, 20-19, at Tampa Stadium in Super Bowl 25 when Bills kicker Scott Norwood missed a 47-yard field goal attempt with eight seconds left. Although Norwood wore the goat horns afterward, his teammates did little early in the contest to prevent the game from coming down to a last-minute kick. A Buffalo offense that had scored a league-high 428 points during the regular season and 95 in the first two playoff games did little in its biggest test of the season. Only running back Thurman Thomas (135 yards rushing) had what could be considered a superior game. The Giants' offense, meanwhile, put together scoring drives of 87, 75 and 74 yards. A 14-play, 75-yard drive that took 9 minutes, 29 seconds off the clock went into the books as the most time-consuming drive in Super Bowl history.

AMERICAN CONFERENCE

EASTERN DIVISION

Team	W	L	T	Pct.	PF	PA
Buffalo*	13	3	0	.813	458	318
N.Y. Jets†	8	8	0	.500	314	293
Miami	8	8	0	.500	343	349
New England	6	10	0	.375	211	305
Indianapolis	1	15	0	.063	143	381

CENTRAL DIVISION

Team	W	L	T	Pct.	PF	PA
Houston*	11	5	0	.688	386	251
Pittsburgh	7	9	0	.438	292	344
Cleveland	6	10	0	.375	293	298
Cincinnati	3	13	0	.188	263	435

WESTERN DIVISION

Team	W	L	T	Pct.	PF	PA
Denver*	12	4	0	.750	304	235
Kansas City†	10	6	0	.625	322	252
L.A. Raiders†	9	7	0	.563	298	297
Seattle	7	9	0	.438	276	261
San Diego	4	12	0	.250	274	342

*Division champion.
†Wild-card team.

NATIONAL CONFERENCE

EASTERN DIVISION

Team	W	L	T	Pct.	PF	PA
Washington*	14	2	0	.875	485	224
Dallas†	11	5	0	.688	342	310
Philadelphia	10	6	0	.625	285	244
N.Y. Giants	8	8	0	.500	281	297
Phoenix	4	12	0	.250	196	344

CENTRAL DIVISION

Team	W	L	T	Pct.	PF	PA
Detroit*	12	4	0	.750	339	295
Chicago†	11	5	0	.688	299	269
Minnesota	8	8	0	.500	301	306
Green Bay	4	12	0	.250	273	313
Tampa Bay	3	13	0	.188	199	365

WESTERN DIVISION

Team	W	L	T	Pct.	PF	PA
New Orleans*	11	5	0	.688	341	211
Atlanta†	10	6	0	.625	361	338
San Francisco	10	6	0	.625	393	239
L.A. Rams	3	13	0	.188	234	390

PLAYOFFS

AFC wild-card playoffs
Kansas City 10 vs. L.A. Raiders 6
Houston 17 vs. N.Y. Jets 10

AFC divisional playoffs
Denver 26 vs. Houston 24
Buffalo 37 vs. Kansas City 14

AFC championship
Buffalo 10 vs. Denver 7

NFC wild-card playoffs
Atlanta 27 at New Orleans 20
Dallas 17 at Chicago 13

NFC divisional playoffs
Washington 24 vs. Atlanta 7
Detroit 38 vs. Dallas 6

NFC championship
Washington 41 vs. Detroit 10

Super Bowl 26
Washington 37 vs. Buffalo 24, at Minneapolis.

AMERICAN CONFERENCE

EASTERN DIVISION

Team	W	L	T	Pct.	PF	PA
Miami*	11	5	0	.688	340	281
Buffalo†	11	5	0	.688	381	283
Indianapolis	9	7	0	.563	216	302
N.Y. Jets	4	12	0	.250	220	315
New England	2	14	0	.125	205	363

CENTRAL DIVISION

Team	W	L	T	Pct.	PF	PA
Pittsburgh*	11	5	0	.688	299	225
Houston†	10	6	0	.625	352	258
Cleveland	7	9	0	.438	272	275
Cincinnati	5	11	0	.313	274	364

WESTERN DIVISION

Team	W	L	T	Pct.	PF	PA
San Diego*	11	5	0	.688	335	241
Kansas City†	10	6	0	.625	348	282
Denver	8	8	0	.500	262	329
L.A. Raiders	7	9	0	.438	249	281
Seattle	2	14	0	.125	140	312

*Division champion.
†Wild-card team.

NATIONAL CONFERENCE

EASTERN DIVISION

Team	W	L	T	Pct.	PF	PA
Dallas*	13	3	0	.813	409	243
Philadelphia†	11	5	0	.688	354	245
Washington†	9	7	0	.563	300	255
N.Y. Giants	6	10	0	.375	306	367
Phoenix	4	12	0	.250	243	332

CENTRAL DIVISION

Team	W	L	T	Pct.	PF	PA
Minnesota*	11	5	0	.688	374	249
Green Bay	9	7	0	.563	276	296
Tampa Bay	5	11	0	.313	267	365
Chicago	5	11	0	.313	295	361
Detroit	5	11	0	.313	273	332

WESTERN DIVISION

Team	W	L	T	Pct.	PF	PA
San Francisco*	14	2	0	.875	431	236
New Orleans†	12	4	0	.750	330	202
Atlanta	6	10	0	.375	327	414
L.A. Rams	6	10	0	.375	313	383

PLAYOFFS

AFC wild-card playoffs
San Diego 17 vs. Kansas City 0
Buffalo 41 vs. Houston 38 (OT)

AFC divisional playoffs
Buffalo 24 at Pittsburgh 3
Miami 31 vs. San Diego 0

AFC championship
Buffalo 29 at Miami 10

NFC wild-card playoffs
Washington 24 at Minnesota 7
Philadelphia 36 at New Orleans 20

NFC divisional playoffs
San Francisco 20 vs. Washington 13
Dallas 34 at Philadelphia 10

NFC championship
Dallas 30 at San Francisco 20

Super Bowl 27
Dallas 52 vs. Buffalo 17, at Pasadena, Calif.

HISTORY *Year-by-year standings*

COWBOYS HIT THE HEIGHTS AGAIN

Three years after hitting the lowest point in franchise history, the Dallas Cowboys were back on top of the football world following a 52-17 romp over Buffalo in Super Bowl 27. In their fourth year under Jimmy Johnson, who replaced legendary coach Tom Landry following an ownership change in February 1989, the Cowboys won a franchise-record 13 regular season games and rolled through the playoffs, beating the Eagles, 49ers and Bills by a combined score of 116-47. Troy Aikman, the first player Johnson drafted after taking over, was superb in the playoffs, compiling a 126.4 passer rating in the three games. With the win Johnson joined Paul Brown as the only men to coach championship teams in both college and the NFL.

AMERICAN CONFERENCE

EASTERN DIVISION

Team	W	L	T	Pct.	PF	PA
Buffalo*	12	4	0	.750	329	242
Miami	9	7	0	.563	349	351
N.Y. Jets	8	8	0	.500	270	247
New England	5	11	0	.313	238	286
Indianapolis	4	12	0	.250	189	378

CENTRAL DIVISION

Team	W	L	T	Pct.	PF	PA
Houston*	12	4	0	.750	368	238
Pittsburgh†	9	7	0	.563	308	281
Cleveland	7	9	0	.438	304	307
Cincinnati	3	13	0	.188	187	319

WESTERN DIVISION

Team	W	L	T	Pct.	PF	PA
Kansas City*	11	5	0	.688	328	291
L.A. Raiders†	10	6	0	.625	306	326
Denver†	9	7	0	.563	373	284
San Diego	8	8	0	.500	322	290
Seattle	6	10	0	.375	280	314

*Division champion.
†Wild-card team.

NATIONAL CONFERENCE

EASTERN DIVISION

Team	W	L	T	Pct.	PF	PA
Dallas*	12	4	0	.750	376	229
N.Y. Giants†	11	5	0	.688	288	205
Philadelphia	8	8	0	.500	293	315
Phoenix	7	9	0	.438	326	269
Washington	4	12	0	.250	230	345

CENTRAL DIVISION

Team	W	L	T	Pct.	PF	PA
Detroit*	10	6	0	.625	298	292
Minnesota†	9	7	0	.563	277	290
Green Bay†	9	7	0	.563	340	282
Chicago	7	9	0	.438	234	230
Tampa Bay	5	11	0	.313	237	376

WESTERN DIVISION

Team	W	L	T	Pct.	PF	PA
San Francisco*	10	6	0	.625	473	295
New Orleans	8	8	0	.500	317	343
Atlanta	6	10	0	.375	316	385
L.A. Rams	5	11	0	.313	221	367

PLAYOFFS

AFC wild-card playoffs
Kansas City 27 vs. Pittsburgh 24 (OT)
L.A. Raiders 42 vs. Denver 24
AFC divisional playoffs
Buffalo 29 vs. L.A. Raiders 23
Kansas City 28 at Houston 20
AFC championship
Buffalo 30 vs. Kansas City 13
NFC wild-card playoffs
Green Bay 28 at Detroit 24
N.Y. Giants 17 vs. Minnesota 10
NFC divisional playoffs
San Francisco 44 vs. N.Y. Giants 3
Dallas 27 vs. Green Bay 17
NFC championship
Dallas 38 vs. San Francisco 21
Super Bowl 28
Dallas 30 vs. Buffalo 13, at Atlanta.

AMERICAN CONFERENCE

EASTERN DIVISION

Team	W	L	T	Pct.	PF	PA
Miami*	10	6	0	.625	389	327
New England†	10	6	0	.625	351	312
Indianapolis	8	8	0	.500	307	320
Buffalo	7	9	0	.438	340	356
N.Y. Jets	6	10	0	.375	264	320

CENTRAL DIVISION

Team	W	L	T	Pct.	PF	PA
Pittsburgh*	12	4	0	.750	316	234
Cleveland†	11	5	0	.688	340	204
Cincinnati	3	13	0	.188	276	406
Houston	2	14	0	.125	226	352

WESTERN DIVISION

Team	W	L	T	Pct.	PF	PA
San Diego*	11	5	0	.688	381	306
Kansas City†	9	7	0	.563	319	298
L.A. Raiders	9	7	0	.563	303	327
Denver	7	9	0	.438	347	396
Seattle	6	10	0	.375	287	323

*Division champion.
†Wild-card team.

NATIONAL CONFERENCE

EASTERN DIVISION

Team	W	L	T	Pct.	PF	PA
Dallas*	12	4	0	.750	414	248
N.Y. Giants	9	7	0	.563	279	305
Arizona	8	8	0	.500	235	267
Philadelphia	7	9	0	.438	308	308
Washington	3	13	0	.188	320	412

CENTRAL DIVISION

Team	W	L	T	Pct.	PF	PA
Minnesota*	10	6	0	.625	356	314
Green Bay†	9	7	0	.563	382	287
Detroit†	9	7	0	.563	357	342
Chicago†	9	7	0	.563	271	307
Tampa Bay	6	10	0	.375	251	351

WESTERN DIVISION

Team	W	L	T	Pct.	PF	PA
San Francisco*	13	3	0	.813	505	296
New Orleans	7	9	0	.438	348	407
Atlanta	7	9	0	.438	317	385
L.A. Rams	4	12	0	.250	286	365

PLAYOFFS

AFC wild-card playoffs
Miami 27 vs. Kansas City 17
Cleveland 20 vs. New England 13
AFC divisional playoffs
Pittsburgh 29 vs. Cleveland 9
San Diego 22 vs. Miami 21
AFC championship
San Diego 17 at Pittsburgh 13
NFC wild-card playoffs
Green Bay 16 vs. Detroit 12
Chicago 35 at Minnesota 18
NFC divisional playoffs
San Francisco 44 vs. Chicago 15
Dallas 35 vs. Green Bay 9
NFC championship
San Francisco 38 vs. Dallas 28
Super Bowl 29
San Francisco 49 vs. San Diego 26 at Miami.

MONTANA IN THE MIDWEST

Although he was unable to take the Chiefs to the same heights he did the San Francisco 49ers a decade earlier, Joe Montana closed out his illustrious career with two relatively productive, if injury-plagued, seasons in Kansas City. Montana, who never completely recovered from injuries suffered in the 1990 NFC title game against the Giants (broken right hand, bruised sternum) that forced him to miss the entire 1991 season and all but one game in '92, played only 38 of 64 quarters for the Chiefs in 1993. Nevertheless, he was the AFC's No. 2-rated quarterback and guided Kansas City to within one game of the Super Bowl. Using the old Montana magic, he spearheaded come-from-behind playoff victories over the Steelers and Oilers before the Chiefs finally succumbed, 30-13, at Buffalo in the AFC championship game.

AMERICAN CONFERENCE

EASTERN DIVISION

Team	W	L	T	Pct.	PF	PA
Buffalo*	10	6	0	.625	350	335
Indianapolis†	9	7	0	.563	331	316
Miami†	9	7	0	.563	398	332
New England	6	10	0	.375	294	377
N.Y. Jets	3	13	0	.188	233	384

CENTRAL DIVISION

Team	W	L	T	Pct.	PF	PA
Pittsburgh*	11	5	0	.689	407	327
Cincinnati	7	9	0	.438	349	374
Houston	7	9	0	.438	348	324
Cleveland	5	11	0	.313	289	356
Jacksonville	4	12	0	.250	275	404

WESTERN DIVISION

Team	W	L	T	Pct.	PF	PA
Kansas City*	13	3	0	.813	358	241
San Diego†	9	7	0	.563	321	323
Seattle	8	8	0	.500	363	366
Denver	8	8	0	.500	388	345
Oakland	8	8	0	.500	348	332

*Division champion.
†Wild-card team.

NATIONAL CONFERENCE

EASTERN DIVISION

Team	W	L	T	Pct.	PF	PA
Dallas*	12	4	0	.750	435	291
Philadelphia†	10	6	0	.625	318	338
Washington	6	10	0	.375	326	359
N.Y. Giants	5	11	0	.313	290	340
Arizona	4	12	0	.250	275	422

CENTRAL DIVISION

Team	W	L	T	Pct.	PF	PA
Green Bay*	11	5	0	.689	404	314
Detroit†	10	6	0	.625	436	336
Chicago	9	7	0	.563	392	360
Minnesota	8	8	0	.500	412	385
Tampa Bay	7	9	0	.438	238	335

WESTERN DIVISION

Team	W	L	T	Pct.	PF	PA
San Francisco*	11	5	0	.688	457	258
Atlanta†	9	7	0	.563	362	349
St. Louis	7	9	0	.438	309	418
Carolina	7	9	0	.438	289	325
New Orleans	7	9	0	.438	319	348

PLAYOFFS

AFC wild-card playoffs
Buffalo 37 vs. Miami 22
Indianapolis 35 at San Diego 20
AFC divisional playoffs
Pittsburgh 40 vs. Buffalo 21
Indianapolis 10 at Kansas City 7
AFC championship
Pittsburgh 20 vs. Indianapolis 16
NFC wild-card playoffs
Philadelphia 58 vs. Detroit 37
Green Bay 37 vs. Atlanta 20
NFC divisional playoffs
Green Bay 27 at San Francisco 17
Dallas 30 vs. Philadelphia 11
NFC championship
Dallas 38 vs. Green Bay 27
Super Bowl 30
Dallas 27 vs. Pittsburgh 17, at Tempe, Ariz.

AMERICAN CONFERENCE

EASTERN DIVISION

Team	W	L	T	Pct.	PF	PA
New England*	11	5	0	.687	418	313
Buffalo†	10	6	0	.625	319	266
Indianapolis†	9	7	0	.563	317	334
Miami	8	8	0	.500	339	325
N.Y. Jets	1	15	0	.063	279	454

CENTRAL DIVISION

Team	W	L	T	Pct.	PF	PA
Pittsburgh*	10	6	0	.625	344	257
Jacksonville†	9	7	0	.563	325	335
Cincinnati	8	8	0	.500	372	369
Houston	8	8	0	.500	345	319
Baltimore	4	12	0	.250	371	441

WESTERN DIVISION

Team	W	L	T	Pct.	PF	PA
Denver*	13	3	0	.813	391	275
Kansas City	9	7	0	.563	297	300
San Diego	8	8	0	.500	310	376
Oakland	7	9	0	.438	340	293
Seattle	7	9	0	.438	317	376

*Division champion.
†Wild-card team.

NATIONAL CONFERENCE

EASTERN DIVISION

Team	W	L	T	Pct.	PF	PA
Dallas*	10	6	0	.625	286	250
Philadelphia†	10	6	0	.625	363	341
Washington	9	7	0	.563	364	312
Arizona	7	9	0	.438	300	397
N.Y. Giants	6	10	0	.375	242	297

CENTRAL DIVISION

Team	W	L	T	Pct.	PF	PA
Green Bay*	13	3	0	.813	456	210
Minnesota†	9	7	0	.563	298	315
Chicago	7	9	0	.438	283	305
Tampa Bay	6	10	0	.375	221	293
Detroit	5	11	0	.313	302	368

WESTERN DIVISION

Team	W	L	T	Pct.	PF	PA
Carolina*	12	4	0	.750	367	218
San Francisco†	12	4	0	.750	398	257
St. Louis	6	10	0	.375	303	409
Atlanta	3	13	0	.188	309	461
New Orleans	3	13	0	.188	229	339

PLAYOFFS

AFC wild-card playoffs
Jacksonville 30 at Buffalo 27
Pittsburgh 42 vs. Indianapolis 14
AFC divisional playoffs
Jacksonville 30 at Denver 27
New England 28 vs. Pittsburgh 3
AFC championship
New England 20 vs. Jacksonville 6
NFC wild-card playoffs
Dallas 40 vs. Minnesota 15
San Francisco 14 vs. Philadelphia 0
NFC divisional playoffs
Green Bay 35 vs. San Francisco 14
Carolina 26 vs. Dallas 17
NFC championship
Green Bay 30 vs. Carolina 13
Super Bowl 31
Green Bay 35, New England 21, at New Orleans.

HISTORY *Year-by-year standings*

LOMBARDI WOULD BE PROUD

Six coaches and 29 years after last winning the Super Bowl, the Green Bay Packers were NFL champions again following a 35-21 victory over New England in Super Bowl 31. The title was not unexpected, despite the many years that had passed since the franchise's last title in Vince Lombardi's final season as coach. The Packers scored the most points of any team and allowed the fewest en route to finishing the 1996 regular season at 13-3. They had the league's best player in quarterback Brett Favre and arguably its best coach (Mike Holmgren) and best general manager (Ron Wolf). Just as important, the '96 Packers were a playoff-hardened team, having lost to Dallas in the NFC title game the previous year and been ousted in the second round in each of the two seasons before that.

1997

AMERICAN CONFERENCE

EASTERN DIVISION

Team	W	L	T	Pct.	PF	PA
New England*	10	6	0	.625	369	289
Miami†	9	7	0	.563	339	327
N.Y. Jets	9	7	0	.563	348	287
Buffalo	6	10	0	.375	255	367
Indianapolis	3	13	0	.188	313	401

CENTRAL DIVISION

Team	W	L	T	Pct.	PF	PA
Pittsburgh*	11	5	0	.688	372	307
Jacksonville†	11	5	0	.688	394	318
Tennessee	8	8	0	.500	333	310
Cincinnati	7	9	0	.438	355	405
Baltimore	6	9	1	.406	326	345

WESTERN DIVISION

Team	W	L	T	Pct.	PF	PA
Kansas City*	13	3	0	.813	375	232
Denver†	12	4	0	.750	472	287
Seattle	8	8	0	.500	365	362
Oakland	4	12	0	.250	324	419
San Diego	4	12	0	.250	266	425

*Division champion.
†Wild-card team.

NATIONAL CONFERENCE

EASTERN DIVISION

Team	W	L	T	Pct.	PF	PA
N.Y. Giants*	10	5	1	.656	307	265
Washington	8	7	1	.531	327	289
Philadelphia	6	9	1	.406	317	372
Dallas	6	10	0	.375	304	314
Arizona	4	12	0	.250	283	379

CENTRAL DIVISION

Team	W	L	T	Pct.	PF	PA
Green Bay*	13	3	0	.813	422	282
Tampa Bay†	10	6	0	.625	299	263
Detroit†	9	7	0	.563	379	306
Minnesota†	9	7	0	.563	354	359
Chicago	4	12	0	.250	263	421

WESTERN DIVISION

Team	W	L	T	Pct.	PF	PA
San Francisco*	13	3	0	.813	375	265
Carolina	7	9	0	.438	265	314
Atlanta	7	9	0	.438	320	361
New Orleans	6	10	0	.375	237	327
St. Louis	5	11	0	.313	299	359

PLAYOFFS

AFC wild-card playoffs
Denver 42 vs. Jacksonville 17
New England 17 vs. Miami 3
AFC divisional playoffs
Pittsburgh 7 vs. New England 6
Denver 14 at Kansas City 10
AFC championship
Denver 24 at Pittsburgh 21
NFC wild-card playoffs
Minnesota 23 at N.Y. Giants 22
Tampa Bay 20 vs. Detroit 10
NFC divisional playoffs
San Francisco 38 vs. Minnesota 22
Green Bay 21 vs. Tampa Bay 7
NFC championship
Green Bay 23 at San Francisco 10
Super Bowl 32
Denver 31 vs. Green Bay 24, at San Diego.

1998

AMERICAN CONFERENCE

EASTERN DIVISION

Team	W	L	T	Pct.	PF	PA
N.Y. Jets*	12	4	0	.750	416	266
Miami†	10	6	0	.625	321	265
Buffalo†	10	6	0	.625	400	333
New England†	9	7	0	.563	337	329
Indianapolis	3	13	0	.188	310	444

CENTRAL DIVISION

Team	W	L	T	Pct.	PF	PA
Jacksonville*	11	5	0	.688	392	338
Tennessee	8	8	0	.500	330	320
Pittsburgh	7	9	0	.438	263	303
Baltimore	6	10	0	.375	269	335
Cincinnati	3	13	0	.188	268	452

WESTERN DIVISION

Team	W	L	T	Pct.	PF	PA
Denver*	14	2	0	.875	501	309
Oakland	8	8	0	.500	288	356
Seattle	8	8	0	.500	372	310
Kansas City	7	9	0	.438	327	363
San Diego	5	11	0	.313	241	342

*Division champion.
†Wild-card team.

NATIONAL CONFERENCE

EASTERN DIVISION

Team	W	L	T	Pct.	PF	PA
Dallas*	10	6	0	.625	381	275
Arizona†	9	7	0	.563	325	378
N.Y. Giants	8	8	0	.500	287	309
Washington	6	10	0	.375	319	421
Philadelphia	3	13	0	.188	161	344

CENTRAL DIVISION

Team	W	L	T	Pct.	PF	PA
Minnesota*	15	1	0	.938	556	296
Green Bay†	11	5	0	.688	408	319
Tampa Bay	8	8	0	.500	314	295
Detroit	5	11	0	.313	306	378
Chicago	4	12	0	.250	276	368

WESTERN DIVISION

Team	W	L	T	Pct.	PF	PA
Atlanta*	14	2	0	.875	442	289
San Francisco†	12	4	0	.750	479	328
New Orleans	6	10	0	.375	305	359
Carolina	4	12	0	.250	336	413
St. Louis	4	12	0	.250	285	378

PLAYOFFS

AFC wild-card playoffs
Miami 24 vs. Buffalo 17
Jacksonville 25 vs. New England 10
AFC divisional playoffs
Denver 38 vs. Miami 3
New York Jets 34 vs. Jacksonville 24
AFC championship
Denver 23 vs. New York Jets 10
NFC wild-card playoffs
Arizona 20 at Dallas 7
San Francisco 30 vs. Green Bay 27
NFC divisional playoffs
Atlanta 20 vs. San Francisco 18
Minnesota 41 vs. Arizona 21
NFC championship
Atlanta 30 at Minnesota 27 (OT)
Super Bowl 33
Denver 34 vs. Atlanta 19, at Miami.

ELWAY, BRONCOS REACH THE TOP

One year after a humbling first-round loss at home to Jacksonville in the 1996 playoffs, the Denver Broncos made sure history did not repeat, whipping the Jaguars, 42-17, in a first-round rematch at Mile High Stadium. That was impressive, but what happened next was more impressive: two straight road playoff victories and the franchise's first-ever Super Bowl title. Prior to the three-game winning streak, the Broncos had won just one other road playoff game in their 37-year history. Although running back Terrell Davis was the Broncos' star and won Super Bowl 32 MVP honors, their leader was veteran quarterback John Elway, who finally scaled the NFL mountaintop after three crushing Super Bowl defeats earlier in his career. Denver thus became the first AFC team in 14 years and only the second wild-card team to win the Super Bowl.

AMERICAN CONFERENCE

EASTERN DIVISION

Team	W	L	T	Pct.	PF	PA
Indianapolis*	13	3	0	.813	423	333
Buffalo†	11	5	0	.688	320	229
Miami†	9	7	0	.563	326	336
N.Y. Jets	8	8	0	.500	308	309
New England	8	8	0	.500	299	284

CENTRAL DIVISION

Team	W	L	T	Pct.	PF	PA
Jacksonville*	14	2	0	.875	396	217
Tennessee†	13	3	0	.813	392	324
Baltimore	8	8	0	.500	324	277
Pittsburgh	6	10	0	.375	317	320
Cincinnati	4	12	0	.250	283	460
Cleveland	2	14	0	.125	217	437

WESTERN DIVISION

Team	W	L	T	Pct.	PF	PA
Seattle*	9	7	0	.563	338	298
Kansas City	9	7	0	.563	390	322
San Diego	8	8	0	.500	269	316
Oakland	8	8	0	.500	390	329
Denver	6	10	0	.375	314	318

*Division champion.
†Wild-card team.

NATIONAL CONFERENCE

EASTERN DIVISION

Team	W	L	T	Pct.	PF	PA
Washington*	10	6	0	.625	443	377
Dallas†	8	8	0	.500	352	276
N.Y. Giants	7	9	0	.438	299	358
Arizona	6	10	0	.375	245	382
Philadelphia	5	11	0	.313	272	357

CENTRAL DIVISION

Team	W	L	T	Pct.	PF	PA
Tampa Bay*	11	5	0	.688	270	235
Minnesota†	10	6	0	.625	399	335
Detroit†	8	8	0	.500	322	323
Green Bay	8	8	0	.500	357	341
Chicago	6	10	0	.375	272	341

WESTERN DIVISION

Team	W	L	T	Pct.	PF	PA
St. Louis*	13	3	0	.813	526	242
Carolina	8	8	0	.500	421	381
Atlanta	5	11	0	.313	285	380
San Francisco	4	12	0	.250	295	453
New Orleans	3	13	0	.188	260	434

PLAYOFFS

AFC wild-card playoffs
Miami 20 at Seattle 17
Tennessee 22 vs. Buffalo 16
AFC divisional playoffs
Tennessee 19 at Indianapolis 16
Jacksonville 62 vs. Miami 7
AFC championship
Tennessee 33 at Jacksonville 14
NFC wild-card playoffs
Minnesota 27 vs. Dallas 10
Washington 27 vs. Detroit 13
NFC divisional playoffs
St. Louis 49 vs. Minnesota 37
Tampa Bay 14 vs. Washington 13
NFC championship
St. Louis 11 vs. Tampa Bay 6
Super Bowl 34
St. Louis 23 vs. Tennessee 16, at Atlanta.

AMERICAN CONFERENCE

EASTERN DIVISION

Team	W	L	T	Pct.	PF	PA
Miami*	11	5	0	.688	323	226
Indianapolis†	10	6	0	.625	429	326
N.Y. Jets	9	7	0	.563	321	321
Buffalo	8	8	0	.500	315	350
New England	5	11	0	.313	276	338

CENTRAL DIVISION

Team	W	L	T	Pct.	PF	PA
Tennessee*	13	3	0	.813	346	191
Baltimore†	12	4	0	.750	333	165
Pittsburgh	9	7	0	.563	321	255
Jacksonville	7	9	0	.438	367	327
Cincinnati	4	12	0	.250	185	359
Cleveland	3	13	0	.188	161	419

WESTERN DIVISION

Team	W	L	T	Pct.	PF	PA
Oakland*	12	4	0	.750	479	299
Denver†	11	5	0	.688	485	369
Kansas City	7	9	0	.438	355	354
Seattle	6	10	0	.375	320	405
San Diego	1	15	0	.063	269	440

*Division champion.
†Wild-card team.

NATIONAL CONFERENCE

EASTERN DIVISION

Team	W	L	T	Pct.	PF	PA
N.Y. Giants*	12	4	0	.750	328	246
Philadelphia†	11	5	0	.688	351	245
Washington	8	8	0	.500	281	269
Dallas	5	11	0	.313	294	361
Arizona	3	13	0	.188	210	443

CENTRAL DIVISION

Team	W	L	T	Pct.	PF	PA
Minnesota*	11	5	0	.688	397	371
Tampa Bay†	10	6	0	.625	388	269
Green Bay	9	7	0	.563	353	323
Detroit	9	7	0	.563	307	307
Chicago	5	11	0	.313	216	355

WESTERN DIVISION

Team	W	L	T	Pct.	PF	PA
New Orleans*	10	6	0	.625	354	305
St. Louis†	10	6	0	.625	540	471
Carolina	7	9	0	.438	310	310
San Francisco	6	10	0	.375	388	422
Atlanta	4	12	0	.250	252	413

PLAYOFFS

AFC wild-card playoffs
Miami 23 vs. Indianapolis 17 (OT)
Baltimore 21 vs. Denver 3
AFC divisional playoffs
Oakland 27 vs. Miami 0
Baltimore 24 at Tennessee 10
AFC championship
Baltimore 16 at Oakland 3
NFC wild-card playoffs
New Orleans 31 vs. St. Louis 28
Philadelphia 21 vs. Tampa Bay 3
NFC divisional playoffs
Minnesota 34 vs. New Orleans 16
N.Y. Giants 20 vs. Philadelphia 10
NFC championship
N.Y. Giants 41 vs. Minnesota 0
Super Bowl 35
Baltimore 34 vs. N.Y. Giants 7, at Tampa.

HISTORY Year-by-year standings

RAMS, RAVENS MAKE DRAMATIC TURNAROUNDS

The ability of teams to turn around their fortunes seemingly overnight was never more evident than during the 1999 and 2000 seasons. The St. Louis Rams, 4-12 in 1998, and the Baltimore Ravens, 8-8 in 1999, rebounded to win Super Bowls the following seasons. The turnaround of the Rams was truly astonishing. In danger of finishing with the NFL's worst record of the 1990s, the Rams—45-99 from 1990 through '98—scored a league-high 526 points (third most in NFL history and 241 more than they had the year before) and won 16 games (including playoffs) by an average score of 33-13. The Ravens, meanwhile, used defense to win their first league championship. Baltimore allowed just 165 points—fewest ever in a 16-game season—en route to becoming the third wild-card team to win the Super Bowl.

AMERICAN CONFERENCE

EASTERN DIVISION

Team	W	L	T	Pct.	PF	PA
New England*	11	5	0	.688	371	272
Miami†	11	5	0	.688	344	290
N.Y. Jets†	10	6	0	.625	308	295
Indianapolis	6	10	0	.375	413	486
Buffalo	3	13	0	.188	265	420

CENTRAL DIVISION

Team	W	L	T	Pct.	PF	PA
Pittsburgh*	13	3	0	.812	352	212
Baltimore†	10	6	0	.625	303	265
Cleveland	7	9	0	.438	285	319
Tennessee	7	9	0	.438	336	388
Jacksonville	6	10	0	.375	294	286
Cincinnati	6	10	0	.375	226	309

WESTERN DIVISION

Team	W	L	T	Pct.	PF	PA
Oakland*	10	6	0	.625	399	327
Seattle	9	7	0	.562	301	324
Denver	8	8	0	.500	340	339
Kansas City	6	10	0	.375	320	344
San Diego	5	11	0	.312	332	321

*Division champion.
†Wild-card team.

NATIONAL CONFERENCE

EASTERN DIVISION

Team	W	L	T	Pct.	PF	PA
Philadelphia*	11	5	0	.688	343	208
Washington	8	8	0	.500	256	303
N.Y. Giants	7	9	0	.438	294	321
Arizona	7	9	0	.438	295	343
Dallas	5	11	0	.312	246	338

CENTRAL DIVISION

Team	W	L	T	Pct.	PF	PA
Chicago*	13	3	0	.812	338	203
Green Bay†	12	4	0	.750	390	266
Tampa Bay†	9	7	0	.562	324	280
Minnesota	5	11	0	.312	290	390
Detroit	2	14	0	.125	270	424

WESTERN DIVISION

Team	W	L	T	Pct.	PF	PA
St. Louis*	14	2	0	.875	503	273
San Francisco†	12	4	0	.750	409	282
New Orleans	7	9	0	.438	333	409
Atlanta	7	9	0	.438	291	377
Carolina	1	15	0	.062	253	410

PLAYOFFS

AFC wild-card playoffs
Oakland 38 vs. N.Y. Jets 24
Baltimore 20 at Miami 3
AFC divisional playoffs
New England 16 vs. Oakland 13 (OT)
Pittsburgh 27 vs. Baltimore 10
AFC championship
New England 24 at Pittsburgh 17
NFC wild-card playoffs
Philadelphia 31 vs. Tampa Bay 9
Green Bay 25 vs. San Francisco 15
NFC divisional playoffs
Philadelphia 33 at Chicago 19
St. Louis 45 vs. Green Bay 17
NFC championship
St. Louis 29 vs. Philadelphia 24
Super Bowl 36
New England 20 vs. St. Louis 17, at New Orleans

AMERICAN CONFERENCE

EAST DIVISION

Team	W	L	T	Pct.	PF	PA
N.Y. Jets*	9	7	0	.563	359	336
New England	9	7	0	.563	381	346
Miami	9	7	0	.563	378	301
Buffalo	8	8	0	.500	379	397

NORTH DIVISION

Team	W	L	T	Pct.	PF	PA
Pittsburgh*	10	5	1	.656	390	345
Cleveland†	9	7	0	.563	344	320
Baltimore	7	9	0	.438	316	354
Cincinnati	2	14	0	.125	279	456

SOUTH DIVISION

Team	W	L	T	Pct.	PF	PA
Tennessee*	11	5	0	.688	367	324
Indianapolis†	10	6	0	.625	349	313
Jacksonville	6	10	0	.375	328	315
Houston	4	12	0	.250	213	356

WEST DIVISION

Team	W	L	T	Pct.	PF	PA
Oakland*	11	5	0	.688	450	304
Denver	9	7	0	.563	392	344
San Diego	8	8	0	.500	333	367
Kansas City	8	8	0	.500	467	399

*Division champion.
†Wild-card team.

NATIONAL CONFERENCE

EAST DIVISION

Team	W	L	T	Pct.	PF	PA
Philadelphia*	12	4	0	.750	415	241
N.Y. Giants†	10	6	0	.625	320	279
Washington	7	9	0	.438	307	365
Dallas	5	11	0	.313	217	329

NORTH DIVISION

Team	W	L	T	Pct.	PF	PA
Green Bay*	12	4	0	.750	398	328
Minnesota	6	10	0	.375	390	442
Chicago	4	12	0	.250	281	379
Detroit	3	13	0	.188	306	451

SOUTH DIVISION

Team	W	L	T	Pct.	PF	PA
Tampa Bay*	12	4	0	.750	346	196
Atlanta†	9	6	1	.594	402	314
New Orleans	9	7	0	.563	432	388
Carolina	7	9	0	.438	258	302

WEST DIVISION

Team	W	L	T	Pct.	PF	PA
San Francisco*	10	6	0	.625	367	351
St. Louis	7	9	0	.438	316	369
Seattle	7	9	0	.438	355	369
Arizona	5	11	0	.313	262	417

PLAYOFFS

AFC wild-card playoffs
N.Y. Jets 41 vs. Indianapolis 0
Pittsburgh 36 vs. Cleveland 33
AFC divisional playoffs
Tennessee 34 vs. Pittsburgh 31 (OT)
Oakland 30 vs. N.Y. Jets 10
AFC championship
Oakland 41 vs. Tennessee 24
NFC wild-card playoffs
Atlanta 27 at Green Bay 7
San Francisco 39 vs. N.Y. Giants 38
NFC divisional playoffs
Philadelphia 20 vs. Atlanta 6
Tampa Bay 31 vs. San Francisco 6
NFC championship
Tampa Bay 27 at Philadelphia 10
Super Bowl 37
Tampa Bay 48 vs. Oakland 21, at San Diego.

THIS ONE WAS TRULY SUPER

The terrorist attacks of September 11, 2001, forced the NFL to move its Week 2 games scheduled for September 16-17 to the end of the regular season, resulting in the first February Super Bowl in league history. And what a Super Bowl it was, as the New England Patriots beat the heavily favored St. Louis Rams, 20-17, on a 48-yard field goal by Adam Vinatieri as time expired. Vinatieri's kick capped a nine-play, 53-yard drive engineered by quarterback Tom Brady (who completed five passes on the march) without the benefit of a timeout after the Rams had scored two touchdowns in final 10 minutes to tie the game at 17-17. At 24 years and 184 days old, Brady became the youngest quarterback to win a Super Bowl and the third-youngest player (after Marcus Allen and Lynn Swann) to be named the game's most valuable player.

AMERICAN CONFERENCE

EAST DIVISION

Team	W	L	T	Pct.	PF	PA
New England*	14	2	0	.875	348	238
Miami	10	6	0	.625	311	261
Buffalo	6	10	0	.375	243	279
N.Y. Jets	6	10	0	.375	283	299

NORTH DIVISION

Team	W	L	T	Pct.	PF	PA
Baltimore*	10	6	0	.625	391	281
Cincinnati	8	8	0	.500	346	384
Pittsburgh	6	10	0	.375	300	327
Cleveland	5	11	0	.313	254	322

SOUTH DIVISION

Team	W	L	T	Pct.	PF	PA
Indianapolis*	12	4	0	.750	447	336
Tennessee†	12	4	0	.750	435	324
Jacksonville	5	11	0	.313	276	331
Houston	5	11	0	.313	255	380

WEST DIVISION

Team	W	L	T	Pct.	PF	PA
Kansas City*	13	3	0	.813	484	332
Denver†	10	6	0	.625	381	301
Oakland	4	12	0	.250	270	379
San Diego	4	12	0	.250	313	

*Division champion.
†Wild-card team.

NATIONAL CONFERENCE

EAST DIVISION

Team	W	L	T	Pct.	PF	PA
Philadelphia*	12	4	0	.750	374	287
Dallas†	10	6	0	.625	289	260
Washington	5	11	0	.313	287	372
N.Y. Giants	4	12	0	.250	243	387

NORTH DIVISION

Team	W	L	T	Pct.	PF	PA
Green Bay*	10	6	0	.625	442	307
Minnesota	9	7	0	.563	416	353
Chicago	7	9	0	.438	283	346
Detroit	5	11	0	.313	270	379

SOUTH DIVISION

Team	W	L	T	Pct.	PF	PA
Carolina*	11	5	0	.688	325	304
New Orleans	8	8	0	.500	340	326
Tampa Bay	7	9	0	.438	301	264
Atlanta	5	11	0	.313	299	422

WEST DIVISION

Team	W	L	T	Pct.	PF	PA
St. Louis*	12	4	0	.750	447	328
Seattle†	10	6	0	.625	404	327
San Francisco	7	9	0	.438	384	337
Arizona	4	12	0	.250	225	452

PLAYOFFS

AFC wild-card playoffs
Tennessee 20 at Baltimore 17
Indianapolis 41 vs. Denver 10
AFC divisional playoffs
New England 17 vs. Tennessee 14
Indianapolis 38 at Kansas City 31
AFC championship
New England 24 vs. Indianapolis 14
NFC wild-card playoffs
Carolina 29 vs. Dallas 10
Green Bay 33 vs. Seattle 27 (OT)
NFC divisional playoffs
Carolina 29 at St. Louis 23 (OT)
Philadelphia 20 vs. Green Bay 17 (OT)
NFC championship
Carolina 14 at Philadelphia 3
Super Bowl 38
New England 32, Carolina 29, at Houston.

SUPER BOWLS

SUMMARIES

SUPER BOWL 1

JANUARY 15, 1967, AT LOS ANGELES

Kansas City (AFL)	0	10	0	0 — 10
Green Bay (NFL)	7	7	14	7 — 35

Winning coach—Vince Lombardi.
Most Valuable Player—Bart Starr.
Attendance—61,946.

SUPER BOWL 2

JANUARY 14, 1968, AT MIAMI

Green Bay (NFL)	3	13	10	7 — 33
Oakland (AFL)	0	7	0	7 — 14

Winning coach—Vince Lombardi.
Most Valuable Player—Bart Starr.
Attendance—75,546.

SUPER BOWL 3

JANUARY 12, 1969, AT MIAMI

New York (AFL)	0	7	6	3 — 16
Baltimore (NFL)	0	0	0	7 — 7

Winning coach—Weeb Ewbank.
Most Valuable Player—Joe Namath.
Attendance—75,389.

SUPER BOWL 4

JANUARY 11, 1970, AT NEW ORLEANS

Minnesota (NFL)	0	0	7	0 — 7
Kansas City (AFL)	3	13	7	0 — 23

Winning coach—Hank Stram.
Most Valuable Player—Len Dawson.
Attendance—80,562.

SUPER BOWL 5

JANUARY 17, 1971, AT MIAMI

Baltimore (AFC)	0	6	0	10 — 16
Dallas (NFC)	3	10	0	0 — 13

Winning coach—Don McCafferty.
Most Valuable Player—Chuck Howley.
Attendance—79,204.

SUPER BOWL 6

JANUARY 16, 1972, AT NEW ORLEANS

Dallas (NFC)	3	7	7	7 — 24
Miami (AFC)	0	3	0	0 — 3

Winning coach—Tom Landry.
Most Valuable Player—Roger Staubach.
Attendance—81,023.

SUPER BOWL 7

JANUARY 14, 1973, AT LOS ANGELES

Miami (AFC)	7	7	0	0 — 14
Washington (NFC)	0	0	0	7 — 7

Winning coach—Don Shula.
Most Valuable Player—Jake Scott.
Attendance—90,182.

SUPER BOWL 8

JANUARY 13, 1974, AT HOUSTON

Minnesota (NFC)	0	0	0	7 — 7
Miami (AFC)	14	3	7	0 — 24

Winning coach—Don Shula.
Most Valuable Player—Larry Csonka.
Attendance—71,882.

SUPER BOWL 9

JANUARY 12, 1975, AT NEW ORLEANS

Pittsburgh (AFC)	0	2	7	7 — 16
Minnesota (NFC)	0	0	0	6 — 6

Winning coach—Chuck Noll.
Most Valuable Player—Franco Harris.
Attendance—80,997.

SUPER BOWL 10

JANUARY 18, 1976, AT MIAMI

Dallas (NFC)	7	3	0	7 — 17
Pittsburgh (AFC)	7	0	0	14 — 21

Winning coach—Chuck Noll.
Most Valuable Player—Lynn Swann.
Attendance—80,187.

SUPER BOWL 11

JANUARY 9, 1977, AT PASADENA, CALIF.

Oakland (AFC)	0	16	3	13 — 32
Minnesota (NFC)	0	0	7	7 — 14

Winning coach—John Madden.
Most Valuable Player—Fred Biletnikoff.
Attendance—103,438.

SUPER BOWL 12

JANUARY 15, 1978, AT NEW ORLEANS

Dallas (NFC)	10	3	7	7 — 27
Denver (AFC)	0	0	10	0 — 10

Winning coach—Tom Landry.
Most Valuable Players—Harvey Martin and Randy White.
Attendance—75,583.

SUPER BOWL 13

JANUARY 21, 1979, AT MIAMI

Pittsburgh (AFC)	7	14	0	14 — 35
Dallas (NFC)	7	7	3	14 — 31

Winning coach—Chuck Noll.
Most Valuable Player—Terry Bradshaw.
Attendance—79,484.

SUPER BOWL 14

JANUARY 20, 1980, PASADENA, CALIF.

Los Angeles (NFC)	7	6	6	0 — 19
Pittsburgh (AFC)	3	7	7	14 — 31

Winning coach—Chuck Noll.
Most Valuable Player—Terry Bradshaw.
Attendance—103,985.

SUPER BOWL 15

JANUARY 25, 1981, AT NEW ORLEANS

Oakland (AFC)	14	0	10	3 — 27
Philadelphia (NFC)	0	3	0	7 — 10

Winning coach—Tom Flores.
Most Valuable Player—Jim Plunkett.
Attendance—76,135.

SUPER BOWL 16

JANUARY 24, 1982, AT PONTIAC, MICH.

San Francisco (NFC)	7	13	0	6 — 26
Cincinnati (AFC)	0	0	7	14 — 21

Winning coach—Bill Walsh.
Most Valuable Player—Joe Montana.
Attendance—81,270.

SUPER BOWL 17

JANUARY 30, 1983, AT PASADENA, CALIF.

Miami (AFC)	7	10	0	0 — 17
Washington (NFC)	0	10	3	14 — 27

Winning coach—Joe Gibbs.
Most Valuable Player—John Riggins.
Attendance—103,667.

SUPER BOWL 18

JANUARY 22, 1984, AT TAMPA

Washington (NFC)	0	3	6	0 — 9
Los Angeles (AFC)	7	14	14	3 — 38

Winning coach—Tom Flores.
Most Valuable Player—Marcus Allen.
Attendance—72,920.

SUPER BOWL 19

JANUARY 20, 1985, AT STANFORD, CALIF.

Miami (AFC)	10	6	0	0 — 16
San Francisco (NFC)	7	21	10	0 — 38

Winning coach—Bill Walsh.
Most Valuable Player—Joe Montana.
Attendance—84,059.

SUPER BOWL 20

JANUARY 26, 1986, AT NEW ORLEANS

Chicago (NFC)	13	10	21	2 — 46
New England (AFC)	3	0	0	7 — 10

Winning coach—MIke Ditka.
Most Valuable Player—Richard Dent.
Attendance—73,818.

SUPER BOWL 21

JANUARY 25, 1987, AT PASADENA, CALIF.

Denver (AFC)	10	0	0	10 — 20
N.Y. Giants (NFC)	7	2	17	13 — 39

Winning coach—Bill Parcells.
Most Valuable Player—Phil Simms.
Attendance—101,063.

SUPER BOWL 22

JANUARY 31, 1988, AT SAN DIEGO

Washington (NFC)	0	35	0	7 — 42
Denver (AFC)	10	0	0	0 — 10

Winning coach—Joe Gibbs.
Most Valuable Player—Doug Williams.
Attendance—73,302.

SUPER BOWL 23

JANUARY 22, 1989, AT MIAMI

Cincinnati (AFC)	0	3	10	3 — 16
San Francisco (NFC)	3	0	3	14 — 20

Winning coach—Bill Walsh.
Most Valuable Player—Jerry Rice.
Attendance—75,179.

SUPER BOWL 24

JANUARY 28, 1990, AT NEW ORLEANS

San Francisco (NFC)	13	14	14	14 — 55
Denver (AFC)	3	0	7	0 — 10

Winning coach—George Seifert.
Most Valuable Player—Joe Montana.
Attendance—72,919.

SUPER BOWL 25

JANUARY 27, 1991, AT TAMPA

Buffalo (AFC)	3	9	0	7 — 19
New York (NFC)	3	7	7	3 — 20

Winning coach—Bill Parcells.
Most Valuable Player—Ottis Anderson.
Attendance—73,813.

SUPER BOWL 26

JANUARY 26, 1992, AT MINNEAPOLIS

Washington (NFC)	0	17	14	6 — 37
Buffalo (AFC)	0	0	10	14 — 24

Winning coach—Joe Gibbs.
Most Valuable Player—Mark Rypien.
Attendance—63,130.

SUPER BOWL 27

JANUARY 31, 1993, AT PASADENA, CALIF.

Buffalo (AFC)	7	3	7	0 — 17
Dallas (NFC)	14	14	3	21 — 52

Winning coach—Jimmy Johnson.
Most Valuable Player—Troy Aikman.
Attendance—98,374.

SUPER BOWL 28

JANUARY 30, 1994, AT ATLANTA

Dallas (NFC)	6	0	14	10 — 30
Buffalo (AFC)	3	10	0	0 — 13

Winning coach—Jimmy Johnson.
Most Valuable Player—Emmitt Smith.
Attendance—72,817.

SUPER BOWL 29

JANUARY 29, 1995, AT MIAMI

San Diego (AFC)	7	3	8	8 — 26
San Francisco (NFC)	14	14	14	7 — 49

Winning coach—George Seifert.
Most Valuable Player—Steve Young.
Attendance—74,107.

SUPER BOWL 30

JANUARY 28, 1996, AT TEMPE, ARIZ.

Dallas (NFC)	10	3	7	7 — 27
Pittsburgh (AFC)	0	7	0	10 — 17

Winning coach—Barry Switzer.
Most Valuable Player—Larry Brown.
Attendance—76,347.

SUPER BOWL 31

JANUARY 26, 1997, AT NEW ORLEANS

New England (AFC)	14	0	7	0 — 21
Green Bay (NFC)	10	17	8	0 — 35

Winning coach—Mike Holmgren.
Most Valuable Player—Desmond Howard.
Attendance—72,301.

SUPER BOWL 32

JANUARY 25, 1998, AT SAN DIEGO

Green Bay (NFC)	7	7	3	7 — 24
Denver (AFC)	7	10	7	7 — 31

Winning coach—Mike Shanahan.
Most Valuable Player—Terrell Davis.
Attendance—68,912.

SUPER BOWL 33

JANUARY 31, 1999, AT MIAMI

Denver (AFC)	7	10	0	17 — 34
Atlanta (NFC)	3	3	0	13 — 19

Winning coach—Mike Shanahan.
Most Valuable Player—John Elway.
Attendance—74,803.

SUPER BOWL 34

JANUARY 30, 2000, AT ATLANTA

St. Louis (NFC)	3	6	7	7 — 23
Tennessee (AFC)	0	0	6	10 — 16

Winning coach—Dick Vermeil.
Most Valuable Player—Kurt Warner.
Attendance—72,625.

SUPER BOWL 35

JANUARY 28, 2001, AT TAMPA

Baltimore (AFC)	7	3	14	10 — 34
N.Y. Giants (NFC)	0	0	7	0 — 7

Winning coach—Brian Billick.
Most Valuable Player—Ray Lewis.
Attendance—71,921.

SUPER BOWL 36

FEBRUARY 3, 2002, AT NEW ORLEANS

St. Louis (NFC)	3	0	0	14 — 17
New England (AFC)	0	14	3	3 — 20

Winning coach—Bill Belichick.
Most Valuable Player—Tom Brady.
Attendance—72,922.

SUPER BOWL 37

JANUARY 26, 2003, AT SAN DIEGO

Oakland (AFC)	3	0	6	12 — 21
Tampa Bay (NFC)	3	17	14	14 — 48

Winning coach—Jon Gruden.
Most Valuable Player—Dexter Jackson.
Attendance—67,603.

SUPER BOWL 38

FEBRUARY 1, 2004, AT HOUSTON

Carolina (NFC)	0	10	0	19 — 29
New England (AFC)	0	14	0	18 — 32

Winning coach—Bill Belichick.
Most Valuable Player—Tom Brady.
Attendance—71,525.

SUPER BOWL 39

FEBRUARY 6, 2005, AT JACKSONVILLE

New England (AFC)	0	7	7	10 — 24
Philadelphia Eagles (NFC)	0	7	7	7 — 21

Winning coach—Bill Belichick.
Most Valuable Player—Deion Branch.
Attendance—78,125.

PRO BOWLS

RESULTS

Date	Site	Winning team, score	Losing team, score	Att.
1-15-39	Wrigley Field, Los Angeles	New York Giants, 13	Pro All-Stars, 10	†20,000
1-14-40	Gilmore Stadium, Los Angeles	Green Bay Packers, 16	NFL All-Stars, 7	†18,000
12-29-40	Gilmore Stadium, Los Angeles	Chicago Bears, 28	NFL All-Stars, 14	21,624
1-4-42	Polo Grounds, New York	Chicago Bears, 35	NFL All-Stars, 24	17,725
12-27-42	Shibe Park, Philadelphia	NFL All-Stars, 17	Washington Redskins, 14	18,671
1943-50	No game was played.			
1-14-51	Los Angeles Memorial Coliseum	American Conference, 28	National Conference, 27	53,676
1-12-52	Los Angeles Memorial Coliseum	National Conference, 30	American Conference, 13	19,400
1-10-53	Los Angeles Memorial Coliseum	National Conference, 27	American Conference, 7	34,208
1-17-54	Los Angeles Memorial Coliseum	East, 20	West, 9	44,214
1-16-55	Los Angeles Memorial Coliseum	West, 26	East, 19	43,972
1-15-56	Los Angeles Memorial Coliseum	East, 31	West, 30	37,867
1-13-57	Los Angeles Memorial Coliseum	West, 19	East, 10	44,177
1-12-58	Los Angeles Memorial Coliseum	West, 26	East, 7	66,634
1-11-59	Los Angeles Memorial Coliseum	East, 28	West, 21	72,250
1-17-60	Los Angeles Memorial Coliseum	West, 38	East, 21	56,876
1-15-61	Los Angeles Memorial Coliseum	West, 35	East, 31	62,971
1-7-62*	Balboa Stadium, San Diego	West, 47	East, 27	20,973
1-14-62	Los Angeles Memorial Coliseum	West, 31	East, 30	57,409
1-13-63*	Balboa Stadium, San Diego	West, 21	East, 14	27,641
1-13-63	Los Angeles Memorial Coliseum	East, 30	West, 20	61,374
1-12-64	Los Angeles Memorial Coliseum	West, 31	East, 17	67,242
1-19-64*	Balboa Stadium, San Diego	West, 27	East, 24	20,016
1-10-65	Los Angeles Memorial Coliseum	West, 34	East, 14	60,598
1-16-65*	Jeppesen Stadium, Houston	West, 38	East, 14	15,446
1-15-66*	Rice Stadium, Houston	AFL All-Stars, 30	Buffalo Bills, 19	35,572
1-15-66	Los Angeles Memorial Coliseum	East, 36	West, 7	60,124
1-21-67*	Oakland-Alameda County Coliseum	East, 30	West, 23	18,876
1-22-67	Los Angeles Memorial Coliseum	East, 20	West, 10	15,062
1-21-68*	Gator Bowl, Jacksonville, Fla.	East, 25	West, 24	40,103
1-21-68	Los Angeles Memorial Coliseum	West, 38	East, 20	53,289
1-19-69*	Gator Bowl, Jacksonville, Fla.	West, 38	East, 25	41,058
1-19-69	Los Angeles Memorial Coliseum	West, 10	East, 7	32,050
1-17-70*	Astrodome, Houston	West, 26	East, 3	30,170
1-18-70	Los Angeles Memorial Coliseum	West, 16	East, 13	57,786
1-24-71	Los Angeles Memorial Coliseum	NFC, 27	AFC, 6	48,222
1-23-72	Los Angeles Memorial Coliseum	AFC, 26	NFC, 13	53,647
1-21-73	Texas Stadium, Irving	AFC, 33	NFC, 28	37,091
1-20-74	Arrowhead Stadium, Kansas City	AFC, 15	NFC, 13	66,918

Date	Site	Winning team, score	Losing team, score	Att.
1-20-75	Orange Bowl, Miami	NFC, 17	AFC, 10	26,484
1-26-76	Louisiana Superdome, New Orleans	NFC, 23	AFC, 20	30,546
1-17-77	Kingdome, Seattle	AFC, 24	NFC, 14	64,752
1-23-78	Tampa Stadium	NFC, 14	AFC, 13	51,337
1-29-79	Los Angeles Memorial Coliseum	NFC, 13	AFC, 7	46,281
1-27-80	Aloha Stadium, Honolulu	NFC, 37	AFC, 27	49,800
2-1-81	Aloha Stadium, Honolulu	NFC, 21	AFC, 7	50,360
1-31-82	Aloha Stadium, Honolulu	AFC, 16	NFC, 13	50,402
2-6-83	Aloha Stadium, Honolulu	NFC, 20	AFC, 19	49,883
1-29-84	Aloha Stadium, Honolulu	NFC, 45	AFC, 3	50,445
1-27-85	Aloha Stadium, Honolulu	AFC, 22	NFC, 14	50,385
2-2-86	Aloha Stadium, Honolulu	NFC, 28	AFC, 24	50,101
2-1-87	Aloha Stadium, Honolulu	AFC, 10	NFC, 6	50,101
2-7-88	Aloha Stadium, Honolulu	AFC, 15	NFC, 6	50,113
1-29-89	Aloha Stadium, Honolulu	NFC, 34	AFC, 3	50,113
2-4-90	Aloha Stadium, Honolulu	NFC, 27	AFC, 21	50,445
2-3-91	Aloha Stadium, Honolulu	AFC, 23	NFC, 21	50,345
2-2-92	Aloha Stadium, Honolulu	NFC, 21	AFC, 15	50,209
2-7-93	Aloha Stadium, Honolulu	AFC, 23 (OT)	NFC, 20	50,007
2-6-94	Aloha Stadium, Honolulu	NFC, 17	AFC, 3	50,026
2-5-95	Aloha Stadium, Honolulu	AFC, 41	NFC, 13	49,121
2-4-96	Aloha Stadium, Honolulu	NFC, 20	AFC, 13	50,034
2-2-97	Aloha Stadium, Honolulu	AFC, 26 (OT)	NFC, 23	50,031
2-1-98	Aloha Stadium, Honolulu	AFC, 29	NFC, 24	49,995
2-7-99	Aloha Stadium, Honolulu	AFC, 23	NFC, 10	50,075
2-6-00	Aloha Stadium, Honolulu	NFC, 51	AFC, 31	50,112
2-4-01	Aloha Stadium, Honolulu	AFC, 38	NFC, 17	50,128
2-9-02	Aloha Stadium, Honolulu	AFC, 38	NFC, 30	50,301
2-2-03	Aloha Stadium, Honolulu	AFC, 45	NFC, 20	50,125
2-8-04	Aloha Stadium, Honolulu	NFC, 55	AFC, 52	50,127
2-13-05	Aloha Stadium, Honolulu	AFC, 38	NFC, 27	50,225

*AFL game.   †Estimated figure.

OUTSTANDING PLAYER AWARDS

Year—Player, team

1951— Otto Graham, Cleveland Browns
1952— Dan Towler, Los Angeles Rams
1953— Dan Doll, Detroit Lions
1954— Chuck Bednarik, Philadelphia Eagles
1955— Billy Wilson, San Francisco 49ers
1956— Ollie Matson, Chicago Cardinals
1957— Bert Rechichar, Baltimore Colts (back)
    Ernie Stautner, Pittsburgh Steelers (lineman)
1958— Hugh McElhenny, San Francisco 49ers (back)
    Gene Brito, Washington Redskins (lineman)
1959— Frank Gifford, New York Giants (back)
    Doug Atkins, Chicago Bears (lineman)
1960— Johnny Unitas, Baltimore Colts (back)
    Gene Lipscomb, Baltimore Colts (lineman)
1961— Johnny Unitas, Baltimore Colts (back)
    Sam Huff, New York Giants (lineman)
1962— Cotton Davidson, Dallas Texans* (offense)
    Jim Brown, Cleveland Browns (back)
    Henry Jordan, Green Bay Packers (lineman)
1963— Curtis McClinton, Dallas Texans* (offense)
    Earl Faison, San Diego Chargers* (defense)
    Jim Brown, Cleveland Browns (back)
    Gene Lipscomb, Pittsburgh Steelers (lineman)
1964— Keith Lincoln, San Diego Chargers* (offense)
    Archie Matsos, Oakland Raiders* (defense)
    Johnny Unitas, Baltimore Colts (back)
    Gino Marchetti, Baltimore Colts (lineman)
1965— Keith Lincoln, San Diego Chargers* (offense)
    Willie Brown, Denver Broncos* (defense)
    Fran Tarkenton, Minnesota Vikings (back)
    Terry Barr, Detroit Lions (lineman)
1966— Joe Namath, New York Jets* (offense)
    Frank Buncom, San Diego Chargers* (defense)
    Jim Brown, Cleveland Browns (back)
    Dale Meinert, St. Louis Cardinals (lineman)
1967— Babe Parilli, Boston Patriots* (offense)
    Verlon Biggs, New York Jets* (defense)
    Gale Sayers, Chicago Bears (back)
    Floyd Peters, Philadelphia Eagles (lineman)
1968— Joe Namath, New York Jets* (offense)
    Don Maynard, New York Jets* (offense)
    Speedy Duncan, San Diego Chargers (defense)
    Gale Sayers, Chicago Bears (back)
    Dave Robinson, Green Bay Packers (lineman)
1969— Len Dawson, Kansas City Chiefs* (offense)
    George Webster, Houston* (defense)

Year—Player, team

    Roman Gabriel, Los Angeles Rams (back)
    Merlin Olsen, Los Angeles Rams (lineman)
1970— John Hadl, San Diego Chargers*
    Gale Sayers, Chicago Bears (back)
    George Andrie, Dallas Cowboys (lineman)
1971— Mel Renfro, Dallas Cowboys (back)
    Fred Carr, Green Bay Packers (lineman)
1972— Jan Stenerud, Kansas City Chiefs (offense)
    Willie Lanier, Kansas City Chiefs (defense)
1973— O.J. Simpson, Buffalo Bills
1974— Garo Yepremian, Miami Dolphins
1975— James Harris, Los Angeles Rams
1976— Billy Johnson, Houston Oilers
1977— Mel Blount, Pittsburgh Steelers
1978— Walter Payton, Chicago Bears
1979— Ahmad Rashad, Minnesota Vikings
1980— Chuck Muncie, New Orleans Saints
1981— Eddie Murray, Detroit Lions
1982— Kellen Winslow, San Diego Chargers
    Lee Roy Selmon, Tampa Bay Buccaneers
1983— Dan Fouts, San Diego Chargers
    John Jefferson, Green Bay Packers
1984— Joe Theismann, Washington Redskins
1985— Mark Gastineau, New York Jets
1986— Phil Simms, New York Giants
1987— Reggie White, Philadelphia Eagles
1988— Bruce Smith, Buffalo Bills
1989— Randall Cunningham, Philadelphia Eagles
1990— Jerry Gray, Los Angeles Rams
1991— Jim Kelly, Buffalo Bills
1992— Michael Irvin, Dallas Cowboys
1993— Steve Tasker, Buffalo Bills
1994— Andre Rison, Atlanta Falcons
1995— Marshall Faulk, Indianapolis Colts
1996— Jerry Rice, San Francisco 49ers
1997— Mark Brunell, Jacksonville Jaguars
1998— Warren Moon, Seattle Seahawks
1999— Ty Law, New England Patriots
    Keyshawn Johnson, New York Jets
2000— Randy Moss, Minnesota Vikings
2001— Rich Gannon, Oakland Raiders
2002— Rich Gannon, Oakland Raiders
2003— Ricky Williams, Miami Dolphins
2004— Marc Bulger, St. Louis Rams
2005— Peyton Manning, Indianapolis Colts
    *AFL game.

RECORDS

INDIVIDUAL SERVICE
PLAYERS

Most years played
26—George Blanda, Chicago Bears, Baltimore, Houston, Oakland, 1949 through 1975, except 1959.

Most years with one club
20—Jackie Slater, L.A. Rams, St. Louis Rams, 1976 through 1995.
Darrell Green, Washington, 1983 through 2002.

Most games played, career
354—Morten Andersen, New Orleans, Atlanta, N.Y. Giants, Kansas City, Minnesota, 1985 through 1989, 1991 through 1995, 1997-98, 2002-04.

Most consecutive games played, career
282—Jim Marshall, Cleveland, Minnesota, Sept. 25, 1960 through Dec. 16, 1979.

COACHES

Most years as head coach
40—George Halas, Chicago Bears, 1920 through 1929, 1933 through 1942, 1946 through 1955 and 1958 through 1967.

Most games won as head coach
328—Don Shula, Baltimore, 1963 through 1969; Miami, 1970 through 1995.

Most games lost as head coach
165—Dan Reeves, Denver, 1981 through 1992; N.Y. Giants, 1993 through 1996; Atlanta, 1997 through 2003.

INDIVIDUAL OFFENSE
RUSHING

YARDS

Most yards, career
18,355—Emmitt Smith, Dallas, Arizona, 1990 through 2004.

Most yards, season
2,105—Eric Dickerson, Los Angeles Rams, 1984.

Most yards, season, by a quarterback
968—Bobby Douglass, Chicago, 1972.

Most years leading league in yards
8—Jim Brown, Cleveland, 1957 through 1965, except 1962.

Most consecutive years leading league in yards
5—Jim Brown, Cleveland, 1957 through 1961.

Most years with 1,000 or more yards
11—Emmitt Smith, Dallas, 1991 through 2001.

Most consecutive years with 1,000 or more yards
11—Emmitt Smith, Dallas, 1991 through 2001.

Most yards, game
295—Jamal Lewis, Baltimore vs. Cleveland, Sept. 14, 2003.

Most games with 200 or more yards, career
6—O.J. Simpson, Buffalo, San Francisco, 1969 through 1979.

Most games with 200 or more yards, season
4—Earl Campbell, Houston, 1980.

Most consecutive games with 200 or more yards, season
2—O.J. Simpson, Buffalo, Dec. 9 through 16, 1973.
O.J. Simpson, Buffalo, Nov. 25 through Dec. 5, 1976.
Earl Campbell, Houston, Oct. 19 through 26, 1980.
Ricky Williams, Miami, Dec. 1 through 9, 2002.

Most games with 100 or more yards, career
78—Emmitt Smith, Dallas, Arizona, 1990 through 2004.

Most games with 100 or more yards, season
14—Barry Sanders, Detroit, 1997.

Most consecutive games with 100 or more yards, career
14—Barry Sanders, Detroit, Sept. 14 through Dec. 21, 1997.

Most consecutive games with 100 or more yards, season
14—Barry Sanders, Detroit, Sept. 14 through Dec. 21, 1997.

Longest run from scrimmage
99 yards—Tony Dorsett, Dallas at Minnesota, Jan. 3, 1983 (TD).

ATTEMPTS

Most attempts, career
4,409—Emmitt Smith, Dallas, Arizona, 1990 through 2004.

Most attempts, season
410—Jamal Anderson, Atlanta, 1998.

Most attempts, game
45—Jamie Morris, Washington at Cincinnati, Dec. 17, 1988 (OT).
43—Butch Woolfolk, New York Giants at Philadelphia, Nov. 20, 1983.
James Wilder, Tampa Bay vs. Green Bay, Sept. 30, 1984 (OT).
Rudi Johnson, Cincinnati vs. Houston, Nov. 9, 2003.

Most years leading league in attempts
6—Jim Brown, Cleveland, 1958 through 1965, except 1960 and 1962.

Most consecutive years leading league in attempts
4—Steve Van Buren, Philadelphia, 1947 through 1950.
Walter Payton, Chicago, 1976 through 1979.

TOUCHDOWNS

Most touchdowns, career
164—Emmitt Smith, Dallas, Arizona, 1990 through 2004.

Most touchdowns, season
27—Priest Holmes, Kansas City, 2003.

Most years leading league in touchdowns
5—Jim Brown, Cleveland, 1957 through 1959, 1963, 1965.

Most consecutive years leading league in touchdowns
3—Steve Van Buren, Philadelphia, 1947 through 1949.
Jim Brown, Cleveland, 1957 through 1959.
Abner Haynes, Dallas Texans, 1960 through 1962.
Cookie Gilchrist, Buffalo, 1962 through 1964.
Leroy Kelly, Cleveland, 1966 through 1968.

Most touchdowns, game
6—Ernie Nevers, Chicago Cardinals vs. Chicago Bears, Nov. 28, 1929.

Most consecutive games with one or more touchdowns, career
13—John Riggins, Washington, Dec. 26, 1982 through Nov. 27, 1983.
George Rogers, Washington, Nov. 24, 1985 through Nov. 2, 1986.

Most consecutive games with one or more touchdowns, season
12—John Riggins, Washington, Sept. 5 through Nov. 27, 1983.

PASSING

PASSER RATING

Highest rating, career (1,500 or more attempts)
96.8—Steve Young, Tampa Bay, San Francisco, 1985 through 1999.

Highest rating, season (qualifiers)
121.1—Peyton Manning, Indianapolis, 2004.

HISTORY *Records*

ATTEMPTS

Most attempts, career
8,358—Dan Marino, Miami, 1983 through 1999.

Most attempts, season
691—Drew Bledsoe, New England, 1994.

Most years leading league in attempts
5—Dan Marino, Miami, 1984, 1986, 1988, 1992, 1997.

Most consecutive years leading league in attempts
3—Johnny Unitas, Baltimore, 1959 through 1961.
George Blanda, Houston, 1963 through 1965.
Drew Bledsoe, New England, 1994 through 1996.

Most attempts, game
70—Drew Bledsoe, New England vs. Minnesota, Nov. 13, 1994 (OT).
69—Vinny Testaverde, N.Y. Jets at Baltimore, Dec. 24, 2000.

COMPLETIONS

Most completions, career
4,967—Dan Marino, Miami, 1983 through 1999.

Most completions, season
418—Rich Gannon, Oakland, 2002.

Most years leading league in completions
6—Dan Marino, Miami, 1984, 1985, 1986, 1988, 1992, 1997.

Most consecutive years leading league in completions
3—George Blanda, Houston, 1963 through 1965.
Dan Marino, Miami, 1984 through 1986.

Most completions, game
45—Drew Bledsoe, New England vs. Minnesota, Nov. 13, 1994 (OT).
43—Rich Gannon, Oakland at Pittsburgh, Sept. 15, 2002.

Most consecutive completions, game
21—Rich Gannon, Oakland at Denver, Nov. 11, 2002.

YARDS

Most yards, career
61,361—Dan Marino, Miami, 1983 through 1999.

Most yards, season
5,084—Dan Marino, Miami, 1984.

Most years leading league in yards
5—Sonny Jurgensen, Philadelphia, Washington, 1961, 1962, 1966, 1967, 1969.
Dan Marino, Miami, 1984 through 1986, 1988, 1992.

Most consecutive years leading league in yards
4—Dan Fouts, San Diego, 1979 through 1982.

Most years with 3,000 or more yards
13—Dan Marino, Miami, 1984 through 1998, except 1993 and 1996.
Brett Favre, Green Bay, 1992 through 2004.

Most yards, game
554—Norm Van Brocklin, Los Angeles vs. New York Yanks, Sept. 28, 1951.

Most games with 400 or more yards, career
13—Dan Marino, Miami, 1983 through 1999.

Most games with 400 or more yards, season
4—Dan Marino, Miami, 1984.

Most consecutive games with 400 or more yards, season
2—Dan Fouts, San Diego, Dec. 11 through 20, 1982.
Dan Marino, Miami, Dec. 2 through 9, 1984.
Phil Simms, New York Giants, Oct. 6 through 13, 1985.

Most games with 300 or more yards, career
63—Dan Marino, Miami, 1983 through 1999.

Most games with 300 or more yards, season
10—Rich Gannon, Oakland, 2002.

Most consecutive games with 300 or more yards, season
6—Steve Young, San Francisco, Sept. 6 through Oct. 18, 1998.
Kurt Warner, St. Louis, Sept. 4 through Oct. 15, 2000.
Rich Gannon, Oakland, Sept. 15 through Oct. 27, 2002.

Longest pass completion
99 yards—Frank Filchock, Washington vs. Pittsburgh, Oct. 15, 1939 (TD).
George Izo, Washington at Cleveland, Sept. 15, 1963 (TD).
Karl Sweetan, Detroit at Baltimore, Oct. 16, 1966 (TD).
Sonny Jurgensen, Washington at Chicago, Sept. 15, 1968 (TD).
Jim Plunkett, Los Angeles Raiders vs. Washington, Oct. 2, 1983 (TD).
Ron Jaworski, Philadelphia vs. Atlanta, Nov. 10, 1985 (TD).
Stan Humphries, San Diego at Seattle, Sept. 18, 1994 (TD).
Brett Favre, Green Bay at Chicago, Sept. 11, 1995 (TD).
Trent Green, Kansas City vs. San Diego, Dec. 22, 2002 (TD).
Jeff Garcia, Cleveland vs. Cincinnati, Oct. 17, 2004 (TD).

YARDS PER ATTEMPT

Most yards per attempt, career (1,500 or more attempts)
8.63—Otto Graham, Cleveland, 1950 through 1955 (13,499 yards, 1,565 attempts).

Most yards per attempt, season (qualifiers)
11.17—Tommy O'Connell, Cleveland, 1957 (1,229 yards, 110 attempts).

Most years leading league in yards per attempt
7—Sid Luckman, Chicago Bears, 1939 through 1943, 1946, 1947.

Most consecutive years leading league in yards per attempt
5—Sid Luckman, Chicago Bears, 1939 through 1943.

Most yards per attempt, game (20 or more attempts)
18.58—Sammy Baugh, Washington vs. Boston, Oct. 31, 1948 (446 yards, 24 attempts).

TOUCHDOWNS

Most touchdowns, career
420—Dan Marino, Miami, 1983 through 1999.

Most touchdowns, season
49—Peyton Manning, Indianapolis, 2004.

Most years leading league in touchdowns
4—Johnny Unitas, Baltimore, 1957 through 1960.
Len Dawson, Dallas Texans, Kansas City, 1962 through 1966, except 1964.
Steve Young, San Francisco, 1992 through 1994, 1998.
Brett Favre, Green Bay, 1995 through 1997, 2003.

Most consecutive years leading league in touchdowns
4—Johnny Unitas, Baltimore, 1957 through 1960.

Most touchdowns, game
7—Sid Luckman, Chicago Bears at New York Giants, Nov. 14, 1943.
Adrian Burk, Philadelphia at Washington, Oct. 17, 1954.
George Blanda, Houston vs. New York Titans, Nov. 19, 1961.
Y.A. Tittle, New York Giants vs. Washington, Oct. 28, 1962.
Joe Kapp, Minnesota vs. Baltimore, Sept. 28, 1969.

INTERCEPTIONS

Most interceptions, career
277—George Blanda, Chicago Bears, Baltimore, Houston, Oakland, 1949 through 1975, except 1959.

Most interceptions, season
42—George Blanda, Houston, 1962.

Most interceptions, game
8—Jim Hardy, Chicago Cardinals vs. Philadelphia, Sept. 24, 1950.

Most attempts with no interceptions, game
70—Drew Bledsoe, New England vs. Minnesota, Nov. 13, 1994 (OT).
63—Rich Gannon, Minnesota at New England, Oct. 20, 1991 (OT).
60—Davey O'Brien, Philadelphia at Washington, Dec. 1, 1940.

INTERCEPTION PERCENTAGE

Lowest interception percentage, career (1,500 or more attempts)
.11—Neil O'Donnell, Pittsburgh, N.Y. Jets, Cincinnati, Tennessee, 1991 through 2003 (3,229 attempts, 68 interceptions).

Lowest interception percentage, season (qualifiers)
.66—Joe Ferguson, Buffalo, 1976 (151 attempts, one interception).

Most years leading league in lowest interception percentage
—Sammy Baugh, Washington, 1940, 1942, 1944, 1945, 1947.

SACKS (SINCE 1963)

Most times sacked, career
516—John Elway, Denver, 1983 through 1998.

Most times sacked, season
76—David Carr, Houston, 2002.

Most times sacked, game
12—Bert Jones, Baltimore vs. St. Louis, Oct. 26, 1980.
  Warren Moon, Houston vs. Dallas, Sept. 29, 1985.

RECEIVING

RECEPTIONS

Most receptions, career
1,549—Jerry Rice, San Francisco, Oakland, 1985 through 2004.

Most receptions, season
143—Marvin Harrison, Indianapolis, 2002.

Most years leading league in receptions
8—Don Hutson, Green Bay, 1936 through 1945, except 1938 and 1940.

Most consecutive years leading league in receptions
5—Don Hutson, Green Bay, 1941 through 1945.

Most receptions, game
20—Terrell Owens, San Francisco vs. Chicago, Dec. 17, 2000.

Most consecutive games with one or more receptions
274—Jerry Rice, San Francisco, Oakland, Dec. 9, 1985 through Sept. 12, 2004.

YARDS

Most yards, career
22,895—Jerry Rice, San Francisco, Oakland, 1985 through 2004.

Most yards, season
1,848—Jerry Rice, San Francisco, 1995.

Most years leading league in yards
7—Don Hutson, Green Bay, 1936 through 1944, except 1937 and 1940.

Most consecutive years leading league in yards
4—Don Hutson, Green Bay, 1941 through 1944.

Most years with 1,000 or more yards
14—Jerry Rice, San Francisco, Oakland, 1986 through 1996, 1998, 2001 through 2002.

Most yards, game
336—Willie Anderson, Los Angeles Rams at New Orleans, Nov. 26, 1989 (OT).
309—Stephone Paige, Kansas City vs. San Diego, Dec. 22, 1985.

Most games with 200 or more yards, career
5—Lance Alworth, San Diego, Dallas, 1962 through 1972.

Most games with 200 or more yards, season
3—Charley Hennigan, Houston, 1961.

Most games with 100 or more yards, career
76—Jerry Rice, San Francisco, Oakland, 1985 through 2004.

Most games with 100 or more yards, season
11—Michael Irvin, Dallas, 1995.

Most consecutive games with 100 or more yards, season
7—Charley Hennigan, Houston, 1961.
  Michael Irvin, Dallas, 1995.

Longest reception
99 yards—Andy Farkas, Washington vs. Pittsburgh, Oct. 15, 1939 (TD).
  Bobby Mitchell, Washington at Cleveland, Sept. 15, 1963 (TD).
  Pat Studstill, Detroit at Baltimore, Oct. 16, 1966 (TD).
  Gerry Allen, Washington at Chicago, Sept. 15, 1968 (TD).
  Cliff Branch, Los Angeles Raiders vs. Washington, Oct. 2, 1983 (TD).
  Mike Quick, Philadelphia vs. Atlanta, Nov. 10, 1985 (TD).
  Tony Martin, San Diego at Seattle, Sept. 18, 1994 (TD).
  Robert Brooks, Green Bay at Chicago, Sept. 11, 1995 (TD).
  Marc Boerigter, Kansas City vs. San Diego, Dec. 22, 2002 (TD).
  Andre Davis, Cleveland vs. Cincinnati, Oct. 17, 2004 (TD).

TOUCHDOWNS

Most touchdowns, career
197—Jerry Rice, San Francisco, Oakland, 1985 through 2004.

Most touchdowns, season
22—Jerry Rice, San Francisco, 1987.

Most years leading league in touchdowns
9—Don Hutson, Green Bay, 1935 through 1944, except 1939.

Most consecutive years leading league in touchdowns
5—Don Hutson, Green Bay, 1940 through 1944.

Most touchdowns, game
5—Bob Shaw, Chicago Cardinals vs. Baltimore, Oct. 2, 1950.
  Kellen Winslow, San Diego at Oakland, Nov. 22, 1981.
  Jerry Rice, San Francisco at Atlanta, Oct. 14, 1990.

Most consecutive games with one or more touchdowns
13—Jerry Rice, San Francisco, Dec. 19, 1986 through Dec. 27, 1987.

COMBINED NET YARDS

(Rushing, receiving, interception returns, punt returns, kickoff returns and fumble returns)

ATTEMPTS

Most attempts, career
4,924—Emmitt Smith, Dallas, Arizona, 1990 through 2004.

Most attempts, season
496—James Wilder, Tampa Bay, 1984.

Most attempts, game
48—James Wilder, Tampa Bay at Pittsburgh, Oct. 30, 1983.

YARDS

Most yards, career
23,330—Brian Mitchell, Washington, Philadelphia, N.Y. Giants, 1990 through 2003.

Most yards, season
2,690—Derrick Mason, Tennessee, 2000.

Most years leading league in yards
5—Jim Brown, Cleveland, 1958 through 1961, 1964.

Most consecutive years leading league in yards
4—Jim Brown, Cleveland, 1958 through 1961.

Most yards, game
404—Glyn Milburn, Denver vs. Seattle, Dec. 10, 1995.

SCORING

POINTS

Most points, career
2,434—Gary Anderson, Pittsburgh, Philadelphia, San Francisco, Minnesota, Tennessee, 1982 through 2004.

Most points, season
176—Paul Hornung, Green Bay, 1960.

Most years leading league in points
5—Don Hutson, Green Bay, 1940 through 1944.
Gino Cappelletti, Boston, 1961 through 1966, except 1962.

Most consecutive years leading league in points
5—Don Hutson, Green Bay, 1940 through 1944.

Most years with 100 or more points
14—Gary Anderson, Pittsburgh, Philadelphia, San Francisco, Minnesota, Tennessee, 1983 through 1985, 1988, 1991 through 1994, 1996 through 2000, 2003.
Morten Andersen, New Orleans, Atlanta, N.Y. Giants, Kansas City, 1985 through 1989, 1991 through 1995, 1997-98, 2002-03.

Most points, game
40—Ernie Nevers, Chicago Cardinals vs. Chicago Bears, Nov. 28, 1929.

Most consecutive games with one or more points
332—Morten Andersen, New Orleans, Atlanta, N.Y. Giants, Kansas City, Minnesota, Dec. 11, 1983 through Jan. 5, 2005 (current).

TOUCHDOWNS

Most touchdowns, career
208—Jerry Rice, San Francisco, Oakland, 1985 through 2004.

Most touchdowns, season
27—Priest Holmes, Kansas City, 2003.

Most years leading league in touchdowns
8—Don Hutson, Green Bay, 1935 through 1938 and 1941 through 1944.

Most consecutive years leading league in touchdowns
4—Don Hutson, Green Bay, 1935 through 1938 and 1941 through 1944.

Most touchdowns, game
6—Ernie Nevers, Chicago Cardinals vs. Chicago Bears, Nov. 28, 1929.
Dub Jones, Cleveland vs. Chicago Bears, Nov. 25, 1951.
Gale Sayers, Chicago vs. San Francisco, Dec. 12, 1965.

Most consecutive games with one or more touchdowns
18—Lenny Moore, Baltimore, Oct. 27, 1963 through Sept. 19, 1965.

EXTRA POINTS

Most extra points attempted, career
959—George Blanda, Chicago Bears, Baltimore, Houston, Oakland, 1949 through 1975, except 1959.

Most extra points made, career
943—George Blanda, Chicago Bears, Baltimore, Houston, Oakland, 1949 through 1975, except 1959.

Most extra points attempted, season
70—Uwe von Schamann, Miami, 1984.

Most extra points made, season
66—Uwe von Schamann, Miami, 1984.

Most extra points attempted, game
10—Charlie Gogolak, Washington vs. New York Giants, Nov. 27, 1966.

Most extra points made, game
9—Pat Harder, Chicago Cardinals at New York Giants, Oct. 17, 1948.
Bob Waterfield, Los Angeles vs. Baltimore, Oct. 22, 1950.
Charlie Gogolak, Washington vs. New York Giants, Nov. 27, 1966.

FIELD GOALS AND FIELD GOAL PERCENTAGE

Most field goals attempted, career
672—Gary Anderson, Pittsburgh, Philadelphia, San Francisco, Minnesota, Tennessee, 1982 through 2004.

Most field goals made, career
538—Gary Anderson, Pittsburgh, Philadelphia, San Francisco, Minnesota, 1982 through 2004.

Most field goals attempted, season
49—Bruce Gossett, Los Angeles, 1966.
Curt Knight, Washington, 1971.

Most field goals made, season
39—Olindo Mare, Miami, 1999.
Jeff Wilkins, St. Louis, 2003.

Most field goals attempted, game
9—Jim Bakken, St. Louis at Pittsburgh, Sept. 24, 1967.

Most field goals made, game
7—Jim Bakken, St. Louis at Pittsburgh, Sept. 24, 1967.
Rich Karlis, Minnesota vs. Los Angeles Rams, Nov. 5, 1989 (OT).
Chris Boniol, Dallas vs. Green Bay, Nov. 18, 1996.
Billy Cundiff, Dallas at N.Y. Giants, Sept. 15, 2003 (OT).

Most field goals made, one quarter
4—Garo Yepremian, Detroit vs. Minnesota, Nov. 13, 1966, second quarter.
Curt Knight, Washington at New York Giants, Nov. 15, 1970, second quarter.
Roger Ruzek, Dallas vs. New York Giants, Nov. 2, 1987, fourth quarter.
Cary Blanchard, Indianapolis at Buffalo, Sept. 21, 1997, second quarter.
Sebastian Janikowski, Oakland at Chicago, Oct. 5, 2003, second quarter.
Jeff Wilkins, St. Louis vs. Baltimore, Nov. 9, 2003, fourth quarter.

Most consecutive games with one or more field goals made, career
38—Matt Stover, Baltimore, Oct. 31, 1999 through Dec. 2, 2001.

Most consecutive field goals made, career
42—Mike Vanderjagt, Indianapolis, Dec. 22, 2002 through Sept. 4, 2004.

Most field goals of 50 or more yards, career
40—Morten Andersen, New Orleans, Atlanta, N.Y. Giants, Kansas City, Minnesota, 1982 through 2004.

Most field goals of 50 or more yards, season
8—Morten Andersen, Atlanta, 1995.

Most field goals of 50 or more yards, game
3—Morten Andersen, Atlanta vs. New Orleans, Dec. 10, 1995.

Longest field goal made
63 yards—Tom Dempsey, New Orleans vs. Detroit, Nov. 8, 1970.
Jason Elam, Denver vs. Jacksonville, Oct. 25, 1998.

Highest field goal percentage, career (100 or more made)
87.0—Mike Vanderjagt, Indianapolis, 1998 through 2004 (223 attempted, 194 made).

Highest field goal percentage, season (qualifiers)
100.00—Tony Zendejas, Los Angeles Rams, 1991 (17 made).
Gary Anderson, Minnesota, 1998 (35 made).
Jeff Wilkins, St. Louis, 2000 (17 made).
Mike Vanderjagt, Indianapolis, 2003 (37 made).

SAFETIES

Most safeties, career
4—Ted Hendricks, Baltimore, Green Bay, Oakland, Los Angeles Raiders, 1969 through 1983.
Doug English, Detroit, 1975 through 1985, except 1980.

Most safeties, season
2—Held by many players.

Most safeties, game
2—Fred Dryer, Los Angeles vs. Green Bay, Oct. 21, 1973.

PUNTING

ost punts, career
367—Sean Landeta, N.Y. Giants, Los Angeles Rams, St. Louis, Tampa Bay, Green Bay, Philadelphia, 1985 through 2004.

ost punts, season
4—Bob Parsons, Chicago, 1981.
Chad Stanley, Houston, 2002.

ost seasons leading league in punting
—Sammy Baugh, Washington, 1940 through 1943.
Jerrel Wilson, Kansas City, 1965, 1968, 1972, 1973.

ost consecutive seasons leading league in punting
—Sammy Baugh, Washington, 1940 through 1943.

ost punts, game
—Leo Araguz, Oakland vs. San Diego, Oct. 11, 1998.

ngest punt
yards—Steve O'Neal, New York Jets at Denver, Sept. 21, 1969.

FUMBLES

ost fumbles, career
1—Warren Moon, Houston, Minnesota, Seattle, Kansas City, 1984 through 2000.

ost fumbles, season
—Kerry Collins, N.Y. Giants, 2001.
Daunte Culpepper, Minnesota, 2002.

ost fumbles, game
—Len Dawson, Kansas City vs. San Diego, Nov. 15, 1964.

PUNT RETURNS

ost punt returns, career
53—Brian Mitchell, Washington, Philadelphia, N.Y. Giants, 1990 through 2003.

ost punt returns, season
—Danny Reece, Tampa Bay, 1979.

ost years leading league in punt returns
—Les "Speedy" Duncan, San Diego, Washington, 1965, 1966, 1971.
Rick Upchurch, Denver, 1976, 1978, 1982.

ost punt returns, game
—Eddie Brown, Washington at Tampa Bay, Oct. 9, 1977.

YARDS

ost yards, career
999—Brian Mitchell, Washington, Philadelphia, N.Y. Giants, 1990 through 2003.

ost yards, season
75—Desmond Howard, Green Bay, 1996.

ost yards, game
7—LeRoy Irvin, Los Angeles at Atlanta, Oct. 11, 1981.

ngest punt return
3 yards—Robert Bailey, Los Angeles Rams at New Orleans, Oct. 23, 1994 (TD).

FAIR CATCHES

ost fair catches, career
31—Brian Mitchell, Washington, Philadelphia, N.Y. Giants, 1990 through 2003.

ost fair catches, season
3—Brian Mitchell, Philadelphia, 2000.

ost fair catches, game
—Lem Barney, Detroit vs. Chicago, Nov. 21, 1976.
Bobby Morse, Philadelphia vs. Buffalo, Dec. 27, 1987.

TOUCHDOWNS

Most touchdowns, career
10—Eric Metcalf, Cleveland, Atlanta, San Diego, Arizona, Carolina, Washington, Green Bay, 1989 through 2002, except 2000.

Most touchdowns, season
4—Jack Christiansen, Detroit, 1951.
Rick Upchurch, Denver, 1976.

Most touchdowns, game
2—Jack Christiansen, Detroit vs. Los Angeles, Oct. 14, 1951.
Jack Christiansen, Detroit vs. Green Bay, Nov. 22, 1951.
Dick Christy, New York Titans vs. Denver, Sept. 24, 1961.
Rick Upchurch, Denver vs. Cleveland, Sept. 26, 1976.
LeRoy Irvin, Los Angeles at Atlanta, Oct. 11, 1981.
Vai Sikahema, St. Louis vs. Tampa Bay, Dec. 21, 1986.
Todd Kinchen, Los Angeles Rams vs. Atlanta, Dec. 27, 1992.
Eric Metcalf, Cleveland vs. Pittsburgh, Oct. 24, 1993.
Eric Metcalf, San Diego at Cincinnati, Nov. 2, 1997.
Darrien Gordon, Denver vs. Carolina, Nov. 9, 1997.
Jermaine Lewis, Baltimore vs. Seattle, Dec. 7, 1997.
Jermaine Lewis, Baltimore vs. N.Y. Jets, Dec. 24, 2000.
Steve Smith, Carolina vs. Cincinnati, Dec. 8, 2002.

KICKOFF RETURNS

Most kickoff returns, career
607—Brian Mitchell, Washington, Philadelphia, N.Y. Giants, 1990 through 2003.

Most kickoff returns, season
82—MarTay Jenkins, Arizona, 2000.

Most years leading league in kickoff returns
3—Abe Woodson, San Francisco, 1959, 1962, 1963.

Most kickoff returns, game
10—Desmond Howard, Oakland at Seattle, Oct. 26, 1997.

YARDS

Most yards, career
14,014—Brian Mitchell, Washington, Philadelphia, N.Y. Giants, 1990 through 2003.

Most yards, season
2,186—MarTay Jenkins, Arizona, 2000.

Most years leading league in yards
3—Bruce Harper, New York Jets, 1977 through 1979.
Tyrone Hughes, New Orleans, 1994 through 1996.

Most yards, game
304—Tyrone Hughes, New Orleans vs. Los Angeles Rams, Oct. 23, 1994.

Longest kickoff return
106 yards—Al Carmichael, Green Bay vs. Chicago Bears, Oct. 7, 1956 (TD).
Noland Smith, K.C. at Denver, Dec. 17, 1967 (TD).
Roy Green, St. Louis at Dallas, Oct. 21, 1979 (TD).

TOUCHDOWNS

Most touchdowns, career
6—Ollie Matson, Chicago Cardinals, Los Angeles Rams, Detroit, Philadelphia, 1952 through 1964, except 1953.
Gale Sayers, Chicago, 1965 through 1971.
Travis Williams, Green Bay, Los Angeles, 1967 through 1971.
Mel Gray, New Orleans, Detroit, Houston, Tennessee, Philadelphia, 1986 through 1997.

Most touchdowns, season
4—Travis Williams, Green Bay, 1967.
Cecil Turner, Chicago, 1970.

Most touchdowns, game
2—Timmy Brown, Philadelphia vs. Dallas, Nov. 6, 1966.
Travis Williams, Green Bay vs. Cleveland, Nov. 12, 1967.
Ron Brown, Los Angeles Rams vs. Green Bay, Nov. 24,

HISTORY *Records*

1985.

Tyrone Hughes, New Orleans vs. Los Angeles Rams, Oct. 23, 1994.

Chad Morton, N.Y. Jets at Buffalo, Sept. 8, 2002 (OT).

COMBINED KICK RETURNS

(KICKOFFS AND PUNTS)

Most kick returns, career
1,070—Brian Mitchell, Washington, Philadelphia, N.Y. Giants, 1990 through 2003.

Most kick returns, season
114—Michael Lewis, New Orleans, 2002.

Most kick returns, game
13—Stump Mitchell, St. Louis at Atlanta, Oct. 18, 1981.
Ronnie Harris, New England at Pittsburgh, Dec. 5, 1993.

YARDS

Most yards, career
19,013—Brian Mitchell, Washington, Philadelphia, N.Y. Giants, 1990 through 2003.

Most yards, season
2,432—Michael Lewis, New Orleans, 2002.

Most yards, game
347—Tyrone Hughes, New Orleans vs. Los Angeles Rams, Oct. 23, 1994.

TOUCHDOWNS

Most touchdowns, career
13—Brian Mitchell, Washington, Philadelphia, N.Y. Giants, 1990 through 2003.

Most touchdowns, season
4—Jack Christiansen, Detroit, 1951.
Emlen Tunnell, New York Giants, 1951.
Gale Sayers, Chicago, 1967.
Travis Williams, Green Bay, 1967.
Cecil Turner, Chicago, 1970.
Billy "White Shoes" Johnson, Houston, 1975.
Rick Upchurch, Denver, 1976.
Dante Hall, Kansas City, 2003.
Eddie Drummond, Detroit, 2004.

Most touchdowns, game
2—Held by many players.

INDIVIDUAL DEFENSE

INTERCEPTIONS

Most interceptions, career
81—Paul Krause, Washington, Minnesota, 1964 through 1979.

Most interceptions, season
14—Dick "Night Train" Lane, Los Angeles, 1952.

Most interceptions, game
4—Held by many players.

Most consecutive games with one or more interceptions
8—Tom Morrow, Oakland, 1962 through 1963.

Most yards on interceptions, career
1,483—Rod Woodson, Pittsburgh, San Francisco, Baltimore, Oakland, 1987 through 2003.

Most yards on interceptions, season
358—Ed Reed, Baltimore, 2004.

Most yards on interceptions, game
177—Charlie McNeil, San Diego vs. Houston, Sept. 24, 1961.

Longest interception return
106—Ed Reed, Baltimore vs. Cleveland, Nov. 7, 2004.

TOUCHDOWNS

Most touchdowns, career
12—Rod Woodson, Pittsburgh, San Francisco, Baltimore, Oakland, 1987 through 2003.

Most touchdowns, season
4—Ken Houston, Houston, 1971.
Jim Kearney, Kansas City, 1972.
Eric Allen, Philadelphia, 1993.

Most touchdowns, game
2—Held by many players.

FUMBLES RECOVERED

Most fumbles recovered (own and opponents'), career
56—Warren Moon, Houston, Minnesota, Seattle, Kansas City, 1984 through 2000.

Most fumbles recovered (own), career
56—Warren Moon, Houston, Minnesota, Seattle, Kansas City, 1984 through 2000.

Most opponents' fumbles recovered, career
29—Jim Marshall, Cleveland, Minnesota, 1960 through 1979.

Most fumbles recovered (own and opponents'), season
12—David Carr, Houston, 2002.

Most fumbles recovered (own), season
12—David Carr, Houston, 2002.

Most opponents' fumbles recovered, season
9—Don Hultz, Minnesota, 1963.

Most fumbles recovered (own and opponents'), game
4—Otto Graham, Cleveland at New York Giants, Oct. 25, 1953.
Sam Etcheverry, St. Louis at New York Giants, Sept. 17, 1961.
Roman Gabriel, Los Angeles at San Francisco, Oct. 12, 1969.
Joe Ferguson, Buffalo vs. Miami, Sept. 18, 1977.
Randall Cunningham, Philadelphia at Los Angeles Raiders, Nov. 30, 1986 (OT).

Most fumbles recovered (own), game
4—Otto Graham, Cleveland at New York Giants, Oct. 25, 1953.
Sam Etcheverry, St. Louis at New York Giants, Sept. 17, 1961.
Roman Gabriel, Los Angeles at San Francisco, Oct. 12, 1969.
Joe Ferguson, Buffalo vs. Miami, Sept. 18, 1977.
Randall Cunningham, Philadelphia at Los Angeles Raiders, Nov. 30, 1986 (OT).

Most opponents' fumbles recovered, game
3—Held by many players.

Longest fumble return
104 yards—Jack Tatum, Oakland at Green Bay, Sept. 24, 1972 (TD).
Aeneas Williams, Arizona vs. Washington, Nov. 5, 2000 (TD).

TOUCHDOWNS

Most touchdowns (own and opponents' recovered), career
5—Jessie Tuggle, Atlanta, 1987 through 2000.

Most touchdowns (own recovered), career
2—Held by many players.

Most touchdowns (opponents' recovered), career
5—Jessie Tuggle, Atlanta, 1987 through 2000.

Most touchdowns (opponents' recovered), season
2—Held by many players.

Most touchdowns (opponents' recovered), game
2—Fred "Dippy" Evans, Chicago Bears vs. Washington, Nov. 28, 1948.

SACKS (SINCE 1982)

Most sacks, career
200—Bruce Smith, Buffalo, Washington, 1985 through 2003.

Most sacks, season
22.5—Michael Strahan, N.Y. Giants, 2001.

Most sacks, game

—Derrick Thomas, Kansas City vs. Seattle, Nov. 11, 1990.

TEAM MISCELLANEOUS
CHAMPIONSHIPS

ost league championships won
—Green Bay, 1929, 1930, 1931, 1936, 1939, 1944, 1961, 1962, 1965, 1966, 1967, 1996.

ost consecutive league championships won
—Green Bay, 1929 through 1931.
Green Bay, 1965 through 1967.

ost first-place finishes during regular season (since 1933)
—Dallas, 1966-71, 1973, 1976-79, 1981, 1985, 1992-96, 1998
N.Y. Giants, 1933-35, 1938-39, 1941, 1944, 1946, 1956, 1958-59, 1961-63, 1986, 1989-90, 1997, 2000.

ost consecutive first-place finishes during regular season (since 1933)
—Los Angeles, 1973 through 1979.

GAMES WON

ost games won, season
—San Francisco, 1984.
Chicago, 1985.
Minnesota, 1998.
Pittsburgh, 2004.

ost consecutive games won, season
—Miami, Sept. 17 through Dec. 16, 1972.
Pittsburgh, Sept. 26, 2004 through Jan. 2, 2005.

ost consecutive games won from start of season
—Miami, Sept. 17 through Dec. 16, 1972 (entire season).

ost consecutive games won at end of season
—Miami, Sept. 17 through Dec. 16, 1972 (entire season).
Pittsburgh, Sept. 26, 2004 through Jan. 2, 2005.

ost consecutive undefeated games, season
—Miami, Sept. 17 through Dec. 16, 1972 (entire season).
Pittsburgh, Sept. 26, 2004 through Jan. 2, 2005.

ost consecutive games won
—New England Patriots, Oct. 5, 2003 through Oct. 24, 2004.

ost consecutive undefeated games
—Canton, 1921 through 1923 (won 22, tied three).

ost consecutive home games won
—Miami, Oct. 17, 1971 through Dec. 15, 1974.

ost consecutive undefeated home games
—Green Bay, 1928 through 1933 (won 27, tied three).

ost consecutive road games won
—San Francisco, Nov. 27, 1988 through Dec. 30, 1990.

ost consecutive undefeated road games
—San Francisco, Nov. 27, 1988 through Dec. 30, 1990 (won 18).

GAMES LOST

ost games lost, season
—New Orleans, 1980.
Dallas, 1989.
New England, 1990.
Indianapolis, 1991.
New York Jets, 1996.
San Diego, 2000.
Carolina, 2001.

ost consecutive games lost
—Tampa Bay, Sept. 12, 1976 through Dec. 4, 1977.

ost consecutive winless games
—Tampa Bay, Sept. 12, 1976 through Dec. 4, 1977 (lost 26).

ost consecutive games lost, season

15—Carolina, Sept. 23, 2001 through Jan. 6, 2002.

Most consecutive games lost from start of season
14—Tampa Bay, Sept. 12 through Dec. 12, 1976 (entire season).
New Orleans, Sept. 7 through Dec. 7, 1980.

Most consecutive games lost at end of season
15—Carolina, Sept. 23, 2001 through Jan. 6, 2002.

Most consecutive winless games, season
15—Carolina, Sept. 23, 2001 through Jan. 6, 2002 (lost 15).

Most consecutive home games lost
14—Dallas, Oct. 9, 1988 through Dec. 24, 1989.

Most consecutive winless home games
14—Dallas, Oct. 9, 1988 through Dec. 24, 1989 (lost 14).

Most consecutive road games lost
24—Detroit, Sept. 9, 2001 through Dec. 21, 2003.

Most consecutive winless road games
24—Detroit, Sept. 9, 2001 through Dec. 21, 2003.

TIE GAMES

Most tie games, season
6—Chicago Bears, 1932.

Most consecutive tie games
3—Chicago Bears, Sept. 25 through Oct. 9, 1932.

TEAM OFFENSE
RUSHING

Most years leading league in rushing
16—Chicago Bears, 1932, 1934, 1935, 1939, 1940, 1941, 1942, 1951, 1955, 1956, 1968, 1977, 1983, 1984, 1985, 1986.

Most consecutive years leading league in rushing
4—Chicago Bears, 1939 through 1942.
Chicago Bears, 1983 through 1986.

ATTEMPTS

Most attempts, season
681—Oakland, 1977.

Most attempts, game
72—Chicago Bears vs. Brooklyn, Oct. 20, 1935.

Most attempts by both teams, game
108—Chicago Cardinals 70, Green Bay 38, Dec. 5, 1948.

Fewest attempts, game
6—Chicago Cardinals at Brooklyn, Oct. 29, 1933.

Fewest attempts by both teams, game
34—Houston 22, Atlanta 12, Dec. 5, 1993.
San Francisco 19, Atlanta 15, Dec. 24, 1995.

YARDS

Most yards, season
3,165—New England, 1978.

Fewest yards, season
298—Philadelphia, 1940.

Most yards, game
426—Detroit vs. Pittsburgh, Nov. 4, 1934.

Most yards by both teams, game
595—Los Angeles 371, New York Yanks 224, Nov. 18, 1951.

Fewest yards, game
-53—Detroit at Chicago Cardinals, Oct. 17, 1943.

Fewest yards by both teams, game
-15—Detroit -53, Chicago Cardinals 38, Oct. 17, 1943.

TOUCHDOWNS

Most touchdowns, season
36—Green Bay, 1962.

Fewest touchdowns, season

1—Brooklyn, 1934.

Most touchdowns, game
8—Kansas City vs. Atlanta, Oct. 24, 2004.

Most touchdowns by both teams, game
8—Los Angeles 6, New York Yanks 2, Nov. 18, 1951.
Chicago Bears 5, Green Bay 3, Nov. 6, 1955.
Cleveland 6, Los Angeles 2, Nov. 24, 1957.
Denver 5, Kansas City 3, Dec. 7, 2003.
Kansas City 8, Atlanta 0, Oct. 24, 2004.

PASSING

ATTEMPTS

Most attempts, season
709—Minnesota, 1981.

Fewest attempts, season
102—Cincinnati, 1933.

Most attempts, game
70—New England vs. Minnesota, Nov. 13, 1994 (OT).
69—N.Y. Jets at Baltimore, Dec. 24, 2000.

Most attempts by both teams, game
112—New England 70, Minnesota 42, Nov. 13, 1994 (OT).
104—Miami 55, New York Jets 49, Oct. 18, 1987 (OT).
N.Y. Jets 58, San Francisco 46, Sept. 6, 1998 (OT).
103—Cincinnati 68, Pittsburgh 35, Dec. 30, 2001 (OT).
102—San Francisco 57, Atlanta 45, Oct. 6, 1985.

Fewest attempts, game
0—Green Bay vs. Portsmouth, Oct. 8, 1933.
Detroit at Cleveland, Sept. 10, 1937.
Pittsburgh vs. Brooklyn, Nov. 16, 1941.
Pittsburgh vs. Los Angeles, Nov. 13, 1949.
Cleveland vs. Philadelphia, Dec. 3, 1950.

Fewest attempts by both teams, game
4—Detroit 3, Chicago Cardinals 1, Nov. 3, 1935.
Cleveland 4, Detroit 0, Sept. 10, 1937.

COMPLETIONS

Most completions, season
432—San Francisco, 1995.

Fewest completions, season
25—Cincinnati, 1933.

Most completions, game
45—New England vs. Minnesota, Nov. 13, 1994 (OT).
43—Washington at Detroit, Nov. 4, 1990 (OT).
Oakland at Pittsburgh, Sept. 15, 2002.

Most completions by both teams, game
71—New England 45, Minnesota 26, Nov. 13, 1994 (OT).
68—San Francisco 37, Atlanta 31, Oct. 6, 1985.
Oakland 34, Denver 34, Nov. 11, 2002.

Fewest completions, game
0—Held by many teams. Last team: Buffalo vs. New York Jets,
Sept. 29, 1974.

Fewest completions by both teams, game
1—Philadelphia 1, Chicago Cardinals 0, Nov. 8, 1936.
Cleveland 1, Detroit 0, Sept. 10, 1937.
Detroit 1, Chicago Cardinals 0, Sept. 15, 1940.
Pittsburgh 1, Brooklyn 0, Nov. 29, 1942.

YARDS

Most yards, season
5,232—St. Louis, 2000.

Most years leading league in yards
10—San Diego, 1965, 1968, 1971, 1978 through 1983, 1985.

Most consecutive years leading league in yards
6—San Diego, 1978 through 1983.

Fewest yards, season

302—Chicago Cardinals, 1934.

Most yards, game
554—Los Angeles vs. New York Yanks, Sept. 28, 1951.

Most yards by both teams, game
884—New York Jets 449, Miami 435, Sept. 21, 1986
(OT).
883—San Diego 486, Cincinnati 397, Dec. 20, 1982.

Fewest yards, game
-53—Denver at Oakland, Sept. 10, 1967.

Fewest yards by both teams, game
-11—Green Bay -10, Dallas -1, Oct. 24, 1965.

TOUCHDOWNS

Most touchdowns, season
51—Indianapolis, 2004.

Fewest touchdowns, season
0—Cincinnati, 1933.
Pittsburgh, 1945.

Most touchdowns, game
7—Chicago Bears at New York Giants, Nov. 14, 1943.
Philadelphia at Washington, Oct. 17, 1954.
Houston vs. New York Titans, Nov. 19, 1961.
Houston vs. New York Titans, Oct. 14, 1962.
New York Giants vs. Washington, Oct. 28, 1962.
Minnesota vs. Baltimore, Sept. 28, 1969.
San Diego at Oakland, Nov. 22, 1981.

Most touchdowns by both teams, game
12—New Orleans 6, St. Louis 6, Nov. 2, 1969.

INTERCEPTIONS

Most interceptions, season
48—Houston, 1962.

Fewest interceptions, season
5—Cleveland, 1960.
Green Bay, 1966.
Kansas City, 1990.
New York Giants, 1990.

Most interceptions, game
9—Detroit vs. Green Bay, Oct. 24, 1943.
Pittsburgh vs. Philadelphia, Dec. 12, 1965.

Most interceptions by both teams, game
13—Denver 8, Houston 5, Dec. 2, 1962.

SACKS

Most sacks allowed, season
104—Philadelphia, 1986.

Most years leading league in fewest sacks allowed
10—Miami, 1973 and 1982 through 1990.

Most consecutive years leading league in fewest sacks allowed
9—Miami, 1982 through 1990.

Fewest sacks allowed, season
7—Miami, 1988.

Most sacks allowed, game
12—Pittsburgh vs. Dallas, Nov. 20, 1966.
Baltimore vs. St. Louis, Oct. 26, 1980.
Detroit vs. Chicago, Dec. 16, 1984.
Houston vs. Dallas, Sept. 29, 1985.

Most sacks allowed by both teams, game
18—Green Bay 10, San Diego 8, Sept. 24, 1978.

SCORING

POINTS

Most points, season
556—Minnesota, 1998.

Most points, game

2—Washington vs. New York Giants, Nov. 27, 1966.
Most points by both teams, game
13—Washington 72, New York Giants 41, Nov. 27, 1966.
Fewest points by both teams, game
—Occurred many times. Last time: New York Giants 0, Detroit 0, Nov. 7, 1943.
Most points in a shutout victory
4—Philadelphia vs. Cincinnati, Nov. 6, 1934.
Fewest points in a shutout victory
—Green Bay at Chicago Bears, Oct. 16, 1932.
Chicago Bears at Green Bay, Sept. 18, 1938.
Most points in first half of game
9—Green Bay vs. Tampa Bay, Oct. 2, 1983.
Most points in first half of game by both teams
0—Houston 35, Oakland 35, Dec. 22, 1963.
Most points in second half of game
9—Chicago Bears at Philadelphia, Nov. 30, 1941.
Most points in second half of game by both teams
5—Washington 38, New York Giants 27, Nov. 27, 1966.
Most points in one quarter
1—Green Bay vs. Detroit, Oct. 7, 1945, second quarter.
Los Angeles vs. Detroit, Oct. 29, 1950, third quarter.
Most points in one quarter by both teams
9—Oakland 28, Houston 21, Dec. 22, 1963, second quarter.
Most points in first quarter
5—Green Bay vs. Cleveland, Nov. 12, 1967.
Most points in first quarter by both teams
2—Green Bay 35, Cleveland 7, Nov. 12, 1967.
Most points in second quarter
1—Green Bay vs. Detroit, Oct. 7, 1945.
Most points in second quarter by both teams
9—Oakland 28, Houston 21, Dec. 22, 1963.
Most points in third quarter
1—Los Angeles vs. Detroit, Oct. 29, 1950.
Most points in third quarter by both teams
8—Los Angeles 41, Detroit 7, Oct. 29, 1950.
Most points in fourth quarter
1—Oakland vs. Denver, Dec. 17, 1960.
Oakland vs. San Diego, Dec. 8, 1963.
Atlanta at Green Bay, Sept. 13, 1981.
Most points in fourth quarter by both teams
2—Chicago Cardinals 28, Philadelphia 14, Dec. 7, 1947.
Green Bay 28, Chicago Bears 14, Nov. 6, 1955.
New York Jets 28, Boston 14, Oct. 27, 1968.
Pittsburgh 21, Cleveland 21, Oct. 18, 1969.
Kansas City 21, New England 21, Sept. 22, 2002.
Most consecutive games without being shut out
20—San Francisco, Oct. 16, 1977 through Sept. 26, 2004.

TIMES SHUT OUT

Most times shut out, season
—Frankford, 1927 (lost six, tied two).
Brooklyn, 1931 (lost eight).
Most consecutive times shut out
—Rochester, 1922 through 1924 (lost eight).

TOUCHDOWNS

Most touchdowns, season
0—Miami, 1984.
Most years leading league in touchdowns
3—Chicago Bears, 1932, 1934, 1935, 1939, 1941, 1942, 1943, 1944, 1946, 1947, 1948, 1956, 1965.
Most consecutive years leading league in touchdowns
—Chicago Bears, 1941 through 1944.
Los Angeles, 1949 through 1952.

San Francisco, 1992 through 1995.
Most touchdowns, game
10—Philadelphia vs. Cincinnati, Nov. 6, 1934.
Los Angeles vs. Baltimore, Oct. 22, 1950.
Washington vs. New York Giants, Nov. 27, 1966.
Most touchdowns by both teams, game
16—Washington 10, New York Giants 6, Nov. 27, 1966.
Most consecutive games with one or more touchdowns
166—Cleveland, 1957 through 1969.

EXTRA POINTS

Most extra points, season
66—Miami, 1984.
Fewest extra points, season
2—Chicago Cardinals, 1933.
Most extra points, game
10—Los Angeles vs. Baltimore, Oct. 22, 1950.
Most extra points by both teams, game
14—Chicago Cardinals 9, New York Giants 5, Oct. 17, 1948.
Houston 7, Oakland 7, Dec. 22, 1963.
Washington 9, New York Giants 5, Nov. 27, 1966.

FIELD GOALS

Most field goals attempted, season
49—Los Angeles, 1966.
Washington, 1971.
Most field goals made, season
39—Miami, 1999.
St. Louis, 2003.
Most field goals attempted, game
9—St. Louis at Pittsburgh, Sept. 24, 1967.
Most field goals made, game
7—St. Louis at Pittsburgh, Sept. 24, 1967.
Minnesota vs. Los Angeles Rams, Nov. 5, 1989 (OT).
Dallas vs. Green Bay, Nov. 18, 1996.
Dallas at N.Y. Giants, Sept. 15, 2003 (OT).
Most field goals attempted by both teams, game
11—St. Louis 6, Pittsburgh 5, Nov. 13, 1966.
Washington 6, Chicago 5, Nov. 14, 1971.
Green Bay 6, Detroit 5, Sept. 29, 1974.
Washington 6, New York Giants 5, Nov. 14, 1976.
Most field goals made by both teams, game
9—San Diego 5, Kansas City 4, Sept. 29, 1996.
Miami 6, New England 3, Oct. 17, 1999.
Most consecutive games with one or more field goals made
38—Baltimore, Oct. 31, 1999 through Dec. 2, 2001.

SAFETIES

Most safeties, season
4—Cleveland, 1927.
Detroit, 1962.
Seattle, 1993.
San Francisco, 1996.
Tennessee, 1999.
Most safeties, game
3—Los Angeles Rams vs. New York Giants, Sept. 30, 1984.
Most safeties by both teams, game
3—Los Angeles Rams 3, New York Giants 0, Sept. 30, 1984.

FIRST DOWNS

Most first downs, season
398—Kansas City, 2004.
Most first downs, game
39—New York Jets vs. Miami, Nov. 27, 1988.
Washington at Detroit, Nov. 4, 1990 (OT).
Most first downs by both teams, game
64—Kansas City 32, Seattle 32, Nov. 24, 2002.

PUNTING

Most punts, season
116—Houston, 2002.

Fewest punts, season
23—San Diego, 1982.

Most punts, game
17—Chicago Bears vs. Green Bay, Oct. 22, 1933.
Cincinnati vs. Pittsburgh, Oct. 22, 1933.

Most punts by both teams, game
31—Chicago Bears 17, Green Bay 14, Oct. 22, 1933.
Cincinnati 17, Pittsburgh 14, Oct. 22, 1933.

Fewest punts, game
0—Held by many teams.

Fewest punts by both teams, game
0—Buffalo 0, San Francisco 0, Sept. 13, 1992.

FUMBLES

Most fumbles, season
56—Chicago Bears, 1938.
San Francisco, 1978.

Fewest fumbles, season
7—Kansas City, 2002.

Most fumbles, game
10—Phil-Pitt vs. New York, Oct. 9, 1943.
Detroit at Minnesota, Nov. 12, 1967.
Kansas City vs. Houston, Oct. 12, 1969.
San Francisco at Detroit, Dec. 17, 1978.

Most fumbles by both teams, game
14—Washington 8, Pittsburgh 6, Nov. 14, 1937.
Chicago Bears 7, Cleveland 7, Nov. 24, 1940.
St. Louis 8, New York Giants 6, Sept. 17, 1961.
Kansas City 10, Houston 4, Oct. 12, 1969.

LOST

Most fumbles lost, season
36—Chicago Cardinals, 1959.

Fewest fumbles lost, season
2—Kansas City, 2002.

Most fumbles lost, game
8—St. Louis at Washington, Oct. 25, 1976.
Cleveland at Pittsburgh, Dec. 23, 1990.

RECOVERED

Most fumbles recovered (own and opponents'), season
58—Minnesota, 1963.

Fewest fumbles recovered (own and opponents'), season
9—San Francisco, 1982.

Most fumbles recovered (own and opponents'), game
10—Denver vs. Buffalo, Dec. 13, 1964.
Pittsburgh vs. Houston, Dec. 9, 1973.
Washington vs. St. Louis, Oct. 25, 1976.

Most fumbles recovered (own), season
37—Chicago Bears, 1938.

Fewest fumbles recovered (own), season
2—Washington, 1958.
Miami, 2000.

TOUCHDOWNS

Most touchdowns on fumbles recovered (own and opponents'), season
5—Chicago Bears, 1942.
Los Angeles, 1952.
San Francisco, 1965.
Oakland, 1978.

Most touchdowns on own fumbles recovered, season
2—Held by many teams. Last team: Buffalo, 2000.

Most touchdowns on fumbles recovered (own and opponents') game
2—Held by many teams.

Most touchdowns on fumbles recovered (own and opponents') both teams, game
3—Detroit 2, Minnesota 1, Dec. 9, 1962.
Green Bay 2, Dallas 1, Nov. 29, 1964.
Oakland 2, Buffalo 1, Dec. 24, 1967.
Oakland 2, Philadelphia 1, Sept. 24, 1995.
Tennessee 2, Pittsburgh 1, Jan. 2, 2000.

Most touchdowns on own fumbles recovered, game
2—Miami vs. New England, Sept. 1, 1996.

Most touchdowns on opponents' fumbles recovered by both teams, game
3—Green Bay 2, Dallas 1, Nov. 29, 1964.
Oakland 2, Buffalo 1, Dec. 24, 1967.
Oakland 2, Philadelphia 1, Sept. 24, 1995.
Tennessee 2, Pittsburgh 1, Jan. 2, 2000.

TURNOVERS

Most turnovers, season
63—San Francisco, 1978.

Fewest turnovers, season
12—Kansas City, 1982.

Most turnovers, game
12—Detroit vs. Chicago Bears, Nov. 22, 1942.
Chicago Cardinals vs. Philadelphia, Sept. 24, 1950.
Pittsburgh vs. Philadelphia, Dec. 12, 1965.

Most turnovers by both teams, game
17—Detroit 12, Chicago Bears 5, Nov. 22, 1942.
Boston 9, Philadelphia 8, Dec. 8, 1946.

PUNT RETURNS

Most punt returns, season
71—Pittsburgh, 1976.
Tampa Bay, 1979.
Los Angeles Raiders, 1985.

Fewest punt returns, season
12—Baltimore, 1981.
San Diego, 1982.

Most punt returns, game
12—Philadelphia at Cleveland, Dec. 3, 1950.

Most punt returns by both teams, game
17—Philadelphia 12, Cleveland 5, Dec. 3, 1950.

YARDS

Most yards, season
875—Green Bay, 1996.

Fewest yards, season
27—St. Louis, 1965.

Most yards, game
231—Detroit vs. San Francisco, Oct. 6, 1963.

Most yards by both teams, game
282—Los Angeles 219, Atlanta 63, Oct. 11, 1981.

TOUCHDOWNS

Most touchdowns, season
5—Chicago Cardinals, 1959.

Most touchdowns, game
2—Held by many teams.

Most touchdowns by both teams, game
2—Occurred many times.

KICKOFF RETURNS

Most kickoff returns, season
9—Cleveland, 1999.
Fewest kickoff returns, season
7—N.Y. Giants, 1944.
Most kickoff returns, game
2—N.Y. Giants at Washington, Nov. 27, 1966.
Most kickoff returns by both teams, game
9—N.Y. Giants 12, Washington 7, Nov. 27, 1966.

YARDS

Most yards, season
2,296—Arizona, 2000.
Fewest yards, season
282—N.Y. Giants, 1940.
Most yards, game
367—Baltimore vs. Minnesota, Dec. 13, 1998.
Most yards by both teams, game
560—Detroit 362, Los Angeles 198, Oct. 29, 1950.

TOUCHDOWNS

Most touchdowns, season
4—Green Bay, 1967.
  Chicago, 1970.
  Detroit, 1994.
Most touchdowns, game
2—Chicago Bears at Green Bay, Sept. 22, 1940.
  Chicago Bears vs. Green Bay, Nov. 9, 1952.
  Philadelphia vs. Dallas, Nov. 6, 1966.
  Green Bay vs. Cleveland, Nov. 12, 1967.
  Los Angeles Rams vs. Green Bay, Nov. 24, 1985.
  New Orleans vs. Los Angeles Rams, Oct. 23, 1994.
  Baltimore vs. Minnesota, Dec. 13, 1998.
  N.Y. Jets at Buffalo, Sept. 8, 2002 (OT).
Most touchdowns by both teams, game (each team scoring)
3—Baltimore (2) vs. Minnesota (1), Dec. 13, 1998.

PENALTIES

Most penalties, season
158—Kansas City, 1998.
Fewest penalties, season
9—Detroit, 1937.
Most penalties, game
22—Brooklyn at Green Bay, Sept. 17, 1944.
  Chicago Bears at Philadelphia, Nov. 26, 1944.
  San Francisco at Buffalo, Oct. 4, 1998.
Most penalties by both teams, game
37—Cleveland 21, Chicago Bears 16, Nov. 25, 1951.
Fewest penalties, game
0—Held by many teams. Last team: Washington at Carolina, Nov. 16, 2003.
Fewest penalties by both teams, game
0—Brooklyn 0, Pittsburgh 0, Oct. 28, 1934.
  Brooklyn 0, Boston 0, Sept. 28, 1936.
  Cleveland 0, Chicago Bears 0, Oct. 9, 1938.
  Pittsburgh 0, Philadelphia 0, Nov. 10, 1940.

YARDS PENALIZED

Most yards penalized, season
1,304—Kansas City, 1998.
Fewest yards penalized, season
39—Detroit, 1937.
Most yards penalized, game
212—Tennessee vs. Baltimore, Oct. 10, 1999.

Most yards penalized by both teams, game
374—Cleveland 209, Chicago Bears 165, Nov. 25, 1951.
Fewest yards penalized, game
0—Held by many teams. Last team: Washington at Carolina, Nov. 16, 2003.
Fewest yards penalized by both teams, game
0—Brooklyn 0, Pittsburgh 0, Oct. 28, 1934.
  Brooklyn 0, Boston 0, Sept. 28, 1936.
  Cleveland 0, Chicago Bears 0, Oct. 9, 1938.
  Pittsburgh 0, Philadelphia 0, Nov. 10, 1940.

TEAM DEFENSE
RUSHING

YARDS ALLOWED

Most yards allowed, season
3,228—Buffalo, 1978.
Fewest yards allowed, season
519—Chicago Bears, 1942.

TOUCHDOWNS ALLOWED

Most touchdowns allowed, season
36—Oakland, 1961.
Fewest touchdowns allowed, season
2—Detroit, 1934.
  Dallas, 1968.
  Minnesota, 1971.

PASSING

YARDS ALLOWED

Most yards allowed, season
4,541—Atlanta, 1995.
Fewest yards allowed, season
545—Philadelphia, 1934.

TOUCHDOWNS ALLOWED

Most touchdowns allowed, season
40—Denver, 1963.
Fewest touchdowns allowed, season
1—Portsmouth, 1932.
  Philadelphia, 1934.

YARDS ALLOWED

(RUSHING AND PASSING)

Most yards allowed rushing and passing, season
6,793—Baltimore, 1981.
Fewest yards allowed rushing and passing, season
1,539—Chicago Cardinals, 1934.

SCORING

POINTS ALLOWED

Most points allowed, season
533—Baltimore, 1981.
Fewest points allowed, season (since 1932)
44—Chicago Bears, 1932.

SHUTOUTS

Most shutouts, season
10—Pottsville, 1926 (won nine, tied one).
  N.Y. Giants, 1927 (won nine, tied one).

Most consecutive shutouts
13—Akron, 1920 through 1921 (won 10, tied three).

TOUCHDOWNS ALLOWED

Most touchdowns allowed, season
68—Baltimore, 1981.

Fewest touchdowns allowed, season (since 1932)
6—Chicago Bears, 1932.
　Brooklyn, 1933.

FIRST DOWNS ALLOWED

Most first downs allowed, season
406—Baltimore, 1981.

Fewest first downs allowed, season
77—Detroit, 1935.

Most first downs allowed by rushing, season
179—Detroit, 1985.

Fewest first downs allowed by rushing, season
35—Chicago Bears, 1942.

Most first downs allowed by passing, season
230—Atlanta, 1995.

Fewest first downs allowed by passing, season
33—Chicago Bears, 1943.

Most first downs allowed by penalties, season
56—Kansas City, 1998.

Fewest first downs allowed by penalties, season
1—Boston, 1944.

INTERCEPTIONS

Most interceptions, season
49—San Diego, 1961.

Fewest interceptions, season
3—Houston, 1982.

Most interceptions, game
9—Green Bay at Detroit, Oct. 24, 1943.
　Philadelphia at Pittsburgh, Dec. 12, 1965.

Most yards returning interceptions, season
929—San Diego, 1961.

Fewest yards returning interceptions, season
5—Los Angeles, 1959.

Most yards returning interceptions, game
325—Seattle vs. Kansas City, Nov. 4, 1984.

Most touchdowns returning interceptions, season
9—San Diego, 1961.

Most touchdowns returning interceptions, game
4—Seattle vs. Kansas City, Nov. 4, 1984.

Most touchdowns returning interceptions by both teams, game
4—Philadelphia 3, Pittsburgh 1, Dec. 12, 1965.
　Seattle 4, Kansas City 0, Nov. 4, 1984.

FUMBLES

Most opponents' fumbles forced, season
50—Minnesota, 1963.
　San Francisco, 1978.

Fewest opponents' fumbles forced, season
11—Cleveland, 1956.
　Baltimore, 1982.
　Tennessee, 1998.

RECOVERED

Most opponents' fumbles recovered, season
31—Minnesota, 1963.

Fewest opponents' fumbles recovered, season
3—Los Angeles, 1974.
　Green Bay, 1995.

Most opponents' fumbles recovered, game
8—Washington vs. St. Louis, Oct. 25, 1976.
　Pittsburgh vs. Cleveland, Dec. 23, 1990.

TOUCHDOWNS

Most touchdowns on opponents' fumbles recovered, season
4—Held by many teams. Last team: Kansas City, 1999.

Most touchdowns on opponents' fumbles recovered, game
2—Held by many teams. Last team: San Diego at St. Louis, Nov. 10, 2002.

TURNOVERS

Most opponents' turnovers, season
66—San Diego, 1961.

Fewest opponents' turnovers, season
11—Baltimore, 1982.

Most opponents' turnovers, game
12—Chicago Bears at Detroit, Nov. 22, 1942.
　Philadelphia at Chicago Cardinals, Sept. 24, 1950.
　Philadelphia at Pittsburgh, Dec. 12, 1965.

SACKS

Most sacks, season
72—Chicago, 1984.

Fewest sacks, season
11—Baltimore, 1982.

Most sacks, game
12—Dallas at Pittsburgh, Nov. 20, 1966.
　St. Louis at Baltimore, Oct. 26, 1980.
　Chicago at Detroit, Dec. 16, 1984.
　Dallas at Houston, Sept. 29, 1985.

PUNTS RETURNED

Most punts returned by opponents, season
71—Tampa Bay, 1976.
　Tampa Bay, 1977.

Fewest punts returned by opponents, season
7—Washington, 1962.
　San Diego, 1982.

Most yards allowed on punts returned by opponents, season
932—Green Bay, 1949.

Fewest yards allowed on punts returned by opponents, season
22—Green Bay, 1967.

Most touchdowns allowed on punts returned by opponents, season
4—New York, 1959.
　Atlanta, 1992.

KICKOFFS RETURNED

Most kickoffs returned by opponents, season
91—Washington, 1983.

Fewest kickoffs returned by opponents, season
10—Brooklyn, 1943.

Most yards allowed on kickoffs returned by opponents, season
2,194—St. Louis, 2001.

Fewest yards allowed on kickoffs returned by opponents, season
225—Brooklyn, 1943.

Most touchdowns allowed on kickoffs returned by opponents, season
4—Minnesota, 1998.

STATISTICAL LEADERS

TOP 20 RUSHERS

ayer	League	Years	Att.	Yds.	Avg.	Long	TD
mitt Smith*	NFL	15	4409	18355	3.9	t75	164
alter Payton	NFL	13	3838	16726	4.4	76	110
rry Sanders	NFL	10	3062	15269	5.0	85	99
rtis Martin*	NFL	10	3298	13366	4.1	t70	85
rome Bettis*	NFL	12	3369	13294	3.9	t71	82
ic Dickerson	NFL	11	2996	13259	4.4	t85	90
ny Dorsett	NFL	12	2936	12739	4.3	t99	77
n Brown	NFL	9	2359	12312	5.2	t80	106
arcus Allen	NFL	16	3022	12243	4.1	t61	123
anco Harris	NFL	13	2949	12120	4.1	t75	91
urman Thomas	NFL	13	2877	12074	4.2	t80	65
arshall Faulk*	NFL	11	2771	11987	4.3	t71	100
hn Riggins	NFL	14	2916	11352	3.9	t66	104
J. Simpson	AFL-NFL	11	2404	11236	4.7	t94	61
cky Watters	NFL	10	2622	10643	4.1	57	78
die George*	NFL	9	2865	10441	3.6	76	68
tis Anderson	NFL	14	2562	10273	4.0	t76	81
e Perry	AAFC-NFL	16	1929	9723	5.0		71
rey Dillon*	NFL	9	2210	9696	4.4	96	57
rl Campbell	NFL	8	2187	9407	4.3	t81	74

*Active through 2004 season.

TOP 20 PASSERS

ayer	League	Years	Att.	Cmp.	Yds.	TD	Int.	Rat.
eve Young	NFL	15	4149	2667	33124	232	107	96.8
rt Warner*	NFL	7	1965	1295	16501	108	69	95.7
aunte Culpepper*	NFL	6	2391	1539	18598	129	74	93.2
yton Manning*	NFL	7	3880	2464	29442	216	120	92.29
e Montana	NFL	15	5391	3409	40551	273	139	92.26
ent Green*	NFL	7	2822	1705	21607	133	82	87.9
m Brady*	NFL	5	2018	1243	13925	97	52	87.5
ett Favre*	NFL	14	7003	4306	49734	376	226	87.4
ff Garcia*	NFL	6	2612	1593	18139	123	65	87.2
to Graham	AAFC-NFL	10	2626	1464	23584	174	135	86.6
an Marino	NFL	17	8358	4967	61361	420	252	86.4
ian Griese*	NFL	7	2144	1351	15208	96	71	85.3
ch Gannon*	NFL	16	4206	2533	28743	180	104	84.7
m Kelly	NFL	11	4779	2874	35467	237	175	84.4
ad Johnson*	NFL	13	3504	2166	23913	143	98	84.0
onovan McNabb*	NFL	6	2586	1507	16926	118	57	83.94
ark Brunell*	NFL	11	3880	2314	26987	151	92	83.86
att Hasselbeck*	NFL	6	1756	1048	12466	72	48	83.7
ger Staubach	NFL	11	2958	1685	22700	153	109	83.42
eve McNair*	NFL	10	3395	2013	23980	140	92	83.38

*Active through 2004 season; minimum 1,500 attempts.

TOP 20 RECEIVERS

ayer	League	Years	No.	Yds.	Avg.	Long	TD
rry Rice*	NFL	20	1549	22895	14.8	t96	197
is Carter	NFL	16	1101	13899	12.6	t80	130
m Brown*	NFL	17	1094	14934	13.7	t80	100
dre Reed	NFL	16	951	13198	13.9	t83	87
t Monk	NFL	16	940	12721	13.5	t79	68
ving Fryar	NFL	17	851	12785	15.0	t80	84
arvin Harrison*	NFL	9	845	11185	13.2	t79	98
rry Centers	NFL	14	827	6797	8.2	54	28
eve Largent	NFL	14	819	13089	16.0	t74	100
annon Sharpe*	NFL	14	815	10060	12.3	t82	62
nry Ellard	NFL	16	814	13777	16.9	t81	65
mmy Smith*	NFL	12	792	11264	14.2	75	61
aac Bruce*	NFL	11	777	11753	15.1	t80	74
mes Lofton	NFL	16	764	14004	18.3	t80	75
enan McCardell*	NFL	13	755	9763	12.9	t76	53

Player	League	Years	No.	Yds.	Avg.	Long	
Charlie Joiner	AFL-NFL	18	750	12146	16.2	t87	6
Michael Irvin	NFL	12	750	11904	15.9	t87	6
Andre Rison	NFL	12	743	10205	13.7	t80	8
Marshall Faulk*	NFL	11	723	6584	9.1	85	3
Rod Smith*	NFL	10	712	9772	13.7	85	5

*Active through 2004 season.

TOP 20 SCORERS

Player	League	Years	TD	XP Made	FG Made	Tota
Gary Anderson*	NFL	23	0	820	538	243
Morten Andersen*	NFL	23	0	798	520	235
George Blanda	NFL-AFL	26	9	943	335	200
Norm Johnson	NFL	18	0	638	366	173
Nick Lowery	NFL	18	0	562	383	171
Jan Stenerud	AFL-NFL	19	0	580	373	169
Lou Groza	AAFC-NFL	21	1	810	264	160
Eddie Murray	NFL	19	0	538	352	159
Al Del Greco	NFL	17	0	543	347	158
John Carney*	NFL	17	0	442	365	153
Matt Stover*	NFL	14	0	431	350	148
Steve Christie*	NFL	15	0	468	336	147
Pat Leahy	NFL	18	0	558	304	147
Jason Elam*	NFL	12	0	491	317	144
Jim Turner	AFL-NFL	16	1	521	304	143
Matt Bahr	NFL	17	0	522	300	142
Mark Moseley	NFL	16	0	482	300	138
Jim Bakken	NFL	17	0	534	282	138
Fred Cox	NFL	15	0	519	282	136
Jason Hanson	NFL	13	0	412	308	133

*Active through 2004 season.

YEAR BY YEAR

AFC

RUSHING
(Based on most net yards)

	Net Yds.	Att.	TD
1960—Abner Haynes, Dallas	875	156	9
1961—Billy Cannon, Houston	948	200	6
1962—Cookie Gilchrist, Buffalo	1096	214	13
1963—Clem Daniels, Oakland	1099	215	3
1964—Cookie Gilchrist, Buffalo	981	230	6
1965—Paul Lowe, San Diego	1121	222	7
1966—Jim Nance, Boston	1458	299	11
1967—Jim Nance, Boston	1216	269	7
1968—Paul Robinson, Cincinnati	1023	238	8
1969—Dick Post, San Diego	873	182	6
1970—Floyd Little, Denver	901	209	3
1971—Floyd Little, Denver	1133	284	6
1972—O.J. Simpson, Buffalo	1251	292	6
1973—O.J. Simpson, Buffalo	2003	332	12
1974—Otis Armstrong, Denver	1407	263	9
1975—O.J. Simpson, Buffalo	1817	329	16
1976—O.J. Simpson, Buffalo	1503	290	8
1977—Mark van Eeghen, Oakland	1273	324	7
1978—Earl Campbell, Houston	1450	302	13
1979—Earl Campbell, Houston	1697	368	19
1980—Earl Campbell, Houston	1934	373	13
1981—Earl Campbell, Houston	1376	361	10
1982—Freeman McNeil, N.Y. Jets	786	151	6
1983—Curt Warner, Seattle	1449	335	13
1984—Earnest Jackson, San Diego	1179	296	8
1985—Marcus Allen, L.A. Raiders	1759	380	11
1986—Curt Warner, Seattle	1481	319	13
1987—Eric Dickerson, Indianapolis	1011	223	5
1988—Eric Dickerson, Indianapolis	1659	388	14
1989—Christian Okoye, Kansas City	1480	370	12
1990—Thurman Thomas, Buffalo	1297	271	11
1991—Thurman Thomas, Buffalo	1407	288	7
1992—Barry Foster, Pittsburgh	1690	390	11
1993—Thurman Thomas, Buffalo	1315	355	6
1994—Chris Warren, Seattle	1545	333	9

	Net Yds.	Att.	T
1995—Curtis Martin, New England	1487	368	1
1996—Terrell Davis, Denver	1538	345	1
1997—Terrell Davis, Denver	1750	369	1
1998—Terrell Davis, Denver	2008	392	2
1999—Edgerrin James, Indianapolis	1553	369	1
2000—Edgerrin James, Indianapolis	1709	387	1
2001—Priest Holmes, Kansas City	1555	327	
2002—Ricky Williams, Miami	1853	383	1
2003—Jamal Lewis, Baltimore	2066	387	1
2004—Curtis Martin, N.Y. Jets	1697	371	1

PASSING
(Based on highest passer rating among qualifiers*)

	Att.	Com.	Yds.	TD	Int.	Ra
1960—Jack Kemp, S.D.	406	211	3018	20	25	67.
1961—George Blanda, Hou.	362	187	3330	36	22	91.
1962—Len Dawson, Dal.	310	189	2759	29	17	98
1963—Tobin Rote, S.D.	286	170	2510	20	17	86.
1964—Len Dawson, K.C.	354	199	2879	30	18	89.
1965—John Hadl, S.D.	348	174	2798	20	21	71.
1966—Len Dawson, K.C.	284	159	2527	26	10	101.
1967—Daryle Lamonica, Oak.	425	220	3228	30	20	80.
1968—Len Dawson, K.C.	224	131	2109	17	9	98.
1969—Greg Cook, Cin.	197	106	1854	15	11	88.
1970—Daryle Lamonica, Oak.	356	179	2516	22	15	76.
1971—Bob Griese, Mia.	263	145	2089	19	9	90.
1972—Earl Morrall, Mia.	150	83	1360	11	7	91.
1973—Ken Stabler, Oak.	260	163	1997	14	10	88.
1974—Ken Anderson, Cin.	328	213	2667	18	10	95.
1975—Ken Anderson, Cin.	377	228	3169	21	11	93.
1976—Ken Stabler, Oak.	291	194	2737	27	17	103.
1977—Bob Griese, Mia.	307	180	2252	22	13	87.
1978—Terry Bradshaw, Pit.	368	207	2915	28	20	84.
1979—Dan Fouts, S.D.	530	332	4082	24	24	82.
1980—Brian Sipe, Cle.	554	337	4132	30	14	91.
1981—Ken Anderson, Cin.	479	300	3754	29	10	98.
1982—Ken Anderson, Cin.	309	218	2495	12	9	95.

	Att.	Com.	Yds.	TD	Int.	Rat.
83— Dan Marino, Mia.	296	173	2210	20	6	96.0
84— Dan Marino, Mia.	564	362	5084	48	17	108.9
85— Ken O'Brien, NYJ	488	297	3888	25	8	96.2
86— Dan Marino, Mia.	623	378	4746	44	23	92.5
87— Bernie Kosar, Cle.	389	241	3033	22	9	95.4
88— Boomer Esiason, Cin.	388	223	3572	28	14	97.4
89— Boomer Esiason, Cin.	455	258	3525	28	11	92.1
90— Jim Kelly, Buf.	346	219	2829	24	9	101.2
91— Jim Kelly, Buf.	474	304	3844	33	17	97.6
92— Warren Moon, Hou.	346	224	2521	18	12	89.3
93— John Elway, Den.	551	348	4030	25	10	92.8
94— Dan Marino, Mia.	615	385	4453	30	17	89.2
95— Jim Harbaugh, Ind.	314	200	2575	17	5	100.7
96— John Elway, Den.	466	287	3328	26	14	89.2
97— Mark Brunell, Jac.†	435	264	3281	18	7	†91.17
98— Vinny Testaverde, NYJ	421	259	3256	29	7	101.6
99— Peyton Manning, Ind.	533	331	4135	26	15	90.7
00— Brian Griese, Den.	336	216	2688	19	4	102.9
01— Rich Gannon, Oak.	549	361	3828	27	9	95.5
02— Chad Pennington, NYJ	399	275	3120	22	6	104.2
03— Steve McNair, Ten.	400	250	3215	24	7	100.4
04— Peyton Manning, Ind.	497	336	4557	49	10	121.1

*This chart includes passer rating points for all leaders, although the
me rating system was not used for determining leading quarterbacks
or to 1973. The old system was less equitable, yet similar to the new
that the rating was based on percentage of completions, touchdown
sses, percentage of interceptions and average gain in yards.

†Brunell and Jeff George of Oakland (521, 290, 3917, 29, 9), tied with
.2 rating points, but rounded to another decimal place, Brunell's rat-
g is higher, 91.17 to 91.15.

RECEIVING
(Based on most receptions)

	No.	Yds.	TD
60—Lionel Taylor, Denver	92	1235	12
61—Lionel Taylor, Denver	100	1176	4
62—Lionel Taylor, Denver	77	908	4
63—Lionel Taylor, Denver	78	1101	10
64—Charley Hennigan, Houston	101	1546	8
65—Lionel Taylor, Denver	85	1131	6
66—Lance Alworth, San Diego	73	1383	13
67—George Sauer, N.Y. Jets	75	1189	6
68—Lance Alworth, San Diego	68	1312	10
69—Lance Alworth, San Diego	64	1003	4
70—Marlin Briscoe, Buffalo	57	1036	8
71—Fred Biletnikoff, Oakland	61	929	9
72—Fred Biletnikoff, Oakland	58	802	7
73—Fred Willis, Houston	57	371	1
74—Lydell Mitchell, Baltimore	72	544	2
75—Reggie Rucker, Cleveland	60	770	3
Lydell Mitchell, Baltimore	60	544	4
76—MacArthur Lane, Kansas City	66	686	1
77—Lydell Mitchell, Baltimore	71	620	4
78—Steve Largent, Seattle	71	1168	8
79—Joe Washington, Baltimore	82	750	3
80—Kellen Winslow, San Diego	89	1290	9
81—Kellen Winslow, San Diego	88	1075	10
82—Kellen Winslow, San Diego	54	721	6
83—Todd Christensen, L.A. Raiders	92	1247	12
84—Ozzie Newsome, Cleveland	89	1001	5
85—Lionel James, San Diego	86	1027	6
86—Todd Christensen, L.A. Raiders	95	1153	8
87—Al Toon, N.Y. Jets	68	976	5
88—Al Toon, N.Y. Jets	93	1067	5
89—Andre Reed, Buffalo	88	1312	9
90—Haywood Jeffires, Houston	74	1048	8
Drew Hill, Houston	74	1019	5
91—Haywood Jeffires, Houston	100	1181	7
92—Haywood Jeffires, Houston	90	913	9
93—Reggie Langhorne, Indianapolis	85	1038	3
94—Ben Coates, New England	96	1174	7
95—Carl Pickens, Cincinnati	99	1234	17
96—Carl Pickens, Cincinnati	100	1180	12
97—Tim Brown, Oakland	104	1408	5

	No.	Yds.	TD
1998—O.J. McDuffie, Miami	90	1050	7
1999—Jimmy Smith, Jacksonville	116	1636	6
2000—Marvin Harrison, Indianapolis	102	1413	14
2001—Rod Smith, Denver	113	1343	11
2002—Marvin Harrison, Indianapolis	143	1722	11
2003—LaDainian Tomlinson, San Diego	100	725	4
2004—Tony Gonzalez, Kansas City	102	1258	7

SCORING
(Based on most total points)

	TD	PAT	FG	Tot.
1960— Gene Mingo, Denver	6	33	18	123
1961— Gino Cappelletti, Boston	8	48	17	147
1962— Gene Mingo, Denver	4	32	27	137
1963— Gino Cappelletti, Boston	2	35	22	113
1964— Gino Cappelletti, Boston	7	36	25	155
1965— Gino Cappelletti, Boston	9	27	17	132
1966— Gino Cappelletti, Boston	6	35	16	119
1967— George Blanda, Oakland	0	56	20	116
1968— Jim Turner, N.Y. Jets	0	43	34	145
1969— Jim Turner, N.Y. Jets	0	33	32	129
1970— Jan Stenerud, Kansas City	0	26	30	116
1971— Garo Yepremian, Miami	0	33	28	117
1972— Bobby Howfield, N.Y. Jets	0	40	27	121
1973— Roy Gerela, Pittsburgh	0	36	29	123
1974— Roy Gerela, Pittsburgh	0	33	20	93
1975— O.J. Simpson, Buffalo	23	0	0	138
1976— Toni Linhart, Baltimore	0	49	20	109
1977— Errol Mann, Oakland	0	39	20	99
1978— Pat Leahy, N.Y. Jets	0	41	22	107
1979— John Smith, New England	0	46	23	115
1980— John Smith, New England	0	51	26	129
1981— Jim Breech, Cincinnati	0	49	22	115
Nick Lowery, Kansas City	0	37	26	115
1982— Marcus Allen, L.A. Raiders	14	0	0	84
1983— Gary Anderson, Pittsburgh	0	38	27	119
1984— Gary Anderson, Pittsburgh	0	45	24	117
1985— Gary Anderson, Pittsburgh	0	40	33	139
1986— Tony Franklin, New England	0	44	32	140
1987— Jim Breech, Cincinnati	0	25	24	97
1988— Scott Norwood, Buffalo	0	33	32	129
1989— David Treadwell, Denver	0	39	27	120
1990— Nick Lowery, Kansas City	0	37	34	139
1991— Pete Stoyanovich, Miami	0	28	31	121
1992— Pete Stoyanovich, Miami	0	34	30	124
1993— Jeff Jaeger, L.A. Raiders	0	27	35	132
1994— John Carney, San Diego	0	33	34	135
1995— Norm Johnson, Pittsburgh	0	39	34	141
1996— Cary Blanchard, Indianapolis	0	27	36	135
1997— Mike Hollis, Jacksonville	0	41	31	134
1998— Steve Christie, Buffalo	0	41	33	140
1999— Mike Vanderjagt, Indianapolis	0	43	34	145
2000— Matt Stover, Baltimore	0	30	35	135
2001— Mike Vanderjagt, Indianapolis	0	41	28	125
2002— Priest Holmes, Kansas City	24	0	0	144
2003— Priest Holmes, Kansas City	27	0	0	162
2004— Adam Vinatieri, New England	0	48	31	141

FIELD GOALS

	No.
1960— Gene Mingo, Denver	18
1961— Gino Cappelletti, Boston	17
1962— Gene Mingo, Denver	27
1963— Gino Cappelletti, Boston	22
1964— Gino Cappelletti, Boston	25
1965— Pete Gogolak, Buffalo	28
1966— Mike Mercer, Oakland-Kansas City	21
1967— Jan Stenerud, Kansas City	21
1968— Jim Turner, N.Y. Jets	34
1969— Jim Turner, N.Y. Jets	32
1970— Jan Stenerud, Kansas City	30
1971— Garo Yepremian, Miami	28
1972— Roy Gerela, Pittsburgh	28
1973— Roy Gerela, Pittsburgh	29

HISTORY *Statistical leaders*

<table>
	No.
1974— Roy Gerela, Pittsburgh	20
1975— Jan Stenerud, Kansas City	22
1976— Jan Stenerud, Kansas City	21
1977— Errol Mann, Oakland	20
1978— Pat Leahy, N.Y. Jets	22
1979— John Smith, New England	23
1980— John Smith, New England	26
Fred Steinfort, Denver	26
1981— Nick Lowery, Kansas City	26
1982— Nick Lowery, Kansas City	19
1983— Raul Allegre, Baltimore	30
1984— Gary Anderson, Pittsburgh	24
Matt Bahr, Cleveland	24
1985— Gary Anderson, Pittsburgh	33
1986— Tony Franklin, New England	32
1987— Dean Biasucci, Indianapolis	24
Jim Breech, Cincinnati	24
1988— Scott Norwood, Buffalo	32
1989— David Treadwell, Denver	27
1990— Nick Lowery, Kansas City	34
1991— Pete Stoyanovich, Miami	31
1992— Pete Stoyanovich, Miami	30
1993— Jeff Jaeger, L.A. Raiders	35
1994— John Carney, San Diego	34
1995— Norm Johnson, Pittsburgh	34
1996— Cary Blanchard, Indianapolis	36
1997— Cary Blanchard, Indianapolis	32
1998— Al Del Greco, Tennessee	36
1999— Olindo Mare, Miami	39
2000— Matt Stover, Baltimore	35
2001— Jason Elam, Denver	31
2002— Adam Vinatieri, New England	27
2003— Mike Vanderjagt, Indianapolis	37
2004— Adam Vinatieri, New England	31
</table>

INTERCEPTIONS

	No.	Yds.
1960— Austin Gonsoulin, Denver	11	98
1961— Bill Atkins, Buffalo	10	158
1962— Lee Riley, N.Y. Titans	11	122
1963— Fred Glick, Houston	12	180
1964— Dainard Paulson, N.Y. Jets	12	157
1965— W.K. Hicks, Houston	9	156
1966— Johnny Robinson, Kansas City	10	136
Bobby Hunt, Kansas City	10	113
1967— Miller Farr, Houston	10	264
Tom Janik, Buffalo	10	222
Dick Westmoreland, Miami	10	127
1968— Dave Grayson, Oakland	10	195
1969— Emmitt Thomas, Kansas City	9	146
1970— Johnny Robinson, Kansas City	10	155
1971— Ken Houston, Houston	9	220
1972— Mike Sensibaugh, Kansas City	8	65
1973— Dick Anderson, Miami	8	136
Mike Wagner, Pittsburgh	8	134
1974— Emmitt Thomas, Kansas City	12	214
1975— Mel Blount, Pittsburgh	11	121
1976— Ken Riley, Cincinnati	9	141
1977— Lyle Blackwood, Baltimore	10	163
1978— Thom Darden, Cleveland	10	200
1979— Mike Reinfeldt, Houston	12	205
1980— Lester Hayes, Oakland	13	273
1981— John Harris, Seattle	10	155
1982— Ken Riley, Cincinnati	5	88
Bobby Jackson, N.Y. Jets	5	84
Dwayne Woodruff, Pittsburgh	5	53
Donnie Shell, Pittsburgh	5	27
1983— Ken Riley, Cincinnati	8	89
Vann McElroy, Los Angeles	8	68
1984— Kenny Easley, Seattle	10	126
1985— Albert Lewis, Kansas City	8	59
Eugene Daniel, Indianapolis	8	53
1986— Deron Cherry, Kansas City	9	150
1987— Mike Prior, Indianapolis	6	57
Mark Kelso, Buffalo	6	25
Keith Bostic, Houston	6	-14
1988— Erik McMillan, N.Y. Jets	8	168
1989— Felix Wright, Cleveland	9	91

	No.	Yds
1990— Richard Johnson, Houston	8	10
1991— Ronnie Lott, L.A. Raiders	8	5
1992— Henry Jones, Buffalo	8	26
1993— Eugene Robinson, Seattle	9	8
Nate Odomes, Buffalo	9	6
1994— Eric Turner, Cleveland	9	19
1995— Willie Williams, Pittsburgh	7	12
1996— Tyrone Braxton, Denver	9	12
1997— Mark McMillian, Kansas City	8	27
Darryl Williams, Seattle	8	17
1998— Ty Law, New England	9	13
1999— Rod Woodson, Baltimore	7	19
Sam Madison, Miami	7	16
James Hasty, Kansas City	7	9
2000— Samari Rolle, Tennessee	7	14
Brian Walker, Miami	7	8
2001— Anthony Henry, Cleveland	10	17
2002— Rod Woodson, Oakland	8	22
2003— Ed Reed, Baltimore	7	13
Marcus Coleman, Houston	7	9
Patrick Surtain, Miami	7	5
2004— Ed Reed, Baltimore	9	35

PUNTING

(Based on highest average yardage per punt by qualifiers)

	No.	Avg
1960— Paul Maguire, L.A. Chargers	43	40.
1961— Bill Atkins, Buffalo	85	44.
1962— Jim Fraser, Denver	55	43.
1963— Jim Fraser, Denver	81	44.
1964— Jim Fraser, Denver	73	44.
1965— Jerrel Wilson, Kansas City	69	45.
1966— Bob Scarpitto, Denver	76	45.
1967— Bob Scarpitto, Denver	105	44.
1968— Jerrel Wilson, Kansas City	63	45.
1969— Dennis Partee, San Diego	71	44.
1970— Dave Lewis, Cincinnati	79	46.
1971— Dave Lewis, Cincinnati	72	44.
1972— Jerrel Wilson, Kansas City	66	44.
1973— Jerrel Wilson, Kansas City	80	45
1974— Ray Guy, Oakland	74	42.
1975— Ray Guy, Oakland	68	43.
1976— Marv Bateman, Buffalo	86	42.
1977— Ray Guy, Oakland	59	43.
1978— Pat McInally, Cincinnati	91	43.
1979— Bob Grupp, Kansas City	89	43.
1980— Luke Prestridge, Denver	70	43
1981— Pat McInally, Cincinnati	72	45.
1982— Luke Prestridge, Denver	45	45.
1983— Rohn Stark, Baltimore	91	45.
1984— Jim Arnold, Kansas City	98	44.
1985— Rohn Stark, Indianapolis	78	45.
1986— Rohn Stark, Indianapolis	76	45.
1987— Ralf Mojsiejenko, San Diego	67	42.
1988— Harry Newsome, Pittsburgh	65	45.
1989— Greg Montgomery, Houston	56	43.
1990— Mike Horan, Denver	58	44.
1991— Reggie Roby, Miami	54	45.
1992— Greg Montgomery, Houston	53	46.
1993— Greg Montgomery, Houston	54	45.
1994— Jeff Gossett, L.A. Raiders	77	43.
1995— Rick Tuten, Seattle	83	45.
1996— John Kidd, Miami	78	46.
1997— Tom Tupa, New England	78	45.
1998— Craig Hentrich, Tennessee	69	47.
1999— Tom Rouen, Denver	84	46.
2000— Darren Bennett, San Diego	92	46.
2001— Shane Lechler, Oakland	73	46.
2002— Chris Hanson, Jacksonville	81	44.
2003— Shane Lechler, Oakland	96	46.
2004— Shane Lechler, Oakland	73	46.

PUNT RETURNS

(Based on most total yards)

	No.	Yds.	Avg
1960—Abner Haynes, Dallas	14	215	15.
1961—Dick Christy, N.Y. Titans	18	383	21.

	No.	Yds.	Avg.
62— Dick Christy, N.Y. Titans	15	250	16.7
63— Claude Gibson, Oakland	26	307	11.8
64— Bobby Jancik, Houston	12	220	18.3
65— Leslie Duncan, San Diego	30	464	15.5
66— Leslie Duncan, San Diego	18	238	13.2
67— Floyd Little, Denver	16	270	16.9
68— Noland Smith, Kansas City	18	270	15.0
69— Bill Thompson, Denver	25	288	11.5
70— Ed Podolak, Kansas City	23	311	13.5
71— Leroy Kelly, Cleveland	30	292	9.7
72— Chris Farasopoulos, N.Y. Jets	17	179	10.5
73— Ron Smith, San Diego	27	352	13.0
74— Lemar Parrish, Cincinnati	18	338	18.8
75— Billy Johnson, Houston	40	612	15.3
76— Rick Upchurch, Denver	39	536	13.7
77— Billy Johnson, Houston	35	539	15.4
78— Rick Upchurch, Denver	36	493	13.7
79— Tony Nathan, Miami	28	306	10.9
80— J.T. Smith, Kansas City	40	581	14.5
81— James Brooks, San Diego	22	290	13.2
82— Rick Upchurch, Denver	15	242	16.1
83— Kirk Springs, N.Y. Jets	23	287	12.5
84— Mike Martin, Cincinnati	24	376	15.7
85— Irving Fryar, New England	37	520	14.1
86— Bobby Joe Edmonds, Seattle	34	419	12.3
87— Bobby Joe Edmonds, Seattle	20	251	12.6
88— Jojo Townsell, N.Y. Jets	35	409	11.7
89— Clarence Verdin, Indianapolis	23	296	12.9
90— Clarence Verdin, Indianapolis	31	396	12.8
91— Rod Woodson, Pittsburgh	28	320	11.4
92— Rod Woodson, Pittsburgh	32	364	11.4
93— Tim Brown, L.A. Raiders	40	465	11.6
94— Tim Brown, L.A. Raiders	40	487	12.2
95— Tamarick Vanover, Kansas City	51	540	10.6
96— David Meggett, New England	52	588	11.3
97— Leon Johnson, N.Y. Jets	51	619	12.1
98— Reggie Barlow, Jacksonville	43	555	12.9
99— Charlie Rogers, Seattle	22	318	14.5
000— Derrick Mason, Tennessee	51	662	13.0
001— Jermaine Lewis, Baltimore	42	519	12.4
002— Santana Moss, N.Y. Jets	25	413	16.5
003— Antwaan Randle El, Pittsburgh	45	542	12.0
004— B.J. Sams, Baltimore	55	575	10.5

KICKOFF RETURNS

(Based on most total yards)

	No.	Yds.	Avg.
960— Ken Hall, Houston	19	594	31.3
961— Dave Grayson, Dallas	16	453	28.3
962— Bobby Jancik, Houston	24	726	30.3
963— Bobby Jancik, Houston	45	1317	29.3
964— Bo Roberson, Oakland	36	975	27.1
965— Abner Haynes, Denver	34	901	26.5
966— Goldie Sellers, Denver	19	541	28.5
967— Zeke Moore, Houston	14	405	28.9
968— George Atkinson, Oakland	32	802	25.1
969— Bill Thompson, Denver	18	513	28.5
970— Jim Duncan, Baltimore	20	707	35.4
971— Mercury Morris, Miami	15	423	28.2
972— Bruce Laird, Baltimore	29	843	29.1
973— Wallace Francis, Buffalo	23	687	29.9
974— Greg Pruitt, Cleveland	22	606	27.5
975— Harold Hart, Oakland	17	518	30.5
976— Duriel Harris, Miami	17	559	32.9
977— Raymond Clayborn, New England	28	869	31.0
978— Keith Wright, Cleveland	30	789	26.3
979— Larry Brunson, Oakland	17	441	25.9
980— Horace Ivory, New England	36	992	27.6
981— Carl Roaches, Houston	28	769	27.5
982— Mike Mosley, Buffalo	18	487	27.1
983— Fulton Walker, Miami	36	962	26.7
984— Bobby Humphery, N.Y. Jets	22	675	30.7
985— Glen Young, Cleveland	35	898	25.7
986— Lupe Sanchez, Pittsburgh	25	591	23.6
987— Paul Palmer, Kansas City	38	923	24.3
988— Tim Brown, L.A. Raiders	41	1098	26.8
989— Rod Woodson, Pittsburgh	36	982	27.3

	No.	Yds.	Avg.
1990— Kevin Clark, Denver	20	505	25.3
1991— Nate Lewis, San Diego	23	578	25.1
1992— Jon Vaughn, New England	20	564	28.2
1993— Clarence Verdin, Indianapolis	50	1050	21.0
1994— Andre Coleman, San Diego	49	1293	26.4
1995— Andre Coleman, San Diego	62	1411	22.8
1996— Mel Gray, Houston	50	1224	24.5
1997— Kevin Williams, Arizona	59	1458	24.7
1998— Vaughn Hebron, Denver	46	1216	26.4
1999— Tremain Mack, Cincinnati	51	1382	27.1
2000— Charlie Rogers, Seattle	66	1629	24.7
2001— Ronney Jenkins, San Diego	58	1541	26.6
2002— Chad Morton, N.Y. Jets	58	1509	26.0
2003— Dante Hall, Kansas City	57	1478	25.9
2004— Dante Hall, Kansas City	68	1718	25.3

SACKS

	No.
1982— Jesse Baker, Houston	7.5
1983— Mark Gastineau, N.Y. Jets	19.0
1984— Mark Gastineau, N.Y. Jets	22.0
1985— Andre Tippett, New England	16.5
1986— Sean Jones, L.A. Raiders	15.5
1987— Andre Tippett, New England	12.5
1988— Greg Townsend, L.A. Raiders	11.5
1989— Lee Williams, San Diego	14.0
1990— Derrick Thomas, Kansas City	20.0
1991— William Fuller, Houston	15.0
1992— Leslie O'Neal, San Diego	17.0
1993— Neil Smith, Kansas City	15.0
1994— Kevin Greene, Pittsburgh	14.0
1995— Bryce Paup, Buffalo	17.5
1996— Michael McCrary, Seattle	13.5
Bruce Smith, Buffalo	13.5
1997— Bruce Smith, Buffalo	14.0
1998— Michael Sinclair, Seattle	16.5
1999— Jevon Kearse, Tennessee	14.5
2000— Trace Armstrong, Miami	16.5
2001— Peter Boulware, Baltimore	15.0
2002— Jason Taylor, Miami	18.5
2003— Adewale Ogunleye, Miami	15.0
2004— Dwight Freeney, Indianapolis	16.0

NFC

RUSHING

(Based on most net yards)

	Net Yds.	Att.	TD
1960— Jim Brown, Cleveland	1257	215	9
1961— Jim Brown, Cleveland	1408	305	8
1962— Jim Taylor, Green Bay	1474	272	19
1963— Jim Brown, Cleveland	1863	291	12
1964— Jim Brown, Cleveland	1446	280	7
1965— Jim Brown, Cleveland	1544	289	17
1966— Gale Sayers, Chicago	1231	229	8
1967— Leroy Kelly, Cleveland	1205	235	11
1968— Leroy Kelly, Cleveland	1239	248	16
1969— Gale Sayers, Chicago	1032	236	8
1970— Larry Brown, Washington	1125	237	5
1971— John Brockington, Green Bay	1105	216	4
1972— Larry Brown, Washington	1216	285	8
1973— John Brockington, Green Bay	1144	265	3
1974— Lawrence McCutcheon, L.A. Rams	1109	236	3
1975— Jim Otis, St. Louis	1076	269	5
1976— Walter Payton, Chicago	1390	311	13
1977— Walter Payton, Chicago	1852	339	14
1978— Walter Payton, Chicago	1395	333	11
1979— Walter Payton, Chicago	1610	369	14
1980— Walter Payton, Chicago	1460	317	6
1981— George Rogers, New Orleans	1674	378	13
1982— Tony Dorsett, Dallas	745	177	5
1983— Eric Dickerson, L.A. Rams	1808	390	18
1984— Eric Dickerson, L.A. Rams	2105	379	14
1985— Gerald Riggs, Atlanta	1719	397	10
1986— Eric Dickerson, L.A. Rams	1821	404	11
1987— Charles White, L.A. Rams	1374	324	11

	Net Yds.	Att.	TD
1988—Herschel Walker, Dallas	1514	361	5
1989—Barry Sanders, Detroit	1470	280	14
1990—Barry Sanders, Detroit	1304	255	13
1991—Emmitt Smith, Dallas	1563	365	12
1992—Emmitt Smith, Dallas	1713	373	18
1993—Emmitt Smith, Dallas	1486	283	9
1994—Barry Sanders, Detroit	1883	331	7
1995—Emmitt Smith, Dallas	1773	377	25
1996—Barry Sanders, Detroit	1553	307	11
1997—Barry Sanders, Detroit	2053	335	11
1998—Jamal Anderson, Atlanta	1846	410	14
1999—Stephen Davis, Washington	1405	290	17
2000—Robert Smith, Minnesota	1521	295	7
2001—Stephen Davis, Washington	1432	356	5
2002—Deuce McAllister, New Orleans	1388	325	13
2003—Ahman Green, Green Bay	1883	355	15
2004—Shaun Alexander, Seattle	1696	353	16

PASSING

(Based on highest passer rating among qualifiers*)

	Att.	Com.	Yds.	TD	Int.	Rat.
1960— Milt Plum, Cle.	250	151	2297	21	5	110.4
1961— Milt Plum, Cle.	302	177	2416	18	10	90.3
1962— Bart Starr, G.B.	285	178	2438	12	9	90.7
1963— Y.A. Tittle, NYG	367	221	3145	36	14	104.8
1964— Bart Starr, G.B.	272	163	2144	15	4	97.1
1965— Rudy Bukich, Chi.	312	176	2641	20	9	93.7
1966— Bart Starr, G.B.	251	156	2257	14	3	105.0
1967— Sonny Jurgensen, Was.	508	288	3747	31	16	87.3
1968— Earl Morrall, Bal.	317	182	2909	26	17	93.2
1969— Sonny Jurgensen, Was.	442	274	3102	22	15	85.4
1970— John Brodie, S.F.	378	223	2941	24	10	93.8
1971— Roger Staubach, Dal.	211	126	1882	15	4	104.8
1972— Norm Snead, NYG	325	196	2307	17	12	84.0
1973— Roger Staubach, Dal.	286	179	2428	23	15	94.6
1974— Sonny Jurgensen, Was.	167	107	1185	11	5	94.5
1975— Fran Tarkenton, Min.	425	273	2994	25	13	91.8
1976— James Harris, L.A.	158	91	1460	8	6	89.6
1977— Roger Staubach, Dal.	361	210	2620	18	9	87.0
1978— Roger Staubach, Dal.	413	231	3190	25	16	84.9
1979— Roger Staubach, Dal.	461	267	3586	27	11	92.3
1980— Ron Jaworski, Phi.	451	257	3529	27	12	91.0
1981— Joe Montana, S.F.	488	311	3565	19	12	88.4
1982— Joe Theismann, Was.	252	161	2033	13	9	91.3
1983— Steve Bartkowski, Atl.	432	274	3167	22	5	97.6
1984— Joe Montana, S.F.	432	279	3630	28	10	102.9
1985— Joe Montana, S.F.	494	303	3653	27	13	91.3
1986— Tommy Kramer, Min.	372	208	3000	24	10	92.6
1987— Joe Montana, S.F.	398	266	3054	31	13	102.1
1988— Wade Wilson, Min.	332	204	2746	15	9	91.5
1989— Joe Montana, S.F.	386	271	3521	26	8	112.4
1990— Phil Simms, NYG	311	184	2284	15	4	92.7
1991— Steve Young, S.F.	279	180	2517	17	8	101.8
1992— Steve Young, S.F.	402	268	3465	25	7	107.0
1993— Steve Young, S.F.	462	314	4023	29	16	101.5
1994— Steve Young, S.F.	461	324	3969	35	10	112.8
1995— Brett Favre, G.B.	570	359	4413	38	13	99.5
1996— Steve Young, S.F.	316	214	2410	14	6	97.2
1997— Steve Young, S.F.	356	241	3029	19	6	104.7
1998— Ran. Cunningham, Min.	425	259	3704	34	10	106.0
1999— Kurt Warner, St.L.	499	325	4353	41	13	109.2
2000— Trent Green, St.L.	240	145	2063	16	5	101.8
2001— Kurt Warner, St.L.	546	375	4830	36	22	101.4
2002— Brad Johnson, T.B.	451	281	3049	22	6	92.9
2003— Daunte Culpepper, Min.	454	295	3479	25	11	96.4
2004— Daunte Culpepper, Min.	548	379	4717	39	11	110.9

*This chart includes passer rating points for all leaders, although the same rating system was not used for determining leading quarterbacks prior to 1973. The old system was less equitable, yet similar to the new in that the rating was based on percentage of completions, touchdown passes, percentage of interceptions and average gain in yards.

RECEIVING

(Based on most receptions)

	No.	Yds.	TD
1960—Raymond Berry, Baltimore	74	1298	10
1961—Jim Phillips, L.A. Rams	78	1092	5

	No.	Yds.	T
1962—Bobby Mitchell, Washington	72	1384	1
1963—Bobby Joe Conrad, St. Louis	73	967	1
1964—Johnny Morris, Chicago	93	1200	1
1965—Dave Parks, San Francisco	80	1344	1
1966—Charley Taylor, Washington	72	1119	1
1967—Charley Taylor, Washington	70	990	
1968—Clifton McNeil, San Francisco	71	994	
1969—Dan Abramowicz, New Orleans	73	1015	
1970—Dick Gordon, Chicago	71	1026	1
1971—Bob Tucker, N.Y. Giants	59	791	
1972—Harold Jackson, Philadelphia	62	1048	
1973—Harold Carmichael, Philadelphia	67	1116	
1974—Charles Young, Philadelphia	63	696	
1975—Chuck Foreman, Minnesota	73	691	
1976—Drew Pearson, Dallas	58	806	
1977—Ahmad Rashad, Minnesota	51	681	
1978—Rickey Young, Minnesota	88	704	
1979—Ahmad Rashad, Minnesota	80	1156	
1980—Earl Cooper, San Francisco	83	567	
1981—Dwight Clark, San Francisco	85	1105	
1982—Dwight Clark, San Francisco	60	913	
1983—Roy Green, St. Louis	78	1227	1
Charlie Brown, Washington	78	1225	
Earnest Gray, N.Y. Giants	78	1139	
1984—Art Monk, Washington	106	1372	
1985—Roger Craig, San Francisco	92	1016	
1986—Jerry Rice, San Francisco	86	1570	1
1987—J.T. Smith, St. Louis	91	1117	
1988—Henry Ellard, L.A. Rams	86	1414	1
1989—Sterling Sharpe, Green Bay	90	1423	1
1990—Jerry Rice, San Francisco	100	1502	1
1991—Michael Irvin, Dallas	93	1523	
1992—Sterling Sharpe, Green Bay	108	1461	1
1993—Sterling Sharpe, Green Bay	112	1274	1
1994—Cris Carter, Minnesota	122	1256	7
1995—Herman Moore, Detroit	123	1686	1
1996—Jerry Rice, San Francisco	108	1254	
1997—Herman Moore, Detroit	104	1293	
1998—Frank Sanders, Arizona	89	1145	
1999—Muhsin Muhammad, Carolina	96	1253	
2000—Muhsin Muhammad, Carolina	102	1183	
2001—Keyshawn Johnson, Tampa Bay	106	1266	1
2002—Randy Moss, Minnesota	106	1347	7
2003—Torry Holt, St. Louis	117	1696	12
2004—Joe Horn, New Orleans	94	1399	11

SCORING

(Based on most total points)

	TD	PAT	FG	Tot.
1960— Paul Hornung, Green Bay	15	41	15	176
1961— Paul Hornung, Green Bay	10	41	15	146
1962— Jim Taylor, Green Bay	19	0	0	114
1963— Don Chandler, N.Y. Giants	0	52	18	106
1964— Lenny Moore, Baltimore	20	0	0	120
1965— Gale Sayers, Chicago	22	0	0	132
1966— Bruce Gossett, L.A. Rams	0	29	28	113
1967— Jim Bakken, St. Louis	0	36	27	117
1968— Leroy Kelly, Cleveland	20	0	0	120
1969— Fred Cox, Minnesota	0	43	26	121
1970— Fred Cox, Minnesota	0	35	30	125
1971— Curt Knight, Washington	0	27	29	114
1972— Chester Marcol, Green Bay	0	29	33	128
1973— David Ray, L.A. Rams	0	40	30	130
1974— Chester Marcol, Green Bay	0	19	25	94
1975— Chuck Foreman, Minnesota	22	0	0	132
1976— Mark Moseley, Washington	0	31	22	97
1977— Walter Payton, Chicago	16	0	0	96
1978— Frank Corral, L.A. Rams	0	31	29	118
1979— Mark Moseley, Washington	0	39	25	114
1980— Eddie Murray, Detroit	0	35	27	116
1981— Eddie Murray, Detroit	0	46	25	121
Rafael Septien, Dallas	0	40	27	121
1982— Wendell Tyler, L.A. Rams	13	0	0	78
1983— Mark Moseley, Washington	0	62	33	161
1984— Ray Wersching, S.F.	0	56	25	131
1985— Kevin Butler, Chicago	0	51	31	144
1986— Kevin Butler, Chicago	0	36	28	120

	TD	PAT	FG	Tot.
87— Jerry Rice, San Francisco	23	0	0	138
88— Mike Cofer, San Francisco	0	40	27	121
89— Mike Cofer, San Francisco	0	49	29	136
90— Chip Lohmiller, Washington	0	41	30	131
91— Chip Lohmiller, Washington	0	56	31	149
92— Morten Andersen, New Orleans	0	33	29	120
Chip Lohmiller, Washington	0	30	30	120
93— Jason Hanson, Detroit	0	28	34	130
94— Fuad Reveiz, Minnesota	0	30	34	132
95— Emmitt Smith, Dallas	25	0	0	150
96— John Kasay, Carolina	0	34	37	145
97— Richie Cunningham, Dallas	0	24	34	126
98— Gary Anderson, Minnesota	0	59	35	164
99— Jeff Wilkins, St. Louis	0	64	20	124
00— Marshall Faulk, St. Louis	26	0	0	*160
01— Marshall Faulk, St. Louis	21	0	0	†128
02— Jay Feely, Atlanta	0	42	32	138
03— Jeff Wilkins, St. Louis	0	46	39	163
04— David Akers, Philadelphia	0	41	27	122

*Includes two 2-Pt. conversions.
†Includes one 2-Pt. conversion.

FIELD GOALS

	No.
60— Tommy Davis, San Francisco	19
61— Steve Myhra, Baltimore	21
62— Lou Michaels, Pittsburgh	26
63— Jim Martin, Baltimore	24
64— Jim Bakken, St. Louis	25
65— Fred Cox, Minnesota	23
66— Bruce Gossett, L.A. Rams	28
67— Jim Bakken, St. Louis	27
68— Mac Percival, Chicago	25
69— Fred Cox, Minnesota	26
70— Fred Cox, Minnesota	30
71— Curt Knight, Washington	29
72— Chester Marcol, Green Bay	33
73— David Ray, L.A. Rams	30
74— Chester Marcol, Green Bay	25
75— Toni Fritsch, Dallas	22
76— Mark Moseley, Washington	22
77— Mark Moseley, Washington	21
78— Frank Corral, L.A. Rams	29
79— Mark Moseley, Washington	25
80— Eddie Murray, Detroit	27
81— Rafael Septien, Dallas	27
82— Mark Moseley, Washington	20
83— Ali Haji-Sheikh, N.Y. Giants	35
84— Paul McFadden, Philadelphia	30
85— Morten Andersen, New Orleans	31
Kevin Butler, Chicago	31
86— Kevin Butler, Chicago	28
87— Morten Andersen, New Orleans	28
88— Mike Cofer, San Francisco	27
89— Rich Karlis, Minnesota	31
90— Chip Lohmiller, Washington	30
91— Chip Lohmiller, Washington	31
92— Chip Lohmiller, Washington	30
93— Jason Hanson, Detroit	34
94— Fuad Reveiz, Minnesota	34
95— Morten Andersen, Atlanta	31
96— John Kasay, Carolina	37
97— Richie Cunningham, Dallas	34
98— Gary Anderson, Minnesota	35
99— Martin Gramatica, Tampa Bay	27
000— Ryan Longwell, Green Bay	33
001— Jay Feely, Atlanta	29
002— Jay Feely, Atlanta	32
Martin Gramatica, Tampa Bay	32
003— Jeff Wilkins, St. Louis	39
004— David Akers, Philadelphia	27

INTERCEPTIONS

	No.	Yds.
960— Dave Baker, San Francisco	10	96
Jerry Norton, St. Louis	10	96
961— Dick Lynch, N.Y. Giants	9	60
1962— Willie Wood, Green Bay	9	132
1963— Dick Lynch, N.Y. Giants	9	251
Rosie Taylor, Chicago	9	172
1964— Paul Krause, Washington	12	140
1965— Bobby Boyd, Baltimore	9	78
1966— Larry Wilson, St. Louis	10	180
1967— Lem Barney, Detroit	10	232
Dave Whitsell, New Orleans	10	178
1968— Willie Williams, N.Y. Giants	10	103
1969— Mel Renfro, Dallas	10	118
1970— Dick LeBeau, Detroit	9	96
1971— Bill Bradley, Philadelphia	11	248
1972— Bill Bradley, Philadelphia	9	73
1973— Bobby Bryant, Minnesota	7	105
1974— Ray Brown, Atlanta	8	164
1975— Paul Krause, Minnesota	10	201
1976— Monte Jackson, L.A. Rams	10	173
1977— Rolland Lawrence, Atlanta	7	138
1978— Ken Stone, St. Louis	9	139
Willie Buchanon, Green Bay	9	93
1979— Lemar Parrish, Washington	9	65
1980— Nolan Cromwell, L.A. Rams	8	140
1981— Everson Walls, Dallas	11	133
1982— Everson Walls, Dallas	7	61
1983— Mark Murphy, Washington	9	127
1984— Tom Flynn, Green Bay	9	106
1985— Everson Walls, Dallas	9	31
1986— Ronnie Lott, San Francisco	10	134
1987— Barry Wilburn, Washington	9	135
1988— Scott Case, Atlanta	10	47
1989— Eric Allen, Philadelphia	8	38
1990— Mark Carrier, Chicago	10	39
1991— Ray Crockett, Detroit	6	141
Deion Sanders, Atlanta	6	119
Aeneas Williams, Phoenix	6	60
Tim McKyer, Atlanta	6	24
1992— Audray McMillian, Minnesota	8	157
1993— Deion Sanders, Atlanta	7	91
1994— Aeneas Williams, Arizona	9	89
1995— Orlando Thomas, Minnesota	9	108
1996— Keith Lyle, St. Louis	9	152
1997— Ryan McNeil, St. Louis	9	127
1998— Kwamie Lassiter, Arizona	8	80
1999— Donnie Abraham, Tampa Bay	7	115
Troy Vincent, Philadelphia	7	91
2000— Darren Sharper, Green Bay	9	109
2001— Ronde Barber, Tampa Bay	10	86
2002— Brian Kelly, Tampa Bay	8	68
2003— Tony Parrish, San Francisco	9	202
Brian Russell, Minnesota	9	185
2004— Ken Lucas, Seattle	6	46
Chris Gamble, Carolina	6	15

PUNTING
(Based on highest average yardage per punt by qualifiers)

	No.	Avg.
1960— Jerry Norton, St. Louis	39	45.6
1961— Yale Lary, Detroit	52	48.4
1962— Tommy Davis, San Francisco	48	45.6
1963— Yale Lary, Detroit	35	48.9
1964— Bobby Walden, Minnesota	72	46.4
1965— Gary Collins, Cleveland	65	46.7
1966— David Lee, Baltimore	49	45.6
1967— Billy Lothridge, Atlanta	87	43.7
1968— Billy Lothridge, Atlanta	75	44.3
1969— David Lee, Baltimore	57	45.3
1970— Julian Fagan, New Orleans	77	42.5
1971— Tom McNeill, Philadelphia	73	42.0
1972— Dave Chapple, L.A. Rams	53	44.2
1973— Tom Wittum, San Francisco	79	43.7
1974— Tom Blanchard, New Orleans	88	42.1
1975— Herman Weaver, Detroit	80	42.0
1976— John James, Atlanta	101	42.1
1977— Tom Blanchard, New Orleans	82	42.4
1978— Tom Skladany, Detroit	86	42.5
1979— Dave Jennings, N.Y. Giants	104	42.7
1980— Dave Jennings, N.Y. Giants	94	44.8

HISTORY *Statistical leaders*

		No.	Avg.
1981—	Tom Skladany, Detroit	64	43.5
1982—	Carl Birdsong, St. Louis	54	43.8
1983—	Frank Garcia, Tampa Bay	95	42.2
1984—	Brian Hansen, New Orleans	69	43.8
1985—	Rick Donnelly, Atlanta	59	43.6
1986—	Sean Landeta, N.Y. Giants	79	44.8
1987—	Rick Donnelly, Atlanta	61	44.0
1988—	Jim Arnold, Detroit	97	42.4
1989—	Rich Camarillo, Phoenix	76	43.4
1990—	Sean Landeta, N.Y. Giants	75	44.1
1991—	Harry Newsome, Minnesota	68	45.5
1992—	Harry Newsome, Minnesota	72	45.0
1993—	Jim Arnold, Detroit	72	44.5
1994—	Sean Landeta, L.A. Rams	78	44.8
1995—	Sean Landeta, St. Louis	83	44.3
1996—	Matt Turk, Washington	75	45.1
1997—	Mark Royals, New Orleans	88	45.9
1998—	Mark Royals, New Orleans	88	45.6
1999—	Mitch Berger, Minnesota	61	45.4
2000—	Mitch Berger, Minnesota	62	44.7
2001—	Todd Sauerbrun, Carolina	93	47.5
2002—	Todd Sauerbrun, Carolina	104	45.5
2003—	Todd Sauerbrun, Carolina	77	44.6
2004—	Tom Tupa, Washington	103	44.1

PUNT RETURNS

(Based on most total yards)

		No.	Yds.	Avg.
1960—	Abe Woodson, San Francisco	13	174	13.4
1961—	Willie Wood, Green Bay	14	225	16.1
1962—	Pat Studstill, Detroit	29	457	15.8
1963—	Dick James, Washington	16	214	13.4
1964—	Tommy Watkins, Detroit	16	238	14.9
1965—	Leroy Kelly, Cleveland	17	265	15.6
1966—	Johnny Roland, St. Louis	20	221	11.1
1967—	Ben Davis, Cleveland	18	229	12.7
1968—	Bob Hayes, Dallas	15	312	20.8
1969—	Alvin Haymond, L.A. Rams	33	435	13.2
1970—	Bruce Taylor, San Francisco	43	516	12.0
1971—	Les Duncan, Washington	22	233	10.6
1972—	Ken Ellis, Green Bay	14	215	15.4
1973—	Bruce Taylor, San Francisco	15	207	13.8
1974—	Dick Jauron, Detroit	17	286	16.8
1975—	Terry Metcalf, St. Louis	23	285	12.4
1976—	Eddie Brown, Washington	48	646	13.5
1977—	Larry Marshall, Philadelphia	46	489	10.6
1978—	Jackie Wallace, L.A. Rams	52	618	11.9
1979—	John Sciarra, Philadelphia	16	182	11.4
1980—	Kenny Johnson, Atlanta	23	281	12.2
1981—	LeRoy Irvin, L.A. Rams	46	615	13.4
1982—	Billy Johnson, Atlanta	24	273	11.4
1983—	Henry Ellard, L.A. Rams	16	217	13.6
1984—	Henry Ellard, L.A. Rams	30	403	13.4
1985—	Henry Ellard, L.A. Rams	37	501	13.5
1986—	Vai Sikahema, St. Louis	43	522	12.1
1987—	Mel Gray, New Orleans	24	352	14.7
1988—	John Taylor, San Francisco	44	556	12.6
1989—	Walter Stanley, Detroit	36	496	13.8
1990—	Johnny Bailey, Chicago	36	399	11.1
1991—	Mel Gray, Detroit	25	385	15.4
1992—	Johnny Bailey, Phoenix	20	263	13.2
1993—	Tyrone Hughes, New Orleans	37	503	13.6
1994—	Brian Mitchell, Washington	32	452	14.1
1995—	Eric Guliford, Carolina	43	475	11.0
1996—	Desmond Howard, Green Bay	58	875	15.1
1997—	Karl Williams, Tampa Bay	46	597	13.0
1998—	Brian Mitchell, Washington	44	506	11.5
1999—	Glyn Milburn, Chicago	30	346	11.5
2000—	Az-Zahir Hakim, St. Louis	32	489	15.3
2001—	Brian Mitchell, Philadelphia	39	467	12.0
2002—	Michael Lewis, New Orleans	44	625	14.2
2003—	Allen Rossum, Atlanta	39	545	14.0
2004—	Allen Rossum, Atlanta	37	457	12.4

KICKOFF RETURNS

(Based on most total yards)

		No.	Yds.	Avg
1960—	Tom Moore, Green Bay	12	397	33.1
1961—	Dick Bass, L.A. Rams	23	698	30.3
1962—	Abe Woodson, San Francisco	37	1157	31.3
1963—	Abe Woodson, San Francisco	29	935	32.2
1964—	Clarence Childs, N.Y. Giants	34	987	29.0
1965—	Tommy Watkins, Detroit	17	584	34.4
1966—	Gale Sayers, Chicago	23	718	31.2
1967—	Travis Williams, Green Bay	18	739	41.1
1968—	Preston Pearson, Baltimore	15	527	35.1
1969—	Bobby Williams, Detroit	17	563	33.1
1970—	Cecil Turner, Chicago	23	752	32.7
1971—	Travis Williams, L.A. Rams	25	743	29.7
1972—	Ron Smith, Chicago	30	924	30.8
1973—	Carl Garrett, Chicago	16	486	30.4
1974—	Terry Metcalf, St. Louis	20	623	31.2
1975—	Walter Payton, Chicago	14	444	31.7
1976—	Cullen Bryant, L.A. Rams	16	459	28.7
1977—	Wilbert Montgomery, Phila.	23	619	26.9
1978—	Steve Odom, Green Bay	25	677	27.1
1979—	Jimmy Edwards, Minnesota	44	1103	25.1
1980—	Rich Mauti, New Orleans	31	798	25.7
1981—	Mike Nelms, Washington	37	1099	29.7
1982—	Alvin Hall, Detroit	16	426	26.6
1983—	Darrin Nelson, Minnesota	18	445	24.7
1984—	Barry Redden, L.A. Rams	23	530	23.0
1985—	Ron Brown, L.A. Rams	28	918	32.8
1986—	Dennis Gentry, Chicago	20	576	28.8
1987—	Sylvester Stamps, Atlanta	24	660	27.5
1988—	Donnie Elder, Tampa Bay	34	772	22.7
1989—	Mel Gray, Detroit	24	640	26.7
1990—	Dave Meggett, N.Y. Giants	21	492	23.4
1991—	Mel Gray, Detroit	36	929	25.8
1992—	Deion Sanders, Atlanta	40	1067	26.7
1993—	Tony Smith, Atlanta	38	948	24.9
1994—	Tyrone Hughes, New Orleans	63	1556	24.7
1995—	Tyrone Hughes, New Orleans	66	1617	24.5
1996—	Tyrone Hughes, New Orleans	70	1791	25.6
1997—	Glyn Milburn, Detroit	55	1315	23.9
1998—	Glyn Milburn, Chicago	62	1550	25.0
1999—	Tony Horne, St. Louis	30	892	29.7
2000—	MarTay Jenkins, Arizona	82	2186	26.7
2001—	Darrick Vaughn, Atlanta	61	1491	24.4
2002—	Michael Lewis, New Orleans	70	1807	25.8
2003—	Josh Scobey, Arizona	73	1684	23.1
2004—	Allen Rossum, Atlanta	58	1250	21.6

SACKS

		No.
1982—	Doug Martin, Minnesota	11.5
1983—	Fred Dean, San Francisco	17.5
1984—	Richard Dent, Chicago	17.5
1985—	Richard Dent, Chicago	17.0
1986—	Lawrence Taylor, N.Y. Giants	20.5
1987—	Reggie White, Philadelphia	21.0
1988—	Reggie White, Philadelphia	18.0
1989—	Chris Doleman, Minnesota	21.0
1990—	Charles Haley, San Francisco	16.0
1991—	Pat Swilling, New Orleans	17.0
1992—	Clyde Simmons, Philadelphia	19.0
1993—	Renaldo Turnbull, New Orleans	13.0
	Reggie White, Green Bay	13.0
1994—	Ken Harvey, Washington	13.5
	John Randle, Minnesota	13.5
1995—	William Fuller, Philadelphia	13.0
	Wayne Martin, New Orleans	13.0
1996—	Kevin Greene, Carolina	14.5
1997—	John Randle, Minnesota	15.5
1998—	Reggie White, Green Bay	16.0
1999—	Kevin Carter, St. Louis	17.0
2000—	La'Roi Glover, New Orleans	17.0
2001—	Michael Strahan, N.Y. Giants	22.5
2002—	Simeon Rice, Tampa Bay	15.5
2003—	Michael Strahan, N.Y. Giants	18.5
2004—	Bertrand Berry, Arizona	14.5

HISTORY *Statistical leaders*

COACHING RECORDS

COACHES WITH 100 OR MORE CAREER VICTORIES

(Ranked according to career wins)

	Yrs.	REGULAR SEASON				POSTSEASON			CAREER			
		Won	Lost	Tied	Pct.	Won	Lost	Pct.	Won	Lost	Tied	Pct.
on Shula	33	328	156	6	.676	19	17	.528	347	173	6	.665
eorge Halas	40	318	148	31	.671	6	3	.667	324	151	31	.671
om Landry	29	250	162	6	.605	20	16	.556	270	178	6	.601
urly Lambeau	33	226	132	22	.624	3	2	.600	229	134	22	.623
huck Noll	23	193	148	1	.566	16	8	.667	209	156	1	.572
an Reeves+	23	190	165	2	.535	11	9	.550	201	174	2	.536
huck Knox	22	186	147	1	.558	7	11	.389	193	158	1	.550
larty Schottenheimer*	19	177	117	1	.602	5	12	.294	182	129	1	.585
aul Brown	21	166	100	6	.621	4	8	.333	170	108	6	.609
ud Grant	18	158	96	5	.620	10	12	.455	168	108	5	.607
ill Parcells*	17	154	116	1	.570	11	7	.611	165	123	1	.573
teve Owen	23	153	100	17	.598	2	8	.200	155	108	17	.584
larv Levy	17	143	112	0	.561	11	8	.579	154	120	0	.562
oe Gibbs^	13	130	70	0	.650	16	5	.762	146	75	0	.661
ill Cowher*	13	130	77	1	.628	8	9	.471	138	86	1	.616
ank Stram	17	131	97	10	.571	5	3	.625	136	100	10	.573
like Holmgren*	13	125	83	0	.601	9	8	.529	134	90	0	.598
Veeb Ewbank	20	130	129	7	.502	4	1	.800	134	130	7	.507
like Ditka	14	121	95	0	.560	6	6	.500	127	101	0	.557
m Mora	15	125	106	0	.541	0	6	.000	125	112	0	.527
eorge Seifert	11	114	62	0	.648	10	5	.667	124	67	0	.649
id Gillman	18	122	99	7	.550	1	5	.167	123	104	7	.541
eorge Allen	12	116	47	5	.705	2	7	.222	118	54	5	.681
like Shanahan*	12	109	71	0	.606	7	4	.636	116	75	0	.607
ick Vermeil*	14	110	103	0	.516	6	5	.545	116	108	0	.518
on Coryell	14	111	83	1	.572	3	6	.333	114	89	1	.561
ohn Madden	10	103	32	7	.750	9	7	.563	112	39	7	.731
uddy Parker	15	104	75	9	.577	3	1	.750	107	76	9	.581
ennis Green*	11	103	72	0	.589	4	8	.333	107	80	0	.572
ince Lombardi	10	96	34	6	.728	9	1	.900	105	35	6	.740
om Flores	12	97	87	0	.527	8	3	.727	105	90	0	.538
ill Walsh	10	92	59	1	.609	10	4	.714	102	63	1	.617

*Active NFL coaches in 2004. +Resigned after 13 games in 2003. ^Returned to coach Redskins in 2004.

2005 COACHES CAREER RECORDS

(Ranked according to career NFL percentages*)

Coach, current team	WITH CURRENT CLUB							CAREER								CAREER TOTALS			
	Regular season				Postseason			Regular season				Postseason			Reg. + Postseason			
	Yrs.	W	L	T	Pct.	App.	W-L	Pct.	Yrs.	W	L	T	Pct.	App.	W-L	Pct.	W	L	T	Pct.
im Mora Jr., Atl.	1	11	5	0	.688	1	1-1	.500	1	11	5	0	.688	1	1-1	.500	12	6	0	.667
oe Gibbs, Wash.	13	130	70	0	.650	8	16-5	.762	13	130	70	0	.650	8	16-5	.762	146	75	0	.661
ndy Reid, Phi.	6	64	32	0	.667	5	7-5	.583	6	64	32	0	.667	5	7-5	.583	71	37	0	.657
like Sherman, G.B.	5	53	27	0	.663	4	2-4	.333	5	53	27	0	.663	4	2-4	.333	55	31	0	.640
like Martz, St.L.	5	51	29	0	.638	4	3-4	.429	5	51	29	0	.638	4	3-4	.429	54	33	0	.621
ill Cowher, Pit.	13	130	77	1	.628	9	8-9	.471	13	130	77	1	.628	9	8-9	.471	138	86	1	.616
like Shanahan, Den.	10	101	59	0	.631	6	7-4	.636	12	109	71	0	.606	6	7-4	.636	116	75	0	.607
like Holmgren, Sea.	6	50	46	0	.521	3	0-3	.000	13	125	83	0	.601	9	9-8	.529	134	90	0	.598
ony Dungy, Ind.	3	34	14	0	.708	3	3-3	.500	9	88	56	0	.611	7	5-7	.417	93	63	0	.596
rian Billick, Bal.	6	56	40	0	.583	3	5-2	.714	6	56	40	0	.583	3	5-2	.714	61	42	0	.592
larty Schottenheimer, S.D.	3	24	24	0	.500	1	0-1	.000	19	177	117	1	.602	12	5-12	.294	182	129	1	.585
ill Belichick, N.E.	5	53	27	0	.663	3	9-0	1.000	10	89	71	0	.556	4	10-1	.909	99	72	0	.579
ill Parcells, Dal.	2	16	16	0	.500	1	0-1	.000	17	154	116	1	.570	9	11-7	.611	165	123	1	.573
ennis Green, Ariz.	1	6	10	0	.375				11	103	72	0	.589	8	4-8	.333	107	80	0	.572
on Gruden, T.B.	3	24	24	0	.500	1	3-0	1.000	7	62	50	0	.554	3	5-2	.714	67	52	0	.563
like Mularkey, Buf.	1	9	7	0	.563				1	9	7	0	.563				9	7	0	.563
eff Fisher, Ten.	11	93	73	0	.560	4	5-4	.556	11	93	73	0	.560	4	5-4	.556	98	77	0	.560
ohn Fox, Car.	3	25	23	0	.521	1	3-1	.750	3	25	23	0	.521	1	3-1	.750	28	24	0	.538
lerman Edwards, NYJ	4	35	29	0	.547	3	2-3	.400	4	35	29	0	.547	3	2-3	.400	37	32	0	.536
teve Mariucci, Det.	2	11	21	0	.344				8	68	60	0	.531	4	3-4	.429	71	64	0	.526
im Haslett, N.O.	5	42	38	0	.525	1	1-1	.500	5	42	38	0	.525	1	1-1	.500	43	39	0	.524
ick Vermeil, K.C.	4	34	30	0	.531	1	0-1	.000	14	110	103	0	.516	6	6-5	.545	116	108	0	.518
om Coughlin, NYG	1	6	10	0	.375				9	74	70	0	.514	4	4-4	.500	78	74	0	.513
Marvin Lewis, Cin.	2	16	16	0	.500				2	16	16	0	.500				16	16	0	.500
like Tice, Min.	4	23	26	0	.469	1	1-1	.500	4	23	26	0	.469	1	1-1	.500	16	19	0	.457
ack Del Rio, Jac.	2	14	18	0	.438				2	14	18	0	.438				14	18	0	.438
Norv Turner, Oak.	1	5	11	0	.313				8	54	70	0	.435	1	1-1	.500	55	71	0	.437
Dom Capers, Hou.	3	16	32	0	.333				7	46	66	0	.411	1	1-1	.500	47	67	0	.412
ovie Smith, Chi.	1	5	11	.0	.313				1	5	11	0	.313				5	11	0	.313

*First year as NFL head coach: Romeo Crennel, Cle.; Mike Nolan, S.F.; Nick Saban, Mia.

HALL OF FAME

ROSTER OF MEMBERS
FOUR NEW INDUCTEES IN 2005

Benny Friedman, Dan Marino, Fritz Pollard and Steve Young were inducted into Pro Football's Hall of Fame in 2005, expanding the list of former stars honored at Canton, Ohio, to 229.

Name	Elec. year	College	Pos.	NFL teams
Adderley, Herb	1980	Michigan State	CB	Green Bay Packers, 1961-69; Dallas Cowboys, 1970-72
Allen, George	2002	Michigan	*	Coach, Los Angeles Rams, 1966-70; Washington Redskins, 1971-77
Allen, Marcus†	2003	Southern California	RB	Los Angeles Raiders, 1982-92; Kansas City Chiefs, 1993-97
Alworth, Lance†	1978	Arkansas	WR	San Diego Chargers, 1962-70; Dallas Cowboys, 1971-72.
Atkins, Doug	1982	Tennessee	DE	Cleveland Browns, 1953-54; Chicago Bears, 1955-66; New Orleans Saints, 1967-69
Badgro, Morris (Red)	1981	Southern California	E	New York Yankees, 1927; New York Giants, 1930-35; Brooklyn Dodgers, 1936
Barney, Lem	1992	Jackson State	CB	Detroit Lions, 1967-77
Battles, Cliff	1968	W. Virginia Wesleyan	HB/QB	Boston Braves, Boston Redskins, Washington Redskins, 1932-37; coach, Brooklyn Dodgers, 1946-47
Baugh, Sammy	1963	Texas Christian	QB	Washington Redskins, 1937-52; coach, New York Titans, 1960-61; Houston Oilers, 1964
Bednarik, Chuck	1967	Pennsylvania	C/LB	Philadelphia Eagles, 1949-62
Bell, Bert	1963	Pennsylvania	*	NFL Commissioner, 1946-59
Bell, Bobby	1983	Minnesota	LB	Kansas City Chiefs, 1963-74
Berry, Raymond†	1973	Southern Methodist	E	Baltimore Colts, 1955-67; coach, New England Patriots, 1984-89
Bethea, Elvin	2003	North Carolina A&T	DE	Houston Oilers, 1968-83
Bidwill, Charles W.	1967	Loyola	*	Owner, Chicago Cardinals, 1933-47
Biletnikoff, Fred	1988	Florida State	WR	Oakland Raiders, 1965-78
Blanda, George†	1981	Kentucky	QB/PK	Chicago Bears, 1949-58; Baltimore Colts, 1950; Houston Oilers, 1960-66; Oakland Raiders, 1967-75
Blount, Mel†	1989	Southern	CB	Pittsburgh Steelers, 1970-83
Bradshaw, Terry†	1989	Louisiana Tech	QB	Pittsburgh Steelers, 1970-83
Brown, Bob	2004	Nebraska	T	Philadelphia Eagles, 1964-68; Los Angeles Rams, 1969-70; Oakland Raiders, 1971-73
Brown, Jim†	1971	Syracuse	FB	Cleveland Browns, 1957-65
Brown, Paul	1967	Miami of Ohio	*	Coach, Cleveland Browns, 1946-62; Cincinnati Bengals, 1968-75
Brown, Roosevelt	1975	Morgan State	T	New York Giants, 1953-65
Brown, Willie†	1984	Grambling	DB	Denver Broncos, 1963-66; Oakland Raiders, 1967-78
Buchanan, Buck	1990	Grambling	DT	Kansas City Chiefs, 1963-75
Buoniconti, Nick	2001	Notre Dame	LB	Boston Patriots, 1962-68; Miami Dolphins, 1969-76
Butkus, Dick†	1979	Illinois	LB	Chicago Bears, 1965-73
Campbell, Earl†	1991	Texas	RB	Houston Oilers, 1978-84; New Orleans Saints, 1984-85
Canadeo, Tony	1974	Gonzaga	HB	Green Bay Packers, 1941-44, 46-52
Carr, Joe	1963		*	NFL President, 1921-39
Casper, Dave	2002	Notre Dame	TE	Oakland Raiders, 1974-80; Houston Oilers, 1980-83; Minnesota Vikings, 1983; Los Angeles Raiders, 1984
Chamberlin, Guy	1965	Nebraska	E*	Player/coach, Canton Bulldogs, Cleveland Bulldogs, Frankford Yellow Jackets, Decatur Staleys, Chicago Staleys, Chicago Cardinals, 1919-28
Christiansen, Jack	1970	Colorado A&M	DB	Detroit Lions, 1951-58; coach, San Francisco 49ers, 1963-67
Clark, Dutch	1963	Colorado College	QB	Portsmouth Spartans, Detroit Lions, 1931-38
Connor, George	1975	Notre Dame	T/LB	Chicago Bears, 1948-55
Conzelman, Jimmy	1964	Washington (Mo.)	HB*	Coach/executive, Decatur, Rock Island, Milwaukee, Detroit, Providence, Chicago Cardinals, 1920-48
Creekmur, Lou	1996	William & Mary	T/G	Detroit Lions, 1950-59
Csonka, Larry	1987	Syracuse	RB	Miami Dolphins, 1968-74, 79; New York Giants, 1976-78
Davis, Al	1992	Syracuse	*	Coach/general manager/president, Oakland-Los Angeles Raiders, 1963-present
Davis, Willie	1981	Grambling	DE	Cleveland Browns, 1958-59; Green Bay Packers, 1960-69
Dawson, Len	1987	Purdue	QB	Pittsburgh Steelers, 1957-59; Cleveland Browns, 1960-61; Dallas Texans, 1962; Kansas City Chiefs, 1963-75
DeLamielleure, Joe	2003	Michigan State	G	Buffalo Bills, 1973-79, 1985; Cleveland Browns, 1980-84
Dickerson, Eric†	1999	Southern Methodist	RB	Los Angeles Rams, 1983-87; Indianapolis Colts, 1987-91; Los Angeles Raiders, 1992; Atlanta Falcons, 1993
Dierdorf, Dan	1996	Michigan	T/C	St. Louis Cardinals, 1971-83
Ditka, Mike	1988	Pittsburgh	TE	Chicago Bears, 1961-66; Philadelphia Eagles, 1967-68; Dallas Cowboys, 1969-72; coach, Chicago Bears, 1982-92; New Orleans Saints, 1997-99
Donovan, Art	1968	Boston College	DT	Baltimore Colts, New York Yanks, Dallas Texans, 1950-61
Dorsett, Tony	1994	Pittsburgh	RB	Dallas Cowboys, 1977-87; Denver Broncos, 1988
Driscoll, Paddy	1965	Northwestern	TB/HB/QB	Player/coach, Hammond Pros, Decatur Staleys, Chicago Cardinals, Chicago Bears, 1919-29, 41-68

Name	Elec. year	College	Pos.	NFL teams
Dudley, Bill	1966	Virginia	HB	Pittsburgh Steelers, Detroit Lions, Washington Redskins, 1942-53
Edwards, Turk	1969	Washington State	T	Boston Braves, Boston Redskins, Washington Redskins, 1932-40
Eller, Carl	2004	Minnesota	DE	Minnesota Vikings, 1964-78; Seattle Seahawks, 1979
Elway, John†	2004	Stanford	QB	Denver Broncos, 1983-1998
Ewbank, Weeb	1978	Miami of Ohio	*	Coach, Baltimore Colts, 1954-62; New York Jets, 1963-73
Fears, Tom	1970	UCLA	E	Los Angeles Rams, 1948-56; coach, New Orleans Saints, 1967-70
Finks, Jim	1995	Tulsa	QB*	Pittsburgh Steelers, 1949-55; administrator, Minnesota Vikings, 1964-73; Chicago Bears, 1974-82; New Orleans Saints, 1986-93
Flaherty, Ray	1976	Gonzaga	E*	Player/coach, Los Angeles Wildcats, New York Yankees, AFL; New York Giants, Boston Redskins, Washington Redskins, New York Yankees, AAFC; Chicago Hornets, 1926-49
Ford, Len	1976	Michigan	E	Los Angeles Dons, Cleveland Browns, Green Bay Packers, 1948-58
Fortmann, Danny	1965	Colgate	G	Chicago Bears, 1936-43
Fouts, Dan†	1993	Oregon	QB	San Diego Chargers, 1973-87
Friedman, Benny	2005	Michigan	QB	Cleveland Bulldogs, 1927; Detroit Wolverines, 1928; New York Giants, 1929-31; Brooklyn Dodgers, 1932-34
Gatski, Frank	1985	Marshall	C	Cleveland Browns, 1946-56; Detroit Lions, 1957
George, Bill	1974	Wake Forest	LB	Chicago Bears, Los Angeles Rams, 1952-66
Gibbs, Joe	1996	San Diego State	*	Washington Redskins, 1981-92
Gifford, Frank	1977	Southern California	HB/E	New York Giants, 1952-60, 62-64
Gillman, Sid	1983	Ohio State	*	Coach, Los Angeles Rams, 1955-59; Los Angeles Chargers, 1960; San Diego Chargers, 1961-69, 71; Houston Oilers, 1973-74
Graham, Otto	1965	Northwestern	QB	Cleveland Browns, 1946-55; coach, Washington Redskins, 1966-68
Grange, Red	1963	Illinois	HB	Chicago Bears, 1925, 29-34; New York Yankees, 1926-27
Grant, Bud	1994	Minnesota	WR*	Philadelphia Eagles, 1951-52; coach, Minnesota Vikings, 1967-83, 1985
Greene, Joe†	1987	North Texas State	DT	Pittsburgh Steelers, 1969-81
Gregg, Forrest†	1977	Southern Methodist	T	Green Bay Packers, Dallas Cowboys, 1956, 58-71; coach, Cleveland Browns 1975-77; Cincinnati Bengals, 1980-83; Green Bay Packers, 1984-87
Griese, Bob	1990	Purdue	QB	Miami Dolphins, 1967-80
Groza, Lou	1974	Ohio State	T/PK	Cleveland Browns, 1946-59, 61-67
Guyon, Joe	1966	Carlisle, Georgia Tech	HB	Canton Bulldogs, Cleveland Indians, Oorang Indians, Rock Island Independents, Kansas City Cowboys, New York Giants, 1919-27
Halas, George	1963	Illinois	E*	Player/coach/ founder, Chicago Bears, 1920-83
Ham, Jack†	1988	Penn State	LB	Pittsburgh Steelers, 1971-82
Hampton, Dan	2002	Arkansas	DT-DE	Chicago Bears, 1979-90
Hannah, John†	1991	Alabama	G	New England Patriots, 1973-85
Harris, Franco†	1990	Penn State	RB	Pittsburgh Steelers, 1972-83; Seattle Seahawks, 1984
Haynes, Mike	1997	Arizona State	CB	New England Patriots, 1976-82; Los Angeles Raiders, 1983-89
Healey, Ed	1964	Dartmouth	T	Rock Island, Chicago Bears, 1920-27
Hein, Mel	1963	Washington State	C	New York Giants, 1931-45
Hendricks, Ted	1990	Miami, Fla.	LB	Baltimore Colts, 1969-73; Green Bay Packers, 1974; Oakland/Los Angeles Raiders, 1975-83
Henry, Wilbur (Pete)	1963	Wash'ton & Jefferson	T	Canton Bulldogs, New York Giants, Pottsville Maroons, 1920-28
Herber, Arnie	1966	Regis	HB/QB	Green Bay Packers, New York Giants, 1930-45
Hewitt, Bill	1971	Michigan	E	Chicago Bears, 1932-36; Philadelphia Eagles, 1937-39; Philadelphia/Pittsburgh, 1943
Hinkle, Clarke	1964	Bucknell	FB	Green Bay Packers, 1932-41
Hirsch, Elroy (Crazylegs)	1968	Wisconsin	E/HB	Chicago Rockets, Los Angeles Rams, 1946-57
Hornung, Paul	1986	Notre Dame	RB	Green Bay Packers, 1957-62, 64-66
Houston, Ken†	1986	Prairie View	DB	Houston Oilers, 1967-72; Washington Redskins, 1973-80
Hubbard, Cal	1963	Centenary, Geneva	T/E	New York Giants, Green Bay Packers, Pittsburgh Pirates, 1927-36
Huff, Sam	1982	West Virginia	LB	New York Giants, 1956-63; Washington Redskins, 1964-67, 69
Hunt, Lamar	1972	Southern Methodist	*	Founder, American Football League, 1959; president, Dallas Texans, 1960-62; Kansas City Chiefs, 1963-present
Hutson, Don	1963	Alabama	E	Green Bay Packers, 1935-45
Johnson, Jimmy	1994	UCLA	DB	San Francisco 49ers, 1961-76
Johnson, John Henry	1987	Arizona State	FB	San Francisco 49ers, 1954-56; Detroit Lions, 1957-59; Pittsburgh Steelers, 1960-65; Houston Oilers, 1966
Joiner, Charlie	1996	Grambling	WR	Houston Oilers, 1969-72; Cincinnati Bengals, 1972-75; San Diego Chargers, 1976-86
Jones, Deacon†	1980	South Carolina State	DE	Los Angeles Rams, 1961-71; San Diego Chargers, 1972-73; Washington Redskins, 1974
Jones, Stan	1991	Maryland	G/DT	Chicago Bears, 1954-65; Washington Redskins, 1966
Jordan, Henry	1995	Virginia	DT	Cleveland Browns, 1957-58; Green Bay Packers, 1959-69
Jurgensen, Sonny	1983	Duke	QB	Philadelphia Eagles, 1957-63; Washington Redskins, 1964-74
Kelly, Jim†	2002	Miami, Fla.	QB	Buffalo Bills, 1986-96
Kelly, Leroy	1994	Morgan State	RB	Cleveland Browns, 1964-73
Kiesling, Walter	1966	St. Thomas (Minn.)	G/T*	Player/coach, Duluth Eskimos, Pottsville Maroons, Chicago Cardinals, Chicago Bears, Green Bay Packers, Pittsburgh Pirates/Steelers, 1926-56
Kinard, Frank (Bruiser)	1971	Mississippi	T	Bro. Dodgers, 1938-43; Bro. Tigers, 1944; N.Y. Yankees, 1946-47
Krause, Paul	1998	Iowa	S	Washington Redskins, 1964-67; Minnesota Vikings, 1968-79
Lambeau, Curly	1963	Notre Dame	TB/FB/E*	Founder/player/coach, Green Bay Packers, 1919-49; Chicago Cardinals, 1950-51; Washington Redskins, 1952-53

Name	Elec. year	College	Pos.	NFL teams
Lambert, Jack†	1990	Kent State	LB	Pittsburgh Steelers, 1974-84
Landry, Tom†	1990	Texas	*	Coach, Dallas Cowboys, 1960-88
Lane, Dick (Night Train)	1974	Scottsbluff J.C.	DB	Los Angeles Rams, Chicago Cardinals, Detroit Lions, 1952-65
Langer, Jim†	1987	South Dakota State	C	Miami Dolphins, 1970-79; Minnesota Vikings, 1980-81
Lanier, Willie	1986	Morgan State	LB	Kansas City Chiefs, 1967-77
Largent, Steve†	1995	Tulsa	WR	Seattle Seahawks, 1976-89
Lary, Yale	1979	Texas A&M	DB	Detroit Lions, 1952-53, 56-64
Lavelli, Dante	1975	Ohio State	E	Cleveland Browns, 1946-56
Layne, Bobby	1967	Texas	QB	Chicago Bears, New York Bulldogs, Detroit Lions, Pittsburgh Steelers, 1948-62
Leemans, Tuffy	1978	George Washington	FB	New York Giants, 1936-43
Levy, Marv†	2001	Coe College	*	Kansas City Chiefs, 1978-82; Buffalo Bills, 1986-97
Lilly, Bob†	1980	Texas Christian	DT	Dallas Cowboys, 1961-74
Little, Larry	1993	Bethune Cookman	G	San Diego Chargers, 1967-68; Miami Dolphins, 1969-80
Lofton, James	2003	Stanford	WR	Green Bay Packers, 1978-86; Los Angeles Raiders, 1987-88; Buffalo Bills, 1989-92; Los Angeles Rams, 1993; Philadelphia Eagles, 1993
Lombardi, Vince	1971	Fordham	*	Coach, Green Bay Packers, 1959-67; Washington Redskins, 1969
Long, Howie	2000	Villanova	DE	Oakland/Los Angeles Raiders, 1981-93
Lott, Ronnie†	2000	Southern California	DB	San Francisco 49ers, 1981-90; Los Angeles Raiders, 1991-92; New York Jets, 1993-94
Luckman, Sid	1965	Columbia	QB	Chicago Bears, 1939-50
Lyman, Roy (Link)	1964	Nebraska	T	Canton Bulldogs, Cleveland Bulldogs, Frankford Yellow Jackets, Chicago Bears, 1922-34
Mack, Tom	1999	Michigan	G	Los Angeles Rams, 1966-78
Mackey, John	1992	Syracuse	TE	Baltimore Colts, 1963-71; San Diego Chargers, 1972
Mara, Tim	1963		*	Founder, New York Giants, 1925-59
Mara, Wellington	1997	Fordham	*	President, New York Giants, 1965-present
Marchetti, Gino†	1972	San Francisco	DE	Dallas Texans, 1952; Baltimore Colts, 1953-66
Marino, Dan†	2005	Pittsburgh	QB	Miami Dolphins, 1983-99
Marshall, George Preston	1963	Randolph-Macon	*	Founder, Washington Redskins, 1932-65
Matson, Ollie†	1972	San Francisco	HB	Chicago Cardinals, 1952, 54-58; Los Angeles Rams, 1959-62; Detroit Lions, 1963; Philadelphia Eagles, 1964-66
Maynard, Don	1987	Texas Western College	WR	New York Giants, 1958; New York Jets, 1960-72; St. Louis Cardinals, 1973
McAfee, George	1966	Duke	HB	Chicago Bears, 1940-41, 45-50
McCormack, Mike	1984	Kansas	T	New York Yanks, 1951; Cleveland Browns, 1954-62
McDonald, Tommy	1998	Oklahoma	WR	Philadelphia Eagles,1957-63; Dallas Cowboys, 1964; Los Angeles Rams, 1965-66; Atlanta Falcons, 1967; Cleveland Browns,1968
McElhenny, Hugh†	1970	Washington	HB	San Francisco 49ers, Minnesota Vikings, New York Giants, Detroit Lions, 1952-64
McNally, Johnny Blood	1963	St. John's (Minn.)	HB	Milwaukee Badgers, Duluth Eskimos, Pottsville Maroons, Green Bay Packers, Pittsburgh Steelers, 1925-38
Michalske, August (Mike)	1964	Penn State	G	New York Yankees, Green Bay Packers, 1927-37
Millner, Wayne	1968	Notre Dame	E	Boston Redskins, Washington Redskins, 1936-41, 45
Mitchell, Bobby	1983	Illinois	RB/FL/WR	Cleveland Browns, 1958-61; Washington Redskins, 1962-68
Mix, Ron	1979	Southern California	T	Los Angeles Chargers, 1960; San Diego Chargers, 1961-69; Oakland Raiders, 1971
Montana, Joe†	2000	Notre Dame	QB	San Francisco 49ers, 1979-92; Kansas City Chiefs, 1993-94
Moore, Lenny	1975	Penn State	HB	Baltimore Colts, 1956-67
Motley, Marion	1968	Nevada	FB/LB	Cleveland Browns, Pittsburgh Steelers, 1946-55
Munchak, Mike	2001	Penn State	G	Houston Oilers, 1982-93
Munoz, Anthony†	1998	Southern California	OT	Cincinnati Bengals, 1980-92
Musso, George	1982	Milliken	G/DT	Chicago Bears, 1933-44
Nagurski, Bronko	1963	Minnesota	FB/T	Chicago Bears, 1930-37, 43
Namath, Joe	1985	Alabama	QB	New York Jets, 1965-76; Los Angeles Rams, 1977
Neale, Earle (Greasy)	1969	W. Virginia Wesleyan	*	Coach, Philadelphia Eagles, 1941-50
Nevers, Ernie	1963	Stanford	FB	Duluth Eskimos, 1926-27; Chicago Cardinals, 1929-31
Newsome, Ozzie†	1999	Alabama	TE	Cleveland Browns, 1978-90
Nitschke, Ray†	1978	Illinois	LB	Green Bay Packers, 1958-72
Noll, Chuck†	1993	Dayton	*	Coach, Pittsburgh Steelers, 1969-91
Nomellini, Leo†	1969	Minnesota	DT	San Francisco 49ers, 1950-63
Olsen, Merlin†	1982	Utah State	DT	Los Angeles Rams, 1962-76
Otto, Jim†	1980	Miami, Fla.	C	Oakland Raiders, 1960-74
Owen, Steve	1966	Phillips	T/G	Player/coach, Kansas City Cowboys, Cleveland Bulldogs, New York Giants, 1924-53
Page, Alan	1988	Notre Dame	DT	Minnesota Vikings, 1967-78; Chicago Bears, 1978-81
Parker, Clarence (Ace)	1972	Duke	HB/QB	Brooklyn Dodgers, 1937-41; Boston Yanks, 1945; New York Yankees, 1946
Parker, Jim†	1973	Ohio State	G	Baltimore Colts, 1957-67
Payton, Walter†	1993	Jackson State	RB	Chicago Bears, 1975-87
Perry, Joe†	1969	Compton J.C.	FB	San Francisco 49ers, Baltimore Colts, 1948-63
Pihos, Pete	1970	Indiana	E	Philadelphia Eagles, 1947-55
Pollard, Fritz	2005	Brown	HB	Akron Pros/Indians, 1919-21, 1925-26; Milwaukee Badgers, 1922-23; Hammond Pros, 1925; Gilberton Cadamounts 1923-24; Providence Steam Roller, 1925
Ray, Hugh (Shorty)	1966	Illinois	*	NFL technical adviser and supervisor of officials, 1938-52

Name	Elec. year	College	Pos.	NFL teams
Reeves, Daniel F.	1967	Georgetown	*	Founder, Cleveland/Los Angeles Rams, 1941-71
Renfro, Mel	1996	Oregon	DB	Dallas Cowboys, 1964-77
Riggins, John	1992	Kansas	HB	New York Jets, 1971-75; Washington Redskins, 1976-85
Ringo, Jim	1981	Syracuse	C	Green Bay Packers, 1953-63; Philadelphia Eagles, 1964-67
Robustelli, Andy	1971	Arnold	DE	Los Angeles Rams, 1951-55; New York Giants, 1956-64
Rooney, Arthur J.	1964	Georgetown	*	Founder, Pittsburgh Steelers, 1933-88
Rooney, Dan	2000	Duquesne	*	Pittsburgh Steelers, 1955-present
Rozelle, Pete	1985	San Francisco	*	NFL Commissioner, 1960-89
St. Clair, Bob	1990	San Francisco	T	San Francisco 49ers, 1953-63
Sanders, Barry†	2004	Oklahoma State	RB	Detroit Lions, 1989-98
Sayers, Gale†	1977	Kansas	RB	Chicago Bears, 1965-71
Schmidt, Joe	1973	Pittsburgh	LB	Detroit Lions, 1953-65; coach, Detroit Lions, 1967-72
Schramm, Tex	1991	Texas	*	President/general manager, Dallas Cowboys, 1960-89
Selmon, Lee Roy	1995	Oklahoma	DE	Tampa Bay Buccaneers, 1976-84
Shaw, Billy	1999	Georgia Tech	G	Buffalo Bills, 1961-69
Shell, Art	1989	Md.-Eastern Shore	T	Oakland-Los Angeles Raiders, 1968-82; coach, Los Angeles Raiders, 1989-94
Shula, Don†	1997	John Carroll	DB*	Cleveland Browns, 1951-52; Baltimore Colts, 1953-56; Washington Redskins, 1957; coach, Baltimore Colts, 1963-69, Miami Dolphins, 1970-95
Simpson, O.J.†	1985	Southern California	RB	Buffalo Bills, 1969-77; San Francisco 49ers, 1978-79
Singletary, Mike†	1998	Baylor	LB	Chicago Bears, 1981-92
Slater, Jackie†	2001	Jackson State	T	Los Angeles Rams, 1976-94; St. Louis Rams, 1995
Smith, Jackie	1994	N'western Louisiana	TE	St. Louis Cardinals, 1963-77; Dallas Cowboys, 1978
Stallworth, John	2002	Alabama A&M	WR	Pittsburgh Steelers, 1974-87
Starr, Bart†	1977	Alabama	QB	Green Bay Packers, 1956-71; coach, Green Bay Packers, 1975-83
Staubach, Roger†	1985	Navy	QB	Dallas Cowboys, 1969-79
Stautner, Ernie†	1969	Boston College	DT	Pittsburgh Steelers, 1950-63
Stenerud, Jan†	1991	Montana State	PK	Kansas City Chiefs, 1967-79; Green Bay Packers, 1980-83; Minnesota Vikings, 1984-85
Stephenson, Dwight	1998	Alabama	C	Miami Dolphins, 1980-87
Stram, Hank	2003	Purdue	*	Dallas Texans, 1960-62; Kansas City Chiefs, 1963-74; New Orleans Saints, 1976-77
Strong, Ken	1967	New York U.	HB/PK	Staten Island Stapletons, New York Yankees, New York Giants, 1929-39, 44-47
Stydahar, Joe	1967	West Virginia	T	Chicago Bears, 1936-42, 45-46
Swann, Lynn	2001	Southern California	WR	Pittsburgh Steelers, 1974-82
Tarkenton, Fran	1986	Georgia	QB	Minnesota Vikings, 1961-66, 72-78; New York Giants, 1967-71
Taylor, Charley	1984	Arizona State	WR	Washington Redskins, 1964-75, 77
Taylor, Jim	1976	Louisiana State	FB	Green Bay Packers, 1958-66; New Orleans Saints, 1967
Taylor, Lawrence†	1999	North Carolina	LB	New York Giants, 1981-93
Thorpe, Jim	1963	Carlisle	HB	Canton Bulldogs, Oorang Indians, Cleveland Indians, Rock Island Independents, New York Giants, Chicago Cardinals 1915-26, 1928
Tittle, Y.A.	1971	Louisiana State	QB	Baltimore Colts, 1948-50; San Francisco 49ers, 1951-60; New York Giants, 1961-64
Trafton, George	1964	Notre Dame	C	Decatur Staleys, Chicago Staleys, Chicago Bears, 1920-32
Trippi, Charley	1968	Georgia	HB	Chicago Cardinals, 1947-55
Tunnell, Emlen	1967	Iowa	DB	New York Giants, Green Bay Packers, 1948-61
Turner, Clyde (Bulldog)	1966	Hardin-Simmons	C/LB	Chicago Bears, 1940-52; coach, New York Titans, 1962
Unitas, John†	1979	Louisville	QB	Baltimore Colts, 1956-72; San Diego Chargers, 1973
Upshaw, Gene†	1987	Texas A&I	G	Oakland Raiders, 1967-81
Van Brocklin, Norm	1971	Oregon	QB	Los Angeles Rams, 1949-57; Philadelphia Eagles, 1958-60; coach, Minnesota Vikings, 1961-66; Atlanta Falcons, 1968-74
Van Buren, Steve	1965	Louisiana State	HB	Philadelphia Eagles, 1944-51
Walker, Doak	1986	Southern Methodist	RB	Detroit Lions, 1950-55
Walsh, Bill	1993	San Jose State	*	Coach, San Francisco 49ers, 1979-88
Warfield, Paul†	1983	Ohio State	WR	Cleveland Browns, 1964-69, 76-77; Miami Dolphins, 1970-74
Waterfield, Bob	1965	UCLA	QB	Cleveland Rams, Los Angeles Rams, 1945-52; coach, Los Angeles Rams, 1960-62
Webster, Mike	1997	Wisconsin	C-G	Pittsburgh Steelers, 1974-88; Kansas City Chiefs, 1989-90
Weinmeister, Arnie	1984	Washington	T	New York Yankees, 1948-49; New York Giants, 1950-53
White, Randy	1994	Maryland	DT	Dallas Cowboys, 1975-88
Wilcox, Dave	2000	Oregon	LB	San Francisco 49ers, 1964-74
Willis, Bill	1977	Ohio State	G	Cleveland Browns, 1946-53
Wilson, Larry†	1978	Utah	DB	St. Louis Cardinals, 1960-72
Winslow, Kellen	1995	Missouri	TE	San Diego Chargers, 1979-87
Wojciechowicz, Alex	1968	Fordham	C/LB	Detroit Lions, Philadelphia Eagles, 1938-50
Wood, Willie	1989	Southern California	S	Green Bay Packers, 1960-71
Yary, Ron	2001	Southern California	OT	Minnesota Vikings, 1968-81; Los Angeles Rams, 1982
Young, Steve†	2005	Brigham Young	QB	Tampa Bay Buccaneers, 1985-86; San Francisco 49ers, 1987-99
Youngblood, Jack	2001	Florida	DE	Los Angeles Rams, 1971-84

*Hall of Fame member was selected for contributions other than as a player.
†Elected in his first year of eligibility.
Abbreviations of positions: C—Center, CB—Cornerback, DB—Defensive back, DE—Defensive end, DT—Defensive tackle, E—End, FB—Fullback, FL—Flanker, G—Guard, HB—Halfback, LB—Linebacker, PK—Placekicker, QB—Quarterback, RB—Running back, S—Safety, T—Tackle, TB—Tailback, TE—Tight end.

THE SPORTING NEWS AWARDS

PLAYER OF THE YEAR

1954—Lou Groza, OT/K, Cleveland
1955—Otto Graham, QB, Cleveland
1956—Frank Gifford, HB, N.Y. Giants
1957—Jim Brown, RB, Cleveland
1958—Jim Brown, RB, Cleveland
1959—Johnny Unitas, QB, Baltimore
1960—Norm Van Brocklin, QB, Philadelphia
1961—Paul Hornung, HB, Green Bay
1962—Y.A. Tittle, QB, N.Y. Giants
1963—Y.A. Tittle, QB, N.Y. Giants
1964—Johnny Unitas, QB, Baltimore
1965—Jim Brown, RB, Cleveland
1966—Bart Starr, QB, Green Bay
1967—Johnny Unitas, QB, Baltimore
1968—Earl Morrall, QB, Baltimore
1969—Roman Gabriel, QB, L.A. Rams
1970—NFC: John Brodie, QB, San Francisco
    AFC: George Blanda, QB/PK, Oakland
1971—NFC: Roger Staubach, QB, Dallas
    AFC: Bob Griese, QB, Miami
1972—NFC: Larry Brown, RB, Washington
    AFC: Earl Morrall, QB, Miami
1973—NFC: John Hadl, QB, L.A. Rams
    AFC: O.J. Simpson, RB, Buffalo
1974—NFC: Chuck Foreman, RB, Minnesota
    AFC: Ken Stabler, QB, Oakland
1975—NFC: Fran Tarkenton, QB, Minnesota
    AFC: O.J. Simpson, RB, Buffalo
1976—NFC: Walter Payton, RB, Chicago
    AFC: Ken Stabler, QB, Oakland
1977—NFC: Walter Payton, RB, Chicago
    AFC: Craig Morton, QB, Denver
1978—NFC: Archie Manning, QB, New Orleans

    AFC: Earl Campbell, RB, Houston
1979—NFC: Ottis Anderson, RB, St. Louis
    AFC: Dan Fouts, QB, San Diego
1980—Brian Sipe, QB, Cleveland
1981—Ken Anderson, QB, Cincinnati
1982—Mark Moseley, PK, Washington
1983—Eric Dickerson, RB, L.A. Rams
1984—Dan Marino, QB, Miami
1985—Marcus Allen, RB, L.A. Raiders
1986—Lawrence Taylor, LB, N.Y. Giants
1987—Jerry Rice, WR, San Francisco
1988—Boomer Esiason, QB, Cincinnati
1989—Joe Montana, QB, San Francisco
1990—Jerry Rice, WR, San Francisco
1991—Thurman Thomas, RB, Buffalo
1992—Steve Young, QB, San Francisco
1993—Emmitt Smith, RB, Dallas
1994—Steve Young, QB, San Francisco
1995—Brett Favre, QB, Green Bay
1996—Brett Favre, QB, Green Bay
1997—Barry Sanders, RB, Detroit
1998—Terrell Davis, RB, Denver
1999—Kurt Warner, QB, St. Louis
2000—Marshall Faulk, RB, St. Louis
2001—Marshall Faulk, RB, St. Louis
2002—Rich Gannon, QB, Oakland
2003—Peyton Manning, QB, Indianapolis
2004—Peyton Manning, QB, Indianapolis
NOTE: From 1970-79, a player was selected as Player of the Year for both the NFC and AFC. In 1980 The Sporting News reinstated the selection of one player as Player of the Year for the entire NFL.

ROOKIE OF THE YEAR

1955—Alan Ameche, FB, Baltimore
1956—J.C. Caroline, HB, Chicago
1957—Jim Brown, FB, Cleveland
1958—Bobby Mitchell, HB, Cleveland
1959—Nick Pietrosante, FB, Detroit
1960—Gail Cogdill, E, Detroit
1961—Mike Ditka, E, Chicago
1962—Ronnie Bull, HB, Chicago
1963—Paul Flatley, WR, Minnesota
1964—Charley Taylor, HB, Washington
1965—Gale Sayers, RB, Chicago
1966—Tommy Nobis, LB, Atlanta
1967—Mel Farr, RB, Detroit
1968—Earl McCullouch, WR, Detroit
1969—Calvin Hill, RB, Dallas
1970—NFC: Bruce Taylor, CB, San Francisco
    AFC: Dennis Shaw, QB, Buffalo
1971—NFC: John Brockington, RB, Green Bay
    AFC: Jim Plunkett, QB, New England
1972—NFC: Chester Marcol, PK, Green Bay
    AFC: Franco Harris, RB, Pittsburgh
1973—NFC: Chuck Foreman, RB, Minnesota
    AFC: Boobie Clark, RB, Cincinnati
1974—NFC: Wilbur Jackson, RB, San Francisco
    AFC: Don Woods, RB, San Diego
1975—NFC: Steve Bartkowski, QB, Atlanta
    AFC: Robert Brazile, LB, Houston
1976—NFC: Sammy White, WR, Minnesota
    AFC: Mike Haynes, CB, New England
1977—NFC: Tony Dorsett, RB, Dallas
    AFC: A.J. Duhe, DT, Miami
1978—NFC: Al Baker, DE, Detroit

    AFC: Earl Campbell, RB, Houston
1979—NFC: Ottis Anderson, RB, St. Louis
    AFC: Jerry Butler, WR, Buffalo
1980—Billy Sims, RB, Detroit
1981—George Rogers, RB, New Orleans
1982—Marcus Allen, RB, L.A. Raiders
1983—Dan Marino, QB, Miami
1984—Louis Lipps, WR, Pittsburgh
1985—Eddie Brown, WR, Cincinnati
1986—Rueben Mayes, RB, New Orleans
1987—Robert Awalt, TE, St. Louis
1988—Keith Jackson, TE, Philadelphia
1989—Barry Sanders, RB, Detroit
1990—Richmond Webb, T, Miami
1991—Mike Croel, LB, Denver
1992—Santana Dotson, DL, Tampa Bay
1993—Jerome Bettis, RB, L.A. Rams
1994—Marshall Faulk, RB, Indianapolis
1995—Curtis Martin, RB, New England
1996—Eddie George, RB, Houston
1997—Warrick Dunn, RB, Tampa Bay
1998—Randy Moss, WR, Minnesota
1999—Edgerrin James, RB, Indianapolis
2000—Brian Urlacher, LB, Chicago
2001—Kendrell Bell, LB, Pittsburgh
2002—Clinton Portis, RB, Denver
2003—Anquan Boldin, WR, Arizona
2004—Ben Roethlisberger, Pittsburgh
NOTE: From 1970-79, a player was selected as Rookie of the Year for both the NFC and AFC. In 1980 The Sporting News reinstated the selection of one player as Rookie of the Year for the entire NFL.

NFL COACH OF THE YEAR

1947—Jimmy Conzelman, Chi. Cardinals
1948—Earle (Greasy) Neale, Philadelphia
1949—Paul Brown, Cleveland (AAFC)
1950—Steve Owen, N.Y. Giants
1951—Paul Brown, Cleveland
1952—J. Hampton Pool, L.A. Rams
1953—Paul Brown, Cleveland
1954—None
1955—Joe Kuharich, Washington
1956—Jim Lee Howell, N.Y. Giants
1961—Vince Lombardi, Green Bay
1962—None
1963—George Halas, Chicago
1964—Don Shula, Baltimore
1965—George Halas, Chicago
1966—Tom Landry, Dallas
1967—George Allen, L.A. Rams
1968—Don Shula, Baltimore
1969—Bud Grant, Minnesota
1970—Don Shula, Miami
1971—George Allen, Washington
1972—Don Shula, Miami
1973—Chuck Knox, L.A. Rams
1974—Don Coryell, St. Louis
1975—Ted Marchibroda, Baltimore
1976—Chuck Fairbanks, New England
1977—Red Miller, Denver
1978—Jack Patera, Seattle

1979—Dick Vermeil, Philadelphia
1980—Chuck Knox, Buffalo
1981—Bill Walsh, San Francisco
1982—Joe Gibbs, Washington
1983—Joe Gibbs, Washington
1984—Chuck Knox, Seattle
1985—Mike Ditka, Chicago
1986—Bill Parcells, N.Y. Giants
1987—Jim Mora, New Orleans
1988—Marv Levy, Buffalo
1989—Lindy Infante, Green Bay
1990—George Seifert, San Francisco
1991—Joe Gibbs, Washington
1992—Bill Cowher, Pittsburgh
1993—Dan Reeves, N.Y. Giants
1994—George Seifert, San Francisco
1995—Ray Rhodes, Philadelphia
1996—Dom Capers, Carolina
1997—Jim Fassel, N.Y. Giants
1998—Dan Reeves, Atlanta
1999—Dick Vermeil, St. Louis
2000—Andy Reid, Philadelphia
2001—Dick Jauron, Chicago
2002—Andy Reid, Philadelphia
2003—Bill Belichick, New England
2004—Bill Cowher, Pittsburgh
NOTE: The Coach of the Year Award was not given from 1957-71.

NFL EXECUTIVE OF THE YEAR

1955—Dan Reeves, L.A. Rams
1956—George Halas, Chicago
1972—Dan Rooney, Pittsburgh
1973—Jim Finks, Minnesota
1974—Art Rooney, Pittsburgh
1975—Joe Thomas, Baltimore
1976—Al Davis, Oakland
1977—Tex Schramm, Dallas
1978—John Thompson, Seattle
1979—John Sanders, San Diego
1980—Eddie LeBaron, Atlanta
1981—Paul Brown, Cincinnati
1982—Bobby Beathard, Washington
1983—Bobby Beathard, Washington
1984—George Young, N.Y. Giants
1985—Mike McCaskey, Chicago
1986—George Young, N.Y. Giants
1987—Jim Finks, New Orleans
1988—Bill Polian, Buffalo

1989—John McVay, San Francisco
1990—George Young, N.Y. Giants
1991—Bill Polian, Buffalo
1992—Ron Wolf, Green Bay
1993—George Young, N.Y. Giants
1994—Carmen Policy, San Francisco
1995—Bill Polian, Carolina
1996—Bill Polian, Carolina
1997—George Young, N.Y. Giants
1998—Jeff Diamond, Minnesota
1999—Bill Polian, Indianapolis
2000—Randy Mueller, New Orleans
2001—Dan Rooney, Pittsburgh
2002—Bruce Allen, Oakland
2003—Scott Pioli, New England
2004—Scott Pioli, New England
NOTE: The Executive of the Year Award was not given from 1957-71.

2004 NFL ALL-PRO TEAM

OFFENSE

WR—Marvin Harrison, Indianapolis
Terrell Owens, Philadelphia
TE—Antonio Gates, San Diego
T—Walter Jones, Seattle
Orlando Pace, St. Louis
G—Alan Faneca, Pittsburgh
Brian Waters, Kansas City
C—Jeff Hartings, Pittsburgh
QB—Peyton Manning, Indianapolis
RB—Edgerrin James, Indianapolis
Curtis Martin, N.Y. Jets

DEFENSE

E—Dwight Freeney, Indianapolis
Julius Peppers, Carolina
T—Richard Seymour, New England
Kevin Williams, Minnesota
LB—James Farrior, Pittsburgh
Ray Lewis, Baltimore
LB—Takeo Spikes, Buffalo
CB—Champ Bailey, Denver
Chris McAlister, Baltimore
S—Brian Dawkins, Philadelphia
Ed Reed, Baltimore

SPECIALISTS

K—Adam Vinatieri, Patriots
P—Shane Lechler, Raiders
KR—Terrence McGee, Bills
PR—Eddie Drummond, Lions

FIRST-ROUND DRAFT CHOICES

(Note: Players in boldface are in Pro Football's Hall of Fame and those in italics are former Heisman Trophy winners. In years in which draft order was not announced, players are arranged alphabetically by team.)

1936
FIRST ROUND—NFL

No.	Team	Player selected	Pos.	College
1.	Philadelphia	*Jay Berwanger*	B	Chicago
2.	Boston	Riley Smith	B	Alabama
3.	Pittsburgh	Bill Shakespeare	B	Notre Dame
4.	Brooklyn	Dick Crayne	B	Iowa
5.	Chi. Cardinals	Jim Lawrence	B	Texas Christian
6.	Chi. Bears	**Joe Stydahar**	T	West Virginia
7.	Green Bay	Russ Letlow	G	San Francisco
8.	Detroit	Sid Wagner	G	Michigan State
9.	New York	Art Lewis	T	Ohio
	Total number of picks in draft: 81.			

OTHER NOTEWORTHY PICKS

Round/Overall—Team, Player selected, Pos., College
2/18—New York, **Tuffy Leemans**, B, George Washington; 3/23—Chi. Cardinals, Eddie Erdelatz, E, St. Mary's (Calif.); 4/31—Brooklyn, Bear Bryant, E, Alabama; 8/65—Boston, **Wayne Millner**, E, Notre Dame; 9/78—Chi. Bears, **Dan Fortmann**, G, Colgate.

1937
FIRST ROUND—NFL

No.	Team	Player selected	Pos.	College
1.	Philadelphia	Sam Francis	B	Nebraska
2.	Brooklyn	Ed Goddard	B	Washington State
3.	Chi. Cardinals	Buzz Buivid	B	Marquette
4.	New York	Ed Widseth	T	Minnesota
5.	Pittsburgh	Mike Basrak	C	Duquesne
6.	Boston	**Sammy Baugh**	QB	Texas Christian
7.	Detroit	Lloyd Cardwell	B	Nebraska
8.	Chi. Bears	Les McDonald	E	Nebraska
9.	Green Bay	Eddie Jankowski	B	Wisconsin
10.	League*	Johnny Drake	B	Purdue

*The league selected for an extra franchise under the likelihood that one would be awarded. The Cleveland Rams received Drake when they were admitted to the league prior to the 1937 season.
Total number of picks in draft: 100.

OTHER NOTEWORTHY PICKS

Round/Overall—Team, Player selected, Pos., College
2/13—Brooklyn, **Ace Parker**, B, Duke; 3/29—Green Bay, Bud Wilkinson, T, Minnesota; 9/87—Detroit, *Larry Kelley*, E, Yale.

1938
FIRST ROUND—NFL

No.	Team	Player selected	Pos.	College
1.	Cleveland	Corbett Davis	B	Indiana
2.	Philadelphia	Jim McDonald	B	Ohio State
3.	Brooklyn	Boyd Brumbaugh	B	Duquesne
4.	Pittsburgh	Whizzer White	B	Colorado
5.	Chi. Cardinals	Jack Robbins	B	Arkansas
6.	Detroit	**Alex Wojciechowicz**	C	Fordham
7.	Green Bay	Cecil Isbell	B	Purdue
8.	New York	George Karamatic	B	Gonzaga
9.	Washington	Andy Farkas	B	Detroit
10.	Chi. Bears	Joe Gray	B	Oregon State
	Total number of picks in draft: 110.			

OTHER NOTEWORTHY PICKS

Round/Overall—Team, Player selected, Pos., College
3/18—Brooklyn, **Frank (Bruiser) Kinard**, T, Mississippi; 12/106—Detroit, *Clint Frank*, B, Yale.

1939
FIRST ROUND—NFL

No.	Team	Player selected	Pos.	College
1.	Chi. Cardinals	Ki Aldrich	C	Texas Christian
2.	Chi. Bears	**Sid Luckman**	QB	Columbia
3.	Cleveland	Parker Hall	B	Mississippi
4.	Philadelphia	*Davey O'Brien*	B	Texas Christian
5.	Brooklyn	Bob MacLeod	B	Dartmouth
6.	Chi. Bears	Bill Osmanski	B	Holy Cross
7.	Detroit	John Pingel	B	Michigan State
8.	Washington	I.B. Hale	T	Texas Christian
9.	Green Bay	Larry Buhler	B	Minnesota
10.	New York	Walt Nielsen	B	Arizona

Team not selecting in first round: Pittsburgh.
Total number of picks in draft: 200.

OTHER NOTEWORTHY PICKS

Round/Overall—Team, Player selected, Pos., College
11/91—Chi. Cardinals, Bowden Wyatt, E, Tennessee.

1940
FIRST ROUND—NFL

No.	Team	Player selected	Pos.	College
1.	Chi. Cardinals	George Cafego	B	Tennessee
2.	Philadelphia	**George McAfee**	B	Duke
3.	Pittsburgh	Kay Eakin	B	Arkansas
4.	Brooklyn	Banks McFadden	B	Clemson
5.	Cleveland	Olie Cordill	B	Rice
6.	Detroit	Doyle Nave	B	USC
7.	Chi. Bears	**Bulldog Turner**	C	Hardin-Simmons
8.	Washington	Ed Boell	B	New York U.
9.	Green Bay	Hal Van Every	B	Minnesota
10.	New York	Grenny Lansdell	B	USC
	Total number of picks in draft: 200.			

OTHER NOTEWORTHY PICKS

Round/Overall—Team, Player selected, Pos., College
2/11—Chi. Cardinals, George (Snuffy) Stirnweiss, B, North Carolina; 2/14—Brooklyn, *Nile Kinnick*, B, Iowa; 4/27—Pittsburgh, Frank (Pop) Ivy, E, Oklahoma; 9/77—Chi. Bears, Hampton Pool, E, Stanford.

1941
FIRST ROUND—NFL

No.	Team	Player selected	Pos.	College
1.	Chi. Bears	*Tom Harmon*	B	Michigan
2.	Chi. Cardinals	John Kimbrough	B	Texas A&M
3.	Chi. Bears	Norm Standlee	B	Stanford
4.	Cleveland	Rudy Mucha	C	Washington
5.	Detroit	Jim Thomason	B	Texas A&M
6.	New York	George Franck	B	Minnesota
7.	Green Bay	George Paskvan	B	Wisconsin
8.	Brooklyn	Dean McAdams	B	Washington
9.	Chi. Bears	Don Scott	B	Ohio State
10.	Washington	Forest Evashevski	B	Michigan

Teams not selecting in first round: Philadelphia, Pittsburgh.
Total number of picks in draft: 200.

OTHER NOTEWORTHY PICKS

Round/Overall—Team, Player selected, Pos., College
2/13—Chi. Cardinals, Paul Christman, QB, Missouri; 9/77—Green Bay, **Tony Canadeo**, B, Gonzaga.

HISTORY *First-round draft choices*

1942
FIRST ROUND—NFL

No. Team	Player selected	Pos.	College
1. Pittsburgh	**Bill Dudley**	B	Virginia
2. Cleveland	Jack Wilson	B	Baylor
3. Philadelphia	Pete Kmetovic	B	Stanford
4. Chi. Cardinals	Steve Lach	B	Duke
5. Detroit	Bob Westfall	B	Michigan
6. Washington	Spec Sanders	B	Texas
7. Brooklyn	Bob Robertson	B	USC
8. New York	Merle Hapes	B	Mississippi
9. Green Bay	Urban Odson	T	Minnesota
10. Chi. Bears	Frankie Albert	B	Stanford

Total number of picks in draft: 200.

OTHER NOTEWORTHY PICKS

Round/Overall—Team, Player selected, Pos., College

7/58—New York, Tommy Prothro, B, Duke; 13/119—Green Bay, Bruce Smith, B, Minnesota; 15/134—Chi. Cardinals, Marv Harshman, B, Pacific Lutheran; 15/135—Detroit, Mac Speedie, E, Utah; 18/167—Brooklyn, Ralph Miller, B, Kansas.

1943
FIRST ROUND—NFL

No. Team	Player selected	Pos.	College
1. Detroit	*Frank Sinkwich*	B	Georgia
2. Philadelphia	Joe Muha	B	Virginia Military
3. Chi. Cardinals	Glenn Dobbs	B	Tulsa
4. Brooklyn	Paul Governali	B	Columbia
5. Cleveland	Mike Holovak	B	Boston College
6. New York	Steve Filipowicz	B	Fordham
7. Pittsburgh	Bill Daley	B	Minnesota
8. Green Bay	Dick Wildung	T	Minnesota
9. Chi. Bears	Bob Steuber	B	Missouri
10. Washington	Jack Jenkins	B	Vanderbilt

Note: Philadelphia and Pittsburgh franchises merged for 1943 season (but after draft); Cleveland franchise suspended operations for one year (but after draft).
Total number of picks in draft: 300.

OTHER NOTEWORTHY PICKS

Round/Overall—Team, Player selected, Pos., College

6/45—Cleveland, *Les Horvath*, B, Ohio State; 13/116—New York, Don McCafferty, T, Ohio State; 17/157—Pittsburgh, Nick Skorich, G, Cincinnati.

1944
FIRST ROUND—NFL

No. Team	Player selected	Pos.	College
1. Boston	*Angelo Bertelli*	QB	Notre Dame
2. Chi. Cardinals	Pat Harder	B	Wisconsin
3. Brooklyn	Creighton Miller	B	Notre Dame
4. Detroit	**Otto Graham**	QB	Northwestern
5. Philadelphia	**Steve Van Buren**	B	Louisiana State
6. New York	Billy Hillenbrand	B	Indiana
7. Green Bay	Merv Pregulman	G	Michigan
8. Washington	Mike Micka	B	Colgate
9. Chi. Bears	Ray Evans	B	Kansas
10. Pittsburgh	Johnny Podesto	B	St. Mary's (Cal.)
11. Cleveland	Tony Butkovich	B	Illinois

Note: Chi. Cardinals and Pittsburgh franchises merged for 1944 season (but after draft).
Total number of picks in draft: 330.

OTHER NOTEWORTHY PICKS

Round/Overall—Team, Player selected, Pos., College

5/42—Cleveland, **Bob Waterfield**, B, UCLA; 8/71—Green Bay, Alex Agase, G, Illinois; 10/88—Chi. Cardinals, Lou Saban, B, Indiana; 12/112—Detroit, Jack Lescoulie, G, UCLA.

1945
FIRST ROUND—NFL

No. Team	Player selected	Pos.	College
1. Chi. Cardinals	**Charley Trippi**	B	Georgia
2. Pittsburgh	Paul Duhart	B	Florida
3. Brooklyn	Joe Renfroe	B	Tulane
4. Boston	Eddie Prokop	B	Georgia Tech
5. Cleveland	**Crazylegs Hirsch**	B	Wisconsin
6. Detroit	Frank Szymanski	C	Notre Dame
7. Chi. Bears	Don Lund	B	Michigan
8. Washington	Jim Hardy	QB	USC
9. Philadelphia	John Yonaker	E	Notre Dame
10. New York	Elmer Barbour	B	Wake Forest
11. Green Bay	Walt Schlinkman	B	Texas Tech

Note: Boston and Brooklyn franchises merged for 1945 season (but after draft).
Total number of picks in draft: 330.

OTHER NOTEWORTHY PICKS

Round/Overall—Team, Player selected, Pos., College

3/25—Philadelphia, Alvin Dark, B, Louisiana State; 5/41—Philadelphia, **Pete Pihos**, E, Indiana; 11/103—Cleveland, **Tom Fears**, E, UCLA; 13/127—Washington, Charlie Conerly, QB, Mississippi; 15/145—Pittsburgh, **George Connor**, T, Notre Dame; 17/166—Brooklyn, **Arnie Weinmeister**, E, Washington.

1946
FIRST ROUND—NFL

No. Team	Player selected	Pos.	College
1. Boston	Frank Dancewicz	QB	Notre Dame
2. Chi. Cardinals	Dub Jones	B	Tulane
3. Pittsburgh	*Doc Blanchard*	B	Army
4. Chi. Bears	*Johnny Lujack*	QB	Notre Dame
5. New York	**George Connor**	T	Notre Dame
6. Green Bay	Johnny Strzykalski	B	Marquette
7. Philadelphia	Leo Riggs	B	USC
8. Detroit	Bill Dellastatious	B	Missouri
9. Washington	Cal Rossi	B	UCLA
10. Los Angeles	Emil Sitko	B	Notre Dame

Total number of picks in draft: 300.

OTHER NOTEWORTHY PICKS

Round/Overall—Team, Player selected, Pos., College

3/19—Chi. Bears, Frank Broyles, QB, Georgia Tech; 9/74—Chi. Bears, Walt Dropo, E, Connecticut.

1947
SPECIAL SELECTIONS—AAFC

These special selections were made prior to the regular AAFC draft and the draft order was not announced.

Team	Player selected	Pos.	College
Brooklyn	*Doc Blanchard*	B	Army
Brooklyn	Choo-Choo Roberts	B	UT-Chattanooga
Buffalo	Bob Fenimore	B	Oklahoma State
Buffalo	Frank Aschenbrenner	B	Northwestern
Buffalo	Cal Richardson	E	Tulsa
Buffalo	Red Cochran	B	Wake Forest
Chicago	*Johnny Lujack*	QB	Notre Dame
Chicago	Bernie Gallagher	T	Pennsylvania
Cleveland	Dick Hoerner	B	Iowa
Cleveland	Robert Lawrence Rice	C	Tulane
Los Angeles	Herman Wedemeyer	B	St. Mary's (Cal.)
Miami	Arnold Tucker	QB	Army
Miami	Ernie Case	B	UCLA
New York	Buddy Young	B	Illinois
New York	**Charley Trippi**	B	Georgia
San Francisco	*Glenn Davis*	B	Army

Note: Miami dropped out of league after draft, but Miami's selections went to new Baltimore franchise formed after draft.
Total number of special selection picks: 16.

FIRST ROUND—AAFC

No.	Team	Player selected	Pos.	College
1.	Miami	Elmer Madar	E	Michigan
2.	Buffalo	Alton Baldwin	E	Arkansas
3.	Brooklyn	Neill Armstrong	E	Oklahoma State
4.	Chicago	George Sullivan	T	Notre Dame
5.	Los Angeles	Burr Baldwin	E	UCLA
6.	San Francisco	Clyde LeForce	B	Tulsa
7.	New York	Ben Raimondi	B	Indiana
8.	Cleveland	Bob Chappuis	B	Michigan

Note: Miami dropped out of league after draft, but Miami's selections went to new Baltimore franchise formed after draft.

Total number of picks in regular rounds of draft (excluding special selections): 170.

OTHER NOTEWORTHY PICKS

Round/Overall—Team, Player selected, Pos., College
2/11—Brooklyn, Charlie Conerly, QB, Mississippi; 6/47—New York, Walt Dropo, E, Connecticut; 10/78—San Francisco, Frank Broyles, QB, Georgia Tech.

FIRST ROUND—NFL

No.	Team	Player selected	Pos.	College
1.	Chi. Bears	Bob Fenimore	B	Oklahoma State
2.	Detroit	*Glenn Davis*	B	Army
3.	Boston	Fritz Barzilauskas	G	Yale
4.	Washington	Cal Rossi	B	UCLA
5.	Pittsburgh	Hub Bechtol	E	Texas
6.	Green Bay	Ernie Case	B	UCLA
7.	Chi. Cardinals	Tex Coulter	T	Army
8.	Philadelphia	Neill Armstrong	E	Oklahoma State
9.	Los Angeles	Herman Wedemeyer	B	St. Mary's (Cal.)
10.	New York	Vic Schwall	B	Northwestern
11.	Chi. Bears	Don Kindt	B	Wisconsin

Note: From 1947-58 one team was granted a "bonus selection," which became the first overall pick in the draft. Each team was allowed only one bonus selection during this period.

Total number of picks in draft: 300.

OTHER NOTEWORTHY PICKS

Round/Overall—Team, Player selected, Pos., College
12/103—Los Angeles, **Dante Lavelli**, E, Ohio State; 13/109—Pittsburgh, Ara Parseghian, B, Miami of Ohio; 20/184—New York, **Tom Landry**, B, Texas; 22/204—New York, **Art Donovan**, T, Boston College; 31/293—Chi. Bears, Ed Ehlers, B, Purdue.

1948

FIRST ROUND—AAFC

No.	Team	Player selected	Pos.	College
1.	Chicago	Tony (Skippy) Minisi	B	Pennsylvania
2.	Baltimore	**Bobby Layne**	QB	Texas
3.	Brooklyn	Harry Gilmer	QB	Alabama
4.	Los Angeles	Vaughn Mancha	C	Alabama
5.	San Francisco	Joe Scott	B	San Francisco
6.	Buffalo	Clyde Scott	B	Arkansas
7.	New York	Lowell Tew	B	Alabama
8.	Cleveland	Jeff Durkota	B	Penn State

Total number of picks in draft: 217.

OTHER NOTEWORTHY PICKS

Round/Overall—Team, Player selected, Pos., College
3/14—Los Angeles, **Len Ford**, E, Michigan; 19/128—New York, **Tom Landry**, B, Texas; 25/177—Cleveland, Ara Parseghian, B, Miami of Ohio; 28/198—Los Angeles, **Lou Creekmur**, T, William & Mary.

FIRST ROUND—NFL

No.	Team	Player selected	Pos.	College
1.	Washington	Harry Gilmer	QB	Alabama
2.	New York	Tony (Skippy) Minisi	B	Pennsylvania

No.	Team	Player selected	Pos.	College
3.	Chi. Bears	Bobby Layne	QB	Texas
4.	Washington	Lowell Tew	B	Alabama
5.	Boston	Vaughn Mancha	C	Alabama
6.	Detroit	**Y.A. Tittle**	QB	Louisiana State
7.	Green Bay	Earl (Jug) Girard	B	Wisconsin
8.	Philadelphia	Clyde Scott	B	Arkansas
9.	Pittsburgh	Dan Edwards	E	Georgia
10.	Chi. Bears	Max Bumgardner	E	Texas
11.	Chi. Cardinals	Jim Spavital	B	Oklahoma State

Note: From 1947-58 one team was granted a "bonus selection," which became the first overall pick in the draft. Each team was allowed only one bonus selection during this period; team not selecting in first round: Los Angeles.

Total number of picks in draft: 300.

OTHER NOTEWORTHY PICKS

Round/Overall—Team, Player selected, Pos., College
26/243—Philadelphia, **Lou Creekmur**, T, William & Mary; 29/274—Pittsburgh, Abe Gibron, G, Purdue.

1949

SECRET DRAFT—AAFC

These players were selected in the first round of a secret two-round draft in July, 1948 in order for the AAFC to have a chance of luring star college players before the NFL could negotiate with them.

Team	Player selected	Pos.	College
Baltimore	Dick Harris	C	Texas
Brooklyn	**Chuck Bednarik**	C	Pennsylvania
Buffalo	Abe Gibron	G	Purdue
Chicago	Terry Brennan	B	Notre Dame
Chicago	Pete Elliott	B	Michigan
Cleveland	Gene Derricotte	B	Michigan
Los Angeles	Dan Dworsky	C	Michigan
San Francisco	**Ernie Stautner**	T	Boston College

Team not selecting in first round: New York.

Total number of picks in secret draft: 16.

FIRST ROUND—AAFC

No.	Team	Player selected	Pos.	College
1.	Chicago	Stan Heath	QB	Nevada
2.	Brooklyn	Joe Sullivan	B	Dartmouth
3.	New York	Bobby Thomason	QB	Virginia Military
4.	Baltimore	George Sims	B	Baylor
5.	Los Angeles	George Taliaferro	B	Indiana
6.	Buffalo	Bill Kay	T	Iowa
7.	San Francisco	Chester Fritz	T	Missouri
8.	Cleveland	Jack Mitchell	QB	Oklahoma

Note: Brooklyn and New York franchises merged for 1949 season (but after draft).

Total number of picks in regular rounds of draft (excluding secret draft selections): 192.

OTHER NOTEWORTHY PICKS

Round/Overall—Team, Player selected, Pos., College
2/9—Chicago, **George Blanda**, QB, Kentucky; 4/22—Chicago, **Jim Finks**, QB, Tulsa; 9/69—Cleveland, *Doak Walker*, B, SMU; 11/78—Chicago, **Norm Van Brocklin**, QB, Oregon.

FIRST ROUND—NFL

No.	Team	Player selected	Pos.	College
1.	Philadelphia	**Chuck Bednarik**	C	Pennsylvania
2.	Detroit	Johnny Rauch	QB	Georgia
3.	Boston	*Doak Walker*	B	SMU
4.	New York	Paul Page	B	SMU
5.	Green Bay	Stan Heath	QB	Nevada
6.	Pittsburgh	Bobby Gage	B	Clemson
7.	Los Angeles	Bobby Thomason	QB	Virginia Military
8.	Washington	Rob Goode	B	Texas A&M
9.	Philadelphia	Frank Tripucka	QB	Notre Dame
10.	Chi. Cardinals	Bill Fischer	G	Notre Dame
11.	Chi. Bears	Dick Harris	C	Texas

Note: From 1947-58 one team was granted a "bonus selection," which became the first overall pick in the draft. Each team was allowed only one bonus selection during this period.
Total number of picks in draft: 251.

OTHER NOTEWORTHY PICKS

Round/Overall—Team, Player selected, Pos., College
/14—New York, Al DeRogatis, T, Duke; 4/37—Los Angeles, Norm Van Brocklin, QB, Oregon; 6/55—New York, Abe Gibron, , Purdue; 12/116—Pittsburgh, Jim Finks, B, Tulsa; 12/119—Chi. Bears, George Blanda, QB, Kentucky; 25/247—Los Angeles, Clay Matthews Sr., T, Georgia Tech.

1950
FIRST ROUND—NFL

No. Team	Player selected	Pos.	College
1. Detroit	Leon Hart	E	Notre Dame
2. Baltimore	Adrian Burk	QB	Baylor
3. Chi. Bears	Chuck Hunsinger	B	Florida
4. Green Bay	Clayton Tonnemaker	C	Minnesota
5. Detroit	Joe Watson	C	Rice
6. Washington	George Thomas	B	Oklahoma
7. N.Y. Giants	Travis Tidwell	B	Auburn
8. Pittsburgh	Lynn Chandnois	B	Michigan State
9. Los Angeles	Ralph Pasquariello	B	Villanova
10. Chi. Bears	Fred (Curly) Morrison	B	Ohio State
11. San Francisco	Leo Nomellini	T	Minnesota
12. Los Angeles	Stan West	G	Oklahoma
13. Cleveland	Ken Carpenter	B	Oregon State
14. Philadelphia	Bud Grant	E	Minnesota

Note: From 1947-58 one team was granted a "bonus selection," which became the first overall pick in the draft. Each team was allowed only one bonus selection during this period; teams not selecting in first round: Chi. Cardinals, N.Y. Bulldogs.
Total number of picks in draft: 391.

OTHER NOTEWORTHY PICKS

Round/Overall—Team, Player selected, Pos., College
2/22—Pittsburgh, Ernie Stautner, T, Boston College; 10/123—Washington, Eddie LeBaron, QB, Pacific; 16/201—Washington, Charlie (Choo-Choo) Justice, B, North Carolina; 20/250—N.Y. Bulldogs, Darrell Royal, B, Oklahoma.

1951
FIRST ROUND—NFL

No. Team	Player selected	Pos.	College
1. N.Y. Giants	Kyle Rote	B	SMU
2. Chi. Bears	Bob Williams	QB	Notre Dame*
3. San Francisco	Y.A. Tittle	QB	Louisiana State*
4. Washington	Leon Heath	B	Oklahoma
5. Green Bay	Bob Gain	T	Kentucky
6. Chi. Cardinals	Jerry Groom	C	Notre Dame
7. Philadelphia	Ebert Van Buren	B	Louisiana State
8. Philadelphia	Chet Mutryn	B	Xavier*
9. Pittsburgh	Butch Avinger	B	Alabama
10. Chi. Bears	Billy Stone	B	Bradley*
11. Los Angeles	Bud McFadin	G	Texas
12. Chi. Bears	Gene Schroeder	E	Virginia
13. N.Y. Giants	Jim Spavital	B	Oklahoma State*
14. Cleveland	Kenny Konz	B	Louisiana State

*Players drafted from Baltimore franchise, which disbanded following 1950 season.
Note: From 1947-58 one team was granted a "bonus selection," which became the first overall pick in the draft. Each team was allowed only one bonus selection during this period; teams not selecting in first round: Detroit, N.Y. Yanks.
Total number of picks in draft: 362.

OTHER NOTEWORTHY PICKS

Round/Overall—Team, Player selected, Pos., College
2/23—Chi. Bears, Bill George, T, Wake Forest; 3/34—N.Y. Yanks, Mike McCormack, T, Kansas; 4/50—Cleveland, Art Donovan, T,

Boston College; 6/69—Detroit, Jack Christiansen, B, Colorado State; 9/110—Cleveland, Don Shula, B, John Carroll; 19/228—Los Angeles, Andy Robustelli, E, Arnold.

1952
FIRST ROUND—NFL

No. Team	Player selected	Pos.	College
1. Los Angeles	Bill Wade	QB	Vanderbilt
2. N.Y. Yanks	Les Richter	G	California
3. Chi. Cardinals	Ollie Matson	B	San Francisco
4. Green Bay	Babe Parilli	QB	Kentucky
5. Philadelphia	Johnny Bright	B	Drake
6. Pittsburgh	Ed Modzelewski	B	Maryland
7. Washington	Larry Isbell	B	Baylor
8. Chi. Bears	Jim Dooley	B	Miami, Fla.
9. San Francisco	Hugh McElhenny	B	Washington
10. Cleveland	Bert Rechichar	B	Tennessee
11. N.Y. Giants	Frank Gifford	B	USC
12. Cleveland	Harry Agganis	QB	Boston University
13. Los Angeles	Bob Carey	E	Michigan State

Note: Shortly after draft, N.Y. Yanks franchise was sold back to league and the club played in 1952 as Dallas Texans; from 1947-58 one team was granted a "bonus selection," which became the first overall pick in the draft. Each team was allowed only one bonus selection during this period; team not selecting in first round: Detroit.
Total number of picks in draft: 360.

OTHER NOTEWORTHY PICKS

Round/Overall—Team, Player selected, Pos., College
2/14—N.Y. Yanks, Gino Marchetti, T, San Francisco; 3/26—Cleveland, Don Klosterman, QB, Loyola, Calif.; 3/34—Detroit, Yale Lary, B, Texas A&M; 4/45—Detroit, Pat Summerall, E, Arkansas; 7/79—Washington, Vic Janowicz, B, Ohio State; 15/176—Chi. Bears, Dick Kazmaier, B, Princeton.

1953
FIRST ROUND—NFL

No. Team	Player selected	Pos.	College
1. San Francisco	Harry Babcock	E	Georgia
2. Baltimore	Billy Vessels	B	Oklahoma
3. Washington	Jack Scarbath	B	Maryland
4. Chi. Cardinals	Johnny Olszewski	B	California
5. Pittsburgh	Ted Marchibroda	QB	Detroit
6. Chi. Bears	Billy Anderson	B	Compton J.C.
7. Green Bay	Al Carmichael	B	USC
8. New York	Bobby Marlow	B	Alabama
9. Los Angeles	Donn Moomaw	C	UCLA
10. San Francisco	Tom Stolhanske	E	Texas
11. Cleveland	Doug Atkins	E	Tennessee
12. Los Angeles	Ed Barker	E	Washington State
13. Detroit	Harley Sewell	G	Texas

Note: From 1947-58 one team was granted a "bonus selection," which became the first overall pick in the draft. Each team was allowed only one bonus selection during this period; team not selecting in first round: Philadelphia.
Total number of picks in draft: 360.

OTHER NOTEWORTHY PICKS

Round/Overall—Team, Player selected, Pos., College
2/17—Chi. Bears, Zeke Bratkowski, QB, Georgia; 2/18—Pittsburgh, John Henry Johnson, B, Arizona State; 3/32—San Francisco, Bob St. Clair, T, Tulsa; 5/54—Chi. Bears, Stan Jones, T, Maryland; 7/79—Green Bay, Jim Ringo, C, Syracuse; 7/81—Philadelphia, Ray Malavasi, G, Mississippi State; 7/85—Detroit, Joe Schmidt, C, Pittsburgh; 10/117—Philadelphia, Tom Brookshier, B, Colorado; 20/239—Cleveland, Chuck Noll, T, Dayton; 25/292—Chi. Cardinals, Haywood Sullivan, B, Florida; 27/321—New York, Roosevelt Brown, T, Morgan State; 30/352—Washington, Bob Mathias, B, Stanford.

HISTORY First-round draft choices

1954
FIRST ROUND—NFL

No. Team	Player selected	Pos.	College
1. Cleveland	Bobby Garrett	QB	Stanford
2. Chi. Cardinals	Lamar McHan	QB	Arkansas
3. Green Bay	Art Hunter	T	Notre Dame
4. Green Bay	Veryl Switzer	B	Kansas State
5. Baltimore	Cotton Davidson	QB	Baylor
6. Chi. Bears	Stan Wallace	B	Illinois
7. Pittsburgh	*Johnny Lattner*	B	Notre Dame
8. Washington	Steve Meilinger	E	Kentucky
9. Philadelphia	Neil Worden	B	Notre Dame
10. Los Angeles	Ed Beatty	C	Mississippi
11. San Francisco	Bernie Faloney	B	Maryland
12. Cleveland	John Bauer	G	Illinois
13. Detroit	Dick Chapman	T	Rice

Note: From 1947-58 one team was granted a "bonus selection," which became the first overall pick in the draft. Each team was allowed only one bonus selection during this period; team not selecting in first round: New York.
Total number of picks in draft: 360.

OTHER NOTEWORTHY PICKS

Round/Overall—Team, Player selected, Pos., College
4/41—New York, Dick Nolan, B, Maryland; 5/51—Green Bay, Max McGee, B, Tulane; 15/174—Chi. Bears, Harlon Hill, E, North Alabama; 20/232—Baltimore, **Raymond Berry**, E, Southern Methodist; 25/293—Baltimore, Pepper Rodgers, B, Georgia Tech.

1955
FIRST ROUND—NFL

No. Team	Player selected	Pos.	College
1. Baltimore	George Shaw	B	Oregon
2. Chi. Cardinals	Max Boydston	E	Oklahoma
3. Baltimore	*Alan Ameche*	B	Wisconsin
4. Washington	Ralph Guglielmi	QB	Notre Dame
5. Green Bay	Tom Bettis	G	Purdue
6. Pittsburgh	Frank Varrichione	T	Notre Dame
7. Los Angeles	Larry Morris	C	Georgia Tech
8. New York	Joe Heap	B	Notre Dame
9. Philadelphia	Dick Bielski	B	Maryland
10. San Francisco	Dickie Moegle	B	Rice
11. Chi. Bears	Ron Drzewiecki	B	Marquette
12. Detroit	Dave Middleton	B	Auburn
13. Cleveland	Kurt Burris	C	Oklahoma

Total number of picks in draft: 360.

OTHER NOTEWORTHY PICKS

Round/Overall—Team, Player selected, Pos., College
3/31—New York, Rosey Grier, T, Penn State; 3/34—San Francisco, Carroll Hardy, B, Colorado; 9/102—Pittsburgh, **Johnny Unitas**, QB, Louisville; 12/139—Los Angeles, Jim Hanifan, E, California; 13/155—Chi. Bears, Norm Cash, B, Sul Ross; 30/354—Los Angeles, K.C. Jones, E, San Francisco.

1956
FIRST ROUND—NFL

No. Team	Player selected	Pos.	College
1. Pittsburgh	Gary Glick	QB	Colorado State
2. San Francisco	Earl Morrall	QB	Michigan State
3. Detroit	*Hopalong Cassady*	B	Ohio State
4. Philadelphia	Bob Pellegrini	C	Maryland
5. Pittsburgh	Art Davis	B	Mississippi State
6. Los Angeles	Joe Marconi	B	West Virginia
7. Chi. Cardinals	Joe Childress	B	Auburn
8. Green Bay	Jack Losch	B	Miami, Fla.
9. Baltimore	**Lenny Moore**	B	Penn State
10. Chi. Bears	Menan (Tex) Schriewer	E	Texas

No. Team	Player selected	Pos.	College
11. Los Angeles	Charlie Horton	B	Vanderbilt
12. Washington	Ed Vereb	B	Maryland
13. Cleveland	Preston Carpenter	B	Arkansas

Note: From 1947-58 one team was granted a "bonus selection," which became the first overall pick in the draft. Each team was allowed only one bonus selection during this period; team not selecting in first round: New York.
Total number of picks in draft: 360.

OTHER NOTEWORTHY PICKS

Round/Overall—Team, Player selected, Pos., College
2/20—Green Bay, **Forrest Gregg**, T, SMU; 3/30—New York, **Sam Huff**, T, West Virginia; 5/54—Philadelphia, Fuzzy Thurston, G, Valparaiso; 15/181—Cleveland, **Willie Davis**, E, Grambling; 16/186—Chi. Cardinals, George Welsh, QB, Navy; 17/200—Green Bay, **Bart Starr**, QB, Alabama; 21/251—Washington, Howard Schnellenberger, E, Kentucky.

1957
FIRST ROUND—NFL

No. Team	Player selected	Pos.	College
1. Green Bay	**Paul Hornung**	QB	Notre Dame
2. Los Angeles	Jon Arnett	B	USC
3. San Francisco	John Brodie	QB	Stanford
4. Green Bay	Ron Kramer	E	Michigan
5. Pittsburgh	Len Dawson	QB	Purdue
6. Cleveland	**Jim Brown**	B	Syracuse
7. Philadelphia	Clarence Peaks	B	Michigan State
8. Baltimore	**Jim Parker**	G	Ohio State
9. Washington	Don Bosseler	B	Miami, Fla.
10. Chi. Cardinals	Jerry Tubbs	C	Oklahoma
11. Los Angeles	Del Shofner	B	Baylor
12. Detroit	Bill Glass	G	Baylor
13. Chi. Bears	Earl Leggett	T	Louisiana State

Note: From 1947-58 one team was granted a "bonus selection," which became the first overall pick in the draft. Each team was allowed only one bonus selection during this period; team not selecting in first round: New York.
Total number of picks in draft: 360.

OTHER NOTEWORTHY PICKS

Round/Overall—Team, Player selected, Pos., College
2/14—Los Angeles, Jack Pardee, B, Texas A&M; 3/31—Philadelphia, **Tommy McDonald**, B, Oklahoma; 4/43—Philadelphia, **Sonny Jurgensen**, QB, Duke; 5/52—Cleveland, **Henry Jordan**, T, Virginia; 5/53—Cleveland, Milt Campbell, B, Indiana; 9/109—New York, **Don Maynard**, B, Texas Western College; 17/203—Detroit, Jack Kemp, QB, Occidental; 29/346—Chi. Cardinals, Lee Corso, B, Florida State.

1958
FIRST ROUND—NFL

No. Team	Player selected	Pos.	College
1. Chi. Cardinals	King Hill	QB	Rice
2. Chi. Cardinals	*John David Crow*	B	Texas A&M
3. Green Bay	Dan Currie	C	Michigan State
4. Los Angeles	Lou Michaels	T	Kentucky
5. Los Angeles	Jim Phillips	E	Auburn
6. Philadelphia	Walt Kowalczyk	B	Michigan State
7. Chi. Bears	Chuck Howley	G	West Virginia
8. San Francisco	Jim Pace	B	Michigan
9. San Francisco	Charlie Krueger	T	Texas A&M
10. Detroit	Alex Karras	T	Iowa
11. Baltimore	Lenny Lyles	B	Louisville
12. New York	Phil King	B	Vanderbilt
13. Cleveland	Jim Shofner	B	Texas Christian

Note: From 1947-58 one team was granted a "bonus selection," which became the first overall pick in the draft. Each team was allowed only one bonus selection during this period; teams not selecting in first round: Pittsburgh, Washington.
Total number of picks in draft: 360.

OTHER NOTEWORTHY PICKS

Round/Overall—Team, Player selected, Pos., College
/15—Green Bay, **Jim Taylor**, B, Louisiana State; 3/36—Green Bay, **Ray Nitschke**, B, Illinois; 4/39—Green Bay, Jerry Kramer, G, Idaho; /84—Cleveland, **Bobby Mitchell**, B, Illinois; 13/154—Baltimore, **Jerry Richardson**, E, Wofford; 19/223—Pittsburgh, Gene Keady, B, Kansas State; 21/244—Philadelphia, John Madden, T, Cal Poly-SLO.

1959
FIRST ROUND—NFL

No. Team	Player selected	Pos.	College
1. Green Bay	Randy Duncan	QB	Iowa
2. Los Angeles	Dick Bass	B	Pacific
3. Chi. Cardinals	Billy Stacy	B	Mississippi State
4. Washington	Don Allard	QB	Boston College
5. San Francisco	Dave Baker	QB	Oklahoma
6. Detroit	Nick Pietrosante	B	Notre Dame
7. Chi. Bears	Don Clark	B	Ohio State
8. San Francisco	Dan James	C	Ohio State
9. Los Angeles	Paul Dickson	T	Baylor
10. New York	Lee Grosscup	QB	Utah
11. Cleveland	Rich Kreitling	E	Illinois
12. Baltimore	Jackie Burkett	C	Auburn

Teams not selecting in first round: Philadelphia, Pittsburgh.
Total number of picks in draft: 360.

OTHER NOTEWORTHY PICKS

Round/Overall—Team, Player selected, Pos., College
/58—Cleveland, Dick LeBeau, B, Ohio State; 18/209—Washington, Joe Kapp, QB, California; 19/222—San Francisco, Tom Osborne, B, Hastings.

1960
AFL

Eight players were selected as territorial picks by the AFL prior to its first draft. The actual draft was held in two stages consisting of a total of 53 rounds. The draft order was not announced. Shortly after the draft, Minneapolis withdrew from the league when it was offered an NFL franchise (to begin play in 1961). Oakland was then allowed to join as the eighth AFL team, and it received the Minneapolis draft list. Before Oakland was admitted to the league, however, other AFL teams had signed a number of players drafted by Minneapolis. The AFL then held an allocation draft for Oakland. Each AFL team protected 11 players and Oakland was allowed to choose 24 unprotected players. Below is the list of AFL territorial picks.

Team	Player selected	Pos.	College
Boston	Gerhard Schwedes	HB	Syracuse
Buffalo	Richie Lucas	QB	Penn State
Dallas	Don Meredith	QB	SMU
Denver	Roger LeClerc	C	Trinity (Ct.)
Houston	*Billy Cannon*	B	Louisiana State
Los Angeles	Monty Stickles	E	Notre Dame
Minneapolis	Dale Hackbart	QB	Wisconsin
New York	George Izo	QB	Notre Dame

Total number of territorial picks: 8.
Total number of regular draft picks (including territorial): 424.
Total number of allocation picks for Oakland franchise: 24

OTHER NOTEWORTHY PICKS

Team, Player selected, Pos., College
Boston, Foge Fazio, C, Pittsburgh; Boston, **Ron Mix**, T, USC; Buffalo, **Larry Wilson**, DB, Utah; Houston, Jim Marshall, T/G, Ohio State; Los Angeles, Paul Maguire, E, The Citadel; Minneapolis, **Jim Otto**, C, Miami, Fla.

FIRST ROUND—NFL

No. Team	Player selected	Pos.	College
1. Los Angeles	*Billy Cannon*	B	Louisiana State
2. Chi. Cardinals	George Izo	QB	Notre Dame
3. Detroit	Johnny Robinson	HB	Louisiana State

No. Team	Player selected	Pos.	College
4. Washington	Richie Lucas	QB	Penn State
5. Green Bay	Tom Moore	B	Vanderbilt
6. Pittsburgh	Jack Spikes	FB	Texas Christian
7. Chi. Bears	Roger Davis	G	Syracuse
8. Cleveland	Jim Houston	E	Ohio State
9. Philadelphia	Ron Burton	HB	Northwestern
10. Baltimore	**Ron Mix**	T	USC
11. San Francisco	Monty Stickles	E	Notre Dame
12. New York	Lou Cordileone	T	Clemson

Note: Chi. Cardinals moved to St. Louis prior to 1960 season (but after draft); expansion Dallas team joined league after draft.
Total number of picks in draft: 240.

OTHER NOTEWORTHY PICKS

Round/Overall—Team, Player selected, Pos., College
3/32—Chi. Bears, Don Meredith, QB, SMU; 4/44—Cleveland, Jim Marshall, T, Ohio State; 7/74—Chi. Cardinals, **Larry Wilson**, DB, Utah.

1961
FIRST ROUND—AFL

Team	Player selected	Pos.	College
Boston	Tommy Mason	HB	Tulane
Buffalo	Ken Rice	T	Auburn
Dallas	E.J. Holub	C	Texas Tech
Denver	Bob Gaiters	HB	New Mexico St.
Houston	**Mike Ditka**	E	Pittsburgh
Los Angeles	Earl Faison	E	Indiana
New York	Tom Brown	G	Minnesota
Oakland	Joe Rutgens	T	Illinois

Note: Los Angeles team moved to San Diego prior to 1961 season (but after draft).
Total number of picks in draft: 240.

OTHER NOTEWORTHY PICKS

Round—Team, Player selected, Pos., College
2—Buffalo, **Billy Shaw**, T, Georgia Tech; 2—Dallas, **Bob Lilly**, T, Texas Christian; 2—New York, **Herb Adderley**, HB, Michigan State; 4—Los Angeles, **Jimmy Johnson**, HB, UCLA; 5—Boston, **Fran Tarkenton**, QB, Georgia; 5—Buffalo, Norm Snead, QB, Wake Forest; 5—Los Angeles, Billy Kilmer, QB, UCLA; 6—Houston, Jake Gibbs, QB, Mississippi; 19—Boston, *Joe Bellino*, B, Navy.

FIRST ROUND—NFL

No. Team	Player selected	Pos.	College
1. Minnesota	Tommy Mason	HB	Tulane
2. Washington	Norm Snead	QB	Wake Forest
3. Washington	Joe Rutgens	T	Illinois
4. Los Angeles	Marlin McKeever	LB	USC
5. Chicago	**Mike Ditka**	E	Pittsburgh
6. San Francisco	**Jimmy Johnson**	B	UCLA
7. Baltimore	Tom Matte	HB	Ohio State
8. St. Louis	Ken Rice	T	Auburn
9. San Francisco	Bernie Casey	B	Bowling Green
10. Cleveland	Bobby Crespino	E	Mississippi
11. San Francisco	Billy Kilmer	QB	UCLA
12. Green Bay	**Herb Adderley**	B	Michigan State
13. Dallas	**Bob Lilly**	T	Texas Christian
14. Philadelphia	Art Baker	FB	Syracuse

Teams not selecting in first round: Dallas, Detroit, New York, Pittsburgh.
Total number of picks in draft: 280.

OTHER NOTEWORTHY PICKS

Round/Overall—Team, Player selected, Pos., College
3/29—Minnesota, **Fran Tarkenton**, QB, Georgia; 9/125—Cleveland, Jake Gibbs, QB, Mississippi; 14/184—Dallas, **Billy Shaw**, T, Georgia Tech; 14/186—Los Angeles, **Deacon Jones**, T, South Carolina State; 17/227—Washington, *Joe Bellino*, B, Navy.

1962

FIRST ROUND—AFL

No. Team	Player selected	Pos.	College
1. Oakland	Roman Gabriel	QB	N. Carolina State
2. Denver	**Merlin Olsen**	T	Utah State
3. Dallas	Ronnie Bull	B	Baylor
4. Buffalo	Ernie Davis	B	Syracuse
5. New York	Sandy Stephens	QB	Minnesota
6. Boston	Gary Collins	E	Maryland
7. Houston	Ray Jacobs	T	Howard Payne
8. San Diego	Bob Ferguson	B	Ohio State

Total number of picks in draft: 272.

OTHER NOTEWORTHY PICKS

Round/Overall—Team, Player selected, Pos., College
2/9—Oakland, **Lance Alworth**, HB, Arkansas; 3/24—San Diego, John Hadl, QB, Kansas; 13/102—Boston, **Nick Buoniconti**, G, Notre Dame.

FIRST ROUND—NFL

No. Team	Player selected	Pos.	College
1. Washington	Ernie Davis	B	Syracuse
2. Los Angeles	Roman Gabriel	QB	N. Carolina State
3. Los Angeles	**Merlin Olsen**	T	Utah State
4. Cleveland	Gary Collins	E	Maryland
5. Pittsburgh	Bob Ferguson	B	Ohio State
6. St. Louis	Fate Echols	T	Northwestern
7. Chicago	Ronnie Bull	B	Baylor
8. San Francisco	**Lance Alworth**	B	Arkansas
9. Baltimore	Wendell Harris	B	Louisiana State
10. Detroit	John Hadl	QB	Kansas
11. Cleveland	Leroy Jackson	B	Western Illinois
12. St. Louis	Irv Goode	C	Kentucky
13. New York	Jerry Hillebrand	E	Colorado
14. Green Bay	Earl Gros	B	Louisiana State

Teams not selecting in first round: Dallas, Minnesota, Philadelphia.
Total number of picks in draft: 280.

OTHER NOTEWORTHY PICKS

Round/Overall—Team, Player selected, Pos., College
7/95—Cleveland, John Havlicek, E, Ohio State; 17/238—Green Bay, **Buck Buchanan**, T, Grambling.

1963

FIRST ROUND—AFL

No. Team	Player selected	Pos.	College
1. Dallas	**Buck Buchanan**	T	Grambling
2. San Diego	Walt Sweeney	E	Syracuse
3. New York	Jerry Stovall	B	Louisiana State
4. Buffalo	Dave Behrman	C	Michigan State
5. Denver	Kermit Alexander	B	UCLA
6. Houston	Danny Brabham	FB	Arkansas
7. Boston	Art Graham	E	Boston College
8. Dallas	Ed Budde	T	Michigan State

Team not selecting in first round: Oakland.
Total number of picks in draft: 232.

OTHER NOTEWORTHY PICKS

Round/Overall—Team, Player selected, Pos., College
5/35—New York, **John Mackey**, E, Syracuse; 7/56—Dallas, **Bobby Bell**, T, Minnesota; 12/90—San Diego, Terry Baker, QB, Oregon State; 24/188—Buffalo, Daryle Lamonica, QB, Notre Dame.

FIRST ROUND—NFL

No. Team	Player selected	Pos.	College
1. Los Angeles	Terry Baker	B	Oregon State
2. St. Louis	Jerry Stovall	B	Louisiana State
3. Minnesota	Jim Dunaway	T	Mississippi

No. Team	Player selected	Pos.	College
4. Philadelphia	Ed Budde	T	Michigan State
5. Baltimore	Bob Vogel	T	Ohio State
6. Dallas	Lee Roy Jordan	LB	Alabama
7. Washington	Pat Richter	E	Wisconsin
8. San Francisco	Kermit Alexander	B	UCLA
9. Cleveland	Tom Hutchinson	E	Kentucky
10. Los Angeles	Rufus Guthrie	G	Georgia Tech
11. Chicago	Dave Behrman	C	Michigan State
12. Detroit	Daryl Sanders	T	Ohio State
13. St. Louis	Don Brumm	DE	Purdue
14. Green Bay	Dave Robinson	E	Penn State

Teams not selecting in first round: New York, Pittsburgh.
Total number of picks in draft: 280.

OTHER NOTEWORTHY PICKS

Round/Overall—Team, Player selected, Pos., College
2/16—Minnesota, **Bobby Bell**, T, Minnesota; 2/19—Baltimore, **John Mackey**, E, Syracuse; 10/129—St. Louis, **Jackie Smith**, E, Northwestern (La.) State; 12/168—Green Bay, Daryle Lamonica, QB, Notre Dame; 19/265—New York, **Buck Buchanan**, T, Grambling

1964

FIRST ROUND—AFL

No. Team	Player selected	Pos.	College
1. Boston	Jack Concannon	QB	Boston College
2. Kansas City	Pete Beathard	QB	USC
3. New York	Matt Snell	FB	Ohio State
4. Denver	Bob Brown	T	Nebraska
5. Buffalo	**Carl Eller**	T	Minnesota
6. Houston	Scott Appleton	T	Texas
7. Oakland	Tony Lorick	HB	Arizona State
8. San Diego	Ted Davis	E	Georgia Tech

Total number of picks in draft: 208.

OTHER NOTEWORTHY PICKS

Round/Overall—Team, Player selected, Pos., College
2/9—Houston, **Charley Taylor**, HB, Arizona State; 4/28—Buffalo, **Paul Warfield**, HB, Ohio State; 6/46—Houston, **Dave Wilcox**, DE, Oregon; 9/67—New York, Sherman Lewis, HB, Michigan State; 10/79—Oakland, **Mel Renfro**, HB, Oregon; 12/89—Denver, **Paul Krause**, DB, Iowa; 14/105—Denver, Bob Hayes, HB, Florida A&M; 16/122—Kansas City, **Roger Staubach**, QB, Navy; 18/140—Boston, Joe Tiller, T, Montana State; 23/183—Oakland, Bill Curry, C, Georgia Tech.

FIRST ROUND—NFL

No. Team	Player selected	Pos.	College
1. San Francisco	Dave Parks	E	Texas Tech
2. Philadelphia	**Bob Brown**	T	Nebraska
3. Washington	**Charley Taylor**	HB	Arizona State
4. Dallas	Scott Appleton	T	Texas
5. Detroit	Pete Beathard	QB	USC
6. Minnesota	**Carl Eller**	T	Minnesota
7. Los Angeles	Bill Munson	QB	Utah State
8. Baltimore	Marv Woodson	HB	Indiana
9. St. Louis	Ken Kortas	T	Louisville
10. Pittsburgh	Paul Martha	HB	Pittsburgh
11. Cleveland	**Paul Warfield**	HB	Ohio State
12. New York	Joe Don Looney	B	Oklahoma
13. Green Bay	Lloyd Voss	T	Nebraska
14. Chicago	Dick Evey	T	Tennessee

Total number of picks in draft: 280.

OTHER NOTEWORTHY PICKS

Round/Overall—Team, Player selected, Pos., College
2/17—Dallas, **Mel Renfro**, B, Oregon; 2/18—Washington, **Paul Krause**, B, Iowa; 3/29—San Francisco, **Dave Wilcox**, DE, Oregon; 7/88—Dallas, Bob Hayes, HB, Florida A&M; 7/89—Detroit, Bill Parcells, T, Wichita State; 8/110—Cleveland, **Leroy Kelly**, HB, Morgan State; 10/129—Dallas, **Roger Staubach**, QB, Navy 18/250—Cleveland, Sherman Lewis, HB, Michigan State.

FIRST ROUND—AFL

Team	Player selected	Pos.	College
Boston	Jerry Rush	T	Michigan State
Buffalo	Jim Davidson	T	Ohio State
Houston	Lawrence Elkins	E	Baylor
Kansas City	**Gale Sayers**	HB	Kansas
New York	**Joe Namath**	QB	Alabama
New York	Tom Nowatzke	FB	Indiana
Oakland	Harry Schuh	T	Memphis State
San Diego	Steve DeLong	DE	Tennessee

Team not selecting in first round: Denver.
Total number of picks in draft: 160.

OTHER NOTEWORTHY PICKS

Round—Team, Player selected, Pos., College
—Denver, **Dick Butkus**, LB, Illinois; 2—New York, *John Huarte*, HB, Notre Dame; 2—Oakland, **Fred Biletnikoff**, E, Florida State; —Buffalo, Marty Schottenheimer, LB, Pittsburgh; 7—San Diego, Jack Snow, E, Notre Dame; 10—Oakland, Craig Morton, HB, California.

REDSHIRT—AFL

The AFL held a separate draft for future picks in 1965 and 1966.

Team	Player selected	Pos.	College
Boston	Dave McCormick	T	Louisiana State
Buffalo	Ken Ambrusko	HB	Maryland
Denver	Miller Farr	HB	Wichita State
Houston	Donny Anderson	HB	Texas Tech
Kansas City	Alphonse Dotson	T	Grambling
New York	Johnny Roland	HB	Missouri
Oakland	Larry Todd	HB	Arizona State
San Diego	Gary Garrison	E	San Diego State

Total number of picks in draft: 96.

OTHER NOTEWORTHY PICKS

Round—Team, Player selected, Pos., College
4—New York, Rich Kotite, E, Wagner.

FIRST ROUND—NFL

No. Team	Player selected	Pos.	College
1. New York	Tucker Frederickson	B	Auburn
2. San Francisco	Ken Willard	FB	North Carolina
3. Chicago	**Dick Butkus**	LB	Illinois
4. Chicago	**Gale Sayers**	HB	Kansas
5. Dallas	Craig Morton	QB	California
6. Chicago	Steve DeLong	DE	Tennessee
7. Green Bay	Donny Anderson	HB	Texas Tech
8. Minnesota	Jack Snow	E	Notre Dame
9. Los Angeles	Clancy Williams	HB	Washington State
10. Green Bay	Lawrence Elkins	E	Baylor
11. Detroit	Tom Nowatzke	FB	Indiana
12. St. Louis	**Joe Namath**	QB	Alabama
13. San Francisco	George Donnelly	B	Illinois
14. Baltimore	Mike Curtis	LB	Duke

Teams not selecting in first round: Cleveland, Philadelphia, Pittsburgh, Washington.
Total number of picks in draft: 280.

OTHER NOTEWORTHY PICKS

Round/Overall—Team, Player selected, Pos., College
3/39—Detroit, **Fred Biletnikoff**, E, Florida State; 4/49—Baltimore, Marty Schottenheimer, LB, Pittsburgh; 6/76—Philadelphia, *John Huarte*, QB, Notre Dame; 17/238—Baltimore, Rick Reichardt, HB, Wisconsin; 19/257—Dallas, Merv Rettenmund, HB, Ball State.

FIRST ROUND—AFL

Team	Player selected	Pos.	College
Boston	Karl Singer	T	Purdue
Buffalo	Mike Dennis	HB	Mississippi
Denver	Jerry Shay	T	Purdue
Houston	Tommy Nobis	LB	Texas
Kansas City	Aaron Brown	E	Minnesota
Miami	Jim Grabowski	FB	Illinois
Miami	Rick Norton	QB	Kentucky
New York	Bill Yearby	T	Michigan
Oakland	Rodger Bird	HB	Kentucky
San Diego	Don Davis	T	Cal State-L.A.

Total number of picks in draft: 181.

OTHER NOTEWORTHY PICKS

Round—Team, Player selected, Pos., College
15—Oakland, Steve Renko, FB, Kansas; 17—Kansas City, Walt Garrison, FB, Oklahoma State; 20—Kansas City, *Mike Garrett*, HB, USC.

REDSHIRT—AFL

The AFL held a separate draft for future picks in 1965 and 1966.

Team	Player selected	Pos.	College
Boston	Willie Townes	T	Tulsa
Buffalo	Jack Gregory	E	UT-Chattanooga
Denver	Nick Eddy	HB	Notre Dame
Houston	Tom Fisher	LB	Tennessee
Kansas City	George Youngblood	E/DB	Cal State-L.A.
Miami	John Roderick	E	SMU
New York	Don Parker	E	Virginia
Oakland	Rod Sherman	HB	USC
San Diego	Bob Windsor	E	Kentucky

Total number of picks in draft: 99.

OTHER NOTEWORTHY PICKS

Round—Team, Player selected, Pos., College
3—Kansas City, **Jan Stenerud**, K, Montana State; Boston, Ray Perkins, E, Alabama.

FIRST ROUND—NFL

No. Team	Player selected	Pos.	College
1. Atlanta	Tommy Nobis	LB	Texas
2. Los Angeles	**Tom Mack**	T	Michigan
3. Pittsburgh	Dick Leftridge	FB	West Virginia
4. Philadelphia	Randy Beisler	DE	Indiana
5. Dallas	John Niland	G	Iowa
6. Washington	Charlie Gogolak	K	Princeton
7. Minnesota	Jerry Shay	T	Purdue
8. St. Louis	Carl McAdams	LB	Oklahoma
9. Green Bay	Jim Grabowski	FB	Illinois
10. New York	Francis Peay	T	Missouri
11. San Francisco	Stan Hindman	T	Mississippi
12. Chicago	George Rice	T	Louisiana State
13. Green Bay	Gale Gillingham	T	Minnesota
14. Cleveland	Milt Morin	E	Massachusetts
15. Baltimore	Sam Ball	T	Kentucky
16. Atlanta	Randy Johnson	QB	Texas A&I

Team not selecting in first round: Detroit.
Total number of picks in draft: 305.

OTHER NOTEWORTHY PICKS

Round/Overall—Team, Player selected, Pos., College
2/18—Los Angeles, *Mike Garrett*, HB, USC; 5/79—Dallas, Walt Garrison, HB, Oklahoma State; 7/110—Baltimore, Ray Perkins, E, Alabama; 20/296—Dallas, Lou Hudson, FL, Minnesota.

HISTORY *First-round draft choices*

1967

FIRST ROUND—AFL-NFL

From 1967 through 1969 the AFL and NFL held a combined draft. The league is noted in parentheses after each team's name.

No.	Team	Player selected	Pos.	College
1.	Baltimore (N)	Bubba Smith	DT	Michigan State
2.	Minnesota (N)	Clint Jones	HB	Michigan State
3.	San Fran. (N)	*Steve Spurrier*	QB	Florida
4.	Miami (A)	**Bob Griese**	QB	Purdue
5.	Houston (A)	George Webster	LB	Michigan State
6.	Denver (A)	Floyd Little	HB	Syracuse
7.	Detroit (N)	Mel Farr	HB	UCLA
8.	Minnesota (N)	Gene Washington	FL	Michigan State
9.	Green Bay (N)	Bob Hyland	G	Boston College
10.	Chicago (N)	Loyd Phillips	DE	Arkansas
11.	San Fran. (N)	Cas Banaszek	TE/LB	Northwestern
12.	N.Y. Jets (A)	Paul Seiler	G	Notre Dame
13.	Wash. (N)	Ray McDonald	FB	Idaho
14.	San Diego (A)	Ron Billingsley	DT	Wyoming
15.	Minnesota (N)	**Alan Page**	DE	Notre Dame
16.	St. Louis (N)	Dave Williams	FL	Washington
17.	Oakland (A)	**Gene Upshaw**	G/T	Texas A&I
18.	Cleveland (N)	Bob Matheson	LB	Duke
19.	Phil. (N)	Harry Jones	HB	Arkansas
20.	Baltimore (N)	Jim Detwiler	HB	Michigan
21.	Boston (A)	John Charles	DB	Purdue
22.	Buffalo (A)	John Pitts	FL/DB	Arizona State
23.	Houston (A)	Tom Regner	G	Notre Dame
24.	Kan. City (A)	Gene Trosch	DT	Miami, Fla.
25.	Green Bay (N)	Don Horn	QB	San Diego State
26.	New Orl. (N)	Les Kelley	HB	Alabama

Teams not selecting in first round: Atlanta (N), Dallas (N), Los Angeles (N), N.Y. Giants (N), Pittsburgh (N).
Total number of picks in draft: 445.

OTHER NOTEWORTHY PICKS

Round/Overall—Team, Player selected, Pos., College
2/34—Detroit (N), **Lem Barney**, DB, Jackson State; 2/50—Kansas City (A), **Willie Lanier**, LB, Morgan State; 9/214—Houston (A), **Ken Houston**, DB, Prairie View A&M; 9/226—Los Angeles, Tommie Smith, HB, San Jose State; 11/285—Dallas (N), Pat Riley, FL, Kentucky; 17/443—Kansas City, Dave Lattin, FL, Texas-El Paso; 17/445—New Orleans, Jimmy Walker, E, Providence.

1968

FIRST ROUND—AFL-NFL

From 1967 through 1969 the AFL and NFL held a combined draft. The league is noted in parentheses after each team's name.

No.	Team	Player selected	Pos.	College
1.	Minnesota (N)	**Ron Yary**	T	USC
2.	Cincinnati (A)	Bob Johnson	C	Tennessee
3.	Atlanta (N)	Claude Humphrey	DE	Tennessee State
4.	San Diego (A)	Russ Washington	T	Missouri
5.	Green Bay (N)	Fred Carr	LB	Texas-El Paso
6.	Boston (A)	Dennis Byrd	DT	N. Carolina State
7.	New Orl. (N)	Kevin Hardy	DE	Notre Dame
8.	Miami (A)	**Larry Csonka**	RB	Syracuse
9.	Buffalo (A)	Haven Moses	E	San Diego State
10.	Pittsburgh (N)	Mike Taylor	T	USC
11.	Detroit (N)	Greg Landry	QB	Massachusetts
12.	Wash. (N)	Jim Smith	DB	Oregon
13.	St. Louis (N)	MacArthur Lane	RB	Utah State
14.	Phil. (N)	Tim Rossovich	DE	USC
15.	San Fran. (N)	Forrest Blue	C	Auburn
16.	Chicago (N)	Mike Hull	RB	USC
17.	N.Y. Jets (A)	Lee White	RB	Weber State
18.	San Diego (A)	Jim Hill	DB	Texas A&I
19.	Kan. City (A)	Mo Moorman	G	Texas A&M
20.	Dallas (N)	Dennis Homan	E	Alabama
21.	Cleveland (N)	Marvin Upshaw	DE	Trinity (Tex.)
22.	Kan. City (A)	George Daney	G	Texas-El Paso

No.	Team	Player selected	Pos.	College
23.	Baltimore (N)	John Williams	T	Minnesota
24.	Detroit (N)	Earl McCullouch	E	USC
25.	Oakland (A)	Eldridge Dickey	QB	Tennessee State
26.	Green Bay (N)	Bill Lueck	G	Arizona
27.	Miami (A)	Doug Crusan	T	Indiana

Teams not selecting in first round: Denver (A), Houston (A), Los Angeles (N), N.Y. Giants (N).
Total number of picks in draft: 462.

OTHER NOTEWORTHY PICKS

Round/Overall—Team, Player selected, Pos., College
2/30—Los Angeles (N), *Gary Beban*, QB, UCLA; 2/31—Denver (A), Curley Culp, DE, Arizona State; 2/52—Oakland (A), Ken Stabler, QB, Alabama; 3/77—Houston (A), **Elvin Bethea**, DE, North Carolina A&T; 3/80—Oakland (A), **Art Shell**, T, Maryland Eastern Shore; 5/118—Miami (A), Jim Kiick, RB, Wyoming; 9/240—Miami (A), Tom Paciorek, DB, Houston; 16/417—Pittsburgh (N), Rocky Bleier, RB, Notre Dame.

1969

FIRST ROUND—AFL-NFL

From 1967 through 1969 the AFL and NFL held a combined draft. The league is noted in parentheses after each team's name.

No.	Team	Player selected	Pos.	College
1.	Buffalo (A)	*O.J. Simpson*	RB	USC
2.	Atlanta (N)	George Kunz	T	Notre Dame
3.	Phil. (N)	Leroy Keyes	RB	Purdue
4.	Pittsburgh (N)	**Joe Greene**	DT	North Texas State
5.	Cincinnati (A)	Greg Cook	QB	Cincinnati
6.	Boston (A)	Ron Sellers	SE	Florida State
7.	San Fran. (N)	Ted Kwalick	TE	Penn State
8.	Los Ang. (N)	Larry Smith	RB	Florida
9.	San Diego (A)	Marty Domres	QB	Columbia
10.	Los Ang. (N)	Jim Seymour	SE	Notre Dame
11.	Miami (A)	Bill Stanfill	DE	Georgia
12.	Green Bay (N)	Rich Moore	DT	Villanova
13.	N.Y. Giants (N)	Fred Dryer	DE	San Diego State
14.	Chicago (N)	Rufus Mayes	T	Ohio State
15.	Houston (A)	Ron Pritchard	LB	Arizona State
16.	San Fran. (N)	Gene Washington	FL	Stanford
17.	New Orl. (N)	John Shinners	G	Xavier
18.	San Diego (A)	Bob Babich	LB	Miami of Ohio
19.	St. Louis (N)	Roger Wehrli	DB	Missouri
20.	Cleveland (N)	Ron Johnson	RB	Michigan
21.	Los Ang. (N)	Bob Klein	TE	USC
22.	Oakland (A)	Art Thoms	DT	Syracuse
23.	Kan. City (A)	Jim Marsalis	DB	Tennessee State
24.	Dallas (N)	Calvin Hill	RB	Yale
25.	Baltimore (N)	Eddie Hinton	FL	Oklahoma
26.	N.Y. Jets (A)	Dave Foley	T	Ohio State

Teams not selecting in first round: Denver (A), Detroit (N), Minnesota (N), Washington (N).
Total number of picks in draft: 442.

OTHER NOTEWORTHY PICKS

Round/Overall—Team, Player selected, Pos., College
2/33—Baltimore (N), **Ted Hendricks**, LB, Miami, Fla.; 2/39—Minnesota (N), Ed White, G, California; 3/63—Miami (A), Mercury Morris, RB, West Texas State; 4/80—Philadelphia (N), Bob Kuechenberg, G, Notre Dame; 4/93—Houston (A), **Charlie Joiner**, DB, Grambling; 8/192—Buffalo (A), James Harris, QB, Grambling; 10/238—Pittsburgh (A), L.C. Greenwood, LB, Arkansas-Pine Bluff; 17/429—N.Y. Giants (N), Ken Riley, LB, Texas-Arlington.

1970

FIRST ROUND—NFL

No.	Team	Player selected	Pos.	College
1.	Pittsburgh	**Terry Bradshaw**	QB	Louisiana Tech
2.	Green Bay	Mike McCoy	DT	Notre Dame

No. Team	Player selected	Pos.	College
3. Cleveland	Mike Phipps	QB	Purdue
4. Boston	Phil Olsen	DT	Utah State
5. Buffalo	Al Cowlings	DE	USC
6. Philadelphia	Steve Zabel	TE	Oklahoma
7. Cincinnati	Mike Reid	DT	Penn State
8. St. Louis	Larry Stegent	RB	Texas A&M
9. San Francisco	Cedrick Hardman	DE	North Texas State
0. New Orleans	Ken Burrough	WR	Texas Southern
1. Denver	Bobby Anderson	RB	Colorado
2. Atlanta	John Small	LB	The Citadel
3. N.Y. Giants	Jim Files	LB	Oklahoma
4. Houston	Doug Wilkerson	G	N.C. Central
5. San Diego	Walker Gillette	WR	Richmond
6. Green Bay	Rich McGeorge	TE	Elon
7. San Francisco	Bruce Taylor	DB	Boston University
8. Baltimore	Norm Bulaich	RB	Texas Christian
9. Detroit	*Steve Owens*	RB	Oklahoma
0. N.Y. Jets	Steve Tannen	DB	Florida
1. Cleveland	Bob McKay	T	Texas
2. Los Angeles	Jack Reynolds	LB	Tennessee
3. Dallas	Duane Thomas	RB	West Texas State
4. Oakland	Raymond Chester	TE	Morgan State
5. Minnesota	John Ward	T	Oklahoma State
6. Kansas City	Sid Smith	T	USC

Teams not selecting in first round: Chicago, Miami, Washington.
Total number of picks in first draft: 442.

OTHER NOTEWORTHY PICKS

ound/Overall—Team, Player selected, Pos., College
'53—Pittsburgh, **Mel Blount**, DB, Southern (La.); 3/66—Dallas, harlie Waters, DB, Clemson; 7/159—Miami, Jake Scott, DB, eorgia; 8/201—St. Louis, Mike Holmgren, QB, USC; 14/346—hiladelphia, Mark Moseley, K, Stephen F. Austin.

1971
FIRST ROUND—NFL

No. Team	Player selected	Pos.	College
1. Boston	*Jim Plunkett*	QB	Stanford
2. New Orleans	Archie Manning	QB	Mississippi
3. Houston	Dan Pastorini	QB	Santa Clara
4. Buffalo	J.D. Hill	WR	Arizona State
5. Philadelphia	Richard Harris	DE	Grambling
6. N.Y. Jets	**John Riggins**	RB	Kansas
7. Atlanta	Joe Profit	RB	N.E. Louisiana
8. Pittsburgh	Frank Lewis	WR	Grambling
9. Green Bay	John Brockington	RB	Ohio State
0. Los Angeles	Isiah Robertson	LB	Southern (La.)
1. Chicago	Joe Moore	RB	Missouri
2. Denver	Marv Montgomery	T	USC
3. San Diego	Leon Burns	RB	Long Beach State
4. Cleveland	Clarence Scott	DB	Kansas State
5. Cincinnati	Vernon Holland	T	Tennessee State
6. Kansas City	Elmo Wright	WR	Houston
7. St. Louis	Norm Thompson	DB	Utah
8. N.Y. Giants	Rocky Thompson	WR	West Texas State
9. Oakland	Jack Tatum	DB	Ohio State
0. Los Angeles	**Jack Youngblood**	DE	Florida
1. Detroit	Bob Bell	DT	Cincinnati
2. Baltimore	Don McCauley	RB	North Carolina
3. San Francisco	Tim Anderson	DB	Ohio State
4. Minnesota	Leo Hayden	RB	Ohio State
5. Dallas	Tody Smith	DE	USC
6. Baltimore	Leonard Dunlap	DB	North Texas State

Note: Boston franchise changed its name to New England (but ter draft); teams not selecting in first round: Miami, Washington.
Total number of picks in draft: 442.

OTHER NOTEWORTHY PICKS

ound/Overall—Team, Player selected, Pos., College
/27—Boston, Julius Adams, DT, Texas Southern; 2/34—Pittsurgh, **Jack Ham**, LB, Penn State; 2/43—St. Louis, **Dan**

Dierdorf, T, Michigan; 3/67—Cincinnati, Ken Anderson, QB, Augustana (Ill.); 4/79—Denver, Lyle Alzado, DE, Yankton; 4/99—Miami, Joe Theismann, QB, Notre Dame; 6/147—St. Louis, Mel Gray, WR, Missouri; 7/161—Philadelphia, Harold Carmichael, WR, Southern (La.).

1972
FIRST ROUND—NFL

No. Team	Player selected	Pos.	College
1. Buffalo	Walt Patulski	DE	Notre Dame
2. Cincinnati	Sherman White	DE	California
3. Chicago	Lionel Antoine	T	Southern Illinois
4. St. Louis	Bobby Moore	WR	Oregon
5. Denver	Riley Odoms	TE	Houston
6. Houston	Gregory Sampson	DE	Stanford
7. Green Bay	Willie Buchanon	DB	San Diego State
8. New Orleans	Royce Smith	G	Georgia
9. N.Y. Jets	Jerome Barkum	WR	Jackson State
10. Minnesota	Jeff Siemon	LB	Stanford
11. Green Bay	Jerry Tagge	QB	Nebraska
12. Chicago	Craig Clemons	DB	Iowa
13. Pittsburgh	**Franco Harris**	RB	Penn State
14. Philadelphia	John Reaves	QB	Florida
15. Atlanta	Clarence Ellis	DB	Notre Dame
16. Detroit	Herb Orvis	DE	Colorado
17. N.Y. Giants	Eldridge Small	DB	Texas A&I
18. Cleveland	Thom Darden	DB	Michigan
19. San Francisco	Terry Beasley	WR	Auburn
20. N.Y. Jets	Mike Taylor	LB	Michigan
21. Oakland	Mike Siani	WR	Villanova
22. Baltimore	Tom Drougas	T	Oregon
23. Kansas City	Jeff Kinney	RB	Nebraska
24. N.Y. Giants	Larry Jacobson	DE	Nebraska
25. Miami	Mike Kadish	DT	Notre Dame
26. Dallas	Bill Thomas	RB	Boston College

Teams not selecting in first round: Los Angeles, New England, San Diego, Washington.
Total number of picks in draft: 442.

OTHER NOTEWORTHY PICKS

Round/Overall—Team, Player selected, Pos., College
2/27—Buffalo, Reggie McKenzie, G, Michigan; 2/40—Atlanta, *Pat Sullivan*, QB, Auburn; 2/50—Minnesota, Ed Marinaro, RB, Cornell; 4/98—Oakland, Cliff Branch, WR, Colorado; 5/110—St. Louis, Conrad Dobler, G, Wyoming; 7/167—Chicago, Jim Fassel, QB, Long Beach State; 13/330—Cleveland, Brian Sipe, QB, San Diego State.

1973
FIRST ROUND—NFL

No. Team	Player selected	Pos.	College
1. Houston	John Matuszak	DE	Tampa
2. Baltimore	Bert Jones	QB	Louisiana State
3. Philadelphia	Jerry Sisemore	T	Texas
4. New England	**John Hannah**	G	Alabama
5. St. Louis	Dave Butz	DT	Purdue
6. Philadelphia	Charle Young	TE	USC
7. Buffalo	Paul Seymour	T	Michigan
8. Chicago	Wally Chambers	DE	Eastern Kentucky
9. Denver	Otis Armstrong	RB	Purdue
10. Baltimore	Joe Ehrmann	DT	Syracuse
11. New England	Sam Cunningham	RB	USC
12. Minnesota	Chuck Foreman	RB	Miami, Fla.
13. N.Y. Jets	Burgess Owens	DB	Miami, Fla.
14. Houston	George Amundson	RB	Iowa State
15. Cincinnati	Isaac Curtis	WR	San Diego State
16. Cleveland	Steve Holden	WR	Arizona State
17. Detroit	Ernest Price	DE	Texas A&I
18. San Francisco	Mike Holmes	DB	Texas Southern
19. New England	Darryl Stingley	WR	Purdue
20. Dallas	Billy Joe DuPree	TE	Michigan State
21. Green Bay	Barry Smith	WR	Florida State

No. Team	Player selected	Pos.	College
22.Cleveland	Pete Adams	T	USC
23. Oakland	Ray Guy	P	Southern Miss
24. Pittsburgh	J.T. Thomas	DB	Florida State
25. San Diego	*Johnny Rodgers*	WR	Nebraska
26. Buffalo	**Joe DeLamielleure**	G	Michigan State

Teams not selecting in first round: Atlanta, Kansas City, Los Angeles, Miami, New Orleans, N.Y. Giants, Washington.
Total number of picks in draft: 442.

OTHER NOTEWORTHY PICKS

Round/Overall—Team, Player selected, Pos., College
2/30—Cleveland, Greg Pruitt, RB, Oklahoma; 2/37—Los Angeles, Ron Jaworski, QB, Youngstown State; 3/53—Dallas, Harvey Martin, DE, East Texas State; 3/57—Buffalo, Joe Ferguson, QB, Arkansas; 3/84—San Diego, **Dan Fouts**, QB, Oregon; 4/88—Denver, Tom Jackson, LB, Louisville; 4/91—Detroit, Dick Jauron, RB, Yale; 17/423—Buffalo, John Stearns, DB, Colorado; 17/429—Minnesota, Dave Winfield, TE, Minnesota.

1974
FIRST ROUND—NFL

No. Team	Player selected	Pos.	College
1. Dallas	Ed Jones	DE	Tennessee State
2. San Diego	Bo Matthews	RB	Colorado
3. N.Y. Giants	John Hicks	G	Ohio State
4. Chicago	Waymond Bryant	LB	Tennessee State
5. Baltimore	John Dutton	DE	Nebraska
6. N.Y. Jets	Carl Barzilauskas	DT	Indiana
7. St. Louis	J.V. Cain	TE	Colorado
8. Detroit	Ed O'Neil	LB	Penn State
9. San Francisco	Wilbur Jackson	RB	Alabama
10. San Francisco	Bill Sandifer	DT	UCLA
11. Los Angeles	*John Cappelletti*	RB	Penn State
12. Green Bay	Barty Smith	RB	Richmond
13. New Orleans	Rick Middleton	LB	Ohio State
14. Denver	Randy Gradishar	LB	Ohio State
15. San Diego	Don Goode	LB	Kansas
16. Kansas City	Woody Green	RB	Arizona State
17. Minnesota	Fred McNeill	LB	UCLA
18. Buffalo	Reuben Gant	TE	Oklahoma State
19. Oakland	Henry Lawrence	T	Florida A&M
20. Chicago	Dave Gallagher	DL	Michigan
21. Pittsburgh	**Lynn Swann**	WR	USC
22. Dallas	Charley Young	RB	N. Carolina State
23. Cincinnati	Bill Kollar	DT	Montana State
24. Baltimore	Roger Carr	WR	Louisiana Tech
25. Minnesota	Steve Riley	T	USC
26. Miami	Donald Reese	DE	Jackson State

Teams not selecting in first round: Atlanta, Cleveland, Houston, New England, Philadelphia, Washington.
Total number of picks in draft: 442.

OTHER NOTEWORTHY PICKS

Round/Overall—Team, Player selected, Pos., College
2/45—Oakland, **Dave Casper**, TE, Notre Dame; 2/46—Pittsburgh, **Jack Lambert**, LB, Kent State; 3/53—Dallas, Danny White, QB, Arizona State; 3/78—Miami, Nat Moore, WR, Florida; 4/82—Pittsburgh, **John Stallworth**, WR, Alabama A&M; 5/125—Pittsburgh, **Mike Webster**, C, Wisconsin; 10/236—N.Y. Giants, Ray Rhodes, WR, Tulsa; 15/365—Houston, Billy (White Shoes) Johnson, WR, Widener; 15/376—Green Bay, Dave Wannstedt, T, Pittsburgh.

1975
FIRST ROUND—NFL

No. Team	Player selected	Pos.	College
1. Atlanta	Steve Bartkowski	QB	California
2. Dallas	**Randy White**	DE/LB	Maryland
3. Baltimore	Ken Huff	G	North Carolina
4. Chicago	**Walter Payton**	RB	Jackson State
5. Cleveland	Mack Mitchell	DE	Houston
6. Houston	Robert Brazile	LB	Jackson State

No. Team	Player selected	Pos.	College
7. New Orleans	Larry Burton	WR	Purdue
8. San Diego	Gary Johnson	DT	Grambling
9. Los Angeles	Mike Fanning	DT	Notre Dame
10. San Francisco	Jimmy Webb	DT	Mississippi Stat
11. Los Angeles	Dennis Harrah	T	Miami, Fla.
12. New Orleans	Kurt Schumacher	T	Ohio State
13. Detroit	Lynn Boden	G	South Dakota St
14. Cincinnati	Glenn Cameron	LB	Florida
15. Houston	Don Hardeman	RB	Texas A&I
16. New England	Russ Francis	TE	Oregon
17. Denver	Louis Wright	DB	San Jose State
18. Dallas	Thomas Henderson	LB	Langston
19. Buffalo	Tom Ruud	LB	Nebraska
20. Los Angeles	Doug France	T	Ohio State
21. St. Louis	Tim Gray	DB	Texas A&M
22. San Diego	Mike Williams	DB	Louisiana State
23. Miami	Darryl Carlton	T	Tampa
24. Oakland	Neal Colzie	DB	Ohio State
25. Minnesota	Mark Mullaney	DE	Colorado State
26. Pittsburgh	Dave Brown	DB	Michigan

Teams not selecting in first round: Green Bay, Kansas City, N. Giants, N.Y. Jets, Philadelphia, Washington.
Total number of picks in draft: 442.

OTHER NOTEWORTHY PICKS

Round/Overall—Team, Player selected, Pos., College
4/95—Denver, Rick Upchurch, WR, Minnesota; 5/116—Ne England, Steve Grogan, QB, Kansas State; 7/176—Los Angeles, F Haden, QB, USC.

1976
FIRST ROUND—NFL

No. Team	Player selected	Pos.	College
1. Tampa Bay	**Lee Roy Selmon**	DE	Oklahoma
2. Seattle	Steve Niehaus	DT	Notre Dame
3. New Orleans	Chuck Muncie	RB	California
4. San Diego	Joe Washington	RB	Oklahoma
5. New England	**Mike Haynes**	DB	Arizona State
6. N.Y. Jets	Richard Todd	QB	Alabama
7. Cleveland	Mike Pruitt	RB	Purdue
8. Chicago	Dennis Lick	T	Wisconsin
9. Atlanta	Bubba Bean	RB	Texas A&M
10. Detroit	James Hunter	DB	Grambling
11. Cincinnati	Billy Brooks	WR	Oklahoma
12. New England	Pete Brock	C	Colorado
13. N.Y. Giants	Troy Archer	DE	Colorado
14. Kansas City	Rod Walters	G	Iowa
15. Denver	Tom Glassic	G	Virginia
16. Detroit	Lawrence Gaines	RB	Wyoming
17. Miami	Larry Gordon	LB	Arizona State
18. Buffalo	Mario Clark	DB	Oregon
19. Miami	Kim Bokamper	LB	San Jose State
20. Baltimore	Ken Novak	DT	Purdue
21. New England	Tim Fox	DB	Ohio State
22. St. Louis	Mike Dawson	DT	Arizona
23. Green Bay	Mark Koncar	T	Colorado
24. Cincinnati	*Archie Griffin*	RB	Ohio State
25. Minnesota	James White	DT	Oklahoma State
26. Los Angeles	Kevin McLain	LB	Colorado State
27. Dallas	Aaron Kyle	DB	Wyoming
28. Pittsburgh	Bennie Cunningham	TE	Clemson

Teams not selecting in first round: Houston, Oaklan Philadelphia, San Francisco, Washington.
Total number of picks in draft: 487.

OTHER NOTEWORTHY PICKS

Round/Overall—Team, Player selected, Pos., College
2/42—San Francisco, Randy Cross, C, UCLA; 3/86—Los Angele **Jackie Slater**, G, Jackson State; 4/105—N.Y. Giants, Harry Carso LB, South Carolina State; 4/117—Houston, **Steve Largent**, W Tulsa; 14/393—Washington, Quinn Buckner, DB, Indiana.

1977

FIRST ROUND—NFL

. Team	Player selected	Pos.	College
. Tampa Bay	Ricky Bell	RB	USC
. Dallas	*Tony Dorsett*	RB	Pittsburgh
. Cincinnati	Eddie Edwards	DT	Miami, Fla.
. N.Y. Jets	Marvin Powell	T	USC
. N.Y. Giants	Gary Jeter	DT	USC
. Atlanta	Wilson Faumuina	T	Kentucky
. New Orleans	Joe Campbell	DE	Maryland
. Cincinnati	Wilson Whitley	DT	Houston
. Green Bay	Mike Butler	DE	Kansas
. Kansas City	Gary Green	DB	Baylor
. Houston	Morris Towns	T	Missouri
. Buffalo	Phil Dokes	DT	Oklahoma State
. Miami	A.J. Duhe	DT	Louisiana State
. Seattle	Steve August	G	Tulsa
. Chicago	Ted Albrecht	T	California
. New England	Raymond Clayborn	DB	Texas
. Cleveland	Robert Jackson	LB	Texas A&M
. Denver	Steve Schindler	G	Boston College
. St. Louis	Steve Pisarkiewicz	QB	Missouri
. Atlanta	Wilson Faumina	DT	San Jose State
. Pittsburgh	Robin Cole	LB	New Mexico
. Cincinnati	Mike Cobb	TE	Michigan State
. Los Angeles	Bob Brudzinski	LB	Ohio State
. San Diego	Bob Rush	C	Memphis State
. New England	Stanley Morgan	WR	Tennessee
. Baltimore	Randy Burke	WR	Kentucky
. Minnesota	Tommy Kramer	QB	Rice
. Green Bay	Ezra Johnson	DE	Morris Brown

Teams not selecting in first round: Detroit, Oakland, Philadelphia, San Francisco, Washington.
Total number of picks in draft: 335.

OTHER NOTEWORTHY PICKS

und/Overall—Team, Player selected, Pos., College
31—Los Angeles, Nolan Cromwell, DB, Kansas; 4/91—Los geles, Vince Ferragamo, QB, Nebraska; 6/140—Chicago, Vince ans, QB, USC; 6/144—N.Y. Jets, Joe Klecko, DT, Temple; 54—Philadelphia, Wilbert Montgomery, RB, Abilene Christian; /275—Dallas, Steve DeBerg, QB, San Jose State; 11/295—San ancisco, Brian Billick, TE, Brigham Young.

1978

FIRST ROUND—NFL

. Team	Player selected	Pos.	College
. Houston	*Earl Campbell*	RB	Texas
. Kansas City	Art Still	DE	Kentucky
. New Orleans	Wes Chandler	WR	Florida
. N.Y. Jets	Chris Ward	T	Ohio State
. Buffalo	Terry Miller	RB	Oklahoma State
. Green Bay	**James Lofton**	WR	Stanford
. San Francisco	Ken MacAfee	TE	Notre Dame
. Cincinnati	Ross Browner	DE	Notre Dame
. Seattle	Keith Simpson	DB	Memphis State
. N.Y. Giants	Gordon King	T	Stanford
. Detroit	Luther Bradley	DB	Notre Dame
. Cleveland	Clay Matthews	LB	USC
. Atlanta	Mike Kenn	T	Michigan
. San Diego	John Jefferson	WR	Arizona State
. St. Louis	Steve Little	K	Arkansas
. Cincinnati	Blair Bush	C	Washington
. Tampa Bay	Doug Williams	QB	Grambling
. New England	Bob Cryder	G	Alabama
. St. Louis	Ken Greene	DB	Washington State
. Los Angeles	Elvis Peacock	RB	Oklahoma
. Minnesota	Randy Holloway	DE	Pittsburgh
. Pittsburgh	Ron Johnson	DB	Eastern Michigan

No.	Team	Player selected	Pos.	College
23.	Cleveland	**Ozzie Newsome**	WR	Alabama
24.	San Francisco	Dan Bunz	LB	Long Beach State
25.	Baltimore	Reese McCall	TE	Auburn
26.	Green Bay	John Anderson	LB	Michigan
27.	Denver	Don Latimer	DT	Miami, Fla.
28.	Dallas	Larry Bethea	DE	Michigan State

Teams not selecting in first round: Chicago, Miami, Oakland, Philadelphia, Washington.
Total number of picks in draft: 334.

OTHER NOTEWORTHY PICKS

Round/Overall—Team, Player selected, Pos., College
2/56—Dallas, Todd Christensen, RB, Brigham Young; 8/206—Detroit, Jim Breech, K, California; 8/215—New England, Mosi Tatupu, RB, USC.

1979

FIRST ROUND—NFL

No.	Team	Player selected	Pos.	College
1.	Buffalo	Tom Cousineau	LB	Ohio State
2.	Kansas City	Mike Bell	DE	Colorado State
3.	Cincinnati	Jack Thompson	QB	Washington State
4.	Chicago	**Dan Hampton**	DT	Arkansas
5.	Buffalo	Jerry Butler	WR	Clemson
6.	Baltimore	Barry Krauss	LB	Alabama
7.	N.Y. Giants	Phil Simms	QB	Morehead State
8.	St. Louis	Ottis Anderson	RB	Miami, Fla.
9.	Chicago	Al Harris	DE	Arizona State
10.	Detroit	Keith Dorney	T	Penn State
11.	New Orleans	Russell Erxleben	K/P	Texas
12.	Cincinnati	Charles Alexander	RB	Louisiana State
13.	San Diego	**Kellen Winslow**	TE	Missouri
14.	N.Y. Jets	Marty Lyons	DE	Alabama
15.	Green Bay	Eddie Lee Ivery	RB	Georgia Tech
16.	Minnesota	Ted Brown	RB	N. Carolina State
17.	Atlanta	Don Smith	DE	Miami, Fla.
18.	Seattle	Manu Tuiasosopo	DT	UCLA
19.	Los Angeles	George Andrews	LB	Nebraska
20.	Cleveland	Willis Adams	WR	Houston
21.	Philadelphia	Jerry Robinson	LB	UCLA
22.	Denver	Kelvin Clark	T	Nebraska
23.	Kansas City	Steve Fuller	QB	Clemson
24.	Miami	Jon Giesler	T	Michigan
25.	New England	Rick Sanford	DB	South Carolina
26.	Los Angeles	Kent Hill	G	Georgia Tech
27.	Dallas	Robert Shaw	C	Tennessee
28.	Pittsburgh	Greg Hawthorne	RB	Baylor

Teams not selecting in first round: Houston, Oakland, San Francisco, Tampa Bay, Washington.
Total number of picks in draft: 330.

OTHER NOTEWORTHY PICKS

Round/Overall—Team, Player selected, Pos., College
2/41—N.Y. Jets, Mark Gastineau, DE, East Central Oklahoma; 2/51—Buffalo, Jim Haslett, LB, Indiana, Pa.; 2/52—New England, Bob Golic, LB, Notre Dame; 3/82—San Francisco, **Joe Montana**, QB, Notre Dame; 6/165—Pittsburgh, Matt Bahr, K, Penn State; 7/173—St. Louis, Kirk Gibson, WR, Michigan State; 10/249—San Francisco, Dwight Clark, WR, Clemson, 12/328—Los Angeles, Drew Hill, WR, Georgia Tech.

1980

FIRST ROUND—NFL

No.	Team	Player selected	Pos.	College
1.	Detroit	*Billy Sims*	RB	Oklahoma
2.	N.Y. Jets	Johnny (Lam) Jones	WR	Texas
3.	Cincinnati	**Anthony Munoz**	T	USC
4.	Green Bay	Bruce Clark	DE	Penn State
5.	Baltimore	Curtis Dickey	RB	Texas A&M

No. Team	Player selected	Pos.	College
6. St. Louis	Curtis Greer	DE	Michigan
7. Atlanta	Junior Miller	TE	Nebraska
8. N.Y. Giants	Mark Haynes	DB	Colorado
9. Minnesota	Doug Martin	DT	Washington
10. Seattle	Jacob Green	DE	Texas A&M
11. Kansas City	Brad Budde	G	USC
12. New Orleans	Stan Brock	T	Colorado
13. San Francisco	Earl Cooper	RB	Rice
14. New England	Roland James	DB	Tennessee
15. Oakland	Marc Wilson	QB	Brigham Young
16. Buffalo	Jim Ritcher	C	N. Carolina State
17. Los Angeles	Johnnie Johnson	DB	Texas
18. Washington	Art Monk	WR	Syracuse
19. Chicago	Otis Wilson	LB	Louisville
20. San Francisco	Jim Stuckey	DT	Clemson
21. Miami	Don McNeal	DB	Alabama
22. Tampa Bay	Ray Snell	G	Wisconsin
23. Philadelphia	Roynell Young	DB	Alcorn State
24. Baltimore	Derrick Hatchett	DB	Texas
25. New England	Vagas Ferguson	RB	Notre Dame
26. Green Bay	George Cumby	LB	Oklahoma
27. Cleveland	*Charles White*	RB	USC
28. Pittsburgh	Mark Malone	QB	Arizona State

Teams not selecting in first round: Dallas, Denver, Houston, San Diego.

Total number of picks in draft: 333.

OTHER NOTEWORTHY PICKS

Round/Overall—Team, Player selected, Pos., College
2/29—Buffalo, Joe Cribbs, RB, Auburn; 2/43—Oakland, Matt Millen, LB, Penn State; 2/48—Miami, **Dwight Stephenson**, C, Alabama; 3/73—New England, Steve McMichael, DT, Texas; 7/166—Detroit, Eddie Murray, K, Tulane.

1981

FIRST ROUND—NFL

No. Team	Player selected	Pos.	College
1. New Orleans	*George Rogers*	RB	South Carolina
2. N.Y. Giants	**Lawrence Taylor**	LB	North Carolina
3. N.Y. Jets	Freeman McNeil	RB	UCLA
4. Seattle	Kenny Easley	DB	UCLA
5. St. Louis	E.J. Junior	LB	Alabama
6. Green Bay	Rich Campbell	QB	California
7. Tampa Bay	Hugh Green	LB	Pittsburgh
8. San Francisco	**Ronnie Lott**	DB	USC
9. Los Angeles	Mel Owens	LB	Michigan
10. Cincinnati	David Verser	WR	Kansas
11. Chicago	Keith Van Horne	T	USC
12. Baltimore	Randy McMillan	RB	Pittsburgh
13. Miami	David Overstreet	RB	Oklahoma
14. Kansas City	Willie Scott	TE	South Carolina
15. Denver	Dennis Smith	DB	USC
16. Detroit	Mark Nichols	WR	San Jose State
17. Pittsburgh	Keith Gary	DE	Oklahoma
18. Baltimore	Donnell Thompson	DT	North Carolina
19. New England	Brian Holloway	T	Stanford
20. Washington	Mark May	T	Pittsburgh
21. Oakland	Ted Watts	DB	Texas Tech
22. Cleveland	Hanford Dixon	DB	Southern Miss
23. Oakland	Curt Marsh	T	Washington
24. San Diego	James Brooks	RB	Auburn
25. Atlanta	Bobby Butler	DB	Florida State
26. Dallas	Howard Richards	T	Missouri
27. Philadelphia	Leonard Mitchell	DE	Houston
28. Buffalo	Booker Moore	RB	Penn State

Teams not selecting in first round: Houston, Minnesota.

Total number of picks in draft: 332.

OTHER NOTEWORTHY PICKS

Round/Overall—Team, Player selected, Pos., College
2/34—Tampa Bay, James Wilder, RB, Missouri; 2/37—Cincinnati, Cris Collinsworth, WR, Florida; 2/38—Chicago, **Mike Singletary**,

LB, Baylor; 2/48—Oakland, **Howie Long**, DT, Villanova; 3/69—Washington, Russ Grimm, C, Pittsburgh; 5/119—Washing Dexter Manley, DE, Oklahoma State; 7/177—Chicago, Jeff Fishe DB, USC; 8/210—Minnesota, Wade Wilson, QB, East Texas Sta 8/213—N.Y. Jets, J.C. Watts, DB, Oklahoma; Supplemental—Ne Orleans, Dave Wilson, QB, Illinois.

1982

FIRST ROUND—NFL

No. Team	Player selected	Pos.	College
1. New England	Ken Sims	DT	Texas
2. Baltimore	Johnie Cooks	LB	Mississippi Stat
3. Cleveland	Chip Banks	LB	USC
4. Baltimore	Art Schlichter	QB	Ohio State
5. Chicago	Jim McMahon	QB	Brigham Young
6. Seattle	Jeff Bryant	DE	Clemson
7. Minnesota	Darrin Nelson	RB	Stanford
8. Houston	**Mike Munchak**	G	Penn State
9. Atlanta	Gerald Riggs	RB	Arizona State
10. Oakland	*Marcus Allen*	RB	USC
11. Kansas City	Anthony Hancock	WR	Tennessee
12. Pittsburgh	Walter Abercrombie	RB	Baylor
13. New Orleans	Lindsay Scott	WR	Georgia
14. Los Angeles	Barry Redden	RB	Richmond
15. Detroit	Jimmy Williams	LB	Nebraska
16. St. Louis	Luis Sharpe	T	UCLA
17. Tampa Bay	Sean Farrell	G	Penn State
18. N.Y. Giants	Butch Woolfolk	RB	Michigan
19. Buffalo	Perry Tuttle	WR	Clemson
20. Philadelphia	Mike Quick	WR	N. Carolina Stat
21. Denver	Gerald Willhite	RB	San Jose State
22. Green Bay	Ron Hallstrom	G	Iowa
23. N.Y. Jets	Bob Crable	LB	Notre Dame
24. Miami	Roy Foster	G	USC
25. Dallas	Rod Hill	DB	Kentucky State
26. Cincinnati	Glen Collins	DE	Mississippi Sta
27. New England	Lester Williams	DT	Miami, Fla.

Note: Oakland franchise moved to Los Angeles (but after draf teams not selecting in first round: San Diego, San Francisc Washington.

Total number of picks in draft: 334.

OTHER NOTEWORTHY PICKS

Round/Overall—Team, Player selected, Pos., College
2/41—New England, Andre Tippett, LB, Iowa; 2/45—N.Y. Giant Joe Morris, RB, Syracuse; 2/52—Miami, Mark Duper, W Northwestern (La.) State; 4/86—New Orleans, Morten Andersen, Michigan State; 5/131—Denver, Sammy Winder, RB, Southe Mississippi; 7/171—Buffalo, Gary Anderson, K, Syracuse.

1983

FIRST ROUND—NFL

No. Team	Player selected	Pos.	College
1. Baltimore	**John Elway**	QB	Stanford
2. L.A. Rams	**Eric Dickerson**	RB	SMU
3. Seattle	Curt Warner	RB	Penn State
4. Denver	Chris Hinton	G	Northwestern
5. San Diego	Billy Ray Smith	LB	Arkansas
6. Chicago	Jimbo Covert	T	Pittsburgh
7. Kansas City	Todd Blackledge	QB	Penn State
8. Philadelphia	Michael Haddix	RB	Mississippi Sta
9. Houston	Bruce Matthews	G	USC
10. N.Y. Giants	Terry Kinard	DB	Clemson
11. Green Bay	Tim Lewis	DB	Pittsburgh
12. Buffalo	Tony Hunter	TE	Notre Dame
13. Detroit	James Jones	RB	Florida
14. Buffalo	**Jim Kelly**	QB	Miami, Fla.
15. New England	Tony Eason	QB	Illinois
16. Atlanta	Mike Pitts	DE	Alabama

o. Team	Player selected	Pos.	College
7. St. Louis	Leonard Smith	DB	McNeese State
8. Chicago	Willie Gault	WR	Tennessee
9. Minnesota	Joey Browner	DB	USC
0. San Diego	Gary Anderson	WR	Arkansas
1. Pittsburgh	Gabriel Rivera	DT	Texas Tech
2. San Diego	Gill Byrd	DB	San Jose State
3. Dallas	Jim Jeffcoat	DE	Arizona State
4. N.Y. Jets	Ken O'Brien	QB	UC Davis
5. Cincinnati	Dave Rimington	C	Nebraska
6. L.A. Raiders	Don Mosebar	T	USC
7. Miami	**Dan Marino**	QB	Pittsburgh
8. Washington	Darrell Green	DB	Texas A&I

Teams not selecting in first round: Cleveland, New Orleans, San rancisco, Tampa Bay.
Total number of picks in draft: 335.

OTHER NOTEWORTHY PICKS

ound/Overall—Team, Player selected, Pos., College

'32—L.A. Rams, Henry Ellard, WR, Fresno State; 2/37—N.Y. iants, Leonard Marshall, DT, Louisiana State; 2/49—San rancisco, Roger Craig, RB, Nebraska; 3/84—Washington, harles Mann, DE, Nevada; 6/167—Miami, Reggie Roby, P, Iowa; '203—Chicago, Richard Dent, DE, Tennessee State; 8/223— liami, Mark Clayton, WR, Louisville; 12/334—Miami, Anthony arter, WR, Michigan.

1984
FIRST ROUND—NFL

o. Team	Player selected	Pos.	College
1. New England	Irving Fryar	WR	Nebraska
2. Houston	Dean Steinkuhler	T	Nebraska
3. N.Y. Giants	Carl Banks	LB	Michigan State
4. Philadelphia	Kenny Jackson	WR	Penn State
5. Kansas City	Bill Maas	DT	Pittsburgh
6. San Diego	Mossy Cade	DB	Texas
7. Cincinnati	Ricky Hunley	LB	Arizona
8. Indianapolis	Leonard Coleman	DB	Vanderbilt
9. Atlanta	Rick Bryan	DT	Oklahoma
0. N.Y. Jets	Russell Carter	DB	SMU
1. Chicago	Wilber Marshall	LB	Florida
2. Green Bay	Alphonso Carreker	DE	Florida State
3. Minnesota	Keith Millard	DE	Washington State
4. Miami	Jackie Shipp	LB	Oklahoma
5. N.Y. Jets	Ron Faurot	DE	Arkansas
6. Cincinnati	Pete Koch	DE	Maryland
7. St. Louis	Clyde Duncan	WR	Tennessee
8. Cleveland	Don Rogers	DB	UCLA
9. Indianapolis	Ron Solt	G	Maryland
0. Detroit	David Lewis	TE	California
1. Kansas City	John Alt	T	Iowa
2. Seattle	Terry Taylor	DB	Southern Illinois
3. Pittsburgh	Louis Lipps	WR	Southern Miss
4. San Francisco	Todd Shell	LB	Brigham Young
5. Dallas	Billy Cannon Jr.	LB	Texas A&M
6. Buffalo	Greg Bell	RB	Notre Dame
7. N.Y. Giants	Bill Roberts	T	Ohio State
8. Cincinnati	Brian Blados	T	North Carolina

Teams not selecting in first round: Denver, L.A. Raiders, L.A. ams, New Orleans, Tampa Bay, Washington.
Total number of picks in draft: 336.

OTHER NOTEWORTHY PICKS

ound/Overall—Team, Player selected, Pos., College

'38—Cincinnati, Boomer Esiason, QB, Maryland; 3/59—N.Y. iants, Jeff Hostetler, QB, West Virginia; 10/280—Cleveland, Earnest yner, RB, East Carolina.

FIRST ROUND—NFL SUPPLEMENTAL

In 1984, the NFL held a three-round supplemental draft for he contract rights to USFL and CFL players.

o. Team	Player selected	Pos.	College
1. Tampa Bay	**Steve Young**	QB	Brigham Young
2. Houston	*Mike Rozier*	RB	Nebraska

No. Team	Player selected	Pos.	College
3. N.Y. Giants	Gary Zimmerman	G	Oregon
4. Philadelphia	Reggie White	DE	Tennessee
5. Kansas City	Mark Adickes	T	Baylor
6. San Diego	Lee Williams	DE	Bethune-Cookman
7. Cincinnati	Wayne Peace	QB	Florida
8. Indianapolis	Paul Bergmann	TE	UCLA
9. Atlanta	Joey Jones	WR	Alabama
10. N.Y. Jets	Ken Hobart	QB	Idaho
11. Cleveland	Kevin Mack	RB	Clemson
12. Green Bay	Buford Jordan	RB	McNeese State
13. Minnesota	Allanda Smith	DB	Texas Christian
14. Buffalo	Dwight Drane	DB	Oklahoma
15. New Orleans	Vaughan Johnson	LB	N. Carolina State
16. New England	Ricky Sanders	WR/PR	SW Texas State
17. St. Louis	Mike Ruether	C	Texas
18. Cleveland	Mike Johnson	LB	Virginia Tech
19. Denver	Freddie Gilbert	DE	Georgia
20. Detroit	Alphonso Williams	WR	Nevada
21. L.A. Rams	William Fuller	DE	North Carolina
22. Seattle	Gordon Hudson	TE	Brigham Young
23. Pittsburgh	Duane Gunn	WR	Indiana
24. San Francisco	Derrick Crawford	WR	Memphis State
25. Dallas	Todd Fowler	TE	Stephen F. Austin
26. Miami	Danny Knight	WR	Mississippi State
27. Washington	Tony Zendejas	K	Nevada
28. L.A. Raiders	Chris Woods	WR	Auburn

Team not selecting in first round: Chicago.
Total number of picks in supplemental draft: 84.

1985
FIRST ROUND—NFL

No. Team	Player selected	Pos.	College
1. Buffalo	Bruce Smith	DE	Virginia Tech
2. Atlanta	Bill Fralic	T	Pittsburgh
3. Houston	Ray Childress	DE	Texas A&M
4. Minnesota	Chris Doleman	LB	Pittsburgh
5. Indianapolis	Duane Bickett	LB	USC
6. Detroit	Lomas Brown	T	Florida
7. Green Bay	Ken Ruettgers	T	USC
8. Tampa Bay	Ron Holmes	DE	Washington
9. Philadelphia	Kevin Allen	T	Indiana
10. N.Y. Jets	Al Toon	WR	Wisconsin
11. Houston	Richard Johnson	DB	Wisconsin
12. San Diego	Jim Lachey	G	Ohio State
13. Cincinnati	Eddie Brown	WR	Miami, Fla.
14. Buffalo	Derrick Burroughs	DB	Memphis State
15. Kansas City	Ethan Horton	RB	North Carolina
16. San Francisco	Jerry Rice	WR	Miss Valley
17. Dallas	Kevin Brooks	DE	Michigan
18. St. Louis	Freddie Joe Nunn	LB	Mississippi
19. N.Y. Giants	George Adams	RB	Kentucky
20. Pittsburgh	Darryl Sims	DE	Wisconsin
21. L.A. Rams	Jerry Gray	DB	Texas
22. Chicago	William Perry	DT	Clemson
23. L.A. Raiders	Jessie Hester	WR	Florida State
24. New Orleans	Alvin Toles	LB	Tennessee
25. Cincinnati	Emanuel King	LB	Alabama
26. Denver	Steve Sewell	RB	Oklahoma
27. Miami	Lorenzo Hampton	RB	Florida
28. New England	Trevor Matich	C	Brigham Young

Teams not selecting in first round: Cleveland, Seattle, Washington.
Total number of picks in draft: 336.

OTHER NOTEWORTHY PICKS

Round/Overall—Team, Player selected, Pos., College

2/37—Philadelphia, Randall Cunningham, QB/P, UNLV; 3/68—New Orleans, Jack Del Rio, LB, USC; 4/86—Buffalo, Andre Reed, WR, Kutztown; 4/100—N.Y. Giants, Mark Bavaro, TE, Notre Dame; 5/114—Dallas, *Herschel Walker*, RB, Georgia; 6/158—St. Louis, Jay Novacek, TE, Wyoming; 11/285—L.A. Rams, *Doug Flutie*, QB, Boston College; Supplemental—Cleveland, Bernie Kosar, QB, Miami, Fla.

1986
FIRST ROUND—NFL

No.	Team	Player selected	Pos.	College
1.	Tampa Bay	*Bo Jackson*	RB	Auburn
2.	Atlanta	Tony Casillas	NT	Oklahoma
3.	Houston	Jim Everett	QB	Purdue
4.	Indianapolis	Jon Hand	DE	Alabama
5.	St. Louis	Anthony Bell	LB	Michigan State
6.	New Orleans	Jim Dombrowski	T	Virginia
7.	Kansas City	Brian Jozwiak	T	West Virginia
8.	San Diego	Leslie O'Neal	DE	Oklahoma State
9.	Pittsburgh	John Rienstra	G	Temple
10.	Philadelphia	Keith Byars	RB	Ohio State
11.	Cincinnati	Joe Kelly	LB	Washington
12.	Detroit	Chuck Long	QB	Iowa
13.	San Diego	James Fitzpatrick	T	USC
14.	Minnesota	Gerald Robinson	DE	Auburn
15.	Seattle	John L. Williams	RB	Florida
16.	Buffalo	Ronnie Harmon	RB	Iowa
17.	Atlanta	Tim Green	LB	Syracuse
18.	Dallas	Mike Sherrard	WR	UCLA
19.	N.Y. Giants	Eric Dorsey	DE	Notre Dame
20.	Buffalo	Will Wolford	T	Vanderbilt
21.	Cincinnati	Tim McGee	WR	Tennessee
22.	N.Y. Jets	Mike Haight	T	Iowa
23.	L.A. Rams	Mike Schad	T	Queens (Canada)
24.	L.A. Raiders	Bob Buczkowski	DE	Pittsburgh
25.	Tampa Bay	Roderick Jones	DB	SMU
26.	New England	Reggie Dupard	RB	SMU
27.	Chicago	Neal Anderson	RB	Florida

Teams not selecting in first round: Cleveland, Denver, Green Bay, Miami, San Francisco, Washington.
Total number of picks in draft: 333.

OTHER NOTEWORTHY PICKS

Round/Overall—Team, Player selected, Pos., College
2/51—N.Y. Giants, Pepper Johnson, LB, Ohio State; 3/56—San Francisco, Tom Rathman, RB, Nebraska; 3/60—New Orleans, Pat Swilling, LB, Georgia Tech; 3/76—San Francisco, John Taylor, WR, Delaware State; 4/96—San Francisco, Charles Haley, LB, James Madison; 6/146—Washington, Mark Rypien, QB, Washington State; 9/233—Philadelphia, Clyde Simmons, DE, Western Carolina; 12/327—L.A. Rams, Marcus Dupree, RB, Oklahoma.

1987
FIRST ROUND—NFL

No.	Team	Player selected	Pos.	College
1.	Tampa Bay	*Vinny Testaverde*	QB	Miami, Fla.
2.	Indianapolis	Cornelius Bennett	LB	Alabama
3.	Houston	Alonzo Highsmith	RB	Miami, Fla.
4.	Green Bay	Brent Fullwood	RB	Auburn
5.	Cleveland	Mike Junkin	LB	Duke
6.	St. Louis	Kelly Stouffer	QB	Colorado State
7.	Detroit	Reggie Rogers	DE	Washington
8.	Buffalo	Shane Conlan	LB	Penn State
9.	Philadelphia	Jerome Brown	DT	Miami, Fla.
10.	Pittsburgh	Rod Woodson	DB	Purdue
11.	New Orleans	Shawn Knight	DT	Brigham Young
12.	Dallas	Danny Noonan	DT	Nebraska
13.	Atlanta	Chris Miller	QB	Oregon
14.	Minnesota	D.J. Dozier	RB	Penn State
15.	L.A. Raiders	John Clay	T	Missouri
16.	Miami	John Bosa	DE	Boston College
17.	Cincinnati	Jason Buck	DE	Brigham Young
18.	Seattle	Tony Woods	LB	Pittsburgh
19.	Kansas City	Paul Palmer	RB	Temple
20.	Houston	Haywood Jeffires	WR	N. Carolina State
21.	N.Y. Jets	Roger Vick	RB	Texas A&M
22.	San Francisco	Harris Barton	T	North Carolina
23.	New England	Bruce Armstrong	T	Louisville
24.	San Diego	Rod Bernstine	TE	Texas A&M
25.	San Francisco	Terrence Flagler	RB	Clemson

No.	Team	Player selected	Pos.	College
26.	Chicago	Jim Harbaugh	QB	Michigan
27.	Denver	Ricky Nattiel	WR	Florida
28.	N.Y. Giants	Mark Ingram	WR	Michigan State

Teams not selecting in first round: L.A. Rams, Washington.
Total number of picks in draft: 335.

OTHER NOTEWORTHY PICKS

Round/Overall—Team, Player selected, Pos., College
2/53—San Diego, Louis Brock, DB, USC; 4/98—New England Rich Gannon, QB, Delaware; 4/110—L.A. Raiders, Steve Beuerlein QB, Notre Dame; 5/117—Washington, Timmy Smith, RB, Texas Tech; 5/122—Pittsburgh, Hardy Nickerson, LB, California; 7/183— L.A. Raiders, *Bo Jackson*, RB, Auburn; 10/255—Green Bay, Don Majkowski, QB, Virginia; 10/261—Pittsburgh, Merril Hoge, RB Idaho State; 12/313—Tampa Bay, Mike Shula, QB, Alabama Supplemental—Seattle, Brian Bosworth, LB, Oklahoma; Supplemental—Philadelphia, Cris Carter, WR, Ohio State.

1988
FIRST ROUND—NFL

No.	Team	Player selected	Pos.	College
1.	Atlanta	Aundray Bruce	LB	Auburn
2.	Kansas City	Neil Smith	DE	Nebraska
3.	Detroit	Bennie Blades	DB	Miami, Fla.
4.	Tampa Bay	Paul Gruber	T	Wisconsin
5.	Cincinnati	Rickey Dixon	DB	Oklahoma
6.	L.A. Raiders	*Tim Brown*	WR	Notre Dame
7.	Green Bay	Sterling Sharpe	WR	South Carolina
8.	N.Y. Jets	Dave Cadigan	T	USC
9.	L.A. Raiders	Terry McDaniel	DB	Tennessee
10.	N.Y. Giants	Eric Moore	T	Indiana
11.	Dallas	Michael Irvin	WR	Miami, Fla.
12.	Phoenix	Ken Harvey	LB	California
13.	Philadelphia	Keith Jackson	TE	Oklahoma
14.	L.A. Rams	Gaston Green	RB	UCLA
15.	San Diego	Anthony Miller	WR	Tennessee
16.	Miami	Eric Kumerow	DE	Ohio State
17.	New England	John Stephens	RB	NW (La.) State
18.	Pittsburgh	Aaron Jones	DE	Eastern Kentucky
19.	Minnesota	Randall McDaniel	G	Arizona State
20.	L.A. Rams	Aaron Cox	WR	Arizona State
21.	Cleveland	Clifford Charlton	LB	Florida
22.	Houston	Lorenzo White	RB	Michigan State
23.	Chicago	Brad Muster	RB	Stanford
24.	New Orleans	Craig Heyward	RB	Pittsburgh
25.	L.A. Raiders	Scott Davis	DE	Illinois
26.	Denver	Ted Gregory	NT	Syracuse
27.	Chicago	Wendell Davis	WR	Louisiana State

Teams not selecting in first round: Buffalo, Indianapolis, San Francisco, Seattle, Washington.
Total number of picks in draft: 333.

OTHER NOTEWORTHY PICKS

Round/Overall—Team, Player selected, Pos., College
2/29—Detroit, Chris Spielman, LB, Ohio State; 2/30— Philadelphia, Eric Allen, DB, Arizona State; 2/36—N.Y. Giants John (Jumbo) Elliott, T, Michigan; 2/40—Buffalo, Thurman Thomas, RB, Oklahoma State; 2/41—Dallas, Ken Norton Jr., LB UCLA; 2/44—Pittsburgh, Dermontti Dawson, G, Kentucky 2/46—L.A. Rams, Willie (Flipper) Anderson, WR, UCLA; 3/76— Indianapolis, Chris Chandler, QB, Washington; 3/80—San Francisco, Bill Romanowski, LB, Boston College.

1989
FIRST ROUND—NFL

No.	Team	Player selected	Pos.	College
1.	Dallas	Troy Aikman	QB	UCLA
2.	Green Bay	Tony Mandarich	T	Michigan State
3.	Detroit	*Barry Sanders*	RB	Oklahoma State

. Team	Player selected	Pos.	College
1. Kansas City	Derrick Thomas	LB	Alabama
5. Atlanta	Deion Sanders	CB	Florida State
6. Tampa Bay	Broderick Thomas	LB	Nebraska
7. Pittsburgh	Tim Worley	RB	Georgia
8. San Diego	Burt Grossman	DE	Pittsburgh
9. Miami	Sammie Smith	RB	Florida State
9. Phoenix	Eric Hill	LB	Louisiana State
1. Chicago	Donnell Woolford	CB	Clemson
2. Chicago	Trace Armstrong	DE	Florida
3. Cleveland	Eric Metcalf	RB	Texas
4. N.Y. Jets	Jeff Lageman	LB	Virginia
5. Seattle	Andy Heck	T	Notre Dame
5. New England	Hart Lee Dykes	WR	Oklahoma State
7. Phoenix	Joe Wolf	G	Boston College
3. N.Y. Giants	Brian Williams	G	Minnesota
9. New Orleans	Wayne Martin	DE	Arkansas
0. Denver	Steve Atwater	S	Arkansas
1. L.A. Rams	Bill Hawkins	DE	Miami, Fla.
2. Indianapolis	Andre Rison	WR	Michigan State
3. Houston	David Williams	T	Florida
4. Pittsburgh	Tom Ricketts	T	Pittsburgh
5. Miami	Louis Oliver	S	Florida
6. L.A. Rams	Cleveland Gary	RB	Miami, Fla.
7. Atlanta	Shawn Collins	WR	Northern Arizona
8. San Francisco	Keith DeLong	LB	Tennessee

Teams not selecting in first round: Buffalo, Cincinnati, L.A. Raiders, Minnesota, Philadelphia, Washington.

Total number of picks in draft: 335.

OTHER NOTEWORTHY PICKS

ound/Overall—Team, Player selected, Pos., College

34—Pittsburgh, Carnell Lake, DB, UCLA; 2/39—Dallas, Daryl hnston, RB, Syracuse; 2/56—San Francisco, Wesley Walls, TE, ississippi; 7/173—Buffalo, Brian Jordan, DB, Richmond; Supemental—Dallas, Steve Walsh, QB, Miami, Fla.; Supplemental— enver, Bobby Humphrey, RB, Alabama; Supplemental—Phoenix, m Rosenbach, QB, Washington State.

1990
FIRST ROUND—NFL

0. Team	Player selected	Pos.	College
1. Indianapolis	Jeff George	QB	Illinois
2. N.Y. Jets	Blair Thomas	RB	Penn State
3. Seattle	Cortez Kennedy	DT	Miami, Fla.
4. Tampa Bay	Keith McCants	LB	Alabama
5. San Diego	Junior Seau	LB	USC
6. Chicago	Mark Carrier	DB	USC
7. Detroit	*Andre Ware*	QB	Houston
8. New England	Chris Singleton	LB	Arizona
9. Miami	Richmond Webb	T	Texas A&M
0. New England	Ray Agnew	DE	N. Carolina State
1. L.A. Raiders	Anthony Smith	DE	Arizona
2. Cincinnati	James Francis	LB	Baylor
3. Kansas City	Percy Snow	LB	Michigan State
4. New Orleans	Renaldo Turnbull	DE	West Virginia
5. Houston	Lamar Lathon	LB	Houston
6. Buffalo	James Williams	DB	Fresno State
7. Dallas	Emmitt Smith	RB	Florida
8. Green Bay	Tony Bennett	LB	Mississippi
9. Green Bay	Darrell Thompson	RB	Minnesota
0. Atlanta	Steve Broussard	RB	Washington State
1. Pittsburgh	Eric Green	TE	Liberty, Va.
2. Philadelphia	Ben Smith	DB	Georgia
3. L.A. Rams	Bern Brostek	C	Washington
4. N.Y. Giants	Rodney Hampton	RB	Georgia
5. San Francisco	Dexter Carter	RB	Florida State

Teams not selecting in first round: Cleveland, Denver, Minnesota, hoenix, Washington.

Total number of picks in draft: 331.

OTHER NOTEWORTHY PICKS

Round/Overall—Team, Player selected, Pos., College

2/48—Green Bay, LeRoy Butler, DB, Florida State; 3/70—Pittsburgh, Neil O'Donnell, QB, Maryland; 5/115—Phoenix, Larry Centers, RB, Stephen F. Austin; 5/130—Washington, Brian Mitchell, RB, Southwestern Louisiana; 7/180—Kansas City, Dave Szott, G, Penn State; 7/192—Denver, Shannon Sharpe, WR, Savannah State; 9/241—Minnesota, Terry Allen, RB, Clemson; 10/265—Buffalo, Mike Lodish, DT, UCLA; 12/329—N.Y. Giants, Matt Stover, K, Louisiana Tech.

1991
FIRST ROUND—NFL

No. Team	Player selected	Pos.	College
1. Dallas	Russell Maryland	DL	Miami, Fla.
2. Cleveland	Eric Turner	S	UCLA
3. Atlanta	Bruce Pickens	CB	Nebraska
4. Denver	Mike Croel	LB	Nebraska
5. L.A. Rams	Todd Lyght	CB	Notre Dame
6. Phoenix	Eric Swann	DL	No college
7. Tampa Bay	Charles McRae	T	Tennessee
8. Philadelphia	Antone Davis	T	Tennessee
9. San Diego	Stanley Richard	CB	Texas
10. Detroit	Herman Moore	WR	Virginia
11. New England	Pat Harlow	T	USC
12. Dallas	Alvin Harper	WR	Tennessee
13. Atlanta	Mike Pritchard	WR	Colorado
14. New England	Leonard Russell	RB	Arizona State
15. Pittsburgh	Huey Richardson	DE	Florida
16. Seattle	Dan McGwire	QB	San Diego State
17. Washington	Bobby Wilson	DT	Michigan State
18. Cincinnati	Alfred Williams	LB	Colorado
19. Green Bay	Vincent Clark	DB	Ohio State
20. Dallas	Kelvin Pritchett	DT	Mississippi
21. Kansas City	Harvey Williams	RB	Louisiana State
22. Chicago	Stan Thomas	T	Texas
23. Miami	Randal Hill	WR	Miami, Fla.
24. L.A. Raiders	Todd Marinovich	QB	USC
25. San Francisco	Ted Washington	DL	Louisville
26. Buffalo	Henry Jones	S	Illinois
27. N.Y. Giants	Jarrod Bunch	FB	Michigan

Teams not selecting in first round: Houston, Indianapolis, Minnesota, New Orleans, N.Y. Jets.

Total number of picks in draft: 334.

OTHER NOTEWORTHY PICKS

Round/Overall—Team, Player selected, Pos., College

2/33—Atlanta, Brett Favre, QB, Southern Mississippi; 2/45—San Francisco, Ricky Watters, RB, Notre Dame; 3/59—Phoenix, Aeneas Williams, DB, Southern; 3/70—Dallas, Erik Williams, T, Central (Ohio) State; 3/83—N.Y. Giants, Ed McCaffrey, WR, Stanford; 4/100—L.A. Raiders, Rocket Ismail, WR, Notre Dame; 5/113—Miami, Bryan Cox, LB, Western Illinois; 5/124—New England, Ben Coates, TE, Livingstone; 7/173—Dallas, Leon Lett, DT, Emporia State; 12/326—Washington, Keenan McCardell, WR, UNLV.

1992
FIRST ROUND—NFL

No. Team	Player selected	Pos.	College
1. Indianapolis	Steve Emtman	DL	Washington
2. Indianapolis	Quentin Coryatt	LB	Texas A&M
3. L.A. Rams	Sean Gilbert	DL	Pittsburgh
4. Washington	*Desmond Howard*	WR	Michigan
5. Green Bay	Terrell Buckley	DB	Florida State
6. Cincinnati	David Klingler	QB	Houston
7. Miami	Troy Vincent	DB	Wisconsin
8. Atlanta	Bob Whitfield	OL	Stanford

No. Team	Player selected	Pos.	College
9. Cleveland	Tommy Vardell	FB	Stanford
10. Seattle	Ray Roberts	OL	Virginia
11. Pittsburgh	Leon Searcy	T	Miami, Fla.
12. Miami	Marco Coleman	LB	Georgia Tech
13. New England	Eugene Chung	OL	Virginia Tech
14. N.Y. Giants	Derek Brown	TE	Notre Dame
15. N.Y. Jets	Johnny Mitchell	TE	Nebraska
16. L.A. Raiders	Chester McGlockton	DT	Clemson
17. Dallas	Kevin Smith	DB	Texas A&M
18. San Francisco	Dana Hall	DB	Washington
19. Atlanta	Tony Smith	RB	Southern Miss
20. Kansas City	Dale Carter	DB	Tennessee
21. New Orleans	Vaughn Dunbar	RB	Indiana
22. Chicago	Alonzo Spellman	DL	Ohio State
23. San Diego	Chris Mims	DL	Tennessee
24. Dallas	Robert Jones	LB	East Carolina
25. Denver	Tommy Maddox	QB	UCLA
26. Detroit	Robert Porcher	DL	S. Carolina State
27. Buffalo	John Fina	OL	Arizona
28. Cincinnati	Darryl Williams	DB	Miami, Fla.

Teams not selecting in first round: Houston, Minnesota, Philadelphia, Phoenix, Tampa Bay.
Total number of picks in draft: 336.

OTHER NOTEWORTHY PICKS

Round/Overall—Team, Player selected, Pos., College
2/31—Cincinnati, Carl Pickens, WR, Tennessee; 2/36—Dallas, Jimmy Smith, WR, Jackson State; 2/37—Dallas, Darren Woodson, DB, Arizona State; 2/56—Detroit, Jason Hanson, K, Washington; 3/62—Green Bay, Robert Brooks, WR, South Carolina; 5/132—Tampa Bay, Santana Dotson, DE, Baylor; 6/166—N.Y. Jets, Jeff Blake, QB, East Carolina; 9/227—Minnesota, Brad Johnson, QB, Florida State; 9/230—Green Bay, *Ty Detmer*, QB, Brigham Young; Supplemental—N.Y. Giants, Dave Brown, QB, Duke.

1993

FIRST ROUND—NFL

No. Team	Player selected	Pos.	College
1. New England	Drew Bledsoe	QB	Washington State
2. Seattle	Rick Mirer	QB	Notre Dame
3. Phoenix	Garrison Hearst	RB	Georgia
4. N.Y. Jets	Marvin Jones	LB	Florida State
5. Cincinnati	John Copeland	DE	Alabama
6. Tampa Bay	Eric Curry	DE	Alabama
7. Chicago	Curtis Conway	WR	USC
8. New Orleans	Willie Roaf	T	Louisiana Tech
9. Atlanta	Lincoln Kennedy	T	Washington
10. L.A. Rams	Jerome Bettis	RB	Notre Dame
11. Denver	Dan Williams	DE	Toledo
12. L.A. Raiders	Patrick Bates	DB	Texas A&M
13. Houston	Brad Hopkins	T	Illinois
14. Cleveland	Steve Everitt	C	Michigan
15. Green Bay	Wayne Simmons	LB	Clemson
16. Indianapolis	Sean Dawkins	WR	California
17. Washington	Tom Carter	DB	Notre Dame
18. Phoenix	Ernest Dye	T	South Carolina
19. Philadelphia	Lester Holmes	T	Jackson State
20. New Orleans	Irv Smith	TE	Notre Dame
21. Minnesota	Robert Smith	RB	Ohio State
22. San Diego	Darrien Gordon	DB	Stanford
23. Pittsburgh	Deon Figures	DB	Colorado
24. Philadelphia	Leonard Renfro	DT	Colorado
25. Miami	O.J. McDuffie	WR	Penn State
26. San Francisco	Dana Stubblefield	DT	Kansas
27. San Francisco	Todd Kelly	DE	Tennessee
28. Buffalo	Thomas Smith	DB	North Carolina
29. Green Bay	George Teague	DB	Alabama

Teams not selecting in first round: Dallas, Detroit, Kansas City, N.Y. Giants.
Total number of picks in draft: 224.

OTHER NOTEWORTHY PICKS

Round/Overall—Team, Player selected, Pos., College
2/40—N.Y. Giants, Michael Strahan, DE, Texas Southern; 2/44—Pittsburgh, Chad Brown, LB, Colorado; 3/65—Indianapolis, Ray Buchanan, DB, Louisville; 3/70—Denver, Jason Elam, K, Hawaii; 3/82—Tampa Bay, John Lynch, DB, Stanford; 5/118—Green Bay, Mark Brunell, QB, Washington; 6/160—Washington, Frank Wycheck, TE, Maryland; 7/192—Minnesota, *Gino Torretta*, QB, Miami, Fla.; 8/207—N.Y. Giants, Jessie Armstead, LB, Miami, Fla.; 8/219—San Francisco, Elvis Grbac, QB, Michigan; 8/222—San Diego, Trent Green, QB, Indiana.

1994

FIRST ROUND—NFL

No. Team	Player selected	Pos.	College
1. Cincinnati	Dan Wilkinson	DT	Ohio State
2. Indianapolis	Marshall Faulk	RB	San Diego State
3. Washington	Heath Shuler	QB	Tennessee
4. New England	Willie McGinest	DE	USC
5. Indianapolis	Trev Alberts	LB	Nebraska
6. Tampa Bay	Trent Dilfer	QB	Fresno State
7. San Francisco	Bryant Young	DT	Notre Dame
8. Seattle	Sam Adams	DE	Texas A&M
9. Cleveland	Antonio Langham	DB	Alabama
10. Arizona	Jamir Miller	LB	UCLA
11. Chicago	John Thierry	LB	Alcorn State
12. N.Y. Jets	Aaron Glenn	DB	Texas A&M
13. New Orleans	Joe Johnson	DE	Louisville
14. Philadelphia	Bernard Williams	T	Georgia
15. L.A. Rams	Wayne Gandy	T	Auburn
16. Green Bay	Aaron Taylor	T	Notre Dame
17. Pittsburgh	Charles Johnson	WR	Colorado
18. Minnesota	Dewayne Washington	CB	N. Carolina State
19. Minnesota	Todd Steussie	T	California
20. Miami	Tim Bowens	DT	Mississippi
21. Detroit	Johnnie Morton	WR	USC
22. L.A. Raiders	Rob Fredrickson	LB	Michigan State
23. Dallas	Shante Carver	DE	Arizona State
24. N.Y. Giants	Thomas Lewis	WR	Indiana
25. Kansas City	Greg Hill	RB	Texas A&M
26. Houston	Henry Ford	DE	Arkansas
27. Buffalo	Jeff Burris	DB	Notre Dame
28. San Francisco	William Floyd	RB	Florida State
29. Cleveland	Derrick Alexander	WR	Michigan

Teams not selecting in first round: Atlanta, Denver, San Diego.
Total number of picks in draft: 222.

OTHER NOTEWORTHY PICKS

Round/Overall—Team, Player selected, Pos., College
2/33—L.A. Rams, Isaac Bruce, WR, Memphis State; 2/36—Seattle, Kevin Mawae, C, Louisiana State; 2/42—Philadelphia, Charlie Garner, RB, Tennessee; 2/46—Dallas, Larry Allen, G, Sonoma State; 2/59—N.Y. Giants, Jason Sehorn, DB, USC; 5/145—San Diego, Rodney Harrison, DB, Western Illinois; 5/149—Green Bay, Dorsey Levens, RB, Georgia Tech; 7/197—Washington, Gus Frerotte, QB, Tulsa; 7/201—Atlanta, Jamal Anderson, RB, Utah; 7/218—Denver, Tom Nalen, C, Boston College.

1995

FIRST ROUND—NFL

No. Team	Player selected	Pos.	College
1. Cincinnati	Ki-Jana Carter	RB	Penn State
2. Jacksonville	Tony Boselli	T	USC
3. Houston	Steve McNair	QB	Alcorn State
4. Washington	Michael Westbrook	WR	Colorado
5. Carolina	Kerry Collins	QB	Penn State
6. St. Louis	Kevin Carter	DE	Florida
7. Philadelphia	Mike Mamula	DE	Boston College
8. Seattle	Joey Galloway	WR	Ohio State

. Team	Player selected	Pos.	College
). N.Y. Jets	Kyle Brady	TE	Penn State
. San Francisco	J.J. Stokes	WR	UCLA
. Minnesota	Derrick Alexander	DE	Florida State
. Tampa Bay	Warren Sapp	DT	Miami, Fla.
. New Orleans	Mark Fields	LB	Washington State
. Buffalo	Ruben Brown	G	Pittsburgh
. Indianapolis	Ellis Johnson	DT	Florida
. N.Y. Jets	Hugh Douglas	DE	Central State (Ohio)
. N.Y. Giants	Tyrone Wheatley	RB	Michigan
. Los Angeles	Napoleon Kaufman	RB	Washington
. Jacksonville	James Stewart	RB	Tennessee
. Detroit	Luther Elliss	DT	Utah
. Chicago	*Rashaan Salaam*	RB	Colorado
. Carolina	Tyrone Poole	DB	Ft. Valley (Ga.) St.
. New England	Ty Law	DB	Michigan
. Minnesota	Korey Stringer	T	Ohio State
. Miami	Billy Milner	T	Houston
. Atlanta	Devin Bush	DB	Florida State
. Pittsburgh	Mark Bruener	TE	Washington
. Tampa Bay	Derrick Brooks	LB	Florida State
. Carolina	Blake Brockermeyer	T	Texas
. Cleveland	Craig Powell	LB	Ohio State
. Kansas City	Trezelle Jenkins	T	Michigan
. Green Bay	Craig Newsome	DB	Arizona State

Note: Los Angeles franchise moved to Oakland (but after draft); ams not selecting in first round: Arizona, Dallas, Denver, San ego.
Total number of picks in draft: 249.

OTHER NOTEWORTHY PICKS

ound/Overall—Team, Player selected, Pos., College
50—Philadelphia, Bobby Taylor, DB, Notre Dame; 2/60— ttsburgh, Kordell Stewart, QB, Colorado; 3/74—New England, rtis Martin, RB, Pittsburgh; 3/90—Green Bay, Antonio eeman, WR, Virginia Tech; 6/196—Denver, Terrell Davis, RB, eorgia; 7/230—Green Bay, Adam Timmerman, G, South Dakota 'ate.

1996

FIRST ROUND—NFL

). Team	Player selected	Pos.	College
1. N.Y. Jets	Keyshawn Johnson	WR	USC
2. Jacksonville	Kevin Hardy	LB	Illinois
3. Arizona	Simeon Rice	DE	Illinois
4. Baltimore	Jonathan Ogden	T	UCLA
5. N.Y. Giants	Cedric Jones	DE	Oklahoma
6. St. Louis	Lawrence Phillips	RB	Nebraska
7. New England	Terry Glenn	WR	Ohio State
8. Carolina	Tim Biakabutuka	RB	Michigan
9. Oakland	Rickey Dudley	TE	Ohio State
0. Cincinnati	Willie Anderson	T	Auburn
1. New Orleans	Alex Molden	DB	Oregon
2. Tampa Bay	Regan Upshaw	DE	California
3. Chicago	Walt Harris	DB	Miss. State
4. Houston	*Eddie George*	RB	Ohio State
5. Denver	John Mobley	LB	Kutztown, Pa.
6. Minnesota	Duane Clemons	DE	California
7. Detroit	Reggie Brown	LB	Texas A&M
8. St. Louis	Eddie Kennison	WR	Louisiana State
9. Indianapolis	Marvin Harrison	WR	Syracuse
0. Miami	Daryl Gardener	DT	Baylor
1. Seattle	Pete Kendall	T	Boston College
2. Tampa Bay	Marcus Jones	DT	North Carolina
3. Detroit	Jeff Hartings	G	Penn State
4. Buffalo	Eric Moulds	WR	Miss. State
5. Philadelphia	Jermane Mayberry	T	Tex. A&M-K'ville
6. Baltimore	Ray Lewis	LB	Miami, Fla.
7. Green Bay	John Michels	T	USC
8. Kansas City	Jerome Woods	DB	Memphis
9. Pittsburgh	Jamain Stephens	T	N. Carolina A&T
0. Washington	Andre Johnson	T	Penn State

Teams not selecting in first round: Atlanta, Dallas, San Diego, an Francisco.
Total number of picks in draft: 254.

OTHER NOTEWORTHY PICKS

Round/Overall—Team, Player selected, Pos., College
2/33—Jacksonville, Tony Brackens, DE, Texas; 2/34—N.Y. Giants, Amani Toomer, WR, Michigan; 2/35—Tampa Bay, Mike Alstott, RB, Purdue; 2/36—New England, Lawyer Milloy, DB, Washington; 2/61—Philadelphia, Brian Dawkins, DB, Clemson; 3/89—San Francisco, Terrell Owens, WR, UT-Chattanooga; 4/102—Washington, Stephen Davis, RB, Auburn; 5/135—Kansas City, Joe Horn, WR, Itawamba JC; 5/154—Miami, Zach Thomas, LB, Texas Tech.

1997

FIRST ROUND—NFL

No. Team	Player selected	Pos.	College
1. St. Louis	Orlando Pace	T	Ohio State
2. Oakland	Darrell Russell	DT	USC
3. Seattle	Shawn Springs	CB	Ohio State
4. Baltimore	Peter Boulware	DE	Florida State
5. Detroit	Bryant Westbrook	DB	Texas
6. Seattle	Walter Jones	T	Florida State
7. N.Y. Giants	Ike Hilliard	WR	Florida
8. N.Y. Jets	James Farrior	LB	Virginia
9. Arizona	Tom Knight	DB	Iowa
10. New Orleans	Chris Naeole	G	Colorado
11. Atlanta	Michael Booker	DB	Nebraska
12. Tampa Bay	Warrick Dunn	RB	Florida State
13. Kansas City	Tony Gonzalez	TE	California
14. Cincinnati	Reinard Wilson	LB	Florida State
15. Miami	Yatil Green	WR	Miami, Fla.
16. Tampa Bay	Reidel Anthony	WR	Florida
17. Washington	Kenard Lang	DE	Miami, Fla.
18. Houston	Kenny Holmes	DE	Miami, Fla.
19. Indianapolis	Tarik Glenn	T	California
20. Minnesota	Dwayne Rudd	LB	Alabama
21. Jacksonville	Renaldo Wynn	DT	Notre Dame
22. Dallas	David LaFleur	TE	Louisiana State
23. Buffalo	Antowain Smith	RB	Houston
24. Pittsburgh	Chad Scott	DB	Maryland
25. Philadelphia	Jon Harris	DE	Virginia
26. San Francisco	Jim Druckenmiller	QB	Virginia Tech
27. Carolina	Rae Carruth	WR	Colorado
28. Denver	Trevor Pryce	DT	Clemson
29. New England	Chris Canty	DB	Kansas State
30. Green Bay	Ross Verba	T	Iowa

Teams not selecting in first round: Chicago, San Diego.
Total number of picks in draft: 240.

OTHER NOTEWORTHY PICKS

Round/Overall—Team, Player selected, Pos., College
2/34—Baltimore, Jamie Sharper, LB, Virginia; 2/36—N.Y. Giants, Tiki Barber, RB, Virginia; 2/42—Arizona, Jake Plummer, QB, Arizona State; 2/43—Cincinnati, Corey Dillon, RB, Washington; 2/44—Miami, Sam Madison, DB, Louisville; 2/60—Green Bay, Darren Sharper, DB, William & Mary; 3/71—Philadelphia, Duce Staley, RB, South Carolina; 3/73—Miami, Jason Taylor, DE, Akron; 4/99—New Orleans, *Danny Wuerffel*, QB, Florida.

1998

FIRST ROUND—NFL

No. Team	Player selected	Pos.	College
1. Indianapolis	Peyton Manning	QB	Tennessee
2. San Diego	Ryan Leaf	QB	Washington State
3. Arizona	Andre Wadsworth	DE	Florida State
4. Oakland	*Charles Woodson*	DB	Michigan
5. Chicago	Curtis Enis	RB	Penn State
6. St. Louis	Grant Wistrom	DE	Nebraska
7. New Orleans	Kyle Turley	T	San Diego State
8. Dallas	Greg Ellis	DE	North Carolina
9. Jacksonville	Fred Taylor	RB	Florida
10. Baltimore	Duane Starks	DB	Miami, Fla.
11. Philadelphia	Tra Thomas	T	Florida State

No.	Team	Player selected	Pos.	College
12.	Atlanta	Keith Brooking	LB	Georgia Tech
13.	Cincinnati	Takeo Spikes	LB	Auburn
14.	Carolina	Jason Peter	DT	Nebraska
15.	Seattle	Anthony Simmons	LB	Clemson
16.	Tennessee	Kevin Dyson	WR	Utah
17.	Cincinnati	Brian Simmons	LB	North Carolina
18.	New England	Robert Edwards	RB	Georgia
19.	Green Bay	Vonnie Holliday	DT	North Carolina
20.	Detroit	Terry Fair	DB	Tennessee
21.	Minnesota	Randy Moss	WR	Marshall
22.	New England	Tebucky Jones	DB	Syracuse
23.	Oakland	Mo Collins	T	Florida
24.	N.Y. Giants	Shaun Williams	DB	UCLA
25.	Jacksonville	Donovin Darius	DB	Syracuse
26.	Pittsburgh	Alan Faneca	G	Louisiana State
27.	Kansas City	Victor Riley	T	Auburn
28.	San Francisco	R.W. McQuarters	DB	Oklahoma State
29.	Miami	John Avery	RB	Mississippi
30.	Denver	Marcus Nash	WR	Tennessee

Teams not selecting in first round: Buffalo, N.Y. Jets, Tampa Bay, Washington.
Total number of picks in draft: 241.

OTHER NOTEWORTHY PICKS

Round/Overall—Team, Player selected, Pos., College
2/38—Dallas, Flozell Adams, T, Michigan State; 2/39—Buffalo, Sam Cowart, LB, Florida State; 2/60—Detroit, Charlie Batch, QB, Eastern Michigan; 3/76—Seattle, Ahman Green, RB, Nebraska; 3/91—Denver, Brian Griese, QB, Michigan; 3/92—Pittsburgh, Hines Ward, WR, Georgia; 5/150—Green Bay, Corey Bradford, WR, Jackson State; 6/173—Minnesota, Matt Birk, C, Harvard; 6/187—Green Bay, Matt Hasselbeck, QB, Boston College; 7/226—Arizona, Pat Tillman, DB, Arizona State.

1999
FIRST ROUND—NFL

No.	Team	Player selected	Pos.	College
1.	Cleveland	Tim Couch	QB	Kentucky
2.	Philadelphia	Donovan McNabb	QB	Syracuse
3.	Cincinnati	Akili Smith	QB	Oregon
4.	Indianapolis	Edgerrin James	RB	Miami, Fla.
5.	New Orleans	*Ricky Williams*	RB	Texas
6.	St. Louis	Torry Holt	WR	N. Carolina State
7.	Washington	Champ Bailey	DB	Georgia
8.	Arizona	David Boston	WR	Ohio State
9.	Detroit	Chris Claiborne	LB	USC
10.	Baltimore	Chris McAlister	DB	Arizona
11.	Minnesota	Daunte Culpepper	QB	Central Florida
12.	Chicago	Cade McNown	QB	UCLA
13.	Pittsburgh	Troy Edwards	WR	Louisiana Tech
14.	Kansas City	John Tait	T	Brigham Young
15.	Tampa Bay	Anthony McFarland	DT	Louisiana State
16.	Tennessee	Jevon Kearse	DE	Florida
17.	New England	Damien Woody	C	Boston College
18.	Oakland	Matt Stinchcomb	T	Georgia
19.	N.Y. Giants	Luke Petitgout	T	Notre Dame
20.	Dallas	Ebenezer Ekuban	DE	North Carolina
21.	Arizona	L.J. Shelton	T	Eastern Michigan
22.	Seattle	Lamar King	DE	Saginaw Valley St.
23.	Buffalo	Antoine Winfield	DB	Ohio State
24.	San Francisco	Reggie McGrew	DT	Florida
25.	Green Bay	Antuan Edwards	DB	Clemson
26.	Jacksonville	Fernando Bryant	DB	Alabama
27.	Detroit	Aaron Gibson	T	Wisconsin
28.	New England	Andy Katzenmoyer	LB	Ohio State
29.	Minnesota	Dimitrius Underwood	DE	Michigan State
30.	Atlanta	Patrick Kerney	DE	Virginia
31.	Denver	Al Wilson	LB	Tennessee

Teams not selecting in first round: Carolina, Miami, N.Y. Jets, San Diego.
Total number of picks in draft: 253.

OTHER NOTEWORTHY PICKS

Round/Overall—Team, Player selected, Pos., College
2/36—Indianapolis, Mike Peterson, LB, Florida; 2/41—St. Louis, Dre' Bly, DB, North Carolina; 2/53—Buffalo, Peerless Price, WR, Tennessee; 3/73—Pittsburgh, Joey Porter, LB, Colorado State; 3/78—Chicago, Marty Booker, WR, Northeast Louisiana; 3/80—Tampa Bay, Martin Gramatica, K, Kansas State; 4/131—Green Bay, Aaron Brooks, QB, Virginia; 7/213—Green Bay, Donald Driver, WR, Alcorn State.

2000
FIRST ROUND—NFL

No.	Team	Player selected	Pos.	College
1.	Cleveland	Courtney Brown	DE	Penn State
2.	Washington	LaVar Arrington	LB	Penn State
3.	Washington	Chris Samuels	T	Alabama
4.	Cincinnati	Peter Warrick	WR	Florida State
5.	Baltimore	Jamal Lewis	RB	Tennessee
6.	Philadelphia	Corey Simon	DT	Florida State
7.	Arizona	Thomas Jones	RB	Virginia
8.	Pittsburgh	Plaxico Burress	WR	Michigan State
9.	Chicago	Brian Urlacher	LB	New Mexico
10.	Baltimore	Travis Taylor	WR	Florida
11.	N.Y. Giants	Ron Dayne	RB	Wisconsin
12.	N.Y. Jets	Shaun Ellis	DE	Tennessee
13.	N.Y. Jets	John Abraham	LB	South Carolina
14.	Green Bay	Bubba Franks	TE	Miami, Fla.
15.	Denver	Deltha O'Neal	DB	California
16.	San Francisco	Julian Peterson	LB	Michigan State
17.	Oakland	Sebastian Janikowski	K	Florida State
18.	N.Y. Jets	Chad Pennington	QB	Marshall
19.	Seattle	Shaun Alexander	RB	Alabama
20.	Detroit	Stockar McDougle	T	Oklahoma
21.	Kansas City	Sylvester Morris	WR	Jackson State
22.	Seattle	Chris McIntosh	T	Wisconsin
23.	Carolina	Rashard Anderson	DB	Jackson State
24.	San Francisco	Ahmed Plummer	DB	Ohio State
25.	Minnesota	Chris Hovan	DT	Boston College
26.	Buffalo	Erik Flowers	DE	Arizona State
27.	N.Y. Jets	Anthony Becht	TE	West Virginia
28.	Indianapolis	Rob Morris	LB	Brigham Young
29.	Jacksonville	R. Jay Soward	WR	USC
30.	Tennessee	Keith Bulluck	LB	Syracuse
31.	St. Louis	Trung Canidate	RB	Arizona

Teams not selecting in first round: Atlanta, Dallas, Miami, New England, New Orleans, San Diego, Tampa Bay.
Total number of picks in draft: 254.

OTHER NOTEWORTHY PICKS

Round/Overall—Team, Player selected, Pos., College
2/33—New Orleans, Darren Howard, DE, Kansas State; 3/78—N.Y. Jets, Laveranues Coles, WR, Florida State; 3/80—Seattle, Darrell Jackson, WR, Florida; 5/142—Oakland, Shane Lechler, T, Texas A&M; 5/149—Green Bay, Kabeer Gbaja-Biamila, DE, San Diego State; 5/153—Kansas City, Dante Hall, RB, Texas A&M; 6/168—New Orleans, Marc Bulger, QB, West Virginia; 6/174—Chicago, Paul Edinger, K, Michigan State; 6/199—New England, Tom Brady, QB, Michigan.

2001
FIRST ROUND—NFL

No.	Team	Player selected	Pos.	College
1.	Atlanta	Michael Vick	QB	Virginia Tech
2.	Arizona	Leonard Davis	T	Texas
3.	Cleveland	Gerard Warren	DT	Florida
4.	Cincinnati	Justin Smith	DE	Missouri
5.	San Diego	LaDainian Tomlinson	RB	Texas Christian
6.	New England	Richard Seymour	DT	Georgia
7.	San Francisco	Andre Carter	DE	California
8.	Chicago	David Terrell	WR	Michigan
9.	Seattle	Koren Robinson	WR	North Carolina St.
10.	Green Bay	Jamal Reynolds	DE	Florida State
11.	Carolina	Dan Morgan	LB	Miami, Fla.
12.	St. Louis	Damione Lewis	DT	Miami, Fla.
13.	Jacksonville	Marcus Stroud	DT	Georgia
14.	Tampa Bay	Kenyatta Walker	T	Florida
15.	Washington	Rod Gardner	WR	Clemson
16.	N.Y. Jets	Santana Moss	WR	Miami, Fla.
17.	Seattle	Steve Hutchinson	G	Michigan
18.	Detroit	Jeff Backus	T	Michigan
19.	Pittsburgh	Casey Hampton	DT	Texas
20.	St. Louis	Adam Archuleta	DB	Arizona State
21.	Buffalo	Nate Clements	DB	Ohio State
22.	N.Y. Giants	Will Allen	DB	Syracuse
23.	New Orleans	Deuce McAllister	RB	Mississippi
24.	Denver	Willie Middlebrooks	DB	Minnesota
25.	Philadelphia	Freddie Mitchell	WR	UCLA
26.	Miami	Jamar Fletcher	DB	Wisconsin
27.	Minnesota	Michael Bennett	RB	Wisconsin
28.	Oakland	Derrick Gibson	DB	Florida State
29.	St. Louis	Ryan Pickett	DT	Ohio State

. Team	Player selected	Pos.	College
). Indianapolis	Reggie Wayne	WR	Miami, Fla.
I. Baltimore	Todd Heap	TE	Arizona State

Teams not selecting in first round: Dallas, Kansas City, nnessee.
Total number of picks in draft: 246.

OTHER NOTEWORTHY PICKS

und/Overall—Team, Player selected, Pos., College
32—San Diego, Drew Brees, QB, Purdue; 2/36—Cincinnati, ad Johnson, WR, Oregon State; 2/39—Pittsburgh, Kendrell ell, LB, Georgia; 2/52—Miami, Chris Chambers, WR, isconsin; 2/53—Dallas, Quincy Carter, QB, Georgia; 2/58— ffalo, Travis Henry, RB, Tennessee; 3/74—Carolina, Steve nith, WR, Utah; 3/80—San Francisco, Kevan Barlow, RB, tsburgh; 4/100—Cincinnati, Rudi Johnson, RB, Auburn; 106—Carolina, *Chris Weinke*, QB, Florida State;.

2002
FIRST ROUND—NFL

. Team	Player selected	Pos.	College
1. Houston	David Carr	QB	Fresno State
2. Carolina	Julius Peppers	DE	North Carolina
3. Detroit	Joey Harrington	QB	Oregon
4. Buffalo	Mike Williams	T	Texas
5. San Diego	Quentin Jammer	DB	Texas
6. Kansas City	Ryan Sims	DT	North Carolina
7. Minnesota	Bryant McKinnie	T	Miami, Fla.
8. Dallas	Roy Williams	DB	Oklahoma
9. Jacksonville	John Henderson	DT	Tennessee
0. Cincinnati	Levi Jones	T	Arizona State
1. Indianapolis	Dwight Freeney	DE	Syracuse
2. Arizona	Wendell Bryant	DT	Wisconsin
3. New Orleans	Donte' Stallworth	WR	Tennessee
4. N.Y. Giants	Jeremy Shockey	TE	Miami, Fla.
5. Tennessee	Albert Haynesworth	DT	Tennessee
6. Cleveland	William Green	RB	Boston College
7. Oakland	Phillip Buchanon	DB	Miami, Fla.
8. Atlanta	T.J. Duckett	RB	Michigan State
9. Denver	Ashley Lelie	WR	Hawaii
0. Green Bay	Javon Walker	WR	Florida State
1. New England	Daniel Graham	TE	Colorado
2. N.Y. Jets	Bryan Thomas	DE	Ala.-Birmingham
3. Oakland	Napoleon Harris	LB	Northwestern
4. Baltimore	Ed Reed	S	Miami, Fla.
5. New Orleans	Charles Grant	DE	Georgia
6. Philadelphia	Lito Sheppard	DB	Florida
7. San Francisco	Mike Rumph	DB	Miami, Fla.
8. Seattle	Jerramy Stevens	TE	Washington
9. Chicago	Marc Colombo	T	Boston College
0. Pittsburgh	Kendall Simmons	G	Auburn
1. St. Louis	Robert Thomas	LB	UCLA
2. Washington	Patrick Ramsey	QB	Tulane

Teams not selecting in first round: Miami, Tampa Bay.
Total number of picks in draft: 261.

OTHER NOTEWORTHY PICKS

ound/Overall—Team, Player selected, Pos., College
'36—Buffalo, Josh Reed, WR, Louisiana State; 2/51—Denver, inton Portis, RB, Miami, Fla.; 2/62—Pittsburgh, Antwaan Randle , WR, Indiana; 3/81—Arizona, Josh McCown, QB, Sam Houston tate; 3/91—Philadelphia, Brian Westbrook, RB, Villanova; 3/92— reen Bay, Marques Anderson, DB, UCLA; 3/95—St. Louis, *Eric rouch*, WR, Nebraska; 4/114—Miami, Randy McMichael, TE, eorgia.

2003
FIRST ROUND—NFL

. Team	Player selected	Pos.	College
1. Cincinnati	*Carson Palmer*	QB	USC
2. Detroit	Charles Rogers	WR	Michigan State
3. Houston	Andre Johnson	WR	Miami, Fla.
4. N.Y. Jets	Dwayne Robertson	DT	Kentucky
5. Dallas	Terence Newman	DB	Kansas State
6. New Orleans	Johnathan Sullivan	DT	Georgia
7. Jacksonville	Byron Leftwich	QB	Marshall
8. Carolina	Jordan Gross	T	Utah
9. Minnesota	Kevin Williams	DT	Oklahoma State
0. Baltimore	Terrell Suggs	DE	Arizona State
1. Seattle	Marcus Trufant	DB	Washington State

No. Team	Player selected	Pos.	College
12. St. Louis	Jimmy Kennedy	DT	Penn State
13. New England	Ty Warren	DT	Texas A&M
14. Chicago	Michael Haynes	DE	Penn State
15. Philadelphia	Jerome McDougle	DE	Miami, Fla.
16. Pittsburgh	Troy Polamalu	DB	USC
17. Arizona	Bryant Johnson	WR	Penn State
18. Arizona	Calvin Pace	DE	Wake Forest
19. Baltimore	Kyle Boller	QB	California
20. Denver	George Foster	T	Georgia
21. Cleveland	Jeff Faine	C	Notre Dame
22. Chicago	Rex Grossman	QB	Florida
23. Buffalo	Willis McGahee	RB	Miami, Fla.
24. Indianapolis	Dallas Clark	TE	Iowa
25. N.Y. Giants	William Joseph	DT	Miami, Fla.
26. San Francisco	Kwame Harris	T	Stanford
27. Kansas City	Larry Johnson	RB	Penn State
28. Tennessee	Andre Woolfolk	DB	Oklahoma
29. Green Bay	Nick Barnett	LB	Oregon State
30. San Diego	Sammy Davis	DB	Texas A&M
31. Oakland	Nnamdi Asomugha	DB	California
32. Oakland	Tyler Brayton	DE	Colorado

Teams not selecting in first round: Atlanta, Miami, Tampa Bay, Washington.
Total number of picks in draft: 262.

OTHER NOTEWORTHY PICKS

Round/Overall—Team, Player selected, Pos., College
2/54—Arizona, Anquan Boldin, WR, Florida State; 3/82—Carolina, Ricky Manning, CB, UCLA; 3/97—Tampa Bay, Chris Simms, QB, Texas; 4/101—Houston, Domanick Davis, RB, LSU; 4/105—Minnesota, Onterrio Smith, RB, Oregon; 6/192—Houston, Drew Henson, QB, Michigan; 7/241—San Francisco, Ken Dorsey, QB, Miami, Fla.

2004
FIRST ROUND—NFL

No. Team	Player selected	Pos.	College
1. San Diego*	Eli Manning	QB	Mississippi
2. Oakland	Robert Gallery	T	Iowa
3. Arizona	Larry Fitzgerald	WR	Pittsburgh
4. N.Y. Giants*	Philip Rivers	QB	N.C. State
5. Washington	Sean Taylor	S	Miami
6. Cleveland	Kellen Winslow	TE	Miami
7. Detroit	Roy Williams	WR	Texas
8. Atlanta	DeAngelo Hall	DB	Virginia Tech
9. Jacksonville	Reggie Williams	WR	Washington
10. Houston	Dunta Robinson	DB	South Carolina
11. Pittsburgh	Ben Roethlisberger	QB	Miami (Ohio)
12. N.Y. Jets	Jonathan Vilma	LB	Miami
13. Buffalo	Lee Evans	WR	Wisconsin
14. Chicago	Tommie Harris	DT	Oklahoma
15. Tampa Bay	Michael Clayton	WR	LSU
16. Philadelphia	Shawn Andrews	T	Arkansas
17. Denver	D.J. Williams	LB	Miami
18. New Orleans	Will Smith	DE	Ohio State
19. Miami	Vernon Carey	T	Miami
20. Minnesota	Kenechi Udeze	DE	USC
21. New England	Vince Wilfork	DT	Miami
22. Buffalo	J.P. Losman	QB	Tulane
23. Seattle	Marcus Tubbs	DT	Texas
24. St. Louis	Steven Jackson	RB	Oregon State
25. Green Bay	Ahmad Carroll	DB	Arkansas
26. Cincinnati	Chris Perry	RB	Michigan
27. Houston	Jason Babin	LB	Western Michigan
28. Carolina	Chris Gamble	DB	Ohio State
29. Atlanta	Michael Jenkins	WR	Ohio State
30. Detroit	Kevin Jones	RB	Virginia Tech
31. San Francisco	Rashaun Woods	WR	Oklahoma State
32. New England	Ben Watson	TE	Georgia

Teams not selecting in first round: Baltimore, Dallas, Indianapolis, Kansas City, Tennessee.
Total number of picks in draft: 255.
*New York traded the rights to Philip Rivers to San Diego for the rights to Eli Manning.

OTHER NOTEWORTHY PICKS

Round/Overall—Team, Player selected, Pos., College
2/33—Karlos Dansby, LB, Auburn; 2/43—Dallas, Julius Jones, RB, Notre Dame; 2/43—Seattle, Michael Boulware, LB, Florida State; 2/62—Carolina, Keary Colbert, WR, Southern California; 5/148—Chicago, Craig Krenzel, QB, Ohio State; 7/202—Arizona, John Navarre, QB, Michigan.

TEAM BY TEAM

ARIZONA CARDINALS
YEAR-BY-YEAR RECORDS

	REGULAR SEASON							PLAYOFFS			
Year	W	L	T	Pct.	PF	PA	Finish	W	L	Highest round	Coach
1920*	6	2	2	.750	...	...	T4th				Paddy Driscoll
1921*	3	3	2	.500	...	...	T8th				Paddy Driscoll
1922*	8	3	0	.727	...	...	3rd				Paddy Driscoll
1923*	8	4	0	.667	...	...	6th				Arnold Horween
1924*	5	4	1	.556	...	...	8th				Arnold Horween
1925*	11	2	1	.846	...	...	1st				Norman Barry
1926*	5	6	1	.455	...	...	10th				Norman Barry
1927*	3	7	1	.300	...	...	9th				Guy Chamberlin
1928*	1	5	0	.167	...	...	9th				Fred Gillies
1929*	6	6	1	.500	...	...	T4th				Dewey Scanlon
1930*	5	6	2	.455	...	...	T7th				Ernie Nevers
1931*	5	4	0	.556	...	...	4th				LeRoy Andrews, E. Nevers
1932*	2	6	2	.250	...	...	7th				Jack Chevigny
1933*	1	9	1	.100	52	101	5th/Western Div.	—	—		Paul Schissler
1934*	5	6	0	.455	80	84	4th/Western Div.	—	—		Paul Schissler
1935*	6	4	2	.600	99	97	T3rd/Western Div.	—	—		Milan Creighton
1936*	3	8	1	.273	74	143	4th/Western Div.	—	—		Milan Creighton
1937*	5	5	1	.500	135	165	4th/Western Div.	—	—		Milan Creighton
1938*	2	9	0	.182	111	168	5th/Western Div.	—	—		Milan Creighton
1939*	1	10	0	.091	84	254	5th/Western Div.	—	—		Ernie Nevers
1940*	2	7	2	.222	139	222	5th/Western Div.	—	—		Jimmy Conzelman
1941*	3	7	1	.300	127	197	4th/Western Div.	—	—		Jimmy Conzelman
1942*	3	8	0	.273	98	209	4th/Western Div.	—	—		Jimmy Conzelman
1943*	0	10	0	.000	95	238	4th/Western Div.	—	—		Phil Handler
1944†	0	10	0	.000	108	328	5th/Western Div.	—	—		P. Handler-Walt Kiesling
1945*	1	9	0	.100	98	228	5th/Western Div.	—	—		Phil Handler
1946*	6	5	0	.545	260	198	T3rd/Western Div.	—	—		Jimmy Conzelman
1947*	9	3	0	.750	306	231	1st/Western Div.	1	0	NFL champ	Jimmy Conzelman
1948*	11	1	0	.917	395	226	1st/Western Div.	0	1	NFL championship game	Jimmy Conzelman
1949*	6	5	1	.545	360	301	3rd/Western Div.	—	—		P. Handler-Buddy Parker
1950*	5	7	0	.417	233	287	5th/American Conf.	—	—		Curly Lambeau
1951*	3	9	0	.250	210	287	6th/American Conf.	—	—		Curly Lambeau
1952*	4	8	0	.333	172	221	T5th/American Conf.	—	—		P. Handler-Cecil Isbell, Joe Kuharich
1953*	1	10	1	.091	190	337	6th/Eastern Conf.	—	—		Joe Stydahar
1954*	2	10	0	.167	183	347	6th/Eastern Conf.	—	—		Joe Stydahar
1955*	4	7	1	.364	224	252	T4th/Eastern Conf.	—	—		Ray Richards
1956*	7	5	0	.583	240	182	2nd/Eastern Conf.	—	—		Ray Richards
1957*	3	9	0	.250	200	299	6th/Eastern Conf.	—	—		Ray Richards
1958*	2	9	1	.182	261	356	T5th/Eastern Conf.	—	—		Pop Ivy
1959*	2	10	0	.167	234	324	6th/Eastern Conf.	—	—		Pop Ivy
1960‡	6	5	1	.545	288	230	4th/Eastern Conf.	—	—		Pop Ivy
1961‡	7	7	0	.500	279	267	4th/Eastern Conf.	—	—		Pop Ivy
1962‡	4	9	1	.308	287	361	6th/Eastern Conf.	—	—		Wally Lemm
1963‡	9	5	0	.643	341	283	3rd/Eastern Conf.	—	—		Wally Lemm
1964‡	9	3	2	.750	357	331	2nd/Eastern Conf.	—	—		Wally Lemm
1965‡	5	9	0	.357	296	309	T5th/Eastern Conf.	—	—		Wally Lemm
1966‡	8	5	1	.615	264	265	4th/Eastern Conf.	—	—		Charley Winner
1967‡	6	7	1	.462	333	356	3rd/Century Div.	—	—		Charley Winner
1968‡	9	4	1	.692	325	289	2nd/Century Div.	—	—		Charley Winner
1969‡	4	9	1	.308	314	389	3rd/Century Div.	—	—		Charley Winner
1970‡	8	5	1	.615	325	228	3rd/NFC Eastern Div.	—	—		Charley Winner
1971‡	4	9	1	.308	231	279	4th/NFC Eastern Div.	—	—		Bob Hollway
1972‡	4	9	1	.308	193	303	4th/NFC Eastern Div.	—	—		Bob Hollway
1973‡	4	9	1	.308	286	365	4th/NFC Eastern Div.	—	—		Don Coryell
1974‡	10	4	0	.714	285	218	1st/NFC Eastern Div.	0	1	NFC div. playoff game	Don Coryell
1975‡	11	3	0	.786	356	276	1st/NFC Eastern Div.	0	1	NFC div. playoff game	Don Coryell
1976‡	10	4	0	.714	309	267	3rd/NFC Eastern Div.	—	—		Don Coryell
1977‡	7	7	0	.500	272	287	3rd/NFC Eastern Div.	—	—		Don Coryell
1978‡	6	10	0	.375	248	296	4th/NFC Eastern Div.	—	—		Bud Wilkinson
1979‡	5	11	0	.313	307	358	5th/NFC Eastern Div.	—	—		B. Wilkinson, Larry Wilson
1980‡	5	11	0	.313	299	350	4th/NFC Eastern Div.	—	—		Jim Hanifan
1981‡	7	9	0	.438	315	408	5th/NFC Eastern Div.	—	—		Jim Hanifan
1982‡	5	4	0	.556	135	170	6th/NFC	0	1	NFC first-round pl. game	Jim Hanifan
1983‡	8	7	1	.531	374	428	3rd/NFC Eastern Div.	—	—		Jim Hanifan
1984‡	9	7	0	.563	423	345	3rd/NFC Eastern Div.	—	—		Jim Hanifan
1985‡	5	11	0	.313	278	414	5th/NFC Eastern Div.	—	—		Jim Hanifan
1986‡	4	11	1	.281	218	351	5th/NFC Eastern Div.	—	—		Gene Stallings
1987‡	7	8	0	.467	362	368	3rd/NFC Eastern Div.	—	—		Gene Stallings

Year	W	L	T	Pct.	PF	PA	Finish	W	L	Highest round	Coach
1988§	7	9	0	.438	344	398	4th/NFC Eastern Div.	—	—		Gene Stallings
1989§	5	11	0	.313	258	377	4th/NFC Eastern Div.	—	—		G. Stallings, Hank Kuhlmann
1990§	5	11	0	.313	268	396	5th/NFC Eastern Div.	—	—		Joe Bugel
1991§	4	12	0	.250	196	344	5th/NFC Eastern Div.	—	—		Joe Bugel
1992§	4	12	0	.250	243	332	5th/NFC Eastern Div.	—	—		Joe Bugel
1993§	7	9	0	.438	326	269	4th/NFC Eastern Div.	—	—		Joe Bugel
1994	8	8	0	.500	235	267	3rd/NFC Eastern Div.	—	—		Buddy Ryan
1995	4	12	0	.250	275	422	5th/NFC Eastern Div.	—	—		Buddy Ryan
1996	7	9	0	.438	300	397	4th/NFC Eastern Div.	—	—		Vince Tobin
1997	4	12	0	.250	283	379	5th/NFC Eastern Div.	—	—		Vince Tobin
1998	9	7	0	.563	325	378	2nd/NFC Eastern Div.	1	1	NFC div. playoff game	Vince Tobin
1999	6	10	0	.375	245	382	4th/NFC Eastern Div.	—	—		Vince Tobin
2000	3	13	0	.188	210	443	5th/NFC Eastern Div.	—	—		V. Tobin, Dave McGinnis
2001	7	9	0	.438	295	343	4th/NFC Eastern Div.	—	—		Dave McGinnis
2002	5	11	0	.313	262	417	4th/NFC West Div.	—	—		Dave McGinnis
2003	4	12	0	.250	225	452	4th/NFC West Div.	—	—		Dave McGinnis
2004	6	10	0	.375	284	322	3rd/NFC West Div.	—	—		Dennis Green

*Chicago Cardinals.
†Card-Pitt, a combined squad of Chicago Cardinals and Pittsburgh Steelers.
‡St. Louis Cardinals.
§Phoenix Cardinals.

FIRST-ROUND DRAFT PICKS

1936—Jim Lawrence, B, Texas Christian
1937—Ray Buivid, B, Marquette
1938—Jack Robbins, B, Arkansas
1939—Charles Aldrich, C, Texas Christian*
1940—George Cafego, B, Tennessee*
1941—John Kimbrough, B, Texas A&M
1942—Steve Lach, B, Duke
1943—Glenn Dobbs, B, Tulsa
1944—Pat Harder, B, Wisconsin
1945—Charley Trippi, B, Georgia*
1946—Dub Jones, B, Tulane
1947—DeWitt (Tex) Coulter, T, Army
1948—Jim Spavital, B, Oklahoma State
1949—Bill Fischer, G, Notre Dame
1950—None
1951—Jerry Groom, C, Notre Dame
1952—Ollie Matson, B, San Francisco
1953—Johnny Olszewski, QB, California
1954—Lamar McHan, B, Arkansas
1955—Max Boydston, E, Oklahoma
1956—Joe Childress, B, Auburn
1957—Jerry Tubbs, C, Oklahoma
1958—King Hill, B, Rice*
　　　John David Crow, B, Texas A&M
1959—Billy Stacy, B, Mississippi State
1960—George Izo, QB, Notre Dame
1961—Ken Rice, T, Auburn
1962—Fate Echols, DT, Northwestern
　　　Irv Goode, C, Kentucky
1963—Jerry Stovall, B, Louisiana State
　　　Don Brumm, E, Purdue
1964—Ken Kortas, DT, Louisville
1965—Joe Namath, QB, Alabama
1966—Carl McAdams, LB, Oklahoma
1967—Dave Williams, WR, Washington
1968—MacArthur Lane, RB, Utah State
1969—Roger Wehrli, DB, Missouri
1970—Larry Stegent, RB, Texas A&M
1971—Norm Thompson, DB, Utah
1972—Bobby Moore, RB, Oregon

1973—Dave Butz, DT, Purdue
1974—J.V. Cain, TE, Colorado
1975—Tim Gray, DB, Texas A&M
1976—Mike Dawson, DT, Arizona
1977—Steve Pisarkiewicz, QB, Missouri
1978—Steve Little, K, Arkansas
　　　Ken Greene, DB, Washington St.
1979—Ottis Anderson, RB, Miami, Fla.
1980—Curtis Greer, DE, Michigan
1981—E.J. Junior, LB, Alabama
1982—Luis Sharpe, T, UCLA
1983—Leonard Smith, DB, McNeese State
1984—Clyde Duncan, WR, Tennessee
1985—Freddie Joe Nunn, LB, Mississippi
1986—Anthony Bell, LB, Michigan St.
1987—Kelly Stouffer, QB, Colorado St.
1988—Ken Harvey, LB, California
1989—Eric Hill, LB, Louisiana State
　　　Joe Wolf, G, Boston College
1990—None
1991—Eric Swann, DL, None
1992—None
1993—Garrison Hearst, RB, Georgia
　　　Ernest Dye, T, South Carolina
1994—Jamir Miller, LB, UCLA
1995—None
1996—Simeon Rice, DE, Illinois
1997—Tom Knight, DB, Iowa
1998—Andre Wadsworth, DE, Florida State
1999—David Boston, WR, Ohio State
　　　L.J. Shelton, T, Eastern Michigan
2000—Thomas Jones, RB, Virginia
2001—Leonard Davis, T, Texas
2002—Wendell Bryant, DT, Wisconsin
2003—Bryant Johnson, WR, Penn State
　　　Calvin Pace, DE, Wake Forest
2004—Larry Fitzgerald, WR, Pittsburgh
2005—Antrel Rolle, CB, Miami
　　　*First player chosen in draft.

HISTORY Team by team

FRANCHISE RECORDS

Most rushing yards, career
7,999—Ottis Anderson
Most rushing yards, season
1,605—Ottis Anderson, 1979
Most rushing yards, game
214—LeShon Johnson at N.O., Sept. 22, 1996

Most rushing touchdowns, season
14—John David Crow, 1962
Most passing attempts, season
560—Neil Lomax, 1984
Most passing attempts, game
61—Neil Lomax at S.D., Sept. 20, 1987
Most passes completed, season

345—Neil Lomax, 1984
Most passes completed, game
37—Neil Lomax at Was., Dec. 16, 1984
　Kent Graham vs. St.L., Sept. 29, 1996 (OT)
Most passing yards, career
34,639—Jim Hart

Most passing yards, season
4,614—Neil Lomax, 1984
Most passing yards, game
522—Boomer Esiason at Was., Nov. 10,
1996 (OT)
468—Neil Lomax at Was., Dec. 16, 1984
Most touchdown passes, season
28—Charley Johnson, 1963
Neil Lomax, 1984
Most pass receptions, career
535—Larry Centers
Most pass receptions, season
101—Larry Centers, 1995
Anquan Boldin, 2003

Most pass receptions, game
16—Sonny Randle at NYG, Nov. 4, 1962
Most receiving yards, career
8,497—Roy Green
Most receiving yards, season
1,598—David Boston, 2001
Most receiving yards, game
256—Sonny Randle vs. NYG, Nov. 4, 1962
Most receiving touchdowns, season
16—Sonny Randle, 1960
Most touchdowns, career
69—Roy Green
Most field goals, season
30—Greg Davis, 1995

Longest field goal
55 yards—Greg Davis at Sea., Dec. 19,
1993
Greg Davis at Det., Sept. 17,
1995
Most interceptions, career
52—Larry Wilson
Most interceptions, season
12—Bob Nussbaumer, 1949
Most sacks, career
66—Freddie Joe Nunn
Most sacks, season
16.5—Simeon Rice, 1999

SERIES RECORDS

Arizona vs.: Atlanta 13-9; Baltimore 1-2; Buffalo 3-5; Carolina 2-3; Chicago 26-54-6; Cincinnati 3-5; Cleveland 11-33-3; Dallas 28-5? 1; Denver 0-6-1; Detroit 21-30-5; Green Bay 22-41-4; Indianapolis 6-6; Jacksonville 0-1; Kansas City 2-6-1; Miami 1-8; Minnesota ? 8; New England 6-5; New Orleans 13-11; N.Y. Giants 41-77-2; N.Y. Jets 2-4; Oakland 2-4; Philadelphia 52-52-5; Pittsburgh 22-31-? St. Louis 22-26-2; San Diego 3-7; San Francisco 10-17; Seattle 7-5; Tampa Bay 8-7; Tennessee 4-3; Washington 44-70-2.
NOTE: Includes records for entire franchise, from 1920 to present; does not include records when team combined with Pittsburg squad and was known as Card-Pitt in 1944.

COACHING RECORDS

LeRoy Andrews, 0-1-0; Norman Barry, 16-8-2; Joe Bugel, 20-44-0; Guy Chamberlain, 3-7-1; Jack Chevigny, 2-6-2; Jimmy Conzelman, 34-31-3 (1-1); Don Coryell, 42-27-1 (0-2); Milan Creighton, 16-26-4; Paddy Driscoll, 17-8-4; Chuck Drulis-Ray Prochaska-Ray Willsey*, 2-0-0; Fred Gillies, 1-5-0; Dennis Green, 6-10; Phil Handler, 1-29-0; Phil Handler-Cecil Isbell*, 1-1-0; Phil Handler-Buddy Parker*, 2-4-0; Jim Hanifan, 39-49-1 (0-1); Bob Hollway, 8-18-2; Arnold Horween, 13-8-1; Frank Ivy, 17-29-2; Joe Kuharich, 4-8-0; Hank Kuhlmann, 0-5-0; Curly Lambeau, 7-15-0; Wally Lemm, 27-26-3; Dave McGinnis, 17-40-0; Ernie Nevers, 13-19-2; Buddy Parker, 4-1-1; Ray Richards, 14-21-1; Buddy Ryan, 12-20-0; Dewey Scanlon, 6-6-1; Paul Schissler, 6-15-1; Gene Stallings, 23-34-1; Joe Stydahar, 3-20-1; Vince Tobin, 28-43-0 (1-1); Bud Wilkinson, 9-20-0; Larry Wilson, 2-1-0; Charley Winner, 35-30-5.
NOTE: Playoff games in parentheses.
*Co-coaches.

RETIRED UNIFORM NUMBERS

No.	Player
8	Larry Wilson
40	Pat Tillman
77	Stan Mauldin
88	J.V. Cain
99	Marshall Goldberg

ATLANTA FALCONS
YEAR-BY-YEAR RECORDS

		REGULAR SEASON						PLAYOFFS		
Year	W	L	T	Pct.	PF	PA	Finish	W	L	Highest round	Coach
1966	3	11	0	.214	204	437	7th/Eastern Conf.	—	—		Norb Hecker
1967	1	12	1	.077	175	422	4th/Coastal Div.	—	—		Norb Hecker
1968	2	12	0	.143	170	389	4th/Coastal Div.	—	—		N. Hecker, N. Van Brockli
1969	6	8	0	.429	276	268	3rd/Coastal Div.	—	—		Norm Van Brocklin
1970	4	8	2	.333	206	261	3rd/NFC Western Div.	—	—		Norm Van Brocklin
1971	7	6	1	.538	274	277	3rd/NFC Western Div.	—	—		Norm Van Brocklin
1972	7	7	0	.500	269	274	2nd/NFC Western Div.	—	—		Norm Van Brocklin
1973	9	5	0	.643	318	224	2nd/NFC Western Div.	—	—		Norm Van Brocklin
1974	3	11	0	.214	111	271	4th/NFC Western Div.	—	—		N. Van Brocklin, M. Campbe
1975	4	10	0	.286	240	289	3rd/NFC Western Div.	—	—		Marion Campbell
1976	4	10	0	.286	172	312	3rd/NFC Western Div.	—	—		M. Campbell, Pat Pepple
1977	7	7	0	.500	179	129	2nd/NFC Western Div.	—	—		Leeman Bennett
1978	9	7	0	.563	240	290	2nd/NFC Western Div.	1	1	NFC div. playoff game	Leeman Bennett
1979	6	10	0	.375	300	388	3rd/NFC Western Div.	—	—		Leeman Bennett
1980	12	4	0	.750	405	272	1st/NFC Western Div.	0	1	NFC div. playoff game	Leeman Bennett
1981	7	9	0	.438	426	355	2nd/NFC Western Div.	—	—		Leeman Bennett
1982	5	4	0	.556	183	199	5th/NFC	0	1	NFC first-round pl. game	Leeman Bennett
1983	7	9	0	.438	370	389	4th/NFC Western Div.	—	—		Dan Henning
1984	4	12	0	.250	281	382	4th/NFC Western Div.	—	—		Dan Henning
1985	4	12	0	.250	282	452	4th/NFC Western Div.	—	—		Dan Henning
1986	7	8	1	.469	280	280	3rd/NFC Western Div.	—	—		Dan Henning
1987	3	12	0	.200	205	436	4th/NFC Western Div.	—	—		Marion Campbell
1988	5	11	0	.313	244	315	4th/NFC Western Div.	—	—		Marion Campbell
1989	3	13	0	.188	279	437	4th/NFC Western Div.	—	—		M. Campbell, Jim Hanifa
1990	5	11	0	.313	348	365	4th/NFC Western Div.	—	—		Jerry Glanville
1991	10	6	0	.625	361	338	2nd/NFC Western Div.	1	1	NFC div. playoff game	Jerry Glanville
1992	6	10	0	.375	327	414	3rd/NFC Western Div.	—	—		Jerry Glanville

				REGULAR SEASON				PLAYOFFS			
ar	W	L	T	Pct.	PF	PA	Finish	W	L	Highest round	Coach
993	6	10	0	.375	316	385	3rd/NFC Western Div.	—	—		Jerry Glanville
994	7	9	0	.438	317	385	3rd/NFC Western Div.	—	—		June Jones
995	9	7	0	.563	362	349	2nd/NFC Western Div.	0	1	NFC wild-card game	June Jones
996	3	13	0	.188	309	461	4th/NFC Western Div.	—	—		June Jones
997	7	9	0	.438	320	361	3rd/NFC Western Div.	—	—		Dan Reeves
998	14	2	0	.875	442	289	1st/NFC Western Div.	2	1	Super Bowl	Dan Reeves
999	5	11	0	.313	285	380	3rd/NFC Western Div.	—	—		Dan Reeves
000	4	12	0	.250	252	413	5th/NFC Western Div.	—	—		Dan Reeves
001	7	9	0	.438	291	377	4th/NFC Western Div.	—	—		Dan Reeves
002	9	6	1	.594	402	314	2nd/NFC South Div.	1	1	NFC div. playoff game	Dan Reeves
003	5	11	0	.313	299	422	4th/NFC South Div.	—	—		Dan Reeves, Wade Phillips
004	11	5	0	.688	340	337	1st/NFC South Div.	1	1	NFC championship game	Jim Mora Jr.

FIRST-ROUND DRAFT PICKS

966—Tommy Nobis, LB, Texas*
    Randy Johnson, QB, Texas A&I
967—None
968—Claude Humphrey, DE, Tennessee State
969—George Kunz, T, Notre Dame
970—John Small, LB, Citadel
971—Joe Profit, RB, Northeast Louisiana State
972—Clarence Ellis, DB, Notre Dame
973—None
974—None
975—Steve Bartkowski, QB, California*
976—Bubba Bean, RB, Texas A&M
977—Warren Bryant, T, Kentucky
    Wilson Faumuina, DT, San Jose State
978—Mike Kenn, T, Michigan
979—Don Smith, DE, Miami, Fla.
980—Junior Miller, TE, Nebraska
981—Bobby Butler, DB, Florida State
982—Gerald Riggs, RB, Arizona State
983—Mike Pitts, DE, Alabama
984—Rick Bryan, DT, Oklahoma
985—Bill Fralic, T, Pittsburgh
986—Tony Casillas, DT, Oklahoma
    Tim Green, LB, Syracuse

1987—Chris Miller, QB, Oregon
1988—Aundray Bruce, LB, Auburn*
1989—Deion Sanders, DB, Florida State
    Shawn Collins, WR, Northern Arizona
1990—Steve Broussard, RB, Washington State
1991—Bruce Pickens, CB, Nebraska
    Mike Pritchard, WR, Colorado
1992—Bob Whitfield, T, Stanford
    Tony Smith, RB, Southern Mississippi
1993—Lincoln Kennedy, T, Washington
1994—None
1995—Devin Bush, DB, Florida State
1996—None
1997—Michael Booker, DB, Nebraska
1998—Keith Brooking, LB, Georgia Tech
1999—Patrick Kerney, DE, Virginia
2000—None
2001—Michael Vick, QB, Virginia Tech*
2002—T.J. Duckett, FB, Michigan State
2003—None
2004—DeAngelo Hall, CB, Virginia Tech
    Michael Jenkins, WR, Ohio State
2005—Sharod "Roddy" White, WR, Alabama-Birmingham
    *First player chosen in draft.

FRANCHISE RECORDS

Most rushing yards, career
,631—Gerald Riggs
Most rushing yards, season
,846—Jamal Anderson, 1998
Most rushing yards, game
202—Gerald Riggs at N.O., Sept. 2, 1984
Most rushing touchdowns, season
14—Jamal Anderson, 1998
Most passing attempts, season
557—Jeff George, 1995
Most passing attempts, game
66—Chris Miller vs. Det., Dec. 24, 1989
Most passes completed, season
336—Jeff George, 1995
Most passes completed, game
37—Chris Miller vs. Det., Dec. 24, 1989
Most passing yards, career
23,470—Steve Bartkowski
Most passing yards, season
4,143—Jeff George, 1995

Most passing yards, game
431—Chris Chandler vs. Buf., Dec. 23, 2001
Most touchdown passes, season
31—Steve Bartkowski, 1980
Most pass receptions, career
573—Terance Mathis
Most pass receptions, season
111—Terance Mathis, 1994
Most pass receptions, game
15—William Andrews vs. Pit., Nov. 15, 1981
Most receiving yards, career
7,349—Terance Mathis
Most receiving yards, season
1,358—Alfred Jenkins, 1981
Most receiving yards, game
198—Terance Mathis at N.O., Dec. 13, 1998

Most receiving touchdowns, season
15—Andre Rison, 1993
Most touchdowns, career
57—Terance Mathis
Most field goals, season
32—Jay Feely, 2002
Longest field goal
59 yards—Morten Andersen vs. S.F., Dec. 24, 1995
Most interceptions, career
39—Rolland Lawrence
Most interceptions, season
10—Scott Case, 1988
Most sacks, career
94.5—Claude Humphrey
Most sacks, season
16—Joel Williams, 1980

SERIES RECORDS

Atlanta vs.: Arizona 9-13; Baltimore 1-1; Buffalo 4-4; Carolina 14-6; Chicago 10-11; Cincinnati 3-7; Cleveland 2-9; Dallas 7-12; Denver 4-7; Detroit 8-22; Green Bay 10-11; Houston 0-1; Indianapolis 1-12; Jacksonville 1-2; Kansas City 1-5; Miami 2-7; Minnesota 7-14; New England 6-4; New Orleans 41-30; N.Y. Giants 10-7; N.Y. Jets 4-4; Oakland 4-7; Philadelphia 9-11-1; Pittsburgh 1-11-1; St. Louis 24-46-2; San Diego 6-1; San Francisco 26-44-1; Seattle 2-7; Tampa Bay 10-13; Tennessee 5-6; Washington 4-14-1.

HISTORY — Team by team

COACHING RECORDS

Leeman Bennett, 46-41-0 (1-3); Marion Campbell, 17-51-0; Jerry Glanville, 27-37-0 (1-1); Jim Hanifan, 0-4-0; Norb Hecker, 4-26-1; Dan Henning, 22-41-1; June Jones, 19-29-0 (0-1); Jim Mora Jr., 11-5-0 (1-1); Pat Peppler, 3-6-0; Wade Phillips, 2-1-0; Dan Reeves, 49-59-1 (3-2); Norm Van Brocklin, 37-49-3.
NOTE: Playoff games in parentheses.

BALTIMORE RAVENS
YEAR-BY-YEAR RECORDS

	REGULAR SEASON							PLAYOFFS			
Year	W	L	T	Pct.	PF	PA	Finish	W	L	Highest round	Coach
1996	4	12	0	.250	371	441	5th/AFC Central Div.	—	—		Ted Marchibroda
1997	6	9	1	.406	326	345	5th/AFC Central Div.	—	—		Ted Marchibroda
1998	6	10	0	.375	269	335	4th/AFC Central Div.	—	—		Ted Marchibroda
1999	8	8	0	.500	324	277	3rd/AFC Central Div.	—	—		Brian Billick
2000	12	4	0	.750	333	165	2nd/AFC Central Div.	4	0	Super Bowl champ	Brian Billick
2001	10	6	0	.625	303	265	2nd/AFC Central Div.	1	1	AFC div. playoff game	Brian Billick
2002	7	9	0	.438	316	354	3rd/AFC North Div.	—	—		Brian Billick
2003	10	6	0	.625	391	281	1st/AFC North Div.	0	1	AFC wild-card game	Brian Billick
2004	9	7	0	.562	317	268	2nd/AFC North Div.	—	—		Brian Billick

FIRST-ROUND DRAFT PICKS

1996—Jonathan Ogden, T, UCLA
    Ray Lewis, LB, Miami, Fla.
1997—Peter Boulware, DE, Florida State
1998—Duane Starks, DB, Miami, Fla.
1999—Chris McAlister, DB, Arizona
2000—Jamal Lewis, RB, Tennessee
    Travis Taylor, WR, Florida

2001—Todd Heap, TE, Arizona State
2002—Ed Reed, S, Miami, Fla.
2003—Terrell Suggs, DE, Arizona State
    Kyle Boller, QB, California
2004—None
2005—Mark Clayton, WR, Oklahoma

FRANCHISE RECORDS

Most rushing yards, career
5,763—Jamal Lewis
Most rushing yards, season
2,066—Jamal Lewis, 2003
Most rushing yards, game
295—Jamal Lewis vs. Cle., Sept. 14, 2003
Most rushing touchdowns, season
14—Jamal Lewis, 2003
Most passing attempts, season
549—Vinny Testaverde, 1996
Most passing attempts, game
63—Elvis Grbac at Cin., Sept. 23, 2001
Most passes completed, season
325—Vinny Testaverde, 1996
Most passes completed, game
33—Elvis Grbac at Cin., Sept. 23, 2001
Most passing yards, career
7,148—Vinny Testaverde
Most passing yards, season
4,177—Vinny Testaverde, 1996

Most passing yards, game
429—Vinny Testaverde vs. St.L., Oct. 27, 1996 (OT)
366—Vinny Testaverde vs. Jac., Nov. 24, 1996 (OT)
353—Vinny Testaverde vs. N.E., Oct. 6, 1996
Most touchdown passes, season
33—Vinny Testaverde, 1996
Most pass receptions, career
204—Travis Taylor
Most pass receptions, season
76—Michael Jackson, 1996
Most pass receptions, game
13—Priest Holmes vs. Ten., Oct. 11, 1998
Most receiving yards, career
2,819—Qadry Ismail
Most receiving yards, season
1,201—Michael Jackson, 1996

Most receiving yards, game
258—Qadry Ismail at Pit., Dec. 12, 1999
Most receiving touchdowns, season
14—Michael Jackson, 1996
Most touchdowns, career
34—Jamal Lewis
Most field goals, season
35—Matt Stover, 2000
Longest field goal
56 yards—Wade Richey vs. Cle., Sept. 14, 2003
Most interceptions, career
21—Ed Reed
Most interceptions, season
9—Ed Reed, 2004
Most sacks, career
67.5—Peter Boulware
Most sacks, season
15—Peter Boulware, 2001

SERIES RECORDS

Baltimore vs.: Arizona 2-1; Atlanta 1-1; Buffalo 1-1; Carolina 0-2; Chicago 1-1; Cincinnati 12-6; Cleveland 8-4; Dallas 2-0; Denver 3-1; Detroit 1-0; Green Bay 0-2; Houston 1-0; Indianapolis 2-3; Jacksonville 6-8; Kansas City 0-3; Miami 1-4; Minnesota 1-1; New England 0-3; New Orleans 2-1; N.Y. Giants 2-0; N.Y. Jets 3-1; Oakland 2-1; Philadelphia, 0-1-1; Pittsburgh 6-12; St. Louis 1-2; San Diego 2-2; San Francisco 1-1; Seattle 2-0; Tampa Bay 0-2; Tennessee 7-6; Washington 2-1.

COACHING RECORDS

Brian Billick, 56-40-0 (5-2); Ted Marchibroda, 16-31-1.
NOTE: Playoff games in parentheses.

YEAR-BY-YEAR RECORDS

	REGULAR SEASON						PLAYOFFS			
Year	W	L	T	Pct.	PF	PA	Finish	W	L	Highest round	Coach
1960*	5	8	1	.385	296	303	3rd/Eastern Div.	—	—		Buster Ramsey
1961*	6	8	0	.429	294	342	4th/Eastern Div.	—	—		Buster Ramsey
1962*	7	6	1	.538	309	272	3rd/Eastern Div.	—	—		Lou Saban
1963*	7	6	1	.538	304	291	2nd/Eastern Div.	0	1	E. Div. championship game	Lou Saban
1964*	12	2	0	.857	400	242	1st/Eastern Div.	1	0	AFL champ	Lou Saban
1965*	10	3	1	.769	313	226	1st/Eastern Div.	1	0	AFL champ	Lou Saban
1966*	9	4	1	.692	358	255	1st/Eastern Div.	0	1	AFL championship game	Joe Collier
1967*	4	10	0	.286	237	285	T3rd/Eastern Div.	—	—		Joe Collier
1968*	1	12	1	.077	199	367	5th/Eastern Div.	—	—		J. Collier, H. Johnson
1969*	4	10	0	.286	230	359	T3rd/Eastern Div.	—	—		John Rauch
1970	3	10	1	.231	204	337	4th/AFC Eastern Div.	—	—		John Rauch
1971	1	13	0	.071	184	394	5th/AFC Eastern Div.	—	—		Harvey Johnson
1972	4	9	1	.321	257	377	4th/AFC Eastern Div.	—	—		Lou Saban
1973	9	5	0	.643	259	230	2nd/AFC Eastern Div.	—	—		Lou Saban
1974	9	5	0	.643	264	244	2nd/AFC Eastern Div.	0	1	AFC div. playoff game	Lou Saban
1975	8	6	0	.571	420	355	3rd/AFC Eastern Div.	—	—		Lou Saban
1976	2	12	0	.143	245	363	5th/AFC Eastern Div.	—	—		Lou Saban, Jim Ringo
1977	3	11	0	.214	160	313	5th/AFC Eastern Div.	—	—		Jim Ringo
1978	5	11	0	.313	302	354	4th/AFC Eastern Div.	—	—		Chuck Knox
1979	7	9	0	.438	268	279	4th/AFC Eastern Div.	—	—		Chuck Knox
1980	11	5	0	.688	320	260	1st/AFC Eastern Div.	0	1	AFC div. playoff game	Chuck Knox
1981	10	6	0	.625	311	276	3rd/AFC Eastern Div.	1	1	AFC div. playoff game	Chuck Knox
1982	4	5	0	.444	150	154	9th/AFC	—	—		Chuck Knox
1983	8	8	0	.500	283	351	3rd/AFC Eastern Div.	—	—		Kay Stephenson
1984	2	14	0	.125	250	454	5th/AFC Eastern Div.	—	—		Kay Stephenson
1985	2	14	0	.125	200	381	5th/AFC Eastern Div.	—	—		Kay Stephenson, Hank Bullough
1986	4	12	0	.250	287	348	4th/AFC Eastern Div.	—	—		H. Bullough, M. Levy
1987	7	8	0	.467	270	305	4th/AFC Eastern Div.	—	—		Marv Levy
1988	12	4	0	.750	329	237	1st/AFC Eastern Div.	1	1	AFC championship game	Marv Levy
1989	9	7	0	.563	409	317	1st/AFC Eastern Div.	0	1	AFC div. playoff game	Marv Levy
1990	13	3	0	.813	428	263	1st/AFC Eastern Div.	2	1	Super Bowl	Marv Levy
1991	13	3	0	.813	458	318	1st/AFC Eastern Div.	2	1	Super Bowl	Marv Levy
1992	11	5	0	.688	381	283	2nd/AFC Eastern Div.	3	1	Super Bowl	Marv Levy
1993	12	4	0	.750	329	242	1st/AFC Eastern Div.	2	1	Super Bowl	Marv Levy
1994	7	9	0	.438	340	356	4th/AFC Eastern Div.	—	—		Marv Levy
1995	10	6	0	.625	350	335	1st/AFC Eastern Div.	1	1	AFC div. playoff game	Marv Levy
1996	10	6	0	.625	319	266	2nd/AFC Eastern Div.	0	1	AFC wild-card game	Marv Levy
1997	6	10	0	.375	255	367	4th/AFC Eastern Div.	—	—		Marv Levy
1998	10	6	0	.625	400	333	3rd/AFC Eastern Div.	0	1	AFC wild-card game	Wade Phillips
1999	11	5	0	.688	320	229	2nd/AFC Eastern Div.	0	1	AFC wild-card game	Wade Phillips
2000	8	8	0	.500	315	350	4th/AFC Eastern Div.	—	—		Wade Phillips
2001	3	13	0	.188	265	420	5th/AFC Eastern Div.	—	—		Gregg Williams
2002	8	8	0	.500	379	397	4th/AFC East Div.	—	—		Gregg Williams
2003	6	10	0	.375	243	279	3rd/AFC East Div.	—	—		Gregg Williams
2004	9	7	0	.562	395	284	3rd/AFC East Div.	—	—		Mike Mularkey

*American Football League.

HISTORY *Team by team*

FIRST-ROUND DRAFT PICKS

1960—Richie Lucas, QB, Penn State
1961—Ken Rice, T, Auburn* (AFL)
1962—Ernie Davis, RB, Syracuse
1963—Dave Behrman, C, Michigan State
1964—Carl Eller, DE, Minnesota
1965—Jim Davidson, T, Ohio State
1966—Mike Dennis, RB, Mississippi
1967—John Pitts, DB, Arizona State
1968—Haven Moses, WR, San Diego St.
1969—O.J. Simpson, RB, Southern California*
1970—Al Cowlings, DE, Southern California
1971—J.D. Hill, WR, Arizona State
1972—Walt Patulski, DE, Notre Dame*
1973—Paul Seymour, T, Michigan
　　　Joe DeLamielleure, G, Michigan State
1974—Reuben Gant, TE, Oklahoma State
1975—Tom Ruud, LB, Nebraska
1976—Mario Clark, DB, Oregon
1977—Phil Dokes, DT, Oklahoma State
1978—Terry Miller, RB, Oklahoma State

1979—Tom Cousineau, LB, Ohio State*
　　　Jerry Butler, WR, Clemson
1980—Jim Ritcher, C, North Carolina State
1981—Booker Moore, RB, Penn State
1982—Perry Tuttle, WR, Clemson
1983—Tony Hunter, TE, Notre Dame
　　　Jim Kelly, QB, Miami, Fla.
1984—Greg Bell, RB, Notre Dame
1985—Bruce Smith, DE, Virginia Tech*
　　　Derrick Burroughs, DB, Memphis State
1986—Ronnie Harmon, RB, Iowa
　　　Will Wolford, T, Vanderbilt
1987—Shane Conlan, LB, Penn State
1988—None
1989—None
1990—James Williams, DB, Fresno State
1991—Henry Jones, S, Illinois
1992—John Fina, T, Arizona
1993—Thomas Smith, DB, North Carolina
1994—Jeff Burris, DB, Notre Dame

1995—Ruben Brown, G, Pittsburgh
1996—Eric Moulds, WR, Mississippi State
1997—Antowain Smith, RB, Houston
1998—None
1999—Antoine Winfield, DB, Ohio State
2000—Erik Flowers, DE, Arizona State
2001—Nate Clements, DB, Ohio State

2002—Mike Williams, T, Texas
2003—Willis McGahee, RB, Miami, Fla.
2004—Lee Evans, WR, Wisconsin
       J.P. Losman, QB, Tulane
2005—None
*First player chosen in draft.

FRANCHISE RECORDS

Most rushing yards, career
11,938—Thurman Thomas
Most rushing yards, season
2,003—O.J. Simpson, 1973
Most rushing yards, game
273—O.J. Simpson at Det., Nov. 25, 1976
Most rushing touchdowns, season
16—O.J. Simpson, 1975
Most pass attempts, season
610—Drew Bledsoe, 2002
Most passing attempts, game
55—Joe Ferguson at Mia., Oct. 9, 1983
Most passes completed, season
375—Drew Bledsoe, 2002
Most passes completed, game
38—Joe Ferguson at Mia., Oct. 9, 1983
Most passing yards, career
35,467—Jim Kelly
Most passing yards, season
4,359—Drew Bledsoe, 2002

Most passing yards, game
463—Drew Bledsoe at Min., Sept. 15, 2002 (OT)
419—Joe Ferguson at Mia., Oct. 9, 1983 (OT)
403—Jim Kelly at S.F., Sept. 13, 1992
Most touchdown passes, season
33—Jim Kelly, 1991
Most pass receptions, career
941—Andre Reed
Most pass receptions, season
100—Eric Moulds, 2002
Most pass receptions, game
15—Andre Reed vs. G.B., Nov. 20, 1994
Most receiving yards, career
13,095—Andre Reed
Most receiving yards, season
1,368—Eric Moulds, 1998
Most receiving yards, game
255—Jerry Butler vs. NYJ, Sept. 23, 1979

Most receiving touchdowns, season
11—Bill Brooks, 1995
Most touchdowns, career
87—Andre Reed
     Thurman Thomas
Most field goals, season
33—Steve Christie, 1998
Longest field goal
59 yards—Steve Christie vs. Mia., Sept. 26, 1993
Most interceptions, career
40—George Byrd
Most interceptions, season
10—Billy Atkins, 1961
     Tom Janik, 1967
Most sacks, career
171—Bruce Smith
Most sacks, season
19—Bruce Smith, 1990

SERIES RECORDS

Buffalo vs.: Arizona 5-3; Atlanta 4-4; Baltimore 1-1; Carolina 3-0; Chicago 4-5; Cincinnati 12-9; Cleveland 5-7; Dallas 3-4; Denver 17-13-1; Detroit 3-3-1; Green Bay 6-3; Houston 1-1; Indianapolis 34-29-1; Jacksonville 3-2; Kansas City 18-16-1; Miami 29-48-1; Minnesota 3-7; New England 40-48-1; New Orleans 4-3; N.Y. Giants 6-3; N.Y. Jets 48-40; Oakland 15-18; Philadelphia 5-5; Pittsburgh 8-10; St. Louis 5-4; San Diego 9-18-2; San Francisco 5-4; Seattle 4-6; Tampa Bay 2-5; Tennessee 14-23; Washington 6-4.

COACHING RECORDS

Hank Bullough, 4-17-0; Joe Collier, 13-16-1 (0-1); Harvey Johnson, 2-23-1; Chuck Knox, 37-36-0 (1-2); Marv Levy, 112-70-0 (11-8); Mike Mularkey, 9-7-0; Wade Phillips, 29-19-0 (0-2); Buster Ramsey, 11-16-1; John Rauch, 7-20-1; Jim Ringo, 3-20-0; Lou Saban, 68-45-4 (2-2); Kay Stephenson, 10-26-0; Gregg Williams, 17-31-0. NOTE: Playoff games in parentheses.

RETIRED UNIFORM NUMBERS

No.	Player
12	Jim Kelly

CAROLINA PANTHERS
YEAR-BY-YEAR RECORDS

	REGULAR SEASON						PLAYOFFS			
Year	W	L	T	Pct.	PF	PA	Finish	W	L	Highest round	Coach
1995	7	9	0	.438	289	325	4th/NFC Western Div.	—	—		Dom Capers
1996	12	4	0	.750	367	218	1st/NFC Western Div.	1	1	NFC championship game	Dom Capers
1997	7	9	0	.438	265	314	2nd/NFC Western Div.	—	—		Dom Capers
1998	4	12	0	.250	336	413	4th/NFC Western Div.	—	—		Dom Capers
1999	8	8	0	.500	421	381	2nd/NFC Western Div.	—	—		George Seifert
2000	7	9	0	.438	310	310	3rd/NFC Western Div.	—	—		George Seifert
2001	1	15	0	.063	253	410	5th/NFC Western Div.	—	—		George Seifert
2002	7	9	0	.438	258	302	4th/NFC South Div.	—	—		John Fox
2003	11	5	0	.688	325	304	1st/NFC South Div.	3	1	Super Bowl	John Fox
2004	7	9	0	.438	355	339	3rd/NFC South Div.	—	—		John Fox

FIRST-ROUND DRAFT PICKS

1995—Kerry Collins, QB, Penn State
     Tyrone Poole, DB, Fort Valley (Ga.) St.
     Blake Brockermeyer, T, Texas
1996—Tim Biakabutuka, RB, Michigan
1997—Rae Carruth, WR, Colorado
1998—Jason Peter, DT, Nebraska
1999—None

2000—Rashard Anderson, DB, Jackson State
2001—Dan Morgan, LB, Miami, Fla.
2002—Julius Peppers, DE, North Carolina
2003—Jordan Gross, T, Utah
2004—Chris Gamble, CB, Ohio State
2005—Thomas Davis, FS, Georgia

Most rushing yards, career
2,530—Tim Biakabatuka
Most rushing yards, season
1,444—Stephen Davis, 2003
Most rushing yards, game
178—Stephen Davis at. N.O., Oct. 26, 2003
Most rushing touchdowns, season
8—Stephen Davis, 2003
Most passing attempts, season
571—Steve Beuerlein, 1999
Most passing attempts, game
63—Chris Weinke vs. Ari., Dec. 30, 2001
Most passes completed, season
343—Steve Beuerlein, 1999
Most passes completed, game
36—Chris Weinke vs. Ari., Dec. 30, 2001
Most passing yards, career
12,690—Steve Beuerlein

Most passing yards, season
4,436—Steve Beuerlein, 1999
Most passing yards, game
373—Steve Beuerlein at Green Bay, Dec. 12, 1999
Most touchdown passes, season
36—Steve Beuerlein, 1999
Most pass receptions, career
578—Muhsin Muhammad
Most pass receptions, season
102—Muhsin Muhammad, 2000
Most pass receptions, game
11—Muhsin Muhammad vs. S.F., Dec. 18, 1999
Muhsin Muhammad vs. G.B., Nov. 27, 2000
Most receiving yards, career
7,751—Muhsin Muhammad
Most receiving yards, season
1,405—Muhsin Muhammad, 2004

Most receiving yards, game
192—Muhsin Muhammad at N.O., Sept. 13, 1998
Most receiving touchdowns, season
16—Muhsin Muhammad, 2004
Most touchdowns, career
44—Muhsin Muhammad
Wesley Walls
Most field goals, season
37—John Kasay, 1996
Longest field goal
56 yards—John Kasay vs. G.B., Sept. 27, 1998
Most interceptions, career
25—Eric Davis
Most interceptions, season
8—Doug Evans, 2001
Most sacks, career
41.5—Kevin Greene
Most sacks, season
15—Kevin Greene, 1998

SERIES RECORDS

Carolina vs.: Arizona 3-2; Atlanta 6-14; Baltimore 2-0; Buffalo 0-3; Chicago 1-1; Cincinnati 2-0; Cleveland 2-0; Dallas 1-4; Denver 0-2; Detroit 2-1; Green Bay 2-5; Houston 0-1; Indianapolis 3-0; Jacksonville 1-2; Kansas City 1-2; Miami 0-2; Minnesota 2-3; New England 2-0; New Orleans 10-10; N.Y. Giants 2-0; N.Y. Jets 1-2; Oakland 1-2; Philadelphia 1-3; Pittsburgh 1-2; St. Louis 8-7; San Diego 2-1; San Francisco 8-7; Seattle 1-1; Tampa Bay 5-4; Tennessee 1-1; Washington 1-6.

COACHING RECORDS

Dom Capers, 30-34-0 (1-1); John Fox, 25-23-0 (3-1); George Seifert, 16-32-0.
NOTE: Playoff games in parentheses.

RETIRED UNIFORM NUMBERS

No.   Player
None

HISTORY Team by team

CHICAGO BEARS
YEAR-BY-YEAR RECORDS

			REGULAR SEASON						PLAYOFFS		
Year	W	L	T	Pct.	PF	PA	Finish	W	L	Highest round	Coach
1920*	10	1	2	.909	...	...	2nd				George Halas
1921†	9	1	1	.900	...	...	1st				George Halas
1922	9	3	0	.750	...	...	2nd				George Halas
1923	9	2	1	.818	...	...	2nd				George Halas
1924	6	1	4	.857	...	...	2nd				George Halas
1925	9	5	3	.643	...	...	7th				George Halas
1926	12	1	3	.923	...	...	2nd				George Halas
1927	9	3	2	.750	...	...	3rd				George Halas
1928	7	5	1	.583	...	...	5th				George Halas
1929	4	9	2	.308	...	...	9th				George Halas
1930	9	4	1	.692	...	...	3rd				Ralph Jones
1931	8	5	0	.615	...	...	3rd				Ralph Jones
1932	7	1	6	.875	...	...	1st				Ralph Jones
1933	10	2	1	.833	133	82	1st/Western Div.	1	0	NFL champ	George Halas
1934	13	0	0	1.000	286	86	1st/Western Div.	0	1	NFL championship game	George Halas
1935	6	4	2	.600	192	106	T3rd/Western Div.	—	—		George Halas
1936	9	3	0	.750	222	94	2nd/Western Div.	—	—		George Halas
1937	9	1	1	.900	201	100	1st/Western Div.	0	1	NFL championship game	George Halas
1938	6	5	0	.545	194	148	3rd/Western Div.	—	—		George Halas
1939	8	3	0	.727	298	157	2nd/Western Div.	—	—		George Halas
1940	8	3	0	.727	238	152	1st/Western Div.	1	0	NFL champ	George Halas
1941	10	1	0	.909	396	147	1st/Western Div.	2	0	NFL champ	George Halas
1942	11	0	0	1.000	376	84	1st/Western Div.	0	1	NFL championship game	George Halas, Hunk Anderson-Luke Johnsos
1943	8	1	1	.889	303	157	1st/Western Div.	1	0	NFL champ	H. Anderson-L. Johnsos
1944	6	3	1	.667	258	172	T2nd/Western Div.	—	—		H. Anderson-L. Johnsos
1945	3	7	0	.300	192	235	4th/Western Div.	—	—		H. Anderson-L. Johnsos
1946	8	2	1	.800	289	193	1st/Western Div.	1	0	NFL champ	George Halas

						REGULAR SEASON			PLAYOFFS	
Year	W	L	T	Pct.	PF	PA	Finish	W	L	Highest round	Coach
1947	8	4	0	.667	363	241	2nd/Western Div.	—	—		George Halas
1948	10	2	0	.833	375	151	2nd/Western Div.	—	—		George Halas
1949	9	3	0	.750	332	218	2nd/Western Div.	—	—		George Halas
1950	9	3	0	.750	279	207	2nd/National Conf.	0	1	Nat. Conf. champ. game	George Halas
1951	7	5	0	.583	286	282	4th/National Conf.	—	—		George Halas
1952	5	7	0	.417	245	326	5th/National Conf.	—	—		George Halas
1953	3	8	1	.273	218	262	T4th/Western Conf.	—	—		George Halas
1954	8	4	0	.667	301	279	2nd/Western Conf.	—	—		George Halas
1955	8	4	0	.667	294	251	2nd/Western Conf.	—	—		George Halas
1956	9	2	1	.818	363	246	1st/Western Conf.	0	1	NFL championship game	Paddy Driscoll
1957	5	7	0	.417	203	211	5th/Western Conf.	—	—		Paddy Driscoll
1958	8	4	0	.667	298	230	T2nd/Western Conf.	—	—		George Halas
1959	8	4	0	.667	252	196	2nd/Western Conf.	—	—		George Halas
1960	5	6	1	.455	194	299	5th/Western Conf.	—	—		George Halas
1961	8	6	0	.571	326	302	T3rd/Western Conf.	—	—		George Halas
1962	9	5	0	.643	321	287	3rd/Western Conf.	—	—		George Halas
1963	11	1	2	.917	301	144	1st/Western Conf.	1	0	NFL champ	George Halas
1964	5	9	0	.357	260	379	6th/Western Conf.	—	—		George Halas
1965	9	5	0	.643	409	275	3rd/Western Conf.	—	—		George Halas
1966	5	7	2	.417	234	272	5th/Western Conf.	—	—		George Halas
1967	7	6	1	.538	239	218	2nd/Central Div.	—	—		George Halas
1968	7	7	0	.500	250	333	2nd/Central Div.	—	—		Jim Dooley
1969	1	13	0	.071	210	339	4th/Central Div.	—	—		Jim Dooley
1970	6	8	0	.429	256	261	3rd/NFC Central Div.	—	—		Jim Dooley
1971	6	8	0	.429	185	276	3rd/NFC Central Div.	—	—		Jim Dooley
1972	4	9	1	.321	225	275	4th/NFC Central Div.	—	—		Abe Gibron
1973	3	11	0	.214	195	334	4th/NFC Central Div.	—	—		Abe Gibron
1974	4	10	0	.286	152	279	4th/NFC Central Div.	—	—		Abe Gibron
1975	4	10	0	.286	191	379	3rd/NFC Central Div.	—	—		Jack Pardee
1976	7	7	0	.500	253	216	2nd/NFC Central Div.	—	—		Jack Pardee
1977	9	5	0	.643	255	253	2nd/NFC Central Div.	0	1	NFC div. playoff game	Jack Pardee
1978	7	9	0	.438	253	274	4th/NFC Central Div.	—	—		Neill Armstrong
1979	10	6	0	.625	306	249	2nd/NFC Central Div.	0	1	NFC wild-card game	Neill Armstrong
1980	7	9	0	.438	304	264	3rd/NFC Central Div.	—	—		Neill Armstrong
1981	6	10	0	.375	253	324	5th/NFC Central Div.	—	—		Neill Armstrong
1982	3	6	0	.333	141	174	12th/NFC	—	—		Mike Ditka
1983	8	8	0	.500	311	301	3rd/NFC Central Div.	—	—		Mike Ditka
1984	10	6	0	.625	325	248	1st/NFC Central Div.	1	1	NFC championship game	Mike Ditka
1985	15	1	0	.938	456	198	1st/NFC Central Div.	3	0	Super Bowl champ	Mike Ditka
1986	14	2	0	.875	352	187	1st/NFC Central Div.	0	1	NFC div. playoff game	Mike Ditka
1987	11	4	0	.733	356	282	1st/NFC Central Div.	0	1	NFC div. playoff game	Mike Ditka
1988	12	4	0	.750	312	215	1st/NFC Central Div.	1	1	NFC championship game	Mike Ditka
1989	6	10	0	.375	358	377	4th/NFC Central Div.	—	—		Mike Ditka
1990	11	5	0	.688	348	280	1st/NFC Central Div.	1	1	NFC div. playoff game	Mike Ditka
1991	11	5	0	.688	299	269	2nd/NFC Central Div.	0	1	NFC wild-card game	Mike Ditka
1992	5	11	0	.313	295	361	4th/NFC Central Div.	—	—		Mike Ditka
1993	7	9	0	.438	234	230	4th/NFC Central Div.	—	—		Dave Wannstedt
1994	9	7	0	.563	271	307	4th/NFC Central Div.	1	1	NFC div. playoff game	Dave Wannstedt
1995	9	7	0	.563	392	360	3rd/NFC Central Div.	—	—		Dave Wannstedt
1996	7	9	0	.438	283	305	3rd/NFC Central Div.	—	—		Dave Wannstedt
1997	4	12	0	.250	263	421	5th/NFC Central Div.	—	—		Dave Wannstedt
1998	4	12	0	.250	276	368	5th/NFC Central Div.	—	—		Dave Wannstedt
1999	6	10	0	.375	272	341	5th NFC Central Div.	—	—		Dick Jauron
2000	5	11	0	.313	216	355	5th/NFC Central Div.	—	—		Dick Jauron
2001	13	3	0	.813	338	203	1st/NFC Central Div.	0	1	NFC div. playoff game	Dick Jauron
2002	4	12	0	.250	281	379	3rd/NFC North Div.	—	—		Dick Jauron
2003	7	9	0	.438	283	346	3rd/NFC North Div.	—	—		Dick Jauron
2004	5	11	0	.312	231	331	4th/NFC North Div.	—	—		Lovie Smith

*Decatur Staleys.
†Chicago Staleys.

FIRST-ROUND DRAFT PICKS

1936—Joe Stydahar, T, West Virginia
1937—Les McDonald, E, Nebraska
1938—Joe Gray, B, Oregon State
1939—Sid Luckman, QB, Columbia
       Bill Osmanski, B, Holy Cross
1940—C. Turner, C, Hardin-Simmons
1941—Tom Harmon, B, Michigan*
       Norm Standlee, B, Stanford
       Don Scott, B, Ohio State

1942—Frankie Albert, B, Stanford
1943—Bob Steuber, B, Missouri
1944—Ray Evans, B, Kansas
1945—Don Lund, B, Michigan
1946—Johnny Lujack, QB, Notre Dame
1947—Bob Fenimore, B, Oklahoma State*
       Don Kindt, B, Wisconsin
1948—Bobby Layne, QB, Texas
       Max Bumgardner, E, Texas

949—Dick Harris, C, Texas
950—Chuck Hunsinger, B, Florida
951—Bob Williams, B, Notre Dame
　　　Billy Stone, B, Bradley
　　　Gene Schroeder, E, Virginia
952—Jim Dooley, B, Miami
953—Billy Anderson, B, Compton (Ca.) J.C.
954—Stan Wallace, B, Illinois
955—Ron Drzewiecki, B, Marquette
956—Menan (Tex) Schriewer, E, Texas
957—Earl Leggett, DT, Louisiana State
958—Chuck Howley, G, West Virginia
959—Don Clark, B, Ohio State
960—Roger Davis, G, Syracuse
961—Mike Ditka, E, Pittsburgh
962—Ron Bull, RB, Baylor
963—Dave Behrman, C, Michigan State
1964—Dick Evey, DT, Tennessee
965—Dick Butkus, LB, Illinois
　　　Gale Sayers, RB, Kansas
　　　Steve DeLong, DE, Tennessee
1966—George Rice, DT, Louisiana State
1967—Loyd Phillips, DE, Arkansas
1968—Mike Hull, RB, Southern California
1969—Rufus Mayes, T, Ohio State
1970—None
1971—Joe Moore, RB, Missouri
1972—Lionel Antoine, T, Southern Illinois
　　　Craig Clemons, DB, Iowa
1973—Wally Chambers, DE, Eastern Kentucky
1974—Waymond Bryant, LB, Tennessee State
　　　Dave Gallagher, DE, Michigan
1975—Walter Payton, RB, Jackson State
1976—Dennis Lick, T, Wisconsin
1977—Ted Albrecht, T, California

1978—None
1979—Dan Hampton, DT, Arkansas
　　　Al Harris, DE, Arizona State
1980—Otis Wilson, LB, Louisville
1981—Keith Van Horne, T, Southern California
1982—Jim McMahon, QB, Brigham Young
1983—Jimbo Covert, T, Pittsburgh
　　　Willie Gault, WR, Tennessee
1984—Wilber Marshall, LB, Florida
1985—William Perry, DT, Clemson
1986—Neal Anderson, RB, Florida
1987—Jim Harbaugh, QB, Michigan
1988—Brad Muster, RB, Stanford
　　　Wendell Davis, WR, Louisiana State
1989—Donnell Woolford, DB, Clemson
　　　Trace Armstrong, DE, Florida
1990—Mark Carrier, DB, Southern California
1991—Stan Thomas, T, Texas
1992—Alonzo Spellman, DE, Ohio State
1993—Curtis Conway, WR, Southern California
1994—John Thierry, LB, Alcorn State
1995—Rashaan Salaam, RB, Colorado
1996—Walt Harris, DB, Mississippi State
1997—None
1998—Curtis Enis, RB, Penn State
1999—Cade McNown, QB, UCLA
2000—Brian Urlacher, LB, New Mexico
2001—David Terrell, WR, Michigan
2002—Marc Colombo, T, Boston College
2003—Michael Haynes, DE, Penn State
　　　Rex Grossman, QB, Florida
2004—Tommie Harris, DT, Oklahoma
2005—Cedric Benson, RB, Texas
*First player chosen in draft.

FRANCHISE RECORDS

Most rushing yards, career
16,726—Walter Payton
Most rushing yards, season
1,852—Walter Payton, 1977
Most rushing yards, game
275—Walter Payton vs. Min., Nov. 20, 1977
Most rushing touchdowns, season
14—Gale Sayers, 1965
　　　Walter Payton, 1977
　　　Walter Payton, 1979
Most passing attempts, season
522—Erik Kramer, 1995
Most passing attempts, game
60—Erik Kramer vs. NYJ, Nov. 16, 1997
Most passes completed, season
315—Erik Kramer, 1995
Most passes completed, game
34—Jim Miller vs. Min., Nov. 14, 1999 (OT)
33—Bill Wade at Was., Oct. 25, 1964

Most passing yards, career
14,686—Sid Luckman
Most passing yards, season
3,838—Erik Kramer, 1995
Most passing yards, game
468—Johnny Lujack vs. Chi. Cards, Dec. 11, 1949
Most touchdown passes, season
29—Erik Kramer, 1995
Most pass receptions, career
492—Walter Payton
Most pass receptions, season
100—Marty Booker, 2001
Most pass receptions, game
14—Jim Keane at NYG, Oct. 23, 1949
Most receiving yards, career
5,059—Johnny Morris
Most receiving yards, season
1,400—Marcus Robinson, 1999
Most receiving yards, game
214—Harlon Hill at S.F., Oct. 31, 1954

Most receiving touchdowns, season
13—Ken Kavanaugh, 1947
　　　Dick Gordon, 1970
Most touchdowns, career
125—Walter Payton
Most field goals, season
31—Kevin Butler, 1985
Longest field goal
55 yards—Bob Thomas at L.A. Rams, Nov. 23, 1975
　　　Kevin Butler vs. Min., Oct. 25, 1993
　　　Kevin Butler at T.B., Dec. 12, 1993
Most interceptions, career
38—Gary Fencik
Most interceptions, season
10—Mark Carrier, 1990
Most sacks, career
124.5—Richard Dent
Most sacks, season
17.5—Richard Dent, 1984

SERIES RECORDS

Chicago vs.: Arizona 54-26-6; Atlanta 11-10; Baltimore 1-1; Buffalo 5-4; Carolina 1-1; Cincinnati 3-4; Cleveland 4-8; Dallas 8-10; Denver 6-6; Detroit 83-62-5; Green Bay 84-78-6; Houston 0-1; Indianapolis 17-22; Jacksonville 2-2; Kansas City 5-4; Miami 3-6; Minnesota 38-47-2; New England 3-6; New Orleans 10-11; N.Y. Giants 26-17-2; N.Y. Jets 5-3; Oakland 5-6; Philadelphia 24-8-1; Pittsburgh 16-6-1; St. Louis 47-34-3; San Diego 5-4; San Francisco 27-27-1; Seattle 2-6; Tampa Bay 33-17; Tennessee 5-4; Washington 20-16-1. NOTE: Includes records as Decatur Staleys in 1920 and Chicago Staleys in 1921.

COACHING RECORDS

Hunk Anderson-Luke Johnsos*, 23-11-2 (1-1); Neill Armstrong, 30-34-0 (0-1); Mike Ditka, 106-62-0 (6-6); Jim Dooley, 20-36-0; Paddy Driscoll, 14-9-1 (0-1); Abe Gibron, 11-30-1; George Halas, 318-148-31 (6-3); Dick Jauron, 35-45-0 (0-1); Ralph Jones, 24-10-7; Jack Pardee, 20-22-0 (0-1); Lovie Smith, 5-11-0; Dave Wannstedt, 40-56-0 (1-1).
NOTE: Playoff games in parentheses.
*Co-coaches.

RETIRED UNIFORM NUMBERS

No.	Player	No.	Player
3	Bronko Nagurski	42	Sid Luckman
5	George McAfee	51	Dick Butkus
7	George Halas	56	Bill Hewitt
28	Willie Galimore	61	Bill George
34	Walter Payton	66	Bulldog Turner
40	Gale Sayers	77	Red Grange
41	Brian Piccolo		

CINCINNATI BENGALS
YEAR-BY-YEAR RECORDS

		REGULAR SEASON							PLAYOFFS		
Year	W	L	T	Pct.	PF	PA	Finish	W	L	Highest round	Coach
1968*	3	11	0	.214	215	329	5th/Western Div.	—	—		Paul Brown
1969*	4	9	1	.308	280	367	5th/Western Div.	—	—		Paul Brown
1970	8	6	0	.571	312	255	1st/AFC Central Div.	0	1	AFC div. playoff game	Paul Brown
1971	4	10	0	.286	284	265	4th/AFC Central Div.	—	—		Paul Brown
1972	8	6	0	.571	299	229	3rd/AFC Central Div.	—	—		Paul Brown
1973	10	4	0	.714	286	231	1st/AFC Central Div.	0	1	AFC div. playoff game	Paul Brown
1974	7	7	0	.500	283	259	2nd/AFC Central Div.	—	—		Paul Brown
1975	11	3	0	.786	340	246	2nd/AFC Central Div.	0	1	AFC div. playoff game	Paul Brown
1976	10	4	0	.714	335	210	2nd/AFC Central Div.	—	—		Bill Johnson
1977	8	6	0	.571	238	235	3rd/AFC Central Div.	—	—		Bill Johnson
1978	4	12	0	.250	252	284	4th/AFC Central Div.	—	—		B. Johnson, H. Rice
1979	4	12	0	.250	337	421	4th/AFC Central Div.	—	—		Homer Rice
1980	6	10	0	.375	244	312	4th/AFC Central Div.	—	—		Forrest Gregg
1981	12	4	0	.750	421	304	1st/AFC Central Div.	2	1	Super Bowl	Forrest Gregg
1982	7	2	0	.778	232	177	3rd/AFC	0	1	AFC first-round pl. game	Forrest Gregg
1983	7	9	0	.438	346	302	3rd/AFC Central Div.	—	—		Forrest Gregg
1984	8	8	0	.500	339	339	2nd/AFC Central Div.	—	—		Sam Wyche
1985	7	9	0	.438	441	437	2nd/AFC Central Div.	—	—		Sam Wyche
1986	10	6	0	.625	409	394	2nd/AFC Central Div.	—	—		Sam Wyche
1987	4	11	0	.267	285	370	4th/AFC Central Div.	—	—		Sam Wyche
1988	12	4	0	.750	448	329	1st/AFC Central Div.	2	1	Super Bowl	Sam Wyche
1989	8	8	0	.500	404	285	4th/AFC Central Div.	—	—		Sam Wyche
1990	9	7	0	.563	360	352	1st/AFC Central Div.	1	1	AFC div. playoff game	Sam Wyche
1991	3	13	0	.188	263	435	4th/AFC Central Div.	—	—		Sam Wyche
1992	5	11	0	.313	274	364	4th/AFC Central Div.	—	—		David Shula
1993	3	13	0	.188	187	319	4th/AFC Central Div.	—	—		David Shula
1994	3	13	0	.188	276	406	3rd/AFC Central Div.	—	—		David Shula
1995	7	9	0	.438	349	374	2nd/AFC Central Div.	—	—		David Shula
1996	8	8	0	.500	372	369	3rd/AFC Central Div.	—	—		D. Shula, B. Coslet
1997	7	9	0	.438	355	405	4th/AFC Central Div.	—	—		Bruce Coslet
1998	3	13	0	.188	268	452	5th/AFC Central Div.	—	—		Bruce Coslet
1999	4	12	0	.250	283	460	5th/AFC Central Div.	—	—		Bruce Coslet
2000	4	12	0	.250	185	359	4th/AFC Central Div.	—	—		B. Coslet, Dick LeBeau
2001	6	10	0	.375	226	309	6th/AFC Central Div.	—	—		Dick LeBeau
2002	2	14	0	.125	279	456	4th/AFC North Div.	—	—		Dick LeBeau
2003	8	8	0	.500	346	384	2nd/AFC North Div.	—	—		Marvin Lewis
2004	8	8	0	.500	374	372	3rd/AFC North Div.	—	—		Marvin Lewis

*American Football League.

FIRST-ROUND DRAFT PICKS

1968—Bob Johnson, C, Tennessee
1969—Greg Cook, QB, Cincinnati
1970—Mike Reid, DT, Penn State
1971—Vernon Holland, T, Tennessee State
1972—Sherman White, DE, California
1973—Issac Curtis, WR, San Diego State
1974—Bill Kollar, DT, Montana State
1975—Glenn Cameron, LB, Florida
1976—Billy Brooks, WR, Oklahoma
　　　Archie Griffin, RB, Ohio State
1977—Eddie Edwards, DT, Miami, Fla.
　　　Wilson Whitley, DT, Houston
　　　Mike Cobb, TE, Michigan State
1978—Ross Browner, DE, Notre Dame
　　　Blair Bush, C, Washington
1979—Jack Thompson, QB, Washington State
　　　Charles Alexander, RB, Louisiana State

1980—Anthony Munoz, T, Southern California
1981—David Verser, WR, Kansas
1982—Glen Collins, DE, Mississippi State
1983—Dave Rimington, C, Nebraska
1984—Ricky Hunley, LB, Arizona
　　　Pete Koch, DE, Maryland
　　　Brian Blados, T, North Carolina
1985—Eddie Brown, WR, Miami, Fla.
　　　Emanuel King, LB, Alabama
1986—Joe Kelly, LB, Washington
　　　Tim McGee, WR, Tennessee
1987—Jason Buck, DE, Brigham Young
1988—Rickey Dixon, S, Oklahoma
1989—None
1990—James Francis, LB, Baylor
1991—Alfred Williams, LB, Colorado
1992—David Klingler, QB, Houston
　　　Darryl Williams, DB, Miami, Fla.

993—John Copeland, DE, Alabama
994—Dan Wilkinson, DT, Ohio State*
995—Ki-Jana Carter, RB, Penn State*
996—Willie Anderson, T, Auburn
997—Reinard Wilson, LB, Florida State
998—Takeo Spikes, LB, Auburn
    Brian Simmons, LB, North Carolina
999—Akili Smith, QB, Oregon

2000—Peter Warrick, WR, Florida State
2001—Justin Smith, DE, Missouri
2002—Levi Jones, T, Arizona State
2003—Carson Palmer, QB, Southern California*
2004—Chris Perry, RB, Michigan
2005—David Pollack, DE, Georgia
*First player chosen in draft.

FRANCHISE RECORDS

Most rushing yards, career
8,061—Corey Dillon
Most rushing yards, season
1,454—Rudi Johnson, 2004
Most rushing yards, game
278—Corey Dillon vs. Den., Oct. 22, 2000
Most rushing touchdowns, season
15—Ickey Woods, 1988
Most passing attempts, season
581—Jon Kitna, 2001
Most passing attempts, game
58—Jon Kitna vs. Pit., Dec. 30, 2001 (OT)
56—Ken Anderson at S.D., Dec. 20, 1982
Most passes completed, season
326—Jeff Blake, 1995
Most passes completed, game
40—Ken Anderson at S.D., Dec. 20, 1982

Most passing yards, career
32,838—Ken Anderson
Most passing yards, season
3,959—Boomer Esiason, 1986
Most passing yards, game
490—Boomer Esiason at L.A. Rams, Oct. 7, 1990
Most touchdown passes, season
29—Ken Anderson, 1981
Most pass receptions, career
530—Carl Pickens
Most pass receptions, season
100—Carl Pickens, 1996
Most pass receptions, game
13—Carl Pickens vs. Pit., Oct. 11, 1998
Most receiving yards, career
7,101—Isaac Curtis
Most receiving yards, season
1,355—Chad Johnson, 2003

Most receiving yards, game
216—Eddie Brown vs. Pit., Nov. 16, 1988
Most receiving touchdowns, season
17—Carl Pickens, 1995
Most touchdowns, career
70—Pete Johnson
Most field goals, season
29—Doug Pelfrey, 1995
Longest field goal
55 yards—Chris Bahr vs. Hou., Sept. 23, 1979
Most interceptions, career
65—Ken Riley
Most interceptions, season
9—Ken Riley, 1976
Most sacks, career
83.5—Eddie Edwards
Most sacks, season
22—Coy Bacon, 1976

SERIES RECORDS

Cincinnati vs.: Arizona 5-3; Atlanta 7-3; Baltimore 6-12; Buffalo 9-12; Carolina 0-2; Chicago 4-3; Cleveland 30-33; Dallas 4-5; Denver 8-15; Detroit 5-3; Green Bay 4-5; Houston 2-0; Indianapolis 8-12; Jacksonville 5-10; Kansas City 10-11; Miami 4-12; Minnesota 4-5; New England 8-11; New Orleans 5-5; N.Y. Giants 5-2; N.Y. Jets 6-12; Oakland 7-17; Philadelphia 7-3; Pittsburgh 28-41; St. Louis 5-5; San Diego 10-17; San Francisco 3-7; Seattle 8-8; Tampa Bay 3-5; Tennessee 29-38-1; Washington 3-4.

COACHING RECORDS

Paul Brown, 55-56-1 (0-3); Bruce Coslet, 21-39-0; Forrest Gregg, 32-25-0 (2-2); Bill Johnson, 18-15-0; Dick LeBeau, 12-33-0; Marvin Lewis, 16-16-0; Homer Rice, 8-19-0; Dave Shula, 19-52-0; Sam Wyche, 61-66-0 (3-2).
NOTE: Playoff games in parentheses.

RETIRED UNIFORM NUMBERS

No.	Player
54	Bob Johnson

CLEVELAND BROWNS
YEAR-BY-YEAR RECORDS

| | | | REGULAR SEASON | | | | | | PLAYOFFS | |
Year	W	L	T	Pct.	PF	PA	Finish	W	L	Highest round	Coach
1946*	12	2	0	.857	423	137	1st/Western Div.	1	0	AAFC champ	Paul Brown
1947*	12	1	1	.923	410	185	1st/Western Div.	1	0	AAFC champ	Paul Brown
1948*	14	0	0	1.000	389	190	1st/Western Div.	1	0	AAFC champ	Paul Brown
1949*	9	1	2	.900	339	171	1st	2	0	AAFC champ	Paul Brown
1950	10	2	0	.833	310	144	1st/American Conf.	2	0	NFL champ	Paul Brown
1951	11	1	0	.917	331	152	1st/American Conf.	0	1	NFL championship game	Paul Brown
1952	8	4	0	.667	310	213	1st/American Conf.	0	1	NFL championship game	Paul Brown
1953	11	1	0	.917	348	162	1st/Eastern Conf.	0	1	NFL championship game	Paul Brown
1954	9	3	0	.750	336	162	1st/Eastern Conf.	1	0	NFL champ	Paul Brown
1955	9	2	1	.818	349	218	1st/Eastern Conf.	1	0	NFL champ	Paul Brown
1956	5	7	0	.417	167	177	4th/Eastern Conf.	—	—		Paul Brown
1957	9	2	1	.818	269	172	1st/Eastern Conf.	0	1	NFL championship game	Paul Brown
1958	9	3	0	.750	302	217	2nd/Eastern Conf.	0	1	E. Conf. championship game	Paul Brown
1959	7	5	0	.583	270	214	T2nd/Eastern Conf.	—	—		Paul Brown
1960	8	3	1	.727	362	217	2nd/Eastern Conf.	—	—		Paul Brown
1961	8	5	1	.615	319	270	3rd/Eastern Conf.	—	—		Paul Brown
1962	7	6	1	.538	291	257	3rd/Eastern Conf.	—	—		Paul Brown
1963	10	4	0	.714	343	262	2nd/Eastern Conf.	—	—		Blanton Collier
1964	10	3	1	.769	415	293	1st/Eastern Conf.	1	0	NFL champ	Blanton Collier
1965	11	3	0	.786	363	325	1st/Eastern Conf.	0	1	NFL championship game	Blanton Collier

– 403 –

Year	W	L	T	Pct.	PF	PA	Finish	W	L	Highest round	Coach
				REGULAR SEASON						**PLAYOFFS**	
1966	9	5	0	.643	403	259	T2nd/Eastern Conf.	—	—		Blanton Collier
1967	9	5	0	.643	334	297	1st/Century Div.	0	1	E. Conf. championship game	Blanton Collier
1968	10	4	0	.714	394	273	1st/Century Div.	1	1	NFL championship game	Blanton Collier
1969	10	3	1	.769	351	300	1st/Century Div.	1	1	NFL championship game	Blanton Collier
1970	7	7	0	.500	286	265	2nd/AFC Central Div.	—	—		Blanton Collier
1971	9	5	0	.643	285	273	1st/AFC Central Div.	0	1	AFC div. playoff game	Nick Skorich
1972	10	4	0	.714	268	249	2nd/AFC Central Div.	0	1	AFC div. playoff game	Nick Skorich
1973	7	5	2	.571	234	255	3rd/AFC Central Div.	—	—		Nick Skorich
1974	4	10	0	.286	251	344	4th/AFC Central Div.	—	—		Nick Skorich
1975	3	11	0	.214	218	372	4th/AFC Central Div.	—	—		Forrest Gregg
1976	9	5	0	.643	267	287	3rd/AFC Central Div.	—	—		Forrest Gregg
1977	6	8	0	.429	269	267	4th/AFC Central Div.	—	—		F. Gregg, Dick Modzelewski
1978	8	8	0	.500	334	356	3rd/AFC Central Div.	—	—		Sam Rutigliano
1979	9	7	0	.563	359	352	3rd/AFC Central Div.	—	—		Sam Rutigliano
1980	11	5	0	.688	357	310	1st/AFC Central Div.	0	1	AFC div. playoff game	Sam Rutigliano
1981	5	11	0	.313	276	375	4th/AFC Central Div.	—	—		Sam Rutigliano
1982	4	5	0	.444	140	182	8th/AFC	0	1	AFC first-round pl. game	Sam Rutigliano
1983	9	7	0	.563	356	342	2nd/AFC Central Div.	—	—		Sam Rutigliano
1984	5	11	0	.313	250	297	3rd/AFC Central Div.	—	—		Rutigliano, Schottenheimer
1985	8	8	0	.500	287	294	1st/AFC Central Div.	0	1	AFC div. playoff game	Marty Schottenheimer
1986	12	4	0	.750	391	310	1st/AFC Central Div.	1	1	AFC championship game	Marty Schottenheimer
1987	10	5	0	.667	390	239	1st/AFC Central Div.	1	1	AFC championship game	Marty Schottenheimer
1988	10	6	0	.625	304	288	2nd/AFC Central Div.	0	1	AFC wild-card game	Marty Schottenheimer
1989	9	6	1	.594	334	254	1st/AFC Central Div.	1	1	AFC championship game	Bud Carson
1990	3	13	0	.188	228	462	4th/AFC Central Div.	—	—		Bud Carson, Jim Shofner
1991	6	10	0	.375	293	298	3rd/AFC Central Div.	—	—		Bill Belichick
1992	7	9	0	.438	272	275	3rd/AFC Central Div.	—	—		Bill Belichick
1993	7	9	0	.438	304	307	3rd/AFC Central Div.	—	—		Bill Belichick
1994	11	5	0	.688	340	204	2nd/AFC Central Div.	1	1	AFC div. playoff game	Bill Belichick
1995	5	11	0	.313	289	356	4th/AFC Central Div.	—	—		Bill Belichick
1999	2	14	0	.125	217	437	6th/AFC Central Div.	—	—		Chris Palmer
2000	3	13	0	.188	161	419	6th/AFC Central Div.	—	—		Chris Palmer
2001	7	9	0	.438	285	319	3rd/AFC Central Div.	—	—		Butch Davis
2002	9	7	0	.563	344	320	2nd/AFC North Div.	0	1	AFC wild-card game	Butch Davis
2003	5	11	0	.313	254	322	4th/AFC North Div.	—	—		Butch Davis
2004	4	12	0	.250	276	390	4th/AFC North Div.	—	—		B. Davis, Terry Robiskie

*All-America Football Conference.

FIRST-ROUND DRAFT PICKS

1950—Ken Carpenter, B, Oregon State
1951—Ken Konz, B, Louisiana State
1952—Bert Rechichar, DB, Tennessee
    Harry Agganis, QB, Boston University
1953—Doug Atkins, DT, Tennessee
1954—Bobby Garrett, QB, Stanford*
    John Bauer, G, Illinois
1955—Kent Burris, C, Oklahoma
1956—Preston Carpenter, B, Arkansas
1957—Jim Brown, B, Syracuse
1958—Jim Shofner, DB, Texas Christian
1959—Rich Kreitling, DE, Illinois
1960—Jim Houston, DE, Ohio State
1961—Bobby Crespino, E, Mississippi
1962—Gary Collins, WR, Maryland
    Leroy Jackson, B, Western Illinois
1963—Tom Hutchinson, TE, Kentucky
1964—Paul Warfield, WR, Ohio State
1965—None
1966—Milt Morin, TE, Massachusetts
1967—Bob Matheson, LB, Duke
1968—M. Upshaw, DE, Trinity (Tex.)
1969—Ron Johnson, RB, Michigan
1970—Mike Phipps, QB, Purdue
    Bob McKay, T, Texas
1971—Clarence Scott, DB, Kansas State
1972—Thom Darden, DB, Michigan
1973—Steve Holden, WR, Arizona State
    Pete Adams, G, Southern California
1974—None
1975—Mack Mitchell, DE, Houston

1976—Mike Pruitt, RB, Purdue
1977—Robert Jackson, LB, Texas A&M
1978—Clay Matthews, LB, Southern California
    Ozzie Newsome, WR, Alabama
1979—Willis Adams, WR, Houston
1980—Charles White, RB, Southern California
1981—Hanford Dixon, CB, Southern Mississippi
1982—Chip Banks, LB, Southern California
1983—None
1984—Don Rogers, DB, UCLA
1985—None
1986—None
1987—Mike Junkin, LB, Duke
1988—Clifford Charlton, LB, Florida
1989—Eric Metcalf, RB, Texas
1990—None
1991—Eric Turner, S, UCLA
1992—Tommy Vardell, FB, Stanford
1993—Steve Everitt, C, Michigan
1994—Antonio Langham, DB, Alabama
    Derrick Alexander, WR, Michigan
1995—Craig Powell, LB, Ohio State
1999—Tim Couch, QB, Kentucky*
2000—Courtney Brown, DE, Penn State*
2001—Gerard Warren, DT, Florida
2002—William Green, RB, Boston College
2003—Jeff Faine, C, Notre Dame
2004—Kellen Winslow, TE, Miami, Fla.
2005—Braylon Edwards, WR, Michigan
    *First player chosen in draft.

Most rushing yards, career
2,312—Jim Brown
Most rushing yards, season
1,863—Jim Brown, 1963
Most rushing yards, game
237—Jim Brown vs. L.A., Nov. 24, 1957
Jim Brown vs. Phi., Nov. 19, 1961
Most rushing touchdowns, season
17— Jim Brown, 1958
Jim Brown, 1965
Most passing attempts, season
567—Brian Sipe, 1981
Most passing attempts, game
57—Brian Sipe vs. S.D., Sept. 7, 1981
Most passes completed, season
337—Brian Sipe, 1980
Most passes completed, game
36—Tim Couch at Ten., Sept. 22, 2002
(OT)

33—Brian Sipe vs. S.D., Dec. 5, 1982
Most passing yards, career
23,713—Brian Sipe
Most passing yards, season
4,132—Brian Sipe, 1980
Most passing yards, game
444—Brian Sipe vs. Bal., Oct. 25, 1981
Most touchdown passes, season
30—Brian Sipe, 1980
Most pass receptions, career
662—Ozzie Newsome
Most pass receptions, season
89— Ozzie Newsome, 1983
Ozzie Newsome, 1984
Most pass receptions, game
14—Ozzie Newsome vs. NYJ, Oct. 14, 1984
Most receiving yards, career
7,980—Ozzie Newsome
Most receiving yards, season
1,236—Webster Slaughter, 1989

Most receiving yards, game
191—Ozzie Newsome vs. NYJ, Oct. 14, 1984
Most receiving touchdowns, season
13—Gary Collins, 1963
Most touchdowns, career
126—Jim Brown
Most field goals, season
29—Matt Stover, 1995
Longest field goal
60 yards—Steve Cox at Cin., Oct. 21, 1984
Most interceptions, career
45—Thom Darden
Most interceptions, season
10—Thom Darden, 1978
Anthony Henry, 2001
Most sacks, career
76.5—Clay Matthews
Most sacks, season
14.5—Bill Glass, 1965

SERIES RECORDS

Cleveland vs.: Arizona 33-11-3; Atlanta 9-2; Baltimore 4-8; Buffalo 7-5; Carolina 0-2; Chicago 8-4; Cincinnati 33-30; Dallas 15-10; Denver 5-15; Detroit 4-12; Green Bay 6-9; Houston 2-0; Indianapolis 13-10; Jacksonville 2-7; Kansas City 8-9-2; Miami 4-7; Minnesota 3-8; New England 11-8; New Orleans 11-3; N.Y. Giants 25-19-2; N.Y. Jets 10-7; Oakland 5-9; Philadelphia 31-14-1; Pittsburgh 55-49; St. Louis 8-9; San Diego 7-12-1; San Francisco 10-6; Seattle 4-11; Tampa Bay 5-1; Tennessee 32-26; Washington 33-9-1.

COACHING RECORDS

Bill Belichick, 36-44-0 (1-1); Paul Brown, 158-48-8 (9-5); Bud Carson, 11-13-1 (1-1); Blanton Collier, 76-34-2 (3-4); Butch Davis, 24-35-0 (0-1); Forrest Gregg 18-23-0; Dick Modzelewski, 0-1-0; Chris Palmer, 5-27-0; Terry Robiskie, 1-4-0; Sam Rutigliano, 47-50-0 (0-2); Marty Schottenheimer, 44-27-0 (2-4); Jim Shofner, 1-6-0; Nick Skorich, 30-24-2 (0-2).
NOTE: Playoff games in parentheses.

RETIRED UNIFORM NUMBERS

No.	Player
14	Otto Graham
32	Jim Brown
45	Ernie Davis
46	Don Fleming
76	Lou Groza

HISTORY *Team by team*

DALLAS COWBOYS
YEAR-BY-YEAR RECORDS

	REGULAR SEASON						PLAYOFFS			
Year	W	L	T	Pct.	PF	PA	Finish	W	L	Highest round	Coach
1960	0	11	1	.000	177	369	7th/Western Conf.	—	—		Tom Landry
1961	4	9	1	.308	236	380	6th/Eastern Conf.	—	—		Tom Landry
1962	5	8	1	.385	398	402	5th/Eastern Conf.	—	—		Tom Landry
1963	4	10	0	.286	305	378	5th/Eastern Conf.	—	—		Tom Landry
1964	5	8	1	.385	250	289	5th/Eastern Conf.	—	—		Tom Landry
1965	7	7	0	.500	325	280	T2nd/Eastern Conf.	—	—		Tom Landry
1966	10	3	1	.769	445	239	1st/Eastern Conf.	0	1	NFL championship game	Tom Landry
1967	9	5	0	.643	342	268	1st/Capitol Div.	1	1	NFL championship game	Tom Landry
1968	12	2	0	.857	431	186	1st/Capitol Div.	0	1	E. Conf. championship game	Tom Landry
1969	11	2	1	.846	369	223	1st/Capitol Div.	0	1	E. Conf. championship game	Tom Landry
1970	10	4	0	.714	299	221	1st/NFC Eastern Div.	2	1	Super Bowl	Tom Landry
1971	11	3	0	.786	406	222	1st/NFC Eastern Div.	3	0	Super Bowl champ	Tom Landry
1972	10	4	0	.714	319	240	2nd/NFC Eastern Div.	1	1	NFC championship game	Tom Landry
1973	10	4	0	.714	382	203	1st/NFC Eastern Div.	1	1	NFC championship game	Tom Landry
1974	8	6	0	.571	297	235	3rd/NFC Eastern Div.	—	—		Tom Landry
1975	10	4	0	.714	350	268	2nd/NFC Eastern Div.	2	1	Super Bowl	Tom Landry
1976	11	3	0	.786	296	194	1st/NFC Eastern Div.	0	1	NFC div. playoff game	Tom Landry
1977	12	2	0	.857	345	212	1st/NFC Eastern Div.	3	0	Super Bowl champ	Tom Landry
1978	12	4	0	.750	384	208	1st/NFC Eastern Div.	2	1	Super Bowl	Tom Landry
1979	11	5	0	.688	371	313	1st/NFC Eastern Div.	0	1	NFC div. playoff game	Tom Landry
1980	12	4	0	.750	454	311	2nd/NFC Eastern Div.	2	1	NFC championship game	Tom Landry
1981	12	4	0	.750	367	277	1st/NFC Eastern Div.	1	1	NFC championship game	Tom Landry
1982	6	3	0	.667	226	145	2nd/NFC	2	1	NFC championship game	Tom Landry
1983	12	4	0	.750	479	360	2nd/NFC Eastern Div.	0	1	NFC wild-card game	Tom Landry

	REGULAR SEASON						PLAYOFFS			
Year	W	L	T	Pct.	PF	PA	Finish	W	L	Highest round	Coach
1984	9	7	0	.563	308	308	4th/NFC Eastern Div.	—	—		Tom Landry
1985	10	6	0	.625	357	333	1st/NFC Eastern Div.	0	1	NFC div. playoff game	Tom Landry
1986	7	9	0	.438	346	337	3rd/NFC Eastern Div.	—	—		Tom Landry
1987	7	8	0	.467	340	348	2nd/NFC Eastern Div.	—	—		Tom Landry
1988	3	13	0	.188	265	381	5th/NFC Eastern Div.	—	—		Tom Landry
1989	1	15	0	.063	204	393	5th/NFC Eastern Div.	—	—		Jimmy Johnson
1990	7	9	0	.438	244	308	4th/NFC Eastern Div.	—	—		Jimmy Johnson
1991	11	5	0	.688	342	310	2nd/NFC Eastern Div.	1	1	NFC div. playoff game	Jimmy Johnson
1992	13	3	0	.813	409	243	1st/NFC Eastern Div.	3	0	Super Bowl champ	Jimmy Johnson
1993	12	4	0	.750	376	229	1st/NFC Eastern Div.	3	0	Super Bowl champ	Jimmy Johnson
1994	12	4	0	.750	414	248	1st/NFC Eastern Div.	1	1	NFC championship game	Barry Switzer
1995	12	4	0	.750	435	291	1st/NFC Eastern Div.	3	0	Super Bowl champ	Barry Switzer
1996	10	6	0	.625	286	250	1st/NFC Eastern Div.	1	1	NFC div. playoff game	Barry Switzer
1997	6	10	0	.375	304	314	4th/NFC Eastern Div.	—	—		Barry Switzer
1998	10	6	0	.625	381	275	1st/NFC Eastern Div.	0	1	NFC wild-card game	Chan Gailey
1999	8	8	0	.500	352	276	2nd/NFC Eastern Div.	0	1	NFC wild-card game	Chan Gailey
2000	5	11	0	.313	294	361	4th/NFC Eastern Div.	—	—		Dave Campo
2001	5	11	0	.313	246	338	5th/NFC Eastern Div.	—	—		Dave Campo
2002	5	11	0	.313	217	329	4th/NFC East Div.	—	—		Dave Campo
2003	10	6	0	.625	289	260	2nd/NFC East Div.	0	1	NFC wild-card game	Bill Parcells
2004	6	10	0	.375	293	405	3rd/NFC East Div.				Bill Parcells

FIRST-ROUND DRAFT PICKS

1961—Bob Lilly, DT, Texas Christian
1962—None
1963—Lee Roy Jordan, LB, Alabama
1964—Scott Appleton, DT, Texas
1965—Craig Morton, QB, California
1966—John Niland, G, Iowa
1967—None
1968—Dennis Homan, WR, Alabama
1969—Calvin Hill, RB, Yale
1970—Duane Thomas, RB, West Texas State
1971—Tody Smith, DE, Southern California
1972—Bill Thomas, RB, Boston College
1973—Billy Joe DuPree, TE, Michigan State
1974—Ed Jones, DE, Tennessee State*
      Charles Young, RB, North Carolina State
1975—Randy White, LB, Maryland
      Thomas Henderson, LB, Langston
1976—Aaron Kyle, DB, Wyoming
1977—Tony Dorsett, RB, Pittsburgh
1978—Larry Bethea, DE, Michigan State
1979—Robert Shaw, C, Tennessee
1980—None
1981—Howard Richards, T, Missouri
1982—Rod Hill, DB, Kentucky State
1983—Jim Jeffcoat, DE, Arizona State
1984—Billy Cannon Jr., LB, Texas A&M

1985—Kevin Brooks, DE, Michigan
1986—Mike Sherrard, WR, UCLA
1987—Danny Noonan, DT, Nebraska
1988—Michael Irvin, WR, Miami, Fla.
1989—Troy Aikman, QB, UCLA*
1990—Emmitt Smith, RB, Florida
1991—Russell Maryland, DL, Miami, Fla.*
      Alvin Harper, WR, Tennessee
      Kelvin Pritchett, DT, Mississippi
1992—Kevin Smith, DB, Texas A&M
      Robert Jones, LB, East Carolina
1993—None
1994—Shante Carver, DE, Arizona State
1995—None
1996—None
1997—David LaFleur, TE, Louisiana State
1998—Greg Ellis, DE, North Carolina
1999—Ebenezer Ekuban, DE, North Carolina
2000—None
2001—None
2002—Roy Williams, DB, Oklahoma
2003—Terence Newman, DB, Kansas State
2004—None
2005—Demarcus Ware, DE, Troy State
      Marcus Spears, DE, LSU
*First player chosen in draft.

FRANCHISE RECORDS

Most rushing yards, career
17,162—Emmitt Smith
Most rushing yards, season
1,773—Emmitt Smith, 1995
Most rushing yards, game
237—Emmitt Smith at Phi., Oct. 31, 1993
Most rushing touchdowns, season
25—Emmitt Smith, 1995
Most passing attempts, season
533—Danny White, 1983
Most passing attempts, game
57—Troy Aikman vs. Min., Nov. 26, 1998
Most passes completed, season
334—Danny White, 1983
Most passes completed, game
34—Troy Aikman at NYG, Oct. 5, 1997
      Troy Aikman vs. Min., Nov. 26, 1998
Most passing yards, career
32,942—Troy Aikman

Most passing yards, season
3,980—Danny White, 1983
Most passing yards, game
460—Don Meredith at S.F., Nov. 10, 1963
Most touchdown passes, season
29—Danny White, 1983
Most pass receptions, career
750—Michael Irvin
Most pass receptions, season
111—Michael Irvin, 1995
Most pass receptions, game
13—Lance Rentzel vs. Was., Nov. 19, 1967
Most receiving yards, career
11,904—Michael Irvin
Most receiving yards, season
1,603—Michael Irvin, 1995
Most receiving yards, game
246—Bob Hayes at Was., Nov. 13, 1966

Most receiving touchdowns, season
14—Frank Clarke, 1962
Most touchdowns, career
164—Emmitt Smith
Most field goals, season
34—Richie Cunningham, 1997
Longest field goal
54 yards—Toni Fritsch at NYG,
      Sept. 24, 1972
      Ken Willis at Cle., Sept. 1, 1991
      Richie Cunningham at Den.,
      Sept. 13, 1998
Most interceptions, career
52—Mel Renfro
Most interceptions, season
11—Everson Walls, 1981
Most sacks, career
113—Harvey Martin
Most sacks, season
23—Harvey Martin, 1977

Dallas vs.: Arizona 53-28-1; Atlanta 12-7; Baltimore 0-2; Buffalo 4-3; Carolina 4-1; Chicago 10-8; Cincinnati 5-4; Cleveland 10-15; Denver 4-4; Detroit 9-8; Green Bay 10-10; Houston 0-1; Indianapolis 7-5; Jacksonville 2-1; Kansas City 4-3; Miami 3-7; Minnesota 9-0; New England 7-2; New Orleans 14-7; N.Y. Giants 50-33-2; N.Y. Jets 6-2; Oakland 3-5; Philadelphia 49-39; Pittsburgh 14-12; St. Louis 9-9; San Diego 5-2; San Francisco 8-14-1; Seattle 6-3; Tampa Bay 6-3; Tennessee 6-5; Washington 54-32-2.

COACHING RECORDS

Dave Campo, 15-33-0; Chan Gailey, 18-14-0 (0-2); Jimmy Johnson, 44-36-0 (7-1); Tom Landry, 250-162-6 (20-16); Bill Parcells, 16-16-0 (0-1); Barry Switzer, 40-24-0 (5-2). NOTE: Playoff games in parentheses.

RETIRED UNIFORM NUMBERS

No.	Player
None	

DENVER BRONCOS
YEAR-BY-YEAR RECORDS

		REGULAR SEASON						PLAYOFFS			
Year	W	L	T	Pct.	PF	PA	Finish	W	L	Highest round	Coach
1960*	4	9	1	.308	309	393	4th/Western Div.	—	—		Frank Filchock
1961*	3	11	0	.214	251	432	3rd/Western Div.	—	—		Frank Filchock
1962*	7	7	0	.500	353	334	2nd/Western Div.	—	—		Jack Faulkner
1963*	2	11	1	.154	301	473	4th/Western Div.	—	—		Jack Faulkner
1964*	2	11	1	.154	240	438	4th/Western Div.	—	—		J. Faulkner, M. Speedie
1965*	4	10	0	.286	303	392	4th/Western Div.	—	—		Mac Speedie
1966*	4	10	0	.286	196	381	4th/Western Div.	—	—		M. Speedie, Ray Malavasi
1967*	3	11	0	.214	256	409	4th/Western Div.	—	—		Lou Saban
1968*	5	9	0	.357	255	404	4th/Western Div.	—	—		Lou Saban
1969*	5	8	1	.385	297	344	4th/Western Div.	—	—		Lou Saban
1970	5	8	1	.385	253	264	4th/AFC Western Div.	—	—		Lou Saban
1971	4	9	1	.308	203	275	4th/AFC Western Div.	—	—		Lou Saban, Jerry Smith
1972	5	9	0	.357	325	350	3rd/AFC Western Div.	—	—		John Ralston
1973	7	5	2	.571	354	296	2nd/AFC Western Div.	—	—		John Ralston
1974	7	6	1	.536	302	294	2nd/AFC Western Div.	—	—		John Ralston
1975	6	8	0	.429	254	307	2nd/AFC Western Div.	—	—		John Ralston
1976	9	5	0	.643	315	206	2nd/AFC Western Div.	—	—		John Ralston
1977	12	2	0	.857	274	148	1st/AFC Western Div.	2	1	Super Bowl	Red Miller
1978	10	6	0	.625	282	198	1st/AFC Western Div.	0	1	AFC div. playoff game	Red Miller
1979	10	6	0	.625	289	262	2nd/AFC Western Div.	0	1	AFC wild-card game	Red Miller
1980	8	8	0	.500	310	323	4th/AFC Western Div.	—	—		Red Miller
1981	10	6	0	.625	321	289	2nd/AFC Western Div.	—	—		Dan Reeves
1982	2	7	0	.222	148	226	12th/AFC	—	—		Dan Reeves
1983	9	7	0	.563	302	327	3rd/AFC Western Div.	0	1	AFC wild-card game	Dan Reeves
1984	13	3	0	.813	353	241	1st/AFC Western Div.	0	1	AFC div. playoff game	Dan Reeves
1985	11	5	0	.688	380	329	2nd/AFC Western Div.	—	—		Dan Reeves
1986	11	5	0	.688	378	327	1st/AFC Western Div.	2	1	Super Bowl	Dan Reeves
1987	10	4	1	.700	379	288	1st/AFC Western Div.	2	1	Super Bowl	Dan Reeves
1988	8	8	0	.500	327	352	2nd/AFC Western Div.	—	—		Dan Reeves
1989	11	5	0	.688	362	226	1st/AFC Western Div.	2	1	Super Bowl	Dan Reeves
1990	5	11	0	.313	331	374	5th/AFC Western Div.	—	—		Dan Reeves
1991	12	4	0	.750	304	235	1st/AFC Western Div.	1	1	AFC championship game	Dan Reeves
1992	8	8	0	.500	262	329	3rd/AFC Western Div.	—	—		Dan Reeves
1993	9	7	0	.563	373	284	3rd/AFC Western Div.	0	1	AFC wild-card game	Wade Phillips
1994	7	9	0	.438	347	396	4th/AFC Western Div.	—	—		Wade Phillips
1995	8	8	0	.500	388	345	4th/AFC Western Div.	—	—		Mike Shanahan
1996	13	3	0	.813	391	275	1st/AFC Western Div.	0	1	AFC div. playoff game	Mike Shanahan
1997	12	4	0	.750	472	287	2nd/AFC Western Div.	4	0	Super Bowl champ	Mike Shanahan
1998	14	2	0	.875	501	309	1st/AFC Western Div.	3	0	Super Bowl champ	Mike Shanahan
1999	6	10	0	.375	314	318	5th/AFC Western Div.	—	—		Mike Shanahan
2000	11	5	0	.688	485	369	2nd/AFC Western Div.	0	1	AFC wild-card game	Mike Shanahan
2001	8	8	0	.500	340	339	3rd/AFC Western Div.	—	—		Mike Shanahan
2002	9	7	0	.563	392	344	2nd/AFC West Div.	—	—		Mike Shanahan
2003	10	6	0	.625	381	301	2nd/AFC West Div.	0	1	AFC wild-card game	Mike Shanahan
2004	10	6	0	.625	381	304	2nd/AFC West Div.	0	1	AFC wild-card game	Mike Shanahan

*American Football League.

HISTORY *Team by team*

FIRST-ROUND DRAFT PICKS

1960—Roger Leclerc, C, Trinity (Conn.)
1961—Bob Gaiters, RB, New Mexico State
1962—Merlin Olsen, DT, Utah State
1963—Kermit Alexander, DB, UCLA
1964—Bob Brown, T, Nebraska
1965—None
1966—Jerry Shay, DT, Purdue

1967—Floyd Little, RB, Syracuse
1968—None
1969—None
1970—Bob Anderson, RB, Colorado
1971—Marv Montgomery, T, Southern California
1972—Riley Odoms, TE, Houston
1973—Otis Armstrong, RB, Purdue

1974—Randy Gradishar, LB, Ohio State
1975—Louis Wright, DB, San Jose State
1976—Tom Glassic, G, Virginia
1977—Steve Schindler, G, Boston College
1978—Don Latimer, DT, Miami, Fla.
1979—Kelvin Clark, T, Nebraska
1980—None
1981—Dennis Smith, DB, Southern California
1982—Gerald Willhite, RB, San Jose State
1983—Chris Hinton, G, Northwestern
1984—None
1985—Steve Sewell, RB, Oklahoma
1986—None
1987—Ricky Nattiel, WR, Florida
1988—Ted Gregory, DT, Syracuse
1989—Steve Atwater, DB, Arkansas

1990—None
1991—Mike Croel, LB, Nebraska
1992—Tommy Maddox, QB, UCLA
1993—Dan Williams, DE, Toledo
1994—None
1995—None
1996—John Mobley, LB, Kutztown (Pa.)
1997—Trevor Pryce, DT, Clemson
1998—Marcus Nash, WR, Tennessee
1999—Al Wilson, LB, Tennessee
2000—Deltha O'Neal, DB, California
2001—Willie Middlebrooks, DB, Minnesota
2002—Ashley Lelie, WR, Hawaii
2003—George Foster, T, Georgia
2004—D.J. Williams, LB, Miami, Fla.
2005—None

FRANCHISE RECORDS

Most rushing yards, career
7,607—Terrell Davis
Most rushing yards, season
2,008—Terrell Davis, 1998
Most rushing yards, game
251—Mike Anderson at N.O., Dec. 3, 2000
Most rushing touchdowns, season
21—Terrell Davis, 1998
Most passing attempts, season
605—John Elway, 1985
Most passing attempts, game
59—John Elway at G.B., Oct. 10, 1993
Most passes completed, season
348—John Elway, 1993
Most passes completed, game
36—John Elway vs. S.D., Sept. 4, 1994
Gus Frerotte vs. S.D., Nov. 19, 2000
Most passing yards, career
51,475—John Elway
Most passing yards, season
4,089—Jake Plummer, 2004

Most passing yards, game
462—Gus Frerotte vs. S.D., Nov. 19, 2000
Most touchdown passes, season
27—John Elway, 1997
Jake Plummer, 2004
Most pass receptions, career
712—Rod Smith
Most pass receptions, season
113—Rod Smith, 2001
Most pass receptions, game
14—Rod Smith at Ari., Sept. 23, 2001
Most receiving yards, career
9,772—Rod Smith
Most receiving yards, season
1,602—Rod Smith, 2000
Most receiving yards, game
214—Shannon Sharpe at K.C., Oct. 20,
2002 (OT)
199—Lionel Taylor vs. Buf., Nov. 27, 1960

Most receiving touchdowns, season
14—Anthony Miller, 1995
Most touchdowns, career
65—Terrell Davis
Most field goals, season
31—Jason Elam, 1995, 2001
Longest field goal
63 yards—Jason Elam vs. Jac., Oct. 25,
1998
Most interceptions, career
44—Steve Foley
Most interceptions, season
11—Goose Gonsoulin, 1960
Most sacks, career
97.5—Simon Fletcher
Most sacks, season
16—Simon Fletcher, 1992

SERIES RECORDS

Denver vs.: Arizona 6-0-1; Atlanta 7-4; Baltimore 1-3; Buffalo 13-17-1; Carolina 2-0; Chicago 6-6; Cincinnati 15-8; Cleveland 15-5; Dallas 4-4; Detroit 6-3; Green Bay 5-4-1; Houston 1-0; Indianapolis 11-4; Jacksonville 2-2; Kansas City 39-50; Miami 3-9-1; Minnesota 4-7; New England 22-15; New Orleans 6-2; N.Y. Giants 4-4; N.Y. Jets 14-14-1; Oakland 34-53-2; Philadelphia 3-6; Pittsburgh 11-6-1; St. Louis 5-5; San Diego 50-39-1; San Francisco 6-4; Seattle 33-17; Tampa Bay 4-2; Tennessee 12-20-1; Washington 5-4.

COACHING RECORDS

Jack Faulkner, 9-22-1; Frank Filchock, 7-20-1; Ray Malavasi, 4-8-0; Red Miller, 40-22-0 (2-3); Wade Phillips, 16-16-0 (0-1); John Ralston, 34-33-3; Dan Reeves, 110-73-1 (7-6); Lou Saban, 20-42-3; Mike Shanahan, 101-59-0 (7-4); Jerry Smith, 2-3-0; Mac Speedie, 6-19-1. NOTE: Playoff games in parentheses.

RETIRED UNIFORM NUMBERS

No.	Player
7	John Elway
18	Frank Tripucka
44	Floyd Little

DETROIT LIONS
YEAR-BY-YEAR RECORDS

			REGULAR SEASON						PLAYOFFS		
Year	W	L	T	Pct.	PF	PA	Finish	W	L	Highest round	Coach
1930*	5	6	3	.455	...	...	T7th				Tubby Griffen
1931*	11	3	0	.786	...	...	2nd				Potsy Clark
1932*	6	2	4	.750	...	...	3rd				Potsy Clark
1933*	6	5	0	.545	128	87	2nd/Western Div.	—	—		Potsy Clark
1934	10	3	0	.769	238	59	2nd/Western Div.	—	—		Potsy Clark
1935	7	3	2	.700	191	111	1st/Western Div.	1	0	NFL champ	Potsy Clark
1936	8	4	0	.667	235	102	3rd/Western Div.	—	—		Potsy Clark
1937	7	4	0	.636	180	105	T2nd/Western Div.	—	—		Dutch Clark
1938	7	4	0	.636	119	108	2nd/Western Div.	—	—		Dutch Clark
1939	6	5	0	.545	145	150	3rd/Western Div.	—	—		Gus Henderson

				REGULAR SEASON				PLAYOFFS		
ear	W	L	T	Pct.	PF	PA	Finish	W' L	Highest round	Coach
940	5	5	1	.500	138	153	3rd/Western Div.	— —		Potsy Clark
941	4	6	1	.400	121	195	3rd/Western Div.	— —		Bill Edwards
942	0	11	0	.000	38	263	5th/Western Div.	— —		B. Edwards, John Karcis
943	3	6	1	.333	178	218	3rd/Western Div.	— —		Gus Dorais
944	6	3	1	.667	216	151	T2nd/Western Div.	— —		Gus Dorais
945	7	3	0	.700	195	194	2nd/Western Div.	— —		Gus Dorais
946	1	10	0	.091	142	310	5th/Western Div.	— —		Gus Dorais
947	3	9	0	.250	231	305	5th/Western Div.	— —		Gus Dorais
948	2	10	0	.167	200	407	5th/Western Div.	— —		Bo McMillin
949	4	8	0	.333	237	259	4th/Western Div.	— —		Bo McMillin
950	6	6	0	.500	321	285	4th/National Conf.	— —		Bo McMillin
951	7	4	1	.636	336	259	T2nd/National Conf.	— —		Buddy Parker
952	9	3	0	.750	344	192	1st/National Conf.	2 0	NFL champ	Buddy Parker
953	10	2	0	.833	271	205	1st/Western Conf.	1 0	NFL champ	Buddy Parker
954	9	2	1	.818	337	189	1st/Western Conf.	0 1	NFL championship game	Buddy Parker
955	3	9	0	.250	230	275	6th/Western Conf.	— —		Buddy Parker
956	9	3	0	.750	300	188	2nd/Western Conf.	— —		Buddy Parker
957	8	4	0	.667	251	231	1st/Western Conf.	2 0	NFL champ	George Wilson
958	4	7	1	.364	261	276	5th/Western Conf.	— —		George Wilson
959	3	8	1	.273	203	275	5th/Western Conf.	— —		George Wilson
960	7	5	0	.583	239	212	T2nd/Western Conf.	— —		George Wilson
961	8	5	1	.615	270	258	2nd/Western Conf.	— —		George Wilson
962	11	3	0	.786	315	177	2nd/Western Conf.	— —		George Wilson
963	5	8	1	.385	326	265	T4th/Western Conf.	— —		George Wilson
964	7	5	2	.583	280	260	4th/Western Conf.	— —		George Wilson
965	6	7	1	.462	257	295	6th/Western Conf.	— —		Harry Gilmer
966	4	9	1	.308	206	317	T6th/Western Conf.	— —		Harry Gilmer
967	5	7	2	.417	260	259	3rd/Central Div.	— —		Joe Schmidt
968	4	8	2	.333	207	241	4th/Central Div.	— —		Joe Schmidt
969	9	4	1	.692	259	188	2nd/Central Div.	— —		Joe Schmidt
970	10	4	0	.714	347	202	2nd/NFC Central Div.	0 1	NFC div. playoff game	Joe Schmidt
971	6	5	3	.583	341	286	2nd/NFC Central Div.	— —		Joe Schmidt
972	8	5	1	.607	339	290	2nd/NFC Central Div.	— —		Joe Schmidt
973	6	7	1	.464	271	247	2nd/NFC Central Div.	— —		Don McCafferty
974	7	7	0	.500	256	270	2nd/NFC Central Div.	— —		Rick Forzano
975	7	7	0	.500	245	262	2nd/NFC Central Div.	— —		Rick Forzano
976	6	8	0	.429	262	220	3rd/NFC Central Div.	— —		R. Forzano, T. Hudspeth
977	6	8	0	.429	183	252	3rd/NFC Central Div.	— —		Tommy Hudspeth
978	7	9	0	.438	290	300	3rd/NFC Central Div.	— —		Monte Clark
979	2	14	0	.125	219	365	5th/NFC Central Div.	— —		Monte Clark
980	9	7	0	.563	334	272	2nd/NFC Central Div.	— —		Monte Clark
981	8	8	0	.500	397	322	2nd/NFC Central Div.	— —		Monte Clark
982	4	5	0	.444	181	176	8th/NFC	0 1	NFC first-round pl. game	Monte Clark
983	9	7	0	.563	347	286	1st/NFC Central Div.	0 1	NFC div. playoff game	Monte Clark
984	4	11	1	.281	283	408	4th/NFC Central Div.	— —		Monte Clark
985	7	9	0	.438	307	366	4th/NFC Central Div.	— —		Darryl Rogers
986	5	11	0	.313	277	326	3rd/NFC Central Div.	— —		Darryl Rogers
987	4	11	0	.267	269	384	5th/NFC Central Div.	— —		Darryl Rogers
988	4	12	0	.250	220	313	4th/NFC Central Div.	— —		Darryl Rogers
989	7	9	0	.438	312	364	3rd/NFC Central Div.	— —		Wayne Fontes
990	6	10	0	.375	373	413	3rd/NFC Central Div.	— —		Wayne Fontes
991	12	4	0	.750	339	295	1st/NFC Central Div.	1 1	NFC championship game	Wayne Fontes
992	5	11	0	.313	273	332	5th/NFC Central Div.	— —		Wayne Fontes
993	10	6	0	.625	298	292	1st/NFC Central Div.	0 1	NFC wild-card game	Wayne Fontes
994	9	7	0	.563	357	342	3rd/NFC Central Div.	0 1	NFC wild-card game	Wayne Fontes
995	10	6	0	.625	436	336	2nd/NFC Central Div.	0 1	NFC wild-card game	Wayne Fontes
996	5	11	0	.313	302	368	5th/NFC Central Div.	— —		Wayne Fontes
997	9	7	0	.563	379	306	3rd/NFC Central Div.	0 1	NFC wild-card game	Bobby Ross
998	5	11	0	.313	306	378	4th/NFC Central Div.	— —		Bobby Ross
999	8	8	0	.500	322	323	3rd/NFC Central Div.	0 1	NFC wild-card game	Bobby Ross
2000	9	7	0	.563	307	307	4th/NFC Central Div.	— —		B. Ross, Gary Moeller
2001	2	14	0	.125	270	424	5th/NFC Central Div.	— —		Marty Mornhinweg
2002	3	13	0	.188	306	451	4th/NFC North Div.	— —		Marty Mornhinweg
2003	5	11	0	.313	270	379	4th/NFC North Div.	— —		Steve Mariucci
2004	6	10	0	.375	296	350	3rd/NFC North Div.	— —		Steve Mariucci

*Portsmouth Spartans.

FIRST-ROUND DRAFT PICKS

1936—Sid Wagner, G, Michigan State
1937—Lloyd Cardwell, B, Nebraska
1938—Alex Wojciechowicz, C, Fordham
1939—John Pingel, B, Michigan State

1940—Doyle Nave, B, Southern California
1941—Jim Thomason, B, Texas A&M
1942—Bob Westfall, B, Michigan
1943—Frank Sinkwich, B, Georgia*

1944—Otto Graham, B, Northwestern	1976—James Hunter, DB, Grambling State
1945—Frank Szymanski, C, Notre Dame	Lawrence Gaines, FB, Wyoming
1946—Bill Dellastatious, B, Missouri	1977—None
1947—Glenn Davis, B, Army	1978—Luther Bradley, DB, Notre Dame
1948—Y.A. Tittle, B, Louisiana State	1979—Keith Dorney, T, Penn State
1949—John Rauch, B, Georgia	1980—Billy Sims, RB, Oklahoma*
1950—Leon Hart, E, Notre Dame*	1981—Mark Nichols, WR, San Jose State
Joe Watson, C, Rice	1982—Jimmy Williams, LB, Nebraska
1951—None	1983—James Jones, RB, Florida
1952—None	1984—David Lewis, TE, California
1953—Harley Sewell, G, Texas	1985—Lomas Brown, T, Florida
1954—Dick Chapman, T, Rice	1986—Chuck Long, QB, Iowa
1955—Dave Middleton, B, Auburn	1987—Reggie Rogers, DE, Washington
1956—Hopalong Cassady, B, Ohio State	1988—Bennie Blades, S, Miami, Fla.
1957—Bill Glass, G, Baylor	1989—Barry Sanders, RB, Oklahoma State
1958—Alex Karras, T, Iowa	1990—Andre Ware, QB, Houston
1959—Nick Pietrosante, B, Notre Dame	1991—Herman Moore, WR, Virginia
1960—John Robinson, DB, Louisiana State	1992—Robert Porcher, DE, South Carolina State
1961—None	1993—None
1962—John Hadl, QB, Kansas	1994—Johnnie Morton, WR, Southern California
1963—Daryl Sanders, T, Ohio State	1995—Luther Elliss, DT, Utah
1964—Pete Beathard, QB, Southern California	1996—Reggie Brown, LB, Texas A&M
1965—Tom Nowatzke, RB, Indiana	Jeff Hartings, G, Penn State
1966—None	1997—Bryant Westbrook, DB, Texas
1967—Mel Farr, RB, UCLA	1998—Terry Fair, DB, Tennessee
1968—Greg Landry, QB, Massachusetts	1999—Chris Claiborne, LB, Southern California
Earl McCullouch, E, Southern California	Aaron Gibson, T, Wisconsin
1969—None	2000—Stockar McDougle, T, Oklahoma
1970—Steve Owens, RB, Oklahoma	2001—Jeff Backus, T, Michigan
1971—Bob Bell, DT, Cincinnati	2002—Joey Harrington, QB, Oregon
1972—Herb Orvis, DE, Colorado	2003—Charles Rogers, WR, Michigan State
1973—Ernie Price, DE, Texas A&I	2004—Roy Williams, WR, Texas
1974—Ed O'Neil, LB, Penn State	Kevin Jones, RB, Virginia Tech
1975—Lynn Boden, G, South Dakota State	2005—Mike Williams, WR, Southern California
	*First player chosen in draft.

FRANCHISE RECORDS

Most rushing yards, career
15,269—Barry Sanders

Most rushing yards, season
2,053—Barry Sanders, 1997

Most rushing yards, game
237—Barry Sanders vs. T.B., Nov. 13, 1994

Most rushing touchdowns, season
16—Barry Sanders, 1991

Most passing attempts, season
583—Scott Mitchell, 1995

Most passing attempts, game
62—Charlie Batch at Ari., Nov. 18, 2001

Most passes completed, season
346—Scott Mitchell, 1995

Most passes completed, game
36—Charlie Batch at Ari., Nov. 18, 2001

Most passing yards, career
15,710—Bobby Layne

Most passing yards, season
4,338—Scott Mitchell, 1995

Most passing yards, game
436—Charlie Batch at Ari., Nov. 18, 2001

Most touchdown passes, season
32—Scott Mitchell, 1995

Most pass receptions, career
670—Herman Moore

Most pass receptions, season
123—Herman Moore, 1995

Most pass receptions, game
14—Herman Moore vs. Chi., Dec. 4, 1995

Most receiving yards, career
9,174—Herman Moore

Most receiving yards, season
1,686—Herman Moore, 1995

Most receiving yards, game
302—Cloyce Box vs. Bal., Dec. 3, 1950

Most receiving touchdowns, season
15—Cloyce Box, 1952

Most touchdowns, career
109—Barry Sanders

Most field goals, season
34—Jason Hanson, 1993

Longest field goal
56 yards—Jason Hanson vs. Cle., Oct. 8, 1995

Most interceptions, career
62—Dick LeBeau

Most interceptions, season
12—Don Doll, 1950
Jack Christiansen, 1953

Most sacks, career
95.5—Robert Porcher

Most sacks, season
23—Al Baker, 1978

SERIES RECORDS

Detroit vs.: Arizona 30-21-5; Atlanta 22-8; Baltimore 0-1; Buffalo 3-3-1; Carolina 1-2; Chicago 62-83-5; Cincinnati 3-5; Cleveland 12-4; Dallas 8-9; Denver 3-6; Green Bay 63-79-7; Houston 1-0; Indianapolis 18-19-2; Jacksonville 1-2; Kansas City 3-7; Miami 2-6; Minnesota 29-56-2; New England 4-4; New Orleans 8-8-1; N.Y. Giants 20-17-1; N.Y. Jets 6-4; Oakland 3-6; Philadelphia 12-12-2; Pittsburgh 14-13-1; St. Louis 37-40-1; San Diego 3-5; San Francisco 26-31-1; Seattle 4-5; Tampa Bay 26-23; Tennessee 3-6; Washington 10-25. NOTE: Includes records as Portsmouth Spartans from 1930 through 1933.

COACHING RECORDS

Dutch Clark, 14-8-0; Monte Clark, 43-61-1 (0-2); Potsy Clark, 53-25-7 (1-0); Gus Dorais, 20-31-2; Bill Edwards, 4-9-1; Wayne Fontes, 66-67-0 (1-4); Rick Forzano, 15-17-0; Harry Gilmer, 10-16-2; Hal Griffen, 5-6-3; Elmer Henderson, 6-5-0; Tommy Hudspeth, 11-13-0; John Karcis, 0-8-0; Steve Mariucci, 11-21-0; Don McCafferty, 6-7-1; Alvin McMillin, 12-24-0; Gary Moeller, 4-3-0; Marty Mornhinweg, 5-27-0; Buddy Parker, 47-23-2 (3-1); Darryl Rogers, 18-40-0; Bobby Ross, 27-30-0 (0-2); Joe Schmidt, 43-34-7 (0-1); George Wilson, 53-45-6 (2-0). NOTE: Playoff games in parentheses.

RETIRED UNIFORM NUMBERS

No.	Player
7	Dutch Clark
20	Lem Barney, Barry Sanders, Billy Sims
22	Bobby Layne
37	Doak Walker
56	Joe Schmidt

						REGULAR SEASON			PLAYOFFS	
ar	W	L	T	Pct.	PF	PA	Finish	W	L	Highest round	Coach
21	3	2	1	.600	...	...	T6th				Curly Lambeau
22	4	3	3	.571	...	...	T7th				Curly Lambeau
23	7	2	1	.778	...	...	3rd				Curly Lambeau
24	7	4	0	.636	...	...	6th				Curly Lambeau
25	8	5	0	.615	...	...	9th				Curly Lambeau
26	7	3	3	.700	...	...	5th				Curly Lambeau
27	7	2	1	.778	...	...	2nd				Curly Lambeau
28	6	4	3	.600	...	...	4th				Curly Lambeau
29	12	0	1	1.000	...	...	1st				Curly Lambeau
30	10	3	1	.769	...	...	1st				Curly Lambeau
31	12	2	0	.857	...	...	1st				Curly Lambeau
32	10	3	1	.769	...	...	2nd				Curly Lambeau
33	5	7	1	.417	170	107	3rd/Western Div.	—	—		Curly Lambeau
34	7	6	0	.538	156	112	3rd/Western Div.	—	—		Curly Lambeau
35	8	4	0	.667	181	96	2nd/Western Div.	—	—		Curly Lambeau
36	10	1	1	.909	248	118	1st/Western Div.	1	0	NFL champ	Curly Lambeau
37	7	4	0	.636	220	122	T2nd/Western Div.	—	—		Curly Lambeau
38	8	3	0	.727	223	118	1st/Western Div.	0	1	NFL championship game	Curly Lambeau
39	9	2	0	.818	233	153	1st/Western Div.	1	0	NFL champ	Curly Lambeau
40	6	4	1	.600	238	155	2nd/Western Div.	—	—		Curly Lambeau
41	10	1	0	.909	258	120	2nd/Western Div.	0	1	W. Div. championship game	Curly Lambeau
42	8	2	1	.800	300	215	2nd/Western Div.	—	—		Curly Lambeau
43	7	2	1	.778	264	172	2nd/Western Div.	—	—		Curly Lambeau
44	8	2	0	.800	238	141	1st/Western Div.	1	0	NFL champ	Curly Lambeau
45	6	4	0	.600	258	173	3rd/Western Div.	—	—		Curly Lambeau
46	6	5	0	.545	148	158	T3rd/Western Div.	—	—		Curly Lambeau
47	6	5	1	.545	274	210	3rd/Western Div.	—	—		Curly Lambeau
48	3	9	0	.250	154	290	4th/Western Div.	—	—		Curly Lambeau
49	2	10	0	.167	114	329	5th/Western Div.	—	—		Curly Lambeau
50	3	9	0	.250	244	406	T5th/National Conf.	—	—		Gene Ronzani
51	3	9	0	.250	254	375	5th/National Conf.	—	—		Gene Ronzani
52	6	6	0	.500	295	312	4th/National Conf.	—	—		Gene Ronzani
53	2	9	1	.182	200	338	6th/Western Conf.	—	—		Gene Ronzani, Hugh Devore-S. McLean
54	4	8	0	.333	234	251	5th/Western Conf.	—	—		Lisle Blackbourn
55	6	6	0	.500	258	276	3rd/Western Conf.	—	—		Lisle Blackbourn
56	4	8	0	.333	264	342	5th/Western Conf.	—	—		Lisle Blackbourn
57	3	9	0	.250	218	311	6th/Western Conf.	—	—		Lisle Blackbourn
58	1	10	1	.091	193	382	6th/Western Conf.	—	—		Scooter McLean
59	7	5	0	.583	248	246	T3rd/Western Conf.	—	—		Vince Lombardi
60	8	4	0	.667	332	209	1st/Western Conf.	0	1	NFL championship game	Vince Lombardi
61	11	3	0	.786	391	223	1st/Western Conf.	1	0	NFL champ	Vince Lombardi
62	13	1	0	.929	415	148	1st/Western Conf.	1	0	NFL champ	Vince Lombardi
63	11	2	1	.846	369	206	2nd/Western Conf.	—	—		Vince Lombardi
64	8	5	1	.615	342	245	T2nd/Western Conf.	—	—		Vince Lombardi
65	10	3	1	.769	316	224	1st/Western Conf.	2	0	NFL champ	Vince Lombardi
66	12	2	0	.857	335	163	1st/Western Conf.	2	0	Super Bowl champ	Vince Lombardi
67	9	4	1	.692	332	209	1st/Central Div.	3	0	Super Bowl champ	Vince Lombardi
68	6	7	1	.462	281	227	3rd/Central Div.	—	—		Phil Bengtson
69	8	6	0	.571	269	221	3rd/Central Div.	—	—		Phil Bengtson
70	6	8	0	.429	196	293	4th/NFC Central Div.	—	—		Phil Bengtson
71	4	8	2	.333	274	298	4th/NFC Central Div.	—	—		Dan Devine
72	10	4	0	.714	304	226	1st/NFC Central Div.	0	1	NFC div. playoff game	Dan Devine
73	5	7	2	.429	202	259	3rd/NFC Central Div.	—	—		Dan Devine
74	6	8	0	.429	210	206	3rd/NFC Central Div.	—	—		Dan Devine
75	4	10	0	.286	226	285	4th/NFC Central Div.	—	—		Bart Starr
76	5	9	0	.357	218	299	4th/NFC Central Div.	—	—		Bart Starr
77	4	10	0	.286	134	219	4th/NFC Central Div.	—	—		Bart Starr
78	8	7	1	.531	249	269	2nd/NFC Central Div.	—	—		Bart Starr
79	5	11	0	.313	246	316	4th/NFC Central Div.	—	—		Bart Starr
80	5	10	1	.344	231	371	5th/NFC Central Div.	—	—		Bart Starr
81	8	8	0	.500	324	361	3rd/NFC Central Div.	—	—		Bart Starr
82	5	3	1	.611	226	169	3rd/NFC	1	1	NFC second-round pl. game	Bart Starr
83	8	8	0	.500	429	439	2nd/NFC Central Div.	—	—		Bart Starr
84	8	8	0	.500	390	309	2nd/NFC Central Div.	—	—		Forrest Gregg
85	8	8	0	.500	337	355	2nd/NFC Central Div.	—	—		Forrest Gregg
86	4	12	0	.250	254	418	4th/NFC Central Div.	—	—		Forrest Gregg
87	5	9	1	.367	255	300	3rd/NFC Central Div.	—	—		Forrest Gregg
88	4	12	0	.250	240	315	5th/NFC Central Div.	—	—		Lindy Infante

						REGULAR SEASON				PLAYOFFS	
Year	W	L	T	Pct.	PF	PA	Finish	W	L	Highest round	Coach
1989	10	6	0	.625	362	356	2nd/NFC Central Div.	—	—		Lindy Infante
1990	6	10	0	.375	271	347	4th/NFC Central Div.	—	—		Lindy Infante
1991	4	12	0	.250	273	313	4th/NFC Central Div.	—	—		Lindy Infante
1992	9	7	0	.563	276	296	2nd/NFC Central Div.	—	—		Mike Holmgren
1993	9	7	0	.563	340	282	3rd/NFC Central Div.	1	1	NFC div. playoff game	Mike Holmgren
1994	9	7	0	.563	382	287	2nd/NFC Central Div.	1	1	NFC div. playoff game	Mike Holmgren
1995	11	5	0	.689	404	314	1st/NFC Central Div.	2	1	NFC championship game	Mike Holmgren
1996	13	3	0	.813	456	210	1st/NFC Central Div.	3	0	Super Bowl champ	Mike Holmgren
1997	13	3	0	.813	422	282	1st/NFC Central Div.	2	1	Super Bowl	Mike Holmgren
1998	11	5	0	.688	408	319	2nd/NFC Central Div.	0	1	NFC wild-card game	Mike Holmgren
1999	8	8	0	.500	357	341	4th/NFC Central Div.	—	—		Ray Rhodes
2000	9	7	0	.563	353	323	3rd/NFC Central Div.	—	—		Mike Sherman
2001	12	4	0	.750	390	266	2nd/NFC Central Div.	1	1	NFC div. playoff game	Mike Sherman
2002	12	4	0	.750	398	328	1st/NFC North Div.	0	1	NFC wild-card game	Mike Sherman
2003	10	6	0	.625	442	307	1st/NFC North Div.	1	1	NFC div. playoff game	Mike Sherman
2004	10	6	0	.625	424	380	1st/NFC North Div.	0	1	NFC wild-card game	Mike Sherman

FIRST-ROUND DRAFT PICKS

1936—Russ Letlow, G, San Francisco
1937—Ed Jankowski, B, Wisconsin
1938—Cecil Isbell, B, Purdue
1939—Larry Buhler, B, Minnesota
1940—Hal Van Every, B, Minnesota
1941—George Paskvan, B, Wisconsin
1942—Urban Odson, T, Minnesota
1943—Dick Wildung, T, Minnesota
1944—Merv Pregulman, G, Michigan
1945—Walt Schlinkman, G, Texas Tech
1946—Johnny Strzykalski, B, Marquette
1947—Ernie Case, B, UCLA
1948—Earl Girard, B, Wisconsin
1949—Stan Heath, B, Nevada
1950—Clayton Tonnemaker, C, Minnesota
1951—Bob Gain, T, Kentucky
1952—Babe Parilli, QB, Kentucky
1953—Al Carmichael, B, Southern California
1954—Art Hunter, T, Notre Dame
      Veryl Switzer, B, Kansas State
1955—Tom Bettis, G, Purdue
1956—Jack Losch, B, Miami
1957—Paul Hornung, B, Notre Dame*
      Ron Kramer, E, Michigan
1958—Dan Currie, C, Michigan State
1959—Randy Duncan, B, Iowa*
1960—Tom Moore, RB, Vanderbilt
1961—Herb Adderley, DB, Michigan State
1962—Earl Gros, RB, Louisiana State
1963—Dave Robinson, LB, Penn State
1964—Lloyd Voss, DT, Nebraska
1965—Donny Anderson, RB, Texas Tech
      Larry Elkins, E, Baylor
1966—Jim Grabowski, RB, Illinois
      Gale Gillingham, T, Minnesota
1967—Bob Hyland, C, Boston College
      Don Horn, QB, San Diego State
1968—Fred Carr, LB, Texas-El Paso
      Bill Lueck, G, Arizona
1969—Rich Moore, DT, Villanova
1970—Mike McCoy, DT, Notre Dame
      Rich McGeorge, TE, Elon

1971—John Brockington, RB, Ohio State
1972—Willie Buchanon, DB, San Diego State
      Jerry Tagge, QB, Nebraska
1973—Barry Smith, WR, Florida State
1974—Barty Smith, RB, Richmond
1975—None
1976—Mark Koncar, T, Colorado
1977—Mike Butler, DE, Kansas
      Ezra Johnson, DE, Morris Brown
1978—James Lofton, WR, Stanford
      John Anderson, LB, Michigan
1979—Eddie Lee Ivery, RB, Georgia Tech
1980—Bruce Clark, DE, Penn State
      George Cumby, LB, Oklahoma
1981—Rich Campbell, QB, California
1982—Ron Hallstrom, G, Iowa
1983—Tim Lewis, DB, Pittsburgh
1984—Alphonso Carreker, DE, Florida State
1985—Ken Ruettgers, T, Southern California
1986—None
1987—Brent Fullwood, RB, Auburn
1988—Sterling Sharpe, WR, South Carolina
1989—Tony Mandarich, T, Michigan State
1990—Tony Bennett, LB, Mississippi
      Darrell Thompson, RB, Minnesota
1991—Vincent Clark, DB, Ohio State
1992—Terrell Buckley, DB, Florida State
1993—Wayne Simmons, LB, Clemson
      George Teague, DB, Alabama
1994—Aaron Taylor, T, Notre Dame
1995—Craig Newsome, DB, Arizona State
1996—John Michels, T, Southern California
1997—Ross Verba, T, Iowa
1998—Vonnie Holliday, DT, North Carolina
1999—Antuan Edwards, DB, Clemson
2000—Bubba Franks, TE, Miami, Fla.
2001—Jamal Reynolds, DE, Florida State
2002—Javon Walker, WR, Florida State
2003—Nick Barnett, LB, Oregon State
2004—Ahmad Carroll, CB, Arkansas
2005—Aaron Rodgers, QB, California
*First player chosen in draft.

FRANCHISE RECORDS

Most rushing yards, career
8,207—Jim Taylor

Most rushing yards, season
1,883—Ahman Green, 2003

Most rushing yards, game
218—Ahman Green vs. Den., Dec. 28, 2003

Most rushing touchdowns, season
19—Jim Taylor, 1962

Most passing attempts, season
599—Don Majkowski, 1989

Most passing attempts, game
61—Brett Favre vs. S.F., Oct. 14, 1996 (OT)
59—Don Majkowski at Det., Nov. 12, 1989

Most passes completed, season
363—Brett Favre, 1994

Most passes completed, game
36—Brett Favre at Chi., Dec. 5, 1993

Most passing yards, career
49,734—Brett Favre

Most passing yards, season
4,458—Lynn Dickey, 1983

Most passing yards, game
418—Lynn Dickey at T.B., Oct. 12, 1980

Most touchdown passes, season
39—Brett Favre, 1996

st pass receptions, career
5—Sterling Sharpe
st pass receptions, season
2—Sterling Sharpe, 1993
st pass receptions, game
—Don Hutson at NYG, Nov. 22, 1942
st receiving yards, career
56—James Lofton
st receiving yards, season
97—Robert Brooks, 1995

Most receiving yards, game
257—Bill Howton vs. L.A. Rams, Oct. 21, 1956
Most receiving touchdowns, season
18—Sterling Sharpe, 1994
Most touchdowns, career
105—Don Hutson
Most field goals, season
33—Chester Marcol, 1972
Ryan Longwell, 2000

Longest field goal
54 yards—Chris Jacke at Det., Jan. 2, 1994
Ryan Longwell at Ten., Dec. 16, 2001
Most interceptions, career
52—Bobby Dillon
Most interceptions, season
10—Irv Comp, 1943
Most sacks, career
84—Ezra Johnson
Most sacks, season
20.5—Ezra Johnson, 1978

SERIES RECORDS

een Bay vs.: Arizona 41-22-4; Atlanta 11-10; Baltimore 2-0; Buffalo 3-6; Carolina 5-2; Chicago 78-84-6; Cincinnati 5-4; Cleveland 9- Dallas 11-9; Denver 4-5-1; Detroit 79-63-7; Houston 1-0; Indianapolis 19-20-1; Jacksonville 2-1; Kansas City 1-6-1; Miami 2-9; nnesota 44-42-1; New England 4-3; New Orleans 13-5; N.Y. Giants 24-21-2; N.Y. Jets 2-7; Oakland 4-5; Philadelphia 22-11; Pittsburgh -12; St. Louis 40-44-2; San Diego 7-1; San Francisco 27-25-1; Seattle 5-4; Tampa Bay 29-18-1; Tennessee 4-5; Washington 16-12-1.

COACHING RECORDS

il Bengtson, 20-21-1; Lisle Blackbourn, 17-31-0; Dan Devine, 25-27-4 (0-1); Hugh vore-Ray (Scooter) McLean, 0-2-0; Forrest Gregg, 25-37-1; Mike Holmgren, 75-37-0 -5); Lindy Infante, 24-40-0; Curly Lambeau, 209-104-21 (3-2); Vince Lombardi, 89-29- 9-1); Ray (Scooter) McLean, 1-10-1; Ray Rhodes, 8-8-0; Gene Ronzani, 14-31-1; Mike erman, 53-27-0 (2-4); Bart Starr, 52-76-3 (1-1). NOTE: Playoff games in parentheses.

RETIRED UNIFORM NUMBERS

No.	Player
3	Tony Canadeo
14	Don Hutson
15	Bart Starr
66	Ray Nitschke

HOUSTON TEXANS
YEAR-BY-YEAR RECORDS

| | REGULAR SEASON | | | | | | PLAYOFFS | | | |
ar	W	L	T	Pct.	PF	PA	Finish	W	L	Highest round	Coach
02	4	12	0	.250	213	356	4th/AFC South Div.	—	—		Dom Capers
03	5	11	0	.313	255	380	4th/AFC South Div.	—	—		Dom Capers
04	7	9	0	.438	309	339	3rd/AFC South Div.	—	—		Dom Capers

FIRST-ROUND DRAFT PICKS

02—David Carr, QB, Fresno State*
03—Andre Johnson, WR, Miami, Fla.
04—Dunta Robinson, CB, South Carolina

Jason Babin, LB, Western Michigan
2005—Travis Johnson, DT, Florida State
*First player chosen in draft.

FRANCHISE RECORDS

st rushing yards, career
219—Domanick Davis
st rushing yards, season
88—Domanick Davis, 2004
st rushing yards, game
9—Domanick Davis vs. N.Y. Jets, Oct. 19, 2003
st rushing touchdowns, season
—Domanick Davis, 2004
st passing attempts, season
4—David Carr, 2002
st passing attempts, game
—David Carr at Ten., Oct. 12, 2003
st passes completed, season
3—David Carr, 2002
st passes completed, game
—David Carr at Ten., Oct. 12, 2003
st passing yards, career
36—David Carr

Most passing yards, season
3,531—David Carr, 2004
Most passing yards, game
371—David Carr at Ten., Oct. 12, 2003
Most touchdown passes, season
16—David Carr, 2004
Most pass receptions, career
145—Andre Johnson
Most pass receptions, season
79—Andre Johnson, 2004
Most pass receptions, game
10—James Allen at Ind., Dec. 1, 2002
Most receiving yards, career
2,112—Andre Johnson
Most receiving yards, season
1,136—Andre Johnson, 2004
Most receiving yards, game
127—Corey Bradford at Ten., Oct. 12, 2003

Most receiving touchdowns, season
6—Corey Bradford, 2002
Most touchdowns, career
22—Domanick Davis
Most field goals, season
18—Kris Brown, 2003
Longest field goal
51 yards—Kris Brown at Ten., Nov. 10, 2002
Most interceptions, career
11—Aaron Glenn
Most interceptions, season
7—Marcus Coleman, 2003
Most sacks, career
11.5—Jamie Sharper
Most sacks, season
8—Jeff Posey, 2002

SERIES RECORDS

uston vs.: Atlanta 1-0; Baltimore 0-1; Buffalo 1-1; Carolina 1-0; Chicago 1-0; Cincinnati 0-2; Cleveland 0-2; Dallas 1-0; Denver 0-1; Detroit ; Green Bay 0-1; Indianapolis 0-6; Jacksonville 4-2; Kansas City 1-1; Miami 1-0; Minnesota 0-1; New England 0-1; New Orleans 0-1; N.Y. nts 1-0; N.Y. Jets 0-2; Oakland 1-0; Philadelphia 0-1; Pittsburgh 1-0; San Diego 0-2; Tampa Bay 0-1; Tennessee 2-4; Washington 0-1.

HISTORY Team by team

INDIANAPOLIS COLTS
YEAR-BY-YEAR RECORDS

			REGULAR SEASON						PLAYOFFS		
Year	W	L	T	Pct.	PF	PA	Finish	W	L	Highest round	Coach
1953*	3	9	0	.250	182	350	5th/Western Conf.	—	—		Keith Molesworth
1954*	3	9	0	.250	131	279	6th/Western Conf.	—	—		Weeb Ewbank
1955*	5	6	1	.455	214	239	4th/Western Conf.	—	—		Weeb Ewbank
1956*	5	7	0	.417	270	322	4th/Western Conf.	—	—		Weeb Ewbank
1957*	7	5	0	.583	303	235	3rd/Western Conf.	—	—		Weeb Ewbank
1958*	9	3	0	.750	381	203	1st/Western Conf.	1	0	NFL champ	Weeb Ewbank
1959*	9	3	0	.750	374	251	1st/Western Conf.	1	0	NFL champ	Weeb Ewbank
1960*	6	6	0	.500	288	234	4th/Western Conf.	—	—		Weeb Ewbank
1961*	8	6	0	.571	302	307	T3rd/Western Conf.	—	—		Weeb Ewbank
1962*	7	7	0	.500	293	288	4th/Western Conf.	—	—		Weeb Ewbank
1963*	8	6	0	.571	316	285	3rd/Western Conf.	—	—		Don Shula
1964*	12	2	0	.857	428	225	1st/Western Conf.	0	1	NFL championship game	Don Shula
1965*	10	3	1	.769	389	284	2nd/Western Conf.	0	1	W. Conf. champ. game	Don Shula
1966*	9	5	0	.643	314	226	2nd/Western Conf.	—	—		Don Shula
1967*	11	1	2	.917	394	198	2nd/Coastal Div.	—	—		Don Shula
1968*	13	1	0	.929	402	144	1st/Coastal Div.	2	1	Super Bowl	Don Shula
1969*	8	5	1	.615	279	268	2nd/Coastal Div.	—	—		Don Shula
1970*	11	2	1	.846	321	234	1st/AFC Eastern Div.	3	0	Super Bowl champ	Don McCafferty
1971*	10	4	0	.714	313	140	2nd/AFC Eastern Div.	1	1	AFC championship game	Don McCafferty
1972*	5	9	0	.357	235	252	3rd/AFC Eastern Div.	—	—		McCafferty, John Sandusky
1973*	4	10	0	.286	226	341	4th/AFC Eastern Div.	—	—		Howard Schnellenberger
1974*	2	12	0	.143	190	329	5th/AFC Eastern Div.	—	—		H. Schnellenberger, Joe Thomas
1975*	10	4	0	.714	395	269	1st/AFC Eastern Div.	0	1	AFC div. playoff game	Ted Marchibroda
1976*	11	3	0	.786	417	246	1st/AFC Eastern Div.	0	1	AFC div. playoff game	Ted Marchibroda
1977*	10	4	0	.714	295	221	1st/AFC Eastern Div.	0	1	AFC div. playoff game	Ted Marchibroda
1978*	5	11	0	.313	239	421	5th/AFC Eastern Div.	—	—		Ted Marchibroda
1979*	5	11	0	.313	271	351	5th/AFC Eastern Div.	—	—		Ted Marchibroda
1980*	7	9	0	.438	355	387	4th/AFC Eastern Div.	—	—		Mike McCormack
1981*	2	14	0	.125	259	533	4th/AFC Eastern Div.	—	—		Mike McCormack
1982*	0	8	1	.056	113	236	14th/AFC	—	—		Frank Kush
1983*	7	9	0	.438	264	354	4th/AFC Eastern Div.	—	—		Frank Kush
1984	4	12	0	.250	239	414	4th/AFC Eastern Div.	—	—		Frank Kush, Hal Hunter
1985	5	11	0	.313	320	386	4th/AFC Eastern Div.	—	—		Rod Dowhower
1986	3	13	0	.188	229	400	5th/AFC Eastern Div.	—	—		Rod Dowhower, Ron Meyer
1987	9	6	0	.600	300	238	1st/AFC Eastern Div.	0	1	AFC div. playoff game	Ron Meyer
1988	9	7	0	.563	354	315	2nd/AFC Eastern Div.	—	—		Ron Meyer
1989	8	8	0	.500	298	301	2nd/AFC Eastern Div.	—	—		Ron Meyer
1990	7	9	0	.438	281	353	3rd/AFC Eastern Div.	—	—		Ron Meyer
1991	1	15	0	.063	143	381	5th/AFC Eastern Div.	—	—		Ron Meyer, Rick Venturi
1992	9	7	0	.563	216	302	3rd/AFC Eastern Div.	—	—		Ted Marchibroda
1993	4	12	0	.250	189	378	5th/AFC Eastern Div.	—	—		Ted Marchibroda
1994	8	8	0	.500	307	320	3rd/AFC Eastern Div.	—	—		Ted Marchibroda
1995	9	7	0	.563	331	316	2nd/AFC Eastern Div.	2	1	AFC championship game	Ted Marchibroda
1996	9	7	0	.563	317	334	3rd/AFC Eastern Div.	0	1	AFC wild-card game	Lindy Infante
1997	3	13	0	.188	313	401	5th/AFC Eastern Div.	—	—		Lindy Infante
1998	3	13	0	.188	310	444	5th/AFC Eastern Div.	—	—		Jim Mora
1999	13	3	0	.813	423	333	1st/AFC Eastern Div.	0	1	AFC div. playoff game	Jim Mora
2000	10	6	0	.625	429	326	2nd/AFC Eastern Div.	0	1	AFC wild-card game	Jim Mora
2001	6	10	0	.375	413	486	4th/AFC Eastern Div.	—	—		Jim Mora
2002	10	6	0	.625	349	313	2nd/AFC South Div.	0	1	AFC wild-card game	Tony Dungy
2003	12	4	0	.750	447	336	1st/AFC South Div.	2	1	AFC championship game	Tony Dungy
2004	12	4	0	.750	522	351	1st/AFC South Div.	1	1	AFC div. playoff game	Tony Dungy

*Baltimore Colts.

FIRST-ROUND DRAFT PICKS

1953—Billy Vessels, B, Oklahoma
1954—Cotton Davidson, B, Baylor
1955—George Shaw, B, Oregon*
      Alan Ameche, B, Wisconsin
1956—Lenny Moore, B, Penn State
1957—Jim Parker, G, Ohio State

1958—Lenny Lyles, B, Louisville
1959—Jackie Burkett, C, Auburn
1960—Ron Mix, T, Southern California
1961—Tom Matte, RB, Ohio State
1962—Wendell Harris, DB, Louisiana State
1963—Bob Vogel, T, Ohio State

64—Marv Woodson, DB, Indiana
65—Mike Curtis, LB, Duke
66—Sam Ball, T, Kentucky
67—Bubba Smith, DT, Michigan State*
   Jim Detwiler, RB, Michigan
68—John Williams, G, Minnesota
69—Eddie Hinton, WR, Oklahoma
70—Norm Bulaich, RB, Texas Christian
71—Don McCauley, RB, North Carolina
   Leonard Dunlap, DB, North Texas State
72—Tom Drougas, T, Oregon
73—Bert Jones, QB, Louisiana State
   Joe Ehrmann, DT, Syracuse
74—John Dutton, DE, Nebraska
   Roger Carr, WR, Louisiana Tech
75—Ken Huff, G, North Carolina
76—Ken Novak, DT, Purdue
77—Randy Burke, WR, Kentucky
78—Reese McCall, TE, Auburn
79—Barry Krauss, LB, Alabama
80—Curtis Dickey, RB, Texas A&M
   Derrick Hatchett, DB, Texas
81—Randy McMillan, RB, Pittsburgh
   Donnell Thompson, DT, North Carolina
82—Johnie Cooks, LB, Mississippi State
   Art Schlichter, QB, Ohio State

1983—John Elway, QB, Stanford*
1984—L. Coleman, DB, Vanderbilt
   Ron Solt, G, Maryland
1985—Duane Bickett, LB, Southern California
1986—Jon Hand, DE, Alabama
1987—Cornelius Bennett, LB, Alabama
1988—None
1989—Andre Rison, WR, Michigan State
1990—Jeff George, QB, Illinois*
1991—None
1992—Steve Emtman, DE, Washington*
   Quentin Coryatt, LB, Texas A&M
1993—Sean Dawkins, WR, California
1994—Marshall Faulk, RB, San Diego State
   Trev Alberts, LB, Nebraska
1995—Ellis Johnson, DT, Florida
1996—Marvin Harrison, WR, Syracuse
1997—Tarik Glenn, T, California
1998—Peyton Manning, QB, Tennessee*
1999—Edgerrin James, RB, Miami, Fla.
2000—Rob Morris, LB, Brigham Young
2001—Reggie Wayne, WR, Miami, Fla.
2002—Dwight Freeney, DE, Syracuse
2003—Dallas Clark, TE, Iowa
2004—None
2005—Marlin Jackson, CB, Michigan
   *First player chosen in draft.

FRANCHISE RECORDS

ost rushing yards, career
720—Edgerrin James
ost rushing yards, season
709—Edgerrin James, 2000
ost rushing yards, game
9—Edgerrin James at Sea., Oct. 15,
   2000
ost rushing touchdowns, season
—Lenny Moore, 1964
ost passing attempts, season
1—Peyton Manning, 2002
ost passing attempts, game
—Jeff George at Was., Nov. 7, 1993
ost passes completed, season
2—Peyton Manning, 2002
ost passes completed, game
—Jeff George at Was., Nov. 7, 1993
   Peyton Manning vs. Ten., Nov. 3,
   2002
ost passing yards, career
,768—Johnny Unitas
ost passing yards, season
557—Peyton Manning, 2004

Most passing yards, game
440—Peyton Manning vs. Jac., Sept.
   25, 2000
Most touchdown passes, season
49—Peyton Manning, 2004
Most pass receptions, career
845—Marvin Harrison
Most pass receptions, season
143—Marvin Harrison, 2002
Most pass receptions, game
14—Marvin Harrison at Cle., Dec. 26, 1999
   Marvin Harrison vs. Dal., Nov. 17,
   2002
Most receiving yards, career
11,185—Marvin Harrison
Most receiving yards, season
1,722—Marvin Harrison, 2002
Most receiving yards, game
224—Raymond Berry at Was., Nov. 10,
   1957
Most receiving touchdowns, season
15—Marvin Harrison, 2001
   Marvin Harrison, 2004

Most touchdowns, career
113—Lenny Moore
Most field goals, season
37—Mike Vanderjagt, 2003
Longest field goal
58 yards—Dan Miller at S.D., Dec. 26,
   1982
Most interceptions, career
57—Bob Boyd
Most interceptions, season
11—Tom Keane, 1953
Most sacks, career
56.5—Fred Cook
Most sacks, season
17—John Dutton, 1975

SERIES RECORDS

dianapolis vs.: Arizona 6-6; Atlanta 12-1; Baltimore 3-2; Buffalo 29-34-1; Carolina 0-3; Chicago 22-17; Cincinnati 12-8; Cleveland
-13; Dallas 5-7; Denver 4-11; Detroit 20-18-2; Green Bay 20-19-1; Houston 6-0; Jacksonville 6-2; Kansas City 8-7; Miami 22-44;
nnesota 13-7-1; New England 24-41; New Orleans 4-5; N.Y. Giants 6-6; N.Y. Jets 39-25; Oakland 3-7; Philadelphia 9-6; Pittsburgh
13; St. Louis 21-17-2; San Diego 8-12; San Francisco 22-18; Seattle 5-3; Tampa Bay 6-4; Tennessee 11-9; Washington 17-10.
TE: Includes records as Baltimore Colts from 1953 through 1983.

COACHING RECORDS

d Dowhower, 5-24-0; Tony Dungy, 34-14-0 (3-3); Weeb Ewbank, 59-52-1 (2-0); Hal
nter, 0-1-0; Lindy Infante, 12-20-0 (0-1); Frank Kush, 11-28-1; Ted Marchibroda, 71-
-0 (2-4); Don McCafferty, 22-10-1 (4-1); Mike McCormack, 9-23-0; Ron Meyer, 36-35-
(0-1); Keith Molesworth, 3-9-0; Jim Mora, 32-32-0 (0-2); John Sandusky, 4-5-0;
ward Schnellenberger, 4-13-0; Don Shula, 71-23-4 (2-3); Joe Thomas, 2-9-0; Rick
nturi, 1-10.
TE: Playoff games in parentheses.

RETIRED UNIFORM NUMBERS

No.	Player
19	Johnny Unitas
22	Buddy Young
24	Lenny Moore
70	Art Donovan
77	Jim Parker
82	Raymond Berry
89	Gino Marchetti

JACKSONVILLE JAGUARS
YEAR-BY-YEAR RECORDS

	REGULAR SEASON							PLAYOFFS			
Year	W	L	T	Pct.	PF	PA	Finish	W	L	Highest round	Coach
1995	4	12	0	.250	275	404	5th/AFC Central Div.	—	—		Tom Coughlin
1996	9	7	0	.563	325	335	2nd/AFC Central Div.	2	1	AFC championship game	Tom Coughlin
1997	11	5	0	.688	394	318	2nd/AFC Central Div.	0	1	AFC wild-card game	Tom Coughlin
1998	11	5	0	.688	392	338	1st/AFC Central Div.	1	1	AFC div. playoff game	Tom Coughlin
1999	14	2	0	.875	396	217	1st/AFC Central Div.	1	1	AFC championship game	Tom Coughlin
2000	7	9	0	.438	367	327	4th/AFC Central Div.	—	—		Tom Coughlin
2001	6	10	0	.375	294	286	5th/AFC Central Div.	—	—		Tom Coughlin
2002	6	10	0	.375	328	315	3rd/AFC South Div.	—	—		Tom Coughlin
2003	5	11	0	.313	276	331	3rd/AFC South Div.	—	—		Jack Del Rio
2004	9	7	0	.562	261	280	2nd/AFC South Div.	—	—		Jack Del Rio

FIRST-ROUND DRAFT PICKS

1995—Tony Boselli, T, Southern California
    James Stewart, RB, Tennessee
1996—Kevin Hardy, LB, Illinois
1997—Renaldo Wynn, DT, Notre Dame
1998—Fred Taylor, RB, Florida
    Donovin Darius, DB, Syracuse
1999—Fernando Bryant, DB, Alabama

2000—R. Jay Soward, WR, Southern California
2001—Marcus Stroud, DT, Georgia
2002—John Henderson, DT, Tennessee
2003—Byron Leftwich, QB, Marshall
2004—Reggie Williams, WR, Washington
2005—Matt Jones, WR, Arkansas

FRANCHISE RECORDS

Most rushing yards, career
7,580—Fred Taylor
Most rushing yards, season
1,572—Fred Taylor, 2003
Most rushing yards, game
234—Fred Taylor at Pit., Nov. 19, 2000
Most rushing touchdowns, season
14—Fred Taylor, 1998
Most passing attempts, season
557—Mark Brunell, 1996
Most passing attempts, game
52—Mark Brunell at St.L., Oct. 20, 1996
Most passes completed, season
353—Mark Brunell, 1996
Most passes completed, game
37—Mark Brunell at St.L., Oct. 20, 1996
Most passing yards, career
25,698—Mark Brunell
Most passing yards, season
4,367—Mark Brunell, 1996

Most passing yards, game
432—Mark Brunell at N.E., Sept. 22, 1996
Most touchdown passes, season
20—Mark Brunell, 1998, 2000
Most pass receptions, career
792—Jimmy Smith
Most pass receptions, season
116—Jimmy Smith, 1999
Most pass receptions, game
16—Keenan McCardell at St.L., Oct. 20, 1996
Most receiving yards, career
11,264—Jimmy Smith
Most receiving yards, season
1,636—Jimmy Smith, 1999
Most receiving yards, game
291—Jimmy Smith at Bal., Sept. 10, 2000
Most receiving touchdowns, season
8—Jimmy Smith, 1998, 2000, 2001

Most touchdowns, career
63—Jimmy Smith
Most field goals, season
31—Mike Hollis, 1997
    Mike Hollis, 1999
Longest field goal
53 yards—Mike Hollis vs. Pit., Oct. 8, 19??
    Mike Hollis vs. Car., Sept. 29, 1996
    Seth Marler vs. S.D., Oct. 5, 2003
Most interceptions, career
15—Aaron Beasley
Most interceptions, season
6—Aaron Beasley, 1999
    Marlon McCree, 2002
Most sacks, career
55—Tony Brackens
Most sacks, season
12—Tony Brackens, 1999

SERIES RECORDS

Jacksonville vs.: Arizona 1-0; Atlanta 2-1; Baltimore 8-6; Buffalo 2-3; Carolina 2-1; Chicago 2-2; Cincinnati 10-5; Cleveland 7-2; Dall?? 1-2; Denver 2-2; Detroit 2-1; Green Bay 1-2; Houston 2-4; Indianapolis 2-6; Kansas City 4-1; Miami 1-1; Minnesota 1-2; New Engla?? 0-3; New Orleans 2-1; N.Y. Giants 1-2; N.Y. Jets 3-2; Oakland 2-1; Philadelphia 2-0; Pittsburgh 8-8; St. Louis 0-1; San Diego 1-1; S?? Francisco 1-0; Seattle 1-3; Tampa Bay 2-1; Tennessee 8-12; Washington 1-2.

COACHING RECORDS

Tom Coughlin, 68-60-0 (4-4); Jack Del Rio, 14-18-0.
NOTE: Playoff games in parentheses.

RETIRED UNIFORM NUMBER??

No.	Player
	None

KANSAS CITY CHIEFS
YEAR-BY-YEAR RECORDS

	REGULAR SEASON							PLAYOFFS			
Year	W	L	T	Pct.	PF	PA	Finish	W	L	Highest round	Coach
1960*†	8	6	0	.571	362	253	2nd/Western Div.	—	—		Hank Stram
1961*†	6	8	0	.429	334	343	2nd/Western Div.	—	—		Hank Stram
1962*†	11	3	0	.786	389	233	1st/Western Div.	1	0	AFL champ	Hank Stram
1963*	5	7	2	.417	347	263	3rd/Western Div.	—	—		Hank Stram
1964*	7	7	0	.500	366	306	2nd/Western Div.	—	—		Hank Stram

	REGULAR SEASON							PLAYOFFS			
Year	W	L	T	Pct.	PF	PA	Finish	W	L	Highest round	Coach
1965*	7	5	2	.583	322	285	3rd/Western Div.	—	—		Hank Stram
1966*	11	2	1	.846	448	276	1st/Western Div.	1	1	Super Bowl	Hank Stram
1967*	9	5	0	.643	408	254	2nd/Western Div.	—	—		Hank Stram
1968*	12	2	0	.857	371	170	2nd/Western Div.	0	1	W. Div. champ. game	Hank Stram
1969*	11	3	0	.786	359	177	2nd/Western Div.	3	0	Super Bowl champ	Hank Stram
1970	7	5	2	.583	272	244	2nd/AFC Western Div.	—	—		Hank Stram
1971	10	3	1	.769	302	208	1st/AFC Western Div.	0	1	AFC div. playoff game	Hank Stram
1972	8	6	0	.571	287	254	2nd/AFC Western Div.	—	—		Hank Stram
1973	7	5	2	.571	231	192	3rd/AFC Western Div.	—	—		Hank Stram
1974	5	9	0	.357	233	293	3rd/AFC Western Div.	—	—		Hank Stram
1975	5	9	0	.357	282	341	3rd/AFC Western Div.	—	—		Paul Wiggin
1976	5	9	0	.357	290	376	4th/AFC Western Div.	—	—		Paul Wiggin
1977	2	12	0	.143	225	349	5th/AFC Western Div.	—	—		Paul Wiggin, Tom Bettis
1978	4	12	0	.250	243	327	5th/AFC Western Div.	—	—		Marv Levy
1979	7	9	0	.438	238	262	5th/AFC Western Div.	—	—		Marv Levy
1980	8	8	0	.500	319	336	3rd/AFC Western Div.	—	—		Marv Levy
1981	9	7	0	.563	343	290	3rd/AFC Western Div.	—	—		Marv Levy
1982	3	6	0	.333	176	184	11th/AFC	—	—		Marv Levy
1983	6	10	0	.375	386	367	5th/AFC Western Div.	—	—		John Mackovic
1984	8	8	0	.500	314	324	4th/AFC Western Div.	—	—		John Mackovic
1985	6	10	0	.375	317	360	5th/AFC Western Div.	—	—		John Mackovic
1986	10	6	0	.625	358	326	2nd/AFC Western Div.	0	1	AFC wild-card game	John Mackovic
1987	4	11	0	.267	273	388	5th/AFC Western Div.	—	—		Frank Gansz
1988	4	11	1	.281	254	320	5th/AFC Western Div.	—	—		Frank Gansz
1989	8	7	1	.531	318	286	2nd/AFC Western Div.	—	—		Marty Schottenheimer
1990	11	5	0	.688	369	257	2nd/AFC Western Div.	0	1	AFC wild-card game	Marty Schottenheimer
1991	10	6	0	.625	322	252	2nd/AFC Western Div.	1	1	AFC div. playoff game	Marty Schottenheimer
1992	10	6	0	.625	348	282	2nd/AFC Western Div.	0	1	AFC wild-card game	Marty Schottenheimer
1993	11	5	0	.688	328	291	1st/AFC Western Div.	2	1	AFC championship game	Marty Schottenheimer
1994	9	7	0	.563	319	298	2nd/AFC Western Div.	0	1	AFC wild-card game	Marty Schottenheimer
1995	13	3	0	.813	358	241	1st/AFC Western Div.	0	1	AFC div. playoff game	Marty Schottenheimer
1996	9	7	0	.563	297	300	2nd/AFC Western Div.	—	—		Marty Schottenheimer
1997	13	3	0	.813	375	232	1st/AFC Western Div.	0	1	AFC div. playoff game	Marty Schottenheimer
1998	7	9	0	.438	327	363	4th/AFC Western Div.	—	—		Marty Schottenheimer
1999	9	7	0	.563	390	322	2nd/AFC Western Div.	—	—		Gunther Cunningham
2000	7	9	0	.438	355	354	3rd/AFC Western Div.	—	—		Gunther Cunningham
2001	6	10	0	.375	320	344	4th/AFC Western Div.	—	—		Dick Vermeil
2002	8	8	0	.500	467	399	4th/AFC West Div.	—	—		Dick Vermeil
2003	13	3	0	.813	484	332	1st/AFC West Div.	0	1	AFC div. playoff game	Dick Vermeil
2004	7	9	0	.438	483	435	3rd/AFC West Div.	—	—		Dick Vermeil

*American Football League.
†Dallas Texans.

FIRST-ROUND DRAFT PICKS

1960—Don Meredith, QB, Southern Methodist
1961—E.J. Holub, C, Texas Tech
1962—Ronnie Bull, RB, Baylor
1963—Buck Buchanan, DT, Grambling* (AFL)
　　　Ed Budde, G, Michigan State
1964—Pete Beathard, QB, Southern California
1965—Gale Sayers, RB, Kansas
1966—Aaron Brown, DE, Minnesota
1967—Gene Trosch, DE, Miami
1968—Mo Moorman, G, Texas A&M
　　　George Daney, G, Texas-El Paso
1969—Jim Marsalis, DB, Tennessee State
1970—Sid Smith, T, Southern California
1971—Elmo Wright, WR, Houston
1972—Jeff Kinney, RB, Nebraska
1973—None
1974—Woody Green, RB, Arizona State
1975—None
1976—Rod Walters, G, Iowa
1977—Gary Green, DB, Baylor
1978—Art Still, DE, Kentucky
1979—Mike Bell, DE, Colorado State
　　　Steve Fuller, QB, Clemson
1980—Brad Budde, G, Southern California
1981—Willie Scott, TE, South Carolina
1982—Anthony Hancock, WR, Tennessee

1983—Todd Blackledge, QB, Penn State
1984—Bill Maas, DT, Pittsburgh
　　　John Alt, T, Iowa
1985—Ethan Horton, RB, North Carolina
1986—Brian Jozwiak, T, West Virginia
1987—Paul Palmer, RB, Temple
1988—Neil Smith, DE, Nebraska
1989—Derrick Thomas, LB, Alabama
1990—Percy Snow, LB, Michigan State
1991—Harvey Williams, RB, Louisiana State
1992—Dale Carter, DB, Tennessee
1993—None
1994—Greg Hill, RB, Texas A&M
1995—Trezelle Jenkins, T, Michigan
1996—Jerome Woods, DB, Memphis
1997—Tony Gonzalez, TE, California
1998—Victor Riley, T, Auburn
1999—John Tait, T, Brigham Young
2000—Sylvester Morris, WR, Jackson State
2001—None
2002—Ryan Sims, DT, North Carolina
2003—Larry Johnson, RB, Penn State
2004—None
2005—Derrick Johnson, OLB, Texas
　　　*First player chosen in draft.

FRANCHISE RECORDS

Most rushing yards, career
6,374—Priest Holmes
Most rushing yards, season
1,615—Priest Holmes, 2002
Most rushing yards, game
200—Barry Word vs. Det., Oct. 14, 1990
Most rushing touchdowns, season
27—Priest Holmes, 2003
Most passing attempts, season
603—Bill Kenney, 1983
Most passing attempts, game
55—Joe Montana at S.D., Oct. 9, 1994
Steve Bono at Mia., Dec. 12, 1994
Most passes completed, season
346—Bill Kenney, 1983
Most passes completed, game
39—Elvis Grbac at Oak., Nov. 5, 2000
Most passing yards, career
28,507—Len Dawson

Most passing yards, season
4,591—Trent Green, 2004
Most passing yards, game
504—Elvis Grbac at Oak., Nov. 5, 2000
Most touchdown passes, season
30—Len Dawson, 1964
Most pass receptions, career
570—Tony Gonzalez
Most pass receptions, season
102—Tony Gonzalez, 2004
Most pass receptions, game
12—Ed Podolak vs. Den., Oct. 7, 1973
Most receiving yards, career
7,306—Otis Taylor
Most receiving yards, season
1,391—Derrick Alexander, 2000
Most receiving yards, game
309—Stephone Paige vs. S.D., Dec. 22, 1985

Most receiving touchdowns, season
12—Chris Burford, 1962
Most touchdowns, career
76—Priest Holmes
Most field goals, season
34—Nick Lowery, 1990
Longest field goals
58 yards—Nick Lowery at Was., Sept. 18 1983
Nick Lowery vs. L.A. Raiders, Sept. 12, 1985
Most interceptions, career
58—Emmitt Thomas
Most interceptions, season
12—Emmitt Thomas, 1974
Most sacks, career
126.5—Derrick Thomas
Most sacks, season
20—Derrick Thomas, 1990

SERIES RECORDS

Kansas City vs.: Arizona 6-2-1; Atlanta 5-1; Baltimore 3-0; Buffalo 16-18-1; Carolina 2-1; Chicago 4-5; Cincinnati 11-10; Cleveland 9-8-2; Dallas 3-4; Denver 50-39; Detroit 7-3; Green Bay 6-1-1; Houston 1-1; Indianapolis 7-8; Jacksonville 1-4; Miami 11-10; Minnesota 4-4; New England 15-11-3; New Orleans 4-4; N.Y. Giants 2-8; N.Y. Jets 15-14-1; Oakland 45-42-2; Philadelphia 2-2; Pittsburgh 8-16; St. Louis 4-4; San Diego 47-41-1; San Francisco 3-6; Seattle 30-18; Tampa Bay 5-4; Tennessee 25-18; Washington 5-1.
NOTE: Includes records as Dallas Texans from 1960 through 1962.

COACHING RECORDS

Tom Bettis, 1-6-0; Gunther Cunningham, 16-16-0; Frank Gansz, 8-22-1; Marv Levy, 31-42-0; John Mackovic, 30-34-0 (0-1); Marty Schottenheimer, 101-58-1 (3-7); Hank Stram, 124-76-10 (5-3); Dick Vermeil, 34-30-0 (0-1); Paul Wiggin, 11-24-0. NOTE: Playoff games in parentheses.

RETIRED UNIFORM NUMBERS

No.	Player	No.	Player
3	Jan Stenerud	36	Mack Lee Hill
16	Len Dawson	63	Willie Lanier
28	Abner Haynes	78	Bobby Bell
33	Stone Johnson	86	Buck Buchanan

MIAMI DOLPHINS
YEAR-BY-YEAR RECORDS

		REGULAR SEASON						PLAYOFFS		
Year	W	L	T	Pct.	PF	PA	Finish	W	L	Highest round	Coach
1966*	3	11	0	.214	213	362	T4th/Eastern Div.	—	—		George Wilson
1967*	4	10	0	.286	219	407	T3rd/Eastern Div.	—	—		George Wilson
1968*	5	8	1	.385	276	355	3rd/Eastern Div.	—	—		George Wilson
1969*	3	10	1	.231	233	332	5th/Eastern Div.	—	—		George Wilson
1970	10	4	0	.714	297	228	2nd/AFC Eastern Div.	0	1	AFC div. playoff game	Don Shula
1971	10	3	1	.769	315	174	1st/AFC Eastern Div.	2	1	Super Bowl	Don Shula
1972	14	0	0	1.000	385	171	1st/AFC Eastern Div.	3	0	Super Bowl champ	Don Shula
1973	12	2	0	.857	343	150	1st/AFC Eastern Div.	3	0	Super Bowl champ	Don Shula
1974	11	3	0	.786	327	216	1st/AFC Eastern Div.	0	1	AFC div. playoff game	Don Shula
1975	10	4	0	.714	357	222	2nd/AFC Eastern Div.	—	—		Don Shula
1976	6	8	0	.429	263	264	3rd/AFC Eastern Div.	—	—		Don Shula
1977	10	4	0	.714	313	197	2nd/AFC Eastern Div.	—	—		Don Shula
1978	11	5	0	.688	372	254	2nd/AFC Eastern Div.	0	1	AFC wild-card game	Don Shula
1979	10	6	0	.625	341	257	1st/AFC Eastern Div.	0	1	AFC div. playoff game	Don Shula
1980	8	8	0	.500	266	305	3rd/AFC Eastern Div.	—	—		Don Shula
1981	11	4	1	.719	345	275	1st/AFC Eastern Div.	0	1	AFC div. playoff game	Don Shula
1982	7	2	0	.778	198	131	2nd/AFC	3	1	Super Bowl	Don Shula
1983	12	4	0	.750	389	250	1st/AFC Eastern Div.	0	1	AFC div. playoff game	Don Shula
1984	14	2	0	.875	513	298	1st/AFC Eastern Div.	2	1	Super Bowl	Don Shula
1985	12	4	0	.750	428	320	1st/AFC Eastern Div.	1	1	AFC championship game	Don Shula
1986	8	8	0	.500	430	405	3rd/AFC Eastern Div.	—	—		Don Shula
1987	8	7	0	.533	362	335	3rd/AFC Eastern Div.	—	—		Don Shula
1988	6	10	0	.375	319	380	5th/AFC Eastern Div.	—	—		Don Shula
1989	8	8	0	.500	331	379	3rd/AFC Eastern Div.	—	—		Don Shula
1990	12	4	0	.750	336	242	2nd/AFC Eastern Div.	1	1	AFC div. playoff game	Don Shula
1991	8	8	0	.500	343	349	3rd/AFC Eastern Div.	—	—		Don Shula
1992	11	5	0	.688	340	281	1st/AFC Eastern Div.	1	1	AFC championship game	Don Shula

REGULAR SEASON

ear	W	L	T	Pct.	PF	PA	Finish	W	L	Highest round	Coach
993	9	7	0	.563	349	351	2nd/AFC Eastern Div.	—	—		Don Shula
994	10	6	0	.625	389	327	1st/AFC Eastern Div.	1	1	AFC div. playoff game	Don Shula
995	9	7	0	.563	398	332	3rd/AFC Eastern Div.	0	1	AFC wild-card game	Don Shula
996	8	8	0	.500	339	325	4th/AFC Eastern Div.	—	—		Jimmy Johnson
997	9	7	0	.563	339	327	2nd/AFC Eastern Div.	0	1	AFC wild-card game	Jimmy Johnson
998	10	6	0	.625	321	265	2nd/AFC Eastern Div.	1	1	AFC div. playoff game	Jimmy Johnson
999	9	7	0	.563	326	336	3rd/AFC Eastern Div.	1	1	AFC div. playoff game	Jimmy Johnson
000	11	5	0	.688	323	226	1st/AFC Eastern Div.	1	1	AFC div. playoff game	Dave Wannstedt
001	11	5	0	.688	344	290	2nd/AFC Eastern Div.	0	1	AFC wild-card game	Dave Wannstedt
002	9	7	0	.563	378	301	3rd/AFC East Div.	—	—		Dave Wannstedt
003	10	6	0	.625	311	261	2nd/AFC East Div.	—	—		Dave Wannstedt
004	4	12	0	.250	275	354	4th/AFC East Div.	—	—		D. Wannstedt, Jim Bates

*American Football League.

FIRST-ROUND DRAFT PICKS

966—Jim Grabowski, RB, Illinois*
  Rick Norton, QB, Kentucky
967—Bob Griese, QB, Purdue
968—Larry Csonka, RB, Syracuse
  Doug Crusan, T, Indiana
969—Bill Stanfill, DE, Georgia
970—None
971—None
972—Mike Kadish, DT, Notre Dame
973—None
974—Don Reese, DE, Jackson State
975—Darryl Carlton, T, Tampa
976—Larry Gordon, LB, Arizona State
  Kim Bokamper, LB, San Jose State
977—A.J. Duhe, DT, Louisiana State
978—None
979—Jon Giesler, T, Michigan
980—Don McNeal, DB, Alabama
981—David Overstreet, RB, Oklahoma
982—Roy Foster, G, Southern California
983—Dan Marino, QB, Pittsburgh
984—Jackie Shipp, LB, Oklahoma
985—Lorenzo Hampton, RB, Florida

1986—None
1987—John Bosa, DE, Boston College
1988—Eric Kumerow, DE, Ohio State
1989—Sammie Smith, RB, Florida State
  Louis Oliver, DB, Florida
1990—Richmond Webb, T, Texas A&M
1991—Randal Hill, WR, Miami, Fla.
1992—Troy Vincent, DB, Wisconsin
  Marco Coleman, LB, Georgia Tech
1993—O.J. McDuffie, WR, Penn State
1994—Tim Bowens, DT, Mississippi
1995—Billy Milner, T, Houston
1996—Daryl Gardener, DT, Baylor
1997—Yatil Green, WR, Miami, Fla.
1998—John Avery, RB, Mississippi
1999—None
2000—None
2001—Jamar Fletcher, DB, Wisconsin
2002—None
2003—None
2004—Vernon Carey, OT, Miami, Fla.
2005—Ronnie Brown, RB, Auburn
  *First player chosen in draft.

HISTORY — Team by team

FRANCHISE RECORDS

Most rushing yards, career
6,737—Larry Csonka
Most rushing yards, season
1,853—Ricky Williams, 2002
Most rushing yards, game
228—Ricky Williams at Buf., Dec. 1, 2002
Most rushing touchdowns, season
16—Ricky Williams, 2002
Most passing attempts, season
623—Dan Marino, 1986
Most passing attempts, game
60—Dan Marino vs. NYJ, Oct. 23, 1988
  Dan Marino at N.E., Nov. 23, 1997
Most passes completed, season
385—Dan Marino, 1994
Most passes completed, game
39—Dan Marino at Buf., Nov. 16, 1986
Most passing yards, career
61,361—Dan Marino

Most passing yards, season
5,084—Dan Marino, 1984
Most passing yards, game
521—Dan Marino vs. NYJ, Oct. 23, 1988
Most touchdown passes, season
48—Dan Marino, 1984
Most pass receptions, career
550—Mark Clayton
Most pass receptions, season
90—O.J. McDuffie, 1998
Most pass receptions, game
12—Jim Jensen at N.E., Nov. 6, 1988
Most receiving yards, career
8,869—Mark Duper
Most receiving yards, season
1,389—Mark Clayton, 1984
Most receiving yards, game
217—Mark Duper vs. NYJ, Nov. 10, 1985

Most receiving touchdowns, season
18—Mark Clayton, 1984
Most touchdowns, career
82—Mark Clayton
Most field goals, season
39—Olindo Mare, 1999
Longest field goal
59 yards—Pete Stoyanovich at NYJ, Nov. 12, 1989
Most interceptions, career
35—Jake Scott
Most interceptions, season
10—Dick Westmoreland, 1967
Most sacks, career
80.5—Jason Taylor
Most sacks, season
18.5—Bill Stanfill, 1973
  Jason Taylor, 2002

SERIES RECORDS

Miami vs.: Arizona 8-1; Atlanta 7-2; Baltimore 4-1; Buffalo 48-29-1; Carolina 2-0; Chicago 6-3; Cincinnati 12-4; Cleveland 7-4; Dallas 5-3; Denver 9-3-1; Detroit 6-2; Green Bay 9-2; Houston 0-1; Indianapolis 44-22; Jacksonville 1-1; Kansas City 10-11; Minnesota 4-4; New England 45-31; New Orleans 5-3; N.Y. Giants 2-3; N.Y. Jets 37-40-1; Oakland 10-15-1; Philadelphia 7-4; Pittsburgh 9-8; St. Louis 5-2; San Diego 10-10; San Francisco 5-4; Seattle 6-3; Tampa Bay 4-3; Tennessee 15-13; Washington 6-3.

COACHING RECORDS

Jim Bates, 3-4-0; Jimmy Johnson, 36-28-0 (2-3); Don Shula, 257-133-2 (17-14); Dave Wannstedt, 42-31-0 (1-2); George Wilson, 15-39-2.
NOTE: Playoff games in parentheses.

RETIRED UNIFORM NUMBERS

No.	Player
12	Bob Griese
13	Dan Marino
39	Larry Csonka

MINNESOTA VIKINGS
YEAR-BY-YEAR RECORDS

	REGULAR SEASON							PLAYOFFS		
Year	W	L	T	Pct.	PF	PA	Finish	W	L	Highest round	Coach
1961	3	11	0	.214	285	407	7th/Western Conf.	—	—		Norm Van Brocklin
1962	2	11	1	.154	254	410	6th/Western Conf.	—	—		Norm Van Brocklin
1963	5	8	1	.385	309	390	T4th/Western Conf.	—	—		Norm Van Brocklin
1964	8	5	1	.615	355	296	T2nd/Western Conf.	—	—		Norm Van Brocklin
1965	7	7	0	.500	383	403	5th/Western Conf.	—	—		Norm Van Brocklin
1966	4	9	1	.308	292	304	T6th/Western Conf.	—	—		Norm Van Brocklin
1967	3	8	3	.273	233	294	4th/Central Div.	—	—		Bud Grant
1968	8	6	0	.571	282	242	1st/Central Div.	0	1	W. Conf. champ. game	Bud Grant
1969	12	2	0	.857	379	133	1st/Central Div.	2	1	Super Bowl	Bud Grant
1970	12	2	0	.857	335	143	1st/NFC Central Div.	0	1	NFC div. playoff game	Bud Grant
1971	11	3	0	.786	245	139	1st/NFC Central Div.	0	1	NFC div. playoff game	Bud Grant
1972	7	7	0	.500	301	252	3rd/NFC Central Div.	—	—		Bud Grant
1973	12	2	0	.857	296	168	1st/NFC Central Div.	2	1	Super Bowl	Bud Grant
1974	10	4	0	.714	310	195	1st/NFC Central Div.	2	1	Super Bowl	Bud Grant
1975	12	2	0	.857	377	180	1st/NFC Central Div.	0	1	NFC div. playoff game	Bud Grant
1976	11	2	1	.821	305	176	1st/NFC Central Div.	2	1	Super Bowl	Bud Grant
1977	9	5	0	.643	231	227	1st/NFC Central Div.	1	1	NFC championship game	Bud Grant
1978	8	7	1	.531	294	306	1st/NFC Central Div.	0	1	NFC div. playoff game	Bud Grant
1979	7	9	0	.438	259	337	3rd/NFC Central Div.	—	—		Bud Grant
1980	9	7	0	.563	317	308	1st/NFC Central Div.	0	1	NFC div. playoff game	Bud Grant
1981	7	9	0	.438	325	369	4th/NFC Central Div.	—	—		Bud Grant
1982	5	4	0	.556	187	198	4th/NFC	1	1	NFC second-round pl. game	Bud Grant
1983	8	8	0	.500	316	348	4th/NFC Central Div.	—	—		Bud Grant
1984	3	13	0	.188	276	484	5th/NFC Central Div.	—	—		Les Steckel
1985	7	9	0	.438	346	359	3rd/NFC Central Div.	—	—		Bud Grant
1986	9	7	0	.563	398	273	2nd/NFC Central Div.	—	—		Jerry Burns
1987	8	7	0	.533	336	335	2nd/NFC Central Div.	2	1	NFC championship game	Jerry Burns
1988	11	5	0	.688	406	233	2nd/NFC Central Div.	1	1	NFC div. playoff game	Jerry Burns
1989	10	6	0	.625	351	275	1st/NFC Central Div.	0	1	NFC div. playoff game	Jerry Burns
1990	6	10	0	.375	351	326	5th/NFC Central Div.	—	—		Jerry Burns
1991	8	8	0	.500	301	306	3rd/NFC Central Div.	—	—		Jerry Burns
1992	11	5	0	.688	374	249	1st/NFC Central Div.	0	1	NFC wild-card game	Dennis Green
1993	9	7	0	.563	277	290	2nd/NFC Central Div.	0	1	NFC wild-card game	Dennis Green
1994	10	6	0	.625	356	314	1st/NFC Central Div.	0	1	NFC wild-card game	Dennis Green
1995	8	8	0	.500	412	385	4th/NFC Central Div.	—	—		Dennis Green
1996	9	7	0	.563	298	315	2nd/NFC Central Div.	0	1	NFC wild-card game	Dennis Green
1997	9	7	0	.563	354	359	4th/NFC Central Div.	1	1	NFC div. playoff game	Dennis Green
1998	15	1	0	.938	556	296	1st/NFC Central Div.	1	1	NFC championship game	Dennis Green
1999	10	6	0	.625	399	335	2nd/NFC Central Div.	1	1	NFC div. playoff game	Dennis Green
2000	11	5	0	.688	397	371	1st/NFC Central Div.	1	1	NFC championship game	Dennis Green
2001	5	11	0	.313	290	390	4th/NFC Central Div.	—	—		Dennis Green, Mike Tice
2002	6	10	0	.375	390	442	2nd/NFC North Div.	—	—		Mike Tice
2003	9	7	0	.563	416	353	2nd/NFC North Div.	—	—		Mike Tice
2004	8	8	0	.500	405	395	2nd/NFC North Div.	1	1	NFC div. playoff game	Mike Tice

FIRST-ROUND DRAFT PICKS

1961—Tommy Mason, RB, Tulane*
1962—None
1963—Jim Dunaway, T, Mississippi
1964—Carl Eller, DE, Minnesota
1965—Jack Snow, WR, Notre Dame
1966—Jerry Shay, DT, Purdue
1967—Clint Jones, RB, Michigan State
      Gene Washington, WR, Michigan State
      Alan Page, DT, Notre Dame
1968—Ron Yary, T, Southern California*
1969—None
1970—John Ward, DT, Oklahoma State
1971—Leo Hayden, RB, Ohio State
1972—Jeff Siemon, LB, Stanford
1973—Chuck Foreman, RB, Miami, Fla.

1974—Fred McNeill, LB, UCLA
      Steve Riley, T, Southern California
1975—Mark Mullaney, DE, Colorado State
1976—James White, DT, Oklahoma State
1977—Tommy Kramer, QB, Rice
1978—Randy Holloway, DE, Pittsburgh
1979—Ted Brown, RB, North Carolina State
1980—Doug Martin, DT, Washington
1981—None
1982—Darrin Nelson, RB, Stanford
1983—Joey Browner, DB, Southern California
1984—Keith Millard, DE, Washington State
1985—Chris Doleman, LB, Pittsburgh
1986—Gerald Robinson, DE, Auburn
1987—D.J. Dozier, RB, Penn State

88—Randall McDaniel, G, Arizona State
89—None
90—None
91—None
92—None
93—Robert Smith, RB, Ohio State
94—DeWayne Washington, CB, North Carolina State
    Todd Steussie, T, California
95—Derrick Alexander, DE, Florida State
    Korey Stringer, T, Ohio State
96—Duane Clemons, DE, California
97—Dwayne Rudd, LB, Alabama

1998—Randy Moss, WR, Marshall
1999—Daunte Culpepper, QB, Central Florida
    Dimitrius Underwood, DE, Michigan State
2000—Chris Hovan, DT, Boston College
2001—Michael Bennett, RB, Wisconsin
2002—Bryant McKinnie, T, Miami, Fla.
2003—Kevin Williams, DT, Oklahoma State
2004—Kenechi Udeze, DE, Southern California
2005—Troy Williamson, WR, South Carolina
    Erasmus James, DE, Wisconsin
*First player chosen in draft.

FRANCHISE RECORDS

Most rushing yards, career
6,818—Robert Smith
Most rushing yards, season
1,521—Robert Smith, 2000
Most rushing yards, game
200—Chuck Foreman at Phi., Oct. 24, 1976
Most rushing touchdowns, season
13—Chuck Foreman, 1975
    Chuck Foreman, 1976
    Terry Allen, 1992
Most passing attempts, season
606—Warren Moon, 1995
Most passing attempts, game
58—Rich Gannon at N.E., Oct. 20, 1991
Most passes completed, season
377—Warren Moon, 1995
Most passes completed, game
36—Tommy Kramer vs. Cle., Dec. 14, 1980
    Tommy Kramer vs. G.B., Nov. 29, 1981
Most passing yards, career
33,098—Fran Tarkenton

Most passing yards, season
4,717—Daunte Culpepper, 2004
Most passing yards, game
490—Tommy Kramer at Was., Nov. 2, 1986 (OT)
456—Tommy Kramer vs. Cle., Dec. 14, 1980
Most touchdown passes, season
39—Daunte Culpepper, 2004
Most pass receptions, career
1,004—Cris Carter
Most pass receptions, season
122—Cris Carter, 1994, 1995
Most pass receptions, game
15—Rickey Young at N.E., Dec. 16, 1979
Most receiving yards, career
12,383—Cris Carter
Most receiving yards, season
1,632—Randy Moss, 2003
Most receiving yards, game
210—Sammy White vs. Det., Nov. 7, 1976

Most receiving touchdowns, season
17—Cris Carter, 1995
    Randy Moss, 1998
    Randy Moss, 2003
Most touchdowns, career
110—Cris Carter
Most field goals, season
35—Gary Anderson, 1998
Longest field goal
54 yards—Jan Stenerud vs. Atl., Sept. 16, 1984
Most interceptions, career
53—Paul Krause
Most interceptions, season
10—Paul Krause, 1975
Most sacks, career
130—Carl Eller
Most sacks, season
21—Chris Doleman, 1989

SERIES RECORDS

Minnesota vs.: Arizona 8-9; Atlanta 14-7; Baltimore 1-1; Buffalo 7-3; Carolina 3-2; Chicago 47-38-2; Cincinnati 5-4; Cleveland 8-3; Dallas 10-9; Denver 7-4; Detroit 56-29-2; Green Bay 42-44-1; Houston 1-0; Indianapolis 7-13-1; Jacksonville 2-1; Kansas City 4-4; Miami 4-4; New England 4-5; New Orleans 16-7; N.Y. Giants 9-8; N.Y. Jets 1-6; Oakland 3-8; Philadelphia 11-8; Pittsburgh 8-5; St. Louis 16-13-2; San Diego 4-5; San Francisco 18-17-1; Seattle 3-6; Tampa Bay 31-18; Tennessee 7-3; Washington 5-7.

COACHING RECORDS

Jerry Burns, 52-43-0 (3-3); Bud Grant, 158-96-5 (10-12); Dennis Green, 97-62-0 (4-8); Les Steckel, 3-13-0; Mike Tice, 23-26-0 (1-1); Norm Van Brocklin, 29-51-4.
NOTE: Playoff games in parentheses.

RETIRED UNIFORM NUMBERS

No.	Player
10	Fran Tarkenton
53	Mick Tingelhoff
70	Jim Marshall
77	Korey Stringer
80	Cris Carter
88	Alan Page

NEW ENGLAND PATRIOTS
YEAR-BY-YEAR RECORDS

		REGULAR SEASON						PLAYOFFS		
Year	W	L	T	Pct.	PF	PA	Finish	W	L	Highest round	Coach
1960*†	5	9	0	.357	286	349	4th/Eastern Div.	—	—		Lou Saban
1961*†	9	4	1	.692	413	313	2nd/Eastern Div.	—	—		Lou Saban, Mike Holovak
1962*†	9	4	1	.692	346	295	2nd/Eastern Div.	—	—		Mike Holovak
1963*†	7	6	1	.538	327	257	1st/Eastern Div.	1	1	AFL championship game	Mike Holovak
1964*†	10	3	1	.769	365	297	2nd/Eastern Div.	—	—		Mike Holovak
1965*†	4	8	2	.333	244	302	3rd/Eastern Div.	—	—		Mike Holovak
1966*†	8	4	2	.667	315	283	2nd/Eastern Div.	—	—		Mike Holovak
1967*†	3	10	1	.231	280	389	5th/Eastern Div.	—	—		Mike Holovak
1968*†	4	10	0	.286	229	406	4th/Eastern Div.	—	—		Mike Holovak
1969*†	4	10	0	.286	266	316	T3rd/Eastern Div.	—	—		Clive Rush
1970†	2	12	0	.143	149	361	5th/AFC Eastern Div.	—	—		Clive Rush, John Mazur
1971	6	8	0	.429	238	325	3rd/AFC Eastern Div.	—	—		John Mazur
1972	3	11	0	.214	192	446	5th/AFC Eastern Div.	—	—		J. Mazur, Phil Bengtson
1973	5	9	0	.357	258	300	3rd/AFC Eastern Div.	—	—		Chuck Fairbanks

			REGULAR SEASON					PLAYOFFS			
Year	W	L	T	Pct.	PF	PA	Finish	W	L	Highest round	Coach
1974	7	7	0	.500	348	289	3rd/AFC Eastern Div.	—	—		Chuck Fairbanks
1975	3	11	0	.214	258	358	4th/AFC Eastern Div.	—	—		Chuck Fairbanks
1976	11	3	0	.786	376	236	2nd/AFC Eastern Div.	0	1	AFC div. playoff game	Chuck Fairbanks
1977	9	5	0	.643	278	217	3rd/AFC Eastern Div.	—	—		Chuck Fairbanks
1978	11	5	0	.688	358	286	1st/AFC Eastern Div.	0	1	AFC div. playoff game	Chuck Fairbanks, Hank Bullough-R. Erhard
1979	9	7	0	.563	411	326	2nd/AFC Eastern Div.	—	—		Ron Erhardt
1980	10	6	0	.625	441	325	2nd/AFC Eastern Div.	—	—		Ron Erhardt
1981	2	14	0	.125	322	370	5th/AFC Eastern Div.	—	—		Ron Erhardt
1982	5	4	0	.556	143	157	7th/AFC	0	1	AFC first-round pl. game	Ron Meyer
1983	8	8	0	.500	274	289	2nd/AFC Eastern Div.	—	—		Ron Meyer
1984	9	7	0	.563	362	352	2nd/AFC Eastern Div.	—	—		R. Meyer, R. Berry
1985	11	5	0	.688	362	290	3rd/AFC Eastern Div.	3	1	Super Bowl	Raymond Berry
1986	11	5	0	.688	412	307	1st/AFC Eastern Div.	0	1	AFC div. playoff game	Raymond Berry
1987	8	7	0	.533	320	293	2nd/AFC Eastern Div.	—	—		Raymond Berry
1988	9	7	0	.563	250	284	3rd/AFC Eastern Div.	—	—		Raymond Berry
1989	5	11	0	.313	297	391	4th/AFC Eastern Div.	—	—		Raymond Berry
1990	1	15	0	.063	181	446	5th/AFC Eastern Div.	—	—		Rod Rust
1991	6	10	0	.375	211	305	4th/AFC Eastern Div.	—	—		Dick MacPherson
1992	2	14	0	.125	205	363	5th/AFC Eastern Div.	—	—		Dick MacPherson
1993	5	11	0	.313	238	286	4th/AFC Eastern Div.	—	—		Bill Parcells
1994	10	6	0	.625	351	312	2nd/AFC Eastern Div.	0	1	AFC wild-card game	Bill Parcells
1995	6	10	0	.375	294	377	4th/AFC Eastern Div.	—	—		Bill Parcells
1996	11	5	0	.687	418	313	1st/AFC Eastern Div.	2	1	Super Bowl	Bill Parcells
1997	10	6	0	.625	369	289	1st/AFC Eastern Div.	1	1	AFC div. playoff game	Pete Carroll
1998	9	7	0	.563	337	329	4th/AFC Eastern Div.	0	1	AFC wild-card game	Pete Carroll
1999	8	8	0	.500	299	284	5th/AFC Eastern Div.	—	—		Pete Carroll
2000	5	11	0	.313	276	338	5th/AFC Eastern Div.	—	—		Bill Belichick
2001	11	5	0	.688	371	272	1st/AFC Eastern Div.	3	0	Super Bowl champ	Bill Belichick
2002	9	7	0	.563	381	346	2nd/AFC East Div.	—	—		Bill Belichick
2003	14	2	0	.875	348	238	1st/AFC East Div.	3	0	Super Bowl champ	Bill Belichick
2004	14	2	0	.875	437	260	1st/AFC East Div.	3	0	Super Bowl champ	Bill Belichick

*American Football League.
†Boston Patriots.

FIRST-ROUND DRAFT PICKS

1960—Ron Burton, RB, Northwestern
1961—Tommy Mason, RB, Tulane
1962—Gary Collins, WR, Maryland
1963—Art Graham, E, Boston College
1964—Jack Concannon, QB, Boston College* (AFL)
1965—Jerry Rush, DE, Michigan State
1966—Karl Singer, T, Purdue
1967—John Charles, DB, Purdue
1968—Dennis Byrd, DE, North Carolina State
1969—Ron Sellers, WR, Florida State
1970—Phil Olsen, DT, Utah State
1971—Jim Plunkett, QB, Stanford*
1972—None
1973—John Hannah, G, Alabama
    Sam Cunningham, RB, Southern California
    Darryl Stingley, WR, Purdue
1974—None
1975—Russ Francis, TE, Oregon
1976—Mike Haynes, DB, Arizona State
    Pete Brock, C, Colorado
    Tim Fox, DB, Ohio State
1977—Raymond Clayborn, DB, Texas
    Stanley Morgan, WR, Tennessee
1978—Bob Cryder, G, Alabama
1979—Rick Sanford, DB, South Carolina
1980—Roland James, DB, Tennessee
    Vagas Ferguson, RB, Notre Dame
1981—Brian Holloway, T, Stanford
1982—Kenneth Sims, DT, Texas*
    Lester Williams, DT, Miami, Fla.

1983—Tony Eason, QB, Illinois
1984—Irving Fryar, WR, Nebraska*
1985—Trevor Matich, C, Brigham Young
1986—Reggie Dupard, RB, Southern Methodist
1987—Bruce Armstrong, T, Louisville
1988—J. Stephens, RB, Northwestern Louisiana State
1989—Hart Lee Dykes, WR, Oklahoma State
1990—Chris Singleton, LB, Arizona
    Ray Agnew, DE, North Carolina State
1991—Pat Harlow, T, Southern California
    Leonard Russell, RB, Arizona State
1992—Eugene Chung, T, Virginia Tech
1993—Drew Bledsoe, QB, Washington State*
1994—Willie McGinest, DE, Southern California
1995—Ty Law, DB, Michigan
1996—Terry Glenn, WR, Ohio State
1997—Chris Canty, DB, Kansas State
1998—Robert Edwards, RB, Georgia
    Tebucky Jones, DB, Syracuse
1999—Damien Woody, C, Boston College
    Andy Katzenmoyer, LB, Ohio State
2000—None
2001—Richard Seymour, DT, Georgia
2002—Daniel Graham, TE, Colorado
2003—Ty Warren, NT, Texas A&M
2004—Vince Wilfork, DT, Miami, Fla.
    Ben Watson, TE, Georgia
2005—Logan Mankins, G, Fresno State
*First player chosen in draft.

FRANCHISE RECORDS

Most rushing yards, career
5,453—Sam Cunningham
Most rushing yards, season
1,635—Corey Dillon, 2004

Most rushing yards, game
212—Tony Collins vs. NYJ, Sept. 18, 1983
Most rushing touchdowns, season
14—Curtis Martin, 1995

Curtis Martin, 1996
Most passing attempts, season
691—Drew Bledsoe, 1994

ost passing attempts, game
)—Drew Bledsoe vs. Min., Nov. 13,
    1994 (OT)
—Drew Bledsoe at Pit., Dec. 16, 1995
ost passes completed, season
)0—Drew Bledsoe, 1994
ost passes completed, game
5—Drew Bledsoe vs. Min., Nov. 13,
    1994 (OT)
—Drew Bledsoe at Pit., Dec. 16, 1995
    Tom Brady vs. K.C., Sept. 22, 2002
    (OT)
ost passing yards, career
9,657—Drew Bledsoe
ost passing yards, season
555—Drew Bledsoe, 1994
ost passing yards, game
26—Drew Bledsoe vs. Min., Nov. 13,
    1994 (OT)

423—Drew Bledsoe vs. Mia., Nov. 23,
    1998
Most touchdown passes, season
31—Babe Parilli, 1964
Most pass receptions, career
534—Stanley Morgan
Most pass receptions, season
101—Troy Brown, 2001
Most pass receptions, game
16—Troy Brown vs. K.C., Sept. 22, 2002
    (OT)
13—Terry Glenn at Cle., Oct. 3, 1999
Most receiving yards, career
10,352—Stanley Morgan
Most receiving yards, season
1,491—Stanley Morgan, 1986
Most receiving yards, game
214—Terry Glenn at Cle., Oct. 3, 1999

Most receiving touchdowns, season
12—Stanley Morgan, 1979
Most touchdowns, career
68—Stanley Morgan
Most field goals, season
32—Tony Franklin, 1986
Longest field goal
57 yards—Adam Vinatieri at Chi., Nov. 10,
    2002
Most interceptions, career
36—Raymond Clayborn
Most interceptions, season
11—Ron Hall, 1964
Most sacks, career
100—Andre Tippett
Most sacks, season
18.5—Andre Tippett, 1984

SERIES RECORDS

ew England vs.: Arizona 5-6; Atlanta 4-6; Baltimore 3-0; Buffalo 48-40-1; Carolina 0-2; Chicago 6-3; Cincinnati 11-8; Cleveland 8-11;
allas 2-7; Denver 15-22; Detroit 4-4; Green Bay 3-4; Houston 1-0; Indianapolis 41-24; Jacksonville 3-0; Kansas City 11-15-3; Miami
4-45; Minnesota 5-4; New Orleans 7-3; N.Y. Giants 4-3; N.Y. Jets 41-47-1; Oakland 12-14-1; Philadelphia 3-6; Pittsburgh 5-12; St.
ouis 4-5; San Diego 17-12-2; San Francisco 3-7; Seattle 7-7; Tampa Bay 3-2; Tennessee 19-15-1; Washington 1-6.
OTE: Includes records as Boston Patriots from 1960 through 1970.

COACHING RECORDS

ill Belichick, 53-27-0 (9-0); Phil Bengtson, 1-4-0; Raymond Berry, 48-39-0 (3-2); Hank
ullough, 0-1-0; Pete Carroll, 27-21-0 (1-2); Ron Erhardt, 21-27-0; Chuck Fairbanks, 46-
9-0 (0-2); Mike Holovak, 52-46-9 (1-1); Dick MacPherson, 8-24-0; John Mazur, 9-21-
' Ron Meyer, 18-15-0 (0-1); Bill Parcells, 32-32-0 (2-2); Clive Rush, 5-16-0; Rod Rust,
-15-0; Lou Saban, 7-12-0.
OTE: Playoff games in parentheses.

RETIRED UNIFORM NUMBERS

No.	Player
20	Gino Cappelletti
40	Mike Haynes
57	Steve Nelson
73	John Hannah
78	Bruce Armstrong
79	Jim Hunt
89	Bob Dee

NEW ORLEANS SAINTS
YEAR-BY-YEAR RECORDS

		REGULAR SEASON							PLAYOFFS		
ear	W	L	T	Pct.	PF	PA	Finish	W	L	Highest round	Coach
967	3	11	0	.214	233	379	4th/Capitol Div.	—	—		Tom Fears
968	4	9	1	.308	246	327	3rd/Century Div.	—	—		Tom Fears
969	5	9	0	.357	311	393	3rd/Capitol Div.	—	—		Tom Fears
970	2	11	1	.154	172	347	4th/NFC Western Div.	—	—		Tom Fears, J.D. Roberts
971	4	8	2	.333	266	347	4th/NFC Western Div.	—	—		J.D. Roberts
972	2	11	1	.179	215	361	4th/NFC Western Div.	—	—		J.D. Roberts
973	5	9	0	.357	163	312	3rd/NFC Western Div.	—	—		John North
974	5	9	0	.357	166	263	3rd/NFC Western Div.	—	—		John North
975	2	12	0	.143	165	360	4th/NFC Western Div.	—	—		J. North, Ernie Hefferle
976	4	10	0	.286	253	346	4th/NFC Western Div.	—	—		Hank Stram
977	3	11	0	.214	232	336	4th/NFC Western Div.	—	—		Hank Stram
978	7	9	0	.438	281	298	3rd/NFC Western Div.	—	—		Dick Nolan
979	8	8	0	.500	370	360	2nd/NFC Western Div.	—	—		Dick Nolan
980	1	15	0	.063	291	487	4th/NFC Western Div.	—	—		Dick Nolan, Dick Stanfel
981	4	12	0	.250	207	378	4th/NFC Western Div.	—	—		Bum Phillips
982	4	5	0	.444	129	160	9th/NFC	—	—		Bum Phillips
983	8	8	0	.500	319	337	3rd/NFC Western Div.	—	—		Bum Phillips
984	7	9	0	.438	298	361	3rd/NFC Western Div.	—	—		Bum Phillips
985	5	11	0	.313	294	401	3rd/NFC Western Div.	—	—		B. Phillips, Wade Phillips
986	7	9	0	.438	288	287	4th/NFC Western Div.	—	—		Jim Mora
987	12	3	0	.800	422	283	2nd/NFC Western Div.	0	1	NFC wild-card game	Jim Mora
988	10	6	0	.625	312	283	3rd/NFC Western Div.	—	—		Jim Mora
989	9	7	0	.563	386	301	3rd/NFC Western Div.	—	—		Jim Mora
990	8	8	0	.500	274	275	2nd/NFC Western Div.	0	1	NFC wild-card game	Jim Mora
991	11	5	0	.688	341	211	1st/NFC Western Div.	0	1	NFC wild-card game	Jim Mora
992	12	4	0	.750	330	202	2nd/NFC Western Div.	0	1	NFC wild-card game	Jim Mora
993	8	8	0	.500	317	343	2nd/NFC Western Div.	—	—		Jim Mora
994	7	9	0	.438	348	407	2nd/NFC Western Div.	—	—		Jim Mora
995	7	9	0	.438	319	348	5th/NFC Western Div.	—	—		Jim Mora

	REGULAR SEASON							PLAYOFFS			
Year	W	L	T	Pct.	PF	PA	Finish	W	L	Highest round	Coach
1996	3	13	0	.188	229	339	5th/NFC Western Div.	—	—		Jim Mora, Rick Venturi
1997	6	10	0	.375	237	327	4th/NFC Western Div.	—	—		Mike Ditka
1998	6	10	0	.375	305	359	3rd/NFC Western Div.	—	—		Mike Ditka
1999	3	13	0	.188	260	434	5th/NFC Western Div.	—	—		Mike Ditka
2000	10	6	0	.625	354	305	1st/NFC Western Div.	1	1	NFC div. playoff game	Jim Haslett
2001	7	9	0	.438	333	409	3rd/NFC Western Div.	—	—		Jim Haslett
2002	9	7	0	.563	432	388	3rd/NFC South Div.	—	—		Jim Haslett
2003	8	8	0	.500	340	326	2nd/NFC South Div.	—	—		Jim Haslett
2004	8	8	0	.500	348	405	2nd/NFC South Div.	—	—		Jim Haslett

FIRST-ROUND DRAFT PICKS

1967—Les Kelley, RB, Alabama
1968—Kevin Hardy, DE, Notre Dame
1969—John Shinners, G, Xavier (Ohio)
1970—Ken Burrough, WR, Texas Southern
1971—Archie Manning, QB, Mississippi
1972—Royce Smith, G, Georgia
1973—None
1974—Rick Middleton, LB, Ohio State
1975—Larry Burton, WR, Purdue
    Kurt Schumacher, T, Ohio State
1976—Chuck Muncie, RB, California
1977—Joe Campbell, DE, Maryland
1978—Wes Chandler, WR, Florida
1979—Russell Erxleben, P, Texas
1980—Stan Brock, T, Colorado
1981—George Rogers, RB, South Carolina*
1982—Lindsay Scott, WR, Georgia
1983—None
1984—None
1985—Alvin Toles, LB, Tennessee
1986—Jim Dombrowski, T, Virginia
1987—Shawn Knight, DT, Brigham Young

1988—Craig Heyward, RB, Pittsburgh
1989—Wayne Martin, DE, Arkansas
1990—Renaldo Turnbull, DE, West Virginia
1991—None
1992—Vaughn Dunbar, RB, Indiana
1993—Willie Roaf, T, Louisiana Tech
    Irv Smith, TE, Notre Dame
1994—Joe Johnson, DE, Louisville
1995—Mark Fields, LB, Washington State
1996—Alex Molden, DB, Oregon
1997—Chris Naeole, G, Colorado
1998—Kyle Turley, T, San Diego State
1999—Ricky Williams, RB, Texas
2000—None
2001—Deuce McAllister, RB, Mississippi
2002—Donte' Stallworth, WR, Tennessee
    Charles Grant, DE, Georgia
2003—Johnathan Sullivan, DT, Georgia
2004—Will Smith, DE, Ohio State
2005—Jammal Brown, OT, Oklahoma
*First player chosen in draft.

FRANCHISE RECORDS

Most rushing yards, career
4,267—George Rogers
Most rushing yards, season
1,674—George Rogers, 1981
Most rushing yards, game
206—George Rogers vs. St.L., Sept. 4, 1983
Most rushing touchdowns, season
13—George Rogers, 1981
    Dalton Hilliard, 1989
    Deuce McAllister, 2002
Most passing attempts, season
567—Jim Everett, 1995
Most passing attempts, game
55—Jim Everett at S.F., Sept. 25, 1994
Most passes completed, season
346—Jim Everett, 1994
Most passes completed, game
33—Archie Manning at G.B., Sept. 10, 1978
    Jeff Blake at S.D., Sept. 10, 2000

Most passing yards, career
21,734—Archie Manning
Most passing yards, season
3,970—Jim Everett, 1995
Most passing yards, game
441—Aaron Brooks vs. Den., Dec. 3, 2000
Most touchdown passes, season
27—Aaron Brooks, 2002
Most pass receptions, career
532—Eric Martin
Most pass receptions, season
94—Joe Horn, 2000
    Joe Horn, 2004
Most pass receptions, game
14—Tony Galbreath at G.B., Sept. 10, 1978
Most receiving yards, career
7,854—Eric Martin
Most receiving yards, season
1,399—Joe Horn, 2004

Most receiving yards, game
205—Wes Chandler vs. Atl., Sept. 2, 197
Most receiving touchdowns, season
10—Joe Horn, 2003
Most touchdowns, career
53—Dalton Hilliard
Most field goals, season
31—Morten Andersen, 1985
    John Carney, 2002
Longest field goal
63 yards—Tom Dempsey vs. Det., Nov. 8, 1970
Most interceptions, career
37—Dave Waymer
Most interceptions, season
10—Dave Whitsell, 1967
Most sacks, career
123—Rickey Jackson
Most sacks, season
17—Pat Swilling, 1991
    La'Roi Glover, 2000

SERIES RECORDS

New Orleans vs.: Arizona 11-13; Atlanta 30-41; Baltimore 1-2; Buffalo 3-4; Carolina 10-10; Chicago 11-10; Cincinnati 5-5; Clevelan 3-11; Dallas 7-14; Denver 2-6; Detroit 8-8-1; Green Bay 5-13; Houston 1-0; Indianapolis 5-4; Jacksonville 1-2; Kansas City 4-4; Miam 3-5; Minnesota 7-16; New England 3-7; N.Y. Giants 9-13; N.Y. Jets 4-5; Oakland 4-5-1; Philadelphia 8-14; Pittsburgh 6-6; St. Louis 29- 36; San Diego 2-7; San Francisco 20-45-2; Seattle 4-5; Tampa Bay 17-9; Tennessee 4-6-1; Washington 7-13.

COACHING RECORDS

Mike Ditka, 15-33-0; Tom Fears, 13-34-2; Jim Haslett, 42-38-0 (1-1); Ernie Hefferle, 1-7-0; Jim Mora, 93-74-0 (0-4); Dick Nolan, 15-29-0; John North, 11-23-0; Bum Phillips, 27-42-0; Wade Phillips, 1-3-0; J.D. Roberts, 7-25-3; Dick Stanfel, 1-3-0; Hank Stram, 7-21-0; Rick Venturi, 1-7-0.
NOTE: Playoff games in parentheses.

RETIRED UNIFORM NUMBERS

No.	Player
31	Jim Taylor
81	Doug Atkins

			REGULAR SEASON						PLAYOFFS		
ear	W	L	T	Pct.	PF	PA	Finish	W	L	Highest round	Coach
925	8	4	0	.667	122	67	T4th				Bob Folwell
926	8	4	0	.667	147	51	T6th				Joe Alexander
927	11	1	1	.917	197	20	1st				Earl Potteiger
928	4	7	2	.364	79	136	6th				Earl Potteiger
929	13	1	1	.929	312	86	2nd				LeRoy Andrews
930	13	4	0	.765	308	98	2nd				L. Andrews, Benny Friedman-Steve Owen
931	7	6	1	.538	154	100	5th				Steve Owen
932	4	6	2	.400	93	113	5th				Steve Owen
933	11	3	0	.786	244	101	1st/Eastern Div.	0	1	NFL championship game	Steve Owen
934	8	5	0	.615	147	107	1st/Eastern Div.	1	0	NFL champ	Steve Owen
935	9	3	0	.750	180	96	1st/Eastern Div.	0	1	NFL championship game	Steve Owen
936	5	6	1	.455	115	163	3rd/Eastern Div.	—	—		Steve Owen
937	6	3	2	.667	128	109	2nd/Eastern Div.	—	—		Steve Owen
938	8	2	1	.800	194	79	1st/Eastern Div.	1	0	NFL champ	Steve Owen
939	9	1	1	.900	168	85	1st/Eastern Div.	0	1	NFL championship game	Steve Owen
940	6	4	1	.600	131	133	3rd/Eastern Div.	—	—		Steve Owen
941	8	3	0	.727	238	114	1st/Eastern Div.	0	1	NFL championship game	Steve Owen
942	5	5	1	.500	155	139	3rd/Eastern Div.	—	—		Steve Owen
943	6	3	1	.667	197	170	2nd/Eastern Div.	0	1	E. Div. champ. game	Steve Owen
944	8	1	1	.889	206	75	1st/Eastern Div.	0	1	NFL championship game	Steve Owen
945	3	6	1	.333	179	198	T3rd/Eastern Div.	—	—		Steve Owen
946	7	3	1	.700	236	162	1st/Eastern Div.	0	1	NFL championship game	Steve Owen
947	2	8	2	.200	190	309	5th/Eastern Div.	—	—		Steve Owen
948	4	8	0	.333	297	388	T3rd/Eastern Div.	—	—		Steve Owen
949	6	6	0	.500	287	298	3rd/Eastern Div.	—	—		Steve Owen
950	10	2	0	.833	268	150	2nd/American Conf.	0	1	Am. Conf. champ. game	Steve Owen
951	9	2	1	.818	254	161	2nd/American Conf.	—	—		Steve Owen
952	7	5	0	.583	234	231	T2nd/American Conf.	—	—		Steve Owen
953	3	9	0	.250	179	277	5th/Eastern Conf.	—	—		Steve Owen
954	7	5	0	.583	293	184	3rd/Eastern Conf.	—	—		Jim Lee Howell
955	6	5	1	.545	267	223	3rd/Eastern Conf.	—	—		Jim Lee Howell
956	8	3	1	.727	264	197	1st/Eastern Conf.	1	0	NFL champ	Jim Lee Howell
957	7	5	0	.583	254	211	2nd/Eastern Conf.	—	—		Jim Lee Howell
958	9	3	0	.750	246	183	1st/Eastern Conf.	1	1	NFL championship game	Jim Lee Howell
959	10	2	0	.833	284	170	1st/Eastern Conf.	0	1	NFL championship game	Jim Lee Howell
960	6	4	2	.600	271	261	3rd/Eastern Conf.	—	—		Jim Lee Howell
961	10	3	1	.769	368	220	1st/Eastern Conf.	0	1	NFL championship game	Allie Sherman
962	12	2	0	.857	398	283	1st/Eastern Conf.	0	1	NFL championship game	Allie Sherman
963	11	3	0	.786	448	280	1st/Eastern Conf.	0	1	NFL championship game	Allie Sherman
964	2	10	2	.167	241	399	7th/Eastern Conf.	—	—		Allie Sherman
965	7	7	0	.500	270	338	T2nd/Eastern Conf.	—	—		Allie Sherman
966	1	12	1	.077	263	501	8th/Eastern Conf.	—	—		Allie Sherman
967	7	7	0	.500	369	379	2nd/Century Div.	—	—		Allie Sherman
968	7	7	0	.500	294	325	2nd/Capitol Div.	—	—		Allie Sherman
969	6	8	0	.429	264	298	2nd/Century Div.	—	—		Alex Webster
970	9	5	0	.643	301	270	2nd/NFC Eastern Div.	—	—		Alex Webster
971	4	10	0	.286	228	362	5th/NFC Eastern Div.	—	—		Alex Webster
972	8	6	0	.571	331	247	3rd/NFC Eastern Div.	—	—		Alex Webster
973	2	11	1	.179	226	362	5th/NFC Eastern Div.	—	—		Alex Webster
974	2	12	0	.143	195	299	5th/NFC Eastern Div.	—	—		Bill Arnsparger
975	5	9	0	.357	216	306	4th/NFC Eastern Div.	—	—		Bill Arnsparger
976	3	11	0	.214	170	250	5th/NFC Eastern Div.	—	—		B. Arnsparger, J. McVay
977	5	9	0	.357	181	265	5th/NFC Eastern Div.	—	—		John McVay
978	6	10	0	.375	264	298	5th/NFC Eastern Div.	—	—		John McVay
979	6	10	0	.375	237	323	4th/NFC Eastern Div.	—	—		Ray Perkins
980	4	12	0	.250	249	425	5th/NFC Eastern Div.	—	—		Ray Perkins
981	9	7	0	.563	295	257	3rd/NFC Eastern Div.	1	1	NFC div. playoff game	Ray Perkins
982	4	5	0	.444	164	160	10th/NFC	—	—		Ray Perkins
983	3	12	1	.219	267	347	5th/NFC Eastern Div.	—	—		Bill Parcells
984	9	7	0	.563	299	301	2nd/NFC Eastern Div.	1	1	NFC div. playoff game	Bill Parcells
1985	10	6	0	.625	399	283	2nd/NFC Eastern Div.	1	1	NFC div. playoff game	Bill Parcells
1986	14	2	0	.875	371	236	1st/NFC Eastern Div.	3	0	Super Bowl champ	Bill Parcells

	REGULAR SEASON							PLAYOFFS			
Year	W	L	T	Pct.	PF	PA	Finish	W	L	Highest round	Coach
1987	6	9	0	.400	280	312	5th/NFC Eastern Div.	—	—		Bill Parcells
1988	10	6	0	.625	359	304	2nd/NFC Eastern Div.	—	—		Bill Parcells
1989	12	4	0	.750	348	252	1st/NFC Eastern Div.	0	1	NFC div. playoff game	Bill Parcells
1990	13	3	0	.813	335	211	1st/NFC Eastern Div.	3	0	Super Bowl champ	Bill Parcells
1991	8	8	0	.500	281	297	4th/NFC Eastern Div.	—	—		Ray Handley
1992	6	10	0	.375	306	367	4th/NFC Eastern Div.	—	—		Ray Handley
1993	11	5	0	.688	288	205	2nd/NFC Eastern Div.	1	1	NFC div. playoff game	Dan Reeves
1994	9	7	0	.563	279	305	2nd/NFC Eastern Div.	—	—		Dan Reeves
1995	5	11	0	.313	290	340	4th/NFC Eastern Div.	—	—		Dan Reeves
1996	6	10	0	.375	242	297	5th/NFC Eastern Div.	—	—		Dan Reeves
1997	10	5	1	.656	307	265	1st/NFC Eastern Div.	0	1	NFC wild-card game	Jim Fassel
1998	8	8	0	.500	287	309	3rd/NFC Eastern Div.	—	—		Jim Fassel
1999	7	9	0	.438	299	358	3rd/NFC Eastern Div.	—	—		Jim Fassel
2000	12	4	0	.750	328	246	1st/NFC Eastern Div.	2	1	Super Bowl	Jim Fassel
2001	7	9	0	.438	294	321	3rd/NFC Eastern Div.	—	—		Jim Fassel
2002	10	6	0	.625	320	279	2nd/NFC East Div.	0	1	NFC wild-card game	Jim Fassel
2003	4	12	0	.250	243	387	4th/NFC East Div.	—	—		Jim Fassel
2004	6	10	0	.375	303	347	2nd/NFC East Div.	—	—		Tom Coughlin

FIRST-ROUND DRAFT PICKS

1936—Art Lewis, T, Ohio
1937—Ed Widseth, T, Minnesota
1938—George Karamatic, B, Gonzaga
1939—Walt Nielsen, B, Arizona
1940—Grenville Lansdell, B, Southern California
1941—George Franck, B, Minnesota
1942—Merle Hapes, B, Mississippi
1943—Steve Filipowicz, B, Fordham
1944—Billy Hillenbrand, B, Indiana
1945—Elmer Barbour, B, Wake Forest
1946—George Connor, T, Notre Dame
1947—Vic Schwall, B, Northwestern
1948—Tony Minisi, B, Pennsylvania
1949—Paul Page, B, Southern Methodist
1950—Travis Tidwell, B, Auburn
1951—Kyle Rote, B, Southern Methodist*
     Jim Spavital, B, Oklahoma State
1952—Frank Gifford, B, Southern California
1953—Bobby Marlow, B, Alabama
1954—None
1955—Joe Heap, B, Notre Dame
1956—None
1957—None
1958—Phil King, B, Vanderbilt
1959—Lee Grosscup, B, Utah
1960—Lou Cordileone, G, Clemson
1961—None
1962—Jerry Hillebrand, LB, Colorado
1963—None
1964—Joe Don Looney, RB, Oklahoma
1965—Tucker Frederickson, RB, Auburn*
1966—Francis Peay, T, Missouri
1967—None
1968—None
1969—Fred Dryer, DE, San Diego State
1970—Jim Files, LB, Oklahoma
1971—Rocky Thompson, RB, West Texas State

1972—Eldridge Small, DB, Texas A&I
     Larry Jacobson, DE, Nebraska
1973—None
1974—John Hicks, G, Ohio State
1975—None
1976—Troy Archer, DE, Colorado
1977—Gary Jeter, DT, Southern Cal
1978—Gordon King, T, Stanford
1979—Phil Simms, QB, Morehead State
1980—Mark Haynes, DB, Colorado
1981—Lawrence Taylor, LB, North Carolina
1982—Butch Woolfolk, RB, Michigan
1983—Terry Kinard, DB, Clemson
1984—Carl Banks, LB, Michigan State
     Bill Roberts, T, Ohio State
1985—George Adams, RB, Kentucky
1986—Eric Dorsey, DE, Notre Dame
1987—Mark Ingram, WR, Michigan State
1988—Eric Moore, T, Indiana
1989—Brian Williams, G, Minnesota
1990—Rodney Hampton, RB, Georgia
1991—Jarrod Bunch, FB, Michigan
1992—Derek Brown, TE, Notre Dame
1993—None
1994—Thomas Lewis, WR, Indiana
1995—Tyrone Wheatley, RB, Michigan
1996—Cedric Jones, DE, Oklahoma
1997—Ike Hilliard, WR, Florida
1998—Shaun Williams, DB, UCLA
1999—Luke Petitgout, T, Notre Dame
2000—Ron Dayne, RB, Wisconsin
2001—Will Allen, DB, Syracuse
2002—Jeremy Shockey, TE, Miami, Fla.
2003—William Joseph, DT, Miami, Fla.
2004—Philip Rivers, QB, North Carolina State
2005—None
*First player chosen in draft.

FRANCHISE RECORDS

Most rushing yards, career
6,927—Tiki Barber

Most rushing yards, season
1,518—Tiki Barber, 2004

Most rushing yards, game
218—Gene Roberts vs. Chi. Cardinals,
     Nov. 12, 1950

Most rushing touchdowns, season
21—Joe Morris, 1985

Most passing attempts, season
568—Kerry Collins, 2001

Most passing attempts, game
62—Phil Simms at Cin., Oct. 13, 1985

Most passes completed, season
335—Kerry Collins, 2002

Most passes completed, game
40—Phil Simms at Cin., Oct. 13, 1985

Most passing yards, career
33,462—Phil Simms

HISTORY *Team by team*

Most passing yards, season
073—Kerry Collins, 2002

Most passing yards, game
13—Phil Simms at Cin., Oct. 13, 1985

Most touchdown passes, season
6—Y.A. Tittle, 1963

Most pass receptions, career
74—Tiki Barber

Most pass receptions, season
2—Amani Toomer, 2002

Most pass receptions, game
3—Tiki Barber at Dal., Jan. 2, 2000

Most receiving yards, career
7,113—Amani Toomer

Most receiving yards, season
1,343—Amani Toomer, 2002

Most receiving yards, game
269—Del Shofner vs. Was., Oct. 28, 1962

Most receiving touchdowns, season
13—Homer Jones, 1967

Most touchdowns, career
78—Frank Gifford

Most field goals, season
35—Ali Haji-Sheikh, 1983

Longest field goal
56 yards—Ali Haji-Sheikh vs. G.B., Sept. 26, 1983
Ali Haji-Sheikh at Det., Nov. 7, 1983

Most interceptions, career
74—Emlen Tunnell

Most interceptions, season
11—Otto Schellbacher, 1951
Jimmy Patton, 1958

Most sacks, career
132.5—Lawrence Taylor

Most sacks, season
22.5—Michael Strahan, 2001

SERIES RECORDS

.Y. Giants vs.: Arizona 77-41-2; Atlanta 7-10; Baltimore, 0-2; Buffalo 3-6; Carolina 0-2; Chicago 17-26-2; Cincinnati 2-5; Cleveland 9-25-2; Dallas 33-50-2; Denver 4-4; Detroit 17-20-1; Green Bay 21-24-2; Houston 0-1; Indianapolis 6-6; Jacksonville 2-1; Kansas City -2; Miami 3-2; Minnesota 8-9; New England 3-4; New Orleans 13-9; N.Y. Jets 6-4; Oakland 2-7; Philadelphia 73-65-2; Pittsburgh 43- 8-3; St. Louis 11-25; San Diego 5-3; San Francisco 11-13; Seattle 7-3; Tampa Bay 9-6; Tennessee 5-3; Washington 81-59-4.

COACHING RECORDS

oe Alexander, 8-4-1; LeRoy Andrews, 24-5-1; Bill Arnsparger, 7-28-0; om Coughlin, 6-10-0; Jim Fassel, 58-53-1 (2-3); Bob Folwell, 8-4-0; enny Friedman, 2-0-0; Ray Handley, 14-18-0; Jim Lee Howell, 53-27- (2-2); John McVay, 14-23-0; Steve Owen, 153-100-17 (2-8); Bill arcells, 77-49-1 (8-3); Ray Perkins, 23-34-0 (1-1); Earl Potteiger, 15- -3; Dan Reeves, 31-33-0 (1-1); Allie Sherman, 57-51-4 (0-3); Alex Webster, 29-40-1. NOTE: Playoff games in parentheses.

RETIRED UNIFORM NUMBERS

No.	Player	No.	Player
1	Ray Flaherty	32	Al Blozis
4	Tuffy Leemans	40	Joe Morrison
7	Mel Hein	42	Charlie Conerly
11	Phil Simms	50	Ken Strong
14	Y.A. Tittle	56	Lawrence Taylor
16	Frank Gifford		

NEW YORK JETS
YEAR-BY-YEAR RECORDS

	REGULAR SEASON							PLAYOFFS			
Year	W	L	T	Pct.	PF	PA	Finish	W	L	Highest round	Coach
1960*†	7	7	0	.500	382	399	2nd/Eastern Div.	—	—		Sammy Baugh
1961*†	7	7	0	.500	301	390	3rd/Eastern Div.	—	—		Sammy Baugh
1962*†	5	9	0	.357	278	423	4th/Eastern Div.	—	—		Bulldog Turner
1963*	5	8	1	.385	249	399	4th/Eastern Div.	—	—		Weeb Ewbank
1964*	5	8	1	.385	278	315	3rd/Eastern Div.	—	—		Weeb Ewbank
1965*	5	8	1	.385	285	303	2nd/Eastern Div.	—	—		Weeb Ewbank
1966*	6	6	2	.500	322	312	3rd/Eastern Div.	—	—		Weeb Ewbank
1967*	8	5	1	.615	371	329	2nd/Eastern Div.	—	—		Weeb Ewbank
1968*	11	3	0	.786	419	280	1st/Eastern Div.	2	0	Super Bowl champ	Weeb Ewbank
1969*	10	4	0	.714	353	269	1st/Eastern Div.	0	1	Div. playoff game	Weeb Ewbank
1970	4	10	0	.286	255	286	3rd/AFC Eastern Div.	—	—		Weeb Ewbank
1971	6	8	0	.429	212	299	4th/AFC Eastern Div.	—	—		Weeb Ewbank
1972	7	7	0	.500	367	324	2nd/AFC Eastern Div.	—	—		Weeb Ewbank
1973	4	10	0	.286	240	306	5th/AFC Eastern Div.	—	—		Weeb Ewbank
1974	7	7	0	.500	279	300	4th/AFC Eastern Div.	—	—		Charley Winner
1975	3	11	0	.214	258	433	5th/AFC Eastern Div.	—	—		C. Winner, Ken Shipp
1976	3	11	0	.214	169	383	4th/AFC Eastern Div.	—	—		Lou Holtz, Mike Holovak
1977	3	11	0	.214	191	300	4th/AFC Eastern Div.	—	—		Walt Michaels
1978	8	8	0	.500	359	364	3rd/AFC Eastern Div.	—	—		Walt Michaels
1979	8	8	0	.500	337	383	3rd/AFC Eastern Div.	—	—		Walt Michaels
1980	4	12	0	.250	302	395	5th/AFC Eastern Div.	—	—		Walt Michaels
1981	10	5	1	.656	355	287	2nd/AFC Eastern Div.	0	1	AFC wild-card game	Walt Michaels
1982	6	3	0	.667	245	166	6th/AFC	2	1	AFC championship game	Walt Michaels
1983	7	9	0	.438	313	331	5th/AFC Eastern Div.	—	—		Joe Walton
1984	7	9	0	.438	332	364	3rd/AFC Eastern Div.	—	—		Joe Walton
1985	11	5	0	.688	393	264	2nd/AFC Eastern Div.	0	1	AFC wild-card game	Joe Walton
1986	10	6	0	.625	364	386	2nd/AFC Eastern Div.	1	1	AFC div. playoff game	Joe Walton
1987	6	9	0	.400	334	360	5th/AFC Eastern Div.	—	—		Joe Walton
1988	8	7	1	.531	372	354	4th/AFC Eastern Div.	—	—		Joe Walton
1989	4	12	0	.250	253	411	5th/AFC Eastern Div.	—	—		Joe Walton
1990	6	10	0	.375	295	345	4th/AFC Eastern Div.	—	—		Bruce Coslet
1991	8	8	0	.500	314	293	2nd/AFC Eastern Div.	0	1	AFC wild-card game	Bruce Coslet
1992	4	12	0	.250	220	315	4th/AFC Eastern Div.	—	—		Bruce Coslet
1993	8	8	0	.500	270	247	3rd/AFC Eastern Div.	—	—		Bruce Coslet
1994	6	10	0	.375	264	320	5th/AFC Eastern Div.	—	—		Pete Carroll
1995	3	13	0	.188	233	384	5th/AFC Eastern Div.	—	—		Rich Kotite
1996	1	15	0	.063	279	454	5th/AFC Eastern Div.	—	—		Rich Kotite

				REGULAR SEASON					PLAYOFFS		
Year	W	L	T	Pct.	PF	PA	Finish	W	L	Highest round	Coach
1997	9	7	0	.563	348	287	3rd/AFC Eastern Div.	—	—		Bill Parcells
1998	12	4	0	.750	416	266	1st/AFC Eastern Div.	1	1	AFC championship game	Bill Parcells
1999	8	8	0	.500	308	309	4th/AFC Eastern Div.	—	—		Bill Parcells
2000	9	7	0	.563	321	321	3rd/AFC Eastern Div.	—	—		Al Groh
2001	10	6	0	.625	308	295	3rd/AFC Eastern Div.	0	1	AFC wild-card game	Herman Edwards
2002	9	7	0	.563	359	336	1st/AFC East Div.	1	1	AFC div. playoff game	Herman Edwards
2003	6	10	0	.375	283	299	4th/AFC East Div.	—	—		Herman Edwards
2004	10	6	0	.625	333	261	2nd/AFC East Div.	1	1	AFC div. playoff game	Herman Edwards

*American Football League.
†New York Titans.

FIRST-ROUND DRAFT PICKS

1960—George Izo, QB, Notre Dame
1961—Tom Brown, G, Minnesota
1962—Sandy Stephens, QB, Minnesota
1963—Jerry Stovall, HB, Louisiana State
1964—Matt Snell, RB, Ohio State
1965—Joe Namath, QB, Alabama
    Tom Nowatzke, RB, Indiana
1966—Bill Yearby, DT, Michigan
1967—Paul Seiler, G, Notre Dame
1968—Lee White, RB, Weber State
1969—Dave Foley, T, Ohio State
1970—Steve Tannen, DB, Florida
1971—John Riggins, RB, Kansas
1972—Jerome Barkum, WR, Jackson State
1972—Mike Taylor, LB, Michigan
1973—Burgess Owens, DB, Miami
1974—Carl Barzilauskas, DT, Indiana
1975—None
1976—Richard Todd, QB, Alabama
1977—Marvin Powell, T, Southern California
1978—Chris Ward, T, Ohio State
1979—Marty Lyons, DE, Alabama
1980—Lam Jones, WR, Texas
1981—Freeman McNeil, RB, UCLA
1982—Bob Crable, LB, Notre Dame
1983—Ken O'Brien, QB, California-Davis
1984—Russell Carter, DB, Southern Methodist

    Ron Faurot, DE, Arkansas
1985—Al Toon, WR, Wisconsin
1986—Mike Haight, T, Iowa
1987—Roger Vick, RB, Texas A&M
1988—Dave Cadigan, T, Southern California
1989—Jeff Lageman, LB, Virginia
1990—Blair Thomas, RB, Penn State
1991—None
1992—Johnny Mitchell, TE, Nebraska
1993—Marvin Jones, LB, Florida State
1994—Aaron Glenn, DB, Texas A&M
1995—Kyle Brady, TE, Penn State
    Hugh Douglas, DE, Central State (Ohio)
1996—Keyshawn Johnson, WR, Southern California*
1997—James Farrior, LB, Virginia
1998—None
1999—None
2000—Shaun Ellis, DE, Tennessee
    John Abraham, LB, South Carolina
    Chad Pennington, QB, Marshall
    Anthony Becht, TE, West Virginia
2001—Santana Moss, WR, Miami, Fla.
2002—Bryan Thomas, DE, Alabama-Birmingham
2003—Dewayne Robertson, DT, Kentucky
2004—Jonathan Vilma, LB, Miami, Fla.
2005—None
*First player chosen in draft.

FRANCHISE RECORDS

Most rushing yards, career
9,567—Curtis Martin
Most rushing yards, season
1,697—Curtis Martin, 2004
Most rushing yards, game
203—Curtis Martin vs. Ind., Dec. 3, 2000
Most rushing touchdowns, season
12—Curtis Martin, 2004
Most passing attempts, season
590—Vinny Testaverde, 2000
Most passing attempts, game
69—Vinny Testaverde at Bal., Dec. 24, 2000
Most passes completed, season
328—Vinny Testaverde, 2000
Most passes completed, game
42—Richard Todd vs. S.F., Sept. 21, 1980
    Vinny Testaverde vs. Sea., Dec. 6, 1998

Most passing yards, career
27,057—Joe Namath
Most passing yards, season
4,007—Joe Namath, 1967
Most passing yards, game
496—Joe Namath at Bal., Sept. 24, 1972
Most touchdown passes, season
29—Vinny Testaverde, 1998
Most pass receptions, career
627—Don Maynard
Most pass receptions, season
93—Al Toon, 1988
Most pass receptions, game
17—Clark Gaines vs. S.F., Sept. 21, 1980
Most receiving yards, career
11,732—Don Maynard
Most receiving yards, season
1,434—Don Maynard, 1967
Most receiving yards, game
228—Don Maynard at Oak., Nov. 17, 1968

Most receiving touchdowns, season
14—Art Powell, 1960
    Don Maynard, 1965
Most touchdowns, career
88—Don Maynard
Most field goals, season
34—Jim Turner, 1968
Longest field goal
55 yards—Pat Leahy vs. Chi., Dec. 14, 1985
    John Hall at Sea., Aug. 31, 1997
Most interceptions, career
34—Bill Baird
Most interceptions, season
12—Dainard Paulson, 1964
Most sacks, career
107.5—Mark Gastineau
Most sacks, season
22—Mark Gastineau, 1984

SERIES RECORDS

N.Y. Jets vs.: Arizona 4-2; Atlanta 4-4; Baltimore 1-3; Buffalo 40-48; Carolina 2-1; Chicago 3-5; Cincinnati 12-6; Cleveland 7-10; Dallas 2-6; Denver 14-14-1; Detroit 4-6; Green Bay 7-2; Houston 2-0; Indianapolis 25-39; Jacksonville 2-3; Kansas City 14-15-1; Miami 37-1; Minnesota 6-1; New England 47-41-1; New Orleans 5-4; N.Y. Giants 4-6; Oakland 12-19-2; Philadelphia 0-7; Pittsburgh 2-15; St Louis 2-9; San Diego 11-17-1; San Francisco 2-8; Seattle 8-8; Tampa Bay 7-1; Tennessee 14-20-1; Washington 1-7.
NOTE: Includes records as New York Titans from 1960 through 1962.

COACHING RECORDS

ammy Baugh, 14-14-0; Pete Carroll, 6-10-0; Bruce Coslet, 26-38-0 (0-1); Herman dwards, 35-29-0 (2-3); Weeb Ewbank, 71-77-6 (2-1); Al Groh, 9-7-0; Mike Holovak, 0- -0; Lou Holtz, 3-10-0; Rich Kotite, 4-28-0; Walt Michaels, 39-47-1 (2-2); Bill Parcells, 9-19-0 (1-1); Ken Shipp, 1-4-0; Clyde Turner, 5-9-0; Joe Walton, 53-57-1 (1-2); harley Winner, 9-14-0.
NOTE: Playoff games in parentheses.

RETIRED UNIFORM NUMBERS

No.	Player
12	Joe Namath
13	Don Maynard
73	Joe Klecko

OAKLAND RAIDERS
YEAR-BY-YEAR RECORDS

Year	W	L	T	Pct.	PF	PA	Finish	W	L	Highest round	Coach
1960*	6	8	0	.429	319	388	3rd/Western Div.	—	—		Eddie Erdelatz
1961*	2	12	0	.143	237	458	4th/Western Div.	—	—		E. Erdelatz, Marty Feldman
1962*	1	13	0	.071	213	370	4th/Western Div.	—	—		M. Feldman, Red Conkright
1963*	10	4	0	.714	363	288	2nd/Western Div.	—	—		Al Davis
1964*	5	7	2	.417	303	350	3rd/Western Div.	—	—		Al Davis
1965*	8	5	1	.615	298	239	2nd/Western Div.	—	—		Al Davis
1966*	8	5	1	.615	315	288	2nd/Western Div.	—	—		John Rauch
1967*	13	1	0	.929	468	233	1st/Western Div.	1	1	Super Bowl	John Rauch
1968*	12	2	0	.857	453	233	1st/Western Div.	1	1	AFL championship game	John Rauch
1969*	12	1	1	.923	377	242	1st/Western Div.	1	1	AFL championship game	John Madden
1970	8	4	2	.667	300	293	1st/AFC Western Div.	1	1	AFC championship game	John Madden
1971	8	4	2	.667	344	278	2nd/AFC Western Div.	—	—		John Madden
1972	10	3	1	.750	365	248	1st/AFC Western Div.	0	1	AFC div. playoff game	John Madden
1973	9	4	1	.679	292	175	1st/AFC Western Div.	1	1	AFC championship game	John Madden
1974	12	2	0	.857	355	228	1st/AFC Western Div.	1	1	AFC championship game	John Madden
1975	11	3	0	.786	375	255	1st/AFC Western Div.	1	1	AFC championship game	John Madden
1976	13	1	0	.929	350	237	1st/AFC Western Div.	3	0	Super Bowl champ	John Madden
1977	11	3	0	.786	351	230	2nd/AFC Western Div.	1	1	AFC championship game	John Madden
1978	9	7	0	.563	311	283	2nd/AFC Western Div.	—	—		John Madden
1979	9	7	0	.563	365	337	4th/AFC Western Div.	—	—		Tom Flores
1980	11	5	0	.688	364	306	2nd/AFC Western Div.	4	0	Super Bowl champ	Tom Flores
1981	7	9	0	.438	273	343	4th/AFC Western Div.	—	—		Tom Flores
1982†	8	1	0	.889	260	200	1st/AFC	1	1	AFC second-round pl. game	Tom Flores
1983†	12	4	0	.750	442	338	1st/AFC Western Div.	3	0	Super Bowl champ	Tom Flores
1984†	11	5	0	.688	368	278	3rd/AFC Western Div.	0	1	AFC wild-card game	Tom Flores
1985†	12	4	0	.750	354	308	1st/AFC Western Div.	0	1	AFC div. playoff game	Tom Flores
1986†	8	8	0	.500	323	346	4th/AFC Western Div.	—	—		Tom Flores
1987†	5	10	0	.333	301	289	4th/AFC Western Div.	—	—		Tom Flores
1988†	7	9	0	.438	325	369	3rd/AFC Western Div.	—	—		Mike Shanahan
1989†	8	8	0	.500	315	297	3rd/AFC Western Div.	—	—		Mike Shanahan, Art Shell
1990†	12	4	0	.750	337	268	1st/AFC Western Div.	1	1	AFC championship game	Art Shell
1991†	9	7	0	.563	298	297	3rd/AFC Western Div.	0	1	AFC wild-card game	Art Shell
1992†	7	9	0	.438	249	281	4th/AFC Western Div.	—	—		Art Shell
1993†	10	6	0	.625	306	326	2nd/AFC Western Div.	1	1	AFC div. playoff game	Art Shell
1994†	9	7	0	.563	303	327	3rd/AFC Western Div.	—	—		Art Shell
1995	8	8	0	.500	348	332	5th/AFC Western Div.	—	—		Mike White
1996	7	9	0	.438	340	293	4th/AFC Western Div.	—	—		Mike White
1997	4	12	0	.250	324	419	4th/AFC Western Div.	—	—		Joe Bugel
1998	8	8	0	.500	288	356	2nd/AFC Western Div.	—	—		Jon Gruden
1999	8	8	0	.500	390	329	4th/AFC Western Div.	—	—		Jon Gruden
2000	12	4	0	.750	479	299	1st/AFC Western Div.	1	1	AFC championship game	Jon Gruden
2001	10	6	0	.625	399	327	1st/AFC Western Div.	1	1	AFC div. playoff game	Jon Gruden
2002	11	5	0	.688	450	304	1st/AFC West Div.	2	1	Super Bowl	Bill Callahan
2003	4	12	0	.250	270	379	3rd/AFC West Div.	—	—		Bill Callahan
2004	5	11	0	.312	320	442	4th/AFC West Div.	—	—		Norv Turner

*American Football League.
†Los Angeles Raiders.

HISTORY Team by team

FIRST-ROUND DRAFT PICKS

1960—Dale Hackbart, DB, Wisconsin
1961—Joe Rutgens, DT, Illinois
1962—Roman Gabriel, QB, North Carolina State* (AFL)
1963—None
1964—Tony Lorick, RB, Arizona State
1965—Harry Schuh, T, Memphis State
1966—Rodger Bird, DB, Kentucky
1967—Gene Upshaw, G, Texas A&I
1968—Eldridge Dickey, QB, Tenn. State

1969—Art Thoms, DT, Syracuse
1970—Raymond Chester, TE, Morgan State
1971—Jack Tatum, DB, Ohio State
1972—Mike Siani, WR, Villanova
1973—Ray Guy, P, So. Mississippi
1974—Henry Lawrence, T, Florida A&M
1975—Neal Colzie, DB, Ohio State
1976—None
1977—None

1978—None
1979—None
1980—Marc Wilson, QB, Brigham Young
1981—Ted Watts, DB, Texas Tech
    Curt Marsh, T, Washington
1982—Marcus Allen, RB, Southern California
1983—Don Mosebar, T, Southern California
1984—None
1985—Jessie Hester, WR, Florida State
1986—Bob Buczkowski, DE, Pittsburgh
1987—John Clay, T, Missouri
1988—Tim Brown, WR, Notre Dame
    Terry McDaniel, CB, Tennessee
    Scott Davis, DE, Illinois
1989—None
1990—Anthony Smith, DE, Arizona
1991—Todd Marinovich, QB, Southern California
1992—Chester McGlockton, DT, Clemson

1993—Patrick Bates, DB, Texas A&M
1994—Rob Fredrickson, LB, Michigan State
1995—Napoleon Kaufman, RB, Washington
1996—Rickey Dudley, TE, Ohio State
1997—Darrell Russell, DT, Southern California
1998—Charles Woodson, DB, Michigan
    Mo Collins, T, Florida
1999—Matt Stinchcomb, T, Georgia
2000—Sebastian Janikowski, PK, Florida State
2001—Derrick Gibson, DB, Florida State
2002—Phillip Buchanon, DB, Miami, Fla.
    Napoleon Harris, LB, Northwestern
2003—Nnamdi Asomugha, DB, California
    Tyler Brayton, DE, Colorado
2004—Robert Gallery, T, Iowa
2005—Fabian Washington, CB, Nebraska
*First player chosen in draft.

FRANCHISE RECORDS

Most rushing yards, career
8,545—Marcus Allen
Most rushing yards, season
1,759—Marcus Allen, 1985
Most rushing yards, game
227—Napoleon Kaufman vs. Den., Oct. 19, 1997
Most rushing touchdowns, season
16—Pete Banaszak, 1975
Most passing attempts, season
618—Rich Gannon, 2002
Most passing attempts, game
64—Rich Gannon at Pit., Sept. 15, 2002
Most passes completed, season
418—Rich Gannon, 2002
Most passes completed, game
43—Rich Gannon at Pit., Sept. 15, 2002
Most passing yards, career
19,078—Ken Stabler

Most passing yards, season
4,689—Rich Gannon, 2002
Most passing yards, game
424—Jeff Hostetler vs. S.D., Oct. 18, 1993
Most touchdown passes, season
34—Daryle Lamonica, 1969
Most pass receptions, career
1,070—Tim Brown
Most pass receptions, season
104—Tim Brown, 1997
Most pass receptions, game
14—Tim Brown vs. Jac., Dec. 21, 1997
Most receiving yards, career
14,734—Tim Brown
Most receiving yards, season
1,408—Tim Brown, 1997
Most receiving yards, game
247—Art Powell vs. Hou., Dec. 22, 1963
Most receiving touchdowns, season
16—Art Powell, 1964

Most touchdowns, career
104—Tim Brown
Most field goals, season
35—Jeff Jaeger, 1993
Longest field goal
55 yards—Sebastian Janikowski at Det., Nov. 2, 2003
Most interceptions, career
39—Willie Brown
    Lester Hayes
Most interceptions, season
13—Lester Hayes, 1980
Most sacks, career
107.5—Greg Townsend
Most sacks, season
17.5—Tony Cline, 1970

SERIES RECORDS

Oakland vs.: Arizona 4-2; Atlanta 7-4; Baltimore 1-2; Buffalo 18-15; Carolina 2-1; Chicago 6-5; Cincinnati 17-7; Cleveland 9-5; Dallas 5-3; Denver 53-34-2; Detroit 6-3; Green Bay 5-4; Houston 0-1; Indianapolis 7-3; Jacksonville 1-2; Kansas City 42-45-2; Miami 15-10-1; Minnesota 8-3; New England 14-12-1; New Orleans 5-4-1; N.Y. Giants 7-2; N.Y. Jets 19-12-2; Philadelphia 4-4; Pittsburgh 8-8; St. Louis 7-3; San Diego 54-34-2; San Francisco 6-4; Seattle 27-22; Tampa Bay 5-1; Tennessee 22-17; Washington 6-3.
NOTE: Includes records as Los Angeles Raiders from 1982 through 1994.

COACHING RECORDS

Joe Bugel, 4-12-0; Bill Callahan, 15-17-0 (2-1); Red Conkright, 1-8-0; Al Davis, 23-16-3; Eddie Erdelatz, 6-10-0; Marty Feldman, 2-15-0; Tom Flores, 83-53-0 (8-3); Jon Gruden, 38-26-0 (2-2); John Madden, 103-32-7 (9-7); John Rauch, 33-8-1 (2-2); Mike Shanahan, 8-12-0; Art Shell, 54-38-0 (2-3); Norv Turner, 5-11-0; Mike White, 15-17-0. NOTE: Playoff games in parentheses.

RETIRED UNIFORM NUMBERS

No.	Player
None	

PHILADELPHIA EAGLES
YEAR-BY-YEAR RECORDS

		REGULAR SEASON							PLAYOFFS		
Year	W	L	T	Pct.	PF	PA	Finish	W	L	Highest round	Coach
1933	3	5	1	.375	77	158	4th/Eastern Div.	—	—		Lud Wray
1934	4	7	0	.364	127	85	T3rd/Eastern Div.	—	—		Lud Wray
1935	2	9	0	.182	60	179	5th/Eastern Div.	—	—		Lud Wray
1936	1	11	0	.083	51	206	5th/Eastern Div.	—	—		Bert Bell
1937	2	8	1	.200	86	177	5th/Eastern Div.	—	—		Bert Bell
1938	5	6	0	.455	154	164	4th/Eastern Div.	—	—		Bert Bell
1939	1	9	1	.100	105	200	T4th/Eastern Div.	—	—		Bert Bell
1940	1	10	0	.091	111	211	5th/Eastern Div.	—	—		Bert Bell

Year	W	L	T	Pct.	PF	PA	Finish	W	L	Highest round	Coach
							REGULAR SEASON			**PLAYOFFS**	
1941	2	8	1	.200	119	218	4th/Eastern Div.	—	—		Greasy Neale
1942	2	9	0	.182	134	239	5th/Eastern Div.	—	—		Greasy Neale
1943*	5	4	1	.556	225	230	3rd/Eastern Div.	—	—		G. Neale-Walt Kiesling
1944	7	1	2	.875	267	131	2nd/Eastern Div.	—	—		Greasy Neale
1945	7	3	0	.700	272	133	2nd/Eastern Div.	—	—		Greasy Neale
1946	6	5	0	.545	231	220	2nd/Eastern Div.	—	—		Greasy Neale
1947	8	4	0	.667	308	242	1st/Eastern Div.	1	1	NFL championship game	Greasy Neale
1948	9	2	1	.818	376	156	1st/Eastern Div.	1	0	NFL champ	Greasy Neale
1949	11	1	0	.917	364	134	1st/Eastern Div.	1	0	NFL champ	Greasy Neale
1950	6	6	0	.500	254	141	T3rd/American Conf.	—	—		Greasy Neale
1951	4	8	0	.333	234	264	5th/American Conf.	—	—		Bo McMillin, Wayne Millner
1952	7	5	0	.583	252	271	T2nd/American Conf.	—	—		Jim Trimble
1953	7	4	1	.636	352	215	2nd/Eastern Conf.	—	—		Jim Trimble
1954	7	4	1	.636	284	230	2nd/Eastern Conf.	—	—		Jim Trimble
1955	4	7	1	.364	248	231	T4th/Eastern Conf.	—	—		Jim Trimble
1956	3	8	1	.273	143	215	6th/Eastern Conf.	—	—		Hugh Devore
1957	4	8	0	.333	173	230	5th/Eastern Conf.	—	—		Hugh Devore
1958	2	9	1	.182	235	306	T5th/Eastern Conf.	—	—		Buck Shaw
1959	7	5	0	.583	268	278	T2nd/Eastern Conf.	—	—		Buck Shaw
1960	10	2	0	.833	321	246	1st/Eastern Conf.	1	0	NFL champ	Buck Shaw
1961	10	4	0	.714	361	297	2nd/Eastern Conf.	—	—		Nick Skorich
1962	3	10	1	.231	282	356	7th/Eastern Conf.	—	—		Nick Skorich
1963	2	10	2	.167	242	381	7th/Western Conf.	—	—		Nick Skorich
1964	6	8	0	.429	312	313	T3rd/Eastern Conf.	—	—		Joe Kuharich
1965	5	9	0	.357	363	359	T5th/Eastern Conf.	—	—		Joe Kuharich
1966	9	5	0	.643	326	340	T2nd/Eastern Conf.	—	—		Joe Kuharich
1967	6	7	1	.462	351	409	2nd/Capitol Div.	—	—		Joe Kuharich
1968	2	12	0	.143	202	351	4th/Capitol Div.	—	—		Joe Kuharich
1969	4	9	1	.308	279	377	4th/Capitol Div.	—	—		Jerry Williams
1970	3	10	1	.231	241	332	5th/NFC Eastern Div.	—	—		Jerry Williams
1971	6	7	1	.462	221	302	3rd/NFC Eastern Div.	—	—		J. Williams, Ed Khayat
1972	2	11	1	.179	145	352	5th/NFC Eastern Div.	—	—		Ed Khayat
1973	5	8	1	.393	310	393	3rd/NFC Eastern Div.	—	—		Mike McCormack
1974	7	7	0	.500	242	217	4th/NFC Eastern Div.	—	—		Mike McCormack
1975	4	10	0	.286	225	302	5th/NFC Eastern Div.	—	—		Mike McCormack
1976	4	10	0	.286	165	286	4th/NFC Eastern Div.	—	—		Dick Vermeil
1977	5	9	0	.357	220	207	4th/NFC Eastern Div.	—	—		Dick Vermeil
1978	9	7	0	.563	270	250	2nd/NFC Eastern Div.	0	1	NFC wild-card game	Dick Vermeil
1979	11	5	0	.688	339	282	2nd/NFC Eastern Div.	1	1	NFC div. playoff game	Dick Vermeil
1980	12	4	0	.750	384	222	1st/NFC Eastern Div.	2	1	Super Bowl	Dick Vermeil
1981	10	6	0	.625	368	221	2nd/NFC Eastern Div.	0	1	NFC wild-card game	Dick Vermeil
1982	3	6	0	.333	191	195	13th/NFC	—	—		Dick Vermeil
1983	5	11	0	.313	233	322	4th/NFC Eastern Div.	—	—		Marion Campbell
1984	6	9	1	.406	278	320	5th/NFC Eastern Div.	—	—		Marion Campbell
1985	7	9	0	.438	286	310	4th/NFC Eastern Div.	—	—		M. Campbell, Fred Bruney
1986	5	10	1	.344	256	312	4th/NFC Eastern Div.	—	—		Buddy Ryan
1987	7	8	0	.467	337	380	4th/NFC Eastern Div.	—	—		Buddy Ryan
1988	10	6	0	.625	379	319	1st/NFC Eastern Div.	0	1	NFC div. playoff game	Buddy Ryan
1989	11	5	0	.688	342	274	2nd/NFC Eastern Div.	0	1	NFC wild-card game	Buddy Ryan
1990	10	6	0	.625	396	299	2nd/NFC Eastern Div.	0	1	NFC wild-card game	Buddy Ryan
1991	10	6	0	.625	285	244	3rd/NFC Eastern Div.	—	—		Rich Kotite
1992	11	5	0	.688	354	245	2nd/NFC Eastern Div.	1	1	NFC div. playoff game	Rich Kotite
1993	8	8	0	.500	293	315	3rd/NFC Eastern Div.	—	—		Rich Kotite
1994	7	9	0	.438	308	308	4th/NFC Eastern Div.	—	—		Rich Kotite
1995	10	6	0	.625	318	338	2nd/NFC Eastern Div.	1	1	NFC div. playoff game	Ray Rhodes
1996	10	6	0	.625	363	341	2nd/NFC Eastern Div.	0	1	NFC wild-card game	Ray Rhodes
1997	6	9	1	.406	317	372	3rd/NFC Eastern Div.	—	—		Ray Rhodes
1998	3	13	0	.188	161	344	5th/NFC Eastern Div.	—	—		Ray Rhodes
1999	5	11	0	.313	272	357	5th/NFC Eastern Div.	—	—		Andy Reid
2000	11	5	0	.688	351	245	2nd/NFC Eastern Div.	1	1	NFC div. playoff game	Andy Reid
2001	11	5	0	.688	343	208	1st/NFC Eastern Div.	2	1	NFC championship game	Andy Reid
2002	12	4	0	.750	415	241	1st/NFC East Div.	1	1	NFC championship game	Andy Reid
2003	12	4	0	.750	374	287	1st/NFC East Div.	1	1	NFC championship game	Andy Reid
2004	13	3	0	.812	386	260	1st/NFC East Div.	2	1	Super Bowl	Andy Reid

*Phil-Pitt "Steagles," a combined squad of Philadelphia Eagles and Pittsburgh Steelers.

FIRST-ROUND DRAFT PICKS

1936—Jay Berwanger, B, Chicago*
1937—Sam Francis, B, Nebraska*
1938—Jim McDonald, B, Ohio State

1939—Davey O'Brien, B, Texas Christian
1940—George McAfee, B, Duke
1941—None

1942—Pete Kmetovic, B, Stanford
1943—Joe Muha, B, Virginia Military
1944—Steve Van Buren, B, Louisiana State
1945—John Yonaker, E, Notre Dame
1946—Leo Riggs, B, Southern California
1947—Neill Armstrong, E, Oklahoma State
1948—Clyde Scott, B, Arkansas
1949—Chuck Bednarik, C, Pennsylvania*
     Frank Tripucka, QB, Notre Dame
1950—Bud Grant, E, Minnesota
1951—Ebert Van Buren, B, Louisiana State
     Chet Mutryn, B, Xavier
1952—John Bright, B, Drake
1953—None
1954—Neil Worden, B, Notre Dame
1955—Dick Bielski, B, Maryland
1956—Bob Pellegrini, C, Maryland
1957—Clarence Peaks, B, Michigan State
1958—Walter Kowalczyk, B, Michigan State
1959—None
1960—Ron Burton, B, Northwestern
1961—Art Baker, B, Syracuse
1962—None
1963—Ed Budde, T, Michigan State
1964—Bob Brown, T, Nebraska
1965—None
1966—Randy Beisler, DE, Indiana
1967—Harry Jones, RB, Arkansas
1968—Tim Rossovich, DE, Southern California
1969—Leroy Keyes, RB, Purdue
1970—Steve Zabel, E, Oklahoma
1971—Richard Harris, DE, Grambling State
1972—John Reaves, QB, Florida
1973—Jerry Sisemore, T, Texas
     Charle Young, TE, Southern California

1974—None
1975—None
1976—None
1977—None
1978—None
1979—Jerry Robinson, LB, UCLA
1980—Roynell Young, DB, Alcorn State
1981—Leonard Mitchell, DE, Houston
1982—Mike Quick, WR, North Carolina State
1983—Michael Haddix, RB, Mississippi State
1984—Kenny Jackson, WR, Penn State
1985—Kevin Allen, T, Indiana
1986—Keith Byars, RB, Ohio State
1987—Jerome Brown, DT, Miami, Fla.
1988—Keith Jackson, TE, Oklahoma
1989—None
1990—Ben Smith, DB, Georgia
1991—Antone Davis, T, Tennessee
1992—None
1993—Lester Holmes, T, Jackson State
     Leonard Renfro, DT, Colorado
1994—Bernard Williams, T, Georgia
1995—Mike Mamula, DE, Boston College
1996—Jermane Mayberry, T, Texas A&M-Kingsville
1997—Jon Harris, DE, Virginia
1998—Tra Thomas, T, Florida State
1999—Donovan McNabb, QB, Syracuse
2000—Corey Simon, DT, Florida State
2001—Freddie Mitchell, WR, UCLA
2002—Lito Sheppard, DB, Florida
2003—Jerome McDougle, DE, Miami, Fla.
2004—Shawn Andrews, T, Arkansas
2005—Mike Patterson, DT, Southern California
*First player chosen in draft.

FRANCHISE RECORDS

Most rushing yards, career
6,538—Wilbert Montgomery
Most rushing yards, season
1,512—Wilbert Montgomery, 1979
Most rushing yards, game
205—Steve Van Buren vs. Pit., Nov. 27, 1949
Most rushing touchdowns, season
15—Steve Van Buren, 1945
Most passing attempts, season
569—Donovan McNabb, 2000
Most passing attempts, game
62—Randall Cunningham at Chi., Oct. 2, 1989
Most passes completed, season
330—Donovan McNabb, 2000
Most passes completed, game
34—Randall Cunningham at Was., Sept. 17, 1989
Most passing yards, career
26,963—Ron Jaworski

Most passing yards, season
3,875—Donovan McNabb, 2004
Most passing yards, game
447—Randall Cunningham at Was., Sept. 17, 1989
Most touchdown passes, season
32—Sonny Jurgensen, 1961
Most pass receptions, career
589—Harold Carmichael
Most pass receptions, season
88—Irving Fryar, 1996
Most pass receptions, game
14—Don Looney at Was., Dec. 1, 1940
Most receiving yards, career
8,978—Harold Carmichael
Most receiving yards, season
1,409—Mike Quick, 1983
Most receiving yards, game
237—Tommy McDonald vs. NYG, Dec. 10, 1961

Most receiving touchdowns, season
14—Terrell Owens, 2004
Most touchdowns, career
79—Harold Carmichael
Most field goals, season
30—Paul McFadden, 1984
     David Akers, 2002
Longest field goal
59 yards—Tony Franklin at Dal., Nov. 12, 1979
Most interceptions, career
34—Eric Allen
     Bill Bradley
Most interceptions, season
11—Bill Bradley, 1971
Most sacks, career
124—Reggie White
Most sacks, season
21—Reggie White, 1987

SERIES RECORDS

Philadelphia vs.: Arizona 52-52-5; Atlanta 11-9-1; Baltimore, 1-0-1; Buffalo 5-5; Carolina 3-1; Chicago 8-24-1; Cincinnati 3-7; Cleveland 14-31-1; Dallas 39-49; Denver 6-3; Detroit 12-12-2; Green Bay 11-22; Houston 1-0; Indianapolis 6-9; Jacksonville 0-2; Kansas City 2-2; Miami 4-7; Minnesota 8-11; New England 6-3; New Orleans 14-8; N.Y. Giants 65-73-2; N.Y. Jets 7-0; Oakland 4-4; Pittsburgh 45-27-3; St. Louis 15-17-1; San Diego 3-5; San Francisco 7-16-1; Seattle 6-3; Tampa Bay 5-4; Tennessee 6-2; Washington 62-72-5.
NOTE: Does not include records when team combined with Pittsburgh squad and was known as Phil-Pitt in 1943.

ert Bell, 10-44-2; Fred Bruney, 1-0-0; Marion Campbell, 17-29-1; Hugh Devore, 7-16-
; Ed Khayat, 8-15-2; Rich Kotite, 36-28-0 (1-1); Joe Kuharich, 28-41-1; Mike
cCormack, 16-25-1; Alvin McMillin, 2-0-0; Wayne Millner, 2-8-0; Earle (Greasy) Neale,
3-43-5 (3-1); Andy Reid, 64-32-0 (7-5); Ray Rhodes, 29-34-1 (1-2); Buddy Ryan, 43-
5-1 (0-3); Buck Shaw, 19-16-1 (1-0); Nick Skorich, 15-24-3; Jim Trimble, 25-20-3; Dick
ermeil, 54-47-0 (3-4); Jerry Williams, 7-22-2; Lud Wray, 9-21-1.
OTE: Playoff games in parentheses.

RETIRED UNIFORM NUMBERS

No.	Player
15	Steve Van Buren
40	Tom Brookshier
44	Pete Retzlaff
60	Chuck Bednarik
70	Al Wistert
92	Reggie White
99	Jerome Brown

PITTSBURGH STEELERS
YEAR-BY-YEAR RECORDS

	REGULAR SEASON							PLAYOFFS			
ear	W	L	T	Pct.	PF	PA	Finish	W	L	Highest round	Coach
933*	3	6	2	.333	67	208	5th/Eastern Div.	—	—		Jap Douds
934*	2	10	0	.167	51	206	5th/Eastern Div.	—	—		Luby DiMello
935*	4	8	0	.333	100	209	3rd/Eastern Div.	—	—		Joe Bach
936*	6	6	0	.500	98	187	2nd/Eastern Div.	—	—		Joe Bach
937*	4	7	0	.364	122	145	3rd/Eastern Div.	—	—		Johnny Blood
938*	2	9	0	.182	79	169	5th/Eastern Div.	—	—		Johnny Blood
939*	1	9	1	.100	114	216	T4th/Eastern Div.	—	—		J. Blood-W. Kiesling
940*	2	7	2	.222	60	178	4th/Eastern Div.	—	—		Walt Kiesling
1941	1	9	1	.100	103	276	5th/Eastern Div.	—	—		Bert Bell-Buff Donelli-Walt Kiesling
1942	7	4	0	.636	167	119	2nd/Eastern Div.	—	—		Walt Kiesling
1943†	5	4	1	.556	225	230	3rd/Eastern Div.	—	—		W. Kiesling-Greasy Neale
1944‡	0	10	0	.000	108	328	5th/Western Div.	—	—		W. Kiesling-Phil Handler
1945	2	8	0	.200	79	220	5th/Eastern Div.	—	—		Jim Leonard
1946	5	5	1	.500	136	117	T3rd/Eastern Div.	—	—		Jock Sutherland
1947	8	4	0	.667	240	259	2nd/Eastern Div.	0	1	E. Div. champ. game	Jock Sutherland
1948	4	8	0	.333	200	243	T3rd/Eastern Div.	—	—		John Michelosen
1949	6	5	1	.545	224	214	2nd/Eastern Div.	—	—		John Michelosen
1950	6	6	0	.500	180	195	T3rd/American Conf.	—	—		John Michelosen
1951	4	7	1	.364	183	235	4th/American Conf.	—	—		John Michelosen
1952	5	7	0	.417	300	273	4th/American Conf.	—	—		Joe Bach
1953	6	6	0	.500	211	263	4th/Eastern Conf.	—	—		Joe Bach
1954	5	7	0	.417	219	263	4th/Eastern Conf.	—	—		Walt Kiesling
1955	4	8	0	.333	195	285	6th/Eastern Conf.	—	—		Walt Kiesling
1956	5	7	0	.417	217	250	5th/Eastern Conf.	—	—		Walt Kiesling
1957	6	6	0	.500	161	178	3rd/Eastern Conf.	—	—		Buddy Parker
1958	7	4	1	.636	261	230	3rd/Eastern Conf.	—	—		Buddy Parker
1959	6	5	1	.545	257	216	4th/Eastern Conf.	—	—		Buddy Parker
1960	5	6	1	.455	240	275	5th/Eastern Conf.	—	—		Buddy Parker
1961	6	8	0	.429	295	287	5th/Eastern Conf.	—	—		Buddy Parker
1962	9	5	0	.643	312	363	2nd/Eastern Conf.	—	—		Buddy Parker
1963	7	4	3	.636	321	295	4th/Eastern Conf.	—	—		Buddy Parker
1964	5	9	0	.357	253	315	6th/Eastern Conf.	—	—		Buddy Parker
1965	2	12	0	.143	202	397	7th/Eastern Conf.	—	—		Mike Nixon
1966	5	8	1	.385	316	347	6th/Eastern Conf.	—	—		Bill Austin
1967	4	9	1	.308	281	320	4th/Century Div.	—	—		Bill Austin
1968	2	11	1	.154	244	397	4th/Century Div.	—	—		Bill Austin
1969	1	13	0	.071	218	404	4th/Century Div.	—	—		Chuck Noll
1970	5	9	0	.357	210	272	3rd/AFC Central Div.	—	—		Chuck Noll
1971	6	8	0	.429	246	292	2nd/AFC Central Div.	—	—		Chuck Noll
1972	11	3	0	.786	343	175	1st/AFC Central Div.	1	1	AFC championship game	Chuck Noll
1973	10	4	0	.714	347	210	2nd/AFC Central Div.	0	1	AFC div. playoff game	Chuck Noll
1974	10	3	1	.750	305	189	1st/AFC Central Div.	3	0	Super Bowl champ	Chuck Noll
1975	12	2	0	.857	373	162	1st/AFC Central Div.	3	0	Super Bowl champ	Chuck Noll
1976	10	4	0	.714	342	138	1st/AFC Central Div.	1	1	AFC championship game	Chuck Noll
1977	9	5	0	.643	283	243	1st/AFC Central Div.	0	1	AFC div. playoff game	Chuck Noll
1978	14	2	0	.875	356	195	1st/AFC Central Div.	3	0	Super Bowl champ	Chuck Noll
1979	12	4	0	.750	416	262	1st/AFC Central Div.	3	0	Super Bowl champ	Chuck Noll
1980	9	7	0	.563	352	313	3rd/AFC Central Div.	—	—		Chuck Noll
1981	8	8	0	.500	356	297	2nd/AFC Central Div.	—	—		Chuck Noll
1982	6	3	0	.667	204	146	4th/AFC	0	1	AFC first-round pl. game	Chuck Noll
1983	10	6	0	.625	355	303	1st/AFC Central Div.	0	1	AFC div. playoff game	Chuck Noll
1984	9	7	0	.563	387	310	1st/AFC Central Div.	1	1	AFC championship game	Chuck Noll
1985	7	9	0	.438	379	355	3rd/AFC Central Div.	—	—		Chuck Noll
1986	6	10	0	.375	307	336	3rd/AFC Central Div.	—	—		Chuck Noll
1987	8	7	0	.533	285	299	3rd/AFC Central Div.	—	—		Chuck Noll
1988	5	11	0	.313	336	421	4th/AFC Central Div.	—	—		Chuck Noll
1989	9	7	0	.563	265	326	3rd/AFC Central Div.	1	1	AFC div. playoff game	Chuck Noll
1990	9	7	0	.563	292	240	3rd/AFC Central Div.	—	—		Chuck Noll

HISTORY *Team by team*

		REGULAR SEASON							PLAYOFFS		
Year	W	L	T	Pct.	PF	PA	Finish	W	L	Highest round	Coach
1991	7	9	0	.438	292	344	2nd/AFC Central Div.	—	—		Chuck Noll
1992	11	5	0	.688	299	225	1st/AFC Central Div.	0	1	AFC div. playoff game	Bill Cowher
1993	9	7	0	.563	308	281	2nd/AFC Central Div.	0	1	AFC wild-card game	Bill Cowher
1994	12	4	0	.750	316	234	1st/AFC Central Div.	1	1	AFC championship game	Bill Cowher
1995	11	5	0	.689	407	327	1st/AFC Central Div.	2	1	Super Bowl	Bill Cowher
1996	10	6	0	.625	344	257	1st/AFC Central Div.	1	1	AFC div. playoff game	Bill Cowher
1997	11	5	0	.688	372	307	1st/AFC Central Div.	1	1	AFC championship game	Bill Cowher
1998	7	9	0	.438	263	303	3rd/AFC Central Div.	—	—		Bill Cowher
1999	6	10	0	.375	317	320	4th/AFC Central Div.	—	—		Bill Cowher
2000	9	7	0	.563	321	255	3rd/AFC Central Div.	—	—		Bill Cowher
2001	13	3	0	.813	352	212	1st/AFC Central Div.	1	1	AFC championship game	Bill Cowher
2002	10	5	1	.656	390	345	1st/AFC North Div.	1	1	AFC div. playoff game	Bill Cowher
2003	6	10	0	.375	300	327	3rd/AFC North Div.	—	—		Bill Cowher
2004	15	1	0	.938	372	251	1st/AFC North Div.	1	1	AFC championship game	Bill Cowher

*Pittsburgh Pirates.
†Phil-Pitt "Steagles," a combined squad of Philadelphia Eagles and Pittsburgh Steelers.
‡Card-Pitt, a combined squad of Chicago Cardinals and Pittsburgh Steelers.

FIRST-ROUND DRAFT PICKS

1936—Bill Shakespeare, B, Notre Dame
1937—Mike Basrak, C, Duquesne
1938—Byron White, B, Colorado
    Frank Filchock, B, Indiana
1939—None
1940—Kay Eakin, B, Arkansas
1941—Chet Gladchuk, C, Boston College
1942—Bill Dudley, B, Virginia*
1943—Bill Daley, B, Minnesota
1944—Johnny Podesto, B, St. Mary's (Calif.)
1945—Paul Duhart, B, Florida
1946—Doc Blanchard, B, Army
1947—Hub Bechtol, E, Texas
1948—Dan Edwards, E, Georgia
1949—Bobby Gage, B, Clemson
1950—Lynn Chandnois, B, Michigan State
1951—Clarence Avinger, B, Alabama
1952—Ed Modzelewski, B, Maryland
1953—Ted Marchibroda, QB, St. Bonaventure
1954—John Lattner, B, Notre Dame
1955—Frank Varrichione, T, Notre Dame
1956—Gary Glick, B, Colorado State*
    Art Davis, B, Mississippi State
1957—Len Dawson, QB, Purdue
1958—None
1959—None
1960—Jack Spikes, B, Texas Christian
1961—None
1962—Bob Ferguson, RB, Ohio State
1963—None
1964—Paul Martha, RB, Pittsburgh
1965—None
1966—Dick Leftridge, RB, West Virginia
1967—None
1968—Mike Taylor, T, Southern California
1969—Joe Greene, DT, North Texas State
1970—Terry Bradshaw, QB, Louisiana Tech*

1971—Frank Lewis, WR, Grambling State
1972—Franco Harris, RB, Penn State
1973—James Thomas, DB, Florida State
1974—Lynn Swann, WR, Southern California
1975—Dave Brown, DB, Michigan
1976—Bennie Cunningham, TE, Clemson
1977—Robin Cole, LB, New Mexico
1978—Ron Johnson, DB, Eastern Michigan
1979—Greg Hawthorne, RB, Baylor
1980—Mark Malone, QB, Arizona State
1981—Keith Gary, DE, Oklahoma
1982—Walter Abercrombie, RB, Baylor
1983—Gabriel Rivera, DT, Texas Tech
1984—Louis Lipps, WR, Southern Mississippi
1985—Darryl Sims, DT, Wisconsin
1986—John Rienstra, G, Temple
1987—Rod Woodson, DB, Purdue
1988—Aaron Jones, DE, Eastern Kentucky
1989—Tim Worley, RB, Georgia
    Tom Ricketts, T, Pittsburgh
1990—Eric Green, TE, Liberty (Va.)
1991—Huey Richardson, DE, Florida
1992—Leon Searcy, T, Miami, Fla.
1993—Deon Figures, DB, Colorado
1994—Charles Johnson, WR, Colorado
1995—Mark Bruener, TE, Washington
1996—Jermain Stephens, T, North Carolina A&T
1997—Chad Scott, DB, Maryland
1998—Alan Faneca, G, Louisiana State
1999—Troy Edwards, WR, Louisiana Tech
2000—Plaxico Burress, WR, Michigan State
2001—Casey Hampton, DT, Texas
2002—Kendall Simmons, G, Auburn
2003—Troy Polamalu, DB, Southern California
2004—Ben Roethlisberger, QB, Miami (Ohio)
2005—Heath Miller, TE, Virginia
    *First player chosen in draft.

FRANCHISE RECORDS

Most rushing yards, career
11,950—Franco Harris
Most rushing yards, season
1,690—Barry Foster, 1992
Most rushing yards, game
218—John Fuqua at Phi., Dec. 20, 1970
Most rushing touchdowns, season
14—Franco Harris, 1976
Most passing attempts, season
519—Tommy Maddox, 2003

Most passing attempts, game
57—Tommy Maddox vs. Hou., Dec. 8, 2002
Most passes completed, season
298—Tommy Maddox, 2003
Most passes completed, game
34—Neil O'Donnell at Chi., Nov. 5, 1995 (OT)
33—Neil O'Donnell at G.B., Dec. 24, 1995
Most passing yards, career
27,989—Terry Bradshaw

Most passing yards, season
3,724—Terry Bradshaw, 1979
Most passing yards, game
473—Tommy Maddox vs. Atl., Nov. 10, 2002 (OT)
409—Bobby Layne vs. Chi. Cardinals, Dec. 13, 1958
Most touchdown passes, season
28—Terry Bradshaw, 1978
Most pass receptions, career
537—John Stallworth

ost pass receptions, season
2—Hines Ward, 2002
ost pass receptions, game
—Courtney Hawkins vs. Ten., Nov. 1, 1998
ost receiving yards, career
723—John Stallworth
lost receiving yards, season
.398—Yancey Thigpen, 1997
lost receiving yards, game
53—Plaxico Burress vs. Atl., Nov. 10,
    2002 (OT)
35—Buddy Dial vs. Cle., Oct. 22, 1961

Most receiving touchdowns, season
12—Buddy Dial, 1961
    Louis Lipps, 1985
    Hines Ward, 2002
Most touchdowns, career
100—Franco Harris
Most field goals, season
34—Norm Johnson, 1995
Longest field goal
55 yards—Gary Anderson vs. S.D.,
    Nov. 25, 1984
    Kris Brown at K.C., Oct. 14, 2001

Most interceptions, career
57—Mel Blount
Most interceptions, season
11—Mel Blount, 1975
Most sacks, career
77—Jason Gildon
Most sacks, season
15—Mike Merriweather, 1984

SERIES RECORDS

ittsburgh vs.: Arizona 31-22-3; Atlanta 11-1-1; Baltimore 12-6; Buffalo 10-8; Carolina 2-1; Chicago 6-16-1; Cincinnati 41-28; Cleveland 9-55; Dallas 12-14; Denver 6-11-1; Detroit 13-14-1; Green Bay 12-18; Houston 0-1; Indianapolis 13-4; Jacksonville 8-8; Kansas City 6-8; Miami 8-9; Minnesota 5-8; New England 12-5; New Orleans 6-6; N.Y. Giants 28-43-3; N.Y. Jets 15-2; Oakland 8-8; Philadelphia 27-5-3; St. Louis 5-15-2; San Diego 18-5; San Francisco 8-10; Seattle 6-8; Tampa Bay 6-1; Tennessee 37-28; Washington 30-42-3.
OTE: Includes records as Pittsburgh Pirates from 1933 through 1940; does not include records when team combined with Philadelphia quad and was known as Phil-Pitt in 1943 and when team combined with Chicago Cardinals squad and was known as Card-Pitt in 1944.

COACHING RECORDS

ill Austin, 11-28-3; Joe Bach, 21-27-0; Bert Bell, 0-2-0; Bill Cowher, 130-77-1 (8-9); uby DiMelio, 2-10-0; Aldo Donelli, 0-5-0; Forrest Douds, 3-6-2; Walt Kiesling, 30-55-5; im Leonard, 2-8-0; Johnny (Blood) McNally, 6-19-0; Johnny Michelosen, 20-26-2; Mike Nixon, 2-12-0; Chuck Noll, 193-148-1 (16-8); Buddy Parker, 51-47-6 (0-1); Jock utherland, 13-9-1 (0-1).
IOTE: Playoff games in parentheses.

RETIRED UNIFORM NUMBERS

No.	Player
70	Ernie Stautner

ST. LOUIS RAMS
YEAR-BY-YEAR RECORDS

| | | REGULAR SEASON | | | | | | PLAYOFFS | | |
Year	W	L	T	Pct.	PF	PA	Finish	W	L	Highest round	Coach
1937*	1	10	0	.091	75	207	5th/Western Div.	—	—		Hugo Bezdek
1938*	4	7	0	.364	131	215	4th/Western Div.	—	—		Hugo Bezdek, Art Lewis
1939*	5	5	1	.500	195	164	4th/Western Div.	—	—		Dutch Clark
1940*	4	6	1	.400	171	191	4th/Western Div.	—	—		Dutch Clark
1941*	2	9	0	.182	116	244	5th/Western Div.	—	—		Dutch Clark
1942*	5	6	0	.455	150	207	3rd/Western Div.	—	—		Dutch Clark
1943*			Rams did not play in 1943.								
1944*	4	6	0	.400	188	224	4th/Western Div.	—	—		Buff Donelli
1945*	9	1	0	.900	244	136	1st/Western Div.	1	0	NFL champ	Adam Walsh
1946†	6	4	1	.600	277	257	2nd/Western Div.	—	—		Adam Walsh
1947†	6	6	0	.500	259	214	4th/Western Div.	—	—		Bob Snyder
1948†	6	5	1	.545	327	269	3rd/Western Div.	—	—		Clark Shaughnessy
1949†	8	2	2	.800	360	239	1st/Western Div.	0	1	NFL championship game	Clark Shaughnessy
1950†	9	3	0	.750	466	309	1st/National Conf.	1	1	NFL championship game	Joe Stydahar
1951†	8	4	0	.667	392	261	1st/National Conf.	1	0	NFL champ	Joe Stydahar
1952†	9	3	0	.750	349	234	2nd/National Conf.	0	1	Nat. Conf. champ. game	J. Stydahar, Hamp Pool
1953†	8	3	1	.727	366	236	3rd/Western Conf.	—	—		Hamp Pool
1954†	6	5	1	.545	314	285	4th/Western Conf.	—	—		Hamp Pool
1955†	8	3	1	.727	260	231	1st/Western Conf.	0	1	NFL championship game	Sid Gillman
1956†	4	8	0	.333	291	307	6th/Western Conf.	—	—		Sid Gillman
1957†	6	6	0	.500	307	278	4th/Western Conf.	—	—		Sid Gillman
1958†	8	4	0	.667	344	278	2nd/Western Conf.	—	—		Sid Gillman
1959†	2	10	0	.167	242	315	6th/Western Conf.	—	—		Sid Gillman
1960†	4	7	1	.364	265	297	6th/Western Conf.	—	—		Bob Waterfield
1961†	4	10	0	.286	263	333	6th/Western Conf.	—	—		Bob Waterfield
1962†	1	12	1	.077	220	334	7th/Western Conf.	—	—		B. Waterfield, H. Svare
1963†	5	9	0	.357	210	350	6th/Western Conf.	—	—		Harland Svare
1964†	5	7	2	.417	283	339	5th/Western Conf.	—	—		Harland Svare
1965†	4	10	0	.286	269	328	7th/Western Conf.	—	—		Harland Svare
1966†	8	6	0	.571	289	212	3rd/Western Conf.	—	—		George Allen
1967†	11	1	2	.917	398	196	1st/Coastal Div.	0	1	W. Conf. champ. game	George Allen
1968†	10	3	1	.769	312	200	2nd/Coastal Div.	—	—		George Allen
1969†	11	3	0	.786	320	243	1st/Coastal Div.	0	1	W. Conf. champ. game	George Allen
1970†	9	4	1	.692	325	202	2nd/NFC Western Div.	—	—		George Allen
1971†	8	5	1	.615	313	260	2nd/NFC Western Div.	—	—		Tommy Prothro
1972†	6	7	1	.464	291	286	3rd/NFC Western Div.	—	—		Tommy Prothro
1973†	12	2	0	.857	388	178	1st/NFC Western Div.	0	1	NFC div. playoff game	Chuck Knox

HISTORY   Team by team

REGULAR SEASON / PLAYOFFS

Year	W	L	T	Pct.	PF	PA	Finish	W	L	Highest round	Coach
1974†	10	4	0	.714	263	181	1st/NFC Western Div.	1	1	NFC championship game	Chuck Knox
1975†	12	2	0	.857	312	135	1st/NFC Western Div.	1	1	NFC championship game	Chuck Knox
1976†	10	3	1	.750	351	190	1st/NFC Western Div.	1	1	NFC championship game	Chuck Knox
1977†	10	4	0	.714	302	146	1st/NFC Western Div.	0	1	NFC div. playoff game	Chuck Knox
1978†	12	4	0	.750	316	245	1st/NFC Western Div.	1	1	NFC championship game	Ray Malavasi
1979†	9	7	0	.563	323	309	1st/NFC Western Div.	2	1	Super Bowl	Ray Malavasi
1980†	11	5	0	.688	424	289	2nd/NFC Western Div.	0	1	NFC wild-card game	Ray Malavasi
1981†	6	10	0	.375	303	351	3rd/NFC Western Div.	—	—		Ray Malavasi
1982†	2	7	0	.222	200	250	14th/NFC	—	—		Ray Malavasi
1983†	9	7	0	.563	361	344	2nd/NFC Western Div.	1	1	NFC div. playoff game	John Robinson
1984†	10	6	0	.625	346	316	2nd/NFC Western Div.	0	1	NFC wild-card game	John Robinson
1985†	11	5	0	.688	340	277	1st/NFC Western Div.	1	1	NFC championship game	John Robinson
1986†	10	6	0	.625	309	267	2nd/NFC Western Div.	0	1	NFC wild-card game	John Robinson
1987†	6	9	0	.400	317	361	3rd/NFC Western Div.	—	—		John Robinson
1988†	10	6	0	.625	407	293	2nd/NFC Western Div.	0	1	NFC wild-card game	John Robinson
1989†	11	5	0	.688	426	344	2nd/NFC Western Div.	2	1	NFC championship game	John Robinson
1990†	5	11	0	.313	345	412	3rd/NFC Western Div.	—	—		John Robinson
1991†	3	13	0	.188	234	390	4th/NFC Western Div.	—	—		John Robinson
1992†	6	10	0	.375	313	383	4th/NFC Western Div.	—	—		Chuck Knox
1993†	5	11	0	.313	221	367	4th/NFC Western Div.	—	—		Chuck Knox
1994†	4	12	0	.250	286	365	4th/NFC Western Div.	—	—		Chuck Knox
1995	7	9	0	.438	309	418	3rd/NFC Western Div.	—	—		Rich Brooks
1996	6	10	0	.375	303	409	3rd/NFC Western Div.	—	—		Rich Brooks
1997	5	11	0	.313	299	359	5th/NFC Western Div.	—	—		Dick Vermeil
1998	4	12	0	.250	285	378	5th/NFC Western Div.	—	—		Dick Vermeil
1999	13	3	0	.813	526	242	1st/NFC Western Div.	3	0	Super Bowl champ	Dick Vermeil
2000	10	6	0	.625	540	471	2nd/NFC Western Div.	0	1	NFC wild-card game	Mike Martz
2001	14	2	0	.875	503	273	1st/NFC Western Div.	2	1	Super Bowl	Mike Martz
2002	7	9	0	.438	316	369	2nd/NFC West Div.	—	—		Mike Martz
2003	12	4	0	.750	447	328	1st/NFC West Div.	0	1	NFC div. playoff game	Mike Martz
2004	8	8	0	.500	319	392	2nd/NFC West Div.	1	1	NFC div. playoff game	Mike Martz

*Cleveland Rams.
†Los Angeles Rams.

FIRST-ROUND DRAFT PICKS

1937—Johnny Drake, B, Purdue
1938—Corbett Davis, B, Indiana*
1939—Parker Hall, B, Mississippi
1940—Ollie Cordill, B, Rice
1941—Rudy Mucha, C, Washington
1942—Jack Wilson, B, Baylor
1943—Mike Holovak, B, Boston College
1944—Tony Butkovich, B, Illinois
1945—Elroy Hirsch, B, Wisconsin
1946—Emil Sitko, B, Notre Dame
1947—Herman Wedemeyer, B, St. Mary's (Cal.)
1948—None
1949—Bobby Thomason, B, Virginia Military
1950—Ralph Pasquariello, B, Villanova
　　　Stan West, G, Oklahoma
1951—Bud McFadin, G, Texas
1952—Bill Wade, QB, Vanderbilt*
　　　Bob Carey, E, Michigan State
1953—Donn Moomaw, C, UCLA
　　　Ed Barker, E, Washington State
1954—Ed Beatty, C, Mississippi
1955—Larry Morris, C, Georgia Tech
1956—Joe Marconi, B, West Virginia
　　　Charlie Horton, B, Vanderbilt
1957—Jon Arnett, B, Southern California
　　　Del Shofner, B, Baylor
1958—Lou Michaels, T, Kentucky
　　　Jim Phillips, E, Auburn
1959—Dick Bass, B, Pacific
　　　Paul Dickson, G, Baylor
1960—Billy Cannon, RB, Louisiana State*
1961—Marlin McKeever, LB, Southern California
1962—Roman Gabriel, QB, North Carolina State
　　　Merlin Olsen, DT, Utah State
1963—Terry Baker, QB, Oregon State*
　　　Rufus Guthrie, G, Georgia Tech

1964—Bill Munson, QB, Utah State
1965—Clancy Williams, DB, Washington State
1966—Tom Mack, G, Michigan
1967—None
1968—None
1969—Larry Smith, RB, Florida
　　　Jim Seymour, E, Notre Dame
　　　Bob Klein, TE, Southern California
1970—Jack Reynolds, LB, Tennessee
1971—Isiah Robertson, LB, Southern
　　　Jack Youngblood, DE, Florida
1972—None
1973—None
1974—John Cappelletti, RB, Penn State
1975—Mike Fanning, DT, Notre Dame
　　　Dennis Harrah, G, Miami, Fla.
　　　Doug France, T, Ohio State
1976—Kevin McLain, LB, Colorado State
1977—Bob Brudzinski, LB, Ohio State
1978—Elvis Peacock, RB, Oklahoma
1979—George Andrews, LB, Nebraska
　　　Kent Hill, G, Georgia Tech
1980—Johnnie Johnson, DB, Texas
1981—Mel Owens, LB, Michigan
1982—Barry Redden, RB, Richmond
1983—Eric Dickerson, RB, Southern Methodist
1984—None
1985—Jerry Gray, DB, Texas
1986—Mike Schad, T, Queens College (Ont.)
1987—None
1988—Gaston Green, RB, UCLA
　　　Aaron Cox, WR, Arizona State
1989—Bill Hawkins, DE, Miami, Fla.
　　　Cleveland Gary, RB, Miami, Fla.
1990—Bern Brostek, C, Washington
1991—Todd Lyght, CB, Notre Dame

992—Sean Gilbert, DE, Pittsburgh
993—Jerome Bettis, RB, Notre Dame
994—Wayne Gandy, T, Auburn
995—Kevin Carter, DE, Florida
996—Lawrence Phillips, RB, Nebraska
     Eddie Kennison, WR, Louisiana State
997—Orlando Pace, T, Ohio State*
998—Grant Wistrom, DE, Nebraska
999—Torry Holt, WR, North Carolina State

2000—Trung Canidate, RB, Arizona
2001—Damione Lewis, DT, Miami, Fla.
     Adam Archuleta, DB, Arizona State
     Ryan Pickett, DT, Ohio State
2002—Robert Thomas, LB, UCLA
2003—Jimmy Kennedy, DT, Penn State
2004—Steven Jackson, RB, Oregon State
2005—Alex Barron, OT, Florida State
    *First player chosen in draft.

FRANCHISE RECORDS

Most rushing yards, career
,245—Eric Dickerson
Most rushing yards, season
2,105—Eric Dickerson, 1984
Most rushing yards, game
247—Willie Ellison vs. N.O., Dec. 5, 1971
Most rushing touchdowns, season
18—Eric Dickerson, 1983
    Marshall Faulk, 2000
Most passing attempts, season
554—Jim Everett, 1990
Most passing attempts, game
55—Mark Rypien vs. Buf., Dec. 10, 1995
Most passes completed, season
375—Kurt Warner, 2001
Most passes completed, game
36—Marc Bulger vs. S.D., Nov. 10, 2002
Most passing yards, career
23,758—Jim Everett

Most passing yards, season
4,830—Kurt Warner, 2001
Most passing yards, game
554—Norm Van Brocklin at N.Y. Yanks,
    Sept. 28, 1951
Most touchdown passes, season
41—Kurt Warner, 1999
Most pass receptions, career
777—Isaac Bruce
Most pass receptions, season
119—Isaac Bruce, 1995
Most pass receptions, game
18—Tom Fears vs. G.B., Dec. 3, 1950
Most receiving yards, career
11,753—Isaac Bruce
Most receiving yards, season
1,781—Isaac Bruce, 1995
Most receiving yards, game
336—Willie Anderson at N.O., Nov. 26,
    1989

Most receiving touchdowns, season
17—Elroy Hirsch, 1951
Most touchdowns, career
84—Marshall Faulk
Most field goals, season
39—Jeff Wilkins, 2003
Longest field goal
57 yards—Jeff Wilkins vs. Ari., Sept. 27,
    1998
Most interceptions, career
46—Ed Meador
Most interceptions, season
14—Night Train Lane, 1952
Most sacks, career
159.5—Deacon Jones
Most sacks, season
22—Deacon Jones, 1964
    Deacon Jones, 1968

SERIES RECORDS

St. Louis vs.: Arizona 26-22-2; Atlanta 46-24-2; Baltimore 2-1; Buffalo 4-5; Carolina 7-8; Chicago 34-47-3; Cincinnati 5-5; Cleveland 9-8; Dallas 9-9; Denver 5-5; Detroit 40-37-1; Green Bay 44-40-2; Indianapolis 17-21-2; Jacksonville 1-0; Kansas City 4-4; Miami 2-8; Minnesota 13-16-2; New England 5-4; New Orleans 36-29; N.Y. Giants 25-11; N.Y. Jets 9-2; Oakland 3-7; Philadelphia 17-15-1; Pittsburgh 15-5-2; San Diego 5-3; San Francisco 58-50-2; Seattle 9-4; Tampa Bay 9-6; Tennessee 5-3; Washington 6-19-1.
NOTE: Includes records as Cleveland Rams from 1937 through 1945 and Los Angeles Rams from 1946 through 1994.

COACHING RECORDS

George Allen, 47-17-4 (2-2); Hugo Bezdek, 1-13-0; Rich Brooks, 13-19-0; Dutch Clark, 16-26-2; Aldo Donelli, 4-6-0; Sid Gillman, 28-31-1 (0-1); Chuck Knox, 69-48-1 (3-5); Art Lewis, 4-4-0; Ray Malavasi, 40-33-0 (3-3); Mike Martz, 51-29-0 (3-4); Hamp Pool, 23-10-2 (0-1); Tommy Prothro, 14-12-2; John Robinson, 75-68-0 (4-6); Clark Shaughnessy, 14-7-3 (0-1); Bob Snyder, 6-6-0; Joe Stydahar, 17-8-0 (2-1); Harland Svare, 14-31-3; Dick Vermeil, 22-26-0 (3-0); Adam Walsh, 15-5-1 (1-0); Bob Waterfield, 9-24-1.
NOTE: Playoff games in parentheses.

RETIRED UNIFORM NUMBERS

No.	Player
7	Bob Waterfield
29	Eric Dickerson
74	Merlin Olsen
78	Jackie Slater
85	Jack Youngblood

SAN DIEGO CHARGERS
YEAR-BY-YEAR RECORDS

		REGULAR SEASON							PLAYOFFS		
Year	W	L	T	Pct.	PF	PA	Finish	W	L	Highest round	Coach
1960*†	10	4	0	.714	373	336	1st/Western Div.	0	1	AFL championship game	Sid Gillman
1961*	12	2	0	.857	396	219	1st/Western Div.	0	1	AFL championship game	Sid Gillman
1962*	4	10	0	.286	314	392	3rd/Western Div.	—	—		Sid Gillman
1963*	11	3	0	.786	399	256	1st/Western Div.	1	0	AFL champ	Sid Gillman
1964*	8	5	1	.615	341	300	1st/Western Div.	0	1	AFL championship game	Sid Gillman
1965*	9	2	3	.818	340	227	1st/Western Div.	0	1	AFL championship game	Sid Gillman
1966*	7	6	1	.538	335	284	3rd/Western Div.	—	—		Sid Gillman
1967*	8	5	1	.615	360	352	3rd/Western Div.	—	—		Sid Gillman
1968*	9	5	0	.643	382	310	3rd/Western Div.	—	—		Sid Gillman
1969*	8	6	0	.571	288	276	3rd/Western Div.	—	—		S. Gillman, C. Waller
1970	5	6	3	.455	282	278	3rd/AFC Western Div.	—	—		Charlie Waller
1971	6	8	0	.429	311	341	3rd/AFC Western Div.	—	—		S. Gillman, H. Svare
1972	4	9	1	.308	264	344	4th/AFC Western Div.	—	—		Harland Svare
1973	2	11	1	.179	188	386	4th/AFC Western Div.	—	—		H. Svare, Ron Waller
1974	5	9	0	.357	212	285	4th/AFC Western Div.	—	—		Tommy Prothro

	REGULAR SEASON							PLAYOFFS			
Year	W	L	T	Pct.	PF	PA	Finish	W	L	Highest round	Coach
1975	2	12	0	.143	189	345	4th/AFC Western Div.	—	—		Tommy Prothro
1976	6	8	0	.429	248	285	3rd/AFC Western Div.	—	—		Tommy Prothro
1977	7	7	0	.500	222	205	3rd/AFC Western Div.	—	—		Tommy Prothro
1978	9	7	0	.563	355	309	4th/AFC Western Div.	—	—		T. Prothro, Don Coryell
1979	12	4	0	.750	411	246	1st/AFC Western Div.	0	1	AFC div. playoff game	Don Coryell
1980	11	5	0	.688	418	327	1st/AFC Western Div.	1	1	AFC championship game	Don Coryell
1981	10	6	0	.625	478	390	1st/AFC Western Div.	1	1	AFC championship game	Don Coryell
1982	6	3	0	.667	288	221	5th/AFC	1	1	AFC second-round pl. game	Don Coryell
1983	6	10	0	.375	358	462	4th/AFC Western Div.	—	—		Don Coryell
1984	7	9	0	.438	394	413	5th/AFC Western Div.	—	—		Don Coryell
1985	8	8	0	.500	467	435	4th/AFC Western Div.	—	—		Don Coryell
1986	4	12	0	.250	335	396	5th/AFC Western Div.	—	—		D. Coryell, Al Saunders
1987	8	7	0	.533	253	317	3rd/AFC Western Div.	—	—		Al Saunders
1988	6	10	0	.375	231	332	4th/AFC Western Div.	—	—		Al Saunders
1989	6	10	0	.375	266	290	5th/AFC Western Div.	—	—		Dan Henning
1990	6	10	0	.375	315	281	4th/AFC Western Div.	—	—		Dan Henning
1991	4	12	0	.250	274	342	5th/AFC Western Div.	—	—		Dan Henning
1992	11	5	0	.688	335	241	1st/AFC Western Div.	1	1	AFC div. playoff game	Bobby Ross
1993	8	8	0	.500	322	290	4th/AFC Western Div.	—	—		Bobby Ross
1994	11	5	0	.688	381	306	1st/AFC Western Div.	2	1	Super Bowl	Bobby Ross
1995	9	7	0	.563	321	323	2nd/AFC Western Div.	0	1	AFC wild-card game	Bobby Ross
1996	8	8	0	.500	310	376	3rd/AFC Western Div.	—	—		Bobby Ross
1997	4	12	0	.250	266	425	5th/AFC Western Div.	—	—		Kevin Gilbride
1998	5	11	0	.313	241	342	5th/AFC Western Div.	—	—		K. Gilbride, June Jones
1999	8	8	0	.500	269	316	3rd/AFC Western Div.	—	—		Mike Riley
2000	1	15	0	.063	269	440	5th/AFC Western Div.	—	—		Mike Riley
2001	5	11	0	.313	332	321	5th/AFC Western Div.	—	—		Mike Riley
2002	8	8	0	.500	333	367	3rd/AFC West Div.	—	—		Marty Schottenheimer
2003	4	12	0	.250	313	441	4th/AFC West Div.	—	—		Marty Schottenheimer
2004	12	4	0	.750	446	313	1st/AFC West Div	0	1	AFC wild-card game	Marty Schottenheimer

*American Football League.
†Los Angeles Chargers.

FIRST-ROUND DRAFT PICKS

1960—Monty Stickles, E, Notre Dame
1961—Earl Faison, E, Indiana
1962—Bob Ferguson, RB, Ohio State
1963—Walt Sweeney, E, Syracuse
1964—Ted Davis, E, Georgia Tech
1965—Steve DeLong, DE, Tennessee
1966—Don Davis, T, Los Angeles State
1967—Ron Billingsley, DT, Wyoming
1968—Russ Washington, T, Missouri
    Jim Hill, DB, Texas A&I
1969—Marty Domres, QB, Columbia
    Bob Babich, LB, Miami of Ohio
1970—Walker Gillette, WR, Richmond
1971—Leon Burns, RB, Long Beach State
1972—None
1973—Johnny Rodgers, WR, Nebraska
1974—Bo Matthews, RB, Colorado
    Don Goode, LB, Kansas
1975—Gary Johnson, DT, Grambling State
    Mike Williams, DB, Louisiana State
1976—Joe Washington, RB, Oklahoma
1977—Bob Rush, C, Memphis State
1978—John Jefferson, WR, Arizona State
1979—Kellen Winslow, TE, Missouri
1980—None
1981—James Brooks, RB, Auburn
1982—None
1983—Billy Ray Smith, LB, Arkansas

    Gary Anderson, WR, Arkansas
    Gill Byrd, DB, San Jose State
1984—Mossy Cade, DB, Texas
1985—Jim Lachey, G, Ohio State
1986—Leslie O'Neal, DE, Oklahoma State
    Jim FitzPatrick, T, Southern California
1987—Rod Bernstine, TE, Texas A&M
1988—Anthony Miller, WR, Tennessee
1989—Burt Grossman, DE, Pittsburgh
1990—Junior Seau, LB, Southern California
1991—Stanley Richard, CB, Texas
1992—Chris Mims, DT, Tennessee
1993—Darrien Gordon, DB, Stanford
1994—None
1995—None
1996—None
1997—None
1998—Ryan Leaf, QB, Washington State
1999—None
2000—None
2001—LaDainian Tomlinson, RB, Texas Christian
2002—Quentin Jammer, DB, Texas
2003—Sammy Davis, DB, Texas A&M
2004—Eli Manning, QB, Mississippi*
2005—Shawne Merriman, OLB, Maryland
    Luis Castillo, DT, Northwestern
    *First player chosen in draft.

FRANCHISE RECORDS

Most rushing yards, career
5,899—LaDainian Tomlinson
Most rushing yards, season
1,683—LaDainian Tomlinson, 2002
Most rushing yards, game
243—LaDainian Tomlinson vs. Oak., Dec. 28, 2003

Most rushing touchdowns, season
19—Chuck Muncie, 1981
Most passing attempts, season
609—Dan Fouts, 1981
Most passing attempts, game
58—Mark Herrmann at K.C., Dec. 22, 1985

Most passes completed, season
360—Dan Fouts, 1981
Most passes completed, game
37—Dan Fouts vs. Mia., Nov. 18, 1984
    (OT)
    Mark Herrmann at K.C., Dec. 22, 1985

Most passing yards, career
43,040—Dan Fouts
Most passing yards, season
4,802—Dan Fouts, 1981
Most passing yards, game
444—Dan Fouts vs. NYG, Oct. 19, 1980
Dan Fouts at S.F., Dec. 11, 1982
Most touchdown passes, season
33—Dan Fouts, 1981
Most pass receptions, career
586—Charlie Joiner
Most pass receptions, season
100—LaDainian Tomlinson, 2003
Most pass receptions, game
15—Kellen Winslow at G.B., Oct. 7, 1984

Most receiving yards, career
9,584—Lance Alworth
Most receiving yards, season
1,602—Lance Alworth, 1965
Most receiving yards, game
260—Wes Chandler vs. Cin., Dec. 20, 1982
Most receiving touchdowns, season
14—Lance Alworth, 1965
Tony Martin, 1996
Most touchdowns, career
83—Lance Alworth
Most field goals, season
34—John Carney, 1994

Longest field goal
54 yards—John Carney vs. Sea., Nov. 10, 1991
John Carney vs. Buf., Sept. 6, 1998
John Carney at K.C., Sept. 17, 2000
Most interceptions, career
42—Gill Byrd
Most interceptions, season
9—Charlie McNeil, 1961
Most sacks, career
105.5—Leslie O'Neal
Most sacks, season
17.5—Gary Johnson, 1980

SERIES RECORDS

San Diego vs.: Arizona 7-3; Atlanta 1-6; Baltimore 2-2; Buffalo 18-9-2; Carolina 1-2; Chicago 4-5; Cincinnati 17-10; Cleveland 12-7-1; Dallas 2-5; Denver 39-50-1; Detroit 5-3; Green Bay 1-7; Houston 2-0; Indianapolis 12-8; Jacksonville 1-1; Kansas City 41-47-1; Miami 10-10; Minnesota 5-4; New England 12-17-2; New Orleans 7-2; N.Y. Giants 3-5; N.Y. Jets 17-11-1; Oakland 34-54-2; Philadelphia 5-3; Pittsburgh 5-18; St. Louis 3-5; San Francisco 4-6; Seattle 22-25; Tampa Bay 7-1; Tennessee 20-13-1; Washington 1-6.
NOTE: Includes records as Los Angeles Chargers in 1960.

COACHING RECORDS

Don Coryell, 69-56-0 (3-4); Kevin Gilbride, 6-16-0; Sid Gillman, 86-53-6 (1-4); Dan Henning, 16-32-0; June Jones, 3-7-0; Tommy Prothro, 21-39-0; Mike Riley, 14-34-0; Bobby Ross, 47-33-0 (3-3); Al Saunders, 17-22-0; Marty Schottenheimer, 24-24-0 (0-1); Harland Svare, 7-17-2; Charlie Waller, 9-7-3; Ron Waller, 1-5-0.
NOTE: Playoff games in parentheses.

RETIRED UNIFORM NUMBERS

No.	Player
14	Dan Fouts

SAN FRANCISCO 49ERS
YEAR-BY-YEAR RECORDS

		REGULAR SEASON						PLAYOFFS			
Year	W	L	T	Pct.	PF	PA	Finish	W	L	Highest round	Coach
1946*	9	5	0	.643	307	189	2nd/Western Div.	—	—		Buck Shaw
1947*	8	4	2	.667	327	264	2nd/Western Div.	—	—		Buck Shaw
1948*	12	2	0	.857	495	248	2nd/Western Div.	—	—		Buck Shaw
1949*	9	3	0	.750	416	227	2nd	—	—		Buck Shaw
1950	3	9	0	.250	213	300	T5th/National Conf.	—	—		Buck Shaw
1951	7	4	1	.636	255	205	T2nd/National Conf.	—	—		Buck Shaw
1952	7	5	0	.583	285	221	3rd/National Conf.	—	—		Buck Shaw
1953	9	3	0	.750	372	237	2nd/Western Conf.	—	—		Buck Shaw
1954	7	4	1	.636	313	251	3rd/Western Conf.	—	—		Buck Shaw
1955	4	8	0	.333	216	298	4th/Western Conf.	—	—		Red Strader
1956	5	6	1	.455	233	284	3rd/Western Conf.	—	—		Frankie Albert
1957	8	4	0	.667	260	264	2nd/Western Conf.	0	1	W. Conf. champ. game	Frankie Albert
1958	6	6	0	.500	257	324	4th/Western Conf.	—	—		Frankie Albert
1959	7	5	0	.583	255	237	T3rd/Western Conf.	—	—		Red Hickey
1960	7	5	0	.583	208	205	T2nd/Western Conf.	—	—		Red Hickey
1961	7	6	1	.538	346	272	5th/Western Conf.	—	—		Red Hickey
1962	6	8	0	.429	282	331	5th/Western Conf.	—	—		Red Hickey
1963	2	12	0	.143	198	391	7th/Western Conf.	—	—		R. Hickey, J. Christiansen
1964	4	10	0	.286	236	330	7th/Western Conf.	—	—		Jack Christiansen
1965	7	6	1	.538	421	402	4th/Western Conf.	—	—		Jack Christiansen
1966	6	6	2	.500	320	325	4th/Western Conf.	—	—		Jack Christiansen
1967	7	7	0	.500	273	337	3rd/Coastal Div.	—	—		Jack Christiansen
1968	7	6	1	.538	303	310	3rd/Coastal Div.	—	—		Dick Nolan
1969	4	8	2	.333	277	319	4th/Coastal Div.	—	—		Dick Nolan
1970	10	3	1	.769	352	267	1st/NFC Western Div.	1	1	NFC championship game	Dick Nolan
1971	9	5	0	.643	300	216	1st/NFC Western Div.	1	1	NFC championship game	Dick Nolan
1972	8	5	1	.607	353	249	1st/NFC Western Div.	0	1	NFC div. playoff game	Dick Nolan
1973	5	9	0	.357	262	319	4th/NFC Western Div.	—	—		Dick Nolan
1974	6	8	0	.429	226	236	2nd/NFC Western Div.	—	—		Dick Nolan
1975	5	9	0	.357	255	286	2nd/NFC Western Div.	—	—		Dick Nolan
1976	8	6	0	.571	270	190	2nd/NFC Western Div.	—	—		Monte Clark
1977	5	9	0	.357	220	260	3rd/NFC Western Div.	—	—		Ken Meyer
1978	2	14	0	.125	219	350	4th/NFC Western Div.	—	—		P. McCulley, F. O'Connor
1979	2	14	0	.125	308	416	4th/NFC Western Div.	—	—		Bill Walsh

	REGULAR SEASON							PLAYOFFS			
Year	W	L	T	Pct.	PF	PA	Finish	W	L	Highest round	Coach
1980	6	10	0	.375	320	415	3rd/NFC Western Div.	—	—		Bill Walsh
1981	13	3	0	.813	357	250	1st/NFC Western Div.	3	0	Super Bowl champ	Bill Walsh
1982	3	6	0	.333	209	206	11th/NFC	—	—		Bill Walsh
1983	10	6	0	.625	432	293	1st/NFC Western Div.	1	1	NFC championship game	Bill Walsh
1984	15	1	0	.938	475	227	1st/NFC Western Div.	3	0	Super Bowl champ	Bill Walsh
1985	10	6	0	.625	411	263	2nd/NFC Western Div.	0	1	NFC wild-card game	Bill Walsh
1986	10	5	1	.656	374	247	1st/NFC Western Div.	0	1	NFC div. playoff game	Bill Walsh
1987	13	2	0	.867	459	253	1st/NFC Western Div.	0	1	NFC div. playoff game	Bill Walsh
1988	10	6	0	.625	369	294	1st/NFC Western Div.	3	0	Super Bowl champ	Bill Walsh
1989	14	2	0	.875	442	253	1st/NFC Western Div.	3	0	Super Bowl champ	George Seifert
1990	14	2	0	.875	353	239	1st/NFC Western Div.	1	1	NFC championship game	George Seifert
1991	10	6	0	.625	393	239	3rd/NFC Western Div.	—	—		George Seifert
1992	14	2	0	.875	431	236	1st/NFC Western Div.	1	1	NFC championship game	George Seifert
1993	10	6	0	.625	473	295	1st/NFC Western Div.	1	1	NFC championship game	George Seifert
1994	13	3	0	.813	505	296	1st/NFC Western Div.	3	0	Super Bowl champ	George Seifert
1995	11	5	0	.688	457	258	1st/NFC Western Div.	0	1	NFC div. playoff game	George Seifert
1996	12	4	0	.750	398	257	2nd/NFC Western Div.	1	1	NFC div. playoff game	George Seifert
1997	13	3	0	.813	375	265	1st/NFC Western Div.	1	1	NFC championship game	Steve Mariucci
1998	12	4	0	.750	479	328	2nd/NFC Western Div.	1	1	NFC div. playoff game	Steve Mariucci
1999	4	12	0	.250	295	453	4th/NFC Western Div.	—	—		Steve Mariucci
2000	6	10	0	.375	388	422	4th/NFC Western Div.	—	—		Steve Mariucci
2001	12	4	0	.750	409	282	2nd/NFC Western Div.	0	1	NFC wild-card game	Steve Mariucci
2002	10	6	0	.625	367	351	1st/NFC West Div.	1	1	NFC div. playoff game	Steve Mariucci
2003	7	9	0	.438	384	337	3rd/NFC West Div.	—	—		Dennis Erickson
2004	2	14	0	.125	259	452	4th/NFC West Div.	—	—		Dennis Erickson

*All-America Football Conference.

FIRST-ROUND DRAFT PICKS

1950—Leo Nomellini, T, Minnesota
1951—Y.A. Tittle, QB, Louisiana State
1952—Hugh McElhenny, RB, Washington
1953—Harry Babcock, E, Georgia*
    Tom Stolhandske, E, Texas
1954—Bernie Faloney, QB, Maryland
1955—Dick Moegel, HB, Rice
1956—Earl Morrall QB, Michigan State
1957—John Brodie, QB, Stanford
1958—Jim Pace, RB, Michigan
    Charles Krueger, T, Texas A&M
1959—Dave Baker, RB, Oklahoma
    Dan James, C, Ohio State
1960—Monty Stickles, E, Notre Dame
1961—Jim Johnson, RB, UCLA
    Bernie Casey, RB, Bowling Green State
    Billy Kilmer, QB, UCLA
1962—Lance Alworth, RB, Arkansas
1963—Kermit Alexander, RB, UCLA
1964—Dave Parks, E, Texas Tech*
1965—Ken Willard, RB, North Carolina
    George Donnelly, DB, Illinois
1966—Stan Hindman, DE, Mississippi
1967—Steve Spurrier, QB, Florida
    Cas Banaszek, LB, Northwestern
1968—Forrest Blue, C, Auburn
1969—Ted Kwalick, TE, Penn State
    Gene Washington, WR, Stanford
1970—Cedrick Hardman, DE, North Texas State
    Bruce Taylor, DB, Boston University
1971—Tim Anderson, DB, Ohio State
1972—Terry Beasley, WR, Auburn
1973—Mike Holmes, DB, Tex. Southern
1974—Wilbur Jackson, RB, Alabama
    Bill Sandifer, DT, UCLA
1975—Jimmy Webb, DT, Mississippi State
1976—None

1977—None
1978—Ken McAfee, TE, Notre Dame
    Dan Bunz, LB, Long Beach State
1979—None
1980—Earl Cooper, RB, Rice
    Jim Stuckey, DT, Clemson
1981—Ronnie Lott, DB, Southern California
1982—None
1983—None
1984—Todd Shell, LB, Brigham Young
1985—Jerry Rice, WR, Misssssippi Valley State
1986—None
1987—Harris Barton, T, North Carolina
    Terrence Flager, RB, Clemson
1988—None
1989—Keith DeLong, LB, Tennessee
1990—Dexter Carter, RB, Florida State
1991—Ted Washington, DL, Louisville
1992—Dana Hall, DB, Washington
1993—Dana Stubblefield, DT, Kansas
    Todd Kelly, DE, Tennessee
1994—Bryant Young, DT, Notre Dame
    William Floyd, RB, Florida State
1995—J.J. Stokes, WR, UCLA
1996—None
1997—Jim Druckenmiller, QB, Virginia Tech
1998—R.W. McQuarters, DB, Oklahoma State
1999—Reggie McGrew, DT, Florida
2000—Julian Peterson, LB, Michigan State
    Ahmed Plummer, DB, Ohio State
2001—Andre Carter, DE, California
2002—Mike Rumph, CB, Miami, Fla.
2003—Kwame Harris, T, Stanford
2004—Rashaun Woods, WR, Oklahoma State
2005—Alex Smith, QB, Utah*
*First player chosen in draft.

FRANCHISE RECORDS

Most rushing yards, career
7,344—Joe Perry

Most rushing yards, season
1,570—Garrison Hearst, 1998

Most rushing yards, game
201—Charlie Garner at Dal., Sept. 24, 2000

ost rushing touchdowns, season
)—Joe Perry, 1953
   J.D. Smith, 1959
   Billy Kilmer, 1961
   Ricky Watters, 1993
   Derek Loville, 1995

ost passing attempts, season
78—Steve DeBerg, 1979

ost passing attempts, game
)—Joe Montana at Was., Nov. 17, 1986

ost passes completed, season
55—Jeff Garcia, 2000

ost passes completed, game
7—Joe Montana at Atl., Nov. 6, 1985

ost passing yards, career
5,124—Joe Montana

ost passing yards, season
,278—Jeff Garcia, 2000

Most passing yards, game
476—Joe Montana at Atl., Oct. 14, 1990

Most touchdown passes, season
36—Steve Young, 1998

Most pass receptions, career
1,281—Jerry Rice

Most pass receptions, season
122—Jerry Rice, 1995

Most pass receptions, game
20—Terrell Owens vs. Chi., Dec. 17, 2000

Most receiving yards, career
19,247—Jerry Rice

Most receiving yards, season
1,848—Jerry Rice, 1995

Most receiving yards, game
289—Jerry Rice vs. Min., Dec. 18, 1995

Most receiving touchdowns, season
22—Jerry Rice, 1987

Most touchdowns, career
187—Jerry Rice

Most field goals, season
30—Jeff Wilkins, 1996

Longest field goal
56 yards—Mike Cofer at Atl., Oct. 14, 1990

Most interceptions, career
51—Ronnie Lott

Most interceptions, season
10—Dave Baker, 1960
   Ronnie Lott, 1986

Most sacks, career
112.5—Cedrick Hardman

Most sacks, season
18—Cedrick Hardman, 1971

SERIES RECORDS

an Francisco vs.: Arizona 17-10; Atlanta 44-26-1; Baltimore 1-1; Buffalo 4-5; Carolina 7-8; Chicago 27-27-1; Cincinnati 7-3; Cleveland -10; Dallas 14-8-1; Denver 4-6; Detroit 31-26-1; Green Bay 25-27-1; Indianapolis 18-22; Jacksonville 0-1; Kansas City 6-3; Miami 4-, Minnesota 17-18-1; New England 7-3; New Orleans 45-20-2; N.Y. Giants 13-11; N.Y. Jets 8-2; Oakland 4-6; Philadelphia 16-7-1; ittsburgh 10-8; St. Louis 50-58-2; San Diego 6-4; Seattle 6-6; Tampa Bay 13-3; Tennessee 7-3; Washington 13-8-1.
OTE: Includes records only from 1950 to present.

COACHING RECORDS

rankie Albert, 19-16-1 (0-1); Jack Christiansen, 26-38-3; Monte Clark, 8- -0; Dennis Erickson, 9-23-0; Red Hickey, 27-27-1; Steve Mariucci, 57- 9-0 (3-4); Pete McCulley, 1-8-0; Ken Meyer, 5-9-0; Dick Nolan, 54-53-5 2-3); Fred O'Connor, 1-6-0; George Seifert, 98-30-0 (10-5); Buck Shaw, 3-25-2; Red Strader, 4-8-0; Bill Walsh, 92-59-1 (10-4).
OTE: Playoff games in parentheses.

RETIRED UNIFORM NUMBERS

No.	Player	No.	Player
12	John Brodie	42	Ronnie Lott
16	Joe Montana	70	Charlie Krueger
34	Joe Perry	73	Leo Nomellini
37	Jimmy Johnson	79	Bob St. Clair
39	Hugh McElhenny	87	Dwight Clark

SEATTLE SEAHAWKS
YEAR-BY-YEAR RECORDS

	REGULAR SEASON							PLAYOFFS			
ear	W	L	T	Pct.	PF	PA	Finish	W	L	Highest round	Coach
976	2	12	0	.143	229	429	5th/NFC Western Div.	—	—		Jack Patera
977	5	9	0	.357	282	373	4th/AFC Western Div.	—	—		Jack Patera
978	9	7	0	.563	345	358	3rd/AFC Western Div.	—	—		Jack Patera
979	9	7	0	.563	378	372	3rd/AFC Western Div.	—	—		Jack Patera
980	4	12	0	.250	291	408	5th/AFC Western Div.	—	—		Jack Patera
981	6	10	0	.375	322	388	5th/AFC Western Div.	—	—		Jack Patera
982	4	5	0	.444	127	147	10th/AFC	—	—		J. Patera, Mike McCormack
983	9	7	0	.562	403	397	2nd/AFC Western Div.	2	1	AFC championship game	Chuck Knox
984	12	4	0	.750	418	282	2nd/AFC Western Div.	1	1	AFC div. playoff game	Chuck Knox
985	8	8	0	.500	349	303	3rd/AFC Western Div.	—	—		Chuck Knox
986	10	6	0	.625	366	293	3rd/AFC Western Div.	—	—		Chuck Knox
987	9	6	0	.600	371	314	2nd/AFC Western Div.	0	1	AFC wild-card game	Chuck Knox
988	9	7	0	.563	339	329	1st/AFC Western Div.	0	1	AFC div. playoff game	Chuck Knox
989	7	9	0	.438	241	327	4th/AFC Western Div.	—	—		Chuck Knox
990	9	7	0	.563	306	286	3rd/AFC Western Div.	—	—		Chuck Knox
991	7	9	0	.438	276	261	4th/AFC Western Div.	—	—		Chuck Knox
992	2	14	0	.125	140	312	5th/AFC Western Div.	—	—		Tom Flores
993	6	10	0	.375	280	314	5th/AFC Western Div.	—	—		Tom Flores
994	6	10	0	.375	287	323	5th/AFC Western Div.	—	—		Tom Flores
995	8	8	0	.500	363	366	3rd/AFC Western Div.	—	—		Dennis Erickson
996	7	9	0	.438	317	376	5th/AFC Western Div.	—	—		Dennis Erickson
997	8	8	0	.500	365	362	3rd/AFC Western Div.	—	—		Dennis Erickson
998	8	8	0	.500	372	310	3rd/AFC Western Div.	—	—		Dennis Erickson
999	9	7	0	.563	338	298	1st/AFC Western Div.	0	1	AFC wild-card game	Mike Holmgren
2000	6	10	0	.375	320	405	4th/AFC Western Div.	—	—		Mike Holmgren
2001	9	7	0	.563	301	324	2nd/AFC Western Div.	—	—		Mike Holmgren
2002	7	9	0	.438	355	369	3rd/NFC West Div.	—	—		Mike Holmgren
2003	10	6	0	.625	404	327	2nd/NFC West Div.	0	1	NFC wild-card game	Mike Holmgren
2004	9	7	0	.562	371	373	1st/NFC West Div.	0	1	NFC wild-card game	Mike Holmgren

FIRST-ROUND DRAFT PICKS

1976—Steve Niehaus, DT, Notre Dame
1977—Steve August, G, Tulsa
1978—Keith Simpson, DB, Memphis State
1979—Manu Tuiasosopo, DT, UCLA
1980—Jacob Green, DE, Texas A&M
1981—Kenny Easley, DB, UCLA
1982—Jeff Bryant, DE, Clemson
1983—Curt Warner, RB, Penn State
1984—Terry Taylor, DB, Southern Illinois
1985—None
1986—John L. Williams, RB, Florida
1987—Tony Woods, LB, Pittsburgh
1988—None
1989—Andy Heck, T, Notre Dame
1990—Cortez Kennedy, DT, Miami, Fla.
1991—Dan McGwire, QB, San Diego State
1992—Ray Roberts, T, Virginia

1993—Rick Mirer, QB, Notre Dame
1994—Sam Adams, DE, Texas A&M
1995—Joey Galloway, WR, Ohio State
1996—Pete Kendall, T, Boston College
1997—Shawn Springs, CB, Ohio State
        Walter Jones, T, Florida State
1998—Anthony Simmons, LB, Clemson
1999—Lamar King, DE, Saginaw Valley State
2000—Shaun Alexander, RB, Alabama
        Chris McIntosh, T, Wisconsin
2001—Koren Robinson, WR, North Carolina State
        Steve Hutchinson, G, Michigan
2002—Jerramy Stevens, TE, Washington
2003—Marcus Trufant, DB, Washington State
2004—Marcus Tubbs, DT, Texas
2005—Chris Spencer, C, Mississippi

FRANCHISE RECORDS

Most rushing yards, career
6,706—Chris Warren
Most rushing yards, season
1,696—Shaun Alexander, 2004
Most rushing yards, game
266—Shaun Alexander vs. Oak., Nov. 11, 2001
Most rushing touchdowns, season
16—Shaun Alexander, 2002
        Shaun Alexander, 2004
Most passing attempts, season
532—Dave Krieg, 1985
Most passing attempts, game
55—Matt Hasselbeck at S.F., Dec. 1, 2002
Most passes completed, season
313—Warren Moon, 1997
        Matt Hasselbeck, 2003
Most passes completed, game
36—Matt Hasselbeck at S.D., Dec. 29, 2002 (OT)
33—Dave Krieg vs. Atl., Oct. 13, 1985

Most passing yards, career
26,132—Dave Krieg
Most passing yards, season
3,841—Matt Hasselbeck, 2003
Most passing yards, game
449—Matt Hasselbeck at S.D., Dec. 29, 2002 (OT)
427—Matt Hasselbeck at S.F., Dec. 1, 2002
Most touchdown passes, season
32—Dave Krieg, 1984
Most pass receptions, career
819—Steve Largent
Most pass receptions, season
87—Darrell Jackson, 2004
Most pass receptions, game
15—Steve Largent vs. Det., Oct. 18, 1987
Most receiving yards, career
13,089—Steve Largent
Most receiving yards, season
1,287—Steve Largent, 1985

Most receiving yards, game
261—Steve Largent vs. Det., Oct. 18, 198
Most receiving touchdowns, season
13—Daryl Turner, 1985
Most touchdowns, career
101—Steve Largent
Most field goals, season
34—Todd Peterson, 1999
Longest field goal
58 yards—Josh Brown at G.B., Oct. 5, 2003
Most interceptions, career
50—Dave Brown
Most interceptions, season
10—John Harris, 1981
        Kenny Easley, 1984
Most sacks, career
116—Jacob Green
Most sacks, season
16.5—Michael Sinclair, 1998

SERIES RECORDS

Seattle vs.: Arizona 5-7; Atlanta 7-2; Baltimore 0-2; Buffalo 6-4; Carolina 1-1; Chicago 6-2; Cincinnati 8-8; Cleveland 11-4; Dallas 3-6; Denver 17-33; Detroit 5-4; Green Bay 4-5; Indianapolis 3-5; Jacksonville 3-1; Kansas City 18-30; Miami 3-6; Minnesota 6-3; New England 7-7; New Orleans 5-4; N.Y. Giants 3-7; N.Y. Jets 8-8; Oakland 22-27; Philadelphia 3-5; Pittsburgh 8-6; St. Louis 4-9; San Diego 25-22; San Francisco 6-6; Tampa Bay 5-1; Tennessee 8-4; Washington 4-8.

COACHING RECORDS

Dennis Erickson, 31-33-0; Tom Flores, 14-34-0; Mike Holmgren, 50-46-0 (0-3); Chuck Knox, 80-63-0 (3-4); Mike McCormack, 4-3-0; Jack Patera, 35-59-0.
NOTE: Playoff games in parentheses.

RETIRED UNIFORM NUMBERS

No.	Player
12	Fans/the twelfth man
80	Steve Largent

TAMPA BAY BUCCANEERS
YEAR-BY-YEAR RECORDS

		REGULAR SEASON						PLAYOFFS		
Year	W	L	T	Pct.	PF	PA	Finish	W	L	Highest round	Coach
1976	0	14	0	.000	125	412	5th/AFC Western Div.	—	—		John McKay
1977	2	12	0	.143	103	223	5th/NFC Central Div.	—	—		John McKay
1978	5	11	0	.313	241	259	5th/NFC Central Div.	—	—		John McKay
1979	10	6	0	.625	273	237	1st/NFC Central Div.	1	1	NFC championship game	John McKay
1980	5	10	1	.344	271	341	4th/NFC Central Div.	—	—		John McKay
1981	9	7	0	.563	315	268	1st/NFC Central Div.	0	1	NFC div. playoff game	John McKay
1982	5	4	0	.556	158	178	7th/NFC	0	1	NFC first-round pl. game	John McKay
1983	2	14	0	.125	241	380	5th/NFC Central Div.	—	—		John McKay

REGULAR SEASON | PLAYOFFS

Year	W	L	T	Pct.	PF	PA	Finish	W	L	Highest round	Coach
1984	6	10	0	.375	335	380	3rd/NFC Central Div.	—	—		John McKay
1985	2	14	0	.125	294	448	5th/NFC Central Div.	—	—		Leeman Bennett
1986	2	14	0	.125	239	473	5th/NFC Central Div.	—	—		Leeman Bennett
1987	4	11	0	.267	286	360	4th/NFC Central Div.	—	—		Ray Perkins
1988	5	11	0	.313	261	350	3rd/NFC Central Div.	—	—		Ray Perkins
1989	5	11	0	.313	320	419	5th/NFC Central Div.	—	—		Ray Perkins
1990	6	10	0	.375	264	367	2nd/NFC Central Div.	—	—		R. Perkins, R. Williamson
1991	3	13	0	.188	199	365	5th/NFC Central Div.	—	—		Richard Williamson
1992	5	11	0	.313	267	365	3rd/NFC Central Div.	—	—		Sam Wyche
1993	5	11	0	.313	237	376	5th/NFC Central Div.	—	—		Sam Wyche
1994	6	10	0	.375	251	351	5th/NFC Central Div.	—	—		Sam Wyche
1995	7	9	0	.438	238	335	5th/NFC Central Div.	—	—		Sam Wyche
1996	6	10	0	.375	221	293	4th/NFC Central Div.	—	—		Tony Dungy
1997	10	6	0	.625	299	263	2nd/NFC Central Div.	1	1	NFC div. playoff game	Tony Dungy
1998	8	8	0	.500	314	295	3rd/NFC Central Div.	—	—		Tony Dungy
1999	11	5	0	.688	270	235	* 1st/NFC Central Div.	1	1	NFC championship game	Tony Dungy
2000	10	6	0	.625	388	269	2nd/NFC Central Div.	0	1	NFC wild-card game	Tony Dungy
2001	9	7	0	.563	324	280	3rd/NFC Central Div.	0	1	NFC wild-card game	Tony Dungy
2002	12	4	0	.750	346	196	1st/NFC South Div.	3	0	Super Bowl champ	Jon Gruden
2003	7	9	0	.438	301	264	3rd/NFC South Div.	—	—		Jon Gruden
2004	5	11	0	.312	301	304	4th/NFC South Div.	—	—		Jon Gruden

FIRST-ROUND DRAFT PICKS

1976—Lee Roy Selmon, DE, Oklahoma*
1977—Ricky Bell, RB, Southern California*
1978—Doug Williams, QB, Grambling State
1979—None
1980—Ray Snell, G, Wisconsin
1981—Hugh Green, LB, Pittsburgh
1982—Sean Farrell, G, Penn State
1983—None
1984—None
1985—Ron Holmes, DE, Washington
1986—Bo Jackson, RB, Auburn*
    Rod Jones, DB, Southern Methodist
1987—Vinny Testaverde, QB, Miami, Fla.*
1988—Paul Gruber, T, Wisconsin
1989—Broderick Thomas, LB, Nebraska
1990—Keith McCants, LB, Alabama
1991—Charles McRae, T, Tennessee
1992—None

1993—Eric Curry, DE, Alabama
1994—Trent Dilfer, QB, Fresno State
1995—Warren Sapp, DT, Miami, Fla.
    Derrick Brooks, LB, Florida State
1996—Regan Upshaw, DE, California
    Marcus Jones, DT, North Carolina
1997—Warrick Dunn, RB, Florida State
    Reidel Anthony, WR, Florida
1998—None
1999—Anthony McFarland, DT, Louisiana State
2000—None
2001—Kenyatta Walker, T, Florida
2002—None
2003—None
2004—Michael Clayton, WR, LSU
2005—Carnell "Cadillac" Williams, RB, Auburn
    *First player chosen in draft.

FRANCHISE RECORDS

Most rushing yards, career
5,957—James Wilder

Most rushing yards, season
1,544—James Wilder, 1984

Most rushing yards, game
219—James Wilder at Min., Nov. 6, 1983

Most rushing touchdowns, season
13—James Wilder, 1984

Most passing attempts, season
570—Brad Johnson, 2003

Most passing attempts, game
51—Brad Johnson vs. Car., Sept. 14, 2003

Most passes completed, season
354—Brad Johnson, 2003

Most passes completed, game
40—Brad Johnson vs. Chi., Nov. 18, 2001

Most passing yards, career
14,820—Vinny Testaverde

Most passing yards, season
3,811—Brad Johnson, 2003

Most passing yards, game
486—Doug Williams at Min., Nov. 16, 1980

Most touchdown passes, season
26—Brad Johnson, 2003

Most pass receptions, career
430—James Wilder

Most pass receptions, season
106—Keyshawn Johnson, 2001

Most pass receptions, game
13—James Wilder vs. Min., Sept. 15, 1985

Most receiving yards, career
5,018—Mark Carrier

Most receiving yards, season
1,422—Mark Carrier, 1989

Most receiving yards, game
212—Mark Carrier at N.O., Dec. 6, 1987

Most receiving touchdowns, season
9—Kevin House, 1981
   Bruce Hill, 1988
   Mark Carrier, 1989

Most touchdowns, career
61—Mike Alstott

Most field goals, season
32—Martin Gramatica, 2002

Longest field goal
57 yards—Michael Husted at L.A. Raiders, Dec. 19, 1993

Most interceptions, career
31—Donnie Abraham

Most interceptions, season
10—Ronde Barber, 2001

Most sacks, career
78.5—Lee Roy Selmon

Most sacks, season
16.5—Warren Sapp, 2000

SERIES RECORDS

Tampa Bay vs.: Arizona 7-8; Atlanta 13-10; Baltimore 2-0; Buffalo 5-2; Carolina 4-5; Chicago 17-33; Cincinnati 5-3; Cleveland 1-5; Dallas 3-6; Denver 2-4; Detroit 23-26; Green Bay 18-29-1; Houston 1-0; Indianapolis 4-6; Jacksonville 1-2; Kansas City 4-5; Miami 3-4; Minnesota 18-31; New England 2-3; New Orleans 9-17; N.Y. Giants 6-9; N.Y. Jets 1-7; Oakland 1-5; Philadelphia 4-5; Pittsburgh 1-5; St. Louis 6-9; San Diego 1-7; San Francisco 3-13; Seattle 1-5; Tennessee 1-7; Washington 5-7.

HISTORY Team by team

COACHING RECORDS

Leeman Bennett, 4-28-0; Tony Dungy, 54-42-0 (2-4); Jon Gruden, 24-24-0 (3-0); John McKay, 44-88-1 (1-3); Ray Perkins, 19-41-0; Richard Williamson, 4-15-0; Sam Wyche, 23-41-0.
NOTE: Playoff games in parentheses.

TENNESSEE TITANS
YEAR-BY-YEAR RECORDS

		REGULAR SEASON						PLAYOFFS			
Year	W	L	T	Pct.	PF	PA	Finish	W	L	Highest round	Coach
1960*†	10	4	0	.714	379	285	1st/Eastern Div.	1	0	AFL champ	Lou Rymkus
1961*†	10	3	1	.769	513	242	1st/Eastern Div.	1	0	AFL champ	L. Rymkus, Wally Lemm
1962*†	11	3	0	.786	387	270	1st/Eastern Div.	0	1	AFL championship game	Pop Ivy
1963*†	6	8	0	.429	302	372	3rd/Eastern Div.	—	—		Pop Ivy
1964*†	4	10	0	.286	310	355	4th/Eastern Div.	—	—		Sammy Baugh
1965*†	4	10	0	.286	298	429	4th/Eastern Div.	—	—		Hugh Taylor
1966*†	3	11	0	.214	335	396	T4th/Eastern Div.	—	—		Wally Lemm
1967*†	9	4	1	.692	258	199	1st/Eastern Div.	0	1	AFL championship game	Wally Lemm
1968*†	7	7	0	.500	303	248	2nd/Eastern Div.	—	—		Wally Lemm
1969*†	6	6	2	.500	278	279	2nd/Eastern Div.	0	1	Div. playoff game	Wally Lemm
1970†	3	10	1	.231	217	352	4th/AFC Central Div.	—	—		Wally Lemm
1971†	4	9	1	.308	251	330	3rd/AFC Central Div.	—	—		Ed Hughes
1972†	1	13	0	.071	164	380	4th/AFC Central Div.	—	—		Bill Peterson
1973†	1	13	0	.071	199	447	4th/AFC Central Div.	—	—		B. Peterson, S. Gillman
1974†	7	7	0	.500	236	282	3rd/AFC Central Div.	—	—		Sid Gillman
1975†	10	4	0	.714	293	226	3rd/AFC Central Div.	—	—		Bum Phillips
1976†	5	9	0	.357	222	273	4th/AFC Central Div.	—	—		Bum Phillips
1977†	8	6	0	.571	299	230	2nd/AFC Central Div.	—	—		Bum Phillips
1978†	10	6	0	.625	283	298	2nd/AFC Central Div.	2	1	AFC championship game	Bum Phillips
1979†	11	5	0	.688	362	331	2nd/AFC Central Div.	2	1	AFC championship game	Bum Phillips
1980†	11	5	0	.688	295	251	2nd/AFC Central Div.	0	1	AFC wild-card game	Bum Phillips
1981†	7	9	0	.438	281	355	3rd/AFC Central Div.	—	—		Ed Biles
1982†	1	8	0	.111	136	245	13th/AFC	—	—		Ed Biles
1983†	2	14	0	.125	288	460	4th/AFC Central Div.	—	—		Ed Biles, Chuck Studley
1984†	3	13	0	.188	240	437	4th/AFC Central Div.	—	—		Hugh Campbell
1985†	5	11	0	.313	284	412	4th/AFC Central Div.	—	—		H. Campbell, J. Glanville
1986†	5	11	0	.313	274	329	4th/AFC Central Div.	—	—		Jerry Glanville
1987†	9	6	0	.600	345	349	2nd/AFC Central Div.	1	1	AFC div. playoff game	Jerry Glanville
1988†	10	6	0	.625	424	365	3rd/AFC Central Div.	1	1	AFC div. playoff game	Jerry Glanville
1989†	9	7	0	.563	365	412	2nd/AFC Central Div.	0	1	AFC wild-card game	Jerry Glanville
1990†	9	7	0	.563	405	307	2nd/AFC Central Div.	0	1	AFC wild-card game	Jack Pardee
1991†	11	5	0	.688	386	251	1st/AFC Central Div.	1	1	AFC div. playoff game	Jack Pardee
1992†	10	6	0	.625	352	258	2nd/AFC Central Div.	0	1	AFC wild-card game	Jack Pardee
1993†	12	4	0	.750	368	238	1st/AFC Central Div.	0	1	AFC div. playoff game	Jack Pardee
1994†	2	14	0	.125	226	352	4th/AFC Central Div.	—	—		Jack Pardee, Jeff Fisher
1995†	7	9	0	.438	348	324	3rd/AFC Central Div.	—	—		Jeff Fisher
1996†	8	8	0	.500	345	319	4th/AFC Central Div.	—	—		Jeff Fisher
1997‡	8	8	0	.500	333	310	3rd/AFC Central Div.	—	—		Jeff Fisher
1998‡	8	8	0	.500	330	320	2nd/AFC Central Div.	—	—		Jeff Fisher
1999	13	3	0	.813	392	324	2nd/AFC Central Div.	3	1	Super Bowl	Jeff Fisher
2000	13	3	0	.813	346	191	1st/AFC Central Div.	0	1	AFC div. playoff game	Jeff Fisher
2001	7	9	0	.438	336	388	4th/AFC Central Div.	—	—		Jeff Fisher
2002	11	5	0	.688	367	324	1st/AFC South Div.	1	1	AFC championship game	Jeff Fisher
2003	12	4	0	.750	435	324	2nd/AFC South Div.	1	1	AFC div. playoff game	Jeff Fisher
2004	5	11	0	.312	344	439	4th/AFC South Div.	—	—		Jeff Fisher

*American Football League.
†Houston Oilers.
‡Tennessee Oilers.

FIRST-ROUND DRAFT PICKS

1960—Billy Cannon, RB, Louisiana State
1961—Mike Ditka, E, Pittsburgh
1962—Ray Jacobs, DT, Howard Payne
1963—Danny Brabham, LB, Arkansas
1964—Scott Appleton, DT, Texas
1965—Lawrence Elkins, WR, Baylor* (AFL)
1966—Tommy Nobis, LB, Texas
1967—George Webster, LB, Michigan State
          Tom Regner, G, Notre Dame
1968—None
1969—Ron Pritchard, LB, Arizona State

1970—Doug Wilkerson, G, North Carolina Central
1971—Dan Pastorini, QB, Santa Clara
1972—Greg Sampson, DE, Stanford
1973—John Matuszak, DE, Tampa*
          George Amundson, RB, Iowa State
1974—None
1975—Robert Brazile, LB, Jackson State
          Don Hardeman, RB, Texas A&I
1976—None
1977—Morris Towns, T, Missouri
1978—Earl Campbell, RB, Texas*